S0-AWP-245

Invite Your Students Back to Business

Business

Pride Hughes Kapoor

5th Edition

Dear Business Instructor:

Increase enrollments. . . . Improve grades. . . . Attract majors. . . .

A business textbook has to do more these days, just like you do. You have to attract students to your courses and keep them there. You have to capture their interest and generate enthusiasm for business. You have to make sure they perform well. And you have to give them a reason to walk away from your course satisfied, and hopefully headed for more courses in your department.

This is an Introduction to Business textbook that does more. It invites students into the study of business, and helps you make them satisfied, successful, and enthusiastic business students (and perhaps even majors!). With these goals in mind, we've revised this edition of *Business* to emphasize:

- **Real-World Relevance:** Thorough and timely coverage of global issues, ethics, changes in the workplace, and small business.
- **A Skills and Career Emphasis:** Exercises in critical thinking and writing, *Enhancing Career Skills* boxes and a complete chapter, *Careers in Business.*
- **Features That Make Business Inviting:** Interesting examples, video cases, vignettes, and learning aids designed to help students succeed.

And to make your job easier, Pride/Hughes/Kapoor's extensive support package includes:

- **Powerful Teaching Resources:** An Instructor's Resource Manual, an Electronic Lecture Manager, Transparencies, Video Cases, a Laserdisc, and print and computerized Test Banks.
- **Powerful Learning Resources:** A Study Guide, a Computerized Tutorial, and numerous simulations and project books (including career development materials).

We invite you to examine the seven-page visual guide that follows. You'll see more of how Pride/Hughes/Kapoor can help you invite students into business, help them succeed, and make them stay.

Sincerely,

William M. Pride

William M. Pride

Bob Hughes

Robert J. Hughes

Jack R. Kapoor

Jack R. Kapoor

R.S.V.P.

Business

5th Edition   Pride Hughes Kapoor

INVITE YOUR STUDENTS BACK TO BUSINESS

We've revised *Business* with this goal in mind: to help you invite students into the study of business and keep them there. Here are some of the many ways the Fifth Edition can make business accessible and relevant to your students.

A TEXT WITH THE RIGHT EMPHASIS

REAL-WORLD RELEVANCE

Pride/Hughes/Kapoor is thoroughly updated to go beyond the basics and show students what matters in business today.

■■■■ **GLOBAL PERSPECTIVES**

Marketing Food Around the World

In Bucharest, Romania, a young couple looks forward to a quiet evening at home. They prepare a traditional homemade Romanian dinner of stuffed cabbage and sit down to watch not-so-traditional MTV and *Beverly Hills, 90210*. Even though American cuisine is not as popular overseas as American television, this couple could soon be substituting frozen pizza or microwaveable burritos for cabbage. Consumers around the world want more and better packaged foods, and U.S. food companies such as Coca-Cola, Campbell Soup, Tropicana, and Gerber Baby Food, just to name a few, are eager

To succeed in glob more than knowing a lit Companies need to be a tions, and taboos of ea Foreign Agricultural Se United States Departme some general advice to ing into forei

regulations. In the Netherlands, spicy Tex-Mex foods are big sellers, and in Denmark, demand is increasing for low-fat foods like turkey and chicken. In Singapore, consumers are hungry for bite-size snack foods like chips, candy, popcorn, and crackers, which they can buy everywhere from gourmet supermarkets to the corner gas station. Polish consumers crave American packaged food, but the government requires that products of U.S. origin be clearly marked and all lab be in Polish. Canadian labeling must be in b French and English, and all weights must

■■■■ **CHANGE IN THE WORKPLACE**

Workplace Diversity: Benefits for B Businesses

We tried everything for so many years, but our business did not perform better until we had a diverse management group." This remark, made recently by the CEO of a major chemical manufacturing company, sums up the growing conviction that workplace diversity is a vital and positive force. In the past, corporate officers and managers approached diversity as a legal responsibility. Are we complying with affirmative action? Have we hired enough women? Are we actively recruiting minorities? Today, companies are seeking out "work force diversity m

ing "diversity and cultural sen common in the workplace as coffee br longer just a legal or moral imperative, di an important issue in building effective strategies.

For those organizations that va strengths of different cultures, diversity to better morale, better qual customer servi

diverse work forces are likely to be highly productive. Companies that market products worldwide reap the benefits of being knowledgeable about and sensitive to cultural differences. When an organization's representatives are trying to close a sale in Japan, it helps if they are aware that there are sixteen ways to say "no" in Japanese!

Prominent companies like Avon, Burger King, Levi Strauss, Xerox, and AT&T lead the way in corporate commitment to work force diversity, even in the face of layoffs and restructuring. Many s are finding diversity a plus. work force diversity asserted nt for our customers to look ple like them. If they can't, it he prospect of them

AT A GLANCE

Cleanup

100
80
60
40
20
0%

Recycling at home / Buying biodegradable products / Recycling at work / Supporting environmental groups

How Americans are contributing to cleaning up the environment.

Source: Opinion Research Corporation

■ Small business issues covered in Chapter 5: *Small Business, Entrepreneurship, and Franchises,* and in examples throughout the text

■ Global issues covered early in Chapter 3: *Global Business,* in *Global Perspectives* boxes, and in examples and photos throughout

NEW!

■ A NEW boxed feature, *Changes in the Workplace,* focusing on diversity, technology, TQM, and cultural changes in business

■ Marginal *At a Glance* features providing visual descriptions of current business statistics

■ *Ethical Challenges* and *Business Journal* boxes highlighting important workplace issues

Exercises

 1. Study the sample application letter illustrated in Figure 23.4 and the résumé illustrated in Figure 23.5. Then develop your own personal application letter and résumé that could be mailed to a prospective employer.

2. In a role-play situation with one of your classmates, answer the interview questions presented in Table 23.4. Then analyze your answers to determine those that need improvement.

3. Interview someone you consider to be a successful person. In the interview, determine how

STRONG SKILLS AND CAREER EMPHASIS

Pride/Hughes/Kapoor provides the practical applications that make a business education so valuable for your students.

■ Skill-building exercises throughout, with **critical thinking** and **writing** exercises in each chapter identified by icons

■ A complete chapter, Chapter 23: *Careers in Business,* that prepares students to identify and pursue career opportunities

■ *Career Profiles* at the end of each part identifying specific skills for different career paths

■ A NEW boxed feature, *Enhancing Career Skills,* that provides specific tips for succeeding in the workplace

CAREER PROFILE

PART 2   Career Opportunities in Management and Organization

The figure in the salary column approximates the expected annual income after two or three years of service.
1 = $12,000–$15,000; 2 = $16,000–$20,000; 3 = $21,000–$27,000; 4 = $28,000–$35,000; 5 = $36,000 and up.

Job Title	Job Description	Salary Range	Educational Requirements	Skills Required	Prospects for Growth
First-line supervisor	Ensure that workers, equipment, and materials are used properly and efficiently; make sure machinery is set up correctly; schedule maintenance of machinery; tell workers what to do and make sure it's done safely, correctly, and on time; enforce safety regulations; evaluate employees; recommend wage increases; and make sure union rules are followed	3–4	High school diploma; some college helpful	Organizational; leadership; technical; conceptual; interpersonal; decision making	Average
Food service manager	Select menu items; determine food, labor, and overhead costs and assign menu prices; order supplies; maintain equipment; repair; interview, hire, fire; schedule workers' hours; supervise kitchen and dining room; resolve customer complaints; during busy hours, managers may help in kitchen or dining room; and manage bookkeeping and payroll tax reports	3	Two years of college or trade school; on-the-job experience	Decision making; interviewing; interpersonal; clerical	Above average
Health service manager	Plan, coordinate, and supervise the delivery of health care; speak before civic groups; promote public participation in health programs; and coordinate the activities of the organization with those of government or community agencies	4–5	Bachelor's degree in business or hospital administration; master's degree preferred	Communication; interpersonal; conceptual; public speaking; decision making	Greatest
Hotel manager	Set room rates; allocate funds; approve expenditures; control food quality; and oversee all assistant managers	5	Some college helpful; bachelor's degree preferred; on-the-job experience	Decision making; communication; interpersonal; problem solving	Above average
Management analyst	Varies from employer to employer and project to project; collect, review, and analyze information, make recommendations, and assist in the implementation of proposals; analyze annual revenues and expenditures; interview employees and observe the operations of organizational unit	4–5	Bachelor's degree in management; on-the-job experience	Communication; problem solving; interpersonal; conceptual	Above average
Operation research analyst	Help organizations plan and operate in the most efficient and effective manner; solve problems by using mathematical models; work closely with managers; identify and analyze problems; and	4			

ENHANCING CAREER SKILLS

Moving Up the Corporate Ladder

Today's employees face many more challenges than previous generations when it comes to climbing the corporate ladder. Once, company loyalty and the ability to take on increasing job responsibilities usually assured advancement within an organization. The reasons for wanting to advance, such as the desire for a better-paying position, for more prestige, and for job satisfaction, haven't changed. But in today's business environment, rather than just relying on being recognized as loyal and competent by one's supervisors in order to move up, a person has to know how to package and market his or her abilities to those in authority.

BUILD YOUR OWN LADDER

1. Constantly improve your skills by taking advantage of everything you can learn on the job, by enrolling in continuing education classes, staying informed of technology in the workplace.

4. Widen your circle of professional and personal acquaintances. Show interest in everyone you meet by asking questions, opening up opportunities to learn of changes in the business climate and allowing other people to know you and your opinions.

5. Compile a portfolio of reference letters from customers and clients with whom you have developed working relationships. Add anything you receive in the way of praise and commendation from your current boss or other managers.

6. Recognize when it is time to move on. A company that hires from the outside with no promotions from within, an employer who takes you for granted, and your gradual dissatisfaction with your job are typical early warning signs.

NETWORKING

A TEXT THAT MAKES BUSINESS INVITING

■■■■ INSIDE BUSINESS

Motivating Basketball Stars and Business Executives

A roomful of *Fortune* 500 executives is waiting to hear a talk about motivating and empowering their employees, establishing goals, and implementing teamwork. The speaker steps onto the stage. He's wearing a chic tie and an Armani suit. Is he a high-powered business consultant? No. He's Pat Riley, then coach of the New York Knicks. Riley piloted the Los Angeles Lakers to four National Basketball Association championships, guided the Knicks to the best record in the Eastern Conference, and was twice named NBA Coach of the Year.

Addressing a ...
said, "I have a b...
one from IBM h...
down to the san...
Riley's basketbal...
that people are ...
their best if they ...
For example ...

Getting personal with small business. The owners of retail shops such as this sailboard store know their customers by name. Personal service is a major competitive edge for small business. This owner believes that, by offering customers a high quality sailboard along with efficient, courteous service, the world will beat a path to his door.

Pride/Hughes/Kapoor invites your students into the study of business and provides the tools that help make their first business course a success.

■ Trademark informal, highly readable writing style

■ Diverse, up-to-date examples that really interest today's students, including all-new *Inside Business* chapter-opening vignettes

■ Video cases, vignettes, photos, and references carefully chosen to appeal to students from a wide range of backgrounds

■ Learning features designed to help students succeed, like page references for key terms and chapter summaries based on learning objectives

LEARNING OBJECTIVES

After studying this chapter, you shou...

1 Understand what is meant by *bu...*

2 Identify the types of ethical conc... the business world.

3 Discuss the factors that affect the... behavior in organizations.

4 Explain how ethical decision ma... encouraged.

5 Describe how our current views ... responsibility of business have ev...

6 Explain the two views on social ... business and understand the argu... against increased social responsi...

7 Discuss the factors that led to the... movement and list some...

8 Ana...

■■■■ CHAPTER REVIEW

Summary

1 Understand what is meant by *business ethics.*

Ethics is the study of right and wrong and of the morality of choices. Business ethics is the application of moral standards to business situations.

2 Identify the types of ethical concerns that arise in the business world.

Ethical issues arise often in business situations out of relationships with investors, customers, employees, creditors, or competitors. Business people should make every effort to be fair, to consider the welfare of customers and others within the firm, to avoid conflicts of interest, and to communicate honestly.

3 Discuss the factors that affect the level of ethical behavior in organizations.

Individual, social, and opportunity factors all affect the level of ethical behavior in an organization. Individual factors include knowledge level, moral values and attitudes, and personal goals. Social factors include cultural norms and the actions and values of

coworkers and significant others. Opportunity factors refer to the amount of leeway that exists in an organization for employees to behave unethically if they so choose.

4 Explain how ethical decision making can be encouraged.

Governments, trade associations, and individual firms can all establish guidelines for defining ethical behavior. Governments can pass stricter regulations. Trade associations provide ethical guidelines for their members. Companies provide codes of ethics, written guides to acceptable and ethical behavior as defined by an organization, and create an atmosphere in which ethical behavior is encouraged. An ethical employee working in an unethical environment may resort to whistle blowing to bring a questionable practice to light.

5 Describe how our current views on the social responsibility of business have evolved.

In a socially responsible business, management realizes that its activities have an impact on society and considers that impact in the decision-making process. Before the 1930s, workers, consumers, a... government had very little influen...

INVITE YOUR STUDENTS BACK TO BUSINESS

A POWERFUL SUPPLEMENT PACKAGE

We've assembled a support package that focuses on generating enthusiasm in your classes and inspiring student success.

INSTRUCTOR'S RESOURCE MANUAL

Written by the authors to make your lectures accessible and exciting, this comprehensive teaching resource with a new easy-to-use design includes:

- Completely revised lecture outlines (12–15 pages per chapter), plus updated supplemental lectures on current issues
- Brief outline and learning objectives for each chapter
- *Teaching Idea Exchange* with over 40 innovative project ideas contributed by instructors across the nation
- Video notes and activity suggestions for videos tied to the first case at the end of each chapter
- Guide to using the full-color transparencies
- Answers to review, discussion, quiz, end-of-chapter, and case questions
- Two quizzes for each chapter containing true/false and multiple choice questions
- *Debate Issues* with discussion questions for inspiring participation and critical thinking
- Introductory notes from the authors for each chapter
- Film suggestions

INVITE YOUR STUDENTS BACK TO BUSINESS

ELECTRONIC LECTURE MANAGER

Allows you to use a computer to create and bring together materials for a multimedia lecture presentation:

- Edit and display the comprehensive lecture outline
- Add any or all of the transparency images
- Incorporate segments from the laserdisc
- Add your own presentation materials

TRANSPARENCIES

300 color transparencies specifically designed to project well, even in large lecture halls. They include debate issues, class exercises, chapter quizzes, and definitions and figures from outside the text.

VIDEOS

Each of these 23 video segments is tied to the first case at the end of each chapter. Notes, suggestions, and activities for each video are in the *Instructor's Resource Manual*.

INVITE YOUR STUDENTS BACK TO BUSINESS

LASERDISC

Five interactive video segments are included on this dramatic lecture-enhancing supplement. A guide with teaching notes and suggestions is included.

TEST BANK/COMPUTERIZED TEST BANK

The authors have personally written these 3,000 test items, including essay, true/false, and multiple choice questions. The computerized version allows you to customize your own tests.

FOR STUDENTS

STUDY GUIDE

Prepared by Kathy Hegar, the *Study Guide* focuses on student understanding and retention by providing key term exercises, and three examinations for each chapter (including answers at the back).

COMPUTERIZED TUTORIAL

Includes learning objectives with page references, chapter overviews, key term exercises and chapter examinations (with questions that differ from those in the printed *Study Guide*).

Invite Your Students Back to Business

ADDITIONAL MATERIALS

Encourage your students to get down to business with these simulations and project books:

- The Job Hunter's Guidebook
- Get the Job You Want
- Toward a Career in Business
- Investing in Business
- Opening a Business
- Business Careers
- Entrepreneur: A Simulation
- Manager: A Simulation

R.S.V.P.

**We invite you to examine
Pride/Hughes/Kapoor, *Business*,
Fifth Edition, in greater detail.
For more information, please contact your
Houghton Mifflin Sales Representative,
or contact:
Houghton Mifflin Faculty Services Center
1900 South Batavia Avenue
Geneva, IL 60134
1-800-733-1717 FAX 1-800-733-1810
http://www.hmco.com**

Business

5th Edition   Pride Hughes Kapoor

Business

Business

Fifth Edition

William M. Pride
Texas A & M University

Robert J. Hughes
Dallas County Community College

Jack R. Kapoor
College of DuPage

Houghton Mifflin Company   **Boston**   **Toronto**
Geneva, Illinois   Palo Alto   Princeton, New Jersey

To Nancy, Allen, and Michael Pride

To Peggy Hughes

To my parents, Ram and Sheela; my wife, Theresa; and my children, Karen, Kathy, and Dave

Sponsoring Editor: Jennifer B. Speer
Senior Associate Editor: Susan M. Kahn
Senior Project Editor: Cathy Labresh Brooks
Senior Production/Design Coordinator: Jill Haber
Senior Manufacturing Coordinator: Marie Barnes

Cover design: Harold Burch, Harold Burch Design, New York
Cover image: Illustration by David Lesh

Text credits begin on page A-30.
Photo credits begin on page A-34.

Printed in the U.S.A.

Library of Congress Catalog Card Number: 95-77046

ISBN
Student text: 0-395-74461-X
Examination text: 0-395-74894-1
Library edition: 0-395-76127-1

123456789-DW-99 98 97 96 95

BRIEF CONTENTS ▪ ▪ ▪ ▪ ▪ ▪ ▪

v

CONTENTS ▪ ▪ ▪ ▪ ▪ ▪ ▪ ▪ ▪ ▪ ▪ ▪ ▪ ▪

vii

PREFACE ■ ■ ■ ■ ■ ■ ■ ■ ■

Change. That six-letter word says a lot about the world in which we live. Think for a moment about the remarkable changes we have seen in just the last three years, and consider how those changes have affected the business environment. Since the last edition of *Business* was published,

- The U.S. gross national product (GNP) grew from $5.6 trillion to $6.4 trillion.

- The amount spent by business and government to control water and air pollution and to clean up toxic waste has increased to over $70 billion a year.

- The North American Free Trade Agreement was enacted to encourage trade between the United States, Canada, and Mexico.

- Health and allied services has become the fastest-growing industry in the United States.

- Many American firms have established total quality management (TQM) programs in order to improve customer satisfaction.

- The ability to communicate well, use a computer, and solve problems with critical-thinking skills has become increasingly important for people trying to get their first job or to climb the corporate ladder.

These important changes along with many more that are just as important are discussed in the new fifth edition of *Business*. In fact, the primary impetus behind this edition is to provide our customers—the students and instructors who use this book—with the latest information available.

As authors, we're especially proud of the fifth edition, but we also realize that it is impossible to rest on past performance. Although *Business* has now been revised and improved four times since it was introduced in 1985, each time we have tried to incorporate not only the latest changes and newest topics affecting the world of business, but also suggestions from both instructors and students who have used the book. With each of the previous editions, our objective has always been to provide both students and instructors with the *best* textbook possible: one that is relevant, accurate, up-to-date, and interesting—just like business itself. And we worked hard to make sure that this new, fifth edition of *Business* continues the same tradition of providing quality instructional materials that can be used to introduce students to the exciting world of business. In the next several sections, we describe the distinctive features that are unique to the fifth edition of *Business* and ultimately make this book different from any other book available today.

xix

■■ NEW TO THE FIFTH EDITION

- The overall chapter sequence has been changed slightly in this edition. The international business chapter (previously Chapter 23) has been repositioned to be closer to the front of the text. Now Chapter 3, it is entitled "Global Business." This new positioning sets the stage for coverage of international issues throughout the text.

- "Business Law" and "Government Assistance, Regulation, and Taxation," previously Chapters 21 and 22, have been combined into one chapter, now Chapter 22.

- All of the chapter opening Inside Business vignettes are new to this edition.

- The use of video cases is new to this edition. At the end of each chapter, the first of two cases is a video case. Over half of all the cases are new to this edition.

- There are five types of boxed features in the fifth edition: Change in the Workplace, Global Perspectives, Ethical Challenges, Enhancing Career Skills, and Business Journal. Almost all of these individual features are new. The issues discussed in the boxes are more fully described in the next section.

- The chapter summaries appear in a new format. Each summary is organized according to the learning objectives presented at the beginning of each chapter.

- New to this edition are critical-thinking and writing exercises located in the end-of-chapter material. One critical-thinking exercise and one writing exercise apply to each chapter and are designated with icons.

■■ EXCITING BOXED FEATURES

To help us highlight today's important issues and to keep the book as lively as possible, we have included a variety of boxed features. There are five types of boxes throughout the book: Change in the Workplace, Global Perspectives, Ethical Challenges, Enhancing Career Skills, and Business Journal.

Change in the Workplace

Nothing is more certain in today's business environment than change. And the changes taking place are dramatic. Although viewpoints vary considerably about whether the changes are positive or negative, businesspeople must deal with the benefits and challenges of these changes. The workplace changes on which we focus fall into several broad areas, including cultural diversity, total quality management, technology, and changes in business practices. Specific topics include

- The Information Superhighway
- Workplace Diversity: Benefits for People and Business

- Customer Satisfaction at Any Price?
- Why Corporations Downsize

Global Perspectives

This series of boxes, together with Chapter 3 and other global examples and photos throughout the text, is designed to enhance students' awareness of the globalization of the business world. Boxes include

- EuroDisney: Cultural Realities Invade Fantasy Land
- The Pepsi Challenge Goes Global
- World Market Quality Standards: ISO 9000
- Is GATT a Good Deal?

Ethical Challenges

Following up on the foundation of Chapter 2, "Ethics and Social Responsibility," the Ethical Challenges special features are designed to develop students' abilities to think critically about typical ethical dilemmas that can arise in the business arena. Examples of topics discussed are

- Codes of Ethics: Doing the Right Thing
- Crossing the Picket Line: A Matter of Ethics
- Do Banks Discriminate When Making Loans?
- Insurance Fraud: We All Pay

Enhancing Career Skills

Enhancing Career Skills presents students with practical advice they can use now. Many students are employed in a variety of businesses while going to school. This special feature provides skill tips that can help them on the job today, next week, next year, and throughout their business careers. Among the topics are

- Improving Your Team Skills
- Moving Up the Corporate Ladder
- Helping to Protect Your Company from Negative Publicity
- Managing a Scarce Resource: Your Time

These boxed features, along with the end-of-part Career Profiles and Chapter 23, "Careers in Business," will help students with practical advice and show the relevance of text material to real-world applications.

Business Journal

The Business Journal series explores a wide range of organizations and contemporary business topics that include business trends, technology, social issues, and success stories. Selected topics include

- Is It Safe to Go to Work?
- Union-Management Partnerships: Old Foes Become Friends
- Lo and Behold, It's the WonderBra!
- The Wired Organization

■■ EFFECTIVE PEDAGOGICAL AIDS

We have worked to make *Business, Fifth Edition*, the most interesting and most pedagogically effective introductory business text available. Many of the following pedagogical features in the text have been evaluated and recommended by reviewers with years of teaching experience.

Part Introductions

Each of the text's seven parts begins with a concise description of the materials to follow. From the outset of each part, a student not only is made aware of what's in each part but also has a better understanding of how the chapters in that part fit with the chapters in the rest of the text.

Learning Objectives

A student with a purpose will learn more effectively than a student wandering aimlessly through the text. Therefore, each chapter of *Business* contains clearly stated learning objectives that signal important concepts to be mastered. Together, the chapter previews and learning objectives enable the student to see where each chapter is going. To aid instructors, questions in the *Test Bank* are keyed to the learning objectives.

Chapter Previews

Each chapter is introduced with a preview—a capsule summary of what to expect in the chapter. The student can grasp quickly the major topics in the chapter and the sequence in which they are covered. Each chapter preview also serves as a useful reminder of that chapter's contents when the student is ready to review.

Inside Business

Chapter opening vignettes, entitled "Inside Business," bring business concepts alive for students. With Inside Business we introduce the theme of each chapter focusing on pertinent activities of a real organization, including Johnson & Johnson, Birkenstock, Starbucks, and Microsoft. The decisions and activities of these and other familiar organizations not only demonstrate what companies are actually doing but also make the materials in each chapter relevant and absorbing for students. When students become involved in the chapter material, critical thinking and active participation replace passive acceptance, and real learning takes place.

Margin Notes

Two types of margin notes help students understand and retain important concepts. First, to aid the student in building a basic business vocabulary, the definition of each key term (in contrasting color) is placed in the margin near the introduction of the term in the text. Second, each learning objective is positioned near the beginning of the section in which that objective is emphasized. This easy reference to terms and objectives reinforces the learning of business fundamentals.

Stimulating Writing Style

One of our major objectives in *Business, Fifth Edition,* is to communicate to students our enthusiasm for business in a direct, engaging manner. Throughout the book we have used a lucid writing style that builds interest and facilitates students' understanding of the concepts discussed. To ensure that the text is stimulating and easy for students to use, we have given special attention to word choice, sentence structure, and the presentation of business language.

Real-World Examples and Illustrations

Numerous real-world examples drawn from familiar organizations and recognizable products are used in each chapter. How does Southwest Airlines manage to attract and keep such upbeat, effective employees? How can warehouse clubs offer products at such a significant discount? Why has Motorola increased spending for training from $7 million a decade ago to $120 million today? What are the fastest-growing industries in the small business sector? Examples such as these from today's business world catch students' attention and enable them to apply the concepts and issues of each chapter.

Complete End-of-Chapter Materials

Each end-of-chapter summary is based on the chapter's learning objectives and brings important ideas together for the student. A list of key terms with page references and a complete set of review questions reinforce the learning of definitions and concepts. Discussion questions and exercises encourage careful consideration of selected issues presented in the chapter. Some of the exercises ask students to engage in critical thinking and writing about chapter issues.

Cases

Each chapter ends with two cases—one of them a video case—focusing on recognizable organizations. The cases offer descriptions of current business issues and activities, allowing students to consider the real-world implications associated with the concepts covered in the chapter. Related questions suitable for class discussion or individual assignment follow each case. Sample case titles include

- Blockbuster Entertainment: More Than Just Videos
- Ben and Jerry's: Being a Good Corporate Citizen Isn't Easy
- Saturn Corporation: A Different Kind of Car Company
- Woolworth Corporation's Commitment to Hiring the Disabled
- Digital Equipment Corporation's AIDS Program
- Ryka Athletic Shoes: By Women, For Women, Helping Women
- The Advertising Council: Advertising for Good, Not for Gain

Glossary

A glossary containing nearly 750 fundamental business terms appears at the end of our text. The glossary serves as a convenient reference tool to reinforce students' learning of basic business vocabulary.

■■ COMPLETE PACKAGE OF SUPPORT MATERIALS

Accompanying the fifth edition of *Business* is a full array of supplementary materials—instructional tools that both augment learning for students and increase the effectiveness of instructors.

Instructor's Resource Manual

The two-volume *Instructor's Resource Manual* features the following items for each chapter:

- Note from the authors
- Learning objectives
- Brief chapter outline
- Video Guide (with video overview and multiple-choice questions)
- Guide for using transparency acetates
- Comprehensive lecture outline
- Supplemental lecture
- Answers to the text Review Questions
- Answers to the text Discussion Questions
- Answers to the case Questions
- Two chapter quizzes with answer keys
- Answer key for class exercise and quiz transparencies

The manual also includes a Teaching Idea Exchange, which profiles innovative project ideas contributed by instructors across the nation. In addition, the *Instructor's Resource Manual* provides an extensive listing, by chapter, of suggested films and videos for classroom use and instructions for using the student enrichment project manuals.

Electronic Lecture Manager

The *Electronic Lecture Manager* is a Windows-based software package that allows instructors to create customized, multimedia lecture presentations that can be displayed on computer-based projection systems. The software makes available lecture outlines from the *Instructor's Resource Manual* and figures and tables from the transparencies, and also allows for access to laserdisc sequences and screens from other Windows-based software. Instructors can quickly and easily integrate all of these components and create their own screens to prepare a seamless classroom presentation with minimal in-class tinkering.

Test Bank

Written and class-tested by the text's authors themselves, the *Test Bank* contains over 3,000 test items. Each chapter contains a variety of essay, true/false, and multiple-choice questions. An item-information column in the *Test Bank* specifies details about each question, such as learning objective tie-in and learning level (knowledge or application). Specific information appears in the introduction to the *Test Bank*.

Computerized Test Bank

This electronic version of the printed *Test Bank* allows instructors to generate and change tests easily on the computer. The program also includes On-Line Testing and Gradebook, by which instructors can administer tests via a network system, modem, or personal computer. The grading function lets users set up a new class, record grades from tests or assignments, and analyze grades and produce class and individual statistics.

Transparencies

The instructional package for *Business, Fifth Edition,* includes 300 color transparencies—some drawn from the text and over 150 from outside sources. In addition to selected figures and tables from the fifth edition, the transparencies for each chapter include a chapter outline, a class exercise useful for stimulating class discussion, a debate issue excellent for generating fast-paced class interaction, and a multiple-choice chapter quiz. Additional transparencies for each chapter include definitions and figures not found in the text.

Videos

The twenty-three video segments, one for each chapter in *Business,* can help instructors bring lectures to life by providing thought-provoking insights into real-world companies, products, and issues. These videos present information about the organizations featured in the video cases at the ends of the chapters. A description of each case video—the title, organization, video length, and an overview—is provided in the *Instructor's Resource Manual.* Multiple-choice questions are also supplied.

Laserdisc

Five interactive video segments are included on this dramatic lecture-enhancing supplement. Instructors can present video clips as desired simply by using the electronic scanner to read a barcode or by accessing material through the *Electronic Lecture Manager*. Also available is an Instructor's Guide with teaching notes and suggestions that summarizes the video material.

Study Guide

Written by Kathryn Hegar of Mountain View College, the *Study Guide* is a self-help tool for students to use in learning definitions, concepts, and relationships in each chapter. The exercises and questions are especially useful for self-evaluation and review purposes. For each chapter in the text, the *Study Guide* provides the following:

- Key terms
- Matching questions
- True/false questions
- Multiple-choice questions
- Completion questions
- Answer key

PC Study/Computerized Tutorial

This study disk is a computer-aided instructional program that helps students review and assess their knowledge of the concepts, issues, and applications discussed in each chapter of the text. The disk gives students the opportunity for active, not passive, learning. Each chapter is supported with a brief chapter overview; learning objectives; and multiple-choice, true/false, and matching questions. In the case of the multiple-choice questions, after the student responds to each item, the easy-to-use program provides reinforcement for correct answers and reasons why incorrect answers are inappropriate. Material in this supplement is not contained in the print *Study Guide*.

This menu-driven, user-friendly program includes a help screen with complete documentation and supports a mouse. Students can choose questions in the order given or in random order and can time their work with a timer function. After completing a test, students can print their score, the questions, and the answers. A screen indicates the percentage and number of questions answered correctly and the number of attempts the student made to answer each question correctly.

Entrepreneur: A Business Simulation

This business simulation, written by Jerald R. Smith and Peggy Golden of the University of Louisville, allows student players to make business decisions through simulated real-world experiences. *Entrepreneur* involves the planning, start-up, and continuing operation of a retail store. Acting as management teams, students encounter many factors as they make decisions for each phase of the business. Additional support materials are provided for instructors.

Student Enrichment Project Manuals

Written by Kathryn Hegar of Mountain View College, the three project manuals are entitled *Toward a Career in Business*, *Investing in Business*, and *Opening a Business*.

Toward a Career in Business guides students through the four stages of getting a job: self-assessment, occupational search, employment tools, and success techniques.

Investing in Business helps students learn how to invest money and how to maximize returns on their investments. Students who use *Investing in Business* become familiar with the advantages and disadvantages of various investment instruments and develop skills in acquiring financial information.

Opening a Business introduces students to the details of starting a company. Part One guides students through the process of gathering and analyzing essential information about business ownership. Part Two contains worksheets for students to complete based on their findings in Part One. After completing this project, students should be able to evaluate their skills as entrepreneurs and managers, calculate the capital needed to start a business, determine applicable state and federal regulations, and begin the planning process.

Business Careers

Business Careers, by Robert H. Luke, Southwest Missouri State University, is a supplement that helps students define career interests in accounting, computer information systems, finance, management, marketing, and entrepreneurship. Each chapter features detailed information on job categories, duties, qualifications, and salaries, plus helpful readings from leading business publications. Useful material on résumés, interviews, dress codes, and more prepares the student to enter today's workplace.

The Job Hunter's Guidebook

The Job Hunter's Guidebook, by Susan Greene of Sterling Communications Ltd., and Melanie Martel of Hesser College, is a brief, clear manual containing abundant examples of and practical advice on each of the job hunter's major tasks: résumés, cover letters, job applications, interviewing, and follow-up. The guide also covers handling rejection, networking, evaluating job offers, and tips for interview attire.

William M. Pride
Robert J. Hughes
Jack R. Kapoor

ACKNOWLEDGMENTS ■ ■ ■ ■ ■

We wish to express a great deal of appreciation to Kathryn Hegar of Mountain View College, for developing the *Study Guide* and the three student enrichment projects. For creating *Entrepreneur: A Business Simulation*, we wish to thank Jerald R. Smith and Peggy Golden of the University of Louisville. For her assistance in editing and manuscript development, we are indebted to Pam Swartz. Finally, we wish to thank the following people for technical assistance: Eric Horton, Theresa and Dave Kapoor, David Pierce, Prema Ramnath, Denise Rutledge, Patricia Thomas, Kathryn Thumme, and Karen Tucker.

We appreciate the assistance and suggestions of numerous individuals who have helped improve and refine this text and instructional package. For the generous gift of their time and for their thoughtful and useful comments and suggestions, we are indebted to the following reviewers of this and previous editions:

David V. Aiken
Hocking College

Phyllis C. Alderdice
Jefferson Community College

Harold Amsbaugh
North Central Technical College

Carole Anderson
Clarion University

James O. Armstrong, II
John Tyler Community College

Ed Atzenhoefer
Clark State Community College

Xenia P. Balabkins
Middlesex County College

Charles Bennett
Tyler Junior College

Robert W. Bitter
Southwest Missouri State University

Mary Jo Boehms
Jackson State Community College

Stewart Bonem
Cincinnati Technical College

James Boyle
Glendale Community College

Steve Bradley
Austin Community College

Lyle V. Brenna
Pikes Peak Community College

Tom Brinkman
Cincinnati Technical College

Harvey S. Bronstein
Oakland Community College

Edward Brown
Franklin University

Joseph Brum
Fayetteville Technical Institute

Janice Bryan
Jacksonville College

Howard R. Budner
Manhattan Community College

Clara Buitenbos
Pan American University

C. Alan Burns
Lee College

Frank Busch
Louisiana Technical University

Joseph E. Cantrell
DeAnza College

Don Cappa
Chabot College

Robert Carrel
Vincennes University

Richard M. Chamberlain
Lorain County Community College

Bruce H. Charnov
Hofstra University

Lawrence Chase
Tompkins Cortland Community College

Michael Cicero
Highline Community College

William Clarey
Bradley University

Robert Coiro
LaGuardia Community College

Don Coppa
Chabot College

Robert J. Cox
Salt Lake Community College

Bruce Cudney
Middlesex Community College

Andrew Curran
Antonelli Institute of Art and Photography

Rex R. Cutshall
Vincennes University

John Daily
St. Edward's University

Helen M. Davis
Jefferson Community College

Harris D. Dean
Lansing Community College

Wayne H. Decker
Memphis State University

William M. Dickson
Green River Community College

M. Dougherty
Madison Area Technical College

Sam Dunbar
Delgado Community College

Robert Elk
Seminole Community College

Pat Ellebracht
Northeast Missouri State University

John H. Espey
Cecil Community College

Carleton S. Everett
Des Moines Area Community College

Frank M. Falcetta
Middlesex County College

Thomas Falcone
Indiana University of Pennsylvania

Janice Feldbauer
Austin Community College

Coe Fields
Tarrant County Junior College

Gregory F. Fox
Erie Community College—City

Michael Fritz
Portland Comm. College at Rock Creek

Fred Fry
Bradley University

Eduardo F. Garcia
Laredo Junior College

Arlen Gastineau
Valencia Community College

Carmine Paul Gibaldi
St. John's University

Edwin Giermak
College of DuPage

R. Gillingham
Vincennes University

Robert Googins
Shasta College

W. Michael Gough
DeAnza College

Cheryl Davisson Gracie
Washtenaw Community College

Joseph Gray
Nassau Community College

Ricky W. Griffin
Texas A & M University

Stephen W. Griffin
Tarrant County Junior College

Roy Grundy
College of DuPage

John Gubbay
Moraine Valley Community College

Rick Guidicessi
Des Moines Area Community College

Ronald Hadley
St. Petersburg Junior College

Carnella Hardin
Glendale Community College

Aristotle Haretos
Flagler College

Richard Hartley
Solano Community College

Sanford Helman
Middlesex County College

Victor B. Heltzer
Middlesex County College

Ronald L. Hensell
Mendocino College

Leonard Herzstein
Skyline College

Donald Hiebert
Northern Oklahoma College

Nathan Himelstein
Essex Community College

L. Duke Hobbs
Texas A & M University

Marie R. Hodge
Bowling Green State University

Townsend Hopper

Joseph Hrebenak
Community College of Allegheny County—Allegheny

James L. Hyek
Los Angeles Valley College

Sally Jefferson
Western Illinois University

Jenna Johannpeter
Belleville Area College

Gene E. A. Johnson
Clark College

Pat Jones
Eastern New Mexico University

Robert Kegel
Cypress College

Isaac W. J. Keim, III
Delta College

George Kelley
Erie Community College

Marshall Keyser
Moorpark College

Betty Ann Kirk
Tallahassee Community College

Edward Kirk
Vincennes University

Clyde Kobberdahl
Cincinnati Technical College

Robert Kreitner
Arizona State University

Patrick Kroll
University of Minnesota, General College

Kenneth Lacho
University of New Orleans

John Lathrop
New Mexico Junior College

R. Michael Lebda
DeVry Institute of Technology

George Leonard
St. Petersburg Junior College

Marvin Levine
Orange County Community College

Chad Lewis
Everett Community College

William M. Lindsay
Northern Kentucky University

Carl H. Lippold
Embry-Riddle Aeronautical University

Thomas Lloyd
Westmoreland County Community College

Paul James Londrigan
Mott Community College

Kathleen Lorencz
Oakland Community College

Fritz Lotz
Southwestern College

Robert C. Lowery
Brookdale Community College

Anthony Lucas
Community College of Allegheny County—Allegheny

Sheldon A. Mador
Los Angeles Trade and Technical College

Gayle J. Marco
Robert Morris College

John Martin
Mt. San Antonio Community College

Irving Mason
Herkimer County Community College

John F. McDonough
Menlo College

Catherine McElroy
Bucks County Community College

L. J. McGlamory
North Harris County College

Charles Meiser
Lake Superior State University

Ina Midkiff-Kennedy
Austin Community College—Northridge

Edwin Miner
Phoenix College

Linda Morable
Richland College

Charles Morrow
Cuyahoga Community College

W. Gale Mueller
Spokane Community College

C. Mullery
Humboldt State University

Robert J. Mullin
Orange County Community College

Patricia Murray
Virginia Union University

Robert Nay
Stark Technical College

James Nead
Vincennes University

Jerry Novak
Alaska Pacific University

Gerald O'Bryan
Danville Area Community College

Larry Olanrewaju
Virginia Union University

David G. Oliver
Edison Community College

Dennis Pappas
Columbus Technical Institute

Roberta F. Passenant
Berkshire Community College

Clarissa M. H. Patterson
Bryant College

Constantine Petrides
Manhattan Community College

Donald Pettit
Suffolk County Community College

Norman Petty
Central Piedmont Community College

Joseph Platts
Miami-Dade Community College

Gloria D. Poplawsky
University of Toledo

Fred D. Pragasam
SUNY at Cobleskill

Kenneth Robinson
Wesley College

John Roisch
Clark County Community College

Rick Rowray
Ball State University

Jill Russell
Camden County College

Karl C. Rutkowski
Pierce Junior College

Martin S. St. John
Westmoreland County Community College

Eddie Sanders, Jr.
Chicago State University

P. L. Sandlin
East Los Angeles College

Nicholas Sarantakes
Austin Community College

Jon E. Seely
Tulsa Junior College

John E. Seitz
Oakton Community College

J. Gregory Service
Broward Community College, North Campus

Dennis Shannon
Belleville Area College

Richard Shapiro
Cuyahoga Community College

Raymond Shea
Monroe Community College

Lynette Shishido
Santa Monica College

Anne Smevog
Cleveland Technical College

Carl Sonntag
Pikes Peak Community College

John Spence
University of Southwestern Louisiana

Nancy Z. Spillman
President, Economic Education Enterprises

Richard J. Stanish
Tulsa Junior College

Jeffrey Stauffer
Ventura College

E. George Stook
Anne Arundel Community College

W. Sidney Sugg
Lakeland Community College

Lynn Suksdorf
Salt Lake Community College

Richard L. Sutton
University of Nevada—Las Vegas

Robert E. Swindle
Glendale Community College

William A. Syvertsen
Fresno City College

Raymond D. Tewell
American River College

George Thomas
Johnston Technical College

Judy Thompson
Briar Cliff College

William C. Thompson
Foothill Community College

Karen Thoms
St. Cloud University

James B. Thurman
George Washington University

Patric S. Tillman
Grayson County College

Jay Todes
North Lake College

Charles E. Tychsen
Northern Virginia Community College—Annandale

Ted Valvoda
Lakeland Community College

Robert H. Vaughn
Lakeland Community College

Frederick A. Viohl
Troy State University

C. Thomas Vogt
Allan Hancock College

Loren K. Waldman
Franklin University

Stephen R. Walsh
Providence College

John Warner
The University of New Mexico—Albuquerque

W. J. Waters, Jr.
Central Piedmont Community College

Philip A. Weatherford
Embry-Riddle Aeronautical University

Jerry E. Wheat
Indiana University, Southeast Campus

Benjamin Wieder
Queensborough Community College

Ralph Wilcox
Kirkwood Community College

Larry Williams
Palomar College

Paul Williams
Mott Community College

Steven Winter
Orange County Community College

Wallace Wirth
South Suburban College

Nathaniel Woods
Columbus State Community College

Gregory J. Worosz
Schoolcraft College

Marilyn Young
Tulsa Junior College

For sharing their pedagogical suggestions in the Teaching Idea Exchange section of the Instructor's Resource Manual, we thank the following contributors:

Stephen R. Ahrens
L. A. Pierce College

Dave Aiken
Hocking Technical College

Frederick J. Bartelheim
Truckee Meadow Community College

Catherine Ann Beegan
Winona State University

Mary Jo Boehms
Jackson State Community College

Sanford Boswell
Coastal Carolina Community College

Roy K. Boutwell
Midwestern State University

Sallie Branscom
Virginia Western Community College

John Buckley
Orange County Community College

Michael Cicero
Highline Community College

Thomas F. Collins
Central Florida Community College

Allen Commander
University of Houston, Downtown

Bruce L. Conners
Kaskaskia College

Nancy Copeland
Eastern Michigan University

Robert J. Cox
Salt Lake Community College

Rex R. Cutshall
Vincennes University

John DeNisco
Buffalo State College

James Eason
Coastal Carolina College

Pat Ellebracht
Northeast Missouri State University

Elinor Garely
Rus Hotels

Martin Gerber
Kalamazoo Valley Community College

Wynell Goddard
Tyler Junior College

Patricia A. Green
Nassau Community College

Donald Gren
Salt Lake Community College

Gene E. A. Johnson
Clark College

Ted Johnson
Tarrant County Junior College, NE

Jim Kennedy
Angelina College

Edward J. Kirk
Vincennes University

Chad Lewis
Everett Community College

Ann Maddox
Angelo State University

Normand Martin
Oklahoma State University

T. D. McConnell
Manchester Community College

D. Dwain McInnis
Palo Alto College

John Q. McMillian
Walters State Community College

Robert R. Meyer
Brookhaven College

Sylvia Meyer
Scottsdale Community College

Rebecca W. Mihelcic
Howard Community College

James Miles
Anoka-Ramsey Community College

Charles A. Miller
L. A. Southwest College

Craig Miller
Normandale Community College

Robert A. Moore
South Utah State College

Lewis J. Neisner
SUNY College at Buffalo

Fred D. Pragasam
State University of New York

Larry J. Seibert
Purdue University, North Central

Dennis G. Shine
Fresno City College

Lee Sutherland
Suffolk University

Laura Turano
Mohegan Community College

H. R. Werrell
Rose State College

Diane Williams
Baker College

Blaine R. Wilson
Central Washington University

Lance Wrzesinski
South Puget Sound Community College

Nancy Zeliff
Northwest Missouri State University

Business

PART ONE

American Business Today

This introductory part of *Business* is an overview of American business. We begin with an examination of the American business system, its basis, and its function within our society. Second, we discuss the responsibilities of business as part of that society. Then we explore the increasing importance of international business opportunities and practices. Next we move to an important and very practical aspect of business: how businesses are owned and by whom. Finally, because the vast majority of businesses are small, we look at American small business in some detail. Included in this part are

CHAPTER 1

Foundations of Business

LEARNING OBJECTIVES

1 Define *business* and identify potential risks and rewards.

2 Describe the important reasons for studying business.

3 Understand the two types of economic systems, capitalism and planned economy.

4 Identify the ways to measure economic performance.

5 Outline the four types of competition.

6 Summarize the development of America's business system.

7 Discuss the challenges that American businesses will encounter in the future.

CHAPTER PREVIEW

In this chapter, we look briefly at what business is and how it got that way. First, we define *business*, noting how business organizations satisfy needs and earn profits. Then we discuss important reasons for studying business. Next we examine how capitalistic and planned economies answer the four basic economic questions. Also, we take a closer look at capitalism in the United States. Then our focus shifts to the four types of competitive situations—pure competition, monopolistic competition, oligopoly, and monopoly. Next we look back into American history to see how events have shaped today's business system. We conclude this chapter with a discussion of the challenges that businesses face.

Mattel's Barbie Endures

Teenage Mutant Ninja Turtles are fading fast. Mighty Morphin Power Rangers are in. Toys are a notoriously fickle business, and last year's hit can become this year's loser. Mattel's Barbie doll, however, goes on and on. Best friend to millions of girls around the world, the foot-high doll with the improbable figure generates annual sales of more than $1 billion worldwide. When Mattel introduced Barbie, named for the owner's daughter, in 1959 at the New York Toy Fair, toy buyers dismissed her as a passing fad. More than thirty-five years have passed since then, and 800 million Barbies have been sold, enough to circle the earth more than three and a half times if laid head-to-pointed-toe. What makes Barbie such an unparalleled success? By continually reinventing Barbie and by introducing imaginative brand extensions, Mattel keeps Barbie forever young.

Although the best-selling Barbie in history is Totally Hair Barbie, a doll with floor-length hair that turns pink when sprayed, shoppers can choose among more than ninety versions of the doll, priced anywhere from $8 to $250. You can get Barbie as a teacher, a doctor, a horsewoman, a presidential candidate, an air force officer, or even an Egyptian queen. When she turned 35, Mattel introduced a reproduction of the original model complete with ponytail and black and white striped bathing suit. Barbie's outfits all have catchy names like "Easter Parade" and "Roman Holiday," some of which are created by fashion designers like Christian Dior or Yves St. Laurent.

To keep Barbie company, you can get her loyal boyfriend Ken and an ever-expanding and diverse group of siblings and friends. There are Barbie doll houses, Barbie sports cars, Barbie fast-food restaurants, Barbie cruise ships and Barbie motor homes that come with camping equipment.

After conquering the hearts of preteen girls in the United States and Western Europe, Barbie went to Asia. When Mattel first introduced her to Japan in 1979, the toy manufacturer had to make some changes to the all-American doll. Her face was too sophisticated and her makeup too heavy for Japanese tastes, so Barbie acquired a more wide-eyed, innocent look. Encouraged by Barbie's global successes, Mattel is now getting ready to launch Barbie in Argentina, Venezuela, Portugal, and thirty-one other countries.

Barbie is aging well. She is the most successful brand-name toy ever sold, and her appeal spans generations. In this era of computer games and high-tech toys, a doll from the 1950s still accounts for over 35 percent of Mattel's sales.

■ ■ ■ ■

3

■ ■ ■ ■ ■ ■ ■ ■ ■ ■ ■

Perhaps the most important characteristic of American business is the freedom of individuals to start a business, to work for a business, to buy or sell ownership shares in a business, and to sell a business outright. Within certain limits imposed mainly to ensure public safety, the owners of a business can produce any legal good or service they choose and attempt to sell it at the price they set. This system of business, in which individuals decide what to produce, how to produce it, and at what price to sell it, is called **free enterprise**. It is rooted in our traditional and constitutional right to own property.

Our free-enterprise system ensures, for example, that Mattel can introduce other Barbie-related products, license the Barbie name for other companies to use, change the doll's price and the method of distribution, and attempt to produce and market Barbie in other countries. Our system also gives executives the right to manage the company, compete with other toy makers, and distribute earnings to stockholders who share in the success of the company. Finally, our system allows customers the right to choose between Mattel's products and those produced by competitors.

free enterprise the system of business in which individuals are free to decide what to produce, how to produce it, and at what price to sell it

An appetite for free enterprise. These entrepreneurs (former Blockbuster executives) started Boston Chicken just a few years ago. They believe in providing their managers with information and technology that allows most decisions to be made at the store level, not at corporate headquarters.

Competition like that between Mattel and other toy manufacturers is a necessary and an extremely important by-product of free enterprise. Because many individuals and groups can open businesses, there are usually a number of firms offering similar products. But a potential customer may want only one such product. Each of the firms offering similar products must therefore try to convince the potential customer to buy its product rather than a similar item made by someone else. In other words, these firms must compete with each other for sales. Business **competition**, then, is essentially a rivalry among businesses for sales to potential customers. In free enterprise, competition works to ensure the efficient and effective operation of American business. Competition also ensures that a firm will survive only if it serves its customers well.

competition   a rivalry among businesses for sales to potential customers

In the next section we begin with a definition of business. We also discuss why a business must be organized, satisfy needs, and earn a profit.

■■ BUSINESS: A DEFINITION

business   the organized effort of individuals to produce and sell, for a profit, the goods and services that satisfy society's needs

LEARNING OBJECTIVE 1
Define *business* and identify potential risks and rewards.

Business is the organized effort of individuals to produce and sell, for a profit, the goods and services that satisfy society's needs. The general term *business* refers to all such efforts within a society (as in "American business") or within an industry (as in "the steel business"). However, *a business* is a particular organization, such as American Airlines, Inc., or Sunnyside Country Store & Gas Pumps, Inc. To be successful, a business must be organized and satisfy needs.

The Organized Effort of Individuals

No person or group of people actually organized American business as we know it today. Rather, over the years individuals have organized their own particular businesses for their own particular reasons. All these individual businesses have given rise to what we call American business.

entrepreneur   a person who risks time, effort, and money to start and operate a business

A person who risks his or her time, effort, and money to start and operate a business is called an **entrepreneur.** To organize a business, an entrepreneur must combine four kinds of resources: material, human, financial, and informational. *Material* resources include the raw materials used in manufacturing processes, as well as buildings and machinery. *Human* resources are the people who furnish their labor to the business in return for wages. The *financial* resource is the money required to pay employees, purchase materials, and generally keep the business operating. And *information* is the resource that tells the managers of the business how effectively the other resources are being combined and used (see Figure 1.1).

Today, businesses are usually classified as one of three specific types. *Manufacturing businesses* are organized to process various materials into tangible goods, such as delivery trucks or towels. *Service businesses* produce services, such as haircuts or legal advice. And some firms—called *marketing middlemen*—are organized to buy the goods produced by manufacturers and then resell them. For example, Sony Corp. is a manufacturer that produces stereo equipment, among other things. These products may be sold to a marketing middleman such as Kmart Corp., which then resells them to

FIGURE 1.1
Combining Resources
A business must effectively combine all four resources to be successful.

consumers   individuals who purchase goods or services for their own personal use rather than to resell or to use in producing goods and services that will be sold

consumers in its retail stores. **Consumers** are individuals who purchase goods or services for their own personal use rather than to resell or to use them in producing other goods and services that will be sold.

Satisfying Needs

The ultimate objective of every firm must be to satisfy the needs of its customers. People generally don't buy goods and services simply to own them; they buy products to satisfy particular needs. People rarely buy an automobile solely to store it in a garage; they do, however, buy automobiles to satisfy their need for transportation. Some of us may feel that this need is best satisfied by an air-conditioned BMW with stereo compact-disc player, automatic transmission, power seats and windows, and remote-control side mirrors. Others may believe that a Ford Escort with a stick shift and an AM radio will do just fine. Both products are available to those who want them, along with a wide variety of other products that satisfy the need for transportation.

When firms lose sight of their customers' needs, they are likely to find the going rough. This is especially true for firms involved in international trade when they are not sure who their customers are or what their customers want. But when the businesses that produce and sell goods and services understand their customers' needs and work to satisfy those needs, they are usually successful. Arkansas-based Wal-Mart Stores, Inc., provides the products its customers want and offers excellent prices. This highly successful discount-store organization continues to expand throughout the United States.

Business Profit

In the course of normal operations, a business receives money (sales revenue) from its customers in exchange for goods or services. It must also pay out money to cover the various expenses involved in doing business. If the firm's sales revenue is greater than its expenses, it has earned a profit. More specifically, as shown in Figure 1.2, **profit** is what remains after all business expenses have been deducted from sales revenue. (A negative profit, which results when a firm's expenses are greater than its sales revenue, is called a *loss*.)

profit   what remains after all business expenses have been deducted from sales revenue

The profit earned by a business becomes the property of its owners. So in one sense profit is the return, or reward, that business owners receive for producing goods and services that consumers want.

FIGURE 1.2
The Relationship Between Sales Revenue and Profit
Profit is what remains after all business expenses have been deducted from sales revenue.

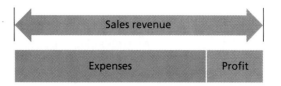

Sales revenue

Expenses

Profit

Profit is also the payment that business owners receive for assuming the considerable risks of ownership. One of these is the risk of not being paid. Everyone else—employees, suppliers, and lenders—must be paid before the owners. And if there is no profit, there can be *no* payments to owners. A second risk that owners run is the risk of losing whatever they have put into the business. A business that cannot earn a profit is very likely to fail, in which case the owners lose whatever money, effort, and time they have invested.

■■ WHY STUDY BUSINESS?

LEARNING OBJECTIVE 2
Describe the important reasons for studying business.

Most people take American business for granted. And yet there are at least three reasons why you should study business.

To Be a Better-Informed Consumer and Investor

The world of business surrounds you. You cannot buy a home from a building contractor, a new Trans Am from the local Pontiac dealer, or a Black & Decker electric sander at the Home Depot without entering a business transaction. These and thousands of similar transactions describe the true nature of our American business system. (Remember, satisfying society's needs is

Hard at work at home. Many people start businesses in their homes. A number of these home-based businesses remain there rather than relocating to commercial buildings.

one part of the definition of business presented earlier in this chapter.) By studying our business system, you become a more fully informed consumer, which means that you will be able to make more intelligent buying decisions and spend your money more wisely. This same basic understanding of business will also make you a better-informed investor.

To Be a Better Employee

Most consumers and investors are also workers. Today, people are looking for a rewarding career that will provide personal satisfaction and the opportunity to be self-sufficient. The information contained in this text will help you select that "ideal" career. Most workers in the United States work for private enterprise, but there are also employment opportunities with the government and not-for-profit organizations. Each of these areas is discussed in more detail in other chapters of this text.

After you select your career, you must obtain the skills required to be successful. Today's employers are looking for job applicants who can *do something,* not just fill a spot on an organizational chart. Employers expect you to have both the technical skills needed to accomplish a specific task and the ability to work well with many types of people in a culturally diverse work force (see Change in the Workplace). These skills, plus a working knowledge of our business system, can give you an inside edge when you compete against other job applicants.

To Start Your Own Business

Some people prefer to work for themselves, and they open their own businesses. To be successful, business owners must possess many of the same skills that successful employees have. And they must be willing to work hard for long hours. Unfortunately, many small-business firms fail. Seventy percent of new businesses fail within the first five years. The material in Chapter 5 and selected topics and examples throughout this text will help you decide whether you want to open a small business.

■■ TYPES OF ECONOMIC SYSTEMS

LEARNING OBJECTIVE 3
Understand the two types of economic systems, capitalism and planned economy.

economics   the study of how wealth is created and distributed

economy   the system through which a society answers the two economic questions—how wealth is created and distributed

Economics is the study of how wealth is created and distributed. By *wealth* we mean anything of value, including the products produced and sold by business. *How wealth is distributed* simply means "who gets what." The way in which people deal with these two issues determines the kind of economic system, or **economy,** that a society has. In the United States, our particular answers have provided us with an economy that is based on capitalism, or private enterprise.

A nation's economic system—capitalistic or planned—significantly affects all the economic activities of its individuals and organizations. This far-reaching impact becomes more apparent when we consider that a country's economic system provides answers to four basic economic questions.

■ ■ ■ ■ CHANGE IN THE WORKPLACE

Workplace Diversity: Benefits for People and Businesses

"We tried everything for so many years, but our business did not perform better until we had a diverse management group." This remark, made recently by the CEO of a major chemical manufacturing company, sums up the growing conviction that workplace diversity is a vital and positive force. In the past, corporate officers and managers approached diversity as a legal responsibility. Are we complying with affirmative action? Have we hired enough women? Are we actively recruiting minorities? Today, companies are seeking out "work force diversity managers" and making "diversity and cultural sensitivity training" as common in the workplace as coffee breaks. No longer just a legal or moral imperative, diversity is an important issue in building effective business strategies.

For those organizations that value the strengths of different cultures, diversity can lead to better morale, better quality products, better customer service, and better job performance. In a society as pluralistic as the United States, companies with the broadest appeal will be the most successful. It makes sense, for example, that a multicultural marketplace will respond more positively to a multicultural sales force. In addition, recent academic studies suggest that diversity enhances performance and productivity. Heterogeneous groups approach situations from a wider range of perspectives and produce more innovative solutions to problems. Factories with

diverse work forces are likely to be highly productive. Companies that market products worldwide reap the benefits of being knowledgeable about and sensitive to cultural differences. When an organization's representatives are trying to close a sale in Japan, it helps if they are aware that there are sixteen ways to say "no" in Japanese!

Prominent companies like Avon, Burger King, Levi Strauss, Xerox, and AT&T lead the way in corporate commitment to work force diversity, even in the face of layoffs and restructuring. Many other organizations are finding diversity a plus. IBM's director of work force diversity asserted that "it is important for our customers to look inside and see people like them. If they can't, it seems to me that the prospect of them becoming or staying our customers diminishes." Responding to research revealing that its lack of internal diversity meant it was not well-positioned to penetrate important cultural markets, Prudential Insurance Co. of America established a Managing Diversity Program. When U.S. Bancorp, a financial services corporation, resolved to improve service to its Pacific Rim customers, company executives recognized that it was essential for employees to become more sensitive to the cultural differences they would be encountering. Experts continue to insist that effective workplace diversity is a key to success in the twenty-first century. If everyone in business thinks and acts the same, they warn, businesses will die.

1. What goods and services—and how much of each—will be produced?
2. How will these goods and services be produced?
3. For whom will these goods and services be produced?
4. Who owns and who controls the major **factors of production:**

factors of production natural resources, labor, capital, and entrepreneurship

- *Natural resources*—elements in their natural state that can be used in production such as land, water, forests, and minerals.
- *Labor*—human resources such as managers and workers.
- *Capital*—facilities, equipment, machinery, and money used in the operation of organizations.
- *Entrepreneurship*—the willingness to take risks and the knowledge and ability to use the other factors of production efficiently.

Capitalism

capitalism an economic system in which individuals own and operate the majority of businesses that provide goods and services

Capitalism is an economic system in which individuals own and operate the majority of businesses that provide goods and services. Capitalism—our economic system—stems from the theories of the eighteenth-century economist Adam Smith, a Scot. In his 1776 book *The Wealth of Nations,* Smith argued that a society's interests are best served when the individuals within that society are allowed to pursue their own self-interest.

> Every individual endeavors to employ his capital so that its produce may be of greatest value. . . . And he is in this led by an INVISIBLE HAND to promote an end which was no part of his intention. By pursuing his own interest he frequently promotes that of Society more effectually than when he really intends to promote it.

In other words, Smith believed that each person should be allowed to work toward his or her *own* economic gain, without interference from government. And, according to Smith, society would benefit most when there was the least interference with the individual's pursuit of economic self-interest. Government should therefore leave the economy to its citizens. The French term *laissez faire* describes Smith's capitalistic system and implies that there shall be no interference in the economy. Loosely translated, it means "let them do" (as they see fit).

Smith's laissez-faire capitalism is based on four fundamental issues. First, Smith argued that the creation of wealth (including products) is properly the concern of private individuals, not of government. Hence the resources that are used to create wealth must be owned by private individuals. Second, Smith argued that the owners of resources should be free to determine how these resources are used. They should also be free to enjoy the income and other benefits they might derive from the ownership of these resources. Third, Smith contended that economic freedom ensures the existence of competitive markets that allow sellers and buyers to enter and exit as they choose. This freedom to enter or leave a market at will has given rise to the name **free-market economy** for the capitalism that Smith described. Finally, in Smith's view, the role of government should be limited to providing defense against foreign enemies, ensuring internal order, and furnishing public works and education. With regard to the economy, government should act only as rule maker and umpire.

free-market economy an economic system in which individuals and firms are free to enter and leave markets at will

Capitalism in the United States

Our economic system is rooted in the laissez-faire capitalism of Adam Smith. However, our real-world economy is not as "laissez faire" as Smith

mixed economy an economy that exhibits elements of both capitalism and socialism

would have liked, because government participates as more than umpire and rule maker. Ours is, in fact, a **mixed economy,** one that exhibits elements of both capitalism and socialism.

In today's economy, the four basic economic questions are answered through the interaction of the following three groups:

1. *Households,* made up of consumers who seek the best value for their money and the best prices for the economic resources they own

2. *Businesses,* which seek to make profits through the sale of products

3. *Federal, state, and local governments,* which seek to promote public safety and welfare and to serve the public interest

The interactions among these three groups are shown in Figure 1.3.

Households Households are both consumers of goods and services, and owners of some of the factors of production. As *resource owners,* the members of households provide businesses with the means of production. In return, businesses pay wages, rent, and interest, which households receive as income.

As *consumers,* household members use their income to purchase the goods and services produced by business. Today almost two-thirds of our nation's total production consists of **consumer products:** goods and services purchased by individuals for personal consumption. (The remaining

consumer products goods and services purchased by individuals for personal consumption

FIGURE 1.3
The Circular Flow in Our Modified Capitalist System
Our economic system is guided by the interplay of buyers and sellers, with the role of government being taken into account.

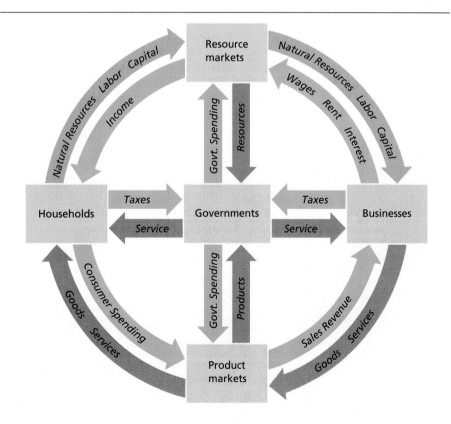

one-third is purchased by businesses and governments.) This means that consumers, as a group, are the biggest customer of American business.

Businesses   Like households, businesses are engaged in two exchanges. They exchange money for resources and use these resources to produce goods and services. Then they exchange their products for sales revenue. This sales revenue, in turn, is exchanged for additional resources, which are used to produce and sell more products. So the circular flow of Figure 1.3 is continuous. Businesses pay *wages, rent, and interest,* which become *household income,* which becomes *consumer spending,* which becomes *sales revenue,* which again becomes *wages, rent, and interest.* And so on.

Along the way, of course, business owners would like to remove something from the circular flow in the form of profits. And households try to retain some income as savings. But are profits and savings really removed from the flow? Usually not! When the economy is running smoothly, households are willing to invest their savings in businesses. They can do so directly, by buying ownership shares in businesses or by lending money to businesses. They can also invest indirectly, by placing their savings in bank accounts; banks then invest these savings as part of their normal business operations. In either case, savings usually find their way back into the circular flow.

When business profits are distributed to business owners, these profits become household income. (Business owners are, after all, members of households.) And, as we saw, household income is retained in the circular flow as either consumer spending or invested savings. So business profits, too, are retained in the business system, and the circular flow is complete. How, then, does government fit in?

Governments   The framers of our Constitution desired as little government interference with business as possible. At the same time, the Preamble to the Constitution sets forth the responsibility of government to protect and promote the public welfare. Local, state, and federal governments discharge this responsibility through regulation and the provision of services. Government regulation of business has already been mentioned; specific regulations are discussed in detail in various chapters of this book. In addition, governments provide numerous services that are considered important but either (1) would not be produced by private firms in a free-enterprise system or (2) would be produced only for those who could afford them. Among these services are

- National defense
- Police and fire protection
- Welfare payments and retirement income
- Education
- National and state parks, forests, and wilderness areas
- Roads and highways
- Disaster relief
- Unemployment insurance programs

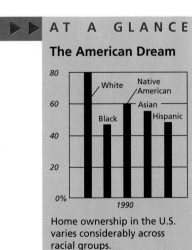

▶▶ AT A GLANCE

The American Dream

Home ownership in the U.S. varies considerably across racial groups.

Source: *U.S. Department of Commerce, Bureau of the Census*

■ ■ ■ ■ ETHICAL CHALLENGES

Is Always Winning Always Ethical?

General Electric Company is the fifth-largest industrial manufacturer in the United States. Its revenues total $60.5 billion, and over 200,000 GE employees in about 100 countries around the world manufacture everything from jet engines and locomotives to lightbulbs. While other prominent firms such as Sears and IBM struggle, GE is prospering. Industry experts aren't questioning the company's genius for making a profit; however, they *are* questioning whether or not it operates according to its own CEO's published declaration, "Integrity is clearly the most important value." A recent study conducted by the Project on Government Oversight, for example, reveals that with sixteen criminal and civil convictions since 1990, GE has been involved in more instances of Pentagon fraud than any other military contractor.

In 1985 GE pleaded guilty to fraud for overcharging the U.S. Air Force on a Minuteman missile contract. In 1989 the company settled four civil suits alleging that GE, by issuing faulty timecards, cheated the government out of millions of dollars. In 1990, GE was convicted of defrauding the Defense Department by overcharging the army for a battlefield computer system. In 1992 the company pleaded guilty to defrauding the Pentagon of over $30 million in the sale of military jet engines. Recently the company faced charges that it conspired with the diamond giant DeBeers to fix the price of industrial diamonds. In addition, the Justice Department, the Federal Avi-

ation Administration, and the Defense Department are all investigating a whistle blower's accusation that GE ignored warnings about electrical problems that could jeopardize aircraft engine safety worldwide, including engines on *Air Force One.* At GE, the cumulative effect of all of these transgressions, whether proven or not, is high turnover, low morale, and the growing public conviction that the company sacrifices ethical operating procedures in pursuit of profits.

Many business analysts believe much of the blame for GE's problems rests on the shoulders of its CEO, Jack Welch. Although he is one of the most admired corporate officers in America, Welch is often reproached for failing to articulate a clear set of corporate values. What he has made clear, insist his critics, is the importance of being number one. Instead of providing GE's management with a framework of organizational ethics goals, he has conveyed the message that, no matter the cost, winning is paramount.

Welch argues that GE's standards are among the most ethical in American industry and denies that his emphasis on winning encourages employees to cheat or cut corners to achieve corporate goals. He defends his aggressive methods by asking how, in the race to be the most successful, he can tell his organization to run slower. Here is the advice from those most concerned about improving General Electric's business ethics image: GE doesn't have to run slower, just better.

- Medical research
- Development of purity standards for foods and drugs

This list could go on and on, but the point is clear: governments are deeply involved in business life. To pay for all these services, governments collect a variety of taxes from households (such as personal income taxes and sales taxes) and from businesses (corporate income taxes).

Figure 1.3 shows this exchange of taxes for government services. It also shows government spending of tax dollars for resources and products required to provide these services. In other words, governments, too, return their incomes to the business system through the resource and product markets.

Actually, with government included, our circular flow looks more like a combination of several flows. And in reality it is. The important point is that, together, the various flows make up a single unit—a complete economic system that effectively provides answers to the basic economic questions. Simply put, the system works.

Planned Economies

Before we discuss how to measure a nation's economic performance, we look quickly here at two other economic systems that contrast sharply with capitalism. These systems are sometimes called **planned economies,** because the answers to the four basic economic questions are determined, at least to some degree, through centralized government planning.

planned economy an economy in which the answers to the basic economic questions are determined, to some degree, through centralized government planning

Socialism   In a *socialist* economy, the key industries are owned and controlled by the government. Such industries usually include transportation, utilities, communications, and those producing important materials such as steel. (Banking, too, is considered extremely important to a nation's economy. In France, the major banks are *nationalized*, or

Consumer goods shortage. Citizens in planned economies sometimes experience shortages of products, as occurred in this store in Havana, Cuba.

transferred to government control.) Land and raw materials may also be the property of the state in a socialist economy. Depending on the country, private ownership of real property (such as land and buildings) and smaller or less vital businesses is permitted to varying degrees. People usually may choose their own occupations, but many work in state-owned industries.

What to produce and how to produce it are determined in accordance with national goals, which are based on projected needs and the availability of resources—at least for government-owned industries. The distribution of goods and services—who gets what—is also controlled by the state to the extent that it controls rents and wages. Among the professed aims of socialist countries are the equitable distribution of income, the elimination of poverty, the distribution of social services (such as medical care) to all who need them, smooth economic growth, and elimination of the economic waste that supposedly accompanies capitalistic competition.

Britain, France, Sweden, and India are democratic countries whose economies include a very visible degree of socialism. Other, more authoritarian countries may actually have socialist economies; however, we tend to think of them as communist because of their almost total lack of freedom.

Communism If Adam Smith was the father of capitalism, Karl Marx was the father of communism. In his writings (during the mid-nineteenth century), Marx advocated a classless society whose citizens together owned all economic resources. He believed that such a society would come about as the result of a class struggle between the owners of capital and the workers they had exploited. All workers would then contribute to this *communist* society according to their ability and would receive benefits according to their need.

The People's Republic of China and Cuba are generally considered to have communist economies. Almost all economic resources are owned by the government in these countries. The basic economic questions are answered through centralized state planning, which sets prices and wages as well. In this planning, the needs of the state generally outweigh the needs of individual citizens. Emphasis is placed on the production of goods the government needs rather than on the products that consumers might want, so there are frequent shortages of consumer goods. Workers have little choice of jobs, but special skills or talents seem to be rewarded with special privileges. Various groups of professionals (bureaucrats, university professors, and athletes, for example) fare much better than, say, factory workers.

Today, the so-called communist economies thus hardly conform to Marx's vision of communism. Rather they seem to practice a strictly controlled kind of socialism. They even allow a bit of free enterprise here and there. Like all real economies, these economies are neither pure nor static. Every operating economy is a constantly changing mixture of various idealized economic systems. Some, like ours, evolve slowly. Others change more quickly, through either evolution or revolution. And, over many years, a nation may move first in one direction and then in the opposite direction. It is impossible to say whether any real economy will ever closely resemble Marx's communism.

■■ MEASURING ECONOMIC PERFORMANCE

LEARNING OBJECTIVE 4
Identify the ways to measure
economic performance.

productivity   the average level
of output per worker per hour

One way to measure a nation's economic performance is to assess its productivity. **Productivity** is the average level of output per worker per hour. It is a measure of the efficiency of production for an economic system. An increase in productivity results in economic growth because a larger number of goods and services are produced by a given labor force. Although U.S. workers produce more than many workers in other countries, the rate of growth in productivity has declined in the United States and has been surpassed in recent years by workers in Japan and the United Kingdom. We discuss productivity in detail in Chapter 7.

gross national product (GNP)
the total dollar value of all
goods and services produced by
all citizens of a country for a
given time period

A general measure of a country's national economic output is called its gross national product. **Gross national product (GNP)** is the total dollar value of all goods and services produced by *all* citizens of a country for a given time period. In 1993, the U.S. gross national product was $6.4 trillion. Comparing the GNP for several different time periods allows observers to determine the extent to which a country is experiencing economic growth.

To make accurate comparisons of GNP figures for two different years, we must adjust the figures for inflation, that is, higher price levels. By using inflation-adjusted figures, we are able to measure real gross national product. **Real gross national product** is the total dollar value, adjusted for price increases, of all goods and services produced by all citizens of a country during a given time period. Comparisons of real gross national product information allow us to measure accurately the differences in output from one time period to another. Figure 1.4 depicts the gross national product of the United States in current dollars and in constant 1982 dollars. The real gross national product figures are represented in the adjusted figures. Note that between 1978 and 1994 America's real gross national product grew from $3.1 trillion to $4.5 trillion.

real gross national product
the total dollar value, adjusted
for price increases, of all goods
and services produced by all
citizens of a country during a
given time period

gross domestic product
(GDP)   the total dollar value
of all goods and services
produced by citizens physically
located within a country

Economists also often refer to another popular economic measure— gross domestic product. **Gross domestic product (GDP)** is the total dollar value of all goods and services produced by citizens physically located within a country. The definition of GDP is very similar to the definition of gross national product, but with one exception. GDP excludes production amounts for U.S. citizens working abroad in foreign nations. For 1993, the gross domestic product for the United States was $6.39 trillion, a figure slightly lower than the GNP ($6.40 trillion) for the same year.

■■ TYPES OF COMPETITION

LEARNING OBJECTIVE 5
Outline the four types of
competition.

As we have noted, a free-market system implies competition among sellers of products and resources. Economists recognize four different degrees of competition, ranging from ideal, complete competition to no competition at all. These are pure competition, monopolistic competition, oligopoly, and monopoly.

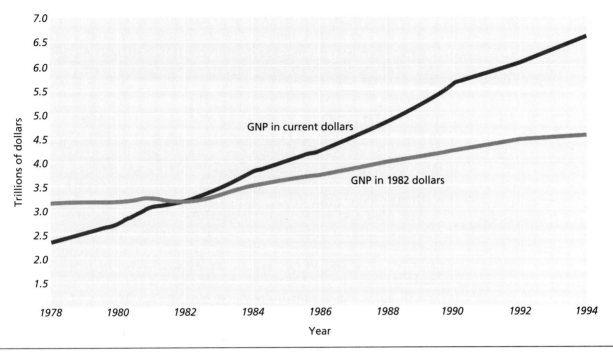

FIGURE 1.4 **GNP in Current Dollars and in Inflation-adjusted Dollars**
The changes in real gross national product from one time period to another can be
used to measure economic performance. *(Source:* Survey of Current Business, *July
1994;* Business Statistics 1963–91; *U.S. Department of Commerce, Bureau of Economic
Analysis)*

Pure Competition

pure competition the market
situation in which there are
many buyers and sellers of a
product, and no single buyer or
seller is powerful enough to
affect the price of that product

Pure (or perfect) competition is the complete form of competition. **Pure
competition** is the market situation in which there are many buyers and
sellers of a product, and no single buyer or seller is powerful enough to affect
the price of that product. Note that this definition includes several important ideas. First, we are discussing the market for a single product—say,
bushels of wheat. (The definition also applies to markets for resources, but
we'll limit our discussion here to product markets.) Second, all sellers offer
essentially the same product for sale; a buyer would be just as satisfied with
seller *A*'s wheat as with that offered by seller *B* or seller *Z*. Third, all buyers
and sellers know everything there is to know about the market (including, in
our example, the prices that all sellers are asking for their wheat). And
fourth, the market is not affected by the actions of any one buyer or seller.

When pure competition exists, every seller should ask the same price
that every other seller is asking. Why? Because if one seller wanted 50 cents
more per bushel of wheat than all the others, that seller would not be able
to sell a single bushel. Buyers could—and would—do better by purchasing
wheat from the competition. On the other hand, a firm willing to sell below
the going price would sell all its wheat quickly. But that seller would lose
sales revenue (and profit), because buyers are actually willing to pay more.

In pure competition, then, sellers—and buyers as well—must accept the going price. But who or what determines this price? Actually, everyone does. The price of each product is determined by the actions of *all buyers and all sellers together*, through the forces of supply and demand. It is this interaction of buyers and sellers, working individually for their own best interests, that Adam Smith referred to as the "invisible hand" of competition. Let us see how it operates.

The Basics of Supply and Demand   The **supply** of a particular product is the quantity of the product that producers are willing to sell at each of various prices. Producers are rational people, so we would expect them to offer more of a product for sale at higher prices and to offer less of the product at lower prices, as illustrated in Figure 1.5.

supply   the quantity of a product that producers are willing to sell at each of various prices

The **demand** for a particular product is the quantity that buyers are willing to purchase at each of various prices. Buyers, too, are usually rational, so we would expect them—as a group—to buy more of a product when its price is low and to buy less of the product when its price is high, as depicted in Figure 1.5. This is exactly what happens when the price of wheat rises dramatically. People buy other grains or do without and reduce their purchases of wheat. They buy more wheat only when the price drops.

demand   the quantity of a product that buyers are willing to purchase at each of various prices

The Equilibrium, or Market, Price   There is always one certain price at which the demanded quantity of a product is exactly equal to the produced quantity of that product. Suppose producers are willing to *supply* 2 million bushels of wheat at a price of $5 per bushel, and buyers are willing to *purchase* 2 million bushels at a price of $5 per bushel. In other words, supply and demand are in balance, or *in equilibrium,* at the price of $5. Economists call this price the *equilibrium price* or *market price.* Under pure competition, the **market price** of any product is the price at which the quantity demanded is exactly equal to the quantity supplied. If suppliers produce 2 million bushels, then no one who is willing to pay $5 per bushel will have to

market price   in pure competition, the price at which the quantity demanded is exactly equal to the quantity supplied

FIGURE 1.5
Supply Curve and Demand Curve
The intersection of a supply curve and a demand curve indicates a single price and quantity at which suppliers will sell products and buyers will purchase them.

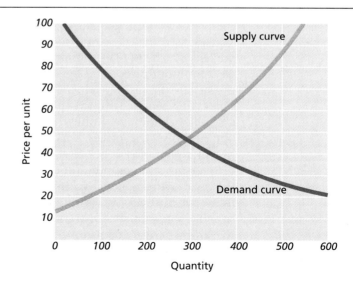

go without wheat, and no producer who is willing to sell at $5 per bushel will be stuck with unsold wheat.

In theory and in the real world, market prices are affected by anything that affects supply and demand. The *demand* for wheat, for example, might change if researchers suddenly discovered that it offered a previously unknown health benefit. Then users would demand more wheat at every price. Or, the *supply* of wheat might change if new technology permitted the production of greater quantities of wheat from the same amount of acreage. In that case, producers would be willing to supply more wheat at each price. Either of these changes would result in a new market price. Other changes that can affect competitive prices are shifts in buyer tastes, the development of new products that satisfy old needs, and fluctuations in income due to inflation or recession.

Monopolistic Competition

monopolistic competition a market situation in which there are many buyers along with a relatively large number of sellers who differentiate their products from the products of competitors

Pure competition is quite rare in today's world. Some specific markets (such as auctions of farm products) may come close, but no real market totally exhibits perfect competition. Many real markets, however, are examples of monopolistic competition. **Monopolistic competition** is a market situation in which there are many buyers along with a relatively large number of sellers. (Today, monopolistic competition is characterized by fewer sellers than would be found in pure competition, but enough sellers to ensure a highly competitive market.) The various products available in a monopolistically competitive market are very similar in nature, and they are all intended to satisfy the same need. However, each seller attempts to make its product somewhat different from the others by providing unique product features— an attention-getting brand name, unique packaging, or services such as free delivery or a "lifetime" warranty. For example, Hanes originally differentiated L'eggs pantyhose from numerous competing brands through unique branding and packaging.

Product differentiation is a fact of life for the producers of many consumer goods, from soaps to clothing to personal computers. An individual producer like Hanes sees what looks like a mob of competitors, all trying to chip away at its market. By differentiating each of its products from all similar products, the producer obtains some limited control over the market price of its product. For example, the prices of various brands of pantyhose vary. Under pure competition, the price of all pantyhose brands would simply be the equilibrium price of pantyhose products.

Oligopoly

oligopoly a market situation (or industry) in which there are few sellers

An **oligopoly** is a market situation (or industry) in which there are few sellers. Generally these sellers are quite large, and sizable investments are required to enter into their market. For this reason, oligopolistic industries tend to remain oligopolistic. Examples of oligopolies are the American automobile, industrial chemical, and farm implement industries.

Because there are few sellers in an oligopoly, each seller has considerable control over price. At the same time, the market actions of each seller can have a strong effect on competitors' sales. If General Motors, for example, reduces its automobile prices, Ford, Chrysler, and even foreign manufacturers usually do the same to retain their market shares. If one firm raises its price, the others may wait and watch the market for a while, to see whether their lower price tag gives them a competitive advantage, and then eventually follow suit. As a result, similar products eventually have similar prices. In the absence of much price competition, product differentiation becomes the major competitive weapon; this is very evident in the advertising of the major American auto manufacturers. For example, when General Motors began offering low-interest financing for all of its cars, Ford and Chrysler also launched competitive financing deals.

Monopoly

monopoly a market (or industry) with only one seller

A **monopoly** is a market (or industry) with only one seller. Because only one firm is the supplier of a product, it has complete control over price. However, no firm can set its price at some astronomical figure just because there is no competition; the firm would soon find it had no sales revenue, either. Instead, the firm in a monopoly position must consider the demand for its product and set the price at the most profitable level.

natural monopoly an industry requiring huge investments in capital and within which duplication of facilities would be wasteful and thus not in the public interest

The best examples of monopolies in the United States are public utilities, such as electric power companies. Each utility firm operates in a **natural monopoly,** an industry that requires a huge investment in capital and within which any duplication of facilities would be wasteful. Natural monopolies are permitted to exist because the public interest is best served by their existence, but they operate under the scrutiny and control of various state and federal agencies.

A legal monopoly—sometimes referred to as a *limited monopoly*—is created when the federal government issues a copyright, patent, and trademark. A copyright, patent, or trademark exists for a specific period of time and can be used to protect the owners of written materials, ideas, or product brands from unauthorized use by competitors that have not shared in the time, effort, and expense required for their development.

Except for natural monopolies and monopolies created by copyrights, patents, and trademarks, federal laws prohibit both monopolies and attempts to form monopolies. A recent amendment to the Sherman Antitrust Act of 1890 made any such attempt a criminal offense, and the Clayton Antitrust Act of 1914 prohibited a number of specific actions that could lead to monopoly. The goal of these and other antitrust laws is to ensure the competitive environment of American business and thereby to protect American consumers.

■■ THE DEVELOPMENT OF AMERICAN BUSINESS

American business and the free-enterprise system developed together with the nation itself. All three have their roots in the knowledge, skills, and values that were brought to this country by the earliest settlers. Refer to Figure 1.6 for an overall view of the relationship between our history, the development of our business system, and some major inventions that influenced them both.

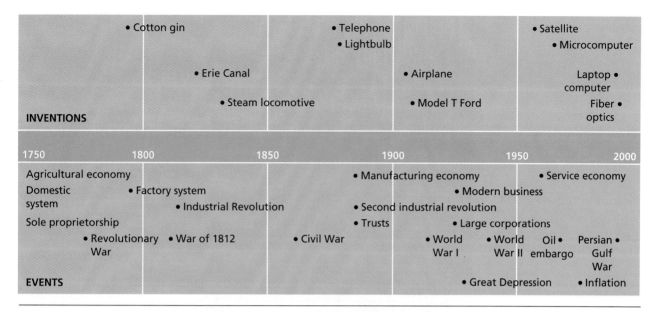

FIGURE 1.6   Time Line of American Business
Notice that invention and innovation naturally led to changes in transportation. This trend in turn caused a shift to more of a manufacturing economy.

The Colonial Period

LEARNING OBJECTIVE 6
Summarize the development of America's business system.

The first settlers in the New World were concerned mainly with providing themselves with basic necessities—food, clothing, and shelter. Almost all families lived on farms, and the entire family worked at the business of surviving.

The colonists did indeed survive, and eventually they were able to produce more than they consumed. They used their surplus for trading, mainly by barter, among themselves and with the English trading ships that called at the colonies. **Barter** is a system of exchange in which goods or services are traded directly for other goods and/or services—without using money. As this trade increased, small-scale business enterprises began to appear. Most of these businesses produced farm products, primarily rice and tobacco for export. Other industries that had been founded by 1700 were shipbuilding, lumbering, fur trading, rum manufacturing, and fishing. These industries also produced mainly for export. International trade with England grew, but British trade policies heavily favored British merchants.

barter   a system of exchange in which goods or services are traded directly for other goods and/or services—without using money

As late as the Revolutionary War period, 90 percent of the population lived on farms and were engaged primarily in activities to meet their own needs. Some were able to use their skills and their excess time to work under the domestic system of production. The **domestic system** was a method of manufacturing in which an entrepreneur distributed raw materials to various homes, where families would process them into finished goods. The goods were then offered for sale by the merchant entrepreneur.

domestic system   a method of manufacturing in which an entrepreneur distributed raw materials to various homes, where families would process them into finished goods to be offered for sale by the merchant entrepreneur

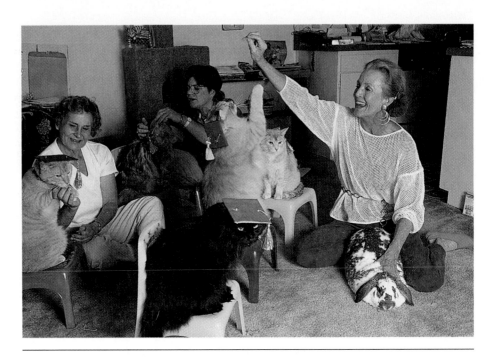

Serving all kinds of customers. Much of the growth in American business today is through service businesses. This service business, located in Woodland Hills, California, offers cat training.

During and after the Revolutionary War, Americans began to produce a wider variety of goods, including gunpowder, tools, hats, and cutlery. Later, after the War of 1812, domestic manufacturing and trade became much more important as trade with England and other nations declined.

The Industrial Revolution

In 1790 a young English apprentice mechanic named Samuel Slater decided to sail to America. At this time, to protect the English textile industry, British law forbade the export of machinery, technology, and skilled workers. To get around the law, Slater painstakingly memorized the plans for Arkwright's water-powered spinning machine and left England disguised as a farmer. A year later he set up a textile factory in Pawtucket, Rhode Island, to spin raw cotton into thread. Slater's ingenuity resulted in America's first use of the **factory system** of manufacturing, in which all the materials, machinery, and workers required to manufacture a product are assembled in one place. The Industrial Revolution in America was born.

By 1814 Francis Cabot Lowell had established a factory in Waltham, Massachusetts, to spin, weave, and bleach cotton all under one roof. He organized the various manufacturing steps into one uninterrupted sequence, hired professional managers, and was able to produce 30 miles of cloth each day! In doing so, Lowell seems to have used a manufacturing technique called specialization. **Specialization** is the separation of a manu-

factory system a system of manufacturing in which all the materials, machinery, and workers required to manufacture a product are assembled in one place

specialization the separation of a manufacturing process into distinct tasks and the assignment of different tasks to different individuals

facturing process into distinct tasks and the assignment of different tasks to different individuals. The purpose of specialization is to increase the efficiency of industrial workers.

The three decades from 1820 to 1850 were the golden age of invention and innovation in machinery. The cotton gin of Eli Whitney greatly increased the supply of cotton for the textile industry. Elias Howe's sewing machine became available to convert materials into clothing. The agricultural machinery of John Deere and Cyrus McCormick revolutionized farm production.

At the same time, new means of transportation greatly expanded the domestic markets for American products. The Erie Canal was opened in the 1820s. Soon afterward, thanks to Robert Fulton's engine, steamboats could move upstream against the current and use the rivers as highways for hauling bulk goods. During the 1830s and 1840s, the railroads began to extend the existing transportation system to the West, carrying goods and people much farther than was possible by waterways alone. Between 1860 and 1880, the number of miles of railroad track tripled; by 1900 it had doubled again.[2]

Many business historians view the period from 1870 to 1900 as the second industrial revolution; certainly, many characteristics of our modern business system took form during these three decades. In this period, for example, the nation shifted from a farm economy to a manufacturing economy. The developing oil industry provided fuel for light, heat, and energy. Greatly increased immigration furnished labor for expanded production. New means of communication brought sophistication to banking and finance. During this time, the United States became not only an industrial giant but a leading world power as well.

Early Twentieth Century

Industrial growth and prosperity continued well into the twentieth century. Henry Ford's moving assembly line, which brought the work to the worker, refined the concept of specialization and spawned the mass production of consumer goods. By the 1920s the automobile industry had begun to influence the entire economy. The steel industry, which supplies materials to the auto industry, grew along with it. The oil and chemical industries grew just as fast and provided countless new synthetic products—novel ways to satisfy society's wants. And the emerging airplane and airline industries promised convenient and faster transportation.

Fundamental changes occurred in business ownership and management as well. The largest businesses were no longer owned by one individual; instead, ownership was in the hands of thousands of corporate shareholders who were willing to invest in—but not to operate—a business.

Certain modern marketing techniques are products of this era, too. Large corporations developed new methods of advertising and selling. Time payment plans made it possible for the average consumer to purchase costly durable goods such as automobiles, appliances, and furnishings. Advertisements counseled the public to "buy now and pay later." A higher standard of living was created for most people—but it was not to last.

The Great Depression

The Roaring Twenties ended with the sudden crash of the stock market in 1929 and the near collapse of the economy. The Great Depression that followed in the 1930s was a time of misery and human suffering. The unemployment rate varied between 16 and 25 percent in the years 1931 through 1939, and the value of goods and services produced in America fell by almost half. People lost their faith in business and its ability to satisfy the needs of society without government interference.

After the election of President Franklin D. Roosevelt, the federal government devised a number of programs to get the economy moving again. In implementing these programs, the government got deeply involved in business for the first time. Many business people opposed this intervention, but they reluctantly accepted the new government regulations.

Recovery and Beyond

The economy was on the road to recovery when World War II broke out in Europe in 1939. The need for vast quantities of war materials—first for our allies and then for the American military as well—spurred business activity and technological development. This rapid economic pace continued after the war, and the 1950s and 1960s witnessed both increasing production and a rising standard of living. **Standard of living** is a loose, subjective measure of how well off an individual or a society is, mainly in terms of want satisfaction through goods and services.

standard of living a loose, subjective measure of how well off an individual or a society is, mainly in terms of want satisfaction through goods and services

In the mid-1970s, however, a shortage of crude oil led to a new set of problems for business. Petroleum products supply most of the energy required to produce goods and services and to transport goods around the world. As the cost of petroleum products increased, a corresponding increase took place in the cost of energy and the cost of goods and services. The result was **inflation,** a general rise in the level of prices, at a rate well over 10 percent per year during the early 1980s. Interest rates also increased dramatically, so both businesses and consumers reduced their borrowing. Business profits fell as the consumer's purchasing power was eroded by inflation and high interest rates, and unemployment reached alarming levels. By the mid-1980s, many of these problem areas showed signs of improvement. Unfortunately, many managers now had something else to worry about—corporate mergers and takeovers. Also, a large number of bank failures, coupled with an increasing number of bankruptcies, again made people uneasy about our business system.

inflation a general rise in the level of prices

At the time of this writing, the U.S. economy does show some signs of improvement. Service businesses have become a dominant part of our economy, and we now devote more effort to the production of services than to the production of goods. Because well over half of the American work force is involved in service industries, ours is called a **service economy.** And American businesses are beginning to realize that to be successful, they must enter the global marketplace. In short, American firms must meet the needs not only of American consumers but also of foreign consumers. See Global Perspectives for a description of one American firm's misunderstanding about foreign consumers' needs. (Both our service economy and our place

service economy an economy in which the majority of the work force is involved in service industries and in which more effort is devoted to the production of services than to the production of goods

■ ■ ■ ■ GLOBAL PERSPECTIVES

EuroDisney: Cultural Realities Invade Fantasy Land

When Disney's first European theme park opened on a 4,800-acre site fifteen miles from Paris, France, the company hoped that Europeans would open their hearts and their wallets to the magic of Disney. After all, for over a decade, Tokyo Disneyland had been a phenomenal success, attracting 125 million visitors since opening. However, in its first full year of operation, EuroDisney lost $900 million. Said Disney's CEO Michael Eisner in response to the park's dismal performance, "We found out we weren't as smart as we thought we were."

Home to about 120 million more people than the United States, the European market seemed like the perfect place to plant a Disney attraction. Europeans flock to Disney's American parks and spend millions of dollars on merchandise like Mickey Mouse T-shirts and *Aladdin* tapes. The French Magic Kingdom incorporates European flavor and themes. Unfortunately for Disney, planners found that convincing the French to come to EuroDisney was much harder than translating "Sleeping Beauty" into "La Belle au Bois Dormant."

What went wrong? No one predicted that a European recession would keep visitors away or, when they did come, keep them from spending very much on park food and souvenirs. But EuroDisney's problems stem as much from cultural misunderstandings as from frugal tourists. French intellectuals branded Disney as a "culture contaminator," protesting its presence with signs demanding "Mickey Go Home." Labor groups protested the very strict employee dress code that prohibits facial hair and eye shadow. In a country where people drink wine with almost every meal, Disney banned alcohol in park restaurants. Standing in long lines for snacks and rides dismayed European visitors. Most Europeans eat lunch at the same time, and for them, lining up was an unpleasant reminder of World War II. Finally, traveling somewhere on an airplane and staying a while is the French idea of a real vacation; driving fifteen miles to an amusement park for a one-day outing is not.

Hoping to turn things around, EuroDisney is making some changes. The organization introduced seasonal pricing, mailed discount coupons to thousands of Parisians, initiated Supervalue hotel rates during the winter, and began offering lower-priced food items. And because Disney changed its alcohol policy, French visitors can now sip a glass of wine with their chicken fingers and pizza. Says EuroDisney's CEO, "We're learning about foreign culture—we're getting there." However, Disney is delaying indefinitely its plans to add an adjoining French MGM park, and Disney watchers should probably not look for a European Epcot Center any time soon.

in the global marketplace are discussed more fully later in the text.) Finally, politicians say that economic recovery is just around the corner. Only time will tell if their predictions are accurate.

■■ THE CHALLENGES AHEAD

LEARNING OBJECTIVE 7
Discuss the challenges that American businesses will encounter in the future.

There it is—the American business system in brief. When it works well, it provides jobs for those who are willing to work, a standard of living that few countries can match, and many opportunities for personal advancement. But, like every other system devised by humans, it is far from perfect. Our business system may give us prosperity, but it also gave us the Great Depression of the 1930s and the economic problems of the 1970s and early 1990s.

Obviously, the system can be improved. It may need no more than a bit of fine-tuning, or it may require more extensive overhauling. Certainly there are plenty of people who are willing to tell us exactly what *they* think the American economy needs. But these people provide us only with conflicting opinions. Who is right and who is wrong? Even the experts cannot agree.

The experts do agree, however, that several key issues will challenge our economic system over the next decade or two. Some of the questions to be resolved are these:

- How much government involvement in our economy is necessary for its continued well-being? In what areas should there be less involvement? In what areas, more?
- How can we manage economic growth and at the same time continue to conserve natural resources and protect our environment?
- How can we meet the challenges of managing culturally diverse work forces to meet the needs of a culturally diverse marketplace?
- How can we evaluate the long-term economic costs and benefits of existing and proposed government programs?
- How can we hold down inflation and yet stimulate the economy to provide jobs for all who want to work?
- How can we preserve the benefits of competition in our American economic system and still meet the needs of the less fortunate?
- How can we make American manufacturers more productive and more competitive with foreign producers who have lower labor costs?
- How can we market American-made products in foreign nations and thus reduce our trade deficit?
- How can we ensure that domestic business organizations will keep pace with the technological advancements of firms in other countries?

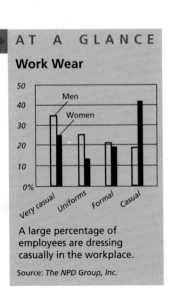

AT A GLANCE

Work Wear

A large percentage of employees are dressing casually in the workplace.

Source: *The NPD Group, Inc.*

The answers to the problems described in this section are anything but simple. In the past, Americans have always been able to solve their economic problems through ingenuity and creativity. Now, as we approach the year

2000, we need that same ingenuity and creativity not only to solve our current problems but also to compete in the global marketplace.

According to economic experts, if we as a nation can become more competitive, we may solve many of our current domestic problems. As an added bonus, increased competitiveness will also enable us to meet the economic challenges posed by other industrialized nations of the world. The way we solve these problems will affect our own future, our children's future, and that of our nation. Within the American economic and political system, the answers are ours to provide.

The American business system is not perfect by any means, but it does work reasonably well. We discuss some of its problems in Chapter 2, as we examine the role of business as part of American society.

■ ■ ■ ■ CHAPTER REVIEW

Summary

1 Define *business* and identify potential risks and rewards.

Business is the organized effort of individuals to produce and sell, for a profit, the goods and services that satisfy society's needs. Four kinds of resources—material, human, financial, and informational—must be combined to start and operate a business. The three general types of businesses are manufacturers, service businesses, and marketing middlemen. Profit is what remains after all business expenses are deducted from sales revenue. It is the payment that owners receive for assuming the risks of business—primarily the risks of not receiving payment and of losing whatever has been invested in the firm. Most often, a business that is operated to satisfy its customers earns a reasonable profit.

2 Describe the important reasons for studying business.

By studying business, you can become a better-informed consumer and investor and be a better employee. And with a sound working knowledge of business, you may decide to open your own business.

3 Understand the two types of economic systems, capitalism and planned economy.

Economics is the study of how wealth is created and distributed. An economy is a system through which a society decides those two issues. An economic system must answer four questions: What goods and services will be produced? How will they be produced? For whom will they be produced? Who owns and who controls the major factors of production? Capitalism (on which our economic system is based) is an economic system in which individuals own and operate the majority of businesses that provide goods and services. Capitalism stems from the theories of Adam Smith. Smith's pure laissez-faire capitalism is an economic system in which these decisions are made by individuals and businesses as they pursue their own self-interest. In a laissez-faire capitalist system, the factors of production are owned by private entities, and all individuals are free to use (or not to use) their resources as they see fit; prices are determined by the workings of supply and demand in competitive markets; and the economic role of government is limited to protecting competition.

Our economic system today is a mixed economy. Although our present business system is essentially capitalist in nature, government takes part, along with households and businesses. In the circular flow that characterizes our business system, households and businesses exchange resources for goods and services, using money as the medium of exchange. Government collects taxes from businesses and households and purchases products with which to provide services.

In a planned economy, government, rather than individuals, owns the factors of production and provides the answers to the three other economic questions. Socialist and communist economies are—at least in theory—planned economies. In the real world, however, no economy attains "theoretical perfection."

4   Identify the ways to measure economic performance.

One criterion for evaluating the performance of an economic system is to assess changes in productivity, which is the average level of output per worker per hour. A more general economic performance measure is gross national product (GNP), which is the total dollar value of all goods and services produced by all the citizens of a country for a given period of time. For comparison purposes, these figures are often adjusted for inflation, a total called the real GNP. Similar to GNP, the gross domestic product (GDP) is the total dollar value of all goods and services produced by citizens physically located within a country.

5   Outline the four types of competition.

Economists recognize four degrees of competition. Ranging from most to least competitive, the four degrees are pure competition, monopolistic competition, oligopoly, and monopoly. The factors of supply and demand generally influence the price that consumers pay producers for goods and services.

6   Summarize the development of America's business system.

Since its beginnings in the seventeenth century, American business has been based on private ownership of property and freedom of enterprise. And from this beginning, through the Industrial Revolution of the early nineteenth century, to the phenomenal expansion of American industry in the nineteenth and early twentieth centuries, our government maintained an essentially laissez-faire attitude toward business. However, during the Great Depression of the 1930s, the federal government began to provide a number of social services to its citizens. Government's role in business has expanded considerably since that time.

7   Discuss the challenges that American businesses will encounter in the future.

Today, American businesses face a number of significant challenges. Among the issues to be contended with are the level of government involvement in business; the extent of business's environmental and social responsibilities; the effective management of cultural diversity in the workplace;

the problem of holding down inflation while stimulating the economy; competition with foreign producers; trade deficit reduction; and technological innovation. If we as a nation can become more competitive, we may solve many of our domestic economic problems. As an added bonus, increased competitiveness will enable us to meet the challenges posed by foreign nations.

Key Terms

You should now be able to define and give an example relevant to each of the following terms:

free enterprise (4)
competition (5)
business (5)
entrepreneur (5)
consumers (6)
profit (6)
economics (8)
economy (8)
factors of production (9)
capitalism (10)
free-market economy (10)
mixed economy (11)
consumer products (11)
planned economy (14)
productivity (16)
gross national product (GNP) (16)
real gross national product (16)
gross domestic product (GDP) (16)
pure competition (17)
supply (18)
demand (18)
market price (18)
monopolistic competition (19)
oligopoly (19)
monopoly (20)
natural monopoly (20)
barter (21)
domestic system (21)
factory system (22)
specialization (22)
standard of living (24)
inflation (24)
service economy (24)

Questions

Review Questions

1. What basic rights are accorded to individuals and businesses in our free-enterprise system?
2. What is meant by free enterprise? Why does free enterprise naturally lead to competition among sellers of products?
3. Describe the four resources that must be combined to organize and operate a business. How do they differ from the economist's factors of production?
4. What distinguishes consumers from other buyers of goods and services?
5. Describe the relationship among profit, business risk, and the satisfaction of customers' needs.
6. What are the four basic economic questions? How are they answered in a capitalist economy? in a planned economy?
7. Describe the four main ingredients of a laissez-faire capitalist economy.
8. Why is the American economy called a mixed economy?
9. Outline the economic interactions between government and business in our business system. Outline those between government and households.
10. What is the difference between gross national product and gross domestic product? Why are these economic measures significant?
11. Identify and compare the four forms of competition that economists recognize.
12. Explain how the market price of a product is determined under pure competition.
13. Trace the steps that led from farming for survival in the American colonial period to today's mass production.

Discussion Questions

1. Most toys reach their peak of popularity within a few years, and then decline. Why has Mattel's Barbie been a successful product for over 35 years?
2. What products are direct competitors of the Barbie doll?
3. Three specific reasons for studying business were included in this chapter. How does each of these reasons affect your life?
4. What factors caused American business to develop into a mixed economic system rather than some other type of system?
5. Does any individual consumer really have a voice in answering the basic economic questions?
6. Is gross national product a reliable indicator of a nation's standard of living? What might be a better indicator?

7. Discuss this statement: "Business competition encourages efficiency of production and leads to improved product quality."
8. In our business system, how is government involved in answering the four basic economic questions? Does government participate in the system or interfere with it?

Exercises

1. Choose a type of business that you are familiar with or interested in. Then write a list of the *specific* material, human, financial, and informational resources you would need to start such a business.
2. Cite four methods (other than pricing) that American auto manufacturers use to differentiate their products. (The best way to do this is to scan their magazine and newspaper ads.) Rate these methods from least effective to most effective, using your own judgment and experience.
3. A marketing middleman like Kmart does not process goods in any way, yet it helps satisfy consumer wants. List and explain several ways in which it does so.

VIDEO CASE 1.1

Baldrige Award Winners: Success Through Customer Service

In America, an outstanding movie can win an Oscar. A superior company can win a Malcolm Baldrige National Quality Award. Since the U.S. Congress established the Baldrige Award in 1987, Motorola, Xerox, Cadillac Motor Car Division, Federal Express, Ritz-Carlton Hotels, and seventeen other companies have received the prestigious honor. Administered by the National Institute of Standards and Technology (NIST), the Baldrige Award recognizes U.S. companies for excellence in quality management. An independent board of quality experts judges applicants on many quality-related factors, not the least of which is customer focus and satisfaction. Of the seventy-one companies competing for the 1994 Baldrige award, the winners— AT&T Consumer Communications Services, Wainwright Industries, and GTE Directories Corp.— were all acclaimed for their exceptional commitment to improving customer service.

AT&T Consumer Communications Services supplies long-distance services to more than 80 million customers worldwide. Competing with over 500 other long-distance providers, AT&T distinguishes itself by considering its customers' needs when shaping products and services. The company asks questions such as: What do our customers want? How can we give it to them? Are they really satisfied with our services? To get answers, AT&T teams regularly measure the success of their efforts. To test the sound quality of "True Voice," the company put consumers in simulated sound environments and asked them to judge what they heard. To respond quickly to customers' problems, AT&T's Market Intelligence Management System studies their comments daily. Whenever customers call in, a computer system puts the message into a common database so that all parts of the company know what customers are saying.

Wainwright Industries, a family-owned parts manufacturer, attributes its success to dedication to customer service and expertise in measuring customer satisfaction. At the company's "Mission Control," managers and employees work together on strategies that can translate into total customer satisfaction. By employing a "customer satisfaction index" to measure customer service and product improvement, Wainwright has boosted customer satisfaction from 84 to 95 percent. Insists the company's president, "Customers, not management, grade service."

Adopting that same philosophy helped GTE Directories win its Baldrige Award. Each time someone at GTE Directories receives customer input, says a company vice president, GTE gets a chance to improve what it does. One of the world's largest telephone directory companies, GTE Directories came up with its Customer Satisfaction Measurement Program to help it attain 100 percent customer satisfaction. One of the first lessons the program taught the company is that satisfying customers requires providing excellent service, not just offering a highly regarded product. To let customers know exactly what they were getting for their money, for example, GTE will hook up metered phones to track the number of calls a specific ad in the Yellow Pages generates.

Too many managers in corporate America believe that researching customer satisfaction wastes time and money. They believe that management knows best how to improve quality. Recent studies, however, indicate that attention to customer service *can* improve quality throughout the company, help achieve quality program requirements, create loyal customers, and earn the company a reputation for caring. As in the cases of these three winners, it might even earn the company a Baldrige Award.

Questions

1. Should a government agency be involved in encouraging and rewarding businesses for excellence in quality management? Explain.

2. What advantages accrue to our economic system when companies achieve excellence in quality management?

3. Why is excellence in customer service of major concern to those involved in quality management?

CASE 1.2

Blockbuster Entertainment: More Than Just Videos

H. Wayne Huizenga, CEO of Florida-based Blockbuster Entertainment Corp., watches only about four videos a year, but he rents more than 10 million videos a week to other people. More people—about 30 million—carry Blockbuster rental memberships than carry American Express Cards, and with more than 3,400 stores, the Blockbuster Video chain is larger than the next 350 video chains combined. However, new telecommunication and cable technologies, which threaten to make a trip to the video store obsolete, have prompted Huizenga to expand Blockbuster into a global multimedia entertainment company.

In just a few years, video sales and rentals have grown into a multibillion dollar business. Going to the video store is as much a part of American life as going to the supermarket. Although he rarely went to the movies, Huizenga appreciated the potential of the video business early on. After launching and running Waste Management, Inc., for twenty years, he bought a small Dallas video chain and quickly transformed it into a forty-eight-state, ten-country operation. With sales revenue of over $1 billion a year and annual sales growth of over 80 percent, Blockbuster continues to expand its empire.

Although Blockbuster Video offers more than 80,000 titles, the chain attracts families by banning movies with NC-17 and X ratings. The company even has a youth-restricted policy: children under 17 cannot rent unrated movies without a parent's written permission. Using its extensive database to track movie and star preferences, Blockbuster is adept at predicting and stocking the movies most in demand.

By purchasing Sound Warehouse and Music Plus chains, Blockbuster is becoming a music retailing powerhouse as well. In one year alone, the company plans to open 100 new outlets across the United States, all sharing the familiar movie-ticket trademark of Blockbuster Video. Although some experts warn that customers will be confused by this strategy, Blockbuster marketers hope that the same people who recognize the logo and trust the video stores will frequent the music stores, too. To better serve customers, Blockbuster is working with IBM to develop a system that will make

CDs right in the store. Customers will be able to individually select and receive CDs from a library of 80,000 titles by using a touch-sensitive computer screen.

In addition, Blockbuster's 35 percent interest in Republic Pictures Corporation and majority control of Spelling Entertainment Group make the company a competitor in film production and distribution and in theater and television entertainment. Huizenga also purchased the Florida Marlins professional baseball team, the Florida Panthers NHL hockey team, and Discovery Zone, developer of children's indoor playgrounds. Recently, he was granted permission from the National Football League to purchase the Miami Dolphins football franchise.

In a joint venture with the British firm Virgin Retail Group, Blockbuster is opening what it calls "mega-stores," multilevel entertainment supermarkets offering CDs, audiocassettes, videos, computer and virtual reality games, and books. Taking a page from family-entertainment king Walt Disney's book, Huizenga plans to open a $150-million, 500-acre sports/entertainment village in Florida. Included will be a 48,000-seat, retractable-dome stadium for the Florida Marlins; a 20,000-seat arena for the Panthers; music production studios; a virtual reality center; a sports museum; a water sports lake; and a little league ballpark.

With a full plate of expansion plans, Blockbuster Entertainment is more profitable than ever, and most of those profits still come from video rentals. However, as Blockbuster increasingly positions itself as a family-entertainment company, customers will have many ways to "make it a Blockbuster night."[4]

Questions

1. Describe Blockbuster's video-rental customers.
2. There are four major types of competition. In which type of competition does Blockbuster participate with respect to the video-rental business?
3. What effects would an economic recession have on Blockbuster's video-rental business? Assuming it is built, what effects would an economic recession have on Blockbuster's mammoth sports/entertainment village in Florida?

■■■■ CHAPTER 2

Ethics and Social Responsibility

LEARNING OBJECTIVES

After studying this chapter, you should be able to

1 Understand what is meant by *business ethics*.

2 Identify the types of ethical concerns that arise in the business world.

3 Discuss the factors that affect the level of ethical behavior in organizations.

4 Explain how ethical decision making can be encouraged.

5 Describe how our current views on the social responsibility of business have evolved.

6 Explain the two views on social responsibility of business and understand the arguments for and against increased social responsibility.

7 Discuss the factors that led to the consumer movement and list some of its results.

8 Analyze how present employment practices are being used to counteract past abuses.

9 Describe the major types of pollution, their causes, and their cures.

10 Identify the steps a business must take to implement a program of social responsibility.

CHAPTER PREVIEW

We begin by defining *business ethics*. Next we look at the factors that affect the standards of behavior in organizations and how ethical behavior can be encouraged. Then we initiate our discussion of social responsibility. We compare and contrast two present-day models of social responsibility and present arguments for and against increasing the social responsibility of business. Next we present the major elements of the consumer movement. We discuss how social responsibility in business has affected employment practices and environmental concerns. Finally, we consider the commitment, planning, and funding that go into a firm's program of social responsibility.

Bausch & Lomb Contact Lenses: Is the Price Right?

During World War I, Bausch & Lomb supplied the U.S. military with lenses for binoculars, search-lights, and telescopes. In the 1950s, Bausch & Lomb won an Oscar for enhancing the quality of motion pictures by developing the Cinemascope lens. In the 1960s, the company contributed the latest lens technology to U.S. satellite and missile systems. However, recent allegations about the ethics of the company's contact lens pricing practices are threatening to tarnish its admirable image.

For years, Bausch & Lomb had a monopoly on soft contact lenses, sales of which propelled the company into the *Fortune* 500. With brand names such as Medalist, SeeQuence, and Optima, varieties of Bausch & Lomb lenses were priced differently, apparently according to their type of use. Conventional daily-wear lenses cost between $50 and $100 a pair, adding up to about $250 a year including cleaners. Frequent-replacement lenses run about $350 a year, and disposable lenses between $400 and $500 a year. What a recent *Business Week* investigation contends, however, is that Bausch & Lomb is selling identical lenses for varying prices; the only real difference among them is packaging. For example, customers are paying $40 a lens for the company's Optima FW, $9 a lens for its Medalist, and $4 a lens for its See-Quence 2, but all of these lenses are exactly the same product.

Largely as a result of this investigation, a group of Bausch & Lomb customers has initiated a law-suit against the company, alleging that Bausch & Lomb has committed fraud by misrepresenting its lenses. Bausch & Lomb concedes that the lenses are the same, but it asserts that eye-care professionals are the ones who direct patients to

wear them varying lengths of time and set the final price that customers pay.

Several ethical questions remain. Is Bausch & Lomb encouraging eye-care professionals to hide from customers the fact that the lenses are all alike? Is it ethical for Bausch & Lomb to assign different names—and different prices—to one product? Aren't customers, who logically assume that a different name signifies a different product, being deceived into paying more than necessary? Although at this time Bausch & Lomb isn't addressing these questions, the courts may force the company to do so. The potential costs to Bausch & Lomb are not only money but also a diminished reputation and loss of customer trust.

■ ■ ■ ■

33

■ ■ ■ ■ ■ ■ ■ ■ ■ ■ ■

$\int$ learly, the management at Bausch & Lomb is concerned that the company's pricing practices could be viewed as ethically questionable. In many organizations, business people have taken steps to encourage socially responsible and ethical decisions and actions. However, not all firms have taken these steps. Some managers still regard ethical and socially responsible business practices as a poor investment, in which the cost is not worth the return. Other managers—indeed, most managers—view the cost of these practices as a necessary business expense, similar to wages or rent. An increasing number of firms are making ethics and social responsibility an essential part of their business operations.

■■ BUSINESS ETHICS DEFINED

LEARNING OBJECTIVE 1
Understand what is meant by *business ethics.*

ethics   the study of right and wrong and of the morality of choices individuals make

business ethics   the application of moral standards to business situations

Ethics is the study of right and wrong and of the morality of choices that individuals make. An ethical decision or action is one that is "right" according to some standard of behavior. **Business ethics** is the application of moral standards to business situations. Recent court cases of unethical behavior such as the Sears, Roebuck and Company scandal involving inflated auto repair bills and the questionable pricing tactics of federal defense contractor General Dynamics Corporation and others have helped to make business ethics a matter of public concern.

■■ ETHICAL ISSUES

LEARNING OBJECTIVE 2
Identify the types of ethical concerns that arise in the business world.

Ethical issues often arise out of a business's relationship with investors, customers, employees, creditors, or competitors. Each of these groups has specific concerns and usually exerts pressure on the organization's managers. For example, investors want management to make sensible financial decisions that will boost sales, profits, and returns on their investments. Customers expect a firm's products to be safe, reliable, and reasonably priced. Employees demand to be treated fairly in hiring, promotion, and compensation decisions. Creditors require accounts to be paid on time and the accounting information furnished by the firm to be accurate. Competitors expect the firm's competitive practices to be fair and honest.

Business people face ethical issues every day. In some instances, employees may experience difficulty in assessing ethical issues (see Enhancing Career Skills). Although some types of issues arise infrequently, others occur regularly. Let's take a closer look at several ethical issues.

Fairness and Honesty

Fairness and honesty in business are two important ethical concerns. Besides obeying all laws and regulations, business persons are expected to refrain from knowingly deceiving, misrepresenting, or intimidating others.

34

ENHANCING CAREER SKILLS

How Do You Know If It's Ethical?

- Who will find out if I pad my expense account?

- Sexual harassment? I was just kidding with her, and besides, that's the way we've always acted around here.

- I just realized that I made an error in my sales forecast! Should I tell my supervisor, regardless of the consequences?

- Everyone else uses the office phones to make personal long-distance calls; should I go ahead and make one?

- I saw my coworker take some office equipment home. Should I confront him, tell my supervisor, or forget it?

Most people ask such questions from time to time. But there is no formula for knowing right and wrong. Laws help only with questions of legality. Sometimes, you can rely on formal company ethics codes, but when you face a personal ethical decision at work, you often have to make it yourself. How will you know what to do?

GUIDELINES FOR DOING THE RIGHT THING

- Choosing the ethical thing to do is your personal responsibility.
    Don't believe "it's not my job."
    No one else can or should choose for you.
    Live by the same set of rules and values at work that you follow at home.

- Examine each situation carefully.
    Acknowledge that sometimes there is a right and a wrong choice.
    Identify the ethical issues—examine how you feel and recognize the consequences of your decision.
    Create some options for yourself and decide which choice will increase your self-respect.
    Test each choice against your standards of understanding, caring, fairness, and honesty.
    Remember that unethical actions usually don't stand up to close examination.

- Consider how your actions affect other people.
    Think through who else will be affected by the decision you make.
    Ask yourself how your decision will influence the quality of life of others.
    Be sensitive to the effect your words and actions have on those with whom you work.

- Take action.
    Doing nothing is not an ethical choice.
    The problem won't go away.
    No matter how ethical you are, ethics count only if you use them.

HOW YOUR EMPLOYER CAN HELP YOU

- Companies should establish clear standards of conduct that are applicable to your daily work responsibilities.

- Ethics officers should investigate alleged violations and make sure that everyone at the organization is abiding by the formal ethics code.

- Companies can set up "ethics help lines" that offer advice to those who are having trouble deciding the right thing to do.

If you think that you probably won't have to face tough ethical decisions at work, think again. The results of a recent survey of 10,000 employees at aerospace, telecommunications, health care, and consumer product companies reveal that

55 percent rarely found company standards of conduct helpful in guiding their own decisions and actions.

63 percent said they are pressured regularly to compromise their standards to achieve business goals.

42 percent reported that they have witnessed ethics violations, and almost half of these people refused to report the incidents.

Recently, for example, Deloitte and Touche, a major accounting firm, agreed to pay $312 million for allegedly issuing clean audits for banks and savings institutions that were in fact on the brink of insolvency.[2]

Organizational Relationships

A business person may be tempted to place his or her personal welfare above the welfare of others or the welfare of the organization. Relationships with customers and coworkers often create ethical problems, since confidential information is expected to be kept secret and all obligations should be honored. Unethical behavior in these areas includes taking credit for others' ideas or work, not meeting one's commitments in a mutual agreement, and pressuring others to behave unethically.

Conflict of Interest

Conflict of interest results when a business person takes advantage of a situation for his or her own personal interest rather than for the employer's interest. Such conflict may occur when payments and gifts make their way into business deals. A wise rule to remember is that anything given to a person that might unfairly influence that person's business decision is a bribe, and all bribes are unethical.

Communications

Business communications, especially advertising, can present ethical questions. False and misleading advertising is illegal and unethical, and it can infuriate customers. Sponsors of advertisements aimed at children must be especially careful to avoid misleading messages. Advertisers of health-related products must also take precautions to guard against deception when using such descriptive terms as "low fat," "fat free," and "light." In fact, recent guidelines on the use of these labels have been issued by the Federal Trade Commission.

■■ FACTORS AFFECTING ETHICAL BEHAVIOR

LEARNING OBJECTIVE 3
Discuss the factors that affect the level of ethical behavior in organizations.

Is it possible for an individual with strong moral values to make ethically questionable decisions in a business setting? What affects a person's inclination to make either ethical or unethical decisions in a business organization? Although the answers to these questions are not entirely clear, there appear to be three general sets of factors that influence the standards of behavior in an organization. As shown in Figure 2.1, the sets consist of individual factors, social factors, and opportunity.[3]

FIGURE 2.1
Factors That Affect the Level of Ethical Behavior in an Organization
(Source: Based on O. C. Ferrell and Larry Gresham, "A Contingency Framework for Understanding Ethical Decision Making in Marketing," Journal of Marketing, *Summer 1985, p. 89.)*

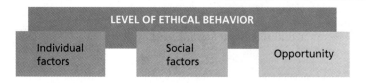

Several individual factors influence the level of ethical behavior in an organization. An individual's knowledge level regarding an issue can help to determine ethical behavior. A decision maker with a greater amount of knowledge regarding an object or situation may take steps to avoid ethical problems, whereas a less-informed person may unknowingly take action that leads to an ethical quagmire. One's moral values and central, value-related attitudes clearly influence his or her business behavior. Most people join organizations to accomplish personal goals. The types of personal goals an individual aspires to and the manner in which these goals are pursued have a significant impact on that individual's behavior in an organization.

A person's behavior in the workplace is, to some degree, determined by cultural norms, and these social factors vary from one culture to another. For example, in some countries it is acceptable and ethical for customs agents to receive gratuities for performing ordinary, legal tasks that are a part of their jobs, whereas in other countries these practices would be viewed as unethical and perhaps illegal. The actions and decisions of coworkers is another social factor believed to shape a person's sense of business ethics. For example, if your coworkers make long-distance telephone calls on company time and at company expense, you might view that behavior as acceptable and ethical because everyone does it. Significant others are persons to whom someone is emotionally attached—spouses, friends, and relatives, for instance. Their moral values and attitudes can also affect an employee's perception of what is ethical and unethical behavior in the workplace.

Opportunity refers to the amount of freedom an organization gives an employee to behave unethically if he or she makes that choice. In some organizations, certain company policies and procedures reduce the opportunity to be unethical. For example, at some fast-food restaurants, one person takes your order and receives your payment and another person fills the order. This procedure reduces the opportunity to be unethical because the person handling the money is not dispensing the product, and the person giving out the product is not handling the money. The existence of an ethical code and the importance management places on this code are other determinants of opportunity (codes of ethics are discussed in more detail later in this chapter). The degree of enforcement of company policies, procedures, and ethical codes is a major force affecting opportunity. When violations are dealt with consistently and firmly, the opportunity to be unethical is reduced.

Now that we have considered some of the factors believed to influence the level of ethical behavior in the workplace, let's explore what can be done to encourage ethical behavior and discourage unethical behavior.

■ ■ ENCOURAGING ETHICAL BEHAVIOR

LEARNING OBJECTIVE 4
Explain how ethical decision making can be encouraged.

Most authorities agree that there is room for improvement in business ethics. A more problematic question is, Can business be made more ethical in the real world? The majority opinion on this issue suggests that government, trade associations, and individual firms can indeed establish acceptable levels of ethical behavior.

Code of Ethics and
Standards of Conduct

Martin Marietta Corporation believes in the highest
ethical standards. We demonstrate these beliefs through
our commitments — commitments we are dedicated
to fulfill.

■ **To our EMPLOYEES** we are committed to just management and
equality for all, providing a safe and healthy workplace, and respecting
the dignity and privacy due all human beings.

■ **To our CUSTOMERS** we are committed to produce reliable products
and services at a fair price that are delivered on time and within budget.

■ **To the COMMUNITIES in which we live** we are committed to be
responsible neighbors, reflecting all aspects of good citizenship.

■ **To our SHAREHOLDERS** we are committed to pursuing sound
growth and earnings objectives and to exercising prudence in the use
of our assets and resources.

■ **To our SUPPLIERS** we are committed to fair competition and the
sense of responsibility required of a good customer.

Defining acceptable behavior. Martin Marietta encourages ethical behavior through an
extensive training program and the use of a written code of ethics.

The government can do so by legislating more stringent regulations. But
rules require enforcement, and the unethical business person frequently
seems to "slip something by" without getting caught. Increased regulation
may help, but it surely cannot solve the entire ethics problem.

Trade associations can and often do provide ethical guidelines for their
members. These organizations within particular industries are in an excellent position to exert pressure on members that stoop to questionable business practices. However, enforcement and authority vary from association
to association. And because trade associations exist for the benefit of their
members, harsh measures may be self-defeating.

Employees can more easily determine and adopt acceptable behavior
when companies provide them with a code of ethics. Such codes are perhaps
the most effective way to encourage ethical behavior. A **code of ethics** is a
written guide to acceptable and ethical behavior (as defined by an organization) that outlines uniform policies, standards, and punishments for violations. Because employees know what is expected of them and what will
happen if they violate the rules, a code of ethics goes a long way toward
encouraging ethical behavior. However, codes cannot possibly cover every
situation. Companies must also create an environment in which employees
recognize the importance of complying with the written code. Managers

code of ethics a guide to
acceptable and ethical behavior
as defined by an organization

must provide direction by fostering communication, actively modeling and encouraging ethical decision making, and training employees to make ethical decisions. (Codes of ethics are explored in more detail in Ethical Challenges.)

Assigning an ethics officer who coordinates ethical conduct gives employees someone to consult if they aren't sure of the right thing to do. An ethics officer meets with employees and top management to provide ethical advice; establishes and maintains an anonymous confidential service to answer questions about ethical issues; and takes action on ethics code violations.

Sometimes, even employees who want to act ethically may find it difficult to do so. Unethical practices can become ingrained in an organization. Employees with high personal ethics may then take a controversial step called whistle blowing. **Whistle blowing** is informing the press or government officials about unethical practices within one's organization. Whistle blowing could have averted disaster and prevented needless deaths in the *Challenger* space shuttle disaster, for example. How could employees have known about life-threatening problems and let them pass? Whistle blowing, on the other hand, can have serious repercussions for employees: those who "make waves" sometimes lose their jobs.

When firms set up anonymous hotlines to handle ethically questionable situations, employees may actually be less reluctant to speak up. When firms instead create an environment that educates employees and nurtures ethical behavior, fewer ethical problems arise, and ultimately the need for whistle blowing is greatly reduced.

It is difficult for an organization to develop ethics codes, policies, and procedures to deal with all relationships and every situation. When no company policy or procedures exists or applies, a quick test to determine if a behavior is ethical is to see if others—coworkers, customers, suppliers—approve of it. Ethical decisions will always withstand scrutiny. Openness and communication about choices will often build trust and strengthen business relationships. Table 2.1 provides some general guidelines for making ethical decisions.

whistle blowing informing the press or government officials about unethical practices within one's organization

■■ SOCIAL RESPONSIBILITY

social responsibility the recognition that business activities have an impact on society and the consideration of that impact in business decision making

Social responsibility is the recognition that business activities have an impact on society and the consideration of that impact in business decision making. Obviously, social responsibility costs money. It is perhaps not so obvious—except in isolated cases—that social responsibility is also good business. Customers eventually find out which firms are acting responsibly and which are not. And, just as easily as they cast their dollar votes for a product produced by a company that is socially responsible, they can vote against the firm that is not.

Consider the following examples of organizations that are attempting to be socially responsible.

- To curb violence, the owner of a New York City carpet store offered a $100 Toys "R" Us gift certificate for every gun turned in to the 34th

■ ■ ■ ■ ETHICAL CHALLENGES

Codes of Ethics: Doing the Right Thing

You work for a computer software manufacturer. Your boss gives you a deadline that will be almost impossible for you to meet. Then you discover that by incorporating someone else's program into your own, you can save yourself hours of work. Should you include the program? You work at an employment agency, and your client asks you to screen qualified applicants so that whites have priority over minorities and men over women. Should you do what your client wants? Your coworker takes supplies from his office home to his daughter. Should you tell your supervisor?

To help employees resolve dilemmas like these, as well as a multitude of other moral and ethical questions, businesses institute formal codes of ethics. A code of ethics is a set of written commitments, outlining the rules and ideals that clarify a company's ethical standards, professional responsibilities, and methods of enforcing compliance. Although unable to resolve every ethical dilemma, codes of ethics *do* provide guidelines that employees can follow in a variety of situations.

No one has designed the universally applicable business code of ethics, but there are some features that most organizations include. A formal code usually begins with a general statement about the company—its purpose, goals, philosophy, responsibilities, and reputation. Codes often specify the organization's obligations to society, such as environmental responsibilities and contributions to the community. A company usually affirms its commitment to uphold and promote the code's principles. Employee issues including rights, expectations, and other specific ethical concerns make up the heart of most codes. Here, the company can offer employees guidance in making ethical decisions dealing with privacy, confidentiality, quality of work, fairness and discrimination, or conflict of interest. Finally, a code of ethics must state clearly how the organization will ensure compliance with the code, detailing procedures for dealing with violations. Without enforcement, an ethics code will be ineffective.

During the 1980s, increasing numbers of organizations created and implemented ethics codes. In a recent Conference Board survey of *Fortune* 1000 firms, 93 percent of the companies that responded reported having a formal code of ethics. For example, the Healthcare Financial Management Association recently took steps to strengthen its accountability. The association's revised code designates specific organization leaders to contact to report ethics violations, emphasizes how its board of directors handles violation of business ethics, and guarantees a fair hearing process. Consumer goods manufacturer S.C. Johnson & Son, makers of Pledge, Drāno, Windex, and many other household products, recognizes that it must behave in ways that the public perceives as ethical. Its code includes expectations for employees and its commitment to consumers, the community, and society in general. Included in the ethics code of electronics giant Texas Instruments Incorporated are issues relating to policies and procedures; laws and regulations; relationships with customers, suppliers, and competitors; conflict of interest; handling of proprietary information; and code enforcement.

Maintaining a formal policy of ethics makes good business sense. By clarifying responsibilities to society, holding professionals accountable, and helping people make good decisions, a code of ethics enhances consumer trust and goodwill. Experts warn, however, that forced compliance with the code, "or else," is not the best way to make ethical behavior an instinctive part of the work environment. Education and socialization, they contend, are far more effective ways to get everyone to do the right thing.

TABLE 2.1   Guidelines for Making Ethical Decisions

1. **Listen and learn.**
Recognize the problem or decision-making opportunity that confronts your company, team, or unit. Don't argue, criticize, or defend yourself—keep listening and reviewing until you are sure you understand others.

2. **Identify the ethical issues.**
Examine how coworkers and consumers are affected by the situation or decision at hand. Examine how you feel about the situation and understand the viewpoint of those who are involved in the decision or the consequences of the decision.

3. **Create and analyze options.**
Try to put aside strong feelings such as anger or desire for power and prestige and come up with as many alternatives as possible before developing an analysis. Ask everyone involved for ideas about which options offer the best long-term results for you and the company. Which option will increase your self-respect even if, in the long run, things don't work out the way you hope?

4. **Identify the best option from your point of view.**
Consider it and test it against some established criteria, such as respect, understanding, caring, fairness, honesty, and openness.

5. **Explain your decision and resolve any differences that arise.**
This may require neutral arbitration from a trusted manager or taking "time out" to reconsider, consult, or exchange written proposals before a decision is reached.

Source: Tom Rusk with D. Patrick Miller, "Doing the Right Thing," *Sky* (Delta Airlines), Aug. 1993, pp. 18–22.

precinct police station in Washington Heights. Within a month the offer brought in more than 1,000 weapons, including semi-automatic uzis, submachine guns, rifles, and 9-millimeter handguns.[4]

- To reduce the incidence of inhalant abuse, H. B. Fuller Company redesigned its adhesives (such as rubber cement) to replace solvents with water-based materials.[5]

- It is estimated that 5 million U.S. children are too hungry to go to school and concentrate in the classroom. Quaker Oats Company donates money and food to support Kids' Cafes (located in inner-city areas), which serve free breakfasts to children five days a week. Some Kids' Cafes serve free evening meals several times a week.[6]

- The Starbucks Coffee Company donates $100,000 a year to CARE, the international aid and relief organization.[7]

- The John Hancock Mutual Life Insurance Company donates funds to Habitat for Humanity in Boston specifically to buy down the mortgages on local condominiums renovated by Habitat. As a result, the residents of these condominiums pay only $1 a month for the first ten years and then $197 a month for the remaining ten years of their mortgages.[8]

- Hurricane Andrew damaged over 75,000 homes in Dade County, Florida. Rather than increasing their prices to make higher profits, as some retailers did, Home Depot teamed up with Georgia Pacific, the

Save a giraffe. British Airways expresses concern and sensitivity toward the environment by helping to preserve over ninety threatened species. The company's Assisting Nature Conservation effort supports field studies and educational projects around the world. This project is only one component of British Airways' program to preserve the environment.

nation's largest plywood producer, to cut the price of plywood to help residents make their homes liveable more quickly.[9]

These are just a few illustrations from the long list of companies that attempt to behave in socially responsible ways. In general, people are more likely to want to work for and buy from such organizations.

■■ SOCIAL RESPONSIBILITY EVOLVES FROM A DYNAMIC BUSINESS ENVIRONMENT

LEARNING OBJECTIVE 5
Describe how our current views on the social responsibility of business have evolved.

Business is far from perfect in many respects, but its social responsibility record today is much better than in past decades. In fact, present demands for social responsibility have their roots in outraged reactions to the abusive business practices of the early 1900s.

During the first quarter of the twentieth century, businesses were free to operate pretty much as they chose. Government protection of workers and consumers was minimal. As a result, people either accepted what business had to offer or they did without. Working conditions were often deplorable

Baltimore, Maryland, vegetable cannery, 1912. During the early part of the twentieth century, children as well as adults worked long hours for low wages in a crowded, unsafe work environment.

by today's standards. The average workweek in most industries exceeded sixty hours, no minimum-wage law existed, and employee benefits were almost nonexistent. Work areas were crowded and unsafe, and industrial accidents were the rule rather than the exception. To improve working conditions, employees organized and joined labor unions. But during the early 1900s, businesses—with the help of government—were able to use such weapons as court orders, brute force, and even the few existing antitrust laws to defeat union attempts to improve working conditions.

During this period, consumers were generally subject to the doctrine of **caveat emptor,** a Latin phrase meaning "let the buyer beware." In other words, "what you see is what you get," and if it's not what you expected, too bad. Although victims of unscrupulous business practices could take legal action, going to court was very expensive and consumers rarely won their cases. Moreover, there were no consumer groups or government agencies to publicize their discoveries or hold sellers accountable for their actions.

Prior to the 1930s, most people believed that competition and the action of the marketplace would correct abuses in time. Government therefore became involved in day-to-day business activities only in cases of obvious abuse of the free-market system. Six of the more important business-related federal laws passed between 1887 and 1914 are described in Table 2.2. As you can see, these laws were aimed more at encouraging competition than at correcting abuses, although two of them did deal with the purity of food and drug products.

caveat emptor   a Latin phrase meaning "let the buyer beware"

TABLE 2.2   Early Government Regulations That Affected American Business

Government Regulation	Major Provisions
Interstate Commerce Act (1887)	First federal act to regulate business practices; provided regulation of railroads and shipping rates
Sherman Antitrust Act (1890)	Prevented monopolies or mergers where competition was endangered
Pure Food and Drug Act (1906)	Established limited supervision of interstate sale of food and drugs
Meat Inspection Act (1906)	Provided for limited supervision of interstate sale of meat and meat products
Federal Trade Commission Act (1914)	Created the Federal Trade Commission to investigate illegal trade practices
Clayton Antitrust Act (1914)	Eliminated many forms of price discrimination that gave large businesses a competitive advantage over smaller firms

The collapse of the stock market on October 29, 1929, triggered the Great Depression and years of dire economic problems for the United States. Factory production fell by almost one-half, and up to 25 percent of the nation's work force was unemployed. Before long, public pressure mounted for government to "do something" about the economy and about worsening social conditions.

Soon after Franklin Roosevelt was inaugurated as president in 1933, he instituted programs to restore the economy and to improve social conditions. Laws were passed to correct what many viewed as the monopolistic abuses of big business, and various social services were provided for individuals. These massive federal programs became the foundation for increased government involvement in the dealings between business and society.

As government involvement has increased, so has everyone's awareness of the social responsibility of business. Today's business owners are concerned about the return on their investment, but at the same time most of them demand ethical behavior from employees. In addition, employees demand better working conditions, and consumers want safe, reliable products. Various advocacy groups echo these concerns and also call for careful consideration of our earth's delicate ecological balance. Managers must therefore operate in a complex business environment—one in which they are just as responsible for their managerial actions as for their actions as individual citizens.

■■ TWO VIEWS OF SOCIAL RESPONSIBILITY

LEARNING OBJECTIVE 6
Explain the two views on social responsibility of business and understand the arguments for and against increased social responsibility.

Government regulation and public awareness are *external* forces that have increased the social responsibility of business. But business decisions are made *within* the firm—and there, social responsibility begins with the attitude of management. Two contrasting philosophies, or models, define the range of management attitudes toward social responsibility.

The Economic Model

According to the traditional concept of business, a firm exists to produce quality goods and services, earn a reasonable profit, and provide jobs. In line with this concept, the **economic model of social responsibility** holds that society will benefit most when business is left alone to produce and market profitable products that society needs. The economic model has its origins in the eighteenth century when businesses were owned primarily by entrepreneurs or owner-managers. Competition was vigorous among small firms, and short-run profits and survival were the primary concerns.

economic model of social responsibility the view that society will benefit most when business is left alone to produce and market profitable products that society needs

To the manager who adopts this traditional attitude, social responsibility is someone else's job. After all, stockholders invest in a corporation to earn a return on their investment, not because the firm is socially responsible, and the firm is legally obligated to act in the economic interest of its stockholders. Moreover, profitable firms pay federal, state, and local taxes that are used to meet the needs of society. Thus, managers who concentrate on profit believe they fulfill their social responsibility indirectly, through the taxes paid by their firms. As a result, social responsibility becomes the problem of government, various environmental groups, charitable foundations, and similar organizations.

Expression of social responsiveness. JCPenney engages in socially responsible behavior by encouraging minority-owned business enterprises to become JCPenney suppliers. Almost 20 percent of JCPenney's 10,000 suppliers are minority-owned businesses.

socioeconomic model of social responsibility the concept that business should emphasize not only profits but the impact of its decisions on society

The Socioeconomic Model

In contrast, some managers believe they have a responsibility not only to stockholders but also to customers, employees, suppliers, and the general public. This broader view is referred to as the **socioeconomic model of social responsibility.** It places emphasis not only on profits but also on the impact of business decisions on society.

Recently, increasing numbers of managers and firms have adopted the socioeconomic model, and they have done so for at least three reasons. First, business is dominated by the corporate form of ownership, and the corporation is a creation of society. If a corporation doesn't perform as a good citizen, society can and will demand changes. Second, many firms are beginning to take pride in their social responsibility records. IBM, Arco, Ben & Jerry's, and Johnson & Johnson are very proud of their commitment to social responsibility. And, of course, many other corporations are much more socially responsible today than they were ten years ago. Third, many business people believe it is in their best interest to take the initiative in this area. The alternative may be legal action brought against the firm by some special-interest group; in such a situation, the firm may lose control of its activities.

The Pros and Cons of Social Responsibility

The merits of the economic and socioeconomic models have been debated for years by business owners, managers, customers, and government officials. Each side seems to have four major arguments to reinforce its viewpoint.

Arguments for Increased Social Responsibility   Proponents of the socioeconomic model maintain that a business must do more than simply seek profits. To support their position, they offer the following arguments:

1. Business cannot ignore social issues because business is a part of our society.
2. Business has the technical, financial, and managerial resources that are needed to tackle today's complex social issues.
3. By helping resolve social issues, business can create a more stable environment for long-term profitability.
4. Socially responsible decision making by firms can prevent increased government intervention, which would force businesses to do what they fail to do voluntarily.

These arguments are based on the assumption that a business has a responsibility not only to stockholders but also to customers, employees, suppliers, and the general public.

Arguments Against Increased Social Responsibility   Opponents of the socioeconomic model argue that business should do what it does best: earn a profit by manufacturing and marketing products that people want. Those who support their position argue as follows:

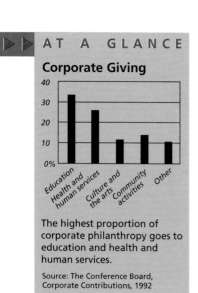

▶▷ AT A GLANCE

Corporate Giving

The highest proportion of corporate philanthropy goes to education and health and human services.

Source: The Conference Board, Corporate Contributions, 1992

1. Business managers are primarily responsible to stockholders, so management must be concerned with providing a return on owners' investments.

2. Corporate time, money, and talent should be used to maximize profits, not to solve society's problems.

3. Social problems affect society in general, so individual businesses should not be expected to solve these problems.

4. Social issues are the responsibility of government officials who are elected for that purpose and who are accountable to the voters for their decisions.

These arguments are obviously based on the assumption that the primary objective of business is to earn profits, whereas government and social institutions should deal with social problems.

Table 2.3 compares the economic and socioeconomic viewpoints in terms of business emphasis. Today, few firms are either purely economic or purely socioeconomic in outlook; most have chosen some middle ground between the two extremes. However, our society generally seems to want—and even to expect—some degree of social responsibility from business. Thus, within this middle ground, businesses are leaning toward the socioeconomic view. In the next several sections, we look at some results of this movement in four specific areas: consumerism, employment practices, concern for the environment, and implementation of social responsibility programs.

■ ■ CONSUMERISM

consumerism all those activities intended to protect the rights of consumers

Consumerism consists of all those activities that are undertaken to protect the rights of consumers. The fundamental issues pursued by the consumer movement fall into three categories: environmental protection, product performance and safety, and information disclosure. Although consumerism

---

TABLE 2.3   A Comparison of the Economic and Socioeconomic Models of Social Responsibility as Implemented in Business

Economic Model			Socioeconomic Model
Primary emphasis is on			Primary emphasis is on
1. Production	M	G	1. Quality of life
2. Exploitation of natural resources	I	R	2. Conservation of natural resources
3. Internal, market-based decisions	D	O	3. Market-based decisions, with some community controls
4. Economic return (profit)	D	U	4. Balance of economic return and social return
5. Firm's or manager's interest	L	N	5. Firm's and community's interests
6. Minor role for government	E	D	6. Active government involvement

Source: Adapted from Keith Davis, William C. Frederick, and Robert L. Blomstrom, *Business and Society: Concepts and Policy Issues* (New York: McGraw-Hill, 1980), p. 9. Used by permission of McGraw-Hill Book Company.

has been with us to some extent since the early nineteenth century, the consumer movement became stronger in the 1960s. It was then that President John F. Kennedy declared that the consumer was entitled to a new "bill of rights."

The Four Basic Rights of Consumers

LEARNING OBJECTIVE 7
Discuss the factors that led to the consumer movement and list some of its results.

President Kennedy's consumer bill of rights asserted that consumers have a right to safety, to be informed, to choose, and to be heard. These four rights are the basis of much of the consumer-oriented legislation that has been passed during the last thirty years. These rights also provide an effective outline of the objectives and accomplishments of the consumer movement.

The Right to Safety   The consumers' right to safety means that products they purchase must be safe for their intended use, must include thorough and explicit directions for proper use, and must be tested by the manufacturer to ensure product quality and reliability. There are several reasons why American business firms must be concerned about product safety. Federal agencies such as the Food and Drug Administration and the Consumer Product Safety Commission have the power to force businesses that make or sell defective products to take corrective actions. Such actions include offering refunds, recalling defective products, issuing public warnings, and reimbursing consumers—all of which can be expensive. Business firms should also be aware that consumers and the government have been winning an increasing number of product-liability lawsuits against sellers of defective products. Moreover, the amount of the awards in these suits has been steadily increasing. The total settlement costs of the class action breast implant suit against sixty companies could be as high as $4.2 billion. Dow Corning Corporation will be responsible for the largest burden—about $2 billion. Approximately 145,000 women have registered for possible claims.[10] Yet another major reason for improving product safety is the consumer's demand for safe products. People will simply stop buying a product they believe is unsafe or unreliable.

The Right to Be Informed   The right to be informed means that consumers must have access to complete information about a product before they buy it. Detailed information about ingredients and nutrition must be provided on food containers, information about fabrics and laundering methods must be attached to clothing, and lenders must disclose the true cost of borrowing the money they make available to customers who purchase merchandise on credit.

In addition, manufacturers must inform consumers about the potential dangers of using their products. Manufacturers that fail to provide such information can be held responsible for personal injuries suffered because of their products. For example, Maytag provides customers with a lengthy booklet that describes how they should use an automatic clothes washer. Sometimes such warnings seem excessive, but they are necessary if user injuries (and resulting lawsuits) are to be avoided.

The Right to Choose   The right to choose means that consumers have a choice of products, offered by different manufacturers and sellers, to satisfy a particular need. The government has done its part by encouraging competition through antitrust legislation. The higher the competition, the greater the choice available to consumers.

Competition and the resulting freedom of choice provide additional benefits for customers by reducing prices. For example, when electronic calculators were initially introduced, they cost over $200. Thanks to intense competition and technological advancements, calculators today can be purchased for less than $10.

The Right to Be Heard   This fourth right means that someone will listen and take appropriate action when customers complain. Actually, management began to listen to consumers after World War II, when competition between businesses that manufactured and sold consumer goods increased. One way firms got a competitive edge was to listen to consumers and provide the products they said they wanted and needed. Today, businesses are listening even more attentively, and many larger firms have consumer relations departments that can be easily contacted via toll-free phone numbers. Other groups listen, too. Most large cities and some states have consumer affairs offices to act on citizens' complaints.

Major Consumerism Forces

The major consumerism forces are individual consumer advocates and organizations, consumer education programs, and consumer laws.

Consumer advocates, such as Ralph Nader, take it upon themselves to protect the rights of consumers. They band together into consumer organizations, either independently or under government sponsorship. Some organizations, such as the National Consumers' League and the Consumer Federation of America, operate nationally, whereas others are active at state and local levels. They inform and organize other consumers, raise issues, help businesses develop consumer-oriented programs, and pressure lawmakers to enact consumer protection laws. Some consumer advocates and organizations encourage consumers to boycott products and businesses to which they have objections. Today, the consumer movement has adopted corporate-style marketing and addresses a broad range of issues. Current campaigns include (1) reduction in the rise of animals for testing purposes, (2) efforts to reduce liquor and cigarette billboard advertising in low-income, inner-city neighborhoods, and (3) efforts to encourage recycling.

Educating consumers to make wiser purchasing decisions is perhaps one of the most far-reaching aspects of consumerism. Increasingly, consumer education is becoming a part of high school and college curricula and adult education programs. These programs cover many topics—for instance, what major factors should be considered when buying specific products, such as insurance, real estate, automobiles, appliances and furniture, clothes, and food; the provisions of certain consumer protection laws; and the sources of information that can help individuals become knowledgeable consumers.

Major advances in consumerism have come through federal legislation. Some laws that have been passed in the last thirty-six years to protect your

TABLE 2.4   Major Federal Legislation Protecting Consumers Since 1960

Legislation	Major Provisions
Federal Hazardous Substances Labeling Act (1960)	Requires warning labels on household chemicals if they are highly toxic.
Kefauver-Harris Drug Amendments (1962)	Established testing practices for drugs and requires manufacturers to label drugs with generic names in addition to trade names.
Cigarette Labeling Act (1965)	Requires manufacturers to place standard warning labels on all cigarette packages and advertising.
Fair Packaging and Labeling Act (1966)	Calls for all products sold across state lines to be labeled with net weight, ingredients, and manufacturer's name and address.
Motor Vehicle Safety Act (1966)	Established standards for safer cars.
Wholesome Meat Act (1967)	Requires states to inspect meat (but not poultry) sold within the state.
Flammable Fabrics Act (1967)	Strengthened flammability standards for clothing to include children's sleepwear in sizes 0 to 6X.
Truth in Lending Act (1968)	Requires lenders and credit merchants to disclose the full cost of finance charges in both dollars and annual percentage rates.
Child Protection and Toy Act (1969)	Bans from interstate commerce toys with mechanical or electrical defects.
Credit Card Liability Act (1970)	Limits credit card holder's liability to $50 per card and stops credit card companies from issuing unsolicited cards.
Fair Credit Reporting Act (1971)	Requires credit bureaus to provide credit reports to consumers regarding their own credit files; also provides for correction of incorrect information.
Consumer Product Safety Commission Act (1972)	Established the Consumer Product Safety Commission.
Trade Regulation Rule (1972)	Established a "cooling-off" period of 72 hours for door-to-door sales.
Fair Credit Billing Act (1974)	Amended the Truth in Lending Act to enable consumers to challenge billing errors.
Equal Credit Opportunity Act (1974)	Provides equal credit opportunities for males and females and for married and single individuals.
Magnuson-Moss Warranty-Federal Trade Commission Act (1975)	Provides for minimum disclosure standards for written consumer product warranties for products that cost more than $15.
Amendment to Equal Credit Opportunity Act (1976)	Prevents discrimination based on race, creed, color, religion, age, and income when granting credit.
Fair Debt Collection Practices Act (1977)	Outlaws abusive collection practices by third parties.
Drug Price Competition and Patent Restoration Act (1984)	Established an abbreviated procedure for registering certain generic drugs.
Orphan Drug Act (1985)	Amended the original 1983 Orphan Drug Act and extends tax incentives to encourage the development of drugs for rare diseases.
Nutrition Labeling and Education Act (1990)	Requires the FDA to review current food labeling and packaging focusing on nutrition label content, label format, ingredient labeling, food descriptors and standards, and health messages.
Telephone Consumer Protection Act (1991)	Prohibits the use of automated dialing and prerecorded-voice calling equipment to make calls or deliver messages.

rights as a consumer are listed and described in Table 2.4. In addition to federal legislation, most business people now realize that they ignore consumer issues only at their own peril. Managers know that improper handling of consumer complaints can mean lost sales, bad publicity, and lawsuits.

■■ EMPLOYMENT PRACTICES

LEARNING OBJECTIVE 8
Analyze how present employment practices are being used to counteract past abuses.

We have seen that a combination of managers who subscribe to the socioeconomic view of business's social responsibility and significant government legislation enacted to protect the buying public has broadened the rights of consumers. The last two decades have seen similar progress in affirming the rights of employees to equal treatment in the workplace.

Everyone who works for a living should have the opportunity to land a job for which he or she is qualified and to be rewarded on the basis of ability and performance. This is an important issue for society, and it also makes good business sense. Yet, over the years, this opportunity has been denied to members of various minority groups. A **minority** is a racial, religious, political, national, or other group regarded as different from the larger group of which it is a part, often singled out for unfavorable treatment.

minority   a racial, religious, political, national, or other group regarded as different from the larger group of which it is a part, often singled out for unfavorable treatment

The federal government responded to the outcry of minority groups during the 1960s and 1970s by passing a number of laws forbidding discrimination in the workplace. (These laws are discussed in Chapter 9 in the context of human resources management.) Now, thirty years after passage of the first of these (the Civil Rights Act of 1964), abuses still exist. An example is the disparity in income levels for whites, blacks, and Hispanics, as illustrated in Figure 2.2. Lower incomes and higher unemployment rates also affect Native Americans, handicapped persons, and women. Responsible managers have instituted a number of programs to counteract the results of discrimination.

Affirmative Action Programs

affirmative action program
a plan designed to increase the number of minority employees at all levels within an organization

An **affirmative action program** is a plan designed to increase the number of minority employees at all levels within an organization. Employers with federal contracts of more than $50,000 per year must have written affirmative action plans. The objective of such programs is to ensure that minorities are represented within the organization in approximately the same proportion as in the surrounding community. If 25 percent of the electricians in a geographic area in which a company is located are black, then approximately 25 percent of the electricians it employs should also be black. Affirmative action plans encompass all areas of human resources management: recruiting, hiring, training, promotion, and pay.

FIGURE 2.2
Comparative Income Levels
Figure represents the median household incomes of the total population and of white, black, and Hispanic workers in 1991. (Hispanic persons may be of any race.)
(Source: Statistical Abstract of the United States, *1993, U.S. Bureau of the Census, p. 462.)*

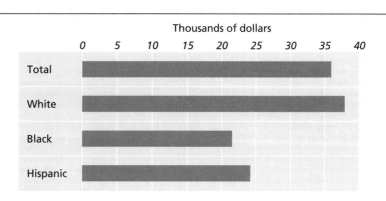

Unfortunately, affirmative action programs have been plagued by two problems. The first involves quotas. In the beginning, many firms pledged to recruit and hire a certain number of minority members by a specific date. To achieve this goal, they were forced to consider only minority applicants for job openings; if they hired nonminority workers, they would be defeating their own purpose. But the courts have ruled that such quotas are unconstitutional even though their purpose is commendable. They are, in fact, a form of discrimination called reverse discrimination.

The second problem is that although most such programs have been reasonably successful, not all business people are in favor of affirmative action programs. Managers not committed to these programs can "play the game" and still discriminate against workers. To help solve this problem, Congress created (and later strengthened) the **Equal Employment Opportunity Commission (EEOC),** a government agency with power to investigate complaints of employment discrimination and power to sue firms that practice it. In 1993 approximately 88,000 charges were filed with EEOC, of which 27 percent dealt with sex discrimination and over one-third focused on racial discrimination.[11]

The threat of legal action has persuaded some corporations to amend their hiring and promotional policies, but the discrepancy between men's and women's salaries has not really been affected, as illustrated in Figure 2.3. For more than thirty years, women have consistently earned only about 60 cents for each dollar earned by men.

Equal Employment Opportunity Commission (EEOC) a government agency with the power to investigate complaints of employment discrimination and the power to sue firms that practice it

Training Programs for the Hard-Core Unemployed

For some firms, social responsibility extends far beyond placing a help-wanted ad in the local newspaper. These firms have assumed the task of helping the **hard-core unemployed:** workers with little education or vocational training and a long history of unemployment. In the past, such

hard-core unemployed workers with little education or vocational training and a long history of unemployment

FIGURE 2.3
Relative Earnings of Male and Female Workers
For more than three decades, the ratio of women's to men's annual, full-time earnings has remained fixed at about the 60 percent level. (Indeed, some observers claim this ratio goes back to biblical times, citing that for purposes of tithing an adult woman was valued at 30 shekels of silver, compared with a man's 50 shekels.) *(Source:* Statistical Abstract of the United States, *1993, U.S. Bureau of the Census, p. 467.)*

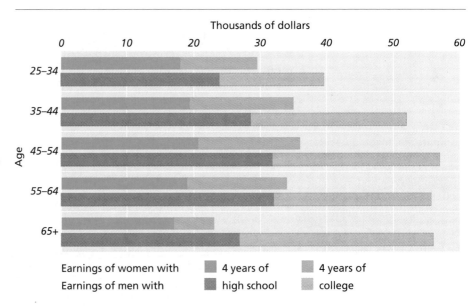

workers were often routinely turned down by personnel managers, even for the most menial jobs.

Obviously, such workers require training; just as obviously, this training can be expensive and time-consuming. To share the costs, business and government have joined together in a number of cooperative programs. One particularly successful partnership is the **National Alliance of Business (NAB),** a joint business-government program to train the hard-core unemployed. The NAB is sponsored by participating corporations, whose executives contribute their talents to do the actual training. The government's responsibilities include setting objectives, establishing priorities, offering the right incentives, and providing limited financing.

National Alliance of Business (NAB)   a joint business-government program to train the hard-core unemployed

■■ CONCERN FOR THE ENVIRONMENT

LEARNING OBJECTIVE 9
Describe the major types of pollution, their causes, and their cures.

The social consciousness of responsible managers and the encouragement of a concerned government have also made the public and the business community partners in a major effort to reduce environmental pollution, conserve natural resources, and reverse some of the worst effects of past negligence in this area.

pollution   the contamination of water, air, or land through the actions of people in an industrialized society

Pollution is the contamination of water, air, or land through the actions of people in an industrialized society. For several decades, environmentalists have been warning us about the dangers of industrial pollution. Unfortunately, business and government leaders either ignored the problem or weren't concerned about it until pollution became a threat to life and health in America. Today Americans expect business and government leaders to take swift action to clean up our environment—and to keep it clean.

Effects of Environmental Legislation

As in other areas of concern to our society, legislation and regulations play a crucial role in pollution control. The laws outlined in Table 2.5 reflect the scope of current environmental legislation. Of major importance was the creation of the Environmental Protection Agency (EPA), the federal agency charged with enforcing laws designed to protect the environment.

When they are aware of a pollution problem, many firms respond to it rather than wait to be cited by the EPA. But other owners and managers take the position that environmental standards are too strict. (Loosely translated, this means that compliance with present standards is too expensive.) Consequently, it has often been necessary for the EPA to take legal action to force firms to install antipollution equipment and clean up waste storage areas.

Experience has shown that the combination of environmental legislation, voluntary compliance, and EPA action can succeed in cleaning up the environment and keeping it clean. However, much still remains to be done.

Water Pollution   Although the quality of our nation's rivers, lakes, and streams has improved significantly in recent years, many of these surface waters remain severely polluted. Currently, one of the most serious water-quality problems results from the high level of toxic pollutants found in these waters. The EPA estimates that 554.7 million pounds of toxic materials were discharged to surface waters in just one year.[12]

TABLE 2.5 Summary of Major Environmental Laws

Legislation	Major Provisions
National Environmental Policy Act (1970)	Established the Environmental Protection Agency (EPA) to enforce federal laws that involve the environment.
Clean Air Amendment (1970)	Provides stringent automotive, aircraft, and factory emission standards.
Water Quality Improvement Act (1970)	Strengthened existing water pollution regulations and provides for large monetary fines against violators.
Resource Recovery Act (1970)	Enlarged the solid-waste disposal program and provides for enforcement by the EPA.
Water Pollution Control Act Amendment (1972)	Established standards for cleaning navigable streams and lakes and eliminating all harmful waste disposal by 1985.
Noise Control Act (1972)	Established standards for major sources of noise and required the EPA to advise the Federal Aviation Administration on standards for airplanes.
Clean Air Act Amendment (1977)	Established new deadlines for cleaning up polluted areas; also required review of existing air-quality standards.
Resource Conservation and Recovery Act (1984)	Amended the original 1976 act and required federal regulation of potentially dangerous solid-waste disposal.
Clean Air Act Amendment (1987)	Established a national air-quality standard for ozone.
Oil Pollution Act (1990)	Expanded the nation's oil spill prevention and response activities; also established the Oil Spill Liability Trust Fund.
Clean Air Act Amendments (1990)	Required that motor vehicles be equipped with onboard systems to control about 90 percent of refueling vapors.

Among the serious threats to people posed by these pollutants are respiratory irritation, cancer, kidney and liver damage, anemia, and heart failure. Toxic pollutants also damage fish and other forms of wildlife. In fish, they cause tumors or reproductive problems; shellfish and wildlife living in or drinking from toxin-infested waters have also suffered genetic defects.

In addition to its adverse impacts on human health and aquatic life, toxic water pollution inflicts significant economic damages. According to the EPA, toxic discharges to surface waters cause losses of approximately $800 million per year in recreational fishing, swimming, and boating opportunities.[13]

The task of water cleanup has proved to be extremely complicated and costly because of pollution runoff and toxic contamination. And yet, improved water quality is not only necessary; it is also achievable. Consider Cleveland's Cuyahoga River. A few years ago the river was so contaminated by industrial wastes that it burst into flames one hot summer day! Now, after a sustained community cleanup effort, the river is pure enough for fish to thrive in.

Another serious issue is acid rain, which is contributing significantly to the deterioration of coastal waters, lakes, and marine life in the eastern United States. Acid rain forms when sulfur emitted by smokestacks in industrialized areas combines with moisture in the atmosphere to form acids that are spread by winds. The acids eventually fall to the earth in rain, which finds its way into streams, rivers, and lakes. The acid rain problem has spread rapidly in recent years, and experts fear the situation will worsen if the nation begins to burn more coal to generate electricity. To solve the problem, investigators must first determine where the sulfur is being emitted. The expenses that this vital investigation and cleanup entail are going to be high. The human costs of having ignored the problem so long may be higher still.

Air Pollution   Usually two or three factors combine to form air pollution in any given location. The first factor is large amounts of carbon monoxide and hydrocarbons emitted by motor vehicles concentrated in a relatively small area. The second is the smoke and other pollutants emitted by manufacturing

Good uses for solid waste. Drink-box recycling helps to significantly reduce land pollution. Over 1,400 schools in a thirteen-state area participate in the drink-box recycling program.

facilities. These two factors can be partially eliminated through pollution-control devices on cars, trucks, and smokestacks.

The third factor that contributes to air pollution—one that cannot be changed—is the combination of weather and geography. The Los Angeles basin, for example, combines just the right weather and geographic conditions for creating dense smog. Los Angeles has strict regulations regarding air pollution. Even so, Los Angeles still struggles with air pollution problems because of uncontrollable conditions.

How effective is air pollution control? Most authorities agree that we are seeing improvement in air quality. A number of cities have cleaner air today than they did twenty years ago. Numerous chemical companies have recognized that they must take responsibility for operating their plants in an environmentally safe manner. Some of them now devote considerable capital expenditures to purchasing antipollution devices. However, air levels of sulfur dioxide and nitrogen dioxide—the main components of acid rain—as well as of soot continue to increase.

Land Pollution Air and water quality may be improving, but land pollution is still a serious problem in many areas. The fundamental issues are (1) how to restore damaged or contaminated land at a reasonable cost and (2) how to protect unpolluted land from future damage.

The land pollution problem has been worsening over the past few years, as modern technology has continued to produce increasing amounts of chemical and radioactive waste. U.S. manufacturers produce an estimated 40 to 60 million tons of contaminated oil, solvents, acids, and sludges each year. Service businesses, utility companies, hospitals, and other industries dump vast amounts of wastes into the environment.

Individuals in the United States also contribute to the waste disposal problem. The U.S. population generated 306,866,000 tons of solid waste in 1993. Of that amount 71 percent was landfilled, 19 percent was recycled, and 10 percent was incinerated.[14] A shortage of landfills, owing to stricter regulations, makes garbage disposal a serious problem in some areas. Incinerators help to solve the landfill shortage problem, but they bring with them their own problems. They reduce the amounts of garbage but also leave tons of ash to be buried—ash that often has a higher concentration of toxicity than the original garbage. Other causes of land pollution include strip-mining of coal, nonselective cutting of forests, and the development of agricultural land for housing and industry.

To help pay the enormous costs of cleaning up land polluted with chemicals and toxic wastes, Congress created a $1.6 billion Superfund in 1980. Originally, money was to flow into the Superfund from a tax paid by 800 oil and chemical companies that produce toxic waste. Then the EPA was to use the money in the Superfund to finance the cleanup of hazardous waste sites across the nation. To replenish the Superfund, the EPA had two options: it could sue the companies that were guilty of dumping chemicals at specific waste sites, or it could negotiate with guilty companies and thus completely avoid the legal system. During the 1980s, officials at the EPA came under fire because they preferred negotiated settlements. Critics referred to these settlements as "sweetheart deals" with industry. They felt the EPA should be

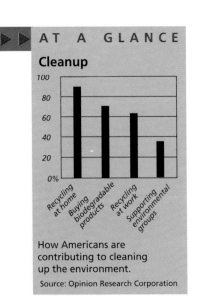

▶▶ AT A GLANCE

Cleanup

How Americans are contributing to cleaning up the environment.

Source: Opinion Research Corporation

much more aggressive in reducing land pollution in the United States. Of course, most corporate executives believe that cleanup efficiency and quality might be improved if companies were more involved. Since the Superfund was established, the EPA has identified 1,270 toxic waste sites but only 49 have been completely cleaned. Much of the $12 billion spent by the EPA has been on lawsuits to force companies to pay for cleanups.[15]

Noise Pollution   Excessive noise caused by traffic, aircraft, and machinery can do physical harm to human beings. Research has shown that people who are exposed to loud noises for long periods of time can suffer permanent hearing loss. The Noise Control Act of 1972 established noise emission standards for aircraft and airports, railroads, and interstate motor carriers. The act also provides funding for noise research at state and local levels.

Noise levels can be reduced by two methods. The source of noise pollution can be isolated as much as possible. (Thus, many metropolitan airports are located outside the cities.) And engineers can modify machinery and equipment to reduce noise levels. If it is impossible to reduce industrial noise to acceptable levels, workers should be required to wear earplugs to guard against permanent hearing damage.

Who Should Pay for a Clean Environment?

Governments and businesses are spending billions of dollars annually to reduce pollution—approximately $35 billion to control air pollution, $25 billion to control water pollution, and $12 billion to treat hazardous wastes.

To make matters worse, much of the money required to purify the environment is supposed to come from already depressed industries, such as the chemical industry. And a few firms have discovered that it is cheaper to pay a fine than to install expensive pollution control equipment.

Who, then, will pay for the environmental cleanup? Many business leaders offer one answer—tax money should be used to clean up the environment and keep it clean. They reason that business is not the only source of pollution, so business should not be forced to absorb the entire cost of the cleanup. Environmentalists disagree. They believe that the cost of proper treatment and disposal of industrial wastes is an expense of doing business. In either case, consumers may have to pay a large part of the cost—either as taxes or in the form of higher prices for goods and services.

■■ IMPLEMENTING A SOCIAL RESPONSIBILITY PROGRAM

LEARNING OBJECTIVE 10
Identify the steps a business must take to implement a program of social responsibility.

A firm's decision to be socially responsible is a step in the right direction—but only the first step. The firm must then develop and implement a tangible program to reach this goal. Consider the scope of the Body Shop's program and the questions that have arisen about this program (see Global Perspectives). A particular firm's social responsibility program will be affected by its size, financial resources, past record in the area of social responsibility, and competition. But above all, the program must have the firm's total commitment or it will fail.

The Body Shop: Practices Versus Promises

In 1976 Anita and T. Gordon Roddick opened the Body Shop, a small cosmetics store, in Brighton, England. Today the Body Shop is a 1,128-outlet retail cosmetics firm operating in forty-five countries. From the start, the Body Shop committed itself to environmental and social responsibility and to ethical business practices. Although annual sales now top $700 million, the Roddicks assert that their company is not just about making money.

For years, it seemed that the Body Shop was living up to the sign posted in Anita Roddick's office: "The Body Shop is the world's most honest company." In addition to offering "100 percent pure and natural" soaps and lotions never tested on animals, the Body Shop is famous for its social activism. Its Trade Not Aid program helps developing countries by purchasing their natural ingredients. In England, the company donated $450,000 to start a newspaper that homeless people now publish and sell.

Recently, however, questions about some of its practices contradict the Body Shop's carefully crafted image as a business with a conscience. Are all of its products natural? A close look into its products uncovered extensive use of artificial colors and fragrances, synthetic preservatives, and petroleum products. Does the Body Shop, as it claims, microbiologically analyze and test all of its raw materials? Reports from unannounced Federal Drug Administration inspectors turned up many quality control problems. For example, to save time during a recent Christmas rush, the Body Shop suspended microbial tests on its banana shampoo. After sending shipments to two distribution centers, the company resumed testing on the product and discovered *E coli* bacteria levels at 1,000 percent above industry standards. Does the company shun animal testing? The Body Shop's purchasing manager recently acknowledged that although the firm's retail products aren't tested on animals, about 47 percent of the ingredients that go into these products are.

Is the Body Shop an environmentally progressive company? The former head of the firm's United States environmental department contends that the company has never recycled as fully as it claims and that, on several occasions, Body Shop plants have failed to report that they leaked waste into local sewage systems. Are the Body Shop's trade practices a model of ethics for businesses around the world? According to a recent report from a meeting of fair trade organizations, the Body Shop's highly touted Trade Not Aid sourcing program accounts for less than 1 percent of the firm's ingredients. In addition, the company does not pay "first-world wages for third-world products," as its advertising maintains. Finally, does the Body Shop donate an "inordinately high percentage of pretax profits to often controversial charitable campaigns," as a company fact sheet reports? A review of public records reveals that the organization's donations have been well below the average annual donations for American companies.

These revelations have raised customers' eyebrows and caused a commotion in the press. Why are so many people so upset? They believe the Body Shop has failed to live up to the socially conscious image the company itself cultivated. If the same disclosures were made about firms that do not claim to be paragons of social responsibility, the story probably wouldn't make headlines or the evening news. For example, no one would be shocked or feel betrayed to learn that Du Pont doesn't obtain its ingredients from the Brazilian rain forest. Experts insist that to maintain the public's trust, companies must live up to their own standards and ideals. To try to regain that trust, the Body Shop is taking action. The company published a rebuttal to the claims tarnishing its reputation, and its new head of information audit has been given the job of making sure that the British firm acts as ethically and responsibly as it says it does.

Commitment by top-level executives. This CEO of GE Capital not only helps to raise funds for the Stamford, Connecticut, Boys and Girls Clubs, but also sends books to the school and donates time to help students learn computing skills.

Developing a Social Responsibility Program

An effective program for social responsibility takes time, money, and organization. In most cases, developing and implementing such a program will require four steps: securing the commitment of top executives, planning, appointing a director, and preparing a social audit.

Commitment of Top Executives   Without the support of top executives, any program will soon falter and become ineffective. As evidence of their commitment to social responsibility, top managers should develop a policy statement that outlines key areas of concern. This statement sets a tone of positive enthusiasm and will later serve as a guide for other employees as they become involved in the program.

Planning   Next, a committee of managers should be appointed to plan the program. Whatever form their plan takes, it should deal with each of the issues described in the top management policy statement. If necessary, outside consultants can be hired to help develop the plan.

Appointment of a Director   After the social responsibility plan is established, a top-level executive should be appointed to direct the organization's activities in implementing it. This individual should be charged with recommending specific policies and helping individual departments understand and live up to the social responsibilities the firm has assumed. Depending on the size of the firm, the director may require a staff to handle the program on a day-to-day basis.

social audit a comprehensive report of what an organization has done, and is doing, with regard to social issues that affect it

The Social Audit At specified intervals, the program director should prepare a social audit for the firm. A **social audit** is a comprehensive report of what an organization has done, and is doing, with regard to social issues that affect it. This document provides the information the firm needs to evaluate and revise its social responsibility program. Typical subject areas include human resources, community involvement, the quality and safety of products, business practices, and efforts to reduce pollution and improve the environment. The information included in a social audit should be as accurate and as quantitative as possible, and the audit should reveal both positive and negative aspects of the program.

Funding the Program

We have noted that social responsibility costs money. Thus, just like any other corporate undertaking, a program to improve social responsibility must be funded. Funding can come from three sources: (1) Management can pass the cost on to consumers in the form of higher prices; (2) The corporation may be forced to absorb the cost of the program if, for example, the competitive situation does not permit a price increase. In this case, the cost is treated as a business expense, and profit is reduced; (3) The federal government may pay for all or part of the cost through tax reductions or other incentives.

■ ■ ■ ■ CHAPTER REVIEW

Summary

1 Understand what is meant by *business ethics.*

Ethics is the study of right and wrong and of the morality of choices. Business ethics is the application of moral standards to business situations.

2 Identify the types of ethical concerns that arise in the business world.

Ethical issues arise often in business situations out of relationships with investors, customers, employees, creditors, or competitors. Business people should make every effort to be fair, to consider the welfare of customers and others within the firm, to avoid conflicts of interest, and to communicate honestly.

3 Discuss the factors that affect the level of ethical behavior in organizations.

Individual, social, and opportunity factors all affect the level of ethical behavior in an organization. Individual factors include knowledge level, moral values and attitudes, and personal goals. Social factors include cultural norms and the actions and values of

coworkers and significant others. Opportunity factors refer to the amount of leeway that exists in an organization for employees to behave unethically if they so choose.

4 Explain how ethical decision making can be encouraged.

Governments, trade associations, and individual firms can all establish guidelines for defining ethical behavior. Governments can pass stricter regulations. Trade associations provide ethical guidelines for their members. Companies provide codes of ethics, written guides to acceptable and ethical behavior as defined by an organization, and create an atmosphere in which ethical behavior is encouraged. An ethical employee working in an unethical environment may resort to whistle blowing to bring a questionable practice to light.

5 Describe how our current views on the social responsibility of business have evolved.

In a socially responsible business, management realizes that its activities have an impact on society and considers that impact in the decision-making process. Before the 1930s, workers, consumers, and government had very little influence on business activities; as a result, business leaders gave little thought to social responsibility. All this changed with the Great Depression. Government regulations, employee demands, and consumer awareness combined to create a demand that businesses act in socially responsible ways.

6   Explain the two views on social responsibility of business and understand the arguments for and against increased social responsibility.

The basic premise of the economic model of social responsibility is that society benefits most when business is left alone to produce profitable goods and services. According to the socioeconomic model, business has as much responsibility to society as it has to its owners. Most managers adopt a viewpoint somewhere between these two extremes.

7   Discuss the factors that led to the consumer movement and list some of its results.

Consumerism consists of all those activities that are undertaken to protect the rights of consumers. The consumer movement has generally demanded—and received—attention from business in the areas of product safety, product information, product choices through competition, and in the resolution of complaints about products and business practices. Although concerns over consumer rights have been around to some extent since the early nineteenth century, the movement became more powerful in the 1960s when President John F. Kennedy initiated the consumer "bill of rights." The four basic rights of consumers include the right to safety, the right to be informed, the right to choose, and the right to be heard.

8   Analyze how present employment practices are being used to counteract past abuses.

Legislation and public demand have prompted some businesses to correct past abuses in employment practices—mainly with regard to minority groups. Affirmative action and training of the hard-core unemployed are two types of programs that have been used successfully.

9   Describe the major types of pollution, their causes, and their cures.

Industry has contributed to the pollution of our land and water through the dumping of wastes, and to air pollution through vehicle and smokestack emissions. This contamination can be cleaned up and controlled, but the big question is, Who will pay? Present cleanup efforts are funded partly by government tax revenues, partly by business, and, in the long run, by consumers.

10   Identify the steps a business must take to implement a program of social responsibility.

A program to implement social responsibility in a business begins with total commitment by top management. The program should be carefully planned, and a capable director should be appointed to implement it. Social audits should be prepared periodically as a means of evaluating and revising the program. Programs may be funded through federal incentives or through price increases.

Key Terms

You should now be able to define and give an example relevant to each of the following terms:

ethics (34)
business ethics (34)
code of ethics (38)
whistle blowing (39
social responsibility (39)
caveat emptor (43)
economic model of social responsibility (45)
socioeconomic model of social responsibility (46)
consumerism (47)
minority (51)
affirmative action program (51)
Equal Employment Opportunity Commission (EEOC) (52)
hard-core unemployed (52)
National Alliance of Business (NAB) (53)
pollution (53)
social audit (60)

Questions

Review Questions

1. Why might an individual with high ethical standards act less ethically in business than in his or her personal life?
2. How would an organizational code of ethics help ensure ethical business behavior?
3. How and why did the American business environment change after the Great Depression?
4. What are the major differences between the economic model of social responsibility and the socioeconomic model?

5. What are the arguments for and against increased social responsibility for business?

6. Describe and give an example of each of the four basic rights of consumers.

7. There are more women than men in the United States. Why, then, are women considered a minority with regard to employment?

8. What is the goal of affirmative action programs? How is this goal achieved?

9. What is the primary function of the Equal Employment Opportunity Commission?

10. How do businesses contribute to each of the four forms of pollution? How can they avoid polluting the environment?

11. Our environment *can* be cleaned up and kept clean. Why haven't we simply done so?

12. Describe the steps involved in developing a social responsibility program within a large corporation.

Discussion Questions

1. Are Bausch & Lomb's contact lens pricing policies ethical? Explain.

2. When a company acts in an ethically questionable manner, what types of problems are caused for the organization and its customers?

3. How can an employee take an ethical stand regarding a business decision when his or her superior has already taken a different position?

4. Overall, would it be more profitable for a business to follow the economic model or the socioeconomic model of social responsibility?

5. Why should business take on the task of training the hard-core unemployed?

6. To what extent should the blame for vehicular air pollution be shared by manufacturers, consumers, and government?

7. Why is there so much government regulation involving social responsibility issues? Should there be less?

Exercises

1. Write out four "guidelines" that could be included as part of the code of ethics that prevails at your school or at a firm where you have worked.

2. Research one case in which the EEOC or the EPA successfully brought suit against one or more firms. Report on that case, giving your own evaluation of the merits of the agency's position.

3. List some items that should be included in a social audit for a small business that is not a retail store.

VIDEO CASE 2.1

R. J. Reynolds Tobacco Company: Joe Camel Under Fire

The surgeon general of the United States reports that every year about 400,000 Americans lose their lives because of smoking cigarettes. Further, the average male smoker is fifteen times more likely to die of lung cancer than a nonsmoker. Despite these grim statistics, Americans continue to spend about $42 billion a year on cigarettes. Ever since the colonial citizens of Jamestown, Virginia, planted the first U.S. commercial tobacco crop in 1612, cigarettes have been part of American life, and the tobacco industry a powerful force in the American economy.

Although Americans continue to light up in large numbers, sales of older cigarette brands, such as R. J. Reynolds's Camel Filters, have declined significantly. However, in 1987 Reynolds introduced an updated advertising campaign featuring the cartoon camel known as Old Joe. In five years, the brand's market share grew from 2.7 percent to 4.1 percent, a notable rise for a 75-year-old brand in a sagging market. Industry analysts attribute the Camel sales increase to the popularity of advertisements and sales promotions featuring Old Joe. The news for RJR Tobacco, however, is not all good. Antismoking activists criticize the manufacturer for creating a campaign that they say targets underage smokers and demand the demise of Old Joe Camel.

When Federal Trade Commission regulations banned radio and television advertising of cigarettes, R. J. Reynolds, along with other tobacco manufacturers, turned to print and direct mail for the bulk of its promotion. Despite more than a decade of these efforts, sales of the venerable Camels continued declining until ads featuring Old Joe rejuvenated the brand. Whether dressed for adventure or a night on the town, Old Joe is depicted as a "Smooth Character" with style and class. For the first time since the campaign began, Reynolds recently added females to the cast of Camel characters. In four-page, full-color ads appearing in *People*, *Us*, *Glamour*, *Redbook*, and *Sports Illustrated*, Josephine Camels crowd Joe's Place, the bar setting of other Joe Camel ads. Male and female camels shoot pool, throw darts, and play cards, all the while smoking or holding lighted cigarettes.

RJR executives openly admit picking a "spokescartoon" with a contemporary image to attract younger consumers, but the question many critics are raising is just how young. Three studies recently published in the *Journal of the American Medical Association* suggest that Old Joe's audience is far too young, that recognition of the character is lower among adults than children, and that cartoon camel ads and promotions encourage children to smoke. Among all age groups, children aged 12 and 13 are the most familiar with the Smooth Character campaign, and a majority of 6-year-olds associate Old Joe with cigarettes as clearly as they do Mickey Mouse with the Disney Channel.

R. J. Reynolds disputes all three of the studies. Company officials contend that the statistics are inaccurate, deny that the Old Joe campaign targets children, and assert that just because children can identify Old Joe doesn't mean they will buy the product. The company cites its own studies showing that despite increased awareness of Joe Camel among children, kids still don't like smoking.

The results of the JAMA studies fanned the fire of controversy surrounding the Old Joe campaign. Several health-related groups insisted that R. J. Reynolds get rid of the Old Joe character, and the American Medical Association and the U.S. Surgeon General requested that RJR voluntarily remove Joe from all advertising and promotion for Camel cigarettes. The Coalition on Smoking and Health petitioned the Federal Trade Commission to take action against the company's cartoon camel, as did some FTC staff.

Reynolds continues to defend its right to advertise a legal product and has no plans to put the brakes on the Old Joe bandwagon. The American Association of Advertisers supports the company, decrying what it terms unconstitutional restrictions on advertising. According to the results of a recent *Advertising Age* poll, it seems that many Americans agree. Over half the respondents who believe that Old Joe strongly influences children to smoke also believe that RJR should not bow to outside pressures to derail him.

The FTC commissioners recently voted three to two against pursuing the case, giving R. J. Reynolds and Old Joe a reprieve. In response to the vote, a spokesperson for the coalition condemned the FTC's decision, calling it a disservice to the children of America.[16]

Questions

1. Would a ban on cigarette advertising violate a tobacco company's First Amendment constitutional rights?
2. Even though the sale of tobacco products is legal, is it ethical for a company to promote a product that kills about 400,000 people in the United States annually? Discuss.
3. Is it ethical for RJR to use a promotional campaign that is so highly effective in reaching children?

4. Evaluate RJR's response to the criticisms of its Old Joe Camel campaign.

CASE 2.2

Ben & Jerry's: Being a Good Corporate Citizen Isn't Easy

"This carton contains some of the finest ice cream available anywhere. We know because we're the guys who make it. We start with lots of fresh Vermont cream and the finest flavorings available. We never use any fillers or artificial ingredients of any kind. With our specially modified equipment, we stir less air into the ice cream creating a denser, richer, creamier product of uncompromisingly high quality. It costs more and it's worth it." Every container of Ben & Jerry's Homemade ice cream carries this message because company founders Ben Cohen and Jerry Greenfield want you to know they are committed to top quality in every one of their flavors—from Wavy Gravy, Cherry Garcia, and Chunky Monkey to Heath Bar Crunch, White Russian, and just plain vanilla. Although not announced on cartons, Ben & Jerry's is equally pledged to its social mission: "to operate the company in a way that actively recognizes the central role that business plays in the structure of society by initiating innovative ways to improve the quality of life of a broad community, local, national, and international." What the company has learned over the years is that making and selling a good product and being a good corporate citizen at the same time isn't easy.

In the summer of 1978, Ben and Jerry opened a homemade ice cream parlor in an abandoned filling station in Burlington, Vermont. By the end of their first summer in business, sales of Ben & Jerry's homemade averaged $650 a day. By the time the first franchise outlet opened in 1981, the ice cream's fame had spread enough to warrant a story in *Time* magazine. The company launched what has become its best-selling flavor, Chocolate Chip Cookie Dough, and in 1992 *Fortune* put that treat on its list of Products of the Year. With annual sales now nearing $150 million, Ben & Jerry's is number two behind Haagen-Dazs in the superpremium ice cream segment.

From the beginning, the company's founders believed that they could care for employees, customers, and the planet, and still make a profit. Ben & Jerry's therefore established an ambitious social responsibility agenda. The company contributes extensively to environmental programs, and gives 7.5 percent of its pretax earnings to nonprofit and charitable groups. To support Vermont family farmers, the company pays them higher than the market rate for milk; to support native tribes in the Amazon rain forest, the company buys their Brazil nuts. If you buy a poster of its new print ad featuring political activists such as Spike Lee, Bobby Seale, Buffy Saint-Marie, and Carlos Santana enjoying Ben & Jerry's new smooth line of ice cream, your money goes to charity.

Although it is often held up as a model of profitable and socially responsible business, the company has plenty of problems maintaining that reputation. Public perception makes it hard for Ben & Jerry's to keep its nice-guy image. Even though people often suspect that the company's socially responsible actions are really public relations gimmicks, they also seem to think that Ben & Jerry's doesn't have the right to be as "ruthless" as other companies. For example, when Ben & Jerry's went to court to stop competitors from distributing other brands of ice cream in some geographic areas, critics were quick to point out the discrepancy between the company's soft image and its hard actions.

People come to work at Ben & Jerry's expecting flexibility, autonomy, and informality along with their paychecks. Many employees are later shocked to learn that the company is not a model of democracy. Asserted one company officer, "Having a voice is not equal to having a vote." In addition, employees have had to cope with outmoded equipment and suffer a relatively high rate of worker injury.

Over the years, Ben & Jerry's has discovered that having a social conscience doesn't necessarily translate into having business skills. For example, the company has had problems with quality control, which was often left to Ben himself, who tested flavors by lining them up, eating them, and deciding how they tasted. His

method failed with Ben & Jerry's "light" brand extension, which customers found icy and grainy. In addition, the same policies that make Ben & Jerry's such an admirable organization make it cost more to run. Pollution control equipment, daycare subsidies, and paying Vermont farmers and Amazon Indians are all expensive.

Recently, given increasing competition and Ben & Jerry's slumping stocks, the company's leaders hired the firm's first ever chief executive officer, Robert Holland. Unfortunately, this plunge into mainstream business brought to an end a practice that had made Ben & Jerry's famous for fairness. The public and experts alike were disappointed that the company decided to abandon its policy of paying no executive more than seven times the salary of the lowest paid employee. (What this means is that while the CEO of General Mills earns $1,407,491 a year, Ben Cohen took home $133,212.) The company knew it would have trouble finding qualified executives who would settle for such a relatively low salary. Cohen insists, however, that he expects no changes in style or social commitment at Ben & Jerry's with the arrival of the new CEO.[17]

Questions

1. Do firms that attempt to be socially responsible experience higher costs? Why or why not?
2. Is there an upper limit on the extent to which a firm can be socially responsible? Explain.
3. In the future, will Ben & Jerry's be able to maintain its high-profile image as a good neighbor to the community and the world? Discuss.

■■■■CHAPTER 3

Global Business

LEARNING OBJECTIVES

After studying this chapter you should be able to

1 Explain the economic basis for international business.

2 Discuss the restrictions that nations place on international trade, the objectives of these restrictions, and their results.

3 Outline the extent of international trade and the organizations that are working to foster it.

4 Define the methods by which a firm can organize for, and enter, international markets.

5 Describe the various sources of export assistance.

6 Identify the institutions that help firms and nations finance international business.

CHAPTER PREVIEW

We describe international trade in this chapter in terms of specialization, whereby each country trades the surplus goods and services it produces most efficiently for products in short supply. We also outline the restrictions that nations place on products from other countries and present some of the advantages and disadvantages of such restrictions. In addition, we discuss the social, cultural, legal, and economic factors that must be considered by firms intending to sell products in other countries. Finally, we list some of the institutions that provide the complex financing necessary for modern international trade.

Exporting Pays Off

A Mesa, Arizona, manufacturer of test equipment for the telecommunications industry has found that national trade shows for telecommunications equipment thoroughly introduce a market.

"In overseas markets, you need a sampling to find out where you get your biggest response and to indicate what kind of demographics is best for your products," says Bruce Nelson, international sales manager for Progressive Electronics, Inc., a fifty-employee firm in Mesa, Arizona. "Our first step is to get a clear picture of where we should focus our attention and exert effort."

"If you are not sure about a country, national trade shows for your industry are a good introduction," he advises. "Going to a trade show is like going to the mall. Everybody's there—your competitors, and in our case, representatives of the telephone company. You walk for three or four days, and you get a pretty good handle on the market. And you get lots of leads." The first major trade show Nelson attended for Progressive Electronics was Telecom 91 in Geneva, Switzerland, attended by 700,000 industry reps.

Jefferson Industries, Inc., a manufacturer of area rugs, mats, and runners based in Chicago, determined that Asia is a promising market. "We are looking at Asia, because—with the greatest concentration of people in the world—it is the up and coming marketplace," says Howard Schnair, president and CEO of Jefferson Industries. The firm makes floor coverings at plants in Chicago and Chatsworth, Georgia.

"The economies in Asia are dynamic and sophisticated," Schnair observes. "Much to my surprise the Asian people want American goods. However, U.S. companies have to offer products that are competitive in price and quality.

"We realized we had a product that enjoyed widespread acceptance, and we knew would be competitive, so we pursued exports," he explains.

Besides Asia, Jefferson Industries exports to Latin America, Europe, and the Middle East. In the past five years, the firm has increased its exports from zero to 12 to 15 percent of sales. Schnair believes that the North American Free Trade Agreement (NAFTA) will be a "big help" in increasing his firm's sales to Mexico and Canada.

Ford Motor Company is the world's third-largest industrial corporation and the second-largest producer of cars and trucks. With manufacturing, assembly, or sales affiliates in twenty-nine countries outside the United States, Ford companies in 1993 employed approximately 322,200 people.

Ford's products were displayed at the 1993 Tokyo Motor Show because growth in Asian markets is important to the company's future. Ford will begin selling the American-built, left-hand-drive 1994 Ford Mustang in Japan, marking the pony car's return to that market for the first time in ten years. The automaker will also begin selling right-hand-drive versions of the domestic-built Ford Probe and the European-built Ford Mondeo. Looking ahead, Ford plans to sell right-hand-drive versions of its popular Taurus and Explorer model lines.[1]

■　■　■　■　■　■　■　■　■　■　■

Although international activities of firms like Ford Motor Company and Progressive Electronics, Inc., receive publicity in the media, international trade is not, of course, limited to the sale of American products in foreign countries. Every nation is involved in international business to some degree.

Theoretically, international trade is every bit as logical and worthwhile as, say, trade between Indiana and Ohio. Yet nations tend to restrict the import of certain goods for a variety of reasons, just as the United States effectively restricted the import of Chinese wrenches and steel pipe made by forced labor.

In spite of such restrictions, international trade has increased almost steadily since World War II. Many of the industrialized nations have signed trade agreements that are intended to eliminate problems in international business and to help less developed nations participate in world trade. Individual firms around the world have seized the opportunity to compete in foreign markets by exporting and increasing foreign production, as well as by other means.

■■ THE BASIS FOR INTERNATIONAL BUSINESS

LEARNING OBJECTIVE 1
Explain the economic basis for international business.

international business all business activities that involve exchanges across national boundaries

International business encompasses all business activities that involve exchanges across national boundaries. Thus a firm is engaged in international business when it buys some portion of its input from, or sells some portion of its output to, an organization located in a foreign country. (A small retail store may sell goods produced in some other country. However, because it purchases these goods from American distributors, it is not considered to be engaged in international trade.)

Absolute and Comparative Advantage

Some countries are better equipped than other countries to produce particular goods or services. The reason may be a country's natural resources, its labor supply, or even customs or a historical accident. Such a country would be best off if it could *specialize* in the production of such products, because it can produce them most efficiently. The country could use what it needed of these products and then trade the surplus for products it could not produce efficiently on its own.

absolute advantage the ability to produce a specific product more efficiently than any other nation

Saudi Arabia has thus specialized in the production of crude oil and petroleum products, South Africa in diamonds, and Australia in wool. Each of these countries is said to have an absolute advantage with regard to a particular product. An **absolute advantage** is the ability to produce a specific product more efficiently than any other nation.

One country may have an absolute advantage with regard to several products, whereas another country may have no absolute advantage at all. Yet it is still worthwhile for these two countries to specialize and trade with

67

each other. To see why this is so, consider the following situation: You are the president of a successful manufacturing firm, and you can accurately type ninety words per minute. Your assistant can type eighty words per minute but would run the business poorly. You thus have an absolute advantage over your assistant in both typing and managing. But you cannot afford to type your own letters because your time is better spent in managing the business. That is, you have a comparative advantage in managing. A **comparative advantage** is the ability to produce a specific product more efficiently than any other product.

comparative advantage the ability to produce a specific product more efficiently than any other product

Your assistant, on the other hand, has a comparative advantage in typing because he or she can do that better than managing the business. So you spend your time managing, and you leave the typing to your assistant. Overall, the business is run as efficiently as possible, because you are each working in accordance with your own comparative advantage.

The same is true for nations. Goods and services are produced more efficiently when each country specializes in the products for which it has a comparative advantage. Moreover, by definition, every country has a comparative advantage in *some* product. The United States has many comparative advantages—in research and development, high technology industries, and identifying new markets, for instance.

Exporting and Importing

Suppose the United States specializes in producing corn. It will then produce a surplus of corn, but perhaps it will have a shortage of wine. France, on the other hand, specializes in producing wine but experiences a shortage of corn. To satisfy both needs—for corn and for wine—the two countries should trade with each other. The United States should export corn and import wine. France should export wine and import corn.

exporting selling and shipping raw materials or products to other nations

Exporting is selling and shipping raw materials or products to other nations. The Boeing Co., for example, exports its airplanes to a number of countries, for use by their airlines. Figure 3.1 shows the top ten merchandise-exporting states.

importing purchasing raw materials or products in other nations and bringing them into one's own country

Importing is purchasing raw materials or products in other nations and bringing them into one's own country. Thus, buyers for Macy's department stores may purchase rugs in India or raincoats in England and have them shipped back to the United States for resale.

balance of trade the total value of a nation's exports less the total value of its imports, over some period of time

Importing and exporting are the principal activities involved in international trade. They give rise to an important concept called the balance of trade. A nation's **balance of trade** is the total value of its exports *less* the total value of its imports, over some period of time. If a country imports more than it exports, its balance of trade is negative and is said to be *unfavorable*. (A negative balance of trade is unfavorable because the country must export money to pay for its excess imports.) In 1993, the United States imported $581 billion worth of merchandise and exported $465 billion worth. It thus had a trade deficit of $116 billion. A **trade deficit** is an unfavorable balance of trade (see Figure 3.2). However, as shown in Figure 3.3, the United States has consistently enjoyed a large and rapidly growing surplus in services. For example, in 1993 the United States imported

trade deficit an unfavorable balance of trade

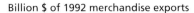

FIGURE 3.1
The Top Ten Merchandise-Exporting States
California and Texas account for almost one-fourth of all the 1992 U.S. merchandise exports.   (*Source:* Business America, *April 1994, p. 6.*)

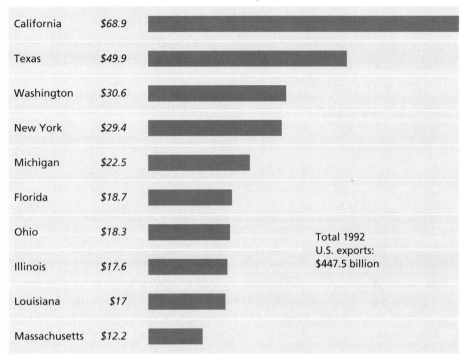

Billion $ of 1992 merchandise exports

California	$68.9
Texas	$49.9
Washington	$30.6
New York	$29.4
Michigan	$22.5
Florida	$18.7
Ohio	$18.3
Illinois	$17.6
Louisiana	$17
Massachusetts	$12.2

Total 1992
U.S. exports:
$447.5 billion

$116 billion worth and exported over $174 billion worth, thus creating a favorable balance in services of $58 billion.[2]

On the other hand, when a country exports more than it imports, it is said to have a *favorable* balance of trade. This has consistently been the case for Japan over the last two decades or so.

FIGURE 3.2
U.S. International Trade in Goods
If a country imports more goods than it exports, the balance of trade is said to be negative, as it was in the United States in 1993.
(Source: U.S. Department of Commerce, Bureau of Economic Analysis, National Income and Product Accounts, Survey of Current Business, *June 1994, p. 95, and* Business America, *March 1994, p. 3.)*

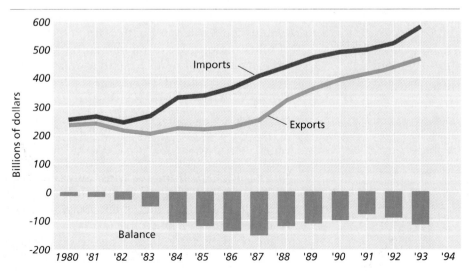

FIGURE 3.3
U.S. International Trade in Goods and Services and the Combined Balance
Even though the United States has a positive balance of trade in services, the combined effect is still a deficit in our balance of trade.
(Source: Business America, *June 1994, p. 33.)*

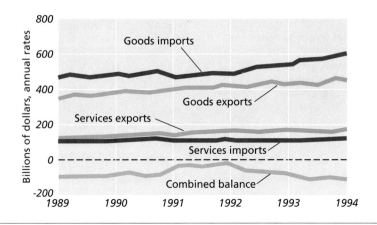

balance of payments the total flow of money into the country less the total flow of money out of the country, over some period of time

AT A GLANCE

U.S. Services Exports

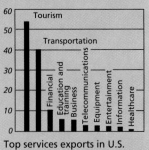

Top services exports in U.S. for 1992

Installation, maintenance and repair. (In billions of dollars)

Source: Dept. of Commerce

LEARNING OBJECTIVE 2
Discuss the restrictions that nations place on international trade, the objectives of these restrictions, and their results.

import duty (tariff) a tax levied on a particular foreign product entering a country

A nation's **balance of payments** is the total flow of money into the country *less* the total flow of money out of the country, over some period of time. Balance of payments is thus a much broader concept than balance of trade. It includes imports and exports, of course. But it also includes investments, money spent by foreign tourists, payments by foreign governments and aid to foreign governments, and all other receipts and payments.

A continual deficit in a nation's balance of payments (a negative balance) can cause other nations to lose confidence in its economy. A continual surplus can indicate that the country encourages exports but limits imports by imposing trade restrictions. As Figure 3.4 shows, the United States has consistently suffered a deficit in its balance of payments since 1984.

■■ RESTRICTIONS TO INTERNATIONAL BUSINESS

Specialization and international trade can result in the efficient production of want-satisfying goods and services on a worldwide basis. As we have noted, total international business is generally increasing. Yet the nations of the world continue to erect barriers to free trade. They do so for reasons ranging from internal political and economic pressures to simple mistrust of other nations. We examine first the types of restrictions that are applied and then the arguments for and against trade restrictions.

Types of Trade Restrictions

Nations are generally eager to export their products. They want to provide markets for their industries and to develop a favorable balance of trade. Hence, most trade restrictions are applied to imports from other nations.

Tariffs   Perhaps the most commonly applied trade restriction is the customs (or import) duty. An **import duty** (also called a **tariff**) is a tax levied on a particular foreign product entering a country. The two types of tariffs are revenue tariffs and protective tariffs; both have the effect of raising the price of the product in the importing nations, but for different reasons. *Revenue tariffs* are imposed solely to generate income for the government. For example, the United States imposes a duty on Scotch whiskey solely for revenue

FIGURE 3.4
U.S. Balance of Payments
Although deficits in the U.S. balance of payments have improved somewhat since 1987, the United States has consistently run large deficits since 1984.   *(Source: U.S. Department of Commerce, Bureau of Economic Analysis, and* Survey of Current Business, *June 1994, p. 95.)*

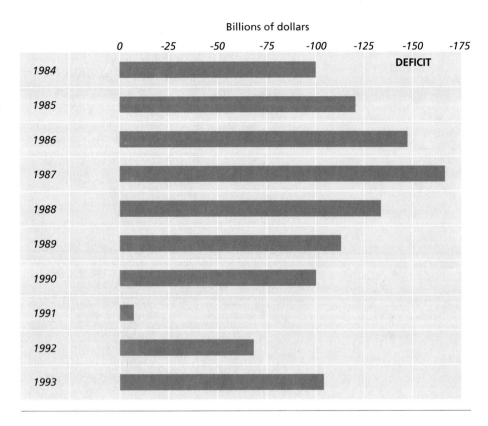

purposes. *Protective tariffs,* on the other hand, are imposed to protect a domestic industry from competition by keeping the price of competing imports level with or higher than the price of similar domestic products. Because fewer units of the product will be sold at the increased price, fewer units will be imported. The French and Japanese agricultural sectors would both shrink drastically if their nations abolished the protective tariffs that keep the price of imported farm products high. Today, U.S. tariffs are the lowest in history, with average tariff rates on all imports under 4 percent. However, certain tariffs are still very high. For example, tariffs on low-priced watches are 151.2 percent and importers of some low-priced shoes must pay 67 percent duty. Tobacco stems importers must pay a 458.3 percent customs penalty.[3]

Some countries rationalize their protectionist policies as a way of offsetting a practice by other nations called dumping. **Dumping** is exportation of large quantities of a product at a price lower than that of the same product in the home market. Thus, dumping drives down the price of the domestic item. In 1993, for example, the Pencil Makers Association, which represents eight U.S. pencil manufacturers, charged that low-priced pencils from Thailand and the People's Republic of China were being sold in the United States at less than fair value prices. Unable to compete with these inexpensive imports, several domestic manufacturers have had to shut down.[4] To protect themselves, domestic manufacturers can obtain an antidumping duty through the government to offset the advantage of the foreign product.

dumping exportation of large quantities of a product at a price lower than that of the same product in the home market

From California farmers to Japanese supermarkets. These Japanese shoppers are purchasing chicken parts and beef steaks imported from the U.S.—the U.S. meat exporters must battle local government regulations and overcome strong traditional relationships between retailers and wholesalers to gain entrance into Japanese markets.

Nontariff Barriers   A **nontariff barrier** is a nontax measure imposed by a government to favor domestic over foreign suppliers. Nontariff barriers create obstacles to the marketing of foreign goods in a country and increase costs for exporters. The following are a few examples of nontariff barriers:

nontariff barrier a nontax measure imposed by a government to favor domestic over foreign suppliers

- An **import quota** is a limit on the amount of a particular good that may be imported into a country during a given period of time. The limit may be set in terms of either quantity (so many pounds of beef) or value (so many dollars' worth of shoes). Quotas may also be set on individual products imported from specific countries. Once an import quota has been reached, imports are halted until the specified time has elapsed.

    U.S. agricultural import quotas permit each American citizen to consume in a year the equivalent of one teaspoon of imported ice cream, two imported peanuts, and one pound of imported cheese.[5]

import quota a limit on the amount of a particular good that may be imported into a country during a given period of time

embargo a complete halt to trading with a particular nation or in a particular product

- An **embargo** is a complete halt to trading with a particular nation or in a particular product. The embargo is used most often as a political weapon. At present, the United States has import embargoes against Cuba and Iraq—both as a result of extremely poor political relations.

foreign-exchange control a restriction on the amount of a particular foreign currency that can be purchased or sold

currency devaluation the reduction of the value of a nation's currency relative to the currencies of other countries

- A **foreign-exchange control** is a restriction on the amount of a particular foreign currency that can be purchased or sold. By limiting the amount of foreign currency that importers can obtain, a government limits the amount of goods that importers can purchase with that currency. This has the effect of limiting imports from the country whose foreign exchange is being controlled.

- A nation can increase or decrease the value of its money relative to the currency of other nations. **Currency devaluation** is the reduction of the value of a nation's currency relative to the currencies of other countries.

   Devaluation increases the cost of foreign goods, while it decreases the cost of domestic goods to foreign firms. For example, suppose the English pound is worth $2. Then an American-made $2,000 computer can be purchased for £1,000. But if the United Kingdom devalues the pound so that it is worth only $1, that same computer will cost £2,000. The increased cost, in pounds, will reduce the import of American computers—and all foreign goods—into England.

   On the other hand, before devaluation, a £500 set of English bone china costs an American $1,000. After the devaluation, the set of china will cost only $500. The decreased cost will make the china—and all English goods—much more attractive to U.S. purchasers.

- Cultural barriers can impede acceptance of products in foreign countries. For example, illustrations of feet are regarded as despicable in Thailand.

   When customers are unfamiliar with particular products from another country, their general perceptions of the country itself affect their attitude toward the product and help determine whether they will adopt it. Because Mexican cars have not been viewed by the world as being quality products, Volkswagen, for example, may not want to advertise that some of its models sold in the United States are made in Mexico.[6]

- Bureaucratic red tape is more subtle than the other forms of nontariff barriers. Yet it can be the most frustrating trade barrier of all. A few examples are unnecessarily restrictive application of standards and complex requirements related to testing, labeling, and certification.

Reasons for Trade Restrictions

Various reasons are advanced for trade restrictions either on the import of specific products or on trade with particular countries. We have noted that political considerations are usually involved in trade embargoes. Other frequently cited reasons for restricting trade include the following:

- *To equalize a nation's balance of payments.* This may be considered necessary to restore confidence in the country's monetary system and in its ability to repay its debts.

- *To protect new or weak industries.* A new, or *infant*, industry may not be strong enough to withstand foreign competition. Temporary trade

▶▶▶ **AT A GLANCE**

Export Obstacles

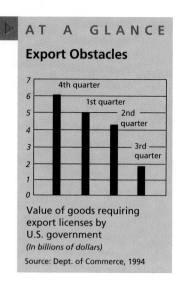

Value of goods requiring
export licenses by
U.S. government
(In billions of dollars)

Source: Dept. of Commerce, 1994

restrictions may be used to give it a chance to grow and become self-sufficient. The problem is that once an industry is protected from foreign competition, it may refuse to grow and "temporary" trade restrictions will become permanent. Consider the Jones Act of 1920, which was enacted to protect the infant U.S. shipping industry. The Jones Act requires all shipping between U.S. ports to be carried on American-built, American-owned, and American-crewed ships. Shipping has long been one of America's weakest industries. A recent U.S. International Trade Commission study concluded that abolishing the Jones Act would save consumers as much as $10.5 billion as a result of lower shipping costs, whereas U.S. maritime operators would lose only $630 million in profits. Thus, the Jones Act could be costing consumers $17 for every $1 of domestic shippers' profits.[7]

- *To protect national security.* Restrictions in this category are generally on exports, to keep the nation's technology out of the hands of potential enemies. For example, strategic and defense-related goods cannot be exported to unfriendly nations.

- *To protect the health of citizens.* Products that are dangerous or unhealthy (for example, farm products contaminated with insecticides) may be embargoed for this reason.

- *To retaliate for another nation's trade restrictions.* A country whose exports are taxed by another country may respond by imposing tariffs on imports from that country.

- *To protect domestic jobs.* By restricting imports, a nation can protect jobs in domestic industries. However, protecting these jobs can be expensive. For example, consumers spend about $25 billion a year to protect jobs in the textile and apparel industry—about $50,000 annually per job.[8] And to protect 9,000 jobs in the carbon steel industry, it costs $6.8 billion, or $750,000 per job.[9]

Reasons Against Trade Restrictions

Trade restrictions have immediate and long-term economic consequences—both within the restricting nation and in world-trade patterns. These include

- *Higher prices for consumers.* Higher prices may result from the imposition of tariffs or the elimination of foreign competition. For example, imposing quota restrictions on Japanese cars means that the average American family must work even longer to earn the price of the average car. Inflation and the effect of prior restrictions on Japanese cars already have pushed the time it takes the average family to earn the price of an average car from twenty-five weeks in 1981 to about thirty weeks now. Further trade restrictions could add another half week or more to that time.[10]

- *Restriction of consumers' choices.* Again, this is a direct result of the elimination of some foreign products from the marketplace and of the artificially high prices that importers must charge for products that *are* still imported.

- *Misallocation of international resources.* The protection of weak industries results in the inefficient use of limited resources. The economies of both the restricting nation and other nations eventually suffer because of this waste.
- *Loss of jobs.* The restriction of imports by one nation must lead to cutbacks—and the loss of jobs—in the export-oriented industries of other nations. Furthermore, trade protection has a significant effect on the composition of employment. U.S. trade restrictions—whether on textiles, apparel, steel, or automobiles—benefit only a few industries while harming many others. The gains in employment accrue to the protected industries and their primary suppliers, and the losses are spread across all other industries. Few states gain employment, but many other states lose employment.[11] In 1992, U.S. exports of goods and services created a total of 10.5 million jobs in the United States. Every $1 billion in U.S. merchandise exports creates 20,000 American jobs.[12]

■■ THE EXTENT OF INTERNATIONAL BUSINESS

LEARNING OBJECTIVE 3
Outline the extent of international trade and the organizations that are working to foster it.

Restrictions or not, international business is growing, although the worldwide recession in 1991 has slowed the rate of growth. During 1993, the world economy expanded by only about 2 percent, less than the average annual increase in world output during the 1980s. Sluggish growth in the developed industrial countries and continued economic decline in the

No empty dishes. Asia's television market is considered one of the biggest in the world—with over three billion entertainment-starved viewers. Here in Medan, Indonesia, the U.S. television programmers are fiercely competing to reach this vast audience by satellite and cable and through local broadcasting companies. News media mogul Rupert Murdoch, who controls Star TV in Hong Kong, beams five channels via satellite free of charge to thirty-nine countries.

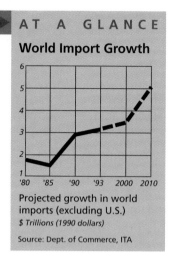

AT   A   GLANCE

World Import Growth

Projected growth in world
imports (excluding U.S.)
$ Trillions (1990 dollars)

Source: Dept. of Commerce, ITA

former Soviet Union and in parts of Eastern Europe (although those areas are progressing in their transition to market-based economies) have held back the world economy.

In contrast, most of the world's developing areas continue to show economic strength. According to the International Monetary Fund (IMF), the contribution of these countries to world output accounts for approximately 35 percent of total world production.

Foreign economic growth is important to the export success of many U.S. companies. The strong correlation between increasing American exports and the economic growth of foreign countries is shown in Figure 3.5. All the top purchasers of U.S. manufactures with above-average growth from 1987 to 1992 were in Asia. As a result, the United States now trades more with its Pacific Rim neighbors than with its traditional trading partners across the Atlantic.[13]

With one of the world's fastest growing economies and a population of 1.2 billion, the People's Republic of China is becoming an increasingly important player in the world trading system. Between 1980 and 1992, the two-way trade between the United States and China tripled as a percentage of total U.S. trade. U.S. exports to China totaled $7.5 billion in 1992, while imports from China amounted to $27.4 billion. That year, the United States was China's third-largest trading partner, and China's trade with the United States represented about 21 percent of Chinese world trade of $16.8 billion.[14] A 1993 IMF study concluded that China's economy is now the world's third largest, after those of the United States and Japan.

The U.S. Department of Commerce has started a new program called Destination ASEAN to promote exports to the booming markets of Southeast Asia. The Association of Southeast Asian Nations (ASEAN) was established to promote political, economic, and social cooperation among its six member countries: Brunei, Indonesia, Malaysia, the Philippines, Singapore, and Thailand. According to Secretary of Commerce Ronald Brown, "ASEAN is now one of the fastest growing and most lucrative economic areas in the world. We have chosen it for special attention because of its vast potential for U.S. exporters."[15]

The developing nations' role in the global trade is growing. In the first three years of this decade, the developing nations accounted for 70 percent of global GDP growth—and 50 percent of the growth in world trade. About 25 percent of industrial countries' exports, and 15 million jobs, now depend on trade with the developing nations.[16] Production in the developing countries is projected to grow an average 4.8 percent per year in the next decade, compared with 3.5 percent in the 1980s, predicts the World Bank. East Asia is likely to continue the fastest growth of all developing regions—7 percent annually.[17]

AT   A   GLANCE

Global Market-Sharing

*33%
Japan*

*26%
United
States*

*15%
United
Kingdom*

*11%
Germany*

*11%
France*

*5%
Italy*

Country share of global
high-tech markets (%)

Source: National Science Board,
Science & Engineering Indicators, 1993

After World War II, trade between the United States and Eastern Europe was minimal. The United States maintained high tariff barriers on imports from most of the Eastern European countries and also restricted its own exports to these countries. But with the disintegration of the Soviet Union, the trade between the United States and Eastern Europe has expanded substantially.

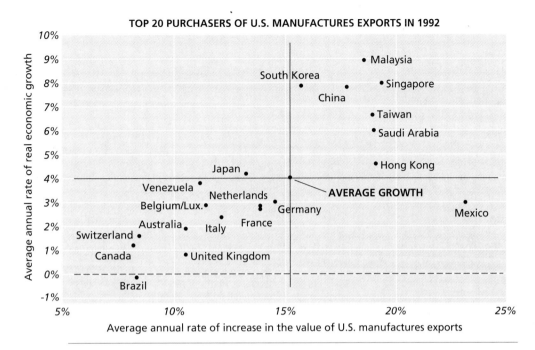

FIGURE 3.5   Average Annual Increase of U.S. Exports and Foreign Markets, from 1987 to 1992.
Foreign economic growth is important to the export success of many U.S.-based companies. *(Source: U.S. Department of Commerce, International Trade Administration, U.S. Foreign Trade Highlights, 1992; IMF, World Economic Outlook, May 1993; and U.S. Industrial Outlook, 1994, p. 16.)*

U.S. exports to and investment in this region will increase as demand for capital goods and technology opens new markets for U.S. products. There has been a substantial expansion in trade between the United States and the Czech and Slovak Federal Republic (CSFR), Hungary, and Poland. Between 1988 and 1993, U.S. imports from these countries grew by 58 percent and our exports to the region increased by 278 percent.[18]

Many more U.S. firms need to take advantage of the almost limitless potential in exporting. At present, only one-third of all U.S. companies export. About fifty of these account for more than 40 percent of American exports. No industrial nation has greater potential for export expansion than the United States. A mere 15 percent growth in export sales would put 1 million Americans to work.

In the United States, an export boom has revived domestic manufacturing and made a significant contribution to U.S. economic growth. After suffering declines and sluggish growth throughout most of the 1980s, U.S. merchandise exports are accelerating rapidly (see Figure 3.6).

Moreover, as Figure 3.7 shows, the importance of exports to the U.S. economy has more than doubled since 1970. And our exports to developing and newly industrialized countries are on the rise (see Figure 3.8).

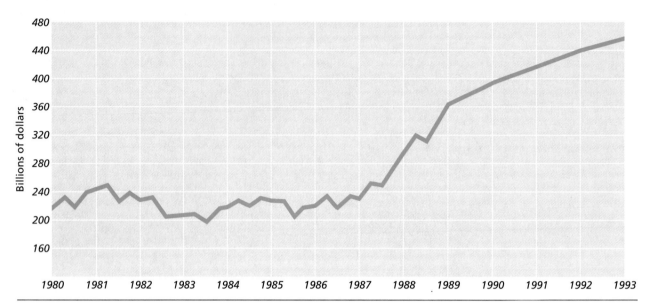

FIGURE 3.6   A Surge in U.S. Merchandise Exports
The current surge in U.S. exports began in 1987, when they reached a record high of $250 billion.   *(Source: Bureau of the Census and* Business America, *June 1994, p. 95.)*

Table 3.1 shows the value of U.S. merchandise exports to, and imports from, each of its ten major trading partners. Figure 3.9 categorizes American exports and imports. Our major exports are manufactured goods (85 percent), agricultural products (9 percent), and mineral fuels (7 percent); our major imports are manufactured goods (82 percent), mineral fuels (10 percent), and agricultural products (8 percent).

General Agreement on Tariffs and Trade (GATT) an international organization of 120 nations whose goal is to reduce or eliminate tariffs and other barriers to world trade

The General Agreement on Tariffs and Trade (1947)

At the end of World War II, the United States and twenty-two other nations organized the body that came to be known as GATT. The **General Agree-**

FIGURE 3.7
Importance of Exports for U.S. Economy (Percentage of GDP)
Exports as a percentage of U.S. GDP have increased from less than 6% in 1970 to almost 12% today.
(Source: U.S. Department of Commerce and The Southwest Economy, *Federal Reserve Bank of Dallas, May 1994, p. 5.)*

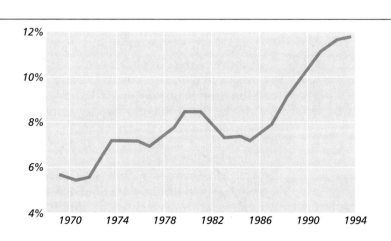

FIGURE 3.8
U.S. Exports to Developing and Newly Industrialized Countries
Markets for U.S. goods and services are growing rapidly in developing and newly industrialized countries.
(Source: U.S. Department of Commerce and The Southwest Economy, *Federal Reserve Bank of Dallas, May 1994, p. 6.)*

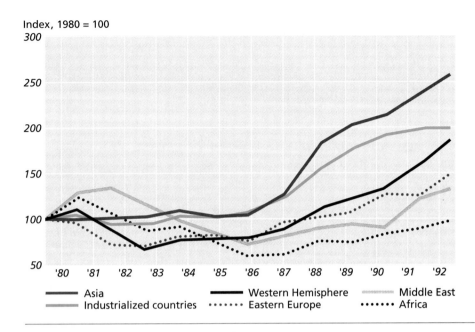

Index, 1980 = 100

Legend:
— Asia
— Industrialized countries
— Western Hemisphere
•••••• Eastern Europe
— Middle East
•••••• Africa

ment on Tariffs and Trade (GATT) is an international organization of 120 nations whose goal is to reduce or eliminate tariffs and other barriers to world trade. These 120 nations account for 90 percent of the world's merchandise trade. GATT, headquartered in Geneva, Switzerland, provides a forum for tariff negotiations and a means for settling international trade disputes and problems. Most-favored-nation status (MFN) is the famous principle of GATT. It means that each GATT member nation must be treated

TABLE 3.1 Leading U.S. Markets and Suppliers, 1993

U.S. Markets		U.S. Suppliers	
Rank/Country	Merchandise Exports (billions)	Rank/Country	Merchandise Imports (billions)
Total Exports	$465.0	Total Imports	$581.0
1. Canada	100.2	1. Canada	110.9
2. Japan	48.0	2. Japan	107.3
3. Mexico	41.6	3. Mexico	39.9
4. United Kingdom	26.4	4. China	31.5
5. Germany	19.0	5. Germany	28.6
6. Taiwan	16.3	6. Taiwan	25.1
7. South Korea	14.8	7. United Kingdom	21.7
8. France	13.3	8. South Korea	17.1
9. Netherlands	12.8	9. France	15.2
10. Singapore	11.7	10. Italy	13.2

Source: Adapted from *Business America,* April 1994, p. 39.

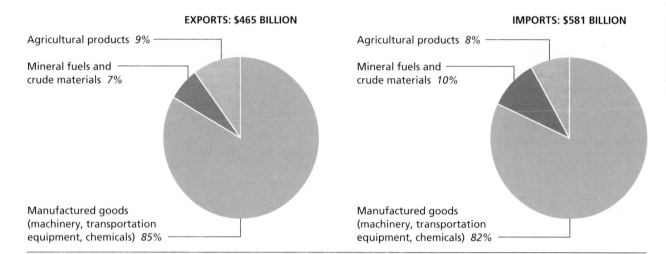

FIGURE 3.9   Selected U.S. Exports and Imports by Major Categories, 1993
Our major exports are machinery, other manufactured goods, and transportation equipment. Our major imports are machinery, other manufactured goods, transportation equipment, and crude materials.   (*Source:* Business America, *April 1994, p. 40.)*

equally by all contracting nations. MFN, therefore, assures that any tariff reductions or other trade concessions are automatically extended to all GATT members. Since 1947 the body has sponsored eight rounds of negotiations to reduce trade restrictions. Three of the most fruitful were the Kennedy Round, the Tokyo Round, and the Uruguay Round.

The Kennedy Round (1964–1967)   In 1962 the U.S. Congress passed the *Trade Expansion Act*. This law gave President John F. Kennedy the authority to negotiate reciprocal trade agreements that could reduce U.S. tariffs by as much as 50 percent. Armed with this authority, which was granted for a period of five years, President Kennedy called for a round of negotiations through GATT.

These negotiations, which began in 1964, have since become known as the *Kennedy Round*. They were aimed at reducing tariffs and other barriers to trade in both industrial and agricultural products. The participants were very successful in reducing tariffs—by an average of more than 35 percent. Representatives were less successful in removing other types of trade barriers.

The Tokyo Round (1973–1979)   In 1973 representatives of approximately one hundred nations gathered in Tokyo for another round of GATT negotiations—the *Tokyo Round,* which was completed in 1979. The participants negotiated tariff cuts of 30 to 35 percent, which were to be implemented over an eight-year period. In addition, they were able to remove or ease such nontariff barriers as import quotas, unrealistic quality standards for imports, and unnecessary red tape in customs procedures.

The Uruguay Round (1986–1993)   In 1986 the *Uruguay Round* was launched to extend trade liberalization and to widen the GATT treaty to include textiles, agricultural products, business services, and intellectual property rights.

This most ambitious and comprehensive global commercial agreement in history concluded overall negotiations on December 15, 1993, with delegations on hand from 109 nations. Calling the 22,000-page agreement "truly momentous," U.S. Vice President Albert Gore said it will "bring the global trading system into the twenty-first century." Gore said that, in developed countries alone, the agreement could raise GDP as much as 3.5 percent in the coming decade. The agreement will lower tariffs by greater than one-third; reform trade in agricultural goods; write new rules of trade for intellectual property and services; and strengthen the dispute-settlement process, among other provisions. These reforms should expand the world economy by an estimated $200 billion annually.

On January 1, 1995, GATT was replaced by a more powerful successor, the World Trade Organization (WTO). WTO incorporates trade in goods, services, and ideas and exerts more binding authority. (See Global Perspectives for some of the benefits of GATT.)

International Economic Communities

economic community an organization of nations formed to promote the free movement of resources and products among its members and to create common economic policies

The primary objective of GATT is to remove barriers to trade on a worldwide basis. On a smaller scale, an **economic community** is an organization of nations formed to promote the free movement of resources and products among its members and to create common economic policies. A number of economic communities now exist. Table 3.2 lists the members of the four that are most familiar.

The *European Union (EU),* also known as the *European Community* and the *Common Market,* was formed in 1957 by six countries—France, the

TABLE 3.2   Members of Major International Economic Communities
European Union and OPEC have been in existence for decades but NAFTA and AFTA are new international economic communities.

European Union (EU)	North American Free Trade Agreement (NAFTA)	ASEAN Free Trade Area (AFTA)	Organization of Petroleum Exporting Countries (OPEC)
France	United States	Indonesia	Venezuela
Germany	Canada	Malaysia	Algeria
Italy	Mexico	Philippines	Libya
Belgium		Singapore	Iraq
Netherlands		Thailand	Iran
Luxembourg		Brunei	United Arab Emirates
United Kingdom			Ecuador
Ireland			Nigeria
Denmark			Gabon
Greece			Saudi Arabia
Portugal			Kuwait
Spain			Qatar
			Indonesia

■ ■ ■ ■ GLOBAL PERSPECTIVES

Is GATT a Good Deal?

Will the Uruguay Round of the General Agreement on Tariffs and Trade (GATT) benefit the United States? Undoubtedly, that is the bottom-line question for all Americans. The answer is, simply, yes. GATT will be an exceptional deal for the United States.

Although the new agreement will not completely liberalize world trade, it will do more for free trade than most analysts thought possible when negotiations began nearly eight years ago in Punte del Este, Uruguay. Granted, the accord has not given the American film industry greater access to the highly guarded French market, nor has it been able to deliver new rules for expanding trade in financial services. But it has opened markets in many areas never before addressed by a free trade agreement.

The latest GATT provisions will mean a higher U.S. standard of living and faster economic growth. Unlike previous GATT agreements, it opens trade in commercial services and agriculture. Moreover, it streamlines the management of the world trading system by unifying customs rules and fine-tuning the mechanism for settling disputes.

For the first time, intellectual property trade is covered by GATT, a move that the U.S. computer, software, telecommunications, and pharmaceutical industries welcome.

More fundamentally, GATT will make products more accessible and less expensive for American consumers—the bottom line of freer trade. The United States, Canada, Japan, and Europe, which account for three-quarters of world trade, are set to eliminate tariffs on pharmaceuticals, construction materials, agricultural equipment, furniture, paper products, steel, and medical equipment.

The accord also holds promise for each sector of the U.S. economy. For business, GATT will open more markets and reduce the risks involved in conducting global trade. For labor, the agreement will provide greater opportunities to specialize in the areas of service and production in which we are the undisputed leader. And for consumers, it will provide access to less expensive goods from around the world. The 1993 GATT accord is indeed a good deal for the United States. But much more than that, it opens the door for the world to take a decisive step toward freer trade and a higher standard of living.

Federal Republic of Germany, Italy, Belgium, the Netherlands, and Luxembourg. Its objective was freely conducted commerce among these nations and others that might later join. As shown in Table 3.2, six more nations have joined the EU.

The EU and the United States account for more than 30 percent of world trade and for more than 70 percent of the industrialized world's gross domestic product. Therefore, together they are major players in the world economic and trading system. Overall, however, the EU is more dependent on foreign trade, with 22 percent of its GDP devoted to international trade, compared with 15 percent for the United States.

A second community in Europe, the *European Economic Area (EEA)*, became effective in January 1994. This pact consists of Austria, Finland, Iceland, Norway, Sweden, and the twelve member nations of the European

Union. The EEA, encompassing an area inhabited by 370 million people, allows for the free movement of goods throughout all seventeen countries.

The *North American Free Trade Agreement (NAFTA)* joined the United States with its first- and third-largest trading partners, Canada and Mexico. Implementation of NAFTA on January 1, 1994, created a market of about 374.2 million people. This market consists of Canada (population 27.3 million), the United States (254.5 million), and Mexico (92.4 million). Given the estimated annual output for this trade area of $7 trillion, NAFTA has major implications for developing business opportunities in the United States.[19]

NAFTA is built on the Canadian Free Trade Agreement (FTA) signed by the United States and Canada in 1989, and on the substantial trade and investment reforms undertaken by Mexico since the mid-1980s. Initiated by the Mexican government, formal negotiations on NAFTA began in June 1991 between the three governments. The support of NAFTA by President Bill Clinton, past U.S. presidents Ronald Reagan and Jimmy Carter, and Nobel Prize–winning economists provided the impetus for U.S. congressional ratification of NAFTA in November 1993.[20]

NAFTA gradually eliminates all tariffs on goods produced and traded between Canada, Mexico, and the United States to provide for a totally free

The NAFTA signing ceremony. In 1994, the North American Free Trade Agreement created a huge market of over 374 million consumers in the United States, Canada, and Mexico. Even though President Bill Clinton, past U.S. presidents Ronald Reagan and Jimmy Carter, and Nobel Prize–winning economists supported NAFTA, many organized-labor and consumer groups opposed the agreement.

trade area by 2009. (See Global Perspectives for more information about NAFTA.)

The *Association of Southeast Asian Nations (ASEAN)*, with headquarters located in Jakarta, Indonesia, was established in 1967 to promote political, economic, and social cooperation among its six member countries: Indonesia, Malaysia, Philippines, Singapore, Thailand, and Brunei. In January 1992, ASEAN agreed to create a free trade area, ASEAN Free Trade Area (AFTA).

The *Pacific Rim*, referring to countries and economies bordering the Pacific Ocean, is an informal, flexible term generally regarded as a reference to East Asia, Canada, and the United States. At a minimum, the Pacific Rim includes Canada, Japan, the People's Republic of China, Taiwan, and the United States. It may also include Australia, Brunei, Cambodia, Hong Kong/Macau, Indonesia, Laos, North Korea, South Korea, Malaysia, New Zealand, the Pacific Islands, the Philippines, Russia (or the Commonwealth of Independent States), Singapore, Thailand, and Vietnam.

The *Commonwealth of Independent States (CIS)* was established in December 1991 as an association of eleven republics of the former Soviet Union: Russia, Ukraine, Belarus (formerly Byelorussia), Moldova (formerly Moldavia), Armenia, Azerbaijan, Uzbekistan, Turkmenistan, Tajikistan,

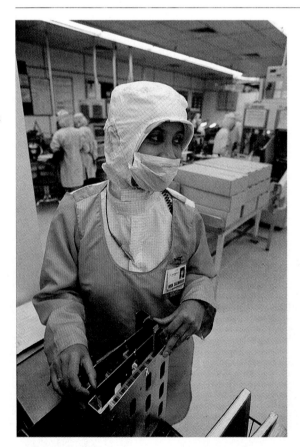

Destination ASEAN. U.S. companies such as Motorola Integrated Circuit Manufacturing are establishing their presence in one of the fastest growing and most lucrative areas in the world. The U.S. Department of Commerce has started Destination ASEAN to promote exports to the booming markets of Southeast Asia. This woman is employed at the Motorola facility in Kuala Lumpur, Malaysia.

■ ■ ■ ■ GLOBAL PERSPECTIVES

North American Free Trade Agreement

In 1993 negotiations for a North American Free Trade Agreement (NAFTA) were completed. This historic agreement builds on the U.S.-Canadian Free Trade Agreement, implemented in 1989, and creates a North American free trade area consisting of Mexico, Canada, and the United States.

NAFTA will create a $6.5 trillion market of 370 million people. It unites the United States with its first- and third-largest trading partners. Canada is our largest market. Mexico is our fastest growing export market, our second-largest market for manufactured exports, and our third-largest market for agricultural products.

NAFTA eliminates tariffs and other barriers to trade between the United States, Mexico, and Canada. It removes barriers to investment, strengthens the protection of intellectual property, and allows most services to be freely provided, even across borders.

- **Tariffs**—Over a fifteen-year period, all tariffs will be eliminated on North American products traded among the three countries. All trade between the United States and Canada will be duty-free by 1998. Mexican tariffs will be eliminated on all U.S. exports of industrial products within ten years. Tariffs on a few remaining agricultural items, such as corn and beans, will be phased out over fifteen years.

- **Rules of Origin**—Goods traded duty-free under NAFTA must contain substantial North American content (parts and labor).

- **Safeguards**—NAFTA provides relief to American workers and firms needing time to adjust to imports from Mexico. Tariff rates can be tem-

porarily raised to pre-NAFTA levels if imports threaten to injure, or actually injure, U.S. producers, workers, or farmers.

- **Services**—NAFTA opens Mexico's $146 billion services market to U.S. and Canadian firms. It allows U.S. firms to provide services in Mexico without relocating their operations and employees.

- **Government Procurement**—NAFTA gives U.S. suppliers immediate and growing access to the $19 billion Mexican government procurement market including state-controlled enterprises (*parastatals*) such as PEMEX, Mexico's oil company, and CFE, Mexico's electricity company.

- **Standards**—NAFTA allows each country and each state or province to establish whatever health, safety, or environmental standards they deem necessary. No U.S. standard will have to be lowered as a result of NAFTA.

- **Land Transportation**—NAFTA opens the international markets in Mexico for U.S. motor carriers. U.S. truck and bus companies will have, for the first time, the right to use their own drivers and equipment in Mexico, which will increase efficiency and reliability and reduce costs to the consumer. NAFTA does not change U.S. safety and highway standards. Mexican and Canadian operators will continue to be subject to all federal and state safety and operating requirements, including size and weight limits and driver qualifications.

- **Benefits**—NAFTA will help expand U.S. exports, generating U.S. jobs. It will promote better environmental and labor laws. It will ensure that American consumers get the highest quality and safest products at the best price.

Kazakhstan, and Kirgizstan (formerly Kirghiziya). The Baltic states did not join. Georgia maintained observer status before joining the CIS in November 1993.

In the Western Hemisphere, the *Caribbean Basin Initiative (CBI)* is an inter-American program, led by the United States, of increased economic assistance and trade preferences to Caribbean and Central American countries. CBI provides duty-free access to the U.S. market for most products from the region, and promotes private sector development in member nations.

The *Organization of Petroleum Exporting Countries (OPEC)* was founded in 1960 in response to reductions in the prices that oil companies were willing to pay for crude oil. The organization was conceived as a collective bargaining unit, to provide oil-producing nations with some control over oil prices.

Finally, the *Organization for Economic Cooperation and Development (OECD)* is a group of twenty-four industrialized market economy countries of North America, Europe, the Far East, and the South Pacific. OECD, headquartered in Paris, was established in 1961 to promote economic development and international trade.

Given the marked increase in international business that these affiliations and market communities reflect, it is important to understand cultural differences, as noted in Change in the Workplace.

■■ LEVELS OF INVOLVEMENT IN INTERNATIONAL BUSINESS

LEARNING OBJECTIVE 4
Define the methods by which a firm can organize for, and enter, international markets.

A firm that has decided to enter international markets can do so in several ways. We shall discuss five different methods (or, more accurately, organizational structures): licensing, exporting, joint ventures, totally owned facilities, and multinational firms. These different approaches require varying degrees of involvement in international business. Typically, a firm begins its international operations at the simplest level. Then, depending on its goals, it may progress to higher levels of involvement.

Licensing

licensing a contractual agreement in which one firm permits another to produce and market its product and use its brand name in return for a royalty or other compensation

At a fairly basic level of international business is licensing. **Licensing** is a contractual agreement in which one firm permits another to produce and market its product and use its brand name in return for a royalty or other compensation. For example, Yoplait yogurt is a French yogurt licensed for production in the United States. The Yoplait brand maintains an appealing French image, and in return, the U.S. producer pays the French firm a percentage of its income from sales of the product.

Licensing is especially advantageous for small manufacturers wanting to launch a well-known brand internationally. For example, all Spalding sporting products are licensed worldwide. The licensor, the Questor Corporation, owns the Spalding name but produces no goods itself. Lowenbrau has used licensing agreements, including one with Miller in the United States, to increase its beer sales worldwide without committing capital to building breweries.[21]

Another advantage of licensing is that it provides a simple method of expanding into a foreign market with virtually no investment. On the other

■ ■ ■ ■ CHANGE IN THE WORKPLACE

Respect Cultural Differences

Going abroad on a business trip? You'll save yourself some embarrassment (and maybe some failed business opportunities) if you do your cultural homework. For example, you must never touch the head of a Thai or pass an object over it, because the head is considered sacred in Thailand. Likewise, in Thailand you never point the bottoms of your feet in the direction of another person or cross your legs while sitting, especially in the presence of an older person. And in Hong Kong, Korea, or Taiwan, you must avoid using triangular shapes—the triangle is considered a negative shape in those countries.

Perhaps your destination is Africa. If so, remember that the number 7 is considered bad luck in Kenya and has magical connotations in Benin, although it's good luck in Czechoslovakia and the United States. Red, which is a positive color in Denmark, represents witchcraft and death in many African countries.

It's only a short trip to Bulgaria? Be prepared— a nod means "no" in Bulgaria, and shaking the head side-to-side means "yes." If you're not prepared, you may agree when you meant to disagree!

Understanding and heeding cultural variables such as these can be critical to success in international business. Lack of familiarity with the business practices, social customs, and etiquette of a country can weaken a company's position in the market, prevent it from accomplishing its objectives, and ultimately lead to failure.

American firms must pay close attention to different styles of doing business and the degree of importance placed on developing business relationships. In some countries, business people have a very direct style, whereas in others style is much more subtle.

Attitudes toward punctuality vary greatly from one culture to another, and misunderstandings can cause confusion. Romanians, Japanese, and Germans are very punctual, whereas many Latin Americans have a more relaxed attitude toward time. The Japanese consider it rude to be late for a business meeting, but it is acceptable—even fashionable—to be late for a social occasion. In Guatemala, on the other hand, a luncheon at a specified time means that some guests might be ten minutes early, whereas others may be forty-five minutes late.

The form of greeting also differs from culture to culture. Traditional greetings may be a handshake, hug, nose rub, kiss, forming the hands into a praying position, or various other gestures. If you aren't aware of the country's accepted form of greeting, you may unknowingly instigate awkward encounters.

Americans have not had a good track record of being sensitive to cultural distinctions. However, as business has become more global, Americans have become more sensitive to cultural differences and the importance of dealing with them effectively.

---

hand, if the licensee does not maintain the licensor's product standards, the product's image may be damaged. Another disadvantage is that a licensing arrangement does not usually provide the original producer with any foreign marketing experience.

Exporting

A firm may also manufacture its products in its home country and export them for sale in foreign markets. Like licensing, exporting can be a relatively low-risk method of entering foreign markets. Unlike licensing, however, it is not a simple method; it opens up several levels of involvement to the exporting firm.

At the most basic level, the exporting firm may sell its products to an *export/import merchant,* which is essentially a merchant wholesaler. The merchant assumes all the risks of product ownership, distribution, and sale. It may even purchase the goods in the producer's home country and assume responsibility for exporting the goods.

The exporting firm may instead ship its products to an *export/import agent,* which arranges the sale of the products to foreign intermediaries for a commission or fee. The agent is an independent firm—like other agents—that sells and may perform other marketing functions for the exporter. The exporter, however, retains title to the products during shipment and until they are sold.

An exporting firm may also establish its own *sales offices,* or *branches,* in foreign countries. These installations are international extensions of the firm's distribution system. They represent a deeper involvement in international business than the other exporting techniques that we have discussed—and thus they carry a greater risk. The exporting firm maintains control over sales, and it gains both experience and knowledge of foreign markets. Eventually, the firm might also develop its own sales force to operate in conjunction with foreign sales offices or branches.

Joint Ventures

A joint venture is a partnership formed to achieve a specific goal or to operate for a specific period of time. A joint venture with an established firm in a foreign country provides immediate market knowledge and access, reduced risk, and control over product attributes. However, joint-venture agreements established across national borders can become extremely complex. As a result, joint-venture agreements generally require a very high level of commitment from all the parties involved. Global Perspectives gives one example of a joint venture between a U.S. firm and a Japanese firm.

A joint venture may be used to produce and market an existing product in a foreign nation or to develop an entirely new product. Florida-based International Development Group, Inc., signed a joint-venture agreement with the largest construction company in Nizhny-Novgorod, Russia. The U.S. company, which invested a 50 percent share in the Nizhny firm, expects to do over $20 million in business in 1994.[22]

In 1993 Unilever, one of the largest consumer goods businesses in the world, entered into joint ventures for the manufacture of ice cream in Beijing, for tea in Guangzhou, and for the construction of a fabric detergent factory in Shanghai. Also, Unilever has a 60 percent stake in a joint venture with China's largest toothpaste company.[23]

■ ■ ■ ■   GLOBAL PERSPECTIVES

Borland Company Ltd.: A Success Story

Borland Company Ltd. (BCL) is among the top five software suppliers in the fiercely competitive Japanese market. The wholly owned, Japanese subsidiary of U.S.-based Borland International Inc., BCL has moved aggressively to develop and market Japanese versions of the parent's world-leading, relational database systems like Paradox and its popular Quattro Pro spreadsheet program.

Borland International Inc. was established in California in 1983. Not long afterward, the U.S. software house appointed Micro Software Associates (MSA) of Japan as its Japan agent. By 1984, MSA had released the Japanese version of Borland's Turbo Pascal programming tool and was busy developing and distributing other Borland products.

In 1989 Borland and MSA teamed up to form Borland Japan. The joint move was spurred in part by the parent's desire to take greater control of marketing and distribution—and to promote the widespread recognition of the Borland brand name by marketing its software under Borland's logo rather than the local agent's. By January 1992, the parent opted to take full control of local operations and distribution by establishing wholly owned Borland Company Ltd.

Kogo Shinohara, vice president of BCL, says that the move was instrumental in gaining pub-licity and name recognition for Borland. "That's important in Japan," he claims, "because consumers tend to rely on name value or recommendations from friends when making purchasing decisions."

Although intensified competition is helping to bring PCs and software systems into wider use, it has also squeezed profit margins throughout the industry. Even BCL feels the heat. This year Shinohara believes BCL will need to rethink its policy of providing free software support by telephone, fax, and on-line services.

BCL's task won't be easy. Japanese consumers tend to demand more after-purchase services than U.S. counterparts, and creating those uniquely Japanese functions and add-ons takes time and money. Promoting mail-order sales is also difficult due to high postage costs in Japan, a reluctance by domestic firms to sell customer lists, and a preference among consumers to buy at service-oriented stores.

Despite these problems, BCL seems committed to providing its customers with user-friendly, high-quality products at affordable prices. The firm has apparently done a great job so far. In 1993 BCL posted $33.3 million in sales, up sharply from the $6.6 million reported in fiscal 1990.

Totally Owned Facilities

At a still deeper level of involvement in international business, a firm may develop its own production and marketing facilities in one or more foreign nations. This *direct investment* provides complete control over operations, but it carries a greater risk than the joint venture. The firm is really establishing a subsidiary in a foreign country. Most firms do so only after they have acquired some knowledge of the host country's markets.

Direct investment may take either of two forms. In the first, the firm builds or purchases manufacturing and other facilities in the foreign country. It uses these facilities to produce its own established products and to market them in that country and perhaps in neighboring countries. Firms such as General Motors, Du Pont, Union Carbide, and Colgate-Palmolive are multinational companies with worldwide manufacturing facilities. Colgate-Palmolive factories are becoming *Euro-factories*, supplying neighboring countries as well as their own local markets.[24]

A second form of direct investment in international business is the purchase of an existing firm in a foreign country under an arrangement that allows it to operate independently of the parent company. When Sony Corporation (a Japanese firm) decided to enter the motion-picture business in the United States, it chose to purchase Columbia Pictures Entertainment Inc., rather than start a new motion-picture studio from scratch.[25]

Strategic Alliances

strategic alliance partnership formed to create competitive advantage on a worldwide basis

Strategic alliances, the newest form of international business structure, are partnerships formed to create competitive advantage on a worldwide basis. They are very similar to joint ventures. The number of strategic alliances is growing at an estimated rate of about 20 percent per year. In fact, in such industries as automaking and computers, strategic alliances are becoming the predominant means of competing. International competition is so fierce and the costs of competing on a global basis so high that few firms have the individual resources to do it alone. Thus individual firms that lack all the internal resources essential for international success may seek to collaborate with other companies.

An example of such an alliance is the New United Motor Manufacturing, Inc. (NUMMI), formed by Toyota and General Motors to make Chevrolet Novas and Toyota Tercels. This enterprise united the quality engineering of Japanese cars with the marketing expertise and market access of General Motors.[26]

Trading Companies

trading company provides a link between buyers and sellers in different countries

A **trading company** provides a link between buyers and sellers in different countries. A trading company, as its name implies, is not involved in manufacturing or owning assets related to manufacturing. It buys in one country at the lowest price consistent with quality and sells to buyers in another country. An important function of trading companies is taking title to products and performing all the activities necessary to move the products from the domestic country to a foreign country. For example, large grain-trading companies operating out of home offices in both the United States and overseas control a major portion of the world's trade in basic food commodities. These trading companies sell homogeneous agricultural commodities that can be stored and moved rapidly in response to market conditions. The best-known U.S. trading company is Sears World Trade, which specializes in consumer goods, light industrial items, and processed foods.[27]

Countertrade

countertrade an international
barter transaction

In the early 1990s, many developing nations had major restrictions on converting domestic currency into foreign currency. Therefore, exporters had to resort to barter agreements with importers. **Countertrade** is essentially an international barter transaction in which goods and services are exchanged for different goods and services. Recent examples are Saudi Arabia's purchase of ten 747 jets from Boeing with payment in crude oil; Philip Morris's sale of cigarettes to the Russian Republic in return for chemicals used to make fertilizers; and Iraq's barter of crude oil for warships from Italy.

The volume of countertrade is growing. In 1992, 20 percent of world trade by value was in the form of countertrade. Some experts predict that at the beginning of the twenty-first century, countertrade may account for up to 50 percent of world trade (see Figure 3.10).

Given the importance of countertrade as a means of financing world trade, prospective exporters will undoubtedly have to engage in this technique from time to time to gain access to international markets.

Multinational Firms

multinational enterprise
a firm that operates on a
worldwide scale, without ties to
any specific nation or region

A **multinational enterprise** is a firm that operates on a worldwide scale, without ties to any specific nation or region. The multinational firm represents the highest level of involvement in international business. It is equally "at home" in most countries of the world. In fact, as far as the operations of the multinational enterprise are concerned, national boundaries exist only on maps. It is, however, organized under the laws of its home country.

Table 3.3 lists the ten largest U.S. industrial, multinational corporations; Table 3.4 shows the fifteen largest public companies outside the United States. Notice that thirteen of the foreign-based multinational companies are located in Japan. Table 3.5 shows the fifteen largest foreign and U.S. public multinational companies. Notice that the largest five

FIGURE 3.10
The Growing Importance of Countertrade
In 1975 only 2 percent of the world's trade by value was in the form of countertrade. In 1992, this figure jumped to more than 20 percent.
(Source: G. Platt, "Worldwide Cash, Credit Crunch Lifts Countertrade," Journal of Commerce, April 21, 1992, pp. 1A, 2A. Adapted by permission.)

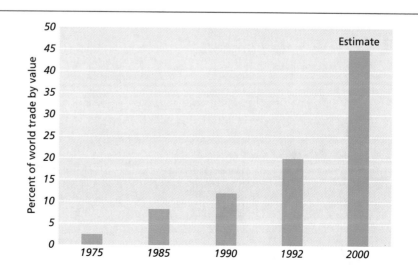

TABLE 3.3   The Ten Largest U.S. Multinational Corporations

1993 Rank	Company	Revenue Foreign (in millions)	Total (in millions)	Foreign as % of Total
1	Exxon	$75,639	$97,825	77.3
2	General Motors	38,646	138,220	28.0
3	Mobil	38,535	57,077	67.5
4	IBM	37,013	62,716	59.0
5	Ford Motor	32,860	108,521	30.3
6	Texaco	24,292	45,395	53.5
7	Citicorp	20,762	32,196	64.5
8	El du Pont de Nemours	16,756	32,621	51.4
9	Chevron	16,601	40,352	41.1
10	Procter & Gamble	15,856	30,433	52.1

Source: From *Forbes* magazine, July 18, 1994, p. 276. Reprinted by permission of FORBES magazine. © Forbes Inc., 1994.

multinationals in the world are Japanese. Table 3.6 describes steps in entering international markets.

According to the chairman of the board of Dow Chemical Co., a multinational firm of United States origin, "The emergence of a world economy and of the multinational corporation has been accomplished hand in hand."[28] He sees multinational enterprises moving toward what he calls the "anational company," a firm that has no nationality but belongs to all coun-

TABLE 3.4   The Fifteen Largest Public Companies Outside the United States

Company	Business	Country	Revenue (in millions)
Mitsui & Co	Trading	Japan	$163,529
Mitsubishi	Trading	Japan	160,184
Sumitomo	Trading	Japan	157,624
Itochu	Trading	Japan	155,229
Marubeni	Trading	Japan	144,570
Nissho Iwai	Trading	Japan	95,507
Royal Dutch/Shell Group	Energy	Netherlands	95,153
Toyota Motor	Automobiles	Japan	85,273
Hitachi	Elec & Electron	Japan	68,614
Tomen	Trading	Japan	64,903E
Nippon Tel & Tel	Telecomm	Japan	61,680
Matsushita Electric Indl	Appliances	Japan	61,413
Daimler-Benz Group	Automobiles	Germany	59,116
Nissan Motor	Automobiles	Japan	53,785
Kanematsu	Trading	Japan	52,771

Source: From *Forbes* magazine, July 18, 1994, p. 222. Reprinted by permission of FORBES Magazine. © Forbes Inc., 1994.

TABLE 3.5   The Fifteen Largest Foreign and U.S. Public Companies

Rank	Company	Country	Revenue (in millions)
1	Mitsui & Co	Japan	$163,529
2	Mitsubishi	Japan	160,184
3	Sumitomo	Japan	157,624
4	Itochu	Japan	155,229
5	Marubeni	Japan	144,570
6	General Motors	United States	138,220
7	Ford Motor	United States	108,521
8	Exxon	United States	97,825
9	Nissho Iwai	Japan	95,507
10	Royal Dutch/Shell Group	Netherlands	95,153
11	Toyota Motor	Japan	85,273
12	Hitachi	Japan	68,614
13	Wal-Mart Stores	United States	67,392
14	AT&T	United States	67,156
15	Tomen	Japan	64,903E

Source: From *Forbes* magazine, July 18, 1994, p. 222. Reprinted by permission of FORBES Magazine. © Forbes Inc., 1994.

tries. In recognition of this movement, there have already been international conferences devoted to the question of how such enterprises would be controlled.

■■ SOURCES OF EXPORT ASSISTANCE

LEARNING OBJECTIVE 5
Describe the various sources of export assistance.

In September 1993, President Bill Clinton announced the *National Export Strategy (NES)* to revitalize U.S. exports. Under the NES, the *Trade Promotion Coordinating Committee (TPCC)* assists U.S. firms in developing export promotion programs. The export services and programs of the nineteen TPCC agencies can help American firms compete in foreign markets and create new jobs in the United States. An overview of selected export assistance programs follows.

- *U.S. Export Assistance Centers (USEACs)*—USEACs are federal export assistance offices. USEACs provide export marketing and trade finance assistance by integrating in a single location the counselors and services of the U.S. and Foreign Commercial Service of the Department of Commerce, the Export-Import Bank, the Small Business Administration, and the U.S. Agency for International Development.
- *International Trade Administration (ITA), U.S. Department of Commerce*—ITA offers assistance and information to help exporters. ITA units include (1) domestic and overseas commercial officers, (2) country experts, and (3) industry experts. Each unit promotes products and offers services and programs for the U.S. exporting community.

TABLE 3.6   Steps in Entering International Markets

Step	Activity	Marketing Tasks
1	Identify exportable products	Identify key selling features Identify needs that they satisfy Identify the selling constraints that are imposed
2	Identify key foreign markets for the products	Determine who the customers are Pinpoint what, when they will buy Do market research Establish priority, or "target," countries
3	Analyze how to sell in each priority market (methods will be affected by product characteristics and unique features of country/market)	Locate available government and private-sector resources Determine service and back-up sales requirements
4	Set export prices and payment terms, methods, and techniques	Establish methods of export pricing Establish sales terms, quotations; invoices, conditions of sale Determine methods of international payments, secured and unsecured
5	Estimate resource requirements and returns	Estimate financial requirements Estimate human resources requirements (full- or part-time export department or operation?) Estimate plant production capacity Determine necessary product adaptations
6	Establish overseas distribution network	Determine distribution agreement and other key marketing decisions (price, repair policies, returns, territory, performance, and termination) Know your customer (use U.S. Department of Commerce international marketing services)
7	Determine shipping, traffic, documentation procedures and requirements	Determine methods of shipments (air or ocean freight, truck, rail?) Finalize containerization Obtain validated export license Follow export-administration documentation procedures
8	Promote, sell, and be paid	Use international media, communications, advertising, trade shows, and exhibitions Determine the need for overseas travel (when, where, how often?) Initiate customer follow-up procedures
9	Continuously analyze current marketing, economic, and political situations	Recognize changing factors influencing marketing strategies Constantly re-evaluate

Source: U.S. Department of Commerce, International Trade Administration, Washington, D.C.

- *U.S. and Foreign Commercial Services (US&FCS)*—To help U.S. firms compete more effectively in the global marketplace, the US&FCS has a network of trade specialists in sixty-nine U.S. cities and sixty-nine countries worldwide. US&FCS offices provide information on foreign markets, agent/distributor location services, trade leads, and counseling on business opportunities, trade barriers, and prospects abroad.

- *Export Legal Assistance Network (ELAN), Small Business Administration*—ELAN is a nationwide group of attorneys with experience in international trade who provide free initial consultations to small businesses on export-related matters.

- *Advocacy Center*—The Advocacy Center, established in November 1993, facilitates high-level U.S. official advocacy to assist U.S. firms competing for major projects and procurements worldwide. The center is directed by the Trade Promotion Coordinating Committee.

- *American Business Center (ABC)*—The ABC program provides U.S. companies that are exploring or establishing commercial opportunities in the Newly Independent States (NIS) of the former Soviet Union with business services such as telephone and fax, temporary office space, market information, and assistance in making business contacts. An ABC operates in Bratislava, Slovakia, under the direction of the Commerce Department's International Trade Administration in cooperation with the Agency for International Development. Additional centers are being opened in Russia, Ukraine, Kazakhstan, and Uzbekistan.

- *Business Information Service for the Newly Independent States (BISNIS)*—BISNIS is the U.S. Department of Commerce information service that provides "one-stop shopping" for U.S. firms interested in doing business in the former Soviet Union. With a staff of international trade specialists available by phone or appointment, BISNIS provides information, answers questions, and assists U.S. companies in exploring business prospects in the NIS markets.

  BISNIS maintains the latest information on current trade regulations and legislation, economic and industrial market data, up-to-date lists of NIS government officials, potential business contacts, available financing, trade promotion activities, and other practical market and business reports.

- *Eastern Europe Business Information Center (EEBIC)*—The EEBIC provides information on trade and investment opportunities, trade regulations and legislations, sources of financing, and government and industry contacts in the former Eastern Bloc. The center is a Department of Commerce service that was initiated in January 1990.

- *National Trade Data Bank (NTDB)*—The NTDB contains international economic and export promotion information supplied by 19 U.S. agencies. Data are updated monthly and are presented in one of three standard formats: text, time series, or matrix. The NTDB contains data from the Departments of Agriculture (Foreign Agriculture Service), Commerce (Bureau of Census, Bureau of Economic Analysis, International Trade Administration, and National Institute for Standards and

Technology), Energy, and Labor (Bureau of Labor Statistics); the Central Intelligence Agency; Eximbank; Federal Reserve System; U.S. International Trade Commission; Overseas Private Investment Corporation; Small Business Administration; the U.S. Trade Representative; and the University of Massachusetts (MISER data on state origins of exports).

These and other sources of export information enhance the business opportunities of U.S. firms seeking to enter expanding foreign markets. Another vital entry factor is financing.

■■ FINANCING INTERNATIONAL BUSINESS

LEARNING OBJECTIVE 6
Identify the institutions that help firms and nations finance international business.

International trade compounds the concerns of financial managers. Currency exchange rates, tariffs and foreign-exchange controls, and the tax structures of host nations all affect international operations and the flow of cash. In addition, financial managers must be concerned both with the financing of their international operations and with the means available to their customers to finance purchases.

Fortunately, along with business in general, a number of larger banks have become international in scope. Many have established branches in major cities around the world. Thus, like firms in other industries, they are able to provide their services where and when they are needed. In addition, financial assistance is available from U.S. government and international sources.

Several of today's international financial organizations were founded many years ago to facilitate free trade and the exchange of currencies among nations. Some, such as the Inter-American Development Bank, have a regional focus, and others, like the Export-Import Bank, are operated by one country but provide international financing.

The Export-Import Bank of the United States

Export-Import Bank of the United States an independent agency of the U.S. government whose function it is to assist in financing the exports of American firms

The **Export-Import Bank of the United States** is an independent agency of the U.S. government whose function it is to assist in financing the exports of American firms. *Eximbank,* as it is commonly called, extends and guarantees credit to overseas buyers of American goods and services, guarantees short-term financing for exports, and discounts negotiable instruments that arise from export transactions. It also cooperates with commercial banks by helping American exporters to offer credit to their overseas customers. Recently, the Eximbank provided credit to Saudi Arabia in a $4 billion contract awarded to AT&T to update the Saudis' communication system.[29]

Multilateral Development Banks

multilateral development bank (MDB) an internationally supported bank that provides loans to developing countries to help them grow

A **multilateral development bank (MDB)** is an internationally supported bank that provides loans to developing countries to help them grow. The most familiar is the World Bank, which operates worldwide. Four other MDBs operate primarily in Africa, Asia, Central and South America, and eastern and central Europe. All five are supported by the industrialized nations, including the United States.

Inter-American Development Bank (IDB) was created in 1959 by ten Latin American countries and the United States. Twenty-six Latin American and fifteen other countries now own the bank, which is headquartered in Washington, D.C. The IDB makes loans and guarantees and provides technical advice and assistance to countries.

With fifty-two member nations, the *Asian Development Bank (ADB)* promotes economic and social progress in Asian and Pacific regions. The U.S. government is the second-largest contributor to ADB's capital, after Japan. Recently, ADB approved $903 million in loans to China for environmental protection, natural resource conservation, and poverty reduction.

African Development Bank (AFDB) was established in 1963 with headquarters in Abidjan, Ivory Coast. Its members include fifty African and twenty-six non-African countries. The AFDB's goal is to foster the economic and social development of its African members. The bank pursues this goal through loans, research, technical assistance, and the development of trade programs.

Established in 1990 to encourage reconstruction and development in the eastern and central European countries, the London-based *European Bank for Reconstruction and Development (EBRD)* has more than forty members. Its loans are geared toward developing market-oriented economies and promoting private enterprise.

The International Monetary Fund

International Monetary Fund (IMF) an international bank with more than 150 member nations; makes short-term loans to countries experiencing balance-of-payment deficits

The **International Monetary Fund (IMF)** with more than 150 member nations is an international bank that makes short-term loans to countries experiencing balance-of-payment deficits. This financing is contributed by member nations, and it must be repaid with interest. Loans are provided primarily to fund international trade.

In the next chapter, we take a look at the various forms of business ownership.

■ ■ ■ ■ CHAPTER REVIEW

Summary

1 Explain the economic basis for international business.

International business encompasses all business activities that involve exchanges across national boundaries. International trade is based on specialization, whereby each country produces those goods and services that it can produce more efficiently than any other goods and services. A nation is said to have a comparative advantage relative to these goods. International trade develops when each nation trades its surplus products for those that are in short supply.

A nation's balance of trade is the difference between the value of its exports and the value of its imports. Its balance of payments is the difference between the flow of money into and out of the nation. Generally, a negative balance of trade is considered unfavorable.

2 Discuss the restrictions that nations place on international trade, the objectives of these restrictions, and their results.

In spite of the benefits of world trade, nations tend to use tariffs and nontariff barriers (import quotas, embargoes, and other restrictions) to limit trade. These restrictions are typically justified as being needed to protect a nation's economy, industries, citizens, or security. They can result in the loss of jobs, higher prices, fewer choices in the marketplace, and the misallocation of resources.

3 Outline the extent of international trade and the organizations that are working to foster it.

World trade is generally increasing. Trade between the United States and other nations is increasing in dollar value but decreasing in terms of our share of the world market. The General Agreement on Tariffs and Trade (GATT) and various economic communities have been formed to dismantle trade barriers and provide an environment in which international business can grow even faster.

4 Define the methods by which a firm can organize for, and enter, international markets.

A firm may enter international markets in several ways. It may license a foreign firm to produce and market its products. It may export its products and sell them through foreign intermediaries or its own sales organization. It may enter into a joint venture with a foreign firm. It may establish its own foreign subsidiaries. Or it may develop into a multinational enterprise. Generally, each of these methods represents a deeper involvement in international business than those that precede it in this list.

5 Describe the various sources of export assistance.

Many government and international agencies provide export assistance to U.S. and foreign firms. The export services and programs of the nineteen U.S. government agencies can help U.S. firms compete in foreign markets and create new jobs in the United States. Sources of export assistance include U.S. Export Assistance Centers, International Trade Administration, U.S. and Foreign Commercial Services, Export Legal Assistance Network, Advocacy Center, American Business Center, Business Information Service for the Newly Independent States, Eastern Europe Business Information Center, and National Trade Data Bank.

6 Identify the institutions that help firms and nations finance international business.

The financing of international trade is more complex than that of domestic trade. Institutions such as Eximbank and the International Monetary Fund have been established to provide financing and ultimately increase world trade for American and international firms.

Key Terms

You should now be able to define and give an example relevant to each of the following terms:

international business (67)
absolute advantage (67)
comparative advantage (68)
exporting (68)
importing (68)
balance of trade (68)
trade deficit (68)
balance of payments (70)
import duty (tariff) (70)
dumping (71)
nontariff barrier (72)
import quota (72)
embargo (72)
foreign-exchange control (73)
currency devaluation (73)
General Agreement on Tariffs and Trade (GATT) (78)
economic community (81)
licensing (86)
strategic alliance (90)
trading company (90)
countertrade (91)
multinational enterprise (91)
Export-Import Bank of the United States (96)
multilateral development bank (MDB) (96)
International Monetary Fund (IMF) (97)

Questions

Review Questions

1. Why do firms engage in international trade?
2. What is the difference between an absolute and a comparative advantage in international trade? How are both types of advantages related to the concept of specialization?
3. What is a favorable balance of trade? In what way is it "favorable"?
4. List and briefly describe the principal restrictions that may be applied to a nation's imports.
5. What reasons are generally given for imposing trade restrictions?
6. What are the general effects of import restrictions on trade?

7. Define and describe the major objectives of the following:
   a. GATT
   b. Economic communities
8. Which nations are the principal trading partners of the United States? What are the major U.S. imports and exports?
9. The methods of engaging in international business may be categorized as either direct or indirect. How would you classify each of the methods described in this chapter? Why?
10. In what ways is a multinational enterprise different from a large corporation that does business in several countries?
11. List some key sources of export assistance. How can these sources be useful to small business firms?
12. In what ways do Eximbank, multilateral development banks, and the IMF enhance international trade?

Discussion Questions

1. What might be the future growth prospects of firms like Progressive Electronics, Inc., which manufacture test equipment for the communications industry?
2. Why are companies such as Jefferson Industries, Inc., looking at Asia as their growth market?
3. The United States restricts imports but, at the same time, supports GATT and international banks whose objective is to enhance world trade. As a member of Congress, how would you justify this contradiction to your constituents?
4. What effects might the devaluation of a nation's currency have on its business firms? on its consumers? on the debts it owes to other nations?
5. Should imports to the United States be curtailed by, say, 20 percent to eliminate our trade deficit? What might happen if this were done?
6. When should a firm consider expanding from strictly domestic trade to international trade? When should it consider becoming further involved in international trade? What factors might affect the firm's decisions in each case?
7. How can a firm obtain the expertise needed to produce and market its products in, for example, the EU?

Exercises

1. In recent years, the United States has used import quotas to reduce the number of automobiles imported from Japan. Prepare a list of the arguments for and against this practice using concepts you learned in this chapter. Then write an essay describing your position regarding future import quotas for Japan, Korea, or any other country that is providing stiff competition for the American auto industry.

2. Arrange an interview with a local export executive or other manager of a firm involved in international trade. Find out what prompted the firm to sell overseas. What are the risks and rewards of exporting?

3. Learn the opinions of a local union leader regarding international trade, and compare them with those of the importer or exporter you interviewed for Exercise 2. With whom do you agree and why?

VIDEO CASE 3.1

Colgate-Palmolive Co.: An International Giant

American oral care firm Colgate-Palmolive Co. is a $7.1 billion consumer products company that markets its products in more than 160 countries. In the last decade, the company has increased its share of the global market to more than 45 percent.

In many growth markets around the world, Colgate is building new facilities to manufacture and sell its products. For example, the company recently built toothpaste plants in Turkey and in Eastern Europe, a bleach plant in the Dominican Republic, a fully automated warehouse in Germany, a new soap manufacturing facility in India, and a new detergent complex in Australia.

Central to Colgate's success is its flexible approach to the rapid rate of change and globalization in the world marketplace. Colgate's strong 1993 financial performance confirms the company's ability to succeed in today's diverse and fast-changing world.

As shown in the following figures, more than half of the company's 1993 net sales, operating profit, and assets are attributable to overseas operations.

Net sales	**In millions**	**Percent**
U.S. and Canada	$2,533.1	35
Europe	1,903.7	27
Latin America	1,525.8	21
Asia and Africa	1,178.7	17
TOTAL	$7,141.3	100

Operating profit		
U.S. and Canada	$ 332.3	38
Europe	171.8	19
Latin America	249.6	28
Asia and Africa	134.7	15
TOTAL	$ 888.4	100

Assets	In millions	Percent
U.S. and Canada	$2,861.0	51
Europe	1,197.1	22
Latin America	804.4	14
Asia and Africa	698.4	13
TOTAL	$5,560.9	100

The firm is continually adding to Colgate's already powerful global presence, especially in developing countries. In 1993 Colgate established new business ventures in Cambodia, Laos, and Bulgaria; set up operations in Tanzania and Mozambique; began manufacturing in Hungary; and broke ground for additional manufacturing plants in Thailand, China, and Mexico. Furthermore, the company increased its stake in Colgate-India from 40 percent to 51 percent, allowing fuller participation in the growth of this market of 900 million people.

Now Colgate is tapping the promising Eastern European markets. With the reunification of East and West Germany, East Germans clamored for the western products available in West Germany. The East German consumers were well aware of the western goods because they had been receiving West German broadcasts of product advertisements for over twenty-five years. Their own state-produced consumer products were noticeably inferior in quality and packaging. Over 17 million consumers in East Germany, and about 38 million in Poland, have still not had their needs satisfied, but Colgate-Palmolive is working to meet them.

Questions

1. Why are Colgate's consumer products in great demand around the world, and especially in the former East Germany?
2. What makes Eastern Europe such an attractive market for Colgate?
3. What opportunities exist for Colgate and other American businesses in the international marketplace?

CASE 3.2

Harley-Davidson Japan

Harley-Davidson, Inc., the U.S. maker of the acclaimed Harley-Davidson motorcycle, recently celebrated its ninetieth anniversary. The company has a lot to celebrate. Its motorcycles have won the hearts and loyalties of "big bike" riders around the world. In Japan, the bike is so popular that Harley's wholly owned local unit—Harley-Davidson Japan KK—need not advertise for customers. The 3,500 units it imports into the country each year are snapped up as soon as they reach the salesroom floor.

In the Beginning

Messrs. Harley and Davidson created their first motorized bike in 1903. Only four units were produced that year; but by the 1920s, the H-D assembly lines were turning out 28,000 bikes annually. Today, production is up to 80,000 vehicles per year and steadily climbing.

H-D bikes first arrived in Japan in 1952. From then until 1981, a domestic trading company acted as the general sales agent for the motorcycles. But Harley wanted more control. So in 1989 it bought a 51 percent controlling share, and by the end of 1991 took over 100 percent ownership to form Harley-Davidson Japan KK.

Give Us More

Tateo Ueno, marketing superintendent for H-D Japan, wants to boost yearly imports of the bike above 3,500 units. "We could sell more," he reasons, "but production in the U.S. is limited. We need to sell 5,000 a year to maintain our 15 percent share in the Japanese market for motorcycles in the seven hundred fifty-one cc category. So we hope that U.S. production will continue to increase."

H-D Japan has a network of thirty-five authorized dealers plus another sixty-five corporate dealers who supply the bikes to long waiting lists of customers year after year. But who are these Japanese bikers who prefer a Harley over so many competing domestic brands?

"We did a market survey," Ueno says, "and came up with some surprises. There are two kinds of Harley owners in Japan. One kind is fairly old, bikers over the age of 50 who love a big bike, especially one with a sidecar. On the other hand, we have very young people who want nothing but a Harley."

H-D Heaven

The mecca for die-hard Harley fans is the H-D showroom in Mita, Tokyo. Here, the big bikes are proudly displayed along with a mountain of other H-D gear ranging from jackets and motor oil to emblazoned helmets and Harley's own model train sets.

Easy Riders, a shop located in Tokyo's Shinjuku ward, is another place where enthusiasts can stock up on Harley gear—and accessories for other foreign bikes—including caps, patches, leather jackets, and coffee mugs. Manager Yasue Noguchi remarks, "We move a lot of Harley merchandise. It's very popular."

Harley the Heartwinner

Harley owners in Japan don't fit the common image of bikers as brawny, tattooed hell-raisers. Indeed, the Harley-Davidson Motorcycle Riders Club, one of the various local H-D owner groups, turns the rough-rider image on its head. Members of the club are Japanese and foreign white-collar executives who commute to their offices on the roaring machines.

Owners may spend as much as Y150,000 ($1,364) a month to maintain their bikes. But nobody's complaining. As one owner put it, "You've got to have heart to have a Harley. Sure, it costs money to keep one. But who's counting? You love the machine so much that money doesn't matter."[31]

Questions

1. Why doesn't Harley-Davidson Japan KK have to advertise for customers?
2. What motivated Harley-Davidson first to acquire 51 percent control of a domestic trading company and then to buy it completely?
3. Who are these Japanese bikers who prefer a Harley over so many competing domestic brands?

CHAPTER 4

The Forms of Business Ownership

LEARNING OBJECTIVES

After studying this chapter, you should be able to

1 Describe the basic differences among the three most common forms of business ownership: sole proprietorships, partnerships, and corporations.

2 Explain the advantages and disadvantages of proprietorships, partnerships, and corporations.

3 Summarize how a corporation is formed, who owns it, and who is responsible for its operation.

4 Describe the basic structure of a corporation.

5 Name three types of corporations organized for special purposes, and explain how they differ from the more typical open or close corporation.

6 Identify how corporations grow.

7 Discuss three additional forms of ownership: cooperatives, joint ventures, and syndicates.

CHAPTER PREVIEW

Our initial focus in this chapter is on three common forms of business ownership: sole proprietorships, partnerships, and corporations. We discuss how these types of businesses are formed and note the advantages and disadvantages of each. Next, we consider several types of corporations organized for special purposes, including S-corporations, government-owned corporations, and not-for-profit corporations. We also describe corporate patterns of growth, which may result from internal expansion or from mergers with other corporations. We conclude the chapter with a discussion of cooperatives, joint ventures, and syndicates—forms of business ownership that are less common but useful in special situations.

Good Stuff Sportswear

Good Stuff Sportswear founder Alan Marcosson got into sportswear because of a lifelong talent and passion for bicycle racing. The Amateur Bicycle League of America named him Best-All-Around Rider in 1971, and he just missed making the Olympic cycling team in 1972. Many serious bicycling enthusiasts wind up in bicycle-related jobs, but Marcosson jokes, "I decided I was going to try and be normal." After graduating from Michigan State with a degree in engineering, he took a job in electrical engineering. "It was fascinating for about ten minutes," he recalls. "After that the biggest problem was staying awake." He quit after three months.

Out of necessity, Marcosson began making his own cycling clothes for races and found he had a knack for it. In 1976 he started making clothes for others as a hobby, liked the feeling, and soon expanded his efforts. In 1980 he was able to quit the ski shop, although he still had to go back seasonally for a few years. He might have gone on this way indefinitely except that an overzealous neighbor noticed the UPS van making frequent fabric deliveries to the apartment and turned him in for violating the local zoning law.

City officials gave Alan Marcosson an ultimatum: move out or shut down the business. Unwilling to quit, he rented a storefront in Cleveland, but paying two expensive rents for his home and business was a losing proposition. He faced a choice of "downtown or way out in the country."

In 1985, Marcosson relocated to southeastern Ohio. While visiting relatives in the region, he had been impressed by the hills that offered a vigorous challenge to bicycle training. He also found that the economic climate was receptive to his entrepreneurship. He was able to purchase a house with a five-year mortgage just two blocks from the county courthouse, with no restrictions on work-

ing out of the home. As another bonus, a recently closed shirt factory had left a large pool of skilled laborers.

Since the move, Marcosson's business has grown steadily: Good Stuff sportswear now employs thirteen full-time workers and expects to gross a half-million dollars in sales this year. The community has welcomed the entrepreneur, and he returns the favor by sponsoring races and tours that bring visitors to the area.

Of his livelihood Alan Marcosson says, "There's nothing else I'd rather do. I've never handled authority figures very well, but with customers, you're on an equal footing. And selling something that you did gives more satisfaction than a paycheck. A lot of the time I forget the purpose is to make money—the doing it is the most important thing. . . . I'm not sure whether fact follows philosophy or vice-versa, but I'm doing what I do because I could figure out no other way to do it."[1]

■ ■ ■ ■

103

■　■　■　■　■　■　■　■　■　■　■

LEARNING OBJECTIVE 1
Describe the basic differences
among the three most common
forms of business ownership:
sole proprietorships,
partnerships, and corporations.

Even though Alan Marcosson experienced problems with the zoning officials, he did not need special permits to start his sole proprietorship. His firm is growing and in the near future he may incorporate his business.

Many, but not all, businesses choose the sole proprietorship form of organization. Others choose to organize as the corporate or partnership forms of organization. The type of organization that is right for a particular business depends on a number of factors discussed in this chapter. In reality, some businesses start as a sole proprietorship, change to a partnership, and then change again to a corporation. That is exactly what happened in the case of Sears, Roebuck and Co., the well-known department store chain.

■■ SOLE PROPRIETORSHIPS

sole proprietorship a
business that is owned (and
usually operated) by one person

A **sole proprietorship** is a business that is owned (and usually operated) by one person. Sole proprietorship is the simplest form of business ownership and the easiest to start. In most instances, the owner (the *sole* proprietor) simply decides he or she is in business and begins operations. Some of today's largest corporations, including Ford Motor Company, H. J. Heinz Company, and J. C. Penney Company, started out as tiny—and, in many cases, struggling—sole proprietorships.

As you can see in Figure 4.1, there are more than 15.1 million sole proprietorships in the United States. They account for almost three-fourths of the country's business firms. Sole proprietorships are most common in retailing, service, and agriculture. Thus the clothing boutique, corner grocery, and television repair shop down the street are likely to be sole proprietorships.

Advantages of Sole Proprietorships

LEARNING OBJECTIVE 2
Explain the advantages and
disadvantages of
proprietorships, partnerships,
and corporations.

Most of the advantages of sole proprietorships arise from the two main characteristics of this form of ownership: simplicity and individual control.

Ease and Low Cost of Formation and Dissolution　No contracts, agreements, or other legal documents are required to start a sole proprietorship. Most are established without even an attorney. A state or city license may be required for certain types of businesses, such as restaurants or catering services, that are regulated in the interest of public safety. But beyond that, a sole proprietor pays no special start-up fees or taxes. Nor are there any minimum capital requirements.

If the enterprise does not succeed, or if the owner decides to enter another line of business, the firm can be closed as easily as it was opened.

FIGURE 4.1
Relative Percentages of Sole Proprietorships, Partnerships, and Corporations in the United States
Sole proprietorships, the most common form of business ownership, are most common in retailing, agriculture, and the service industries.
(Source: U.S. Department of Commerce, U.S. Department of the Treasury, Internal Revenue Service, Statistics of Income Bulletin (Spring 1992), Table 19, and the State of Small Business: A Report of the President, 1993, p. 37.)

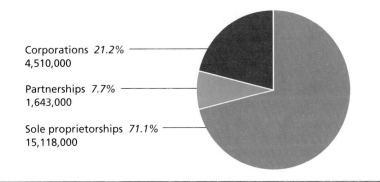

Corporations *21.2%*
4,510,000

Partnerships *7.7%*
1,643,000

Sole proprietorships *71.1%*
15,118,000

Creditors must be paid, of course. But generally, the owner does not have to go through any legal procedure before hanging up an "Out of Business" sign.

Retention of All Profits   Because all profits earned by a sole proprietorship become the personal earnings of the owner, the owner has a strong—perhaps the strongest—incentive to succeed. This direct financial reward attracts many entrepreneurs to the sole proprietorship form of business and, if the business succeeds, is a source of great satisfaction.

Flexibility   The sole owner of a business is completely free to make decisions about the firm's operations. Without asking or waiting for anyone's approval, a sole proprietor can switch from retailing to wholesaling, move a shop's location, open a new store, or close an old one.

A sole owner can also respond to changes in market conditions much more quickly than the partnership or corporate forms of business. Suppose the sole owner of an appliance store finds that many customers now prefer to shop on Sunday afternoons. He or she can make an immediate change in business hours to take advantage of that information (provided that state laws allow such stores to open on Sunday). The manager of one store in a large corporate chain may have to seek the approval of numerous managers before making such a change. Furthermore, a sole proprietor can quickly switch suppliers to take advantage of a lower price, whereas such a switch could take weeks in a more complex business.

Possible Tax Advantages   The sole proprietorship's profits are taxed as personal income of the owner. Thus a sole proprietorship does not pay the special state and federal income taxes that corporations pay. (As you will see later, the result of these special taxes is that a corporation's profits are taxed twice. A sole proprietorship's profits are taxed only once.) Also, recent changes in federal tax laws have resulted in higher tax rates for corporations than for individuals at some income levels.

Secrecy   Sole proprietors are not required by federal or state governments to publicly reveal their business plans, profits, or other vital facts. Therefore, competitors cannot get their hands on this information. Of course, sole proprietorships must report certain financial information on their personal tax forms, but that information is kept secret by taxing authorities.

Repairing a cello. A sole proprietor in St. Paul, Minnesota, makes and repairs cellos, violins, and violas. It is the direct financial award that attracts many entrepreneurs to the sole proprietorship form of business. This craftsman probably enjoys the independence and the ability to control the quality of his work.

Given these advantages of sole proprietorships, do the exercise in Enhancing Career Skills to determine whether you might have what it takes to run a business.

Disadvantages of Sole Proprietorships

The disadvantages of a sole proprietorship stem from the fact that these businesses are owned by one person. For a profitable business run by a capable owner, many of the following disadvantages cause no problems. Individuals who start out with few management skills or little money are most at risk in these areas.

unlimited liability a legal concept that holds a sole proprietor personally responsible for all the debts of his or her business

Unlimited Liability   **Unlimited liability** is a legal concept that holds a sole proprietor personally responsible for all the debts of his or her business. This means there is no legal difference between the debts of the business and the debts of the proprietor. If the business fails, the owner's personal property—including house, savings, and other assets—can be seized (and sold if necessary) to pay creditors.

Unlimited liability is thus the other side of the owner-keeps-the-profits coin. It is perhaps the major factor that tends to discourage would-be entrepreneurs with substantial personal assets from using this form of business organization.

Will You Be Successful in Running Your Own Business?

THINKING OF STARTING A BUSINESS? ASK YOURSELF THESE QUESTIONS.

For each question, check the answer that comes closest to expressing your feelings. Be honest with yourself.

Are you a self-starter?

1. I do things on my own. Nobody has to tell me to get going.
2. If someone gets me started I keep going all night.
3. Easy does it. I don't put myself out until I have to.

How do you feel about other people?

1. I like people—I can get along with just about anybody.
2. I have plenty of friends—I don't need anyone else.
3. Most people irritate me.

Can you lead others?

1. I can get most people to go along when I start something.
2. I can give the orders if someone tells me what we should do.
3. I let someone else get things moving. Then I go along if I feel like it.

Can you take responsibility?

1. I like to take charge of things and see them through.
2. I'll take over if I have to, but I'd rather let someone else be responsible.
3. There's always some eager beaver around wanting to show how smart he is. I say let him.

How good an organizer are you?

1. I like to have a plan before I start. I'm usually the one to get things lined up when the group wants to do something.
2. I do all right unless things get too confused.
3. You get all set and then something comes along and presents too many problems. So I just take things as they come.

How good a worker are you?

1. I can keep going as long as I have to. I don't mind working hard for something I want.
2. I'll work hard for a while, but when I've had enough, that's it.
3. I can't see that hard work gets you anywhere.

Can you make decisions?

1. I can make up my mind in a hurry if I have to. It usually turns out O.K., too.
2. I can if I have plenty of time. If I have to make up my mind fast, I think later I should have decided the other way.
3. I don't like to be the one who has to decide things.

Can people trust what you say?

1. You bet they can. I don't say things I don't mean.
2. I try to be on the level most of the time, but sometimes I just say what's easiest.
3. Why bother if the other fellow doesn't know the difference?

Can you stick with it?

1. If I make up my mind to do something, I don't let *anything* stop me.
2. I usually finish what I start—if it goes well.
3. If it doesn't go right away, I quit. Why beat your brains out?

Now count the checks you made.

How many checks are there beside the *first* answer to each question?

How many checks are there beside the *second* answer to each question?

How many checks are there beside the *third* answer to each question?

If most of your checks are beside the first answers, you probably have what it takes to run a business. If not, you're likely to have more trouble than you can handle by yourself. Better find a partner who is strong on the points you're weak on. If many checks are beside the third answer, not even a good partner will be able to shore you up.

107

Lack of Continuity   Legally, the sole proprietor *is* the business. If the owner dies or is declared legally incompetent, the business essentially ceases to exist. In many cases, however, the owner's heirs take over the business and either sell it or continue to operate it. This is especially true if it is a profitable enterprise.

Limited Ability to Borrow   Banks, suppliers, and other lenders are usually unwilling to lend large sums to sole proprietorships. Only one person—the sole proprietor—can be held responsible for repaying such loans, and the assets of most sole proprietors are fairly limited. Moreover, these assets may already have been used as the basis for personal borrowing (a home mortgage or car loan) or for short-term credit from suppliers. Lenders also worry about the lack of continuity of sole proprietorships: who will repay a loan if the sole proprietor is incapacitated or dies?

The limited ability to borrow can prevent a sole proprietorship from growing. It is the main reason why many business owners change from the sole proprietorship to some other ownership form when they need relatively large amounts of capital.

Limited Business Skills and Knowledge   In Parts 2, 3, 4, and 5 of this text, we will see that managers perform a variety of management functions in such areas as finance, marketing, human resources management, and operations. The sole proprietor is often the sole manager—in addition to being the sole salesperson, buyer, accountant, and, on occasion, janitor.

Even the most experienced business owner is unlikely to have expertise in all these areas. Consequently, unless he or she obtains the necessary expertise by hiring assistants or consultants, the business can suffer in the areas in which the owner is less knowledgeable.

Lack of Opportunity for Employees   The sole proprietor may find it hard to attract and keep competent help. Potential employees may feel that there is no room for advancement in a firm whose owner assumes all managerial responsibilities. And when those who *are* hired are ready to take on added responsibility, they may find that the only way to do so is to quit the sole proprietorship and work for a larger firm or start up their own businesses.

Beyond the Sole Proprietorship

The major disadvantages of a sole proprietorship stem from its one-person control—and the limited amount that one person can do in a workday. One way to reduce the effect of these disadvantages (and retain many of the advantages) is to have more than one owner.

■■ PARTNERSHIPS

Throughout our lives, we form partnerships with family members, friends, and spouses. Business partnerships do not usually entail as much affection as these other relationships, but to some people they are equally natural. A person who would not think of starting and running a business alone may enthusiastically seize the opportunity to enter into a business partnership.

The Uniform Partnership Act, which has been adopted by all states except Georgia and Louisiana, defines a **partnership** as an association of two or more persons to act as co-owners of a business for profit. For example, in 1973, two young black pharmacists named Cornell McBride and Therman McKenzie each put up $250 and, together, went into business making a hair spray for black men. They worked from the tiny basement of McBride's three-room house, mixing their first batch in a 55-gallon drum and stirring it with a pool cue. Their company—M & M Products—became one of the ten largest black-owned businesses in the country. Eventually, the two partners sold their business to BML Associates, Inc.—another black-owned business—for a price in excess of $25 million.[2]

There are approximately 1.6 million partnerships in the United States. As shown in Figure 4.2, partnerships account for about $465 billion in receipts. Note, however, that this form of ownership is much less common than the sole proprietorship or the corporation. In fact, partnerships represent only about 8 percent of all American businesses. (Refer back to Figure 4.1.)

partnership an association of two or more persons to act as co-owners of a business for profit

Partnerships made in heaven. Partners Henry W. Morton, age 82, and Henry R. Morton pose with the sleds manufactured by their partnership, PARIS Industries, in Maine. Like sole proprietorships, partnerships are relatively easy to form and all profits belong to the owners of the partnership.

FIGURE 4.2
Total Sales Receipts of American Businesses
Although corporations account for only 21.2 percent of U.S. businesses, they bring in 90 percent of the sales receipts. *(Source: U.S. Department of Commerce, Bureau of the Census,* Statistical Abstract of the United States, *1993, p. 531.)*

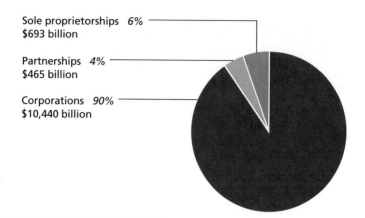

Sole proprietorships 6%
$693 billion

Partnerships 4%
$465 billion

Corporations 90%
$10,440 billion

Although there is no legal maximum, most partnerships have only two partners. (An exception to this statement is found in accounting, law, and advertising, fields in which most of the largest partnerships have many more than two partners.) Often a partnership represents a pooling of special managerial skills and talents; at other times, it results when a sole proprietor takes on a partner for the purpose of obtaining more capital.

Types of Partners

All partners need not be equal. Some may be fully active in running the business, whereas others may have a much more limited role.

general partner   a person who assumes full or shared responsibility for operating a business

General Partners   A **general partner** is one who assumes full or shared responsibility for operating a business. He or she also assumes unlimited liability for its debts, including debts incurred by any other general partner without his or her knowledge or consent. To ensure that the liabilities of the business are legally assumed by at least one person, the Uniform Partnership Act requires every partnership to have at least one general partner.

General partners are active in day-to-day business operations, and each partner can enter into contracts on behalf of all the others. Although a partnership business pays no income tax, each partner is taxed on his or her share of the profit—in the same way a sole proprietor is taxed. To avoid future liability, a general partner who withdraws from the partnership must give notice to creditors, customers, and suppliers.

limited partner   a person who contributes capital to a business but is not active in managing it; this partner's liability is limited to the amount he or she invested in the business

Limited Partners   A **limited partner** is a person who contributes capital to a business but is not active in managing it; this partner's liability is *limited* to the amount he or she has invested in the business. In return for their investment, limited partners share in the firm's profits.

Because of potential liability problems, not all states allow limited partnerships. In those that do, the prospective partners must file formal articles of partnership and publish a notice regarding the limitation in at least one newspaper. They must also ensure that at least one partner is a general partner. The goal of these requirements is to protect the customers and creditors of the limited partnership.

Partners can also be silent, secret, dormant, or nominal, depending on the individual's involvement in the business or the special abilities he or she brings to the firm. The four types of partners have the following characteristics:

1. *Silent partner*—Not active in management, but may be known to the public as a partner.
2. *Secret partner*—Active in management, but not known to the public or held out as a partner.
3. *Dormant partner*—Neither active nor known or held out as a partner.
4. *Nominal partner*—Not a party to the partnership agreement or a true partner in any sense. By adding his or her name to the partnership, a nominal partner becomes liable as if he or she were a partner if persons have given credit to the firm because of such representation.

The Partnership Agreement

Some states require partners to draw up *articles of partnership* and file them with the secretary of state. Articles of partnership are a written agreement listing and explaining the terms of the partnership. Even when it is not required, an oral or written agreement among partners is legal and can be enforced in the courts. A written agreement has an obvious advantage—it is not subject to lapses of memory.

Figure 4.3 shows a typical partnership agreement. The partnership agreement should state who will make the final decisions, what each partner's duties will be, the contribution each partner will make, and what happens if a partner wants to dissolve the partnership or dies. The breakup of a partnership can be as complicated and traumatic as a divorce, and it is never too early to consider what could happen in the future.

When entering into a partnership agreement, partners would be wise to agree to let a neutral third party—a consultant, an accountant, a lawyer, or a mutual friend—assist with any disputes that might arise. With no intense personal stake in the dispute, a third party can look beyond personal opinion and emotions to seek the best solution for the company. Each partner should agree to abide by the third party's decisions. See Ethical Challenges to glimpse a partnership at work through ups and downs.

Advantages of Partnerships

Partnerships have many advantages that cause business owners to choose this type of ownership. The most important advantages are described below.

Ease and Low Cost of Formation   Like sole proprietorships, partnerships are relatively easy to form. The legal requirements are often limited to registering the name of the business and purchasing any necessary licenses or permits. It may not even be necessary to prepare written articles of partnership. However, it is generally a good idea to get the advice and assistance of an attorney when forming a partnership.

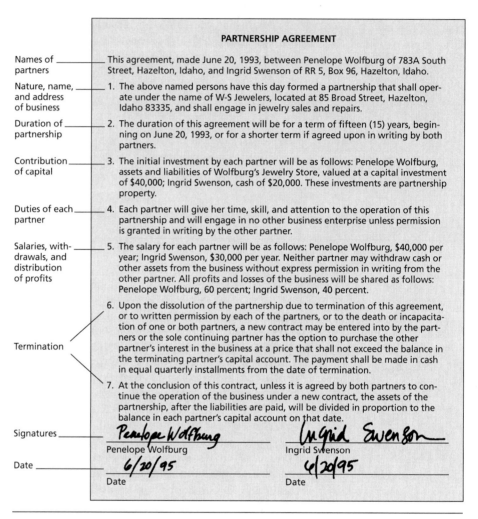

PARTNERSHIP AGREEMENT

Names of partners — This agreement, made June 20, 1993, between Penelope Wolfburg of 783A South Street, Hazelton, Idaho, and Ingrid Swenson of RR 5, Box 96, Hazelton, Idaho.

Nature, name, and address of business — 1. The above named persons have this day formed a partnership that shall operate under the name of W-S Jewelers, located at 85 Broad Street, Hazelton, Idaho 83335, and shall engage in jewelry sales and repairs.

Duration of partnership — 2. The duration of this agreement will be for a term of fifteen (15) years, beginning on June 20, 1993, or for a shorter term if agreed upon in writing by both partners.

Contribution of capital — 3. The initial investment by each partner will be as follows: Penelope Wolfburg, assets and liabilities of Wolfburg's Jewelry Store, valued at a capital investment of $40,000; Ingrid Swenson, cash of $20,000. These investments are partnership property.

Duties of each partner — 4. Each partner will give her time, skill, and attention to the operation of this partnership and will engage in no other business enterprise unless permission is granted in writing by the other partner.

Salaries, withdrawals, and distribution of profits — 5. The salary for each partner will be as follows: Penelope Wolfburg, $40,000 per year; Ingrid Swenson, $30,000 per year. Neither partner may withdraw cash or other assets from the business without express permission in writing from the other partner. All profits and losses of the business will be shared as follows: Penelope Wolfburg, 60 percent; Ingrid Swenson, 40 percent.

6. Upon the dissolution of the partnership due to termination of this agreement, or to written permission by each of the partners, or to the death or incapacitation of one or both partners, a new contract may be entered into by the partners or the sole continuing partner has the option to purchase the other partner's interest in the business at a price that shall not exceed the balance in the terminating partner's capital account. The payment shall be made in cash in equal quarterly installments from the date of termination.

Termination —

7. At the conclusion of this contract, unless it is agreed by both partners to continue the operation of the business under a new contract, the assets of the partnership, after the liabilities are paid, will be divided in proportion to the balance in each partner's capital account on that date.

Signatures — *Penelope Wolfburg*   *Ingrid Swenson*
Penelope Wolfburg   Ingrid Swenson

Date — 6/20/95   6/20/95
Date   Date

FIGURE 4.3 Articles of Partnership
Articles of partnership are a written agreement that lists and explains the terms of the partnership. *(Source: Arnold J. Goldman and William D. Sigismond,* Business Law, *3d ed. Copyright © 1992 by Houghton Mifflin Company. All rights reserved.)*

▶▶ AT A GLANCE

U.S. Partnerships, 1990

In thousands, based on tax returns filed

Source: U.S. Internal Revenue Service

Availability of Capital and Credit Partners can pool their funds so that their business has more capital than would be available to a sole proprietorship. This additional capital, coupled with the general partners' unlimited liability, can form the basis for a good credit rating. Banks and suppliers may be more willing to extend credit or grant sizable loans to such a partnership than to an individual owner.

This does not mean that partnerships can borrow easily all the money they need. Many partnerships have found it hard to get long-term financing simply because lenders worry about the possibility of management disagreements and lack of continuity. But, in general, partnerships have greater assets and so stand a better chance of obtaining the loans they need.

■ ■ ■ ■ **ETHICAL CHALLENGES**

Ben & Jerry's Homemade, Inc.

Ben Greenfield and Jerry Cohen opened their first scoop shop in a converted gas station in Burlington, Vermont, in 1977, investing $12,000 in some secondhand equipment. Their rich, all-natural ice cream, full of crunchy bits of cookies and candies, soon became popular. Before long, they were packaging more and more ice cream to sell in local restaurants and grocery stores, quickly gaining shelf space in 150 stores across the state. By 1990, Ben & Jerry's Homemade, Inc., topped $70 million in sales revenue on 6 million gallons of ice cream.

Cohen and Greenfield have made it their business not only to taste sweet success but to give something back to their employees, their community, and the world at large. The company's rapid growth, however, caused several crises for the two "hippies," who had never envisioned themselves in three-piece business suits. In fact, when Cohen and Greenfield first went into business together, they vowed to write their own rules. Among these was a mission statement that called for "innovative ways to improve the quality of life of a broad community—local, national, and international."

But by the early 1980s, Cohen and Greenfield feared their company's growth was uncontrollably veering away from their 1960s values; Greenfield even dropped out of the business for a time. When Cohen then considered selling the company, a friend convinced him to reconsider and suggested that Cohen could shape the company into whatever he wanted it to be. Cohen in turn developed the idea of "caring capitalism," which involved devoting part of the company's profits toward worthy causes as well as finding creative ways to improve the life of the company's employees and its community. Greenfield rejoined the company soon after.

Ben & Jerry's social concern can be seen in many of its products. One percent of the profits from the Peace Pop, an ice cream bar on a stick, go to programs that build awareness for peace worldwide. To help preserve endangered rain forests, the company buys rain forest nuts for its Rainforest Crunch ice cream. Homeless people bake brownies for its Chocolate Fudge Brownie ice cream and Brownie Bars.

Each year, Ben & Jerry's conducts a social audit to measure whether the company is fulfilling its self-imposed obligations. Nonetheless, the company will continue to struggle in its attempts to balance growth and profits with social responsibility; in 1995, a new CEO, Robert Holland, was chosen from among thousands of applicants to continue the company's efforts in this direction. And Ben & Jerry's customers—mostly ice cream lovers 25 to 45 years old—continue to buy its products with the satisfaction that they are doing something good not only for their taste buds but for society.

Retention of Profits   As in a sole proprietorship, all profits belong to the owners of the partnership. The partners share directly in the financial rewards and therefore are highly motivated to do their best to make the firm succeed.

Personal Interest   General partners are very concerned with the operation of the firm—perhaps even more so than sole proprietors. After all, they are responsible for the actions of all other general partners, as well as for their own.

Combined Business Skills and Knowledge   Partners often have complementary skills. The weakness of one partner—in finance, for example—may be offset by another partner's strength in that area. Moreover, the ability to discuss important decisions with another concerned individual often takes some of the pressure off everyone and leads to more effective decision making.

Possible Tax Advantages   Like sole proprietors, partners are taxed only on their individual incomes from the business. The special taxes (such as the state franchise tax) that corporations must pay are not imposed on partnerships. Also, at certain levels of income, the new federal tax rates are lower for individuals than for corporations.

Disadvantages of Partnerships

Although partnerships have many advantages when compared with sole proprietorships and corporations, they also have some disadvantages, which anyone thinking of forming a partnership should consider.

Unlimited Liability   As we have noted, each general partner is personally responsible for all debts of the business, even if that particular partner did not incur those debts. General partners thus run the risk of having to use their personal assets to pay creditors. Limited partners, however, risk only their original investment.

Lack of Continuity   Partnerships are terminated if any one of the general partners dies, withdraws, or is declared legally incompetent. However, that partner's ownership share can be purchased by the remaining partners. In other words, the law does not automatically provide that the business shall continue, but the articles of partnership may do so. For example, the partnership agreement may permit surviving partners to continue the business after buying a deceased partner's interest from his or her estate. However, if the partnership loses an owner whose specific skills cannot be replaced, it is not likely to survive.

Effects of Management Disagreements   Not all partnerships work, and very few work smoothly all the time. Business partners—with egos, ambitions, and money on the line—are especially susceptible to friction. If the division of responsibilities among several partners is to be successful, the partners must work together as a team. They must have great trust in each other. When partners begin to disagree about decisions, policies, or ethics, distrust may build and get worse as time passes—often to the point where it is impossible to operate the business successfully. To help avert such disagreements, a number of issues can be settled before forming the partnership (see Table 4.1).

Frozen Investment   It is easy to invest money in a partnership, but it is sometimes quite difficult to get it out. This is the case, for example, when

TABLE 4.1   Questions to Ask When Forming a Partnership

Money
- Where will the start-up money come from?
- How and when will it be repaid?
- How will the partners be compensated?
- When and how will this remuneration change?
- How are employees hired, and how much will they be paid?
- How are spending priorities set?
- Who approves payments and signs the checks?
- What are the profit goals?
- How are profit goals set, and when will they be revised?
- Are profits plowed back into the business or distributed to the partners?
- If profits are taken out, at what rate are they distributed?

Goals
- What are the short-term and long-term goals of the partnership?
- Are the partners totally committed to these goals?

Separation of Responsibilities
- Who will handle personnel matters?
- Which employees report to which partners?
- How are the responsibilities divided for accounting, acquisition of new equipment and office space, new business, marketing, and other functions?
- What happens if one partner is dissatisfied with the way another partner handles a particular responsibility?

Decision Making
- Which matters require joint decisions?
- In which areas can partners act independently?
- What criteria are used to evaluate decisions?

Individual Contributions
- How much time will each partner be required to devote to the business?
- Do all the partners value each other's contributions as much as their own?

Growth
- How will areas for growth be chosen?
- How will growth be financed?
- Who will manage the additional work created by the growth?
- If a new venture loses money, how will the partners decide whether to give up or to keep trying?

Disagreement
- What are the ground rules for resolving disagreements?
- Will conflicts be ended by deferring to the partner with the most expertise in the matter, by using facts and figures, or by an expert third party?
- Which matters require complete agreement before any action can be taken?

Communication
- How and when will information be shared?
- Will communication with employees be through the chain of command?

Source: Adapted from Patricia O'Toole, *Savvy,* January 1982, p. 63. Reprinted with permission from *Savvy* magazine. Copyright by Family Media, Inc.

remaining partners are unwilling to buy the share of the business that belongs to the partner who retires or wants to relocate to another city. To avoid such difficulties, the partnership agreement should include some procedure for buying out a partner.

In some cases, a partner must find someone outside the firm to buy his or her share. How easy or difficult it is to find an outsider depends on how successful the business is.

Beyond the Partnership

The advantages of a partnership over a sole proprietorship derive mainly from the added capital and management expertise of the partners. However, some of the basic disadvantages of the sole proprietorship also plague the general partnership. Two problems in particular—unlimited liability and management disagreements—can cause problems. A third form of business ownership, the corporation, successfully overcomes these disadvantages.

■■ CORPORATIONS

LEARNING OBJECTIVE 3
Summarize how a corporation is formed, who owns it, and who is responsible for its operation.

corporation an artificial person created by law, with most of the legal rights of a real person, including the rights to start and operate a business, to own or dispose of property, to borrow money, to sue or be sued, and to enter into binding contracts

Perhaps the best definition of a corporation was given by Chief Justice John Marshall in a famous Supreme Court decision in 1819. A corporation, he said, "is an artificial being, invisible, intangible, and existing only in contemplation of the law." In other words, a **corporation** is an artificial person created by law, with most of the legal rights of a real person. These include the rights to start and operate a business, to own or dispose of property, to borrow money, to sue or be sued, and to enter into binding contracts. Unlike a real person, however, a corporation exists only on paper.

There are more than 4.5 million corporations in the United States. They comprise only about one-fifth of all businesses, but they account for nine-tenths of all sales revenues and more than three-quarters of all business profits. Table 4.2 lists the twenty largest U.S. industrial corporations, ranked according to sales.

Corporate Ownership

stock the shares of ownership of a corporation

stockholder a person who owns a corporation's stock

The shares of ownership of a corporation are called its **stock.** The people who own a corporation's stock—and thus own part of the corporation—are called its **stockholders,** or sometimes its *shareholders*. Once a corporation has been formed, it may sell its stock to individuals. It may also issue stock as a reward to key employees in return for certain services, or as a return to investors (in place of cash payments).

close corporation a corporation whose stock is owned by relatively few people and is not traded in stock markets

A **close corporation** is a corporation whose stock is owned by relatively few people and is not traded openly (that is, in stock markets). As an example, Mr. and Mrs. DeWitt Wallace owned virtually all the stock of Reader's Digest Association, making it one of the largest corporations of this kind. A person who wishes to sell the stock of a close corporation generally arranges to sell it *privately,* to another stockholder or a close acquaintance.

open corporation a corporation whose stock is traded openly in stock markets and can be purchased by any individual

An **open corporation** is one whose stock is traded openly in stock markets and can be purchased by any individual. General Motors Corp., the largest industrial company in the United States, is an example. Most large firms are open corporations, and their stockholders may number in the millions. For example, AT&T is owned by 3 million shareholders.

Forming a Corporation

incorporation   the process of
forming a corporation

The process of forming a corporation is called **incorporation.** The people who actually start the corporation are its *incorporators.* They must make several decisions about the corporation before and during the incorporation process.

Where to Incorporate   A business is allowed to incorporate in any state it chooses. Most small and medium-sized businesses are incorporated in the state where they do the most business. The founders of larger corporations, or of those that will do business nationwide, often compare the benefits that various states provide to corporations. Some states are more hospitable than others, and some offer low taxes and other benefits to attract new firms. Delaware offers the most lenient tax structure, and a huge number of firms (more than 75,000) have incorporated there, even though their corporate headquarters may be located in another state. Figure 4.4 shows the best and worst "business climates" among the states, according to one group of experts. Best or worst business climate includes such factors as fiscal policies of state and local governments, state-regulated employment costs, labor costs, availability and productivity of labor, and other manufacturing criteria such as energy and environmental costs.

domestic corporation   a
corporation in the state in
which it is incorporated

An incorporated business is called a **domestic corporation** in the state in which it is incorporated. In all other states where it does business, it is

TABLE 4.2   The Twenty Largest U.S. Industrial Corporations, Ranked by Sales

Rank		Company	Sales	Profits	Assets
1993	1992		($ millions)	($ millions)	($ millions)
1	1	GENERAL MOTORS Detroit	133,621.9	2,465.8	188,200.9
2	3	FORD MOTOR Dearborn, Mich.	108,521.0	2,529.0	198,938.0
3	2	EXXON Irving, Texas	97,825.0	5,280.0	84,145.0
4	4	INTL. BUSINESS MACHINES Armonk, N.Y.	62,716.0	(8,101.0)	81,113.0
5	5	GENERAL ELECTRIC Fairfield, Conn.	60,823.0	4,315.0	251,506.0
6	6	MOBIL Fairfax, Va.	56,576.0	2,084.0	40,585.0
7	7	PHILIP MORRIS New York	50,621.0	3,091.0	51,205.0
8	11	CHRYSLER Highland Park, Mich.	43,600.0	(2,551.0)	43,830.0
9	10	TEXACO White Plains, N.Y.	34,359.0	1,068.0	26,626.0
10	9	E.I. DU PONT DE NEMOURS Wilmington, Del.	32,621.0	555.0	37,053.0
11	8	CHEVRON San Francisco	32,123.0	1,265.0	34,736.0
12	13	PROCTER & GAMBLE Cincinnati	30,433.0	(656.0)	24,935.0
13	14	AMOCO Chicago	25,336.0	1,820.0	28,486.0
14	12	BOEING Seattle	25,285.0	1,244.0	20,450.0
15	15	PEPSICO Purchase, N.Y.	25,020.7	1,587.9	23,705.8
16	17	CONAGRA Omaha	21,519.1	270.3	9,988.7
17	18	SHELL OIL Houston	20,853.0	781.0	26,851.0
18	16	UNITED TECHNOLOGIES Hartford	20,736.0	487.0	15,618.0
19	24	HEWLETT-PACKARD Palo Alto	20,317.0	1,177.0	16,736.0
20	19	EASTMAN KODAK Rochester, N.Y.	20,059.0	(1,515.0)	20,325.0

Source: *Fortune,* April 18, 1994, p. 230. Copyright © 1994 Time Inc. Used by permission. All rights reserved.

FIGURE 4.4
The Best and Worst States in Which to Incorporate a Manufacturing Firm
Number 1 represents the best, number 48 the worst. Data are not available for Alaska and Hawaii.
(Source: Adapted with permission from Grant Thornton.)

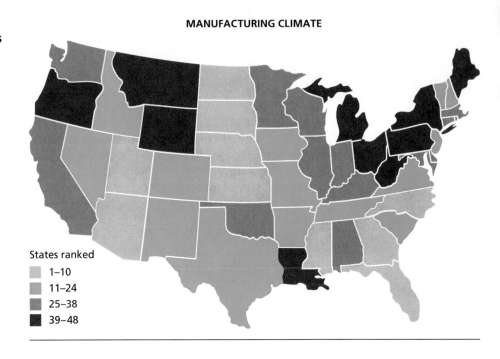

MANUFACTURING CLIMATE

States ranked
- 1–10
- 11–24
- 25–38
- 39–48

foreign corporation a corporation in any state in which it does business except the one in which it is incorporated

alien corporation a corporation chartered by a foreign government and conducting business in the United States

corporate charter a contract between the corporation and the state, in which the state recognizes the formation of the artificial person that is the corporation

called a **foreign corporation.** Sears, Roebuck, for example, is incorporated in New York, where it is a domestic corporation. In the remaining forty-nine states, Sears is a foreign corporation. A corporation chartered by a foreign government and conducting business in the United States is an **alien corporation.** Volkswagen, Sony Corp., and Lever Brothers Co. are examples of alien corporations.

The Corporate Charter   Once a "home state" has been chosen, the incorporators submit *articles of incorporation* to the secretary of state. If the articles of incorporation are approved, they become the firm's corporate charter. A **corporate charter** is a contract between the corporation and the state, in which the state recognizes the formation of the artificial person that is the corporation. Usually the charter (and thus the articles of incorporation) includes the following information:

- Firm's name and address
- Incorporators' names and addresses
- Purpose of the corporation
- Maximum amount of stock and types of stock to be issued
- Rights and privileges of shareholders
- Length of time the corporation is to exist (usually without limit)

Each of these key details is the result of decisions the incorporators must make as they organize the firm—before they submit the articles of incorporation. Let's look at one such area: stockholders' rights.

Stockholders' Rights   There are two basic types of stock (some variations on these two types are discussed in Chapters 19 and 20). Each entitles the owner to a different set of rights and privileges. Owners of **common stock** may vote on corporate matters, but their claims on profit and assets are subordinate to the claims of others. Generally, an owner of common stock has one vote for each share owned. The owners of **preferred stock** usually have no voting rights, but their claims on profit and assets take precedence over those of common-stock owners.

Perhaps the most important right of owners of both common and preferred stock is to share in the profit earned by the corporation through the payment of dividends. A **dividend** is a distribution of earnings to the stockholders of a corporation. Other rights include being offered additional stock in advance of a public offering (*pre-emptive rights*); examining corporate records; voting on the corporate charter; and attending the corporation's annual stockholders' meeting, where they may exercise their right to vote.

Because common stockholders usually live all over the nation, very few actually attend the annual meeting. Instead, they vote by proxy. A **proxy** is a legal form listing issues to be decided and requests that stockholders transfer their voting rights to some other individual or individuals. The stockholder can register a vote and transfer voting rights simply by signing and returning the form.

Organizational Meeting   As the last step in forming a corporation, the original stockholders meet to elect their first board of directors. (Later, directors will be elected or re-elected at the corporation's annual meetings.) The board members are directly responsible to the stockholders for the way they operate the firm.

Corporate Structure

The organizational structure for most corporations is more complicated than the sole proprietorship or partnership form of organization. In a corporation, both the board of directors and the corporate officers are involved in management.

Board of Directors   As an artificial person, a corporation can act only through its directors, who represent the corporation's owners. The **board of directors** is the top governing body of a corporation, and, as we noted, directors are elected by the shareholders. Board members can be chosen from within the corporation or from outside it.

Directors who are elected from within the corporation are usually its top managers—the president and executive vice presidents, for example. Those elected from outside the corporation are generally experienced managers or entrepreneurs with proven leadership ability and/or specific talents the organization seems to need. In smaller corporations, majority stockholders may also serve as board members.

The major responsibilities of the board of directors are to set company goals and develop general plans (or strategies) for meeting those goals. They are also responsible for the firm's overall operation.

---

common stock   stock owned by individuals or firms who may vote on corporate matters, but whose claims on profit and assets are subordinate to the claims of others

preferred stock   stock owned by individuals or firms who usually do not have voting rights, but whose claims on profit and assets take precedence over those of common-stock owners

dividend   a distribution of earnings to the stockholders of a corporation

proxy   a legal form listing issues to be decided at a stockholders' meeting and requests that stockholders transfer their voting rights to some other individual or individuals

LEARNING OBJECTIVE 4
Describe the basic structure of a corporation.

board of directors   the top governing body of a corporation, the members of which are elected by the stockholders

corporate officer the chairman of the board, president, executive vice presidents, corporate secretary and treasurer, or any other top executive appointed by the board of directors

Corporate Officers   A **corporate officer** is appointed by the board of directors. The chairman of the board, president, executive vice presidents, and corporate secretary and treasurer are all corporate officers. They help the board make plans, carry out strategies established by the board, and manage day-to-day business activities. Periodically (usually each month), they report to the board of directors. And, at the annual meeting, the directors report to the stockholders. In theory, then, the stockholders are able to control the activities of the entire corporation through its directors (see Figure 4.5).

Advantages of Corporations

Because a corporation is an artificial person or legal entity, it has some definite advantages when compared with other forms of ownership.

Limited Liability   One of the most attractive features of corporate ownership is **limited liability.** With few exceptions, each owner's financial liability is limited to the amount of money she or he has paid for the corporation's stock. This feature arises from the fact that the corporation is itself a legal being, separate from its owners. If a corporation fails, creditors have a claim only on the corporation's assets, not on the owners' personal assets.

limited liability a feature of corporate ownership that limits each owner's financial liability to the amount of money she or he has paid for the corporation's stock

Ease of Raising Capital   The corporation is by far the most effective form of business ownership for raising capital. Like sole proprietorships and partnerships, corporations can borrow from lending institutions. However, they can also raise additional sums of money by selling stock. Individuals are more willing to invest in corporations than in other forms of business because their liability is limited and they can sell their stock easily.

Ease of Transfer of Ownership   A telephone call to a stockbroker is all that is required to put stock up for sale. Willing buyers are available for most stocks, at the market price. Ownership is transferred automatically when the sale is made, and practically no restrictions apply to the sale and purchase of stock issued by an open corporation.

Perpetual Life   A corporation, as essentially a legal "person," exists independently of its owners and survives them. Unless its charter specifies otherwise, a corporation has perpetual life. The withdrawal, death, or incompetence of a key executive or owner does not cause the corporation to be terminated. Sears, Roebuck, which started as a partnership in 1886 and incorporated in 1906, is the nation's third-largest retailing corporation, even though its original owners, Richard Sears and Alvah Roebuck, have been dead for decades.

AT A GLANCE

Shareholder Census

Number of shareholders in public corporations.
(In millions of dollars)

Source: N.Y. Stock Exchange (from data available as of April 1994)

FIGURE 4.5   **Hierarchy of Corporate Structure**
Stockholders exercise a great deal of influence through their right to vote and elect directors.

Stockholders (owners) → *Elect* → Board of directors → *Appoints* → Officers → *Hire* → Workers

Specialized Management   Typically, corporations are able to recruit more skilled and knowledgeable managers than proprietorships and partnerships. This is because they have more available capital and are large enough to offer considerable opportunity for advancement. Within the corporate structure, administration, human resources, finance, marketing, and operations are placed in the charge of experts in these fields.

Disadvantages of Corporations

Like its advantages, a corporation's disadvantages stem from its legal definition as a person. The most serious disadvantages are described below.

Difficulty and Expense of Formation   Forming a corporation can be a relatively complex and costly process. The use of an attorney may be necessary to complete the legal forms and apply to the state for a charter. Charter fees, attorney's fees, registration costs associated with selling stock, and other organizational costs can amount to thousands of dollars for even a medium-sized corporation. The costs of incorporating, in both time and money, discourage many owners of smaller businesses from forming corporations.

Government Regulation   Most government regulation of business is directed at corporations. A corporation must meet various government standards before it can sell its stock to the public. Then it must file many reports on its business operations and finances with local, state, and federal governments. In addition, the corporation must make periodic reports to its stockholders about various aspects of the business. Also, its activities are restricted by law to those spelled out in its charter.

Double Taxation   Unlike sole proprietorships and partnerships, corporations must pay a tax on their profits. Then stockholders must pay a personal income tax on profits received as dividends. As a result, corporate profits are taxed twice—once as corporate income and again as the personal income of stockholders.

Lack of Secrecy   Because open corporations are required to submit detailed reports to government agencies and to stockholders, they cannot keep their operations confidential. Competitors can study these required corporate reports and then use the information to compete more effectively. In effect, every public corporation has to share some of its secrets with its competitors.

Table 4.3 summarizes and compares some characteristics of sole proprietorships, partnerships, and corporations.

■■ SPECIAL TYPES OF CORPORATIONS

LEARNING OBJECTIVE 5
Name three types of corporations organized for special purposes, and explain how they differ from the more typical open or close corporation.

Although most corporations are organized for the purpose of earning business profits, some are organized for special purposes. Among them are S-corporations, government-owned corporations, and not-for-profit corporations.

TABLE 4.3   Forms of Doing Business

Characteristics	Sole Proprietorship	Partnership	Corporation
Instrument of creation	None	Agreement—oral or written	Articles of incorporation
Tax rates	Individual	Individual	Corporate
Organizational documents	None	Partnership agreement	Articles of incorporation, bylaws, minutes
Limited liability	No	No	Yes
Recognition of losses	Owner	Partners	Corporation

Source: John A. Anderson, "The Business Entity That's Best For You," *Panorama*, No. 13, 2nd Quarter, 1982. Reprinted by permission of Pannell Kerr Forster and the author.

S-Corporations

If a corporation meets certain requirements, its directors may apply to the Internal Revenue Service for status as an S-corporation (formerly known as a subchapter-S corporation). An **S-corporation** is a corporation that is taxed as though it were a partnership. In other words, the corporation's income is taxed only as the personal income of shareholders.

S-corporation   a corporation that is taxed as though it were a partnership

Becoming an S-corporation can be an effective way to avoid double taxation while retaining the legal benefits of incorporation. Moreover, shareholders can personally claim their share of losses incurred by the corporation to offset their own personal income.

To qualify for the special status of an S-corporation, a firm must meet the following criteria:

1. The firm must have no more than thirty-five shareholders.
2. The shareholders must be individuals, estates, or certain trusts, and they must be citizens or permanent residents of the United States.
3. There can be only one class of outstanding stock.
4. The firm must not own 80 percent or more of the stock of any other corporation.
5. Income from passive sources—such as interest, rent, and royalties—cannot exceed 25 percent of the firm's gross income.

Government-Owned Corporations

government-owned corporation   a corporation owned and operated by a local, state, or federal government

A **government-owned corporation** is owned and operated by a local, state, or federal government. The Tennessee Valley Authority (TVA), the National Aeronautics and Space Administration (NASA), and the Federal Deposit Insurance Corporation (FDIC) are all government-owned corporations. They are operated by the U.S. government. Most municipal bus lines and

Not all corporations are created equal. Hoover Dam in Nevada is a government-owned corporation. Profit is secondary in government-owned corporations; their main objective is to ensure that a particular service is available to citizens.

subways are run by city-owned corporations. A government corporation usually provides a service the business sector is reluctant or unable to offer. (It is doubtful, for instance, whether private enterprise could have secured the financial resources needed to put astronauts on the moon.) Profit is secondary in such corporations. In fact, they may continually operate at a loss, particularly in the area of public transportation. Their main objective is to ensure that a particular service is available to citizens.

In certain cases, a government will invite citizens or firms to invest in a government corporation as part owners. A business owned partly by the government and partly by private citizens or firms is called a **quasi-government corporation.** COMSAT (Communications Satellite Corporation), the Federal National Mortgage Association (Fannie Mae), and the Student Loan Marketing Association (Sallie Mae) are examples of quasi-government corporations.

quasi-government corporation a business owned partly by the government and partly by private citizens or firms

Not-for-Profit Corporations

not-for-profit corporation a corporation organized to provide a social, educational, religious, or other service, rather than to earn a profit

A **not-for-profit corporation** is a corporation organized to provide a social, educational, religious, or other service, rather than to earn a profit. Various charities, museums, private schools, and colleges are organized in this way, primarily to ensure limited liability. The Great Woods Corporation, one such

When profits are not the goal. Churches are one of the most familiar types of not-for-profit corporations. This Congregational Church in Coral Gables, Florida, is a not-for-profit and an income tax–exempt corporation. Churches and social or educational organizations do not issue stock certificates because no dividends are paid.

example, was formed to provide outdoor camping experiences for disabled children. Even though this corporation may receive more money than it spends, any surplus funds are "reinvested" in camping activities for disabled children. It is a not-for-profit corporation because its primary purpose is to provide a social service. The statutes of most states contain separate provisions dealing with the organization and operation of not-for-profit corporations. These organizations do not issue stock certificates because no dividends are paid and no one is interested in buying or selling their stock. They are also exempted from income taxes.

Occasionally, some not-for-profit organizations are inspired with entrepreneurial zeal. The Children's Television Workshop, for example, netted $7.7 million a few years ago by licensing Sesame Street products. In the same year, the New York Museum of Modern Art sold air rights in Manhattan for $17 million to allow the construction of a private forty-four-story residential tower. Tax-free income from the sale helped finance a new wing, doubling the size of the museum.[3]

■■ CORPORATE GROWTH AND MERGERS

LEARNING OBJECTIVE 6
Identify how corporations grow.

Growth seems to be a basic characteristic of business, at least for firms that can obtain the capital needed to finance growth. One reason for seeking growth has to do with profit: a larger firm generally has greater sales revenue and thus greater profit. Another reason is that, in a growing economy, a business that does not grow is actually shrinking relative to the economy. A third reason is that business growth is a means by which some executives boost their power, prestige, and reputation.

Going for growth from within. Bausch & Lomb is expanding the sale of contact lenses and lens-care products to new geographic markets. In China, Bausch & Lomb created a brand-new market by teaching opticians to fit lenses.

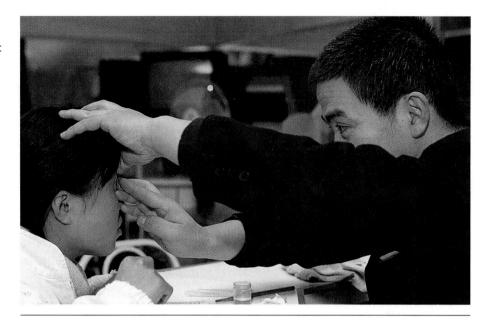

Should all firms grow? Certainly not until they are ready. Growth poses new problems and requires additional resources that must first be available and must then be used effectively. The main ingredient in growth is capital—and, as we have noted, capital is most readily available to corporations. Thus, to a great extent, business growth means corporate growth.

Growth from Within

Most corporations grow by expanding their present operations. Some introduce and sell new but related products, such as Chrysler Corporation's minivan or IBM's personal computers. Others expand the sale of present products to new geographic markets or new groups of consumers in geographic markets already served. Currently, Wal-Mart Stores, Inc., serves customers in forty-nine states and Puerto Rico and has long-range plans for expanding into international markets.

Growth from within, especially when carefully planned and controlled, can have relatively little adverse effect on a firm. For the most part, the firm continues to do what it has been doing (and doing successfully), but it does so on a larger scale. Because this type of growth is anticipated, it can be gradual and the firm can usually adapt to it easily.

Growth Through Mergers

merger the purchase of one corporation by another

Another way for a firm to grow is by purchasing some other company. The purchase of one corporation by another is called a **merger.** (The term *acquisition* means essentially the same thing, but it is usually reserved for large corporations buying other corporations.) The firm that is expanding simply buys the stock of the purchased corporation. (This is not always as simple as it sounds. In some cases, the management and stockholders of the firm targeted for acquisition are unwilling to let their company become a subsidiary of the purchasing firm. The results may be greatly inflated stock prices, legal battles, and—at the least—general ill will between the two firms.) The underlying reason for growth by merger is the supposition that the merged companies can produce benefits for the shareholders that the individual companies cannot offer on their own.

Horizontal Mergers   A *horizontal merger* is a merger between firms that make and sell similar products in similar markets (see Figure 4.6). The purchase of Telecom USA by MCI Communications is an example of a horizontal merger. The rash of mergers between large American companies in the 1980s resulted in many horizontal mergers. This type of merger tends to reduce the number of firms in an industry—and thus may reduce competition. For this reason, each merger may be reviewed carefully by federal agencies before it is permitted.

Firms may use horizontal mergers to accomplish goals other than growth. For example, the major goal of the oil-company mergers that occurred in the 1980s was to acquire large petroleum reserves. It was actually less costly to obtain petroleum by buying a firm that owned oil than by exploring, drilling, and pumping oil from the ground.

Vertical Mergers   A *vertical merger* is a merger between firms that operate at different but related levels in the production and marketing of a product. Generally, one of the merging firms is either a supplier or a customer of the other. A vertical merger occurred when Pepsico—a major soft drink producer—acquired Pizza Hut. After this merger, only Pepsi drinks were sold in Pizza Hut restaurants.

Conglomerate Mergers   A *conglomerate merger* takes place between firms in completely unrelated industries. Several years ago, Xerox Corporation

FIGURE 4.6
Three Types of Growth by Merger
An automobile manufacturer acquiring another automobile manufacturer is a horizontal merger. If the same auto manufacturer buys out the company that makes its tires, a vertical merger takes place. A conglomerate merger results when the auto manufacturer buys a sports equipment firm.

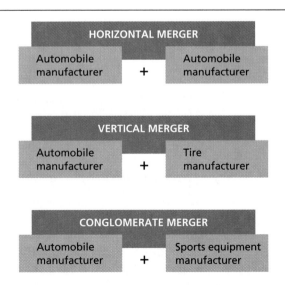

purchased Crum and Forster, Inc. (an insurance firm), and Brown-Forman Distillers Corporation purchased Lenox, Inc., a producer of china. Both acquisitions were conglomerate mergers, and both enlarged the product base from which the purchasing firm receives its sales revenue.

Current Merger Trends

Future historians may focus on the explosion in mergers and company acquisitions as the most important economic trend of the 1980s. Companies gobbled each other up and sold off subsidiaries at an unprecedented rate. Although some results of this merger-and-acquisition mania are already evident, business experts can only guess at the long-term consequences of this major reshuffling of corporate America.

Economists, financial analysts, corporate managers, and stockholders still hotly debate whether takeovers will be good for the economy—or for individual companies—in the long run. But one thing is clear: there are two sides to the takeover question. Takeover advocates argue that in companies that have been taken over, the purchasers have been able to make the company more profitable and productive by changing the top management team and by forcing the company to concentrate on one main business. Subsidiaries and divisions not aligned with the company's main business were sold off and the proceeds used to either pay off debt or enhance the company.

Takeover opponents argue that takeovers do nothing to enhance corporate profitability or productivity. These critics argue that threats of takeovers have forced managers to devote valuable time to defending their companies from takeover attempts, thus robbing time from new product development and other vital business activities. As a result, U.S. companies are less competitive with companies in such countries as Japan, West Germany, and South Korea, where takeovers rarely occur. Finally, the opposition argues that the only people who benefit from takeovers are investment bankers, brokerage firms, and takeover artists. These people receive financial rewards by manipulating U.S. corporations, rather than by producing tangible products or services.

Most experts now predict that merger-and-acquisition activity will be more routine, as cash-rich companies look for smaller companies that complement existing business operations. Analysts also look for more mergers that involve companies or investors from other countries. European and Japanese companies were involved in fifteen of the fifty largest mergers in the first part of the 1990s.[4] The mergers that involve foreign investors are typically conglomerate mergers. For example, Matsushita Electric's acquisition of the American entertainment company MCA, Inc., was a conglomerate merger that enabled Matsushita to diversify into something totally different from its usual business operations. Finally, most experts predict less debt financing will be used to pay for mergers and acquisitions. Bankers and lenders of the 1990s seem to be far more skeptical than those of the 1980s when they consider possible merger deals.

■■ OTHER FORMS OF BUSINESS OWNERSHIP

LEARNING OBJECTIVE 7
Discuss three additional forms of ownership: cooperatives, joint ventures, and syndicates.

Sole proprietorships, partnerships, and corporations are by far the most common forms of business ownership in the United States. Other forms of ownership do exist, however. Like the nonstandard corporate forms, they are used primarily to serve their owners' special needs.

Cooperatives

cooperative an association of individuals or firms whose purpose is to perform some business function for all its members

A **cooperative** is an association of individuals or firms whose purpose is to perform some business function for all its members. The cooperative's members pay membership fees, which cover its operating costs. Members also pay for services provided by the cooperative as they use them. Members benefit from the activities of the cooperative because it can perform its function more effectively than any member could by acting alone. For example, when *buying cooperatives* purchase goods in bulk and distribute them to members, the unit cost is lower than it would be if each member bought the goods in a much smaller quantity.

Cooperatives such as credit unions are owned by their members, and they may or may not be incorporated. When they are, the corporation is usually not for profit. Therefore, surplus funds are either returned to the members or set aside to finance future needs. Cooperatives generally have unlimited life; they need not be dissolved when a member leaves the organization. Cooperatives that are incorporated also obtain such advantages as limited liability.

Although cooperatives are found in all segments of our economy, they are most prevalent in agriculture. Farmers use cooperatives to purchase supplies, to buy services such as trucking and storage, and to market their products. The trademark *Ocean Spray*, for example, is owned by Ocean Spray Cranberries, Inc., a cooperative of some seven hundred cranberry growers and more than one hundred citrus growers spread throughout the country.

Joint Ventures

joint venture a partnership that is formed to achieve a specific goal or to operate for a specific period of time

A **joint venture** is a partnership formed to achieve a specific goal or to operate for a specific period of time. Both the scope of the firm and the liabilities of the partners are limited. Once the goal is reached or the period of time elapses, the joint venture is dissolved.

Corporations, as well as individuals, may enter into joint ventures. A number of these joint ventures were formed by major oil producers in the 1970s and 1980s to share the extremely high cost of exploring for offshore petroleum deposits.

Syndicates

syndicate a temporary association of individuals or firms organized to perform a specific task that requires a large amount of capital

A **syndicate** is a temporary association of individuals or firms organized to perform a specific task that requires a large amount of capital. The syndicate is formed because no one person or firm is willing to put up the entire amount required for the undertaking. Like a joint venture, a syndicate is dissolved as soon as its purpose has been accomplished. However, the participants in a syndicate do not form a separate firm, as do the members of a joint venture.

Syndicates are most commonly used to underwrite large insurance policies, loans, and investments. Banks have formed syndicates to provide loans to developing countries, to share the risk of default. Stock brokerage firms usually join together in the same way to market a new issue of stock.

Whether they are sole proprietorships, partnerships, or corporations, most U.S. businesses are small. In the next chapter, we focus on these small businesses. We examine, among other things, the meaning of the word *small* as it applies to business and the place of small business in the American economy.

■ ■ ■ ■ CHAPTER REVIEW

Summary

1   Describe the basic differences among the three most common forms of business ownership: sole proprietorships, partnerships, and corporations.

The three major forms of business in the United States are the sole proprietorship, the partnership, and the corporation. A sole proprietorship is a business that is owned by one person. In essence, the owner and the business are one. A partnership is an association of two or more individuals who act as co-owners of a business for profit. A corporation is an artificial "person" created by law, with most of the legal rights of an actual person.

2   Explain the advantages and disadvantages of proprietorships, partnerships, and corporations.

In the sole proprietorship, all business profits become the property of the owner, and all business debts are the responsibility of the owner. Sole proprietorship is the simplest form of business to enter, control, and leave. It also has possible tax advantages. Perhaps for these reasons, more than two-thirds of all American business firms are sole proprietorships. They nevertheless have disadvantages, such as limits on one person's ability to borrow or to be an expert in all areas.

Although partnership eliminates some of the disadvantages of sole proprietorship, it is the least popular of the major forms of business. Like sole proprietors, general partners are responsible for running the business and for all business debts.

Limited partners receive a share of the profit in return for investing in the business. However, they are not responsible for business debts beyond the amount they have invested. A partnership agreement (or articles of partnership) is a written document setting forth the terms of a partnership.

Perhaps the major advantage of the corporate form is limited liability: stockholders are not liable for the corporation's debts beyond the amount they have paid for its stock. Another important advantage is the perpetual life of the corporation. A major disadvantage is double taxation. The corporation's earnings are taxed once as corporate income and again as personal income (when earnings are distributed to stockholders).

3   Summarize how a corporation is formed, who owns it, and who is responsible for its operation.

Corporations are artificial beings created by law. These artificial beings have the right to start and operate a business, own property, and enter into contracts. Although corporations comprise only one-fifth of all American businesses, they account for nine-tenths of all business receipts. The largest businesses in the United States are organized as corporations.

4   Describe the basic structure of a corporation.

Shares of ownership of a corporation are called stock, and owners are called stockholders. A corporation must be chartered, or formally recognized, by a particular state. Once the corporation has received a charter, its original stockholders elect a board of directors. The board of directors then appoints corporate officers. Once each year, all stockholders have the right to vote for the firm's directors—either in person at the firm's annual meeting or by proxy.

5 Name three types of corporations organized for special purposes, and explain how they differ from the more typical open or close corporation.

The stock of open corporations is available to anyone who wants to buy it; the stock of close corporations is not. S-corporations are corporations that are taxed as though they were partnerships. Various criteria must be met to qualify for this status. Government-owned corporations provide particular services, such as public transportation, to citizens. Not-for-profit corporations are formed to provide social services rather than to earn profits, but they are not owned by governments.

6 Identify how corporations grow.

A corporation may grow by expanding its present operations or through merger—the purchase of another corporation.

7 Discuss three additional forms of ownership: cooperatives, joint ventures, and syndicates.

Three additional forms of business ownership are the cooperative, the joint venture, and the syndicate. All are used by their owners to meet special needs, and each may be owned by either individuals or firms.

Key Terms

You should now be able to define and give an example relevant to each of the following terms:

sole proprietorship (104)
unlimited liability (106)
partnership (109)
general partner (110)
limited partner (110)
corporation (116)
stock (116)
stockholder (116)
close corporation (116)
open corporation (116)
incorporation (117)
domestic corporation (117)
foreign corporation (118)
alien corporation (118)
corporate charter (118)
common stock (119)
preferred stock (119)
dividend (119)
proxy (119)
board of directors (119)
corporate officer (120)
limited liability (120)
S-corporation (122)
government-owned corporation (122)
quasi-government corporation (123)
not-for-profit corporation (123)
merger (125)
cooperative (128)
joint venture (128)
syndicate (128)

Questions

Review Questions

1. What is a sole proprietorship? What are the major advantages and disadvantages of this form of business ownership?
2. How does a partnership differ from a sole proprietorship? Which disadvantages of sole proprietorship does the partnership tend to eliminate or reduce?
3. Why is sole proprietorship the most popular form of business ownership? Why is partnership the least popular?
4. What is the difference between general partners and limited partners?
5. Explain the difference between
   a. An open corporation and a close corporation
   b. A domestic corporation, a foreign corporation, and an alien corporation
   c. A government-owned corporation, a quasi-government corporation, and a not-for-profit corporation
6. Outline the incorporation process and describe the basic corporate structure.
7. What rights do stockholders have?
8. What are the primary duties of a corporation's board of directors? How are directors elected?
9. What are the major advantages and disadvantages associated with the corporate form of business ownership?
10. How does an S-corporation differ from the usual open or close corporation?
11. Describe the three types of mergers.
12. Why are cooperatives formed? Explain how they operate.
13. In what ways are joint ventures and syndicates alike? In what ways do they differ?

Discussion Questions

1. For what reasons did Alan Marcosson quit his electrical engineering job after just three months?
2. How would you describe Marcosson's entrepreneurial spirit? Do you believe he has the characteristics of a successful entrepreneur?
3. If you were to start a business, which ownership form would you use? What factors might affect your choice of ownership form?
4. Why might an investor choose to become a limited partner instead of purchasing the stock of an open corporation?
5. Discuss the following statement: "Corporations are not really run by their owners."
6. Is growth a good thing for all firms? How can management tell when a firm is ready to grow?
7. What kinds of services do government-owned corporations provide? How might such services be provided without government involvement?

Exercises

1. Suppose you are a part-time employee working for the sole proprietor of a car wash. The owner has offered you a 29 percent partnership, and you are going to accept. Write out at least six articles of a partnership agreement that would cover your partnership.

2. You and your partner in the car wash of Exercise 1 have decided to incorporate. List the steps you would follow to form the corporation, and include specific decisions you must make at each step. Include at least six articles of incorporation (or, if you prefer, obtain and fill out a standard articles-of-incorporation form for your state).

3. Research a recent merger and determine the specific reasons why each of the two firms sought, or agreed to, the merger.

VIDEO CASE 4.1

General Motors Annual Stockholders Meeting

In the 1980s and early 1990s, U.S. domestic automobile manufacturers, especially General Motors, were in turmoil. Dire headlines in business newspapers and magazines predicted a gloomy future: "Can GM Remodel Itself?" "May We Help You Kick the Tires," "Rude Awakening: The Rise, Fall, and Struggle for Recovery of General Motors," "GM Is Spreading the Gospel According to Toyota," "War, Recession, Gas Hikes . . . GM's Turn-around Will Have to Wait," "General Motors: What Went Wrong?" and "Can GM Fix Itself?" The list is endless. According to John F. Smith, Jr., chief executive officer and president of General Motors, "All of the well-publicized difficulties we faced in the past few years were in a sense the overdue wake-up call. GM's success had made it easy to ignore the significance of change and the signs of potential future problems."

To try to solve its problems and increase competitiveness, in 1984 GM created a new division that focused on larger luxury cars—the Buicks, Oldsmobiles, and Cadillacs. The result was that by 1987 all the cars produced by this division began to look alike and buyers grew wary of GM's products. Cadillac buyers did not know why they were paying more for a car that looked just like GM's other less expensive models, like Buicks, and sales of Cadillacs plummeted.

Realizing their mistake, GM's top management reorganized the company to give control of engineering and design back to the separate divisions. The Cadillac division benefited the most from this restructuring. To turn the division around, Cadillac was granted its own engineering team in 1988 and moved quickly to create a new identity for the line. Once again in control of its decision making, Cadillac managers lengthened the cars two inches, totally restyled them, increased advertising, and used direct mail to promote test drives. By 1990 Cadillac had gross profit margins of 40 to 50 percent, compared to 30 percent for the rest of GM's divisions. The Cadillac division had become very successful, launching redesigned models in 1991, 1992, and 1993. Their sales have been growing steadily, especially as the rising value of the yen has made Japanese luxury cars like the Lexus and Infiniti relatively expensive.

In 1990 GM's Cadillac division won the prestigious 1990 Malcolm Baldrige Quality Award. According to David A. Garvin and Robert and Jane Cizik, professors of business administration at the Harvard Business School, the award "has become the most important catalyst for transforming American business." In 1992 GM introduced the very successful Cadillac Seville STS and successfully marketed the model against Toyota's Lexus and Germany's Mercedes. Even after all the improvements, however, the plant that produced the Cadillac Seville STS still ran at only 50 percent capacity. But Cadillac continued its leadership of the luxury car market for the forty-fifth year with 1993 sales again exceeding 200,000 units.

What follows is the summary of remarks made by John Grettenberger, vice president and general manager of GM's Cadillac Motor Division, to the shareholders who attended the annual meeting on May 20, 1994.

Our Cadillac team has come a long way, and we are now stronger than ever. We have been spending the last six years transforming our product to prepare for the challenges of the twenty-first century. Our quality and reliability have been recognized by customers and industry analysts. Recently Cadillac was named number 1 in vehicle dependability by J. D. Power & Associates, the industry analysts. It is the first time that a domestic car has topped that list. In a five-year ownership rating, Cadillac holds the number-1 ranking among the luxury cars. Cadillac was the only company in the industry to redesign its entire product line. Eight all-new models hit the market in just three years. The 1992 Seville and the Eldorado were first of the new generation to reach dealers, and 1992 Seville STS won the most prestigious awards in the industry, including the Motor Trend Car of the Year. In the following year, GM introduced the Northstar system to the Seville Touring Sedan and the Eldorado Touring Coupe, and the car won another fifteen editorial awards.

The Northstar system has established Cadillac's tradition for innovation and technological leadership. Customers know the Northstar system by name and use it as a benchmark when comparison shopping.

The year 1995 marked the eightieth anniversary of the first Cadillac V8, and eighty years later it is still setting the industry standards in power-train technology. Cadillac's world-class vehicle systems are the key to the sales success of the Seville and the Eldorado, and the model year sales have improved over 110 percent between 1991 and 1993. Continued improvement is expected for the 1994 model year.

The Cadillac division has successfully attracted new buyers to Cadillac. The division made major inroads with young, affluent buyers who tend to prefer imports. The average age of buyers is decreasing. These young buyers, both male and female, are import-oriented and prefer sporty, contemporary cars with a feel-of-the-road handling. Two important new groups of Cadillac buyers are affluent women and African Americans.

Cadillac is setting new standards for the capability, competency, and overall balance of the large luxury sedan with the introduction of the all-new 1994 Cadillac DeVille Concours. The DeVille Concours is a fully equipped, six-passenger sedan with Cadillac's exclusive Northstar system. The 270-horsepower Northstar V8 engine establishes the DeVille Concours as the most powerful front-wheel-drive, six-passenger sedan in the world. The DeVille Concours is newly designed, with comprehensive climate controls, precision instrumentation, ergonomically designed leather seating areas, and an all-new, eleven-speaker Delco Electronics Active Audio System. The base price? $37,990.

Questions

1. Why was the U.S. automobile industry in a tailspin during the 1980s and the early 1990s?
2. What was GM's focus in 1984 to solve its problems? What were the results?
3. How did GM reorganize the company to bring a turnaround at the Cadillac division?
4. Comment on this John Grettenberger remark to GM shareholders at the 1994 annual meeting: "Our Cadillac team has come a long way, and we are now stronger than ever." Do you agree or disagree? Defend your position.

CASE 4.2

Unilever's Thomas J. Lipton Company

In 1993 Thomas J. Lipton Company, traditionally known for its market-leading teas and soup mixes, became the nation's largest ice cream producer. The company accomplished this feat by acquiring ice cream makers Klondike, Breyers, and Sealtest during the year. Lipton's ice cream business, now known as Good Humor-Breyers, successfully integrated the new brands into the existing Good Humor and Popsicle operations and achieved record sales and profits.

The Pepsi/Lipton Tea Partnership, a joint venture to market Lipton ready-to-drink teas through Pepsico's extensive production and distribution network, also had an excellent year. Through this partnership, the company exceeded its ambitious goals, selling to tea drinkers more than 1 billion individual Lipton bottles, cans, and fountain servings. Within its Beverage Division, Lipton regular tea bags maintained their strong leadership position and sales volume despite a highly competitive year. Moreover, Lipton convenience teas gained market share in all iced tea mix and instant tea categories.

Lipton's Foods Division continued its successful performance in side dishes, demonstrating market leadership all year, and sales of Lipton Recipe Secrets also increased. Lawry's Foods significantly improved its market share in spice blends and specialty sauces and won both Clio and Effie Awards for its seasoned salt advertising. Lipton's Foodservice Group achieved record sales through full-line foodservice distributor channels, with particularly healthy performances in Lipton Tea and Wish-Bone salad dressings.

The year 1994 was a vital year for Thomas J. Lipton's employees as the company intensified its focus on growth through innovation. By systematically analyzing its products, processes, and services, Lipton is working diligently to deliver value to its customers and consumers.

Lipton's parent, Unilever United States, Inc., is one of the largest consumer goods firms in the world, employing 294,000 people and operating through some 400 companies in 80 countries. In 1993 corporate sales totaled $41.9 billion worldwide. In the United States, Unilever offers a broad range of foods, soaps and detergents, personal care products, and specialty chemicals through Lever Brothers, Thomas J. Lipton, Van den Bergh Foods, Chesebrough-Pond's, Elizabeth Arden, Calvin Klein Cosmetics, National Starch and Chemical, and a number of other companies.[6]

Questions

1. Is Thomas J. Lipton Company an open or close corporation? Explain your answer.
2. Lipton is a corporation; what might be some advantages and disadvantages of this form of organizational structure?
3. What strategies have propelled Lipton's growth?
4. What was the purpose of Thomas J. Lipton Company's joint venture with Pepsico?

CHAPTER 5

Small Business, Entrepreneurship, and Franchises

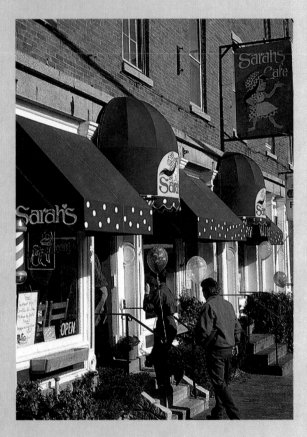

LEARNING OBJECTIVES

After studying this chapter, you should be able to

1 Define what a small business is and recognize the fields in which small businesses are concentrated.

2 Identify the people who start small businesses and the reasons why some succeed and many fail.

3 Assess the contributions of small businesses to our economy.

4 Judge the advantages and disadvantages of operating a small business.

5 Explain how the Small Business Administration helps small businesses.

6 Appraise the concept and types of franchising.

7 Analyze the growth of franchising and its advantages and disadvantages.

CHAPTER PREVIEW

In this chapter we do not take small businesses for granted. Instead we look closely at this important business sector—beginning with a definition of *small business,* a description of industries that often attract small businesses, and a profile of some of the people who start small businesses. Next we consider the importance of small businesses in our economy. We also present the advantages and disadvantages of smallness in business. Then we describe services provided by the Small Business Administration, a government agency formed to assist owners and managers of small businesses. We conclude the chapter with a discussion of the pros and cons of franchising, an approach to small business ownership that has become very popular in the last two decades.

Essex Industries, Inc.

More than fifty years ago, Harold Guller was delivering groceries in St. Louis, Missouri, for his father's store. Just three years ago, he was inducted into the St. Louis Small Business Administration Hall of Fame, another in a long list of honors and awards he has earned.

Harold Guller's success story is based on personal initiative, hard work, and dedication. He truly is a "self-made person." Today he is chairman emeritus and chief executive officer of Essex Industries, Inc., headquartered in St. Louis. Essex's ten distinct companies design, engineer, and manufacture components for a wide variety of uses. Customers range from the military, aerospace, and aircraft industries to medical, automotive, and general manufacturers.

Initially, Guller's dream of attending college was dampened by his family's modest means and lack of resources. He managed to scrape together the $125 tuition for entrance into Washington University, but his education was interrupted by World War II. After serving in Europe during the war, he returned home to St. Louis in 1946. With two friends, Guller formed Essex Industries in an abandoned mortuary and produced airplane radio noise filters. The rest, as they say, is history.

Essex has grown over the years into ten subsidiaries and divisions and now employs about 450 workers. In its founder's words, "I am intensely proud of Essex, its people, its products and its history of growth from rather shaky beginnings. The memories of our sweat, the warmth of our friendships, the glow of our dreams are all as vivid to me now as they were 45 years ago. These

are exciting times . . . a coming together of diverse personalities, working hard to make a shared dream come true. Every day is a fulfillment of that dream."

In 1972 Harold Guller's company received the National Small Business Subcontractor of the Year award. His many other honors culminated in his induction into the Small Business Administration Hall of Fame. Harold Guller—dramatic testimony that there is nothing small about small business.[1]

■ ■ ■ ■

■ ■ ■ ■ ■ ■ ■ ■ ■ ■ ■

The kind of growth enjoyed by Harold Guller is unusual. Most businesses start small, and those that survive usually stay small. Nevertheless, small businesses provide a solid foundation for our economy—as employers, as suppliers and purchasers of goods and services, and as taxpayers.

■■ SMALL BUSINESS: A PROFILE

LEARNING OBJECTIVE 1
Define what a small business is and name the fields in which small businesses are concentrated.

The Small Business Administration (SBA) defines a **small business** as "one which is independently owned and operated for profit and is not dominant in its field." How small must a firm be not to dominate its field? That depends on the particular industry it is in. The SBA has developed the following specific "smallness" guidelines for the various industries:[2]

- *Manufacturing*—a maximum number of employees ranging from 500 to 1,500, depending on the products manufactured
- *Wholesaling*—a maximum number of employees not to exceed 500
- *Retailing*—maximum yearly sales or receipts ranging from $10 million to $13.5 million, depending on the industry
- *General construction*—average annual receipts ranging from $9.5 million to $17 million, depending on the industry
- *Special trade construction*—annual sales ranging up to $7 million
- *Agriculture*—maximum annual receipts of $0.5 million to $3.5 million
- *Services*—maximum annual receipts ranging from $2.5 million to $14.5 million, depending on the type of service

A new standard, based only on the number of employees, has been proposed but not yet adopted by the SBA.

Annual sales in the millions of dollars may not seem very small. However, for many firms, profit is only a small percentage of total sales. Thus a firm may earn only $30,000 or $40,000 on yearly sales of $1 million—and that *is* small in comparison to the profits earned by most medium-sized and large firms. Moreover, most small firms have annual sales well below the maximum limits in the SBA guidelines.

The Small-Business Sector

A surprising number of Americans take advantage of their freedom to start a business. There are, in fact, about 21.3 million businesses in this country. Only about 14,000 of these employ more than 500 workers—enough to be considered large.

Over 734,000 new businesses are incorporated in a typical year.[3] At the same time that new firms are being created, however, others are going out of business. Statistically, over 70 percent of new businesses can be expected to fail within their first five years.[4] The primary reason for these failures is mismanagement resulting from a lack of business know-how. The makeup of the small-business sector is thus constantly changing. In spite of the high failure rate, many small businesses succeed modestly. Some, like Apple Computer, Inc., are extremely successful—to the point where they can no longer be considered small. Taken together, small businesses are also responsible for providing a high percentage of the jobs in the United States. According to some estimates, the figure is well over 50 percent.

Industries That Attract Small Businesses

Some industries, such as auto manufacturing, require huge investments in machinery and equipment. Businesses in such industries are big from the day they are started—if an entrepreneur or group of entrepreneurs can gather the capital required to start one.

By contrast, a number of other industries require only a low initial investment and some special skills or knowledge. It is these industries that tend to attract new businesses. Growing industries, such as outpatient care facilities, are attractive because of their profit potential. However, knowledgeable entrepreneurs choose areas with which they are familiar, and these

A personal touch. Service firms, such as this furniture repair shop in North Carolina, require a low initial capital investment. Knowledgeable entrepreneurs, such as this expert furniture repairman, who choose areas with which they are familiar, can provide personal service to their customers.

are most often the more established industries. Consider the example of Asher Benjamin & Company of Sheffield, Massachusetts, which specializes in producing high-quality, Shaker-style furniture that gives many years of service and pleasure. The firm's owners, Peter and Meg Strattner, build furniture the old-fashioned way—one piece at a time. Founded in 1981, the company manufactures a full line of handsome wood tables, chairs, chests, cupboards, and beds for both domestic and foreign markets. Initial sales in 1981 were over $31,000, increased to $620,000 in 1989, and skyrocketed to $3 million in 1992. The company currently employs twenty-seven people, and the Strattners have recently expanded their sales to markets in Canada, England, and Germany.[5]

Small enterprise spans the gamut from corner newspaper vending to the development of optical fibers. The owners of small businesses sell gasoline, flowers, and coffee to go. They publish magazines, haul freight, teach languages, and program computers. They make wines, movies, and high-fashion clothes. They build new homes and restore old ones. They fix appliances, recycle metals, and sell used cars. They drive cabs and fly planes. They make us well when we are ill, and they sell us the products of corporate giants.

As Figure 5.1 shows, the various kinds of businesses generally fall into three broad categories of industries: distribution, service, and production. Within these categories, small businesses tend to cluster in the service industries and in retailing. Table 5.1 shows the fastest growing industries in the small-business sector.

Distribution Industries This category includes retailing, wholesaling, transportation, and communications—industries that are concerned with the movement of goods from producers to consumers. Distribution industries account for approximately 33 percent of all small businesses. Of these,

FIGURE 5.1
Relative Proportions of Small Businesses by Industry
Small businesses are found in three major industries; most are in service and distribution. *(Source: Adapted from* The State of Small Business: A Report of the President [Washington D.C.: GPO, 1993], *pp. 48–51.)*

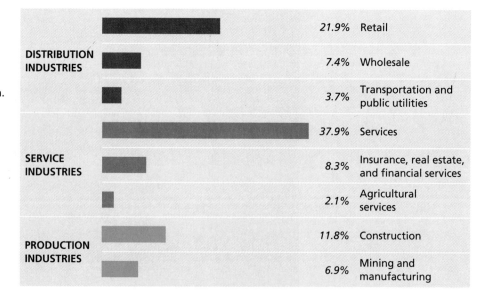

	21.9%	Retail
DISTRIBUTION INDUSTRIES	7.4%	Wholesale
	3.7%	Transportation and public utilities
	37.9%	Services
SERVICE INDUSTRIES	8.3%	Insurance, real estate, and financial services
	2.1%	Agricultural services
PRODUCTION INDUSTRIES	11.8%	Construction
	6.9%	Mining and manufacturing

TABLE 5.1   Fastest Growing Industries in Small Business by Percent of Employment, September 1991 to September 1992

Industry	Employment Change (Thousands)	Employment Change (Percent)
Miscellaneous health and allied services	64.2	26.9
Child day-care services	37.4	8.9
Title abstract offices	2.2	7.5
Meat and fish markets	3.5	7.3
School buses	9.1	7.3
Miscellaneous investing	8.2	7.0
Social services	11.4	6.5
Job training and vocational rehabilitation services	15.9	6.4
Residential care	28.0	5.5
Miscellaneous food stores	5.4	5.4
Individual and family social services	23.2	4.6
Museums, botanical and zoological gardens	3.2	4.6
Air transportation, nonscheduled	1.3	4.6
Miscellaneous amusement and recreation services	35.4	4.4
Credit unions	5.8	4.3

Source: Adapted by the U.S. Small Business Administration, Office of Advocacy, from the U.S. Department of Labor, Bureau of Labor Statistics, *Employment and Earnings* (November 1992), Table B.2 (size distribution by industry taken from special tabulations prepared by the U.S. Department of Commerce, Bureau of the Census, 1993), and *The State of Small Business: A Report of the President* (Washington, D.C.: GPO, 1993), p. 58.

almost three-quarters are involved in retailing, the sale of goods directly to consumers. Clothing and jewelry stores, pet shops, bookstores, and grocery stores, for example, are all retailing firms. Slightly less than one-quarter of the small distribution firms are wholesalers. Wholesalers purchase products in quantity from manufacturers and then resell them to retailers.

Service Industries   This category accounts for over 48 percent of all small businesses. Of these, about three-quarters provide such nonfinancial services as medical and dental care; watch, shoe, and TV repairs; hair-cutting and styling; restaurant meals; and dry cleaning. About 8 percent of the small service firms offer financial services, such as accounting, insurance, real estate, and investment counseling.

Production Industries   This last category includes the construction, mining, and manufacturing industries. Only about 19 percent of all small businesses are in this group, mainly because these industries require relatively large initial investments. Small firms that do venture into production generally make parts and subassemblies for larger manufacturing firms or supply special skills to larger construction firms. Consider Aegir Systems, Inc., an Oxnard, California, company headed by Ella D. Williams. With a lot of hard work, perseverance, a strong belief in herself, a second mortgage on her home, and a little help from her friends, Williams started Aegir in 1981. She soon landed her first contract for $8 million with the Pacific Missile Test Center at Point Mugu. Aegir began by providing engineering support for existing defense programs, monitoring weapons to make sure they functioned properly. It soon expanded into computer processing and management consulting. Today Aegir Systems employs seventy-two people, earns annual revenue of $4 million, and has offices in Los Angeles and Washington, D.C. Williams was one of five entrepreneurs to receive the 1991 Women of Enterprise award given by the SBA and Avon Products, Inc., to women who have overcome adversity to succeed in the business world.[6]

The People in Small Businesses: The Entrepreneurs

Small businesses are typically managed by the people who started and own them. Most of these people have held jobs with other firms and could still be so employed if they wanted. Yet owners of small businesses would rather take the risk of starting and operating their own firms, even if the money they make is less than the salaries they might otherwise earn.

Entrepreneurship: no guts, no glory. It takes a very special person to be a successful entrepreneur, like this owner-entrepreneur of the Whole Earth store in Laramie, Wyoming, pictured here with his employees. Entrepreneurs need tremendous drive and total commitment to a single goal to make an idea profitable.

Researchers have suggested a variety of personal factors as reasons why individuals go into business. One that is often cited is the "entrepreneurial spirit"—the desire to create a new business. Other factors, such as independence, the desire to determine one's own destiny, and the willingness to find and accept a challenge, certainly play a part. Background may exert an influence as well. In particular, researchers think that people whose families have been in business (successfully or not) are most apt to start and run their own businesses. Those who start their own businesses also tend to cluster around certain ages—more than 70 percent are between 24 and 44 years old (see Figure 5.2). Women own 5.3 million businesses and are starting new businesses at twice the rate of men.[7]

Finally, there must be some motivation to start a business. A person may decide she has simply "had enough" of working and earning a profit for someone else. Another may lose his job for some reason and decide to start the business he has always wanted rather than seek another job. Still another person may have an idea for a new product or a new way to sell an existing product. Or the opportunity to go into business may arise suddenly, perhaps as a result of a hobby, as was the case with Cheryl Strand. Strand started baking and decorating cakes from her home while working full-time as a word processor at Clemson University. Her cakes became so popular that she soon found herself working through her lunch breaks and late into the night to meet customer demand.

After deciding in July 1989 to start her own business, Strand contacted the Clemson University Small Business Development Center. The center helped her prepare for the business start-up and develop a loan package—complete with a detailed business plan and financial statements for presentation at local banks. Strand obtained the $10,000 she needed.

FIGURE 5.2
How Old Is the Average Entrepreneur?
People in all age groups become entrepreneurs, but more than 70 percent are between 24 and 44.   *(Source: Data developed and provided by the NFIB Foundation and sponsored by the American Express Travel Related Services Company, Inc.)*

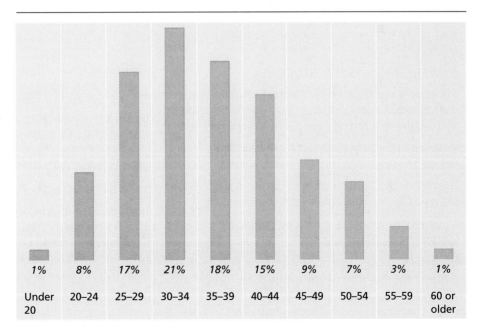

| 1% | 8% | 17% | 21% | 18% | 15% | 9% | 7% | 3% | 1% |
| Under 20 | 20–24 | 25–29 | 30–34 | 35–39 | 40–44 | 45–49 | 50–54 | 55–59 | 60 or older |

What It Takes to Be an Entrepreneur

The following quiz is designed to help you find out if you have what it takes to be an entrepreneur. If you score better than 50 percent, maybe you should start working on your business plan.

1. WAS ONE OF YOUR PARENTS AN ENTREPRENEUR?

An entrepreneur in the family is the single most telling indicator of successful entrepreneurs. In fact, counting such businesses as law practices, farms, or ministerships, fully 80 percent of today's entrepreneurs come from a family heritage of individual businesses.

2. ARE YOU AN IMMIGRANT?

There is a high correlation between immigrants and entrepreneurs. "Immigrant" includes not only those born outside the United States but also those who moved from farm to city or, for example, from the Midwest to the West Coast.

3. DID YOU HAVE A PAPER ROUTE?

Yes? Fine. An entrepreneurial streak shows up early in life. And an even more indicative sign of entrepreneurial tendencies would be that you had subcontracted the deliveries to a younger sibling and dickered with the news company for an adjoining route.

4. WERE YOU A GOOD STUDENT?

There is no indication that entrepreneurs are less well educated than others, but the entrepreneur often has an expulsion listed on school records.

5. WHAT IS YOUR FAVORITE SPECTATOR SPORT?

Entrepreneurs are poor spectators; they excel at individual sports such as sailing and skiing.

6. WHAT IS THE SIZE OF THE COMPANY WHERE YOU NOW WORK?

Statistics show that many entrepreneurs have come from medium-sized companies—those with 30 to 500 employees.

7. HAVE YOU EVER BEEN FIRED?

Having been fired may not look good on your résumé for a job at General Foods, but it indicates that you may have entrepreneurial timber. Entrepreneurs make poor employees—that's why they become entrepreneurs.

8. IN YOUR NEW BUSINESS WOULD YOU BE WILLING TO DISCUSS PROBLEMS WITH YOUR EMPLOYEES?

An open communication policy may be good business, but the typical entrepreneur has a secretive streak. If he or she confides in anyone, it will probably be another entrepreneur.

9. ARE YOU AN INVENTOR? A PH.D.?

These are not positive indicators. Inventors fall in love with their products; Ph.D.s with their research. Entrepreneurs are less enamored of their products than in pricing them right and getting them into the marketplace.

10. HOW OLD ARE YOU?

Although people of all ages start new businesses, the ideal age seems to be 32–35. It takes a certain number of years of building business self-confidence to carry the entrepreneur beyond the adversity certain to be encountered in a new venture. It also takes time to develop a critical mass of frustration with being an employee. As a person reaches the early 30s, not only finances but family life may stabilize, and those with children are not yet facing college tuition bills. The person who waits much beyond these years may have figured out a way of dealing with the frustration.

11. WHEN DO YOU PLAN TO RETIRE?

It doesn't much matter what you answer. If you're an entrepreneur, you won't retire. The real distinction between the entrepreneur and the nonentrepreneur is that no matter what the stage of life, the entrepreneur is out there starting businesses.

Since its start, Cakes by Cheryl has increased sales by approximately 56 percent per year, has doubled in size, and now offers fresh breads, deli sandwiches, a tempting line of baked goods, and catering and carry-out services.[8]

To help determine if you might have the characteristics of an entrepreneur, see Enhancing Career Skills.

In some people the motivation to start a business develops slowly, as they gain the knowledge and ability required for success as a business owner. Knowledge and ability—especially management ability—are probably the most important factors involved. A new firm is very much built around the entrepreneur. The owner must be able to manage the firm's finances, its personnel (if there are any employees), and its day-to-day operations. He or she must handle sales, advertising, purchasing, pricing, and a variety of other business functions. The knowledge and ability to do so are most often acquired through experience working for other firms in the same area of business.

Successful small business owner Bill Masters is a true entrepreneur in every sense of the word. From modest beginnings in a small mill town in South Carolina, Masters turned a $50 investment in early 1976 into the world's largest kayak manufacturing business for both the whitewater and touring markets. By 1983 his company, Perception, Inc., of Easley, South Carolina, was logging annual sales of $2 million. Perception is also the world leader in kayak innovation. Masters is responsible for several improvements in the design and manufacturing of kayaks, including his HD-1 design, which took first place in three of six divisions of the U.S. Open Canoe Championships in 1977. (The following year a separate division was created for the HD-1!)

Masters also developed a process for making one-piece, molded polyethylene kayak hulls, which are stronger than the fiberglass versions. When he couldn't get satisfactory work from an existing plastics company, Masters designed and built his own rotational molding machine to produce the polyethylene kayaks.

In 1981 Masters began expanding overseas and now has franchise operations in Great Britain and New Zealand, where Perception currently enjoys about 30 percent of the market. Perception kayaks are also the bestsellers in the United States and Japan with more than 50 percent of both markets.[9]

Why Small Businesses Fail

Small businesses are prone to failure. Capital, management, and planning are the key ingredients in the survival of a small business, and also the most common reasons for failure. Businesses can experience a number of money-related problems. It may take several years before a business begins to show a profit. Entrepreneurs need to have not only the capital to open a business but also the money to operate it in its possibly lengthy start-up phase. One cash-flow obstacle often leads to others. And a series of cash-flow predicaments usually ends in a business failure.

Many entrepreneurs lack the management skills required to run a business. Money, time, personnel, and inventory all need to be effectively managed if a small business is to succeed. Starting a small business requires much more than optimism and a good idea.

Success and expansion sometimes lead to problems. Frequently entrepreneurs with successful small businesses make the mistake of overexpansion. But fast growth often results in dramatic changes in a business. Thus the entrepreneur must plan carefully and adjust competently to potentially new and disruptive situations.

Every day, and in every part of the country, people open new businesses. Though many will fail, others represent well-conceived ideas developed by entrepreneurs who have the expertise, resources, and determination to make their businesses succeed. As these well-prepared entrepreneurs pursue their individual goals, our society benefits in many ways from their work and creativity. Such billion-dollar companies as Apple Computer, McDonald's Corporation, and Procter & Gamble are all examples of small businesses that expanded into industry giants.

■■ THE IMPORTANCE OF SMALL BUSINESSES IN OUR ECONOMY

LEARNING OBJECTIVE 3
Assess the contributions of small business to our economy.

This country's economic history abounds with stories of ambitious men and women who turned their ideas into business dynasties. The Ford Motor Company started as a one-man operation with an innovative method for industrial production. L.L. Bean, Inc., can trace its beginnings to a basement shop on Maine Street in Freeport, Maine. Both Xerox and Polaroid began as small firms with a better way to do a job.

Providing Technical Innovation

Invention and innovation are among the foundations of our economy. The increases in productivity that have characterized the past two hundred years of our history are all rooted in one principal source: new ways to do a job with less effort for less money. Studies show that the incidence of innovation among small-business workers is significantly higher than among workers in large businesses. Small firms produce two and a half times as many innovations as large firms, relative to the number of persons employed.

According to the U.S. Office of Management and Budget, more than half the major technological advances of this century originated with individual inventors and small companies. A sampling of those innovations is remarkable.

- Air conditioning
- Automatic transmission
- Ball-point pen
- FM radio
- Helicopter
- Instant camera
- Insulin
- Jet engine
- Penicillin
- Power steering
- Xerography
- Zipper

Creating employment opportunities for the young and the old. Small businesses have traditionally provided the thrust to keep our nation's economy running smoothly and prosperously. Ninety-nine percent of all firms in the United States are small, and they employ 57 percent of the private work force. Nearly 71 percent of future employment in the nation's fastest-growing industries is likely to come from small firms. Two of every three new workers find their first jobs in small business.

Perhaps even more remarkable—and important—is the fact that many of these inventions sparked major new U.S. industries.

Providing Employment

Small businesses employ 57 percent of the nation's private work force. Between September 1991 and September 1992, jobs in small business–dominated industries increased by 177,700, helping to offset a 400,000-job decline in industries dominated by large businesses.[10] Small businesses have thus contributed significantly to solving unemployment problems. Historically, small businesses have created the bulk of new jobs. Table 5.2 shows the small-business industries that are generating the most new jobs. Furthermore, nearly 71 percent of future employment in the nation's fastest-growing industries is likely to come from small-business firms.[11]

TABLE 5.2 Small Business Industries Generating Most New Jobs Between September 1991 and September 1992

Industry	Employment Increase (Thousands)
Miscellaneous health and allied services	64.2
Offices and clinics of doctors of medicine	37.7
Child day-care services	37.4
Miscellaneous amusement and recreation services	35.4
Eating and drinking places	28.7
Residential care	28.0
Individual and family social services	23.2
Motor vehicle dealers, new and used	19.2
Management and public relations services	17.8
Job training and vocational rehabilitation services	15.9
Civic, social, and fraternal organizations	14.1
Miscellaneous shopping goods stores	12.6
Lumber and other building materials dealers	12.4
Social services	11.4
Millwork, veneer, plywood, and structural wood members	9.3
Total, Top 15 Industries	367.3

Source: Adapted by the U.S. Small Business Administration, Office of Advocacy, from the U.S. Department of Labor, Bureau of Labor Statistics, *Employment and Earnings* (November 1992), Table B.2 (size distribution by industry taken from special tabulations prepared by the U.S. Department of Commerce, Bureau of the Census, 1993), and *The State of Small Business: A Report of the President* (Washington, D.C.: GPO, 1993), p. 57.

Providing Competition

Small businesses challenge larger, established firms in many ways, causing them to become more efficient and more responsive to consumer needs. A small business cannot, of course, compete with a large firm in all respects. But a number of small firms, each competing in its own particular area and its own particular way, together have the desired competitive effect. Thus, several small janitorial companies together add up to reasonable competition for the no-longer-small ServiceMaster.

Filling Needs of Society and Other Businesses

By their nature, large firms must operate on a large scale. Many may be unwilling or unable to meet the special needs of smaller groups of consumers. Such groups create almost perfect markets for small companies, which can tailor their products to these groups and fill their needs profitably. A prime example is a firm that modifies automobile controls to accommodate handicapped drivers.

Small firms also provide a variety of goods and services to each other and to much larger firms. Sears, Roebuck purchases merchandise from approximately 12,000 suppliers—and most of them are small businesses. General Motors relies on more than 32,000 companies for parts and supplies and depends on more than 11,000 independent dealers to sell its automobiles and trucks. Large firms generally buy parts and assemblies from smaller firms for one very good reason: it is less expensive than manufacturing the parts in their own factories. This lower cost is eventually reflected in the price that consumers pay for their products.

Centennial One, Inc., is a highly successful janitorial company based in Prince George's County, Md. The company's founder and president, Lillian H. Lincoln-Youman, proudly counts among her clients Westinghouse, IBM, Comsat, and Dulles International Airport in Washington, D.C. (In 1988, President Reagan presented Centennial One's president with the National Minority Entrepreneur of the Year Award.)[12]

It is clear that small businesses are a vital part of our economy and that, as consumers and as members of the labor force, we all benefit enormously from their existence. Now let us look at the situation from the viewpoint of the owners of small businesses.

■■ THE PROS AND CONS OF SMALLNESS

LEARNING OBJECTIVE 4
Judge the advantages and disadvantages of operating a small business.

Do most owners of small businesses dream of their firms growing into giant corporations—managed by professionals—while they serve only on the board of directors? Or would they rather stay small, in a firm where they have the opportunity (and the responsibility) to do everything that needs to be done? The answers depend on the personal characteristics and motivations of the individual owners. For many, the advantages of remaining small far outweigh the disadvantages.

Advantages of Small Business

Small-business owners often must struggle to enter competitive new markets with limited resources and face increasing international competition. However, they enjoy several unique advantages.

Personal Relationships with Customers and Employees   For those who like dealing with people, small business is the place to be. The owners of retail shops get to know many of their customers by name and deal with them on a personal basis. Through such relationships, small-business owners often become involved in the social, cultural, and political life of the community.

Relationships between owner-managers and employees also tend to be closer in smaller businesses. To many an employee, the owner is a friend and counselor as well as the boss.

These personal relationships provide an important business advantage. The personal service small businesses offer to customers is a major competitive weapon—one that larger firms try to match but often cannot. In addition, close relationships with employees often help the small-business owner keep effective workers who might earn more with a larger firm.

Getting personal with small business. The owners of retail shops such as this sailboard store know their customers by name. Personal service is a major competitive edge for small business. This owner believes that, by offering customers a high-quality sailboard along with efficient, courteous service, the world will beat a path to his door.

Ability to Adapt to Change   Being his or her own boss, the owner-manager of a small business does not need anyone's permission to adapt to change. An owner may add or discontinue merchandise or services, change store hours, and experiment with various price strategies in response to changes in market conditions. Moreover, through personal relationships with customers, the owners of small businesses quickly become aware of changes in people's needs and interests—as well as in the activities of competing firms.

Simplified Recordkeeping   Many small firms need only a simple set of records. Recordkeeping might consist of a checkbook, a cash-receipts journal in which to record all sales, and a cash-disbursements journal in which to record all amounts that are paid out. Obviously, enough records must be kept to allow for producing and filing accurate tax returns.

Independence   Small-business owners don't have to punch in and out, bid for vacation times, take orders from superiors, or worry about being fired or laid off. They are the masters of their own destinies—at least with regard to employment. For many people, this is the prime advantage of owning a small business.

Other Advantages   According to the Small Business Administration, the most profitable companies in the United States are small firms that have been in business for more than ten years and employ fewer than twenty people.[13] Small-business owners also enjoy a number of the advantages of sole proprietorships, which are discussed in Chapter 4. These include being able to keep all profits, the ease and low cost of going into business and (if necessary) going out of business, and being able to keep business information secret.

Disadvantages of Small Business

Personal contacts with customers, closer relationships with employees, being one's own boss, less cumbersome recordkeeping chores, and independence are the bright side of small business. In contrast, the dark side reflects problems unique to these firms.

Risk of Failure   As we have noted, small businesses (especially newer ones) run a heavy risk of going out of business—about two out of three close their doors within the first five years. Older, well-established but small firms can be hit hard by a business recession, mainly because they do not have the financial resources to weather an extended difficult period.

Limited Potential   Small businesses that survive do so with varying degrees of success. Many are simply the means of making a living for the owner and his or her family. The owner may have some technical skill—as a hair stylist or an electrician does—and may have started a business to practice his or her trade. Such a business is unlikely to grow into a big business. Also, employees' potential for advancement is limited.

Limited Ability to Raise Capital   Small businesses typically have a limited ability to obtain capital. Figure 5.3 shows that most small-business

FIGURE 5.3   Sources of Capital for Entrepreneurs
Small businesses get financing from various sources, but the most important is personal resources.   *(Source: Data developed and provided by the NFIB Foundation and sponsored by the American Express Travel Related Services Company, Inc.)*

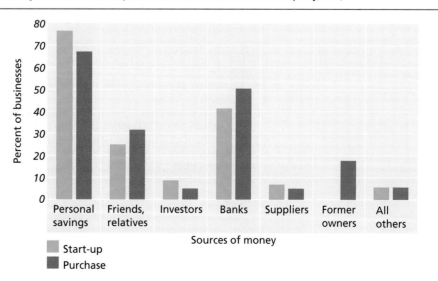

financing comes out of the owner's pocket. Personal loans from lending institutions provide only about one-fourth of the capital required by small businesses.

Although every person who considers starting a small business should be aware of the hazards and pitfalls we have noted, a well-conceived business plan may help avoid the risk of failure. The U.S. government is also dedicated to helping small businesses make it. It expresses this aim most actively through the Small Business Administration.

■■ DEVELOPING A BUSINESS PLAN

Lack of planning can be as deadly as a lack of money to a new small business. Planning is important to any business, large or small, and should never be overlooked or taken lightly. A **business plan** is a carefully constructed guide for the person starting a business. It also serves as a concise document that potential investors can examine to see if they would like to invest in or assist in financing a new venture.

Table 5.3 shows the ten sections that a business plan should include. When constructing a business plan, the business person should strive to keep it easy to read, uncluttered, and complete. Officials of financial institutions just don't have the time to flip through pages of facts and figures.

business plan a carefully constructed guide for the person starting a business

TABLE 5.3   Components of a Business Plan

1. **Introduction**   Basic information such as name and address of the business, nature of the business, statement of the business's financial needs (if any), and statement of confidentiality (to keep important information away from potential competitors)
2. **Executive summary**   Summary of the entire business plan (a convenience for busy investors), including a justification stating why the business will succeed
3. **Industry analysis**   Examination of the potential "customer," current competitors, and business's future
4. **Detailed description of the business**   Information on the products or services to be offered, size and location of the business, personnel and office equipment needed, and brief history of the business
5. **Production plan**   Description and cost analysis of the manufacturing process, plus an outline of the raw materials, physical plant, and heavy machinery needed
6. **Marketing plan**   Discussion of pricing, promotion, distribution, and product forecasts
7. **Organizational plan**   Description of the form of ownership of the venture and responsibilities of all members of the organization
8. **Assessment of risk**   Evaluation of the weaknesses of the business and how the company plans to deal with these and other business problems
9. **Financial plan**   Summary of the investment needed, forecasts of sales, cash-flow forecasts, breakeven analysis, estimated balance sheet, and sources of funding
10. **Appendix**   Supplementary information such as market research results, copies of leases, and supplier price lists

Source: Adapted from Robert D. Hisrich and Michael P. Peters, *Entrepreneurship* (Homewood, Ill.: BPI/Irwin, 1989), pp. 126–140. Reprinted by permission.

In the business plan, the business person should be sure to answer the four questions that banking officials and investors are most interested in: (1) What exactly is the nature and mission of the new venture? (2) Why is this new enterprise a good idea? (3) What are the business person's goals? (4) How much will the new venture cost?[14]

The great amount of time and consideration that should go into creating a business plan will probably end up saving time later. Sharon Burch, who was running a computer software business while earning a degree in business administration, had to write a business plan as part of one course. Burch has said, "I wish I'd taken the class before I started my business. I see a lot of things I could have done differently. But it has helped me since I've been using the business plan as a guide for my business."[15]

Accuracy and realistic expectations are crucial to an effective business plan. It is unethical to deceive investors and loan officers, and it is unwise to deceive yourself.

■■ THE SMALL BUSINESS ADMINISTRATION

Small Business Administration (SBA) a governmental agency that assists, counsels, and protects the interests of small businesses in the United States

LEARNING OBJECTIVE 5
Explain how the Small Business Administration helps small businesses.

The **Small Business Administration (SBA),** created by Congress in 1953, is a governmental agency that assists, counsels, and protects the interests of small businesses in the United States. It helps people get into business and stay in business. The agency provides assistance to owners and managers of prospective, new, and established small businesses. Through more than one hundred offices throughout the nation, the SBA provides both financial assistance and management counseling. It helps small firms bid for and obtain government contracts, and it helps them prepare to enter foreign markets.

SBA Management Assistance

Statistics show that most failures in small business are related to poor management. For this reason, the SBA places special emphasis on improving the management ability of the owners and managers of small businesses. The SBA's Management Assistance Program is extensive and diversified. It includes free individual counseling, courses, conferences, workshops, and a wide range of publications. During a recent year the SBA indicated that it counseled or trained more than 404,000 people and answered over 300,000 calls.[16]

Management Courses and Workshops The management courses offered by the SBA cover all the functions, duties, and roles of managers. Instructors may be teachers from local colleges and universities or professionals such as management consultants, bankers, lawyers, and accountants. Fees for these courses are quite low. The most popular such course is a general survey of eight to ten different areas of business management. In follow-up studies, business people may concentrate in depth on one or more of these areas, depending on their particular strengths and weaknesses. The SBA occasionally offers one-day conferences. These conferences are aimed at keeping owner-managers up-to-date on new management developments, tax laws, and the like.

The SBA also invites prospective owners of small businesses to workshops at which management problems and good management practices are discussed. A major goal of these sessions is to emphasize the need for sufficient preparation before starting a new venture. Sometimes the sessions convince eager but poorly prepared entrepreneurs to slow down and wait until they are ready for the difficulties that lie ahead.

SCORE and ACE   The **Service Corps of Retired Executives (SCORE)** is a group of 14,000 retired business people who volunteer their services to small businesses through the SBA. The collective experience of SCORE volunteers spans the full range of American enterprise.

A small-business owner who has a particular problem can request free counseling from SCORE. An assigned counselor visits the owner in his or her establishment and, through careful observation, analyzes the business situation and the problem. If the problem is complex, the counselor may call on other volunteer experts to assist. Finally, the counselor offers a plan for solving the problem and helping the owner through the critical period.

Consider the plight of Elizabeth Halvorsen, a mystery writer from Minneapolis. Her husband had built up the family advertising and graphic arts firm for seventeen years when he was called into active duty and assigned to the Persian Gulf. The only one left behind who could run the business was Mrs. Halvorsen, who admittedly had no business experience. Enter SCORE. With a SCORE management expert at her side, she kept the business on track.[17]

In a recent year, SCORE held over 3,808 training sessions attended by more than 114,000 people and provided individual counseling to 172,000 small-business owners.[18]

The **Active Corps of Executives (ACE)** is a group of active managers who counsel small-business owners on a volunteer basis. ACE was established to supplement the services available through SCORE and to keep the SBA's management counseling as current as possible. ACE volunteers come from major corporations, trade associations, educational institutions, and various professions.

Help for Minority-Owned Small Businesses   Americans who are members of minority groups have had difficulty entering the nation's economic mainstream. Raising money is a nagging problem for minority business owners, who may also lack adequate training. Members of minority groups are, of course, eligible for all SBA programs, but the SBA makes a special effort to assist those who want to start small businesses or expand existing ones. For example, the Minority Business Development Agency awards grants to develop and increase business opportunities for members of racial and ethnic minorities.

Helping women become entrepreneurs is also a special goal of the SBA. Women make up more than half of America's population, but they own about one-fourth of its businesses. In 1980 an SBA Assistant Administrator for Women's Business Enterprise was appointed, and programs directed specifically toward this group were expanded.

Service Corps of Retired Executives (SCORE)   a group of retired business people who volunteer their services to small businesses through the SBA

Active Corps of Executives (ACE)   a group of active managers who counsel small-business owners on a volunteer basis

▶▶ **AT A GLANCE**

Women's Ownership

Industries with the largest percentage of companies owned by women.

Source: *The State of Small Business: A Report of the President,* 1993, p. 63.

Small Business Institute (SBI) a group of senior and graduate students in business administration who provide management counseling to small businesses

Small Business Institutes   A **Small Business Institute (SBI)** is a group of senior and graduate students in business administration who provide management counseling to small businesses. SBIs have been organized on almost 520 college campuses as another way to help business owners. The students work in small groups guided by faculty advisers and SBA management-assistance experts. Like SCORE volunteers, they analyze and help solve the problems of small-business owners at their business establishments.

Small Business Development Center (SBDC) university-based group that provides individual counseling and practical training to owners of small businesses

Small Business Development Centers   A **Small Business Development Center (SBDC)** is one of fifty-seven university-based groups that provide individual counseling and practical training to owners of small businesses. SBDCs draw from the resources of local, state, and federal governments; private business; and universities. These groups can provide managerial and technical help, data from research studies, and other types of specialized assistance that are of value to small businesses.

According to a recent report by the U.S. Senate Committee on Small Business, 69 percent of clients were satisfied overall with the counseling they received. Similarly, 76 percent of the clients indicated they would contact the SBDC for future help and 82 percent said they would recommend the SBDC program to others.[19]

SBA Publications   The SBA issues management, marketing, and technical publications dealing with hundreds of topics of interest to present and prospective managers of small firms. Most of these publications are available from the SBA free of charge. Others can be obtained for a small fee from the U.S. Government Printing Office.

SBA Financial Assistance

Small businesses seem to be constantly in need of money. An owner may have enough capital to start and operate the business. But then he or she may require more money to finance increased operations during peak selling seasons, to pay for required pollution-control equipment, to mop up after a natural disaster such as a flood, or to finance an expansion. The SBA offers special financial-assistance programs that cover all these situations. However, its primary financial function is to guarantee loans to eligible businesses.

Regular Business Loans   Most of the SBA's business loans are actually made by private lenders such as banks, but repayment is partially guaranteed by the agency. That is, the SBA may guarantee that it will repay the lender up to 90 percent of the loan if the borrowing firm cannot repay it. Guaranteed loans may be as large as $750,000. The average size of an SBA-guaranteed business loan is $208,000 and its average duration is about eight years.

venture capital money that is invested in small (and sometimes struggling) firms that have the potential to become very successful

Small Business Investment Companies   **Venture capital** is money that is invested in small (and sometimes struggling) firms that have the potential to become very successful. In many cases, only a lack of capital keeps these firms from rapid and solid growth. The people who invest in such firms expect that their investments will grow with the firms and become quite profitable.

The popularity of these investments has increased over the past ten years, but most small firms still have difficulty in obtaining venture capital. To help such businesses, the SBA licenses, regulates, and provides financial assistance to Small Business Investment Companies. A **Small Business Investment Company (SBIC)** is a privately owned firm that provides venture capital to small enterprises that meet its investment standards. SBICs are intended to be profit-making organizations. However, SBA aid allows them to invest in small businesses that would not otherwise attract venture capital.

Recently, the 322 SBICs held capital resources of $2.5 billion. Since the SBIC program began in 1958, about 57,000 small businesses have received $8.9 billion in venture capital financing.[20]

We have discussed the importance of the small-business segment of our economy. We have weighed the advantages and drawbacks of operating a small business as compared with a large one. But is there a way to achieve the best of both worlds? Can one preserve one's independence as a business owner and still enjoy some of the benefits of "bigness"? Let's take a close look at franchising.

Small Business Investment Company (SBIC) privately owned firm that provides venture capital to small enterprises that meet its investment standards

■■ FRANCHISING

A **franchise** is a license to operate an individually owned business as if it were part of a chain of outlets or stores. Often the business itself is also called a franchise. Among the most familiar franchises are McDonald's, H & R Block, AAMCO Transmissions, GNC (General Nutrition Centers) Franchising, and Mail Boxes Etc. Many other franchises carry familiar names; this method of doing business has become very popular in the last twenty-five years or so. It is an attractive means of starting and operating a small business.

franchise a license to operate an individually owned business as though it were part of a chain of outlets or stores

franchising the actual granting of a franchise

franchisor an individual or organization granting a franchise

franchisee a person or organization purchasing a franchise

LEARNING OBJECTIVE 6
Appraise the concept and types of franchising.

What Is Franchising?

Franchising is the actual granting of a franchise. A **franchisor** is an individual or organization granting a franchise. A **franchisee** is a person or organization purchasing a franchise. The franchisor supplies a known and advertised business name, management skills, the required training and materials, and a method of doing business. The franchisee supplies labor and capital, operates the franchised business, and agrees to abide by the provisions of the franchise agreement. Table 5.4 lists some items that would be covered in a typical franchise agreement.

Types of Franchising Arrangements

Franchising arrangements fall into three general categories. In the first approach, a manufacturer authorizes a number of retail stores to sell a certain brand-name item. This franchising arrangement, one of the oldest, is prevalent in sales of passenger cars and trucks, farm equipment, shoes, paint, earth-moving equipment, and petroleum. About 90 percent of all

AT A GLANCE

Franchising in the United States

1920	The Ben Franklin Company
1925	A&W Root Beer
1938	Arthur Murray Dance Studios
1940	Baskin–Robbins Ice Cream

Early franchises in the U.S. that are still in business.

TABLE 5.4   McDonald's Conventional Franchise Agreement as of July 1994

McDonald's (Franchisor) Provides	Individual (Franchisee) Supplies
1. Nationally recognized trademarks and established reputation for quality 2. Designs and color schemes for restaurants, signs, and equipment 3. Formulas and specifications for certain food products 4. Proven methods of inventory and operations control 5. Bookkeeping, accounting, and policies manuals specially geared toward a franchised restaurant 6. A franchise term of up to 20 years 7. Formal training program completed on a part-time basis in approximately 18-24 months in a McDonald's restaurant 8. Five weeks of classroom training, including two weeks at Hamburger University 9. Ongoing regional support services and field service staff 10. Research and development into labor-saving equipment and methods 11. Monthly bulletins, periodicals, and meetings to inform franchisees about management and marketing techniques	1. Total investment of approximately $445,000 to $580,000 includes initial franchise fee of $45,000 and refundable security deposit of $15,000 2. Approximate cash requirement of 40 percent of total investment 3. A minimum of 4 percent of gross sales annually for marketing and advertising 4. Payment of 8.5 percent of gross sales monthly to McDonald Corp. 5. Kitchen equipment, seating, decor, lighting, and signs in conformity with McDonald's standards (included in total investment figure) 6. Willingness to relocate 7. Taxes, insurance, and maintenance costs 8. Commitment to assuring high-quality standards and upholding McDonald's reputation

Source: *McDonald's Franchising,* McDonald's Corporation, July 1994. Used with permission from McDonald's Corporation.

gasoline is sold through franchised, independent, retail service stations, and franchised dealers handle virtually all sales of new cars and trucks. In the second type of franchising arrangement, a producer licenses distributors to sell a given product to retailers. This arrangement is common in the soft-drink industry. Most national manufacturers of soft-drink syrups—The Coca-Cola Company, Dr Pepper/Seven-Up Companies, Pepsico, Royal Crown Companies Inc.—franchise independent bottlers who then serve retailers. In a third form of franchising, a franchisor supplies brand names, techniques, or other services instead of a complete product. Although the franchisor may provide certain production and distribution services, its primary role is the careful development and control of marketing strategies. This approach to franchising, which is the most typical today, is used by Holiday Inns Inc., Howard Johnson Co., AAMCO Transmissions, McDonald's, Dairy Queen, Avis, Inc., The Hertz Corporation, KFC (Kentucky Fried Chicken) Corporation, and H & R Block, to name a few.

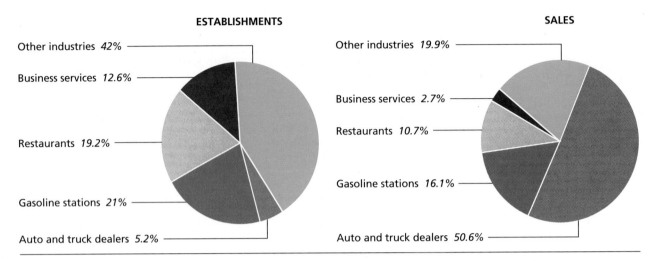

FIGURE 5.4   Distribution of Franchised Establishments and Sales, 1992
*(Source: U.S. Department of Commerce, Bureau of the Census, Statistical Abstract of
the United States 1988 [Washington, D.C.: U.S. Government Printing Office, 1988],
p. 742; Idem., Statistical Abstract of the United States 1992 [Washington, D.C.: U.S. Government Printing Office, 1992], p. 778; and The State of Small Business: A Report of the
President, 1993, p. 115.)*

The Growth of Franchising

LEARNING OBJECTIVE 7
Analyze the growth of
franchising and its advantages
and disadvantages

Franchising, which began in the United States around the time of the Civil
War, was originally used by large firms, such as the Singer Sewing Company,
to distribute their products. Franchising has been steadily increasing in popularity since the early 1900s, primarily for filling stations and car dealerships; however, this retailing strategy has experienced enormous growth
since the mid-1970s (see Figures 5.4 and 5.5). The franchise proliferation
has generally paralleled the expansion of the fast-food industry—the field
that uses franchises to the greatest extent. As Table 5.5 shows, *Entrepreneur*
magazine's top-rated franchises were nearly all in this category.

TABLE 5.5   Top Ten Franchises (ranked by *Entrepreneur* magazine)

Rank	Name of Franchise	Minimum Start-up Costs
1	Subway	$43,000–$85,500
2	McDonald's	$400,000–$535,000
3	Burger King	$73,000–$511,000
4	Hardee's	$497,200–$722,800
5	7-Eleven Convenience Stores	$12,500+
6	Dunkin' Donuts	$181,600–$255,100
7	Mail Boxes Etc.	$68,500–$112,400
8	Choice Hotels International	$1,500,000–$4,000,000
9	Snap-On Inc.	$79,300–$162,000
10	Dairy Queen	$370,000–$715,000

Source: "The Top Ten Franchises for 1995," *Entrepreneur* magazine, January 1995, p. 135.

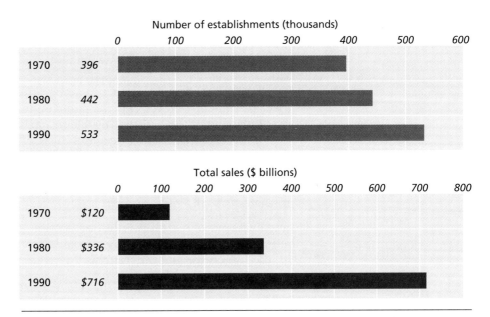

FIGURE 5.5   Number and Sales of Franchised Establishments in 1970, 1980, and 1990
(Sources: U.S. Department of Commerce, Franchising in the Economy, 1986–1988; *the International Franchise Association, Education Foundation, Inc., and Horwath International,* Franchising in the Economy, 1988–1990, *and* Franchising in the Economy, 1991; *and* The State of Small Business: A Report of the President, *1993, p. 113.)*

Of course, franchising is not limited to fast foods. Hair salons, tanning parlors, and professionals such as dentists and lawyers are expected to participate in franchising arrangements in growing numbers. Franchised health clubs, exterminators, and campgrounds are already widespread, as are franchised tax preparers and travel agencies. The real estate industry has also experienced a rapid increase in franchising. In 1990, approximately $716 billion in sales at over 533,000 franchised outlets accounted for 35 percent of all retail sales in the United States (see Figure 5.5). The Department of Commerce estimates that by the year 2000, franchising will generate more than half of all sales.[21]

Also, women-owned franchises are growing. For example, in 1994 the LubePro oil change service licensed its first female-owned franchise. Franchisers like Precision Tune Inc. and Creative Colors International are starting a trend toward courting female franchisers in traditionally male-oriented industries.[22]

Recently, ten franchisers were nominated for the Franchise Hall of Fame. Among the winners: McDonald's, H & R Block tax services, and Blockbuster Video rental outlets.[23]

Are Franchises Successful?

Franchising is designed to provide a tested formula for success, along with ongoing advice and training. The success rate for businesses owned and operated by franchisees is significantly higher than the success rate for other independently owned small businesses. Only 5 to 8 percent of franchised businesses fail during the first two years of operation, whereas approximately 54 percent of independent businesses fail during that time period.[24]

Nevertheless, franchising is not a guarantee of success for either franchisees or franchisors. Too rapid expansion, inadequate capital or management skills, and a host of other problems can cause failure for both. Thus, for example, the Dizzy Dean's Beef and Burger franchise is no longer in business. If you are considering buying a franchise, Enhancing Career Skills lists several questions you should consider.

Advantages of Franchising

Franchising plays a vital role in our economy and may soon become the dominant form of retailing. Why? Because franchising offers advantages to both the franchisor and the franchisee.

To the Franchisor   The franchisor gains fast and selective distribution of its products without incurring the high cost of constructing and operating its

One way to begin: franchising. Victor Aron and his wife, Lundy Edwards, are the owners of this Body Shop franchise. For them, franchising offers an exciting entry into the world of small business. An established brand name, operating systems, ongoing services, and continuing development are available to these franchisees.

Evaluating a Franchise

How can you protect yourself against making a mistake in buying a franchise? No answer is 100 percent reliable, but there are several important steps you can take before making a commitment to buy a franchise.

EXAMINE THE FRANCHISE OPPORTUNITY ITSELF

1. Did your lawyer approve the franchise contract after he or she studied it, paragraph by paragraph?
2. Does the franchise call on you to take any steps which are, according to your lawyer, unwise or illegal in your state, county, or city?
3. Does the franchise give you an exclusive territory for the length of the franchise, or can the franchisor sell a second or third franchise in your territory?
4. Is the franchisor connected in any way with any other franchise companies handling similar merchandise or services?
5. If the answer to the last question is yes, what is your protection against this second franchisor organization?
6. Under what circumstances and at what cost can you pull out of the franchise contract?
7. If you sell your franchise, will you be paid for your goodwill, or will the goodwill you have built into the business be lost to you?

TAKE A HARD LOOK AT THE FRANCHISOR

1. For how many years has the franchisor been in business?
2. Does the franchisor have a reputation for honesty and fair dealing among the local entrepreneurs holding its franchise?
3. Has the franchisor shown you any certified figures indicating exact net profits of one or more going franchises, which you yourself checked with the franchisee?
4. Will the franchisor help you with
   a. A management training program?
   b. An employee training program?
   c. A public relations program?
   d. Merchandising ideas?
   e. Financing?

5. Will the franchisor help you find a good location for your franchise?
6. Is the franchisor adequately financed so that it can carry out its stated plan of financial help and expansion?
7. Is the franchisor a one-person company or a larger company with a trained and experienced management team so that there is always an experienced person as its head?
8. Exactly what can the franchisor offer you that you cannot do for yourself?
9. Has the franchisor investigated you carefully enough to ensure that you can successfully operate one of its franchises at a profit, both to the franchisor and to you?

TAKE AN EQUALLY HARD LOOK AT YOURSELF AND YOUR EXPECTATIONS

1. How much capital will you need to buy the franchise and operate it until your sales revenues equal your expenses?
2. Where are you going to get the capital you need?
3. Are you prepared to give up some independence of action to get the advantages offered by the franchise?
4. Do you really believe you have the ability, training, and experience to work smoothly and profitably with the franchisor, your employees, and your customers?
5. Are you ready to spend much or all of the rest of your business life with this franchisor, offering its product or service to your customers?

IS THERE A MARKET FOR YOUR PRODUCT?

1. Have you made any study to find out whether the product or service you propose to sell under franchise has a market in your territory at the prices you will have to charge?
2. Will the population in your territory increase, remain static, or decrease over the next five years?
3. Will the demand for the product or service you are considering be greater, about the same, or less in five years?
4. What competition exists in your territory for the product or service, either from nonfranchise firms or franchise firms?

own outlets. The franchisor thus has more capital available to expand production and to use for advertising. At the same time, it can ensure, through the franchise agreement, that outlets are maintained and operated according to its own standards.

The franchisor also benefits from the fact that the franchisee—a sole proprietor in most cases—is likely to be very highly motivated to succeed. The success of the franchise means more sales, which translate into higher royalties for the franchisor.

To the Franchisee   The franchisee gets the opportunity to start a business with limited capital and to make use of the business experience of others. Moreover, an outlet with a nationally advertised name, such as Radio Shack, McDonald's, or Century 21 Real Estate, has guaranteed customers as soon as it opens.

If business problems arise, the franchisor gives the franchisee guidance and advice. This counseling is primarily responsible for the very high degree of success enjoyed by franchises. In most cases, the franchisee does not pay for such help.

The franchisee also receives materials to use in local advertising and can take part in national promotional campaigns sponsored by the franchisor. McDonald's and its franchisees, for example, constitute one of the nation's top twenty purchasers of advertising. Finally, the franchisee may be able to minimize the cost of advertising, supplies, and various business necessities by purchasing them in cooperation with other franchisees.

Disadvantages of Franchising

The disadvantages of franchising mainly affect the franchisee because the franchisor retains a great deal of control. The franchisor's contract can dictate every aspect of the business: decor, design of employee uniforms, types of signs, and all the details of business operations. All Burger King french fries taste the same because all Burger King franchisees have to make them the same way.

Contract disputes are the cause of many lawsuits. For example, in 1994 nine 7-Eleven franchisees filed a lawsuit against their franchisor, the Southland Corporation, alleging violation of franchise agreements. The franchisees charged that Southland failed to advertise, remodel stores, and provide other support services.[25] Some franchisees claim that contracts are unfairly tilted toward the franchisors. Others have charged that they lost their franchise and investment because their franchisor would not approve the sale of the business when they found a buyer.[26]

To arbitrate disputes between franchisors and franchisees, the National Franchise Mediation Program was established in 1993 by thirty member firms, including Burger King Corporation, McDonald Corporation, and Wendy's International Inc. Negotiators have already resolved thirty cases through mediation.

Franchise-holders pay for their security, usually with a one-time franchise fee and continuing royalty and advertising fees, collected as a percentage of sales. As Table 5.4 shows, a McDonald's franchisee pays an initial

■ ■ ■ ■ **GLOBAL PERSPECTIVES**

Eastern Enterprises

When Edward and Linda Holt opened their small tree-cutting operation in 1977, they had no idea how fast the company would grow.

In 1981 yearly sales were about $300,000. This year, Eastern Enterprises reaped nearly $6 million in sales and has become remarkably successful in the international market, with 95 percent of its sales to Japan, Taiwan, Italy, and Germany.

As a timber exporter, Eastern Enterprises buys logs for resale worldwide for use in furniture making and other specialty woods businesses. The company also acts as a purchasing agent for customers who have special wood needs.

Eastern Enterprises has participated in SBA's Export Revolving Line of Credit (ERLC) program since 1984. The ERLC program is designed to help small businesses develop export markets for their products and services by allowing them to make unlimited withdrawals and repayments during a specified maturity period. SBA guarantees 85 percent of the ERLC loans up to $750,000.

The Holts attribute Eastern's success to their considerable knowledge of the international specialty wood market. For example, Eastern deals only with hardwoods, selling primarily oak, ash, poplar, walnut, and paulownia. Each year they visit customers around the globe to learn their needs and desires.

"I believe that I have been able to feel out the market, identify the needs of my customers, and deliver a product of superior quality at a price they can afford," Holt confirms. "I have always worked hard to keep the trust and confidence of my customers and the goodwill of my employees."

franchise fee of $45,000, a $15,000 franchise security deposit, an annual fee of 4 percent of gross sales (for advertising), and a monthly fee of at least 8.5 percent of gross sales. In Table 5.5 you can see how much money a franchisee needs to start a new franchise for selected organizations. In some fields, franchise agreements are not uniform: one franchisee may pay more than another for the same services.

Even success can cause problems. Sometimes a franchise is so successful that the franchisor opens its own outlet nearby, in direct competition—although franchisees may fight back. For example, a court recently ruled that Burger King could not enter into direct competition with the franchisee because the contract was not specific on the issue.[27] A spokesperson for one franchisor contends that the company "gives no geographical protection" to its franchise-holders and thus is free to move in on them. Thus, in a 1994 Taco Bell case, the court ruled that the language of the contract specifically gave the franchisor permission to enter into competition with its own Taco Bell franchisee.[28]

Franchise operators work hard. They often put in ten- and twelve-hour days, six days a week. The International Franchise Association advises prospective franchise purchasers to investigate before investing and to approach buying a franchise cautiously. Franchises vary widely in approach as well as in products. Some, like Dunkin' Donuts and Baskin-Robbins ice cream stores, demand long hours. Others, like Command Performance hair salons and Uncle John's Family Restaurants, are more appropriate for those who don't want to spend many hours at their stores.

■■ GLOBAL PERSPECTIVES IN SMALL BUSINESS

For American small businesses, the world is becoming smaller. National and international economies are growing more and more interdependent as political leadership and national economic directions change and trade barriers diminish or disappear. Globalization plus instant worldwide communications are rapidly shrinking distances at the same time they are expanding business opportunities.

Even the U.S. Small Business Administration is offering to help the nation's small-business owners enter the world markets. The SBA's efforts include counseling small firms on how and where to market overseas, matching U.S. small-business executives with potential overseas customers, and helping exporters secure financing. The agency brings small U.S. firms into direct contact with potential overseas buyers and partners. Global Perspectives gives one example of a small business that received assistance from the SBA.

International trade will become more important to small-business owners as they face unique challenges in the new century. Small businesses, which are expected to remain the dominant form of organization in this country, must be prepared to adapt to significant international demographic and economic changes in the world marketplace.

This chapter ends our discussion of the foundations of American business. From here on, we shall be looking closely at various aspects of business operations. We begin, in the next chapter, with a discussion of management—what management is, what managers do, and how they work to coordinate the basic economic resources within a business organization.

■ ■ ■ ■ ■ CHAPTER REVIEW

Summary

1   Define what a small business is and recognize the fields in which small businesses are concentrated.

A small business is one that is independently owned and operated for profit and is not dominant in its field. There are about 21.3 million businesses in this country, and more than 90 percent of them are small businesses. Small businesses employ more than one-half of the nation's private work force, in spite of the fact that about 70 percent of new businesses can be expected to fail within five years. More than half of all small businesses are retailing and service businesses.

2   Identify the people who start small businesses and the reasons why some succeed and many fail.

Such personal characteristics as independence, desire to create a new enterprise, and willingness to accept a challenge may impel individuals to start small businesses. Various external circumstances, such as special expertise or even the loss of a job, can also supply the motivation to strike out on one's own. Lack of capital and of management experience and poor planning are the major causes of failure.

3   Assess the contributions of small businesses to our economy.

Small businesses have been responsible for a wide variety of inventions and innovations, some of which have given rise to new industries. Historically, small businesses have created the bulk of the new jobs, and they employ more than half the nation's private work force. Further, they have mounted effective competition to larger firms. They provide things that society needs, act as suppliers to larger firms, and serve as customers of other businesses, both large and small.

4 Judge the advantages and disadvantages of operating a small business.

The advantages of smallness in business include the opportunity to establish personal relationships with customers and employees, the ability to adapt to changes quickly, independence, and simplified recordkeeping. The major disadvantages are the high risk of failure and the limited potential for growth.

A business plan—a carefully constructed guide for a person starting a new business—should be easy to read, uncluttered, and complete. Potential investors will examine the plan to decide whether to assist in financing.

5 Explain how the Small Business Administration helps small businesses.

The U.S. Small Business Administration was created in 1953 to assist and counsel the millions of small-business owners. The SBA offers management courses and workshops; managerial help, including one-to-one counseling through SCORE and ACE; various publications; and financial assistance through guaranteed loans and SBICs. It places special emphasis on aid to minority-owned businesses, including those owned by women.

6 Appraise the concept and types of franchising.

A franchise is a license to operate an individually owned business as though it were part of a chain. The franchisor provides a known business name, management skills, a method of doing business, training, and required materials. The franchisee contributes labor and capital, operates the franchised business, and agrees to abide by the provisions of the franchise agreement. There are three major categories of franchise agreements. Franchising has grown tremendously since the mid-1970s.

7 Analyze the growth of franchising and its advantages and disadvantages.

The franchisor's major advantage in franchising is fast and well-controlled distribution of products, with minimal capital outlay. In return, the franchisee has

the opportunity to open a business with limited capital, to make use of the business experience of others, and to sell to an existing clientele. For this, the franchisee must usually pay both an initial franchise fee and a continuing royalty based on sales. He or she must also follow the dictates of the franchise with regard to operation of the business.

Worldwide business opportunities are expanding for small businesses. Even the U.S. Small Business Administration is assisting small business owners in penetrating foreign markets. The next century will present unique challenges and opportunities for small-business owners.

Key Terms

You should now be able to define and give an example relevant to each of the following terms:

small business (136)
business plan (150)
Small Business Administration (SBA) (151)
Service Corps of Retired Executives (SCORE) (152)
Active Corps of Executives (ACE) (152)
Small Business Institute (SBI) (153)
Small Business Development Center (SBDC) (153)
venture capital (153)
Small Business Investment Company (SBIC) (154)
franchise (154)
franchising (154)
franchisor (154)
franchisee (154)

Questions

Review Questions

1. What information would you need to determine whether a particular business is small according to SBA guidelines?
2. Which two areas of business generally attract the most small businesses? Why are these areas attractive to small business?
3. Distinguish among service industries, distribution industries, and production industries.
4. What kinds of factors impel certain people to start new businesses?
5. What are the major causes of small-business failure? Do these causes also apply to larger businesses?
6. Briefly describe four contributions of small business to the American economy.

7. What are the major advantages and disadvantages of smallness in business?

8. What are the major components of a business plan? Why should an individual develop a business plan?

9. Identify five ways in which the SBA provides management assistance to small businesses.

10. Identify two ways in which the SBA provides financial assistance to small businesses.

11. Why does the SBA concentrate on providing management and financial assistance to small businesses?

12. What is venture capital? How does the SBA help small businesses obtain it?

13. Explain the relationships among a franchise, the franchisor, and the franchisee.

14. What does the franchisor receive in a franchising agreement? What does the franchisee receive? What does each provide?

15. Cite one major benefit of franchising for the franchisor. Cite one major benefit of franchising for the franchisee.

Discussion Questions

1. What is the secret of Harold Guller's success?

2. For what reasons was Guller inducted into the Small Business Administration Hall of Fame?

3. Most people who start small businesses are aware of the high failure rate and the reasons for it. Why, then, do some take no steps to protect their firms from failure? What steps should they take?

4. Are the so-called advantages of small business really advantages? Wouldn't every small-business owner like his or her business to grow into a large firm?

5. Do average citizens benefit from the activities of the SBA, or is the SBA just another way to spend our tax money?

6. Would you rather own your own business independently or become a franchisee? Why?

Exercises

✎ **1.** From a sampling of twenty-five small businesses in your community, calculate the percentage in service industries, distribution industries, and production industries. Explain any major differences between your findings and Figure 5.1.

● **2.** Devise a plan for opening a new bicycle sales and repair shop in your community. Consider each of the components described in the business plan. Also give some thought to how you will avoid the major causes of small-business failure.

VIDEO CASE 5.1

Sir Speedy, Inc.: The Business Printers

Sir Speedy, Inc., a California corporation launched in 1968, is a leading franchisor of printing centers. Sir Speedy provides full-service printing, and its franchisees enjoy the highest average gross sales volume per store in the fast-printing and copying industry. In fact, Sir Speedy's top twenty-five centers average over $1 million in annual sales even though, remarkably, 97 percent of its franchisees have no previous experience in the printing industry.

In the past ten years, the quick-printing industry in the United States has grown an impressive 170 percent in sales volume. By contrast, the Sir Speedy network has mushroomed over 700 percent. As of December 31, 1994, a total of 838 franchised Sir Speedy Printing Centers dotted 46 states and 12 foreign countries.

All Sir Speedy Printing Centers are owned by franchisees. To ensure their franchisees' success, Sir Speedy provides comprehensive training, guidance, and support.

Training begins with an intensive two-week course at Sir Speedy–Copies Now University at corporate offices in California, where franchisees learn the four-part operating system. The first part covers how to develop a business plan and how to maintain daily financial control. For example, franchisees learn about pricing, estimating, forecasting, budgeting, and accounting procedures.

Next, franchisees study how to prepare local marketing, advertising, and public relations plans. Then, franchisees receive training in prepress, printing, and finishing methods and in how to deal with suppliers. The operating system concludes with sessions on how to hire, compensate, train, and develop staff.

The training continues with on-site instruction and counseling during the first two weeks at the franchisee's printing center. When the center opens for business, franchisees have on hand all the equipment and supplies they need to start generating sales.

The franchisor provides continuous support to help each center run smoothly and prosper. For example, the franchisees receive regular visits from Sir Speedy's business management consultants. In addition, Sir Speedy offers various communications programs, such as newsletters, seminars, regional franchise meetings, franchisees' advisory councils, local advertising associations, and an annual international convention.

The franchise package cost of a Sir Speedy Printing Center is $160,000, plus working capital. The costs are allocated as follows:

Franchise fee: $17,500.00
The Franchise Fee includes the use of the trade names, logos, trademarks, and methods of doing business.

Start-up costs: $32,500.00
This amount includes training, travel and lodging in connection with training, first year's accounting service, market survey, lease negotiation assistance, grand opening promotion, small equipment items, supplies and initial inventory.

Equipment: $110,000.00
The package includes an impressive list of equipment, cabinets, counters, shelving and furniture—all color coordinated to attract customers and provide pleasant working conditions.

Working capital: $65,000.00
It is recommended that a franchisee have a minimum amount set aside to cover pre-opening expenses and operating capital. This may vary depending on location of business, etc., but these amounts are generally sufficient for total working capital requirements. In addition, living expenses will be necessary. No provision is made for living expenses in the working capital amount.

Questions

1. Give some examples of the types of services provided by Sir Speedy Printing Centers.
2. Why would entrepreneurs buy a Sir Speedy franchise when they have the resources to open a center on their own?
3. Must a prospective Sir Speedy franchisee know about the quick-printing and copying business? Explain.

4. Can Sir Speedy, Inc., guarantee that a Sir Speedy Printing Center will be successful?

CASE 5.2

Wu & Associates, Inc.

Raymond Wu came to the United States from Taiwan in 1973. Seventeen years later he struck out on his own to pursue the American dream of being his own boss. Captured by the entrepreneurial spirit that drives small-business owners to contribute so much to the nation's economy, he founded his general contracting business, Wu & Associates, Inc.

Like many small-business owners, Wu and his company had all the technical skills needed for success, but selling these capabilities to skeptical federal government buyers was a problem. Wu has two engineering degrees and is a licensed professional engineer. He served as project engineer on highway construction projects in the Far East and since arriving in this country has managed multimillion dollar contracts with public and private agencies.

Following the start-up of his firm in 1990, Wu was low bidder on a succession of contracts for the U.S. Navy but was rejected. When a small business is the low bidder on a government contract and is rejected because the firm's responsibility or eligibility is questioned, the bidder can appeal to SBA for a Certificate of Competency (COC), which requires the contracting officer to award the contract to the lowest bidder. Congress has given SBA the final word in such cases.

SBA's procurement assistance staff performed an independent study of Wu & Associates' credentials, found the fledgling company fully capable of performing the contracts, and issued the COC. Since then, Wu has received six additional contracts from the navy without SBA help.

In 1991 Wu & Associates' revenues amounted to about $450,000, and Wu estimated $1.5 million to $2 million in total sales in 1992. "Now that I've got a track record, I am no longer a 'nonresponsible' bidder. I'm very thankful for the SBA's help. Without the SBA, I wouldn't be here."[30]

Questions

1. To what do you attribute Wu's success?
2. What role did education play in Wu's success?
3. Why did the navy reject Wu's bids? How did he go about winning the navy's contracts?

CAREER PROFILE ■ ■ ■ ■ ■ ■ ■ ■ ■ ■ ■

CAREER PLANNING

The future looks bright for individuals who possess the training and skills needed for the technological challenges of the future. The courses that you take in college, your early employment experience, and early career exploration are all important as you plan your own career.

CAREER INFORMATION FOR EACH MAJOR PART OF *BUSINESS*

To help you explore different employment opportunities and plan for your future, we have included specific career information at the end of each major part in your textbook. Most of this career information is from the U.S. Department of Labor's *Occupational Outlook Handbook* and is presented in an easy-to-use grid format.

CHAPTER 23—CAREERS IN BUSINESS

We also include detailed career coverage in the last chapter of the book. We chose to place this chapter last so that it will be a capstone activity crowning all you have examined in the areas of management, marketing, finance, accounting, and international business. Chapter 23 topics include the importance of career choices, trends in employment, occupational search activities, career planning and preparation, résumé writing, and interviewing techniques. We also provide information on the traits that characterize successful and sought-after employees.

ADDITIONAL CAREER PUBLICATIONS

Two additional sources of career information are available from Houghton Mifflin—the publisher of your text. *Toward a Career in Business*, by Kathryn Hegar, provides students with job-search techniques. Constructed in a workbook format, this project book provides hands-on experience in these areas: (1) self-assessment; (2) occupational search; (3) employment tools; and (4) success techniques. *Business Careers*, by Robert Luke, provides specific, detailed information for the areas of accounting, computer information systems, finance, management, marketing, entrepreneurship, and international business.

PART 1   Sample Career Table

Job Title	Job Description	Salary Range
Accountant–Corporate	Analyze source documents and journalize accounting entries for a private business; post journal entries to ledger accounts; prepare a trial balance and financial statements for each accounting period; close the accounting books at the end of each accounting period	3–4
Computer Operator	Use available software programs to process data into information; prepare reports based on original input data; communicate with managers and other personnel who need processed information	1–2
First-line Supervisor	Ensure that workers, equipment, and materials are used properly and efficiently; make sure machinery is set up correctly; schedule maintenance of machinery; tell workers what to do and make sure it's done safely, correctly, and on time; keep employee records; enforce safety regulations; recommend wage increases; make sure union rules are followed	3

■ ■ ■ ■ ■ ■ ■ ■ ■ ■ ■ ■ ■ ■ ■

A FINAL NOTE ON CAREERS

Throughout the fifth edition of *Business* we have made a special effort to emphasize that the business environment is undergoing rapid changes. Your success in career planning will be based to some extent on your ability to adapt to these changes. Good luck!

EXPLANATION OF SAMPLE CAREER TABLE

Job Title

This column lists common job titles that correspond to job opportunities in the employment world today. Entries are alphabetized for easy reference.

Job Description

This column lists the elements that an individual in this type of job would perform on a regular basis.

Salary Range

Salary ranges for each job title are included here. Of course, actual salary will be determined by employee qualifications, geographical differences in salary levels, and other factors.

Educational Requirements

Here the general educational level for each job title in column one is shown. In some cases, on-the-job experience is also necessary.

Skills Required

Typical skills that an employee in this type of job or position would need for success are listed.

Prospects for Growth

Employment prospects for each job title are indicated by a relative scale. In descending order, the scale ranges from greatest growth through average growth to no growth.

The figure in the salary column approximates the expected annual income after two or three years of service.
1 = $14,000–$16,000; 2 = $17,000–$21,000; 3 = $22,000–$28,000; 4 = $29,000–$36,000; 5 = higher than $36,000.

Educational Requirements	Skills Required	Prospects for Growth
Bachelor's degree in accounting; master's degree preferred	Computer; problem solving; quantitative; analytical; diagnostic; conceptual; critical thinking	Greatest
Two years of college in data processing; on-the-job experience	Computer; problem solving; quantitative; technical	Greatest
High school diploma; some college preferred	Organizational; leadership; technical; decision making	Below average

167

▣▪▪▪▪
PART TWO

Management and Organization

This part of the book deals with the organization—the "thing" that is a business. We begin with a discussion of the management functions involved in developing and operating a business. Then we analyze the organization itself, to see what makes it tick. Next we put the two together, to examine the part of a business that is concerned with manufacturing finished products. Included in this part are

■■■■ CHAPTER 6

The Management Process

LEARNING OBJECTIVES

After studying this chapter you should be able to

1 Define what management is.

2 Describe the four basic management functions: planning, organizing, leading and motivating, and controlling.

3 Distinguish among the various kinds of managers, in terms of both level and area of management.

4 Identify the key management skills and the managerial roles.

5 Explain the different types of leadership.

6 Discuss the steps in the managerial decision-making process.

7 Describe how total quality management can improve customer satisfaction.

8 Summarize what it takes to become a successful manager today.

CHAPTER PREVIEW

In this chapter we define *management* and describe the four basic management functions of planning, organizing, leading and motivating, and controlling. Then we focus on the types of managers with respect to levels of responsibility and areas of expertise. Next we focus on the skills of effective managers and the different roles managers must play. We examine several styles of leadership and explore the process by which managers make decisions. We also describe how total quality management can improve customer satisfaction. We conclude the chapter with a discussion of what it takes to be a successful manager today.

Johnson & Johnson Manages for Excellence

Johnson & Johnson, often referred to as J&J, is the world's largest manufacturer of health care products, generating annual sales that exceed $15 billion. Its phenomenal success, though, is no accident of just being in the right place at the right time. Instead, executives at J&J have developed a different way of doing business built on management techniques that encourage managers to set their own goals, take risks when developing new products, and make important decisions at lower levels within the firm.

Johnson & Johnson's success can be traced to its Credo—a 308-word statement that describes what sets J&J apart from the pack. This statement tells managers who they are and what they should care about. For example, the first two sentences of the Credo state the number 1 priority for Johnson & Johnson.

> We believe our first responsibility is to the doctors, nurses, and patients, to mothers and fathers and all others who use our products and services. In meeting their needs everything we do must be of high quality.

After dedication to customers, J&J's responsibilities to employees and to the communities in which the firm operates are described in the second and third paragraphs of the Credo. The *last* paragraph describes the firm's accountability to its stockholders. In one short sentence, J&J declares that if it adheres to the basic principles described in the Credo, the stockholders should realize a "fair return." To the surprise of materialistic industry analysts and even some of its own stockholders, J&J's philosophy works extremely well. Last year, the firm earned almost $2 billion. Return on stockholders' equity was an amazing 32 percent. And investors have more than doubled their investments in the past five years.

While most corporations have trouble managing a handful of subsidiaries, Johnson & Johnson uses a decentralized management approach to control a vast product mix that ranges from baby shampoo to bandages to advanced surgical equipment and prescription drugs. According to Ralph S. Larsen, chairman and CEO, the people who manage each of J&J's 168 operating companies in over fifty countries around the world need the freedom and autonomy to run their companies. Only with the authority to make major decisions can they be creative, look for ways to improve existing products, and develop new products. At first glance, it almost seems that the people at headquarters couldn't care less if the smaller companies are successful or not. Nothing could be further from the truth. J&J wants each of the 168 companies to succeed and will do everything possible to help them achieve success, expand sales, and increase profits. Rest assured that a company manager who calls "home" and asks for help gets all of the expertise J&J has to offer.[1]

■ ■ ■ ■

171

■ ■ ■ ■ ■ ■ ■ ■ ■ ■ ■

Just the thought of managing Johnson & Johnson's 168 operating companies in over fifty countries would worry most corporate managers. And Ralph Larsen, J&J's chairman and CEO, does worry. But he also knows that he has the "best" people on board to help him accomplish the corporation's goals. In fact, Larsen would be the first to admit that J&J is too large for *any* one person to manage. In some ways, his realization that he needs help, and that he can't do the whole job alone, is a major reason why J&J, or any corporation, hires managers today.

Without a doubt, management is one of the most exciting, challenging, and rewarding professions available to graduates today. The men and women who manage business firms play an important part in shaping the world we live in. Depending on its size, a business firm like The Home Depot, Inc., may employ a number of specialized managers who are responsible for particular areas of management, such as marketing, finance, and operations. That same organization also includes managers at several levels within the firm. For Home Depot, what is important is not the number of managers it employs but the ability of these managers to achieve the organization's goals. As you will see in this chapter, today's managers wear many hats and perform a variety of different jobs.

LEARNING OBJECTIVE 1
Define what management is.

management the process of coordinating people and other resources of an organization to achieve the goals of the organization

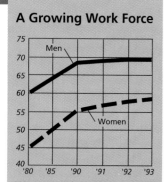
■■ WHAT IS MANAGEMENT?

Management is the process of coordinating people and other resources to achieve the goals of the organization. As we saw in Chapter 1, most organizations make use of four kinds of resources: material, human, financial, and informational (see Figure 6.1).

Material resources are the tangible, physical resources an organization uses. For example, General Motors uses steel, glass, and fiberglass to produce cars and trucks on complex machine-driven assembly lines. A college or university uses books, classroom buildings, desks, and computers to educate students. And the Mayo Clinic uses beds, operating room equipment, and diagnostic machines to provide health care.

FIGURE 6.1   The Four Main Resources of Management
Managers coordinate an organization's resources to achieve the goals of the organization.

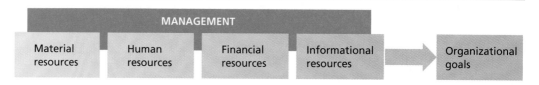

172

Is Herb Kelleher America's best CEO? The fact that Southwest Airlines' CEO Herb Kelleher is ranked as "one of the best" CEOs is a testimony to his ability to manage people. Seen here at an employee dinner, Kelleher (center) is an enthusiastic, down-to-earth manager known to give employees the same respect and attention that he gives Southwest's passengers.

Perhaps the most important resources of any organization are its *human resources*—people. In fact, some firms live by the philosophy that their employees are their most important assets. One such firm is Southwest Airlines. Southwest treats its employees with the same respect and attention that it gives its passengers. Southwest selectively seeks employees with upbeat attitudes and promotes from within its own ranks 80 percent of the time. And when it's time for making decisions, everyone who will be affected is encouraged to get involved in the process. In an industry in which deregulation, recession, and skyrocketing fuel costs killed off Eastern, Pan Am, and Braniff, Southwest keeps on growing and making a profit because of its valuable 12,000 employees.

Financial resources are the funds the organization uses to meet its obligations to investors and creditors. A 7-Eleven convenience store obtains money from customers at the check-out counters and uses a portion of that money to pay its suppliers. Citicorp, a large New York bank, borrows and lends money. Your college obtains money in the form of tuition, income from its endowments, and state and federal grants. It uses the money to pay utility bills, insurance premiums, and professors' salaries.

Finally, many organizations increasingly find they cannot afford to ignore *information*. External environmental conditions—including the economy, consumer markets, technology, politics, and cultural forces—are all changing so rapidly that a business that does not adapt will probably not survive. And, to adapt to change, the business must know what is changing and how it is changing. Companies are finding it increasingly important to gather information about their competitors in today's business environment. Companies such as Ford Motor Company and General Electric are known to collect information about their competitors. These companies are technology based, but other types of companies, such as Kraft and J. C. Penney, collect information as well. To see how managers cope with the problem of too much information, read Change in the Workplace.

It is important to realize that the four types of resources described above are only general categories of resources. Within each category are hundreds or thousands of more specific resources. It is this complex mix of

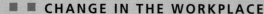

■ ■ ■ ■ CHANGE IN THE WORKPLACE

How Managers Cope With Information Overload

Back in Chapter 1, we defined *information* as the business resource that tells managers how effectively their other resources (material, human, and financial) are being combined and used. On the surface, it's hard to argue that *more* information could be bad. And yet today's managers often find themselves trapped in an infobog. *Infobog* is a new term coined to describe information overload.

SYMPTOMS OF INFORMATION OVERLOAD

Twenty years ago experts predicted that the information revolution would make employees more efficient. Computerized electronic mail—or simply E-mail—would tie people together. Information galore would help people make decisions, slash manufacturing times, and speed the process of introducing new products. Now that employees all have their own personal computers (PCs) wired to the network and in touch with the world, many managers wonder if we have gone too far. The facts below depict just how widespread the infobog problem may be:

> Today, Americans possess almost 320 million E-mail addresses, cellular phones, pagers, fax machines, voice mailboxes, answering machines, and standard-issue telephones.

> In some "wired" companies, employees must spend over three hours each day processing over one hundred E-mail messages.

> Industry experts believe that as much as 80 percent of the E-mail employees receive is junk mail.

At a time when managers are struggling just to keep up with the technical changes in their own field, having to cope with excess information, or "E-mail trash," leads to frustration and reduced productivity.

HOW TO SURVIVE INFORMATION OVERLOAD

Although there is no easy way to pull yourself out of the infobog, successful executives recommend the following three methods to manage the flood of information. First, experts suggest that you begin by looking at what's really important to you. Set specific goals that you want to accomplish during the next twelve months and then develop a plan to reach those goals. Once you know where you are headed, you may be able simply to delete as much as 50 percent of unwanted information irrelevant to your goals.

Second, many people have found that it helps to handle E-mail messages only at certain times of the day. By checking your E-mail early in the morning, at noon, and at the end of the day, you can commit the majority of your time to more important tasks, ones that help you obtain your goals.

Finally, the PC may be the largest single cause of information overload, but it may also be the best solution to the problem. Today, software is available to filter and sort your E-mail messages. These programs can delete unwanted messages and rank incoming messages according to names you have entered. For example, you could instruct the computer to place any messages from your boss at the top of the list and to put messages about a company exercise program at the bottom. Be forewarned: A filtered-out message may be really important, but if it comes from a person who is not on your approved list, the software might scrap it.

specific resources—and not simply "some of each" of the four general categories—that managers must coordinate to produce goods and services.

Another interesting way to look at management is in terms of the different functions managers perform. These functions have been identified as planning, organizing, leading and motivating employees, and controlling. We look at each of these management functions in the next section.

■■ BASIC MANAGEMENT FUNCTIONS

LEARNING OBJECTIVE 2
Describe the four basic management functions: planning, organizing, leading and motivating, and controlling.

When Lee Iacocca took the reins at Chrysler Corporation in 1978, the firm was on the brink of bankruptcy. One of Iacocca's first moves was to establish specific goals for sales growth and a written plan for achieving them. He changed the basic structure of the organization. Then he provided effective leadership by working for $1 a year until he had turned the company around. He also developed an elaborate control system to keep Chrysler on track.

Iacocca performed at least four different management functions while at the helm of Chrysler. First, he established goals and developed plans to achieve those goals. Next, he organized people and other resources into an efficient "well-oiled machine." Then, he led and motivated employees to work effectively to help achieve Chrysler's goals. Finally, he maintained control to ensure that the organization was working steadily toward its goals.

Management functions like those described above do not occur according to some rigid, preset timetable. Managers don't plan in January, organize in February, lead and motivate in March, and control in April. At any given time, managers may engage in a number of functions at the same time. However, each function tends to lead naturally to others. Figure 6.2 provides a visual framework for a more detailed discussion of the four basic management functions. How well managers perform these key functions determines whether a corporation is successful. The five "world-class" corporations described in the Business Journal are not only successful, they are also the most admired corporations in the United States. Their managers, you can be sure, are largely responsible for their esteemed status.

FIGURE 6.2   The Management Process
Note that management is not a step-by-step procedure but a process with a feedback loop that represents a flow.

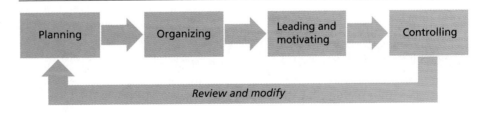

World-Class Corporations

For the last twelve years, *Fortune* magazine has conducted a nationwide survey to determine America's most and least admired companies from the viewpoint of senior executives, outside directors, and financial analysts. This year's survey polled 404 companies in 42 industry groups. More than ten thousand individuals were asked to rate the ten largest companies within their own industry. The survey focused on the following eight attributes:

- Quality of management
- Quality of products or services
- Innovativeness
- Long-term investment value
- Financial soundness
- Ability to attract, develop, and keep talented people
- Responsibility to the community and the environment
- Wise use of corporate assets

In every survey *Fortune* magazine has conducted, the most admired corporations have been those with reputations for outstanding financial performance, and almost all have succeeded because they are premier innovators.

THE TOP FIVE MOST ADMIRED CORPORATIONS

Rubbermaid Inc.

As manufacturers of plastic and rubber products for consumer and institutional markets, Rubbermaid achieved first place with its reputation for producing quality products and services, its innovativeness marked by introducing an average of one new product every day, and its awareness of community and environmental responsibility

The Home Depot, Inc.

With 270 retail warehouse stores offering a wide assortment of building materials and home-improvement items for the "do-it-yourselfer," The Home Depot is most admired for its quality of management and its ability to attract, develop, and keep talented people. Its 53,000 employees are trained to always bear in mind that "you can never do enough for a customer."

The Coca-Cola Company

The world's largest producer and distributor of soft drinks and fruit juice products, Coca-Cola is admired for its financial soundness and its value as a long-term investment. Probably the most famous brand name in the world, the soft drink invented in Atlanta, Georgia, in 1886 is now sold in 195 countries. In the United States alone, it is estimated that each person drinks an average of 296 servings of Coca-Cola's beverages yearly.

Microsoft Corporation

The world's leading developer of personal computer software has introduced almost 100 new products in the past two years. Recognized primarily for dominating the office PC market, Microsoft is now moving into software for the home and for children. The ratings on its financial soundness and profitability, its use of corporate assets, and its ability to attract, develop, and keep talented people ranked Microsoft as tied with Coca-Cola for third place in the survey.

Minnesota Mining and Manufacturing Company

3M is a worldwide producer of a variety of products, the most famous being Scotch-brand tape and Post-it Notes. The company's innovativeness in industrial and consumer products, imaging and electronic products, and life sciences earned 3M the Number 5 spot. Even though there are more than 60,000 3M products on the market today, management has been looking to the year 2000 and beyond by investing, in just the last five years, almost $5 billion on research and development.

Planning

planning establishing organizational goals and deciding how to accomplish them

Planning, in its simplest form, is establishing organizational goals and deciding how to accomplish them. It is often referred to as the "first" management function because all other management functions depend on planning. Organizations like Texaco, Houston Community Colleges, and the U.S. Secret Service begin the planning process by developing a mission statement.

mission a statement of the basic purpose that makes a business different from other firms

An organization's **mission** is a statement of the basic purpose that makes this business different from other firms. The mission of Texaco Inc. is to earn a profit for its owners by refining and selling petroleum products. Houston Community College System's mission is to provide an education for local citizens. The mission of the Secret Service is to protect the life of the president. Once an organization's mission has been described in a mission statement, the next step is to develop organizational goals and objectives.

goal an end result that the organization is expected to achieve over a one-to-ten-year period of time

objective a specific statement detailing what the organization intends to accomplish over a shorter period of time

Establishing Goals and Objectives A **goal** is an end result that the organization is expected to achieve over a one-to-ten-year period of time. For example, Rubbermaid Inc. has established a goal of obtaining 25 percent of its sales revenues from markets outside the United States by the year 2000.[2] An **objective** is a specific statement detailing what the organization intends to accomplish over a shorter period of time. Compared to goals, objectives have a much narrower time frame—usually one year or less. For McDonald's, one objective might be to increase sales of french fries by 5 percent over the next nine months. Sears, Roebuck might adopt the objective of increasing sales by 7 percent this year. For IBM, one objective might be to reduce the average delivery time for personal computers to retailers by four days next year.

Goals and objectives can deal with a variety of factors, such as sales, company growth, costs, customer satisfaction, and employee morale. Whereas a small manufacturer may focus primarily on sales objectives for the next six months, Exxon Corporation may be more interested in goals for the year 2000. Finally, goals are set at every level of the organization. Every member of the organization—the president of the company, the head of a department, and an operating employee at the lowest level—has a set of goals he or she hopes to achieve.

The goals developed for these different levels must be consistent with one another. However, it is likely that some conflict will arise. A production department, for example, may have a goal of minimizing costs. One way to do this is to produce only one type of product and offer "no frills." Marketing, on the other hand, may have a goal of maximizing sales. And one way to implement this goal is to offer prospective customers a wide range of products with many options. As part of his or her own goal setting, the manager who is ultimately responsible for *both* departments must achieve some sort of balance between conflicting goals. This balancing process is called *optimization.*

The optimization of conflicting goals requires insight and ability. Faced with the marketing-versus-production conflict just described, most managers would probably not adopt either viewpoint completely. Instead, they might decide on a reasonably diverse product line offering only the most widely sought-after options. Such a compromise would seem to be best for the organization as a whole.

Establishing Plans to Accomplish Goals and Objectives   Once goals and objectives have been set for the organization, managers must develop plans for achieving them. A **plan** is an outline of the actions by which the organization intends to accomplish its goals and objectives. Just as it has different goals and objectives, the organization also develops several types of plans.

An organization's **strategy** is its broadest set of plans, developed as a guide for major policy setting and decision making. These plans are set by the board of directors and top management and are generally designed to achieve the long-term goals of the organization. Thus, a firm's strategy defines what business the company is in or wants to be in and the kind of company it is or wants to be. When the U.S. Surgeon General issued a report linking smoking and cancer in the 1950s, top management at Philip Morris Companies recognized that the company's very survival was being threatened. Executives needed to develop a strategy to diversify into nontobacco products.

In addition to strategies, most organizations also employ several narrower kinds of plans. A **tactical plan** is a smaller-scale plan developed to implement a strategy. Most tactical plans cover a one-to-three-year time period. If a strategic plan will take five years to complete, the firm may develop five tactical plans, one covering each year. Tactical plans may be updated periodically as conditions and experience dictate. Their more limited scope permits them to be changed more easily than strategies. In an attempt to fulfill its strategy of diversification, Philip Morris developed individual tactical plans to purchase several nontobacco-related companies such as General Foods, Kraft Foods, and Miller Brewing.

An **operational plan** is a type of plan designed to implement tactical plans. Operational plans are usually established for one year or less and deal with how to accomplish the organization's specific objectives. Assume that after Philip Morris purchased Kraft Foods, managers adopted the objective of increasing sales of Kraft's Cheez Whiz by 5 percent the first year. A sales increase of this size does not just happen, however. Management must develop an operational plan that describes certain activities the firm can undertake over the next year to bring about the increased sales. Specific components of the Kraft Cheez Whiz operational plan might include newspaper and television advertising, reduced prices, and coupon offers—all designed to increase consumer sales.

Regardless of how hard managers try, sometimes business activities don't go as planned. Today, most corporations also develop contingency plans along with strategies, tactical plans, and operational plans. A **contingency plan** is a plan that outlines alternative courses of action that may be taken if the organization's other plans are disrupted or become ineffective. Remember that one reason for Philip Morris's purchase of Kraft was to diversify into nontobacco products. If it became impossible to purchase Kraft, Philip Morris could fall back on contingency plans to purchase other nontobacco companies.

plan   an outline of the actions by which the organization intends to accomplish its goals and objectives

strategy   an organization's broadest set of plans, developed as a guide for major policy setting and decision making

tactical plan   a smaller-scale plan developed to implement a strategy

operational plan   a type of plan designed to implement tactical plans

contingency plan   a plan that outlines alternative courses of action that may be taken if the organization's other plans are disrupted or become ineffective

Organizing the Enterprise

After goal setting and planning, the second major function of the manager is organization. **Organizing** is the grouping of resources and activities to accomplish some end result in an efficient and effective manner. Consider the case of an inventor who creates a new product and goes into business to sell it. At first, she will probably do everything herself—purchase raw materials, make the product, advertise it, sell it, and keep her business records up-to-date. Eventually, as business grows, she will find that she needs help. To begin with, she might hire a professional sales representative and a part-time bookkeeper. Later she might need to hire full-time sales staff, other people to assist with production, and an accountant. As she hires new personnel, she must decide what each person will do, to whom that person will report, and generally how that person can best take part in the organization's activities. In a similar fashion, Saturn, a subsidiary of General Motors, must decide what resources will be needed and how they will be organized to produce Saturn automobiles in its Spring Hill, Tennessee, plant. We discuss these and other facets of the organizing function in much more detail in the next chapter.

organizing the grouping of resources and activities to accomplish some end result in an efficient and effective manner

Leading and Motivating

The leading and motivating function is concerned with the human resources within the organization. Specifically, **leading** is the process of influencing people to work toward a common goal. **Motivating** is the process of providing reasons for people to work in the best interests of the organization. Together, leading and motivating are often referred to as **directing.**

leading the process of influencing people to work toward a common goal

motivating the process of providing reasons for people to work in the best interests of the organization

directing the combined processes of leading and motivating

We have already noted the importance of an organization's human resources. Because of this importance, leading and motivating are critical activities. Obviously, different people do things for different reasons—that is, they have different *motivations*. Some are primarily interested in earning as much money as they can. Others may be spurred on by opportunities to get ahead in an organization. Part of the manager's job, then, is to determine what factors motivate workers and to try to provide those incentives in a way that encourages effective performance.

Quite a bit of research has been done on both motivation and leadership. As you will see in Chapter 9, research on motivation has yielded very useful information. Research on leadership has been less successful. In spite of decades of study, no one has discovered a general set of personal traits or characteristics that makes a good leader. Later in this chapter, we discuss leadership in more detail.

Controlling Ongoing Activities

controlling the process of evaluating and regulating ongoing activities to ensure that goals are achieved

Controlling is the process of evaluating and regulating ongoing activities to ensure that goals are achieved. To see how controlling works, consider a rocket launched by NASA to place a satellite in orbit. Do NASA personnel simply fire the rocket and then check back in a few days to find out whether the satellite is in place? Of course not. The rocket is constantly monitored, and its course is regulated and adjusted as needed to get the satellite to its destination.

The control function includes three steps (see Figure 6.3). The first is *setting standards* to which performance can be compared. The second is *measuring actual performance* and comparing it with the standard. And the third is *taking corrective action* as necessary. Notice that the control function is circular in nature. The steps in the control function must be repeated periodically until the goal is achieved. For example, suppose that United Air Lines, Inc., establishes a goal of increasing its profit by 12 percent next year. To ensure that this goal is reached, United's management might monitor its profit on a monthly basis. After three months, if profit has increased by 3 percent, management might be able to assume that plans are going according to schedule. Probably no action will be taken. However, if profit has increased by only 1 percent after three months, some corrective action would be needed to get the firm on track. The particular action that is required depends on the reason for the small increase in profit.

■ ■ KINDS OF MANAGERS

LEARNING OBJECTIVE 3
Distinguish among the various kinds of managers, in terms of both level and area of management.

Managers can be classified two ways: according to their level within the organization and according to their area of management. In this section we use both perspectives to explore the various types of managers.

Levels of Management

For the moment, think of an organization as a three-story structure (as illustrated in Figure 6.4). Each story corresponds to one of the three general levels of management: top managers, middle managers, and first-line managers.

top manager an upper-level executive who guides and controls the overall fortunes of the organization

Top Managers   A **top manager** is an upper-level executive who guides and controls the overall fortunes of the organization. Top managers constitute a small group. In terms of planning, they are generally responsible for developing the organization's mission. They also determine the firm's strategy. It

FIGURE 6.3
The Control Function
The control function includes the three steps of setting standards, measuring actual performance, and taking corrective action.

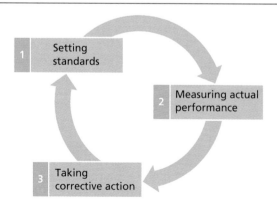

FIGURE 6.4
Management Levels Found in Most Companies
The coordinated effort of all three levels of managers is required to implement the goals of any company.

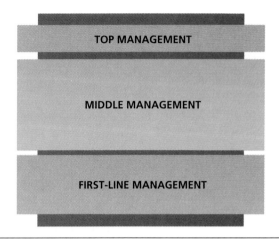

takes years of hard work, long hours, and perseverance, as well as talent and no small share of good luck, to reach the ranks of top management in large companies. Common job titles associated with top managers are president, vice president, chief executive officer (CEO), and chief operating officer (COO).

Middle Managers   Middle management probably comprises the largest group of managers in most organizations. A **middle manager** is a manager who implements the strategy developed by top managers. Middle managers develop tactical plans and operational plans, and they coordinate and supervise the activities of first-line managers. Titles at the middle-management level include division manager, department head, plant manager, and operations manager.

middle manager a manager who implements the strategy and major policies developed by top management

First-Line Managers   A **first-line manager** is a manager who coordinates and supervises the activities of operating employees. First-line managers spend most of their time working with and motivating their employees, answering questions, and solving day-to-day problems. Most first-line managers are former operating employees who, owing to their hard work and potential, were promoted into management. Many of today's middle and top managers began their careers on this first management level. Common titles for first-line managers include office manager, supervisor, and foreman.

first-line manager a manager who coordinates and supervises the activities of operating employees

Areas of Management

Organizational structure can also be divided into areas of management specialization (see Figure 6.5). The most common areas are finance, operations, marketing, human resources, and administration. Depending on its mission, goals, and objectives, an organization may include other areas as well—research and development, for example.

financial manager a manager who is primarily responsible for the organization's financial resources

Financial Managers   A **financial manager** is primarily responsible for the organization's financial resources. Accounting and investment are specialized areas within financial management. Because financing affects the

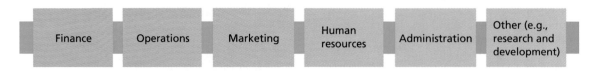

FIGURE 6.5   **Areas of Management Specialization**
Other areas may have to be added, depending on the nature of the firm and the industry.

operation of the entire firm, many of the CEOs and presidents of this country's largest companies are people who got their "basic training" as financial managers.

operations manager
a manager who manages the systems that convert resources into goods and services

Operations Managers   An **operations manager** manages the systems that convert resources into goods and services. Traditionally, operations management has been equated with manufacturing—the production of goods. However, in recent years many of the techniques and procedures of operations management have been applied to the production of services and to a variety of nonbusiness activities. Like financial management, operations management has produced a large percentage of today's company CEOs and presidents.

marketing manager
a manager who is responsible for facilitating the exchange of products between the organization and its customers or clients

Marketing Managers   A **marketing manager** is responsible for facilitating the exchange of products between the organization and its customers or clients. Specific areas within marketing are marketing research, advertising, promotion, sales, and distribution. A sizable number of today's company presidents have risen from the ranks of marketing management.

human resources manager
a person charged with managing the organization's human resources programs

Human Resources Managers   A **human resources manager** is charged with managing the organization's human resources programs. He or she engages in human resources planning; designs systems for hiring, training, and evaluating the performance of employees; and ensures that the organization follows government regulations concerning employment practices. Because human resources management is a relatively new area of specialization in many organizations, few top managers have this kind of background. However, this situation should change with the passage of time.

administrative manager
a manager who is not associated with any specific functional area but who provides overall administrative guidance and leadership

Administrative Managers   An **administrative manager** (also called a *general manager*) is not associated with any specific functional area but provides overall administrative guidance and leadership. A hospital administrator is a good example of an administrative manager. He or she does not specialize in operations, finance, marketing, or human resources management but instead coordinates the activities of specialized managers in all these areas. In many respects, most top managers are really administrative managers.

Whatever their level in the organization and whatever area they specialize in, successful managers generally exhibit certain key skills and are able to play certain managerial roles. But, as we shall see, some skills are likely to be more critical at one level of management than at another.

■■ WHAT MAKES EFFECTIVE MANAGERS?

In general, effective managers are those who (1) possess certain important skills and (2) are able to use these skills in a number of managerial roles. Probably no manager is called on to use any particular skill *constantly* or to play a particular role *all the time*. However, these skills and abilities must be available when they are needed.

Key Management Skills

LEARNING OBJECTIVE 4
Identify the key management skills and the managerial roles.

technical skill a specific skill needed to accomplish a specialized activity

The skills that typify effective managers tend to fall into three general categories: technical, conceptual, and interpersonal.

Technical Skills   A **technical skill** is a specific skill needed to accomplish a specialized activity. For example, the skills engineers and machinists need to do their jobs are technical skills. First-line managers (and, to a lesser extent, middle managers) need the technical skills relevant to the activities they manage. Although these managers may not have to perform the technical tasks themselves, they must be able to train subordinates, answer questions, and otherwise provide guidance and direction. A first-line manager in the accounting department for the Hyatt Corporation, for example, must be able to perform computerized accounting transactions *and* be able to help employees complete the same accounting task. In general, top managers do not rely on technical skills as heavily as do managers at other levels. Still, understanding the technical side of a business is an aid to effective management at every level.

conceptual skill the ability to think in abstract terms

Conceptual Skills   **Conceptual skill** is the ability to think in abstract terms. Conceptual skill allows the manager to see the "big picture" and to understand how the various parts of an organization or an idea can fit together. In 1951 a man named Charles Wilson decided to take his family on a cross-country vacation. All along the way, the family was forced to put up with high-priced but shabby hotel accommodations. Wilson reasoned that most travelers would welcome a chain of moderately priced, good-quality road-side hotels. You are probably familiar with the solution he conceived: Holiday Inns. Wilson was able to identify a number of isolated factors (existing accommodation patterns, the need for a different kind of hotel, and his own investment interests) to "dream up" the new business opportunity and to carry it through to completion.

Conceptual skills are useful in a wide range of situations, including the optimization of goals described earlier. They appear, however, to be more crucial for top managers than for middle or first-line managers.

interpersonal skill the ability to deal effectively with other people

Interpersonal Skills   An **interpersonal skill** is the ability to deal effectively with other people, both inside and outside the organization. Examples of interpersonal skills are the ability to relate to people, understand their needs and motives, and show genuine compassion. One reason why Mary Kay Ash, founder and former CEO of Mary Kay Cosmetics, has been so successful is her ability to motivate her employees and to inspire their loyalty and devotion to her vision for the firm. And although it is obvious that a CEO like Mary Kay Ash must be able to work with employees throughout the

ENHANCING CAREER SKILLS

Tips for the New Supervisor

All too often, people who get promoted to supervisory or management positions have no idea how to do their new jobs, and in many cases there is no one to turn to for help. New supervisors are often chosen on the basis of their technical skills rather than their interpersonal or human skills. They may be proficient in accounting, in computer programming, or in operating complicated machinery. But the one thing they *don't* have is expertise in dealing with people. Make no mistake: managing people is a brand-new—and often difficult—experience for first-time supervisors.

Although there is no quick and easy way to gain the experience required to become a seasoned supervisor, the following suggestions can help you do a better job of working with people.

1. Realize That People Work for Different Reasons. Many new supervisors believe that the paycheck is the key reason why employees show up for work each day. Granted, compensation is a very important reason for working, but it may not be most important. Study after study has demonstrated that many workers feel full appreciation for work done, being included on decisions, and doing jobs or tasks that make a difference may be just as important a reward—or even more important—than money.

2. Develop Two-Way Communication with Your Employees. A large part of any supervisor's job is communication—listening to employees, answering questions, providing directions, and giving encouragement and praising workers. When communicating with employees, make eye contact and try to "read" what employees are really thinking. Above all, allow workers to verbalize their concerns and complaints. Once problems are clearly defined, you can take corrective action, if needed.

3. Learn How to Deal with Problems. Dealing with a problem is delicate business. On the one hand, you don't want to alienate your employees by being too harsh; on the other, you must confront each problem head on. To deal with a problem effectively, management experts suggest the following three steps. First, make a special effort to identify clearly the *real* problem. Second, pinpoint the individual factors that may be causing the problem. Finally, take definite steps to correct the problem.

4. Don't Be Afraid to Praise Workers. Ironically, new supervisors often feel uneasy about giving praise to hardworking employees. And yet the ability to praise workers for a job well done is an essential part of any supervisor's job. Start with specific achievements. For example, "Congratulations—you exceeded your production quota by 15 percent, more than anyone else in the department," means more than "You did a good job." Although words of praise, thank-you notes, and expressions of confidence can let workers know that you appreciate their work, use these only when they are deserved. Used too often, they lose their meaning.

organization, what is not so obvious is that middle and first-line managers must also possess interpersonal skills. For example, a first-line manager on an assembly line at Procter & Gamble must rely on employees to manufacture Tide laundry detergent. The better the manager's interpersonal skills, the more likely the manager will be able to lead and motivate those employees. When all other things are equal, the manager able to exhibit these skills will be more successful than the arrogant and brash manager who doesn't care about others. Before examining the different types of managerial roles, read Enhancing Career Skills.

Managerial Roles

Research suggests that managers must, from time to time, act in ten different roles if they are to be successful.[3] (By *role* we mean a part that someone plays.) These ten roles can be grouped into three broad categories: decisional, interpersonal, and informational.

decisional role   a role that involves various aspects of management decision making

Decisional Roles   As you might suspect, a **decisional role** is one that involves various aspects of management decision making. The decisional role can be subdivided into the following four specific managerial roles. In the role of *entrepreneur,* the manager is the voluntary initiator of change. For example, a manager for Coca-Cola who develops a new strategy or expands the sales force into a new market is playing the entrepreneur's role. A second role is that of *disturbance handler.* A manager who settles a strike is handling a disturbance. Third, the manager also occasionally plays the role of *resource allocator.* In this role, the manager might have to decide which departmental budgets to cut and which expenditure requests to approve. The fourth role is that of *negotiator.* Being a negotiator might involve settling a dispute between a manager and a worker assigned to the manager's work group.

Providing information: One of a manager's most important jobs. A manager must use technical, conceptual, and interpersonal skills to perform different managerial roles. Here a manager for Pacific Gas and Electric Company is acting as a spokesperson to convey information to people outside of the organization.

interpersonal role a role in which the manager deals with people

Interpersonal Roles Dealing with people is an integral part of the manager's job. An **interpersonal role** is one in which the manager deals with people. Like the decisional role, the interpersonal role can be broken down according to three managerial functions. The manager may be called on to serve as a *figurehead*, perhaps by attending a ribbon-cutting ceremony or taking an important client to dinner. The manager may also have to play the role of *liaison* by serving as a go-between for two different groups. As a liaison, a manager might represent his or her firm at meetings of an industry-wide trade organization. Finally, the manager often has to serve as a *leader*. Playing the role of leader includes being an example for others in the organization as well as developing the skills, abilities, and motivation of employees.

informational role a role in which the manager either gathers or provides information

Informational Roles An **informational role** is one in which the manager either gathers or provides information. The informational role can be subdivided as follows. In the role of *monitor*, the manager actively seeks information that may be of value to the organization. For example, a manager who hears about a good business opportunity is engaging in the role of monitor. The second informational role is that of *disseminator*. In this role, the manager transmits key information to those who can use it. As a disseminator, the above-mentioned manager would tip off the appropriate marketing manager about the business opportunity. The third informational role is that of *spokesperson*. In this role, the manager provides information to people outside the organization, such as the press, television reporters, and the public.

■■ LEADERSHIP

LEARNING OBJECTIVE 5
Explain the different types of leadership.

leadership the ability to influence others

Leadership has been broadly defined as the ability to influence others. A leader has power and can use it to affect the behavior of others. Leadership is different from management in that a leader strives for voluntary cooperation, whereas a manager may depend on coercion to change employee behavior.

Formal and Informal Leadership

Some experts make a distinction between formal leadership and informal leadership. Formal leaders have legitimate power of position; that is, they have *authority* within an organization and influence others to work for the organization's objectives. Informal leaders usually have no such authority and may or may not exert their influence in support of the organization. Both formal and informal leaders make use of several kinds of power, including the ability to grant rewards or impose punishments, the possession of expert knowledge, and personal attraction or charisma. Informal leaders who identify with the organization's goals are a valuable asset to any organization. On the other hand, a business can be brought to its knees by informal leaders who turn work groups against management.

Styles of Leadership

For many years leadership was viewed as a combination of personality traits, such as self-confidence, concern for people, intelligence, and dependability. Achieving a consensus on which traits were most important was difficult, however, and attention turned to styles of leadership behavior. In the last few decades several styles of leadership have been identified: authoritarian, laissez-faire, and democratic.[4] The **authoritarian leader** holds all authority and responsibility, with communication usually moving from top to bottom. This leader assigns workers to specific tasks and expects orderly, precise results. The leaders at United Parcel Service employ authoritarian leadership. At the other extreme is the **laissez-faire leader,** who gives authority to employees. With the laissez-faire style, subordinates are allowed to work as they choose with a minimum of interference. Communication flows horizontally among group members. Leaders at Apple Computer are known to employ a laissez-faire leadership style in order to give employees as much freedom as possible to develop new products. The **democratic leader** holds final responsibility but also delegates authority to others, who participate in determining work assignments. In this leadership style, communication is active both upward and downward. Employee commitment is high because of participation in the decision-making process. Managers for both Wal-Mart and Southwest Airlines have used the democratic leadership style to encourage employees to become more than just rank-and-file workers.

authoritarian leader one who holds all authority and responsibility, with communication usually moving from top to bottom

laissez-faire leader one who gives authority to employees and allows subordinates to work as they choose with a minimum of interference; communication flows horizontally among group members

democratic leader one who holds final responsibility but also delegates authority to others, who help determine work assignments; communication is active upward and downward

Which Managerial Leadership Style Is Best?

Today, most management experts agree that no one "best" managerial leadership style exists. Each of the styles described above—authoritarian, laissez-faire, and democratic—has advantages and disadvantages. For example, democratic leadership can motivate employees to work effectively because they are implementing *their own* decisions. On the other hand, the decision-making process associated with democratic leadership takes time that subordinates could otherwise be devoting to the work itself.

Although hundreds of research studies have been conducted to prove which leadership style is best, there are still no definite conclusions. The "best" leadership seems to occur when the leader's style matches the situation. Actually, each of the three leadership styles can be effective in the right situation. The style that is *most* effective depends on the interaction among the employees, the characteristics of the work situation, and the manager's personality.

LEARNING OBJECTIVE 6
Discuss the steps in the managerial decision-making process.

decision making the act of choosing one alternative from among a set of alternatives

■■ MANAGERIAL DECISION MAKING

Decision making is the act of choosing one alternative from among a set of alternatives.[5] In ordinary, everyday situations our decisions are made casually and informally. We encounter a problem, mull it over for a way out, settle on a likely solution, and go on. Managers, however, require a more

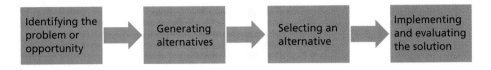

FIGURE 6.6   Major Steps in the Managerial Decision-Making Process
Managers require a systematic method for solving problems in a variety of ways.
(Source: Robert Kreitner, Management, 6th ed. Copyright © 1995 by Houghton Mifflin Company. Adapted with permission.)

systematic method for solving complex problems in a variety of situations. As shown in Figure 6.6, managerial decision making involves four steps: (1) identifying the problem or opportunity, (2) generating alternatives, (3) selecting an alternative, and (4) implementing and evaluating the solution.[6]

Identifying the Problem or Opportunity

problem   the discrepancy between an actual condition and a desired condition

A **problem** is the discrepancy between an actual condition and a desired condition—the difference between what is occurring and what one wishes to occur. For example, a marketing manager for Campbell Soup Company has a problem if sales revenues for Campbell's Hungry Man frozen dinners are declining (the actual condition). In order to solve this problem, the marketing manager must take steps to increase sales revenues (desired

Managing change. The ability to manage change may be one of the most important skills a manager can have. At the Eugene, Oregon, Water and Electric board—a public utility with $115 million in annual revenue—general manager Randy Berggren is using information and effective management decision-making techniques to lead a corporate revolution.

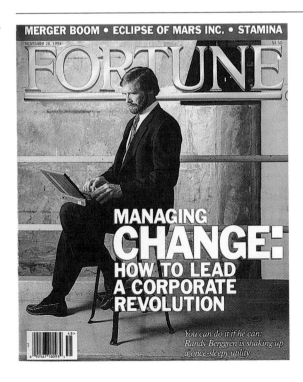

condition). Most people consider a problem to be "negative"; however, a problem can also be "positive": a positive problem should be viewed as an "opportunity."

Although accurate identification of a problem is essential before the problem can be solved, this stage of decision making creates many difficulties for managers. Sometimes managers' preconceptions of the problem prevent them from seeing the situation as it actually is. They produce an answer before the proper question has ever been asked. In other cases, managers overlook truly significant issues by focusing on unimportant matters. Also, managers may mistakenly analyze problems in terms of symptoms rather than underlying causes.

Effective managers learn to look ahead so that they are prepared when decisions must be made. They clarify situations and examine the causes of problems, asking whether the presence or absence of certain variables alters a given situation. Finally, they consider how individual behaviors and values affect the way problems or opportunities are defined.

Generating Alternatives

After a problem has been suitably defined, the next task is to generate alternatives. Generally, the more important the decision, the more attention is devoted to this stage. Managers should be open to fresh, innovative ideas as well as to more obvious answers.

Certain techniques can aid in the generation of creative alternatives. Brainstorming, commonly used in group discussions, encourages participants to come up with as many new ideas as possible, no matter how outrageous. Other group members are not permitted to criticize or ridicule. Another approach to generating alternatives, developed by the U.S. Navy, is called "Blast! Then Refine." Group members tackle a recurring problem afresh, erasing from their minds all solutions and procedures tried in the past. The group then re-evaluates its original objectives, modifies them if necessary, and devises new solutions to the problem. Other techniques—including trial and error—are also useful in this stage of decision making.

Selecting an Alternative

A final decision is influenced by a number of considerations, including financial constraints, human and information resources, time limits, legal obstacles, and political factors. Managers must select the alternative that will be most effective and practical under the circumstances. At times two or more alternatives, or some combination of alternatives, will be equally appropriate.

Managers may choose solutions to problems on several levels. The word *satisfice* has been coined to describe solutions that are only adequate and not the best possible. Managers often make decisions that satisfice if they lack time or information, even though this is not the most productive approach in the long run. In other situations, managers should try to carefully investigate alternatives and select the one that best solves the problem.

Implementing and Evaluating the Solution

Implementation of a decision requires time, planning, preparation of personnel, and evaluation of the results. Managers must usually deal with unforeseen consequences as well, even when they have carefully considered the alternatives.

The final step in managerial decision making entails evaluating the effectiveness of a decision. If the alternative that was chosen removes the difference between the actual condition and the desired condition, the decision is judged effective. If the problem still exists, managers may

- Decide to give the chosen alternative more time to work.
- Adopt a different alternative.
- Start the problem identification process all over again.

Failure to evaluate decisions may have serious consequences. Back in 1988, The Clorox Company entered the laundry detergent business. After being battered by industry giants Procter & Gamble and Unilever, and losing money on its new laundry detergent line, Clorox evaluated the decision. The result was a halt in the production of laundry detergent products in the early 1990s. According to management, Clorox had decided to back up and concentrate on its core business.[7]

■■ MANAGING TOTAL QUALITY

total quality management (TQM)   the coordination of efforts directed at improving customer satisfaction, increasing employee participation, strengthening supplier partnerships, and facilitating an organizational atmosphere of continuous quality improvement

A high priority in some organizations today is the management of quality. Major reasons for a greater focus on quality include foreign competition, more demanding customers, and poor financial performance resulting from reduced market shares and higher costs. Over the last few years, several U.S. firms have lost the dominant, competitive positions they had held for decades.

Total quality management is a much broader concept than just controlling the quality of the product itself (which is discussed in Chapter 8). **Total quality management (TQM)** is the coordination of efforts directed at improving customer satisfaction, increasing employee participation, strengthening supplier partnerships, and facilitating an organizational atmosphere of continuous quality improvement. For total quality management programs to be effective, management must address each of the following components:

- *Customer satisfaction*—Improving customer satisfaction can occur by producing higher quality products, providing better customer service, and showing customers that the company really cares about them.
- *Employee participation*—Increasing employee participation can occur when employees are allowed to contribute to decisions, develop self-managed work teams, and assume responsibility and accountability for improving the quality of their work.

It takes everybody to manage total quality management. By using TQM techniques, these Allied Chemical employees at the Hopewell, Virginia, plant found a new way to increase productivity and reduce costs while refining ammonium sulfate, used in the manufacturing of fertilizer.

- *Forming and strengthening supplier relationships*—Working with suppliers can lead to obtaining the right supplies and materials on time at lower costs.

Quality improvement should not be viewed as achievable through one single program that has a target objective. Instead, a program based on continuous improvement has proved to be the most effective long-term approach. American Express, AT&T, Hewlett-Packard, and Motorola have all used TQM to improve quality and ultimately customer satisfaction.

The costs of poor quality—remanufacturing, repairs, and reperformance of service—can range from 25 to 40 percent of sales. Fortunately, there is considerable evidence that the quality of U.S. products is improving. In 1981, for example, over 70 percent of new U.S. cars displayed defects within six months; a decade later, fewer than 40 percent had defects. Today's figure is closer to the 30 percent defects figure achieved by Japanese car makers.

Although many factors influence the effectiveness of a total quality management program, two issues are crucial. First, top management must make a strong commitment to a TQM program by treating quality improvement as a top priority and giving it frequent attention. Firms that establish a total quality management program but then focus on other priorities will find that their quality improvement initiatives will fail. Second, management must coordinate the specific elements of a TQM program so that they work in harmony with each other.

Although only about one-fourth of U.S. companies have total quality management programs, these programs provide many benefits. Overall financial benefits include lower operating costs, higher return on sales and on investment, and an improved ability to use premium pricing rather than competitive pricing. Additional benefits include faster development of innovations, improved access to global markets, higher levels of customer retention, and an enhanced reputation.[8]

■■ WHAT IT TAKES TO BECOME A SUCCESSFUL MANAGER TODAY

LEARNING OBJECTIVE 8
Summarize what it takes to become a successful manager today.

Everyone hears stories about the corporate elite who make salaries in excess of $250,000 a year, travel to and from work in chauffeur-driven limousines, and enjoy lucrative pension plans that provide for a luxurious lifestyle even after they retire. Although management can obviously be a very rewarding career, what is not so obvious is the amount of time and hard work that managers invest in order to achieve the impressive salaries and perks that come with the job.

A Day in the Life of a Manager

Organizations don't pay managers to look good behind an expensive wood desk. Organizations pay for performance. As we already pointed out in this chapter, managers coordinate the organization's resources. They also perform the four basic management functions: planning, organizing, leading and motivating, and controlling. And managers make decisions and then implement and evaluate those decisions. This heavy workload requires that managers work long hours, and most don't get paid overtime for work in excess of forty hours a week. Typically, the number of hours increases as managers move up the corporate ladder.

Make no mistake about it: today's managers work hard in a tough and demanding job. The pace is hectic. Managers spend a great deal of time talking with people on an individual basis. The purpose of these conversations is usually to obtain information or to resolve problems. (Remember, a problem can be either negative or positive and is a discrepancy between an actual condition and a desired condition.) In addition to talking with individuals, a manager often spends a large part of the workday in meetings with other managers and employees. In most cases, the purpose of the meetings—some brief and some lengthy—is to resolve problems. And if the work is not com-

Managers at work. One of the reasons Home Depot is successful is the hard work and dedication of both managers and employees. Here, managers and employees check inventory levels to ensure that the right amount of merchandise is available to meet customer needs.

pleted by the end of the day, the manager usually packs unfinished tasks in a briefcase and totes them home to work on that night.

Personal Skills Required for Success

To be successful in today's competitive business environment, you must possess a number of different skills. Some of these skills—technical, conceptual, and interpersonal skills—were discussed earlier in this chapter. But you also need to develop some "personal" skills in order to be successful. For starters, oral and written communication skills, computer skills, and critical-thinking skills may give you the edge in getting an entry-level management position.

1. *Oral communication skills.*   Because a large part of a manager's day is spent conversing with other managers and employees, the ability to speak *and* listen is critical for success. For example, oral communication skills are used when a manager must make sales presentations, conduct interviews, perform employee evaluations, and hold press conferences.

2. *Written communication skills.*   Managers must be able to write. The manager's ability to prepare letters, memos, sales reports, and other written documents may spell the difference between success and failure.

3. *Computer skills.*   Today, most managers have at their fingertips a computer monitor that is linked to the organization's larger computer system. Most employers do not expect you to be an expert computer

programmer, but they do expect that you should know how to use a computer to prepare written and statistical reports and communicate with other managers and employees in the organization.

4. *Critical-thinking skills.*   Employers expect managers to use the steps for effective managerial decision making that were described earlier in this chapter. They also expect managers to use their critical-thinking skills to ensure that they identify the problem correctly, generate reasonable alternatives, and select the "best" alternative to solve an organization's problem.

The Importance of Education and Experience

Although most experts agree that management skills must be learned on the job, the concepts that you learn in business courses lay the foundation for a successful career. In addition, successful completion of college courses or obtaining a degree can open doors to job interviews and career advancement.

Most applicants who enter the world of work do not have a wealth of work experience. And yet there are methods that you can use to "beef up" your résumé and to capitalize on the work experience you do have. First, obtain summer jobs that will provide opportunities to learn about the field you wish to enter when you finish your formal education. If you choose carefully, part-time jobs during the school year can also provide work experience that other job applicants may not have. (By the way, many colleges and universities sponsor work-cooperative programs that give students college credit for job experience.) Even with a solid academic background and relevant work experience, many would-be managers still find it difficult to land the "right" job. Often, they start in an entry-level position to gain more experience and eventually—after years on the job—reach that "ideal" job. Perseverance does pay!

We include this practical advice not to frighten you but to provide a real-world view of what a manager's job is really like. Once you know what is required of managers today—and how competitive the race is for the top jobs—you can decide whether a career in management is right for you.

In the next chapter, we examine the organizing function of managers in some detail. We look specifically at various organizational forms that today's successful businesses use. Like most factors in management, the form of an organization depends on the organization's goals, strategies, and personnel.

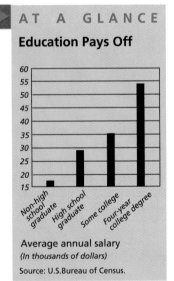

▷▷ **AT A GLANCE**

Education Pays Off

Average annual salary
(In thousands of dollars)

Source: U.S.Bureau of Census.

■ ■ ■ ■ ■ CHAPTER REVIEW

Summary

1   Define what management is.

Management is the process of coordinating people and other resources to achieve the goals of the organization. Managers are concerned with four types of resources—material, human, financial, and informational.

2   Describe the four basic management functions: planning, organizing, leading and motivating, and controlling.

Managers perform four basic functions. Management functions do not occur according to some rigid, preset timetable, though. At any time, managers may engage in a number of functions at the same time. However, each function tends to lead naturally to others. First, managers engage in planning—determining where the firm should be going and how best to get there. Three types of plans, from the broadest to the most specific, are strategies, tactical plans, and operational plans. Next, managers organize resources and activities to accomplish results in an efficient and effective manner. Then, managers lead and motivate others to work in the best interests of the organization. Finally, managers control ongoing activities to keep the organization on course. There are three steps in the control function: (a) setting standards; (b) measuring actual performance; and (c) taking corrective action.

3   Distinguish among the various kinds of managers, in terms of both level and area of management.

Managers—or management positions—may be classified from two different perspectives. From the perspective of level within the organization, there are top managers, who control the fortunes of the organization; middle managers, who implement strategies and major policies; and first-line managers, who supervise the activities of operating employees. From the viewpoint of area of management, managers most often deal with the functions of finance, operations, marketing, human resources, and administration.

4   Identify the key management skills and the managerial roles.

Effective managers tend to possess a specific set of skills and to fill three basic managerial roles. Technical, conceptual, and interpersonal skills are all important, though the relative importance of each varies with the level of management within the organization. The primary managerial roles can be classified as decisional, interpersonal, or informational.

5   Explain the different types of leadership.

Managers' effectiveness often depends on their styles of leadership—that is, their ability to influence others, either formally or informally. Leadership styles include the authoritarian "do-it-my-way" style, the laissez-faire "do-it-your-way" style, and the democratic "let's-do-it-together" style.

6   Discuss the steps in the managerial decision-making process.

Decision making, an integral part of a manager's work, is the process of developing a set of possible alternative solutions and choosing one alternative from among the set. Managerial decision making involves four steps: managers must accurately identify problems, generate several possible solutions, choose the solution that will be most effective under the circumstances, and implement and evaluate the chosen course of action.

7   Describe how total quality management can improve customer satisfaction.

Total quality management (TQM) is the coordination of efforts directed at improving customer satisfaction, increasing employee participation, strengthening supplier partnerships, and facilitating an organizational atmosphere of continuous quality improvement. To have an effective total quality management program, top management must make a strong, sustained commitment to the effort and must be able to coordinate all of the program's elements so that they work in harmony. Overall financial benefits of TQM include lower operating costs, higher returns on sales and investment, and an improved ability to use premium pricing rather than competitive pricing.

8   Summarize what it takes to become a successful manager today.

Organizations pay managers for their performance. Managers coordinate resources; they also plan, organize, lead, motivate, and control. They make decisions that can spell the difference between an organization's success and failure. And in order to complete their tasks, managers work long hours at a hectic pace. In order to succeed, they need personal skills (oral and written communication skills, computer skills, and critical-thinking skills), an academic background that provides a foundation for a management career, and practical work experience.

Key Terms

You should now be able to define and give an example relevant to each of the following terms:

management (172)

planning (177)

mission (177)

goal (177)

objective (177)

plan (178)

strategy (178)

tactical plan (178)

operational plan (178)

contingency plan (178)
organizing (179)
leading (179)
motivating (179)
directing (179)
controlling (179)
top manager (180)
middle manager (181)
first-line manager (181)
financial manager (181)
operations manager (182)
marketing manager (182)
human resources manager (182)
administrative manager (182)
technical skill (183)
conceptual skill (183)
interpersonal skill (183)
decisional role (185)
interpersonal role (186)
informational role (186)
leadership (186)
authoritarian leader (187)
laissez-faire leader (187)
democratic leader (187)
decision making (187)
problem (188)
total quality management (TQM) (190)

Questions

Review Questions

1. Define the term *manager* without using the word *management* in your definition.
2. What is the mission of a neighborhood restaurant? of the Salvation Army? What might be reasonable objectives for these organizations?
3. What does the term *optimization* mean?
4. How do a strategy, a tactical plan, and an operational plan differ? What do they all have in common?
5. What exactly does a manager organize, and for what reason?
6. Why are leadership and motivation necessary in a business in which people are paid for their work?
7. Explain the steps involved in the control function.
8. How are the two perspectives on kinds of managers—that is, level and area—different from each other?

9. In what way are management skills related to the roles managers play? Provide a specific example to support your answer.
10. Compare and contrast the major styles of leadership.
11. Discuss what happens during each of the four steps of the managerial decision-making process.
12. What are the major benefits of a total quality management program?
13. What personal skills should a manager possess in order to be successful?

Discussion Questions

1. Johnson & Johnson's corporate credo places customers, employees, and the communities in which J&J operates, ahead of stockholders. Do you agree with this concept? Why or why not?
2. As the year 2000 approaches, the health care industry is undergoing dramatic changes. How do you think the management style at Johnson & Johnson helps the company to cope with these changes?
3. Does a healthy firm (one that is doing well) have to worry about effective management? Explain.
4. Which of the management functions, skills, and roles do not apply to the owner-operator of a sole proprietorship?
5. Which leadership style might be best suited to each of the three general levels of management within an organization?
6. According to this chapter, the leadership style that is *most* effective depends on the interaction among the employees, the characteristics of the work situation, and the manager's personality. Do you agree or disagree? Explain your answer.
7. Do you think people are really as important to an organization as this chapter seems to indicate?
8. As you learned in this chapter, managers often work long hours at a hectic pace. Would this type of career appeal to you? Explain your answer.

Exercises

✎ **1.** You are the owner and only employee of a firm that you started this morning. Your firm is to produce and sell hand-sewn, canvas work pants to clothing stores. (You, of course, are an expert tailor.)

   a. Write out your firm's mission and at least four of its objectives.
   b. Write out your firm's sales strategy and a tactical plan that follows from the sales strategy. Make sure the strategy is in keeping with your objectives.

c. Write out one operational plan designed to implement the tactical plan described above.

2. Rate yourself on each of the three key management skills and on your proven ability to perform each of the four management functions. (Use a scale of 1 to 5, with 5 being the highest.) Based on your ratings, explain why you would or would not hire yourself for a first-line management position.

VIDEO CASE 6.1

Fluor Corporation: Building a Better Tomorrow

Thinking of adding a family room to your home? Why not call Fluor? Well, not exactly! You see Fluor Daniel Corporation is the largest construction and engineering firm in the world. But even though Fluor's annual sales revenues are $7.9 billion a year, you probably have never even heard of this company. That's because Fluor concentrates on building oil refineries, power plants, and manufacturing facilities for the auto, pharmaceutical, and food industries all over the globe. In addition to construction and engineering, the California-based corporation also helps both businesses and governments improve the environment with state-of-the-art pollution cleanup.

Today's Fluor Daniel Corporation is a combination of two companies started years ago. The original Fluor Corporation was started in 1912 by Si Fluor, a Swiss immigrant carpenter. Daniel International began in 1934 when Charlie Daniel quit his lumber company job and started a contracting firm. The two merged in 1977. Until the mid-1980s, the corporation was primarily involved in projects for petroleum clients, and business was good. But management realized the impact that a drop in oil prices could have on major construction projects. When oil prices did drop in the 1980s, many of the industrial contracts that had become Fluor Daniel's bread and butter were canceled.

Management began to look for ways to cut expenses and to diversify into other construction areas. These cost-cutting measures highlighted the need for a "road map" that would show everybody—both managers and employees—where the company was going. Management also realized that before any organization can really accomplish its objectives, it must define itself. To this end, executives at Fluor Daniel asked three tough questions: (1) What services does Fluor Daniel provide to clients? (2) Where is Fluor Daniel going? and (3) How is Fluor Daniel going to get there?

Answers to those questions resulted in the current Fluor Daniel mission statement—the company's road map. The mission statement is only four lines long, and yet it provides the direction that a global corporation with almost 40,000 employees needs to stay on track.

> As Fluor Daniel employees our mission is to assist clients in attaining a competitive advantage by delivering quality services of unmatched value.

The people at Fluor Daniel believe that the current mission statement is a living document built on ethical conduct, mutual trust, and teamwork. It is also client-focused and stresses the importance of innovation, flexibility, quality, and safety. Although management is quick to point out that there is more to managing a company than just developing a mission statement, it's a good place to start. And more important, Fluor Daniel is counting on this mission statement to guide the company well into the twenty-first century.[9]

Questions

1. Why does Fluor Daniel Corporation—a company with almost 40,000 employees who already know how to perform their jobs—need a mission statement?
2. Describe in your own words the important components of Fluor Daniel's mission statement.
3. Today, Fluor Daniel managers see the world as a global village that is rapidly and constantly changing. In what ways can their current mission statement help their company not only remain competitive but also increase sales and profits?

CASE 6.2

Rubbermaid: America's Most Admired Company

Every year since 1985, Rubbermaid Incorporated has landed in the top ten of *Fortune* magazine's list of most admired corporations in America. Finally, in 1993, the firm became Number 1. According to management experts, Rubbermaid's success is no accident but is built on basic, fundamental management principles that still work in today's competitive business environment.

For starters, a commitment to making quality products is one reason why Rubbermaid is so successful. Improving over 5,000 everyday products—mops, storage boxes, toys, desk organizers, and so on—that most people take for granted may not seem important, but to Rubbermaid's 11,000 employees this commitment is the "stuff that dreams are made of." Two examples illustrate Rubbermaid's level of commitment to details.

According to one story, Rubbermaid's CEO was walking along a New York street one day when he heard a doorman grumbling as he tried to sweep dirt into a Rubbermaid dustpan. He asked the man what was wrong, and the answer persuaded the executive that the lip where the dustpan meets the floor was too thick to catch the dirt. Not long after that, shoppers were buying redesigned Rubbermaid dustpans in stores all over the United States.

Another example further illustrates Rubbermaid's commitment to doing things right. Several times a week, Rubbermaid's employees visit stores that sell the company's products. If they find a lid that doesn't fit or even a wrinkled label, they buy the entire stock, bring it back to headquarters in Wooster, Ohio, and call a meeting to deal with the problem. This hands-on management style makes Rubbermaid's priorities clear to everyone at the company. In fact, all Rubbermaid employees—not just top management—are encouraged to make suggestions or propose changes that will improve the company's products.

In addition to paying attention to the details that make existing products better, Rubbermaid's management is also committed to developing new products. The firm has had phenomenal success with its research and development activities. Because the firm introduces more than 365 new products each year—about one a day—no competitor can match Rubbermaid's record for new product development. To speed new product development, Rubbermaid has established twenty special project teams that are charged with changing concepts and ideas into marketable products. Each team made up of five to seven people (one each from marketing, manufacturing, research and development, finance, and other departments) focuses on developing new products for specific product lines like kitchen gadgets, bathroom accessories, or office products.

One team came up with an idea for a portable "office space": a plastic organizer that holds pens, files, and other materials; supplies a writing surface; and attaches to a car seat. Going into the field together, team members asked customers what features they would like and what price they would be willing to pay. And they must have come up with the right answers because when the new product hit the market, sales quickly doubled original projections.

Another product team created the Sidekick, Rubbermaid's ecological answer to the school lunchbox. Children don't need to throw away paper sacks, cardboard juice boxes, or plastic sandwich bags, because the Sidekick has reusable containers for everything.

Rubbermaid credits top-level management for the company's reputation for quality and excellent customer service. It credits team management for the speedy launch of products. Because management strategies avoid bureaucratic red tape, Rubbermaid is able to develop and market most new products in less than one year. When Rubbermaid puts these two management strategies together, they spell success. Since 1980, company sales have quadrupled, and earnings have increased for thirty-nine consecutive quarters. Perhaps more important, Rubbermaid's dividend payments to stockholders have increased every year for the last thirty-nine years. With this blend of stellar financial performance, a commitment to quality, and an excellent research and development program, it is no wonder that Rubbermaid is the most admired corporation in America.[10]

Questions

1. In Chapter 1, we pointed out that a successful business must produce products or services that meet the needs of society. In what ways does Rubbermaid fulfill the needs of society?
2. What type of leadership style does the top management at Rubbermaid use?
3. Based on the information in this case, how does the total quality management concept operate at Rubbermaid? Explain your answer.

■■■■■ CHAPTER 7

Creating the Organization

LEARNING OBJECTIVES

After studying this chapter you should be able to

1 Identify five characteristics common to all organizations.

2 Explain why job specialization is important.

3 Identify the various bases for departmentalization.

4 Explain how decentralization follows from delegation.

5 Understand how the span of management describes an organization.

6 Distinguish between line and staff management.

7 Describe the three basic forms of organizational structure: bureaucratic, organic, and matrix.

8 Summarize how corporate culture, intrapreneurship, committees, coordination techniques, informal groups, and the grapevine affect an organization.

CHAPTER PREVIEW

We begin this chapter by examining the business organization—what it is and how it functions in today's business environment. Next we focus one by one on five characteristics that shape an organization's structure. We discuss job specialization within a company; the grouping of jobs into manageable units or departments; the delegation of power from management to workers; the span of management; and the differences between line and staff management. Then we step back for an overall view of three approaches to organizational structure—the bureaucratic structure, the organic structure, and the matrix structure. Finally we look at the network of social interactions—the informal organization—that operates within the formal business structure.

General Motors Corporation

Until the late 1970s, General Motors not once suffered a financial setback, even during the Great Depression years. Decentralized divisions for Cadillac, Buick, Oldsmobile, Pontiac, and Chevrolet were responsible for their own operations. Each division focused on an income segment of consumers. The highest-priced model car in each division would be roughly equivalent in value to the lowest-priced model car in the next division, so when consumers were ready to trade, they usually upgraded to the next division. Over the years, GM continued to grow by acquiring other companies and making them successful by means of the same decentralized management systems that worked for the parent organization.

But in time American consumers began to change their buying habits, and by the late 1970s, they were becoming more interested in purchasing products that fit their lifestyles, rather than on what fit their pocketbooks. GM began to widen (and overlap) the price range in each division's cars. They automated their assembly lines, losing $30 million in the process. And they failed to recognize and capitalize on the emerging market that was exploding in the United States for light trucks and minivans.

By the 1980s, GM's primary business—the production and sale of passenger cars—was in deep trouble. Even though the firm was drifting into a financial crisis, it acquired Ross Perot's Electronic Data Systems and Hughes Electronics. The business world was skeptical, but surprisingly, under GM's decentralized management practices, both companies became very successful. Something, however, was definitely wrong: the system was working in the newly acquired acquisitions, but it was no longer working for the GM-established organization. Increasing numbers of American consumers were buying foreign cars;

"Made in the U.S.A." carried no weight. Unable to overcome the competition, GM closed several plants and laid off thousands of workers. In 1990 GM wrote off $2.1 billion to cover plant shutdowns. And between 1990 and 1992, GM lost nearly $30 billion.

Then, in April 1992, John F. Smith, Jr., stepped to the helm as the CEO and president, just as the U.S. automobile market was beginning to rebound. Since taking charge, Smith has concentrated primarily on reorganizing the North American Operations of General Motors, which was losing $500 million a month in 1992. Even though the organization had struggled with financial difficulties for years, executives still used the "old formula for success." Smith changed that by centralizing management and merging GM's divisions so that production, design, and purchasing are under one umbrella. Now, each level of the organization, from engineering to finance, is following the same strategies and operations set out by management to achieve one common ultimate goal—creating cars that consumers will buy.[1]

■ ■ ■ ■

■　　■　　■　　■　　■　　■　　■　　■　　■　　■　　■

ven General Motors, the world's largest industrial organization, must constantly look for ways to improve its method of doing business. And General Motors, like many other companies, is deliberately organized in a way that helps it both to achieve its goals and objectives, and to create products that consumers will buy.

When firms like General Motors are organized, the focus is sometimes on achieving low operating costs. In other cases, the emphasis is on providing high-quality products to ensure customer satisfaction. The way that a firm is organized influences its performance. Thus, the issue of organization is important.

■■ WHAT IS AN ORGANIZATION?

We used the term *organization* throughout Chapter 6 without really defining it, mainly because its everyday meaning is close to its business meaning. Here, however, let us agree that an **organization** is a group of two or more people working together to achieve a common set of goals. A neighborhood dry cleaner owned and operated by a husband-and-wife team is an organization. IBM, Rubbermaid, and The Home Depot, which employ hundreds of thousands of workers worldwide, are also organizations in the very same sense. Although each corporation's organizational structure is vastly more complex than that of the dry-cleaning establishment, each must be organized if it is to achieve its goals.

An inventor who goes into business to produce and market a new invention hires people, decides what each will do, determines who will report to whom, and so on. These activities are the essence of organizing, or creating, the organization. One way to create a "picture" of an organization is to create an organization chart.

organization a group of two or more people working together to achieve a common set of goals

Developing Organization Charts

organization chart a diagram that represents the positions and relationships within an organization

An **organization chart** is a diagram that represents the positions and relationships within an organization. An example of an organization chart is shown in Figure 7.1. What does it tell us?

Each rectangle in the chart represents a particular position or person in the organization. At the top of the chart is the president; at the next level are the vice presidents. The solid vertical lines connecting the vice presidents to the president indicate that the vice presidents are in the chain of command. The **chain of command** is the line of authority that extends from the highest to the lowest levels of the organization. Moreover, each vice president reports directly to the president. Similarly, the plant managers, regional sales managers, and accounting department manager report directly to the vice presidents.

chain of command the line of authority that extends from the highest to the lowest levels of an organization

201

Key

—————— Chain of command

— — — Staff

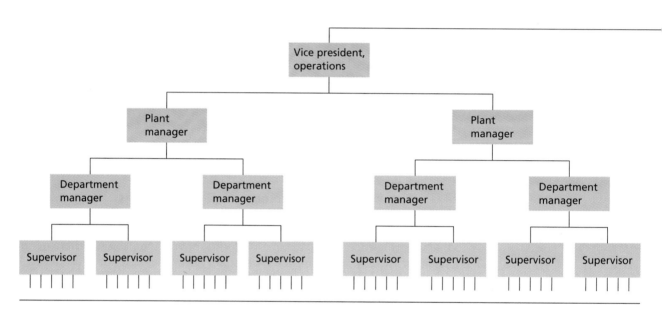

FIGURE 7.1   A Typical Corporate Organization Chart
A company's organization chart represents the positions and relationships within an organization and shows the managerial chains of command.

Top U.S. Corporations

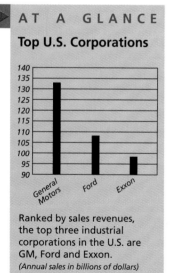

Ranked by sales revenues, the top three industrial corporations in the U.S. are GM, Ford and Exxon.
(Annual sales in billions of dollars)

Source: Fortune, Apr. 18, 1994, p. 220.

Notice that the connections to the directors of legal services, public affairs, and human resources are shown as broken lines; these people are not part of the direct chain of command. Instead, they hold *advisory*, or *staff*, positions. This difference will be made clear later in the chapter, when we discuss line and staff positions.

Most smaller organizations find organization charts useful. They clarify positions and reporting relationships for everyone in the organization, and they help managers track growth and change in the organizational structure. For two reasons, however, many large organizations, such as Exxon, Kellogg, and Procter & Gamble, do not maintain complete, detailed charts. It is difficult to chart accurately even a few dozen positions, much less the thousands that characterize larger firms. And larger organizations are almost always changing one part of their structure or another. An organization chart would probably be outdated before it was completed. Regardless of whether a firm has an organization chart, most employees want to move up the corporate ladder. For suggestions on how to begin the climb, see Enhancing Career Skills.

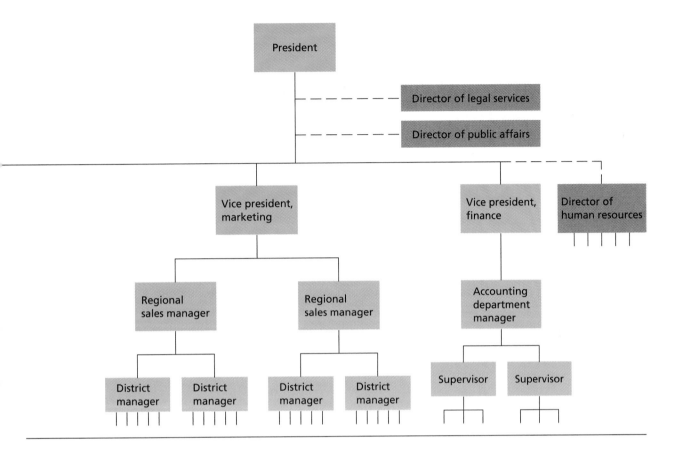

▰▰ FIVE CHARACTERISTICS COMMON TO ALL ORGANIZATIONS

LEARNING OBJECTIVE 1
Identify five characteristics common to all organizations.

When a firm is started, management must decide how to organize the firm. These decisions are all part of five major steps that sum up the organizing process. The five steps are as follows:

1. Divide the work that is to be done by the entire organization into separate parts, and assign those parts to positions within the organization. This step is often called *job design*.
2. Group the various positions into manageable units, or departments. This step is called *departmentalization*.
3. Distribute responsibility and authority within the organization. This step is called *delegation*.
4. Determine the number of subordinates who will report to each manager. This step creates the firm's *span of management*.
5. Distinguish between those positions with direct authority and those that are support positions. This establishes the organization's *chain of command*.

In the next several sections, we describe each of these characteristics and show how they affect today's organizations.

■■ JOB DESIGN

In Chapter 1 we defined *specialization* as the separation of a manufacturing process into distinct tasks and the assignment of different tasks to different people. Here we are extending that concept to *all* the activities that are performed within the organization.

Job Specialization

job specialization the separation of all organizational activities into distinct tasks and the assignment of different tasks to different people

Job specialization is the separation of all organizational activities into distinct tasks and the assignment of different tasks to different people. As we noted in Chapter 1, Adam Smith was the first to emphasize the power of specialization in his book *The Wealth of Nations*. According to Smith, the various tasks in a particular pin factory were arranged so that one worker drew the wire for the pins, another straightened the wire, a third cut it, a fourth ground the point, and a fifth attached the head. Using this method, Smith claimed, ten men were able to produce 48,000 pins per day. Before specialization, they could produce only 200 pins per day because each worker had to perform all five tasks!

The Rationale for Specialization

For a number of reasons, some job specialization is necessary in every organization. First and foremost is the simple fact that the "job" of most

A job is a job is a job. When manufacturing some products like pianos, the job is just too large for one employee. But when job specialization is used, the entire process is broken down into separate distinct tasks. Each task that must be performed—like inserting keys into the piano's keyboard—can be assigned to a different employee.

ENHANCING CAREER SKILLS

Moving Up the Corporate Ladder

Today's employees face many more challenges than previous generations when it comes to climbing the corporate ladder. Once, company loyalty and the ability to take on increasing job responsibilities usually assured advancement within an organization. The reasons for wanting to advance, such as the desire for a better-paying position, for more prestige, and for job satisfaction, haven't changed. But in today's business environment, rather than just relying on being recognized as loyal and competent by one's supervisors in order to move up, a person has to know how to package and market his or her abilities to those in authority.

BUILD YOUR OWN LADDER

1. Constantly improve your skills by taking advantage of everything you can learn on the job, by enrolling in continuing education classes, and by staying informed of technology changes in the workplace. Many skills are transferrable from one career field to another.

2. Familiarize yourself fully with the organization that employs you. Get to know as many people as you can. These relationships may provide information about new job opportunities within the firm.

3. Keep a list of all your business and personal accomplishments and achievements. Set goals for self-improvement and review them periodically. This exercise reinforces your self-confidence.

4. Widen your circle of professional and personal acquaintances. Show interest in everyone you meet by asking questions, opening up opportunities to learn of changes in the business climate and allowing other people to know you and your opinions.

5. Compile a portfolio of reference letters from customers and clients with whom you have developed working relationships. Add anything you receive in the way of praise and commendation from your current boss or other managers.

6. Recognize when it is time to move on. A company that hires from the outside with no promotions from within, an employer who takes you for granted, and your gradual dissatisfaction with your job are typical early warning signs.

NETWORKING

Quietly look for every opportunity to advance yourself; regard everyone you come in contact with as a member of your network base. Volunteer for community projects, join a local political organization, and interact with people from varying business fields. Do not hesitate to ask for business cards from everyone you meet. The people you meet and help along the way can become resources to draw on to open doors throughout the stages of your career.

organizations is simply too large for one person to handle. In a firm like Chrysler Corporation, hundreds or even thousands of people may be needed to manufacture automobiles. Others will be needed to sell the cars, to control the firm's finances, and so on.

Second, when a worker has to learn only a specific, highly specialized task, that individual should be able to learn to do it very efficiently. Third,

Teamwork: An alternative to job specialization. One of the drawbacks to job specialization is that employees often feel bored, dissatisfied, and alone. By using job rotation, job enlargement, or job enrichment, employees often feel they are part of a team and become more productive. Here one employee trains another employee to do a new and "bigger" job—computerized wheel alignment.

the worker who is doing the same job over and over does not lose time changing from one operation to another, as the pin workers probably did when each was producing a complete pin. Fourth, the more specialized the job, the easier it may be to design specialized equipment for those who do it. And finally, the more specialized the job, the easier it is to train new employees when an employee quits or is absent from work.

Alternatives to Job Specialization

Unfortunately, specialization can have some negative consequences as well. The most significant drawback is the boredom and dissatisfaction many employees feel when they do the same job over and over. Monotony can be deadening. Bored employees may be absent from work frequently, may not put much effort into their work, and may even sabotage the company's efforts to produce quality products.

job rotation the systematic shifting of employees from one job to another

To combat these problems, managers often turn to job rotation, job enlargement, or job enrichment. **Job rotation** is the systematic shifting of employees from one job to another. For example, a worker may be assigned to a different job every week for a four-week period and then return to the first job in the fifth week. The idea behind job rotation is to provide a variety of tasks so that workers are less likely to get bored and dissatisfied. Companies that use job rotation include Ford, Xerox, Prudential Insurance Company, and the U.S. Nissan subsidiary. Two other approaches—job enlargement and job enrichment—can also provide solutions to the problems caused by job specialization. These topics, along with other methods used to motivate employees, are discussed in Chapter 9.

■■ DEPARTMENTALIZATION

After jobs are designed, they must be grouped together into "working units," or departments. This process is called departmentalization. More specifically, **departmentalization** is the process of grouping jobs into manageable units. Several departmentalization bases are commonly used. In fact, most firms use more than one.

departmentalization the process of grouping jobs into manageable units.

Departmentalization Bases

LEARNING OBJECTIVE 3
Identify the various bases for departmentalization.

Today, the most common bases for organizing a business into effective departments are by function, by product, by location, and by type of customer.

departmentalization by function grouping jobs that relate to the same organizational activity

By Function   **Departmentalization by function** groups jobs that relate to the same organizational activity. Under this scheme, all marketing personnel are grouped together in the marketing department, all production personnel in the production department, and so on.

Most smaller and newer organizations base their departmentalization on function. Supervision is simplified because everyone is involved in the same kinds of activities, and coordination is fairly easy. The disadvantages of this method of grouping jobs are that it can lead to slow decision making and that it tends to emphasize the department rather than the organization as a whole.

departmentalization by product grouping activities related to a particular product or service

By Product   **Departmentalization by product** groups activities related to a particular product or service. This scheme is often used by older and larger firms that produce and sell a variety of products. Each department handles its own marketing, production, financial management, and human resources activities.

Departmentalization by product or service makes decision making easier and provides for the integration of all activities associated with each product or service. However, it causes some duplication of specialized activities—such as finance—from department to department. And the emphasis is placed on the product rather than on the whole organization.

Digital Equipment Corporation, one of the largest computer manufacturers in the world, was originally organized around eighteen separate product groups. Each group competed with the others and became protective rather than cooperative. Instead of working for the common goals of the company, members of each product group worked for the good of that group. As a result, Digital's efficiency and profits suffered *and* the company changed its organization structure.

departmentalization by location grouping activities according to the defined geographic area in which they are performed

By Location   **Departmentalization by location** groups activities according to the defined geographic area in which they are performed. Departmental areas may range from whole countries (for international firms) to regions within countries (for national firms) to areas of several city blocks (for police departments organized into precincts). Departmentalization by location allows the organization to respond readily to the unique demands or requirements of different locations. Nevertheless, a large administrative staff and an elaborate control system may be needed to coordinate operations in many locations.

One of the ways that the president of Digital Equipment solved its problem of counterproductive product groups was to combine the twelve U.S. product groups into three regional management centers. This helped to clear up communication problems among different departments and consolidated much of the administrative paperwork that had been slowing down important decisions.

By Customer **Departmentalization by customer** groups activities according to the needs of various customer populations. A local Chevrolet dealership, for example, may have one sales staff to deal with individual consumers and a different sales staff to work with corporate fleet buyers. The obvious advantage of this approach is that it allows the firm to deal efficiently with unique customers or customer groups. The biggest drawback is that a larger-than-usual administrative staff is needed.

Another part of Digital Equipment's reorganization was the assigning of the sales force to specific customers rather than to specific markets. Before the reorganization, as many as six salespeople, each from a different product group, could call on one large customer. The situation was confusing and frustrating for customers, and not very profitable for Digital.

Combinations of Bases Many organizations use more than one of these departmentalization bases. For example, General Motors has realigned its divisions on the bases of products into small-vehicle and large-vehicle groups. Each GM division, in turn, is departmentalized by function; Pontiac, for example, has its own marketing, finance, and personnel groups. Production groups might be further departmentalized by plant location.

departmentalization by customer grouping activities according to the needs of various customer populations

---

FIGURE 7.2
Multibase Departmentalization for New-Wave Fashions, Inc.
Most firms use more than one basis for departmentalization to improve efficiency and to avoid overlapping positions.

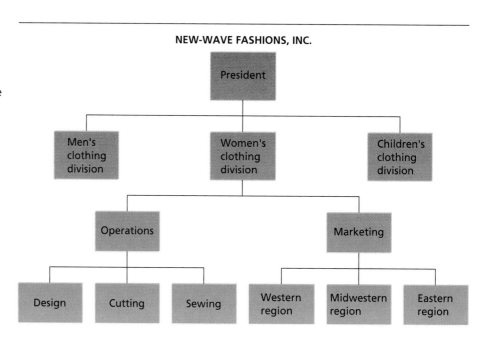

NEW-WAVE FASHIONS, INC.

Similarly, a divisional marketing group might be divided in such a way that one unit handles consumer sales and another handles fleet and corporate sales.

Take a moment to examine Figure 7.2. Notice that departmentalization by customer is used to organize New-Wave Fashions, Inc., into three major divisions: men's clothing, women's clothing, and children's clothing. Then functional departmentalization is used to distinguish the firm's production and marketing activities. Finally, location is used to organize the firm's marketing efforts.

■■ DELEGATION, DECENTRALIZATION, AND CENTRALIZATION

LEARNING OBJECTIVE 4
Explain how decentralization follows from delegation.

delegation assigning part of a manager's work and power to other workers

The third major step in the organizing process is to distribute power in the organization. **Delegation** assigns part of a manager's work and power to other workers. The degree of centralization or decentralization of authority is determined by the overall pattern of delegation within the organization.

Delegation of Authority

Because no manager can do everything, delegation is vital to the completion of a manager's work. Delegation is also important in developing the skills and abilities of subordinates. It allows those who are being groomed for higher-level positions to play increasingly important roles in decision making.

responsibility the duty to do a job or perform a task

authority the power, within the organization, to accomplish an assigned job or task

Steps in Delegation The delegation process generally involves three steps (see Figure 7.3). First, the manager must *assign responsibility*. **Responsibility** is the duty to do a job or perform a task. In most job settings, a manager simply gives the worker a job to do. For example, typical job assignments might range from asking a worker to prepare a report on the status of a new quality-control program to placing the person in charge of a special task force. Second, the manager must *grant authority*. **Authority** is the power, within the organization, to accomplish an assigned job or task. This might include the power to obtain specific information, order supplies, authorize

FIGURE 7.3
Steps in the Delegation Process
To be successful, a good manager must learn how to delegate. No one can do everything alone.

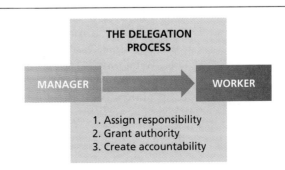

THE DELEGATION PROCESS

MANAGER → WORKER

1. Assign responsibility
2. Grant authority
3. Create accountability

accountability   the obligation of a worker to accomplish an assigned job or task

relevant expenditures, and make certain decisions. Finally, the manager must *create accountability*. **Accountability** is the obligation of a worker to accomplish an assigned job or task.

Note that accountability is created but that it cannot be delegated away. Suppose you are an operations manager for Delta Air Lines and are responsible for performing some job. You, in turn, delegate part of the task to a worker. You nonetheless remain accountable to your immediate supervisor for getting the job done properly. If the worker fails to complete the assignment, you—not the worker—will be called on to account for what has become *your* failure.

Barriers to Delegation   For several reasons, managers may be unwilling to delegate work. One reason was just stated—the person who delegates remains accountable for the work. Many managers are reluctant to delegate simply because they want to be sure the work gets done properly. Another reason for reluctance to delegate stems from the opposite situation. The manager fears the worker will do the work so well that he or she will attract the approving notice of higher-level managers and will therefore become a threat to the manager. Finally, some managers don't delegate because they are so disorganized they simply are not able to plan and assign work effectively.

Decentralization of Authority

decentralized organization   an organization in which management consciously attempts to spread authority widely in the lower levels of the organization

centralized organization   an organization that systematically works to concentrate authority at the upper levels of the organization

The general pattern of delegation throughout an organization determines the extent to which that organization is decentralized or centralized. In a **decentralized organization,** management consciously attempts to spread authority widely in the lower organization levels. A **centralized organization** systematically works to concentrate authority at the upper levels.

A variety of factors can influence the extent to which a firm is decentralized. One is the external environment in which the firm operates. The more complex and unpredictable this environment is, the more likely it is that top management will let lower-level managers make important decisions. After all, lower-level managers are closer to the problems. Another factor is the nature of the decision itself. The riskier or the more important the decision, the greater the tendency to centralize decision making. A third factor is the abilities of lower-level managers. If these managers do not have strong decision-making skills, top managers will be reluctant to decentralize. And, in contrast, strong lower-level decision-making skills encourage decentralization. Finally, a firm that has traditionally practiced centralization is likely to maintain that centralization in the future, and vice versa.

In principle, neither decentralization nor centralization is right or wrong. What works for one organization may or may not work for another. Kmart Corporation and McDonald's have both been very successful—and both practice centralization. By the same token, decentralization has worked very well for General Electric and Sears. Every organization must assess its own situation and then choose the level of centralization or decentralization that it feels will work best in that situation.

■■ THE SPAN OF MANAGEMENT

span of management (or span of control)   the number of workers who report directly to one manager

The fourth major characteristic of organizational structure, the **span of management** (or **span of control**) is the number of workers who report directly to one manager. For hundreds of years, theorists have searched for an ideal span of management. When it became apparent that there is no perfect number of subordinates for a manager to supervise, they turned their attention to the more general issue of whether the span should be wide or narrow. This issue is further complicated by the fact that the span of management may change from one department to another department within the same organization. For example, the span of management at Federal Express varies within the company. Departments in which workers do the same tasks on a regular basis—such as customer service agents, handlers and sorters, and couriers—usually have a span of management of fifteen to twenty employees per manager. Groups performing multiple and different tasks are more likely to have smaller spans of management consisting of five or six employees.[2] Thus, Federal Express uses a wide span of control in some departments and a narrow span of control in others.

Wide and Narrow Spans of Control

LEARNING OBJECTIVE 5
Understand how the span of management describes an organization.

A *wide* span of management exists when a manager has a large number of subordinates. A *narrow* span exists when the manager has only a few subordinates. Several factors determine the span that is better for a particular manager (see Figure 7.4). Generally, the span of control may be wide (1) when the manager and the subordinates are very competent, (2) when the organization has a well-established set of standard operating procedures, and (3) when few new problems are expected to arise. The span

FIGURE 7.4
The Span of Management
Several criteria determine whether a firm uses a wide span of management, in which several workers report to one manager, or a narrow span, in which a manager supervises only a few workers.

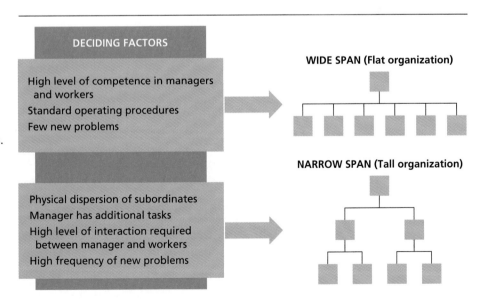

DECIDING FACTORS

High level of competence in managers and workers
Standard operating procedures
Few new problems

WIDE SPAN (Flat organization)

Physical dispersion of subordinates
Manager has additional tasks
High level of interaction required between manager and workers
High frequency of new problems

NARROW SPAN (Tall organization)

should be narrow (1) when workers are physically located far from one another, (2) when the manager has much work to do in addition to supervising workers, (3) when a great deal of interaction is required between supervisor and workers, and (4) when new problems arise frequently.

Another factor that influences an organization's span of control is corporate downsizing—a topic described in Change in the Workplace.

Organizational Height

organizational height   the number of layers, or levels, of management in a firm

The span of management has an obvious impact on relations between managers and workers. It has a more subtle but equally important impact on the height of the organization. **Organizational height** is the number of layers, or levels, of management in a firm. The span of management plays a direct role in determining the height of the organization, as shown in Figure 7.4. If spans of management are wider, fewer levels are needed and the organization is *flat*. If spans of management are generally narrow, more levels are needed and the resulting organization is *tall*.

In a taller organization, administrative costs are higher because more managers are needed. And communication among levels may become distorted because information has to pass up and down through more people. Although flat organizations avoid those problems, their managers may have to perform more administrative duties simply because there are fewer managers. Wide spans of management may also require managers to spend considerably more time supervising and working with subordinates.

■■ LINE AND STAFF MANAGEMENT

line management position   a position that is part of the chain of command and that includes direct responsibility for achieving the goals of the organization

staff management position   a position created to provide support, advice, and expertise within an organization

The last major characteristic that affects organizational structure is the chain of command that reaches from the highest to the lowest levels of management. A **line management position** is part of the chain of command; it is a position in which a person makes decisions and gives orders to subordinates to achieve the goals of the organization. A **staff management position,** by contrast, is a position created to provide support, advice, and expertise to someone in the chain of command. Staff positions are not part of the chain of command but do have authority over their assistants. Staff personnel are not specifically accountable for accomplishing the goals of the firm. A marketing executive for Carnival Cruise Lines is a line manager because marketing is directly related to accomplishing the firm's mission and objectives. A legal adviser at Carnival, however, doesn't actively engage in profit-making activities but rather provides legal support to those who do. Hence the legal adviser occupies a staff position (see Figure 7.5).

Line and Staff Positions Compared

LEARNING OBJECTIVE 6
Distinguish between line and staff management.

Both line and staff managers are needed for effective management, but the two kinds of positions differ in important ways. The basic difference is in terms of authority. Line managers have *line authority*, which means that they can make decisions and issue directives that relate to the organization's goals.

■ ■ ■ ■   CHANGE IN THE WORKPLACE

Why Corporations Downsize

According to the *American Heritage Dictionary,* the term *downsize* means "to make in a smaller size." That is exactly what has happened in some of the largest and most successful U.S. corporations over the last ten years. AT&T, for example, has eliminated 140,000 jobs since 1984. IBM has reduced its work force by over 100,000 employees in just the past four years. And according to a recent American Management Association study, almost 50 percent of companies surveyed are reporting work force reductions. The size of those reductions averages between 9 and 10 percent of each employer's total work force.

Downsizing is almost always described—optimistically—as an opportunity for the corporation to get "lean and mean." It is also referred to as a method of positioning the firm for long-term success. Most employees who have been victims of downsizing know the real reason: to reduce labor costs. When labor costs are reduced, the corporation is more profitable. According to the American Management Association's study, over 50 percent of the corporations that downsized their work force "upsized" their operating profit.

HOW DOWNSIZING AFFECTS REMAINING EMPLOYEES

Because a downsized corporation has a smaller work force, each retained employee must perform more tasks and usually work longer hours. Both employees and managers often complain of more severe emotional stress and more frequent worker burnout. And morale for remaining employees is often low as fatigue and resentment set in. For managers, one of the most difficult parts of downsizing is firing employees. For employees, it's the nagging worry over whether they will survive the next round of layoffs and terminations.

HOW YOU CAN AVOID BEING A VICTIM OF DOWNSIZING

Although many corporations are downsizing, opportunities still abound for valued employees. To keep from becoming a victim of the downsizing spiral, take a few definite steps to increase your value to the organization. For starters,

1. *Work above and beyond the call of duty.* Because there are fewer employees, your employer may ask or expect you to put in longer hours in order to get the job done. You may want to "volunteer" to stay late or work on Saturdays in order to complete important tasks.

2. *Practice time-management skills.* Because more work must be completed by fewer employees, every minute is important. Learn to make lists, prioritize jobs, and finish important projects on time.

3. *Help your boss.* Too often, employees forget that their supervisor is also feeling more outer pressure and inner stress. Talk with your boss to discover tasks you can work on that will help reduce the pressure on both of you. Above all, try to be a problem solver—and not a problem.

Staff managers seldom have this kind of authority. Instead, they usually have either advisory authority or functional authority. *Advisory authority* is simply the expectation that line managers will consult the appropriate staff manager when making decisions. Functional authority is stronger, and in some ways it is like line authority. *Functional authority* is the authority of

FIGURE 7.5
Line and Staff Management
A line manager has direct responsibility for achieving the company's goals and is in the direct chain of command. A staff manager supports and advises the line managers.

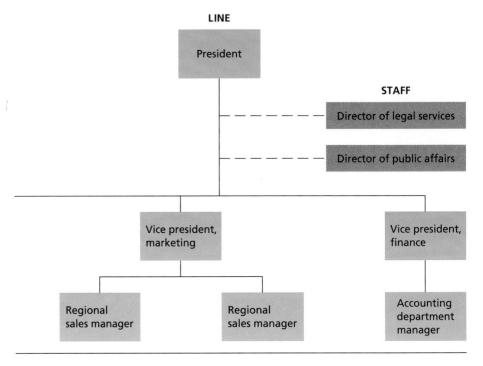

staff managers to make decisions and issue directives, but only about their own areas of expertise. For example, a legal adviser for Minnesota Mining and Manufacturing can decide whether to retain a particular clause in a contract, but not what price to charge for a new product. Contracts are part of the legal adviser's area of expertise; pricing is not.

Line-Staff Conflict

For a variety of reasons, conflict between line managers and staff managers is fairly common in business. Staff managers often have more formal education and are sometimes younger (and perhaps more ambitious) than line managers. Line managers may perceive staff managers as a threat to their own authority and thus may resent them. For their part, staff managers may become annoyed or angry if their expert recommendations—in public relations or human resources management, for example—are not adopted by line management.

Fortunately, there are several ways to minimize the likelihood of such conflict. One way is to integrate line and staff managers into one team working together. Another is to ensure that the areas of responsibility of line and staff managers are clearly defined. Finally, line and staff managers can both be held accountable for the results of their activities.

Before studying the next topic—Forms of Organizational Structure—you may want to review the five organization-shaping characteristics that have been presented in the first part of this chapter. See Table 7.1 for a summary.

TABLE 7.1   Five Characteristics of Organizational Structure

Dimension	Purpose
Job design	To divide the work performed by an organization into parts and assign each part a position within the organization.
Departmentalization	To group various positions in an organization into manageable units. Departmentalization may be based on function, product, location, customer, or a combination of these bases.
Delegation	To distribute part of a manager's work and power to other workers. A deliberate concentration of authority at the upper levels of the organization creates a centralized structure. A wide distribution of authority into the lower levels of the organization creates a decentralized structure.
Span of management	To set the number of workers who report directly to one manager. A narrow span has only a few workers reporting to one manager. A wide span has a large number of workers reporting to one manager.
Line and staff management	To distinguish between those positions that are part of the chain of command and those that provide support, advice, or expertise to those in the chain of command.

■■ FORMS OF ORGANIZATIONAL STRUCTURE

LEARNING OBJECTIVE 7
Describe the three basic forms of organizational structure: bureaucratic, organic, and matrix.

Up to this point, we have focused our attention on the major characteristics of organizational structure. In many ways, this is like discussing the important parts of a jigsaw puzzle one by one. Now it is time to put the puzzle together. In particular, we discuss three basic forms of organizational structure: bureaucratic, organic, and matrix.

The Bureaucratic Structure

The term *bureaucracy* is often used in an unfavorable context, and it tends to suggest rigidity and red tape. This image may be a negative one, but it does somewhat capture the nature of the bureaucratic structure.

bureaucratic structure a management system based on a formal framework of authority that is carefully outlined and precisely followed

A **bureaucratic structure** is a management system based on a formal framework of authority that is carefully outlined and precisely followed. A bureaucracy is likely to have the following characteristics:

1. A high level of job specialization
2. Departmentalization by function
3. Formal patterns of delegation
4. A high degree of centralization
5. Narrow spans of management, resulting in a tall organization
6. Clearly defined line and staff positions, with formal relationships between the two

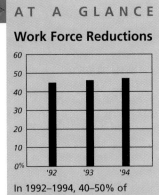

Perhaps the best examples of contemporary bureaucracies are government agencies and colleges and universities. Consider the very rigid and formal college entrance and registration procedures. The reason for such procedures is to ensure that the organization is able to deal with large numbers of people in an equitable and fair manner. We may not enjoy them, but regulations and standard operating procedures pretty much guarantee uniformity.

Another example of a bureaucratic structure is the U.S. Postal Service. Like colleges and universities, the post office relies on procedures and rules to accomplish the organization's goals. However, the postal service has streamlined some of its procedures and initiated new services in order to compete with Federal Express, United Parcel Service, and other delivery systems. As a result, customer satisfaction has begun to improve.

The biggest drawback to the bureaucratic structure is its lack of flexibility. A bureaucracy has trouble adjusting to change and coping with the unexpected. Because today's business environment is dynamic and complex, many firms have found that the bureaucratic structure is not an appropriate organizational structure.

The Organic Structure

organic structure a management system founded on cooperation and knowledge-based authority

An **organic structure** is a management system founded on cooperation and knowledge-based authority. It is much less formal than the bureaucracy and much more flexible. An organic structure tends to have the following structural characteristics:

Not "limited" by the organizational structure. Because The Limited operates in the complex, everchanging retail fashion industry, this nationwide retailer uses an organic structure. While creating an atmosphere of cooperation, this structure allows employees to use knowledge-based authority to make decisions and react quickly to changes.

1. A low level of job specialization
2. Departmentalization by product, location, or customer
3. Informal patterns of delegation
4. A high degree of decentralization
5. Wide spans of management, resulting in a flat organization
6. Less clearly defined line and staff positions, with less formal relationships between the two

The organic structure tends to be more effective when the environment of the firm is complex, dynamic, and changing. This type of organization allows a business firm to monitor the environment and react quickly to changes. Of course, the organic structure requires more cooperation among employees than the bureaucracy does. Employees must be willing and able to work together in an informal atmosphere in which lines of authority may shift according to the situation. Both Motorola and The Limited, Inc., have used the organic structure to manage ongoing change in their respective industries.

The Matrix Structure

The matrix structure is the newest and most complex organizational structure. When the matrix structure is used, individuals report to more than one superior at the same time. The **matrix structure** combines vertical and horizontal lines of authority. The matrix structure occurs when product departmentalization is superimposed on a functionally departmentalized organization. In a matrix organization, authority flows both down and across.

To understand the setup of a matrix organization, first consider the usual functional arrangement, with people working in departments such as marketing and finance. Now suppose we assign people from these departments to a special group that is working on a new project as a team. In reality, most project teams are charged with the responsibility of developing new products. For example, Ford Motor Company assembled a special project team to design and manufacture its new global cars—the Ford Contour and the Mercury Mystique. The manager in charge of the team is usually called a *project manager.* Any individual who is working with the team reports to *both* the project manager and the individual's superior in the functional department (see Figure 7.6).

Many firms have experimented with matrix structures. Notable examples include Texas Instruments, Monsanto, and Ford. Matrix structures offer several advantages over the conventional organizational forms. Added flexibility is probably the most obvious advantage. Motivation also improves because people become more deeply committed to their special projects. In addition, employees experience personal development through doing a variety of jobs. And people communicate more as they become liaisons between their project groups and their functional departments.

The matrix structure also has some disadvantages. Having employees report to more than one supervisor can cause confusion about who is in

matrix structure   an organizational structure that combines vertical and horizontal lines of authority by superimposing product departmentalization on a functionally departmentalized organization

FIGURE 7.6
A Matrix Structure
A matrix is usually the result of combining product departmentalization with function departmentalization. It is a complex structure in which employees have more than one supervisor. *(Source: Ricky W. Griffin,* Management, *4th ed. Copyright © 1993 by Houghton Mifflin Company. Used by permission.)*

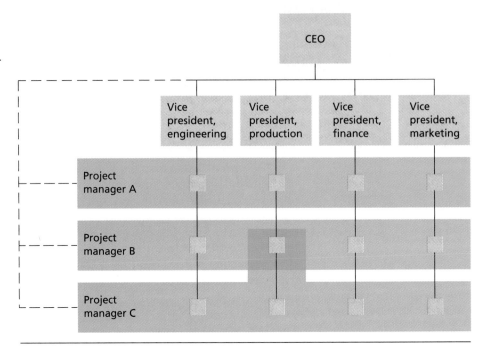

charge in various situations. Like committees, groups may take longer to resolve problems and issues than individuals working alone. And because more managers and support staff may be needed, a matrix structure may be more expensive to maintain than a conventional structure. After years of continued use, Texas Instruments scrapped its complex matrix organization in favor of a more traditional and streamlined organizational structure.

■■ ADDITIONAL FACTORS THAT INFLUENCE AN ORGANIZATION

LEARNING OBJECTIVE 8
Summarize how corporate culture, intrapreneurship, committees, coordination techniques, informal groups, and the grapevine affect an organization.

The Marriott Corporation employs over 195,000 men and women. As you might expect, other factors in addition to the five just covered affect the way a corporation that size operates on a day-to-day basis. In order to get a "true picture" of the organizational structure for Marriott or any other huge organization, you need to consider the topics discussed in the last section of this chapter.

Corporate Culture

corporate culture the inner rites, rituals, heroes, and values of a firm

Managers do not perform their jobs in a vacuum. Most managers function within a corporate culture. A **corporate culture** is generally defined as the inner rites, rituals, heroes, and values of a firm. Rituals that might seem silly to an outsider can have a powerful influence on how the employees of a particular organization think and act. For example, new employees at Honda Motor Co.'s Marysville, Ohio, manufacturing facility are encouraged to plant a small pine tree on the company's property. Symbolically, the growth of each employee's tree represents his or her personal growth and development at Honda.[3]

Terrence Deal (a Harvard University professor) and Allan Kennedy (a management consultant) have identified several key types of cultures.[4] One is the *tough-guy, macho culture,* in which people act as rugged individuals who like to take chances. Another is the *work hard/play hard culture.* Here the emphasis is on fun and action with few risks. Southwest Airlines has this type of culture. A third major form of corporate culture is the *bet-your-company culture.* In this corporate situation, the emphasis is on big-stakes decisions and gambles that may pay off far in the future. Finally, there is the *process culture,* in which the organization functions mechanically, with much "red tape" and little actual exchange of information.

Corporate culture is generally thought to have a very strong influence on a firm's performance over time. Hence it is useful to be able to assess a firm's corporate culture. Common indicators include the physical setting (building, office layouts, and so on); what the company itself says about its corporate culture (in its advertising and news releases, for example); how the company greets its guests (does it have formal or informal reception areas?); and how employees spend their time (working alone in an office most of the time or spending much of the day working with others).

Deal and Kennedy believe that cultural change is needed when the company's environment is changing, when the industry is becoming more competitive, when the company's performance is mediocre, when the company is growing rapidly, or when the company is about to become a truly large corporation. Moreover, they believe organizations of the future will look quite different from those of today. In particular, they predict that tomorrow's business firms will be made up of small task-oriented work groups, each with control over its own activities. These small groups will be coordinated through an elaborate computer network and held together by a strong corporate culture. More information on the "wired" organization is presented in Business Journal.

Intrapreneurship

Since innovations and new product development are important to companies, and entrepreneurs are among the most innovative people around, it seems almost natural that an entrepreneurial character would prominently surface in many of today's larger organizations. An **intrapreneur** is an employee who takes responsibility for pushing an innovative idea, product, or process through the organization.[5] An intrapreneur possesses the confidence and drive of an entrepreneur but is allowed to use organizational resources for idea development.

intrapreneur an employee who pushes an innovative idea, product, or process through the organization

Art Fry, inventor of the colorful Post-it Notes that corporate America can't live without, is a devoted advocate of intrapreneurship. Nurturing his note-pad idea at Minnesota Mining and Manufacturing for years, Fry speaks highly of the intrapreneurial commitment at 3M. On being an intrapreneur, Fry says, "First you need a product champion to get that core vision going. Then, you need the facilities that 3M has and a willingness to pull the concept together."[6] Fry suggests that an intrapreneur is an individual who

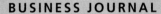

BUSINESS JOURNAL

The Wired Organization

The typical workplace of the 1970s relied on large, clumsy, noisy equipment to help its workers accomplish the goals of the organization. During the day, employees talked primarily with coworkers who were on the same level in the organization. Oh, once in a while they might see the president or vice president of the company in the hallway, but in order to communicate with such top executives, they almost always had to go through the official chain of command. Any company information they received was usually limited to what directly affected their own little niche in the organization. So they most likely kept up with the trends in the business world by scanning newspapers, magazines, and trade journals. If their positions called for them to have any contact with outsiders, it was performed by traveling to another location, sending messages back and forth through the U.S. mail, or spending enormous amounts of time on the telephone.

The workplace of today is far different from the way it was just twenty years ago. Because of technology, the management of organizations is being restructured through the use of computer networks. At the core of this revolution is the personal computer—a hardware and software appliance that connects people and facilitates the flow of information that an organization needs to get the job done. At the touch of a fingertip, this digital form of communication allows employees on a network to be wired to other employees and provides instant access to the latest information about the organization, the competition, or the economy.

Coworkers are now not only the people in the same room; they may be next door, across the country, or even on the other side of the world. With a network, coworkers communicate and exchange ideas through E-mail, voice mail, facsimiles, and teleconferencing. In fact, business transactions are already conducted via worldwide satellite networks and communication devices that circle the globe, reducing travel expense and time away from the office. A company may not even need a large employee parking lot because many workers perform their duties from their homes.

Upper-level managers no longer wait in their "ivory towers" for feedback from middle management but instead point and click their way on-screen to retrieve whatever data they need to plan and budget for the organization. A network provides the means to short-circuit the chain of command (giving all levels of employees access to the top), saves time and money for the organization, and promotes a more open and informal style of managing a company. And electronic bulletin boards and multimedia publications on a network allow members of an organization to stay current with business trends. Using customized intelligent software, users can even filter out extraneous information, so their time is spent more efficiently.

---

doesn't have all the skills to get the job done and, thus, has to work within an organization, making use of its skills and attributes.

Committees

ad hoc committee a committee created for a specific short-term purpose

Today several types of committees are used by business firms that impact their organizational structure. An **ad hoc committee** is created for a spe-

standing committee a relatively permanent committee charged with performing some recurring task

cific short-term purpose, such as reviewing the firm's employee benefits plan. Once its work is finished, the ad hoc committee disbands. A **standing committee** is a relatively permanent committee charged with performing some recurring task. A firm might establish a budget review committee, for example, to review departmental budget requests on an ongoing basis. Finally, a **task force** is a committee established to investigate a major problem or pending decision. A firm contemplating a merger with another company might form a task force to assess the pros and cons of the merger.

task force a committee established to investigate a major problem or pending decision

Committees offer some advantages over individual action. Their several members are, of course, able to bring more information and knowledge to the task at hand. Furthermore, committees tend to make more accurate decisions and to transmit their results through the organization more effectively. However, committee deliberations take much longer than individual actions. Unnecessary compromise may take place within the committee. Or the opposite may occur, as one person dominates (and thus negates) the committee process.

Coordination Techniques

managerial hierarchy the arrangement that provides increasing authority at higher levels of management

A large organization is forced to coordinate organizational resources to minimize duplication and to maximize effectiveness. One technique is simply to make use of the **managerial hierarchy,** which is the arrangement that provides increasing authority at higher levels of management. One manager is placed in charge of all the resources that are to be coordinated. That person

Solving a diverse problem. When properly managed, cultural diversity can provide competitive advantages for an organization. Seen here is a group of Levi Strauss employees that form the firm's Diversity Council. The objective of this committee is to help Levi Strauss to cope with the problems and advantages of a diverse workforce.

is able to coordinate them by virtue of the authority accompanying that position.

Resources can also be coordinated through rules and procedures. For example, a rule can govern how a firm's travel budget is to be allocated. This particular resource, then, would be coordinated in terms of that rule.

In complex situations, more sophisticated coordination techniques may be called for. One approach is to establish a liaison. Recall from Chapter 6 that a liaison is a go-between—a person who coordinates the activities of two groups. Suppose General Motors is negotiating a complicated contract with a supplier of steering wheels. The supplier might appoint a liaison whose primary responsibility is to coordinate the contract negotiations. Finally, for *very* complex coordination needs, a committee could be established. Suppose General Motors is in the process of purchasing the steering-wheel supplier. In this case a committee might be appointed to integrate the new firm into General Motors' larger organizational structure.

The Informal Organization

informal organization
the pattern of behavior and interaction that stems from personal rather than official relationships

So far, we have discussed the organization as a more or less formal structure consisting of interrelated positions. This is the organization that is shown on an organization chart. There is another kind of organization, however, that does not show up on any chart. We define this **informal organization** as the

A not-so formal organization. An informal group is created by the group members themselves to accomplish a task that they feel is important. Here a group of employees from all levels within an organization get together after work to play basketball. The main objective for the players is to have fun. The advantage for the organization is that employees get to know each other.

pattern of behavior and interaction that stems from personal rather than official relationships. Firmly embedded within every informal organization are informal groups and the notorious grapevine.

informal group a group created by the members themselves to accomplish goals that may or may not be relevant to the organization

Informal Groups   An **informal group** is created by the group members themselves to accomplish goals that may or may not be relevant to the organization. Workers may create an informal group to go bowling, form a union, get a particular manager fired or transferred, or have lunch together every day. The group may last for several years or only a few hours.

Employees join informal groups for a variety of reasons. Perhaps the main reason is that people like to be with others who are similar to themselves. Or it may be that the goals of the group appeal to the individual. Others may join informal groups simply because they have a need to be with their associates and to be accepted by them.

Informal groups can be powerful forces in organizations. They can restrict output, or they can help managers through tight spots. They can cause disagreement and conflict, or they can help boost morale and job satisfaction. They can show new people how to contribute to the organization, or they can help people get away with substandard performance. Clearly, managers should be aware of these informal groups. Those who make the mistake of fighting the informal organization have a major obstacle to overcome.

grapevine   the informal communications network within an organization

The Grapevine   The **grapevine** is the informal communications network within an organization. It is completely separate from—and sometimes much faster than—the organization's formal channels of communication. Formal communication usually follows a path that parallels the organizational chain of command. By contrast, information can be transmitted through the grapevine in any direction—up, down, diagonally, or horizontally across the organizational structure. Subordinates may pass information to their bosses, an executive may relay something to a maintenance worker, or there may be an exchange of information between people who work in totally unrelated departments.

Grapevine information may be concerned with topics ranging from the latest management decisions, to the results of today's World Series game, to pure gossip. It can be important or of little interest. And it can be highly accurate or totally distorted.

How should managers treat the grapevine? Certainly they would be making a big mistake if they tried to eliminate it. People working together, day in and day out, are going to communicate. A more rational approach is to recognize the existence of the grapevine as a part—though an unofficial part—of the organization. For example, managers should respond promptly and aggressively to inaccurate grapevine information to minimize the damage that such misinformation might do. Moreover, the grapevine can come in handy when managers are on the receiving end of important communications from the informal organization.

In the next chapter, we apply these and other management concepts to an extremely important business function: the production of goods and services.

■ ■ ■ ■ CHAPTER REVIEW

Summary

1   Identify five characteristics common to all organizations.

An organization is a group of two or more people working together to achieve a common set of goals. The relationships among positions within an organization can be illustrated by means of an organization chart. Five specific characteristics—job design, departmentalization, delegation, span of management, and chain of command—help determine what an organization chart, and ultimately the organization itself, look like.

2   Explain why job specialization is important.

Job specialization is the separation of all the activities within an organization into smaller components and the assignment of those different components to different people. Several factors combine to make specialization a useful technique for designing jobs, but high levels of specialization may cause employee dissatisfaction and boredom. Techniques for overcoming these problems include job enlargement, job rotation, and job enrichment.

3   Identify the various bases for departmentalization.

Departmentalization is the grouping of jobs into manageable units. Typical bases for departmentalization are by function, product, location, or customer. Because each of these bases provides particular advantages, most firms—especially larger ones—use a combination of different bases in different organizational situations.

4   Explain how decentralization follows from delegation.

Delegation is the assigning of part of a manager's work to other workers. It involves the following three steps: (a) assigning responsibility, (b) granting authority, and (c) creating accountability. A decentralized firm is one that delegates as much power as possible to people in the lower management levels. In a centralized firm, on the other hand, power is systematically retained at the upper levels.

5   Understand how the span of management describes an organization.

The span of management is the number of workers who report directly to a manager. Spans are generally characterized as wide (many workers per manager) or narrow (few workers per manager). Wide spans generally result in flat organizations (few layers of management); narrow spans generally result in tall organizations (many layers of management).

6   Distinguish between line and staff management.

A line position is one that is in the organization's chain of command, or line of authority. A manager in a line position makes decisions and gives orders to workers to achieve the goals of the organization. On the other hand, a manager in a staff position provides support, advice, and expertise to someone in the chain of command. Staff positions may carry some authority, but it usually applies only within staff areas of expertise.

7   Describe the three basic forms of organizational structure: bureaucratic, organic, and matrix.

There are three basic forms of organizational structure. The bureaucratic structure is characterized by formality and rigidity. With the bureaucratic structure, rules and procedures are used to ensure uniformity. The less formal organic structure is characterized by cooperation and knowledge-based authority. The newer matrix structure may be visualized as product departmentalization superimposed on functional departmentalization. With the matrix structure, an employee on a team reports to both the project manager and the individual's supervisor in a functional department.

8   Summarize how corporate culture, intrapreneurship, committees, coordination techniques, informal groups, and the grapevine affect an organization.

Corporate culture is the inner rites, rituals, heroes, and values of a firm and is thought to have a very strong influence on a firm's performance over time. An intrapreneur is an employee in an organizational environment who takes responsibility for pushing an innovative idea, product, or process through the organization. Additional elements that influence an organization include the use of committees and development of techniques for achieving coordination among various groups within the organization. Finally, both informal groups created by group members and an informal communication network called the grapevine may affect an organization and its performance.

Key Terms

You should now be able to define and give an example relevant to each of the following terms:

organization (201)
organization chart (201)
chain of command (201)
job specialization (204)
job rotation (206)
departmentalization (207)
departmentalization by function (207)
departmentalization by product (207)
departmentalization by location (207)
departmentalization by customer (208)
delegation (209)
responsibility (209)
authority (209)
accountability (210)
decentralized organization (210)
centralized organization (210)
span of management (or span of control) (211)
organizational height (212)
line management position (212)
staff management position (212)
bureaucratic structure (215)
organic structure (216)
matrix structure (217)
corporate culture (218)
intrapreneur (219)
ad hoc committee (220)
standing committee (221)
task force (221)
managerial hierarchy (221)
informal organization (222)
informal group (223)
grapevine (223)

Questions

Review Questions

1. In what way do organization charts create a picture of an organization?
2. What is the chain of command in an organization?
3. What determines the degree of specialization within an organization?
4. Describe how job rotation can be used to combat the problems caused by job specialization.

5. What are the major differences among the four departmentalization bases?
6. Why do most firms employ a combination of departmentalization bases?
7. What three steps are involved in delegation? Explain each.
8. How does a firm's top management influence its degree of centralization?
9. How is organizational height related to the span of management?
10. What are the key differences between line and staff positions?
11. Contrast the bureaucratic and organic forms of organizational structure.
12. Which form of organizational structure would probably lead to the strongest informal organization? Why?
13. How may the managerial hierarchy be used to coordinate the organization's resources?

Discussion Questions

1. For many years, General Motors was successful with a decentralized management system. What do you think decentralization meant for each division of the automaker?
2. What major change did John Smith introduce to GM's North American Operations? How did he do it?
3. Explain how the five steps of the organizing process determine the characteristics of the resulting organization. Which steps are most important?
4. Which kinds of firms would probably operate most effectively as centralized firms? as decentralized firms?
5. How do decisions concerning span of management, the use of committees, and coordination techniques affect organizational structure?
6. How might a manager go about formalizing the informal organization?

Exercises

1. Draw the organization chart for the academic institution that you are attending. State your assumptions if you must make them.
✎ 2. Assume that a wealthy investor hires you to manage a new computer software store. The store will be located in a shopping mall and will be open from 10:00 A.M. until 9:00 P.M. seven days a week. Prepare a two-page executive report that describes how many employees you will need, the qualifications for each employee, and the type of organization you will use to make this new retail business a success.

3. One of your employees enters your office, closes the door, and tells you that she has heard "through the grapevine" that a worker is stealing money from the cash register. As supervisor, how do you respond to such information obtained through the grapevine? Assuming the information is correct, what would you do to correct this situation?

VIDEO CASE 7.1

3M: Ideas at Hand

Innovation isn't planned—it just happens. But it happens more often when employees know it is their firm's top priority—and 3M employees know it. The St. Paul–based firm is known for its long-term commitment to new product development. And that commitment has been the reason why 3M has introduced products like Scotch cellophane tape and Scotch masking tape, 3M software diskettes, Bufpuf skin-care products, Scotchguard fabric protector, and Post-it Notes. In fact, the above products are just a tiny sampling of the more than 60,000 products manufactured by the 3M Company.

Is 3M's success an accident? Not at all. The commitment to innovation begins with the firm's organizational structure. Currently, the multinational firm is organized into three business segments: industry and consumer products; information imaging and electronics; and life sciences products. Each major division is broken down into product units that operate like small autonomous companies, each with its own mission and personality. These product units are further subdivided into cross-functional teams. Made up of designers, engineers, marketers, accountants, and others, these "action teams" have enormous freedom to outline their own goals and to develop products of their own choosing. There's only one catch. One corporate rule applies consistently throughout the organization: each division must generate 25 percent of its revenues from products introduced within the previous five years.

Because of the importance of new product development to 3M, special attention is devoted to the organization of the firm's research and development (R&D) efforts. For starters, 3M's management always encourages new ideas. When a company scientist devoted energy and hours to an idea for sticky-backed pieces of paper, he wasn't worried that coworkers would complain he was wasting time. Company policy states that researchers may use 15 percent of their time on any project they choose. That freedom resulted in the popular Post-it Notes that now generate millions of dollars a year in sales revenues.

Next, 3M devotes special attention to the way research and development activities are organized. Creating three levels of R&D allows 3M to keep new products coming at the same time it encourages long-range projects. Division laboratories do short-term research geared toward products destined for specific markets. To come up with the technologies and applications needed three to ten years in the future, 3M initiated what it calls sector laboratories. And basic research that may not lead to actual products for ten to twenty years goes on in corporate laboratories.

Finally, 3M supplies the financial resources necessary to fund research and development. In just the last five years, 3M has invested almost $5 billion in R&D. According to management, this type of financial commitment is necessary to develop the products that will be needed in the year 2000 and beyond.

As a result of its flexible organization, its financial commitment, and its speed at turning ideas into products, 3M was recently placed on *Datamation's* elite list of one hundred "world-class" organizations. With 175 factories operating in the United States alone, business dealings in more than 50 countries, and annual net income in excess of $1.3 billion, the "world-class" label is no exaggeration.[7]

Questions

1. Today, the most common bases for organizing a business into effective departments are by function, by product, by location, or by type of customer. Which of these departmentalization bases does 3M use? Explain your answer.
2. How does the organization of the research and development department differ from that of other 3M departments?
3. In the last five years, 3M has invested almost $5 billion in research and development. How does this commitment to new ideas help 3M develop products that will solve customer problems?

CASE 7.2

Kmart Zigzags Through Reorganization

We have all heard the saying, "Get a game plan." Well, that is exactly what Kmart has been doing, again, and again, and again for the past decade. In fact, Kmart's biggest problem may be that it has reorganized too often and in too many directions. In the shuffle the company seems to have lost sight of its core business—discount retailing.

Kmart, the outgrowth of the old Kresge chain of five-and-dime stores, became the pioneer in discount retail merchandising when its first discount store opened in Detroit in 1962. Low- and middle-income American consumers loved the convenience of shopping in one store for a variety of merchandise at reasonable prices, and Kmart eventually opened over 2,000 stores across the United States. By the late 1970s, Kmart was one of the largest retailers in the country, second only to Sears. The corporation sold most of its old Kresge stores in the 1980s and began to diversify, purchasing specialty companies like Borders-Walden Bookstores, Builders Square, Payless Drugstores, and Office Max. Also, Kmart ventured into larger warehouse clubs, launching its chain of Pace membership warehouses.

Just as Kmart was restructuring its existing operations and expanding its retail business, Sam Walton burst onto the scene with his Wal-Mart Stores determined to match or beat Kmart in quality and pricing. Now, Kmart found itself in fierce competition with Sears *and* Wal-Mart. At the same time, Kmart had to finance its expansion into specialty retailing and began to neglect its roots in the discount business. The very stores that built Kmart's reputation as the leader in discount merchandising had fallen, rundown and shabby, into a sea of neglect.

It became obvious that Kmart had to renovate its existing stores. But as the expense for this undertaking became prohibitive and as more and more consumers shunned Kmart for Wal-Mart, the pioneer had to close stores in areas that produced low sales. In 1991 four Super Kmarts opened offering the usual discount assortment plus full-line grocery stores, fancy specialty departments, and pharmacies. This array attracted a wider base of customers and did enjoy limited success, but Kmart continued to lose apparel business to Sears.

And Wal-Mart hammered Kmart on pricing on just about every product in the store. Despite all their efforts—even recruiting celebrities to assist them in upscaling their merchandise image—Kmart officers were unable to recapture the loyal following of lost customers. And Kmart, like all retailers, was hurt by the 1992 fears of a recession that prompted consumers to cut back on purchasing.

In 1993 Kmart's profits were down by 69 percent. As earnings continued to fall, the largest investor rebellion in corporate history occurred in 1994 when Kmart, yet again, wanted to restructure by selling shares in its subsidiary organizations. Soundly defeated by its stockholders, Kmart then began selling off subsidiaries that no longer met its new corporate strategy. Ironically, eight Dallas area Pace stores were acquired by rival Wal-Mart. The stockholders' uprising is not the only outward evidence of disenchantment with current Kmart management. Both management and financial experts are concerned that the lack of a definite leadership plan has resulted in turmoil and morale problems all the way from senior executives down the line to store employees. These same experts believe one more Kmart reorganization is in order—but this time, they suggest, the restructuring should begin at the top.[8]

Questions

1. How effective do you think Kmart's past restructuring efforts have been for the organization? Explain your answer.
2. Are Kmart's current problems primarily organizational? If not, what other factors may have led to Kmart losing market share to Wal-Mart and Sears?

CHAPTER 8

Production and Operations Management

LEARNING OBJECTIVES

After studying this chapter you should be able to

1 Explain the nature of operations management.

2 Outline how the conversion process transforms raw materials, labor, and other resources into finished products.

3 Discuss the need for research and development.

4 Distinguish between design planning and operational planning.

5 Explain the four major areas of operations control: purchasing, inventory control, scheduling, and quality control.

6 Discuss the increasing role of computers and robotics in the production process.

7 Outline the reasons for recent trends in productivity.

CHAPTER PREVIEW

We begin this chapter with an overview of operations management—the activities involved in the conversion of resources into products. We describe the conversion process that makes production possible and also note the growing role of services in our economy. Then we examine more closely three important aspects of operations management: developing ideas for new products, planning product design and production facilities, and effectively controlling operations after production has begun. Next we discuss changes in production as a result of automation, robotics, and computer-aided manufacturing. We close the chapter with a look at productivity trends and ways productivity can be improved.

IBM Goes Soft

International Business Machines (IBM) has long been recognized as the largest computer company in the world. However, in the mid-1980s the giant known as Big Blue sank into a disturbing market-share slump. Back in the 1960s IBM developed its System/360 mainframe computer and had built a solid core business around the manufacture, sales, installation, and maintenance of this high-profit product. But the ever-increasing power and capabilities of personal computers caused the demand for IBM's large, expensive mainframe computers to drop. Even then, the firm was confident that nothing would ever disturb its leadership. But by the early 1990s, sales of mainframes had plummeted by almost 50 percent. IBM was losing sales to customers who scrapped their mainframe computer and minicomputers in favor of networks that used personal computers.

To combat this problem, Louis V. Gerstner, Jr., who took over as IBM's chief executive in 1993, began exploring new methods of manufacturing products. The emerging technology of manufacturing with software and computer networks have now led IBM to adopt the digital factory concept. Called *soft manufacturing*, this trend is a mix of human and computer technology. The emphasis is on customized products utilizing software-controlled continuous flow manufacturing. For example, at a plant in Charlotte, North Carolina, a team of forty people can build twenty-seven different products on one assembly line at the same time. The products could be PCs, bar-code scanners, portable medical computers, satellite communications devices—or any other product IBM manufactures.

Here's how IBM's system works. A customer may call a sales rep on a toll-free telephone num-

ber at IBM's location in North Carolina, and as they discuss the customer's needs, the rep can enter the specifications for the new product directly into the computer. The same computer processes the order to a nearby plant. An employee carrying a bar-code reader around the plant gathers all the needed parts from inventory and delivers them to an employee on the assembly line. While the product is being built, every part and the assembly method are verified against a computer program connected to the factory network to ensure accuracy. The new product is then tested and packaged automatically for delivery to the customer the next day.

This soft manufacturing plant is just one of a new kind of American factory in which production processes have changed because of the exploding information age we live in. IBM is betting that this revolution in American manufacturing will be cost-effective, will make the firm more competitive, will better serve the needs of IBM customers, and ultimately will strengthen its share of the computer marketplace.[1]

■ ■ ■ ■

229

■　■　　■　　■　　■　　■　　■　　■　　■　　■　　■

International Business Machines, most often referred to as IBM, realized long ago that it must constantly seek high levels of productivity and high-quality products in order to remain competitive in the ever-changing computer industry. To achieve these two objectives, organizations like IBM expend considerable resources to ensure that they have effective operations management.

In Chapter 6, operations managers were described as the people who create and manage systems that convert resources into goods and services. In this chapter, we examine the activities that are part of the operations manager's job. **Operations management** consists of all the activities managers engage in to produce goods and services. A number of activities are involved in operations management. First, an organization like Johnson & Johnson may undertake product development in order to develop a new skin treatment like Retin-A. Next, production must be planned. Unfortunately, Johnson & Johnson managers cannot just push the "start button" and immediately begin producing a new product. As you will see, planning takes place both *before* anything is produced and *during* the production process. Finally, managers must concern themselves with the control of operations to ensure that the organization's goals are achieved. For a product like Johnson & Johnson's Retin-A, control of operations deals with a number of important issues including product quality, the amount of inventory of both raw materials and finished product, the manufacturing process, and production costs. We discuss each of these major activities in the sections that follow. But first we need to take a closer look at the nature of production itself.

■■ THE CONVERSION PROCESS

Simply put, production is the conversion of resources into goods and services. The resources are materials, finances, people, and information—the same business resources discussed in Chapters 1 and 6. The goods and services are varied and diverse ranging from small computer chips to heavy manufacturing equipment. The purpose of this transformation of resources into goods and services is to provide utility to customers. **Utility** is the ability of a good or service to satisfy a human need. Although there are four types of utility—form, place, time, and possession—operations management focuses primarily on form utility. **Form utility** is created by converting raw materials, labor, and other resources into finished products.

But how does the conversion take place? How does Ford convert steel and glass, money from previous auto sales and stockholders' investments, production workers and managers, and economic and marketing forecasts into automobiles? How does Aetna Life and Casualty convert office buildings, insurance premiums, actuaries, and mortality tables into life insurance

230

policies? They do so through the use of a conversion process like the one illustrated in Figure 8.1. As indicated by our Aetna Life and Casualty example, the conversion process is not limited to manufacturing products. The conversion process can also be used to produce services and ideas.

The Nature of the Conversion

The conversion of resources into products and services can be described in several ways. We limit our discussion here to three: the focus of the conversion, its magnitude, and the number of production processes employed.

Focus   By the *focus* of a conversion process we mean the resource or resources that comprise the major input. For a bank like Citicorp, financial resources are of prime concern in the conversion process. A refiner such as Texaco concentrates on material resources. A college or university is primarily concerned with information. And a barbershop focuses on the use of human resources.

Magnitude   The *magnitude* of a conversion is the degree to which the resources are physically changed by the conversion. At one extreme lie such processes as the one by which First Brands Corporation produces Glad Wrap. Various chemicals in liquid or powder form are combined to form long, thin sheets of plastic Glad Wrap. Here the input resources are totally unrecognizable in the finished product. At the other extreme, American Airlines produces *no* physical change in its input resources. The airline simply transports people from one place to another.

Number of Production Processes   A single firm may employ one process or many. In general, larger firms that make a variety of products use multiple production processes. For example, General Electric manufactures some of its own products, buys other merchandise from wholesalers, and operates a credit division, an insurance company, and a medical equipment division. Clearly a number of different production processes are involved in these activities. Smaller firms, by contrast, may operate in one fairly narrow market in which few production processes are required.

FIGURE 8.1   The Conversion Process
The conversion process converts resources such as materials, finances, and people into useful goods, services, and ideas. It is a crucial step in the economic development of any nation.

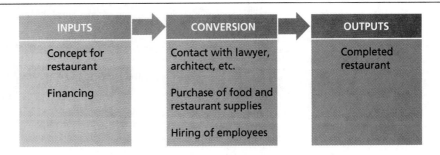

The Increasing Importance of Services

The application of operations management to the production of services has coincided with a dramatic growth in the number and diversity of service organizations. In 1900 only 28 percent of American workers were employed in service organizations. By 1950 this figure had grown to 40 percent, and by July 1994 it had risen to 79 percent.[2] By any yardstick, service firms have become a dominant part of our economy. In fact, the American economy is now characterized as a service economy (see Figure 8.2). A **service economy** is one in which more effort is devoted to the production of services than to the production of goods.

This rapid growth is the primary reason for the increased emphasis on production techniques in service firms. The managers of restaurants, laundries, real estate agencies, banks, movie theaters, airlines, travel bureaus, and other service firms have realized that they can benefit from the experience of manufacturers and construction firms. And yet the production of services is uniquely different from the production of manufactured goods in the following four ways:

1. Services are consumed immediately and, unlike manufactured goods, cannot be stored. For example, a hair stylist cannot store completed haircuts like a manufacturer stores microwave ovens.

service economy an economy in which more effort is devoted to the production of services than to the production of goods

FIGURE 8.2
Service Industries
The growth of service firms has increased so dramatically that we live in what is now referred to as a service economy. *(Source:* Monthly Labor Review, *Bureau of Labor Statistics, Nov. 1994, p. 86.)*

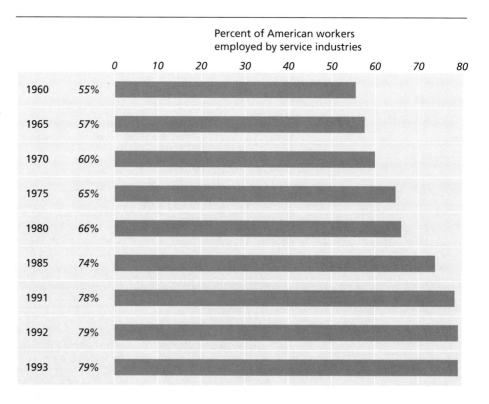

Percent of American workers employed by service industries

Year	Percent
1960	55%
1965	57%
1970	60%
1975	65%
1980	66%
1985	74%
1991	78%
1992	79%
1993	79%

2. Services are provided when and where the customer desires the service. In many cases, customers will not travel as far to obtain a service as they would to purchase a manufactured good.

3. Services are usually labor intensive because the human resource is often the most important resource used in the production of services.

4. Services are intangible and therefore it is more difficult to evaluate customer satisfaction.[3]

Although it is often more difficult to measure customer satisfaction, today's successful service firms work hard at providing the services that customers want. Compared to manufacturers, service firms often listen more carefully to customers and respond more quickly to the market's changing needs. In fact, customer satisfaction is so important that it is one of the criteria used to select winners of the Malcolm Baldrige National Quality Award. For other selection criteria and a discussion of this prestigious award, read Business Journal.

Now that we understand something about the production process that is used to transform resources into goods and services, we can consider three major activities involved in operations management. These are product development, planning for production, and operations control.

■ ■ WHERE DO NEW PRODUCTS AND SERVICES COME FROM?

LEARNING OBJECTIVE 3
Discuss the need for research and development.

No firm can produce a product or service until it has an idea. In other words, someone must first come up with a new way to satisfy a need—a new product or an improvement in an existing product. Only then can the firm begin the variety of activities that make up operations management.

Research and Development

How did we get VCRs, personal computers, and compact-disc players? We got them the same way we got light bulbs and automobile tires: from people working with new ideas. Thomas Edison created the first light bulb and Charles Goodyear discovered the vulcanization process that led to tires. In the same way, scientists and researchers working in businesses and universities have produced many of the newer products we already take for granted.

research and development (R&D) a set of activities intended to identify new ideas that have the potential to result in new goods and services

These activities are generally referred to as research and development. For our purposes, **research and development (R&D)** is a set of activities intended to identify new ideas that have the potential to result in new goods and services.

There are three general types of R&D activities. *Basic research* consists of activities aimed at uncovering new knowledge. The goal of basic research is scientific advancement, without regard for its potential use in the development of goods and services. *Applied research*, in contrast, consists of activities geared to discovering new knowledge with some potential use. *Development and implementation* are research activities undertaken specifi-

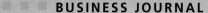

BUSINESS JOURNAL

A New Standard for Quality

In 1987 Congress established the Malcolm Baldrige National Quality Award. This prestigious award, named in honor of a former secretary of commerce, is presented by the president of the United States to those U.S. companies who have demonstrated outstanding and effective quality management practices. The intent of the award is to promote an awareness of how the highest standards in quality management can affect our nation's economy. A maximum of two awards in each of three categories—manufacturing, service, and small business—may be made annually. Between 1988 and 1993 a total of nineteen companies won the 25-pound, 14-inch high, Steuben crystal trophy imbedded with a medallion inscribed "Malcolm Baldrige National Quality Award" and "The Quest for Excellence" on one side and emblazoned with the presidential seal on the other.

ROLE MODELS

One of the purposes of the award is to recognize these outstanding companies as role models, so information about their successful quality improvement strategies is shared with other organizations. Of course, as a plus for the recipients, a significant benefit of winning is the right to tout the award in their advertising. Among this elite group are companies like AT&T's Universal Card Services, Texas Instruments Inc. Defense Systems & Electronics Group, Federal Express Corp., Motorola, Inc., The Ritz-Carlton Hotel Co., Milliken & Company, Xerox Corp. Business Products

and Systems, Cadillac Motor Car Division, IBM Rochester, Granite Rock Company, Ames Rubber Corp., and Eastman Chemical Company.

SELECTION CRITERIA

Every company that applies for the award is examined and evaluated by an independent committee of private- and public-sector quality experts. The seven common criteria for judgment are

- Leadership
- Information and analysis
- Planning
- Human resource use
- Quality assurance of products and services
- Quality results
- Customer satisfaction

In addition to examining written reports that describe a company's success in each of the above areas, the independent committee conducts on-site inspections as part of the evaluation process.

Since the award was first given, the Malcolm Baldrige National Quality Award has become so prestigious that the U.S. Commerce Department has been deluged with requests for criteria information about not only the award itself but also how to establish a total quality management program. To date, the agency has distributed more than 1 million copies of the criteria worldwide in at least nine languages.

Someone from outer space or just space age TV? Manufacturers around the globe have been developing high-definition television. Here a research worker in France is testing a television picture tube that could become part of the next generation of high-tech TVs.

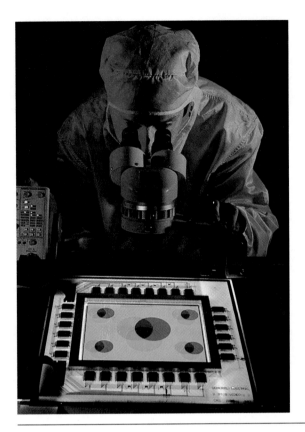

cally to put new or existing knowledge to use in producing goods and services. The 3M Company used development and implementation to combine paper and a special type of adhesive to produce Post-it Notes. In a similar fashion, Genentech, Inc., invested five years and $200 million to develop Activase, a new medication that dissolves clots after an individual suffers a heart attack.[4]

Most firms organize their R&D activities as a staff function, either at the corporate level or within product-based departments. When R&D activities are placed at the corporate level, they are somewhat centralized. This arrangement allows the firm to concentrate research activities in one group, with no duplication of effort among departments. However, a corporate R&D staff may not be sensitive to the needs of each separate department within the corporation. Placing separate R&D staffs within product departments overcomes this problem. But costs are higher because R&D facilities must be duplicated for the various departments. Some firms try to combine the two approaches by centralizing basic research and some applied research but decentralizing the remaining R&D effort.

Product Extension and Refinement

When a brand-new product is first marketed, its sales are zero and slowly increase from that point. If the product is successful, annual sales increase more and more rapidly until they reach some peak. Then, as time passes, annual sales begin to decline, and they continue to decline until it is no longer profitable to manufacture the product. (This rise-and-decline pattern, called the *product life cycle,* is discussed in more detail in Chapter 13.)

If a firm sells only one product, when that product reaches the end of its life cycle, the firm will die too. To stay in business, the firm must, at the very least, find ways to refine or extend the want-satisfying capability of its product. Consider television sets. Since they were first introduced in the late 1930s, television sets have been constantly *refined,* so that they now provide clearer, sharper pictures with less dial adjusting. They are tuned electronically for better picture control and can even compensate for variations in room lighting and picture-tube wear. During the same time, television sets were also *extended.* Full-color as well as black-and-white sets can be purchased. There are television-only sets and others that include VCRs, digital clocks, and telephones. Both manual and remote control models are available.

Each refinement or extension results in an essentially "new" product whose sales make up for the declining sales of a product that was introduced earlier. For example, Jell-O was introduced to the public in 1897 and was acquired by General Foods in 1925. One of General Foods' newer products, Jello Pudding Pops, is still based on Jell-O. Jello Pudding Pops produces sales of more than $100 million annually. For most firms, extension and refinement are expected results of their development and implementation effort. Most often, they result from the application of new knowledge to existing products.

■■ PLANNING FOR PRODUCTION

Only a few of the many ideas for new products, refinements, and extensions ever reach the production stage. But for those ideas that do, the next step in the process of operations management is planning for production. Planning for production involves two major phases: design planning and operational planning.

Design Planning

design planning the development of a plan for converting a product idea into an actual product

product line a group of similar products that differ only in relatively minor characteristics

When the R&D staff at IBM recommended to top management that the firm produce and market an affordable personal computer, the company could not simply swing into production the next day. Instead, a great deal of time and energy had to be invested in determining what the new computer would look like, where and how it would be produced, and what options would be included. These decisions are a part of design planning. **Design planning** is the development of a plan for converting a product idea into an actual product. The major decisions involved in design planning deal with product line, required capacity, use of technology, number and location of facilities, and human resources.

Product Line   A **product line** is a group of similar products that differ only in relatively minor characteristics. During the design-planning stage, management must determine how many different product variations there will be. An automobile manufacturer like General Motors needs to determine how many different models to produce, what major options to offer, and the like. A restaurant chain like Pizza Inn must decide how many menu items to offer.

An important issue in deciding on the product line is to balance customer preferences and production requirements. It is also important to identify the most effective combination of product alternatives. For this reason, marketing managers play an important role in making product-line decisions. Once the product line has been determined, each distinct product within the product line must be designed. **Product design** is the process of creating a set of specifications from which the product can be produced. The need for a careful and complete design of tangible goods is fairly obvious; they cannot be manufactured without it. But services should be carefully designed as well, and *for the same reason.* And with more firms selling in more countries around the globe, specifications for both products and services are more important than ever. For information on world market standards, see Global Perspectives.

product design   the process of creating a set of specifications from which a product can be produced

Required Capacity   **Capacity** is the amount of products or services that an organization can produce in a given period of time. (The capacity of an automobile assembly plant, for instance, might be 500,000 cars per year.) Operations managers—again working with the firm's marketing managers—must determine the required capacity. This in turn determines the size of the production facility. Capacity planning is vitally important. If the facility is built with too much capacity, valuable resources (plant, equipment, and money) will lie idle. If the facility offers insufficient capacity, additional capacity may have to be added later, when it is much more expensive than in the initial building stage. Suppose an automobile assembly plant were constructed with the capacity to produce 500,000 cars per year. If customers then wanted only 400,000 cars per year, 20 percent of the capital invested in the plant would be wasted. If instead customers wanted as many as 600,000 cars per year, the company might have to build a costly addition to the plant to produce all the cars it can sell.

capacity   the amount of products or services that an organization can produce in a given time

Capacity means about the same thing to service businesses. For example, the capacity of a restaurant like the Hard Rock Cafe is the number of patrons it can serve at one time. Like the manufacturing facility described above, if the restaurant is built with too much capacity—too many tables and chairs—valuable resources will be wasted. If the restaurant is too small, customers may have to wait for service; if the wait is too long, they may leave and choose another restaurant.

Use of Technology   During the design-planning stage, operations personnel must determine the degree to which *automation*—including industrial robots—should be enlisted in place of human labor. Here, there is a tradeoff between high initial costs and low operating costs (for automation) and low initial costs and high operating costs (for human labor). Ultimately, management must choose between a labor-intensive technology and a capital-intensive technology. A **labor-intensive technology** is a process in which people must do most of the work. Housecleaning services and professional

labor-intensive technology   a process in which people must do most of the work

When workers do a better job than machines. A hand-made quilt is just one example where people or a labor-intensive technology can be used to produce quality products. The pride in workmanship and the quality of the finished product would be difficult if not impossible to duplicate if these skilled workers were replaced with a high-tech machine.

capital-intensive technology a process in which machines and equipment do most of the work

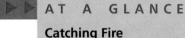

AT   A   GLANCE

Catching Fire

By mid-1994, almost 2,000 certificates had been issued to U.S. firms that meet ISO 9000 world market quality standards.

Source: *Nation's Business,* May 1994, p. 71, and *Fortune,* June 28, 1993, p. 117.

baseball teams, for example, are labor intensive. A **capital-intensive technology** is a process in which machines and equipment do most of the work. An automated assembly plant is capital intensive.

Number and Location of Facilities   A very complex set of design-planning decisions deals with the production facilities to be used in creating products and services. Major decisions include the number of facilities to be used, their locations, and their layouts.

Should all the organization's production capacity be placed in one or two large facilities? Or should it be divided among several smaller facilities? In general, firms that market a wide variety of products find it more economical to have a number of smaller facilities. Firms that produce only a small number of products tend to have fewer but larger facilities. There are many exceptions to this general rule, and decisions concerning facility size are often affected by zoning and other restrictions.

In determining where to locate production facilities, management must consider a number of variables, including the following:

- Geographic locations of suppliers of parts and raw materials
- Locations of major markets for their company's products
- Transportation costs to deliver finished products to customers
- Availability of skilled and unskilled labor in various geographic areas
- Special requirements, such as great amounts of energy or water used in the production process

■ ■ ■ ■ GLOBAL PERSPECTIVES

World Market Quality Standards: ISO 9000

With so many diversified companies and cultures competing in the world marketplace, it is natural to assume everyone's perception of a quality product will not be the same. Without a common standard, however, consumers, wherever they may be—in the United States, Japan, or Germany—are faced with uncertainty when it comes to purchasing a product or service. And without a common base on which to compare quality, consumers are often left at the mercy of the vendor.

Recognizing the seriousness of this problem to world commerce, the International Organization for Standardization in Geneva, Switzerland (a nonprofit standard-setting body with a membership of ninety-five countries), brought together a panel of quality experts to consider and define what methods a company must use to produce a quality product. In 1987 the panel published the ISO 9000 (*iso* is Greek for "equal"), which sets the guidelines for quality management procedures that factories, laboratories, and offices must comply with in order to receive certification. This certification ensures their end-products or services meet a common set of minimum standards in the world marketplace. This certificate, issued by independent auditors, is registered and attests that a company meets the standards for quality control procedures in manufacturing design, production processes, testing of products, training employees, keeping records, and correcting defects.

Although certification is not a legal requirement to do business globally, ninety-five countries have approved the standards, and many European businesses regard the certificate as a sort of "Good Housekeeping Seal of Approval." In fact, ISO 9000 is so prevalent in the European Community that many customers refuse to do business with noncertified companies. From a marketing standpoint, this reluctance provides strong motivation for a company to seek certification. As an added bonus, companies completing the certification process discover major, cost-efficient improvements to their overall quality programs.

Motorola, one of the winners of the prestigious Malcolm Baldrige National Quality Award presented by the president of the United States, is seeking ISO 9000 registration for many of its plants located around the world as an insurance policy for competing in the global marketplace. Other major companies, including Du Pont, General Electric, and Eastman Kodak, are urging their suppliers to adopt ISO 9000 standards, not only because customers are demanding it, but as an attempt to help them run their businesses more efficiently.

Some controversy accompanies these guidelines. Especially loud is the complaint that companies are forced to spend enormous amounts initially to comply. Others say ISO 9000 does not address the quality issue strongly enough and recommend that the Baldrige Award criteria become the standard for international quality. In the meantime, with the ISO 9000 certificate and registration, a common quality system has been established for a vast cross-section of industries and nations that enables equal competition in the export marketplace, achieves cost reductions in quality management, and gives customers quality assurance.

plant layout   the arrangement of machinery, equipment, and personnel within a facility

The choice of a particular location often involves *optimizing*, or balancing, the most important variables for each production facility.

Finally, the **plant layout,** which is the arrangement of machinery, equipment, and personnel within the facility, must be determined. Three general types of plant layout are used (see Figure 8.3).

The *process layout* is used when different operations are required for creating small batches of different products. The plant is arranged so that each operation is performed in its own particular area. Once the task in one area is completed, the work in process is moved to another area. An auto repair shop provides an example of a process layout. The various operations might be engine repair, body work, wheel alignment, and safety inspection. Each operation is performed in a different area. A particular car "visits" only those areas performing the kinds of work it needs.

A *product layout* is used when all products undergo the same operations in the same sequence. Work stations are arranged to match the sequence of operations, and work flows from station to station. An assembly line is the best example of a product layout. For example, Chrysler Corporation uses a product layout to produce automobiles.

A *fixed-position layout* is used when a very large product is produced. Aircraft manufacturers and shipbuilders apply this method because of the difficulty of moving a large product like an airliner or ship. The product remains stationary while people and machines are moved as needed to assemble the product. Boeing, for example, uses the fixed-position layout to build 777 jet aircraft because it is much easier to move people and machines around the airliner than to move the plane during the production process.

Human Resources   In many ways, human resources are more the concern of human resources managers than of operations managers, but the two must work together at the design-planning stage. Several design-planning activities affect the work of human resources managers. For example, suppose a sophisticated production process requiring special skills is called for. The firm will have to recruit employees with the appropriate skills, develop training programs, or do both. Depending on where production facilities are to be located, arrangements may have to be made to transfer skilled workers to the new locations or to train local workers.

Human resources managers can also obtain and provide valuable information on availability of skilled workers in various areas, wage rates, and other factors that may influence choices of the use of technology and plant location.

Operational Planning

Once the production process and facilities have been designed, operational plans must be developed and revised periodically for each facility. The objective of operational planning is to decide on the amount of products or services that each facility will produce. Four steps are required: (1) selecting a planning horizon, (2) estimating market demand, (3) comparing market demand with capacity, and (4) adjusting products or services to meet demand.

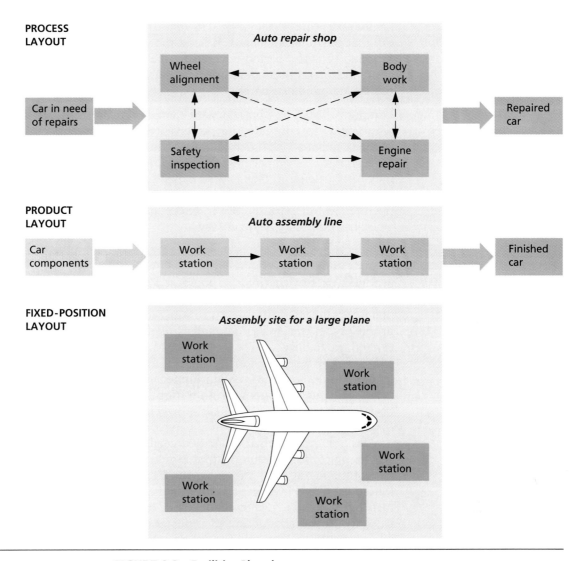

FIGURE 8.3   Facilities Planning
The process layout is used when small batches of different products are created in a different operating sequence. The product layout is used when all products undergo the same operations in the same sequence. The fixed-position layout is used in producing a product too large to move.

planning horizon the period during which a plan will be in effect

Selecting a Planning Horizon   A **planning horizon** is simply the period during which a plan will be in effect. A common planning horizon for production plans is one year. Then, before each year is up, management must plan for the next.

A planning horizon of one year is generally long enough to average out seasonal increases and decreases in sales. At the same time, it is short enough for planners to adjust output to accommodate long-range sales trends. Firms that operate in a rapidly changing business environment may find it best to select a shorter planning horizon to keep their production planning current.

Estimating Market Demand   The *market demand* for a product is the quantity that customers will purchase at the going price. This quantity must be estimated for the period covered by the planning horizon. The sales forecasts and projections developed by marketing managers are the basis for market-demand estimates.

Comparing Market Demand with Capacity   The third step in operational planning is to compare the projected market demand with the facility's capacity to satisfy that demand. Again, demand and capacity must be compared for the same period—the planning horizon. One of three outcomes may result: demand may exceed capacity, capacity may exceed demand, or capacity and demand may be equal. If they are equal, the facility should be operated at full capacity. But if market demand and capacity are not equal, an adjustment may be necessary.

Adjusting Products or Services to Meet Demand   When market demand exceeds capacity, several options are available to the firm. Production of products or services may be increased by operating the facility overtime with existing personnel or by starting a second or third work shift. For manufacturers, another response is to subcontract a portion of the work to other producers. If the excess demand is likely to be permanent, the firm may expand the facility.

Some firms occasionally pursue another option—ignore the excess demand and allow it to remain unmet. For several years, this strategy was used by the Adolph Coors Co. A mystique gradually developed around Coors beer because it was not available in many parts of the country. When the firm's brewing capacity was finally expanded, an eager market was waiting.

What happens when capacity exceeds market demand? Again, there are several options. To reduce output temporarily, workers may be laid off and part of the facility shut down. Or the facility may be operated on a shorter-than-normal workweek for as long as the excess capacity persists. To adjust to a permanently decreased demand, management may shift the excess capacity to the production of other goods or services. The most radical adjustment is to eliminate the excess capacity by selling unused facilities.

■■ OPERATIONS CONTROL

LEARNING OBJECTIVE 5
Explain the four major areas of operations control: purchasing, inventory control, scheduling, and quality control.

So far we have discussed the development of a product idea and the planning that translates that idea into the reality. Now it's time to push the "start button" and put the facility into operation. In this section, we examine four important areas of operations control: purchasing, inventory control, scheduling, and quality control (see Figure 8.4).

FIGURE 8.4 Four Aspects of Operations Control
To implement the operations control system in any business requires the effective use of purchasing, inventory control, scheduling, and quality control by all managerial levels.

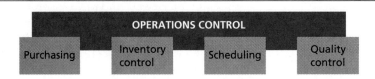

Purchasing

purchasing all the activities involved in obtaining required materials, supplies, and parts from other firms

Purchasing consists of all the activities involved in obtaining required materials, supplies, and parts from other firms. For Levi Strauss, denim cloth, thread, and zippers must be purchased before a single pair of jeans can be produced. Similarly, Nike, Inc., must purchase leather, rubber, cloth for linings, and laces before manufacturing a pair of athletic shoes. For all firms, the purchasing function is far from routine, and its importance should not be underestimated. For some products, purchased materials make up more than 50 percent of their wholesale costs.[5]

The objective of purchasing is to ensure that required materials are available when they are needed, in the proper amounts, and at minimum cost. In order to achieve this objective, management must select suppliers carefully. Purchasing personnel should constantly be on the lookout for new or back-up suppliers, even when their needs are being met by their present suppliers. It may become necessary to change suppliers for a variety of reasons. Or such problems as strikes and equipment breakdowns may cut off the flow of purchased materials from a primary supplier.

The choice of suppliers should result from careful analysis of a number of factors. The following are especially critical:

- *Price*—Comparing prices offered by different suppliers is always an essential part of selecting a supplier. Even tiny differences in price add up to enormous sums when large quantities are purchased. A saving of 2 cents per unit on annual purchases of 100,000 units yields a yearly saving of $2,000.

- *Quality*—Purchasing specialists are always challenged to find the "best" materials at the lowest price. Although the goal is not necessarily to find the highest quality available, purchasing specialists always try to buy materials at a level of quality that is in keeping with their intended use. The minimum acceptable quality is usually specified by product designers. Beyond that, purchasing personnel need to weigh quality against price because higher quality usually costs more.

- *Reliability*—An agreement to purchase high-quality materials at a low price is the purchaser's dream. But such an agreement becomes a nightmare if the supplier doesn't deliver. Purchasing personnel should check the reliability of potential suppliers as well as their ability to meet delivery schedules.

- *Credit terms*—Purchasing specialists should determine if the supplier demands immediate payment or will extend credit. Also, does the supplier offer a cash discount for prompt payment? A cash discount—a topic covered in Chapter 13—is essentially a price reduction and should always be considered when choosing a supplier.

- *Shipping costs*—One of the most overlooked factors in purchasing is geographic location of the supplier. Low prices and favorable credit terms offered by a distant supplier can be wiped out when the buyer must pay the shipping costs to get materials and supplies where they are needed. Above all, the question of who pays the shipping costs should be answered before any supplier is chosen.

Inventory Control

Can you imagine what would happen if a Coca-Cola manufacturing plant ran out of the familiar red and white aluminum cans? Management would be forced to shut the assembly line down until the next shipment of cans arrived from a supplier. It would be impossible to complete the manufacturing process and ship the cases of Coke to retailers. In reality, operations managers for Coca-Cola realize the disasters that a shortage of needed materials can cause and will avoid this type of problem if at all possible. The simple fact is that shutdowns are expensive because costs such as rent, wages, and insurance must still be paid. On the other hand, large stockpiles of materials are also costly because the money invested in stored materials does not contribute to the firm or its operations. The objective of inventory control is to balance these two opposing factors to ensure that sufficient materials are on hand without paying excessive storage costs.

Operations managers are concerned with three types of inventories. A *raw-materials inventory* consists of materials that will become part of the product during the conversion process; these include purchased materials, parts, and subassemblies. The *work-in-process inventory* consists of partially completed products that require further processing. The *finished-goods inventory* consists of completed goods awaiting shipment to customers.

Associated with each type of inventory are a *holding cost,* or storage cost, and a *stock-out cost,* the cost of running out of inventory. **Inventory control** is the process of managing inventories in such a way as to minimize inventory costs, including both holding costs and potential stock-out costs. We have already discussed these costs with regard to raw materials or purchased inventories. For work in process, the stock-out cost is the cost of the resulting shutdown or partial shutdown of a production line or facility. For finished goods, the cost of running out is the resulting loss of sales.

Today, computer systems are being used both to control inventory levels and to record costs. For small firms, microcomputer-based systems can be used to keep track of inventories, provide periodic inventory reports, and alert managers to impending stock-outs. For larger firms, more complex computer-based systems maintain inventories of thousands of individual items, perform routine purchasing chores in accordance with a purchasing plan, and schedule the production of both subassemblies and finished goods.

One of the most sophisticated methods of inventory control used today is materials requirements planning. **Materials requirements planning (MRP)** is a computerized system that integrates manufacturing planning and inventory control. One of the great advantages of an MRP system is its ability to juggle delivery schedules and lead times effectively. For a complex product like an automobile or airplane, it is virtually impossible for individual managers to oversee the hundreds of parts that go into the finished product. But a manager using an MRP system can arrange both order and delivery schedules so that materials, parts, and supplies arrive when they are needed. With MRP, the following steps are used:

1. The materials and parts needed for production are listed on a document called a bill of materials.

inventory control the process of managing inventories in such a way as to minimize inventory costs, including both holding costs and potential stock-out costs

materials requirements planning (MRP) a computerized system that integrates manufacturing planning and inventory control

2. Once the materials and parts that are needed have been identified, the amount of inventory on hand is determined.

3. Managers then determine schedules for ordering needed merchandise.

4. Managers also determine delivery schedules for materials and parts that are needed to produce the finished product.

An extension of materials requirements planning is known as *manufacturing resource planning.* The primary difference between the two systems is that materials requirements planning involves just production and inventory personnel whereas the manufacturing resource planning system involves the entire organization. Thus, manufacturing resource planning, often referred to as *MRP II,* provides a single common set of facts that can be used by all of the organization's managers to make effective decisions.

Because large firms can incur huge inventory costs, much attention has been devoted to inventory control. The "just-in-time" system being used by some businesses is one result of all this attention. A **just-in-time inventory system** is designed to ensure that materials or supplies arrive at a facility just when they are needed so that storage is minimized. The just-in-time system reduces carrying costs and excessive inventory. It requires considerable cooperation between the supplier and the customer. The customer must specify what will be needed, when, and in what amounts. The supplier must be sure the right supplies arrive at the agreed upon time and location.

What is most important, however, is not *how* inventories are controlled but the fact that they *are* controlled. Without proper inventory control, it is impossible for operations managers to schedule the work required to produce goods that can be sold to customers.

just-in-time inventory system a system designed to ensure that materials or supplies arrive at a facility just when they are needed so that storage is minimized

Scheduling

scheduling   the process of ensuring that materials are at the right place at the right time

Scheduling is the process of ensuring that materials are at the right place at the right time. These materials may be raw materials, subassemblies, work in process, or finished goods. They may be moved from the warehouse to the work stations; they may move from station to station along an assembly line; or they may arrive at work stations "just in time" to be made part of the work in process there. For finished goods, scheduling involves both movement into finished-goods inventory and shipment to customers to fill orders.

As our definition implies, both place and time are important to scheduling. (This is no different from, say, the scheduling of classes. You cannot attend your classes unless you know both where and when they are held.) The *routing* of materials is the sequence of work stations that the materials will follow. Assume that Drexel-Heritage—one of America's largest furniture manufacturers—is scheduling production of an oval coffee table made from cherry wood. Operations managers would route the needed materials (wood, screws, packaging materials, and so on) through a series of individual work stations along an assembly line. At each work station, a specific task would be performed and then the partially finished piece would move to the next work station. Once all work is completed, Drexel can either store the completed coffee table in a warehouse or ship it to a retailer. When routing materials, operations managers are especially concerned with the sequence of production. For the coffee table, the top and legs must be cut to specifications before the wood is finished. (If the wood was finished before being cut, the finish would be ruined and the coffee table would have to be restained.)

When scheduling production, managers are also concerned with timing. The *timing* function specifies when the materials will arrive at each station and how long they will remain there. For the cherry coffee table, it may take workers thirty minutes to cut the table top and legs and another thirty minutes to drill the holes and assemble the table. Before packaging the coffee table for shipment, it must be finished with cherry stain and allowed to dry. This last step may take as long as three days depending on weather conditions and humidity.

Although it may not seem so, manufacturing a coffee table for Drexel-Heritage is a relatively easy process. Still, whether production is simple or complex, operations managers are responsible for monitoring schedules—called *follow-up*—to ensure that the work flows according to a timetable. For complex products, many operations managers prefer to use Gantt charts or the PERT technique.

Gantt chart a graphic scheduling device that displays the tasks to be performed on the vertical axis and the time required for each task on the horizontal axis

Scheduling Through Gantt Charts   Developed by Henry L. Gantt, a **Gantt chart** is a graphic scheduling device that displays the tasks to be performed on the vertical axis and the time required for each task on the horizontal axis. A typical Gantt chart that describes the activities required to build three dozen golf carts is illustrated in Figure 8.5. As you see in the figure, completed tasks can also be shown on a Gantt chart, so actual progress can be monitored against planned activities. Gantt charts are generally used for scheduling routine production activities. And they can be used for scheduling the work of one worker or the work of a group of employees. Gantt charts are not particularly suitable for scheduling extremely complex situations. Nevertheless, using them forces a manager to plan the steps required to get a job done and to specify time requirements for each part of the job.[6]

PERT (Program Evaluation and Review Technique) a project scheduling technique that identifies the major activities necessary to complete the project and sequences them based on the time required to perform each one

Scheduling Control via PERT   Another technique for scheduling a process or project and maintaining control of the schedule is **PERT (Program Evaluation and Review Technique).** PERT was developed for use in constructing the *Polaris* submarine in the late 1950s. It has since been applied successfully in a wide range of industries.

To use PERT, we begin by identifying all the major *activities* involved in the project. For example, the activities involved in producing a textbook include editing the manuscript, designing the book, obtaining cost estimates, marking the manuscript for typesetting, setting type, and carrying out other activities. The completion of each of these activities is an *event*.

Next we arrange the events in a sequence. In doing so, we must be sure that an event that must occur before another event in the actual process also occurs before that event in the sequence. For example, the manuscript must be edited before the type is set. Therefore, in our sequence, the event "edit manuscript" must precede the event "set type."

Next we use arrows to connect events that must occur in sequence. We then estimate the time required for each activity and mark it near the cor-

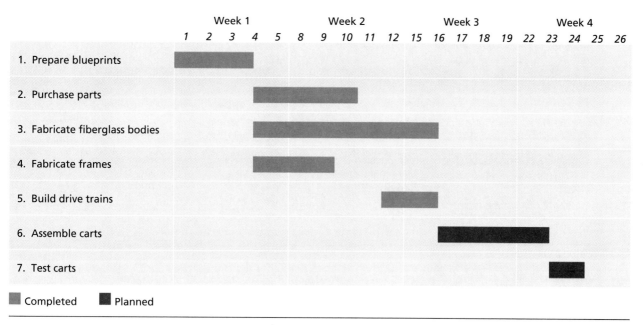

FIGURE 8.5 **A Gantt Chart**
This chart details the job of building three dozen electric golf carts between August 1 and August 25. *(Source: Robert Kreitner,* Management, *6th ed. Copyright © 1995 by Houghton Mifflin Company. Used by permission.)*

responding arrow. The path that takes the longest time from start to finish is called the *critical path.* The activities on this path determine the minimum time in which the process can be completed. These activities are the ones that must be scheduled and controlled carefully. A delay in any one of them will cause a delay in completion of the project as a whole.

Figure 8.6 is a PERT diagram for the production of this book. The critical path runs from event 1 to event 4 to event 5 (which takes 12 weeks) rather than connecting events 1, 2, 3, and 5 (which takes only 10 weeks). It then runs through events 6, 8, and 9 to the finished book at event 10. Note that even a six-week delay in preparing the cover will not delay the production process. However, *any* delay in an activity on the critical path will hold up publication. Thus, if necessary, resources could be diverted from cover preparation to, say, make-up of pages.

Quality Control

quality control the process of ensuring that goods and services are produced in accordance with design specifications

Quality control is the process of ensuring that goods and services are produced in accordance with design specifications for the products. The major objective of quality control is to see that the organization lives up to the standards that it has set for itself on quality. Some firms, such as Mercedes-Benz and Neiman Marcus, have built their reputations on quality. Customers pay more for their products in return for assurances of high quality. Other firms adopt a strategy of emphasizing lower prices along with reasonable (but not particularly high) quality.

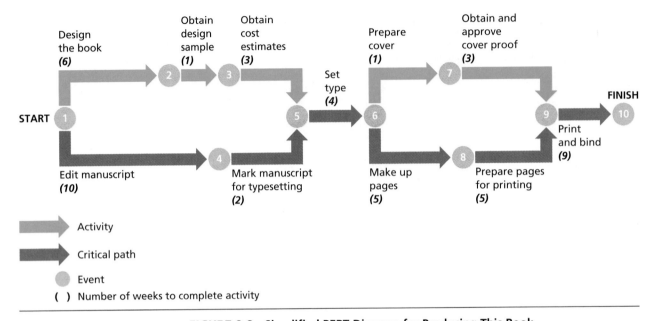

Design
the book
(6)

Obtain
design
sample
(1)

Obtain
cost
estimates
(3)

Set
type
(4)

Prepare
cover
(1)

Obtain and
approve
cover proof
(3)

FINISH

START

Edit manuscript
(10)

Mark manuscript
for typesetting
(2)

Make up
pages
(5)

Prepare pages
for printing
(5)

Print
and bind
(9)

Activity

Critical path

Event

( ) Number of weeks to complete activity

FIGURE 8.6   Simplified PERT Diagram for Producing This Book
A PERT diagram identifies the activities necessary to complete a given project and arranges the activities based on the total time required for each to become an event. The activities on the critical path determine the minimum time required.

quality circle   a group of employees who meet on company time to solve problems of product quality

inspection   the examination of the quality of work in process

American automakers have recently adopted a goal that calls for better quality in their products. The use of a **quality circle,** a group of employees who meet on company time to solve problems of product quality, is one way automakers are achieving this goal at the operations level. Quality circles have also been used successfully in some high-technology companies, such as IBM, the Northrop Corporation, and Digital Equipment.

Increased effort is also being devoted to **inspection,** which is the examination of the quality of work in process. Inspections are performed at various times during production. Purchased materials may be inspected when they arrive at the production facility. Subassemblies and manufactured parts may be inspected before they become part of a finished product. And finished goods may be inspected before they are shipped to customers. Items that are within design specifications continue on their way. Those that are not within design specifications are removed from production.

The method of inspection depends on the item being examined. Visual inspection may be sufficient for products such as furniture or rug-cleaning services. For General Electric, one or two light bulbs may be tested from every hundred produced. At the other extreme, complete x-ray inspection may be required for the vital components of airplanes produced by Cessna.

Historically, efforts to ensure quality increased the costs associated with making that good or service. For that reason, quality and productivity were viewed as conflicting; one was increased at the other's expense. Over the years, more and more managers have realized that quality is an essential

How do you get a job like this? Quality control is part of a sophisticated manufacturing process used at San Antonio–based Pace Foods to transform tomatoes, hot peppers, and seasoning into one of the world's most famous picante sauces. Here workers are using taste testing to ensure that the product measures up to the company's high quality standards.

"ingredient" of the good or service being provided. Viewed in this light, quality becomes an overall approach to doing business and is the concern of all members of the organization (as discussed in Chapter 6). This view of quality provides several benefits. The number of defects decreases, which causes profits to increase. Making products right the first time reduces many of the rejects and much of the rework. And making the employees responsible for quality eliminates the need for inspection. An employee is indoctrinated to accept full responsibility for the quality of his or her work.

■■ THE IMPACT OF COMPUTERS AND ROBOTICS ON PRODUCTION

LEARNING OBJECTIVE 6
Discuss the increasing role of computers and robotics in the production process.

Automation, a development that is revolutionizing the workplace, is the total or near-total use of machines to do work. The rapid increase in automated procedures has been made possible by the microprocessor, a one-quarter-inch square silicon chip that led to the production of desk-top computers for offices and factories. In factories, computers are used in robotics and in computer manufacturing systems.

Robotics

robotics the use of programmable machines to perform a variety of tasks by manipulating materials and tools

Robotics is the use of programmable machines to perform a variety of tasks by manipulating materials and tools. Robots work quickly, accurately, and steadily. They are especially effective in tedious assembly-line jobs and for handling hazardous materials. To date, the automotive industry has made the most extensive use of robotics, but robots have also been used to mine coal, inspect the inner surfaces of pipes, assemble computer components, provide certain kinds of patient care in hospitals, and clean and guard buildings at night. See Change in the Workplace to get a glimpse of U.S. manufacturers hard at work to increase the number of robots used in the workplace.

Computer Manufacturing Systems

computer-aided design (CAD) the use of computers to aid in the development of products

computer-aided manufacturing (CAM) the use of computers to plan and control manufacturing processes

People are quick to point out how computers have changed their everyday life, but most individuals do not realize the impact that computers have had on manufacturing. In simple terms, the factory of the future has already arrived. For most manufacturers, the changeover began with the use of computer-aided design and computer-aided manufacturing. **Computer-aided design (CAD)** is the use of computers to aid in the development of products. Using CAD, Ford speeds up car design, Canon designs new cameras and photocopiers, and American Greetings creates new birthday cards. **Computer-aided manufacturing (CAM)** is the use of computers to plan and control manufacturing processes. A well-designed CAM system allows manufacturers to become much more productive. Not only are a greater number of products produced, but speed and quality also increase. Toyota,

Sewing machine or personal computer? These Italian workers are using a PC to "sew" designer clothing. Here a personal computer is used to not only design clothing but also to cut patterns, make changes in production schedules, and improve overall production efficiency.

■ ■ ■ ■ CHANGE IN THE WORKPLACE

Robots Today and Tomorrow

We were enchanted with R2D2 and C3PO in *Star Wars*. We laughed and cried with Johnny #5 in *Short Circuit*. But those lovable, versatile sci-fi creatures that we watched on the big screen bear no resemblance to the robots used in manufacturing today. Instead, robots are sophisticated machines designed and programmed to do one repetitive task that is too boring for humans. They are also able to maintain consistent quality throughout a process because they never tire and work nonstop, often without supervision. Robots have been used primarily in the United States for assembling automobiles and handling hazardous materials, but now they are slowly popping up in smaller manufacturing operations. Robots still need people to program them, to operate them, to load their parts, and to perform maintenance.

ROBOTS BUILDING PROFITS TODAY

Robots make it possible for companies like Engineering Concepts Unlimited, a small Indiana company, to manufacture palm-sized electronic engine controllers. Worldwide, ECU sells $1 million each year in goods produced by only three employees and four robots. The robots complete one unit every three to four seconds by placing parts in holes, putting boards in a rack, flipping them over, and soldering connections.

The Paramount Corporation, a metal finisher and die caster, uses robots to spray-paint metal boxes that are used to house cable television controls. Paramount had sales last year of around $6 million with fifty employees and two painting robots.

And Kerner Industries of Chico, California, has thirty employees who use robots to manufacture the thermoelectric devices for the modular freezing unit that cools Rubbermaid's 36-quart portable refrigerator. Without robots, Kerner would have to hire fifty additional employees to complete the process.

WHAT IS THE FUTURE OF ROBOTS?

Japanese industry, noted for manufacturing items for far less than we can, uses 400,000 robots compared to the 45,000 robots on U.S. assembly lines today. To close the gap, many U.S. manufacturers are working hard to find new uses for robot technology. Many of the robots being developed and tested today will be used not only in manufacturing but also in farming, health care, and aviation, and possibly as a "robotic housekeeper" for the home.

- ROMPER—robotic melon picker—will identify and harvest round crops like melons, lettuce, cabbage, and pumpkins by imaging and then confirming ripeness by "smell."

- ROBODOC will go into the operating room and bore holes for hip replacements, zap brain tumors with radiation, or operate on unborn babies while a (human) doctor directs the surgery from a computer at a remote location.

- ANDI—automated nondestructive inspector—made of suction cups and a complex pneumatic system, will walk all over an airplane like a fly, even upside-down, to detect tiny but potentially deadly flaws in the plane's skin.

And then there is HOMER, a vacuum cleaner created as a hobby by Frank Jenkins, a computer programmer in Menlo, California. The goal is to develop a robot vacuum cleaner that can free-roam and process sensory information. HOMER still has a way to go: he still needs a neural network that will identify doors, corners, and walls. And he needs to sense where to suck up only the dirt—not a marble, not a sock, and definitely not the cat.

Hasbro, Oneida, and Apple Computer have all used CAM to increase productivity.

If you are thinking that the next logical step is to combine the CAD and CAM computer systems, you are right. Today, the most successful manufacturers have already linked CAD and CAM together to form a computer-integrated manufacturing system. Specifically, **computer-integrated manufacturing (CIM)** is a computer system that not only helps design products but also controls the machinery needed to produce the finished product. For example, Liz Claiborne, Inc., uses CIM to design clothing, establish patterns for the new fashions, and then cut the cloth needed to produce the finished product. Other advantages of using CIM include improved flexibility, more efficient scheduling, and higher product quality—all factors that make a production facility more competitive in today's global economy.

computer-integrated manufacturing (CIM) a computer system that not only helps design products but also controls the machinery needed to produce the finished product

Flexible Manufacturing Systems

Manufacturers have known for a number of years that the old-style, traditional assembly lines used to manufacture products present a number of problems that until now have been difficult to correct. For example, traditional assembly lines turn out extremely large numbers of identical products economically, but the system requires expensive, time-consuming retooling of equipment whenever a new product is to be manufactured. Now, it is possible to use flexible manufacturing systems to solve such problems. A **flexible manufacturing system (FMS)** combines robotics and computer-integrated manufacturing in a single production system. Instead of having to spend vast amounts of time and effort to retool the traditional mechanical equipment on an assembly line for each new product, an FMS is rearranged simply by reprogramming electronic machines. Because FMSs require less time and expense to reprogram, manufacturers can produce smaller batches of a variety of products without raising the production cost.

flexible manufacturing system (FMS) a single production system that combines robotics and computer-integrated manufacturing

In the typical FMS system, robots feed basic wood, metal, or plastic parts into computer-controlled machines and retrieve the parts when they emerge. Automated carts and bins keep the parts moving from one work station to another, while a complex set of electronic controls coordinates the functioning of the entire system. Although the design and installation costs of FMSs are high, the electronic equipment is used more frequently and efficiently than the machinery on a traditional assembly line.

Technological Displacement

Automation is expected to increase productivity by cutting manufacturing time, reducing error, and simplifying retooling procedures. No one knows, however, what the effect will be on the work force. Some experts estimate that automation will bring changes to as many as 45 percent of all jobs by the end of the century. Total unemployment may not increase, but many workers will be faced with the choice of retraining for new jobs or seeking jobs in other sectors of the economy. Institutions of government, business, and education will have to cooperate to prepare workers for new roles in an automated workplace.[7]

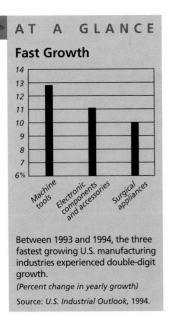

▶ ▶ ▶ **AT A GLANCE**

Fast Growth

Between 1993 and 1994, the three fastest growing U.S. manufacturing industries experienced double-digit growth.
(Percent change in yearly growth)
Source: *U.S. Industrial Outlook*, 1994.

■■ THE MANAGEMENT OF PRODUCTIVITY

No coverage of production and operations management would be complete
without a discussion of productivity. Productivity concerns all managers,
but it is especially important to operations managers, the people who must
oversee the creation of the firm's goods and services. We define **productivity** as a measure of output per unit of time per worker. Hence, if each worker
at plant A produces 75 units per day, and each worker at plant B produces
only 70 units per day, the workers at plant A are more productive. If one
bank teller serves 25 customers per hour and another serves 28 per hour, the
second teller is more productive.

Productivity Trends

Since the early 1960s, the productivity growth rate in the United States has
fallen considerably behind those in other countries. American workers still
produce more than their counterparts in some of the other industrialized
countries, such as Germany, Canada, and Denmark. But our *rate of productivity growth* is lagging behind the productivity growth rates of such other
countries as Sweden and the United Kingdom.[8]

Causes of Productivity Declines

Several factors have been cited as possible causes of America's reduced productivity. First, in recent years the United States has experienced major
changes in the composition of its work force. In particular, many women
and young people have entered the work force for the first time. The majority of these new entrants have relatively little work experience. Therefore,
their productivity might be lower than average. As they develop new skills
and experience, their downward influence on productivity trends should
diminish.

There has also been a shift in the ratio of capital investment to labor
input in American industry. During the last decade, businesses have slowed
their rate of investment in new equipment and technology. As workers have
had to use increasingly outdated equipment, their productivity has naturally
declined.

Yet another factor that may contribute to the decline in productivity
growth is a decrease in spending for research and development. The amount
of money spent for R&D by government and industry, expressed as a percentage of gross national product, has been falling since 1964. As a result,
there have been fewer innovations and new products.

Finally, increased government regulation is frequently cited as a factor
affecting productivity. Federal agencies such as the Occupational Safety and
Health Administration (OSHA) and the Food and Drug Administration
(FDA) are increasingly regulating and intervening in business practices. The
Goodyear Tire & Rubber Company generated 345,000 pages of computer
printout weighing 3,200 pounds to comply with one new OSHA regulation!
Furthermore, the company spends over $35 million each year solely to meet
the requirements of six regulatory agencies.

Danger! This Facility Contains . . . ? One of the reasons for declines in productivity is increased government regulation. Today, all fifty states and many nations around the globe have strict laws that describe proper procedures for handling dangerous chemicals and other hazardous materials. And although business owners often complain about the cost of compliance, they are quick to agree that some government regulation is needed to protect employees, consumers, and the environment.

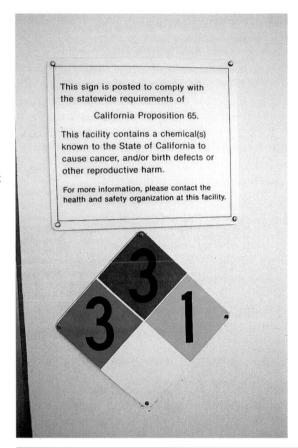

This sign is posted to comply with the statewide requirements of

California Proposition 65.

This facility contains a chemical(s) known to the State of California to cause cancer, and/or birth defects or other reproductive harm.

For more information, please contact the health and safety organization at this facility.

Improving Productivity

Several techniques and strategies have been suggested as possible cures for these downward productivity trends. Some involve the removal of major barriers to productivity growth. For example, research and development could be stimulated by tax credits. Similarly, various government policies that may be hindering productivity could be eliminated or at least modified.

Increased cooperation between management and labor could improve productivity. When unions and management work together, quite often the result is improved productivity.

In a related area, many managers believe that increased employee participation can enhance productivity. A popular method of increasing participation is the quality circle now being used by a number of firms. As we have already noted, quality circles are not only helpful in controlling quality; they can also increase employee morale and motivation through participation in decision making.

Still another potential solution to productivity problems is to change the incentives for work. Many firms simply pay employees for their time, regardless of what or how much they produce. That is, employees are paid by the hour. As long as they produce at some minimal level, everything is fine. By changing the reward system so that people are paid for what they contribute, rather than for the time they put in, it may be possible to motivate employees to produce at higher levels.

The next chapter treats a very important aspect of management in general and of productivity management in particular—employee motivation and morale. In Chapter 9, we discuss a number of major theories of employee motivation. And we see how managers use various reward systems to boost motivation and morale.

■ ■ ■ ■ CHAPTER REVIEW

Summary

1   Explain the nature of operations management.

Operations management consists of all the activities that managers engage in to create products (goods and services). Operations are as relevant to service organizations as to manufacturing firms. Generally, three major activities are involved in producing goods or services: product development, planning for production, and operations control.

2   Outline how the conversion process transforms raw materials, labor, and other resources into finished products.

A business transforms resources into goods and services in order to provide utility to customers. Utility is the ability of a good or service to satisfy a human need. Form utility is created by converting raw materials, labor, and other production inputs into finished products. Conversion processes vary in terms of the major resources used to produce goods and services (focus), the degree to which resources are changed (magnitude), and the number of production processes that a business uses.

3   Discuss the need for research and development.

Operations management often begins with the research and product development effort. The results of R&D may be entirely new products or extensions and refinements of existing products. Research and development activities are classified as basic research (aimed at uncovering new knowledge), applied research (discovering new knowledge with some potential use), and development and implementation

(using new or existing knowledge to produce goods and services).

4   Distinguish between design planning and operational planning.

Planning for production involves two major phases: design planning and operational planning. First, design planning is undertaken to address questions related to the product line, required production capacity, the use of technology, the design of production facilities, and human resources. Next, operational planning focuses on the use of production facilities and resources. The steps for operational planning include (a) selecting the appropriate planning horizon, (b) estimating market demand, (c) comparing market demand and capacity, and (d) adjusting production of products or services to meet demand.

5   Explain the four major areas of operations control: purchasing, inventory control, scheduling, and quality control.

The major areas of operations control are purchasing, inventory control, scheduling, and quality control. Purchasing involves selecting suppliers. The choice of suppliers should result from careful analysis of a number of factors including price, quality, reliability, credit terms, and shipping costs. Inventory control is the management of stocks of raw materials, work in process, and finished goods to minimize the total inventory cost. Today, most firms use a computerized system to maintain inventory records. In addition, many firms use a just-in-time inventory system, in which materials or supplies arrive at a facility just when they are needed so that storage is minimized. Scheduling ensures that materials are at the right place at the right time—for use within the facility or for shipment to customers. Quality control guarantees that products meet their design specifications.

6   Discuss the increasing role of computers and robotics in the production process.

Automation, the total or near-total use of machines to do work, is rapidly changing the way work is done in U.S. factories and offices. A growing number of industries are using programmable machines called robots to perform tasks that are tedious or hazardous to human beings. Computer-aided design, computer-aided manufacturing, and computer-integrated manufacturing use computers to help design and manufacture products. The flexible manufacturing system combines robotics and computer-integrated manufacturing to produce smaller batches of products more efficiently than on the traditional assembly line.

7   Outline the reasons for recent trends in productivity.

In recent years, the productivity growth rate in this country has fallen behind the pace of growth in some of the other industrialized nations. Several factors have been cited as possible causes for this disturbing trend, and managers have begun to explore solutions for overcoming it.

Key Terms

You should now be able to define and give an example relevant to each of the following terms:

operations management (230)
utility (230)
form utility (230)
service economy (232)
research and development (R&D) (234)
design planning (236)
product line (236)
product design (237)
capacity (237)
labor-intensive technology (237)
capital-intensive technology (239)
plant layout (240)
planning horizon (241)
purchasing (243)
inventory control (244)
materials requirements planning (MRP) (244)
just-in-time inventory system (245)
scheduling (245)
Gantt chart (246)

PERT (Program Evaluation and Review Technique) (246)
quality control (247)
quality circle (248)
inspection (248)
robotics (250)
computer-aided design (CAD) (250)
computer-aided manufacturing (CAM) (250)
computer-integrated manufacturing (CIM) (252)
flexible manufacturing system (FMS) (252)
productivity (253)

Questions

Review Questions

1. List all the activities or functions that are involved in operations management.
2. In terms of focus, magnitude, and number, characterize the production processes used by a local pizza parlor, a dry-cleaning establishment, and an auto repair shop.
3. Identify and briefly describe the two major aspects of product development.
4. What are the major elements of design planning?
5. What is the objective of operational planning? What four steps are used to accomplish this objective?
6. If you were an operations manager, what would you do if market demand exceeds the production capacity of your manufacturing facility? What action would you take if the production capacity of your manufacturing facility exceeds market demand?
7. Why is selecting a supplier so important?
8. What costs must be balanced and minimized through inventory control?
9. How can materials requirements planning (MRP) help control inventories?
10. Explain in what sense scheduling is a *control* function of operations managers.
11. How can CAD, CAM, and CIM help a manufacturer produce products?
12. How might productivity be measured in a restaurant? in a department store? in a public school system?

Discussion Questions

1. What developments led IBM to explore new methods of manufacturing products in the early 1990s?

2. For a company like IBM, what are the advantages of soft manufacturing? Are there any disadvantages? Explain.

3. Do certain kinds of firms need to stress particular areas of operations management? Explain.

4. Is it really necessary for service firms to engage in research and development? in operations planning and control?

5. How are the four areas of operations control interrelated?

6. Is operations management relevant to nonbusiness organizations such as colleges and hospitals? Why or why not?

Exercises

1. Assume you have made the decision to go into the business of assembling and selling desk lamps with built-in electronic calculators. Decide whether you would use a process layout or a product layout in your production facility. Then sketch the plant layout.

2. For the calculator lamp in Exercise 1, prepare a two-page executive summary detailing the arrangements you would make in each of the four areas of operations control.

3. Draw a PERT diagram for the development of a term paper. Start with choosing the topic and end with submitting the final draft.

VIDEO CASE 8.1

Saturn Corporation: A Different Kind of Car Company

When the first Saturn car rolled off the assembly line in Spring Hill, Tennessee, on July 30, 1990, the vehicle was the culmination of a revolutionary and exciting dream shared by General Motors Corporation and the United Auto Workers: to work together as equal partners to design and develop a new company that would set an example for American manufacturing excellence. After struggling for over a decade to improve productivity in its automobile manufacturing divisions and being unable to overcome the competition from foreign imports, GM was faced with laying off more than 170,000 blue-collar workers. Its radical solution was to join forces with the unions to create a separate company and, in a whole new way, produce a quality, cost-competitive automobile, while

emphasizing customer satisfaction. The workers, as co-equals with management, are involved in all decision-making aspects of the organization. Through teamwork, newer and more cost-efficient methods of manufacturing, and innovative marketing practices, this partnership has truly become a role model for the industry.

GM first showed the public a prototype of the Saturn in 1984, and in the hopes of reviving the American car industry, the automaker invested more than $4 billion to develop the Saturn Corporation. Saturn's initial success was phenomenal, largely due to outstanding marketing efforts and the fact that the Saturn is an economical car with prices starting under $10,000. Even a fully equipped car costs less than $15,000. Saturn's emphasis on customer satisfaction results in the kind of care and service usually associated with luxury foreign cars like Lexus and Infiniti. The Saturn has the lowest defect rates of any American car on the market. A new distribution system gave dealers franchises in larger geographic areas and allowed them to have multiple showrooms. Sales were so brisk that by summer 1993 dealers were actually unable to keep them in stock. But Saturn's facility in Spring Hill can produce only 300,000 cars per year, and the opening of a second plant was delayed by GM's own financial problems.

Even though Saturn claimed to have broken even in 1993, GM did not agree and put the pressure on the company to turn an operating profit and to revise its manufacturing system. In order to comply, Saturn cut corners drastically by curtailing the expansion of dealerships, slashing advertising, and postponing improvements to aging models. Saturn could not have chosen a worse time to stop being aggressive. It faces tough competition from Chrysler Corporation's new Neon subcompact, as well as from Toyota and Honda. For example, all three offered dual air bags as standard equipment before Saturn.

As a result of the cutbacks, sales began to slow down in early 1994. Granted, it is difficult to overcome GM's ongoing cash problems and its refusal to approve a second facility to boost production to over 500,000 cars per year. Nevertheless, Saturn is trying to recapture its momentum by returning to aggressive advertising, creating new leasing options, and launching new dealerships. Because the Saturn is a good quality car with a high resale value, the company is also considering fleet sales. By late spring 1994 sales began to improve and if they are successful in these new markets, Saturn dealers may again face the same shortages they did in 1993.[9]

Questions

1. Why did General Motors risk more than $4 billion to join forces with the unions in developing the Saturn Corporation?
2. What effect did the decision to slow dealership expansion, cut back on advertising, and postpone product improvements have on the Saturn Corporation?
3. The initial goals of the Saturn Corporation were to produce a quality, cost-competitive automobile and to emphasize customer satisfaction. How did Saturn accomplish these goals?

CASE 8.2

Levi Strauss: A Global Manufacturing Strategy

Make no mistake about it: jeans manufactured by Levi Strauss & Co. have become a status symbol for young, upwardly mobile Europeans and Asians. And customers in Europe and Asia are willing to pay top dollar for a pair of genuine Levis. For example, a pair of Levi's 501 button-fly blue jeans sell for about $80 in European boutiques. The same jeans sell for about $30 at a local J. C. Penney or Sears store in the United States. The demand for Levi Strauss products abroad is also reflected on the firm's financial statements. In 1992—the latest year for which complete financial data are available—Levi Strauss had total sales of $5.6 billion. Of that amount, 38 percent of sales came from outside the United States. Even more important, over half of the firm's $361 million profits came from overseas.

Long ago, management at Levi Strauss developed a corporate strategy that customers—wherever they live—should be supplied with jeans manufactured in nearby factories. To fulfill this goal, Levi Strauss has opened factories in India, Turkey, Korea, Taiwan, Hungary, and Poland. Although *all* manufacturing facilities have their unique problems, management at Levi Strauss has been pleased with its foreign manufacturing operations. For example, Levi's first plant in Eastern Europe was opened in Budapest, Hungary, right next door to Texcoop, a state-owned sweater factory that had gone out of business. In contrast to the outdated equipment collecting dust across the alley, the 350 workers at the Levi Strauss factory use state-of-the-art equipment to stitch seams and sew pockets on more than 1 million jackets and pairs of jeans a year. When employees compare operations at Texcoop with those

at Levi's, they not only praise technological advances but point out that working conditions are better and that materials are always on hand when needed. Workers are also amazed that only eight supervisors oversee the whole factory. Government-run Texcoop employed one manager for every three workers!

In another Levi Strauss plant in Plock, Poland, operations started with the rental and conversion of two football-field-sized warehouses into a factory and the hiring of 600 workers. Despite the fact that factory management has experienced some stumbling blocks—including poor telecommunications and problems obtaining an adequate supply of high-quality thread and certain chemicals—both management and employees are optimistic. They would like to manufacture jeans good enough to be sold in Paris or New York as well as in Warsaw. Since the Levi's trademark has been synonymous with high-quality denim jeans for over a century, this excellence is an especially important goal for any Levi Strauss factory, regardless of its address.

In addition to operating its own manufacturing plants, Levi Strauss pays foreign contractors to produce jeans, jackets, and casual apparel. Before being chosen, contractors must agree to adhere to an extensive set of guidelines that establish acceptable business conduct. Created by Levi Strauss corporate management, the guidelines

- Ensure that wages comply with local laws and are competitive with local businesses.
- Ban the use of child or prison labor.
- Limit working hours and mandate regularly scheduled days off.
- Stipulate certain environmental requirements.
- Establish safe and healthy working conditions.

Since enacting these guidelines, Levi Strauss has terminated its relationship with about 5 percent of its contractors who didn't meet the standards. An additional 25 percent of contractors have been forced to make improvements in the workplace or improve wages paid to employees. Of course, Levi Strauss contractor guidelines can increase manufacturing costs, and these costs are likely to be passed on to Levi Strauss and ultimately to consumers. But according to Robert Haas, chairman and CEO of Levi Strauss, "Ultimately, there are important commercial benefits to be gained from managing your business in a responsible and ethical way that best serves your enterprise's long-term interest. The opposite seems equally clear: the dangers of not doing so are profound."[10]

Questions

1. Why does Levi Strauss want to locate factories in Europe and Asia?

2. Many U.S. businesses choose to manufacture goods in foreign countries because employee wages are lower. Does it seem reasonable then that Levi Strauss should require foreign contractors to adhere to its strict set of guidelines designed to establish acceptable business conduct?

CAREER PROFILE ■ ■ ■ ■ ■ ■ ■ ■ ■ ■ ■ ■ ■

PART 2   Career Opportunities in Management and Organization

Job Title	Job Description	Salary Range
First-line supervisor	Ensure that workers, equipment, and materials are used properly and efficiently; make sure machinery is set up correctly; schedule maintenance of machinery; tell workers what to do and make sure it's done safely, correctly, and on time; enforce safety regulations; evaluate employees; recommend wage increases; and make sure union rules are followed	3–4
Food service manager	Select menu items; determine food, labor, and overhead costs and assign menu prices; order supplies; maintain equipment repairs; interview, hire, fire; schedule workers' hours; supervise kitchen and dining room; resolve customer complaints; during busy hours, managers may help in kitchen or dining room; and manage bookkeeping and payroll tax reports	3
Health service manager	Plan, coordinate, and supervise the delivery of health care; speak before civic groups; promote public participation in health programs; and coordinate the activities of the organization with those of government or community agencies	4–5
Hotel manager	Set room rates; allocate funds; approve expenditures; control food quality; and oversee all assistant managers	5
Management analyst	Varies from employer to employer and project to project; collect, review, and analyze information, make recommendations, and assist in the implementation of proposals; analyze annual revenues and expenditures; interview employees; and observe the operations of organizational unit	4–5
Operation research analyst	Help organizations plan and operate in the most efficient and effective manner; solve problems by using mathematical models; work closely with managers; identify and analyze problems; and build and interpret models	4
Purchasing agent	Purchase the goods, materials, supplies, and services required by an organization; ensure quality and quantity of products; and typically focus on routine purchasing tasks, often specializing in a commodity or a group of related commodities	3–4
Secretarial supervisor	Supervise general secretaries; may also file documents; answer telephones and mail; do research; and prepare statistical reports	3
Traffic manager	Analyze various transportation possibilities and select the methods most suited to the company's needs; select carrier and route; prepare necessary shipping documents; handle damage claims; and consult with company officials about scheduling shipments	4

■ ■ ■ ■ ■ ■ ■ ■ ■ ■ ■ ■ ■ ■ ■

The figure in the salary column approximates the expected annual income after two or three years of service.
1 = $12,000–$15,000; 2 = $16,000–$20,000; 3 = $21,000–$27,000; 4 = $28,000–$35,000; 5 = $36,000 and up.

Educational Requirements	Skills Required	Prospects for Growth
High school diploma; some college helpful	Organizational; leadership; technical; conceptual; interpersonal; decision making	Average
Two years of college or trade school; on-the-job experience	Decision making; interviewing; interpersonal; clerical	Above average
Bachelor's degree in business or hospital administration; master's degree preferred	Communication; interpersonal; conceptual; public speaking; decision making	Greatest
Some college helpful; bachelor's degree preferred; on-the-job experience	Decision making; communication; interpersonal; problem solving	Above average
Bachelor's degree in management; on-the-job experience	Communication; problem solving; interpersonal; conceptual	Above average
Bachelor's degree in math, statistics, or computers	Problem solving; math; interpersonal; conceptual	Above average
Bachelor's degree in business; on-the-job experience helpful	Decision making; budgeting; interpersonal; inspection; conceptual	Average
High school diploma; on-the-job experience; some college preferred	Basic office skills; initiative; writing; interpersonal; organizational	Average
Some college; degree helpful	Conceptual; technical; decision making; communication	Average

261

■■■■ PART THREE

The Human Resource

This part of *Business* is concerned with the most important and least predictable of all resources—people. We begin by discussing various ideas about why people behave as they do, paying special attention to the work environment. Then we apply these ideas to the management of a firm's work force. Finally, we look at organized labor in the United States and probe the sometimes controversial relationship between business management and labor unions. Included in this part are

CHAPTER 9

People and Motivation in Business

LEARNING OBJECTIVES

After studying this chapter you should be able to

1 Explain what motivation is.

2 Recognize some earlier perspectives on motivation: scientific management, Theory X, and Theory Y.

3 Outline Maslow's hierarchy of needs.

4 Discuss Herzberg's motivation-hygiene theory.

5 Describe four contemporary views of motivation: equity theory, expectancy theory, reinforcement theory, and Theory Z.

6 Explain several techniques for increasing employee motivation.

CHAPTER PREVIEW

First, to provide a perspective of current motivational theories, we present several early views of motivation that influenced management practices, including Taylor's ideas of scientific management, Mayo's Hawthorne Studies, and McGregor's Theory X and Theory Y. We also describe two widely known theories of human motivation—Maslow's hierarchy of needs and Herzberg's concepts of satisfaction and dissatisfaction. Then, turning our attention to contemporary ideas, we examine equity theory, expectancy theory, reinforcement theory, and Theory Z, and explain how to apply these motivational theories in an organization's reward system. Finally, we discuss specific techniques managers can use to improve employee motivation.

Motivating Basketball Stars and Business Executives

A roomful of *Fortune* 500 executives is waiting to hear a talk about motivating and empowering their employees, establishing goals, and implementing teamwork. The speaker steps onto the stage. He's wearing a chic tie and an Armani suit. Is he a high-powered business consultant? No. He's Pat Riley, then coach of the New York Knicks. Riley piloted the Los Angeles Lakers to four National Basketball Association championships, guided the Knicks to the best record in the Eastern Conference, and was twice named NBA Coach of the Year.

Addressing a group of IBM executives, Riley said, "I have a basketball in my hands, and someone from IBM has a computer, but it all comes down to the same thing: being part of a team." Riley's basketball experiences have taught him that people are motivated to work hard and do their best if they feel that they are part of a team. For example, when the Lakers signed Magic Johnson to a $25 million contract, other players' jealousy and resentment translated into lackluster playing and a series of losses. Then Riley became head coach, instilled his vision of the importance of teamwork, and turned the Lakers into the team of the decade. At regular team meetings everyone has a chance to speak, and the group decides what it needs to do to win the championship. After setting specific goals, team members monitor one another to make sure everyone is doing his best to meet the standards they have all set.

In addition to teamwork, Riley strongly advocates recognizing and rewarding effort. Insists Riley, "Everyone wants to stand up and be counted." It's not just the glamour of the slam dunk that makes a winning team, Riley asserts, but the more modest contributions that the tele-

vision cameras don't capture. To make sure that all of his players' efforts are noticed, Riley initiated the "Career Best Effort Program." Starting with the player's record when first joining the team, Riley assesses what that player is capable of in the future. Because measuring up against a superstar like Patrick Ewing might make a player feel defeated before he begins, no one's accomplishments are judged against those of his teammates. Every year, Riley compares a player's performance in five areas to his own performance the year before. And it isn't just points, rebounds, and assists that count, but effort too. When a player's statistics improve, Riley posts them on the player's locker for everyone to see.

A recent survey of 3,100 *Fortune* 1000 executives revealed that Riley is among the top five individuals cited as inspiring them to change the way they make business decisions. More than four hundred of them have each paid him $25,000 to speak to groups of their managers.

■ ■ ■ ■

265

■ ■ ■ ■ ■ ■ ■ ■ ■ ■ ■ ■

To achieve organizational goals effectively, employees need more than the right raw materials, adequate facilities, and equipment that works. Whether it's the New York Knicks, IBM, or a local convenience store, organizations must also have motivated employees. Although from time to time some workers may be dissatisfied, other employees are quite satisfied with their jobs and are motivated to meet high performance goals. To some extent, a high level of employee motivation derives from effective management practices.

■ ■ WHAT IS MOTIVATION?

LEARNING OBJECTIVE 1
Explain what motivation is.

motivation the individual, internal process that energizes, directs, and sustains behavior; the personal "force" that causes us to behave in a particular way

morale an employee's feelings toward his or her job and superiors and toward the firm itself

We look at various levels of needs and motivation later in this chapter, but first we must ask, what exactly is motivation? Most often, the term is used to explain people's behavior. Successful athletes are said to be highly motivated. A student who avoids work is said to be unmotivated. (From another viewpoint, the student might be thought of as motivated—to avoid work.)

We define **motivation** as the individual, internal process that energizes, directs, and sustains behavior. Motivation is the personal "force" that causes you or me to behave in a particular way. When we say that job rotation motivates employees, we mean that it activates this process or force within them.

An employee's **morale** is his or her feelings toward the job, toward superiors, and toward the firm itself. High morale results mainly from the satisfaction of needs on the job or as a result of the job. One need that might be satisfied on the job is the need *to be recognized* as an important contributor to the organization. Another need satisfied as a result of the job is the need for *financial security*. High morale, in turn, leads to the dedication and loyalty that are in evidence at the Japanese auto plants in the United States, as well as to the desire to do the job well. Low morale can lead to shoddy work, absenteeism, and high turnover rates as employees leave to seek more satisfying jobs with other firms.

Motivation, morale, and the satisfaction of employees' needs are thus intertwined. Along with productivity, they have been the subject of much study since the end of the nineteenth century. We continue our discussion of motivation by outlining some landmarks of that early research.

■ ■ HISTORICAL PERSPECTIVES ON MOTIVATION

LEARNING OBJECTIVE 2
Recognize some earlier perspectives on motivation: scientific management, Theory X, and Theory Y.

Researchers often begin a study with some fairly narrow goal in mind. But after they develop an understanding of their subject, they realize that both their goal and their research should be broadened. This is exactly what happened when early research into productivity blossomed into the more modern study of employee motivation.

266

Taking pride in your work can be quite motivating. This craftsman is using his skills and expertise to restore this theater facade. His meticulous efforts are largely motivated by the pride that comes from doing excellent work.

Scientific Management

During the early part of the twentieth century, Frederick W. Taylor became interested in improving the efficiency of individual workers. This interest stemmed from his own experiences in manufacturing plants. It eventually led to **scientific management,** the application of scientific principles to management of work and workers.

scientific management   the application of scientific principles to management of work and workers

One of Taylor's first jobs was with the Midvale Steel Company in Philadelphia, where he developed a strong distaste for waste and inefficiency. He also observed a practice he called "soldiering." Workers soldiered, or worked slowly, because they feared if they worked faster, they would run out of work and lose their jobs. Taylor realized managers were not aware of this practice because they had no idea what the workers' productivity level *should* be.

Taylor later left Midvale and spent several years at Bethlehem Steel. It was there that he made his most significant contribution. In particular, he suggested that each job should be broken down into separate tasks. Then management should determine (1) the best way to perform these tasks and (2) the job output to expect when the tasks were performed properly. Next, management should carefully choose the best person for each job and train that person to do the job properly. Finally, management should cooperate with workers to ensure that jobs were performed as planned.

piece-rate system   a compensation system under which employees are paid a certain amount for each unit of output they produce

Taylor also developed the idea that most people work only to earn money. He therefore reasoned that pay should be tied directly to output. The more a person produced, the more he or she should be paid. This gave rise to the **piece-rate system,** under which employees are paid a certain amount for each unit of output they produce. The piece-rate system is used by some firms in the garment industry. Under Taylor's piece-rate system, each employee was assigned an output quota. Those exceeding the quota were paid a higher per-unit rate for *all* units they produced (see Figure 9.1).

Taylor's system was put into practice at Bethlehem Steel, and the results were dramatic. Average earnings per day for steel handlers rose from $1.15 to $1.88. (Don't let the low wages that prevailed at the time obscure the fact that this is an increase of better than 63 percent!) The average amount of steel handled per day increased from 16 to 57 tons.

Taylor's revolutionary ideas had a profound impact on management practice. However, his view of motivation was soon recognized as overly simplistic and narrow. It is true that most people expect to be paid for their work. But it is also true that people work for a variety of reasons other than pay. Simply increasing a person's pay may not increase his or her motivation or productivity.

The Hawthorne Studies

Between 1927 and 1932, two experiments were conducted by Elton Mayo at the Hawthorne plant of the Western Electric Company in Chicago. The original objective of these studies, now referred to as the Hawthorne Studies, was to determine the effects of the work environment on employee productivity.

In the first set of experiments, lighting in the workplace was varied for one group of workers but not for a second group. Then the productivity of both groups was measured to determine the effect of the variations in light. To the amazement of the researchers, productivity increased for *both* groups. And for the group whose lighting was varied, productivity remained high until the light was reduced to the level of moonlight!

The second set of experiments focused on the effectiveness of the piece-rate system in increasing the output of *groups* of workers. Researchers expected that output would increase because faster workers would put pressure on slower workers to produce more. Again, the results were not as expected. Output remained constant, no matter what "standard" rates management set.

FIGURE 9.1
The Piece-Rate System
Workers who exceeded their quota were rewarded by being paid at a higher rate per piece for all the pieces they produced.

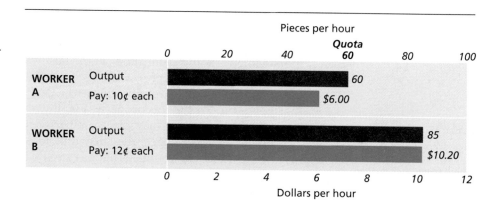

The researchers came to the conclusion that *human factors* were responsible for the results of the two experiments. In the lighting experiments, researchers had given both groups of workers a *sense of involvement* in their jobs merely by asking them to participate in the research. These workers—perhaps for the first time—felt as though they were an important part of the organization. In the piece-rate experiments, each group of workers informally set the acceptable rate of output for the group. To gain or retain the *social acceptance* of the group, each worker had to produce at that rate. Slower or faster workers were pressured to maintain the group's pace.

The Hawthorne Studies showed that such human factors are at least as important to motivation as pay rates. From these and other studies, the *human relations movement* in management was born. Its premise was simple: employees who are happy and satisfied with their work are motivated to perform better. Hence, management would do best to provide a work environment that maximizes employee satisfaction.

Theory X and Theory Y

The concepts of Theory X and Theory Y were advanced by Douglas McGregor in his 1960 book *The Human Side of Enterprise.*[2] They are, in essence, sets of assumptions that underlie management's attitudes and beliefs regarding worker behavior.

Theory X a concept of employee motivation generally consistent with Taylor's scientific management; assumes that employees dislike work and will function only in a highly controlled work environment

Theory X is a concept of employee motivation generally consistent with Taylor's scientific management. Theory X assumes that employees dislike work and will function effectively only in a highly controlled work environment. According to Theory X,

1. People dislike work and try to avoid it.
2. Because people dislike work, managers must coerce, control, and frequently threaten employees to achieve organizational goals.
3. People generally must be led because they have little ambition and will not seek responsibility; they are concerned mainly with security.

The logical outcome of such assumptions will be a highly controlled work environment—one in which managers make all the decisions and employees take all the orders.

Theory Y a concept of employee motivation generally consistent with the ideas of the human relations movement; assumes that employees accept responsibility and work toward organizational goals if by so doing they also achieve personal rewards

On the other hand, **Theory Y** is a concept of employee motivation generally consistent with the ideas of the human relations movement. Theory Y assumes that employees accept responsibility and work toward organizational goals if by so doing they also achieve personal rewards. According to Theory Y,

1. People do not naturally dislike work; in fact, work is an important part of their lives.
2. People will work toward goals to which they are committed.
3. People become committed to goals when it is clear that accomplishing the goals will bring personal rewards.
4. People often seek out and willingly accept responsibility.

5. Employees have the potential to help accomplish organizational goals.

6. Organizations generally do not make full use of their human resources.

Obviously this view is quite different from—and much more positive than—that of Theory X. McGregor argued that most managers behave in accordance with Theory X. But he maintained that Theory Y is more appropriate and effective as a guide for managerial action (see Table 9.1).

The human relations movement and Theories X and Y increased managers' awareness of the importance of social factors in the workplace. However, human motivation is a complex and dynamic process to which there is no simple key—neither money alone nor social factors alone. Rather, a variety of factors must be considered in any attempt to increase motivation. We turn now from research on worker productivity to research that focused directly on human needs.

■■■ MASLOW'S HIERARCHY OF NEEDS

LEARNING OBJECTIVE 3
Outline Maslow's hierarchy of needs.

need   a personal requirement

hierarchy of needs   Maslow's sequence of human needs in the order of their importance

physiological needs   the things human beings require for survival

safety needs   the things human beings require for physical and emotional security

social needs   the human requirements for love and affection and a sense of belonging

The concept of a hierarchy of needs was advanced by Abraham Maslow, a psychologist. A **need** is a personal requirement. Maslow assumed that humans are "wanting" beings who seek to fulfill a variety of needs. He observed that these needs can be arranged according to their importance in a sequence now known as Maslow's **hierarchy of needs** (see Figure 9.2).

At the most basic level are **physiological needs,** the things we require to survive. These needs include food and water, clothing, shelter, and sleep. In the employment context, these needs are usually satisfied through adequate wages.

At the next level are **safety needs,** the things we require for physical and emotional security. Safety needs may be satisfied through job security, health insurance, pension plans, and safe working conditions.

Next are the **social needs,** the human requirements for love and affection and a sense of belonging. To an extent, these needs can be satisfied through relationships in the work environment and the informal organization. But social networks beyond the workplace—with family and friends, for example—are usually needed too.

TABLE 9.1   Theory X and Theory Y Contrasted

Area	Theory X	Theory Y
Attitude toward work	Dislike	Involvement
Control systems	External	Internal
Supervision	Direct	Indirect
Level of commitment	Low	High
Employee potential	Ignored	Identified
Use of human resources	Limited	Not limited

FIGURE 9.2
Maslow's Hierarchy of Needs
Maslow believed that people act to fulfill five categories of needs.

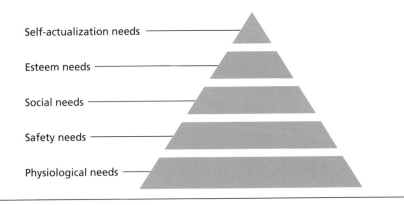

Self-actualization needs

Esteem needs

Social needs

Safety needs

Physiological needs

esteem needs the human requirements for respect, recognition, and a sense of one's own accomplishment and worth

self-actualization needs the needs to grow and develop as people and to become all that we are capable of being

At the level of **esteem needs,** we require respect and recognition (the esteem of others), as well as a sense of our own accomplishment and worth (self-esteem). These needs may be satisfied through personal accomplishment, promotion to more responsible jobs, various honors and awards, and other forms of recognition.

At the uppermost level are **self-actualization needs,** the needs to grow and develop as people and to become all that we are capable of being. These are the most difficult needs to satisfy, and the means of satisfying them tend to vary with the individual. For some people, learning a new skill, starting a new career after retirement, or becoming "the best there is" at some endeavor may be the way to satisfy the self-actualization needs.

Maslow suggested that people work to satisfy their physiological needs first, then their safety needs, and so on up the "needs ladder." In general, they are motivated by the needs at the lowest (most important) level that remain unsatisfied. However, needs at one level do not have to be completely satisfied before needs at the next-higher level come into play. If the majority of a person's physiological and safety needs are satisfied, that person will be motivated primarily by social needs. But any physiological and safety needs that remain unsatisfied will also be important.

Maslow's hierarchy of needs provides a useful way of viewing employee motivation, as well as a guide for management. By and large, American business has been able to satisfy workers' basic needs, but the higher-order needs present more of a challenge. These needs are not satisfied in a simple manner, and the means of satisfaction vary from one employee to another.

■■ HERZBERG'S THEORY

LEARNING OBJECTIVE 4
Discuss Herzberg's motivation-hygiene theory.

In the late 1950s, Frederick Herzberg interviewed approximately two hundred accountants and engineers in Pittsburgh. During the interviews, he asked them to think of a time when they had felt especially good about their jobs and their work. Then he asked them to describe the factor or factors that had caused them to feel that way. Next he did the same regarding a time when they had felt especially bad about their work. He was surprised to find that feeling good and feeling bad resulted from entirely different sets of factors. That is, low pay might have made a particular person feel bad, but it was not high pay that had made him or her feel good. Instead, it was some completely different factor.

Satisfaction and Dissatisfaction

Prior to Herzberg's interviews, the general assumption was that employee satisfaction and dissatisfaction lay at opposite ends of the same scale. People felt satisfied, dissatisfied, or somewhere in between. Herzberg's interviews, however, convinced him that satisfaction and dissatisfaction may be different dimensions altogether. One dimension might range from satisfaction to no satisfaction, and the other might range from dissatisfaction to no dissatisfaction. In other words, the opposite of satisfaction is not dissatisfaction. The idea that satisfaction and dissatisfaction are separate and distinct dimensions is referred to as the **motivation-hygiene theory** (see Figure 9.3).

The job factors that Herzberg found most frequently associated with satisfaction are achievement, recognition, responsibility, advancement, growth, and the work itself. These factors are generally referred to as **motivation factors** because their presence increases motivation. However, their absence does not necessarily result in feelings of dissatisfaction. When motivation factors are present, they act as *satisfiers.*

Job factors cited as causing dissatisfaction are supervision, working conditions, interpersonal relationships, pay, job security, and company policies and administration. These factors, called **hygiene factors,** reduce dissatisfaction when they are present to an acceptable degree. However, they do not necessarily result in high levels of motivation. When hygiene factors are absent, they act as *dissatisfiers.*

Using Herzberg's Theory

Herzberg provides explicit guidelines for using the motivation-hygiene theory of employee motivation. He suggests that the hygiene factors must be present to ensure that a worker can function comfortably. But he warns that

motivation-hygiene theory the idea that satisfaction and dissatisfaction are separate and distinct dimensions

motivation factors job factors that increase motivation, but whose absence does not necessarily result in dissatisfaction, according to the motivation-hygiene theory

hygiene factors job factors that reduce dissatisfaction when present to an acceptable degree, but do not necessarily result in high levels of motivation, according to the motivation-hygiene theory

FIGURE 9.3
Motivation-Hygiene Theory
Herzberg's theory takes into account that there are different dimensions to job satisfaction and dissatisfaction and that these factors do not overlap.

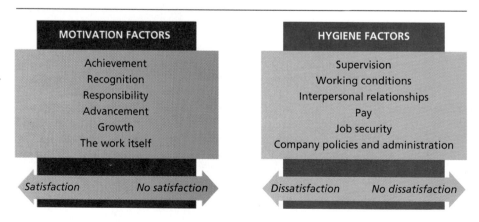

a state of *no dissatisfaction* never exists. In any situation, people will always be dissatisfied with something.

Managers should make hygiene as positive as possible but should then expect only short-term, not long-term, improvement in motivation. Managers must instead focus on providing the motivation factors, which *will* presumably enhance motivation and long-term effort.

We should note that employee pay has more effect than Herzberg's theory indicates. He suggests that pay provides only short-term change and not true motivation. Yet, in many organizations, pay constitutes a form of recognition and reward for achievement—and recognition and achievement are both motivation factors. The effect of pay may depend on how it is distributed. If a pay increase does not depend on performance (as in across-the-board or cost-of-living raises), it may not motivate people. However, if pay is increased as a form of recognition (as in bonuses or incentives), it may play a powerful role in motivating employees to higher performance.

■■ CONTEMPORARY VIEWS ON MOTIVATION

LEARNING OBJECTIVE 5
Describe four contemporary views of motivation: equity theory, expectancy theory, reinforcement theory, and Theory Z.

Maslow's hierarchy of needs and Herzberg's two-factor theory are popular and widely known theories of motivation. Each is also a significant step up from the relatively narrow views of scientific management and Theories X and Y. But they do have one weakness: each attempts to specify *what* motivates people, but neither explains *why* or *how* motivation develops or is sustained over time. In recent years, managers have begun to explore four other models that take a more dynamic view of motivation. These are equity theory, expectancy theory, reinforcement theory, and Theory Z.

Equity Theory

equity theory   a theory of motivation based on the premise that people are motivated first to achieve and then to maintain a sense of equity

The **equity theory** of motivation is based on the premise that people are motivated first to achieve and then to maintain a sense of equity. As used here, *equity* is the distribution of rewards in direct proportion to the contribution of each employee to the organization. Everyone need not receive the *same* rewards, but the rewards should be in accordance with individual contributions.

According to the theory, we tend to implement the idea of equity in the following way. First, we develop our own input-to-outcome ratio. Inputs are the time, effort, skills, education, experience, and so on that we contribute to the organization. Outcomes are the opposite: the rewards we get from the organization, such as pay, benefits, recognition, and promotions. Next, we compare this ratio with what we perceive as the input-to-outcome ratio for some other person. It might be a coworker, a friend who works for another firm, or even an average of all the people in our organization. This person is called the "comparison other." Note that our perception of this person's input-to-outcome ratio may be absolutely correct or completely wrong. However, we believe it is correct.

If the two ratios are roughly the same, we feel that the organization is treating us equitably. In this case we are motivated to leave things as they

FIGURE 9.4
Expectancy Theory
Vroom's theory is based on the idea that motivation depends on how much people want something and on how likely they think they are to get it.

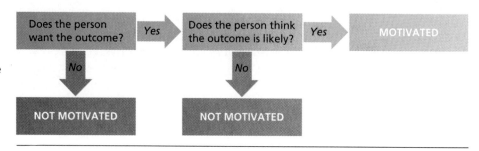

are. However, if our ratio is the higher of the two, we feel underrewarded and are motivated to make changes. We may (1) decrease our own inputs by not working so hard, (2) try to increase our total outcome by asking for a raise in pay, (3) try to get the comparison other to increase some inputs or receive decreased outcomes, (4) leave the work situation, or (5) do a new comparison with a different comparison other.

Equity theory is most relevant to pay as an outcome. Because pay is a very real measure of a person's worth to the organization, comparisons involving pay are a natural part of organizational life. Managers can avoid problems arising from inequity by doing everything possible to avoid inequity. For instance, they can make sure that rewards are distributed on the basis of performance and that everyone clearly understands the basis for his or her own pay.

Expectancy Theory

expectancy theory a model of motivation based on the assumption that motivation depends on how much we want something and on how likely we think we are to get it

Expectancy theory, developed by Victor Vroom, is a very complex model of motivation that is based on a deceptively simple assumption. According to expectancy theory, motivation depends on how much we want something and on how likely we think we are to get it (see Figure 9.4). Consider, for example, the case of three sales representatives who are candidates for promotion to one sales manager's job. Bill has had a very good sales year and always gets good performance evaluations. However, he isn't sure he wants the job because it involves a great deal of travel, long working hours, and much stress and pressure. Paul wants the job badly but doesn't think he has much chance of getting it. He has had a terrible sales year and gets only mediocre performance evaluations from his present boss. Susan wants the job as much as Paul, and she thinks she has a pretty good shot at it. Her sales have improved significantly this past year, and her evaluations are the best in the company.

Expectancy theory would predict that Bill and Paul are not very motivated to seek the promotion. Bill doesn't really want it, and Paul doesn't think he has much of a chance of getting it. Susan, however, is very motivated to seek the promotion because she wants it *and* thinks she can get it.

Expectancy theory is complex because each action we take is likely to lead to several different outcomes, some we may want and others we may not want. For example, a person who works hard and puts in many extra hours may get a pay raise, be promoted, and gain valuable new job skills.

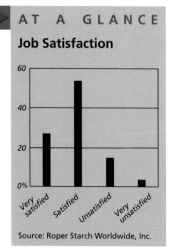

Motivating Workers Takes More Than Money

When *Working Woman* magazine asked 200 CEOs what business would be like in the twenty-first century, 80 percent said that to stay competitive, they'd have to push their workers harder than ever. How will managers persuade their employees to give 110 percent to the company? A recent Roper poll shows that the answer isn't necessarily salary. Asked to define *success,* 80 percent of the 1,027 respondents put "Having a happy family life" first and "Having money and power" dead last on a list of seven choices. Productivity will depend as much on satisfied workers as on state-of-the-art processes and high-tech machinery, and so more businesses will have to motivate people in nontraditional ways.

Managers have typically assumed that employees who want more time for family or for leisure are not highly motivated in their jobs. What they have discovered instead is that workers who have more time to spend with their families or on outside pursuits are actually *more* motivated and *more* productive. Part-time employment, job sharing, flextime, compressed work weeks, and telecommuting are all ways of providing workers with flexible schedules. Job sharing is a type of part-time work in which two people share one job. When you work twenty to twenty-five hours a week instead of forty, you can work harder while you're at work, knowing that you have enough time to concentrate on your personal life. Compressed work weeks, in which people work forty hours in four days instead of five, is another way of giving employees more personal time. Flextime allows workers to start their days early or late, whichever best suits individual needs. Telecommuters don't even have to come to the office at all; they use phone, Fax, and computer to work at home. Recent studies done at companies that encourage telecommuting, such as Hewlitt-Packard, Citicorp, American Express, and Traveler's Insurance, show that employee productivity rose 20 to 30 percent, workers took fewer sick days, and there was more job satisfaction and less job turnover.

Research shows that people who work in an authoritarian environment do only as much work as they have to and leave as soon as they can. Those who are treated with respect, who receive recognition, who are encouraged to be involved in the company, and who function with some measure of independence are more motivated and more productive. Industry experts claim that one of the secrets of Wal-Mart's success is its positive relations with employees. Recognizing employees for their contributions and suggestions motivates them to do more. Many organizations reward workers for suggestions that save money, streamline procedures, or in some way contribute to the company. Workers who feel personally involved with the company are more motivated. By informing workers about the business—trusting them with sales figures and operating costs, for example, rather than keeping such statistics secret—management keeps workers from feeling as if they are on the outside looking in. For example, SuperQuinn, a major grocery chain in Dublin, Ireland, reports the company's sales volume and profits to every employee, including part-time workers.

Recognizing the need to reinvent the workplace, increasing numbers of U.S. businesses are finding new ways to motivate employees. Offering family-friendly scheduling and encouraging a more participative management style are noteworthy examples. Having a written policy and implementing that policy, however, do not always go hand in hand, and conventional attitudes are hard to change. When interviewed, employees at eighty major companies revealed that fewer than 2 percent take advantage of job sharing, telecommuting, or part-time hours. Many people are afraid that by changing the way they work, they will lose seniority, incur the resentment of fellow employees, and jeopardize their jobs. Finding ways to motivate these workers will challenge business into the next century.

But that person may also be forced to spend less time with his or her family and be forced to cut back on social life.

For one person, the promotion may be paramount, the pay raise and new skills fairly important, and the loss of family and social life of negligible importance. For someone else, the family and social life may be the most important, the pay raise of moderate importance, the new skills unimportant, and the promotion undesirable because of the additional hours it would require. The first person would be motivated to work hard and put in the extra hours, whereas the second person would not be at all motivated to do so. In other words, it is the entire bundle of outcomes—and the individual's evaluation of the importance of each outcome—that determines motivation.

Expectancy theory is difficult to apply, but it does provide several useful guidelines for managers. It suggests that managers must recognize that (1) employees work for a variety of different reasons; (2) these reasons, or expected outcomes, may change over time; and (3) it is necessary to clearly show employees how they can attain the outcomes they desire.

Reinforcement Theory

reinforcement theory
a theory of motivation based on the premise that behavior that is rewarded is likely to be repeated, whereas behavior that is punished is less likely to recur

The contemporary motivation theory with perhaps the greatest potential for business application is reinforcement theory. **Reinforcement theory** is based on the premise that behavior that is rewarded is likely to be repeated, whereas behavior that is punished is less likely to recur.

Kinds of Reinforcement A *reinforcement* is an action that follows directly from a particular behavior. It may be a pay raise following a particularly large sale to a new customer or a reprimand for coming to work late. Reinforcements can take a variety of forms and can be used in a number of ways. A *positive reinforcement* is one that strengthens desired behavior by providing a reward. For example, many employees respond well to praise. Recognition from their supervisors for a job well done increases (strengthens) their willingness to perform well in the future.

A *negative reinforcement* strengthens desired behavior by eliminating an undesirable task or situation. Suppose a machine shop must be cleaned thoroughly every month—a dirty, miserable task. During one particular month when the workers do a less-than-satisfactory job at their normal work assignments, the boss requires the workers to clean the factory rather than bringing in the usual private maintenance service. The employees will be motivated to work harder the next month to avoid the unpleasant cleanup duty again.

Punishment is an undesired consequence that follows from undesirable behavior. Common forms of punishment used in organizations include reprimands, reduced pay, disciplinary layoffs, and termination (firing). Punishment often does more harm than good. It tends to create an unpleasant environment, fosters hostility and resentment, and suppresses undesirable behavior only until the supervisor's back is turned.

Managers who rely on *extinction* hope to eliminate undesirable behavior by ignoring it. The idea is that the behavior will eventually become "extinct." Suppose, for example, that an employee has the habit of writing memo after memo to his or her manager about insignificant events. If the manager doesn't respond to any of these memos, the employee will probably stop writing them, and the behavior will have been squelched.

Using Reinforcement The effectiveness of reinforcement depends on which type is used and how it is timed. Each of the four types is best in certain situations. However, many situations lend themselves to the use of more than one type. Generally, positive reinforcement is considered the most effective, and it is recommended when the manager has a choice.

Continual, repetitious reinforcement can become tedious for both manager and employees, especially when the same behavior is being reinforced over and over in the same way. At the start, it may be necessary to reinforce a desired behavior every time it occurs. However, once a desired behavior has become more or less established, occasional reinforcement seems to be most effective.

Theory Z

In the 1970s William Ouchi, a management professor at UCLA, began to study business practices in American and Japanese firms. He concluded that different types of management systems dominate in these two countries.[3] In Japan, Ouchi found what he calls *Type J* firms. They are characterized by lifetime employment for employees, collective (or group) decision making, collective responsibility for the outcomes of decisions, slow evaluation and promotion, implied control mechanisms, nonspecialized career paths, and a holistic concern for employees as people.

American industry is dominated by what Ouchi calls *Type A* firms, which follow a different pattern. They emphasize short-term employment, individual decision making, individual responsibility for the outcomes of decisions, rapid evaluation and promotion, explicit control mechanisms, specialized career paths, and a segmented concern for employees only as employees.

A few very successful American firms represent a blend of the Type J and Type A patterns. These *Type Z* organizations emphasize long-term employment, collective decision making, individual responsibility for the outcomes of decisions, slow evaluation and promotion, informal control along with some formalized measures, moderately specialized career paths, and a holistic concern for employees. Examples of Type Z firms are IBM, Eastman Kodak, Hewlett-Packard, and Ford.

Theory Z is the belief that some middle ground between Ouchi's Type A and Type J practices is best for American business (see Figure 9.5). A major part of Theory Z is the emphasis on participative decision making. The focus is on "we" rather than on "us versus them." Theory Z employees and managers view the organization as a family. This participative spirit fosters cooperation and the dissemination of information and organizational values.

Theory Z the belief that some middle ground between Ouchi's Type A and Type J practices is best for American business

■■ KEY MOTIVATION TECHNIQUES

LEARNING OBJECTIVE 6
Explain several techniques for increasing employee motivation.

Today, it takes more than a generous salary to motivate employees. Increasingly, companies are trying to motivate employees by satisfying their less

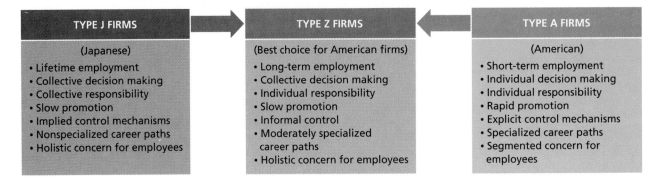

TYPE J FIRMS	TYPE Z FIRMS	TYPE A FIRMS
(Japanese)	(Best choice for American firms)	(American)
• Lifetime employment • Collective decision making • Collective responsibility • Slow promotion • Implied control mechanisms • Nonspecialized career paths • Holistic concern for employees	• Long-term employment • Collective decision making • Individual responsibility • Slow promotion • Informal control • Moderately specialized career paths • Holistic concern for employees	• Short-term employment • Individual decision making • Individual responsibility • Rapid promotion • Explicit control mechanisms • Specialized career paths • Segmented concern for employees

FIGURE 9.5   The Features of Theory Z
The best aspects of Japanese and American management theories combine to form the nucleus of Theory Z.

tangible needs. In this section we discuss several specific techniques that help managers boost employee motivation.

Management by Objectives

management by objectives (MBO) a motivation technique in which managers and employees collaborate in setting goals

Management by objectives (MBO) is a motivation technique in which managers and employees collaborate in setting goals. The primary purpose of MBO is to clarify the roles that the employees are expected to play in reaching the organization's goals. By allowing individuals to participate in goal setting and performance evaluation, MBO increases their motivation. Most MBO programs consist of a series of five steps, as shown in Figure 9.6.

The first step in setting up an MBO program is to secure the acceptance of top management. It is essential that top managers endorse and participate in the program if others in the firm are to accept it. The commitment of top management also provides a natural starting point for educating employees about the purposes and mechanics of MBO.

Next, preliminary goals must be established. Top management also plays a major role in this activity because the preliminary goals reflect the firm's mission and strategy. The intent is to have these goals filter down through the organization.

The third step, which actually consists of several smaller steps, is the heart of MBO.

1. The manager explains to each employee that he or she has accepted certain goals for the group (manager plus employees) and asks the individual to think about how he or she can help achieve these goals.

2. The manager later meets with each employee individually. Together, the two of them establish goals for the employee. Whenever possible, the goals should be measurable and should specify the time frame for completion (usually one year).

3. The manager and the employee decide what resources the employee will need in order to accomplish his or her goals.

As the fourth step, the manager and each employee meet periodically to review the employee's progress. They may agree to modify certain goals during these meetings if circumstances have changed. For example, a sales representative may have accepted a goal of increasing sales by 20 percent. However, an aggressive competitor may have entered the marketplace, making this goal unattainable. In light of this circumstance, the goal may be revised downward to 10 or 15 percent.

The fifth step in the MBO process is evaluation. At the end of the designated time period, the manager and each employee meet again to determine which of the individual's goals were met, which were not met, and why. The employee's reward (in the form of a pay raise, praise, or promotion) is based primarily on the degree of goal attainment.

Like every other management method, MBO has advantages and disadvantages. MBO can motivate employees by involving them actively in the life of the firm. By discussing goals and performance appraisal, communication is improved and employees feel that they are an important part of the organization. Periodic goal setting and consistent review also enhance control within an organization. A major problem with MBO is that it does not work unless the process begins at the top of an organization. In some cases, MBO results in excessive paperwork. In addition, some managers have difficulty sitting down and working out goals with their employees and may instead just assign them goals.[4] Finally, MBO programs prove difficult to implement unless goals are quantifiable.

MBO has proved to be an effective motivational tool in many organizations. Tenneco, Black & Decker, Du Pont, General Foods, RCA, and General Motors all have reported success with MBO. Like any management technique, however, it must be applied with caution and in the right spirit if it is to work.

FIGURE 9.6
The Five Steps of an Effective MBO Program
An MBO program clarifies the roles employees are expected to play in reaching the organization's goals and allows employees to participate in goal setting and performance evaluation.

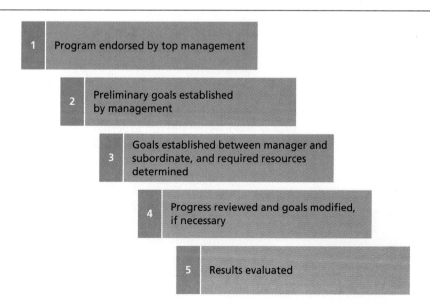

1 Program endorsed by top management

2 Preliminary goals established by management

3 Goals established between manager and subordinate, and required resources determined

4 Progress reviewed and goals modified, if necessary

5 Results evaluated

Motivation to do a better job. Managing a production line at an S.C. Johnson & Sons plant in Wisconsin increases this hourly worker's job satisfaction.

Job Enrichment

job enrichment   a motivating technique that provides employees with more variety and responsibility in their jobs

job enlargement   expanding a worker's assignments to include additional but similar tasks

Job enrichment is an effort to motivate employees by providing them with variety in their tasks while giving them some responsibility for, and control over, their jobs. At the same time, employees gain new skills and acquire a broader perspective about how their individual work contributes to the goals of the organization. Earlier in this chapter, we noted that Herzberg's motivation-hygiene theory is one rationale for the use of job enrichment; that is, the added responsibility and control that job enrichment confers on employees increases their satisfaction and motivation. At times, **job enlargement**—expanding a worker's assignments to include additional but similar tasks—can lead to job enrichment. Job enlargement might mean that a worker on an assembly line who used to connect three wires to components moving down the line now connects five wires. Unfortunately, the added tasks are often just as routine as those that the worker performed before the change. In such cases, enlargement may not be effective. AT&T, IBM, and Maytag Corporation have all experimented with job enlargement.

Whereas job enlargement does not really change the routine and monotonous nature of jobs, job enrichment does. Job enrichment requires that added tasks give an employee more responsibility for what he or she does. It provides workers with both more tasks to do and more control over how they perform them. In particular, job enrichment removes many controls from jobs, gives workers more authority, and assigns work in complete, natural units. Moreover, employees are frequently given fresh and challenging job assignments. By blending more planning and decision making into jobs, job enrichment gives work more depth and complexity. These changes tend to provide motivating opportunities for growth and advancement.

job redesign   type of job
enrichment in which work is
restructured to cultivate the
worker-job match

Job redesign is a type of job enrichment in which work is restructured in ways that cultivate the worker-job match. Job redesign can be achieved by combining tasks, forming work groups, or establishing closer customer association. Employees are often more motivated when jobs are combined because the increased variety of tasks presents more challenge and therefore more reward. Work groups motivate employees by showing them how their jobs fit within the organization as a whole and how they contribute to its success. Establishing client relationships allows employees to interact directly with customers. Not only does this type of redesign add a personal dimension to employment, it provides workers with immediate and relevant feedback about how they are doing their job.

Among the companies that have used job enrichment successfully are General Foods, Texas Instruments, and Chevron Corporation. Chevron evaluates performance by focusing on employee career development, attempting to help employees enhance their effectiveness and job satisfaction. The company's career-enrichment process, now serving as a model for many other organizations, follows a step-by-step procedure that includes preparation, joint planning, plan review, implementation, and end-of-period review.

Job enrichment works best when employees seek more challenging work. Of course not all workers respond positively to job enrichment programs. Employees must desire personal growth and have the skills and knowledge to perform enriched jobs. Lack of self-confidence, fear of failure, or distrust of management's intentions are likely to lead to ineffective performance on enriched jobs. In addition, some workers do not view their jobs as routine and boring, and others even prefer routine jobs because they are satisfying and stress-free. Companies that use job enrichment as an alternative to specialization also face extra expenses, such as the costs of retraining.

Behavior Modification

behavior modification
use of a systematic program of
reinforcement to encourage
desirable behavior

Behavior modification is the use of a systematic program of reinforcement to encourage desirable behavior. Behavior modification involves both rewards to encourage desirable actions and punishments to discourage undesirable actions. However, studies show that rewards, such as compliments and appreciation, are much more effective behavior modifiers than punishments, such as reprimands and scorn.

When applied to management, behavior modification strives to encourage desirable organizational behavior. Use of this technique begins with the identification of a target behavior—the behavior that is to be changed. (It might be low production levels or a high rate of absenteeism, for example.) Existing levels of this behavior are then measured. Next, managers provide positive reinforcement in the form of rewards when employees exhibit the desired behavior (such as increased production or less absenteeism). For example, the supervisor can reward employees whose performance improves. If an individual has a poor attendance record, begin rewarding employees for good attendance. Companies use praise, gifts, meals, trips, and other forms of tangible recognition to reward employees. Finally, the levels of the target behavior are measured again to determine whether the desired changes have been achieved. If they have, the reinforcement is maintained. However, if the target behavior has not changed significantly in the desired direction, the reward system must be changed to one that is likely to be more effective. The key is to devise effective rewards that will not only modify employees' behavior in desired ways but will also motivate them. To that end, experts suggest that management should reward quality, loyalty, and productivity.

Flextime

To most people, work schedule means the standard 9-to-5, forty-hour workweek. In reality, though, many people have work schedules that are quite different from this. Police officers, firefighters, restaurant personnel, airline employees, and medical personnel usually have work schedules that are far from standard. Some manufacturers also rotate personnel from shift to shift. And many professional people—such as managers, artists, and lawyers—work more than forty hours each week because they need extra time to get their work done or simply because they want to.

The needs and lifestyles of today's work force are changing. Dual-income families make up a much larger share of the work force than ever before. Women are the fastest growing sector of the work force. In 1963, 38 percent of American women worked outside the home; in 1993 that number had grown to 60 percent. More employees are responsible for the care of elderly relatives.[5] Recognizing that these changes increase the demand for family time, many employers are offering flexible work schedules that not

Flexible lifestyle. Flextime allows parents to spend more time with children and to manage family and home responsibilities.

only help employees better manage their time but also increase employee motivation and job satisfaction.

One such plan is called **flextime,** a system in which employees set their own work hours within certain limits determined by employers. Typically the firm establishes two bands of time: the *core time,* when all employees must be at work, and the *flexible time,* when employees may choose whether to be at work. The only condition is that every employee must work a total of eight hours each day. For example, the hours between 9 and 11 A.M. and 1 and 3 P.M. might be core time, and the hours between 6 and 9 A.M., between 11 A.M. and 1 P.M., and between 3 and 6 P.M. might be flexible time. This would give employees the option of coming in early and getting off early, coming in later and leaving later, or taking an extra-long lunch break. But flextime also ensures that everyone is present at certain times, when conferences with supervisors and department meetings can be scheduled. Another type of flextime allows employees to work a forty-hour work week in four days instead of five. Workers who put in ten hours a day instead of eight get an extra day off each week.

The sense of independence and autonomy employees gain from having a say in what hours they work can be a motivating factor. In addition, employees who have enough time to deal with nonwork issues often work more productively and with greater satisfaction when they are on the job. Two common problems associated with utilizing flextime are (1) supervisors sometimes find their jobs complicated by having employees who come and go at different times and (2) employees sometimes resent coworkers who are on flextime. Despite potential problems, a recent study performed by Boston-based Work/Family Directions found that one-fourth of the 2.4 million employees in eighty *Fortune* 500 companies use flextime.[6] In another survey, Coopers & Lybrand learned that 60 percent of the firms it polled offer flexible work schedules. By the year 2000, this study predicts, approximately 80 percent of companies will offer flextime as a standard business operation.[7]

Part-Time Work and Job Sharing

Part-time work is permanent employment in which individuals work less than a standard workweek. The specific number of hours worked varies, but part-time jobs are structured so that all responsibilities can be completed in the number of hours that an employee works. Part-time work is of special interest to parents who want more time with their children and people who simply desire more leisure time.

Job sharing (sometimes referred to as work sharing) is an arrangement whereby two people share one full-time position. One job sharer may work from 8 A.M. to noon and the other from 1 to 5 P.M., or they may alternate workdays. For example, at National City Corporation in Cleveland, Ohio, two women share the position of manager of corporate communications. One works Tuesdays and Thursdays and the other works Mondays, Wednesdays, and Fridays. By communicating daily, sharing a portable computer, and using voice mail and fax, these managers are able to handle a challenging administrative position and still have time for their families.[8] Job

flextime   a system in which employees set their own work hours within employer-determined limits

part-time work   permanent employment in which individuals work less than a standard workweek

job sharing   an arrangement whereby two people share one full-time position

sharing thus combines the security of a permanent job with the flexibility of a part-time job.

For firms, job sharing provides a unique opportunity to attract highly skilled employees who might not be available on a full-time basis. In addition, companies can save on expenses by reducing the cost of benefits and avoiding the disruptions of employee turnover. For employees, opting for the flexibility of part-time work or job sharing means giving up some of the benefits received for full-time work. In addition, job sharing is difficult if tasks aren't easily divisible or if two people do not work or communicate well with one another.

Telecommuting

telecommuting working at home all of the time or for a portion of the workweek

A growing number of companies allow **telecommuting**—working at home all of the time or for a portion of the workweek. In 1993 about 3 million full-time employees worked at home as telecommuters. Adding to that figure those who are contract workers or who spend a few days of the week working at home during business hours, the number of U.S. telecommuters reaches 7.5 million.[9] Personal computers, modems, fax machines, voice mail, cellular phones, and overnight couriers all facilitate the work-at-home trend. Working at home means individuals can set their own hours and have more time with their families. Because they spend less time traveling back and forth to a conventional office and have fewer office distractions, many telecommuters report increased productivity. Among the disadvantages to

More than one way to get the job done. Through telecommuting, this Ithaca, New York, businessperson is able to accomplish most of his work out of his home office.

telecommuting are feelings of isolation, putting in longer hours, and being distracted by family or household responsibilities.

Employee Empowerment

empowerment giving employees greater involvement in their jobs by increasing their participation in decision making

Many companies are increasing employee motivation through the use of empowerment. **Empowerment** means giving employees greater involvement in their jobs and in the operations of the organization by increasing their participation in decision making. Replacing top-down total management control, empowered employees have a voice in what they do, and how and when they do it. In some organizations, employees' input is restricted to individual choices, such as when to take breaks. In other companies, their responsibilities might encompass more far-reaching issues, such as production schedules.

For empowerment to work effectively, management must be involved. Managers should set expectations, communicate standards, institute periodic evaluations, and guarantee follow-up.[10] Studies have shown that when effectively implemented, empowerment often leads to increased job satisfaction, improved job performance, higher quality output, increased organizational commitment, lower turnover, and reduced sick leave.[11] For an example of how one company—Levi Strauss—successfully empowers employees, see Ethical Challenges. Obstacles to empowerment include resistance on the part of management, distrust of management on the part

The team that works together smiles together. Most people like being a part of the team, working toward a common goal, supporting each other, and sharing the exhilaration of success. At a Hewlett Packard service center a work team answers phone calls from customers. This team chose its own supervisor, giving team members a strong interest in seeing the supervisor succeed.

■ ■ ■ ■ ETHICAL CHALLENGES

Levi Strauss Links Values to Success

When corporate executives talk about how to make their organizations more successful, the words "empowering workers" and "involvement" are as likely to come up as "sales" and "profits." Few American companies, however, embrace these ideas as wholeheartedly as Levi Strauss & Company. Robert Haas, Levi's CEO, is convinced that a company employing over 30,000 people and selling more than two hundred styles of jeans can still operate ethically and help every worker from the factory floor to the executive suite feel like an essential part of the organization. During the 1920s, Levi Strauss gave free English-language and citizenship lessons to its factory workers, and Levi's was one of the first companies to integrate its factories in the South. Following in his grandfather's, father's, and uncle's footsteps, Haas continues running the company with the belief that a business can make profits and care about people at the same time.

Written by top management, Levi's "Corporate Aspirations" is a set of decision-making guidelines that hangs on office and factory walls throughout the company. If you are in management at Levi Strauss and you want a raise, you'd better be sure that you exhibit "aspirational behavior." One-third of a manager's evaluation is based on it. Managers must show their commitment to the success of others and be willing to acknowledge their own contribution to problems when they arise. They must work hard to recognize individuals and teams for their contributions, whether for creativity and innovation or for less glamorous day-in, day-out operations. Managers must actively empower workers by trusting them with more authority and responsibility. The company's new benefits review plan ensures that workers are included in every stage of assessing their own performance, from goal setting to rewards. The plan's principles include bringing each worker's aspirations to life, linking employees closely to the company's strategy, increasing the emphasis on performance-based pay, rewarding individual contributions, and improving communication.

All of these words look good on paper, but do they translate into empowerment and involvement for the people who work at Levi's? From major decisions to personal encounters, the answer seems to be yes. When Levi's decided to reorganize the company, it asked 6,000 employees for advice on what to do differently. Two hundred managers incorporated that information into the new structure. When a financial planner recently came to work at Levi's, she wasn't too sure about what she called "this touchy-feely" philosophy. She changed her mind when she took a chance and confronted her boss for being too dictatorial. He agreed with her and changed his behavior. When a new rivet setter at a Levi's factory discovered that he could leave his machine to get a drink without permission, he was astonished and very pleased.

Says CEO Haas of Levi's strategy, "We are not doing this because it makes us feel good—although it does. We are not doing this because it is politically correct. We are doing this because we believe in the interconnection between liberating the talents of our people and business success." Levi Strauss is currently measuring success in terms of increased customer and consumer loyalty, a growing reputation for attracting the best employees and keeping their morale high, a talent for launching business in new markets, and five straight years of record sales and earnings.

of workers, insufficient training, and poor communication between management and employees.

Work Teams

work teams groups of employees with the authority and skills to manage themselves

Another method for increasing employee motivation is to introduce self-managed **work teams,** groups of employees with the authority and skills to manage themselves. Experts submit that workers on self-managed teams are more motivated and satisfied because they have more task variety and more job control. On many work teams, members rotate through all of the jobs for which the team is responsible. Some organizations cross-train the entire team so that everyone can perform everyone else's job. In a traditional business structure, management is responsible for hiring and firing employees, establishing budgets, purchasing supplies, conducting performance reviews, and disciplining team members. When teams are in place, they take over some or all of these management functions.

To make the most effective use of teams, it is essential that organizations are committed to the team approach, that team objectives are clear, that training and education is ongoing, and that compensation rewards team-based goals. One such compensation system is *gain sharing,* in which employee bonuses are tied to achievement of team goals, such as increased sales or productivity or improved customer satisfaction.[12]

When correctly implemented, use of work teams can lead to higher employee morale, increased productivity, and often innovation. Both Xerox and Procter & Gamble have earned reputations for successfully implementing the self-directed team strategy. Smaller organizations can also benefit. For example, Allina, a company that operates nonprofit hospitals in Minnesota, has had excellent results since creating management-union teams. One of these teams saved the company $200,000 annually by improving the equipment maintenance procedure.

A recent study found that 47 percent of *Fortune* 1000 companies use self-managed work teams and 60 percent plan to increase their use in the next few years.[13] Although the work team strategy is increasingly popular, it is not without its problems. Lack of support from managers and supervisors and insufficient training in the team approach can minimize or eliminate potential benefits. In addition, companies must be prepared for an initial increase in costs for training and implementation.

Employee Ownership

employee ownership practice of employees owning the company they work for by virtue of being stockholders

Some organizations are discovering that a highly effective technique for motivating employees is **employee ownership**—employees own the company they work for by becoming stockholders. Employee-owned businesses directly reward employees for success. When the company enjoys increased sales or lower costs, employees benefit directly. In the United States today, almost 12 million employees own stock in more than 10,000 companies for which they work.[14] The National Center for Employee Ownership, an organization that studies employee-owned American businesses, reports that employee stock ownership plans (ESOPs) provide considerable employee incentive and increase employee involvement and commitment.

Improving Your Team Skills

Corporate America loves teams—groups of employees with all the technical skills and authority needed to manage themselves. There are many kinds of self-directed teams—quality circles, management teams, work teams, and problem-solving teams are just a few examples. Teams plan, organize, staff, lead, control, and measure. Sometimes they hire and fire, establish budgets, purchase supplies, track expenses, conduct reviews, reward performance, and render discipline. When people take direction from the work itself, rather than relying on procedures and supervision, they often increase productivity and improve quality. By adopting self-managed work teams, Federal Express boosted productivity 40 percent; at Boeing, teams reduced engineering problems by half on the company's new 777 jet. Teams do, however, face many obstacles before they produce results like these. If you're going to be part of a team, work on improving specific skills so that you won't be one of those obstacles to success.

The best team players have acquired, and continue to acquire, skill in three general areas: technical, interpersonal, and conceptual.

TECHNICAL SKILLS

Many organizations require that team members be familiar with the jobs of everyone on the team.

- Learn all of the skills you will need so that you can perform each task for which your team is responsible.
- Be sure you have enough knowledge about specialized tasks so that you are able to step in and do someone else's job.

INTERPERSONAL SKILLS

In self-managed teams, there are no managers to settle conflicts. For your team to be productive, you will need to avoid conflict when possible, and learn to deal with conflict when it arises.

- Become a more effective listener—give and receive honest feedback.
- Improve your problem-solving abilities.
- Learn how to make decisions, both on your own and with a group.
- Learn to run a meeting effectively.
- Become a successful negotiator.
- Improve your communications skills.
- Work on your ability to confront differences constructively and keep focused on team, rather than personal, goals.

CONCEPTUAL SKILLS

Learn more about your company—its products, markets, customers, and competitors. The more you know, the more valuable you become to your team and your organization.

- Develop your ability to analyze strengths and weaknesses. In a self-directed team without managers, members assume this responsibility.
- Make sure you understand how your team fits together with other teams in the company.
- Learn all you can about your company's budgets and sales forecasting.

Of course, you can't acquire all of these skills on your own. To make self-directed teams work, and to provide you and your team members with the needed tools, your company has responsibilities, too. Management must:

- Provide training in working on teams.
- Clearly outline the team's responsibilities.
- Develop distinct standards for performance evaluation based on team goals (for example, increasing sales or improving customer relations).
- Enhance team communication by providing tools like electronic mail, Fax, or even teleconferencing if necessary.
- Foster a climate of trust within the company.

■ ■ ■ ■ CHAPTER REVIEW

Summary

1 Explain what motivation is.

Motivation is the individual, internal process that energizes, directs, and sustains behavior. Motivation is affected by employee morale, the feelings toward the job, superiors, and the firm itself. Motivation, morale, and job satisfaction are closely related.

2 Recognize some earlier perspectives on motivation: scientific management, Theory X, and Theory Y.

One of the first approaches to employee motivation was Frederick Taylor's scientific management. Taylor believed that employees work only for money and that they must be closely supervised and managed. Douglas McGregor labeled this view Theory X and then described an alternative view called Theory Y. Theory Y is more in keeping with the results of the Hawthorne Studies (which showed the importance of social processes in the workplace) and with the human relations movement (which was based on the idea that employees can be motivated to behave as responsible members of the organization).

3 Outline Maslow's hierarchy of needs.

Maslow's hierarchy of needs suggests that people are motivated by five sets of needs. In ascending order of importance, these motivators are physiological, safety, social, esteem, and self-actualization needs. People are motivated by the lowest (most important) set of needs that remains unfulfilled. As needs at one level are satisfied, people try to satisfy needs at the next level.

4 Discuss Herzberg's motivation-hygiene theory.

Frederick Herzberg found that satisfaction and dissatisfaction are influenced by two distinct sets of factors. Motivation factors, including recognition and responsibility, affect an employee's degree of satisfaction, but do not affect dissatisfaction. Hygiene factors, including pay and working conditions, affect an employee's degree of dissatisfaction but do not affect satisfaction.

5 Describe four contemporary views of motivation: equity theory, expectancy theory, reinforcement theory, and Theory Z.

Equity theory maintains that people are motivated to obtain and preserve equitable treatment for themselves. Expectancy theory suggests that our motivation depends on how much we want something and how likely we think we are to get it. Reinforcement theory is based on the idea that people will repeat behavior that is rewarded and will avoid behavior that is punished. Theory Z emphasizes long-term employment, collective decision making, individual responsibility for the outcomes of decisions, informal control, and a holistic concern for employees.

6 Explain several techniques for increasing employee motivation.

Management by objectives is a motivation technique in which managers and employees collaborate in setting goals. MBO motivates employees by getting them more involved in their jobs and in the organization as a whole. Job enrichment seeks to motivate employees by increasing the variety of, responsibility for, and control over their jobs. Job enlargement, expanding a worker's assignments to include additional tasks, is one aspect of job enrichment. Job redesign is a type of job enrichment in which work is restructured to improve the worker-job match.

Behavior modification uses reinforcement to encourage desirable behavior. Rewards for productivity, quality, and loyalty change employees' behavior in desired ways and also increase their motivation. Allowing employees to work more flexible hours is another way to build motivation and job satisfaction. Flextime is a system of work scheduling that allows workers to set their own hours as long as they fall within limits established by employers. Part-time work is permanent employment in which individuals work less than a standard workweek. Job sharing is an arrangement whereby two people share one full-time position. Telecommuting is working at home all or part of the workweek. All of these types of work arrangements allow employees more time outside of the workplace to deal with family responsibilities or to enjoy free time.

Employee empowerment, work teams, and employee ownership are also techniques that boost employee motivation. Empowerment means giving employees greater involvement in their jobs by increasing their decision-making authority. Work teams are groups of self-managing employees. When employees participate in ownership programs such as employee stock ownership plans (ESOPs), they have more incentive to make the company succeed.

Key Terms

You should now be able to define and give an example relevant to each of the following terms:

motivation (266)

morale (266)

scientific management (267)

piece-rate system (267)

Theory X (269)

Theory Y (269)

need (270)

hierarchy of needs (270)

physiological needs (270)

safety needs (270)

social needs (270)

esteem needs (271)

self-actualization needs (271)

motivation-hygiene theory (272)

motivation factors (272)

hygiene factors (272)

equity theory (273)

expectancy theory (274)

reinforcement theory (276)

Theory Z (277)

management by objectives (MBO) (278)

job enrichment (280)

job enlargement (280)

job redesign (281)

behavior modification (281)

flextime (283)

part-time work (283)

job sharing (283)

telecommuting (284)

empowerment (285)

work teams (287)

employee ownership (287)

Questions

Review Questions

1. Compare the two earlier schools of thought on motivation: scientific management and Theory X versus the human relations movement and Theory Y.
2. How did the results of the Hawthorne Studies influence researchers' thinking about employee motivation?

3. What are the five sets of needs in Maslow's hierarchy? How are a person's needs related to motivation?
4. What are the two dimensions in Herzberg's motivation-hygiene theory? What kinds of factors affect each dimension?
5. According to equity theory, how does an employee determine whether he or she is being treated equitably?
6. According to expectancy theory, what two variables determine motivation?
7. What is the fundamental premise of reinforcement theory?
8. Identify and describe the major techniques for motivating employees.
9. Describe the steps involved in the MBO process.
10. What are the objectives of MBO? What do you think might be its disadvantages?
11. How does employee participation increase motivation?
12. Describe the steps in the process of behavior modification.
13. What are the major benefits and most common problems associated with the use of work teams?

Discussion Questions

1. What types of motivation techniques work for Pat Riley?
2. Is motivation more important in an organization like the New York Knicks than at Xerox or Sears? Explain.
3. How might managers make use of the hierarchy of needs in motivating employees? What problems would they encounter?
4. Do the various theories of motivation contradict each other or complement each other? Explain.
5. What combination of motivational techniques do you think would result in the best overall motivation and reward system?
6. Reinforcement theory and behavior modification have been called demeaning because they tend to treat people "like mice in a maze." Do you agree?

Exercises

1. Analyze the system that is used in your school to motivate and reward students. Determine (a) the theory or theories on which it is based and (b) how it could be improved.

2. Suppose you are the owner of a neighborhood hardware store and have two employees besides yourself. Make a list of the motivational problems you might encounter. Write a plan indicating what techniques you could use to minimize these problems.

VIDEO CASE 9.1

Eaton Corporation: Excellence Through People

At the Eaton Corporation plant in Kearney, Nebraska, workers make valves for automobiles and trucks. When the 700 employees arrive at work each day, the plant manager greets most of them by name. The director of human resources often goes out onto the factory floor to help pack boxes of valves for shipment. Recently, all of the top managers joined press operators to scrub the giant, grease-laden forge presses. Everyone at the plant receives the same benefits package, and no one punches a time clock. Even if this plant were a small company's only plant, its atmosphere might come as a surprise. But when you take into account that Eaton Corporation manufactures more than 5,000 products in twenty-two countries for customers like Caterpillar, Mack Trucks, and John Deere, it's downright astonishing. Eaton believes that a company is more likely to succeed if its atmosphere is open and every employee feels important and works together to get the job done—so that's the kind of company Eaton tries to be.

In 1919 Joseph Eaton and his partner started the Eaton Axle Company, manufacturing rear axles for trucks. By 1931 he had purchased eleven more auto parts companies and renamed his firm Eaton Manufacturing. Today, Eaton Corporation makes axles, valve trains, truck transmissions, engine components, brakes, clutches, electrical equipment, air traffic control systems, hydraulic gear, semiconductor equipment, and the landing systems for NASA's space shuttles.

Like most American manufacturers, Eaton used to run its factories in a traditional, autocratic way. Management told workers what to do and how to do it, and not much more. Everyone was constrained by job titles, job descriptions, and work rules. By contrast, Eaton today strives for the mutual trust and respect that comes from openness. The resulting employee involvement translates into a workplace where people do their best and business flourishes. Managers explain to workers why they are doing what they are doing and workers can trust managers to tell them the truth. In turn, workers feel free to talk to their supervisors honestly about ideas for improvement or problems they are having. At one Iowa plant's monthly departmental meetings, executives call employees in to discuss what they like and don't like. Workers new to Eaton are often surprised at how quickly these conversations translate into concrete results. One Eaton worker remarked that he likes working at Eaton because when he comes to work, nobody tells him what to do or when to do it.

Eaton believes that workers are capable of making important contributions to improving the way the company operates. Who can understand problems and potential solutions better than those doing the work? To make sure that its employees have input into decisions that affect their working lives, Eaton relies on quality circles—groups of employees from all levels of the company who work together to improve procedures and solve problems. At a Saginaw, Michigan, plant that makes hydraulic valve lifters, union and management were both skeptical when quality circles were introduced. Now everyone works together instead of quarrelling over changes, employees are more motivated, and operating costs are down. A carpenter at an Eaton electronics plant reports that when his quality circle gets together, they themselves decide what they want to work on, brainstorm together, and solve the problem; they don't get their assignments from higher-ups.

Eaton did not hire professional speakers for its recent Continuous Improvement Seminar. There were no celebrities to warm up the audience or facilitators to stimulate communication. Who got up to talk about how well quality circles were working? One after another, technicians, accountants, machine operators, and maintenance people told their peers about the work they'd done and its impact on the firm's business. An atmosphere like this, plus $4 billion in annual sales and a turnover rate of half the national average for manufacturing plants, confirms that Eaton management's belief in its people is justified.[15]

Questions

1. What type of motivational techniques are being used at Eaton?
2. In what ways does Eaton benefit from the use of these techniques?
3. Would you like to work at Eaton Corporation? Why or why not?

CASE 9.2

Owning the Company Motivates Employees at Reflexite

At the nineteen-year-old Reflexite Corporation in New Britain, Connecticut, employees are excited about their company and their product, a material that reflects light back to its source. Used on highway signs, barricades, life preservers, firefighting gear, and Halloween safety stickers, Reflexite is also woven into fabric as a safety feature on sneakers and backpacks. Thomas Built Buses, a major manufacturer of school buses sold all over the world, uses Reflexite as its vehicle marking material. When Hurricane Andrew struck Florida, knocking out street lights and traffic signals, temporary roll-up traffic signs made of Reflexite helped fleeing residents and emergency service vehicles. What has made Reflexite a profitable company, a serious competitor to corporate giant 3M, and the winner of *Inc.* magazine's "Entrepreneur of the Year" award is more than marketing a great product with lots of uses. At Reflexite, employees own the company; workers are thus intensely motivated because each has a personal stake in the company's success or failure.

After brothers Hugh and Bill Rowland invented a new method for producing retroreflective material, they acquired a patent and set up a business to sell it commercially. By the early 1980s, 3M had heard of the product and offered to buy the Rowlands out for about $5 million. Although the money was tempting, the brothers were well aware that 3M wanted only the technology, not the Connecticut factory or the employees depending on it for their livelihood. Instead of selling to 3M, they hired a new president and offered a stock ownership plan to their employees, who bought the company, kept their jobs, and turned Reflexite into a phenomenal success. Although the company still manufactures its basic material at the original New Britain site, there is now a Reflexite Europa, a Reflexite UK, a Reflexite Deutschland, a Reflexite Mexico, a Reflexite Japan, a Reflexite Italia, and distribution centers in Korea, Singapore, and Taiwan. The company expects that by the year 2000, it will be operating in twenty-five countries around the world.

Together, and as individuals, Reflexite employees own 59 percent of the company, and a monthly owner's bonus check is a tangible reminder of how business is faring. Employee shareholders receive 3 percent of the operating profits that, in a good month, can add several hundred dollars to a paycheck. Of course, in a bad month, no one gets a bonus check. Because the quality of their own work directly affects the amount of money they take home, Reflexite employees are uncommonly motivated to do their best. Every employee participates in an intensive sixty-day Quality Awareness Training Program. One technician reported that he takes extra interest in his work because he knows that if he makes mistakes, it's his own money going out the door.

The longer people remain with the company, the more shares they receive, so experienced employees almost never leave. Turnover among those who stay more than a year is almost nonexistent. What this means for Reflexite is an ability to keep almost all of its people with know-how. In addition, employee enthusiasm about research, development, and problem solving keeps Reflexite on the cutting edge of new technology. The company's Employee-Assistance Request Form creates a feedback system that keeps suggestions from getting lost, and putting new products on the market means more money for each and every employee.

Reflexite employees demonstrated their loyalty when many took voluntary leaves of absence without pay, and top managers took 10 percent pay cuts, to avoid layoffs and losses during the nationwide economic slowdown. People demonstrated their eagerness to work for Reflexite when 1,700 applicants responded to an ad for the position of sales and marketing general manager.

From hourly workers to executive officers, feelings of ownership are strong. When the company president gets nibbles from would-be buyers, he enjoys informing them that the company has already been sold—to its employees.[16]

Questions

1. What benefits accrue to Reflexite as a result of its employee ownership?
2. Are there disadvantages to the company or its work force when employees own a major portion of the firm? Discuss.
3. How would your work behavior and your attitude toward your job be affected if you shared in the ownership of the company you work for?

■ ■ ■ ■ CHAPTER 10

Human Resources Management

LEARNING OBJECTIVES

After studying this chapter you should be able to

1 Describe the major components of human resources management.

2 Identify the steps in human resources planning.

3 Describe cultural diversity and understand some of the challenges and opportunities associated with it.

4 Explain the objectives and uses of job analysis.

5 Describe the processes of recruiting, employee selection, and orientation.

6 Discuss the primary elements of employee compensation and benefits.

7 Explain the purposes and techniques of employee training, development, and performance appraisal.

8 Outline the major legislation affecting human resources management.

CHAPTER PREVIEW

We begin our study of human resources management, or HRM, with an overview of how businesses acquire, maintain, and develop their human resources. After listing the steps by which firms match their human resources needs with the supply of human resources available, we explore several dimensions of cultural diversity. Then we examine the concept of job analysis. Next we focus on a firm's recruiting, selection, and orientation procedures as the means of acquiring employees. We also describe forms of employee compensation that motivate employees to remain with the firm and to work effectively. Then we discuss employee training, management development, and performance appraisal methods. Finally, we consider legislation that affects HRM practices.

293

Respect and Empowerment at Hanna Andersson

Established in Portland, Oregon, in 1984, Hanna Andersson is one of America's most successful catalog marketers of children's clothing. Four catalogs a year offer upscale 100 percent cotton clothing in three hundred styles that range in price from $4 to $90. What makes Hanna Andersson stand out from a crowd of competitors such as L.L. Bean, Lands' End, and OshKosh B'Gosh is the way the firm takes care of its employees. When the company's founders talked about the kind of organization they wanted to run, they envisioned a workplace in which people would feel comfortable in, and fulfilled by, their jobs. Experts agree that Hanna Andersson has turned the vision into reality. The company has won the Business Enterprise Trust Award, *Forbes* magazine's business ethics award, and placed three years running on *Working Mother*'s list of "100 Best Companies for Working Mothers."

What is it about this award-winner that makes people like it so much? Hanna Andersson respects and empowers employees and gives them the kinds of benefits that make a real difference in the quality of their lives. Even part-time workers (at least thirty hours a week) receive full benefits. Employees enjoy an excellent health-care plan, cash bonuses, profit sharing, tuition reimbursement, and hefty discounts on company clothing. If workers donate to charities, Hanna matches their contributions up to $500 a year. Further, Hanna Andersson reimburses employees for half of their child-care expenses. Although this benefit costs the company about $250,000 a year, its owners believe that people are more effective workers when they aren't worrying about their children.

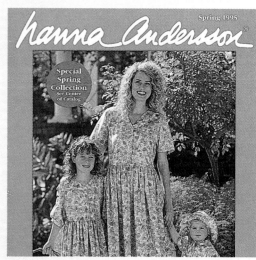

Flexible scheduling and a liberal sick-leave policy also make Hanna Andersson a family-friendly firm.

When its competition intensified and 1990s value-conscious shoppers became less enthusiastic about spending $40 on toddlers' overalls, Hanna Andersson's sales fell. The head of human resources took on the unhappy task of lowering spending by reducing some prized employee benefits. Management now limits the amount of child-care reimbursement and requires employees to contribute to their health-insurance plans. Although the company will buy employees commuter bus passes, it no longer pays for their parking. Company executives realize that being successful means more than motivating employees. At the same time they insist that, although they are modifying their pro-worker orientation, they will never abandon it.

■ ■ ■ ■

■ ■ ■ ■ ■ ■ ■ ■ ■ ■ ■

Hanna Andersson's award-winning employee benefits program is a major component of this organization's human resource efforts. Effective employee benefits programs, like the one at Hanna Andersson, are very important in attracting, motivating, and retaining the appropriate mix of human resources.

■■ HUMAN RESOURCES MANAGEMENT: AN OVERVIEW

LEARNING OBJECTIVE 1
Describe the major components of human resources management.

human resources management (HRM) all the activities involved in acquiring, maintaining, and developing an organization's human resources

The human resource is not only unique and valuable, it is an organization's most important resource. It seems logical that an organization would expend a great deal of effort to acquire and make full use of such a resource, and most organizations do. That effort is now known as human resources management, or HRM. It has also been called *staffing* and *personnel management*.

Human resources management consists of all the activities involved in acquiring, maintaining, and developing an organization's human resources. As the definition implies, HRM begins with acquisition—getting people to work for the organization. Next, steps must be taken to keep these valuable resources. (This is important; after all, they are the only business resources that can leave the organization at will.) Finally, the human resources should be developed to their full capacity to contribute to the firm.

HRM Activities

Each of the three phases of HRM—acquiring, maintaining, and developing human resources—consists of a number of related activities. Acquisition, for example, includes planning, as well as the various activities that lead to hiring new personnel. Altogether, this phase of HRM includes five separate activities. They are

- *Human resources planning*—determining the firm's future human resources needs.
- *Job analysis*—determining the exact nature of the positions to be filled.
- *Recruiting*—attracting people to apply for positions in the firm.
- *Selection*—choosing and hiring the most qualified applicants.
- *Orientation*—acquainting new employees with the firm.

Maintaining human resources consists primarily of motivating employees to remain with the firm and to work effectively. We discussed motivation at length in Chapter 9; here we concentrate on these additional aspects of maintaining human resources:

295

- *Compensation*—rewarding employee effort through monetary payments.
- *Benefits*—providing rewards to ensure employee well-being.

The development phase of HRM is concerned with improving employees' skills and expanding their capabilities. The two important activities within this phase are

- *Training and development*—teaching employees new skills, new jobs, and more effective ways of doing their present jobs.
- *Performance appraisal*—assessing employees' current and potential performance levels.

These activities are discussed in more detail shortly, when we have completed this overview of human resources management.

Responsibility for HRM

In general, human resources management is a shared responsibility of line managers and staff HRM specialists.

In very small organizations, the owner is usually both a line manager and the staff HRM specialist. He or she handles all or most HRM activities. As the firm grows in size, a human resources manager is generally hired to take over most of the staff responsibilities. As growth continues, additional staff positions are added as needed. In firms as large as, say, Bristol-Myers Squibb Co., HRM activities tend to be very highly specialized. There may be separate groups to deal with compensation, training and development programs, and the other staff activities.

Specific HRM activities are assigned to those who are in the best position to perform them. Human resources planning and job analysis are usually done by staff specialists, with input from line managers. Similarly, recruiting and selection are generally handled by staff experts, although line managers are involved in the actual hiring decisions. Orientation programs are usually devised by staff specialists, and the orientation itself is carried out by both staff specialists and line managers. Compensation systems (including benefits) are most often developed and administered by the HRM staff. However, line managers recommend pay increases and promotions. Training and development activities are usually the joint responsibility of staff and line managers. Performance appraisal is the job of the line manager, although HRM staff personnel design the firm's appraisal system in most organizations.

LEARNING OBJECTIVE 2
Identify the steps in human resources planning.

human resources planning
the development of strategies to meet a firm's future human resources needs

■■ HUMAN RESOURCES PLANNING

Human resources planning is the development of strategies to meet the firm's future human resources needs. The starting point for this planning is the organization's overall strategic plan. From this, human resources planners can forecast the firm's future demand for human resources. Next, the planners must determine whether the needed human resources will be available; that is, they must anticipate the supply of human resources within the firm. Finally, they have to take steps to match supply with demand.

Forecasting Human Resources Demand

Planners should base forecasts of the demand for human resources in an organization on as much relevant information as they can gather. The firm's overall strategic plan will provide information about future business ventures, new products, and projected expansions or contractions of particular product lines. Information on past staffing levels, evolving technologies, industry staffing practices, and projected economic trends can also be very helpful.

HRM staff use all this information to determine both the number of employees the firm will require and their qualifications—including skills, experience, and knowledge. Planners use a wide range of methods to forecast specific personnel needs. For example, with one simple method, personnel requirements are projected to increase or decrease in the same proportion as sales revenue. Thus, if a 30 percent increase in sales volume is projected over the next two years, a 30 percent increase in personnel requirements would be expected for the same period. (This method can be applied to specific positions as well as to the work force in general. It is not, however, a very precise forecasting method.) At the other extreme are elaborate, computer-based personnel planning models used by some larger firms such as Exxon Corporation.

Forecasting Human Resources Supply

The human resources supply forecast must take into account both the present work force and any changes or movements that may occur within it. For example, suppose planners project that in five years a firm that currently employs 100 engineers will need to employ a total of 200 engineers. Planners cannot simply assume that they will have to hire 100 engineers over the next five years. During that period, some of the firm's present engineers are likely to be promoted, leave the firm, or move to other jobs within the firm. Thus planners might project the supply of engineers in five years at 87, which means that the firm will have to hire a total of 113 (or more) new engineers.

replacement chart a list of key personnel and their possible replacements within the firm

Two useful techniques for forecasting human resources supply are the replacement chart and the skills inventory. A **replacement chart** is a list of key personnel, along with possible replacements within the firm. The chart is maintained to ensure that top management positions can be filled fairly quickly in the event of an unexpected death, resignation, or retirement. Some firms also provide additional training for employees who might eventually replace top managers.

skills inventory a computerized data bank containing information on the skills and experience of all present employees

A **skills inventory** is a computerized data bank containing information on the skills and experience of all present employees. It is used to search for candidates to fill new or newly available positions. For a special project, a manager might be seeking a current employee with an engineering degree, at least six years of experience, and fluency in French. The skills inventory can quickly identify employees who possess such qualifications.

Matching Supply with Demand

Once they have forecasts of both the demand for personnel and the firm's supply of personnel, planners can devise a course of action for matching the two. When demand is forecast to be greater than supply, plans must be made to recruit and select new employees. The timing of these actions depends on the types of positions to be filled. Suppose we expect to open another plant in five years. Along with other employees, a plant manager and twenty-five maintenance workers will be needed. We can probably wait quite a while before we begin to recruit maintenance personnel. However, because the job of plant manager is so critical, we may start searching for the right person for that position immediately.

When supply is forecast to be greater than demand, the firm must take steps to reduce the size of its work force. Several methods are available, although none of them is especially pleasant for managers or discharged employees. When the oversupply is expected to be temporary, some employees may be *laid off*—dismissed from the work force until they are needed again.

Perhaps the most humane method for making personnel cutbacks is through attrition. *Attrition* is the normal reduction in the work force that occurs when employees leave the firm. If these employees are not replaced, the work force eventually shrinks to the point where supply matches demand. Of course, attrition may be a very slow process—too slow to really help the firm.

Early retirement is another option. Under early retirement, people who are within a few years of retirement are permitted (or encouraged) to retire early with full benefits. Depending on the age makeup of the work force, this may or may not reduce the staff enough.

As a last resort, unneeded employees are sometimes simply *fired*. Because of its negative impact, this method is generally used only when absolutely necessary.

■■ CULTURAL DIVERSITY IN HUMAN RESOURCES

LEARNING OBJECTIVE 3
Describe cultural diversity and understand some of the challenges and opportunities associated with it.

Today's work force is made up of many types of people. Firms can no longer safely assume that every employee walking in the door has similar beliefs or expectations. Whereas North American white males may believe in challenging authority, Asians tend to respect and defer to it. In Hispanic cultures, people often bring music, food, and family members to work, a custom that U.S. businesses have traditionally not allowed. A job applicant who won't make eye contact during an interview may be rejected for being unapproachable, when according to her culture she was just being polite.

As a larger number of women, minorities, and immigrants enter the U.S. work force, the workplace is growing more diverse. Based on the *Work Force 2000 Study* conducted by the Hudson Institute, fewer than one-fifth of all persons entering the work force by the year 2000 will be native-born white males. By then, women will represent approximately 62 percent of all persons entering the work force; approximately 53 percent will be minori-

Cultural diversity in the workplace. Cultural diversity among employees may present a few challenges but many benefits. This is IBM's corporate work force diversity staff, which helps the company ensure that its work force does not become homogeneous.

ties. Hispanics continue to be the fastest growing population in the United States, and it is estimated that they will represent 27 percent of the net growth of the work force through the turn of the century.

cultural (workplace) diversity differences among people in a work force due to race, ethnicity, and gender.

Cultural or **workplace diversity** refers to the differences among people in a work force due to race, ethnicity, and gender. This increasing diversity is forcing managers to learn to supervise and motivate people with a broader range of value systems. The flood of women into the work force, combined with a new emphasis on participative parenting by men, has brought many family-related issues into the workplace. Today's more educated employees also want greater independence and flexibility. In return for their efforts, they want both compensation and a better quality of life.

Although cultural diversity presents a challenge, managers should view it as an opportunity rather than a limitation. When properly managed, cultural diversity can provide competitive advantages for an organization. Table 10.1 shows several such benefits that creative management of cultural diversity can offer. A firm that manages diversity properly can develop cost advantages over firms that do not manage diversity well. Moreover, organizations that manage diversity creatively are in a much better position to attract the best personnel. A culturally diverse organization may gain a marketing edge because it understands different cultural groups. Proper guidance and management of diversity in an organization can also improve the level of productive creativity. Workers who bring fresh viewpoints to problem solving and decision making may enliven these processes substantially.[2]

Because cultural diversity creates challenges along with these advantages, it is important for an organization's employees to know how to cope with it. To accomplish that goal, numerous U.S. firms are taking action to train their managers to respect and manage diversity, according to one recent study. Diversity training programs may include recruiting minorities,

TABLE 10.1   Possible Competitive Advantages of Cultural Diversity

Cost	As organizations become more diverse, the cost of a poor job in integrating workers will increase. Companies that handle this well can thus create cost advantages over those that do a poor job.
Resource acquisition	Companies develop reputations on favorability as prospective employers for women and ethnic minorities. Those with the best reputations for managing diversity will win the competition for the best personnel.
Marketing edge	For multinational organizations, the insight and cultural sensitivity that members with roots in other countries bring to the marketing effort should improve these efforts in important ways. The same rationale applies to marketing to subpopulations domestically.
Creativity	Diversity of perspectives and less emphasis on conformity to norms of the past (which characterize the modern approach to management of diversity) should improve the level of creativity.
Problem solving	Differences within decision-making and problem-solving groups potentially produce better decisions through a wider range of perspectives and more thorough critical analysis of issues.

Source: Adapted from Taylor H. Cox and Stacy Blake, "Managing Cultural Diversity: Implications for Organizational Competitiveness," *Academy of Management Executive,* Vol. 5, No. 3, (1991), p. 46. Used by permission.

training minorities to be managers, training managers to view diversity positively, teaching English as a second language, providing mentoring programs, and facilitating support groups for immigrants. For example, Apple Computer's manager of multicultural programs schedules regular workshops to explore the minority experience in a majority society. At Xerox Corporation, managers are held accountable for the number of minorities employed at every level in every division. Corning Incorporated rotates new minorities through different jobs during their first five years with the firm. Before they are assigned permanent positions at Digital Equipment Corporation, minorities work at one of DEC's two multicultural plants, which provide comfortable learning environments. Procter & Gamble uses a mentoring program to help minorities adjust to the corporate environment.

As is the case with many organizational goals, a diversity program will be successful only if it is systematic and ongoing and has a strong, sustained commitment from top leadership. Cultural diversity is here to stay. Its impact in organizations is widespread and will continue to grow. Management must learn to overcome the obstacles and capitalize on the advantages associated with the varying viewpoints and backgrounds of culturally diverse human resources.

■■ JOB ANALYSIS

LEARNING OBJECTIVE 4
Explain the objectives and uses of job analysis.

job analysis a systematic procedure for studying jobs to determine their various elements and requirements

There is no sense in trying to hire people unless we know what we are hiring them for. In other words, we need to know the exact nature of a job before we can find the right person to do it.

Job analysis is a systematic procedure for studying jobs to determine their various elements and requirements. Consider the position of clerk, for example. In a large corporation, there may be fifty kinds of clerks' positions. They all may be called "clerks," but each may be different from the others in the activities to be performed, the level of proficiency required for each activity, and the particular set of qualifications that the position demands. These distinctions are the focus of job analysis.

job description a list of the elements that make up a particular job

The job analysis for a particular position typically consists of two parts—a job description and a job specification. A **job description** is a list of the elements that make up a particular job. It includes the duties the jobholder must perform, the working conditions under which the job must be performed, the jobholder's responsibilities (including number and types of subordinates, if any), and the tools and equipment that must be used on the job (see Figure 10.1).

job specification a list of the qualifications required to perform a particular job

A **job specification** is a list of the qualifications required to perform a particular job. Included are the skills, abilities, education, and experience that the jobholder must have.

The job analysis is the basis for recruiting and selecting new employees—for either existing positions or new ones. It is also used in other areas of human resources management, including evaluation and the determination of equitable compensation levels.

■■ RECRUITING, SELECTION, AND ORIENTATION

LEARNING OBJECTIVE 5
Describe the processes of recruiting, employee selection, and orientation.

In an organization with jobs waiting to be filled, HRM personnel need to (1) find candidates for those jobs and (2) match the right candidate with each job. Three activities are involved: recruiting, selection, and (for new employees) orientation.

Recruiting

recruiting the process of attracting qualified job applicants

Recruiting is the process of attracting qualified job applicants. Because it is a vital link in a costly process (the average cost of hiring an employee is $6,600),[3] recruiting needs to be a systematic rather than haphazard process. One goal of recruiters is to attract the "right number" of applicants. The right number is enough to allow a good match between applicants and open positions, but not so many that matching them requires too much time and effort. For example, if there are five open positions and five applicants, the firm essentially has no choice. It must hire those five applicants (qualified or not) or the positions will remain open. At the other extreme, if several hundred job seekers apply for the five positions, HRM personnel will have to spend weeks processing their applications.

FIGURE 10.1
Job Description
A job description is a list of the elements that make up a particular position and the tasks that the employee is required to perform.

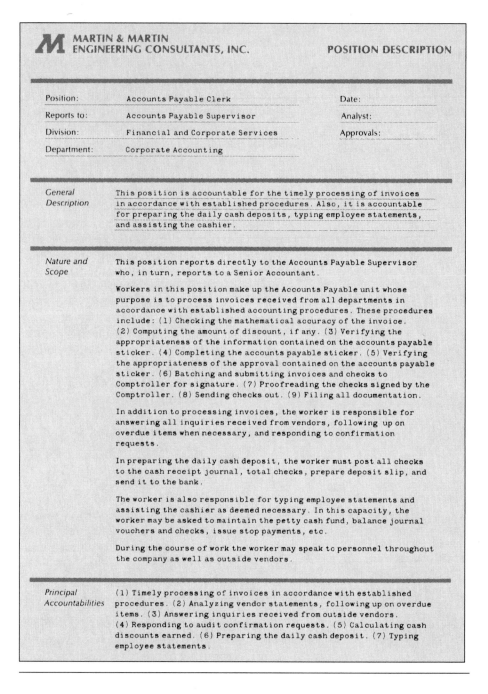

MARTIN & MARTIN
ENGINEERING CONSULTANTS, INC.   POSITION DESCRIPTION

Position:	Accounts Payable Clerk	Date:
Reports to:	Accounts Payable Supervisor	Analyst:
Division:	Financial and Corporate Services	Approvals:
Department:	Corporate Accounting	

General Description

This position is accountable for the timely processing of invoices in accordance with established procedures. Also, it is accountable for preparing the daily cash deposits, typing employee statements, and assisting the cashier.

Nature and Scope

This position reports directly to the Accounts Payable Supervisor who, in turn, reports to a Senior Accountant.

Workers in this position make up the Accounts Payable unit whose purpose is to process invoices received from all departments in accordance with established accounting procedures. These procedures include: (1) Checking the mathematical accuracy of the invoice. (2) Computing the amount of discount, if any. (3) Verifying the appropriateness of the information contained on the accounts payable sticker. (4) Completing the accounts payable sticker. (5) Verifying the appropriateness of the approval contained on the accounts payable sticker. (6) Batching and submitting invoices and checks to Comptroller for signature. (7) Proofreading the checks signed by the Comptroller. (8) Sending checks out. (9) Filing all documentation.

In addition to processing invoices, the worker is responsible for answering all inquiries received from vendors, following up on overdue items when necessary, and responding to confirmation requests.

In preparing the daily cash deposit, the worker must post all checks to the cash receipt journal, total checks, prepare deposit slip, and send it to the bank.

The worker is also responsible for typing employee statements and assisting the cashier as deemed necessary. In this capacity, the worker may be asked to maintain the petty cash fund, balance journal vouchers and checks, issue stop payments, etc.

During the course of work the worker may speak to personnel throughout the company as well as outside vendors.

Principal Accountabilities

(1) Timely processing of invoices in accordance with established procedures. (2) Analyzing vendor statements, following up on overdue items. (3) Answering inquiries received from outside vendors. (4) Responding to audit confirmation requests. (5) Calculating cash discounts earned. (6) Preparing the daily cash deposit. (7) Typing employee statements.

Recruiters may seek applicants outside the firm, within the firm, or both. The source used generally depends on the nature of the position, the situation within the firm, and (sometimes) the firm's established or traditional recruitment policies.

Recruiting at career fairs. Career fairs provide job seekers with an opportunity to become better informed about potential employers and to network with recruiters. Companies benefit by gaining exposure to job seekers and by being able to make contacts with potential employees.

external recruiting the attempt to attract job applicants from outside the organization

External Recruiting   **External recruiting** is the attempt to attract job applicants from outside the organization. Among the means available for external recruiting are newspaper advertising, recruiting on college campuses and in union hiring halls, using employment agencies, and soliciting the recommendations of present employees. In addition, many people who are looking for work simply apply at the firm's employment office.

Clearly, it is best to match the recruiting means with the kind of applicant being sought. For example, private employment agencies most often handle professional people, whereas public employment agencies (operated by state or local governments) are usually more concerned with operations personnel. Hence we might approach a private agency if we were looking for a vice president, but we would be more inclined to contact a public agency if we wanted to hire a machinist.

The primary advantage of external recruiting is that it enables the firm to bring in people with new perspectives and varied business backgrounds. It may also be the only way to attract applicants with the required skills and knowledge. A disadvantage of external recruiting is that it is often expensive, especially if private employment agencies must be used. External recruiting may also provoke resentment among present employees.

internal recruiting considering present employees as applicants for available positions

Internal Recruiting   **Internal recruiting** means considering present employees as applicants for available positions. Generally, current employees are considered for *promotion* to higher-level positions. However, employees may also be considered for *transfer* from one position to another at the same level.

Promoting from within provides strong motivation for current employees and helps the firm to retain quality personnel. General Electric, Exxon, Bell Telephone Laboratories, and Eastman Kodak are companies dedicated to promoting from within. (In cases where there is a strong union, the practice of *job posting,* or informing current employees of upcoming openings, may be required by the union contract.) The primary disadvantage of internal recruiting is that promoting a current employee leaves another position to be filled. Not only does the firm still incur recruiting and selection costs, but it must now train two employees instead of one.

In many situations, it may be impossible to recruit internally. For example, a new position may be such that no current employee is qualified to fill it. Or the firm may be growing so rapidly that there is no time to go through the reassigning of positions that promotion or transfer require.

Selection

selection   the process of gathering information about applicants for a position and then using that information to choose the most appropriate applicant

Selection is the process of gathering information about applicants for a position and then using that information to choose the most appropriate applicant. Note the use of the word *appropriate.* In selection, the idea is not to hire the person with the "most" qualifications but rather to choose the applicant with the qualifications that are most appropriate for the job. The actual selection of an applicant often is made by one or more line managers who have responsibility for the position being filled. However, HRM personnel usually help the selection process by developing a pool of applicants and expediting the assessment of these applicants. Common means of obtaining information about applicants' qualifications are employment applications, tests, interviews, references, and assessment centers.

Employment Applications   Just about everyone who applies for anything must submit an application. You probably filled one out to apply for admission to your school. An employment application is useful in collecting factual information on a candidate's education, work experience, and personal history (see Figure 10.2). The data obtained from applications are usually used for two purposes: to identify candidates who are worthy of further scrutiny and to familiarize interviewers with applicants' backgrounds.

Many job candidates submit résumés to prospective employers, and some firms require them. A *résumé* is a one- or two-page summary of the candidate's background and qualifications. It includes a description of the type of job the applicant is seeking. A résumé may be sent to a firm to request consideration for available jobs, or it may be submitted along with an employment application.

In recent years, HRM experts have developed a technique to determine the relative importance of information provided on applications and résumés. Current employees are asked which factors in their own backgrounds most strongly relate to their current jobs. Then these factors are given extra weight in assessing new applicants' qualifications to perform similar jobs.

Employment Tests   Tests administered to job candidates usually focus on aptitudes, skills, abilities, or knowledge relevant to the jobs that are to be performed. Such tests (word processing tests, for example) indicate how

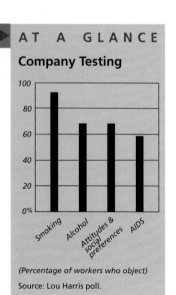

▶ ▶ ▶ A T   A   G L A N C E

Company Testing

(Percentage of workers who object)

Source: Lou Harris poll.

FIGURE 10.2
Typical Employment Application
Employers use applications to collect factual information on a candidate's education, work experience, and personal history. *(Source: Used by permission of CBS Inc.)*

PLEASE PRINT ALL INFORMATION

CBS EMPLOYMENT APPLICATION

CBS POLICY FORBIDS DISCRIMINATION BASED ON AGE, COLOR, RACE, RELIGION, SEX, NATIONAL ORIGIN, ANCESTRY OR ANY OTHER CATEGORY PROTECTED BY APPLICABLE FEDERAL AND STATE LAW. IN ADDITION, CBS POLICY FORBIDS DISCRIMINATION BASED ON SEXUAL ORIENTATION. IF YOU ARE APPLYING FOR A POSITION IN THE FIELD OF BROADCASTING AND BELIEVE THERE HAS BEEN DISCRIMINATION YOU MAY NOTIFY THE FEDERAL COMMUNICATIONS COMMISSION OR OTHER APPROPRIATE AGENCY.

PERSONAL

Last Name | First | Initial | Today's Date | Social Security Number

Present Address (Street, City, State, Zip Code) | Area Code / Home Telephone

Permanent Address if different from above (Street, City, State, Zip Code)

Do you have relatives employed by CBS? ☐ Yes ☐ No | Have you previously applied at CBS? ☐ Yes ☐ No When? | Shift Preferred

If yes, give name and relationship | Were you ever employed by CBS? ☐ Yes ☐ No From To

Have you been convicted of any law violation other than a minor traffic violation? Conviction will not necessarily disqualify you from employment. ☐ Yes ☐ No | Date | Place | Charge

Are there any positions or job duties which you cannot perform because of a physical, mental or medical disability? If so, describe

EMPLOYMENT AND EXPERIENCE

Business telephone number and extension where you can be reached | Position applied for | Salary desired $ | Date you could start

From (Mo. Yr.)	To (Mo. Yr.)	Previous employers' Name, Address (most recent first)	Name of Immediate Supervisor & Title	Your Position	Salary (if applicable) Beginning	Last	Reason for leaving

EDUCATION

From (Mo. Yr.)	To (Mo. Yr.)	Name and Address of School	Type of course or major	Did you Graduate? Yes	No	Degree / Diploma	Year awarded
		High or Prep 1					
		2					
		Business or special					
		College 1					
		2					
		Graduate School					

US MILITARY

From (Mo. Yr.)	To (Mo. Yr.)	Branch of service (if none, write "none")	Highest rank held	Date and type of discharge Dishonorable or general discharge will not necessarily disqualify you from employment.

Please complete reverse side

CBS 199 Rev. 4/97

well the applicant will do on the job. Occasionally companies use general intelligence or personality tests, but these are seldom helpful in predicting specific job performance.

At one time, a number of companies were criticized for using tests that were biased against members of certain minority groups—in particular, African Americans. This practice of testing is not as common today for two reasons. The test results were, to a great extent, unrelated to job performance. And to prove that they are not discriminating, firms must be able to demonstrate that the results of any tests they use are valid predictors of on-the-job performance. Applicants who believe they have been discriminated against in a test may file a complaint with the Equal Employment Opportunity Commission (EEOC).

Interviews   The employment interview is perhaps the most widely used selection technique. Job candidates are usually interviewed by at least one member of the HRM staff and by the person for whom they will be working. Candidates for higher-level jobs may also meet with a department head or vice president and may have several additional interviews.

Interviews provide an opportunity for the applicant and the firm to learn more about each other. Interviewers can pose problems to test the candidate's abilities. They can probe employment history more deeply and learn something about the candidate's attitudes and motivation. The candidate, meanwhile, has a chance to find out more about the job and the people with whom he or she would be working.

Unfortunately, interviewing may be the stage at which discrimination enters the selection process. For example, suppose a female applicant mentions that she is the mother of small children. Her interviewer may (mistakenly) assume that she would not be available for job-related travel. In addition, interviewers may be unduly influenced by factors such as appearance. Or they may ask different questions of different applicants, so that it becomes impossible to compare candidates' qualifications.

Some of these problems can be solved through better interviewer training and the use of structured interviews. In a *structured interview*, the interviewer asks only a prepared set of questions. The firm may also consider using several different interviewers for each applicant, but that solution is likely to be a costly one.

References   A job candidate is generally asked to furnish the names of references—people who can verify background information and provide personal evaluations of the candidate. Naturally, applicants tend to list only references who are likely to say good things about them. Thus personal evaluations obtained from references may not be of much value. However, references are often contacted to verify such information as previous job responsibilities and the reason an applicant chose to leave a former job.

Assessment Centers   A newer selection technique is the assessment center, which is used primarily to select current employees for promotion to higher-level management positions. Typically, a group of employees is sent to the center for two or three days. While there, they participate in activities designed to simulate the management environment and predict managerial effectiveness. Trained observers (usually managers) make recommendations regarding promotion possibilities. Although this technique is gaining popularity, the expense involved limits its use to larger organizations.

Orientation

Once all the available information about job candidates has been collected and analyzed, those involved in the selection decide which candidate they would like to hire. A job offer is extended to the candidate. If it is accepted, the candidate becomes an employee and starts to work for the firm.

Soon after a candidate joins the firm, he or she goes through the firm's orientation program. **Orientation** is the process of acquainting new employees with the organization. Orientation topics range from such basic items as the location of the company cafeteria to concerns about various career paths within the firm. The orientation itself may consist of a half-hour informal presentation by a human resources manager. Or it may be an elaborate program involving dozens of people and lasting several days or weeks.

orientation the process of acquainting new employees with an organization

■■ ■ COMPENSATION AND BENEFITS

LEARNING OBJECTIVE 6
Discuss the primary elements of employee compensation and benefits.

We have noted that an effective employee reward system must (1) enable employees to satisfy their basic needs, (2) provide rewards comparable to those offered by other firms, (3) be distributed fairly within the organization, and (4) recognize that different people have different needs.

The firm's compensation system can be structured to meet the first three of these requirements. The fourth is more difficult in that it must take into account many variables among many people. Most firms offer a number of benefits that, taken together, generally help provide for employees' varying needs.

Compensation Decisions

compensation the payment employees receive in return for their labor

compensation system the policies and strategies that determine employee compensation

Compensation is the payment employees receive in return for their labor. Its importance to employees is obvious. And, because compensation can account for up to 80 percent of a firm's operating costs, it is equally important to management. The firm's **compensation system**—the policies and strategies that determine employee compensation—must therefore be carefully designed to provide for employee needs while keeping labor costs within reasonable limits. For most firms, designing an effective compensation system requires three separate management decisions—about wage level, wage structure, and individual wages.

Wage Level Management must first position the firm's general pay level relative to pay levels of comparable firms. In other words, will the firm pay its employees less than, more than, or about the same as similar organizations? Most firms choose a pay level near the industry average. A firm that is not in good financial shape may pay less than the going rate. Large, prosperous organizations, by contrast, may pay a little more than average to attract and retain the most capable employees.

wage survey a collection of data on prevailing wage rates within an industry or a geographic area

To determine what the average is, the firm may use wage surveys. A **wage survey** is a collection of data on prevailing wage rates within an industry or a geographic area. Such surveys are compiled by industry associations, local governments, personnel associations, and (occasionally) individual firms.

■ ■ ■ ■ CHANGE IN THE WORKPLACE

Workplace Couples: Can Romance and Business Mix?

At Parker Hannifer Corporation, manufacturer of automobile air-conditioning parts, marriage between employees has become so routine that human resources management has coined a name for these couples—"Parker-Parkers." Du Pont encourages dual careers, counting 3,500 couples in its 100,000-person work force. A dozen married couples met and work at Microsoft headquarters in Seattle, including CEO Bill Gates, who wed one of his marketing executives. Companies used to disapprove of, discourage, or even ban romance in the workplace. Management was convinced that people who are attracted to each other at work will be too distracted to get their jobs done. Today, those old notions are disappearing along with the time clock and the typewriter. A recent *Fortune* poll reveals that 75 percent of CEOs questioned believe that romances between workers are "none of the company's business." A study by the Society for Human Resource Management found that 70 percent of companies questioned permit and accept workplace romance.

Why are so many employees using the workplace as an opportunity to meet, date, and even marry people? One answer seems obvious: people who work together are likely to have similar backgrounds and talents. With men and women working longer and longer hours, work is the natural place to meet. But other factors also contribute to the growing acceptance of workplace romance. More women in the work force means more interaction between the sexes in almost every type of job. Empowered employees are less willing to let a company dictate their private lives. Finally, given the spread of AIDS and other diseases, coworkers may seem more appealing (and safer) to date than strangers.

A number of recent studies suggest that, rather than lowering morale and productivity, coworker romances often boost them and increase both partners' job commitment. Research at the University of Wisconsin's Center for Communication reveals that when couples work together, their productivity (as well as that of their other coworkers) remains unaffected or improves. A study of the faculty at five midwestern colleges compared work teams made up entirely of either men or women with those composed of both male and female members. Without exception, the mixed teams were quicker and more creative at problem solving than the single-gender groups.

When office romance does cause problems, it's more likely for the couple to suffer than the company. Sometimes the difficulty is just too much togetherness. Sometimes business demands leave little time for quality family time. Relationships can be jeopardized when one partner gets a promotion and the other doesn't, or one gets transferred and the other has to give up a job to follow. Some couples report that the company treats them as a unit, not as individuals. Anything one of them does at work reflects on both partners, and when considering raises, companies often base decisions on the couple's combined income.

Whatever its benefits and drawbacks, office romance is not going away. More than half of the CEOs interviewed in the *Fortune* study report that they observe many more married couples at the office than they did a decade ago. Asserts the head of Mitchell Energy Corporation, "People meet and get married, and you really can't stop that."

Wage Structure   Next, management must decide on relative pay levels for all the positions within the firm. Will managers be paid more than secretaries? Will secretaries be paid more than custodians? The result of this set of decisions is often called the firm's *wage structure*.

job evaluation   the process of determining the relative worth of the various jobs within a firm

The wage structure is almost always developed on the basis of a job evaluation. **Job evaluation** is the process of determining the relative worth of the various jobs within a firm. Most observers would probably agree that a secretary should make more money than a custodian, but how much more? Twice as much? One and one-half times as much? Job evaluation should provide the answers to such questions.

A number of techniques may be used to evaluate jobs. The simplest is to rank all the jobs within the firm according to their value to the firm. Of course, if there are more than a few jobs, this technique loses its simplicity very quickly. A more frequently used method is based on the job analysis. Points are allocated to each job for each of its elements and requirements, as set forth in the job analysis. For example, "college degree required" might be worth 50 points, whereas the need for a high school education might count for only 25 points. The more points a job is allocated, the more important it is presumed to be (and the higher its level in the firm's wage structure).

Individual Wages   Finally, the specific payments that individual jobholders will receive must be determined. Consider the case of two secretaries working side by side. Job evaluation has been used to determine the relative level of secretarial pay within the firm's wage structure. However, suppose one secretary has fifteen years of experience and can accurately type 80 words per minute. The other has two years of experience and can type only 55 words per minute. In most firms, these people would not receive the same pay. Instead, a wage range would be established for the secretarial position. In this case, the range might be $7 to $9.50 per hour. The more experienced and proficient secretary would then be paid an amount near the top of the range (say, $8.90 per hour); the less experienced secretary would receive an amount that was lower but still within the range (say, $7.75 per hour).

Two wage decisions actually come into play here. First the employee's initial rate must be established. It is based on experience, other qualifications, and expected performance. Later the employee may be given pay increases based on seniority and performance.

Comparable Worth

comparable worth   a concept that seeks equal compensation for jobs requiring about the same level of education, training, and skills

There is growing concern that one reason women in the work force are paid less than men is that a certain proportion of women occupy female-dominated jobs—nurses, clerk typists, and medical records analysts, for example—that require education, skills, and training equal to higher-paid positions but are undervalued by our economic system. **Comparable worth** is a concept that seeks equal compensation for jobs requiring about the same level of education, training, and skills. Several states have enacted laws that require equal pay for comparable work in government positions. Critics of comparable worth argue that the market has determined the worth of these jobs and that laws should not be enacted to tamper with the pricing mechanism of the market. They also point out that artificially inflating salaries for these female-dominated occupations encourages women to keep these jobs rather than to seek out other higher-paying jobs.

Types of Compensation

Compensation can be paid in a variety of forms. Most forms of compensation fall into the following categories: hourly wage, weekly or monthly salary, commissions, bonuses, lump-sum salary increases, and profit sharing.

hourly wage a specific amount of money paid for each hour of work

Hourly Wage   An **hourly wage** is a specific amount of money paid for each hour of work. People who earn wages are paid their hourly wage for the first forty hours worked in any week. They are then paid one and one-half times their hourly wage for time worked in excess of forty hours. (That is, they are paid "time and a half" for overtime.) Workers in retailing and fast-food chains, on assembly lines, and in clerical positions are usually paid an hourly wage.

salary a specific amount of money paid for an employee's work during a set calendar period, regardless of the actual number of hours worked

Weekly or Monthly Salary   A **salary** is a specific amount of money paid for an employee's work during a set calendar period, regardless of the actual number of hours worked. Salaried employees receive no overtime pay, but they do not lose pay when they are absent from work (within reasonable limits). Most professional and managerial positions are salaried.

commission a payment that is a percentage of sales revenue

Commissions   A **commission** is a payment that is a percentage of sales revenue. Sales representatives and sales managers are often paid entirely through commissions or through a combination of commissions and salary.

bonus a payment in addition to wages, salary, or commissions; usually an extra reward for outstanding job performance

Bonuses   A **bonus** is a payment in addition to wages, salary, or commissions. Bonuses are really extra rewards for outstanding job performance. They may be distributed to all employees or only to certain employees within the organization. Some firms distribute bonuses to all employees every Christmas. The size of the bonus depends on the firm's earnings and the particular employee's length of service with the firm. Other firms offer bonuses to employees who exceed specific sales or production goals.

To avoid yearly across-the-board salary increases, some organizations individually reward outstanding workers through merit bonuses. This pay-for-performance approach allows management to control labor costs while encouraging employees to work more efficiently. An employee's merit bonus depends on his or her achievements relative to those of others.

Lump-Sum Salary Increases   In traditional reward systems, an employee who receives an annual pay increase is given part of the increase in each pay period. For example, suppose an employee on a monthly salary gets a 10 percent annual pay hike. He or she actually receives 10 percent of the former monthly salary added to each month's paycheck for a year. Companies that offer **lump-sum salary increases** give the employee the option of taking the entire pay raise in one lump sum at the beginning of the year. The employee then draws his or her "regular" pay for the rest of the year. The lump-sum payment is typically treated as an interest-free loan that must be repaid if

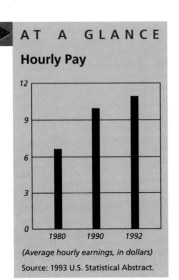

▶▶ **AT A GLANCE**

Hourly Pay

(Average hourly earnings, in dollars)

Source: 1993 U.S. Statistical Abstract.

lump-sum salary increase an entire pay raise taken in one lump sum

profit sharing the distribution of a percentage of the firm's profit among its employees

the employee leaves the firm during the year. B. F. Goodrich, Aetna Life and Casualty, and Timex have all offered variations of this plan.

Profit Sharing **Profit sharing** is the distribution of a percentage of the firm's profit among its employees. The idea is to motivate employees to work effectively by giving them a stake in the company's financial success. Some firms—including Sears, Roebuck and Co.—have linked their profit-sharing plans to employee retirement programs; that is, employees receive their profit-sharing distributions, with interest, when they retire. Olga Company, a maker of lingerie and underwear, places 20 to 25 percent of its annual pre-tax earnings in a profit-sharing plan for its employees.

Employee Benefits

employee benefit a reward in addition to regular compensation that is provided indirectly to employees—mainly a service (such as insurance) paid for by the employer, or an employee expense (such as college tuition) reimbursed by the employer

An **employee benefit** is a reward in addition to regular compensation that is provided indirectly to employees. Employee benefits consist mainly of services (such as insurance) that are paid for partially or totally by employers and employee expenses (such as college tuition) that are reimbursed by employers. Currently, the average cost of these benefits is more than one-third of the total cost of wages and salaries. Thus a person who earns $25,000 a year is likely to receive, in addition, over $7,500 worth of employee benefits.

Types of Benefits Employee benefits take a variety of forms. *Pay for time not worked* covers such absences as vacation time, holidays, and sick leave. *Insurance packages* may include health, life, and dental insurance for employees and their families. Some firms pay the entire cost of the insurance package and others share the cost with the employee. The costs of *pension and retirement programs* may also be borne entirely by the firm or shared with the employee.

Some benefits are required by law. For example, employers must maintain *workers' compensation insurance*, which pays medical bills for injuries that occur on the job. Workers' comp also provides income for employees who are disabled by job-related injuries. Employers must also pay for *unemployment insurance* and must contribute to each employee's federal *Social Security* account.

Other benefits provided by employers include *tuition-reimbursement plans*, *credit unions*, *child care*, company *cafeterias* selling reduced-price meals, various *recreational facilities*, and broad *stock option plans* that are available to all employees, not just to top management.[4]

flexible benefit plan compensation plan whereby employee receives predetermined amount of benefit dollars to spend on a package of benefits that he or she has selected to meet individual needs

Flexible Benefit Plans Through a **flexible benefit plan** an employee receives a predetermined amount of benefit dollars and may allocate these dollars to various categories of benefits in the mix that best fits his or her needs. Some flexible benefit plans offer a broad array of benefit options including health care, dental care, life insurance, accidental death and dismemberment coverage for worker and dependents, long-term disability, vacation, retirement savings, and dependent care. Other firms offer limited options primarily in health and life insurance and retirement plans. Although the cost of administering flexible plans is high, a number of

Training and development at Andersen Consulting. Andersen Consulting employees are provided generous amounts of training. Here, employees are taking a multinational training class.

AT A GLANCE

Health Benefits

(Percentage of firms offering health benefits)

Source: Health Insurance Association of America, employer survey.

LEARNING OBJECTIVE 7
Explain the purposes and techniques of employee training, development, and performance appraisal.

employee training the process of teaching operations and technical employees how to do their present jobs more effectively and efficiently

management development the process of preparing managers and other professionals to assume increased responsibility in both present and future positions

organizations including Quaker Oats and Coca-Cola have implemented this option for several reasons. Because employees' needs are so diverse, flexible plans help firms offer benefit packages that more specifically meet their employees needs. Flexible plans can, in the long run, help a company contain costs because a specified amount is allocated to cover the benefits of each employee. Furthermore, organizations that offer flexible plans with many choices may be perceived as being employee-friendly. Thus, they put themselves in a position to attract and retain qualified employees.[5]

■■ TRAINING AND DEVELOPMENT

Training and development are both aimed at improving employees' skills and abilities. However, the two are usually differentiated as either employee training or management development. **Employee training** is the process of teaching operations and technical employees how to do their present jobs more effectively and efficiently. **Management development** is the process of preparing managers and other professionals to assume increased responsibility in both present and future positions. Thus training and development differ in both who is being taught and the purpose of the teaching. Both are necessary for personal and organizational growth. Companies that hope to stay competitive typically make huge commitments to employee training and development. For example, Motorola, Inc., spends $120 million annually, up from $7 million ten years ago, for employee education and training. Motorola's substantial educational efforts are companywide and range from the basic three R's to technical training, problem solving, and even interpersonal skills.[6]

Training and Development Methods

A variety of methods are available for employee training and management development. Some of these methods may be more suitable for one or the other, but most can be applied to both.

- *On-the-job methods*—the trainee learns by doing the work under the supervision of an experienced employee.
- *Vestibule training*—the work situation is simulated in a separate area so that learning takes place away from the day-to-day pressures of work.
- *Classroom teaching and lectures*—you probably already know these methods quite well.
- *Conferences and seminars*—experts and learners meet to discuss problems and exchange ideas.
- *Role playing*—participants act out the roles of others in the organization for better understanding of these roles (primarily a management development tool).

Evaluation of Training and Development

Training and development are very expensive. The training itself costs quite a bit, and employees are usually not working—or are working at a reduced load and pace—during training sessions. To ensure that training and development are cost effective, the managers responsible should evaluate the company's efforts periodically.

The starting point for this evaluation is a set of verifiable objectives that are developed *before* the training is undertaken. Suppose a training program is expected to improve the skills of machinists. The objective of the program might be stated as follows: "At the end of the training period, each machinist should be able to process thirty parts per hour with no more than one defective part per ninety parts completed." This objective clearly specifies what is expected and how training results may be measured or verified. Evaluation then consists of measuring machinists' output and the ratio of defective parts produced after the training.

The results of training evaluations should be made known to all those involved in the program—including trainees and upper management. For trainees, the results of evaluations can enhance motivation and learning. For upper management, the results may be the basis for making decisions about the training program itself.

Another form of evaluation—performance appraisal—is an equally important part of human resources management.

■ ■ PERFORMANCE APPRAISAL

performance appraisal the evaluation of employees' current and potential levels of performance to allow superiors to make objective human resources decisions

Performance appraisal is the evaluation of employees' current and potential levels of performance to allow managers to make objective human resources decisions. The process has three main objectives. First, performance appraisal allows a manager to let workers know how well they are

■ ■ ■ ■   **BUSINESS JOURNAL**

Is It Safe to Go to Work?

If you're afraid that you'll be harassed, threatened, attacked, or even murdered while at work, you are not paranoid. Since 1986, thirty-four U.S. Postal Service employees have been shot and killed on the job. In a midwestern suburb, an employee stabbed his boss to death when they disagreed over a procedure for handling paperwork. A recently fired technician slipped into his laboratory and opened fire on workers with a semi-automatic pistol.

The National Institute for Occupational Safety and Health (NIOSH) reports that more than one thousand Americans are murdered on the job every year, and over 2 million are attacked. For women, murder is the Number 1 cause of death in the workplace. It's not just violence from strangers during robberies or other crimes that figure into these alarming statistics. It's also the acts of estranged spouses, embittered coworkers, and disgruntled customers. The director of the National Safe Workplace Institute warns that violence directed against employees is the fastest growing category of workplace violence in America.

Why are stories about violence at work becoming such familiar headline news? Many experts believe that workplace assaults, like gun availability and movie and television violence, are another symptom of our increasingly dangerous society. Others blame alcohol and drug abuse. Although these factors contribute significantly to the problem, many experts point to an increasingly harsh work environment as the real culprit. The outrage, depression, and despair resulting from layoffs, firings, frozen wages, overwork, overbearing management, and coworker conflict, experts claim, can push workers over the edge.

Whatever the reasons behind the violence, employers and employees want solutions. U.S. firms are spending about $22 billion a year to hire more guards, install high-tech closed-circuit cameras and magnetic access systems, and run security checks on workers. Stricter screening of potential employees—including reference, credit, and criminal background investigations, and even psychological exams and personality profiles—is becoming standard hiring procedure. Consultants, the FBI, and psychiatrists are advising companies on workplace violence preparation. At one San Francisco law firm, twenty attorneys work full-time on workplace violence. NIOSH publishes a booklet called *Preventing Homicide in the Workplace* and also issues its own guidelines.

Northwestern National Life recently held a conference on workplace violence and came up with this list of recommendations:

- Train both supervisors and employees to negotiate and communicate effectively.
- Develop explicit companywide harassment policies.
- Establish and follow grievance procedures.
- Institute employee-assistance programs.
- Review security procedures regularly.
- Provide safety-education programs for employees.
- Offer counseling and support for laid-off or fired workers.
- Train supervisors to recognize signs of potentially violent employees and signs of substance abuse.
- Set up a crisis plan for dealing with violent events.

doing and how they can do better in the future. Second, it provides an effective basis for distributing rewards such as pay raises and promotions. Third, performance appraisal helps the organization monitor its employee selection, training, and development activities. If large numbers of employees continually perform below expectations, the firm may need to revise its selection process or strengthen its training and development activities.

Common Evaluation Techniques

The various techniques and methods for appraising employee performance are either objective or judgmental in nature.

Objective Methods   Objective appraisal methods use some measurable quantity as the basis for assessing performance. Units of output, dollar volume of sales, number of defective products, and number of insurance claims processed are all objective, measurable quantities. Thus an employee who processes an average of twenty-six claims per week is given a higher evaluation than one whose average is nineteen claims per week.

Such objective measures may require some adjustment for the work environment. Suppose the first of our insurance claims processors works in New York City, whereas the second works in rural Iowa. Both must visit each client, perhaps because they are processing homeowners' insurance claims. The difference in their average weekly output may be due entirely to the long distances the Iowan must travel to visit clients. In this case the two may very well be equally competent and motivated. Thus, a manager must take into account circumstances that may be hidden by a purely statistical measurement.

Judgmental Methods   Judgmental appraisal methods are used much more frequently than objective methods. They require that the manager judge or estimate the employee's performance level, relative to some standard (see the performance appraisal form in Figure 10.3). In one such method, the manager ranks subordinates from best to worst. This approach has a number of drawbacks, including the lack of any absolute standard.

Rating scales comprise the most popular judgmental appraisal technique. A *rating scale* consists of a number of statements. Each employee is rated on the degree to which each statement applies. For example, one statement might be, "This employee always does high-quality work." The supervisor would give the employee a rating, from 5 down to 1, corresponding to gradations ranging from "strongly agree" to "strongly disagree." The ratings on all the statements are added to obtain the employee's total evaluation.

Avoiding Appraisal Errors   Managers must be cautious if they are to avoid making mistakes when appraising employees. It is common to overuse one portion of an evaluation instrument, thus overemphasizing some issues and underemphasizing others. A manager must guard against allowing an employee's poor performance on one activity to influence his or her judgment of that subordinate's work on other activities. Similarly, putting too much weight on recent performance distorts an employee's evaluation. For

FIGURE 10.3
Performance Appraisal Form
Judgmental appraisal methods are used much more often than objective methods. Using judgmental methods requires that the manager estimate the employee's performance level, relative to some standard.   *(Source: Courtesy of Polaroid Corporation.)*

POLAROID CORPORATION

INDIVIDUAL PROGRESS REPORT

PURPOSE

This progress report is issued three times during the member's first year of employment to allow you to give extensive thought to whether the individual is going to be the kind of member we want to continue employing at Polaroid.

PROCEDURE

1. Please judge this member on the characteristics listed below. Base your evaluation on your knowledge of the member's current performance on this job.
2. Concentrate on only one characteristic at a time. Place a check (✓) in the space provided which best expresses your judgement of each characteristic.

This is (3)   (8)   (11)   Month Rating   NAME _____

JOB CLASSIFICATION _____   DATE HIRED _____

SUPERVISOR _____   DATE OF THIS RATING _____

TIME UNDER YOUR SUPERVISION _____   DEPARTMENT _____

QUALITY OF WORK - (Do not consider amount of work). Is work done correctly and accurately? Does work meet the required standards of quality? Is there little waste or spoilage?

| Work is carelessly done or not done correctly. Produces waste or rejected material. | Does not produce work up to standards. Has to be checked frequently to get required results. Work frequently not accurate. | Does acceptable work. Results meet normal standards. Work performed is satisfactory. | Performs work of high quality. Makes few errors. Work can be depended upon. | Work is of highest quality. Very accurate. Does job exactly as it should be done. Never spoils a job or creates waste. |

Additional comments: _____

SAFETY HABITS AND ATTITUDES - Works carefully? Follows safety instructions and rules? Points out unsafe conditions?

| Unsafe; careless. Disregards safety rules. Creates hazards. | Obeys safety rules when recommended. Takes some chances. | Works with reasonable care. Usually and normally safe. | Works carefully. Observes all safety rules. Aware of safety problem. | Very safety-conscious. Considers safety promotion part of job. Makes suggestions. |

Additional comments: _____

ABILITY TO UNDERSTAND AND FOLLOW INSTRUCTIONS - Understands instructions? Remembers what to do? Completes task?

| Dull. Requires repeated and constant instructions. Poor memory. | Needs detailed instructions on every point. Must be reminded of original instructions. | Seems to understand instructions. May require occasional follow-up. | Rarely has to have instructions repeated. Understands and follows instructions as given. | Seems to anticipate instructions. "Catches on" immediately. Understands with great ease and follows through. |

Additional comments: _____

WORK OUTPUT - (Do not consider quality of work). General work habits? Work habits compared to others in the group?

| Slow worker. Lazy. Stalls around. Low production. | Takes it easy. Requires some pushing. Below normal production. Clock watcher. | Works steadily. Does job in reasonable manner. Does normal amount of work. | Works hard. Always steady at job. Does more than others doing same job. | Fast and hard worker. Outstanding for amount of work done. High production. Keeps driving throughout the day. |

Additional comments: _____

POLAROID STOCK NO. 27-094

example, if the employee is being rated on performance over the last year, a manager should not permit last month's disappointing performance to overshadow the quality of the work done in the first eleven months of the year. Finally, a manager must guard against discrimination on the basis of race, age, gender, religion, national origin, or sexual orientation.

Performance Feedback

No matter which appraisal technique is used, the results should be discussed with the employee soon after the evaluation is completed. The manager should explain the basis for present rewards and should let the employee know what he or she can do to be recognized as a better performer in the future. The information provided to an employee in such discussions is called *performance feedback*.

Performance feedback should occur in two stages, not in a single sitting. The first is the *evaluation interview*. At this interview the manager plays the role of the evaluator and makes the employee aware of what he or she is doing right and wrong. The subordinate should understand how the manager reached these decisions and what criteria the manager used. In the second stage, or *feedback interview*, the manager should specify how the employee can improve individual performance. Suggestions should be made regarding methods, techniques, and perhaps training that would boost performance.[7]

Many managers find it difficult to discuss the negative aspects of an appraisal. Unfortunately, they may ignore performance feedback altogether or provide it in a very weak and ineffectual manner. In truth, though, most employees have strengths that can be emphasized to soften the discussion of their weaknesses. An employee may not even be aware of weaknesses and their consequences. If they are not pointed out through performance feedback, they cannot possibly be eliminated. Only through tactful, honest communication can the results of an appraisal be fully utilized.

■■ THE LEGAL ENVIRONMENT OF HRM

LEARNING OBJECTIVE 8
Outline the major legislation affecting human resources management.

Legislation regarding HRM practices has been passed mainly to protect the rights of employees, to promote job safety, and to eliminate discrimination in the workplace. Eight pieces of legislation (see Table 10.2) and one set of executive orders are of primary concern.

National Labor Relations Act and Labor-Management Relations Act

These laws are concerned with dealings between business firms and labor unions. This general area is, in concept, a part of human resources management. However, because of its importance, it is often treated as a separate set of activities. We discuss both labor-management relations and these two acts in detail in Chapter 11.

Fair Labor Standards Act

This act, originally passed in 1938 and amended many times, applies primarily to wages. It establishes such factors as minimum wages and overtime pay rates. Many managers and other professionals, however, are exempt from this law. Managers, for example, seldom get paid overtime when they work more than forty hours in a week.

TABLE 10.2 Federal Legislation That Focuses on Human Resources Management

Law	Purpose
National Labor Relations Act (1935)	Establishes a collective bargaining process in labor-management relations. It also established the National Labor Relations Board (NLRB).
Fair Labor Standards Act (1938)	Establishes a minimum wage and an overtime pay rate for employees working more than forty hours per week.
Labor-Management Relations Act (1947)	Provides a balance between union power and management power. Also known as the Taft-Hartley Act.
Equal Pay Act (1963)	Specifies that men and women who do equal jobs must be paid the same wage.
Title VII of the Civil Rights Act (1964)	Eliminates discrimination in employment practices based on sex, race, color, religion, or national origin.
Age Discrimination in Employment Act (1967/1978)	Outlaws personnel practices that discriminate against people aged 40 to 69. The 1978 amendment outlaws company policies that require employees to retire before age 70.
Occupational Safety and Health Act (1970)	Regulates the degree to which employees can be exposed to hazardous substances and specifies the safety equipment that the employer must provide.
Employment Retirement Income Security Act (1974)	Regulates company retirement programs and provides a federal insurance program for retirement plans that go bankrupt.
Americans with Disabilities Act (1990)	Prohibits discrimination against qualified individuals with disabilities in all employment practices, including job application procedures, hiring, firing, advancement, compensation, training, and other terms, conditions, and privileges of employment.
Civil Rights Act (1991)	Facilitates employees suing employers for sexual discrimination and collecting punitive damages.

Equal Pay Act

Passed in 1963, this law overlaps somewhat with Title VII of the Civil Rights Act (see below). The Equal Pay Act specifies that men and women who are doing equal jobs must be paid the same wage. Equal jobs are jobs that demand equal effort, skill, and responsibility and that are performed under the same conditions. Differences in pay are legal if they can be attributed to differences in seniority, qualifications, or performance. But women cannot be paid less (or more) for the same work solely because they are women.

Civil Rights Acts

Title VII of the Civil Rights Act of 1964 applies directly to selection and promotion. It forbids organizations to discriminate in those areas on the basis of sex, race, color, religion, or national origin. Hence the purpose of Title VII is to ensure that employers make personnel decisions on the basis of employee qualifications only. As a result of this act, discrimination in employment (especially against African Americans) has been reduced in this country.

The Equal Employment Opportunity Commission (EEOC) is charged with enforcing Title VII. A person who believes he or she has been discriminated against can file a complaint with the EEOC. The EEOC investigates the complaint. If it finds that the person has, in fact, been the victim of discrimination, the commission can take legal action on his or her behalf.

The Civil Rights Act of 1991 facilitates an employee's suing and collecting punitive damages for sexual discrimination. Discriminatory promotion and termination decisions as well as on-the-job issues such as sexual harassment are covered by this act.

Age Discrimination in Employment Act

The general purpose of this act, which was passed in 1967 and amended in 1978, is the same as that of Title VII—to eliminate discrimination. However, as the name implies, the Age Discrimination in Employment Act is concerned only with discrimination based on age. In particular, it outlaws personnel practices that discriminate against people aged 40 to 69. (No federal law forbids discrimination against people younger than 40, but several states have adopted age-discrimination laws that apply to a variety of age groups.) Also outlawed are company policies that require employees to retire before age 70.

Protecting older workers.
The Age Discrimination in Employment Act protects older employees from discrimination due to their age.

Occupational Safety and Health Act

Passed in 1970, this act is concerned mainly with issues of employee health and safety. For example, the act regulates the degree to which employees can be exposed to hazardous substances. It also specifies the safety equipment that must be provided.

The Occupational Safety and Health Administration (OSHA) was created to enforce this act. Inspectors from OSHA investigate employee complaints regarding unsafe working conditions. They also make spot checks on companies operating in particularly hazardous industries, such as chemicals and mining, to ensure compliance with the law. A firm that is found to be in violation of federal standards can be heavily fined or shut down.

Employee Retirement Income Security Act

This act was passed in 1974 to protect the retirement benefits of employees. It does not require that firms provide a retirement plan. However, it does specify that *if* a retirement plan is provided, it must be managed in such a way that the interests of employees are protected. It also provides federal insurance for retirement plans that go bankrupt.

Affirmative Action

Affirmative action is not one act but is a series of executive orders, issued by the president of the United States. These orders established the requirement for affirmative action in personnel practices. This stipulation applies to all employers holding contracts with the federal government. It prescribes that such employers (1) actively encourage job applications from members of minority groups and (2) hire qualified employees from minority groups that are not fully represented in their organizations. Many firms that do not hold government contracts voluntarily take part in this affirmative-action program.

Americans with Disabilities Act

The Americans with Disabilities Act (ADA) prohibits discrimination against qualified individuals with disabilities in all employment practices—including job application procedures, hiring, firing, advancement, compensation, training, and other terms and conditions of employment. All private employers and government agencies with fifteen or more employees are covered by the ADA. Defining who is a qualified individual with a disability is of course difficult. Depending on how "qualified individual with a disability" is interpreted, up to 43 million Americans can be included under this law. This law also mandates that all businesses that serve the public must make their facilities accessible to people with disabilities.

Not only are individuals with physical disabilities protected under the ADA; also safeguarded are those with less visible conditions such as heart disease, diabetes, epilepsy, cancer, AIDS, and emotional illnesses. Because of this law, many organizations no longer require job applicants to pass physical examinations as a condition of employment. Within the first two years after this law went into effect in July 1992, approximately 33,000 cases were filed with EEOC charging discrimination under its provisions.

Employing persons with disabilities. The Americans with Disabilities Act prohibits discrimination against qualified individuals with disabilities in all employment practices. Employers are required to provide disabled employees with reasonable accommodations.

Employers are required to provide disabled employees with reasonable accommodation. *Reasonable accommodation* is any modification or adjustment to a job or work environment that will enable a qualified employee with a disability to perform a central job function. Examples of reasonable accommodation include making existing facilities readily accessible to and usable by an individual confined to a wheelchair. Reasonable accommodation might also mean restructuring a job, modifying work schedules, acquiring or modifying equipment, providing qualified readers or interpreters, or changing examinations or training programs.

■ ■ ■ ■ CHAPTER REVIEW

Summary

1   Describe the major components of human resources management.

Human resources management (HRM) is the set of activities involved in acquiring, maintaining, and developing an organization's human resources. Responsibility for HRM is shared by specialized staff and line managers. HRM activities include human resources planning, job analysis, recruiting, selection, orientation, compensation, benefits, training and development, and appraisal.

2   Identify the steps in human resources planning.

Human resources planning consists of forecasting the human resources that the firm will need and those that it will have available and then planning a course of action to match supply with demand. Layoffs, attrition, early retirement, and (as a last resort) firing are ways to reduce the size of the work force. Supply is increased through hiring.

3   Describe cultural diversity and understand some of the challenges and opportunities associated with it.

Cultural diversity refers to the differences among people in a work force related to race, ethnicity, and gender. With the increase of women, minorities, and immigrants entering the U.S. work force, management is posed with both challenges and competitive advantages. Some organizations are implementing diversity-related training programs and working to make the most of cultural diversity. With the proper guidance and management, a culturally diverse organization can prove beneficial to all involved.

4   Explain the objectives and uses of job analysis.

Job analysis provides a job description and a job specification for each position within the firm. A job description is a list of the elements that make up a particular job. A job specification is a list of qualifications required to perform a particular job. Job analysis is used in evaluation and determining compensation levels and serves as the basis for recruiting and selecting new employees.

5   Describe the processes of recruiting, employee selection, and orientation.

Recruiting is the process of attracting qualified job applicants. Candidates for open positions may be recruited from within or outside the firm. In the selection process, information about candidates is obtained from applications, résumés, tests, interviews, references, and assessment centers. This information is then used to select the most appropriate candidate for the job. Newly hired employees will then go through a formal or informal orientation program to acquaint themselves with the firm.

6   Discuss the primary elements of employee compensation and benefits.

Compensation is the payment employees receive in return for their labor. In developing a system for paying employees, management must decide on the firm's general wage level (relative to other firms), the wage structure within the firm, and individual wages. Wage surveys and job analyses are useful in making these decisions. Employees may be paid hourly wages, salaries, or commissions. They may also receive bonuses, lump-sum salary increases, and profit-sharing payments. Employee benefits, which are nonmonetary rewards to employees, add about one-third to the cost of compensation.

7   Explain the purposes and techniques of employee training, development, and performance appraisal.

Employee training and management development programs enhance the ability of employees to contribute to the firm. Several techniques are available. Because training is expensive, an organization should periodically evaluate the effectiveness of its training programs.

Performance appraisal, or evaluation, is used to provide employees with performance feedback, to serve as a basis for distributing rewards, and to monitor selection and training activities. Both objective and judgmental appraisal techniques are used. Their results must be communicated to employees if evaluation is to help eliminate job-related weaknesses.

8   Outline the major legislation affecting human resources management.

A number of laws have been passed that affect HRM practices and that protect the rights and safety of employees. Some of these are the National Labor Relations Act of 1935; the Labor-Management Relations Act of 1947; the Fair Labor Standards Act of 1938; the Equal Pay Act of 1963; Title VII of the Civil Rights Act of 1964; the Age Discrimination in Employment Act of 1967/1978; the Occupational Safety and Health Act of 1970; the Employment Retirement Income Security Act of 1974; and the Americans with Disabilities Act of 1990.

Key Terms

You should now be able to define and give an example relevant to each of the following terms:

human resources management (HRM) (295)

human resources planning (296)

replacement chart (297)

skills inventory (297)

cultural (workplace) diversity (299)

job analysis (301)

job description (301)

job specification (301)

recruiting (301)

external recruiting (303)

internal recruiting (303)

selection (304)

orientation (307)

compensation (307)

compensation system (307)

wage survey (307)

job evaluation (309)

comparable worth (309)

hourly wage (310)

salary (310)

commission (310)

bonus (310)

lump-sum salary increase (310)

profit sharing (311)

employee benefit (311)

flexible benefit plan (311)

employee training (312)

management development (312)

performance appraisal (313)

Questions

Review Questions

1. List the three main HRM activities and their objectives.
2. In general, on what basis is responsibility for HRM divided between line and staff managers?
3. How is a human resources' demand forecast related to the firm's organizational planning?
4. How do human resources managers go about matching the firm's supply of workers with its demand for workers?
5. What are the major challenges and benefits associated with a culturally diverse work force?
6. How are a job analysis, job description, and job specification related?
7. What are the advantages and disadvantages of external recruiting? of internal recruiting?
8. In your opinion, what are the two best techniques for gathering information about job candidates?
9. Why is orientation an important HRM activity?
10. Explain how the three wage-related decisions result in a compensation system.
11. How is a job analysis used in the process of job evaluation?
12. Suppose you have just opened a new Ford auto sales showroom and repair shop. Which of your employees would be paid wages, which would receive salaries, and which would receive commissions?
13. What is the difference between the objective of employee training and the objective of management development?
14. Why is it so important to provide feedback after a performance appraisal?

Discussion Questions

1. How does Hanna Andersson benefit from having an award-winning employee benefits program?
2. In what ways has Hanna Andersson's benefits program changed due to the firm's decline in sales?
3. How accurately can managers plan for future human resources needs?
4. How might an organization's recruiting and selection practices be affected by the general level of employment?
5. Are employee benefits really necessary? Why?
6. What actions would you take, as a manager, if an operations employee with six years of experience on the job refused ongoing training and ignored performance feedback?
7. Why are there so many laws relating to HRM practices? Which are the most important laws, in your opinion?

Exercises

1. Construct a job analysis for the position of "entering first-year student" at your school.
2. Write a newspaper ad to attract applicants for the position of retail salesperson in your small business.
3. Describe the orientation procedure used by a firm that you have worked for or by your school. Then devise an *improved* orientation procedure for that organization.

VIDEO CASE 10.1

Woolworth Corporation's Commitment to Hiring the Disabled

The Americans with Disabilities Act prohibits job discrimination against individuals with physical and mental disabilities ranging from back injuries and epilepsy to cerebral palsy and mental retardation. A recent study shows that since passage of the ADA in 1990, more disabled people are working and their income levels are rising. Workers with disabilities prepare tables and seat customers in restaurants; log in and sort mail; stock shelves; manage currency at commercial banks; lobby Congress; and wait on customers in retail establishments. Of the more than 20 million retail workers in the United States, a growing number have disabilities of one kind or another. At the forefront of the movement to hire developmentally disabled individuals is Woolworth Corporation, one of the leading retailers in the United States. In addition to hiring many disabled workers in a variety of capacities, the company strives to educate other firms about the benefits of such employment practices.

In 1879 Frank Woolworth opened "The Great 5 Cent Store" in Utica, New York. Although this original store failed, Woolworth moved to Pennsylvania, launched America's first "five-and-dime," and started a retailing empire that today generates about $10 billion in annual sales. Woolworth Corporation operates more than 9,000 general merchandise and specialty stores, including Woolworth's, Champs Sports, Foot Locker and Lady Footlocker, Kinney Shoes, Kids' Mart, Afterthoughts, and others, in twelve countries around the world. In 1899 the company's founder authorized store managers to contribute a percentage of their sales to "worthy local welfare enterprises and charities." By establishing an internal program of hiring qualified people with disabilities, Woolworth carries on this long-time commitment to charitable and community service activities that has distinguished it for over a century.

Harold Sells, Woolworth's CEO, explains that hiring developmentally disabled workers not only contributes to those individuals' independence and self-esteem, it also makes good business sense. With retailers facing a dwindling supply of workers, disabled individuals offer a pool of potential employees for manual, clerical, and sales positions. Woolworth's management reports that disabled employees are reliable, eager, hard-working, and productive. In addition, working alongside these individuals fosters an attitude of tolerance, compassion, and mutual respect that permeates and improves the workplace for everyone. Finally, by employing this largely overlooked segment of the population, businesses create consumers and taxpayers while reducing the burden on social services. A person with a regular paycheck doesn't need to collect government entitlements.

Several organizations have recognized Woolworth Corporation, not only for its record of hiring workers with disabilities, but also for its efforts to change the attitudes of leaders in the business community. The ARC, America's largest volunteer organization devoted to serving people with mental retardation, presented Woolworth with its Humanitarian Award. This distinction honors those who show an ongoing commitment to people with disabilities by supporting their employment and integrating them into the workplace. Woolworth also won the National Retail Federation's first American Spirit Award, created to recognize retail members' humanitarianism and community service.

Naturally, there are obstacles to bringing more disabled people into America's work force, but a growing number of business people are finding the effort both rewarding and profitable. At Red Lobster restaurants, United Parcel Service, Johnson & Johnson, and other well-known companies, productive disabled workers are making significant contributions. At AT&T's national headquarters, for example, a young man with Down's syndrome works full-time in the mail room. His coworkers admire his industriousness and positive outlook. In his three years of employment, he has not missed one day of work. He earns $26,000 a year.[8]

Questions

1. In what ways does the Woolworth Corporation benefit from the employment of developmentally disabled persons?
2. Why do you think Woolworth encourages other businesses to hire disabled workers?
3. What are the potential costs associated with hiring people who are developmentally disabled?

CASE 10.2

Digital Equipment Corporation's AIDS Program

Every 54 seconds, someone in the United States contracts the AIDS-causing HIV virus, and 3,000 cases are reported every month. Experts predict these figures will triple in the next few years. Because most of those contracting the virus are of working age—22 to 45 years old—managing AIDS in the workplace is becoming an increasingly critical issue for businesses. Then why do only about 20 percent of large corporations have written AIDS policies? Businesses commonly support programs dealing with socially acceptable chronic illnesses like cancer, but AIDS carries a stigma and attracts few advocates. Pacific Bell and Wells Fargo & Co. defied public opinion years ago by initiating AIDS training programs. Since then, only a handful of major corporations including Levi Strauss, Bank of America, IBM, and Digital Equipment Corp. (DEC) have dared to join them.

Instituting a written AIDS program is good for workers, but it also makes good business sense. Two years after the U.S. Congress passed the Americans with Disabilities Act, making it illegal for employers to discriminate against qualified but disabled workers, the number of AIDS discrimination cases skyrocketed from fewer than 400 to more than 95,000. By implementing a written, documented AIDS program, companies become less vulnerable to discrimination lawsuits. And by reducing fear and prejudice, they keep workers productive. A sound policy should tell managers how to act fairly and should tell employees what to expect. Further, managers must be trained to implement policy and employees educated so that they can reduce the spread of the disease and improve relations with infected coworkers.

For years, DEC executives considered implementing some kind of AIDS program, but until an employee came to them and said, "I have AIDS," they did nothing more than talk. At that time, some DEC workers were even afraid to install computer systems in hospitals caring for AIDS patients, believing they could catch it by breathing the air or touching something in the room. From a company with no AIDS policy and no support system, DEC has gone on to become the only major firm in the United States with a corporate department working full-time on the problems of AIDS in the workplace.

DEC's AIDS policy guidelines are simple: employees with serious illnesses have the right to continue working as long as they can perform their jobs, and medical records are confidential. However, DEC's AIDS Programs office manager is proud of the education program built on this base. The program not only teaches managers to respond skillfully within company guidelines but also creates a sympathetic environment in which workers feel free to tell supervisors about their illnesses. Managers attend mandatory four-hour training sessions that include medical explanations, discussions about employee-relation issues, and videos by medical personnel. Workers learn how the disease is spread and what the law says regarding employee rights. They also learn to deal with psychological problems, such as fear or panic, which can deeply affect personal and professional lives. DEC writes and distributes a pamphlet containing medical facts, company guidelines and benefits, and a list of places to go for help, both inside DEC and in the larger community. To bring the reality of the disease home to its employees, DEC invites people infected with HIV to speak at training sessions. One 35-year-old man relates that when he first came to DEC to talk about his illness, he was one of a panel of three speakers. Of those, he is the only one still alive.

To date, DEC has trained more than half of its 123,000 personnel, both managers and nonmanagers. However, the organization's efforts to halt the spread of AIDS, or at least to alleviate some suffering, don't stop at its own doors. The company sponsors fundraising events and grants money for AIDS research.

Despite DEC's accomplishments and those of other firms, AIDS discrimination is still active in the workplace. When a sports superstar shocks the public by revealing that he has the HIV virus, his teammates and coaches stand behind him. When an average worker comes forward, he or she might be told, "Leave by the end of the day and don't touch anything on your way out."[9]

Questions

1. Do most business organizations need an AIDS policy? Why or why not?
2. DEC's AIDS policy guidelines are rather simple and straightforward. Would a different type of organization (hospital, tire manufacturer, grocery store) need a different kind of AIDS policy? Explain.
3. Should an organization's policies and guidelines for AIDS be different from those regarding other types of medical problems? Discuss.

CHAPTER 11

Union-Management Relations

LEARNING OBJECTIVES

After studying this chapter you should be able to

1 Explain how and why labor unions came into being.

2 Discuss the sources of unions' negotiating power and trends in union membership.

3 Identify the main focus of several major pieces of labor-management legislation.

4 Enumerate the steps involved in forming a union, and show how the National Labor Relations Board is involved in the process.

5 Describe the basic elements in the collective bargaining process.

6 Identify the major issues covered in a union-management contract.

7 Explain the primary bargaining tools available to unions and management.

CHAPTER PREVIEW

We open this chapter by reviewing the history of labor unions in this country. Then we turn our attention to organized labor today, noting current membership trends and summarizing important labor-relations laws. We discuss the unionization process—why employees join unions, how a union is formed, and what the National Labor Relations Board does. Collective bargaining procedures are then explained. Next we consider such issues as employee pay, working hours, security, management rights, and grievance procedures, all of which are issues included in a union-management contract. We close with a discussion of various labor and management negotiating techniques, including strikes, lockouts, mediation, and arbitration.

Union-Management Power Struggle at Caterpillar

Caterpillar, Inc., is in the business of making earth-moving machinery, and business is booming. The company is the world's leading producer of wheel loaders, excavators, motor graders, backhoe loaders, and off-highway trucks. Current earnings are up 16 percent over last year; its biggest competitor, Komatsu, is doing poorly; and its employees earn up to $40 an hour, some of the best hourly pay in the country. No wonder the ongoing bitter battle between Caterpillar and its union, the United Auto Workers, seems bewildering.

In a time of increasing cooperation between management and unions, Caterpillar's relationship with the UAW remains adversarial and combative. Between September 1993 and September 1994, union workers at Caterpillar staged nine wildcat strikes and five spontaneous walkouts. Workers shut down the entire company for three days after managers suspended a union official, and two of Cat's largest plants suffered several one-day strikes. From the fall of 1991 through the summer of 1994, the union filed eighty-nine complaints against the company with the National Labor Relations Board.

In such prosperous times, what are Caterpillar and the union squabbling about? Although workers would like higher wages and a better health plan, what they are really pushing for is increased job security. After the UAW won protection from layoffs for its members at John Deere & Co., the union asked for the same pledge from Caterpillar's management. The company's CEO refused, arguing that Cat's employees already have one of the top pay packages in the country.

What experts contend, however, is that the real struggle is over power and control. Caterpillar, they say, is in a position to offer increased job security but won't, and the union, for its part,

refuses to bargain in good faith. The result of this unwillingness to compromise is a stream of petty punishments by management, dismal worker morale, and 12,600 union members settling the most recent strike only because Caterpillar threatened to replace them permanently if they didn't. Employees complain of harassment by supervisors. Workers are dismissed for wearing anti-Cat buttons. A manager told a shop steward he could no longer write up employee grievances. Said one 27-year veteran at Caterpillar, "It's an awful place to work."

Although union activity is up, and the UAW is calling for a companywide shutdown, Caterpillar doesn't seem concerned. Fearful of losing their jobs to replacements, workers aren't likely to stage a prolonged walkout. And Caterpillar would probably not suffer from a strike anyway—the firm can bring in products from its nonunion overseas plants.

■ ■ ■ ■

■　　■　　■　　■　　■　　■　　■　　■　　■　　■　　■

The labor-management conflicts at Caterpillar have a long history. Labor strife has reduced job satisfaction among workers, made the organization less productive, decreased the firm's ability to compete globally, and threatened workers' job security. Fortunately, not all companies and unions have these types of problems. Many businesses have highly cooperative relationships with unions.

A **labor union** is an organization of workers acting together to negotiate their wages and working conditions with employers. In the United States, nonmanagement employees have the legal right to form unions and to bargain, as a group, with management. The result of the bargaining process is a *labor contract,* a written agreement that is in force for a set period of time (usually one to three years). The dealings between labor unions and business management, both in the bargaining process and beyond it, are called **union-management relations** or, more simply, **labor relations.**

There is a dual relationship between labor and management. The two groups have different goals, a fact that tends to place them at odds with each other. But these goals must be attained by the same means—through the production of goods and services. At contract bargaining sessions, the two groups must work together to attain their goals. Perhaps mainly for this reason, antagonism now seems to be giving way to cooperation in union-management relations.

Before we examine how organized labor operates today, let's take a look at its roots in the history of the labor movement.

■■ THE HISTORICAL DEVELOPMENT OF UNIONS

Until the middle of the nineteenth century, there was very little organization of labor in this country. Groups of workers did occasionally form a **craft union,** which is an organization of skilled workers in a single craft or trade. These alliances were usually limited to a single city, and they often lasted only a short time. The first known strike in the United States involved a group of Philadelphia printers who stopped working over demands for higher wages. When the employers granted the printers a pay increase, the group disbanded.

Early History

In the mid-1800s, improved transportation opened new markets for manufactured goods. Improved manufacturing methods made it possible to supply those markets, and American industry began to grow. The Civil War and the continued growth of the railroads after the war led to further industrial expansion.

328

Large-scale production required more and more skilled industrial workers. As the skilled labor force grew, craft unions emerged in the more industrialized areas. From these craft unions, three significant labor organizations evolved. See Figure 11.1 for a historical overview of unions and their patterns of membership.

Knights of Labor The first significant national labor organization to emerge was the Knights of Labor, which was formed as a secret society in 1869 by Uriah Stephens. Membership reached approximately 700,000 by 1886. One major goal of the Knights was to eliminate the depersonalization of the worker that resulted from mass-production technology. Another was to improve the moral standards of both employees and society. To the detriment of the group, its leaders concentrated so intently on social and economic change that they did not recognize the effects of technological change. Moreover, they assumed that all employees had the same goals as the Knights' leaders—social and moral reform. The major reason for the demise of the Knights was the Haymarket riot of 1886. At a rally (called to demand a reduction in the length of a workday from ten to eight hours) in Chicago's Haymarket Square, a bomb exploded. Several police officers and

FIGURE 11.1 Historical Overview of Unions
The total number of members for all unions has risen dramatically since 1869, when the first truly national union was organized. The dates of major events in the history of labor unions are singled out along the line of membership change. *(Sources: U.S. Bureau of Labor Statistics and Dictionary of U.S. Labor Organizations, 1986–1987; Aaron Bernstein, "Why America Needs Unions," Business Week, May 23, 1994, p. 70.)*

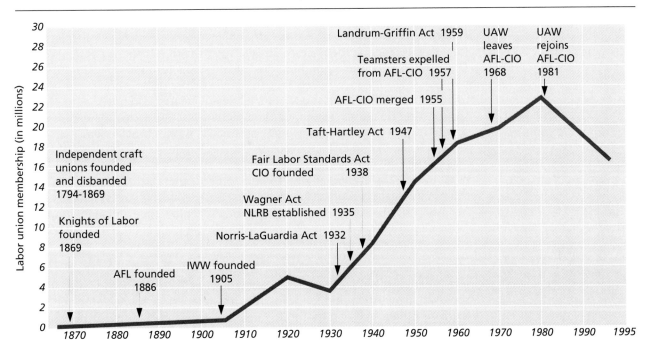

Discouragement of union activities. Mounted police break up a meeting of the Industrial Workers of the World at Union Square in New York City on April 4, 1914.

strike   a temporary work stoppage by employees, calculated to add force to their demands

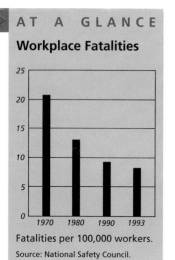

AT A GLANCE

Workplace Fatalities

Fatalities per 100,000 workers.

Source: National Safety Council.

civilians were killed or wounded. The Knights were not directly implicated, but they quickly lost public favor.

American Federation of Labor   In 1886 several leaders of the Knights joined with independent craft unions to form the *American Federation of Labor (AFL)*. Samuel Gompers, one of the AFL's founders, became its first president. Gompers believed that the goals of the union should be those of its members rather than those of its leaders. The AFL did not seek to change the existing business system, as the Knights of Labor had. Instead, its goal was to improve its members' living standards within that system.

Another major difference between the Knights of Labor and the AFL was in their positions regarding strikes. A **strike** is a temporary work stoppage by employees, calculated to add force to their demands. The Knights did not favor the use of strikes, whereas the AFL strongly believed that striking was an effective labor weapon. The AFL also believed that organized labor should play a major role in politics. As we will see, the AFL is still very much a part of the American labor scene.

Industrial Workers of the World   The *Industrial Workers of the World (IWW)* was created in 1905 as a radical alternative to the AFL. Among its goals was the overthrow of capitalism. This revolutionary stance prevented the IWW from gaining much of a foothold. Perhaps its major accomplishment was to make the AFL seem, by comparison, less threatening to the general public and to business leaders.

Labor Unions in the Twentieth Century

During the first two decades of this century, both business and government attempted to keep labor unions from growing. This period was plagued by strikes and violent confrontations between management and unions. In steelworks, garment factories, and auto plants, clashes took place in which striking union members fought bitterly against nonunion workers, police, and private security guards.

The AFL continued to be the major force in organized labor. By 1920 its membership included 75 percent of all those who had joined unions. Throughout its existence, however, the AFL had been unsure of the best way to deal with unskilled and semiskilled workers. Most of its members were skilled workers in specific crafts or trades. But technological changes during World War I had brought about a significant increase in the number of unskilled and semiskilled employees in the work force. These people sought to join the AFL, but they were not well received by its established membership.

industrial union an organization of both skilled and unskilled workers in a single industry

Some unions within the AFL did recognize the need to organize unskilled and semiskilled workers, and they began to penetrate the automotive and steel industries. The type of union they formed was an **industrial union,** an organization of both skilled and unskilled workers in a single industry. Soon workers in the rubber, mining, newspaper, and communications industries were also organized into unions. Eventually these unions left the AFL and formed the *Congress of Industrial Organizations (CIO).*

During this same time (the late 1930s), there was a major upswing in rank-and-file membership—in the AFL, CIO, and independent unions. Strong union leadership, the development of effective negotiating tactics, and favorable legislation combined to increase total union membership to 9 million in 1940. At this point the CIO began to rival the AFL in size and influence. There was another bitter rivalry: the AFL and CIO often clashed over which of them had the right to organize and represent particular groups of employees.

Since World War II, the labor scene has gone through a number of changes. For one thing, during and after the war years there was a downturn in public opinion regarding unions. A few isolated but very visible strikes during the war caused public sentiment to shift against unionism. Perhaps the most significant occurrence, however, was the merger of the AFL and the CIO. After years of bickering, the two groups recognized that they were wasting effort and resources by fighting each other and that a merger would greatly increase the strength of both. The merger took place on December 5, 1955. The resulting organization, called the *AFL-CIO,* had a membership of as many as 16 million workers, which made it the largest labor organization of its kind in the world. Its first president was George Meany, who served until 1979.

■■ ORGANIZED LABOR TODAY

LEARNING OBJECTIVE 2
Discuss the sources of unions' negotiating power and trends in union membership.

The power of unions to negotiate effectively with management is derived from two sources. The first is their membership. The more workers a union represents within an industry, the greater its clout in dealing with firms operating in that industry. The second source of union power is the group of laws that guarantee unions the right to negotiate and, at the same time, regulate the negotiating process.

Union Membership

At present, union members account for a relatively small portion of the American work force: fewer than one-fifth of the nation's workers belong to unions. Union membership is concentrated in a few industries and job categories. Within these industries, though, unions wield considerable power.

The AFL-CIO is still the largest union organization in this country, boasting approximately 13.3 million members. Those represented by the AFL-CIO include actors, barbers, construction workers, carpenters, retail clerks, musicians, teachers, postal workers, painters, steel and iron workers, firefighters, bricklayers, and newspaper reporters. Figure 11.2 shows the organization of the AFL-CIO.

One of the largest unions not associated directly with the AFL-CIO is the Teamsters' Union. The *Teamsters* were originally part of the AFL-CIO, but in 1957 they were expelled for corrupt and illegal practices. The union started out as an organization of professional drivers, but it has recently begun to recruit employees in a wide variety of jobs. Current membership is about 1.3 million workers.

The *United Auto Workers* represents employees in the auto industry. The UAW, too, was originally part of the AFL-CIO, but it left the parent union—of its own accord—in 1968. Currently the UAW has about 748,000 members. For a while, the Teamsters and the UAW formed a semistructured partnership called the Alliance for Labor Action. This partnership was eventually dissolved, and the UAW again became part of the AFL-CIO in 1981.

Membership Trends

The proportion of union members, relative to the size of the nation's work force, has declined over the last twenty years. Moreover, total union membership has dropped since 1980, despite steadily increasing membership in earlier years (see Figure 11.1). To a great extent, this decline in membership is caused by changing trends in business, like the following:

- Heavily unionized industries have either been decreasing in size or have not been growing as fast as nonunionized industries. For example, recent cutbacks in the steel and auto industries have tended to reduce union membership. At the same time, the growth of high-tech industries has increased the ranks of nonunion workers.
- Many firms have moved from the heavily unionized Northeast and Great Lakes regions to the less unionized Southeast and Southwest—the so-called Sunbelt. At the relocated plants, formerly unionized firms tend to hire nonunion workers.
- The largest growth in employment is occurring in the service industries, and these industries are typically not unionized.

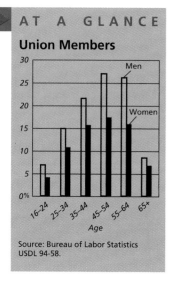

AT A GLANCE

Union Members

Source: Bureau of Labor Statistics USDL 94-58.

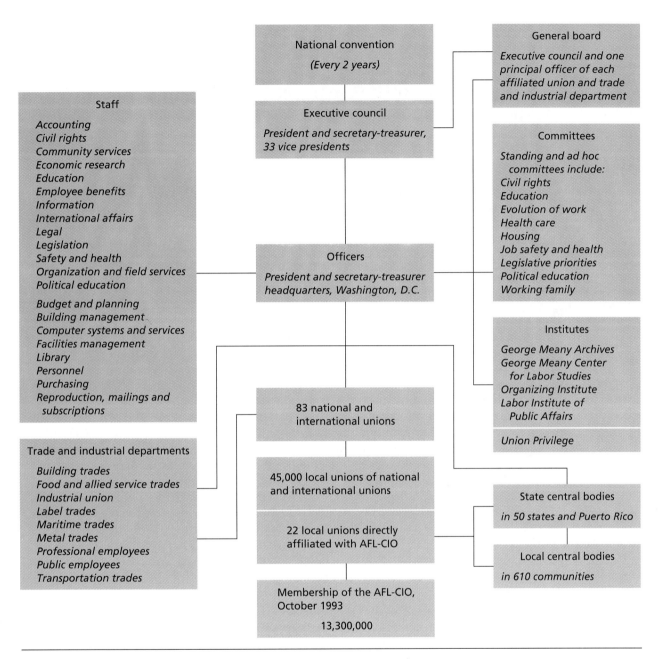

FIGURE 11.2 AFL-CIO Organization Chart
Like a big corporation, the AFL-CIO has organized its chain of command to best attain
its goals as well as the goals of the various unions it represents.   *(Source: "Structure of
the AFL-CIO," American Federation of Labor and Congress of Industrial Organizations,
Washington, D.C., Dec. 1993, p. 2.)*

- Management is providing benefits that tend to reduce employees' need
  for unionization. Increased employee participation and better wages
  and working conditions are goals of unions. When these benefits are
  already supplied by management, workers are less likely to join

BUSINESS JOURNAL

Union-Management Partnerships: Old Foes Become Friends

With their bargaining power and political clout waning and their membership falling, are unions the dinosaurs of the American workplace? Unions have played a significant role in the American economy, serving the needs of both management and workers. From unions came standardized jobs, grievance procedures, higher wages, better benefits, and improved working conditions. However, the mighty unions that ruled an age of manufacturing and mass production seem headed for extinction in the empowered workplace of the future.

There are those who insist that America still needs its unions. Statistics indicate that unions can boost productivity. In construction and in twenty manufacturing industries, unionized companies are about 20 percent more productive, and unionized hospitals are about 16 percent more productive than their nonunion counterparts. Workers who thought they didn't need unions to get good pay and safe working conditions are uneasy in an age of downsizing, massive layoffs, and a widening gap between the lofty salaries of top management and the take-home pay of hourly wage earners. To survive and be effective, however, unions have recognized they need to change. Instead of harboring a traditional feisty "us versus them" mentality, many unions are becoming partners with management, cooperating to enhance the workplace, improve quality, and reduce costs.

From farm equipment builders to clothing manufacturers, from steel to communications, industries are finding ways for managers and union officials to work together. At National Steel Corporation, all union members with one year's seniority are protected from layoffs, and hourly workers have greater say in decision making. As a result of this cooperation, the number of hours needed to make one ton of steel has fallen 30 percent. Over six thousand members of the Amalgamated Clothing and Textile Workers Union have joined with Xerox in a partnership that has brought three hundred jobs back to the United States from abroad and saves the company about $2 million a year. Representatives from union and management at Scott Paper Company have pledged to "work together to meet the needs of employees, customers, shareholders, the union, and the community." Scott's reputation for lowering costs and improving quality has made its management-labor alliance a model for other American paper companies. The willingness of union members to accept lower wages and fewer benefits made it possible for employees to buy United Airlines, now the largest employee-owned American company.

In Europe, most companies perceive unions as allies rather than as enemies, but in the United States, management often seems to wish unions didn't exist at all. The Labor and Commerce departments as well as the AFL-CIO are trying to recast American attitudes in the European mold, and the efforts are showing signs of success. The number of union-management partnerships is increasing. In addition, the Department of Labor recently reported that the average length of labor contracts is at its highest since that agency began keeping records in 1972, a statistic that many experts regard as a symbol of growing trust between management and unions.

existing unions or start new ones. The number of elections to vote on forming new unions is less than one-half the 7,000-a-year pace of the 1970s.

Teamsters convention. The Teamsters union meets periodically to elect officials and focus on union activities and member concerns.

It remains to be seen whether unions will be able to regain the prominence and power they enjoyed between the world wars and during the 1950s. There is little doubt, however, that they will remain a powerful force in particular industries.

■■ LABOR-MANAGEMENT LEGISLATION

LEARNING OBJECTIVE 3
Identify the main focus of several major pieces of labor-management legislation.

As we have noted, business opposed early efforts to organize labor. The federal government generally supported antiunion efforts through the court system, and in some cases federal troops were used to end strikes. Gradually, however, the government began to correct this imbalance through the legislative process.

Norris-LaGuardia Act

The first major piece of legislation to secure rights for unions, the *Norris-LaGuardia Act* of 1932, was considered a landmark in labor-management relations. This act made it difficult for businesses to obtain court orders that banned strikes, picketing, or union membership drives. Previously, courts had issued such orders readily as a means of curbing these activities.

National Labor Relations Act

The *National Labor Relations Act*, also known as the *Wagner Act*, was passed by Congress in 1935. It established procedures by which employees decide whether they want to be represented by a union. If workers choose to be represented, the Wagner Act requires management to negotiate with union representatives. Before this law was passed, union efforts were sometimes interpreted as violating the Sherman Act (1890) because they were viewed as attempts to monopolize. The Wagner Act also forbids certain unfair labor practices on the part of management, such as firing or punishing workers because they are pro-union, spying on union meetings, and bribing employees to vote against unionization.

Finally, the Wagner Act established the **National Labor Relations Board (NLRB)** to enforce the provisions of the law. The NLRB is primarily concerned with (1) overseeing the elections in which employees decide whether they will be represented by a union and (2) investigating complaints lodged by unions or employers.

> **National Labor Relations Board (NLRB)** the federal agency that enforces the provisions of the Wagner Act

Fair Labor Standards Act

In 1938 Congress enacted the *Fair Labor Standards Act.* One major provision of this act permits the federal government to set a minimum wage. The first minimum wage, which was set in the late 1930s and did not include farm workers and retail employees, was $0.25 an hour. Today the minimum wage is $4.25 an hour. Some employees, such as professional, executive, and administrative personnel, are exempt from the minimum wage provisions. The act also requires that employees be paid at overtime rates for work in excess of forty hours a week. Finally, this law prohibits the use of child labor.

Labor-Management Relations Act

The legislation of the 1930s sought to discourage unfair practices on the part of employers. Recall from Figure 11.1 that union membership grew from approximately 2 million in 1910 to almost 12 million by 1945. Unions represented over 35 percent of all nonagricultural employees in 1945. As union membership and power grew, however, the federal government began to examine the practices of labor. Several long and bitter strikes, mainly in the coal and trucking industries in the early 1940s, led to a demand for legislative restraint on unions. As a result, in 1947 Congress passed the *Labor-Management Relations Act,* also known as the *Taft-Hartley Act,* over President Harry Truman's veto.

The objective of the Taft-Hartley Act is to provide a balance between union power and management authority. It lists unfair labor practices that unions are forbidden to use. These include refusal to bargain with management in good faith, charging excessive membership dues, harassing nonunion workers, and using various means of coercion against employers.

The Taft-Hartley Act also gives management more rights during union organizing campaigns. For example, management may outline for employees the advantages and disadvantages of union membership, as long as the information it presents is accurate. The act gives the president of the United States the power to obtain a temporary injunction to prevent or stop a strike that endangers national health and safety. An **injunction** is a court order requiring a person or group either to perform some act or to refrain from performing some act. Finally, the Taft-Hartley Act authorized states to enact

> **injunction** a court order requiring a person or group either to perform some act or to refrain from performing some act

laws to allow employees to work in a unionized firm without joining the union. About twenty states (many in the South) have passed such *right-to-work laws.*

Landrum-Griffin Act

In the 1950s, Senate investigations and hearings exposed labor racketeering in unions and uncovered cases of bribery, extortion, and embezzlement among union leaders. It was discovered that a few union leaders had taken union funds for personal use and accepted payoffs from employers for union protection. Some were involved in arson, blackmail, and murder. Public pressure for reform resulted in the 1959 *Landrum-Griffin Act.*

This law was designed to regulate the internal functioning of labor unions. Provisions of the law require unions to file annual reports with the U.S. Department of Labor regarding their finances, elections, and various decisions made by union officers. The Landrum-Griffin Act also ensures each union member the right to seek, nominate, and vote for each elected position in his or her union. It provides safeguards governing union funds, and it requires management and unions to report the lending of management funds to union officers, union members, or local unions.

The various pieces of legislation we have reviewed here effectively regulate much of the relationship between labor and management after a union has been established. The next section demonstrates that forming a union is also a carefully regulated process.

■■ THE UNIONIZATION PROCESS

LEARNING OBJECTIVE 4
Enumerate the steps involved in forming a union, and show how the National Labor Relations Board is involved in the process.

For a union to be formed at a particular firm, some employees of the firm must first be interested in being represented by a union. They must then take a number of steps to formally declare their desire for a union. To ensure fairness, most of the steps in this unionization process are supervised by the NLRB.

Why Some Employees Join Unions

Obviously, employees start or join a union for a variety of reasons. One commonly cited reason is to combat alienation. Some employees—especially those whose jobs are dull and repetitive—may perceive themselves as merely parts of a machine. They may feel that they lose their individual or social identity at work. Union membership is one way to establish contact with others in the firm.

Another common reason for joining a union is the perception that union membership increases job security. No one wants to live in fear of arbitrary or capricious dismissal from a job. Unions actually have only limited ability to guarantee a member's job, but they can help increase job security by enforcing seniority rules.

Employees may also join a union because of dissatisfaction with one or more elements of their jobs. If they are unhappy with their pay, benefits, or

Local unions in action. Union representatives talk to truck drivers and dock workers in Minneapolis about the closing of the workers' company.

working conditions, they may look to a union to correct the perceived deficiencies.

Some people join unions because of their personal backgrounds. For example, a person whose parents are strong believers in unions might be inclined to feel just as positive about union membership.

In some situations, employees *must* join a union to keep their jobs. Many unions try, through their labor contracts, to require that a firm's new employees join the union after a specified probationary period. Under the Taft-Hartley Act, states may pass right-to-work laws prohibiting this practice.

Steps in Forming a Union

The first step in forming a union is the *organizing campaign* (see Figure 11.3). Its primary objective is to develop widespread employee interest in having a union. To kick off the campaign, a national union may send organ-

FIGURE 11.3   Steps in Forming a Union
The unionization process consists of a campaign, authorization cards, a formal election, and certification of the election by the National Labor Relations Board.

| 1 Organizing campaign | 2 Authorization cards | 3 Election | 4 NLRB certification |

izers to the firm to stir this interest. Alternatively, the employees themselves may decide that they want a union. Then they contact the appropriate national union and ask for organizing assistance.

The organizing campaign can be quite emotional, and it may lead to conflict between employees and management. On the one hand, the employees who want the union will be dedicated to its creation. On the other hand, management will be extremely sensitive to what it sees as a potential threat to its power and control.

At some point during the organizing campaign, employees are asked to sign *authorization cards* (see Figure 11.4) to indicate—in writing—their support for the union. Because of various NLRB rules and regulations, both union organizers and company management must be very careful in their behavior during this authorization drive. For example, employees cannot be asked to sign the cards when they are supposed to be working. And management may not indicate in any way that employees' jobs or job security will be in jeopardy if they *do* sign the cards.

If at least 30 percent of the eligible employees sign authorization cards, the organizers generally request that the firm recognize the union as the employees' bargaining representative. Usually the firm rejects this request, and a *formal election* is held to decide whether to have a union. This election usually involves secret ballots and is conducted by the NLRB. The outcome of the election is determined by a simple majority of eligible employees who choose to vote.

If the union obtains a majority, it becomes the official bargaining agent for its members and the final step, *NLRB certification*, takes place. The union may immediately begin the process of negotiating a labor contract with management. If the union is voted down, the NLRB will not allow another election for one year.

FIGURE 11.4
Sample Authorization Card
Unions must have written authorization to represent employees. *(Source: Reprinted with permission of NLRB.)*

bargaining unit   the specific
group of employees represented
by a union

Several factors can complicate the unionization process. For example, the **bargaining unit,** which is the specific group of employees that the union is to represent, must be defined. Union organizers may want to represent all hourly employees at a particular site (such as all workers at a manufacturing plant). Or they may wish to represent only a specific group of employees (such as all electricians in a large manufacturing plant).

jurisdiction   the right of a
particular union to organize
particular workers

Another issue that may have to be resolved is that of **jurisdiction,** which is the right of a particular union to organize particular workers. When jurisdictions overlap or are unclear, the employees themselves may decide who will represent them. In some cases, two or more unions may be trying to organize some or all of the employees of a firm. Then the election choices may be union A, union B, or no union at all.

The Role of the NLRB

As we have demonstrated, the NLRB is heavily involved in the unionization process. Generally, the NLRB is responsible for overseeing the organizing campaign, conducting the election (if one is warranted), and certifying the election results.

During the organizing campaign, both employers and union organizers can take steps to educate employees regarding the advantages and disadvantages of having a union. However, neither is allowed to use underhanded tactics or distort the truth. If violations occur, the NLRB can stop the questionable behavior, postpone the election, or set aside the results of an election that has already taken place.

The NLRB usually conducts the election within forty-five days after the organizers submit the required number of signed authorization cards. A very high percentage of the eligible voters generally participate in the election, and it is held at the workplace during normal working hours. In certain cases, however, a mail ballot or other form of election may be called for.

Certification of the election involves counting the votes and considering challenges to the election. After the election results are announced, management and the union organizers have five days in which to challenge the election. The basis for a challenge might be improper conduct prior to the election or participation by an ineligible voter. After considering any challenges, the NLRB passes final judgment on the election results.

When union representation is established, union and management get down to the serious business of contract negotiations.

■■ COLLECTIVE BARGAINING

LEARNING OBJECTIVE 5
Describe the basic elements in the collective bargaining process.

collective bargaining   the process of negotiating a labor contract with management

Once certified by the NLRB, a new union's first task is to establish its own identity and structure. It immediately signs up as many members as possible. Then, in an internal election, members choose officers and representatives. A negotiating committee is also chosen to begin **collective bargaining,** the process of negotiating a labor contract with management.

The First Contract

To prepare for its first contract session with management, the negotiating committee decides on its position on the various contract issues and determines the issues that are most important to the union's members. For example, the two most pressing concerns might be a general wage increase and an improved benefits package.

The union then informs management that it is ready to begin negotiations, and the two parties agree on a time and location. Both sides continue to prepare for the session up until the actual date of the negotiations.

Negotiations are occasionally held on company premises, but it is more common for the parties to meet away from the workplace—perhaps in a local hotel. The union is typically represented by the negotiating committee and one or more officials from the regional or national union office. The firm is normally represented by managers from the industrial-relations, operations, HRM, and legal departments. Each side is required by law to negotiate in good faith and not to stall or attempt to extend the bargaining proceedings unnecessarily.

The union normally presents its contract demands first. Management then responds to the demands, often with a counterproposal. The bargaining may move back and forth, from proposal to counterproposal, over a number of meetings. Throughout the process, union representatives constantly keep their members informed of what is going on and how the committee feels about the various proposals and counterproposals.

Each side clearly tries to "get its own way" as much as possible, but each also recognizes the need for compromise. For example, the union may begin the negotiations by demanding a wage increase of $1 per hour but may be willing to accept 60 cents per hour. Management may initially offer 40 cents but may be willing to pay 75 cents. Eventually, the two sides will agree on a wage increase of between 60 and 75 cents per hour.

If an agreement cannot be reached, the union may strike. Strikes are rare during a union's first contract negotiations. In most cases, the initial contract is eventually developed by the negotiating teams.

ratification approval of a labor contract by a vote of the union membership

The final step in collective bargaining is **ratification,** which is approval of the contract by a vote of the union membership. If the membership accepts the terms of the contract, it is signed and becomes a legally binding agreement. If the contract is not ratified, the negotiators must go back and try to iron out a more acceptable agreement.

Later Contracts

A labor contract may cover a period of one to three years or more, but every contract has an expiration date. As that date approaches, both management and the union begin to prepare for new contract negotiations. Now, however, the entire process is likely to be much thornier than the first negotiation.

For one thing, the union and the firm have "lived with each other" for several years during which time some difficulties may have emerged. Each side may see certain issues as being of critical importance, issues that provoke a great deal of emotion at the bargaining table and that are often difficult to resolve. For another thing, each side has learned from the earlier negotiations. Each may take a harder line on certain issues and be less willing to compromise.

The contract deadline itself also produces tension. As the expiration date of the existing contract draws near, each side feels pressure—real or imagined—to reach an agreement. This pressure may nudge the negotiators toward agreement, but it can also have the opposite effect, making an accord more difficult to reach. Moreover, at some point during the negotiations, union leaders are likely to take a *strike vote*. This vote reveals whether union members are willing to strike in the event that a new contract is not negotiated before the old one expires. In almost all cases, this vote supports a strike. So the threat of a strike may add to the pressure mounting on both sides as they go about the business of negotiating.

■■ UNION-MANAGEMENT CONTRACT ISSUES

LEARNING OBJECTIVE 6
Identify the major issues
covered in a union-management
contract.

As you might expect, many diverse issues are negotiated by unions and management and are incorporated into their labor contract. Unions tend to emphasize issues related to members' income, their standard of living, and the strength of the union. Management's primary goals are to retain as much control as possible over the operations of the firm and to maximize its strength relative to that of the union. The balance of power between union and management varies from firm to firm.

Employee Pay

An area of bargaining that is central to union-management relations is employee pay. Three separate issues are usually involved: the forms of pay, the magnitude of pay, and the means by which the magnitude of pay will be determined.

Forms of Pay   The primary form of pay is direct compensation—the wage or salary and benefits that an employee receives in exchange for his or her contribution to the organization. Because direct compensation is a fairly straightforward issue, negotiators often spend much more of their time developing a benefits package for employees. And, as the range of benefits and their costs have escalated over the years, this element of pay has become increasingly important and complex.

We discussed the various employee benefits in Chapter 10. Of these, health, life, disability, and dental insurance are important benefits that unions try to obtain for their members. Deferred compensation, in the form of pension or retirement programs, is also a common focal point.

Other benefits commonly dealt with in the bargaining process include paid vacation time, holidays, and a policy on paid sick leave. Obviously, unions argue for as much paid vacation and holiday time as possible and for liberal sick-leave policies. Management naturally takes the opposite position.

Magnitude of Pay Of considerable importance is the *magnitude,* or amount, of pay that employees receive as both direct and indirect compensation.

The union attempts to ensure that pay is equitable with that received by other employees, both locally and nationally, in the same or similar industries. The union also attempts to include in the contract clauses that provide pay increases over the life of the agreement. The commonest is the *cost-of-living clause,* which ties periodic pay increases to increases in the cost of living, as defined by various economic statistics or indicators.

Of course, the magnitude of pay is also affected by the organization's ability to pay. If the firm has recently posted large profits, the union may expect large pay increases for its members. If the firm has not been very profitable, the union may agree to smaller pay hikes or even to a pay freeze. In an extreme situation (for example, when the firm is bordering on bankruptcy), the union may agree to pay cuts. Very stringent conditions are usually included in any agreement to a pay cut.

Bargaining with regard to magnitude also revolves around employee benefits. At one extreme, unions seek a wide range of benefits, entirely or largely paid for by the firm. At the other extreme, management may be willing to offer the benefits package but may want its employees to bear most of the cost. Again, factors such as equity (with similar firms and jobs) and ability to pay enter into the final agreement.

Pay Determinants Negotiators also address the question of how individual pay will be determined. For management, the ideal arrangement is to tie wages to each employee's productivity. As we saw, this method of payment tends to motivate and reward effort. Unions, on the other hand, feel that this arrangement can also create unnecessary competition among employees. They generally argue that employees should be paid—at least in part—according to seniority. **Seniority** is the length of time an employee has worked for the organization.

seniority the length of time an employee has worked for the organization

Determinants regarding benefits are also negotiated. For example, management may want to provide profit-sharing benefits only to employees who have worked for the firm for a specified number of years. The union may want these benefits provided to all employees.

Working Hours

Of special interest relative to working hours is the matter of overtime. Federal law defines **overtime** as time worked in excess of forty hours in one week. And it specifies that overtime pay must be at least one and one-half times the normal hourly wage. Unions may attempt to negotiate overtime rates for all hours worked beyond eight hours in a single day. Similarly, the union may attempt to obtain higher overtime rates (say, twice the normal hourly wage) for weekend or holiday work. Still another issue is an upper limit to overtime, beyond which employees can refuse to work.

overtime time worked in excess of forty hours in one week; under some union contracts, time worked in excess of eight hours in a single day

In firms with two or more work shifts, workers on less desirable shifts are paid a premium for their time. Both the amount of the premium and the manner in which workers are chosen for (or choose) particular shifts are negotiable issues. Other issues related to working hours are the work starting times and the length of lunch periods and coffee breaks.

■ ■ ■ ■ **CHANGE IN THE WORKPLACE**

Getting Fired May Mean Getting Rich

"You're fired!" Workers have always feared hearing those words, but increasingly, employers fear saying them too. Until the early 1980s, the principle of "employment at will" prevailed in the workplace. Employers could fire someone for a good reason, a bad reason, or no reason at all, as long as they didn't violate any antidiscrimination laws. By 1989, however, the theories of "implied contract" and "good faith and fair dealing" had all but eliminated the "at will" notion, and the number of wrongful termination suits brought by former employees had skyrocketed.

In Los Angeles, a 56-year-old construction company executive was awarded $5.7 million in a wrongful termination suit after claiming that he was forced to quit because of age. When the executive director of a security company was fired shortly after being diagnosed with cancer, he filed a wrongful termination suit. He had received no warnings or disciplinary actions of any kind and was competently handling all of his job responsibilities. In ruling in his favor, the jury was especially concerned that the employer had never talked to him about his ability to do his job. About half of the charges filed under the Americans with Disabilities Act of 1990 claim wrongful termination. For companies, legal defense costs can be significant, sometimes crippling a small business. A recent Rand study on the effects of wrongful termination revealed that many companies are so concerned about wrongful termination suits that they have reduced their staff of full-time employees, turning instead to temporary workers who can never bring charges.

How can organizations minimize the chances that disgruntled former employees will sue them for wrongful termination? Experts advise that companies institute policies and practices to guarantee care and fairness in hiring, evaluating, and terminating employees. When screening and interviewing potential employees, interviewers should ask the kind of open-ended questions that elicit the most information, taking care not to promise permanent employment or exaggerate the potential for promotion. Employee handbooks should clarify offenses that can lead to termination, and employees should sign a statement acknowledging that they have read and understood what is expected of them. Companies should use a progressive system of evaluation and action, making sure to document every step. For example, if an employee does something serious enough to lead to termination, a manager should talk to the employee and put notes on every relevant discussion in writing. Then the manager should set a time limit for correcting the problem. If the problem continues, the company can suspend the worker. Finally, if the problem resumes when the worker returns, termination will be the last step. When it comes time to fire someone, experts warn, be sure more than one employee representative attends the termination interview.

Although these procedures reduce the likelihood of wrongful termination, the best defense is to create a positive working environment. Workers need to be in positions that are most appropriate for their skills and interests. Managers need to be fair and to encourage communication. Experts agree that informed, empowered, and motivated employees are less likely to feel vengeful toward former employers if they lose their jobs.

Security

Security actually covers two issues: the job security of the individual worker and the security of the union as the bargaining representative of the firm's employees.

job security protection against the loss of employment

Job security is protection against the loss of employment. It is, and probably always will be, a major concern of individuals. As we noted earlier, the desire for increased job security is a major reason for joining unions in the first place. In the typical labor contract, job security is based on seniority. If employees must be laid off or dismissed, those with the least seniority are the first to go. Some of the more senior employees may have to move to lower-level jobs, but they remain employed.

union security protection of the union's position as the employees' bargaining agent

Union security is protection of the union's position as the employees' bargaining agent. Union security is frequently a more volatile issue than job security. Unions strive for as much security as possible, but management tends to see an increase in union security as an erosion of its control.

Union security arises directly from its membership. The greater the ratio of union employees to nonunion employees, the more secure the union. In contract negotiations, unions thus attempt to establish various union-membership conditions. The most restrictive of these is the **closed shop,** in which workers must join the union before they are hired. This condition was outlawed by the Taft-Hartley Act, but several other arrangements, including the following, are subject to negotiation:

closed shop a workplace in which workers must join the union before they are hired; outlawed by the Taft-Hartley Act

union shop a workplace in which new employees must join the union after a specified probationary period

agency shop a workplace in which employees can choose not to join the union but must pay dues to the union anyway

maintenance shop a workplace in which an employee who joins the union must remain a union member as long as he or she is employed by the firm

- The **union shop,** in which new employees must join the union after a specified probationary period.
- The **agency shop,** in which employees can choose not to join the union but must pay dues to the union anyway. (The idea is that nonunion employees benefit from union activities and should help support them.)
- The **maintenance shop,** in which an employee who joins the union must remain a union member as long as he or she is employed by the firm.

Management Rights

Of particular interest to the firm are those rights and privileges that are to be retained by management. For example, the firm wants as much control as possible over whom it hires, how work is scheduled, and how discipline is handled. The union, in contrast, would like some control over these and all other matters affecting its members. It is interesting that unions in the United States are making surprisingly rapid progress toward their goal of playing a more direct role in corporate governance. In exchange for union concessions that helped Chrysler Corporation fend off bankruptcy, Douglas Fraser, a high-ranking union official, was given a seat on Chrysler's board of directors. He participated fully in all company business except labor-management strategy. Since that time, union executives have taken seats on a number of corporate boards.

Grievance Procedures

grievance procedure a formally established course of action for resolving employee complaints against management

A **grievance procedure** is a formally established course of action for resolving employee complaints against management. Virtually every labor contract contains one grievance procedure. Procedures vary in scope and detail, but most include the four steps described below (see also Figure 11.5).

Original Grievance   The process begins with an employee who believes that he or she has been treated unfairly, in violation of the labor contract. For example, an employee may be entitled to a formal performance review after six months on the job. If no such review is conducted, the employee may file a grievance. To do so, the employee explains the grievance to a **shop steward,** an employee who is elected by union members to serve as their representative. The employee and the steward then discuss the grievance with the employee's immediate supervisor. Both the grievance and the supervisor's response are put in writing.

shop steward an employee who is elected by union members to serve as their representative

Broader Discussion   In most cases the problem is resolved during the initial discussion with the supervisor. If it is not, a second discussion is held. Now the participants include the original parties (employee, supervisor, and steward); a representative from the union's grievance committee; and the firm's industrial-relations representative. Again a record is kept of the discussion and its results.

Full-Scale Discussion   If the grievance is still not resolved, a full-scale discussion is arranged. This discussion includes everyone involved in the

FIGURE 11.5   Steps in Resolving a Grievance
The employee grievance procedure for most organizations consists of four steps. Each ensuing step involves all the personnel from the preceding step plus at least one higher-level person. The final step is to go to a neutral third party, the arbitrator.

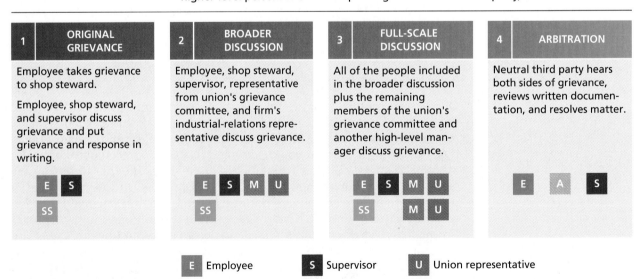

1 ORIGINAL GRIEVANCE	**2 BROADER DISCUSSION**	**3 FULL-SCALE DISCUSSION**	**4 ARBITRATION**
Employee takes grievance to shop steward.	Employee, shop steward, supervisor, representative from union's grievance committee, and firm's industrial-relations representative discuss grievance.	All of the people included in the broader discussion plus the remaining members of the union's grievance committee and another high-level manager discuss grievance.	Neutral third party hears both sides of grievance, reviews written documentation, and resolves matter.
Employee, shop steward, and supervisor discuss grievance and put grievance and response in writing.			

E Employee	S Supervisor	U Union representative
SS Shop steward	M Manager	A Arbitrator

broadened discussion, as well as all remaining members of the union's grievance committee and another high-level manager. As usual, all proceedings are put in writing. All participants are careful not to violate the labor contract during this attempt to resolve the complaint.

arbitration   the step in a grievance procedure by which a neutral third party hears the two sides of a dispute and renders a decision

Arbitration   The final step in almost all grievance procedures is **arbitration,** in which a neutral third party hears the grievance and renders a binding decision. As in a court hearing, each side presents its case with the right to cross-examine witnesses. In addition, the arbitrator reviews the written documentation of all previous steps in the grievance procedure. Both sides may then give summary arguments and/or present briefs. The arbitrator then decides whether a provision of the labor contract has been violated and proposes a remedy. The arbitrator cannot make any decision that would add to, detract from, or modify the terms of the contract. If it can be proved that the arbitrator exceeded the scope of his or her authority, either party may appeal the decision to the courts.

What actually happens when union and management "lock horns" over all the issues we have mentioned? We can answer this question by looking now at the negotiating tools each side can wield.

■■ UNION AND MANAGEMENT NEGOTIATING TOOLS

LEARNING OBJECTIVE 7
Explain the primary bargaining tools available to unions and management.

Management and unions can draw on certain tools to influence one another during contract negotiations. Both sides may use advertising and publicity to gain support for their respective positions. The most extreme tools are strikes and lockouts, but there are other, milder techniques as well.

Strikes

Unions go out on strike only in a very few instances and almost always only after an existing labor contract has expired. (In 1993, there were only 35 major strikes—"major" meaning those involving over 1,000 workers.[2]) Even then, if new contract negotiations seem to be proceeding smoothly, a union does not actually start a strike. The union does take a strike vote, but the vote may be used primarily to show members' commitment to a strike if negotiations fail.

When union members do go out on strike, it is usually because negotiations seem to be stalled. A strike is simply a work stoppage: the employees do not report for work. In addition, striking workers engage in **picketing,** marching back and forth in front of their place of employment with signs informing the public that a strike is in progress. In doing so, they hope that (1) the public will be sympathetic to the strikers and will not patronize the struck firm; (2) nonstriking employees of the firm will honor the picket line and not report to work either; and (3) members of other unions will not cross the picket line (for example, to make deliveries) and will thereby further restrict the operations of the struck firm.

picketing   marching back and forth in front of the place of employment with signs informing the public that a strike is in progress

Obviously, strikes are expensive to both the firm and the strikers. The firm loses business and earnings during the strike. In fact, the main objective of a strike is to put financial pressure on the firm. At the same time, the

Union employees using negotiating tools. In Los Angeles, Local 11 Union members encourage union sympathizers to boycott Canter's Deli.

striking workers lose the wages they would have earned if they had been at their jobs.

Unions try to support striking members as much as possible. Larger unions are able to put a portion of their members' dues into a *strike fund.* The fund is used to provide financial support for striking union members.

At times, workers may go out on a **wildcat strike,** which is a strike that has not been approved by the union. In this situation, union leaders typically work with management to convince the strikers to return to work.

wildcat strike   a strike that has not been approved by the strikers' union

Slowdowns and Boycotts

Almost every labor contract contains a clause that prohibits strikes during the life of the contract. (This is why strikes, if they occur, usually take place after a contract has expired.) However, a union may strike a firm while the contract is in force if members believe management has violated its terms. Workers may also engage in a **slowdown,** which is a technique whereby workers report to their jobs but work at a pace slower than normal.

A **boycott** is a refusal to do business with a particular firm. Unions occasionally bring this strategy to bear by urging their members (and sympathizers) not to purchase the products of a firm with which they are having a dispute. A *primary boycott,* which is aimed at the employer directly involved in the dispute, can be a powerful weapon. A *secondary boycott,* which is aimed at a firm doing business with the employer, is prohibited by the Taft-Hartley Act.

slowdown   a technique whereby workers report to their jobs but work at a slower pace than normal

boycott   a refusal to do business with a particular firm

■ ■ ■ ■ ETHICAL CHALLENGES

Crossing the Picket Line: A Matter of Ethics

In the past, choosing between participating in a strike and crossing the picket line to work was simpler. Workers didn't worry about losing a good job if they went on strike. They knew the factory would shut down during the stoppage and that a job would be waiting when the strike was over. Today, though, many U.S. manufacturers keep up production during strikes by hiring replacement workers or persuading workers to cross the picket line. Many strikers fear that if they strike too long, the company will no longer need or want them. Striking workers, therefore, often face a difficult ethical dilemma.

If you're a union member, you're supposed to support the union. If you honor the picket line too long, however, your finances can suffer. If you abandon the strike, you feel guilty about breaking faith with your fellow workers and letting your union down. When the ethics of honoring an agreement to take part in a union collide with financial survival, workers have a difficult time knowing the right thing to do.

Workers who earn lower wages and are less financially secure are more likely to cross the picket line. During a recent strike at Caterpillar, Inc., for example, a striking welder supporting his wife and six children lost his home-mortgage financing. He admitted that although he still could spare the money to buy his children ice cream, he didn't know how long he could wait around before returning to work. Examples of common statements by workers are, "I don't relish the idea of crossing a picket line, but you've got to work"; "Let's face it, most people need a job"; and "I don't want to be the person that starts a big flood going back, but I don't want to lose my house." Is it unethical to stick with the union when it secures your pay raises or improves your working conditions but to desert it when it becomes inconvenient? The ethics are hardly clear-cut when the choice is between loyalty to the union and feeding your family.

"Should union members cross the picket line?" As complicated as this question is, many other related ethical questions are just as thorny. Is it ethical for nonunion workers to cross the picket line and replace union employees? They aren't breaking a code or agreement, but they could be costing others their jobs and undermining the power of unions to benefit all workers. Should outside workers, both union and nonunion, honor picket lines? Is it ethical for picketers to threaten those who do cross the line? Incidents of violence and harassment are common. Is it ethical for companies to hire replacement workers? Many striking Caterpillar workers, for example, were frightened into crossing picket lines when they read daily newspaper advertisements announcing that the company was hiring new permanent employees. In today's economy, many of these decisions come down to a choice between abstract ethics and concrete practicality.

Lockouts and Strikebreakers

lockout   a firm's refusal to allow employees to enter the workplace

Management's most potent weapon is the lockout. In a **lockout,** the firm refuses to allow employees to enter the workplace. Like strikes, lockouts are expensive for both the firm and its employees. For this reason they are rarely used, and then only in certain special circumstances. A firm that produces perishable goods, for example, may use a lockout if management believes its employees will soon go on strike. The idea is to stop production in time to ensure that there is minimal spoilage of finished goods or work in process.

Management may also attempt to hire strikebreakers. A **strikebreaker** is a nonunion employee who performs the job of a striking union member. Hiring strikebreakers can result in violence when picketing employees confront the nonunion workers at the entrance to the struck facility. The firm also faces the problem of finding qualified replacements for the striking workers. Sometimes management personnel take over the jobs of strikers. Managers at telephone companies have handled the switchboards on more than one occasion.

strikebreaker a nonunion employee who performs the job of a striking union member

Mediation and Arbitration

Strikes and strikebreaking, lockouts and boycotts, all pit one side against the other. Ultimately one side "wins" and the other "loses." Unfortunately, the negative effects of such actions—including resentment, fear, and distrust—may linger for months or years after a dispute has been resolved.

More productive techniques that are being used increasingly are mediation and arbitration. Either one may come into play before a labor contract expires or after some other strategy, such as a strike, has proved ineffective.

mediation the use of a neutral third party to assist management and the union during their negotiations

Mediation is the use of a neutral third party to assist management and the union during their negotiations. This third party (the mediator) listens to both sides, trying to find common ground for agreement. The mediator also tries to facilitate communication between the two sides, to promote compromise, and generally to keep the negotiations moving. At first the mediator may meet privately with each side. Eventually, however, his or her goal is to get the two to settle their differences at the bargaining table.

Unlike mediation, the *arbitration* step is a formal hearing. Just as it may be the final step in a grievance procedure, it may also be used in contract negotiations (perhaps after mediation attempts) when the two sides cannot agree on one or more issues. Here, the arbitrator hears the formal positions of both parties on outstanding, unresolved issues. The arbitrator then analyzes these positions and makes a decision on the possible resolution of the issues. If both sides have agreed in advance that the arbitration will be binding, they must accept the arbitrator's decision.

If mediation and arbitration are unsuccessful, then, under the provisions of the Taft-Hartley Act, the president of the United States can obtain a temporary injunction to prevent or stop a strike if it would jeopardize national health or security.

This chapter ends our discussion of human resources. In the next part of the text, we examine the marketing function of business. We begin, in Chapter 12, by discussing the meaning of the term *marketing* and the various markets for products and services.

■ ■ ■ ■ CHAPTER REVIEW

Summary

1   Explain how and why labor unions came into being.

A labor union is an organization of workers who act together to negotiate wages and working conditions with their employers. Labor relations are the dealings between labor unions and business management.

The first major union in the United States was the Knights of Labor, formed in 1869 to eliminate the depersonalization of workers. The Knights were followed in 1886 by the American Federation of Labor (AFL). The goal of the AFL was to improve its members' living standards within the business system. In 1905 the radical Industrial Workers of the World was formed; its goal was the overthrow of capitalism. Of these three, only the AFL remained when the Congress of Industrial Organizations (CIO) was founded as a body of industrial unions between World War I and World War II. After years of competing, the AFL and CIO merged in 1955. The largest union not affiliated with the AFL-CIO is the Teamsters' Union.

2   Discuss the sources of unions' negotiating power and trends in union membership.

The power of unions to negotiate with management comes from two sources. The first is the size of their membership. The second source is the groups of laws that guarantee unions the right to negotiate and that regulate the negotiation process. At present, union membership accounts for less than one-fifth of the American work force, and it seems to be decreasing for various reasons. Nonetheless, unions wield considerable power in many industries—those in which their members comprise a large proportion of the work force.

3   Identify the main focus of several major pieces of labor-management legislation.

Important laws that affect union power are the Norris-LaGuardia Act (limits management's ability to obtain injunctions against unions), the Wagner Act (forbids certain unfair labor practices by management), the Fair Labor Standards Act (allows the federal government to set the minimum wage and to mandate overtime rates), the Taft-Hartley Act (forbids certain unfair practices by unions), and the Landrum-Griffin Act (regulates the internal functioning of labor unions). The National Labor Relations Board, a federal agency that oversees union-management relations, was created by the Wagner Act.

4   Enumerate the steps involved in forming a union, and show how the National Labor Relations Board is involved in the process.

Attempts to form a union within a firm begin with an organizing campaign to develop widespread employee interest in having a union. Next, employees sign an authorization card indicating in writing their support for the union. The third step is to hold a formal election to decide whether to have a union. Finally, if the union obtains a majority, it receives NLRB certification, making it the official bargaining agent for its members. The entire process is supervised by the NLRB, which oversees the organizing campaign, conducts the election, and certifies the election results.

5   Describe the basic elements in the collective bargaining process.

Once a union is established, it may negotiate a labor contract with management through the process of collective bargaining. First, the negotiating committee decides on its position on the various contract issues. The union informs the management that it is ready to begin negotiations and a time and place are set. The union is represented by the negotiating committee and the organization by managers from several departments in the company. Each side is required to negotiate in good faith and not to stall or attempt to extend the bargaining unnecessarily. The final step is ratification, which is the approval of the contract by a vote of the union membership.

6   Identify the major issues covered in a union-management contract.

Contract issues include employee pay and benefits, working hours, job and union security, management rights, and grievance procedures. As the expiration date of an existing contract approaches, management and the union begin to negotiate a new contract.

7   Explain the primary bargaining tools available to unions and management.

Management and unions can use certain tools to sway one another—and public opinion—during contract negotiations. Advertising and publicity help each side gain support. When contract negotiations do not run smoothly, unions may apply pressure on management through strikes, slowdowns, or boycotts. Management may counter by imposing lockouts or hiring strikebreakers. Less drastic techniques for breaking contract deadlocks are mediation and arbitration. In both, a neutral third party is involved in the negotiations.

Key Terms

You should now be able to define and give an example relevant to each of the following terms:

labor union (328)

union-management (labor) relations (328)

craft union (328)

strike (330)

industrial union (331)

National Labor Relations Board (NLRB) (336)

injunction (336)

bargaining unit (340)

jurisdiction (340)

collective bargaining (340)

ratification (341)

seniority (343)

overtime (343)

job security (345)

union security (345)

closed shop (345)

union shop (345)

agency shop (345)

maintenance shop (345)

grievance procedure (346)

shop steward (346)

arbitration (347)

picketing (347)

wildcat strike (348)

slowdown (348)

boycott (348)

lockout (349)

strikebreaker (350)

mediation (350)

Questions

Review Questions

1. Briefly describe the history of unions in the United States.

2. How has government regulation of union-management relations evolved during this century?

3. For what reasons do employees start or join unions?

4. Describe the process of forming a union, and explain the role of the NLRB in that process.

5. List the major areas that are negotiated in a labor contract.

6. Explain the three issues involved in negotiations concerning employee pay.

7. What is the difference between job security and union security? How do unions attempt to enhance union security?

8. What is a grievance? Describe the typical grievance procedure.

9. What steps are involved in collective bargaining?

10. For what reasons are strikes and lockouts relatively rare nowadays?

11. What are the objectives of picketing?

12. In what ways do the techniques of mediation and arbitration differ?

Discussion Questions

1. What major problems are created by Caterpillar's adversarial relationship with the United Auto Workers?

2. If Caterpillar and the UAW formed a cooperative partnership, how would the workers benefit?

3. Do unions really derive their power mainly from their membership and labor legislation? What are some other sources of union power?

4. Which labor-contract issues are likely to be the easiest to resolve? Which are likely to be the most difficult?

5. Discuss the following statement: Union security means job security for union members.

6. How would you prepare for labor contract negotiations as a member of management? as head of the union negotiating committee?

7. Under what circumstances are strikes and lockouts justified in place of mediation or arbitration?

Exercises

✎ 1. Develop a labor contract to govern student-teacher relations in your school. Include at least four major issues in the written contract.

🗣 2. Find two or more articles describing a recent strike.

a. Try to determine the exact nature of the issue or issues on which negotiators could not agree.

b. Determine the means by which these issues were finally resolved.

c. Explain how these issues might have been resolved without a strike.

3. Find a copy of a labor contract in your library. List the issues that are covered in the contract, and compare them with the issues cited in this chapter.

VIDEO CASE 11.1

Management and Unions Team Up at Xerox

In Xerox Corporation's motto, "Be the Best of the Best Together," *together* is the operative word. Xerox has welded a remarkable partnership with its union, the Amalgamated Clothing and Textile Workers (ACTWU). Thousands of Xerox manufacturing employees belong to the ACTWU, which cooperates with management to cut costs, increase revenues, improve quality, respond to workers' needs, and keep Xerox competitive. The partnership is working out well for both sides. Xerox and the ACTWU recently ratified a contract in which workers agreed to forgo raises in exchange for a seven-year job guarantee. Management in turn gets workers' commitment to increase efforts to raise profits and productivity. This kind of relationship has helped earn Xerox a Malcolm Baldrige Quality Award and more recently *Personnel Journal*'s Optimas Award, also honoring the partnership between Xerox and the ACTWU.

During the 1940s, Xerox was known as the Haloid Company. Its owner's belief in cooperation between management and the union laid the foundation for today's alliance. Management shared profitability with workers by increasing wages and improving benefits. While the company grew during the 1950s and 1960s, this cooperative philosophy continued.

For some time, Xerox reigned supreme in the plain-paper copier market. When you needed something duplicated, you didn't make a copy, you made a "Xerox." During the 1970s, however, Japanese competitors such as Sharp and Canon and U.S. manufacturer IBM grabbed a substantial chunk of Xerox's market share, reducing it from 90 to 43 percent. Japanese companies were selling many copiers for what it cost Xerox just to *make* them. Rework, scrap, excessive inspec-

tions, and lost business were costing the company about $2 billion a year. In addition, a two-week strike in 1973 alerted the company and its workers to the need for avoiding conflict by establishing a genuine partnership.

Instead of saving money by closing plants, subcontracting component parts, and laying off workers, Xerox joined forces with the ACTWU to solve its problems and keep its employees. The company established "Leadership Through Quality," a plan in which unionized workers received extensive training in problem solving and effective team skills, and its "Employee Involvement" program, whose key elements are trust, communication, and training. Union leadership knows that workers can suggest changes and voice ideas without fear of reprisal, and the company knows that the union will cooperate with changes designed to increase productivity and reduce costs. Any group of employees can form a team and are given up to two hours a week on company time to solve a problem.

Xerox's contract with the union states that if management concludes the company is not manufacturing a product cost-effectively, it will work with the union to establish a study action team composed of union officers, hourly workers, and management personnel. The team attempts to restructure the department and cut costs; only if they can't find a way to make a competitive, high-quality product is Xerox free to subcontract.

Xerox had a chance to put its partnership to a dramatic test. To save about $3 million, the company considered subcontracting its wire harness manufacturing operations, a plan that would have eliminated 180 jobs. As mandated in its labor agreement, a study action team proposed alternatives. When implemented, the alternatives not only reduced costs and saved jobs but improved the quality of the wire harnesses, raised worker morale, and intensified worker commitment to Xerox.

At Xerox, whenever a manufacturing glitch or a faulty part threatens product quality, workers are authorized to stop production until they find a remedy. Management is committed to the concept that its employees are human beings who have more to offer than repetitive, circumscribed, unthinking performance; the ACTWU is committed to work jointly with the company to improve quality. This partnership has helped Xerox cut production costs by 30 percent, slash new-product development time in half, increase its return on investment from 8 to

14 percent, and become the first U.S. company to win back market share from the Japanese without government intervention.

What does Xerox's future look like? One of Xerox's most recent innovations is the establishment of focus factories, which replace assembly lines with self-managed teams producing narrow product lines. Without union cooperation, asserts one company executive, this change would have been impossible. The company is also developing Project 2010, its strategy for leading the industry into the next century; it goes without saying that the union is involved even at the early stages of planning.[3]

Questions

1. What benefits does the Xerox Corporation receive from its commitment to partnership with its union?
2. What are the advantages and disadvantages for union members of participating in the partnership?
3. In your judgment, do union-management partnerships like the one at Xerox strengthen or weaken the power of American labor unions? Defend your answer.

CASE 11.2

Elyria Foundry Votes Out Its Union

At the 88-year-old Elyria Foundry just outside of Cleveland, Ohio, workers caste engine frames, air-conditioner compressors, pump housings, manifolds, flywheels, pistons, and other huge iron components, six days a week, twenty-four hours a day. When Gregg L. Foster bought the plant from Chromalloy just over a decade ago, Elyria was a dying operation losing about $3 million a year. Today, it is one of the most profitable foundries in the United States, and its owner is one of *Inc.* magazine's Turnaround Entrepreneurs of the year.

Foster gambled on Elyria at a time when recession was hitting the industry hard and orders from machine tool builders were down. In 1980 Elyria boasted a work force of over four hundred and sales of almost $17 million. At that time, the foundry didn't need its own sales force; customers came to Elyria. By 1983, however, sales had plummeted to $4 million and the work force

to a mere seventy-five. When Foster bought the foundry, he inherited 500,000 square feet of deteriorating buildings, aging machinery, and poor management-labor relations. Despite these grim and seemingly insurmountable conditions, Foster believed that if he could get labor and management to cooperate, Elyria would succeed.

One of Foster's first acts after acquiring the foundry was to shut down operations for three days to decide which workers would stay and which would go. At the end of that time, he eliminated fifteen managerial positions, sixteen company cars, and three country-club memberships. Foster believed it was unjust for a select few to enjoy privileges that were denied to most workers. Instead, he wanted *all* workers to recognize their importance. He also rehired the one hundred employees with the best performance and attendance records, rolled back salaries, and did away with some expensive perks, such as five-week paid vacations. Because of prior union agreements, many of Elyria's employees were restricted to performing only one task: a crane operator, for example, could refuse to work anywhere else in the foundry. Limiting workers to a single job inevitably reduced productivity and often led to conflict. Foster wanted all employees to work wherever needed—including managers working on the line. Faced with what it slammed as "union-busting" changes, the International Molder's and Allied Workers (IMAW—the union that represented Elyria workers) threatened an immediate strike. In a speech promising stable full-time employment and a share of the profits, Foster urged his workers not to strike. The IMAW backed down from its hard line, and shortly afterward, plant workers voted overwhelmingly to decertify the union.

With a turnover rate of less than 1 percent, an attendance rate of 99 percent, and a customer attrition rate of 1 percent, Elyria workers seem to be flourishing without union help. To prove his good faith, Foster handed out profit-sharing checks the first year (even though he needed the money for working capital). He has continued paying 15 percent of the company's pretax earnings in profit sharing every year since. To provide employees with good working conditions, Foster renovated locker rooms, put in new restrooms and a new cafeteria, and even cleaned the windows and whitewashed the walls. The company has also improved and expanded its employee education program and reduced personal injuries.

Elyria's recent yearly sales of $29 million translate into an annual growth rate of over 30 percent. Before Gregg Foster bought the foundry, 391 employees labored to produce 12,000 tons of cast metal. Today, 216 workers turn out the same tonnage. Using labor more effectively keeps Elyria's costs lower and salaries higher than those at any other U.S. foundry. The plant's 256 salaried and hourly workers aren't worried about layoffs, and nobody mentions bringing back the union.[4]

Questions

1. What types of labor problems contributed to Elyria's poor performance before Gregg Foster took over the business?
2. How have workers benefited since the union was voted out?

CAREER PROFILE ■ ■ ■ ■ ■ ■ ■ ■ ■ ■ ■

PART 3   Career Opportunities in Human Resources

Job Title	Job Description	Salary Range
Employment counselor	Help individuals make wise career decisions; help evaluate education, training, work history, interests, skills, personal traits, and physical capacities of an applicant; help applicant develop job-seeking skills	4
Health inspector	Enforce adherence to a wide range of laws, regulations, policies, and procedures; administer regulations that govern the acceptability of persons and products entering the United States from foreign countries	4
Industrial relations director	Formulate labor policy; oversee industrial labor relations; negotiate collective bargaining agreements; coordinate grievance resolutions resulting from disputes under the contract for firms with unionized employees	5
Labor relations specialist	Provide the link between top management and employees; help management make effective use of employees' skills; help employees find satisfaction in their jobs and working conditions; prepare information for management to use during negotiation; interpret and administer the contract with respect to grievances, wages, salaries, employee welfare, health care, pensions, union practices, and other contractual stipulations	4
Mediator	Advise and counsel labor and management to prevent and, when necessary, resolve disputes over labor agreements or other labor relations issues	4
Personnel interviewer	Help job-seekers find employment; help employers find qualified staff; gather information on employer's needs and try to match employees to needs; evaluate and test applicants; help identify best jobs for applicants	3
Human resources manager	Conduct and supervise the employment functions of a company; recruit, hire, and train employees; develop wage and salary scales; administer benefit programs	5
Regulatory inspector	Insure compliance with laws and regulations that protect employees and public welfare	4
Safety inspector	Specialize in foods, feeds and pesticides, weights and measures, cosmetics, or drugs and medical equipment; check firms that produce, handle, store, and market foods, drugs, and cosmetics; look for inaccurate labeling; look for deterioration or decomposition of product; use a variety of special machines to do checking and testing; write reports about findings; testify in court if findings require legal actions	4

■ ■ ■ ■ ■ ■ ■ ■ ■ ■ ■ ■ ■ ■ ■ ■ ■

The figure in the salary column approximates the expected annual income after two or three years of service.
1 = $12,000–$15,000; 2 = $16,000–$20,000; 3 = $21,000–$27,000; 4 = $28,000–$35,000; 5 = $36,000 and up.

Educational Requirements	Skills Required	Prospects for Growth
Degree in business or human resources management	Decision making; analytical; communication; interpersonal	Above average
Degree in medically related field	Communication; detail; basic office	Above average
Bachelor's degree in business or management; on-the-job experience	Communication; problem solving; analytical	Above average
Bachelor's degree; on-the-job experience	Interpersonal; communication; problem solving; analytical	Above average
Bachelor's degree; on-the-job experience	Interpersonal; problem solving	Above average
Some college; degree helpful	Communication; office; interpersonal	Average
Bachelor's degree in human resources management; master's degree helpful	Communication; decision making; interpersonal	Above average
High school diploma; some college preferred	Communication; detail; basic office	Above average
High school diploma; some college preferred	Analytical; communication; interpersonal	Above average

Marketing

The business activities that make up a firm's marketing efforts are those most directly concerned with satisfying customers' needs. In this part, we discuss these activities in some detail. We begin with a general discussion of marketing and the market for consumer goods. Then, in turn, we discuss the four elements that together make up a marketing mix: product, price, distribution, and promotion. Included in this part are

■■■■ CHAPTER 12

An Overview of Marketing

LEARNING OBJECTIVES

After studying this chapter, you should be able to

1 Know the meaning of *marketing*, and explain how it creates utility for purchasers of products.

2 Trace the development of the marketing concept and understand how it is implemented.

3 Understand what markets are and how they are classified.

4 Identify the four elements of the marketing mix, and be aware of their importance in developing a marketing strategy.

5 Explain how the marketing environment affects strategic market planning.

6 Describe how market measurement and sales forecasting are used.

7 Distinguish between a marketing information system and marketing research.

8 Identify several factors that may influence buying behavior.

9 Describe three ways of measuring consumer income.

CHAPTER PREVIEW

In this chapter we examine marketing activities that add value to products. We trace the evolution of the marketing concept and describe how organizations practice it. Next our focus shifts to market classifications and marketing strategy. We analyze the four elements of a marketing mix and also discuss uncontrollable factors in the marketing environment. We consider tools for strategic market planning, including market measurement, sales forecasts, marketing information systems, and marketing research. Last, we look at the forces that influence consumer and organizational buying behavior.

Ford's Mustang for a New Generation

In April 1964, Ford Motor Company introduced an affordable sports car that immediately captured the imaginations of American car buyers—the Mustang. That year almost 500,000 people bought one, and in the decades since, droves of Mustang lovers have come to resemble a devoted cult of true believers. There are five magazines devoted to Mustangmania, including *Mustang Monthly*. Mustang Clubs of America boasts more than 110 active chapters, and over thirty U.S. businesses supply replacement parts to Mustang collectors. The sporty "pony car," as it is affectionately known, has even inspired musical tributes, like the often-recorded song "Mustang Sally."

When Ford decided to stop making the Mustang, many distressed Mustangophiles protested, including the president of Ford's Automotive Group who grumbled, "It was unthinkable to me not to have a Mustang." So instead of putting it out to pasture, Ford decided to spend $700 million to redesign and update the Mustang. Ford's goal was to come up with an inexpensive, attractive, and powerful car that kept the Mustang identity while eliminating some of its quality and handling problems. To help in the revamping, the company's designers solicited input from thirty-three focus groups made up of potential young buyers who weren't even born when Mustang was introduced, as well as from thousands of older Mustang collectors with very firm ideas about what makes a *real* Mustang. When it came time to develop the next generation Mustang, a 450-member team designed and built the car from start to finish in thirty-five months.

A $40 million advertising campaign attracts boomers with nostalgia and young first-time buyers with price appeal. Although at just under $13,000 the new Mustang's sticker price is quite a bit higher than the original's $2,368, the cost is moderate by today's standards. Interspersing images of the 1964 classic and today's model, television ads unveiling the new Mustang conveyed the campaign's theme, "It is what it was and more."

Ford management is glad that it didn't kill the Mustang and hand the market segment it invented to rival General Motors' Camaro and Firebird. Mustang won *Motor Trend*'s "Car of the Year" award and made *Time* magazine's list of the year's best products. Three decades after its introduction, Mustang still appeals to American consumers.

■ ■ ■ ■

■ ■ ■ ■ ■ ■ ■ ■ ■ ■ ■

marketing the process of planning and executing the conception, pricing, promotion, and distribution of ideas, goods, and services to create exchanges that satisfy individual and organizational objectives

LEARNING OBJECTIVE 1
Know the meaning of *marketing,* and explain how it creates utility for purchasers of products.

utility the ability of a good or service to satisfy a human need

ord Motor Company's re-introduction of the Mustang illustrates how an organization can be successful in a highly competitive market. Marketing encompasses a diverse set of decisions and activities performed by individuals and by both business and nonbusiness organizations. Marketing begins and ends with the customer. The American Marketing Association defines **marketing** as "the process of planning and executing the conception, pricing, promotion, and distribution of ideas, goods, and services to create exchanges that satisfy individual and organizational objectives." The marketing process involves eight major functions and numerous related activities (see Table 12.1). All of these functions are essential if the marketing process is to be effective.

■■ UTILITY: THE VALUE ADDED BY MARKETING

As defined in Chapter 8, **utility** is the ability of a good or service to satisfy a human need. A lunch at a Pizza Hut, an overnight stay at a Holiday Inn, and

TABLE 12.1 Major Marketing Functions

Exchange Functions: All companies such as manufacturers, wholesalers, and retailers buy and sell to market their merchandise.
1. **Buying** includes such functions as obtaining raw materials to make products, knowing how much merchandise to keep on hand, and selecting suppliers.
2. **Selling** creates possession utility by transferring the title of a product from seller to customer.

Physical Distribution Functions: These functions involve the flow of goods from producers to customers. Transportation and storage provide time utility and place utility, and require careful management of inventory.
3. **Transporting** involves selecting a mode of transport that provides an acceptable delivery schedule at an acceptable price.
4. **Storing** goods is often necessary to sell them at the best selling time.

Facilitating Functions: These functions help the other functions take place.
5. **Financing** helps at all stages of marketing. To buy raw materials, manufacturers often borrow from banks or receive credit from suppliers. Wholesalers may be financed by manufacturers, and retailers may receive financing from the wholesaler or manufacturer. Finally, retailers often provide financing to customers.
6. **Standardizing** sets uniform specifications for products or services. **Grading** classifies products by size and quality, usually through a sorting process. Together, standardization and grading facilitate production, transportation, storage, and selling.
7. **Risk taking**—even though competent management and insurance can minimize risks—is a constant reality of marketing because of such losses as bad debt expense, obsolescence of products, theft by employees, and product-liability lawsuits.
8. **Gathering market information** is necessary for making all marketing decisions.

a Mercedes 420 SEL all satisfy human needs. Thus, each possesses utility. There are four kinds of utility.

Form utility is created by converting production inputs into finished products. Marketing efforts may indirectly influence form utility because the data gathered as part of marketing research are frequently used to determine the size, shape, and features of a product.

The three kinds of utility that are directly created by marketing are place, time, and possession utility. **Place utility** is created by making a product available at a location where customers wish to purchase it. A pair of shoes is given place utility when it is shipped from a factory to a department store.

Time utility is created by making a product available when customers wish to purchase it. For example, Halloween costumes might be manufactured in April but not displayed until late September, when consumers start buying them. By storing the costumes until they are wanted, the manufacturer or retailer provides time utility.

Possession utility is created by transferring title (or ownership) of a product to the buyer. For a product as simple as a pair of shoes, ownership is usually transferred by means of a sales slip or receipt. For such products as automobiles and homes, the transfer of title is a more complex process. Along with the title to its product, the seller transfers the right to use that product to satisfy a need (see Figure 12.1).

Place, time, and possession utility have real value in terms of both money and convenience. This value is created and added to goods and services through a wide variety of marketing activities—from research indicating what customers want to product warranties ensuring that customers get what they pay for. Overall, these marketing activities account for about half of every dollar spent by consumers. When they are part of an integrated marketing program that delivers maximum utility to the customer, most of us would agree that they are worth the cost.

form utility utility created by converting production inputs into finished products

place utility utility created by making a product available at a location where customers wish to purchase it

time utility utility created by making a product available when customers wish to purchase it

possession utility utility created by transferring title (or ownership) of a product to the buyer

FIGURE 12.1
Types of Utility
Form utility is created by the production process, but marketing creates place, time, and possession utility.

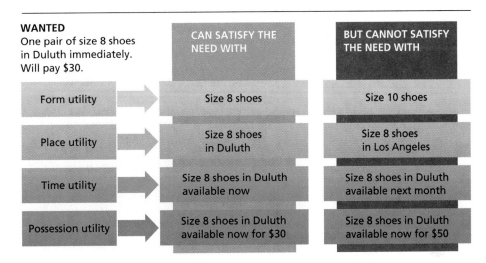

WANTED One pair of size 8 shoes in Duluth immediately. Will pay $30.	CAN SATISFY THE NEED WITH	BUT CANNOT SATISFY THE NEED WITH
Form utility	Size 8 shoes	Size 10 shoes
Place utility	Size 8 shoes in Duluth	Size 8 shoes in Los Angeles
Time utility	Size 8 shoes in Duluth available now	Size 8 shoes in Duluth available next month
Possession utility	Size 8 shoes in Duluth available now for $30	Size 8 shoes in Duluth available now for $50

Place, time, and possession utility are only the most fundamental applications of marketing activities. In recent years, marketing activities have been influenced by a broad business philosophy known as *the marketing concept.*

■■ THE MARKETING CONCEPT

LEARNING OBJECTIVE 2
Trace the development of the marketing concept and understand how it is implemented.

The process that leads any business to success seems simple. First, the firm must talk to its potential customers to assess their needs for its goods or services. Then the firm must develop a good or service to satisfy those needs. Finally, the firm must continue to seek ways to provide customer satisfaction. This process is an application of the marketing concept, or marketing orientation. As simple as it seems, American business has been slow to accept it.

Evolution of the Marketing Concept

From the start of the Industrial Revolution until the early twentieth century, business effort was directed mainly toward the production of goods. Consumer demand for manufactured products was so great that manufacturers could almost bank on selling everything they produced. Business had a strong *production orientation,* in which emphasis was placed on increased output and production efficiency. Marketing was limited to taking orders and distributing finished goods.

Customer satisfaction. Satisfying customers' needs is a major component of the marketing concept. Through its Customer One program, Chrysler makes every customer's satisfaction a number one priority.

In the 1920s, production began to catch up with demand. Now producers had to direct their efforts toward selling goods rather than just producing goods that consumers readily bought. This new *sales orientation* was characterized by increased advertising, enlarged sales forces, and, occasionally, high-pressure selling techniques. Manufacturers produced the goods they expected consumers to want, and marketing consisted primarily of promoting products through personal selling and advertising, taking orders, and delivering goods.

During the 1950s, however, business people started to realize that even enormous advertising expenditures and the most thoroughly proven sales techniques were not enough. Something else was needed if products were to sell as well as expected. It was then that business managers recognized that they were not primarily producers or sellers but rather were in the business of satisfying customers' wants. As a top executive at Whirlpool states, "The key to a whole new technology is to improve customer satisfaction and give them some utility instead of just glitz. I think that's the challenge to us as manufacturers."[2] Marketers realized that the best approach was to adopt a customer orientation—in other words, the organization had to first determine what customers need and then develop goods and services to fill those particular needs (see Table 12.2).

marketing concept   a business philosophy that involves the entire organization in the process of satisfying customers' needs while achieving the organization's goals

This **marketing concept** is a business philosophy that involves the entire organization in the process of satisfying customers' needs while achieving the organization's goals. All functional areas—research and development, production, finance, human resources, and, of course, marketing—are viewed as playing a role in providing customer satisfaction.

Implementing the Marketing Concept

The marketing concept has been adopted by many of the most successful business firms. Some firms, such as Ford Motor Company and Apple Computer, have gone through minor or major reorganizations in the process. Because the marketing concept is essentially a business philosophy, anyone can say, "I believe in it." But to make it work, management must fully adopt and then implement it.

To implement the marketing concept, a firm must first obtain information about its present and potential customers. The firm must determine not

TABLE 12.2   Evolution of Customer Orientation
Business managers recognized that they were not primarily producers or sellers but rather were in the business of satisfying customers' wants.

Production Orientation	Sales Orientation	Customer Orientation
Take orders	Increase advertising	Determine customer needs
Distribute goods	Enlarge sales force	Develop products to fill these needs
	Intensify sales techniques	Achieve the organization's goals

■ ■ ■ ■ ■ CHANGE IN THE WORKPLACE

Customer Satisfaction at Any Price?

In the early 1980s, a scientific equipment manufacturer decided to get on the total quality management (TQM) bandwagon. One thousand managers went through a four-day course on quality, and then the company reinvented the way it did business. While all of the factors on their quality charts rose, ecstatic managers revelled in the glowing statistics. On-time delivery jumped from 42 percent to 92 percent; the radiation equipment division was ranked number 1 in the industry for prompt customer visits. The company, however, was losing market share. The staff in the vacuum equipment department were so determined to meet production schedules, they neglected to return customer phone calls. People in the radiation division felt such deadline pressure that they often failed to provide customers with adequate explanations.

All over the United States, organizations that were TQM disciples have discovered that it doesn't always pay. Few companies measure the cost of quality. According to the Government Accounting Office, of the twenty-two companies that recently reached the final round of the Malcolm Baldrige National Quality Award competition, only five had measured the cost of their programs. Wallace Company, manufacturer of oil field equipment, is an excellent example of a firm that paid too high a price for its quality programs. In 1990 the company won a Malcolm Baldrige Quality Award, and two years later it filed for bankruptcy. To avoid ending up like this organization, many companies are emphasizing ROQ, return on quality, instead of TQM.

Satisfying customers, companies agree, is the key to success. They now recognize, however, that they should focus on quality efforts that improve customer satisfaction at a reasonable cost. By implementing ROQ, companies try to ensure that they get enough return for their investment in quality. For each dollar they spend, firms want to know the effect on customer retention, sales, or market share. A quality effort that has no effect on the bottom line is going to be reconsidered, revamped, or removed. Said one CEO, "If we're not going to make money off it, we're not going to do it."

At AT&T, advocates of every new quality initiative must first demonstrate that the company will realize a minimum 10 percent return on the company's investment from the program. Nations-Bank Corp. now measures every customer service improvement, such as adding tellers or lowering mortgage rates, in terms of added income. Famous for satisfying customers with on-time delivery, Federal Express discovered that the faster it moved packages, the more inaccurate deliveries became—and every redirected package cost the company $50. Even this Baldrige award winner is rethinking some of its quality goals.

What a growing number of organizations are discovering is that listening to customers and learning what they want is the easy part of delivering quality. Providing that quality without spending too much is the difficult part. To do that, advise experts, companies have to learn when *not* to listen to their customers.

only what customers' needs are but also how well those needs are being satisfied by products currently on the market—both its own products and those of competitors. It must ascertain how its products might be improved and what opinions customers have of the firm and its marketing efforts.

The firm must then use this information to pinpoint the specific needs and potential customers toward which it will direct its marketing activities and resources. (Obviously, no firm can expect to satisfy all needs. And not every individual or firm can be considered a potential customer for every product manufactured or sold by a firm.) Next, the firm must mobilize its marketing resources to (1) provide a product that will satisfy its customers; (2) price the product at a level that is acceptable to buyers and that will yield a profit; (3) promote the product so that potential customers will be aware of its existence and its ability to satisfy their needs; and (4) ensure that the product is distributed so that it is available to customers where and when needed.

Finally, the firm must again obtain marketing information—this time regarding the effectiveness of its efforts. Can the product be improved? Is it being promoted properly? Is it being distributed efficiently? Is the price too high or too low? The firm must be ready to modify any or all of its marketing activities based on information about its customers and competitors.

■■ MARKETS AND THEIR CLASSIFICATION

LEARNING OBJECTIVE 3
Understand what markets are and how they are classified.

market a group of individuals, organizations, or both, that have needs for products in a given category and that have the ability, willingness, and authority to purchase such products

A **market** is a group of individuals, organizations, or both that have needs for products in a given category and that have the ability, willingness, and authority to purchase such products. The people or organizations must want the product. They must be able to purchase the product by exchanging money, goods, or services for it. They must be willing to use their buying power. Finally, they must be socially and legally authorized to purchase the product.

Markets are broadly classified as consumer or industrial markets. These classifications are based on the characteristics of the individuals and organizations within each market. Because marketing efforts vary depending on the intended market, marketers should understand the general characteristics of these two groups.

Consumer markets consist of purchasers and/or individual household members who intend to consume or benefit from the purchased products and who do not buy products to make profits.

Industrial markets are grouped broadly into producer, reseller, governmental, and institutional categories. These markets purchase specific kinds of products for use in making other products, for resale, or for day-to-day operations. *Producer markets* consist of individuals and business organizations that buy certain products to use in the manufacture of other products. *Reseller markets* consist of intermediaries such as wholesalers and retailers that buy finished products and sell them for a profit. *Governmental markets* consist of federal, state, county, and local governments. They buy goods and services to maintain internal operations and to provide citizens with such products as highways, education, water, energy, and national defense. Governmental purchases total billions of dollars each year. *Institutional markets* include churches, not-for-profit private schools and hospitals, civic clubs, fraternities and sororities, charitable organizations, and foundations. Their goals are different from such typical business goals as profit, market share, or return on investment.

■■ DEVELOPING MARKETING STRATEGIES

marketing strategy a plan that will enable an organization to make the best use of its resources and advantages to meet its objectives

marketing mix a combination of product, price, distribution, and promotion developed to satisfy a particular target market

target market a group of persons for whom a firm develops and maintains a marketing mix suitable for the specific needs and preferences of that group

A **marketing strategy** is a plan that will enable an organization to make the best use of its resources and advantages to meet its objectives. A marketing strategy consists of (1) the selection and analysis of a target market and (2) the creation and maintenance of an appropriate **marketing mix,** a combination of product, price, distribution, and promotion developed to satisfy a particular target market.

Target Market Selection and Evaluation

A **target market** is a group of persons for whom a firm develops and maintains a marketing mix suitable for the specific needs and preferences of that group. In selecting a target market, marketing managers examine potential markets for their possible effects on the firm's sales, costs, and profits. The managers attempt to determine whether the organization has the resources to produce a marketing mix that meets the needs of a particular target market and whether satisfying those needs is consistent with the firm's overall objectives. They also analyze the strengths and numbers of competitors already marketing to people in this target market. When selecting a target

Targeting products to the young. A growing number of products are aimed at children because children's buying power is rising and they have greater influence on the purchase decisions of many products.

market, marketing managers generally take either the total market approach or the market segmentation approach.

Total Market Approach   A company that designs a single marketing mix and directs it at the entire market for a particular product is using a **total market approach** (see Figure 12.2). This approach, also known as an *undifferentiated approach*, assumes that individual customers in the target market for a specific kind of product have similar needs and, therefore, that the organization can satisfy most customers with a single marketing mix. This single marketing mix consists of one type of product with little or no variation, one price, one promotional program aimed at everyone, and one distribution system to reach all customers in the total market. Products that can be marketed successfully with the total market approach include staple food items, such as sugar and salt, and certain kinds of farm produce. A total market approach is useful only in a limited number of situations because for most product categories, buyers have different needs. When customers' needs vary, a company should use the market segmentation approach.

Market Segmentation Approach   A firm that is marketing 40-foot yachts would not direct its marketing effort toward every person in the total boat market. Some might want a sailboat or a canoe. Others might want a speedboat or an outboard-powered fishing boat. Still others might be looking for something resembling a small ocean liner. Marketing efforts directed toward these boat buyers would be wasted.

Instead, the firm would direct its attention toward a particular portion, or *segment*, of the total market for boats. A **market segment** is a group of individuals or organizations, within a market, that share one or more common characteristics. The process of dividing a market into segments is called **market segmentation.** As Figure 12.2 shows, a firm using this approach directs a marketing mix at a segment rather than at the total

total market approach
a single marketing mix directed at the entire market for a particular product

market segment   a group of individuals or organizations, within a market, that share one or more common characteristics

market segmentation   the process of dividing a market into segments and directing a marketing mix at a particular segment or segments rather than at the total market

FIGURE 12.2   General Approaches for Selecting Target Markets
The total market approach (left) assumes that individual customers have similar needs and that most customers can be satisfied with a single marketing mix. When customers' needs vary, the market segmentation approach (right) should be used.

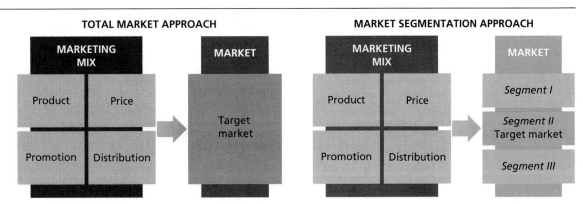

market. In our example, one common characteristic, or *basis*, for segmentation might be "end use of a boat." The firm would be interested primarily in that market segment whose uses for a boat could lead to the purchase of a 40-foot yacht. Another basis for segmentation might be income; still another might be geographic location. Each of these variables can affect the type of boat an individual might purchase. When choosing a basis for segmentation, it is important to select a characteristic that relates to differences in people's needs for a product. The yacht producer, for example, would not use religion to segment the boat market because people's needs for boats do not vary based on religion.

Marketers use a wide variety of segmentation bases. Those bases most commonly applied to consumer markets are shown in Table 12.3. Each may be used as a single basis for market segmentation or in combination with other bases.

Creating a Marketing Mix

LEARNING OBJECTIVE 4
Identify the four elements of the marketing mix, and be aware of their importance in developing a marketing strategy.

A business firm controls four important elements of marketing that it combines in a way that reaches the firm's target market. These are the *product* itself, the *price* of the product, the means chosen for its *distribution,* and the *promotion* of the product. When combined, these four elements form a marketing mix (see the circular area in Figure 12.3).

A firm can vary its marketing mix by changing any one or more of these ingredients. Thus a firm may use one marketing mix to reach one target market and a second, somewhat different marketing mix, to reach another target market. For example, most automakers produce several different types and models of vehicles and aim them at different market segments based on age, income, and other factors.

The *product* ingredient of the marketing mix includes decisions about the product's design, brand name, packaging, warranties, and the like. When McDonald's decides on brand names, package designs, sizes of orders, fla-

TABLE 12.3   Common Bases of Market Segmentation

Demographic	Psychographic	Geographic	Behavioristic
Age	Personality attributes	Region	Volume usage
Gender		Urban, suburban, rural	End use
Race	Motives		Benefit expectations
Ethnicity	Lifestyles	Market density	
Income		Climate	Brand loyalty
Education		Terrain	Price sensitivity
Occupation		City size	
Family size		County size	
Family life cycle		State size	
Religion			
Social class			

Source: Adapted from William M. Pride and O. C. Ferrell, *Marketing: Concepts and Strategies,* Ninth Edition. Copyright © 1995 by Houghton Mifflin Company. Used by permission.

FIGURE 12.3
The Marketing Mix and the Marketing Environment
The marketing mix consists of elements that the firm controls—product, price, distribution, and promotion. The firm generally has no control over marketing environment forces.   *(Source: Adapted from William M. Pride and O. C. Ferrell,* Marketing: Concepts and Strategies, *Ninth Edition. Copyright © 1995 by Houghton Mifflin Company. Used by permission.)*

vors of sauces, and recipes, these choices are all part of the product ingredient.

The *pricing* ingredient is concerned with both base prices and discounts of various kinds. Pricing decisions are intended to achieve particular goals, such as to maximize profit or even to make room for new models. The rebates offered by automobile manufacturers are a pricing strategy developed to boost low auto sales. Product and pricing are discussed in detail in Chapter 13.

The *distribution* ingredient involves not only transportation and storage but also the selection of intermediaries. How many levels of intermediaries should be used in the distribution of a particular product? Should the product be distributed as widely as possible? Or should distribution be restricted to a few specialized outlets in each area? These and other questions related to distribution are considered in Chapter 14.

The *promotion* ingredient focuses on providing information to target markets. The major forms of promotion are advertising, personal selling, sales promotion, and publicity. These four forms are discussed in Chapter 15.

These ingredients of the marketing mix are controllable elements. A firm can vary each of them to suit its organizational goals, marketing goals, and target markets. As we extend our discussion of marketing strategy, we will see that the marketing environment includes a number of *uncontrollable* elements.

Marketing Strategy and the Marketing Environment

LEARNING OBJECTIVE 5
Explain how the marketing environment affects strategic market planning.

The marketing mix consists of elements that a firm controls and uses to reach its target market. In addition, the firm has control over such

Creating a marketing strategy. While numerous marketing environment forces are considered, marketers at Canon pay close attention to technological changes and competition when formulating marketing strategies for their copiers.

For an idea of how much color copier experience we have, push this 1.2 billion times.

Canon

organizational resources as finances and information. These resources, too, may be used to accomplish marketing goals. However, the firm's marketing activities are also affected by a number of external—and generally uncontrollable—forces. As Figure 12.3 illustrates, the forces that make up the external *marketing environment* are

- *Economic forces*—the effects of economic conditions on customers' ability and willingness to buy
- *Sociocultural forces*—influences in a society and its culture that result in changes in attitudes, beliefs, norms, customs, and lifestyles
- *Political forces*—influences that arise through the actions of elected and appointed officials
- *Competitive forces*—the actions of competitors, who are in the process of implementing their own marketing plans
- *Legal and regulatory forces*—laws that protect consumers and competition, and government regulations that affect marketing
- *Technological forces*—technological changes that on one hand can create new marketing opportunities or, on the other, can cause products to become obsolete almost overnight

These forces influence decisions about marketing mix ingredients. Changes in the environment can have a major impact on existing marketing strategies. In addition, changes in environmental forces may lead to abrupt shifts in the needs of people in the target market.

Strategic Market Planning

The development of a marketing strategy begins with an assessment of the marketing environment. Marketers should gather and analyze all available information concerning the marketing environment, the effectiveness of previous marketing programs or strategies, the firm's present and potential markets and their needs, and the availability of resources. Obviously, marketing research and the firm's system for managing its marketing information play an important role in this first stage of the planning process.

Next, the organization should formulate particular and detailed marketing objectives. These objectives should be consistent with organizational goals. They must also be measurable and realistic—in line with both the marketing situation and available resources.

Then the firm must select a target market and design a marketing mix to reach that market. Here, product, pricing, distribution, and promotional decisions need to be coordinated to produce a unified mix. As we have noted, the marketing strategy must be designed to operate effectively in the dynamic marketing environment.

Finally, the organization must evaluate the performance of its marketing strategy. Both marketing research and the marketing information system come into play here as monitoring tools. The information that is obtained should be used to evaluate the strategy and modify it as necessary. This information should also be used to begin the next round of market planning.

■■ MARKET MEASUREMENT AND SALES FORECASTING

LEARNING OBJECTIVE 6
Describe how market measurement and sales forecasting are used.

Measuring the sales potential for specific types of market segments helps an organization make some important decisions. It can evaluate the feasibility of entering new segments. The organization can also decide how best to allocate its marketing resources and activities among market segments in which it is already active. All such estimates should identify the relevant time frame. Short-range estimates cover periods of less than one year; medium-range estimates, one to five years; and long-range estimates, more than five years. The estimates should also define the geographic boundaries of the forecast. For example, sales potential can be estimated for a city, county, state, or group of nations. Finally, analysts should indicate whether their estimates are for a specific product item, a product line, or an entire product category.

sales forecast an estimate of the amount of a product that an organization expects to sell during a certain period of time, based on a specified level of marketing effort

A company **sales forecast** is an estimate of the amount of a product that an organization expects to sell during a certain period of time, based on a specified level of marketing effort. Managers in different divisions of the organization rely on sales forecasts when they purchase raw materials, schedule production, secure financial resources, consider plant or equipment purchases, hire personnel, and plan inventory levels. Because the accuracy of a sales forecast is so important, organizations often use several forecasting methods, including executive judgments, surveys of buyers or

■ ■ ■ ■ GLOBAL PERSPECTIVES

The Pepsi Challenge Goes Global

Remember when Coca-Cola dominated the U.S. soft-drink business? Its closest competitor, Pepsico, trailed 20 percent behind in market share. But feisty Pepsi fought hard enough in the cola wars to win 31 percent of the U.S. market. Outside North America, however, Coke continued to outsell Pepsi by about three to one. According to a Nielsen survey, Coke is the number 1 consumer product sold in Europe. Now, Pepsi is aggressively invading long-held Coke territory all over the world. Pepsi executives assert that Coke is not unbeatable on the global front; the king just had a fifty-year head start.

To appeal to the British, who drink a lot of fruit juice, Pepsi's British marketing director quickly pushed through the development and introduction of Strawberry Wild Bunch Pepsi and Tropical Wild Bunch Pepsi. In Germany, Pepsico bought the rights to bottle and sell Pepsi products to German retailers. In China, Pepsi spent $340 million to build ten new bottling plants. To promote its products throughout Europe, Pepsi sponsored a traveling basketball tournament featuring Magic Johnson. Pepsi pulled out of South Africa in 1985 but is now returning, despite Coca-Cola's 75 percent control of soft-drink sales there. Pepsico is also challenging laws that ban comparative advertising in some of its foreign markets and spending more abroad on vending machines and delivery trucks.

With its introduction of one-calorie Pepsi Max, Pepsi is breaking the cardinal rule of soft-drink marketing: colas are global and marketable under the same brand from Toledo to Tokyo. Pepsi Max, however, will quench the thirsts of soft-drink lovers in Europe, Latin America, and the Far East but will never appear on U.S. supermarket shelves. Research in Britain, Germany, and Australia showed that consumers in those countries want to decrease their sugar intake, so Pepsi came up with a new cola with a new blend of sweeteners and a new name. Pepsi Max is positioned as a sugar-free cola with maximum cola taste.

When Pepsi launched Max in Great Britain, men and women in red and blue outfits rode by in Maxmobile jeeps or rolled by on inline skates giving out free cans. Television spots featured fearless surfers and snowboarders drinking the new soft drink and "living life to the Max." In Mexico, Pepsi held the Pepsi Challenge, the same taste-comparison test that converted so many Coke drinkers in the United States. Of the 100,000 who sampled Coke and Pepsi Max in two months, 55 percent preferred Max.

After Pepsi Max promotions in England, Max's annual British sales totaled $33 million and Pepsi's overall cola share there rose 2 percent. In the two Mexican cities that offered the Pepsi Challenge, sales of cases of Pepsi Max rose 13 percent. Pepsico's executives are excited, but not complacent. Pepsi's global strategy will continue to be the same one that brought success in the United States: take risks, act aggressively, and innovate continually.

sales personnel, time series analyses, correlation analyses, and market tests. The specific methods used depend on the costs involved, type of product, characteristics of the market, time span of the forecast, purposes for which the forecast is used, stability of historical sales data, availability of the required information, and expertise and experience of forecasters.

■ ■ MARKETING INFORMATION

Accurate and timely information is the foundation of effective marketing—
and, in particular, of the marketing concept. A wealth of marketing information is available, both within the firm and from outside sources, but this
information must be gathered, analyzed, and put to use by marketing
personnel.

There are two general approaches to collecting marketing information.
A marketing information system provides information on a continuing
basis, whereas marketing research offers information for specific marketing
projects.

Marketing Information Systems

**marketing information
system**   a system for managing
marketing information that is
gathered continually from
internal and external sources

A **marketing information system** is a system for managing marketing
information that is gathered continually from internal and external sources.
Most systems are computer-based because of the amount of data that the
system must accept, store, sort, and retrieve. *Continual* collection of data is
essential if the system is to incorporate the most up-to-date information.

In concept, the operation of a marketing information system is not complex. Data from a variety of sources are fed into the system. Data from *internal* sources include sales figures, product and marketing costs, inventory
levels, and activities of the sales force. Data from *external* sources relate to

**Marketing information
provider.** Matchmaker/2000
For Windows, with more than
twelve million address ranges,
can help marketers identify
customers and prospects.

**Their idea of
precise geocoding.**   **Ours.**

Matchmaker/2000™
for Windows™ is
the only geocoding
system that matches
street address ranges to latitude and
longitude coordinates. So you end
up with a more precise and useful
picture of where your customers and
prospects are located. Matchmaker/2000
offers nationwide street coverage.

with more than 12 million address
ranges. Other programs offer only
half as many. Matchmaker/2000 is
continuously updated. So your data is
always current. And you'll achieve the
highest match percentage available in
the industry today. Matchmaker/2000
is an invaluable tool for market penetration studies. Point and cluster evaluations. Sales effectiveness analyses.

Scheduling and routing. And custom
zone creation. You'll work smarter.
And faster. The program is offered
with a range of expandable and up-
gradable database options to meet
your specific budget and application.
Contact Geographic Data Technology,
Inc., 13 Dartmouth College Highway,
Lyme, NH 03768-9713. Or call
1-800-331-7881, x1101.

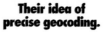

**GEOGRAPHIC DATA
TECHNOLOGY, INC.**   1-800-331-7881 x1101

ENHANCING CAREER SKILLS

How to Develop a Marketing Plan

An extraordinary amount of planning goes into marketing products before you see them at the supermarket or local mall. To market their products effectively, organizations write a marketing plan, which is the document specifying the resources, objectives, strategy, implementation, and control efforts to be used in marketing a specific product or product group. Marketing plans can be short-range (one year or less), moderate-range (two to five years), or long-range (more than five years).

COMPONENTS OF A MARKETING PLAN

Executive Summary

This short statement summarizing the entire report is sometimes easier to write *after* you have completed the marketing plan.

Environmental Analysis

This comprises current information about the environment in which a company will market its product, the target market, and performance objectives.

Assessing the *marketing environment* includes:

1. Looking at forces affecting marketing—competitive, legal, political, economic, technological, and sociocultural.

2. Assessing your organization's marketing resources—availability of human resources, capacity of equipment, and financial resources.

Assessing the *target market* includes asking:

1. What are the current needs of each target market?

2. What changes in these needs do you anticipate?

3. How well are the company's products meeting these needs?

4. What are the relevant aspects of consumer behavior and product use?

Evaluating the firm's *current marketing objectives and performance* includes:

1. Making sure your firm's objectives are consistent with the marketing environment.

2. Analyzing your company's sales volume, market share, and profitability.

Strengths and Weaknesses

Here you focus on the advantages and disadvantages that your organization has in meeting your target market's needs.

- *Example of a strength:* Your company has a highly-trained and capable sales force.

- *Example of a weakness:* Your company's products have a low-quality image even though the actual

the firm's suppliers, intermediaries, and customers; competitors' marketing activities; and economic conditions. All these data are stored and processed within the marketing information system. Its output is a flow of information in the form that is most useful for marketing decision making. This information might include daily sales reports by territory and product, forecasts of sales or buying trends, and reports on changes in market share for the major brands in a specific industry. Both the information

quality is equal to or exceeds the quality of your major competitor's products.

Opportunities and Threats

This section covers factors that exist outside and independent of your company but nonetheless can affect operations.

- *Opportunity:* Favorable conditions in the environment that could produce rewards for the company if you act on them—for example, consumers have less leisure time and demand more convenience products.
- *Threat:* Conditions that may prevent your company from achieving its objectives unless you act—for example, more women are working outside the home, which means that your company's door-to-door sales are suffering.

Marketing Objectives

This section states what your marketing activities are designed to accomplish. Forms of marketing objectives can include:

- Product introduction, improvement, or innovation
- Sales or market share
- Profitability
- Pricing
- Distribution
- Advertising

Marketing objectives must:

- Be expressed in clear, simple terms.
- Be written so that they can be accurately measured.

- Give a time frame for achieving objectives.
- Be consistent with the company's overall marketing strategy.

Marketing Strategies

Marketing strategy includes selecting the target market and developing the marketing mix.

- *Selecting a target market:* Describe the target market in terms of demographic, geographic, psychographic, and product usage characteristics.
- *Determining the marketing mix:* Decide how product, distribution, promotion, and price will satisfy customer needs.

Marketing Implementation

This section describes the process of putting your marketing strategies into action and answers these questions:

- What specific actions will we take?
- How will we perform these activities?
- Who is responsible for completing the activities?
- How much will these activities cost?

Evaluation and Control

How will you measure and evaluate the results of your marketing plan? You should consider and include:

- *Performance standards:* How will you judge your product's performance?
- *Financial controls:* How will you evaluate whether or not the marketing plan is working?
- *Monitoring procedures:* How will you pinpoint the cause of any problems you encounter?

outputs and their form depend on the requirements of the personnel in the organization.

Marketing Research

marketing research the process of systematically gathering, recording, and analyzing data concerning a particular marketing problem

Marketing research is the process of systematically gathering, recording, and analyzing data concerning a particular marketing problem. Thus marketing research is used in specific situations to obtain information that is not otherwise available to decision makers. It is an intermittent, rather than a continual, source of marketing information.

Table 12.4 outlines a six-step procedure for conducting marketing research. This procedure is particularly well suited to testing new products, determining various characteristics of consumer markets, and evaluating promotional activities. General Foods Corporation makes extensive use of marketing research in the form of taste tests to determine whether proposed new products will appeal to consumers.

■■ TYPES OF BUYING BEHAVIOR

buying behavior   the decisions and actions of people involved in buying and using products

consumer buying behavior the purchasing of products for personal or household use, not for business purposes

Buying behavior may be defined as the decisions and actions of people involved in buying and using products.[3] **Consumer buying behavior** refers to the purchasing of products for personal or household use, not for busi-

TABLE 12.4   The Six Steps of Marketing Research

1. Define the problem	In this step, the problem is clearly and accurately stated to determine what issues are involved in the research, what questions to ask, and what types of solutions are needed. This is a crucial step that should not be rushed.
2. Make a preliminary investigation	The objective of preliminary investigation is to develop both a sharper definition of the problem and a set of tentative answers. The tentative answers are developed by examining internal information and published data, and by talking with persons who have some experience with the problem. These answers will be tested by further research.
3. Plan the research	At this stage researchers know what facts are needed to resolve the identified problem and what facts are available. They make plans on how to gather needed but missing data.
4. Gather factual information	Once the basic research plan has been completed, the needed information can be collected by mail, telephone, or personal interviews; by observation; or from commercial or government data sources. The choice depends on the plan and the available sources of information.
5. Interpret the information	Facts by themselves do not always provide a sound solution to a marketing problem. They must be interpreted and analyzed to determine the choices that are available to management.
6. Reach a conclusion	Sometimes the conclusion or recommendation becomes obvious when the facts are interpreted. However, in other cases, reaching a conclusion may not be so easy because of gaps in the information or intangible factors that are difficult to evaluate. If and when the evidence is less than complete, it is important to say so.

Source: Adapted from Small Business Administration (Washington, D.C.), *Small Business Bibliography No. 9.*

organizational buying behavior the purchasing of products by producers, resellers, governmental units, and institutions

ness purposes. **Organizational buying behavior** is the purchasing of products by producers, resellers, governmental units, and institutions. Since a firm's success depends greatly on buyers' reactions to a particular marketing strategy, it is important to understand buying behavior. Marketing managers are better able to predict consumer responses to marketing strategies and to develop a satisfying marketing mix if they are aware of the factors that affect buying behavior.

Consumer Buying Behavior

LEARNING OBJECTIVE 8
Identify several factors that may influence buying behavior.

Consumers' buying behaviors differ when they buy different types of products. For frequently purchased, low-cost items, a consumer employs routine response behavior, involving very little search or decision-making effort. The buyer uses limited decision making for purchases made occasionally or when more information is needed about an unknown product in a well-known product category. When buying an unfamiliar, expensive item or one that is seldom purchased, the consumer engages in extensive decision making.

A person deciding on a purchase goes through some or all of the steps shown in Figure 12.4. First, the consumer acknowledges that a problem exists. Then the buyer looks for information, which may include brand names, product characteristics, warranties, and other features. Next the buyer weighs the various alternatives he or she has discovered and then finally makes a choice and acquires the item. In the after-purchase stage, the consumer evaluates the suitability of the product. This judgment will affect future purchases. As Figure 12.4 shows, the buying process is influenced by

Person-specific influences affect buying behavior. Older customers, such as these cereal buyers, are especially interested in nutritional information.

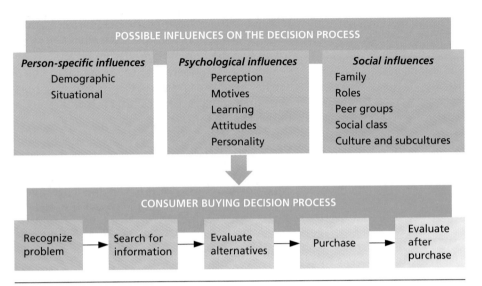

FIGURE 12.4   Consumer Buying Decision Process and Possible Influences on the Process
A buyer goes through some or all of these steps when making a purchase.   *(Source: Adapted from William M. Pride and O. C. Ferrell,* Marketing: Concepts and Strategies, *Ninth Edition. Copyright © 1995 by Houghton Mifflin Company. Used by permission.)*

>> **AT A GLANCE**

Joint Decisions

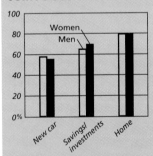

Married men and women report that both spouses have an equal influence on many purchase decisions.

Source: Roper Starch Worldwide, New York, NY.

person-specific factors (demographic, situational), psychological factors (perception, motives, learning, attitudes, personality), and social factors (family, roles, peer groups, social class, culture and subculture).

Organizational Buying Behavior

Organizational buyers consider a product's quality, its price, and the service provided by suppliers. Organizational buyers are usually better informed than consumers about the products they buy and generally buy in larger quantities. In an organization, a committee or group of people, rather than single individuals, often decide on purchases. Committee members must consider the organization's objectives, purchasing policies, resources, and personnel. Organizational buying occurs through description, inspection, sampling, or negotiation.

■■ THE AMERICAN CONSUMER

In this section we examine several measures of consumer income, a major source of buying power. By looking at why, what, where, and when consumers buy, we explain how this income is spent.

Consumer Income

LEARNING OBJECTIVE 9
Describe three ways of measuring consumer income.

Purchasing power is created by income. However, as every taxpayer knows, not all income is available for spending. For this reason, marketers consider

personal income   the income an individual receives from all sources *less* the Social Security taxes the individual must pay

disposable income   personal income *less* all additional personal taxes

discretionary income   disposable income *less* savings and expenditures on food, clothing, and housing

income in three different ways. **Personal income** is the income an individual receives from all sources *less* the Social Security taxes the individual must pay. **Disposable income** is personal income *less* all additional personal taxes. These taxes include income, estate, gift, and property taxes levied by local, state, and federal governments. About 5 percent of all disposable income is saved. **Discretionary income** is disposable income *less* savings and expenditures on food, clothing, and housing. Discretionary income is of particular interest to marketers because consumers have the most choice in spending it. Consumers use their discretionary income to purchase items ranging from automobiles and vacations to movies and pet food.

Why Do Consumers Buy?

Consumers buy with the hope of getting a large amount of current and future satisfaction relative to their buying power. Consumers buy because they would rather have a particular good or service than the money they have to spend to buy it! Here are the major reasons why consumers choose to buy a given product:

1. *They have a use for the product.* Many items fill an immediate "use" need. A family needs pots and pans; a student needs books.

2. *They like the convenience a product offers.* Such items as electric can openers and trash compacters are not essential, but they offer convenience and thus satisfaction.

3. *They believe the purchase will enhance their wealth.* People collect antiques or gold coins as investments as well as for enjoyment. Homeowners buy aluminum siding, landscape services, and fences to add to the value of their property.

4. *They take pride in ownership.* Many consumers purchase items such as a compact-disc player or a Rolex watch because such products provide status and pride of ownership as well as utility.

5. *They buy for safety.* Consumers buy health, life, and fire insurance to protect themselves and their families. Smoke detectors, burglar alarms, traveler's checks, and similar products also provide safety and protection.

What Do Consumers Buy?

Figure 12.5 shows how consumer spending is divided among various categories of products and services. The average American household spent $30,692 in 1993 according to the latest available data from the Bureau of Labor Statistics. As we have noted, the greatest proportion of disposable income is spent on food, clothing, and shelter. The largest share—$9,636—went toward housing and related expenses, such as supplies, utilities, and furnishings. The second-largest expense was transportation, with families spending an average of $5,453 on cars and other vehicles, insurance, repairs, and public transportation. The average household spent $4,399 on food,

FIGURE 12.5
Consumer Spending
What percentage of disposable income is spent on various categories of products and services? *(Source: Based on Consumer Expenditure Survey, Bureau of Labor Statistics, 1994.)*

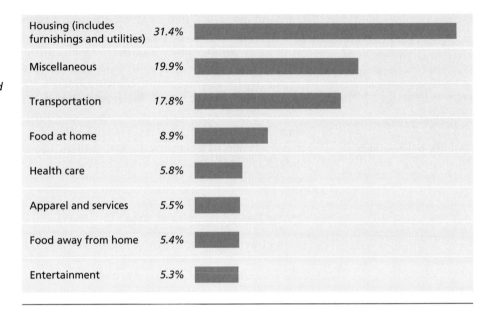

Category	Percentage
Housing (includes furnishings and utilities)	31.4%
Miscellaneous	19.9%
Transportation	17.8%
Food at home	8.9%
Health care	5.8%
Apparel and services	5.5%
Food away from home	5.4%
Entertainment	5.3%

including $2,735 to eat at home. Clothing and related services, such as dry cleaning, used up $1,676. Another $1,626 went toward entertainment, and slightly more than $1,776 was spent on health care.[4] (A mere 1 percent of total disposable income amounts to over $30 billion. Thus none of the categories in Figure 12.5 is really "small" in terms of total dollars spent.)

Where Do Consumers Buy?

Probably the most important factor that influences a consumer's decision about where to buy a particular product is his or her perception of the store. Consumers' general impressions of an establishment's products, prices, and sales personnel can mean the difference between repeat sales and lost business. Consumers distinguish among various types of retail outlets (such as specialty shops, department stores, and discount outlets), and they choose particular types of stores for specific purchases. Many retail outlets go to a great deal of trouble to build and maintain a particular image. Products that do not fit the image are not carried. Consumers also select the businesses they patronize on the basis of location, product assortment, and such services as credit terms, return privileges, and free delivery.

When Do Consumers Buy?

In general, consumers buy when buying is most convenient. Certain business hours have long been standard for establishments that sell consumer products. However, many of these establishments have stretched their hours to include evenings, holidays, and Sundays. Ultimately, within each area, the consumers themselves control when they do their buying.

In the next chapter we discuss two elements of the marketing mix: product and price. Our emphasis will be on the development of product and pricing within a marketing strategy.

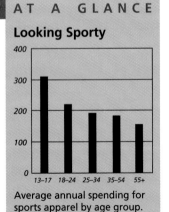

AT A GLANCE
Looking Sporty

Average annual spending for sports apparel by age group. *(In dollars)*

Source: Sporting Goods Manufacturing Association.

■ ■ ■ ■ CHAPTER REVIEW

Summary

1   Know the meaning of *marketing,* and explain how it creates utility for purchasers of products.

Marketing is the process of planning and executing the conception, pricing, promotion, and distribution of ideas, goods, and services to create exchanges that satisfy individual and organizational objectives. Marketing adds value in the form of utility, or the power of a product or service to satisfy a need. It creates place utility by making products available where customers want them, time utility by making products available when customers want them, and possession utility by transferring the ownership of products to buyers.

2   Trace the development of the marketing concept and understand how it is implemented.

From the Industrial Revolution until the early twentieth century, business people focused on the production of goods; from the 1920s to the 1950s, the emphasis moved to the selling of goods. After 1950, however, business people recognized that their enterprises involved not only producing and selling products but also satisfying customers' needs. They began to implement the marketing concept, a business philosophy that involves the entire business organization in the dual processes of meeting the customer's needs and achieving the organization's goals.

Implementation of the marketing concept begins and ends with customers—first to determine what customers' needs are, and later to evaluate how well the firm is meeting those needs.

3   Understand what markets are and how they are classified.

A market consists of people with needs, the ability to buy, and the desire and authority to purchase. Markets are classified as consumer and industrial (producer, reseller, governmental, and institutional) markets.

4   Identify the four elements of the marketing mix, and be aware of their importance in developing a marketing strategy.

A marketing strategy is a plan for the best use of an organization's resources to meet its objectives. Developing a marketing strategy involves selecting and analyzing a target market and creating and maintaining a marketing mix that will satisfy that target market. A target market is chosen through either the total market approach or the market segmentation approach. A market segment is a group of individuals or organizations within a market that have similar characteristics and needs. Businesses that use a total market approach design a single marketing mix and direct it at the entire market for a particular product. The market segmentation approach directs a marketing mix at a segment of a market.

The four elements of a firm's marketing mix are product, price, distribution, and promotion. The product ingredient includes decisions about the product's design, brand name, packaging, and warranties. The pricing ingredient is concerned with both base prices and various types of discounts. Distribution involves not only transportation and storage but also the selection of intermediaries. Promotion focuses on providing information to target markets. The elements of the marketing mix can be varied to suit broad organizational goals, marketing objectives, and target markets.

5   Explain how the marketing environment affects strategic market planning.

Marketing activities are affected by a number of external forces that make up the marketing environment. These forces include economic forces, sociocultural forces, political forces, competitive forces, legal and regulatory forces, and technological forces. Economic forces affect customers' ability and willingness to buy. Sociocultural forces are societal and cultural factors, such as attitudes, beliefs, and lifestyles, that affect customers' buying choices. Political forces and legal and regulatory forces influence marketing planning through laws that protect consumers and regulate competition. Competitive forces are the actions of competitors who are implementing their own marketing plans. Technological forces can create new marketing opportunities or quickly cause a product to become obsolete.

6   Describe how market measurement and sales forecasting are used.

To achieve a firm's marketing objectives, marketing mix strategies must begin with an assessment of the marketing environment, which in turn will influence decisions about marketing mix ingredients. Market measurement and sales forecasting are used to estimate sales potential and predict product sales in specific market segments.

7   Distinguish between a marketing information system and marketing research.

Strategies are monitored and evaluated through marketing research and the marketing information system, which stores and processes internal and external data in a form that aids marketing decision making. A marketing information system is a system for managing marketing information that is gathered continually from internal and external sources. Marketing research is the process of systematically gathering, recording, and analyzing data concerning a particular marketing problem. It is an intermittent, rather than a continual, source of marketing information.

8   Identify several factors that may influence buying behavior.

Buying behavior consists of the decisions and actions of people involved in buying and using products. Consumer buying behavior refers to the purchase of products for personal or household use. Organizational buying behavior is the purchase of products by producers, resellers, governments, and institutions. Understanding buying behavior helps marketers predict how buyers will respond to marketing strategies. Influences on buying behavior fall into three categories: person-specific influences, including demographic and situational; psychological influences, including perception, motives, learning, attitudes, and personality; and social influences, including family, roles, peer groups, social class, and cultures and subcultures.

9   Describe three ways of measuring consumer income.

Personal income is the income an individual receives, less the Social Security taxes he or she must pay. Disposable income is personal income minus all other taxes. Discretionary income is what remains of disposable income after savings and expenditures for necessities. Consumers use discretionary income to buy goods and services that best satisfy their needs.

Key Terms

You should now be able to define and give an example relevant to each of the following terms:

marketing (362)
utility (362)
form utility (363)
place utility (363)
time utility (363)
possession utility (363)
marketing concept (365)
market (367)
marketing strategy (368)
marketing mix (368)
target market (368)
total market approach (369)
market segment (369)
market segmentation (369)
sales forecast (373)
marketing information system (375)
marketing research (377)
buying behavior (378)
consumer buying behavior (378)
organizational buying behavior (379)
personal income (381)
disposable income (381)
discretionary income (381)

Questions

Review Questions

1. How, specifically, does marketing create place, time, and possession utility?
2. How is a marketing-oriented firm different from a production-oriented firm or a sales-oriented firm?
3. What are the major requirements for a group of individuals and organizations to be a market? How does a consumer market differ from an industrial market?
4. What are the major components of a marketing strategy?
5. What is the purpose of market segmentation? What is the relationship between market segmentation and the selection of target markets?
6. What are the four elements of the marketing mix? In what sense are they "controllable"?
7. Describe the forces in the marketing environment that affect an organization's marketing decisions.
8. What major issues should be specified prior to conducting a sales forecast?
9. What is the difference between a marketing information system and a marketing research project? How might the two be related?
10. Why do marketers need to understand buying behavior?
11. How are personal income, disposable income, and discretionary income related? Which is the best indicator of consumer purchasing power?

12. List five reasons why consumers make purchases. What need is satisfied in each case?

Discussion Questions

1. What types of people make up the target market for the Ford Mustang?

2. Describe the marketing mix for the Mustang.

3. In what way is each of the following a marketing activity?
 a. The provision of sufficient parking space for customers at a suburban shopping mall
 b. The purchase by a clothing store of seven dozen sweaters in assorted sizes and colors
 c. The inclusion of a longer and more comprehensive warranty on an automobile

4. How might adoption of the marketing concept benefit a firm? How might it benefit the firm's customers?

5. Is marketing information as important to small firms as it is to larger firms? Explain.

6. How does the marketing environment affect a firm's marketing strategy?

Exercises

1. Describe how a producer of computer hardware could apply the marketing concept.

✎ **2.** Through library research, determine the distribution of income among American households in as much detail as possible. Then write an explanation of how you would use this information if you were marketing 40-foot yachts.

● **3.** How would you develop a marketing strategy for an in-home rug and upholstery cleaning service? What marketing information would you need? How would you obtain it?

VIDEO CASE 12.1

Marketing the New *American Heritage Dictionary*

Do you want to know the exact meaning of *cyberpunk, liposuction, arbitrage, triathlete, sound bite, junk bond,* or *hip-hop*? To find the definitions of these and almost 16,000 other new words, look them up in the latest edition of *The American Heritage Dictionary.* You can also learn about words that have meanings unique to specific U.S. geographical regions, like *bodacious, gum band,* and *hoagie.* Other improvements over previous editions of the dictionary include more than 400 new word histories, better and more complete appendixes, and higher-quality illustrations. People responded so

positively to these changes that the new *American Heritage Dictionary* spent sixteen weeks on *The New York Times* bestseller list. About 250,000 copies of the dictionary were sold in its debut year. How did a reference book join the ranks of best-selling adventure stories, romance novels, and scandal-filled biographies? Industry experts attribute the dictionary's phenomenal success in large part to its publisher's creative and effective marketing strategy.

When Houghton Mifflin Company launched the third edition of *The American Heritage Dictionary,* it took *Merriam-Webster's Collegiate Dictionary,* the industry leader, head on. Long dominating the U.S. dictionary market, the word *Webster* has become almost synonymous with *dictionary.* But Houghton Mifflin was convinced that its dictionary's unique positioning would enable it to win the war of the words. Before the arrival of *The American Heritage Dictionary,* Third Edition, you had basically two choices. You could pay about $90 for a highly-detailed unabridged dictionary with about 4,000 pages, or you could select a much smaller, condensed version for about $20. *The American Heritage Dictionary,* however, is positioned in between. It has just under 1,000 pages and sells for about $40. To make people aware that this dictionary is different from all the others, Houghton chose a black book jacket instead of the red one sported by virtually every other dictionary on the market.

Supporting the positioning strategy was a creative $1.5 million advertising and promotion program designed to deliver the message that *The American Heritage Dictionary* is not just another boring reference book. In fact, television and radio ads for the book carried the tag line, "There Is a Difference." Print ads in *Vanity Fair, New Age Journal, People,* and many other mass publications, carried the same slogan. Bookstores and other retail outlets displayed *The American Heritage Dictionary* on a free-standing kiosk instead of a crowded, cluttered bookshelf.

The list of creative promotions is long. The company set up a toll-free phone line—1-800-NEW-WORD—featuring the voice of actor Tony Randall to answer consumer questions about new words in the dictionary. Houghton Mifflin's marketers composed a rap song that included many of the new words in the dictionary. To understand lyrics like "And prequels, sequels, liposuction, pixels, O-rings, quasers, quarks," you have to look them up in the new *American Heritage Dictionary.* The publisher established connections with popular television games shows, such as *Jeopardy,* in which the dictionary was identified on air as the source for verifying some of the answers, and *Wheel of Fortune,* which not only advertised the dictionary but gave it away as a gift to contestants. The executive editor of the new *American Heritage Dictionary* praised its features on ABC's *Good Morning America*, and *Larry King Live*. Arsenio Hall brought it onto his show to look up *nerd*. In the movie *Wolf*, Jack Nicholson had the dictionary on his desk just in case he needed to check out the word *lycanthropy*.

The new *American Heritage's* early and huge success has spawned a line of related products. *The American Heritage College Dictionary* came out about a year after the original, and other Houghton Mifflin lexicon products have followed the leader, including dictionaries for high school students and children. In addition, the publisher came out with a full-featured electronic version of the dictionary. Available on computer disk, the paperless high-tech *AHD* became a top seller in the retail computer software market. Using the same massive database of words for all publications means that Houghton Mifflin can develop an impressive range of products in little time at low cost. Was all the effort Houghton Mifflin put into its new product worthwhile? After all, it's just a dictionary. Given that dictionaries can generate sales for ten years or more, the publisher answers with a resounding yes.[5]

Questions

1. To what extent did Houghton Mifflin attempt to adopt and use the marketing concept?
2. Describe the marketing mix for the new *American Heritage Dictionary*.
3. What type of decision-making process would a dictionary buyer most likely use?

CASE 12.2

Campbell Soup Serves Up Variety

Over 120 years ago, the Campbell Soup Company introduced canned condensed soup and gave the world its first convenience food. Since then, those well-known red and white labels and the sigh "Mmmm, mmmm, good" have become symbols of American culture. However, today's increasingly health-conscious consumers often spurn canned soup in favor of those made with fresh ingredients. Although sales of the popular brand total $1.1 billion, earning the line 48.9 percent of the canned soup market, Campbell faces declining domestic sales. Turning to global markets, the company's executives hope that by the year 2000, more than half of the firm's profits will come from sales outside the United States.

Experts caution that strong cultural and regional tastes and preferences make food more difficult to translate to foreign markets than soda or laundry detergent. The editor of *Food and Drink Daily* recently stressed the importance of recognizing the unique characteristics of individual global market segments. Just because Americans love to ladle out clam chowder and tomato soup by the bowl full doesn't mean those same flavors appeal to customers around the world. Marketers at Campbell know that demographics, lifestyle, and geography influence customer choices, with diet especially sensitive to local fancies. To avoid potential pitfalls that differences often create, Campbell conducts extensive research in specific consumer segments before generating and marketing brands.

All over the globe, Campbell's research and taste tests are resulting in new, locally pleasing recipes. In Argentina, consumers don't take to the enduring American favorite, chicken noodle soup, but they do like split pea with ham. Emphasizing *Sopa de Campbell's* fresh ingredients, regional ads proclaim it "the real soup." Polish soup lovers, who eat an average of five bowls each week, can choose from eight varieties of Campbell's *zupa*, including *flaki*—tripe soup spiced with lots of pepper. To please Mexican palates, Campbell came up with hot and spicy Cream of Chile Poblano.

In its Hong Kong test kitchen, the company concocted some recipes it hoped would appeal to Asia's 2 billion consumers. What did Campbell chefs come up with? Successes include watercress and duck gizzard soup, radish-carrot soup, fig soup, and date soup, varieties that Americans will probably not look for (or find) on neighborhood grocery shelves. Although willing to experiment even with snake, Campbell balked when it came to using ingredients from endangered species, such as shark's fin. What the company discovered is that Chinese consumers are willing to buy soup in a can if the right soup is inside.

Encouraged by its Hong Kong success, Campbell launched seventeen varieties of soup in the Chinese province of Guangdong. Product sampling suggested that mainland Chinese would buy the same brands already popular in Hong Kong. Campbell's toughest competitor is homemade soup, as much a staple in China as rice. Chinese eat more soup in a few weeks than most Americans eat in a year—they just aren't used to eating canned varieties. Company executives hope that as more Chinese adopt a faster-paced, more Westernized lifestyle, they will come to accept convenience foods in the form of canned soup. Backed by a $465,000 ad campaign, Campbell plans to make its product available in about 570 retail food outlets in Guangdong.

To become a major player in the global soup market, Campbell will face stiff competition. British consumers, for example, have known and preferred Heinz canned soups for many years. To attract more British shoppers, Campbell is creating new products developed specifically to meet English tastes. To expand its Japanese distribution from Tokyo and Osaka to include all of Japan, the soupmaker recently entered a joint venture with Nakano Vinegar Company of Japan.

Is the world ready for Campbell's soup? The company's CEO believes the answer is a resounding yes. His considerable international experience—as a former marketing executive with Colgate-Palmolive in South Africa and with Parke-Davis in Hong Kong—tells him that responding to consumer preferences leads to increased sales.[6]

Questions

1. What fundamental behavioral issue is of greatest importance to marketers at Campbell in introducing canned soup to mainland Chinese?
2. Which buyer behavior variables are most likely to influence preferences for soup flavors?
3. Does the type of consumer decision-making process vary from one culture to another when it comes to buying soup? Discuss.

CHAPTER 13

Product and Price

LEARNING OBJECTIVES

After studying this chapter you should be able to

1 Explain what a product is and how products are classified.

2 Discuss the product life cycle and how it leads to new-product development.

3 Define *product line* and *product mix,* and be able to distinguish between the two.

4 Identify the methods available for changing a product mix.

5 Explain the uses and importance of branding, packaging, and labeling.

6 Describe the economic basis of pricing and the means by which sellers can control prices and buyers' perceptions of prices.

7 Identify the major pricing objectives and the methods that businesses use to implement them.

8 Explain the different strategies available to companies as they set basic prices.

CHAPTER PREVIEW

We look first in this chapter at products. We examine product classifications and describe the four stages, or life cycle, through which every product moves. Next we illustrate how firms manage products effectively by modifying or deleting existing products and by developing new products. Branding, packaging, and labeling of products are also discussed. Then our focus shifts to pricing. We explain competitive factors that influence sellers' pricing decisions and also explore buyers' perceptions of prices. After considering organizational objectives that can be accomplished through pricing, we outline several methods for setting prices. Finally, we describe pricing strategies by which sellers can reach target markets successfully.

Birkis: Not Just for Boomers

Whoopi Goldberg wore them in her *Time* magazine photo. Chelsea Clinton wears them to school. Harrison Ford wears them, and so do Keanu Reeves, Kelly McGillis, and Woody Harrelson. What are showing up on so many feet, famous and otherwise? They're Birkenstocks, or "Birkis"—sandals, clogs, and shoes. Once an icon of the 1960s and 1970s, this classic "hippie" gear has become tony fashion footwear.

When Margot Fraser's firm, California-based Birkenstock Footprint Sandals, Inc., became the exclusive importer of the German-made shoe line, Fraser had no marketing plan. The only willing outlets she found were health-food stores, and the only advertising was word of mouth. The Birkenstock family had been making shoes for over two hundred years. However, it wasn't until Fraser brought them to the United States that Americans began enjoying the comfort of the practical two-strap sandal with the funny-shaped sole. At about $80 a pair, the original plain brown sandal remains the company's bestseller. However, Birkenstocks now come in over a hundred styles, fifty colors, and can cost up to about $200 a pair. Available in such trendy hues as fuchsia, cognac, and forest green, and in such exotic styles as Ibiza, Bali, and Sydney, Birkenstocks are showing up on the covers of *GQ* and *Vogue* instead of in the pages of *Mother Jones* and the *Vegetarian Times*.

To overcome its counterculture image and to attract 1990s comfort-seeking consumers and aging baby boomers, Birkenstock's marketing staff developed a strategy that includes an intensified advertising program, an expanded product line, and increased distribution avenues.

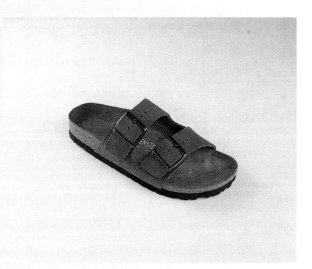

Recently, the company launched its first national sales team. Birki lovers can now buy myriad adult renditions, as well as BirkiKids, a children's line extension, at more than a hundred independent retail outlets, general shoe chains, and department stores including Macy's and Dillard's. They can also order Birkis by mail from L.L. Bean, Sharper Image, and the company's own catalog.

Birkenstock's success has sparked competition in the comfort shoe market. Models from Teva, Mephisto, and Ralph Lauren rival Birkenstock in the upscale price range, and companies like Kinney Shoes, are doing well with very popular $40 to $60 copies. Birkenstock doesn't appear worried about price-conscious shoe shoppers, however. Sales will soon reach $100 million, predicts the company, because people are willing to pay more to get authentic Birkis.

■ ■ ■ ■

■   ■   ■   ■   ■   ■   ■   ■   ■   ■   ■   ■

product everything that one
receives in an exchange,
including all tangible and
intangible attributes and
expected benefits; it may be a
good, service, or idea

A **product** is everything that one receives in an exchange, including all tangible and intangible attributes and expected benefits. A pair of Birkenstocks, for example, includes not only the footwear itself but also care instructions and the status that accrues to the wearer. A car includes a warranty, owner's manual, and perhaps free emergency road service for a year. Some of the intangibles that may go with an automobile include the status associated with ownership and the memories generated from past rides. Developing and managing products effectively is crucial to an organization's ability to maintain successful marketing mixes.

As we noted in Chapter 1, a product may be a good, service, or idea. A *good* is a real, physical thing that we can touch, such as a pair of Birkenstocks. A *service* is the result of applying human or mechanical effort to a person or thing. Basically, a service is a change we pay others to make for us. A real estate agent's services result in a change in the ownership of real property. A barber's services result in a change in your appearance. An *idea* may take the form of philosophies, lessons, concepts, or advice. Often, ideas are included with a good or service. Thus we might buy a book (a good) that provides ideas on how to lose weight. Or we might join Weight Watchers, for both ideas on how to lose weight and help (services) in doing so.

Our definition of the term *product* is based on the concept of an exchange. In a purchase, the product is exchanged for money—an amount of money equal to the *price* of the product. When the product is a good, the price may include such services as delivery, installation, warranties, and training. A good *with* such services is not the same product as the good *without* such services. In other words, sellers set a price for a particular "package" of goods, services, and ideas. When the makeup of that package changes, the price should change as well.

■■ CLASSIFICATION OF PRODUCTS

LEARNING OBJECTIVE 1
Explain what a product is and
how products are classified.

Different classes of products are directed at particular target markets. A product's classification largely determines what kinds of distribution, promotion, and pricing are appropriate in marketing the product.

Products can be grouped into two general categories: consumer and industrial. A product purchased to satisfy personal and family needs is a **consumer product.** A product bought for use in a firm's operations or to make other products is an **industrial product.** The buyer's intent—or the ultimate use of the product—determines the classification of an item. Note that a single item can be both a consumer and an industrial product. A broom is a consumer product if you use it in your home. However, the same broom is an industrial product if you use it in the maintenance of your business. After a product is classified as a consumer or industrial product, it can

consumer product a product
purchased to satisfy personal
and family needs

industrial product a product
bought for use in a firm's
operations or to make other
products

be further categorized as a particular type of consumer or industrial product.

Consumer Product Classifications

The traditional and most widely accepted system of classifying consumer products consists of three categories: convenience, shopping, and specialty products. These groupings are based primarily on characteristics of buyers' purchasing behavior.

convenience product a relatively inexpensive, frequently purchased item for which buyers want to exert only minimal effort

A **convenience product** is a relatively inexpensive, frequently purchased item for which buyers want to exert only minimal effort. Examples include bread, gasoline, newspapers, soft drinks, and chewing gum. The buyer spends little time in planning the purchase of a convenience item or in comparing available brands or sellers.

shopping product an item for which buyers are willing to expend considerable effort on planning and making the purchase

A **shopping product** is an item for which buyers are willing to expend considerable effort on planning and making the purchase. Buyers allocate ample time for comparing stores and brands with respect to prices, product features, qualities, services, and perhaps warranties. Appliances, upholstered furniture, men's suits, bicycles, and cellular phones are examples of shopping products. These products are expected to last for a fairly long time and thus are purchased less frequently than convenience items.

specialty product an item that possesses one or more unique characteristics for which a significant group of buyers is willing to expend considerable purchasing effort

A **specialty product** possesses one or more unique characteristics for which a significant group of buyers is willing to expend considerable purchasing effort. Buyers actually plan the purchase of a specialty product; they know exactly what they want and will not accept a substitute. In searching for specialty products, purchasers do not compare alternatives. Examples

Shopping product. A VCR is usually considered a shopping product because customers are willing to spend time comparing brands, styles, and product features.

include unique sports cars, a specific type of antique dining table, a rare imported beer, or perhaps special handcrafted stereo speakers.

One problem with this approach to classification is that buyers may behave differently when purchasing a specific type of product. Thus, a single product can fit into more than one category. To minimize this problem, marketers think in terms of how buyers are most likely to behave when purchasing a specific item.

Industrial Product Classifications

Based on their characteristics and intended uses, industrial products can be classified into the following categories: raw materials, major equipment, accessory equipment, component parts, process materials, supplies, and services.

A **raw material** is a basic material that actually becomes part of a physical product. It usually comes from mines, forests, oceans, or recycled solid wastes. Raw materials are usually bought and sold according to grades and specifications.

Major equipment includes large tools and machines used for production purposes. Examples of major equipment are lathes, cranes, and stamping machines. Some major equipment is custom-made for a particular organization, but other items are standardized products that perform one or several tasks for many types of organizations.

Accessory equipment is standardized equipment that generally can be used in several ways within a firm's production or office activities. Examples include hand tools, typewriters, fractional-horsepower motors, and calculators. Compared with major equipment, accessory items are usually much less expensive and are purchased routinely with less negotiation.

A **component part** becomes part of a physical product and is either a finished item ready for assembly or a product that needs little processing before assembly. Although it becomes part of a larger product, a component part can often be identified easily. Clocks, tires, and switches are examples of component parts.

A **process material** is used directly in the production of another product; unlike a component part, however, a process material is not readily identifiable. Like component parts, process materials are purchased according to industry standards or to the specifications of the individual purchaser. Examples include industrial glue and food preservatives.

A **supply** facilitates production and operations, but it does not become part of the finished product. Paper, pencils, oils, and cleaning agents are examples.

An **industrial service** is an intangible product that an organization uses in its operations. Examples include financial, legal, marketing research, and janitorial services. Purchasers must decide whether to provide their own services internally or to hire them from outside the organization.

raw material a basic material that actually becomes part of a physical product; usually comes from mines, forests, oceans, or recycled solid wastes

major equipment large tools and machines used for production purposes

accessory equipment standardized equipment used in a variety of ways in a firm's production or office activities

component part an item that becomes part of a physical product and is either a finished item ready for assembly or a product that needs little processing before assembly

process material a material that is used directly in the production of another product and is not readily identifiable in the finished product

supply an item that facilitates production and operations but does not become part of the finished product

industrial service an intangible product that an organization uses in its operations

■■ THE PRODUCT LIFE CYCLE

LEARNING OBJECTIVE 2
Discuss the product life cycle and how it leads to new-product development.

In a way, products are like people. They are born, they live, and they die. Every product progresses through a **product life cycle,** which is a series of

product life cycle a series of stages in which a product's sales revenue and profit increase, reach a peak, and then decline

stages in which its sales revenue and profit increase, reach a peak, and then decline. A firm must be able to launch, modify, and delete products from its offering of products in response to changes in product life cycles. Otherwise, the firm's profit will disappear and the firm will fail. Depending on the product, life cycle stages will vary in length. In this section, we discuss the stages of the life cycle and how marketers can use this information.

Stages of the Product Life Cycle

Generally the product life cycle is assumed to be composed of four stages—introduction, growth, maturity, and decline—as shown in Figure 13.1. Some products progress through these stages rapidly, in a few weeks or months. Others may take years to go through each stage. The Rubicks Cube had a relatively short life cycle. Parker Brothers' *Monopoly* game, which was introduced over fifty years ago, is still going strong.

Introduction   In the *introduction stage,* customer awareness and acceptance of the product are low. Sales rise gradually as a result of promotion and distribution activities, but initially high development and marketing costs result in low profit, or even in a loss. There are relatively few competitors. The price is sometimes high, and purchasers are primarily people who want to be "the first on their block" to own the new product. The marketing challenge at this stage is to make potential customers aware of the product's existence and its features, benefits, and uses.

A new product is seldom an immediate success. Marketers must watch early buying patterns carefully and be prepared to modify the new product promptly if necessary. The product should be priced to attract the particular market segment that has the greatest desire and ability to buy the product. Plans for distribution and promotion should suit the targeted market segment. As with the product itself, the initial price, distribution channels, and promotional efforts may need to be adjusted quickly to maintain sales growth during the introduction stage.

FIGURE 13.1
Product Life Cycle
The graph shows sales volume and profits during the life cycle of a product. *(Source: Adapted from William M. Pride and O. C. Ferrell,* Marketing: Concepts and Strategies, Ninth Edition. *Copyright © 1995 by Houghton Mifflin Company. Used by permission.)*

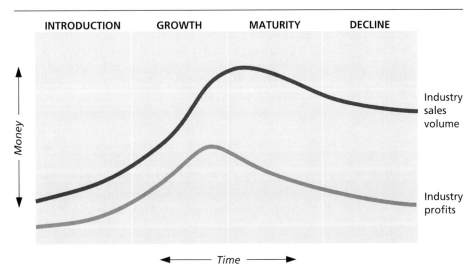

Growth   In the *growth stage,* sales increase rapidly as the product becomes well known. Other firms have probably begun to market competing products. The competition and lower unit costs (due to mass production) result in a lower price, which reduces the profit per unit. Note that industry profits reach a peak and begin to decline during this stage. To meet the needs of the growing market, the originating firm offers modified versions of its product and expands its distribution. The 3M Company, the maker of Post-it Notes, has developed a variety of sizes, colors, and designs.

Management's goal in the growth stage is to stabilize and strengthen the product's position by encouraging brand loyalty. To beat the competition, the company may further improve the product or expand the product line to appeal to specialized market segments. Management may also compete by lowering prices if increased production efficiency has resulted in savings for the company. As the product becomes more widely accepted, marketers may be able to broaden the network of distributors. Marketers can also emphasize customer service and prompt credit for defective products. During this period promotional efforts attempt to build brand loyalty among customers.

Maturity   Sales are still increasing at the beginning of the *maturity stage,* but the rate of increase has slowed. Later in this stage the sales curve peaks and begins to decline. Industry profits decline throughout this stage. Dealers' product lines are simplified, markets are segmented more carefully, and price competition increases. The increased competition forces weaker competitors to leave the industry. Refinements and extensions of the original product continue to appear on the market.

During a product's maturity stage, its market share may be strengthened by redesigned packaging or style changes. Also, consumers may be encouraged to use the product more often or in new ways. Pricing strategies are flexible during this stage. Markdowns and price incentives are not uncommon, although price increases may work to offset production and distribution costs. Marketers may offer incentives and assistance of various kinds to dealers to encourage them to support mature products, especially in the face of competition from private-label brands. New promotional efforts and aggressive personal selling may be necessary during this period of intense competition.

Decline   During the *decline stage,* sales volume decreases sharply. Profits continue to fall. The number of competing firms declines, and the only survivors in the marketplace are those firms that specialize in marketing the product. Production and marketing costs become the most important determinant of profit.

When a product adds to the success of the overall product line, the company may retain it; otherwise, management must determine when to eliminate the product. A product usually declines because of technological advances or environmental factors, or because consumers have switched to competing brands. Therefore, few changes are made in the product itself during this stage. Instead, management may raise the price to cover costs, reprice to maintain market share, or lower the price to reduce inventory. Similarly, management will narrow distribution of the declining product to the most profitable existing markets. During this period the company will not give the product a lot of promotion, although the firm may use advertising and sales incentives to slow the product's decline. The company may choose to eliminate less profitable versions of the product from the product line and, eventually, may decide to drop the product entirely.

Using the Product Life Cycle

Marketers should be aware of the life-cycle stage of each product they are responsible for. And they should try to estimate how long the product is expected to remain in that stage. Both must be taken into account in making decisions about the marketing strategy for a product. If a product is expected to remain in the maturity stage for a long time, a replacement product might be introduced later in the maturity stage. If the maturity stage is expected to be short, however, a new product should be introduced much earlier. In some cases, a firm may be willing to take the chance of speeding up the decline of existing products. In other situations, a company will attempt to extend a product's life cycle. For example, General Mills, Inc., has extended the life of Bisquick baking mix (launched in the mid-1930s) by significantly improving the product's formulation.

■■ PRODUCT LINE AND PRODUCT MIX

LEARNING OBJECTIVE 3
Define *product line* and *product mix*, and be able to distinguish between the two.

product line   a group of similar products that differ only in relatively minor characteristics

product mix   all the products that a firm offers for sale

In Chapter 8, a **product line** was defined as a group of similar products that differ only in relatively minor characteristics. Generally, the products within a product line are related to each other in the way they are produced, marketed, or used. Procter & Gamble, for example, manufactures and markets several shampoos including Prell, Head & Shoulders, Pert Plus, and Ivory.

Many organizations tend to introduce new products within existing product lines. This permits them to apply the experience and knowledge that they have acquired to the production and marketing of new products. Other firms develop entirely new product lines.

A firm's **product mix** consists of all the products that the firm offers for sale. Two "dimensions" are often applied to a firm's product mix. The *width* of the mix is a measure of the number of product lines it contains. The *depth* of the mix is a measure of the average number of individual products within each line. These are somewhat vague measures; we speak of a *broad* or a *narrow* mix, rather than a mix of exactly three or five product lines.

Many firms seek new products that will broaden their product mix, just as Kodak has done with digital cameras. By developing new product lines, firms gain additional experience and expertise. Moreover, firms achieve stability by operating within several different markets. Problems in one particular market do not affect a multiline firm nearly as much as they would affect a firm that depended entirely on a single product line.

■■ MANAGING THE PRODUCT MIX

LEARNING OBJECTIVE 4
Identify the methods available for changing a product mix.

To provide products that both satisfy people in a firm's target market or markets and achieve the organization's objectives, a marketer must develop, adjust, and maintain an effective product mix. Seldom can the same product mix be effective for long. Because customers' product preferences and attitudes change, their desire for a product may diminish or grow. In some cases, a firm needs to alter its product mix to adapt to competition. A marketer may have to eliminate a product from the mix because one or more competitors dominate that product's specific market segment. Similarly, an organization may have to introduce a new product or modify an existing one to compete more effectively. A marketer may expand the firm's product mix to take advantage of excess marketing and production capacity. For whatever reason a product mix is altered, the product mix must be managed to bring about improvements in the mix. There are three major ways to improve a product mix: change an existing product, delete a product, or develop a new product.

Changing Existing Products

product modification   the process of changing one or more of a product's characteristics

Product modification refers to changing one or more of a product's characteristics. For this approach to be effective, several conditions must be met. First, the product must be modifiable. Second, existing customers must be able to perceive that a modification has been made, assuming that the modified item is still directed at the same target market. Third, the modification should make the product more consistent with customers' desires so that it provides greater satisfaction.

Existing products can be altered in three primary ways: in quality, function, and aesthetics. *Quality modifications* are changes that relate to a product's dependability and durability and are usually achieved by alterations in

Changing existing products. Kraft, the maker of Velveeta, has modified an existing product to make it more attractive to customers seeking reduced-fat products.

■ ■ ■ ■ **BUSINESS JOURNAL**

Lo and Behold, It's the Wonderbra!

With all the hoopla of a Hollywood premiere, Playtex, a division of Sara Lee Corp., introduced the Wonderbra. While Wonderbra's marketing manager celebrated its benefits on the *Phil Donahue Show*, armored vehicles delivered the first shipment to three upscale New York department stores. Macy's sold one Wonderbra every fifteen seconds, and many stores had to limit sales to one per customer. What is this underwear item that is causing such a sensation? Likened to a suspension bridge with padding, the Wonderbra is a high-tech bra with forty-six wire, lace, and fabric components that simultaneously push in and push up. Said superthin supermodel Kate Moss of Wonderbras, "I swear, even I can get cleavage with them."

What is making so many women eager to wear a bra that lifts, separates, and creates drop-dead cleavage? Some women concede that they are eager to buy a product that can give them fuller looking breasts without the potential dangers of silicon implants. Aging baby boomers are looking for ways to counteract gravity's relentless pull. Whatever the reasons for their popularity, Playtex is taking advantage of the opportunity to boost U.S. bra sales, which have been flat for years.

To promote the Wonderbra, which comes in sizes 32A to 36C and sells for about $26, Playtex launched a multimillion dollar print and billboard campaign. Double-page ads in *Vanity Fair*, *Mademoiselle*, *Cosmopolitan*, *Vogue*, and *Glamour* feature the Wonderbra model and ask, "Who Cares If It's a Bad Hair Day?" Traffic-stopping billboards in Los Angeles, San Francisco, Miami, Houston, and six other major U.S. cities bear the model and the motto, "Hello Boys." Playtex is even selling posters of the Wonderbra Girl through student catalogs.

Playtex's all-out advertising efforts are part of Wonderbra's frontal assault in what has become the battle of the bras. Its major competitor is the British Super-Uplift bra, whose campaign slogans include "Lock up your sons" and "Say goodbye to your feet." When Super-Uplift made its American debut, department stores sold 1 million in three months. Victoria's Secret offers women the Miracle Bra, promoting it with a television campaign designed to build brand identity. With the tag line, "No other bra measures up," Miracle Bra promises women that they will appear one full size larger. Other contenders in the "clash of the cleavagemakers" include Loveable's IncrediBra, Vanity Fair's It Must Be Magic, Lily's La Lift, and similarly tempting offerings from Warner and Maidenform.

According to the Intimate Apparel Council, push-up bras make up about 10 percent of U.S. bra sales. Playtex believes that Wonderbra will improve that figure. In addition, by bringing back the bra, the firm hopes it has launched a U.S. underwear renaissance. The company plans to make the Wonderbra the first in a whole Wonder line of products, including the bulge-battling Wonder Girdle.

the materials or production process. *Functional modifications* affect a product's versatility, effectiveness, convenience, or safety; they usually require redesign of the product. Typical product categories that have undergone extensive functional modifications include home appliances, office and farm equipment, and consumer electronics. *Aesthetic modifications* are directed at changing the sensory appeal of a product by altering its taste, texture, sound, smell, or visual characteristics. Because a buyer's purchasing decision is affected by how a product looks, smells, tastes, feels, or sounds, an aesthetic modification may have a definite impact on purchases. Through aesthetic modifications, a firm can differentiate its product from competing brands and perhaps gain a sizable market share if customers find the modified product more appealing.

Deleting Products

product deletion the elimination of one or more products from a product line

To maintain an effective product mix, an organization often has to eliminate some products. This is called **product deletion.** A weak product costs a firm too much time, money, and resources that could be available for modifying other products or developing new ones. Also, when a weak product generates an unfavorable image among customers, the negative image may rub off on other products sold by the firm.

Most organizations find it difficult to delete a product. Some firms drop weak products only after they have become severe financial burdens. A better approach is some form of systematic review of the product's impact on the overall effectiveness of a firm's product mix. Such a review should analyze a product's contribution to a company's sales for a given period. It should include estimates of future sales, costs, and profits associated with the product and a consideration of whether changes in the marketing strategy could improve the product's performance.

A product deletion program can definitely improve a firm's performance. For example, Del Monte once claimed that it had the largest assortment of canned fruits and vegetables nationally. The company recently deleted a number of items and significantly improved the firm's profitability.

Developing New Products

Developing and introducing new products is frequently time-consuming, expensive, and risky. Thousands of new products are introduced annually. Depending on how we define it, the failure rate for new products ranges between 60 and 75 percent. Although developing new products is risky, failing to introduce new products can be just as hazardous. New products are generally grouped into three categories on the basis of their degree of similarity to existing products. *Imitations* are products that are designed to be similar to—and to compete with—existing products of other firms. Examples are the various brands of fluoride toothpaste that were developed to compete with Crest. *Adaptations* are variations of existing products that are intended for an established market. Caffeine-free, diet soft drinks are product adaptations. Product refinements and extensions are most often considered adaptations, although imitative products may also include some refinement and extension. *Innovations* are entirely new products. They may give rise to a new industry (such as xerography or television) or revolutionize an existing one. The introduction of sound tracks, for example, permanently changed the motion picture industry. Similarly, compact discs have brought major changes to the recording industry. Innovative products take considerable time, effort, and money to develop. They are therefore less common than adaptations and imitations.

Before a new product is introduced, it goes through seven phases. Figure 13.2 depicts the evolutionary nature of new-product development.

Idea Generation Idea generation involves looking for product ideas that will help a firm achieve its objectives. Although some organizations get their ideas almost by chance, firms trying to maximize product mix effectiveness usually develop systematic approaches for generating new-product ideas. Ideas may come from marketing managers, researchers, engineers, competitors, advertising agencies, management consultants, private research organizations, or customers.

Screening During screening, ideas that do not match organizational resources and objectives are rejected. At this stage, firms must ask whether they have the expertise to develop and market a product. Management may reject a good idea because the company lacks needed skills and abilities. The largest number of product ideas are rejected during the screening phase.

Concept Testing Concept testing is a phase in which a product idea is presented to a small sample of potential buyers through a written or oral description (and perhaps a few drawings) to determine their attitudes and initial buying intentions regarding the product. For a single product idea, an organization can test one or several concepts of the same product. Concept

FIGURE 13.2 Phases of New-Product Development
Generally, marketers follow these seven steps to develop a new product. *(Source: Adapted from William M. Pride and O. C. Ferrell,* Marketing: Concepts and Strategies, Ninth Edition. *Copyright © 1995 by Houghton Mifflin Company. Used by permission.)*

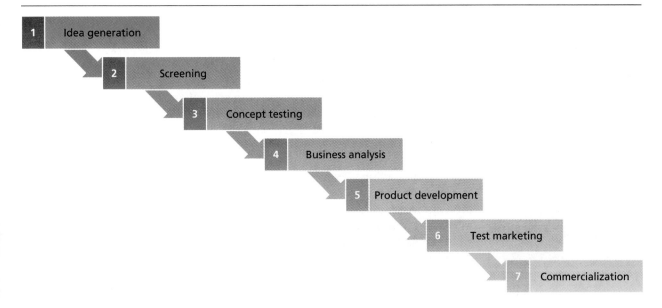

testing is a low-cost means for an organization to determine consumers' initial reactions to a product idea prior to investing considerable resources in product research and development. Product development personnel can use the results of concept testing to improve product attributes and product benefits that are most important to potential customers. The types of questions asked vary considerably depending on the type of product idea being tested. The following are typical questions:

- Which benefits of the proposed product are especially attractive to you?
- Which features are of little or no interest to you?
- What are the primary advantages of the proposed product over the one you currently use?
- If this product were available at an appropriate price, how often would you buy it?
- How could this proposed product be improved?

Business Analysis   Business analysis provides a tentative outline of a product's position in the marketplace, including its probable profitability. During this stage, the firm considers how the new product, if it were introduced, would affect the firm's sales, costs, and profits. Marketing personnel usually work up preliminary sales and cost projections at this point, with the help of R&D and production managers.

Product Development   In the product development phase, the company must find out first if it is technically feasible to produce the product and then if the product can be made at costs low enough to justify a reasonable price. If a product idea makes it to this point, it is transformed into a working model, or *prototype*.

Test Marketing   Test marketing is the limited introduction of a product in several towns or cities chosen to represent the intended market. Its aim is to determine buyers' probable reactions. The product is left in the test markets long enough to give buyers a chance to repurchase the product if they are so inclined. Marketers can experiment with advertising, pricing, and packaging in different test areas and can measure the extent of brand awareness, brand switching, and repeat purchases that result from alterations in the marketing mix.

Commercialization   During commercialization, plans for full-scale manufacturing and marketing must be refined and completed, and budgets for the project must be prepared. In the early part of the commercialization phase, marketing management analyzes the results of test marketing to find out what changes in the marketing mix are needed before the product is introduced. The results of test marketing may tell the marketers, for example, to change one or more of the product's physical attributes, to modify the distribution plans to include more retail outlets, to alter promotional efforts, or

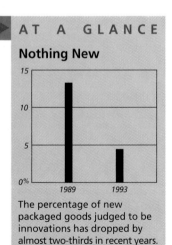

▶ ▶ ▶ **AT A GLANCE**

Nothing New

The percentage of new packaged goods judged to be innovations has dropped by almost two-thirds in recent years.

Source: Superbrands 1995; Adweek Magazine Supplement.

to change the product's price. Products are not usually introduced nation-wide overnight. Most new products are marketed in stages, beginning in selected geographic areas and expanding into adjacent areas over a period of time.

Why Do Products Fail?   In spite of this rigorous process for developing product ideas, the majority of new products end up as failures. In fact, many well-known companies have produced market failures (see Table 13.1).

Why does a new product fail? Mainly because the product and its marketing program are not planned and tested as completely as they should be. For example, to save on development costs, a firm may market-test its product but not its entire marketing mix. Or a firm may market a new product before all the "bugs" have been worked out. Or, when problems show up in the testing stage, a firm may try to recover its product development costs by pushing ahead with full-scale marketing anyway. Finally, some firms try to market new products with inadequate financing.

▮▮ BRANDING, PACKAGING, AND LABELING

LEARNING OBJECTIVE 5
Explain the uses and importance of branding, packaging, and labeling.

Three important features of a product (particularly a consumer product) are its brand, package, and label. These features may be used to associate a product with a successful product line or to distinguish it from existing products. They may be designed to attract customers at the point of sale or to provide information to potential purchasers. Because the brand, package, and label are very real parts of the product, they deserve careful attention during product planning.

TABLE 13.1   Examples of Product Failures

Company	Product
Hunt-Wesson Foods, Inc.	Fresh and Lite low-fat frozen Chinese entrees
RCA	VideoDisc player
Time Warner Inc.	*TV-Cable Week*
The Coca-Cola Company	Tiny soda fountain for office use
NeXT Inc.	Optical drive personal computer
General Motors Corp.	Cadillac Allante luxury sedan
Huffy Corp.	Cross Sport light mountain bike
BIC Corp.	$5 glass flask perfume
Anheuser-Busch Companies	Bud Dry and Michelob Dry beer
Colgate-Palmolive Co.	Fab 1-Shot laundry detergent
Campbell Soup Co.	Fresh Chef fresh salads and soups
Pepsico, Inc.	Pepsi A.M. cola
Polaroid	Polavision camera
IBM	PCjr personal computer
NutraSweet	Simplesse fat substitute
RJR Nabisco, Inc.	Premier smokeless cigarettes

Sources: Christopher Power, "Flops," *Business Week,* Aug. 16, 1993, pp. 76–82; and Cyndee Miller, "Little Relief Seen for New Products Failure Rate," *Marketing News,* June 21, 1993, pp. 1, 10, 11.

What Is a Brand?

brand   a name, term, symbol, design, or any combination of these that identifies a seller's products as distinct from those of other sellers

brand name   the part of a brand that can be spoken

brand mark   the part of a brand that is a symbol or distinctive design

trademark   a brand name or brand mark that is registered with the U.S. Patent and Trademark Office and is thus legally protected from use by anyone except its owner

trade name   the complete and legal name of an organization

manufacturer (or producer) brand   a brand that is owned by a manufacturer

store (or private) brand   a brand that is owned by an individual wholesaler or retailer

A **brand** is a name, term, symbol, design, or any combination of these that identifies a seller's products as distinct from those of other sellers.[2] A **brand name** is the part of a brand that can be spoken. It may include letters, words, numbers, or pronounceable symbols, like the ampersand in *Procter & Gamble*. A **brand mark,** on the other hand, is the part of a brand that is a symbol or distinctive design, like Planters' "Mr. Peanut." A **trademark** is a brand name or brand mark that is registered with the U.S. Patent and Trademark Office and is thus legally protected from use by anyone except its owner. A **trade name** is the complete and legal name of an organization, such as Pizza Hut or Houghton Mifflin Company (the publisher of this text).

Brands are often classified according to who owns them: manufacturers or stores. A **manufacturer** (or **producer**) **brand,** as the name implies, is a brand that is owned by a manufacturer. The majority of foods (Frosted Flakes), major appliances (Whirlpool), gasolines (Exxon), automobiles (Honda), and clothing (Levis), are sold with producer branding. Many consumers prefer producer brands because they are nationally known, offer consistent quality, and are widely available.

A **store** (or **private**) **brand** is one that is owned by an individual wholesaler or retailer. Among the better-known store brands are Kenmore and Craftsman, both owned by Sears, Roebuck and Co. Owners of store brands claim that they can offer lower prices, earn greater profits, and improve customer loyalty with their own brands. Companies that manufacture a private brand often find such operations to be profitable because they can use excess capacity and at the same time avoid most marketing costs. About one-third of all tire, food, and appliance sales are of store-branded items.

Manufacturer brand. Hewlett Packard is a manufacturer brand. The symbol with the HP to the left of the brand is the company's brand mark.

Consumer confidence is the most important element in the success of a branded product, whether the brand is owned by a producer or a retailer. Because branding identifies each product completely, customers can easily repurchase products that provide satisfaction, performance, and quality. And they can just as easily avoid or ignore products that do not. In supermarkets, the products most likely to keep their shelf space are the brands with large market shares and strong customer loyalty.

generic product (or brand)
a product with no brand at all

A **generic product** (sometimes called a **generic brand**) is a product with no brand at all. Its plain package carries only the name of the product—applesauce, peanut butter, potato chips, or whatever—in black type. Generic products, available in supermarkets since 1977, usually are made by the major producers that manufacture name brands. They appeal mainly to consumers who are willing to sacrifice consistency in size or quality for a lower price. However, generic products are not necessarily lower in quality. Even though generic brands may have accounted for as much as 10 percent of all grocery sales several years ago, they currently represent less than 1 percent.

Choosing and Protecting a Brand

A number of issues should be considered when selecting a brand name. The name should be easy for customers to say, spell, and recall. Short, one-syllable names such as *Tide* often satisfy this requirement. The brand name should suggest, in a positive way, the product's uses, special characteristics, and major benefits and should be distinctive enough to set it apart from competing brands. Choosing the right brand name has become a challenge because many obvious product names have already been used. In 1993, the U.S. Patent and Trademark office registered 34,349 new trademarks.

It is important to select a brand that can be protected through registration, reserving it for exclusive use by a specific firm. Some brands, because of their designs, are more easily infringed on than others. Although registration protects trademarks domestically for ten years and can be renewed indefinitely, a firm should develop a system for ensuring that its trademarks will be renewed as needed. To protect its exclusive right to the brand, the company must ensure that the selected brand will not be considered an infringement on any existing brand already registered with the U.S. Patent and Trademark Office. This task may be complicated by the fact that infringement is determined by the courts, which base their decisions on whether a brand causes consumers to be confused, mistaken, or deceived about the source of the product.

A firm must guard against a brand name becoming a generic term that refers to a general category. Generic terms cannot be protected as exclusive brand names. For example, names such as *yo-yo, aspirin, escalator,* and *thermos*—all exclusively brand names at one time—were eventually declared generic terms that refer to product classes. As such, they could no longer be protected. To ensure that a brand name does not become a generic term, the firm should spell the name with a capital letter and use it as an adjective to modify the name of the general product class, as in Jell-O Brand Gelatin. An organization can deal directly with this problem by advertising that its brand is a trademark and should not be used generically. Firms can also use the registered trademark symbol ® to indicate that the brand is trademarked.

Branding Strategies

The basic branding decision for any firm—producer or seller—is whether to brand its products. A producer may market its products under its own brands, private brands, or both. A seller (store) may carry only producer brands, its own brands, or both. Once either type of firm decides to brand, it chooses one of two branding strategies: individual branding or family branding.

individual branding the strategy in which a firm uses a different brand for each of its products

   Individual branding is the strategy in which a firm uses a different brand for each of its products. For example, Procter & Gamble uses individual branding for its line of bar soaps, which includes Ivory, Camay, Lava, Zest, Safeguard, and Coast. Individual branding offers two major advantages. A problem with one product will not affect the good name of the firm's other products. And the different brands can be directed toward different market segments. For example, Holiday Inns' Hampton Inns are directed toward budget-minded travelers, Residence Inns toward apartment dwellers, and Crown Plazas toward upscale customers.

family branding the strategy in which a firm uses the same brand for all or most of its products

   Family branding is the strategy in which a firm uses the same brand for all or most of its products. Sony, General Electric, IBM, and Xerox use family branding for their entire product mix. A major advantage of family branding is that the promotion of any one item that carries the family brand tends to help all other products with the same brand name. In addition, new products have a head start when their brand name is already known and accepted by customers.

Packaging

packaging all the activities involved in developing and providing a container for a product

Packaging consists of all the activities involved in developing and providing a container for a product. The package is a vital part of the product. It can make the product more versatile, safer, or easier to use. Through its shape, appearance, and printed message, a package can influence purchasing decisions.

Packaging Functions   Effective packaging means more than simply putting products in containers and covering them with wrappers. The basic function of packaging materials is to protect the product and maintain its functional form. Fluids such as milk, orange juice, and hair spray need packages that preserve and protect them; the packaging should prevent damage that could affect the product's usefulness and increase costs. Since product tampering has become a problem for marketers of many types of goods, several packaging techniques have been developed to counter this danger. Some packages are also designed to foil shoplifting.

   Another function of packaging is to offer consumer convenience. For example, small aseptic packages—individual-serving boxes or plastic bags that contain liquids and do not require refrigeration—appeal strongly to children and to young adults with active lifestyles. The size or shape of a package may relate to the product's storage, convenience of use, or replacement rate. Small, single-serving cans of vegetables, for instance, may prevent waste and make storage easier. A third function of packaging is to promote a product by communicating its features, uses, benefits, and image. Sometimes, a firm develops a reusable package to make the product more desirable. For example, the Cool Whip package doubles as a food-storage container.

Package Design Considerations   Many factors must be weighed when developing packages. Obviously, one major consideration is cost. Although a variety of packaging materials, processes, and designs are available, some are rather expensive. In recent years, buyers have shown a willingness to pay more for improved packaging, but there are limits.

Marketers must also decide whether to package the product in single or multiple units. Multiple-unit packaging can increase demand by increasing the amount of the product available at the point of consumption (in the home, for example). However, multiple-unit packaging does not work for infrequently used products because buyers do not like to tie up their dollars in an excess supply or to store these products for a long time. Multiple-unit packaging can, however, make storage and handling easier (as in the case of six-packs used for soft drinks); it can also facilitate special price offers, such as two-for-one sales. In addition, multiple-unit packaging may increase consumer acceptance of a product by encouraging the buyer to try it several times. On the other hand, customers may hesitate to try the product at all if they do not have the option to buy just one.

Marketers should consider how much consistency is desirable among an organization's package designs. To promote an overall company image, a firm may decide that all packages must be similar or include one major element of the design. This approach, called *family packaging,* is sometimes used only for lines of products, as with Campbell's soups, Weight Watchers entrees, and Planters nuts. The best policy is sometimes no consistency, especially if a firm's products are unrelated or aimed at vastly different markets.

Packages also play an important promotional role. Through verbal and nonverbal symbols, the package can inform potential buyers about the product's content, uses, features, advantages, and hazards. Firms can create desirable images and associations by choosing particular colors, designs, shapes, and textures. Many cosmetics manufacturers, for example, design their packages to create impressions of richness, luxury, and exclusiveness. The package performs another promotional function when it is designed to be safer or more convenient to use, if such features help stimulate demand.

Packaging must also meet the needs of intermediaries. Wholesalers and retailers consider whether a package facilitates transportation, handling, and storage. Resellers may refuse to carry certain products if their packages are cumbersome.

Finally, firms must consider the issue of environmental responsibility when developing packages. Companies must balance consumers' desires for convenience against desires to preserve the environment. Nearly 50 percent of all garbage consists of discarded plastic packaging, such as Styrofoam containers, plastic soft-drink bottles, carryout bags, and other packaging.

■ ■ ■ ■ GLOBAL PERSPECTIVES

Marketing Food Around the World

In Bucharest, Romania, a young couple looks forward to a quiet evening at home. They prepare a traditional homemade Romanian dinner of stuffed cabbage and sit down to watch not-so-traditional MTV and *Beverly Hills, 90210.* Even though American cuisine is not as popular overseas as American television, this couple could soon be substituting frozen pizza or microwaveable burritos for cabbage. Consumers around the world want more and better packaged foods, and U.S. food companies such as Coca-Cola, Campbell Soup, Tropicana, and Gerber Baby Food, just to name a few, are eager to supply it.

To succeed in global food marketing takes more than knowing a little of the local language. Companies need to be aware of the tastes, traditions, and taboos of each of their markets. The Foreign Agricultural Services, a division of the United States Department of Agriculture, offers some general advice to those companies venturing into foreign food markets. First and foremost, the agency recommends that food producers do marketing research in those countries in which they are involved, learning much about the market and the culture that will be the target of their products. To gather information on competitors, U.S. food producers should participate in foreign trade shows. To find out if consumers want what they have to sell, producers should test-market their products in individual countries. Finally, the agency suggests getting to know local agents and distributors.

What many food producers discover is that almost every country has its own special tastes, as well as specific food labeling and packaging regulations. In the Netherlands, spicy Tex-Mex foods are big sellers, and in Denmark, demand is increasing for low-fat foods like turkey and chicken. In Singapore, consumers are hungry for bite-size snack foods like chips, candy, popcorn, and crackers, which they can buy everywhere from gourmet supermarkets to the corner gas station. Polish consumers crave American packaged food, but the government requires that products of U.S. origin be clearly marked and all labels be in Polish. Canadian labeling must be in both French and English, and all weights must be shown in metric units. In Switzerland, home to some of the world's finest cooking schools, specialty products face a very competitive market.

CPC International, Inc., maker of Knorr soups, Hellman's mayonnaise, and Skippy peanut butter, has been extremely successful in marketing foods all over the world. Buying nearly fifty food companies from Uruguay to Ireland has certainly made catering to local tastes easier. But even with its American brands, CPC pays close attention to national taste differences. For example, in Brazil, Hellman's mayonnaise is more lemony; in Britain, it's more vinegary. Consumers in Thailand prefer Knorr soup's "tom yam" bouillon cubes to the more familiar chicken flavor.

International markets for food are opening fast. Those food companies that tailor their products and marketing efforts to specific cultural needs will win the hearts and stomachs of hungry global consumers. Gerber Baby Food understands that principle: Gerber makes baby food sardines for Japanese babies and baby food artichokes for babies in France.

Plastic packaging material is not biodegradable, and paper necessitates destruction of valuable forest lands. Consequently, many companies are exploring packaging alternatives and recycling more materials.

Labeling

labeling   the presentation of information on a product or its package

Labeling is the presentation of information on a product or its package. The *label* is the part that contains the information. This information may include the brand name and mark, the registered-trademark symbol ®, the package size and contents, product claims, directions for use and safety precautions, a list of ingredients, the name and address of the manufacturer, and the Universal Product Code symbol, which is used for automated check-out and inventory control.

A number of federal regulations specify information that *must* be included in the labeling for certain products; for example,

- Garments must be labeled with the name of the manufacturer, country of manufacture, fabric content, and cleaning instructions;
- Any food product for which a nutritional claim is made must have nutrition labeling that follows a standard format;
- Food product labels must state the number of servings per container, the serving size, the number of calories per serving, the number of calories derived from fat, and amounts of specific nutrients;
- Nonedible items such as shampoos and detergents must carry safety precautions as well as instructions for their use.

Such regulations are aimed at protecting the consumer from both misleading product claims and the improper (and thus unsafe) use of products.

express warranty   a written explanation of the responsibilities of the producer in the event that the product is found to be defective or otherwise unsatisfactory

Labels may also carry the details of written or express warranties. An **express warranty** is a written explanation of the responsibilities of the producer in the event that the product is found to be defective or otherwise unsatisfactory. As a result of consumer discontent (along with some federal legislation), firms have begun to simplify the wording of warranties and to extend their duration. The L.L. Bean warranty states, "Our products are guaranteed to give 100% satisfaction in every way. Return anything purchased from us at any time if it proves otherwise. We will replace it, refund your purchase price or credit your credit card, as you wish."

■■ PRICING PRODUCTS

LEARNING OBJECTIVE 6
Describe the economic basis of pricing and the means by which sellers can control prices and buyers' perceptions of prices.

You should now realize that a product is more than a thing that we can touch or a change that we can see. Rather, a product is a set of attributes and benefits that has been carefully designed to satisfy its market while earning a profit for its seller. But no matter how well a product is designed, it cannot perform its function if it is priced incorrectly. Few people will purchase a product with too high a price, and a product with too low a price will earn little or no profit. Somewhere between too high and too low there is a "proper," effective price for each product. Let's take a closer look at how businesses go about determining a product's right price.

The Meaning and Use of Price

price   the amount of money that a seller is willing to accept in exchange for a product, at a given time and under given circumstances

The **price** of a product is the amount of money that a seller is willing to accept in exchange for the product, at a given time and under given circumstances. At times, the price results from negotiations between buyer and seller. But in many business situations, the price is fixed by the seller. Suppose a seller sets a price of $10 for a particular product. In essence, the seller is saying, "Anyone who wants this product can have it here and now, in exchange for $10."

Each interested buyer then makes a personal judgment regarding the utility of the product, often in terms of some dollar value. A particular person who feels that he or she will get at least $10 worth of want satisfaction (or value) from the product is likely to buy it. But if that person can get more want satisfaction by spending $10 in some other way, he or she will not buy it.

Price thus serves the function of *allocator.* First, it allocates goods and services among those who are willing and able to buy them. (As we noted in Chapter 1, the answer to the economic question "For whom to produce?" depends primarily on prices.) Second, price allocates financial resources (sales revenue) among producers according to how well they satisfy customers' needs. And third, price helps customers to allocate their own financial resources among various want-satisfying products.

Can Firms Control Their Prices?

To focus on the extent to which firms can control their prices, we must take another look at the forces of supply and demand and the actions of firms in a real economy.

supply the quantity of a product that producers are willing to sell at each of various prices

Supply and Demand—Once Again   In Chapter 1, we defined the **supply** of a product as the quantity of the product that producers are willing to sell at each of various prices. We can draw a graph of the supply relationship for a particular product, say, jeans (see the left graph of Figure 13.3). Note that the quantity supplied by producers *increases* as the price increases along this *supply curve.*

demand the quantity of a product that buyers are willing to purchase at each of various prices

As defined in Chapter 1, the **demand** for a product is the quantity that buyers are willing to purchase at each of various prices. We can also draw a graph of the demand relationship (see the middle graph of Figure 13.3).

FIGURE 13.3
Supply and Demand Curves
Supply curve *(left):* The upward slope means that producers will supply more jeans at higher prices. **Demand curve *(middle):*** The downward slope (to the right) means that buyers will purchase fewer jeans at higher prices. **Supply and demand curves together *(right):*** Point E indicates equilibrium in quantity and price for both sellers and buyers.

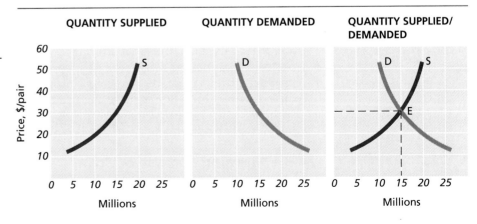

How to Get a Good Price

At the supermarket, you don't bargain with the butcher over the price of hamburger. At Wal-Mart, you don't negotiate with the manager over the price of shampoo. However, when you go to a garage sale or a flea market, haggling over prices is part of the fun. You want to come away feeling that you got a good deal. When it comes to more serious purchases, getting a good deal is even more important, especially with the rising cost of products and services. To get the best bargain, take note of these money-saving strategies.

BUYING A CAR

You walk into the showroom, and there before your eyes is the car of your dreams. You walk over and look at the sticker price in the window. Before you walk out the door and buy a bicycle instead, remember: that's the price of the dealer's dreams. If you plan and negotiate well, you can shave hundreds, even thousands, of dollars off the sticker price.

- Buy at the right time of year: buying late in the model year can lower the price up to 5 percent.
- Negotiate up from the dealer's invoice price (the price the dealer paid), not down from the sticker price. You can get the car's cost to the dealer from sources such as *Edmund's New Car Prices*.
- Get your car loan from a credit union: banks charge about 1 percent more interest, and dealers even more.
- Look for a dealer that offers value pricing: the price is set and includes a package of several popular options such as air-conditioning and automatic transmission.

BUYING A HOUSE

A house is probably the biggest purchase you will ever make. According to financial planners, most first-time buyers pay more than they need to. However, certain home-buying strategies can save you money for carpeting and furniture.

- Don't use the seller's asking price as the starting point for your negotiations: find out what comparable homes in the area are selling for and start with a price 5 to 10 percent below the most recent comparable prices.
- Make your offer only a few percentage points below what you are really prepared to offer: sellers don't take you seriously if your offer is too low.
- Remember where the realtor's loyalty is: realtors represent the seller and usually get paid based on a percentage of the sales price.
- Compare the lender's fees and interest rates: sometimes you can pay less by choosing a higher interest rate with lower fees.
- You don't have to borrow from a local bank: if you can get lower interest rates somewhere else, you can save money in the long run.
- Beware of "no-cost" financing: you can't get a loan without paying interest.

CHOOSING BANKING SERVICES

Most of your regular banking services involve your checking and credit card accounts. With a little effort, you can improve the deal you get from your bank.

- Compare what banks offer before opening an account: do they have free checking with no minimum balance, for example?
- Make sure that there are a minimum number of fees: ATM and overdraft charges can add up.
- Choose a credit card issuer on the basis of how you use your card: if you pay off the balance every month, interest rates don't matter; if you carry over a balance (72 percent of card holders do), go for the lowest interest rate.

If you do your homework and are willing to haggle, you can often save yourself some money. In small shops, offering cash can seal a deal on the spot. Some experts even recommend bargaining in department stores. "If I buy place settings of china for twelve instead of for eight, can I get a discount?"

Note that the quantity demanded by purchasers *increases* as the price decreases along the *demand curve.* The buyers and sellers of a product interact in the marketplace. We can show this interaction by superimposing the supply curve onto the demand curve for our product, as shown in the right graph of Figure 13.3. The two curves intersect at point *E*, which represents a quantity of 15 million pairs of jeans and a price of $30 per pair. Point *E* is on the supply curve; thus producers are willing to supply 15 million pairs at $30 each. Point *E* is also on the demand curve; thus buyers are willing to purchase 15 million pairs at $30 each. Point *E* represents *equilibrium.* If 15 million pairs are produced and priced at $30, they will all be sold. And everyone who is willing to pay $30 will be able to buy a pair of jeans.

Prices in the Real Economy   In a (largely theoretical) system of pure competition, no producer has control over the price of its product: all producers must accept the equilibrium price. If they charge a higher price, they will not sell their products. If they charge a lower price, they will lose sales revenue and profits. In addition, the products of the various producers are indistinguishable from each other when a system of pure competition exists. Every bushel of wheat, for example, is exactly like every other bushel of wheat.

In the real economy, however, producers try to gain some control over price by differentiating their products from similar products. **Product differentiation** is the process of developing and promoting differences between one's product and all similar products. The idea behind product differentiation is to create a specific demand for the firm's product—to take the product out of competition with all similar products. Then, in its own little "submarket," the firm can control price to some degree. Jeans with certain designer labels are a result of product differentiation.

Firms also attempt to gain some control over price through advertising. If the advertising is effective, it will increase the quantity demanded. This may permit a firm to increase the price at which it sells its particular output.

In a real market, firms may reduce prices to obtain a competitive edge. A firm may hope to sell more units at a lower price, thereby increasing its total sales revenue. Although each unit earns less profit, total profit may rise.

Finally, the few large sellers in an oligopoly (an industry in which there are few sellers) have considerable control over price, mainly because each controls a large proportion of the total supply of its product. However, as we pointed out in Chapter 1, this control of price is diluted by each firm's wariness of its competitors.

Overall, then, firms in the real economy do exert some control over prices. How they use this control depends on their pricing goals and their production and marketing costs, as well as on the workings of supply and demand in competitive markets.

product differentiation   the process of developing and promoting differences between one's product and all similar products

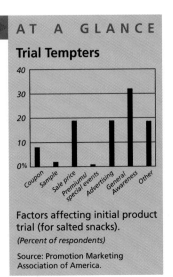

AT A GLANCE

Trial Tempters

Factors affecting initial product trial (for salted snacks).
(Percent of respondents)

Source: Promotion Marketing Association of America.

Price and Nonprice Competition

Before the price of a product can be set, an organization must decide on what basis it will compete—on the basis of price alone or some combination of factors. The choice influences pricing decisions as well as other marketing mix variables.

price competition an emphasis on setting a price equal to or lower than competitors' prices to gain sales or market share

Price competition occurs when a seller emphasizes the low price of a product and sets a price that equals or beats competitors' prices. To use this approach most effectively, a seller must have the flexibility to change prices often and must do so rapidly and aggressively whenever competitors change their prices. Price competition allows a marketer to set prices based on demand for the product or in response to changes in the firm's finances. Competitors can do likewise, however, which is a major drawback of price competition. They, too, can quickly match or outdo an organization's price cuts. In addition, if circumstances force a seller to raise prices, competing firms may be able to maintain their lower prices.

nonprice competition competition based on factors other than price

Nonprice competition is based on factors other than price. It is used most effectively when a seller can make its product stand out from the competition by distinctive product quality, customer service, promotion, packaging, or other features. Buyers must be able to perceive these distinguishing characteristics and consider them desirable. Once customers have chosen a brand for nonprice reasons, they may not be as easily attracted to competing firms and brands. In this way a seller can build customer loyalty to its brand. Price is still an important part of a marketing mix in nonprice competition, but it is possible for a firm to increase a brand's unit sales without lowering its price.

Buyers' Perceptions of Price

In setting prices, managers should consider the price sensitivity of people in the target market. How important is price to them? Is it always "very important"? Members of one market segment may be more influenced by price than members of another. For a particular product, the price may be a

Price is not everything. Brooks Brothers, an exclusive men's clothier, depends on nonprice competition. This retailer competes on the basis of breadth of product offering, product quality, and excellent customer service.

bigger factor to some buyers than to others. For example, buyers may be more sensitive to price when purchasing gasoline than when purchasing running shoes.

Buyers will accept different ranges of prices for different products; that is, they will tolerate a narrow range for certain items and a wider range for others. For example, consider the wide range of prices that consumers pay for soft drinks—from 10 cents per ounce at the movies down to 1.5 cents per ounce on sale at the grocery store. Management should be aware of these limits of acceptability and the products to which they apply. The firm should also take note of buyers' perceptions of a given product in relation to competing products. A premium price may be appropriate if a product is considered superior to others in that category or if the product has inspired strong brand loyalty. On the other hand, if buyers have even a hint of a negative view of a product, a lower price may be necessary.

Sometimes buyers relate price to quality. They may consider a higher price to be an indicator of higher quality. Managers involved in pricing decisions should determine whether this outlook is widespread in the target market. If it is, a higher price may improve the image of a product and, in turn, make the product more desirable.

■■ PRICING OBJECTIVES

LEARNING OBJECTIVE 7
Identify the major pricing objectives and the methods that businesses use to implement them.

Before setting prices for a firm's products, management must decide what it expects to accomplish through pricing. That is, management must set pricing objectives that are in line with both organizational and marketing objectives.

Of course, one objective of pricing is to make a profit, but this may not be a firm's primary objective. One or more of the following factors may be just as important.

Survival

A firm may have to price its products to survive—either as an organization or as a player in a particular market. This usually means that the firm will cut its price to attract customers, even if it then must operate at a loss. Of course, such a goal can hardly be pursued on a long-term basis. Consistent losses would cause the business to fail.

Profit Maximization

Many firms may state that their goal is to maximize profit, but this goal is impossible to define (and thus impossible to achieve). What, exactly, is the "maximum" profit? How does a firm know when it has been reached? Firms that wish to set profit goals should express them as either specific dollar amounts or percentage increases over previous profits.

Target Return on Investment

The *return on investment (ROI)* is the amount earned as a result of that investment. Some firms set an annual-percentage ROI as their pricing goal.

Battling for market share. Most electronics retailers promote price vigorously in an attempt to gain market share. The pricing objective for many electronics retailers is to gain or maintain market share.

ConAgra, the company that produces Healthy Choice meals and a multitude of other products, has a target after-tax ROI of 20 percent.

Market Share Goals

A firm's *market share* is its proportion of total industry sales. Some firms attempt, through pricing, to maintain or increase their share of the market. To gain market share, Ford Motor Company prices its Escort subcompact at $8,888.

Status Quo Pricing

In pricing their products, some firms are guided by a desire to avoid "making waves," or to maintain the status quo. This is especially true in industries that depend on price stability. If such a firm can maintain its profit or market share simply by meeting the competition—charging about the same price as competitors for similar products—then it will do so.

■■ PRICING METHODS

Once a firm has developed its pricing objectives, it must select a pricing method and strategy to reach that goal. The *pricing method* provides a "basic" price for each product. *Pricing strategies* are then used to modify the basic price, depending on pricing objectives and the market situation.

Two factors are important to every firm engaged in setting prices. The first is recognition that the market, and not the firm's costs, ultimately determines the price at which a product will sell. The second is awareness that costs and expected sales can be used only to establish some sort of *price floor*, the minimum price at which the firm can sell its product without incurring a loss.

In this section, we look at three kinds of pricing methods: cost-based, demand-based, and competition-based pricing.

Cost-Based Pricing

Using the simplest method of pricing, cost-based pricing, the seller first determines the total cost of producing (or purchasing) one unit of the product. The seller then adds an amount to cover additional costs (such as insurance or interest) and profit. The amount that is added is called the **markup.** The total of the cost plus the markup is the selling price of the product.

A firm's management can calculate markup as a percentage of its total costs. Suppose, for example, that the total cost of manufacturing and marketing 1,000 portable stereos is $100,000, or $100 per unit. If the manufacturer wants a markup that is 20 percent above its costs, the selling price will be $100 plus 20 percent of $100, or $120 per unit.

Markup pricing is easy to apply, and it is used by many businesses (mostly retailers and wholesalers). However, it has two major flaws. The first is the difficulty of determining an effective markup percentage. If this percentage is too high, the product may be overpriced for its market; then too few units may be sold to return the total cost of producing and marketing the product. In contrast, if the markup percentage is too low, the seller is "giving away" profit it could have earned simply by assigning a higher price. In other words, the markup percentage needs to be set to account for the workings of the market, and that is very difficult to do.

The second problem with markup pricing is that it separates pricing from other business functions. The product is priced *after* production quantities are determined, *after* costs are incurred, and almost without regard for the market or the marketing mix. To be most effective, the various business functions should be integrated. *Each* should have an impact on *all* marketing decisions.

Cost-based pricing can also be facilitated through the use of breakeven analysis. For any product, the **breakeven quantity** is the number of units that must be sold for the total revenue (from all units sold) to equal the total cost (of all units sold). **Total revenue** is the total amount received from the sales of a product. We can estimate projected total revenue as the selling price multiplied by the number of units sold.

The costs involved in operating a business can be broadly classified as either fixed or variable costs. A **fixed cost** is a cost incurred no matter how many units of a product are produced or sold. Rent, for example, is a fixed cost; it remains the same whether 1 unit or 1,000 are produced. A **variable cost** is a cost that depends on the number of units produced. The cost of fab-

markup   the amount that a seller adds to the cost of a product to determine its basic selling price

breakeven quantity   the number of units that must be sold for the total revenue (from all units sold) to equal the total cost (of all units sold)

total revenue   the total amount received from sales of a product

fixed cost   a cost incurred no matter how many units of a product are produced or sold

variable cost   a cost that depends on the number of units produced

total cost the sum of the fixed costs and the variable costs attributed to a product

ricating parts for a stereo receiver is a variable cost. The more units produced, the higher the cost of parts. The **total cost** of producing a certain number of units is the sum of the fixed costs and the variable costs attributed to those units.

If we assume a particular selling price, we can find the breakeven quantity either graphically or by using a formula. Figure 13.4 graphs the total revenue earned and the total cost incurred by the sale of various quantities of a hypothetical product. With fixed costs of $40,000, variable costs of $60 per unit, and a selling price of $120, the breakeven quantity is 667 units. To find the breakeven quantity, first deduct the variable cost from the selling price to determine how much money the sale of one unit contributes to offsetting fixed costs. Then divide that contribution into the total fixed costs to arrive at the breakeven quantity. (The breakeven quantity in Figure 13.4 is the quantity represented by the intersection of the total revenue and total cost axes.) If the firm sells more than 667 units at $120 each, it will earn a profit. If it sells fewer units, it will suffer a loss.

Demand-Based Pricing

Rather than basing the price of a product on its cost, companies sometimes use a pricing method based on the level of demand for the product: *demand-based pricing*. This method results in a high price when product demand is strong and a low price when demand is weak. Most long-distance telephone companies use demand-based pricing. To use this method, a marketer estimates the amounts of a product that customers will demand at different prices and then chooses the price that generates the highest total revenue. Obviously, the effectiveness of this method depends on the firm's ability to estimate demand accurately.

FIGURE 13.4
Breakeven Analysis
Breakeven analysis answers the question, What is the lowest level of production and sales at which a company can break even on a particular product?

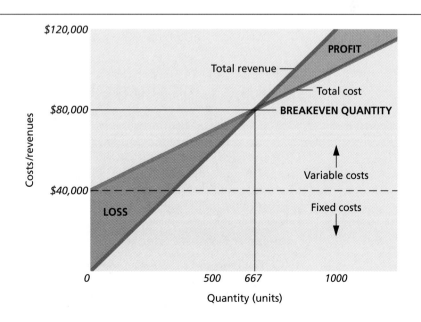

A firm may favor a demand-based pricing method called *price differentiation* if it wants to use more than one price in the marketing of a specific product. Price differentiation can be based on such considerations as time of the purchase, type of customer, or type of distribution channel. Here are several examples. Florida hotel accommodations are more expensive in winter than in summer. A homeowner pays more for air-conditioner filters than does an apartment complex owner purchasing the same size filters in greater quantity. Christmas tree ornaments are usually cheaper on December 26 than on December 16. For price differentiation to work correctly, the company must first be able to segment a market on the basis of different strengths of demand and then to keep the segments separate enough so that segment members who buy at lower prices cannot sell to buyers in segments that are charged a higher price. This isolation could be accomplished, for example, by selling to geographically separated segments.

Compared with cost-based pricing, demand-based pricing places a firm in a better position to attain higher profit levels, assuming that buyers value the product at levels sufficiently above the product's cost. To use demand-based pricing, however, management must be able to estimate demand at different price levels, which may be difficult to do accurately.

Competition-Based Pricing

In using *competition-based pricing*, an organization considers costs and revenue secondary to competitors' prices. The importance of this method increases if competing products are quite similar and the organization is serving markets in which price is the crucial variable of the marketing strategy. A firm that uses competition-based pricing may choose to be below competitors' prices, slightly above competitors' prices, or at the same level. The price that your bookstore paid to the publishing company of this text was determined using competition-based pricing. Competition-based pricing can help attain a pricing objective to increase sales or market share. Competition-based pricing may be combined with other cost approaches to arrive at profitable levels.

■■ PRICING STRATEGIES

LEARNING OBJECTIVE 8
Explain the different strategies available to companies as they set basic prices.

A seller may temporarily or permanently apply various pricing strategies to the basic prices of its individual products or complete product lines (see Figure 13.5). The extent to which a particular seller uses any of the following strategies depends on its pricing and marketing goals, the markets for its products, the degree of product differentiation, the life-cycle stage of the product, and other factors.

New-Product Strategies

The two primary types of new-product pricing strategies are price skimming and penetration pricing. An organization can use either one or even both over a period of time.

FIGURE 13.5   Pricing Strategies
After using a pricing method to set the basic price for a product, the seller adjusts the price according to a pricing strategy.

Price Skimming   Some consumers are willing to pay a high price for an innovative product, either because of its novelty or because of the prestige or status that ownership confers. **Price skimming** is the strategy of charging the highest-possible price for a product during the introduction stage of its life cycle. The seller essentially "skims the cream" off the market, which helps to recover more quickly the high costs of research and development. Also, a skimming policy may hold down demand for the product, which is helpful if the firm's production capacity is limited during the introduction stage. The greatest disadvantage is that a skimming price may make the product appear lucrative to potential competitors, who may then attempt to enter that market.

price skimming the strategy of charging the highest-possible price for a product during the introduction stage of its life cycle

Penetration Pricing   At the opposite extreme, **penetration pricing** is the strategy of setting a low price for a new product. The idea is to earn a large market share for the product quickly. The seller hopes that this approach will sell more units during the early life-cycle stages and thus discourage competitors from entering the market. If the low price stimulates sales, the firm may also be able to order longer production runs, which result in lower production costs per unit. A disadvantage of penetration pricing is that it places a firm in a less flexible position. It is more difficult to raise prices significantly than it is to lower them.

penetration pricing the strategy of setting a low price for a new product

Psychological Pricing Strategies

Psychological pricing strategies encourage purchases based on emotional responses rather than on economically rational responses. They are used primarily for consumer products rather than industrial products.

Odd Pricing   Many retailers believe that consumers respond more positively to odd-number prices like $4.99 than to whole-dollar prices like $5. **Odd pricing** is the strategy of setting prices at odd amounts slightly below a whole number of dollars.

Nine and five are the most popular ending figures for prices, accounting for nearly 80 percent of the marketplace. These odd prices were started

odd pricing the strategy of setting prices at odd amounts slightly below a whole number of dollars

by retailers in the 1890s as clerks had to make change and customers were encouraged to make impulse purchases.

Sellers who use this strategy believe odd prices will increase sales and, hence, total revenue and profit. The strategy is not limited to low-priced items. Auto manufacturers may set the price of a car at $9,999 rather than $10,000. Odd pricing has been the subject of various psychological studies, but the results have not been conclusive.

Multiple-Unit Pricing   Many retailers (and especially supermarkets) practice **multiple-unit pricing,** setting a single price for two or more units, such as two cans for 99 cents rather than 50 cents per can. Especially for frequently purchased products, this strategy can increase sales. Customers who see the single price, and who expect eventually to use more than one unit of the product, regularly purchase multiple units to save money.

multiple-unit pricing the strategy of setting a single price for two or more units

Prestige Pricing   **Prestige pricing** is the strategy of setting a high price to project an aura of quality and status. Because high-quality items are generally more expensive than those of average quality, many buyers believe that high price *means* high quality for certain types of products such as cosmetics, perfumes, and jewelry. High-priced products such as Rolex watches and high-priced stores such as Neiman Marcus tend to attract quality- and prestige-conscious customers.

prestige pricing the strategy of setting a high price to project an aura of quality and status

Price Lining   **Price lining** is selling goods only at certain predetermined prices that reflect definite price breaks. For example, a shop may sell men's ties only at $15 and $24. This strategy is widely used in clothing and accessory stores. It eliminates minor price differences from the buying decision—both for customers and for purchasing managers who buy merchandise to sell in the store.

price lining the strategy of selling goods only at certain predetermined prices that reflect definite price breaks

Geographic Pricing

Geographic pricing strategies deal with delivery costs. The seller may assume all delivery costs, no matter where the buyer is located. This practice is sometimes called *postage-stamp pricing*. The pricing strategy that requires the buyer to pay the delivery costs is called *FOB point of origin pricing*. It stands for "free on board at the point of origin," which means that the buyer will pay the transportation costs from the seller's warehouse to the buyer's place of business. *FOB destination* indicates that the seller will pay the transportation costs to the buyer's location.

Discounting

A **discount** is a deduction from the price of an item. Producers and sellers offer a wide variety of discounts to their customers, including the following:

discount a deduction from the price of an item

- *Trade discounts* are discounts from the list prices that are offered to marketing intermediaries, or middlemen. A furniture retailer, for example, may receive a 40 percent discount from the manufacturer. The retailer would then pay $60 for a lamp carrying a list price of $100. Intermediaries, discussed in Chapter 14, perform various marketing activities in return for trade discounts.

- *Quantity discounts* are discounts given to customers who buy in large quantities. The seller's per-unit selling cost is lower for larger purchases. The quantity discount is a way of passing part of this saving on to the buyer.
- *Cash discounts* are discounts offered for prompt payment. A seller may offer a discount of "2/10, net 30," meaning that the buyer may take a 2 percent discount if the bill is paid within 10 days and that the bill must be paid in full within 30 days.

In this chapter, we discussed two ingredients of the marketing mix—product and pricing. Chapter 14 is devoted to a third element—distribution. As that chapter shows, distribution includes not only the physical movement of products but also the organizations that facilitate exchanges among the producers and users of products.

■ ■ ■ ■ ■ CHAPTER REVIEW

Summary

1 Explain what a product is and how products are classified.

A product is everything that one receives in an exchange, including all attributes and expected benefits. The product may be a manufactured item, a service, an idea, or some combination of these.

Products are classified according to their ultimate use. Classification affects a product's distribution, promotion, and pricing. Consumer products, which include convenience, shopping, and specialty products, are purchased to satisfy personal and family needs. Industrial products are purchased for use in a firm's operations or to make other products. Industrial products can be classified as raw materials, major equipment, accessory equipment, component parts, process materials, supplies, and services.

2 Discuss the product life cycle and how it leads to new-product development.

Every product moves through a series of four stages—introduction, growth, maturity, and decline—which together form the product life cycle. As the product progresses through these stages, its sales and profitability increase, peak, and then decline. Marketers keep track of the life-cycle stage of products in order to estimate when a new product should be introduced to replace a declining one.

3 Define *product line* and *product mix,* and be able to distinguish between the two.

A product line is a group of similar products marketed by a firm. The products in a product line

are related to each other in the way they are produced, marketed, and used. The firm's product mix includes all the products it offers for sale. The width of a mix is a measure of the number of product lines it contains. The depth of the mix is a measure of the average number of individual products within each line.

4 Identify the methods available for changing a product mix.

Customer satisfaction and organizational objectives require marketers to develop, adjust, and maintain an effective product mix. Marketers may improve a product mix by changing existing products, deleting products, and developing new products.

New products are developed through a series of seven steps. The first step, idea generation, involves the accumulation of a pool of possible product ideas. Screening, the second step, removes from consideration those product ideas that do not mesh with organizational goals or resources. Concept testing, the third step, is a phase in which a small sample of potential buyers is exposed to a proposed product through a written or oral description in order to determine their initial reaction and buying intentions. The fourth step, business analysis, generates information about the potential sales, costs, and profits. During the development step, the product idea is transformed into mock-ups and actual prototypes to determine if the product is technically feasible to build and can be produced at reasonable costs. Test marketing is an actual launch of the product into several selected cities. Finally, during commercialization, plans for full-scale production and marketing are refined and implemented. Most product failures result from inadequate product planning and development.

5   Explain the uses and importance of branding, packaging, and labeling.

A brand is a name, term, symbol, design, or any combination of these that identifies a seller's products as distinct from those of other sellers. Brands can be classified as manufacturer brands, store brands, or generic brands. A firm can choose between two branding strategies—individual branding or family branding. Branding strategies are used to associate (or *not* associate) particular products with existing products, producers, or intermediaries. Packaging protects goods, offers consumer convenience, and enhances marketing efforts by communicating product features, uses, benefits, and image. Labeling provides customers with product information, some of which is required by law.

6   Describe the economic basis of pricing and the means by which sellers can control prices and buyers' perceptions of prices.

Under the ideal conditions of pure competition, an individual seller has no control over the price of its products. Prices are determined by the workings of supply and demand. In our real economy, however, sellers do exert some control, primarily through product differentiation. Product differentiation is the process of developing and promoting differences between one's product and all similar products. Firms also attempt to gain some control over pricing through advertising. A few large sellers have considerable control over prices because each controls a large proportion of the total supply of the product. Firms must consider the relative importance of price to buyers in the target market before setting prices. Buyers' perceptions of prices are affected by the importance of the product to them, the range of prices they consider acceptable, their perceptions of competing products, and their association of quality with price.

7   Identify the major pricing objectives and the methods that businesses use to implement them.

Objectives of pricing include survival, profit maximization, target return on investment, achieving market goals, and maintaining the status quo. Firms sometimes have to price products to survive, which usually requires cutting prices to attract customers. Return on investment (ROI) is the amount earned as a result of the investment in developing and marketing the product. The firm sets an annual-percentage ROI as the pricing goal. Some firms use pricing to maintain or increase their market share. And in industries in which price stability is important, firms often price their products by charging about the same as competitors.

8   Explain the different strategies available to companies as they set basic prices.

Prices may be established based on costs, demand, competitors' prices, or some combination of these. Cost- and competition-based pricing are simpler than demand-based pricing, which takes into account additional market factors in the pricing process. Once basic prices are set, the seller may apply various pricing strategies to reach its target markets more effectively. New-product strategies include price skimming and penetration pricing. Psychological strategies include odd pricing, multiple-unit pricing, prestige pricing, and price lining. Geographic strategies include postage-stamp pricing, FOB origin, and FOB destination. Discounting strategies include trade discounts, quantity discounts, and cash discounts.

Key Terms

You should now be able to define and give an example relevant to each of the following terms:

product (390)
consumer product (390)
industrial product (390)
convenience product (391)
shopping product (391)
specialty product (391)
raw material (392)
major equipment (392)
accessory equipment (392)
component part (392)
process material (392)
supply (392)
industrial service (392)
product life cycle (392)
product line (395)
product mix (395)
product modification (396)
product deletion (398)
brand (402)
brand name (402)
brand mark (402)

trademark (402)

trade name (402)

manufacturer (or producer) brand (402)

store (or private) brand (402)

generic product (or brand) (403)

individual branding (404)

family branding (404)

packaging (404)

labeling (407)

express warranty (407)

price (407)

supply (408)

demand (408)

product differentiation (410)

price competition (411)

nonprice competition (411)

markup (414)

breakeven quantity (414)

total revenue (414)

fixed cost (414)

variable cost (414)

total cost (415)

price skimming (417)

penetration pricing (417)

odd pricing (417)

multiple-unit pricing (418)

prestige pricing (418)

price lining (418)

discount (418)

Questions

Review Questions

1. What does the purchaser of a product obtain, besides the good, service, or idea itself?
2. What are the products of (a) a bank, (b) an insurance company, and (c) a university?
3. What major factor determines whether a product is a consumer or an industrial product?
4. Describe each of the classifications of industrial products.
5. What are the four stages of the product life cycle? How can a firm determine which stage a particular product is in?
6. What is the difference between a product line and a product mix? Give an example of each.
7. Under what conditions does product modification work best?

8. Why do products have to be deleted from a product mix?
9. Why must firms introduce new products?
10. Briefly describe the seven new-product development stages.
11. What is the difference between manufacturer brands and store brands; between family branding and individual branding?
12. How can packaging be used to enhance marketing activities?
13. For what purposes is labeling used?
14. What is the primary function of prices in our economy?
15. Compare and contrast the characteristics of price and nonprice competition.
16. How might buyers' perceptions of price influence pricing decisions?
17. List and briefly describe the five major pricing objectives.
18. What are the differences among markup pricing, pricing by breakeven analysis, and competition-based pricing?
19. In what way is demand-based pricing more realistic than markup pricing?
20. Why would a firm use competition-based pricing?
21. Which pricing strategies are used mainly (a) for new products, (b) by retailers, and (c) in sales to intermediaries?

Discussion Questions

1. Why have Birkenstocks become so popular in the U.S.?
2. Is Birkenstock competing on the basis of price?
3. Why is it important to understand how products are classified?
4. What factors might determine how long a product remains in each stage of the product life cycle? What can a firm do to prolong each stage?
5. Some firms do not delete products until they become financially threatening. What problems may result from relying on this practice?
6. Which steps in the evolution of new products are most important? Which are least important? Defend your choices.
7. Do branding, packaging, and labeling really benefit consumers? Explain.
8. To what extent can a firm control its prices in our market economy? What factors limit such control?
9. Under what conditions would a firm be most likely to use nonprice competition?
10. Can a firm have more than one pricing objective? Can it use more than one of the pricing methods discussed in this chapter? Explain.

11. What are the major disadvantages of price skimming?

12. What is an "effective" price?

Exercises

✎ **1.** Suppose you have an idea for a new game called *Oligopoly*. Write a short report explaining how you would shepherd your idea through the product development steps from idea generation to commercialization.

◉ **2.** Develop a package for the game described in Exercise 1. Consider the package material, the package design, and the information you would include on the package.

3. As the manager of a clothing store, you have just received a shipment of new cheesecloth T-shirts. The T-shirts cost you $48 per dozen, and your usual markup is 40 percent. However, yours is the only store in town that will be carrying this fashionable product. What price will you set for the T-shirts? Why?

VIDEO CASE 13.1

Ryka Athletic Shoes: By Women, For Women, Helping Women

Sheri Poe is the founder and CEO of Ryka, Inc., manufacturer of women's shoes for aerobics, step aerobics, walking, running, hiking, and cross training. It wasn't easy for an upstart like Ryka to compete with giants like Reebok and Nike for a share in the $11 billion athletic footwear industry. Poe had to resort to some unusual marketing strategies. She promoted Ryka Ultra-Lite aerobics shoes on the Oprah Winfrey show. She had her company's British distributor deliver several pairs of Rykas with a personal note to fitness enthusiast Princess Diana. A few months later *People* magazine printed a photo of Princess Di strolling down a London street in a pair of Ryka fitness shoes. Her trainer told Ryka that the princess likes the fit and wears them regularly, but she is also moved by the fact that part of the company's profits go toward stopping violence against women. Ryka is Poe's way of fulfilling her dream—running a successful business while finding a way to help women who are victims of rape, assault, and abuse.

The Ryka phenomenon began when Poe and several aerobics classmates realized that they were experiencing back pain because their shoes didn't fit right. Poe surveyed department stores and athletic footwear shops, asking customers and sales people what kinds of shoes they wanted. She discovered that no one was paying attention to the women's market. The majority of women's shoes were simply designed as scaled-down versions of men's shoes. To get a proper and painless fit, women needed athletic shoes with higher arches and thinner heels, but couldn't find them. Poe decided that there was a future for a company that made athletic shoes just for women.

Rather than cater to the ins and outs of fashion trends, Ryka concentrates on manufacturing only high-performance athletic shoes that fit a woman's foot. Rykas are anatomically correct for women's feet, and the company's patented Nitrogen E/S system provides cushioning and shock absorption for the heel and the ball of the foot. Ryka Ultra-Lite aerobics shoes weigh only 7.7 ounces, about one-third that of regular aerobics shoes. An eagerness to listen to suggestions from aerobics instructors and their students not only leads to product improvements, it keeps the company on the cutting edge of aerobics trends. For example, Ryka was the first athletic shoe producer to develop and market lightweight shoes specifically designed for the ups and downs of the increasingly popular step aerobics.

What sets Ryka apart from other athletic shoe companies, though, is not only its unique product line. The real soul of Ryka is its commitment to being a socially responsible company. When Sheri Poe was a young college student, she was assaulted and raped on her way home from work. In launching Ryka, Poe was determined that her company find ways to help women who, like her, have been victims of violent crimes. Seven percent of Ryka Shoes' pretax profits go to the Ryka Rose Foundation, *rose* standing for "restoring one's self-esteem." When women buy a pair of Rykas, they know that some of their money provides educational materials and supports battered women's shelters, violence-prevention programs, and nonprofit treatment centers. A card attached to their laces outlines physical safety tips for women. Ryka tells retailers that carry its shoes, "You and your customers can make a difference."

From the beginning, Ryka has had to struggle for every small success. Until it found a quality manufacturer in Korea, Ryka shoes often either didn't fit or fell apart. Until Poe hired a vice president of marketing and sales who shifted the company's marketing emphasis from its cause to its shoes, many retailers wouldn't carry Ryka because it wasn't a nationally recognized brand. Despite these efforts and Sheri Poe's remarkable energy and devotion to her company and her cause, Ryka has continued to struggle for survival. A planned merger with L.A. Gear in 1995 fell through when L.A. Gear pulled out because of Ryka's disappointing revenues. The merger's failure does not mean that Poe's dream is dying. When women buy Ryka brands, part of the profits continue to support the Ryka Rose Foundation.[3]

Questions

1. Are Ryka shoes a convenience, shopping, or specialty product?
2. Evaluate the marketing vice president's decision to shift the company's marketing focus from its cause (preventing violence against women) to its shoes.
3. Athletics shoes are in which stage of the product life cycle?

CASE 13.2

Effective Pricing Makes Southwest Airlines Profitable

Boasting twenty-one consecutive years of profitability, Southwest Airlines has become a model for the entire airline industry. How does Southwest thrive in a business that sees some airlines barely survive and others, such as venerable Pan Am, fold? The answer is low fares. By rejecting traditional industry practices such as hub flying, connecting flights, assigned seating, and in-flight meals, Southwest keeps its costs down. Low costs for Southwest translate into very low fares for its customers. One analyst jokingly commented that flying Southwest is so inexpensive, traveling by automobile is the airline's only serious competition. For Southwest, however, holding onto its position as low-price leader is no joking matter. Competitors like USAir, Continental, and United are all adopting Southwest's pricing strategies in an effort to beat Southwest at its low-cost, low-price game. To make sure that customers don't lump its low-fare flights together with this new crop of Southwest wanna-bes, Southwest is further reducing the prices of many fares and running ads in national newspapers reminding fliers who was first.

In 1967, Texas businessman Rollin King and lawyer Herb Kelleher established Air Southwest Company. Originally, King and Kelleher planned to fly only within Texas, linking Dallas, San Antonio, and Houston with low-priced, frequent flights. Almost immediately, airline companies serving Texas filed suit against their fledgling competitor, claiming that the market was already being adequately served. However, the Texas Supreme Court ruled in favor of the renamed Southwest Airlines, and in 1971 the company made its initial flight between Dallas and San Antonio. Over the years, Southwest garnered fame for "Friends Fly Free" two-for-one fares, advance-purchase "Fun Fares," and a frequent flyer program based on number of flights instead of accumulated mileage. Today, Southwest owns more than 140 Boeing 737s, flies to over forty U.S. cities, and serves its passengers almost 50 million bags of peanuts a year.

Years ago, the price of an airline ticket prohibited average Americans from flying. Planes carried well-to-do individuals and business travelers, but not very many vacationing families or college students going home for the holidays. Today, 72 percent of Americans have flown, but thanks in large part to Southwest Airlines, high fares are history. Industry experts acknowledge that Southwest Airlines has permanently changed air travel in the United States. Bargain-seeking consumers now drive the market, and Southwest gives them plenty of bargains from which to choose. Without advance purchase, they can fly one-way from Cleveland to Baltimore for $19, or from Chicago to Baltimore for $29. From Los Angeles, commuters can get a one-way ticket to San Jose for $29. The airline also has twenty-one-day advance-purchase fares that are half the price of its fares on all last-minute flights. As part of its sponsorship of ABC television's *Monday Night Football*, Southwest offered $25 nonstop, one-way fares every Monday night during football season. Asserts the airline's vice president of advertising and promotion, "We don't go on sale; our fares stay low."

Industry experts agree that the airline to watch is Southwest. According to the 1994 Airlines Quality Rating, Southwest is now the nation's number 1 major airline based on fares, on-time performance, customer satisfaction, number of accidents, financial viability, baggage complaints, and age of the fleet. Southwest can compete in any market it enters, and its competitors know that Southwest will do almost anything to offer the lowest prices. In a nationally run advertisement, Southwest's CEO Herb Kelleher vows to "nuke" the competition in any and all fare wars.[4]

Questions

1. Price competition within the airline industry has driven many competitors out of business or into bankruptcy protection. Why has Southwest Airlines been successful in competing on the basis of price?
2. What are Southwest's primary pricing objectives?
3. Airline marketers try to gain some control over price by differentiating their products. What are some examples of product differentiation in the airline industry?

■ ■ ■ ■ **CHAPTER 14**

Wholesaling, Retailing, and Physical Distribution

LEARNING OBJECTIVES

After studying this chapter you should be able to

1 Identify the various channels of distribution that are used for consumer and industrial products.

2 Explain the concept of market coverage.

3 Describe what a vertical marketing system is, and identify the types of vertical marketing systems.

4 Discuss the need for wholesalers.

5 Identify the major types of wholesalers, and describe the services they perform for retailers and manufacturers.

6 Distinguish among the major types of retailers.

7 Explain the wheel of retailing hypothesis.

8 Identify the categories of shopping centers and the factors that determine how shopping centers are classified.

9 Explain the five most important physical distribution activities.

CHAPTER PREVIEW

First in this chapter we examine various channels of distribution—the company-to-company paths that products follow as they move from producer to ultimate user. Then we discuss wholesalers and retailers, two important groups of intermediaries operating within these channels. Next we examine the types of shopping centers. Finally, we explore the physical distribution function and the major modes of transportation that are used to move goods.

Starbucks Gourmet Coffee Reaches Customers Through Multiple Channels

If you go to Starbucks for coffee, you don't plunk down fifty cents on the counter and get a cup of the same brew your automatic drip pot dispenses at home. Your *barista* (Italian for "bartender") brings you a *caffe latte*—a shot of espresso and steamed milk topped with milk foam—or a *caffe mocha*—espresso, cocoa, steamed milk, and whipped cream. If you're dieting, you can order a "skinny latte" made with skim milk. After you finish your drink, you can browse around the store and perhaps purchase an espresso machine, some 23-karat-gold coffee filters, or a natural hair brush for cleaning your coffee grinder. Starbucks is the leading marketer of specialty brand coffees in North America. With 425 stores in ten states serving 2 million Americans a week, the Seattle-based chain of trendy coffee bars does for coffee what Haagen-Dazs does for ice cream: cater to a premium niche on a mass scale.

In 1971 Starbucks got its start as a single coffee bean shop in Seattle. Inspired by coffee he enjoyed in Italy, the company's CEO began opening stylish coffee bars serving espresso-type gourmet drinks. By 1987 Seattle coffee-lovers had nine Starbucks full-service coffee bars to choose from. As American coffee drinkers increasingly spurned Maxwell House in favor of gourmet brands, Starbucks exported its chic cafes to cities such as San Diego, Las Vegas, Houston, Atlanta, Minneapolis, New York, and Boston. Experts predict that by the year 2000, Starbucks' annual sales will top $1 billion.

In addition to its own retail outlets, the coffee maker uses other marketing channels to raise brand awareness and increase sales. Traveling Starbucks-lovers can get a cup of their favorite coffee at kiosks and carts in several major airports. Shopping Starbucks fans can indulge in a

cup at Barnes & Noble bookstores, Nordstrom department stores, and other specialty retailers. The coffee company also has agreements with ITT Corp., Sheraton Hotels, and most recently Delta Airlines to serve the Starbucks brand. The Starbucks' House Blend is now offered at the gate and on board Delta shuttle flights between Boston, New York, and Washington, D.C. In addition, Starbucks operates a national direct mail business, making all its coffee flavors and coffee-making and drinking supplies available through a nationally distributed catalog.

With America's thirst for gourmet coffee growing, other coffee makers are competing more intensely with Starbucks. Brother's Gourmet Products, Inc., is opening a chain of Brother's coffee bars, and Seattle's Best Coffee plans to franchise five hundred stores nationwide. By attacking the coffee market on many fronts, however, Starbucks is still the number 1 brand in the $2.1 billion specialty coffee market. According to one industry expert, "There's nobody out there even close to matching them."

■ ■ ■ ■

425

■　■　　■　　■　　■　　■　　■　　■　　■　　■　　■

More than 2 million firms in the United States help move products from producers to consumers. Of all marketers, retail firms that sell directly to consumers are the most visible. Store chains like Starbucks; Sears, Roebuck and Co.; and Wal-Mart Stores, Inc., operate retail outlets where consumers make purchases. Other retailers, like Avon Products and Electrolux, send their salespeople to the homes of customers. Still others, like Lands' End and L.L. Bean, sell through catalogs or through both catalogs and stores.

In addition, there are more than half a million wholesalers that sell merchandise to other firms. Most consumers know little about these firms that work "behind the scenes" and rarely sell directly to consumers.

These and other intermediaries are concerned with the transfer of both products and ownership. They thus help create the time, place, and possession utilities that are critical to marketing. As we will see, they also perform a number of services for their suppliers and their customers.

Before we look closely at some of these important intermediaries, we should get an idea of the various channels—some simple, some complex—through which products are distributed to customers.

■■ CHANNELS OF DISTRIBUTION

A **channel of distribution,** or **marketing channel,** is a sequence of marketing organizations that directs a product from the producer to the ultimate user. Every marketing channel begins with the producer and ends with either the consumer or the industrial user.

A marketing organization that links a producer and user within a marketing channel is called a **middleman,** or **marketing intermediary.** For the most part, middlemen are concerned with the transfer of *ownership* of products. A **merchant middleman** (or, more simply, a *merchant*) is a middleman that actually takes title to products by buying them. A **functional middleman,** on the other hand, helps in the transfer of ownership of products but does not take title to the products.

Different channels of distribution are generally used to move consumer and industrial products. The six most commonly used channels are illustrated in Figure 14.1.

Channels for Consumer Products

Producer to Consumer This channel, which is often called the *direct channel*, includes no marketing intermediaries. Practically all services, but very few consumer goods, are distributed through the direct channel. However, the sellers of some consumer goods, such as Avon Products, Mary Kay Cosmetics, and Fuller Brush, prefer to sell directly to consumers.

channel of distribution (or marketing channel) a sequence of marketing organizations that directs a product from the producer to the ultimate user

middleman (or marketing intermediary) a marketing organization that links a producer and user within a marketing channel

merchant middleman a middleman that actually takes title to products by buying them

functional middleman a middleman that helps in the transfer of ownership of products but does not take title to the products

LEARNING OBJECTIVE 1
Identify the various channels of distribution that are used for consumer and industrial products.

426

FIGURE 14.1
Distribution Channels
Producers use various
channels to distribute their
products.

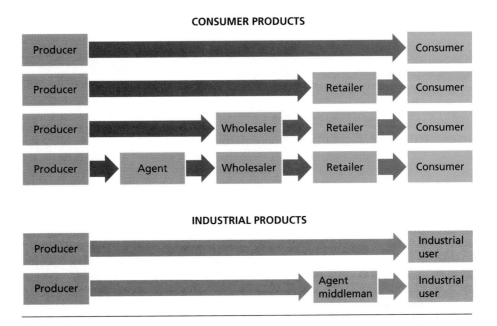

Producers sell directly to consumers for several reasons. They can better control the quality and price of their products. They don't have to pay (through discounts) for the services of intermediaries. And they can maintain closer ties with consumers.

retailer a middleman that buys from producers or other middlemen and sells to consumers

Producer to Retailer to Consumer   A **retailer** is a middleman that buys from producers or other middlemen and sells to consumers. Producers sell directly to retailers when retailers (such as Wal-Mart and Kmart) can buy in large quantities. This channel is most often used for products that are bulky, such as furniture and automobiles, for which additional handling would increase selling costs. It is also the usual channel for perishable products, such as fruits and vegetables, and for high-fashion products that must reach the consumer in the shortest possible time. If you purchased this textbook new, it came to you via this channel.

wholesaler a middleman that sells products to other firms

Producer to Wholesaler to Retailer to Consumer   This channel is known as the *traditional channel* because most consumer goods (especially convenience goods) pass through wholesalers to retailers. A **wholesaler** is a middleman that sells products to other firms. These firms may be retailers, industrial users, or other wholesalers. A producer uses wholesalers when its products are carried by so many retailers that the producer cannot deal with all of them. For example, the maker of Wrigley's gum uses this type of channel.

Producer to Agent to Wholesaler to Retailer to Consumer   Producers may use agents to reach wholesalers. Agents are functional middlemen that do not take title to products and that are compensated by commissions paid by producers. This channel is used for products that are sold through

Direct channel of distribution. An Avon sales representative in Budapest, Hungary, markets products from a table in an office building.

thousands of outlets to millions of consumers. Often, these products are inexpensive, frequently purchased items. For example, to reach a large number of potential customers, a small manufacturer of gas-powered lawn-edgers might choose to use agents who market its product to wholesalers, who in turn sell the lawn-edgers to a large number of retailers. This channel is also used for highly seasonal products (such as Christmas tree decorations) and by producers that do not have their own sales forces.

Multiple Channels for Consumer Goods   Often a manufacturer uses different distribution channels to reach different market segments. A manufacturer uses multiple channels, for example, when the same product is sold to consumers and industrial users. Multiple channels are also used to increase sales or to capture a larger share of the market. With the goal of selling as much merchandise as possible, both Firestone Tire & Rubber Co. and The Goodyear Tire & Rubber Company market their tires through their own retail outlets as well as through independent service stations and department stores.

Channels for Industrial Products

Producers of industrial products generally tend to use short channels. We will outline the two that are most commonly used.

Producer to Industrial User   In this direct channel, the manufacturer's own sales force sells directly to industrial users. Heavy machinery, large computers, and major equipment are usually distributed in this way. The very short channel allows the producer to provide customers with expert and timely services, such as delivery, machinery installation, and repairs.

Manufacturer to Agent Middleman to Industrial User   This channel is employed by manufacturers to distribute such items as operating supplies, accessory equipment, small tools, and standardized parts. The agent is an independent intermediary between the producer and the user. Generally, agents represent sellers.

Market Coverage

LEARNING OBJECTIVE 2
Explain the concept of market coverage.

How does a producer decide which distribution channels (and which particular intermediaries) to use? Like every other marketing decision, this one should be based on all relevant factors. These include the firm's production capability and marketing resources, the target market and buying patterns of potential customers, and the product itself. After evaluating these factors, the producer can choose a particular *intensity of market coverage*. Then the producer selects channels and intermediaries to implement that coverage (see Figure 14.2).

intensive distribution   the use of all available outlets for a product

Intensive distribution is the use of all available outlets for a product. The producer that wants to give its product the widest possible exposure in the marketplace chooses intensive distribution. The manufacturer saturates the market by selling to any intermediary of good financial standing that is willing to stock and sell the product. For the consumer, intensive distribution means being able to shop at a nearby store and spend minimum time finding the product in the store. Many convenience goods, including candy, gum, and cigarettes, are distributed intensively.

selective distribution   the use of only a portion or percentage of the available outlets for a product in each geographic area

Selective distribution is the use of only a portion or percentage of the available outlets for a product in each geographic area. Manufacturers of goods such as furniture, major home appliances, and clothing typically prefer selective distribution. Franchisers also use selective distribution in granting franchises for the sale of their goods and services in a specific geographic area.

exclusive distribution   the use of only a single retail outlet for a product in a large geographic area

Exclusive distribution is the use of only a single retail outlet for a product in a large geographic area. Exclusive distribution is usually limited

FIGURE 14.2
Market Coverage
The number of outlets a producer chooses for a product depends on the type of product. Batteries, for example, are distributed intensively in this area; sports equipment is selectively distributed; and Steubenglass is exclusively distributed.

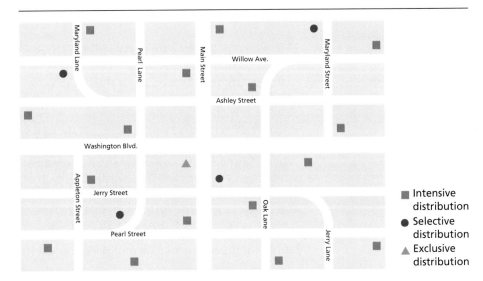

to very prestigious products. It is appropriate, for instance, for specialty goods such as upscale pianos, fine china, and expensive jewelry. The producer usually places many requirements (inventory levels, sales training, service quality, warranty procedures) on exclusive dealers.

Vertical Marketing Systems

LEARNING OBJECTIVE 3
Describe what a vertical marketing system is, and identify the types of vertical marketing systems.

vertical channel integration the combining of two or more stages of a distribution channel under a single firm's management

vertical marketing system (VMS) a centrally managed distribution channel resulting from vertical channel integration

Vertical channel integration occurs when two or more stages of a distribution channel are combined and managed by one firm. A **vertical marketing system (VMS)** is a centrally managed distribution channel resulting from vertical channel integration. This merging eliminates the need for certain intermediaries. One member of a marketing channel may assume the responsibilities of another member, or it may actually purchase the operations of that member. For example, a large-volume discount retailer that ships and warehouses its own stock directly from manufacturers does not need a wholesaler. Total vertical integration occurs when a single management controls all operations from production to final sale. Oil companies that own wells, transportation facilities, refineries, terminals, and service stations exemplify total vertical integration.

There are three types of VMSs: administered, contractual, and corporate. In an *administered VMS*, one of the channel members dominates the other members, perhaps because of its large size. Under its influence, the channel members collaborate on production and distribution. A powerful manufacturer, such as Procter & Gamble, receives a great deal of cooperation from intermediaries that carry its brands. Although the goals of the entire system are considered when decisions are made, control rests with individual channel members, as in conventional marketing channels. Under a *contractual VMS*, cooperative arrangements and the rights and obligations of channel members are defined by contracts or other legal measures. In a *corporate VMS*, actual ownership is the vehicle by which production and distribution are joined. A grocery-store chain, for example, may obtain its bread products from several of its own bakeries. Most vertical marketing systems are organized to improve distribution by combining individual operations.

■■ MARKETING INTERMEDIARIES: WHOLESALERS

LEARNING OBJECTIVE 4
Discuss the need for wholesalers.

Wholesalers may be the most misunderstood of marketing intermediaries. Producers sometimes try to eliminate them from distribution channels by dealing directly with retailers or consumers. Yet wholesalers provide a variety of essential marketing services. Although wholesalers can be eliminated, their functions cannot be eliminated; these functions *must* be performed by other channel members or by the consumer or ultimate user. Eliminating a wholesaler may or may not cut distribution costs.

Justifications for Marketing Intermediaries

The press, consumers, public officials, and other marketers often charge wholesalers, at least in principle, with inefficiency and parasitism. Consumers in particular feel strongly that the distribution channel should be made as short as possible. They assume that the fewer the intermediaries in a distribution channel, the lower the price of the product.

Those who believe that the elimination of wholesalers would bring about lower prices, however, do not recognize that the services wholesalers perform would still be needed. Those services would simply be provided by other means, and consumers would still bear the costs. Moreover, all manufacturers would have to keep extensive records and employ enough personnel to deal with a multitude of retailers individually. Even with direct distribution, products might be considerably more expensive because prices would reflect the costs of producers' inefficiencies. Figure 14.3 shows that sixteen contacts could result from the efforts of four buyers purchasing the products of four producers. With the assistance of an intermediary, only eight contacts would be necessary.

To illustrate further the useful role of wholesalers in the marketing system, assume that all wholesalers in the candy industry were abolished. With more than 1.3 million retail businesses to contact, candy manufacturers could be making as many as a million sales calls or more, regularly, just to maintain the present level of product visibility. Hershey Foods, for example, would have to set up warehouses all over the country, organize a fleet of trucks, purchase and maintain thousands of vending machines, and deliver all of its own candy. Sales and distribution costs for candy would soar. Candy producers would be contacting and shipping products to thousands of small businesses, instead of to a few large wholesalers and retailers. The outrageous costs of this inefficiency would be passed on to consumers. Candy bars would be more expensive and probably in short supply.

Wholesalers often are more efficient and economical not only for manufacturers but also for consumers. Because pressure to eliminate them comes from both ends of the marketing channel, wholesalers should perform only those functions that are genuinely in demand. To stay in business, wholesalers should also take care to be efficient and productive and to provide high-quality services to other channel members.

FIGURE 14.3
Efficiency Provided by an Intermediary
The services of an intermediary reduce the number of contacts, or exchanges, between producers and buyers, thereby increasing efficiency. *(Source: Adapted from William M. Pride and O. C. Ferrell,* Marketing: Concepts and Strategies, Ninth Edition. *Copyright © 1995 by Houghton Mifflin Company. Used by permission.)*

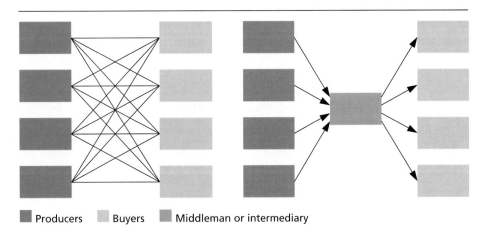

■ Producers   ■ Buyers   ■ Middleman or intermediary

Food wholesaler. This food wholesaler serves medium- and small-grocery retailers in Philadelphia.

Wholesalers' Services to Retailers

Wholesalers help retailers by buying in large quantities and then selling to retailers in smaller quantities and by delivering goods to retailers. They also stock—in one place—the variety of goods that retailers would otherwise have to buy from many producers. And wholesalers provide assistance in three other vital areas: promotion, market information, and financial aid.

Promotion   Some wholesalers help promote the products they sell to retailers. These services are usually either free or performed at cost. Wholesalers, for example, are major sources of display materials designed to stimulate impulse buying. They may also help retailers build effective window, counter, and bin displays; they may even assign their own employees to work on the retail sales floor during special promotions.

Market Information   Wholesalers are a constant source of market information. Wholesalers have numerous contacts with local businesses and distant suppliers. In the course of these dealings, they accumulate information about consumer demand, prices, supply conditions, new developments within the trade, and even industry personnel. Most of this information is relayed to retailers informally, through the wholesaler's sales force. However, some wholesalers distribute bulletins or newsletters to their customers as well.

Information regarding industry sales and competitive prices is especially important to all firms. Dealing with a number of suppliers and many retailers, a wholesaler is a natural clearinghouse for such information. And most wholesalers are willing to pass news on to their customers.

Financial Aid   Most wholesalers provide a type of financial aid that retailers often take for granted. By making prompt and frequent deliveries, wholesalers enable retailers to keep their own inventory investments small in relation to sales. Such indirect financial aid reduces the amount of operating capital retailers need.

In some trades, wholesalers extend direct financial assistance through long-term loans. Most wholesalers also provide help through delayed billing, giving customers thirty to sixty days *after delivery* to pay for merchandise. Wholesalers of seasonal merchandise may offer even longer payment periods. For example, a wholesaler of lawn and garden supplies may deliver seed to retailers in January but not bill them for it until May.

Wholesalers' Services to Manufacturers

Some of the services that wholesalers perform for producers are similar to those provided to retailers. Others are quite different.

Providing an Instant Sales Force   A wholesaler provides its producers with an instant sales force so that producers' sales representatives need not call on retailers. This can result in enormous savings for producers. For example, Lever Brothers and General Foods would have to spend millions of dollars each year to field a sales force that could call on all the retailers that sell their numerous products. Instead, these producers rely on wholesalers to sell and distribute their products to retailers.

Reducing Inventory Costs   Wholesalers purchase goods in sizable quantities from manufacturers and store these goods for resale. By doing so, they reduce the amount of finished goods inventory that producers must hold and, thereby, the cost of carrying inventories.

Assuming Credit Risks   When producers sell through wholesalers, it is the wholesalers who extend credit to retailers, make collections from retailers, and assume the risks of nonpayment. These services reduce the producers' cost of extending credit to customers and the resulting bad debt expense.

Furnishing Market Information   Just as they do for retailers, wholesalers supply market information to the producers they serve. Valuable information accumulated by wholesalers may concern consumer demand, the producers' competition, and buying trends.

Types of Wholesalers

LEARNING OBJECTIVE 5
Identify the major types of wholesalers, and describe the services they perform for retailers and manufacturers.

Wholesalers generally fall into three categories: merchant wholesalers; commission merchants, agents, and brokers; and manufacturers' sales branches and sales offices. Of these, merchant wholesalers constitute the largest portion. They account for about 58 percent of wholesale sales, four-fifths of all wholesale employees, and four out of every five establishments.[2]

merchant wholesaler
a middleman that purchases goods in large quantities and then sells them to other wholesalers or retailers and to institutional, farm, government, professional, or industrial users

Merchant Wholesalers   A **merchant wholesaler** is a middleman that purchases goods in large quantities and then sells them to other wholesalers or retailers and to institutional, farm, government, professional, or industrial users. Merchant wholesalers usually operate one or more warehouses at which they receive, take title to, and store goods. These wholesalers are sometimes called *distributors* or *jobbers*.

Most merchant wholesalers are businesses composed of salespeople, order takers, receiving and shipping clerks, inventory managers, and office personnel. The successful merchant wholesaler must analyze available products and market needs. It must be able to adapt the type, variety, and quality of its products to changing market conditions.

Merchant wholesalers may be classified as full-service or limited-service wholesalers, depending on the number of services they provide. A **full-service wholaler**
a middleman that performs the entire range of wholesaler functions described earlier in this section. These functions include delivering goods, supplying warehousing, arranging for credit, supporting promotional activities, and providing general customer assistance.

full-service wholesaler
a middleman that performs the entire range of wholesaler functions

Under this broad heading are the general merchandise wholesaler, limited-line wholesaler, and specialty-line wholesaler. A **general merchandise wholesaler** deals in a wide variety of products, such as drugs, hardware, nonperishable foods, cosmetics, detergents, and tobacco. A **limited-line wholesaler** stocks only a few product lines. A **specialty-line wholesaler** carries a select group of products within a single line. Food delicacies such as shellfish represent the kind of product handled by this wholesaler.

general merchandise wholesaler   a middleman that deals in a wide variety of products

limited-line wholesaler
a middleman that stocks only a few product lines

specialty-line wholesaler
a middleman that carries a select group of products within a single line

In contrast to a full-service wholesaler, a **limited-service wholesaler** assumes responsibility for a few wholesale services only. Other marketing tasks are left to other channel members or consumers. This category includes cash-and-carry wholesalers, truck wholesalers, drop shippers, and mail-order wholesalers.

limited-service wholesaler
a middleman that assumes responsibility for a few wholesale services only

Commission Merchants, Agents, and Brokers   Commission merchants, agents, and brokers are functional middlemen. Functional middlemen do not take title to products. They perform a small number of marketing activities and are paid a commission that is a percentage of the sales price.

commission merchant
a middleman that carries merchandise and negotiates sales for manufacturers

A **commission merchant** usually carries merchandise and negotiates sales for manufacturers. In most cases, commission merchants have the power to set the prices and terms of sales. After a sale is made, they either arrange for delivery or provide transportation services.

agent   a middleman that expedites exchanges, represents a buyer or a seller, and often is hired permanently on a commission basis

An **agent** is a middleman that expedites exchanges, represents a buyer or a seller, and often is hired permanently on a commission basis. When agents represent producers, they are known as *sales agents* or *manufacturer's agents*. As long as the products represented do not compete, a sales agent may represent one or several manufacturers on a commission basis. The agent solicits orders for the manufacturers within a specific territory. As a rule, the manufacturers ship the merchandise and bill the customers directly. The manufacturers also set the prices and other conditions of the sales. What do the manufacturers gain by using a sales agent? The sales agent provides immediate entry into a territory, regular calls on customers,

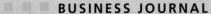

BUSINESS JOURNAL

Frieda's Finest Wholesale Produce

Bringing new ideas to fruit and vegetable wholesaling, Frieda Caplan built Frieda's Finest by offering the kinds of produce that market-dominators such as Dole and Chiquita politely but emphatically decline. Thanks in large part to this trendsetting wholesaler of exotic fruits and vegetables, shoppers throughout the United States and Canada can buy elephant garlic, yellow-meat watermelon, Habanero peppers, prickly pear cactus, Enoki mushrooms, purple potatoes, and dried strawberries, to name a few, in the produce sections of their supermarkets.

There was a time when the only mushrooms available to most grocery shoppers were found in cans. By launching a wholesale produce business specializing in fresh mushrooms, Frieda Caplan helped transform an unusual vegetable into standard fare on American tables. By doing the same for alfalfa sprouts and a variety of squashes, she changed the look of America's supermarket produce sections. When a buyer from a large national supermarket chain asked Frieda if she could supply Chinese gooseberries, she had never heard of them. Soon afterward, however, some New Zealand fruit growers offered her 2,400 pounds of the fuzzy, brown-skinned fruit with the strawberry-banana-melon-pineapple flavor. Frieda took the fruit, renamed it "kiwi" after the national bird of

New Zealand, and sold it to chains throughout the United States.

Today, more than three hundred food and complimentary items carry the Frieda label. What is the key to the company's wholesaling success? Many buyers report that although they could often purchase exotic fruits and vegetables at lower prices from other wholesalers, they buy Frieda's because of the firm's flexibility and excellent service. The company maintains consistent quality standards that produce buyers have come to rely on. Frieda's also offers strong retail support: it holds seminars for produce buyers and managers and provides merchandising bulletins, displays, and promotion packages. Frieda's weekly newsletter keeps produce retailers informed about what is available, what is selling, and what consumers are saying in the hundreds of letters Frieda's receives every week.

Frieda Caplan admits that once a specialty becomes a staple, her company can no longer compete with wholesaling giants. Frieda's Finest kiwis and common mushrooms no longer dominate the market. By turning instead to strange fruits like the jicama and the kiwano, Frieda's records annual sales of over $23 million and continues changing the way America eats.

selling experience, and a known, predetermined selling expense (a commission that is a percentage of sales revenue).

broker a middleman that specializes in a particular commodity, represents either a buyer or a seller, and is likely to be hired on a temporary basis

A **broker** is a middleman that specializes in a particular commodity, represents either a buyer *or* a seller, and is likely to be hired on a temporary basis. However, food brokers, which sell grocery products to resellers, generally have long-term relationships with their clients. Brokers may perform only the selling function or both buying and selling, using established contacts or special knowledge of their fields.

manufacturer's sales branch essentially a merchant wholesaler that is owned by a manufacturer

Manufacturers' Sales Branches and Sales Offices   A **manufacturer's sales branch** is, in essence, a merchant wholesaler that is owned by a manufacturer. Sales branches carry stock, extend credit, deliver goods, and offer help in promoting products. Their customers are retailers, other wholesalers, and industrial purchasers.

Because sales branches are owned by producers, they stock primarily the goods manufactured by their own firms. Selling policies and terms are usually established centrally and then transmitted to branch managers for implementation.

manufacturer's sales office essentially a sales agent owned by a manufacturer

A **manufacturer's sales office** is essentially a sales agent owned by a manufacturer. Sales offices may sell goods manufactured by their own firms and also certain products of other manufacturers that complement their own product lines. For example, Hiram Walker & Sons imports wine from Spain to increase the number of products its sales offices can offer to customers.

■■ MARKETING INTERMEDIARIES: RETAILERS

LEARNING OBJECTIVE 6 Distinguish among the major types of retailers.

Retailers are the final link between producers and consumers. Retailers may buy from either wholesalers or producers. They sell not only goods but also such services as repairs, haircuts, and tailoring. Some retailers sell both. Sears, Roebuck sells consumer goods, financial services, and repair services for home appliances bought at Sears.

Of the more than 1.51 million retail firms in the United States, about 90 percent have annual sales of less than $1 million.[3] On the other hand, there are giants that realize well over $1 million every week in sales revenue. Table 14.1 lists the twenty largest retail firms, the cities where their headquarters are located, and their approximate sales revenues and yearly profits. Figure 14.4 shows retail sales categorized by major merchandise type and the percentage of total sales for each type.

Classes of In-Store Retailers

independent retailer   a firm that operates only one retail outlet

One way to classify retailers is by the number of stores owned and operated by the firm. An **independent retailer** is firm that operates only one retail outlet. Approximately 78 percent of retailers are independent.[4] One-store operators, like all small businesses, generally provide personal service and a convenient location.

chain retailer   a company that operates more than one retail outlet

A **chain retailer** is a company that operates more than one retail outlet. By adding outlets, chain retailers attempt to reach new geographic markets. As sales increase, chains may buy merchandise in larger quantities and thus take advantage of quantity discounts. They also wield more power in their dealings with suppliers. About 22 percent of retailers operate chains.[5]

Another way to classify in-store retailers is by store size and the kind and number of products carried. Let's take a closer look at store types based on these dimensions.

Department Stores   These large retail establishments consist of several sections, or departments, that sell a wide assortment of products. According to

TABLE 14.1   The Twenty Largest Retail Firms in the United States

Rank	Company (Headquarters)	Annual Sales (in millions)	Annual Profits (in millions)
1	Wal-Mart (Bentonville, Ark.)	$67,344.6	$2,333.3
2	Kmart (Troy, Mich)	34,156.0	(1.0)*
3	Sears, Roebuck and Co. (Chicago)	29,564.0	751.6
4	Kroger (Cincinnati)	22,384.3	(12.0)*
5	J. C. Penney (Dallas)	19,578.0	940.0
6	Dayton Hudson (Minneapolis)	19,233.0	375.0
7	American Stores Co. (Salt Lake City)	18,763.4	247.1
8	Safeway Inc. (Oakland, Calif.)	15,214.5	123.3
9	Price/Costco (San Diego)	15,155.0	223.0
10	May Department Stores Co. (St. Louis)	11,529.0	711.0
11	Albertson's (Boise, Idaho)	11,283.7	339.7
12	Winn-Dixie Stores (Jacksonville, Fla.)	10,831.5	236.4
13	Melville (Rye, N.Y.)	10,435.4	331.8
14	A&P (Montvale, N.J.)	10,384.0	3.9
15	Woolworth (New York)	9,626.0	(495.0)*
16	The Home Depot (Atlanta)	9,238.8	457.4
17	Walgreen Co. (Deerfield, Ill.)	8,294.8	221.7
18	Toys "R" Us (Paramus, N. J.)	7,946.0	483.0
19	Army & Air Force Exchange (Dallas)	7,700.0	315.2
20	Food Lion (Salisbury, N.C.)	7,609.8	3.8

*Parentheses indicate losses

Source: "State of the Industry," *Chain Store Age Executive,* August 1994, pp. 3A, 4A. Reprinted by permission from *Chain Store Age Executive* (August 1994), Copyright Lebhar-Friedman, Inc., 425 Park Avenue, New York, NY 10022.

FIGURE 14.4
Retail Sales Categorized by Merchandise Type
The numbers in this graph represent the percentage of total sales for each merchandise type. *(Source:* Monthly Retail Trade: Sales and Inventories, *July 1994, U.S. Bureau of the Census, p. 5.)*

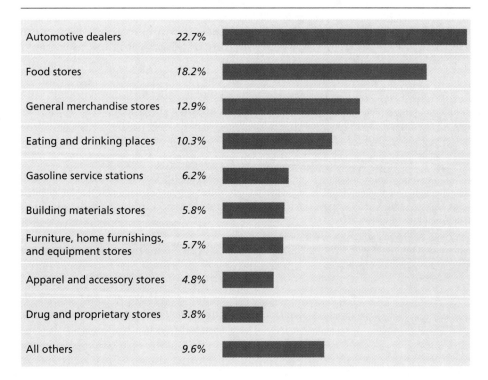

Automotive dealers	22.7%
Food stores	18.2%
General merchandise stores	12.9%
Eating and drinking places	10.3%
Gasoline service stations	6.2%
Building materials stores	5.8%
Furniture, home furnishings, and equipment stores	5.7%
Apparel and accessory stores	4.8%
Drug and proprietary stores	3.8%
All others	9.6%

department store a retail store that (1) employs twenty-five or more persons and (2) sells at least home furnishings, appliances, family apparel, and household linens and dry goods, each in a different part of the store

discount store a self-service, general merchandise outlet that sells goods at lower-than-usual prices

catalog showroom a retail outlet that displays well-known brands and sells them at discount prices through catalogs within the store

warehouse showroom a retail facility in a large, low-cost building with on-premises inventories and minimal services

convenience store a small food store that sells a limited variety of products but remains open well beyond normal business hours

AT A GLANCE

Selective Shoppers

Reasons that female leisure shoppers choose specific stores.

Source: EDK Forecast.

the U.S. Bureau of the Census, a **department store** is a retail store that (1) employs twenty-five or more persons and (2) sells at least home furnishings, appliances, family apparel, and household linens and dry goods, each in a different part of the store. Marshall Fields in Chicago (and several other cities), Harrod's in London, and Au Printemps in Paris are examples of large department stores. Sears, Roebuck and J. C. Penney are also department stores. Department stores are distinctly service oriented. Along with the goods they sell, these retailers provide credit, delivery, personal assistance, liberal return policies, and pleasant shopping atmospheres.

Discount Stores A **discount store** is a self-service, general merchandise outlet that sells goods at lower-than-usual prices. These stores can offer lower prices by operating on smaller markups; locating large retail showrooms in low-rent areas; and offering minimal customer services. To keep prices low, discount stores operate on the basic principle of high turnover of such items as appliances, toys, clothing, automotive products, and sports equipment. To attract customers, many discount stores also offer some food and household items at low prices. Popular discount stores include Kmart, Wal-Mart, Dollar General, and Target.

As competition among discount stores has increased, some discounters have improved their services, store environments, and locations. As a consequence, many of the better-known discount stores have assumed the characteristics of department stores. This upgrading has boosted their prices and blurred the distinction between some discount stores and department stores.[6]

Catalog and Warehouse Showrooms A **catalog showroom** is a retail outlet that displays well-known brands and sells them at discount prices through catalogs within the store. Colorful catalogs are available in the showroom (and sometimes by mail). The customer selects the merchandise, either from the catalog or from the showroom display. The customer fills out an order form provided by the store and hands the form to a clerk. The clerk retrieves the merchandise from a warehouse room that is adjacent to the selling area. Service Merchandise is a well-known catalog showroom.

Warehouse showrooms are retail facilities with five basic characteristics: (1) large, low-cost buildings, (2) warehouse materials-handling technology, (3) vertical merchandise displays, (4) large on-premises inventories, and (5) minimal service. Some of the best-known showrooms are operated by big furniture retailers such as Wickes Furniture and Levitz Furniture Corporation. These operations employ few personnel and offer few services. Most customers carry away purchases in the manufacturer's carton, although some warehouse showrooms will deliver for a fee.

Convenience Stores A **convenience store** is a small food store that sells a limited variety of products but remains open well beyond normal business hours. Almost 70 percent of convenience store customers live within a mile of the store. White Hen Pantry, 7-Eleven, Circle K, and Open Pantry stores, for example, are found in most areas, as are independent convenience stores. Their limited product mixes and the high prices they must charge to stay open long hours, seven days a week, keep convenience stores from becoming a threat to other grocery retailers.

supermarket a large self-service store that sells primarily food and household products

Supermarkets   A **supermarket** is a large self-service store that sells primarily food and household products. It stocks canned, fresh, frozen, and processed foods, paper products, and cleaning goods. Supermarkets may also sell such items as housewares, toiletries, toys and games, drugs, stationery, books and magazines, plants and flowers, and a few clothing items.

Supermarkets are large-scale operations that emphasize low prices and one-stop shopping for household needs. The first self-service food market opened over fifty years ago; it grossed only $5,000 per week, with an average sale of just $1.31.[7] Today, a supermarket has minimum annual sales of at least $2 million. Current top-ranking supermarkets include Safeway Stores, Inc., The Kroger Company, Winn-Dixie Stores, Albertson's, and A & P.

superstore a large retail store that carries not only food and nonfood products ordinarily found in supermarkets but also additional product lines

Superstores   A **superstore** is a large retail store that carries not only food and nonfood products ordinarily found in supermarkets but also additional product lines—housewares, hardware, small appliances, clothing, personal-care products, garden products, and automotive merchandise. Superstores also provide a number of services to entice customers. Typically these include automotive repair, snack bars and restaurants, film developing, and banking.

combination store a store that carries food items and general merchandise

Combination Stores   A **combination store** joins groceries and general merchandise under one roof, with general merchandising generating 25 to 40 percent of sales. Combination stores occupy 30,000 to 100,000 square feet. Because of their huge size and broad assortment, combination stores benefit from an increased number of customers, more impulse purchasing, higher per-customer expenditures, and greater profits from the mix of food items and general merchandise products. Up to one-half of the selling space may be devoted to nonfood products.

warehouse club a large-scale, members-only establishment that combines features of cash-and-carry wholesaling with discount retailing

Warehouse Clubs   The **warehouse club** is a large-scale, members-only operation that combines cash-and-carry wholesaling features with discount retailing. For a nominal annual fee (usually $25), small retailers may purchase products at wholesale prices for business use or for resale. Warehouse clubs also sell to ultimate consumers. Instead of paying a membership fee, individual consumers pay about 5 percent more on each item than do small-business owners. Individual purchasers can usually choose to pay yearly dues for membership cards that allow them to avoid the 5 percent markup.

Warehouse clubs offer the same types of products offered by discount stores, but in a limited range of sizes and styles. Because their product lines are shallow and sales volumes are high, warehouse clubs can offer a broad range of merchandise, including perishable and nonperishable foods, beverages, books, appliances, housewares, automotive parts, hardware, furniture, and sundries. The sales volume of most warehouse clubs is four to five times that of a typical department store. With stock turning over at an average rate of eighteen times each year, warehouse clubs sell their goods before manufacturers' payment periods are up, thus reducing their need for capital.

To keep their prices 20 to 40 percent lower than those of supermarkets and discount stores, warehouse clubs provide few services. They generally advertise only through direct mail. Their facilities often have concrete floors and aisles wide enough for forklifts. Merchandise is stacked on pallets or displayed on pipe racks. All payments must be in cash, and customers must transport purchases themselves. Although at one time there were about twenty competing warehouse clubs, only two major competitors remain: Sam's Club and Price/Costco.

Traditional Specialty Stores   A **traditional specialty store** carries a narrow product mix with deep product lines. Traditional specialty stores are sometimes called *limited-line retailers*. If they carry depth in one particular product category, they may be called *single-line retailers*. Specialty stores usually sell shopping products such as clothing, jewelry, sporting goods, fabrics, computers, flowers, baked goods, books, and pet supplies. Examples of specialty stores include The Gap, Radio Shack, Hickory Farms, and Foot Locker.

traditional specialty store
a store that carries a narrow product mix with deep product lines

Specialty stores usually offer better selections than department stores. They attract customers by emphasizing service, atmosphere, and location. Consumers who are dissatisfied with the impersonal atmosphere of large retailers often find the attention offered by small specialty stores appealing.

Off-Price Retailers   **Off-price retailers** are stores that buy manufacturers' seconds, overruns, returns, and off-season production runs at below-wholesale prices and sell them to consumers at deep discounts. Off-price retailers sell limited lines of national-brand and designer merchandise, usually clothing, shoes, or housewares. Examples of off-price retailers include T.J. Maxx, Stein Mart, Burlington Coat Factory, and Marshalls. Off-price stores charge up to 50 percent less than department stores do for comparable merchandise but offer few customer services. They often include community dressing rooms, central checkout counters, and no credit, returns, or exchanges. Another form of off-price retailing is the manufacturers' outlet mall, which sells manufacturer overstocks and unsold merchandise from

off-price retailer   a store that buys manufacturers' seconds, overruns, returns, and off-season merchandise for resale to consumers at deep discounts

Traditional specialty retailer.
Gap stores are traditional specialty retailers. The Gap specializes in casual clothing for both men and women.

other retail stores. Prices are low and assorted manufacturers sell their products in these malls.

Category Killer   A **category killer** is a very large specialty store that concentrates on a single product line and competes by offering low prices and an enormous number of products. These stores are called category killers because they take business away from smaller, high-cost retail stores. Examples of category killers include The Home Depot (building materials), Office Depot (office supplies and equipment), and Toys "R" Us, the nation's leading toy retailer.

Kinds of Nonstore Retailing

Nonstore retailing is selling that does not take place in conventional store facilities; consumers purchase products without visiting a store. Nonstore retailers use direct selling, direct marketing, and vending machines.

Direct Selling   **Direct selling** is the marketing of products to customers through face-to-face sales presentations at home or in the workplace. Traditionally called door-to-door selling, direct selling has grown to become a vast industry. Instead of the door-to-door approach, many companies today—such as World Book, Mary Kay, Amway, and Avon—identify customers by mail, telephone, or at shopping malls and then make appointments. The party plan method of direct selling takes place in homes or in the workplace. Customers act as hosts and invite friends or coworkers to view products. A salesperson conducts the "party" and demonstrates products. Companies that rely on the party plan are Tupperware, Stanley Home Products, and Sarah Coventry.

Benefits of direct selling include product demonstration, personal attention, and convenience. In fact, personal attention is the foundation on which some direct sellers base their companies. The primary disadvantage of direct selling is the fact that it is the most expensive form of retailing. Overall costs of direct selling are high because of high salesperson commissions and efforts required to locate prospects. In addition, some people view direct selling negatively, and some communities have enacted local ordinances regulating or even banning direct selling.

Direct Marketing   **Direct marketing** is the use of the telephone and nonpersonal media to communicate product and organizational information to customers, who can then buy products by mail or telephone. Catalog marketing, direct-response marketing, telemarketing, home shopping, and computer-interactive marketing are all types of direct marketing.

With **catalog marketing,** an organization provides a catalog from which customers make selections and place orders by mail or telephone. Some companies, such as Spiegel and J. C. Penney, offer a wide range of products. Other catalog companies, such as L.L. Bean and Lands' End, offer one major line of products. Certain catalog companies specialize in only a few products, such as educational toys or specialty foods. Many customers find catalog marketing efficient and convenient. Retailers do not have to invest in expensive store fixtures, and personal selling and operating expenses are significantly reduced. However, catalog marketing provides

category killer   a very large specialty store that concentrates on a single product line and competes on the basis of low prices and product availability

nonstore retailing   a type of retailing where consumers purchase products without visiting a store

direct selling   the marketing of products to ultimate consumers through face-to-face sales presentations at home or in the workplace

direct marketing   the use of the telephone and nonpersonal media to introduce products to consumers, who can then purchase them by mail or telephone

catalog marketing   marketing in which an organization provides a catalog from which customers make selections and place orders by mail or telephone

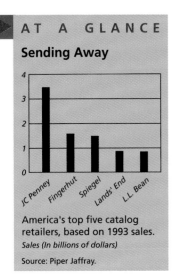

▶▶▶ AT A GLANCE

Sending Away

America's top five catalog retailers, based on 1993 sales.
Sales (In billions of dollars)

Source: Piper Jaffray.

direct-response marketing marketing that occurs when a retailer advertises a product and makes it available through mail or telephone orders

telemarketing the performance of marketing-related activities by telephone

television home shopping selling in which products are displayed to television viewers, who can then order them by calling a toll-free number and paying by credit card

computer-interactive retailing selling that presents products on customers' computer screens; customers place orders through their terminals and modems

automatic vending the use of machines to dispense convenience goods automatically when customers deposit money

limited service and is most effective for only some types of products. Some catalog retailers have reputations for excellent service, but studies show that many catalog customers complain about product quality, delivery times, and shipment errors.

Direct-response marketing occurs when a retailer advertises a product and makes it available through mail or telephone orders. Customers usually use a credit card to make purchases. Examples of direct-response marketing are a television commercial advertising a set of knives available through a toll-free number, a magazine ad for a series of cookbooks available by filling out a coupon, and even billboards promoting travel services by calling 1-800-GO AMTRAK. Sending letters, samples, brochures, or booklets to prospects on a mailing list are also forms of direct-response marketing.

Telemarketing is using the telephone to perform marketing-related activities. Examples of companies that use telemarketing to supplement other marketing methods include Merrill Lynch, Allstate Insurance, Avis, General Motors, and American Express. Some organizations use a prepared list of customers, and others rely on names from telephone directories. Advantages of telemarketing include generating sales leads, improving customer service, speeding up payment on past-due accounts, raising funds for nonprofit organizations, and gathering marketing information.

Television home shopping displays products to television viewers, who can then order them by calling a toll-free number and paying by credit card. There are many home shopping cable channels; some of them specialize in specific product categories. The most common products sold through television home shopping are electronics, clothing, housewares, and jewelry. Benefits of home shopping include time for thorough product demonstration and customer convenience.

Computer-interactive retailing, sometimes called *videotex,* presents products on customers' computer screens. Customers purchase products by ordering them through their terminals and modems. Computer-information services such as Prodigy and CompuServe offer videotex services in addition to financial and travel services.

Automatic Vending **Automatic vending** is the use of machines to dispense convenience goods automatically when customers deposit the appropriate amount of money. Vending machines do not require sales personnel; they permit twenty-four-hour service; and they can be placed in convenient locations in office buildings, educational institutions, motels and hotels, shopping malls, and service stations. The machines make available a wide assortment of goods—candy, cigarettes, soups, sandwiches, fresh fruits, yogurt, chewing gum, postage stamps, hot and cold beverages, perfume and cosmetics, even golf balls! Machines sell travel insurance at airports and offer around-the-clock banking services at convenient urban and suburban locations.

Because vending machines need only a small amount of space and no sales personnel, this retailing method has some advantages over stores. What drawbacks plague the vending-machine business? For one thing, malfunctioning is a costly and frustrating problem, as is vandalism. The

■ ■ ■ ■ ■ GLOBAL PERSPECTIVES

Avon Calling in Emerging Markets

As more and more American women seek permanent full-time jobs, the number of "Avon Ladies" in the United States is steadily declining, and so are the cosmetics giant's U.S. sales. In addition, Avon is no match for retail chains like Wal-Mart that sell similar products at discount prices. Avon faces problems in Europe as well. In Germany, many consumers find direct sellers intrusive. In France, where the fashion and cosmetics industries flourish, many reject what they view as "cheap imitations" of haute couture. And for those who aren't averse to saving a deutschemark or a franc, European "hypermarches" offer discounts just like Wal-Mart's. But in Argentina, Brazil, Hungary, Slovakia, Poland, the Czech Republic, India, and Vietnam, and many other emerging markets around the world, women are delighted to see their Avon representatives at the door offering a full line of powders, polishes, and perfumes.

In 1886 David McConnel created the California Perfume Company, (renamed Avon in 1950), hiring women to sell cosmetics and other beauty-related items door-to-door. It didn't take long for the expression "Avon Calling" to become American household words. Today, Avon is a $4 billion cosmetics and beauty-aids marketer with 1.7 million sales representatives in 112 countries around the world, from Mexico to China. Although you might not picture the Avon lady as someone clutching her sample bag stocked with deodorant, lotion, and perfume and trudging along dirt roads to visit wooden shacks in the tiny villages of Brazil, more than half of Avon's sales come from countries outside the United States and western Europe.

As it expands internationally, Avon's biggest challenge has been to build brand awareness. In isolated regions like Brazil's Amazon, Avon distributes leaflets announcing its arrival. In China, where people are used to shopping at their local markets and are a little suspicious of door-to-door salespeople, Avon opens showrooms where shoppers can sample products such as a skin cream developed specifically for Asian women. To attract Polish customers, Avon advertised in leading women's magazines and local newspapers; the headline declared that Avon is "Twoj Styl"—Your Style. Avon believes that once consumers in these markets are aware of what the company has to offer and once its sales staff get their feet in the door, Avon's personalized service and product knowledge will win customers over and earn their loyalty.

Avon isn't the only direct sales cosmetics company with its eye on emerging markets, however. Sales of rival Mary Kay Cosmetics are growing in Taiwan, Mexico, and Argentina, and soon women in China and Poland will be able to choose between Avon and Mary Kay. In addition, Avon will soon have competition from Wal-Mart in Argentina, China, Brazil, and Hong Kong. With developing markets accounting for more than 35 percent of its total annual sales, Avon remains confident. The company expects that within the next few years, women in Ukraine, Belarus, Romania, and Albania will answer their doorbells and hear the words "Avon Calling" in their native languages.

Easy shopping. Home shopping, a type of direct marketing, allows the customer to shop from the comfort of home. Over the last decade, home shopping has grown significantly as a form of non-store retailing.

machines must also be serviced frequently to operate properly. Together, repairs and servicing result in a very high proportion of the cost of vending-machine selling—often eating up more than one-third of sales revenues.

The Wheel of Retailing

LEARNING OBJECTIVE 7
Explain the wheel of retailing hypothesis.

wheel of retailing
a hypothesis that suggests that new retail operations usually begin at the bottom—in price, profits, and prestige—and gradually move up the cost/price scale, competing with newer businesses that are evolving in the same way

Newly developing retail businesses strive for a secure position in the ever-changing retailing environment. One theory attempts to explain how types of retail stores originate and develop. The **wheel of retailing** hypothesis suggests that new retail operations usually begin at the bottom—in price, profits, and prestige. In time, their facilities become more elaborate, their investments increase, and their operating costs go up. Finally, the retailers emerge at the top of the cost/price scale, competing with newer businesses that are evolving in the same way.[8]

In Figure 14.5, the wheel of retailing illustrates the development of department and discount stores. Department stores such as Sears were originally high-volume, low-cost retailers competing with general stores and other small businesses. As the costs of services rose in department stores, discount stores began to fill the low-price retailing niche. Now many discount stores, in turn, are following the pattern by expanding services, improving locations, upgrading inventories, and raising prices.

Like most hypotheses, the wheel of retailing may not be universally applicable. The theory cannot predict what new retailing developments will occur, or when, for example. In industrialized, expanding economies, however, the hypothesis does help explain retailing patterns.

Telemarketers: Making Sales While Maintaining Privacy

When it costs companies $7 for a telephone sales representative to make the same sale that it costs $300 for a traveling representative to make, it is no wonder that telemarketing is flourishing. Over 500,000 U.S. operations employ about 4.5 million telemarketers who call over 18 million Americans every day and generate $500 billion worth of sales. What many businesses welcome as the future of sales, however, many disgruntled customers resent as "junk calls."

Consumers are upset by much more than just shady or outright illegal telephone solicitations for dream homes or vacations. Privacy advocates are angry that customers' names often appear on lists that companies pass around from one to another. Families are irritated by unsolicited dinnertime callers trying to sell them insurance or children's books. Especially disturbing to many consumers is the recent appearance of autodialing, in which machines call and give the sales pitch. To protect the privacy of residential telephone customers and to minimize consumer dissatisfaction, the U.S. Congress, various states, and the Federal Communications Commission have instituted laws and regulations to control telemarketing.

Passed in 1992, the Telephone Consumer Protection Act prohibits phone solicitation between 9 P.M. and 8 A.M. and stipulates that consumers can stop solicitors from calling them by asking to be put on a company's "do-not-call" list. Firms that continue calling after such a request are subject to legal actions. Many states maintain statewide "no-call" lists. Florida, for example, recently sued a refrigeration and air-conditioning company for allegedly telemarketing to people on its state no-call list. The 1994 Telemarketing and Consumer Fraud and Abuse Prevention Act strengthens the 1992 legislation with rules designed to protect consumers from dishonest telemarketers.

When the caller is a human, you can ask to be put on the list, but what happens when the caller is a machine? To exert tighter controls on autodialing, Congress recently outlined additional telemarketing regulations. Organizations using autodialing must now devise some way for consumers who object to unsolicited calls to get on a do-not-call list; companies must immediately identify themselves, giving a telephone number and address; and the autodialer must release the phone line within five seconds of the party's hanging up. Convinced that these rules do not go far enough, some states have banned autodialing altogether. Although the U.S. Supreme Court affirmed that states have the right to ban businesses from using automatically dialed, recorded messages to make unsolicited sales calls, an Oregon judge recently labeled such a law an unconstitutional infringement of free speech. Because many small businesses cannot afford live operators and depend on prerecorded solicitations, it is unlikely the issue will soon be resolved.

The Direct Marketing Association's Privacy Taskforce advises aggravated consumers to stay on the line long enough to find out who's calling and to get on the no-call list. For a $20 membership fee, you can get your name on a list sent to 1,200 telemarketers by Private Citizen, an Illinois-based citizen's rights group. New technology, such as Caller I.D., may save those who can afford the service from unwanted calls. However, lack of rules stipulating how consumers can prove they asked to be on a no-call list, absence of a national no-call data base, and exclusion of tax-exempt organizations from many regulations all add up to lots of leeway for unsolicited sales calls. So dissatisfied was one consumer that he invented a machine, the "PreFone Filter," that alerts callers that no sales calls are accepted. Although planning to market the device nationally, the inventor will not be making his sales pitch on the phone.

445

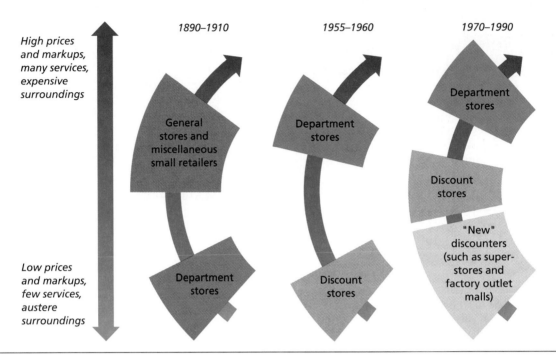

1890–1910   *1955–1960*   *1970–1990*

High prices and markups, many services, expensive surroundings

General stores and miscellaneous small retailers

Department stores

Department stores

Discount stores

"New" discounters (such as super-stores and factory outlet malls)

Low prices and markups, few services, austere surroundings

Department stores

Discount stores

FIGURE 14.5
The Wheel of Retailing
If the "wheel" is considered to be turning slowly in the direction of the arrow, then the department stores around 1900 and the discounters later can be viewed as coming on the scene in the lower part of the wheel. As it slowly turns, they move with it, becoming higher-priced operations and, at the same time, leaving room for lower-priced types of firms to gain entry at the low end of the wheel.
(Source: Adapted from Robert F. Hartley. Copyright © 1984. Used by permission.)

LEARNING OBJECTIVE 8
Identify the categories of shopping centers and the factors that determine how shopping centers are classified.

neighborhood shopping center   a planned shopping center consisting of several small convenience and specialty stores

■■ THE PLANNED SHOPPING CENTER

The planned shopping center is a self-contained retail facility, constructed by private owners and containing various stores. Shopping centers are designed and promoted to serve diverse groups of consumers with widely differing needs. The management of a shopping center strives for a coordinated mix of stores, a comfortable atmosphere, adequate parking, pleasant landscaping, and special events to attract consumers. The convenience of shopping for most family and household needs in a single location is an important part of shopping-center appeal.

A planned shopping center is one of three types: neighborhood, community, or regional. Although shopping centers vary, each offers a complementary mix of stores for the purpose of generating consumer traffic.

Neighborhood Shopping Centers

A **neighborhood shopping center** typically consists of several small convenience and specialty stores. Businesses in neighborhood shopping centers might include small grocery stores, drugstores, gas stations, and fast-food restaurants. These retailers serve consumers who live less than ten minutes away, usually within a two- to three-mile radius of the stores. Because most purchases in the neighborhood shopping center are based on convenience or personal contact, these retailers generally make only limited efforts to coordinate sales activities.

Community Shopping Centers

A **community shopping center** includes one or two department stores and some specialty stores, along with convenience stores. It attracts consumers from a wider geographic area who will drive longer distances to find products and specialty items unavailable in neighborhood shopping centers. Community shopping centers, which are carefully planned and coordinated, generate traffic with special events such as art exhibits, automobile shows, and sidewalk sales. The management of a community shopping center maintains a balance of tenants so that the center can offer wide product mixes and deep product lines.

Regional Shopping Centers

A **regional shopping center** usually has large department stores, numerous specialty stores, restaurants, movie theaters, and sometimes even hotels. It carries most of the merchandise offered by a downtown shopping district. Downtown merchants, in fact, have often renovated their stores and enlarged their parking facilities to meet the competition of successful regional shopping centers. Urban expressways and improved public transportation have also helped many downtown shopping areas to remain vigorous.

Regional shopping centers carefully coordinate management and marketing activities to reach the 150,000 or more customers in their target market. These large centers usually advertise, hold special events, and provide transportation to certain groups of customers. They also maintain a suitable mix of stores. National chain stores can gain leases in regional shopping centers more easily than small independent stores because they are better able to meet the centers' financial requirements.

■■ PHYSICAL DISTRIBUTION

Physical distribution is all those activities concerned with the efficient movement of products from the producer to the ultimate user. Physical distribution is thus the movement of the products themselves—both goods and services—through their channels of distribution. It is a combination of several interrelated business functions. The most important of these are inventory management, order processing, warehousing, materials handling, and transportation.

Not too long ago, each of these functions was considered distinct from all the others. In a fairly large firm, one group or department would handle each function. Each of these groups would work to minimize its own costs and to maximize its own effectiveness, but the result was usually high physical distribution costs.

Various studies of the problem emphasized both the interrelationships among the physical distribution functions *and* the relationships between physical distribution and other marketing functions. Long production runs may reduce per-unit product costs, but they can cause inventory-control and warehousing costs to skyrocket. A new automated warehouse may reduce materials-handling costs to a minimum, but if the warehouse is not located properly, transportation time and costs may increase substantially.

There are many more instances of these interrelationships, and they have been duly noted. Marketers now view physical distribution as an integrated effort that provides an important marketing service: getting the right product to the right place at the right time and at minimal *overall* cost.

Inventory Management

inventory management   the process of managing inventories in such a way as to minimize inventory costs, including both holding costs and potential stock-out costs

In Chapter 8 we discussed inventory management from the standpoint of operations. We defined **inventory management** as the process of managing inventories in such a way as to minimize inventory costs, including both holding costs and potential stock-out costs. Both the definition and the objective of inventory control apply here as well.

Holding costs are the costs of storing products until they are purchased or shipped to customers. *Stock-out costs* are the costs of sales lost when items are not in inventory. Of course, holding costs can be minimized by minimizing inventories, but then stock-out costs would ruin the firm. And stock-out costs can be minimized by carrying very large inventories, but then holding costs would be enormous.

Inventory management is thus a sort of balancing act between stock-out costs and holding costs. The latter include the cost of money invested in inventory, the cost of storage space, insurance costs, and inventory taxes. Often, even a relatively small reduction in inventory investment can provide a relatively large increase in working capital. And sometimes this reduction can best be accomplished through a willingness to incur a reasonable level of stock-out costs.

Order Processing

order processing   activities involved in receiving and filling customers' purchase orders

Order processing consists of activities involved in receiving and filling customers' purchase orders. It may include the means by which customers order products as well as procedures for billing and for granting credit.

Fast, efficient order processing is an important marketing service—one that can provide a dramatic competitive edge. The people who purchase goods for intermediaries are especially concerned with their suppliers' promptness and reliability in order processing. To them it means minimal inventory costs as well as the ability to order goods when they are needed rather than weeks in advance.

Warehousing

warehousing   the set of activities involved in receiving and storing goods and preparing them for reshipment

Warehousing is the set of activities involved in receiving and storing goods and preparing them for reshipment. Goods are stored to create time utility; that is, they are held until they are needed for use or sale. But along with storage, warehousing includes these other activities:[9]

- *Receiving goods*—The warehouse accepts delivered goods and assumes responsibility for them.
- *Identifying goods*—Records are made of the quantity of each item received. Items may be marked, coded, or tagged for identification.

- *Sorting goods*—Delivered goods may have to be sorted before being stored.
- *Dispatching goods to storage*—Items must be moved to specific storage areas, where they can be found later.
- *Holding goods*—The goods are kept in storage under proper protection until needed.
- *Recalling, selecting, or picking goods*—Items that are to leave the warehouse must be efficiently selected from storage.
- *Marshaling shipments*—The items making up each shipment are brought together, and the shipment is checked for completeness. Records are prepared or modified as necessary.
- *Dispatching shipments*—Each shipment is packaged suitably and directed to the proper transport vehicle. Shipping and accounting documents are prepared.

A firm may either use its own warehouses or rent space in public warehouses. A *private warehouse,* owned and operated by a particular firm, can be designed to serve the firm's specific needs. However, the organization must take on the task of financing the facility, determining the best location for it, and ensuring that it is used fully. Generally, only companies that deal in large quantities of goods can justify private warehouses.

Public warehouses offer their services to all individuals and firms. Most are huge, one-story structures on the outskirts of major cities, where rail and truck transportation are easily available. They provide storage facilities, areas for sorting and marshaling shipments, and office and display spaces for wholesalers and retailers. Public warehouses will also hold—and issue receipts for—goods used as collateral for borrowed funds.

Materials Handling

materials handling the actual physical handling of goods, in warehousing as well as during transportation

Materials handling is the actual physical handling of goods, in warehousing as well as during transportation. Proper materials-handling procedures and techniques can increase the usable capacity of a warehouse or that of any means of transportation. Proper handling can reduce breakage and spoilage as well.

Modern materials handling attempts to reduce the number of times a product is handled. One method is called *unit loading.* Several smaller cartons, barrels, or boxes are combined into a single standard-size load that can be handled efficiently by forklift, conveyer, or truck.

Transportation

transportation the shipment of products to customers

As a part of physical distribution, **transportation** is simply the shipment of products to customers. The greater the distance between seller and purchaser, the more important the choice of the means of transportation and the particular carrier.

carrier a firm that offers transportation services

A firm that offers transportation services is called a **carrier.** A *common carrier* is a transportation firm whose services are available to all shippers. Railroads, airlines, and most long-distance trucking firms are common carriers. A *contract carrier* is available for hire by one or several shippers.

Fast worldwide delivery. DHL is a provider of express delivery services to many parts of the world. Although express delivery services are usually limited to small shipments, shippers are willing to pay a higher cost for speed of delivery and assurance of security.

WHEN YOU HAVE THE BEST ON-TIME RECORD IN EUROPE, YOU KNOW HOW TO NAVIGATE THE BACK STREETS.

Whether it's the canals of Venice or the outskirts of Vladivostok, DHL has the most reliable delivery record in Europe. That's the kind of overseas expertise you'd expect from the company with more local people, airplanes and trucks than anyone else in the business. As you can see, we even have our own shipping lanes.

1-800-CALL-DHL

WE'LL TAKE IT FROM HERE

Contract carriers do not serve the general public. Moreover, the number of firms they can handle at any one time is limited by law. A *private carrier* is owned and operated by the shipper.

In addition, a shipper can hire agents called *freight forwarders* to handle its transportation. Freight forwarders pick up shipments from the shipper, ensure that the goods are loaded on selected carriers, and assume responsibility for the safe delivery of the shipments to their destinations. Freight forwarders can often group a number of small shipments into one large load (which is carried at a lower rate). This, of course, saves money for shippers.

The U.S. Postal Service offers *parcel post* delivery, which is widely used by mail-order houses. The post office provides complete geographic coverage at the lowest rates, but it limits the size and weight of the shipments it will accept. United Parcel Service, Inc. (UPS), a privately owned firm, also provides small-parcel services for shippers. Other privately owned carriers, such as Federal Express, DHL, and Airborne, offer fast—often overnight—parcel delivery, both within and outside the United States. There are also many local parcel carriers, including specialized delivery services for various time-sensitive industries, such as publishing.

The six major criteria used for selecting transportation modes are compared in Table 14.2. Obviously the cost of a transportation mode is important to marketers. At times marketers choose higher-cost modes of transportation in order to take advantage of the benefits that they provide. Speed is measured by the total time that a carrier possesses the products, including time required for pickup and delivery, handling, and movement between point of origin and destination. Usually there is a direct relationship between cost and speed; that is, faster modes of transportation are

TABLE 14.2   Relative Ratings of Transportation Modes by Selection Criteria

Selection Criteria						
Mode	Cost	Speed	Dependability	Load Flexibility	Accessibility	Frequency
Railroads	Moderate	Average	Average	High	High	Low
Trucks	High	Fast	High	Average	Very high	High
Airplanes	Very high	Very fast	High	Low	Average	Average
Waterways	Very low	Very slow	Average	Very high	Limited	Very low
Pipelines	Low	Slow	High	Very low	Very limited	Very high

more expensive. A transportation mode's dependability is determined by the consistency of service provided by that mode. Load flexibility is the degree to which a transportation mode can provide appropriate equipment and conditions for moving specific kinds of products and can be adapted for moving other kinds of products. For example, certain types of products may need controlled temperatures or humidity levels. Accessibility refers to a transportation mode's ability to move goods over a specific route or network. Frequency refers to how often a marketer can ship products by a specific transportation mode. Whereas pipelines provide continuous shipments, railroads and waterways follow specific schedules for moving products from one location to another. In Table 14.2 each transportation mode is rated on a relative basis for these six selection criteria. Figure 14.6 shows recent trends and a breakdown by use of the five different modes of transportation.

Railroads   In terms of total freight carried, railroads are America's most important mode of transportation. They are also the least expensive for many products. Almost all railroads are common carriers, although a few coal-mining companies operate their own lines.

Many commodities carried by railroads could not be transported easily by any other means. They include a wide range of foodstuffs, raw materials, and manufactured goods. Coal ranks first by a considerable margin. Other major commodities carried by railroads include grain, paper and pulp products, liquids in tank-car loads, heavy equipment, and lumber.

Trucks   The trucking industry consists of common, contract, and private carriers. It has undergone tremendous expansion since the creation of a national highway system in the 1920s. Trucks can move goods to suburban and rural areas not served by railroads. They can handle freight quickly and economically, and they carry a wide range of shipments. Many shippers favor this mode of transportation because it offers door-to-door service, less stringent packaging requirements than ships and airplanes, and flexible delivery schedules.

Railroad and truck carriers have teamed up to provide a form of transportation called *piggyback*. Truck trailers are carried from city to city on specially equipped railroad flatcars. Within each city, the trailers are then pulled in the usual way by truck tractors.

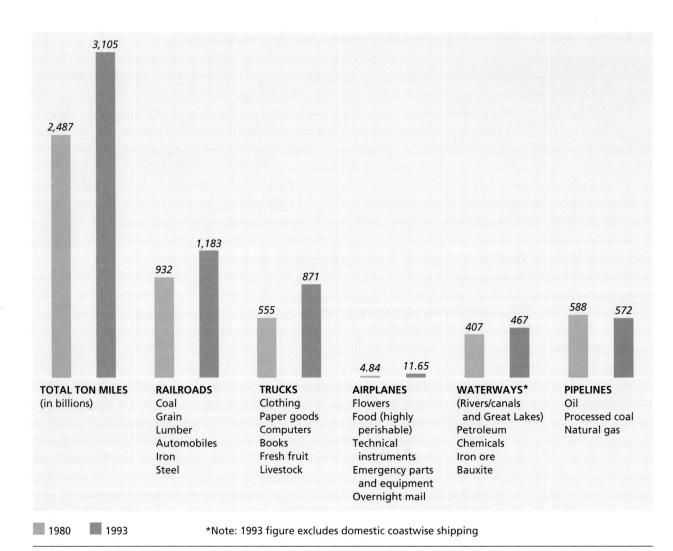

TOTAL TON MILES (in billions): 2,487 (1980), 3,105 (1993)

RAILROADS
Coal
Grain
Lumber
Automobiles
Iron
Steel
932 (1980), 1,183 (1993)

TRUCKS
Clothing
Paper goods
Computers
Books
Fresh fruit
Livestock
555 (1980), 871 (1993)

AIRPLANES
Flowers
Food (highly perishable)
Technical instruments
Emergency parts and equipment
Overnight mail
4.84 (1980), 11.65 (1993)

WATERWAYS*
(Rivers/canals and Great Lakes)
Petroleum
Chemicals
Iron ore
Bauxite
407 (1980), 467 (1993)

PIPELINES
Oil
Processed coal
Natural gas
588 (1980), 572 (1993)

■ 1980   ■ 1993   *Note: 1993 figure excludes domestic coastwise shipping

FIGURE 14.6
Changes in Ton Miles for Various Transportation Modes
Between 1980 and 1993, airline tonnage doubled and truck transportation increased significantly, while pipeline usage declined. Examples of typical products carried by the various modes are shown. *(Source: Rosalyn A. Wilson, "Transportation in America," December 1994, Eno Foundation for Transportation. Reprinted with permission.)*

Airplanes   Air transport is the fastest but most expensive means of transportation. All certified airlines are common carriers. Supplemental or charter lines are contract carriers.

Because of the high cost, lack of airport facilities in many areas, and reliance on weather conditions, airlines carry less than 1 percent of all intercity freight. Only high-value or perishable items, such as flowers, aircraft parts, and pharmaceuticals, or goods that are needed immediately are usually shipped by air.

Waterways   Cargo ships and barges offer the least expensive but slowest form of transportation. They are used mainly for bulky, nonperishable goods such as iron ore, bulk wheat, motor vehicles, and agricultural implements. Of course, shipment by water is limited to cities located on navigable waterways. But ships and barges account for a steady 16 percent of all intercity freight hauling.

Waterway transportation.
Container ships carry sealed containers that can be transferred to truck or rail transportation without unloading the container.

Pipelines   Pipelines are a highly specialized mode of transportation. They are used primarily to carry petroleum and natural gas. Pipelines have become more and more important as the nation's need for petroleum products has increased. Such products as semiliquid coal and wood chips can also be shipped through pipelines continuously, reliably, and with minimal handling.

In the next chapter we discuss the fourth element of the marketing mix—promotion.

■ ■ ■ ■ CHAPTER REVIEW

Summary

1   Identify the various channels of distribution that are used for consumer and industrial products.

A marketing channel is a sequence of marketing organizations that directs a product from producer to ultimate user. The marketing channel for a particular product is concerned with the transfer of ownership of that product. Merchant middlemen (merchants) actually take title to products, whereas functional middlemen simply aid in the transfer of title.

The channels used for consumer products include the direct channel from producer to consumer; the channel from producer to retailer to consumer; the channel from producer to wholesaler to retailer to consumer; and the channel from producer to agent to wholesaler to retailer to consumer. There are two major channels of industrial products: (a) producer to user and (b) producer to agent middleman to user.

2   Explain the concept of market coverage.

Channels and intermediaries are chosen to implement a given level of market coverage. Intensive distribution is the use of all available outlets for a product, providing the widest market coverage. Selective distribution uses only a portion of the available outlets in an area. Exclusive distribution uses only a single retail outlet for a product in a large geographical area.

3 Describe what a vertical marketing system is, and identify the types of vertical marketing systems.

A vertical marketing system (VMS) results from a combination of two or more channel members from different levels under one management. Administered, contractual, and corporate systems represent the three major types of VMSs.

4 Discuss the need for wholesalers.

Wholesalers are intermediaries that purchase from producers or other intermediaries and sell to industrial users, retailers, or other wholesalers. Wholesalers perform many functions in a channel. If they are eliminated, other channel members—such as the producer or retailers—must perform these functions. Wholesalers provide retailers with help in promoting products, collecting information, and financing. They provide manufacturers with sales help, reduce their inventory costs, furnish market information, and extend credit to retailers.

5 Identify the major types of wholesalers, and describe the services they perform for retailers and manufacturers.

Merchant wholesalers buy and then sell products. Commission merchants and brokers are essentially agents and do not take title to the goods they distribute. Sales branches and offices are owned by the manufacturers they represent and resemble merchant wholesalers and agents, respectively.

6 Distinguish among the major types of retailers.

Retailers are intermediaries that buy from producers or wholesalers and sell to consumers. In-store retailers include department stores, discount stores, catalog and warehouse showrooms, convenience stores, supermarkets, superstores, combination stores, warehouse clubs, traditional specialty stores, off-price retailers, and category killers. Nonstore retailers are retailers that do not sell in conventional store facilities and include direct selling, direct marketing, and automatic vending. Types of direct marketing include catalog marketing, direct-response marketing, telemarketing, television home shopping, and computer-interactive retailing.

7 Explain the wheel of retailing hypothesis.

The wheel of retailing hypothesis states that retailers begin as low-status, low-margin, low-priced stores and over time evolve into high-cost, high-priced operations.

8 Identify the categories of shopping centers and the factors that determine how shopping centers are classified.

There are three major types of shopping centers: neighborhood, community, and regional. A center fits one of these categories based on its mix of stores and the size of the geographic area it serves.

9 Explain the five most important physical distribution activities.

Physical distribution consists of activities designed to move products from producers to ultimate users. Its five major functions are inventory management, order processing, warehousing, materials handling, and transportation. These interrelated functions are integrated into the marketing effort.

Key Terms

You should now be able to define and give an example relevant to each of the following terms:

channel of distribution (or marketing channel) (426)
middleman (or marketing intermediary) (426)
merchant middleman (426)
functional middleman (426)
retailer (427)
wholesaler (427)
intensive distribution (429)
selective distribution (429)
exclusive distribution (429)
vertical channel integration (430)
vertical marketing system (VMS) (430)
merchant wholesaler (434)
full-service wholesaler (434)
general merchandise wholesaler (434)
limited-line wholesaler (434)
specialty-line wholesaler (434)
limited-service wholesaler (434)
commission merchant (434)
agent (434)
broker (435)
manufacturer's sales branch (436)
manufacturer's sales office (436)
independent retailer (436)
chain retailer (436)

department store (438)

discount store (438)

catalog showroom (438)

warehouse showroom (438)

convenience store (438)

supermarket (439)

superstore (439)

combination store (439)

warehouse club (439)

traditional specialty store (440)

off-price retailer (440)

category killer (441)

nonstore retailing (441)

direct selling (441)

direct marketing (441)

catalog marketing (441)

direct-response marketing (442)

telemarketing (442)

television home shopping (442)

computer-interactive retailing (442)

automatic vending (442)

wheel of retailing (444)

neighborhood shopping center (446)

community shopping center (447)

regional shopping center (447)

physical distribution (447)

inventory management (448)

order processing (448)

warehousing (448)

materials handling (449)

transportation (449)

carrier (449)

Questions

Review Questions

1. In what ways is a channel of distribution different from the path taken by a product during physical distribution?
2. What are the most common marketing channels for consumer products? for industrial products?
3. What are the three general approaches to market coverage? What types of products is each used for?
4. What is a vertical marketing system? Identify examples of the three types of VMSs.
5. List the services performed by wholesalers. For whom is each service performed?

6. What is the basic difference between a merchant wholesaler and an agent?
7. Identify three kinds of full-service wholesalers. What factors are used to classify wholesalers into one of these categories?
8. Distinguish between (a) commission merchants and agents and (b) manufacturers' sales branches and manufacturers' sales offices.
9. What is the basic difference between wholesalers and retailers?
10. What is the difference between a department store and a discount store with regard to selling orientation and philosophy?
11. How do (a) convenience stores, (b) traditional specialty stores, and (c) category killers compete with other retail outlets?
12. What can nonstore retailers offer their customers that in-store retailers cannot?
13. What does the wheel of retailing hypothesis suggest about new retail operations?
14. Compare and contrast community shopping centers and regional shopping centers.
15. What is physical distribution? Which major functions does it include?
16. What activities besides storage are included in warehousing?
17. List the primary modes of transportation, and cite at least one advantage of each.

Discussion Questions

1. What type of retailer is Starbucks Gourmet Coffee?
2. Evaluate Starbucks management's decision to use multiple forms of retailing.
3. Which distribution channels would producers of services be most likely to use? Why?
4. Many producers sell to consumers both directly and through middlemen. How can such a producer justify competing with its own middlemen?
5. In what situations might a producer use agents or commission merchants rather than its own sales offices or branches?
6. If a middleman is eliminated from a marketing channel, under what conditions will costs decrease? Under what conditions will costs increase? Will the middleman's functions be eliminated? Explain.
7. Which types of retail outlets are best suited to intensive distribution? to selective distribution? to exclusive distribution? Explain your answer in each case.
8. How are the various physical distribution functions related to each other? to the other elements of the marketing mix?

Exercises

1. On the basis of your experience as a consumer, list the services that retailers perform for their customers. Then circle those that could be eliminated easily. Next place a check mark beside those that are most important to you. Finally, summarize your conclusions in a paragraph or two.

2. Suppose you have developed and will produce a new golf tee that increases golfers' accuracy and driving distance. Design a marketing channel (or channels) for your product. Explain why this choice of channels would be most effective for your product.

3. For the golf tees described in Exercise 2, answer the following questions:

   a. How would you package your product for sale and for ease in inventory control and materials handling?

   b. Where would you locate your storage facilities? (Assume nationwide distribution of your product.)

   c. What means of transportation would you use to distribute your product to consumers? Why?

VIDEO CASE 14.1

The Container Store: The Definitive Place to Get Organized

If your life's a mess, head for The Container Store! At this box bonanza, you can find over 16,000 products to put things in, including trash containers and recycling bins, desktop and closet organizers, cartons and wrapping paper, 35 types of shoe racks, 103 varieties of coat hangers, 261 styles of jars and bottles, 500 kinds of pantry organizers, and more. You can spend as little as $1.50 for a child's leak-proof sipper cup or as much as several hundred dollars for a closet-organizing system. Calling itself the "ultimate organization store," the $70-million-a-year retail chain offers its customers storage and organization products in an attractive atmosphere staffed by knowledgeable salespeople. A poll of industry experts unanimously acclaimed The Container Store as "the most innovative storage merchandiser in the nation."

When The Container Store's founders, Garrett Boone and Kip Tindell, opened their first outlet in 1978, they had two employees, an innovative idea, and zero experience owning a retail business. At the time, durable, well-designed, reasonably priced storage and organization merchandise was available only in commercial markets serving offices, factories, and hospitals. Boone and Tindell wanted to provide those same products for home use. Skeptical potential investors responded with, "You're going to open a store that sells empty boxes?" Undaunted, the two persisted, and six months later, sales in their first store hit $200,000.

In the early days, Boone and Tindell worried that, because their operation was very specialized, as soon as people bought what they needed, the market would be saturated. Not so. New stores continue attracting customers, and seasoned customers come back for new products or new ways to use old ones. Experiencing annual growth of some 30 percent, three times the industry average, Container Stores now open their doors to shoppers in Texas, Georgia, Virginia, and Illinois. Florida and California are next in line.

To the company's owners, mass merchandising does not mean a dreary atmosphere. The Container Store customers are treated to blue ceilings over pale gray carpeting and are surrounded by natural light from skylights and floor-to-ceiling windows. Shoppers looking for general purpose items, such as tubs, baskets, and bins, can easily locate them in the center of the store. To find specialized items, they just look for the bold banners that identify such custom sections as Kitchen, Closet, Packaging, Leisure, or Bath. Although store size is growing as the number of products expands, the basic design and layout remain the same.

What distinguishes The Container Store among retailers is the versatility of the products it sells. Because there were few storage products manufactured specifically for home use when Boone and Tindell started out, they often bought commercial products that could double as consumer products. A mason's tool sack made a fine overnight bag, and an egg basket worked well as a carryall. The company's owners recognized the sales potential of offering handy adaptations. Says one company official, "We have all these multipurpose products, and customers need us to tell them the uses." Today, a laundry hamper can easily function as a recycling bin, and a cosmetics organizer works as a tackle box. To encourage creative product use, The Container Store merchandisers display many items in seven or eight sections throughout the store.

From the sales floor to the warehouse, The Container Store reflects its owners' conviction that quality customer service translates into business success. Boone and Tindell like to say that regardless of the job description, every Container Store employee works in customer service. Attracted by the chain's extraordinary success, several major corporations have approached Boone and Tindell with offers to buy the company. The answer is always no. These two want to continue doing business their way: flexible, friendly, and customer-oriented.[10]

Questions

1. What type of retailer is The Container Store?
2. If the Container Store were to get involved in non-store retailing, what type would be most appropriate? Explain.
3. So far, Boone and Tindell have not tried franchising. Would you advise them to start franchising new stores rather than expanding through company stores? Why or why not?

CASE 14.2

Wal-Mart Flexes Its Muscles in Marketing Channels

What do Mr. Coffee, Procter & Gamble, Rubbermaid, Scott Paper, and Royal Appliance all have in common? Although these firms manufacture diverse products, each one sells a surprisingly large percentage of goods through Wal-Mart stores. Super-retailer Wal-Mart attracts these firms and many others with the tantalizing chance to increase sales. One manufacturer's representative admitted that most suppliers would "just do absolutely anything" to sell at Wal-Mart. A universal eagerness among companies to boost sales and profits makes Wal-Mart a powerful leader in the marketing channel.

When Sam Walton opened his first Wal-Mart discount store in Bentonville, Arkansas, in 1962, he irrevocably changed the face of retailing. Walton believed that cooperation among manufacturers, wholesalers, and retailers in the marketing channel would ultimately give American consumers the value they want and deserve. Around two thousand outlets nationwide, about $75 billion in annual sales, and three decades of continuing growth confirm that Walton had a good idea.

Wal-Mart's executives assert that their company's way of doing business eliminates excess distribution and operating costs and passes the savings on to American consumers. Vendors, however, often complain that the company abuses its channel power, demanding discounts for new store openings; levying fines for shipment errors; and telling huge manufacturers which products to make, in what styles and colors, at what price, and when to ship them.

Despite the criticism, many well-known suppliers cater to Wal-Mart's demands. To satisfy Wal-Mart, Rubbermaid modified its product assortment and promotions. To serve Wal-Mart more efficiently, Borden restructured and consolidated its sales and distribution units. To provide Wal-Mart with information and to respond to suggestions, seventy full-time Procter & Gamble employees staff an office near the retailer's Bentonville headquarters.

Basking in the success resulting from close relationships like these, Wal-Mart announced its intention to deal similarly with all two thousand of its vendors. The retailer decided to require customized marketing plans for every item stocked by Wal-Mart. All vendors would receive a vendor planning packet, which not only would request what has always been considered privileged in-house information—such as overall marketing, product mix, and pricing strategies—but also would dictate unique Wal-Mart marketing methods.

The first planning packet went to pet-food vendors. Hoping to increase its pet department sales by 25 percent, Wal-Mart pressured its suppliers to help the chain reach that goal. The packet asked suppliers to detail their product mix and reveal logistical, promotional, and pricing strategies, as well as to project the retail sales and profit Wal-Mart could expect from sales of those products. Reaction to the program among Wal-Mart's pet-food suppliers was extremely negative; many labeled Wal-Mart a "bully." Wal-Mart quickly backed off from the plan, at least for a while.

Wal-Mart's willingness to put its vendor planning system on hold did not stop the organization from flaunting its clout and retail dominance. In a slightly less heavy-handed approach to category management, Wal-Mart sent letters to certain vendors asking them to prepare for category planning meetings to help plot strategy for capturing greater market share. Wal-Mart is also putting the heat on its suppliers. Instead of giving them three days to fill orders, Wal-Mart now demands delivery in only two days. Wal-Mart recently undercut one of its own suppliers, Eastman Kodak, by selling high-end Royal Gold film at lower than the minimum advertised price requested by the company. Finally, Wal-Mart instituted a new policy that eliminates intermediaries. The retailer will no longer trade with independent brokers or manufacturers' representatives but will communicate directly only with manufacturers. By shortening the marketing channel, insist Wal-Mart executives, the new rules lower costs, increase efficiency, and make vendors directly accountable to Wal-Mart for quality, price, and availability.

Where is the cooperative relationship Sam Walton advocated? This is the question many intermediaries are asking. Small manufacturers fret that because they don't have the resources to hire a private sales force, their products will be dumped from Wal-Mart's shelves. Charging that Wal-Mart's new practices amount to "strong-arm tactics," many Davids are organizing to fight the retail Goliath.

As industry experts observe suppliers jumping to restructure their organizations and revamp pricing and promotion to please Wal-Mart, they predict that—all the muttering aside—power will continue to shift in Wal-Mart's direction. Said one manufacturing executive about Wal-Mart, "They're not difficult to deal with. It's very simple. They say, 'We want this. Either you do it, or we'll get it from somebody else.' "[11]

Questions

1. Which type of consumer products marketing channel does Wal-Mart prefer?
2. Wal-Mart operates Sam's Clubs, which sell to businesses and to ultimate consumers. Are Sam's Clubs wholesalers or retailers?
3. Wal-Mart is working to eliminate intermediaries and accumulate information about its suppliers' strategies. Are these steps ethical? Defend your answer.

■■■■ CHAPTER 15

Promotion

LEARNING OBJECTIVES

After studying this chapter you should be able to

1 Understand the role of promotion.

2 Explain the purposes of the three types of advertising.

3 Describe the advantages and disadvantages of the major advertising media.

4 Identify the major steps in developing an advertising campaign.

5 Recognize the various kinds of salespersons, the steps in the personal-selling process, and the major sales management tasks.

6 Describe sales promotion objectives and methods.

7 Discuss the types and uses of publicity and the requirements for effective use of publicity.

8 Identify the factors that influence the selection of promotion mix ingredients.

CHAPTER PREVIEW

In this chapter we introduce four promotion methods and describe how they are used in an organization's marketing plans. First, we examine the role of advertising in the promotion mix. We discuss different types of advertising, the process of developing an advertising campaign, and social and legal concerns in advertising. Next we consider several categories of personal selling, noting the importance of effective sales management. We also look at sales promotion—why firms use it and which sales promotion techniques are most effective. Then we explain how both publicity and public relations can be used to build sales. Finally, we illustrate how these four promotion methods are combined in an effective promotion mix.

459

Just What the Doctor Ordered

Over the years, Dr Pepper has climbed from its lowly position as the "most misunderstood soft drink" to being "just what the Doctor ordered." Today, Dr Pepper is the number 1 noncola soft drink in America, and Diet Dr Pepper is America's top-selling diet noncola. While Coke and Pepsi battle it out for the number 1 cola spot, Dr Pepper uses advertising, sales promotion, and event sponsorship in an aggressive promotional campaign that emphasizes its position as the leading noncola.

Dr Pepper ads appear during such top-rated television shows as *Monday Night Football, Seinfeld,* and *Melrose Place,* communicating the message that this soft drink is a part of mainstream American life. Commercials with the tagline "You're a part of me; you're the heart of me" show sports fans, picnickers, and others being sociable, having fun, and drinking Dr Pepper. Diet Dr Pepper ads highlight the product's claim that it tastes just like regular Dr Pepper. In one commercial, neither a high-tech machine that analyzes a glass of Diet Dr Pepper nor a thirsty human can tell the difference.

Dr Pepper sales promotion efforts have one fundamental objective: to increase sales. These efforts always target specific channels or packages and are always easy to understand. For example, "Peel-a-Pepper" targets the two-liter market by rewarding one out of twelve customers with a free two-liter bottle, and "Twist-a-Pepper" gives away free 16-ounce, 20-ounce, or one-liter bottles of Dr Pepper to those lucky customers who

find specially marked twist-off caps. One of the company's most popular promotions is in conjunction with Footlocker. Soft-drink customers who buy featured 12- and 24-packs of Dr Pepper cans win Footlocker merchandise.

Because it boosts product visibility, event sponsorship is another important segment of Dr Pepper's overall promotional efforts. Dr Pepper has sponsored the Indianapolis 500, World Cup Soccer, the National Basketball Association finals, and other major sporting events. In addition, the soft-drink company backs the festival of *Cinco de Mayo* and the Country Music Awards.

Since 1991, Dr Pepper has increased promotional spending by 135 percent, making Dr Pepper the fourteenth-most-advertised brand sold in grocery stores. Dr Pepper's promotional efforts continue to build brand awareness, increase total sales volume, and persuade more soft-drink consumers to try Dr Pepper.

■■■■

■　■　■　■　■　■　■　■　■　■　■

To maintain its market share in a highly competitive industry, Dr Pepper spends heavily on promotional tools such as advertising, sales promotion, and event sponsorship. An organization can use these and other tools in its promotional programs.

promotion communication intended to inform, persuade, or remind an organization's target markets of the organization or its products

Promotion is communication intended to inform, persuade, or remind an organization's target markets of the organization or its products. The promotion with which we are most familiar—advertising—is intended to inform, persuade, or remind us to buy particular products. But there is more to promotion than advertising, and it is used for other purposes as well. Charities use promotion to inform us of their need for donations, to persuade us to give, and to remind us to do so in case we have forgotten. Even the Internal Revenue Service uses promotion (in the form of publicity) to remind us of its April 15 deadline for filing tax returns.

promotion mix the particular combination of promotion methods a firm uses to reach a target market

A **promotion mix** is the particular combination of promotion methods a firm uses to reach a target market. The makeup of a mix depends on many factors, including the characteristics of the target market. We discuss these factors toward the end of this chapter, after we examine the promotion methods of advertising, personal selling, sales promotion, and publicity and public relations.

■■ THE ROLE OF PROMOTION

LEARNING OBJECTIVE 1
Understand the role of promotion.

Promotion is commonly the object of two misconceptions. On the one hand, people take note of highly visible promotional activities, such as advertising and personal selling, and conclude that these make up the entire field of marketing. On the other hand, people sometimes consider promotional activities to be unnecessary, expensive, and the cause of higher prices. Neither view is accurate.

The role of promotion is to facilitate exchanges directly or indirectly by informing individuals, groups, or organizations and influencing them to accept a firm's products. To expedite exchanges directly, marketers convey information about a firm's goods, services, and ideas to particular market segments. To bring about exchanges indirectly, marketers address interest groups (such as environmental and consumer groups), regulatory agencies, investors, and the general public concerning a company and its products. The broader role of promotion, therefore, is to maintain positive relationships between a company and various groups in the marketing environment.

Marketers frequently design promotional communications, such as advertisements, for specific groups, although some may be directed at wider audiences. Several different messages may be communicated simultaneously to different market segments. For example, Exxon Corporation may

461

Promotion in many forms. This auto dealership is using King Kong to attract attention and to set itself apart from its competitors.

address customers about a new motor oil, inform investors about the firm's financial performance, and update the general public on the firm's environmental efforts to clean up the Alaskan shoreline.

Marketers must carefully plan, implement, and coordinate promotional communications to make the best use of them. The effectiveness of promotional activities depends greatly on the quality and quantity of information available to marketers about the organization's marketing environment (see Figure 15.1). If marketers want to influence customers to buy a certain product, for example, they must know who these customers are likely to be and how they make purchase decisions for that type of product. Marketers must gather and use information about particular audiences to communicate successfully with them.

■■ THE PROMOTION MIX: AN OVERVIEW

Marketers can use several promotional methods to communicate with individuals, groups, and organizations. The methods that are combined to promote a particular product make up the promotion mix for that item.

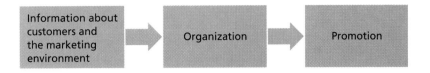

FIGURE 15.1 Information Flows Into and Out of an Organization
A promotional activity's effectiveness depends on the information available to marketers. *(Source: Adapted from William M. Pride and O. C. Ferrell,* Marketing: Concepts and Strategies, *Ninth Edition. Copyright © 1995 by Houghton Mifflin Company. Used by permission.)*

Advertising, personal selling, sales promotion, and publicity are the four major elements in an organization's promotion mix (see Figure 15.2). Two, three, or four of these ingredients are used in a promotion mix, depending on the type of product and target market involved.

Advertising is a paid, nonpersonal message communicated to a select audience through a mass medium. The key words in the definition are *nonpersonal,* which excludes personal selling by a sales force, and *paid,* which excludes publicity. Advertising is flexible enough that it can reach a very large target group or a small, carefully chosen target audience. **Personal selling** is personal communication aimed at informing customers and persuading them to buy a firm's products. It is more expensive to reach one person through personal selling than through advertising, but this method

advertising a paid, nonpersonal message communicated to a select audience through a mass medium

personal selling personal communication aimed at informing customers and persuading them to buy a firm's products

FIGURE 15.2 Possible Ingredients for an Organization's Promotion Mix
Depending on the type of product and target market involved, two or more of these ingredients are used in a promotion mix. *(Source: Adapted from William M. Pride and O. C. Ferrell,* Marketing: Concepts and Strategies, *Ninth Edition. Copyright © 1995 by Houghton Mifflin Company. Used by permission.)*

provides immediate feedback and is often more persuasive than advertising. **Sales promotion** is the use of activities or materials as direct inducements to customers or salespersons. It adds extra value to the product or increases the customer's incentive to buy the product. **Publicity** is a nonpersonal message delivered in news-story form through a mass medium, at no charge. Magazine, newspaper, radio, and television stories about a company's new stores, products, or personnel changes are examples of publicity. Although marketers do not pay outright for such media coverage, there are still definite costs associated with the preparation and distribution of news releases.

■■ ADVERTISING

In 1993 organizations spent $138 billion on advertising in the United States.[2] Figure 15.3 shows how advertising expenditures and employment in advertising have increased since 1972. In recent years, the growth of advertising has subsided to some extent.

FIGURE 15.3   **Growth of Advertising Expenditures and of Employment in Advertising**
Total advertising expenditures and employment in advertising have been steadily increasing since 1972. Both are expected to continue to rise during the rest of the 1990s.   (*Source: Reprinted with permission from* Advertising Age, *May 2, 1994. Copyright © Crain Communications, Inc. All rights reserved; and* U.S. Industrial Outlook, *1994, pp. 51–55.*)

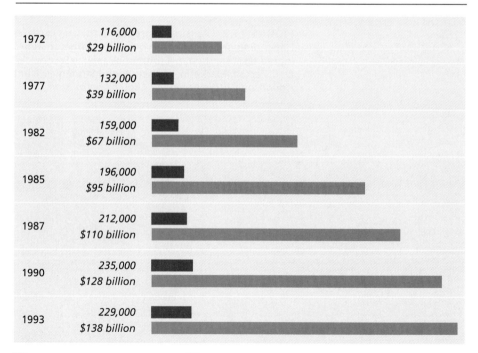

Year	Number of people employed	Amount of money spent
1972	116,000	$29 billion
1977	132,000	$39 billion
1982	159,000	$67 billion
1985	196,000	$95 billion
1987	212,000	$110 billion
1990	235,000	$128 billion
1993	229,000	$138 billion

■ Number of people employed   ■ Amount of money spent

Types of Advertising by Purpose

LEARNING OBJECTIVE 2
Explain the purposes of the
three types of advertising.

**selective (or brand)
advertising** advertising that is
used to sell a particular brand
of product

Depending on its purpose and message, advertising may be classified into three groups: selective, institutional, and primary-demand.

Selective Advertising   **Selective (or brand) advertising** is advertising that is used to sell a particular brand of product. It is by far the most common type of advertising, and it accounts for the lion's share of advertising expenditures. Producers use brand-oriented advertising to convince us to buy their products, from Bubble Yum to Buicks.

Selective advertising that aims at persuading consumers to make purchases within a short time is called *immediate-response advertising*. Most local advertising is of this type. It generally promotes products with immediate appeal, such as fans or air conditioners during an unusually hot summer. Selective advertising aimed at keeping a firm's name or product before the public is called *reminder advertising.*

Comparative advertising, which has become more popular over the last two decades, compares specific characteristics of two or more identified brands. Of course, the comparison shows the advertiser's brand to be as good as or better than the other identified competing brands. Comparisons are often based on the outcome of surveys or research studies. Though competing firms act as effective watchdogs against each other's advertising claims, consumers themselves would do well to cultivate a certain sophistication concerning claims based on "scientific studies" and various statistical manipulations. Comparative advertising is illegal or at least unacceptable in a number of other countries.

institutional advertising
advertising designed to enhance
a firm's image or reputation

Institutional Advertising   **Institutional advertising** is advertising designed to enhance a firm's image or reputation. Many public utilities and larger firms, such as AT&T and the major oil companies, use part of their advertising dollars to build goodwill rather than to stimulate sales directly. A positive public image helps an organization to attract not only customers but also employees and investors.

primary-demand advertising
advertising whose purpose is to
increase the demand for *all*
brands of a product within a
specific industry

Primary-Demand Advertising   **Primary-demand advertising** is advertising aimed at increasing the demand for *all* brands of a product within a specific industry. Trade and industry associations, such as the American Dairy Association ("Milk: Help Yourself"), are the major users of primary-demand advertising. Their advertisements promote broad product categories, such as beef, milk, pork, potatoes, and prunes, without mentioning specific brands.

Advertising Media

LEARNING OBJECTIVE 3
Describe the advantages and
disadvantages of the major
advertising media.

advertising media the
various forms of
communication through which
advertising reaches its audience

The **advertising media** are the various forms of communication through which advertising reaches its audience. They include newspapers, magazines, direct mail, outdoor displays, television, and radio. Figure 15.4 shows how organizations allocate their advertising expenditures among the various media. Note that *electronic media*—television and radio—account for less than 30 percent of all media expenditures.

Stimulating primary demand. Several cattle-related associations in Missouri join together to create an advertising campaign aimed at encouraging people to consume more beef.

Newspapers   Newspaper advertising accounts for almost one-fourth of all advertising expenditures. More than 85 percent is purchased by local retailers. Newspaper advertising is used extensively by retailers because it is relatively inexpensive compared to other media. Furthermore, because it provides only local coverage, advertising dollars are not wasted in reaching people who are outside the organization's market area. It is also timely. Ads can usually be placed the day before they are to appear.

There are some drawbacks, however, to newspaper advertising. It has a short life span; newspapers are generally read through once and then discarded. Color reproduction in newspapers is usually poor; thus most ads must be run in black and white. Finally, marketers cannot target specific demographic groups through newspaper ads because newspapers are read by such a broad spectrum of people.

Newspapers carry more cooperative advertising than other media. **Cooperative advertising** is advertising in which the cost is shared by a producer and one or more local retailers. The costs are shared because the advertising benefits both the producer, whose products are promoted, and the retailer, which reaches its customers through the advertising.

Magazines   The advertising revenues of magazines have been climbing dramatically since 1976. In 1993 they reached $7.4 billion, or about 5.3 percent of all advertising expenditures.

cooperative advertising
advertising in which the cost is shared by a producer and one or more local retailers

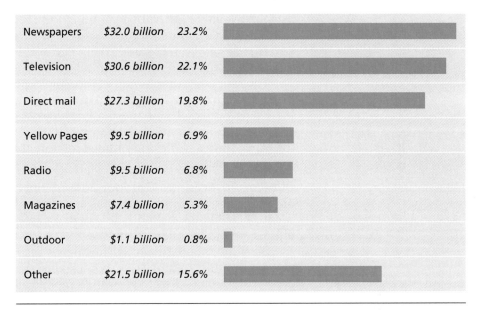

Newspapers	$32.0 billion	23.2%	
Television	$30.6 billion	22.1%	
Direct mail	$27.3 billion	19.8%	
Yellow Pages	$9.5 billion	6.9%	
Radio	$9.5 billion	6.8%	
Magazines	$7.4 billion	5.3%	
Outdoor	$1.1 billion	0.8%	
Other	$21.5 billion	15.6%	

FIGURE 15.4   Distribution of Advertising Expenditures Among Various Advertising Media
About 45 percent (45 cents of every dollar) spent on advertising are consumed in newspaper and television advertising.   *(Source: Reprinted with permission from* Advertising Age, *May 2, 1994. Copyright © Crain Communications, Inc. All rights reserved.)*

Advertisers can reach very specific market segments through ads in special-interest magazines. A boat manufacturer has a ready-made consumer audience in subscribers to *Yachting* or *Sail.* Producers of photographic equipment advertise in *Travel & Leisure* or *Popular Photography.* A number of more general magazines like *Time* and *Cosmopolitan* publish regional editions, which provide advertisers with geographic flexibility as well.

Magazine advertising is more prestigious than newspaper advertising, and it allows for high-quality color reproduction. In addition, magazine advertisements have a longer life span than those in other media. Issues of *National Geographic,* for example, may be kept for months or years by subscribers, and the ads they contain are viewed repeatedly.

The major disadvantages of magazine advertising are high cost and lack of timeliness. Because magazine ads must normally be prepared more than two to three months in advance, they cannot be adjusted to reflect the latest market conditions. Magazine ads—especially full-color ads—are also expensive. Although the cost of reaching a thousand people may compare favorably with that of other media, the cost of a full-page, four-color ad can be very high—$147,000 in *Time.*

direct-mail advertising
promotional material mailed
directly to individuals

Direct Mail   Direct-mail advertising is promotional material mailed directly to individuals. Direct mail is the most selective medium: mailing

Charge It!

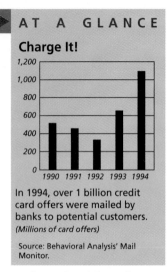

In 1994, over 1 billion credit card offers were mailed by banks to potential customers.
(Millions of card offers)

Source: Behavioral Analysis' Mail Monitor.

outdoor advertising short promotional messages on billboards, posters, and signs

lists are available (or can be compiled) to reach almost any target market, from airplane enthusiasts to zoologists. The effectiveness of direct-mail advertising can be measured easily because recipients either buy or don't buy the product that is advertised.

The success of direct-mail advertising depends to some extent on appropriate and current mailing lists. A direct-mail campaign may fail if the mailing list is outdated and the mailing does not reach the right people. In addition, this medium is relatively costly. Nevertheless, direct-mail advertising expenditures in 1993 amounted to more than $27 billion, almost 20 percent of the total.

Outdoor Advertising   **Outdoor advertising** consists of short promotional messages on billboards, posters, and signs. In 1993 outdoor advertisers spent $1.1 billion, or slightly less than 1 percent of total advertising expenditures, on outdoor advertising.

Sign and billboard advertising allows the marketer to focus on a particular geographic area; it is fairly inexpensive. However, because most outdoor promotion is directed toward a mobile audience, the message must be limited to a few words. The medium is especially suitable for products that lend themselves to pictorial display.

Television   Television ranks second only to newspapers in total advertising revenue. In 1993, 22.1 percent of advertising expenditures, or $30 billion, went to television. Approximately 98 percent of American homes have at least one color television set, which is watched an average of seven hours each day.[3] The average U.S. household can receive nearly twenty-eight TV channels, including cable and pay stations, according to Nielson Media

Outdoor advertising. A Doctor-referral service uses outdoor advertising for promotion. This advertisement was placed to reach a specific target market.

Research. Sixty-three percent of households receive basic cable television.[4] Television obviously provides advertisers with considerable access to consumers.

Television advertising is the primary medium for larger firms whose objective is to reach national or regional markets. A national advertiser may buy *network time,* which guarantees that its message will be broadcast by hundreds of local stations affiliated with the network. However, the opportunity to reach extremely large television audiences has been reduced as a result of the increased availability and popularity of cable channels and home videos. Both national and local firms may buy *local time* on a single station that covers a particular geographic area.

Advertisers may *sponsor* an entire show, participate with other sponsors of a show, or buy *spot time* for a single 10-, 20-, 30-, or 60-second commercial during or between programs. To an extent, they may select their audience by choosing the day of the week and the approximate time of day their ads will be shown. Anheuser-Busch, Inc., advertises Budweiser Beer and Noxell Corporation advertises Noxema shaving cream during TV football games because the majority of viewers are men, who are likely to use these products.

Another option available to television advertisers is the infomercial. An **infomercial** is a program-length (usually a half-hour) televised commercial message resembling an entertainment or consumer affairs program. Infomercials for products such as the Flowbee hair-cutting system and Soloflex exercise equipment tell customers why they need the product, what benefits it provides, in what ways it out-performs its competitors, and how much it costs. Although infomercials were initially aired primarily over cable television, today they are becoming more common on other types of television. Currently infomercials are responsible for marketing over $1 billion worth of products annually. A number of Fortune 500 companies are beginning to use infomercials.

Television advertising rates are based on the number of people expected to be watching when the commercial is aired. In 1995, the cost of a 30-second Superbowl commercial was $1 million. During regular prime-time programs, advertisers spend between $60,000 and $250,000 for a 30-second television commercial.

Unlike magazine advertising, television advertising has a short life. If a viewer misses a commercial, it is missed forever. Viewers may also become indifferent to commercial messages. Or they may use the commercial time as a break from viewing, thus missing the message altogether. Remote-control devices make it especially easy to avoid television commercials.

Radio   Advertisers spent about $9.5 billion, or 6.8 percent of total expenditures, on radio advertising in 1993. Like magazine advertising, radio advertising offers selectivity. Radio stations develop programming for—and are tuned in by—specific groups of listeners. There are almost half a billion radios in the United States (about six per household), which makes radio the most accessible medium.

Radio can be less expensive than other media. Actual rates depend on geographic coverage, the number of commercials contracted for, the time

infomercial   a program-length televised commercial message resembling an entertainment or consumer affairs program

period specified, and whether the station broadcasts on AM, FM, or both. Even small retailers are able to afford radio advertising. A radio advertiser can schedule and change ads on short notice. The disadvantages of using radio are the absence of visual images and (because there are so many stations) the small audience size.

Major Steps in Developing an Advertising Campaign

LEARNING OBJECTIVE 4
Identify the major steps in developing an advertising campaign.

An advertising campaign is developed in several stages. These stages may vary in number and the order in which they are implemented, depending on the company's resources, product, and audiences. A campaign in any organization, however, will include the following steps in some form.

1. Identify and Analyze the Advertising Target   The advertising target is the group of people toward which an organization's advertisements are directed. To pinpoint the advertising target and develop an effective campaign, marketers must analyze such information as the geographic distribution of consumers; their age, sex, race, income, and education; and their attitudes toward both the advertiser's product and competing products. How marketers use this information will be influenced by the features of the product to be advertised and the nature of the competition. Precise identification of the advertising target is crucial to the proper development of subsequent stages and, ultimately, to the success of the campaign itself.

2. Define the Advertising Objectives   The goals of an advertising campaign should be stated precisely and in measurable terms. The objectives should include the current position of the firm, indicate how far and in what direction from that original reference point the company wishes to move, and specify a definite period of time for the achievement of the goals. Advertising objectives that focus on sales will stress increasing sales by a certain percentage or dollar amount, or expanding the firm's market share. Communication objectives will emphasize increasing product or brand awareness, improving consumer attitudes, or conveying product information.

3. Create the Advertising Platform   An advertising platform includes the important selling points or features that an advertiser wishes to incorporate into the advertising campaign. These features should be those that are important to consumers in their selection and use of a product and, if possible, those features that competing products lack. Although research into what consumers view as important issues is expensive, it is the most productive way to determine which issues to include in an advertising platform.

4. Determine the Advertising Appropriation   The advertising appropriation is the total amount of money designated for advertising in a given period. This stage is critical to the success of the campaign because advertising efforts based on an inadequate budget will understimulate customer demand, and a budget too large will waste a company's resources. Advertising appropriations may be based on last year's (or next year's forecasted) sales, on what competitors spend on advertising, or on executive judgment.

Celebrity Endorsers: Star Power Pays Off

Every year, companies pay actors, singers, athletes, and other celebrities millions of dollars to endorse their products. Supermodel Cindy Crawford recommends drinking Pepsi-Cola and using Revlon cosmetics. Robert Redford and Amy Grant remind television viewers that Target Stores are a great place to get gifts for Mother's and Father's Day. And Michael Jordan has endorsed fourteen companies' products, from Wheaties, Gator-Aide, and McDonald's, to Hanes underwear and Nike athletic shoes. Despite studies showing that the overall approval ratings of celebrities appearing in commercials is declining, advertisers still love the stars and remain convinced that the right spokesperson can deliver sales.

"Celebrities are worth it," says Brand Strategy Services, a group that rates celebrities and brands on consumer perceptions. They get lots of attention and generate lots of impact. But not just any celebrity will do. Advertisers insist that the secret to successful product endorsement is pairing the right product with the right celebrity. Research suggests that endorsers should be well-known, well-liked, honest, trustworthy, and have a good reputation. According to marketing experts, consumers will associate these positive qualities with the product, enhancing its image.

Who are the most successful celebrity endorsers? Video Storyboard, which rates the effectiveness and popularity of entertainers and sports figures who appear in commercials, recently came out with its list of the top 10 celebrity endorsers. Leading the list were Cindy Crawford for Pepsi-Cola and Revlon, Candice Bergen for Sprint, Bill Cosby for Jell-O, Elizabeth Taylor for White Diamonds perfume, and Jerry Seinfeld for American Express. Number 1 in the sports category was Michael Jordan.

Although the rush to sign up celebrities isn't abating, companies do face potential pitfalls. Fame is fleeting, so agencies and companies must constantly reevaluate who's in and who's out, hoping to avoid a multimillion dollar contract with someone whose popularity suddenly plummets. For example, figure skater Nancy Kerrigan and speed skaters Dan Jansen and Bonnie Blair were the darlings of advertisers after their successes at the 1994 Olympics, but their sparkle will fade when new heroes shine in the next Olympics. Sometimes the personality overwhelms the brand. A recent survey reveals that consumers often have difficulty recalling the link between celebrities and products. One out of three respondents thought that Candice Bergen endorses MCI or AT&T, rivals of Sprint, the long-distance provider that she does plug. Finally, celebrity endorsers can become caught up in scandals, and advertisers abhor negative publicity. Although some advertisers don't believe that when stars fall from grace their products' reputations are damaged, most won't take any chances. When Michael Jackson's legal problems made daily headlines, PepsiCo dropped his soft-drink commercials. And TV viewers no longer see O. J. Simpson leaping through the Hertz parking lot.

When choosing celebrities to endorse their products, many companies are more likely to pick the person who's on the most recent cover of *People* magazine than do market research. Because of so much adverse media attention, however, industry experts predict that companies will do more research on potential spokespersons and will stick to "solid citizen" types.

5. Develop the Media Plan   A media plan specifies exactly which media will be used in the campaign and when advertisements will appear. The primary concern of the media planner is to reach the largest possible number of persons in the advertising target for each dollar spent, though cost effectiveness is not easy to measure. In addition to cost, media planners must consider the location and demographics of people in the advertising target, the content of the message, and the characteristics of the audiences reached by various media. The media planner begins with general media decisions, selects subclasses within each medium, and finally chooses particular media vehicles for the campaign.

6. Create the Advertising Message   The content and form of a message are influenced by the product's features, the characteristics of people in the advertising target, the objectives of the campaign, and the choice of media. An advertiser must consider these factors to choose words and illustrations that will be meaningful and appealing to persons in the advertising target. The copy, or words, of an advertisement will vary depending on the media choice but should attempt to move the audience through attention, interest, desire, and action. Artwork and visuals should complement copy by attracting the audience's attention and communicating an idea quickly.

7. Execute the Campaign   Execution of an advertising campaign requires extensive planning, scheduling, and coordination because many tasks must be completed on time and the efforts of many people and firms must be coordinated. Production companies, research organizations, media firms, printers, photoengravers, and commercial artists are just a few of the people and firms contributing to a campaign. Advertising management personnel must constantly assess the quality of the work and take corrective action when necessary. In some instances, advertisers make changes during the campaign in order to meet objectives more effectively.

8. Evaluate Advertising Effectiveness   A campaign's success should be measured, in terms of its original objectives, before, during, and/or after the campaign. An advertiser should at least be able to estimate whether sales or market share went up because of the campaign or whether any change occurred in customer attitudes or brand awareness. Data from past and current sales, responses to coupon offers, and customer surveys administered by research organizations are some of the ways in which advertising effectiveness can be evaluated.

Advertising Agencies

advertising agency   an independent firm that plans, produces, and places advertising for its clients

Advertisers can plan and produce their own advertising with help from media personnel, or they can hire advertising agencies. An **advertising agency** is an independent firm that plans, produces, and places advertising for its clients. Many larger ad agencies offer help with sales promotion and publicity as well. The media usually pay a commission of 15 percent to advertising agencies. Thus the cost to the agency's client can be quite moderate. The client may be asked to pay for selected services the agency per-forms. Other methods for compensating agencies are also used.

Firms that do a lot of advertising may use both an in-house advertising department and an independent agency. This approach gives the firm the advantage of being able to call on the agency's expertise in particular areas of advertising. An agency can also bring a fresh viewpoint to the firm's prod-ucts and advertising plans.

Table 15.1 lists the nation's twenty leading advertisers, in all media. In 1994 the number-1 honor went to Procter & Gamble.

Social and Legal Considerations in Advertising

Critics of U.S. advertising have two main complaints—that it is wasteful and that it can be deceptive. Although advertising (like any other activity) can be performed inefficiently, it is far from wasteful. Let's look at the evidence:

- Advertising is the most effective and the least expensive means of communicating product information to millions of individuals and firms.

TABLE 15.1   Advertising Expenditures and Sales Volume for the Top 20 National Advertisers (in millions of dollars)

Rank	Company	Advertising Expenditures	Sales	Advertising Expenditures as Percentage of Sales
1	Procter & Gamble Co.	$2,397.5	$15,362	15.6%
2	Philip Morris Cos.	1,844.3	38,387	4.8
3	General Motors Corp.	1,539.2	109,668	1.4
4	Sears, Roebuck and Co.	1,310.7	29,565	4.4
5	Pepsico Inc.	1,038.9	18,309	5.7
6	Ford Motor Co.	958.3	75,661	1.3
7	AT&T	812.1	61,580	1.3
8	Nestlé SA	793.7	20,163	3.9
9	Johnson & Johnson	762.5	7,203	10.6
10	Chrysler Corp.	761.6	37,847	2.0
11	Warner-Lambert Co.	751.0	2,747	27.3
12	Unilever NV	738.2	8,550	8.6
13	McDonald's Corp.	736.6	3,931	18.7
14	Time Warner	695.1	4,414	15.7
15	Toyota Motor Corp.	690.4	84,873	0.8
16	Walt Disney Co.	675.7	6,711	10.1
17	Grand Metropolitan PLC	652.9	6,862	9.5
18	Kellogg Co.	627.1	3,784	16.6
19	Eastman Kodak Co.	624.7	8,384	7.5
20	Sony Corp.	589.0	9,127	6.5

Source: Reprinted with permission from *Advertising Age,* September 28, 1994. Copyright © Crain Communications, Inc. All rights reserved.

- Advertising encourages competition and is, in fact, a means of competition. It thus leads to the development of new and improved products, wider product choices, and lower prices.
- Advertising revenues support our mass communications media—newspapers, magazines, radio, and television. This means that advertising pays for much of our news coverage and entertainment programming.
- Advertising provides job opportunities in fields ranging from sales to film production.

Along with pure fact, advertising tends to include some exaggeration, stretching of the truth, and occasional deception. Consumers usually spot such distortion in short order. Also, various government and private agencies scrutinize advertising for false or misleading claims or offers. At the national level, the Federal Trade Commission, the Food and Drug Administration, and the Federal Communications Commission oversee advertising practices. Advertising may also be monitored by state and local agencies, Better Business Bureaus, and industry associations. These organizations have varying degrees of control over advertising, but their overall effect has been a positive one.

■■ PERSONAL SELLING

Personal selling is the most adaptable of all promotion methods because the person who is presenting the message can modify it to suit the individual buyer. However, personal selling is also the most expensive promotion method.

Most successful salespeople are able to communicate with others on a one-to-one basis and are strongly motivated. They strive to have a thorough knowledge of the products they offer for sale. And they are willing and able to deal with the details involved in handling and processing orders. Sales managers tend to emphasize these qualities in recruiting and hiring, as well as in the other human resources management activities discussed in Chapter 10.

Many selling situations demand the face-to-face contact and adaptability of personal selling. This is especially true of industrial sales, in which a single purchase may amount to millions of dollars. Obviously, sales of that size must be based on carefully planned sales presentations, personal contact with customers, and thorough negotiations.

Kinds of Salespersons

LEARNING OBJECTIVE 5
Recognize the various kinds of salespersons, the steps in the personal-selling process, and the major sales management tasks.

Because most businesses employ different salespersons to perform different functions, marketing managers must select the kinds of sales personnel that will be most effective in selling the firm's products. Salespersons may be identified as order getters, order takers, and support personnel. A single individual can, and often does, perform all three functions.

Order Getters   An **order getter** is responsible for what is sometimes called **creative selling:** selling the firm's products to new customers and increasing sales to present customers. An order getter must perceive buyers' needs, supply customers with information about the firm's product, and persuade them to buy the product. Order-getting activities may be separated into two groups. In current-customer sales, salespeople concentrate on obtaining additional sales, or leads for prospective sales, from customers who have purchased the firm's products at least once. In new-business sales, sales personnel seek out new prospects and convince them to make an initial purchase of the firm's product. The real estate, insurance, appliance, heavy industrial machinery, and automobile industries in particular depend on new-business sales.

Order Takers   An **order taker** handles repeat sales in ways that maintain positive relationships with customers. An order taker sees that customers have products when and where they are needed and in the proper amounts. *Inside order takers* receive incoming mail and telephone orders in some businesses; they also include salespersons in retail stores. *Outside* (or *field*) *order takers* travel to customers. Often the buyer and the field salesperson develop a mutually beneficial relationship of placing, receiving, and delivering orders. Both inside and outside order takers are active salespersons and often produce most of their companies' sales.

Support Personnel   **Sales support personnel** aid in selling but are more involved in locating *prospects* (likely first-time customers), educating customers, building goodwill for the firm, and providing follow-up service. The most common categories of support personnel are missionary, trade, and technical salespersons.

A **missionary salesperson,** who usually works for a manufacturer, visits retailers to persuade them to buy the manufacturer's products. If the retailers agree, they buy the products from wholesalers, who are the manufacturer's actual customers. Missionary salespersons are often employed by producers of medical supplies and pharmaceuticals to promote these products to retail druggists, physicians, and hospitals.

A **trade salesperson,** who generally works for a food producer or processor, assists customers in promoting products, especially in retail stores. A trade salesperson may obtain additional shelf space for the products, restock shelves, set up displays, and distribute samples. Because trade salespersons are usually order takers as well, they are not strictly support personnel.

A **technical salesperson** assists the company's current customers in technical matters. He or she may explain how to use a product, how it is made, how to install it, or how a system is designed. A technical salesperson should be formally educated in science or engineering. Computers, steel, and chemicals are some of the products handled by technical salespeople.

Marketers usually need sales personnel from several of these categories. Factors that affect hiring and other personnel decisions include the number of customers and their characteristics; the product's attributes, complexity, and price; the distribution channels used by the company; and the company's approach to advertising.

---

order getter a salesperson who is responsible for selling the firm's products to new customers and increasing sales to present customers

creative selling selling products to new customers and increasing sales to present customers

order taker a salesperson who handles repeat sales in ways that maintain positive relationships with customers

sales support personnel employees who aid in selling but are more involved in locating prospects, educating customers, building goodwill for the firm, and providing follow-up service

missionary salesperson a salesperson—generally employed by a manufacturer—who visits retailers to persuade them to buy the manufacturer's products

trade salesperson a salesperson—generally employed by a food producer or processor—who assists customers in promoting products, especially in retail stores

technical salesperson a salesperson who assists the company's current customers in technical matters

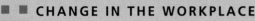

CHANGE IN THE WORKPLACE

Automating the Sales Force

Salespeople using technology in the future may feel more as if they're playing Nintendo than employing a sales tool. They will talk to their computers and their computers will talk back. Acting like digital mentors, the machines will lead them to success by suggesting ideas and strategies. Computers will function as electronic receptionists, taking calls, prioritizing appointments, and reminding sales reps of staff meetings. When reps are ready to make a sales call, their computers will even provide automated driving directions. If you think this high-tech picture of sales is science fiction, you're wrong. Microsoft, AT&T, and other companies are working on advanced technology that will help salespeople increase productivity and better serve their customers. Many sales forces already use computers in some capacity, and personal digital assistants, such as Apple Computer's Newton, are already on the market.

The potential of sales force automation is enormous. Through their databases, sales staff will have access to valuable, up-to-the-minute information on inventory, customer needs, and sales and special promotions. Because information will be at their fingertips, salespeople will no longer lose deals because of slow credit checks, lose customers who go to competitors when their service problems aren't answered promptly, or lose sales because of stock-outs.

One company succeeding with its automated sales force is Gillette, a top marketer of razors and other health and beauty aids such as Noxema cleansers and Cover Girl cosmetics. Two hundred and fifty of the company's retail merchandise sales representatives carry pen-based computers called "GriD PAD Hds." Despite the imposing sounding name, sales reps find these devices easy to use. Remarked one sales manager, "They won't dazzle cyberpunks, but they get the job done." During sales calls, Gillette reps collect data on how products are doing. The pen computer's software tells the sales person which items a store carries and reminds him or her to make sure the store has new products and that point-of-purchase displays are in place. By plugging into a phone jack at the end of the day, sales staff transmit their data—sales figures, customers' needs, product trends, and so on—to Gillette's central database. Gillette's management reports that since equipping the sales staff with the GRiDs, reps spend almost no time in the office. Instead, they're in the field making sales and satisfying customers.

Experts suggest a few guidelines for companies that are leaning toward automating their sales force:

- The technology should meet the needs of the sales force—the "highest-tech" equipment is not necessarily the right choice.

- Get input from the people who will be using the technology.

- No system can be too easy to use.

- Using automation should facilitate gathering, storing, and communicating information.

- Keep the customer in mind—the chosen technology should improve customer service.

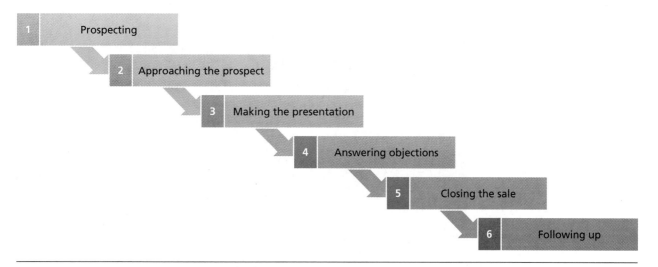

FIGURE 15.5   **The Six Steps of the Personal-Selling Process**
Personal selling is not only the most adaptable of all promotional methods, but also the most expensive.

The Personal-Selling Process

No two selling situations are exactly alike, and no two salespeople perform their jobs in exactly the same way. Most salespeople, however, follow the six-step procedure illustrated in Figure 15.5.

Prospecting   The first step in personal selling is to research potential buyers and choose the most likely customers, or prospects. Sources of prospects include business associates and customers, public records, telephone and trade-association directories, and company files. The salesperson concentrates on those prospects who have the financial resources, willingness, and authority to buy the product.

Approaching the Prospect   First impressions are often lasting impressions. Thus the salesperson's first contact with the prospect is crucial to successful selling. The best approach is one that is based on knowledge—of the prospect, of the prospect's needs, and of how the product can meet those needs. Salespeople who understand each customer's particular situation are likely to make a good first impression—and to make a sale.

Making the Presentation   The next step is the actual delivery of the sales presentation. In many cases, this includes demonstrating the product. The salesperson points out the product's features, its benefits, and how it is superior to competitors' merchandise. If the product has been used successfully by other firms, the salesperson may mention this as part of the presentation.

During a demonstration, the salesperson may suggest that the prospect try out the product personally. The demonstration and product trial should underscore specific points made during the presentation.

Personal selling. Personal selling is commonly used at the retail level for replacement of automobile tires, because customers need detailed information before purchase.

Answering Objections   The prospect is likely to raise objections or ask questions at any time. This gives the salesperson a chance to eliminate objections that might prevent a sale, to point out additional features, or to mention special services the company offers.

Closing the Sale   To close the sale, the salesperson asks the prospect to buy the product. This is considered the critical point in the selling process. Many experienced salespeople make use of a *trial closing*, in which they ask questions that are based on the assumption that the customer is going to buy the product. The questions "When would you want delivery?" and "Do you want the standard or the deluxe model?" are typical of trial closings. They allow the reluctant prospect to make a purchase without having to say, "I'll take it."

Following Up   The salesperson must follow up after the sale to ensure that the product is delivered on time, in the right quantity, in good condition, and in proper operating condition. During follow-up, the salesperson also makes it clear that he or she is available in case problems develop. Follow-up leaves a good impression and eases the way toward future sales. Hence it is essential to the selling process. The salesperson's job does not end with a sale. It continues as long as the seller and the customer maintain a working relationship.

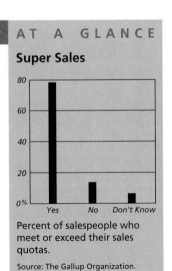

▷▷ AT A GLANCE

Super Sales

Percent of salespeople who meet or exceed their sales quotas.

Source: The Gallup Organization.

Managing Personal Selling

A firm's success often hinges on the competent management of its sales force. Without a strong sales force—and the sales revenue it brings in—a business will soon fail.

Sales managers have responsibilities in a number of areas. They must set sales objectives in concrete, quantifiable terms, specifying a certain period of time and a certain geographic area. They must adjust the size of the sales force to meet changes in the firm's marketing plan and the marketing environment. Sales managers must attract and hire effective salespersons. They must develop a training program and decide where, when, how, and for whom to conduct the training. They must formulate a fair and adequate compensation plan to keep qualified employees. They must motivate salespersons to boost their productivity. They must define sales territories and determine scheduling and routing of the sales force. Finally, sales managers must evaluate the operation as a whole through sales reports, communications with customers, and invoices.

■■ SALES PROMOTION

LEARNING OBJECTIVE 6
Describe sales promotion
objectives and methods.

Sales promotion consists of activities or materials that are direct inducements to customers or salespersons. Sales promotion techniques are used primarily to enhance and supplement other promotion methods. In this role they can have a significant impact on sales of consumer products. The dramatic increase in recent spending for sales promotion shows that marketers have recognized the potential of this marketing method. Many firms now include numerous sales promotion efforts as part of their overall promotion mix.

Sales Promotion Objectives

Sales promotion activities may be used singly or in combination, both offensively and defensively, to achieve one goal or a set of goals. Marketers use sales promotion activities and materials for a number of purposes, including

1. to draw new customers
2. to encourage trial purchases of a new product
3. to invigorate the sales of a mature brand
4. to boost sales to current customers
5. to reinforce advertising
6. to increase traffic in retail stores
7. to steady irregular sales patterns
8. to build up reseller inventories
9. to neutralize competitive promotional efforts
10. to improve shelf space and displays[5]

Any sales promotion objective should be consistent with the organization's general goals and with its marketing and promotion objectives.

Sales Promotion Methods

Most sales promotion methods can be classified as promotion techniques for either consumer sales or trade sales. A **consumer sales promotion method** attracts consumers to particular retail stores and motivates them to purchase certain new or established products. A **trade sales promotion method** encourages wholesalers and retailers to stock and actively promote a manufacturer's products. Incentives such as money, merchandise, marketing assistance, or gifts are commonly awarded to resellers who buy products or respond positively in other ways. Of the total dollars spent on promotion (excluding personal selling) in 1993, 47 percent was spent on trade promotions, 28 percent on consumer promotions, and 25 percent on advertising.[6]

A number of factors enter into marketing decisions about which, and how many, sales promotion methods to use. Of greatest importance are the objectives of the promotional effort. Product characteristics—size, weight, cost, durability, uses, features, and hazards—and target market profiles—age, gender, income, location, density, usage rate, and buying patterns—must likewise be considered. Distribution channels and availability of appropriate resellers also influence the choice of sales promotion methods, as do the competitive and regulatory environments. Let's now discuss a few important sales promotion methods.

consumer sales promotion method a sales promotion method designed to attract consumers to particular retail stores and to motivate them to purchase certain new or established products

trade sales promotion method a sales promotion method designed to encourage wholesalers and retailers to stock and actively promote a manufacturer's product

refund a return of part of the purchase price of a product

Refunds   A **refund** is a return of part of the purchase price of a product. Usually the refund is offered by the producer to consumers who send in a coupon along with a specific proof of purchase. (A refund is sometimes called a *manufacturer's rebate.*) Refunding is a relatively low-cost promotion method. Once used mainly for new product items, it is now applied to a wide variety of products.

cents-off coupon a coupon that reduces the retail price of a particular item by a stated amount at the time of purchase

Coupons   A **cents-off coupon** is a coupon that reduces the retail price of a particular item by a stated amount at the time of purchase. These coupons may be worth anywhere from a few cents to more than $1. They are reproduced in newspapers and magazines and/or sent to consumers by direct mail. More and more firms now use coupons. Some 322 billion coupons were distributed in 1993. Of these, 2.4 percent were redeemed by consumers.[7] The average value of a coupon increased from 29 cents in 1987 to 54 cents in 1993.[8] Coupons seem to work best for new or improved product items. The largest single category of coupons is health and beauty aids, followed by prepared foods, frozen and refrigerated foods, cereals, and household products. Stores in some areas even deduct double or triple the value of manufacturers' coupons from the purchase price, as a sales promotion technique of their own. Coupons may also offer free merchandise, either with or without an additional purchase of the product.

Cashing in on coupons. Instant coupon machines allow customers to obtain coupons at the point of purchase. The machines are convenient for customers and an economical way for the producer to distribute coupons.

Samples   A **sample** is a free package or container of a product. Samples may be offered through coupons, by direct mail, or in stores. Sampling encourages consumers to try the product. It is the most expensive sales promotion technique and is most often used to promote new products.

sample   a free package or container of a product

Premiums   A **premium** is a gift that a producer offers the customer in return for using its product. A producer of packaged foods may, for instance, offer consumers a cookbook as a premium. Premiums are often attached to or enclosed inside packages.

premium   a gift that a producer offers the customer in return for using its product

Point-of-Purchase Displays   A **point-of-purchase display** is promotional material placed within a retail store. The display is usually located near the product being promoted. It may actually hold merchandise (as do L'eggs hosiery displays) or inform customers about what the product offers and encourage them to buy it. Most point-of-purchase displays are prepared and set up by manufacturers and wholesalers.

point-of-purchase display   promotional material placed within a retail store

Trade Shows   A **trade show** is an industrywide exhibit at which many sellers display their products. Some trade shows are organized exclusively for dealers—to permit manufacturers and wholesalers to show their latest lines to retailers. Others are promotions designed to stimulate consumer awareness and interest. Among the latter are boat shows, home shows, and flower shows put on each year in large cities.

trade show   an industrywide exhibit at which many sellers display their products

■■ PUBLICITY AND PUBLIC RELATIONS

LEARNING OBJECTIVE 7
Discuss the types and uses of
publicity and the requirements
for effective use of publicity.

Publicity, as mentioned earlier, is a nonpersonal message in news-story form delivered through a mass medium, free of charge. Publicity differs from advertising in two ways. First, the media do not get paid for communicating the message. And second, its content and timing are not controlled by the firm. When it enhances the image of the firm or its products, publicity can be an effective form of promotion.

public relations   all activities whose objective is to create and maintain a favorable public image

Public relations consists of all activities whose objective is to create and maintain a favorable public image. In one sense, publicity is a part of public relations—the "information" part. Actually, good public relations generally results in good publicity and thus a favorable image.

Public-relations activities are many and varied, including the sponsorship of programs on public television and radio, and the sponsorship of events (including the Olympics). Although a large proportion of the funds spent for event sponsorship support sports events, companies also underwrite festivals, popular music, plays, and social causes. These and other public-relations efforts tend to build sales indirectly by showing that the sponsor is a "good citizen."

Types of Publicity

news release   a typed page of about 300 words provided by an organization to the media as a form of publicity

feature article   a piece (of up to 3,000 words) prepared by an organization for inclusion in a particular publication

captioned photograph   a picture accompanied by a brief explanation

press conference   a meeting at which invited media personnel hear important news announcements and receive supplementary textual materials and photographs

Several approaches to publicity are available to marketers. A **news release,** one of the most widely used types of publicity, is generally one typed page of about 300 words provided by an organization to the media. The release includes the firm's name, address, phone number, and contact person. A **feature article,** which may run as long as 3,000 words, is usually written for inclusion in a particular publication. A **captioned photograph,** a picture accompanied by a brief explanation, is an effective way to illustrate a new or improved product. A **press conference** allows invited media personnel to hear important news announcements and to receive supplementary textual materials and photographs. Finally, letters to the editor, special newspaper or magazine editorials, films, and tapes may be prepared and distributed to appropriate media for possible use.

At times, a single type of publicity will be adequate for a promotion mix. At other times, publicity will predominate in a mix, and the marketer will capitalize on several avenues of publicity. The specific kinds of publicity chosen depend on the composition of the target audience, the response of media personnel, the significance of the news item, and the nature and quantity of information to be communicated.

The Uses of Publicity

Businesses may use publicity for only one purpose or for several purposes. Publicity can raise public awareness of a company's products or activities. It can maintain a desired level of visibility for an organization. It can show a forward-looking company to its best advantage and help to downplay or refute a negative image as well. Table 15.2 lists some of the issues that can be addressed by publicity releases.

Helping to Protect Your Company from Negative Publicity

When General Motors showed that NBC reporters had rigged footage of GM trucks exploding for its *Dateline* news program, the resulting bad publicity lowered the network's credibility. Although an investigation proved that Goodyear tires were *not* responsible for accidents resulting in two deaths, the tire manufacturer suffered a flood of bad publicity. Negative publicity surrounding a major insurance company's policies resulted in a drop in stock prices and several shareholder lawsuits. The effects of negative publicity can have long-lasting consequences for a company, to both its finances and its reputation. Research shows that one negative item of information can negate five positive items. Although it is impossible to prevent all bad publicity, firms can minimize damage by anticipating, preparing for, and controlling events that do occur.

THE BEST WAY TO MINIMIZE NEGATIVE PUBLICITY IS TO AVOID IT

- Whenever your company makes a decision, ask the question, "Is this right?"
- Make sure that providing quality products and/or services is a number 1 priority.
- Respond to customer complaints quickly.
- Communicate your commitment to quality to your target market.
- Identify possible negative incidents by (1) soliciting customer and employee complaints and (2) conducting internal and external environmental scanning.

DETERMINE AN APPROPRIATE RESPONSE WHEN INCIDENTS OCCUR

By acting in an appropriate and timely manner when negative publicity threatens to undermine your company, you can lessen the effects and sometimes even enhance your company's image and create consumer loyalty. Companies usually respond to incidents in one of four ways:

- *Instinctive reaction.* When management reacts instinctively, denial is the most common response. This response is not very effective.
- *Stonewalling.* With this type of response, management refuses to address the problem at all or "fight all the way." Typically, this response is not effective.
- *Formal compliance.* This type of response results from some type of government intervention. A company is under legal obligation to address the problem and does so only to comply with the law. One consequence of this type of response is reduced customer confidence in the organization.
- *Seizing the initiative.* When management seizes the initiative, it moves aggressively to counteract the impact of negative publicity before the news has a chance to affect the company. For example, companies can issue informative press releases, recall products, investigate responsible parties, and take other actions that show customers it takes responsibility for what has occurred and is trying to correct the problem. When organizations respond in this way, they often gain public support and approval.

Proactive strategies are like a vaccination against the potentially damaging effects of negative publicity. To seize the initiative when the need arises, your company must be prepared. Planning to protect the organization from negative publicity includes

- Developing a system that allows the company to respond quickly to customer complaints.
- Structuring and organizing the company to facilitate a rapid response to negative events.
- Installing an emergency plan with designated individuals in charge of efforts to address negative incidents.

The director of public relations for Chrysler Corporation offers one more bit of advice for managing a crisis: "Tell the truth because people will begin to believe you. Keep telling the truth, all of it, and people will believe you."

483

TABLE 15.2   Possible Issues for Publicity Releases

Changes in marketing personnel	Packaging changes
Support of a social cause	New products
Improved warranties	Creation of a new slogan
Reports on industry conditions	Research developments
New uses for established products	Company's history and development
Product endorsements	Employment, production, and sales records
Winning of quality awards	Award of contracts
Company name changes	Opening of new markets
Interviews with company officials	Improvements in financial position
Improved distribution policies	Opening of an exhibit
International business efforts	History of a brand
Athletic event sponsorship	Winners of company contests
Visits by celebrities	Logo changes
Reports on new discoveries	Speeches of top management
Innovative marketing activities	Merit awards to the organization
Economic forecasts	Anniversary of inventions

Using Publicity Effectively

A company's publicity efforts should be thorough, well organized, and regular. The program should be led by a designated individual or department within the business or by a public-relations firm.

Because publicity functions often require personal communications with editors, reporters, and other media personnel, good professional relationships with these individuals are essential. Their advice can help ensure that a business's publicity program meshes well with the workings of the media.

A firm striving for effective publicity should review its news items carefully to avoid releasing those that are insignificant or poorly written. News items that do not meet media standards are usually rejected by media personnel.

The number of news releases actually published or broadcast can give a company a good indication of the effectiveness of its publicity program. As one check on the print media, an organization can pay clipping services to cut out and relay published news stories to the publicity department. No similar service is available, however, for monitoring broadcast news releases. A firm can request that a notification card be returned when a station has broadcast a certain news release, but stations do not always comply with these requests.

■■ PROMOTION PLANNING

promotional campaign a plan for combining and using the four promotion methods—advertising, personal selling, sales promotion, and publicity—in a particular promotion mix to reach one or more marketing goals

A **promotional campaign** is a plan for combining and using the four promotion methods—advertising, personal selling, sales promotion, and publicity—in a particular promotion mix to reach one or more marketing goals. In planning a promotion, marketers must answer these two questions:

- What will be the role of promotion in the overall marketing mix?
- To what extent will each promotion method be used in the promotion mix?

The answer to the first question depends on the firm's marketing objectives, since the role of each element of the marketing mix—product, price, distribution, and promotion—depends on these detailed versions of the firm's marketing goals. The answer to the second question depends on the answer to the first as well as on the target market.

Promotion and Marketing Objectives

Promotion is naturally better suited to certain marketing objectives than to others. For example, promotion can do little to further a marketing objective such as "reduce delivery time by one-third." It can, however, be used to inform customers that delivery is faster. Let's consider some objectives that *would* require the use of promotion as a primary ingredient of the marketing mix.

Providing Information   This is, of course, the main function of promotion. It may be used to communicate to target markets the availability of new products or product features. It may alert them to special sales or offers or give the locations of retailers that carry the firm's products. In other words, promotion can be used to enhance the effectiveness of each of the other ingredients of the marketing mix.

Increasing Market Share   Promotion can be used to convince new customers to try a product, while maintaining the product loyalty of established customers. Comparative advertising, for example, is directed mainly at those who might—but presently do not—use a particular product. Advertising that emphasizes the product's features also assures those who *do* use the product that they have made a smart choice.

Positioning the Product   The sales of a product depend, to a great extent, on its competition. The stronger the competition, the more difficult it is to maintain or increase sales. For this reason, many firms go to great lengths to position their products in the marketplace. **Positioning** is the development of a product image in buyers' minds relative to the images they have of competing products.

> positioning the development of a product image in buyers' minds relative to the images they have of competing products

Promotion is the prime positioning tool. A marketer can use promotion to position a brand away from competitors to avoid competition. Promotion may also be used to position one product directly against another product. For example, Coca-Cola and Pepsi position their products to compete head-to-head against each other.

Stabilizing Sales   Special promotional efforts can be used to increase sales during slack periods, such as the "off season" for certain sports equipment. By stabilizing sales in this way, a firm can use its production facilities more effectively and reduce both capital costs and inventory costs. Promotion is also often used to increase the sales of products that are in the declining stage of their life cycle. The objective is to keep them going for a little while longer.

Developing the Promotion Mix

LEARNING OBJECTIVE 8
Identify the factors that influence the selection of promotion mix ingredients.

Once the role of promotion is established, the various promotion methods may be combined in a promotional campaign. As in so many other areas of business, promotion planning begins with a set of specific objectives. The promotion mix is then designed to accomplish these objectives.

Marketers often use several promotion mixes simultaneously if a firm sells multiple products. The selection of promotion mix ingredients and the degree to which they are used depend on the organization's resources and objectives, the nature of the target market, the characteristics of the product, and the feasibility of various promotion methods.

The amount of promotional resources available in an organization influences the number and intensity of promotion methods that marketers can use. A firm with a limited budget for promotion will probably rely on personal selling, because the effectiveness of personal selling can be measured more easily than that of advertising. An organization's objectives also have an effect on its promotional activities. A company wishing to make a wide audience familiar with a new convenience item will probably depend heavily on advertising and sales promotion. If a company's objective is to communicate information to consumers—on the features of countertop appliances, for example—then the company may develop a promotion mix that includes some advertising, some sales promotion to attract consumers to stores, and much personal selling.

The size, geographic distribution, and socioeconomic characteristics of the target market play a part in the composition of a product's promotion mix. If the market is small, personal selling will probably be the most important element in the promotion mix. This is true of organizations that sell to small industrial markets and businesses that use only a few wholesalers to market their products. Companies that need to contact millions of potential customers, however, will emphasize sales promotion and advertising because these methods are relatively inexpensive. The age, income, and education of the target market will also influence the choice of promotion techniques. For example, with less educated consumers, personal selling may be more effective than ads in newspapers or magazines.

In general, industrial products require a considerable amount of personal selling, whereas consumer goods depend on advertising. This is not true in every case, however. The price of the product also influences the composition of the promotion mix. Because consumers often want the advice of a salesperson on an expensive product, high-priced consumer goods may call for more personal selling. Similarly, advertising and sales promotion may be more crucial to marketers of seasonal items because having a year-round sales force is not always appropriate.

The cost and availability of promotion methods are important factors in the development of a promotion mix. Although national advertising and sales promotion activities are expensive, the cost per customer may be quite small if the campaign succeeds in reaching large numbers of people. In addition, local advertising outlets—newspapers, magazines, radio and television stations, and outdoor displays—may not be that costly for a small, local business. In some situations, a firm may find that no available advertising medium reaches the target market effectively.

This chapter concludes our discussion of marketing. In the next chapter we begin our examination of information for business by discussing management information and computers.

■ ■ ■ ■ CHAPTER REVIEW

Summary

1   Understand the role of promotion.

Promotion is communication intended to inform, persuade, or remind an organization's target market of the organization or its products. The major promotion mix ingredients are advertising, personal selling, sales promotion, and publicity. The role of promotion is to facilitate exchanges directly or indirectly and to help an organization maintain favorable relationships with groups in the marketing environment.

2   Explain the purposes of the three types of advertising.

Advertising is a paid, nonpersonal message communicated to a select audience through a mass medium. Selective advertising promotes a particular brand of product. Institutional advertising is image-building advertising for a firm. Primary-demand advertising promotes the products of an entire industry rather than just a single brand.

3   Describe the advantages and disadvantages of the major advertising media.

The major advertising media are newspapers, magazines, direct mail, outdoor advertising, television, and radio. Newspapers account for the largest share of advertising expenditures, with television running a close second. Newspapers are relatively inexpensive compared to other media, reach only people in the market area, and are timely. Disadvantages include a short life span, poor color reproduction, and inability to target specific demographic groups. Magazine advertising can be quite prestigious. In addition, it can reach very specific market segments, can provide high-quality color reproduction, and has a relatively long life span. Major disadvantages include high cost and lack of timeliness. Outdoor advertising allows marketers to focus on a particular geographic area and is relatively

inexpensive. Messages, though, must be limited to a few words because the audience is usually moving. Television offers marketers the opportunity to broadcast a firm's message nationwide. However, television advertising is very expensive and has a short life span, and the advent of cable channels and home videos has reduced the likelihood of reaching extremely large audiences. Radio advertising offers selectivity, can be less expensive than other media, and is flexible for scheduling purposes. Radio's limitations include no visual presentation and fragmented, small station audiences.

4   Identify the major steps in developing an advertising campaign.

An advertising campaign is developed in several stages. A firm's first task is to identify and analyze its advertising target. The goals of the campaign must also be clearly defined. Then the firm must develop the advertising platform, or statement of important selling points, and determine the size of the advertising budget. The next steps are to develop a media plan, to create the advertising message, and to execute the campaign. Finally, promotion managers must evaluate the effectiveness of the advertising efforts before, during, and/or after the campaign.

5   Recognize the various kinds of salespersons, the steps in the personal-selling process, and the major sales management tasks.

Personal selling is a personal communications process aimed at informing customers and persuading them to buy a firm's products. It is the most adaptable promotion method because the salesperson can modify the message to fit each buyer. Three major kinds of salepersons are order getters, order takers, and support personnel. The six steps in the personal-selling process are prospecting, approaching the prospect, making the presentation, answering objections, closing the sale, and following up. Sales managers are directly involved in setting sales force objectives; recruiting, selecting, and training salespersons; compensating and motivating sales personnel; creating sales territories; and evaluating sales performance.

6 Describe sales promotion objectives and methods.

Sales promotion is the use of activities and materials as direct inducements to customers and salespersons. Some methods of sales promotion include refunds, coupons, samples, premiums, point-of-purchase displays, and trade shows.

7 Discuss the types and uses of publicity and the requirements for effective use of publicity.

Public relations, or image-building, activities include the sponsorship of programs and events that are of interest to the general public. Publicity is a nonpersonal message in news-story form delivered through a mass medium at no charge. The information is transmitted to the media via news releases, feature articles, captioned photographs, and press conferences. To be effective, a company's publicity efforts should be thorough, well organized, and regular.

8 Identify the factors that influence the selection of promotion mix ingredients.

A promotional campaign is a plan for combining and using advertising, personal selling, sales promotion, and publicity to achieve one or more marketing goals. Campaign objectives are developed from marketing objectives. Then the promotion mix is developed based on the organization's marketing objectives, the nature of the target market, the product characteristics, and the feasibility of various promotional methods.

Key Terms

You should now be able to define and give an example relevant to each of the following terms:

promotion (461)
promotion mix (461)
advertising (463)
personal selling (463)
sales promotion (464)
publicity (464)
selective (or brand) advertising (465)
institutional advertising (465)
primary-demand advertising (465)
advertising media (465)
cooperative advertising (466)
direct-mail advertising (467)
outdoor advertising (468)
infomercial (469)
advertising agency (472)
order getter (475)
creative selling (475)
order taker (475)
sales support personnel (475)
missionary salesperson (475)
trade salesperson (475)
technical salesperson (475)
consumer sales promotion method (480)
trade sales promotion method (480)
refund (480)
cents-off coupon (480)
sample (481)
premium (481)
point-of-purchase display (481)
trade show (481)
public relations (482)
news release (482)
feature article (482)
captioned photograph (482)
press conference (482)
promotional campaign (484)
positioning (485)

Questions

Review Questions

1. What is the difference between a marketing mix and a promotion mix? How are they related?
2. What is the major role of promotion?
3. How are selective, institutional, and primary-demand advertising different from one another? Give an example of each.
4. What is cooperative advertising? What sorts of firms use it?
5. List the four major print media, and give an advantage and a disadvantage of each.
6. What types of firms use each of the two electronic media?
7. Outline the main steps involved in developing an advertising campaign.
8. Why would a firm with its own advertising department use an ad agency?
9. Identify and give examples of the three major types of salespersons.

10. Explain how each step in the personal-selling process leads to the next step.

11. What are the major tasks involved in managing a sales force?

12. In your opinion, what are the three most effective techniques for sales promotion? How does each of these techniques supplement advertising?

13. What is the difference between publicity and public relations? What is the purpose of each?

14. Why is promotion particularly effective in positioning a product? in stabilizing or increasing sales?

15. What factors determine the specific promotion mix that a firm should use?

Discussion Questions

1. Is Dr Pepper aiming at the same target audience as it did five years ago?

2. What types of promotional opportunity could arise out of the use of event sponsorship?

3. Discuss the pros and cons of comparative advertising from the viewpoint of (a) the advertiser, (b) the advertiser's competitors, and (c) the target market.

4. Which kinds of advertising—in which media— influence you most? Why?

5. Which kinds of retail outlets or products require mainly order taking by salespeople?

6. Why would a producer offer refunds or cents-off coupons rather than simply lowering the price of its products?

7. During the 1980s, customers were very receptive to certain types of sales promotion methods. Why?

8. How does the publicity that business firms seek help the general public?

9. What steps should a company take to avoid negative publicity?

10. What kind of promotion mix might be used to extend the life of a product that has entered the declining stage of its product life cycle?

Exercises

1. Describe, sketch, or photocopy one example of each of the following types of advertisements. Explain briefly what makes it an example of its particular type.
   a. Immediate-response (selective)
   b. Reminder (selective)
   c. Institutional
   d. Primary-demand
   e. Local
   f. Cooperative

2. Write a description of four different point-of-purchase displays you have seen. For each, give the type of display, the product and brand displayed or promoted, and your evaluation of the effectiveness of the display.

3. Choose a particular product that was not discussed in the chapter. From your overall knowledge of the product, outline a promotion mix for it. That is, determine what percentage of your total promotion budget you would allocate to each promotion method, at whom the promotion would be directed, and the media you would use. Give your reason for each decision.

VIDEO CASE 15.1

The Advertising Council: Advertising for Good, Not for Gain

- "Advertising is sexist or racist."
- "Ads make people want what they don't need and can't afford."
- "Commercials are provocative, explicit, intrusive, irritating, or just plain lies."

Americans have long criticized the advertising industry for promoting greed and consumption. What many don't realize is that advertising sells more than merchandise. From preventive health care such as vaccinations and prenatal check-ups to complex and controversial issues such as racial tolerance, mental illness, and AIDS, the Advertising Council develops campaigns that confront some of America's vital concerns. For over half a century, this nonprofit organization has demonstrated that advertising can inform, educate, and unite people; change attitudes; and combat social problems.

In 1942, after the attack on Pearl Harbor plunged the United States into World War II, the government established the War Advertising Council. Inaugurating public service advertising, the council had as its purpose encouraging Americans to help the war effort by buying war bonds, planting "victory gardens," saving metals and rubber, and conserving fuel. How effective was the campaign? By the end of the war, advertisers and the media had donated about $1 billion in time and space for war-related messages, and Americans had purchased $35 billion worth of war bonds, planted 50 million victory gardens, and salvaged a million pounds of rubber, tin, and steel. Convinced by these results that advertising could be a powerful tool for public good, the War Advertising Council became the Advertising Council and prepared to take on America's postwar problems.

Planning, creating, and implementing advertising nationally, the Advertising Council selects issues that the federal government or nonprofit social agencies suggest. To maintain independence, the council raises all funds from private sources and allows no public officials on its board of directors. Campaigns must address problems faced by all areas of the United States and must suggest specific actions individuals can take to remedy the situation. The Ad Council usually does not promote specific organizations, but rather promotes behaviors consistent with the goals of the organizations. For example, the Ad Council would not promote the American Heart Association, but it might produce an ad that stresses healthy eating as a way to minimize the risk of heart attacks. Over five hundred prominent national manufacturers and marketers, including Johnson & Johnson, RJR Nabisco, Procter & Gamble, and Coca-Cola, sponsor council projects. Advertising agencies create campaigns, with national advertisers directing the process and providing financial support. The media provide about twenty thousand print, broadcast, outdoor, and transit outlets. In one year alone, donations totaled over $1 billion in media space and time, and thousands of hours of advertising agency services.

Over the years, the Advertising Council has developed award-winning campaigns on numerous issues. The council's early crusades dealt with uncomplicated, benign stands. Smokey the Bear cautioned, "Only You Can Prevent Forest Fires" and children sang, "Please, please, don't be a litterbug" to "Keep America Beautiful." In the late 1960s, however, America's concerns changed, and with them the Ad Council's focus. Social ills and controversial issues took center stage—drinking and driving, alcoholism, drugs, child abuse, rape, cancer, and AIDS. Recent council campaigns encourage the study of math and science, give tips on car jacking prevention, and urge education reform; recently, its "Life's Too Short. Stop the Hate" campaign promoted racial harmony.

For those skeptics who doubt that advertising is powerful enough to inspire people to act against inhumanity, discrimination, and spread of disease, the statistics may be convincing. Since the Advertising Council began its "A Mind Is a Terrible Thing to Waste" ads in 1971, money raised for the United Negro College Fund has grown 800 percent. In one year, a million children called the Runaway Teen Hotline after seeing the council's posters and billboards. An Ad Council research study on the effects of its campaign to prevent colon cancer reveals that awareness of the disease rose 30 percent in one year. When the U.S. Senate recently considered new laws requiring health warnings in beer and alcohol advertising, representatives were able to convince senators that the council is so successful in getting the message out that the legislation would be redundant.

The Ad Council continues to explore new ways to publicize today's troublesome, and agonizing, problems. To reach young adults, the council is using nontraditional media, including high school and college newspapers, sports arena signage, movie theater advertising, and MTV. To supplement conventional thirty-second spots and print ads, the council is using talk shows, infomercials, and interactive computer information services. Its first thirty-minute infomercial features the new "Breaking the Cycle of Disadvantage" campaign, designed to improve the health and education of children living in poverty. Subscribers to some interactive computer networks like Prodigy can ask the Ad Council questions about recycling and get immediate answers from the nonprofit environmental group Earth Share.

Impressed by the Advertising Council's success in the United States, a coalition of Russian advertisers and news and social organizations recently formed the Advertising Council in Russia. Its first campaign is called "We're All People." The Russian group hopes to do what the Ad Council has accomplished for over fifty years in the United States—use the power of advertising to turn hundreds of social causes into major national issues.[9]

Questions

1. In what ways would the process for developing Ad Council campaigns differ from the steps discussed in this chapter?
2. Does publicity play a role in the Ad Council campaigns? Explain.
3. How might the effectiveness of Ad Council campaigns be measured?

CASE 15.2

Nabisco's Winning Sales Force

In almost every grocery store in the United States, you will find shelves full of Nabisco's Oreos, Teddy Grahams, Chips Ahoy!, Ritz Crackers, and Wheat Thins. Challengers come and go, but these favorites never get lost in the shuffle. The 97-year-old National Biscuit Company, a subsidiary of RJR Nabisco, Inc., has a knack for coming up with popular products. Eight of the top ten selling brands in the cookie/cracker category are Nabisco offerings, adding up to about 1 billion pounds of snacks sold every year. Does this achievement prove that a really good product "sells itself"? Nabisco's sales force says no. They believe their extraordinary success is the result of extensive training, dedicated customer service, and personal commitment to the product and the company—not just a reputation for supplying delicious cookies. Recently winning *Sales and Marketing Management*'s "Best Sales Force" survey award affirms Nabisco's belief in and reliance on its salespeople.

Thorough training gives Nabisco's people an edge when they go into the field. The company spends about $1 million a year on strategy meetings for sales personnel. At these sessions, salespeople examine current sales figures and set new goals together; plan sales and marketing strategies; find out about new products, upcoming promotions, and advertising campaigns; and work together to improve their selling skills. To continually improve the quality of these training sessions, the company tries to provide pertinent guest speakers and state-of-the-technology visual aids and, most important, to encourage more sales representative participation. Nabisco works hard to ensure that its salespeople leave with knowledge they can put to use.

Equipped with exceptional training, sales personnel in turn provide their customers with exceptional service. Using data from powerful laptop, handheld, or pen-based computers, salespeople often share with outlet managers information to help boost sales, such as who their customers are, what the average purchases are, and how to create the most effective product mix. Eliminating the inconvenience of trips to a central warehouse, Nabisco delivers products directly to its customers, a service that most of its competitors shun. Salespeople will sometimes set up the cookie/cracker department themselves, picking the best location and stocking shelves. Providing neighborhood "mom and pop" operations the same service quality it provides its national supermarket chains is important to Nabisco. When the cost of having sales representatives visit every small customer became prohibitive, the company

designed a computer-based telemarketing network for these accounts. Customer representatives conduct transactions over the phone and send order information directly to Nabisco's distribution center using the company's mainframe computer. Soon, customers will be able to place orders through a voice response unit (VRU) twenty-four hours a day.

Nabisco's salespeople are deeply committed to their company, in part because their personal input and involvement are highly valued. Communication is good between the decision makers in the marketing department and the sales reps. By talking to one another, marketers get frequent feedback, and sales reps get the satisfaction of knowing that their ideas and suggestions carry weight. Nabisco rewards people for a good sales record but breaks with the tradition of giving a gift—an all-expenses-paid vacation, for example—only to the top-selling individuals. Instead, the company ties salaries and bonuses to personalized sales goals. The more that salespeople meet or exceed these goals (and 75 percent of them do), the more money they make. Because the motivation to keep selling is self-directed, every Nabisco salesperson can be a winner.

Nabisco sales personnel are proud of their jobs, their products, and their company. In addition to posting record sales of $6.4 billion and winning the "Best Sales Force" award, Nabisco reps won high marks for retaining existing accounts and bringing in new ones.[10]

Questions

1. What factors contribute to making a sales meeting successful?
2. How does Nabisco motivate its sales force?
3. Why is an effective sales force so important to a company like Nabisco?

CAREER PROFILE ■ ■ ■ ■ ■ ■ ■ ■ ■ ■ ■

PART 4   Career Opportunities in Marketing

Job Title	Job Description	Salary Range
Advertising account executive	Manage the development and implementation of the client's advertising campaign; know client's product and marketing plans and agency's resources for carrying out plans; plan the advertising campaign and create its components; sell the client on the planned advertising campaign; go to location to oversee the production of commercials; ensure that artists, copywriters, and production people meet the schedule	4
Advertising manager	Develop advertising to reach organizations' customers; one-person staff in some companies; responsible for the administration of a large budget; coordinate the activities of the department to meet deadlines and schedules; place the company's advertising in the appropriate media; handle day-to-day administration of the department; represent the company in its dealings with an agency	5
Manufacturer's salesperson	Interest wholesale and retail buyers and purchasing agents in products; spend much time traveling; keep prospective buyers up-to-date with sales promotions and prices; help buyers with technical problems; work with engineers adapting products to customers' needs	4
Marketing researcher	Plan and design research projects; conduct interviews and fact-gathering operations; tabulate and analyze findings	5
Media buyer	Be well informed about costs and audiences of various media; work with account executives to decide how to reach the target audience for the client's product; buy media time and space	2
Public relations specialist	Help business, governments, universities, hospitals, schools, and other organizations build positive relationships with their various publics; handle the press, political campaigns, and employee relations; understand the attitudes and concerns of customers, employees, and various publics and communicates this to management; contact media that might print or air materials; develop information packets	3
Store manager	Manage a multitude of store operations including personnel, ordering, displays, selling, accounting, and advertising	4
Wholesale or retail buyer	Purchase merchandise for resale; specialize in acquiring one or two lines of merchandise; be knowledgeable about the products and what will appeal to consumers; keep up with inventories; check on competitive sales activities; help to determine customer trends and interests; help in planning sales promotions	4

The figure in the salary column approximates the expected annual income after two or three years of service.
1 = $12,000–$15,000; 2 = $16,000–$20,000; 3 = $21,000–$27,000; 4 = $28,000–$35,000; 5 = $36,000 and up.

Educational Requirements	Skills Required	Prospects for Growth
Bachelor's degree in business or liberal arts	Communication; problem solving; interpersonal	Average
Bachelor's degree in business or liberal arts	Communication; decision making; interpersonal; marketing skills	Above average
Some college; degree preferred; on-the-job-experience	Communication; marketing skills; interpersonal; time management	Below average
College degree; on-the-job experience	Analytical; communication	Average
Some college; on-the-job experience	Communication; decision making; interpersonal	Limited
College degree; on-the-job experience	Writing; public speaking; interpersonal; communicaion; time management; problem solving	Average
College degree; on-the-job experience	Office; decision making	Average
Varies; college preferred; on-the-job experience	Communication; interpersonal; decision making; marketing skills	Below average

PART FIVE

Information for Business

The subject of this part is information, the fourth essential resource on which all businesses rely. First we discuss computers and the different kinds of information that are necessary for effective decision making. Then we examine the role of accounting and how financial information is collected, processed, and presented. Included in this part are

CHAPTER 16 Management Information and Computers

CHAPTER 17 Accounting

Management Information and Computers

LEARNING OBJECTIVES

After studying this chapter you should be able to

1 Describe how information differs from data.

2 Summarize the development of the computer.

3 Explain the difference between computer hardware and computer software.

4 Describe the impact that computers have had on business.

5 Explore future business applications of improved computer technology.

6 Discuss management's information requirements.

7 State the four functions of a management information system.

8 Explain how a management information system uses statistics to turn data into information.

CHAPTER PREVIEW

In this chapter, we take a closer look at management information and computers. First, we look at the difference between data and information. Then we see how computers help managers transform data into information. We also consider the present and future impact of computers on business. Next we analyze what types of information managers need. Finally, we examine the components of a management information system (MIS) and show how the system can be used to aid managers in the decision-making process.

Microsoft: What's Next?

Microsoft Corporation, led by thirty-nine-year-old Bill Gates, is the most successful software firm in the world. Founded in 1975, when Gates was just nineteen, the firm now has annual sales revenues in excess of $4.7 billion. And with a 24 percent after-tax profit margin, the firm is debt-free. The firm's early success was tied to a partnership with IBM that began in the early 1980s. When IBM introduced its first personal computer, Microsoft supplied the operating system—MS-DOS—that guides the inner workings of the personal computer.

Microsoft's initial success with operating systems enabled the firm to branch out into application software. And with the introduction of Windows—an all-in-one software program that enables users to integrate electronic mail, graphics, word processing, and other application programs—Microsoft's profits, sales, and stock price have all quadrupled. The phenomenal success of Microsoft over the last twenty years has led industry analysts to wonder what the future holds.

Already, Microsoft is moving onto the information superhighway. In late 1994, Microsoft announced plans to introduce its own on-line services—code-named Marvel. And although Marvel is designed to compete with CompuServe, Prodigy, and America Online, experts admit that Microsoft will have an edge obtaining new customers. Marvel will be an integral part of the new version of the Windows software program that will be introduced in mid-1995. Microsoft is expected to make it *very easy* for computer users who purchase the new Windows program to begin using Microsoft's on-line service.

Developing a successful on-line service is especially important to Microsoft's long-range plans because Gates believes that both businesses and consumers will use computers connected to on-

Operating System Version 3.1

line services to complete everyday business transactions. Clothing boutiques, department stores, travel agencies, brokerage houses, banks, movie theaters, and publishers would advertise their products electronically to consumers. Customers would then use their personal computer to place orders for products and services and use credit card numbers for all transactions. Business firms advertising their products on Microsoft's on-line service would pay a fee—essentially, electronic rent—to Microsoft. Customers, in addition to paying a monthly fee, would pay a transaction charge each time they purchase goods or services. Given the potential for huge revenues generated by on-line services, coupled with the fact that it sells more software products than anyone in the world, Microsoft will be able to maintain its leadership position in the computer industry well beyond the year 2000.[1]

■■■■

497

■　　■　　■　　■　　■　　■　　■　　■　　■　　■　　■

B ill Gates, along with his managers and employees, are optimistic that Microsoft will be able to maintain its number one position in the software industry. While Microsoft operates in an industry that has undergone dramatic changes over the past twenty years, the firm has continued to provide quality, state-of-the-art software programs that meet the needs of their customers. Now, Microsoft is in a position to use profits from software sales to move onto the information superhighway and provide information—a topic discussed throughout this chapter—to an ever-increasing number of customers.

As we noted in Chapter 1, information is one of the four major resources (along with material, human, and financial resources) that managers must combine in order to operate a business. To help their managers obtain and use information, most firms establish management information systems.

■■ THE NEED FOR MANAGEMENT INFORMATION

Many people use the terms *data* and *information* interchangeably, but the two differ in important ways. **Data** are numerical or verbal descriptions that usually result from measurements of some sort. (The word *data* is plural; the singular form is *datum.*) Your current wage level, the amount of last year's after-tax profit for Compaq Computers, and the retail prices for automobiles currently produced by Chrysler Corporation are all data. Most people think of data as being numerical only, but they can be nonnumerical as well. A description of an individual as a "tall, athletic person with short, dark hair" would certainly qualify as data.

Information is data presented in a form that is useful for a specific purpose. Suppose a human resources manager wants to compare the wages paid to male and female employees by the firm over a period of seven years. The manager might begin with a stack of computer printouts listing every person employed by the firm, along with each employee's current and past wages. The manager would be hard-pressed to make any sense of all the names and numbers. Such printouts consist of data rather than information.

Now suppose the manager uses a computer to compute and graph the average wage paid to men and that paid to women in each of the seven years. The resulting graph (see Figure 16.1) is information because the manager can use it for the purpose at hand—to compare wages paid to men with those paid to women over the seven-year period.

The wage data from the printouts became information when they were summarized in the graph. Large sets of data often must be summarized if they are to be at all useful, but this is not always the case. If the manager in our example had wanted to know only the wage history of a specific employee, that information would be contained in the original computer

498

FIGURE 16.1
Data versus Information
Data are numerical or verbal descriptions that usually result from measurements; information is data presented in a form useful for a specific purpose. Thus the computer printout of every employee's wages is data, whereas the graph that compares average wages year by year is information.

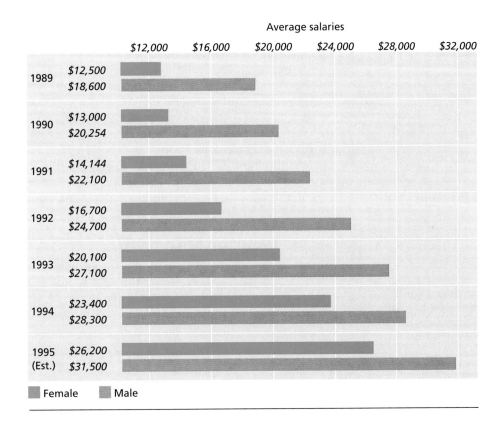

	Jan	Feb	March	April	May	June	July	Aug	Sept	Oct	Nov	Dec	Totals
Female Employees													
Employee 1	1,150	1,150	1,150	1,150	1,150	1,150	1,200	1,200	1,200	1,200	1,200	1,300	$14,200
Employee 2	1,400	1,400	1,400	1,400	1,400	1,400	1,400	1,400	1,400	1,400	1,400	1,400	$16,800
Employee 3	1,600	1,600	1,600	1,600	1,800	1,800	1,800	1,800	1,800	1,900	1,900	1,900	$21,100
Employee 4	1,200	1,200	1,200	1,200	1,200	1,200	1,250	1,250	1,250	1,250	1,250	1,250	$14,700
Male Employees													
Employee 5	1,800	1,800	1,800	1,800	1,800	1,800	1,800	1,800	1,800	1,800	1,800	1,800	$21,600
Employee 6	2,000	2,000	2,000	2,000	2,000	2,000	2,100	2,100	2,100	2,100	2,100	2,100	$24,600
Employee 7	1,900	1,900	1,900	1,900	1,900	1,900	1,950	1,950	1,950	1,950	2,000	2,000	$23,200
Employee 8	2,400	2,400	2,400	2,400	2,400	2,400	2,500	2,500	2,500	2,500	2,500	2,500	$29,400

Average salaries

| | $12,000 | $16,000 | $20,000 | $24,000 | $28,000 | $32,000 |

1989 $12,500 $18,600

1990 $13,000 $20,254

1991 $14,144 $22,100

1992 $16,700 $24,700

1993 $20,100 $27,100

1994 $23,400 $28,300

1995 (Est.) $26,200 $31,500

■ Female   Male

printout. That is, the data (the employee's name and wage history) would already be in the most useful form for the manager's purpose; they would need no further processing.

The average company maintains a great deal of data—personnel, inventory, sales, accounting, and other types—that can be transformed into information. Often, each type of data is stored in separate departments within the organization. In a large organization, each type of data is more effectively used when it is organized into a database. A **database** is a single collection of data that is stored in one place and can be used by people throughout the organization to make decisions. In addition to just storing data in one place, the organization must establish procedures for gathering, updating, and

database a single collection of data that is stored in one place and can be used by people throughout the organization to make decisions

processing facts in the database. Then, computers can help ensure that the facts in a database are up-to-date and available when employees and managers need them.

■■ HISTORICAL DEVELOPMENT OF THE COMPUTER

LEARNING OBJECTIVE 2
Summarize the development of the computer.

Until perhaps twenty-five years ago, most data and information were stored using manual systems. Records were kept in written form, and clerical personnel were responsible for collecting, filing, retrieving, and processing the data required by managers. Today, most clerical tasks are completed with the aid of a computer.

computer an electronic machine that can accept, store, manipulate, and transmit data in accordance with a set of specific instructions

A **computer** is an electronic machine that can accept, store, manipulate, and transmit data in accordance with a set of specific instructions. Moreover, it can store huge amounts of data, process them very rapidly with perfect accuracy, and transmit (or present) results in a variety of ways. For example, California-based Carter Hawley Hale Stores Inc. is a large corporation that owns several retail companies, including The Broadway, Emporium, and Weinstock's on the West Coast. Altogether, Carter's management must keep track of approximately 90 stores and more than 8 million items of merchandise. To deal with this mountain of data, Carter's management invested $75 million in a computer center near Los Angeles to keep track of all the buying, pricing, and inventory-control data and to provide management with the information it needs to run the retail network.

The Evolution of Computers

Today, large firms such as Carter Hawley Hale use computers on a daily basis, and even most small businesses rely on the daily use of computers. This was not always the case, however. Even after computers were developed and mass produced, most were too large and too expensive for most businesses. Although the computer is a relatively recent invention, its development rests on centuries of research (see Figure 16.2).

FIGURE 16.2
A Chronology of Technological Developments
Many significant developments led up to the invention of the electronic computers widely used today.

EARLY TECHNOLOGICAL DEVELOPMENTS

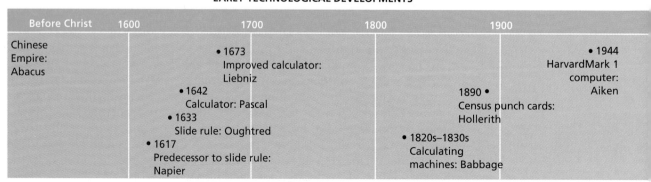

Before Christ	1600	1700	1800	1900
Chinese Empire: Abacus		• 1673 Improved calculator: Liebniz		• 1944 HarvardMark 1 computer: Aiken
		• 1642 Calculator: Pascal	1890 • Census punch cards: Hollerith	
		• 1633 Slide rule: Oughtred		
	• 1617 Predecessor to slide rule: Napier		• 1820s–1830s Calculating machines: Babbage	

Early Technological Developments   One early calculating device, the abacus, was developed by Chinese merchants before the birth of Christ. Composed of several wires, each strung with ten beads, the abacus enabled merchants to calculate solutions to mathematical problems and store the results.

In the seventeenth century, the slide rule was developed through the work of John Napier and William Oughtred. And the first real mechanical "calculator" was developed in 1642 by the French mathematician Blaise Pascal. Later in the same century, the German Gottfried von Liebniz developed a mechanical device that would not only add and subtract but also multiply, divide, and calculate square roots.

In the early 1800s, Charles Babbage, a British mathematician, designed a machine that could perform mathematical calculations and store the intermediate results in a memory unit—the forerunner of today's computer. Later, Babbage designed a similar machine that could perform addition, subtraction, multiplication, or division based on instructions coded on cards. Both machines contained many features similar to those found in today's modern computers. As a result, Babbage is often called the father of modern computer technology.

In the late 1880s, the U.S. government commissioned Herman Hollerith to develop a system that could process the 1890 census data. His punch card system (based on Babbage's original concept) reduced the time required to process the 1890 census data to two and a half years. (It had taken seven and a half years to process the 1880 census data manually.) Later, Hollerith founded the Tabulating Machine Company to manufacture and sell punch card equipment to businesses. The Tabulating Machine Company eventually changed its name and today is known as International Business Machines (IBM).

In 1944 Howard Aiken of Harvard University, in collaboration with IBM and the U.S. War Department, embarked on a joint project to manufacture the Harvard Mark I computer. It was not a true electronic computer because it relied on electromagnetic relays and mechanical counters to perform

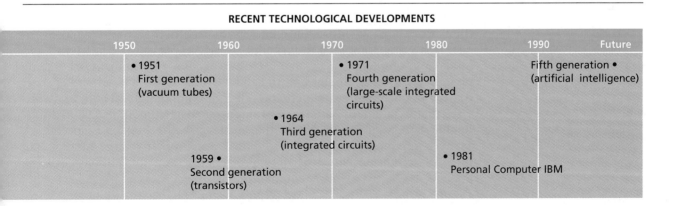

RECENT TECHNOLOGICAL DEVELOPMENTS

1950	1960	1970	1980	1990	Future
• 1951 First generation (vacuum tubes)		• 1971 Fourth generation (large-scale integrated circuits)		Fifth generation • (artificial intelligence)	
	• 1964 Third generation (integrated circuits)				
1959 • Second generation (transistors)			• 1981 Personal Computer IBM		

mathematical calculations. Nevertheless, this device did open the door for the development of the electronic computer.

Recent Technological Developments   Today's electronic computers are the result of five stages (sometimes called generations) of research and development. The first generation of computers (1951 to 1958) relied on glass vacuum tubes to control the internal operations of the computer. The vacuum tubes, which were quite large, generated a great deal of heat. As a result, the overall computer was huge and required special air conditioning to compensate for the excessive heat buildup.

The second generation (1959 to 1963) began when tiny, electronic transistors replaced vacuum tubes. Transistors greatly reduced the size of the computer and were more reliable, required less maintenance, and processed data much faster than had the vacuum tubes. High-speed printers and card readers were introduced during the second generation. Finally, second-generation computers were programmed with high-level languages such as FORTRAN (*FOR*mula *TRAN*slation) and COBOL (*CO*mmon *B*usiness *Ori*ented *L*anguage).

The third generation (1964 to 1970) began when computer manufacturers started using integrated circuits (ICs), small silicon chips containing a network of transistors. Integrated circuits were quite a bit faster and more reliable than the single transistors used in the second generation. Third-generation computers had more storage capacity and greater compatibility of computer components. The concept of remote terminals that communicate with a central computer became a reality at this time.

The fourth generation (1971 to the present) began when computer manufacturers began using large-scale integrated (LSI) circuits. LSI circuits are silicon superchips that contain thousands of small transistors. As a result of LSI circuits, fourth-generation computers are smaller than those manufactured during the third generation. Both the Apple and the IBM personal computers were developed during the fourth generation. Also, increased storage and even greater compatibility were characteristics of computers manufactured during this period.

To date, we have experienced four generations of computer development. Now, many experts believe we are entering the *fifth generation*—computers that can simulate human decision making. Today, researchers are studying the human brain in an attempt to learn how people reason and think. For years, scientists have known that the human brain is more efficient than any computer in terms of storage capacity, data retrieval, and information processing. The researchers' goal is to duplicate the same processes with a computer and thus create a form of artificial intelligence. **Artificial intelligence** is a combination of computer hardware and software that exhibits the same type of intelligence as human beings. Artificial intelligence is currently one of the fastest-growing high-tech specialties. Many companies in the computer field are investing large amounts of money to either develop artificial-intelligence systems or purchase existing systems developed by other companies.

According to John Sculley, Apple's former chairman, "the really interesting stuff begins in the 1990s."[2] Tomorrow's computer technology will be

artificial intelligence
a combination of computer hardware and software that exhibits the same type of intelligence as human beings

everywhere—especially in all sorts of consumer and health products—because personal computers will be as popular as phones. The practical applications for artificial intelligence generated by a computer are unlimited. Later in this chapter, we examine these additional technological developments and how they will affect business and society.

■■ COMPUTER HARDWARE AND SOFTWARE

LEARNING OBJECTIVE 3
Explain the difference between computer hardware and computer software.

The computers used in business today are generally categorized according to size: mainframes, minicomputers, and microcomputers. In this section, we examine each type. Then we discuss the difference between computer hardware and computer software—the two components that are required for a computer to process data into information.

Types of Computers

The *mainframe computer* is the large, powerful, and expensive (usually costing more than $1 million) computer traditionally identified with the largest businesses. IBM established its reputation by manufacturing mainframe computers. Mainframes, which may be as big as a good-sized room, can handle immense quantities of data, perform a variety of operations on these data in fractions of a second, and provide output information in several different forms. Huge organizations, like Exxon Corporation, Ford Motor Co.,

Computers come in all shapes and sizes. Computers are often classified as mainframes, minicomputers, or microcomputers. Shown here is a student at Bergen Community College, Paramus, New Jersey, working on a large mainframe computer.

or the U.S. government, have the most need for mainframe computers. The largest and most powerful mainframe computers are sometimes referred to as *supercomputers*. These machines, which cost between $15 and $20 million, are used almost exclusively by universities and government agencies that are heavily involved in research activities requiring large memories and high-speed processing.

Minicomputers are smaller (more or less desk-sized) computers that revolutionized the industry and made computers available to most firms. These self-contained systems cost between $5,000 and $200,000. With a minicomputer, most businesses can now maintain very sophisticated information systems that were previously beyond their reach. Most minicomputers can process several programs at the same time and can be used by several people simultaneously. Currently, IBM, Hewlett-Packard, and Digital Equipment Corporation account for almost half of all minicomputer sales.

The *microcomputer*, sometimes referred to as a personal computer, is a desktop-sized computer. It was made possible by the development of *microprocessor chips*, a fraction of an inch in size, that contain all the electronic circuitry required to perform large-scale data processing. Microcomputers sell for as little as several hundred dollars or as much as a few thousand dollars and are available in portable, laptop, notebook, and handheld models. Although microcomputers are often purchased for use in the home, many smaller firms find them completely satisfactory for their limited needs. Companies like IBM, Compaq Computer Corporation, and Apple Computer, Inc., make microcomputers for the small-business market.

Computer Hardware

input unit the device used to enter data into a computer

Most computers and computer systems consist of five basic components (see Figure 16.3). The **input unit** is the device used to enter data into a computer. Today, data are entered manually via a keyboard (much like a typewriter keyboard) or electronically through the use of a mouse, light pen, touch pad, touch screen, or optical scanner. Currently, voice recognition as an input device is being developed by a number of manufacturers. When fully developed, voice recognition will make use of a computer easier for almost anyone.

memory (or **storage unit**) the part of a computer that stores all data entered into the computer and processed by it

The **memory** (or **storage unit**) is the part of a computer that stores all data entered into the computer and processed by it. One measure of a computer's power is the amount of data that can be stored within it at one time. This memory capacity is given in bytes: one byte is the capacity to store one character. One kilobyte (1 Kbyte) is the capacity to store 1,024 characters, and one megabyte (1 Mb) is the capacity to store 1,024,000 characters. A personal computer with four megabytes of primary memory is thus capable of storing the information contained in this book. Primary memory is especially important because it determines how big a program can be executed and how much data can be stored in the computer at one time.

control unit the part of a computer that guides the entire operation of the computer

The **control unit** is the part of a computer that guides the entire operation of the computer. It transfers data and sends processing directions to the various other computer components, in the proper sequence to carry out the instructions of the user.

FIGURE 16.3
How a Computer Works
A computer is a machine that accepts, stores, manipulates, and transmits data in accordance with a set of specific instructions. Most computers consist of five basic components.

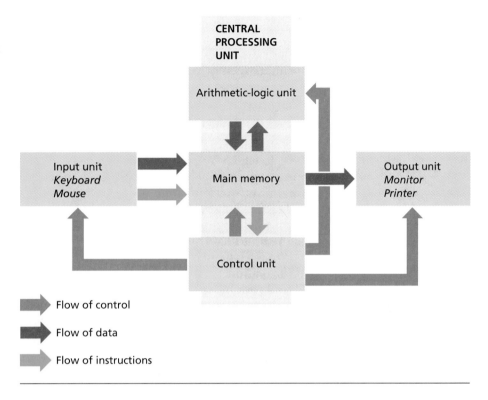

CENTRAL PROCESSING UNIT

Arithmetic-logic unit

Input unit
Keyboard
Mouse

Main memory

Output unit
Monitor
Printer

Control unit

→ Flow of control
→ Flow of data
→ Flow of instructions

arithmetic-logic unit   the part of a computer that performs mathematical operations, comparisons of data, and other types of data transformations

output unit   the mechanism by which a computer transmits processed data to the user

hardware   the electronic equipment used in a computer system

The **arithmetic-logic unit** is the part of a computer that performs mathematical operations, comparisons of data, and other types of data transformations.

The **output unit** is the mechanism by which a computer transmits processed data to the user. Most commonly, computer output is printed on paper or displayed on a monitor, a televisionlike screen.

All these components make up the computer's **hardware,** the electronic equipment used in a computer system. Hence, the keyboard used to enter data; the arithmetic-logic, control, and storage units; and the monitor and printer are all hardware. For tips on purchasing a computer, see Enhancing Career Skills.

Secondary Storage

Although a computer's primary memory can store a large amount of information, that storage capacity is generally used for the particular data that are being processed at any given time (and for the processing instructions). Secondary storage—tape drives, hard disk drives, and floppy disk drives—can be used to store data that are not needed at the moment. With each type of drive, data can be saved on a tape or disk and then fed back into the computer's primary memory when needed. There are three advantages of using secondary storage. First, when secondary storage is used, the computer's primary memory is reserved for data that are being processed at any given time. Second, when data are stored on disks, employees can take work to another location and use a compatible computer to process data and complete assignments. Finally, secondary storage—magnetic tapes and hard or floppy disks—is inexpensive when compared to storing data in a computer's primary memory.

Computer Networks

computer network a system in which several computers can either function individually or communicate with each other

The concept of networking is perhaps the greatest boon to management decision making since the low-cost computer. A **computer network** is a system in which several computers can either function individually or communicate with each other. A typical business network revolves around a mainframe or minicomputer, which serves as the basic computer system for all areas and levels of the firm. In addition, each key manager has her or his own microcomputer. These smaller computers have sufficient capacity to store up-to-date information and maintain records that are of primary interest to a particular manager, who has immediate and personal access to that information.

In addition, each manager can communicate with the mainframe or minicomputer through his or her microcomputer. A manager for Reebok in charge of shipping, for example, may be considering a change in the company's shipping schedule. To make the change, she may need to know something about sales patterns in the various sales territories. Rather than requesting the information from marketing and then waiting for it to be prepared, she can request it electronically from the mainframe.

Similarly, microcomputers can communicate directly with each other. Once the new shipping schedule is drafted, the shipping manager can transmit it to other managers—computer to computer—to get their opinions.

Operating Systems

operating system a set of programs that controls the basic operations of the computer

Before a computer can process data into information, an operating system must be installed in, or *booted* into, the computer. An **operating system** is a set of programs that controls the basic operations of the computer. More specifically, an operating system controls the computer's resources—its keyboard, memory, monitor, and so on. And it also helps manage individual files in the computer's memory. Finally, the operating system oversees the execution of application software—a topic covered later in this chapter.

Today, three operating systems—MS-DOS, OS/2, and UNIX—are commonly used with IBM (or IBM-compatible) computers. Macintosh DOS is the operating system used with Apple's Macintosh line of computers. It is quite common for vendors to sell computer "packages" that include everything you need to get started. As part of the package, the vendor will include an operating system already installed in the computer's memory.

Computer Application Software

application software a computer program designed to solve specific business or personal information problems

Application software is a computer program designed to solve specific business or personal information problems. It is the most popular form of software used today. Although large firms with special software needs may hire employees to develop computer programs, most medium- and

Do You Need A Computer At Home?

It's a fact of life. In order to navigate in the business world today, you must be computer literate. From the top of the corporate ladder all the way down to the mailroom, just getting through the typical workday in the future will require some basic computer skills. In addition, we encounter computers wherever we go, not only in the office but in the classroom, at the bank, even at the supermarket. So it seems reasonable to assume that it will not be very long before we consider the computer as important as the telephone. But the problem for many of us will be to determine if we *really need* a computer at home

Before you purchase a computer, ask yourself, "What uses do I have for a computer?" You have particular needs, and evaluating just what a computer can do for you and what software will meet those needs are the first steps in making the right decision. Students might use word processing to do school reports; small-business owners may find that spreadsheets would help maintain financial records; and sales managers could bring disks home from the office and go on-line at their own computers to complete lists of sales prospects from company databases.

GUIDELINES FOR SELECTING YOUR FIRST PERSONAL COMPUTER

There are many brands of IBM-compatibles that run an impressive selection of user-friendly software programs. And the Apple Macintosh is the most popular brand in America's elementary schools, as well as in many businesses, because of its reputation for being easy to learn. Any brand

of computer provides basically one set of hardware—a keyboard, a monitor, a computer case that holds the electronic circuit boards, and an optional printer. The novice buyer is likely to be confounded by the wide array of choices and will be confronted with package prices ranging from as low as $1,200 to as high as $3,000. Given the options, it would be wise for you to acquaint yourself with some of the technical terms beforehand by reading magazine articles in *Consumer Reports*, *Consumer Research*, and *PC World*. Talking with computer-wise friends can also help. Some of the buzzwords and acronyms used to describe parts of the computer are

- *processor*—the "brain" that does the calculations and controls the software.
- *megahertz*—the speed of the processor
- *RAM*—the amount of random access memory a user can efficiently access at one time
- *hard drive*—an area where software and data are stored
- *diskette drive*—slot on the front of a computer case into which you insert program disks or files stored separately
- *CD-ROM drive*—a multimedia component that operates interactive encyclopedias, talking books, music, and games
- *modem*—a device that links computers through telephone lines for on-line services and fax capabilities
- *printers*—a selection of dot matrix, bubble-jet, ink-jet, and laser, with black only or color printing capabilities

small-sized firms use ready-made software. Both custom- and ready-made software are discussed below.

The Programming Function Writing and testing the program are probably the most critical steps in using a computer to process data. If a computer is not programmed correctly, the information it delivers will be incorrect. The old adage "garbage in, garbage out" captures this very important point.

Computer programmers are in great demand today as a result of the growing use of computers. A **computer programmer** develops the step-by-step instructions contained in a computer program. Generally, the programmer begins by defining the problem and then designing a solution to it. To aid their programming efforts, programmers use flow charts. A **flow chart** is a graphic description of the types and sequences of operations in a computer program. After developing the flow chart, the programmer must translate it into instructions that the computer can follow. Because the computer cannot understand English, all instructions are coded into the computer through the use of a programming language. Once the program is written, it must be debugged and tested. Only after all errors have been corrected can the program be used.

In large companies with specialized needs, programming is usually performed by in-house employees who create new programs, change existing programs when necessary, and maintain the computer system. Programming may also be farmed out to outside consultants who work on a fee or contract basis. In addition to developing their own software, businesses have another option. They can purchase ready-made software.

Ready-made Software Today, ready-made software is available to handle almost any application, ranging from individualized instruction to sophisticated business forecasting. Ready-made software costs range from less than $10 to more than $100,000, and total worldwide software sales exceed $40 billion a year. Using ready-made software offers the user two distinct advantages. First, ready-made software almost always costs less than programs developed in-house. Second, the quality of ready-made software may be higher than programs that are developed by in-house programmers. Before deciding to purchase ready-made software, businesses must consider the following questions:

- Will the ready-made software enable the firm to process data and obtain the information it needs?
- Can the software be adapted or changed to meet the firm's needs?
- Can the software be used with the computer equipment now in place?
- What kind of training is available with the software?
- Can employees contact the vendor if they have questions or encounter problems when they attempt to use the software?
- Do the expected benefits of using the software justify the cost?

Although many ready-made software packages have been extremely successful, others have been dismal failures. For this reason, most computer

computer programmer a person who develops the step-by-step instructions contained in a computer program

flow chart a graphic description of the types and sequences of operations in a computer program

experts suggest that you talk to someone who has used a specific ready-made software package before you decide to purchase it. Ready-made application software is further discussed in the next section: The Impact of Computers on Business.

■■ ■ THE IMPACT OF COMPUTERS ON BUSINESS

LEARNING OBJECTIVE 4
Describe the impact that computers have had on business.

As the cost of computer memory drops and the availability of sophisticated application software grows, more and more businesses are becoming computer literate. The kinds of analyses, research, and recordkeeping that were once available only to the very largest organizations—if they were available at all—are now within reach of even the smallest businesses.

Current Business Applications

Today, application software has been developed to satisfy almost every business need. The most common types of software for business applications include

- Database management
- Graphics
- Spreadsheets

Drawing made easy with the help of a computer. Today, computer-aided design software programs can help industrial engineers design state-of-the-art products.

- Word processing
- Desktop publishing
- Accounting
- Computer-aided design (CAD)
- Computer-aided manufacturing (CAM)
- Computer-integrated manufacturing (CIM)

Six of the most popular packages (database management, graphics, spreadsheets, word processing, desktop publishing, and accounting) are described in the following sections.

Database Management Programs   Earlier in this chapter, we defined a database as a single collection of data stored in one place and used by people throughout the organization to make decisions. Forty years ago, a company like Eastman Kodak stored its data in file cabinets and then retrieved data when needed. Any manipulation to transform the data contained in each file folder into useful information would be completed manually—usually by the manager who needed the information.

Today, database management software allows users to electronically store and transform data into information. Data can be sorted by different criteria; for example, typical data for a firm's personnel department might include criteria such as each worker's age, gender, salary, and years of service. If management needs to know the names of workers who have at least fifteen years of experience and are at least fifty years old, an employee using database management software can print a list of such employees in a matter of minutes. And the same type of manipulation of data for other departments within a business is possible with database management software. In addition to building its own database, a company can also subscribe to on-line computer services that enable users to access large external databases.

Graphics Programs   Whether you play a video game or watch the computerized scoreboard at a football stadium, you are viewing computer-generated graphics. A **graphics program** enables users to display and print pictures, drawings, charts, and diagrams. From a business standpoint, graphics can be used for oral or written presentations of financial analyses, budgets, sales projections, and the like.

graphics program   a software package that enables the user to display and print pictures, drawings, charts, and diagrams

Although visual aids have always been available, their use was restricted because someone had to take the time to draw them. With the aid of a graphics program, the computer can generate drawings in seconds. Typically, graphics software allows the user to select a type of visual aid from a menu of available graphic options. The user enters the numerical data, such as sales figures, to be illustrated. The computer program then converts the data into a graph, bar chart, or pie chart.

spreadsheet program   a software package that allows the user to organize numerical data into a grid of rows and columns

Spreadsheet Programs   A **spreadsheet program** is a software package that allows the user to organize numerical data into a grid of rows and columns. Typically, spreadsheet software such as VisiCalc and Lotus 1-2-3 allows users to build a spreadsheet by using commands such as *create, format, enter, move, insert, compute, save, delete,* and *print.*

Formulas entered into the spreadsheet allow the computer to perform mathematical calculations automatically. For example, a manager for Dallas-based Malone's Cost-Plus Grocery Stores may want to project sales and expenses for the next three-month period. Numerical data for both sales and expenses are entered into the computer, and the spreadsheet software calculates the dollar amount of profit or loss based on the assumptions. Spreadsheet software can also be used to answer "what if" questions. By changing data to match new assumptions, the manager can see how the change will affect other data contained in the spreadsheet. This same manager might want to calculate the firm's profits based on projections that sales will increase 5, 10, and 15 percent. In this case, three additional spreadsheets could be prepared, based on each set of assumptions. In fact, any variable contained in the spreadsheet could be changed and, within seconds, new information could be generated to aid the manager in the decision-making process.

word processing program
a software package that allows the user to store written documents (letters, memos, reports) in the computer memory or on a disk

Word Processing Programs   A **word processing program** allows the user to store written documents (letters, memos, reports) in the computer memory or on a disk. Once stored, the material can be revised, edited, deleted, or printed. No longer is it necessary to spend long hours retyping entire documents. Only the changed portions need to be entered into the computer before the document is reprinted. In addition, materials that have been stored on a disk can be used at a later date. For example, most firms use a collection letter to urge prompt payment of past-due amounts. A word processing program can be used to send a personalized copy of the letter to all overdue accounts through the use of sort and merge features. Mail-order firms and direct-mail marketing firms make extensive use of these features to appeal to customers. Tens, hundreds, or thousands of letters—each sent to a selected individual—can be prepared from one master document.

desktop publishing program
a software package that allows users to prepare text and graphics in high-quality, professional looking reports, newsletters, and pamphlets

Desktop Publishing Programs   In addition to word processing programs, many computer users rely on desktop publishing programs. A **desktop publishing program** is a software package that allows users to prepare text and graphics in high-quality, professional looking reports, newsletters, and pamphlets. Most desktop publishing programs go beyond word processing programs to give the user more control over complex designs and page layout. With the aid of a laser printer, the user can prepare documents that are nearly as good as those produced by a professional printing company.

accounting program   a software package that enables the user to record and report financial information

Accounting Programs   An **accounting program** is a software package that enables the user to record and report financial information. Almost all of the commercially available computerized accounting packages contain three basic modules: general ledger and financial reporting, accounts receivable, and accounts payable. The general ledger and financial reporting module processes routine, daily accounting entries. This module should also prepare financial statements at the end of each accounting period. The accounts receivable module prepares customer invoices, maintains customer balances, allows different payment terms to different customers, and generates past-due notices to slow-paying customers. The accounts payable module records and monitors invoices from vendors or suppliers. It should also take advantage of cash discounts offered by suppliers and vendors for prompt payment. Finally, the better accounting packages prepare checks to pay suppliers, vendors, and employees.

Other Application Programs   Although it is impossible to describe all the application software programs that business firms use today, three programs described in Chapter 8—Production and Operations Management—deserve mention here. Computer-aided design (CAD) programs use computers to aid in the development of products. Computer-aided manufacturing (CAM) uses computers to plan and control manufacturing processes. And computer-integrated manufacturing (CIM) is a computer system that not only helps design products but also controls the machinery needed to produce finished products. Each of these application programs streamlines the manufacturing process and ultimately makes a manufacturer more productive. As you will see in the next section, programs like these will become increasingly popular as business firms move into the next century.

■■ FUTURE COMPUTER APPLICATIONS

LEARNING OBJECTIVE 5
Explore future business applications of improved computer technology.

information society   a society in which large groups of employees generate or depend on information to perform their jobs

Today, the United States is characterized as an information society. An **information society** is one in which large groups of employees generate or depend on information to perform their jobs. And the need for more and better information will continue to increase in the future. Improved computer technology will help meet this need.

New and Improved Computer Technology

Most experts predict that in the future computers will affect every aspect of human life. Already computers are installed in cars, toys, and appliances. They are used by musicians and engineers, artists and bank tellers, students and teachers. In fact, it is virtually impossible to find an individual who is not impacted by a computer or the information generated by a computer. Like it or not, these trends will continue. In the remainder of this section, we describe how improved computer technology will impact the world of business as we approach the year 2000.

Smart Offices and Workplaces   Most modern business offices are already equipped with word processing equipment that electronically sends messages and correspondence to their destinations. This type of communication, sometimes called *electronic mail,* will expand in the future. The use of computer terminals for graphics, accounting, data entry, and other office functions will also grow. The ability to access information will enable more people to work at home with a personal computer linked to the office mainframe or minicomputer. In addition, more information than ever before will be available as more people travel the information superhighway (see Change in the Workplace).

Computers are already being used to control automated manufacturing equipment, but the use of application programs like CAD, CAM, and CIM will spread to many more industries. In fact, some computers are capable of

■ ■ ■ ■ CHANGE IN THE WORKPLACE

The Information Superhighway

It is hard to pick up a newspaper or listen to a newscast these days without coming across some mention of the term *information superhighway*. But most people still wonder what this phenomenon is. In general terms, the information superhighway is a fiber-optic cable that eventually will link every home, business, classroom, and library in the United States. Users can gain access to information contained in libraries, government institutions, private businesses, and giant databases throughout the world. The entrance ramp to this superhighway was paved between 1985 and 1992 when telecommunications companies laid 95,000 miles of fiber-optic cable. But it will require tens of billions of dollars invested by cable, wireless, computer, and other related firms to lay the millions of more miles necessary to accomplish the federal government's goal of a high-speed, fiber-optic transmission system available to *every* American.

CONSUMERS MAY HAVE TO YIELD

Many individuals have looked through the windshield onto the information superhighway when they have used a multimedia encyclopedia, played an interactive game, or shopped from their homes through their computers. Some of us, however, are utterly overwhelmed by the vast array of choices in software and electronic gadgetry on the market today. Well, fasten your seat belt: the ride on the information superhighway will force consumers to learn basic computer skills and attain the ability to communicate effectively in order to keyboard their way through the maze of new products and services that will be dreamed up by innovators and entrepreneurs in the years ahead.

OPENING LANES FOR THE EMPLOYEE

Technologies that didn't even exist until just recently and those that will be developed in the coming years will have a powerful effect on the economy. New uses for this technology in business and industry will spur growth and multiply employment opportunities. Individuals who take the wheel and are able to keep up with the rapid changes by learning more than just fundamental computer skills will find companies eager to hire them to work, either in the office or in their own homes, with other people who live in other states, other time zones, or even other countries. And those who cannot cope or who fail to appreciate the impact of these emerging technologies on the workplace will find themselves left by the wayside, working in minimum wage jobs.

FULL SPEED AHEAD

Venturing forth on this electronic highway are ordinary people like Cynthia Denton of Hobson, Montana. Ms. Denton uses Internet, a global web of computer networks, to teach students in rural sections of the western United States. Even though students are not physically present in her classroom, Denton spends "a lot of personal time with each one of them. They have to write, interact with the instructions, and personally respond to what I key in." Russell Thomas, a financial consultant and writer for business newsletters, logs on to the America Online network to send and receive his mail, to get expert tax advice, to check stock quotes, to trade securities, to download files from a base of 30,000 publications, and to enter into discussions with business leaders, all without ever leaving his home. And today, Texans looking for work can search, in English and Spanish, through more than 1,200 federal and state job listings at any one of the fifty supermarkets at which the Texas State Employment Commission has installed "InfoTexas," an electronic job bank with touch screens, video, audio text, and graphics.

High-tech forestry. It is virtually impossible to find a business or an industry not influenced by a computer or the information generated by a computer. Here an employee for a logging company is using a computer to determine the value of the firm's inventory—trees in a forest.

AT A GLANCE

Home Computers

People use their home computers for a variety of tasks.

Source: Inteco Corporation, *Redbook*, Feb. 1995, p. 54.

controlling entire assembly lines. Robots and robotlike equipment are already common in the automobile, steel, and manufacturing industries. For example, General Motors, Ford, and Chrysler use robots to paint automobiles, weld car bodies, and perform other jobs on assembly lines. And robots are often used when the work is dangerous. Most experts agree that the current computer technology used in manufacturing applications reflects only the "tip of the iceberg." Expect that the factory of the future will increasingly depend on automation and robotics. Thus factories will use fewer employees, and all employees will be required to work with computers.

Smart Homes and Cars   Instead of manufacturing the same old product year after year, the "best" manufacturers improve existing products or create new products. In many cases, new or improved products are closely tied to improved computer technology. For example, consider this list of products that could adorn the typical smart home of tomorrow:

- Computerized protection systems that not only monitor the home for break-ins and fires but also alert the homeowner and authorities when problems occur.

- Computerized heating and cooling systems that lower operating costs.
- Computer-controlled water heaters that operate only during selected hours of the day or night.
- Computer-controlled household appliances (washers, dryers, refrigerators, dishwashers, microwaves) that are far more energy efficient than today's models.
- Videophones, interactive television, video recorders, and stereos that use computerized components to provide improved customer satisfaction.
- Computerized sprinkler systems that water the lawn only when it needs watering.

Of course, many of these conveniences are already available. In the future, they will not only be more popular, even standard, but also improved because of evolving technology.

Like our homes, the cars we drive already incorporate a number of computer components. Computers control the engine, brakes, transmission, suspension, and security system. And computers have enhanced the sound system and climate control in today's more expensive cars. In the future, expect refinements of existing computerized automotive technology along with some new innovations. One interesting proposal is called the Intelligent Vehicle/Highway System, or simply IVHS. Through a system of cameras and sensors, cars of the future may literally drive themselves. As an added bonus, cars on "autopilot" operate with increased fuel efficiency and reduced driver frustration.

Global Economy   In the future, the ability to exchange ideas and complete financial transactions by computer will increase. Already, the banking industry has developed an electronic funds transfer system to ease problems associated with transferring money between banks in different nations. The success of this program may well lead to a cashless society. Instead of using money or checks, you would pay for all of your purchases through computerized transactions. According to the experts, a cashless society would decrease theft and fraud and add a measure of safety to monetary transactions.

The Computer's Impact on Society

The technological trends just described will not only revolutionize twenty-first century business. The advances in medicine, transportation, conservation of natural resources, and all other areas of human life will be just as spectacular. It is safe to say that every aspect of your life will be affected by the changes that will take place in the development of computer technology during your lifetime.

It is also certain that changes brought about by improved computer technology will create new problems for both individuals and businesses. Three such problems will require special attention.

1. Although experts predict a significant number of new jobs in the computer industry and related fields, employees who don't know how

to use a computer, or who refuse to learn, will be at a definite disadvantage. In the future, continued training and skills updating will be a necessity for all employees.

2. Computers themselves don't invade someone else's privacy, but the people who operate computers *can* violate another's privacy. The right to privacy is guaranteed by law, but the emerging information age has already created conflicts that must be resolved in order to protect this right.

3. Computers can be and have been used to commit crimes. Because a computer can become a powerful and hard-to-detect tool in the hands of a dishonest employee, safeguards must be developed to deter computer crime.

With this understanding of how computers affect society and transform data into information, we can now examine a management information system (MIS).

■■ THE MANAGEMENT INFORMATION SYSTEM

management information system (MIS) a system that provides managers with the information they need to perform their jobs as effectively as possible

Where do managers get the information they need? In many organizations, the answer lies in a **management information system (MIS),** which is a system that provides managers with the information they need to perform their jobs as effectively as possible (see Figure 16.4).

If this sounds like the marketing information system discussed in Chapter 12, the similarity is intended. In many firms, the MIS is combined with a marketing information system so that it can provide information based on a wide variety of data. In fact, it makes little sense to have separate information systems for the various management areas. After all, the goal is to provide needed information to all managers.

Managers' Information Requirements

LEARNING OBJECTIVE 6
Discuss management's information requirements.

Managers have to plan for the future, implement their plans in the present, and evaluate the results against what has been accomplished in the past. Thus they need access to information that summarizes future possibilities, the present situation, and past performance. Of course, the specific types of information they need depend on their area of management and on their level within the firm.

In Chapter 6 we identified five areas of management: finance, operations, marketing, human resources, and administration. Financial managers are obviously most concerned with their firm's finances. They study its debts and receivables, cash flow, future capitalization needs, financial ratios, and other accounting information. Of equal importance to financial managers is information about the present state of the economy and predictions of business conditions for the near and long-term future.

Operations managers are concerned with present and future sales levels and with the availability of the resources required to meet sales forecasts. They need to know the cost of producing their firm's goods and services, including inventory costs. And they are involved with new-product plan-

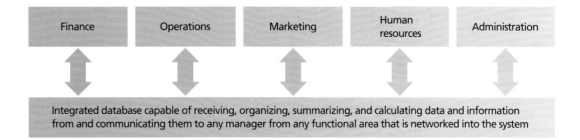

FIGURE 16.4   Management Information System (MIS)
After an MIS is installed, a user can get information directly from the MIS without having to go through other people in the organization.   *(Source: Adapted from Ricky W. Griffin,* Management, *4th ed. Copyright © 1993 by Houghton Mifflin Company, p. 556. Used by permission.)*

ning. They must also keep abreast of any innovative production technology that might be useful to their firm.

Marketing managers need to have detailed information about their firm's product mix and the products offered by competitors. Such information includes prices and pricing strategies, new promotional campaigns, and products that competitors are test marketing. Information concerning target markets, current and projected market share, new and pending product legislation, and developments within channels of distribution is also important to marketing managers.

Human resources managers must be aware of anything that pertains to their firm's employees. Key examples include current wage levels and benefits packages both within their firm and in firms that compete for valuable employees; current legislation and court decisions that affect employment practices; union activities; and their firm's plans for growth, expansion, or mergers.

Administrative managers are responsible for the overall management of their organization. Thus they are concerned with the coordination of information—just as they are concerned with the coordination of material, human, and financial resources. First, administrators must ensure that subordinates have access to the information they need to do their jobs. And second, they must ensure that the information is used in a consistent manner. Suppose, for example, that the operations group for General Electric Co. is designing a plant to manufacture consumer electronic products to be opened in five years. GE's management will want answers to many questions: Is the capacity of the plant consistent with marketing plans based on economic projections? Will human resources managers be able to staff the plant on the basis of their employment forecasts? And will projected sales generate enough income to cover the expected cost?

Size and Complexity of the System

A management information system (MIS) must be tailored to the needs of the organization it serves. In some firms a tendency to save on initial costs may result in a system that is too small or overly simple. Such a system generally ends up serving only one or two management levels or a single department—the one that gets its data into the system first. Managers in other departments "give up" on the system as soon as they find that it cannot accept or process their data. They either look elsewhere for information or do without.

Almost as bad is an MIS that is too large or too complex for the organization. Unused capacity and complexity do nothing but increase the cost of owning and operating the system. In addition, a system that is difficult to use will probably not be used at all. Managers may find that it is easier to maintain their own records. Or, again, they may try to operate without information that could be helpful in their decision making.

Obviously, much is expected of an effective MIS. Let's examine the four functions that an MIS must perform to provide the information that managers need.

■■ FUNCTIONS OF THE MANAGEMENT INFORMATION SYSTEM

LEARNING OBJECTIVE 7
State the four functions of a management information system.

To provide information, a management information system must perform four specific functions. It must collect data; store and then update the data; process data into information; and present information to users (see Figure 16.5).

Collecting Data

The first step in using an MIS is to gather the data needed to establish the firm's *data bank*. This data bank should include all past and current data that may be useful in managing the firm. The data entered into the system must be *relevant* to the needs of the firm's managers. And, perhaps most important, the data must be *accurate*. Irrelevant data are simply useless; inaccurate data can be disastrous. The data can be obtained from within the firm and from outside sources.

Internal Sources of Data   Typically, the majority of the data gathered for an MIS comes from internal sources. The most common internal sources of information include company records, reports, managers, and conferences and meetings.

FIGURE 16.5   Four MIS Functions
Every MIS must be tailored to the organization it serves and must perform four functions.

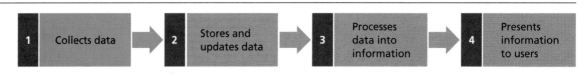

Some employees go to great lengths to gather data. The first step in using an MIS is to gather needed data. Here three municipal employees are using a computer to gather data about water flow in a municipal sewer system.

Past and present accounting data can provide information about the firm's customers, creditors, and suppliers. Similarly, sales reports are a source of data on sales and sales patterns, pricing strategies, and the level and effectiveness of promotional campaigns. Personnel records are useful as a source of data on wage and benefits levels, hiring patterns, employee turnover, and other human resources variables.

Present and past production forecasts should also be included in the MIS, with data indicating how well these forecasts predicted actual events. Similarly, specific plans and management decisions—regarding capital expansion and new-product development, for example—should be incorporated into the system.

External Sources of Data   External sources of management data include customers, suppliers, bankers, trade and financial publications, industry conferences, and firms that specialize in gathering data for organizations.

Like internal data, data from external sources take various forms, depending on the requirements of the firm and its managers. A marketing research company may be used to acquire forecasts pertaining to product

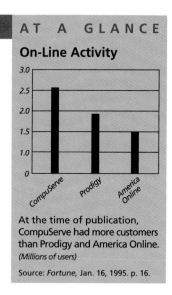

AT A GLANCE

On-Line Activity

At the time of publication,
CompuServe had more customers
than Prodigy and America Online.
(Millions of users)

Source: *Fortune,* Jan. 16, 1995. p. 16.

demand, consumer tastes, and other marketing variables. Suppliers are an excellent source of information about the future availability and costs of raw materials and component parts used by the firm.

Bankers can often provide valuable economic insights and projections. And the information furnished by trade publications and industry conferences is usually concerned as much with future projections as with the present conditions. Both are valuable sources of data on competitors and production technology.

Legal issues and court decisions that may affect the firm are occasionally discussed in local newspapers and, more often, in specialized publications such as the *Wall Street Journal, Fortune,* and *Business Week.* Government publications like the *Monthly Labor Review* and the *Federal Reserve Bulletin* are also quite useful as sources of external data. On-line computer services—like those described in Business Journal—can also provide data from external sources.

Cautions in Collecting Data   Three cautions should be observed in collecting data for an MIS. First, the cost of obtaining data from such external sources as marketing research firms can be quite high. In all cases—whether the data come from internal or external sources—the cost of obtaining data should be weighed against the potential benefits that having the data will confer on the firm.

Second, although computers do not make mistakes, the people who use them can make or cause errors. Simply by pushing the wrong key on a computer keyboard, an employee can change an entire set of data, along with the information it contains. When data (or information) and a manager's judgment disagree, always check the data.

Third, outdated or incomplete data usually yield inaccurate information. Data collection is an ongoing process. New data must be added to the data bank, either as they are obtained or in regularly scheduled updates.

Storing and Updating Data

A management information system must be capable of storing data until they are needed. And an MIS must also be able to update stored data to ensure that the information presented to managers is complete and timely. An operations manager for Goodyear Tire & Rubber Company, for instance, cannot produce finished goods with last week's work-in-process inventory. She or he needs to know what is available *today.*

Computers are especially well suited for both storing and rapidly updating MIS data. When data are stored for an MIS, the computer is used only to transfer the data to magnetic tapes, hard disks, or floppy disks. Usually, the programmer enters the data into the computer, which transfers it to a tape or disk. When the tape or disk is full, the programmer removes it from the machine, adds a label showing which data it contains, stores the tape or disk on a shelf, and (if necessary) continues with another tape or disk. When the data stored on a particular disk are needed, the disk is reinserted into the computer. At this point, the data are ready to be processed by the computer.

Manual Updating   To update stored data manually, a programmer inserts the proper tape or disk into the computer, locates the data that are to be

On-Line Computer Services

Would you like to send and receive electronic mail, search reference materials, access up-to-date news, sports, and financial information, interact with discussion bulletin boards, shop, and play games just by using the keyboard on your personal computer? Well, now you can. All it takes to tap your computer into an on-line service is a modem and payment of a monthly fee. Companies offer basic packages for under $15, and optional services are available at additional hourly rates. You, as the consumer, will find that the services vary widely from one company to another. So you will need to match your decision to go on-line with the service that best meets your personal interests and fits your budget.

WHICH SERVICE IS BEST FOR YOU?

All the major services offer E-mail, and all eventually, for an additional fee, will provide users with gateway access to the Internet—a global system with thousands of computer networks. **CompuServe,** the largest and most popular among business and professional people, provides access to extensive research databases of national and regional publications, stock market quotes, a search and trace feature to locate lost friends, movie reviews, support services from software and hardware manufacturers, and many other features. **Prodigy** is more family-oriented and easier to use. For the casual home computer user, it has a basic encyclopedia, graphics, wire service news, detailed stock market information, *Newsweek* magazine, and *Consumer Reports,* but it has limited research capabilities. Prodigy is

praised for its censoring of bulletin board exchanges and criticized for its extensive advertising. **America Online** is the fastest growing service with its wide selection of news and financial information, games and entertainment, graphics and sound enhancements, lively chat lines and bulletin boards where *anything goes,* and software that can be downloaded. Also, there are small on-line services catering to special-interest groups. For example, **Women's Wire,** based in South San Francisco, offers UPI news, the Small Business Administration's guidelines for starting a business, reports from the U.S. Department of Labor's Women's Bureau, and other issues of interest to working women.

A LOOK AHEAD

As more personal computer users come on-line, the competition for their business will increase, forcing providers to expand services and lower prices. Other companies will emerge to offer more for less, giving the consumer even more choices than they have now. Microsoft Corporation, the industry's software leader, is almost ready to unveil its first on-line service—code-named **Marvel.** It can be programmed into the new Microsoft Windows 95 operating system scheduled for distribution in late 1995. And Ziff-Davis Publishing Company is hoping to launch **Interchange,** which will display all the text and graphics from Z-D's large line of computer publications, including *PC Magazine.* On-line services like this could revolutionize the way we read our newspapers, books, and magazines.

changed, and inputs the new data. The computer automatically replaces the older data with the new.

The frequency with which data are updated depends on how fast they change and how often they are used. When it is vital to have current data, updating may occur daily. Otherwise, new data may be collected and held for updating at a certain time each week or, perhaps, each month.

Automatic Updating   In automatic updating, the system itself updates the existing data bank as new information becomes available. The data bank, usually in the form of hard disks, is permanently connected to the MIS. The computer automatically finds the proper disk and replaces the existing data with the new data.

For example, Giant Food, a Maryland-based grocery store chain, has installed cash registers that automatically transmit, to a central computer, information regarding each item sold. The computer adjusts the store's inventory records accordingly. At any time of the day, the manager can get precise, up-to-the-minute information on the inventory of every item sold by the store. In some systems, the computer may even be programmed to reorder items whose inventories fall below some specified level.

Forms of Updating   We have been discussing the type of updating in which new data are *substituted for* old data. Although this is an efficient type of updating in terms of the use of storage space, it does result in the loss of the old data. In a second form of updating, new data are *added to* the old data— much as a new file folder is placed between two folders that are already in a drawer. (In fact, on a magnetic tape or disk, existing data are actually spread apart by the computer to accommodate the new data.) The form of updating a firm uses will depend entirely on whether the existing data will be needed in the future.

High-tech, working lunch. To get the job done, employees often use portable, laptop computers—even during lunch—to process data into information.

Processing Data

LEARNING OBJECTIVE 8
Explain how a management information system uses statistics to turn data into information.

data processing the transformation of data into a form that is useful for a specific purpose

Data are collected, stored in an MIS, and updated under the assumption that they will be of use to managers. Some data are used in the form in which they are stored. This is especially true of verbal data—a legal opinion, for example. Other data require processing to extract, highlight, or summarize the information they contain. **Data processing** is the transformation of data into a form that is useful for a specific purpose. For verbal data, this processing consists mainly of extracting the pertinent material from storage and combining it into a report.

Most business data, however, are in the form of numbers—large groups of numbers, such as daily sales volumes or annual earnings of workers in a particular city. Such groups of numbers are difficult to handle and to comprehend, but their contents can be summarized through the use of statistics.

statistic a measure that summarizes a particular characteristic for an entire group of numbers

Statistics as Summaries A **statistic** is a measure that summarizes a particular characteristic for an entire group of numbers. In this section we discuss the most commonly used statistics, using the data given in Figure 16.6. This figure contains only eleven items of data, which simplifies our discussion. Most business situations would deal with tens or hundreds of items. Fortunately, computers can be programmed to process such large volumes of numbers quickly. Managers are free to concern themselves mainly with the information that results.

frequency distribution a listing of the number of times each value appears in a set of data

The number of items in a set of data can be reduced by developing a frequency distribution. A **frequency distribution** is a listing of the number of times each value appears in the set of data. For the data in Figure 16.6, the frequency distribution is as follows:

FIGURE 16.6
Statistics
A statistic is a measure that summarizes a particular characteristic for an entire group of numbers.

Rondex Corporation
Employee salaries for
the month of April 199x

Employee	Monthly salary
Thomas P. Ouimet	$ 3,500
Marina Ruiz	3,500
Ronald F. Washington	3,000
Sarah H. Abrams	3,000
Kathleen L. Norton	3,000
Martin C. Hess	2,800
Jane Chang	2,500
Margaret S. Fernandez	2,400
John F. O'Malley	2,000
Robert Miller	2,000
William G. Dorfmann	1,800
Total	$29,500

Monthly salary	Frequency
$3,500	2
3,000	3
2,800	1
2,500	1
2,400	1
2,000	2
1,800	1

It is also possible to obtain a grouped frequency distribution:

Salary range	Frequency
$3,000–$3,500	5
2,500– 2,999	2
2,000– 2,499	3
1,500– 1,999	1

Note that summarizing the data into a grouped frequency distribution has reduced the number of data items by approximately 60 percent.

Measures of Size and Dispersion   The arithmetic mean, median, and mode are statistical measures used to describe the size of numerical values in a set of data. Perhaps the most familiar statistic is the arithmetic mean, which is commonly called the *average.*

arithmetic mean   the sum of all the values of a set of data, divided by the number of items in the set

The **arithmetic mean** of a set of data is the sum of all the data values, divided by the number of items in the set. The sum of employee salaries given in Figure 16.6 is $29,500. The average (arithmetic mean) of employee salaries is $2,681.82 ($29,500 ÷ 11 = $2,681.82).

median   the value that appears at the exact middle of a set of data when the data are arranged in order

The **median** of a set of data is the value that appears at the exact middle of the data when they are arranged in order. The data in Figure 16.6 are already arranged from the highest value to the lowest value. Their median is thus $2,800, which is exactly halfway between the top and bottom values.

mode   the value that appears most frequently in a set of data

The **mode** of a set of data is the value that appears most frequently in the set. In Figure 16.6, the $3,000 monthly salary appears three times, which is more times than any other salary amount appears. Thus, $3,000 is the mode for this set of data.

Although the mean, or arithmetic average, is the most commonly used statistical measure of size, it may be distorted by a few extremely small or large values in the set of data. In this case, a manager may want to rely on the median, mode, or both to describe the values in a set of data. Managers often use the median to describe dollar values or income levels when the arithmetic average for the same numbers is distorted. In a similar fashion, marketers often use the mode to describe a firm's most successful or popular product when average sales amounts for a group of products would be inaccurate or misleading.

range   the difference between the highest value and the lowest value in a set of data

Another characteristic of the items within a set of values is the *dispersion,* or spread. The simplest measure of dispersion is the **range,** which is the difference between the highest value and the lowest value in a set of data. The range of the data in Figure 16.6 is $3,500 – $1,800 = $1,700.

The smaller the range of the numbers in a set of data, the closer the values are to the mean—and, thus, the more effective the mean is as a measure of those values. Other measures of dispersion that are used to describe business data are the *variance* and the *standard deviation*. These are somewhat more complicated than the range, and we shall not define or calculate them here. However, you should remember that larger values of both the variance and the standard deviation indicate a greater spread among the values of the data.

With the proper software, a computer can provide these and other statistical measures almost as fast as a user can ask for them. How they are used is then up to the manager. Although statistics provide information in a much more manageable form than raw data, they can be interpreted incorrectly. Note, for example, that the average of the employee salaries given in Figure 16.6 is $2,681.82, yet not one of the employee salaries is exactly equal to that amount. This distinction between actual data and the statistics that describe them is an important one that you should never disregard.

Presenting Information

A management information system must be capable of presenting the information in a *usable* form. That is, the method of presentation—reports, tables, graphs, or charts, for example—must be appropriate for the information itself and for the uses to which it will be put.

Verbal information may be presented in list or paragraph form. Employees are often asked to prepare formal business reports. A typical business report includes (1) an introduction, (2) the body of the report, (3) the conclusions, and (4) the recommendations.

The *introduction* section, which sets the stage for the remainder of the report, describes the problem to be studied in the report, identifies the research techniques that were used, and previews the material that will be presented in the report. The *body of the report* should objectively describe the facts that were discovered in the process of completing the report. The body should also provide a foundation for the conclusions and the recommendations. The *conclusions* are statements of fact that describe the findings contained in the report. They should be specific, practical, and based on the evidence contained in the report. The *recommendations* section presents suggestions on how the problem might be solved. Like the conclusions, recommendations should be specific, practical, and based on the evidence.

Statistical charts and tabular displays may be necessary in a formal business report. For example, numerical information and combinations of numerical and verbal information may be easier to understand if presented in visual displays and tables.

visual display a diagram that represents several items of information in a manner that makes comparison easier

Visual Displays A **visual display** is a diagram that represents several items of information in a manner that makes comparison easier. The most accurate visual display is a *graph,* in which values are plotted to scale on a set of axes. Graphs are most effective for presenting information about one variable that changes with time (such as variations in sales figures for a business over a ten- or fifteen-year period). Graphs tend to emphasize trends as well as peaks and low points in the value of the variable. Figure 16.7 illustrates examples of visual displays generated by a computer.

In a *bar chart,* each value is represented as a vertical or horizontal bar. The longer the bar, the greater the value. This type of display is useful for

FIGURE 16.7
Typical Visual Displays Used in Business Presentations
Visual displays help business people present information in a form that can be easily understood.

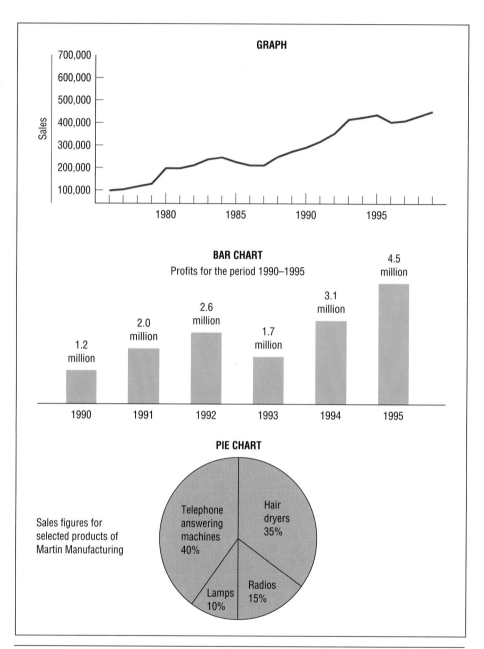

presenting values that are to be compared. The eye can quickly pick out the longest or shortest bar, or even those that seem to be of average size.

A *pie chart* is a circle ("pie") that is divided into "slices," each of which represents a different item. The circle represents the whole—for example, total sales. The size of each slice shows the contribution of that item to the whole. The larger the slice, the larger the contribution. By their nature, pie charts are most effective in displaying the relative size or importance of various items of information.

Tabular Displays   A **tabular display** is used to present verbal or numerical information in columns and rows. It is most useful in presenting information about two or more related variables (for example, variations in both sales volume and size of sales force by territory).

Tabular displays generally have less impact than visual displays. Moreover, the data contained in most two-column tables (like Figure 16.6) can be displayed visually. However, displaying the information that could be contained in a three-column table would require several bar or pie charts. In such cases, the items of information are easier to compare when they are presented in a table. Information that is to be manipulated—for example, to calculate loan payments—is also usually displayed in tabular form.

In this chapter, we have explored the role of the computer in business and have outlined some functions and requirements of an MIS. In Chapter 17, we examine the accounting process, which is a major source of information for business.

■ ■ ■ ■ CHAPTER REVIEW

Summary

1   Describe how information differs from data.

Data are numerical or verbal descriptions, whereas information is data presented in a form that is useful for a specific purpose. Generally, information is more effectively used when it is organized into a database. A database is a single collection of data stored in one place and can be used by people throughout an organization to make decisions.

2   Summarize the development of the computer.

Today, business, government, and other organizations depend on computers to process data and to make information available for decision making. A computer is an electronic machine that can accept, store, manipulate, and transmit data in accordance with a set of specific instructions. Although computers are a relative recent invention, we have already seen four generations of computers mature and are welcoming a fifth. The fifth generation is especially exciting as researchers begin studying the process that leads to a form of artificial intelligence.

3   Explain the difference between computer hardware and computer software.

Currently, firms can choose mainframe computers, minicomputers, or microcomputers to match their information needs. Each of these machines consists of at least one input unit, a memory, a control unit, an arithmetic-logic unit, and an output unit. Firms can also establish a computer network—a system in which several computers can either function individually or communicate with one another. Regardless of the type of computer used, an operating system must be used to control the basic operations of the computer. Application software may be used to solve either business or personal information problems. This type of software can be custom-made, or developed by a computer programmer. It is also possible to purchase ready-made software.

4   Describe the impact that computers have had on business.

Today, application software has been developed to satisfy almost every business need. Database management programs can store and transform data into information. Data contained in a database program can also be sorted by selected criteria. Graphics programs make it possible to create and display pictures, drawings, charts, and diagrams. Spreadsheets are software packages that allow users to organize numerical data into a grid of rows and columns. Spreadsheets also allow managers to answer "what if" questions by changing data to match new assumptions. Word processing programs allow users to store documents in the computer's memory or on a disk. Once entered, the material can be revised, edited, deleted, printed, or simply used at a later date. A desktop publishing program goes beyond the typical word processing program and is a software package that allows users to prepare text and graphics in high-quality, professional-looking reports, newsletters, and pamphlets. An accounting program is a software package that enables the user to record and report financial information.

5 Explore future business applications of improved computer technology.

Most experts predict that in the future computers will affect every aspect of human life. Specific trends that will affect business include the increase of computers in offices and manufacturing facilities, homes, and automobiles. Computers will also have a growing impact on the global economy. It is also safe to say that changes caused by increased use of improved computer technology may create new problems for both individuals and businesses. Three such problems—job displacement, threats to individual privacy, and computer crime—will require special attention.

6 Discuss management's information requirements.

A management information system (MIS) is a means of providing managers with the information they need to perform management functions as effectively as possible. The data that are entered into the system must be relevant, accurate, and timely. The information provided by the system must be all of these—and it must be in usable form as well. The management information system itself should match the firm it serves in capacity and complexity.

7 State the four functions of a management information system.

The four functions performed by an MIS are collecting data, storing and updating data, processing data, and presenting information. Data may be collected from such internal sources as accounting documents and other financial records, conferences and meetings, and sales and production records. External sources include customers, suppliers, bankers, publications, and information-gathering organizations. With a computer, data can be stored on magnetic tapes and disks and used whenever they are needed. Data should be updated regularly to maintain their timeliness and accuracy. Updating can be accomplished manually or via computer.

8 Explain how a management information system uses statistics to turn data into information.

Data processing is the MIS function that transforms stored data into a form that is useful for a specific purpose. Large groups of numerical data are usually processed into summary numbers called statistics.

The arithmetic mean, median, and mode are measures of the size of values in a set of data. The range is a measure of the dispersion, or spread, of the data values. Although statistics can provide information in a manageable form, the user is responsible for correctly interpreting statistics. Finally, the processed data (which can now be called information) must be presented for use. Verbal information is generally presented in list, paragraph, or report form. Typically, the components of a business report are the introduction, the body of the report, the conclusions, and the recommendations. Numerical information is most often displayed in graphs and charts or in tables.

Key Terms

You should now be able to define and give an example relevant to each of the following terms:

data (498)
information (498)
database (499)
computer (500)
artificial intelligence (502)
input unit (504)
memory (or storage unit) (504)
control unit (504)
arithmetic-logic unit (505)
output unit (505)
hardware (505)
computer network (506)
operating system (506)
application software (506)
computer programmer (508)
flow chart (508)
graphics program (510)
spreadsheet program (510)
word processing program (511)
desktop publishing program (511)
accounting program (511)
information society (512)
management information system (MIS) (516)
data processing (523)
statistic (523)
frequency distribution (523)
arithmetic mean (524)
median (524)
mode (524)

range (524)
visual display (525)
tabular display (527)

Questions

Review Questions

1. What is the difference between data and information? Give one example of accounting data and one example of accounting information.
2. In basic terms, what is a database? How is it used in a business?
3. Briefly describe the history of computers.
4. List the five primary components of a computer, and briefly state the function of each.
5. What is meant by the term *computer network?*
6. What are the advantages of ready-made software? What are the disadvantages?
7. How do businesses use database management programs, graphics programs, spreadsheet programs, word processing programs, desktop publishing programs, and accounting programs?
8. Describe how improved computer technology will affect businesses between now and the year 2000.
9. In your own words, define a management information system (MIS).
10. How do the information requirements of managers differ by management area?
11. Why must a management information system (MIS) be tailored to the needs of the organization it serves?
12. List the four functions of an MIS.
13. What kinds of data might be updated by substituting new data for old data? by adding new data to old data?
14. What are the differences among the mean, median, and mode of a set of data? How can a few extremely small or large numbers affect the mean?
15. What are the components of a typical business report?

Discussion Questions

1. Founded just over twenty years ago, Microsoft's annual sales revenues are now in excess of $4.7 billion. What factors led to Microsoft's phenomenal success?
2. Microsoft's vision of the information superhighway provides a new method of conducting everyday business transactions "on-line" with the use of personal computers. Does this idea of on-line business transactions appeal to you? Explain your answer.
3. How can confidential data (such as the wages of individual employees) be kept confidential but be made available to managers who need them?
4. Why are computers so well suited to management information systems? What are some things that computers *cannot* do in dealing with data and information?
5. Do managers really need all the kinds of information discussed in this chapter? If not, which kinds can they do without?
6. Assume that you have been out of college for ten years and are unemployed. Unfortunately, your computer skills are seriously outdated. How would you go about updating your computer skills?

Exercises

1. Leaf through a few magazines to find advertisements for three different brands of computers. For each brand, list the product attributes stressed in the ads. Then prepare a two-page report describing why one particular brand of computer is a better buy than the other two. (*Note:* Your report should include all of the components discussed in this chapter—an introduction, the body of the report, conclusions, and recommendations.)
2. Choose a bar chart, a pie chart, or a graph, and display the data given in Figure 16.6. Why did you choose this method of presentation?

VIDEO CASE 16.1

The Information Revolution at Frito-Lay

For most people, it's hard to push a grocery cart through the snack food section of the supermarket without reaching for a bag of Fritos, Wavy Lay's, Doritos, Tostitos, or Ruffles—all brands produced by Frito-Lay. And with a 25 percent share of the world market for snack chip foods, annual sales revenues of $4.5 billion, and over 26,000 employees, Texas-based Frito-Lay is the largest snack chip company in the world. According to management, a large part of Frito-Lay's financial success is tied to a revolution in information technology that began almost ten years ago.

Today, Frito-Lay relies on a sophisticated computer network to connect 40 manufacturing facilities, 1,900 warehouses, 200 distribution centers, and 400,000 retail stores to corporate headquarters. This same system tracks over 4.5 billion packages of Frito-

Lay snack foods that are sold each year. In fact, every facet of the organization—from purchasing raw commodities to managing finished inventories—is served by the computerized information system.

The heart of this network is a small, hand-held computer. All of the firm's 10,000 sales people carry their own units to monitor store inventory, process sales receipts, and report sales data to the national headquarters. Here's how the system works. First, after checking current inventory levels at a retail store, a sales person keys in orders for each customer. Next, the sales person returns to the truck and fills the customer's order while the computer prints out an error-free sales receipt complete with tax, discounts, and special promotions. At the end of the day, each sales person's hand-held computer can also link up with the mainframe computer at Frito-Lay's national headquarters to download the day's sales data and upload information for the following day's route. Because salespeople don't have to spend time completing invoices by hand, management estimates that Frito-Lay saves between 30,000 and 50,000 worker-hours each week. And that's time that sales reps can use to call on new customers.

In addition to making employees more productive, management can zero in on sales information immediately. For example, a marketing manager may be concerned that sales for Doritos are decreasing. The manager can use Frito-Lay's computerized information system to isolate sales information for this specific product. She or he can also look at sales information by type of store and specific geographic regions. With these figures, the marketing manager may decide to lower prices, increase television advertising in a geographic region, or offer special promotional discounts to retailers. And because the information is current—usually never more than twenty-four hours old—the manager's decisions can take advantage of opportunities immediately without having to wait days or weeks to gather the facts.[3]

Questions

1. Back in 1987, Frito-Lay began investing millions of dollars to revolutionize its management information system (MIS). Based on the information presented in this case, do you feel the investment was a good one? Why?
2. How does Frito-Lay's computerized information system help the sales force sell more snack foods?
3. It is obvious that hand-held computers can help the sales force. How can supervisors and top managers use information provided by the system to make important decisions?

CASE 16.2

The Chips Are Down at Intel

Since the introduction of personal computers, small microprocessor chips—the brains inside computers—have dramatically transformed banking, transportation, communication, education, and just about every other industry, almost overnight. And although people recognize popular computer names like IBM, Apple, Compaq, Dell, and Packard Bell, many have never heard of Intel Corporation—the company that manufactures between 70 and 80 percent of all the chips used in personal computers.

California-based Intel Corporation was founded in 1968 by three engineers: Robert Noyce, the co-inventor of the integrated circuit; Gordon Moore; and Andrew Grove, Intel's current chief executive officer. During the 1970s, as the small company began to grow, it used initial profits to fund an aggressive research and development program. In 1981 the firm's research efforts paid off when IBM chose the Intel 8088 chip for its personal computer. During the early 1980s, IBM's PCs became the standard for the computer industry. As a result, the demand for Intel's chips soared, and so did Intel's sales and profits. Again, Intel invested in research, and in 1985 it introduced the 386 chip. Between 1985 and the end of 1991, Intel sold an estimated 14 million 386 chips and earned over $2 billion in profits.

To stay on top, Intel continued to spend between 10 and 15 percent of annual revenues on research. Again, the commitment to research paid off. Its fourth generation chip—the new, improved 486—became the preferred chip for personal computers during the first part of the 1990s. Then in 1993, Intel introduced its current and most powerful chip—the fifth generation Pentium. This chip has the power of a mainframe computer and is about five times as fast as the 486 model. Quickly, the Pentium chip became the benchmark for the personal computer industry.

For Intel, everything seemed to be right on track until November 1994. That's when news began to surface that Intel's Pentium chip contained a minor flaw. According to Intel, the flaw affects only those users who work with high-level scientific or spreadsheet calculations. Intel downplays the chances of error, estimating that the likelihood of error is one in 9 billion calculations or once in 27,000 years. Nevertheless, two problems were obvious after news of the flawed chip became widespread. First, IBM—one of Intel's largest and most respected customers—stopped selling personal computers containing the flawed Pentium chip. According to IBM's research studies, a calculation error caused by the flawed chip could occur as often as every

24 days. Fortunately for Intel, other manufacturers like Compaq, Dell, and Apple did not follow IBM's lead; they all continued to sell personal computers containing Pentium chips.

Second, the flawed Pentium chip quickly became a public relations nightmare for Intel. Although the chances of error may be remote, consumers were still concerned about quality. Bowing to increased pressure from both consumers and manufacturers, Intel finally announced it would replace flawed chips for any buyer who wanted a new Pentium chip, no questions asked. Unfortunately, Intel took almost six weeks to make the announcement.[4]

Questions

1. Intel invests between 10 and 15 percent of annual sales on research and development. How has the company's R&D effort enabled Intel to compete in the computer-information industry?

2. When it became obvious that the Pentium chip was flawed, six weeks passed before Intel offered to replace the chips. Do you think the chipmaker should have responded more quickly? Explain your answer.

CHAPTER 17

Accounting

LEARNING OBJECTIVES

After studying this chapter you should be able to

1 Explain what accounting is and what accountants do.

2 Discuss the accounting equation and the concept of double-entry bookkeeping.

3 Read and interpret a balance sheet.

4 Read and interpret an income statement.

5 Describe business activities that affect a firm's cash flow.

6 Summarize why managers, lenders, and investors compare present financial statements with those prepared for past accounting periods.

7 Use financial ratios to reveal how a business is doing.

CHAPTER PREVIEW

We begin this chapter with an overview of the accounting process. We identify different types of accountants and see how their work is important both to a firm's managers and to individuals and groups outside a firm. Then we focus on the basics of an accounting system—the accounting equation, double-entry bookkeeping, and the process by which raw data are organized into financial statements. Next we examine the three most important financial statements: the balance sheet, the income statement, and the statement of cash flows. Finally, we show how ratios can measure a firm's financial health.

Deloitte & Touche versus IDB Communications

Today, many investors trust that the financial data reported by a firm in its annual report or quarterly earnings report is accurate and beyond question. In fact, the "really good" investors, creditors, and government officials recognize that a company can put a favorable spin on the numbers. According to its auditors, that's exactly what IDB Communications—an up-and-coming telecommunications company—did in 1994. Believing that IDB exceeded what is normally considered acceptable accounting practices, Deloitte & Touche—one of America's Big Six accounting firms—simply resigned as the firm's auditors.

Although there are generally accepted accounting principles that are supposed to be followed, many firms can *and* do "adjust" their financial statements to increase profits. The confrontation between Deloitte & Touche and IDB began when auditors questioned expense and revenue items accounting for more than half of the firm's profit for the first quarter in 1994. Once challenged, management at IDB dropped the questionable amounts. But in order to maintain the same amount of profit, IDB then came up with new expense and revenue items to replace the ones that had been scrapped. The auditors at Deloitte & Touche raised a second red flag. Again, IDB introduced replacement items. And because the entries in IDB's last calculations produced even higher total profits than the firm had originally reported, IDB increased its expenses—one more time—and finally reported profits just about the same as those submitted in the first place. At this point, the auditors for Deloitte & Touche said enough is enough and promptly resigned.

According to Jeffrey P. Sudikoff, IDB's chairman and chief executive officer, the confrontation

was no more than a misunderstanding over a few small accounting issues. But according to Deloitte & Touche, the accounting issues in question were not "small." Specifically, Deloitte & Touche questioned (1) the value of inventory reported by IDB; (2) the proper time when $5 million in revenues that resulted from the sale of leasing options to another communications firm should be reported; and (3) the increase in IDB's reserve for bad debt expense.

Although the confrontation between IDB and Deloitte & Touche is over, IDB's investors may still be trying to decide if they can believe the financial information reported by management at IDB. As each investor wrestles with this question, it should be pointed out that the dollar value for a share of IDB stock immediately dropped by approximately 50 percent of its market value upon the announcement of Deloitte & Touche's resignation. Based on this fact, it appears that investors consider trustworthy financial information—like profits—to be extremely important.[1]

■■■■

Just the thought that either a firm's management or its accountants have "cooked the books" sends chills through investors, creditors, and government officials. As a result, large accounting firms like Deloitte & Touche have taken steps to ensure that the information they provide not only to corporate executives, but also to investors, creditors, and government officials, is accurate. After all, the basic product that an accounting firm sells is information—information that must meet clients' needs.

Today, it is impossible to manage a business operation without accurate and up-to-date accounting information. Managers and employees, lenders, suppliers, stockholders, and government agencies all rely on the information contained in two financial statements, each no more than one page in length. These two reports—the balance sheet and the income statement—are concise summaries of a firm's activities during a specific time period. Together, they represent the results of perhaps tens of thousands of transactions that have occurred during the accounting period. Moreover, the form of the financial statements is pretty much the same for all businesses, from a neighborhood video arcade to giant conglomerates like Disney, General Motors, and Coca-Cola. This information has a variety of uses, both within the firm and outside it. However, first and foremost, accounting information is management information. As such, it is of most use to those who manage the business.

LEARNING OBJECTIVE 1
Explain what accounting is and what accountants do.

accounting the process of systematically collecting, analyzing, and reporting financial information

private (or nonpublic) accountant an accountant who is employed by a specific organization

n n ACCOUNTING AND ACCOUNTANTS

Accounting is the process of systematically collecting, analyzing, and reporting financial information. Because of its great value, business owners have been concerned with financial information for hundreds of years: the first book of accounting principles was written in 1494, by an Italian monk named Paciolo.

Modern accounting in the United States can be traced back to the establishment of the American Institute of Certified Public Accountants (AICPA) in 1887. By the early 1900s, accounting instruction was offered at many colleges and universities. Today, accounting courses are required for virtually every type of business degree.

Careers in Accounting

Accountants are generally classified as private or public accountants. A **private (or nonpublic) accountant** is employed by a specific organization. A medium-sized or large firm may employ one or several private accountants to design its accounting system, manage its accounting department, and provide managers with advice and assistance. Private accountants also provide the following services for their employers:

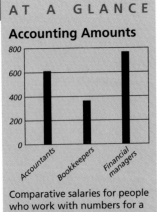

▷ ▷ AT A GLANCE

Accounting Amounts

Comparative salaries for people who work with numbers for a living.
(Weekly income in dollars)

Source: Bureau of Labor Statistics (reported in *Business Almanac and Sourcebook*, 1995, p. 321).

534

It's hard to disguise poor financial performance when an accountant looks at the numbers. The primary users of accounting information are the owners and managers of a firm. Here an accountant explains to the owner of a small costume shop how much profit the business earned during the last accounting period.

1. *General accounting*—Recording business transactions and preparing financial statements.
2. *Budgeting*—Helping managers to develop budgets for sales and operating expenses.
3. *Cost accounting*—Determining the cost of producing specific products or services.
4. *Tax accounting*—Planning tax strategy and preparing tax returns for the firm.

Smaller and medium-sized firms that don't require full-time accountants can hire the services of public accountants. A **public accountant** is an accountant whose services may be hired on a fee basis by individuals or firms. Public accountants may be self-employed or may work for accounting firms. Accounting firms range in size from one-person operations to huge, international firms with hundreds of accounting partners and thousands of employees. Table 17.1 lists the six largest public accounting firms in the world and some of their clients.

Most accounting firms include on their staffs at least one **certified public accountant (CPA),** an individual who has met state requirements for accounting education and experience and has passed a rigorous two-day accounting examination. The examination is prepared by the American Institute of Certified Public Accountants and covers accounting practice, accounting theory, auditing, and business law. State requirements usually include a college degree in accounting and from one to three years of on-the-job experience. Once an individual becomes a CPA, he or she must

public accountant an accountant whose services may be hired on a fee basis by individuals or firms

certified public accountant (CPA) an individual who has met state requirements for accounting education and experience and has passed a rigorous two-day accounting examination

TABLE 17.1   Accounting's "Big Six" Certified Public Accounting Firms

Firm	Worldwide Revenues (in billions)	Major Clients
Arthur Andersen & Company	$6.1	Blockbuster, Fiat, First Chicago Tenneco, U.S. Shoe
KPMG Peat Marwick	6.0	Apple Computer, BMW, Citicorp, Hasbro, J. C. Penney, Xerox
Ernst & Young	5.8	BankAmerica, Coca-Cola, McDonald's, Mobil, Wal-Mart
Coopers & Lybrand	5.2	American Brands, Glaxo, Johnson & Johnson, 3M
Deloitte and Touche	5.0	BASF, Chrysler, Dow Chemical, General Motors, RJR Nabisco
Price Waterhouse	3.9	Amoco, Compaq, IBM, Kmart, Nike, Scott, Disney, Woolworth

Source: Gary Hoover, ed., *Hoover's Handbook of American Business 1995.* Copyright © 1994. Published by The Reference Press, Inc., Austin, Texas, 800-486-8666. Used with permission.

participate in continuing-education programs to remain certified in most states. These specialized programs are designed to provide the current training needed in today's changing business environment. Today, CPAs are also required to take an ethics course in order to satisfy their continuing-education requirement. Details regarding specific requirements for practice as a CPA in a particular state can be obtained by contacting the appropriate State Board of Accountancy.

Certification as a CPA brings both status and responsibility. Only an independent CPA can audit the financial contents of a corporation's annual report and express an opinion—as required by law—regarding the acceptability of the corporation's accounting practices. And because CPAs have a great deal of experience, they are often asked to consult with business firms troubled by financial and/or management difficulties. Fees for the services provided by CPAs generally range from $50 to $300 an hour.

Users of Accounting Information

As we have noted, the primary users of accounting information are *managers.* The firm's accounting system provides a range of information that can be compiled for the entire firm; for each product; for each sales territory, store, or individual salesperson; for each division or department; and generally in any way that will help those who manage the organization. At a company like Kraft General Foods, Inc. (a division of Philip Morris Incorporated), for example, financial information is gathered for all of its hundreds of food products: Maxwell House Coffee, Tombstone Pizza, Post Cereals, Jell-O Desserts, Kool Aid, and so on. The president of the company would be interested in total sales for all these products. The vice president for marketing would be interested in national sales for Tombstone Pizza and

Jell-O Desserts. The northeastern sales manager might want to look at sales figures for Kool Aid in New England. For a large, complex organization like Kraft General Foods, the accounting system must be complete and yet flexible because managers at different levels must be able to get the information they need.

Much of this accounting information is *proprietary;* it is not divulged to anyone outside the firm. However, certain financial information is demanded by outside individuals and organizations that the firm must deal with (see Table 17.2).

- *Lenders* require at least the information contained in the firm's financial statements before they will commit themselves to either short- or long-term loans. *Suppliers* generally ask for such information before they will extend trade credit to a firm.
- *Stockholders* must, by law, be provided with a summary of the firm's financial position in quarterly and annual reports. In addition, *potential investors* must be provided with financial statements in the prospectus for each securities issue.
- *Government agencies* require a variety of information pertaining to the firm's tax liabilities, payroll deductions for employees, and new issues of stocks and bonds.

The firm's accounting system must be able to provide all this information, in the required form. An important function of accountants is to ensure that such information is accurate and thorough enough to satisfy these outside groups. To see what can happen when accounting records are questionable, read Ethical Challenges.

■■ THE ACCOUNTING PROCESS

LEARNING OBJECTIVE 2
Discuss the accounting equation and the concept of double-entry bookkeeping.

Accounting can be viewed as a system for transforming raw financial *data* into useful financial *information*. In this section, we see how such a system

TABLE 17.2   Users of Accounting Information
The primary users of accounting information are managers, but financial information is also demanded by outside individuals and organizations that the company deals with.

Management	Lenders and Suppliers	Stockholders and Potential Investors	Government Agencies
Plan and set goals	Evaluate credit risks before committing to short-term or long-term financing	Evaluate the financial health of the firm before purchasing stocks or bonds	Confirm tax liabilities
Organize			Confirm payroll deductions
Lead and motivate			Approve new issues of stocks and bonds
Control			

▪ ▪ ▪ ▪ ETHICAL CHALLENGES

Accounting Records "Doctored"

On January 29, 1993, John J. Pomerantz, CEO of Leslie Fay Companies, found out that the firm's accounting records had been "doctored" to overstate the value of inventory and understate the cost of making clothes for as far back as 1990. According to Pomerantz, neither he nor other top management officials for the nation's second-largest maker of women's apparel sold to department stores knew of any irregularities until the end of January 1993. While the financial scandal—the largest reported in the 1990s—is still unfolding, all evidence points at the company's now-suspended controller Donald F. Kenia. If convicted, Kenia could face up to ten years in prison and $500,000 in fines for reporting false company earnings to the Securities and Exchange Commission.

One month after discovering the deception, it was estimated that instead of earning $23.9 million in 1992, the companies actually lost $13.7 million. And the earnings figures for 1991 were 42 percent less than reported. In just weeks, as the value of the stock plummeted from $12.38 to $5.25, stockholders filed dozens of lawsuits against Leslie Fay. And it wasn't very long before its lenders, suppliers, and subcontractors demanded the monies owed them and refused to extend further credit or services. In order to protect its $440 million in assets, the Leslie Fay Companies were forced to file Chapter 11 under the U.S. Bankruptcy Code. With liabilities of $260 million, they needed to buy time to reorganize and, at the same time, obtain the financing and materials needed to continue to operate their businesses. Eighteen months after filing, the companies announced they will discontinue or sell off some of their less profitable clothing lines and will split the remaining lines into separate divisions operated under separate management teams. In the meantime, their creditors do receive payments for work done under bankruptcy protection but still have to wait for a repayment plan on Leslie Fay's previous outstanding debts.

In August 1994, an independent auditing committee cleared Pomerantz, other top management executives, and members of the board of directors of any knowledge or participation in the fraud. However, Pomerantz, the son of the founder of Leslie Fay and a graduate of the Wharton School of Finance, was criticized for seldom visiting his base of operations in Wilkes Barre, Pennsylvania, and for focusing on the sales figures instead of analyzing the volumes of financial information he received. And other officers of the companies fell short of their obligations when they gave only cursory attention to the important details in the firm's financial statements. Finally, the committee also noted that even before the fraud was uncovered, Leslie Fay's outside auditing firm, BDO Seidman, was negligent in its duties by failing to discover irregular accounting entries that did not conform to general accounting standards. The reasons for Kenia's manipulation of the records is still a mystery because examiners have found that none of the companies' funds are missing.

operates. Then, in the next three sections, we describe the three most important financial statements provided by the accounting process.

The Accounting Equation

The accounting equation is a simple statement that forms the basis for the accounting process. It shows the relationship among the firm's assets, liabilities, and owners' equity.

- **Assets** are the resources that a firm owns—cash, inventories, land, equipment, buildings, patents, and the like.
- **Liabilities** are the firm's debts and obligations—what it owes to others.
- **Owners' equity** is the difference between a firm's assets and its liabilities—what would be left over for the firm's owners if its assets were used to pay off its liabilities.

The relationship among these three terms is almost self-evident: *owners' equity = assets – liabilities*. By moving terms algebraically, we obtain the standard form of the **accounting equation:**

$$\text{assets} = \text{liabilities} + \text{owners' equity}$$

In addition to assets, liabilities, and owners' equity, two additional accounts also affect the accounting equation. **Revenues** are the dollar amounts received by a firm. For most firms, revenues result from the sale of merchandise or services and increase the owners' equity account. **Expenses** are the costs incurred in operating a business. Typical expenses include wage expense, utility expense, delivery expense, and rent expense. The opposite of revenues, expenses always decrease the owners' equity account.

Implementation of this equation begins with the recording of raw data—that is, the firm's day-to-day financial transactions. It is accomplished through the double-entry system of bookkeeping.

The Double-Entry Bookkeeping System

Double-entry bookkeeping is a system in which each financial transaction is recorded as two separate accounting entries to maintain the balance shown in the accounting equation. Suppose Maria Martin invests $50,000 in cash to start a new business called Maple Tree Software. Before she makes this investment, both sides of the accounting equation equal zero. The firm has no assets, no liabilities, and no owners' equity. The results of Martin's investment are shown as transaction *A* in Figure 17.1. Cash (an asset) is increased by $50,000; owners' equity is also increased by $50,000 to balance the increase in assets.

Note that the entries for this transaction are not lumped together as one asset increase and one owners' equity increase. Instead, the entries are placed in separate *accounts*, which show exactly what is being increased. Here the investments are cash, so the *Cash* account is increased. Similarly, under owners' equity, there is one account for Martin's owners' equity.

Five additional transactions are shown in Figure 17.1:

- In transaction *B*, a bank loan of $10,000 was used to purchase equipment. The loan is a liability, and the equipment is an asset.
- In transaction *C*, inventory worth $5,000 was purchased on credit. The inventory is an asset, and the amount owed is a liability.
- In transaction *D*, $5,000 in cash was used to pay off part of the bank loan. The payoff decreases cash, an asset; the reduction of the loan amount also decreases a liability.
- In transaction *E*, Maple Tree Software provides computer services for $3,000 to its first customer. As a result, the cash account is increased and the owners' equity account is increased.
- In transaction *F*, $1,000 in cash was used to pay the rent expense. The payment decreases cash, an asset; the payment also equally reduces owners' equity.

Follow through each of these transactions in Figure 17.1 to make sure you understand why each entry is recorded as shown. Also note that, after all six transactions, assets total $62,000, and liabilities and owners' equity

FIGURE 17.1   Six Business Transactions Recorded Using the Double-Entry System
Double-entry bookkeeping is used to balance the accounting equation (assets = liabilities + owners' equity).

MAPLE TREE SOFTWARE

	Cash		Equipment		Inventory	=	Bank Loans		Suppliers	+	Martin
Transaction A *(cash investment)*	+$50,000		–0–		–0–	=	–0–		–0–		+$50,000
	$50,000	+	–0–	+	–0–	=	–0–	+	–0–	+	$50,000
Transaction B *(equipment purchase via bank loan)*	–0–		+$10,000		–0–	=	+$10,000		–0–		–0–
	$50,000	+	$10,000	+	–0–	=	$10,000	+	–0–	+	$50,000
Transaction C *(credit purchase of inventory)*	–0–		–0–		+$ 5,000	=	–0–		+$ 5,000		–0–
	$50,000	+	$10,000	+	$ 5,000	=	$10,000	+	$ 5,000	+	$50,000
Transaction D *(partial payoff of loan)*	–$ 5,000		–0–		–0–	=	–$ 5,000		–0–		–0–
	$45,000	+	$10,000	+	$ 5,000	=	$ 5,000	+	$ 5,000	+	$50,000
Transaction E *(sales revenues)*	+$ 3,000		–0–		–0–	=	–0–		–0–		$ 3,000
	$48,000	+	$10,000	+	$ 5,000	=	$ 5,000	+	$ 5,000	+	$53,000
Transaction F *(payment of rent expense)*	–$ 1,000		–0–		–0–	=	–0–		–0–		–$ 1,000
	$47,000	+	$10,000	+	$ 5,000	=	$ 5,000	+	$ 5,000	+	$52,000

total $62,000. Thus the books are still balanced. That is, assets are indeed equal to liabilities plus owners' equity.

The Accounting Cycle

In the typical accounting system, raw data are transformed into financial statements in five steps. The first three—analyzing, journalizing, and posting—are performed on a continual basis throughout the accounting period. The last two—preparation of the trial balance and of the financial statements—are performed at the end of the accounting period.

Analyzing Source Documents   The basic accounting data are contained in *source documents*, which are the receipts, invoices, sales slips, and other documents that show the dollar values of day-to-day business transactions. The accounting cycle begins with the analysis of each of these documents. The purpose of the analysis is to determine which accounts are affected by the documents and how they are affected.

Journalizing the Transactions   Every financial transaction is then recorded in a journal—a process called *journalizing*. Transactions must be recorded in the firm's general journal or in specialized journals. The **general journal** is a book of original entry in which typical transactions are recorded in order of their occurrence. An accounting system may also include *specialized journals* for specific types of transactions that occur frequently. Thus a retail store might have cash receipts, cash disbursements, purchases, and sales journals in addition to its general journal. Today, large, medium-sized, and even small businesses use a computer when journalizing accounting entries.

general journal   a book of original entry in which typical transactions are recorded in order of their occurrence

High-tech accounting help. Today many business owners use a personal computer and accounting software to transform raw data into financial information.

general ledger   a book of
accounts containing a separate
sheet or section for each
account

posting   the process of
transferring journal entries to
the general ledger

trial balance   a summary of
the balances of all general
ledger accounts at the end of
the accounting period

Posting Transactions   Next the information recorded in the general journal
or specialized journals is transferred to the general ledger. The **general
ledger** is a book of accounts containing a separate sheet or section for each
account. The process of transferring journal entries to the general ledger is
called **posting.**

Preparing the Trial Balance   A **trial balance** is a summary of the balances
of all general ledger accounts at the end of the accounting period. To prepare
a trial balance, the accountant determines and lists the balances for all
ledger accounts at the end of each accounting period. If the trial balance
totals are correct and the accounting equation is still in balance, the accountant can proceed to the financial statements. If not, a mistake has occurred
somewhere, which the accountant must find and correct before proceeding.

Preparing Financial Statements and Closing the Books   The firm's financial
statements are prepared from the information contained in the trial balance. This information is presented in a standardized format to make the
statements as accessible as possible to the various parties who may be interested in the firm's financial affairs.

Once these statements have been prepared and checked, the firm's
books are "closed" for the accounting period. A new accounting cycle is then
begun for the next period.

Now let us consider the three most important financial statements generated by the accounting process: the balance sheet, the income statement,
and the statement of cash flows.

■■ THE BALANCE SHEET

LEARNING OBJECTIVE 3
Read and interpret a balance
sheet.

**balance sheet (or statement
of financial position)**   a
summary of the dollar amounts
for a firm's assets, liabilities,
and owners' equity accounts at
a particular time

A **balance sheet** (or **statement of financial position**) is a summary of the
dollar amounts for a firm's assets, liabilities, and owners' equity accounts at
a particular time. The balance sheet must demonstrate that the accounting
equation does indeed balance. That is, it must show that the firm's assets are
equal to its liabilities plus its owners' equity. As previously noted, the balance sheet is prepared at least once a year. Most firms also have balance
sheets prepared semiannually, quarterly, or monthly.

Figure 17.2 shows the balance sheet for Northeast Art Supply, a small
corporation that sells picture frames, paints, canvases, and other artists'
supplies to retailers in New England. Note that assets are reported at the top
of the statement, followed by liabilities and owners' (or stockholders')
equity. Let us work through the different accounts in Figure 17.2, from top
to bottom.

Assets

liquidity   the ease with which
an asset can be converted into
cash

current assets   cash and other
assets that can quickly be
converted into cash or that will
be used in one year or less

On a balance sheet, assets are listed in order, from the *most liquid* to the *least
liquid*. The **liquidity** of an asset is the ease with which it can be converted
into cash.

Current Assets   **Current assets** are cash and other assets that can quickly
be converted into cash or that will be used in one year or less. Because cash

FIGURE 17.2
Balance Sheet
A balance sheet summarizes a firm's accounts at a particular time, showing the various dollar amounts that enter into the accounting equation and showing that the equation balances. Note that assets ($340,000) equal liabilities plus owners' equity ($340,000).

NORTHEAST ART SUPPLY, INC.

Balance Sheet
December 31, 199x

ASSETS

Current assets			
Cash		$ 59,000	
Marketable securities		10,000	
Accounts receivable	$ 40,000		
Less allowance for doubtful accounts	2,000	38,000	
Notes receivable		32,000	
Merchandise inventory		41,000	
Prepaid expenses		2,000	
Total current assets			$182,000
Fixed assets			
Delivery equipment	$110,000		
Less accumulated depreciation	20,000	$ 90,000	
Furniture and store equipment	62,000		
Less accumulated depreciation	15,000	47,000	
Total fixed assets			137,000
Intangible assets			
Patents		$ 6,000	
Goodwill		15,000	
Total intangible assets			21,000
Total assets			$340,000

LIABILITIES AND STOCKHOLDERS' EQUITY

Current liabilities			
Accounts payable	$ 35,000		
Notes payable	25,000		
Salaries payable	4,000		
Taxes payable	6,000		
Total current liabilities		$ 70,000	
Long-term liabilities			
Mortgage payable on store equipment	$ 40,000		
Total long-term liabilities		40,000	
Total liabilities			$110,000
Stockholders' equity			
Common stock, 10,000 shares at $15 Par value		$150,000	
Retained earnings		80,000	
Total owners' equity			230,000
Total liabilities and owners' equity			$340,000

is the most liquid asset, it is listed first. Following that are *marketable securities*—stocks, bonds, and other liquid investments—that can be converted into cash in a matter of days. These are temporary investments of excess cash that Northeast Art Supply doesn't need immediately.

Next are the firm's receivables. Its *accounts receivables,* which result from the issuance of trade credit to customers, are generally due within thirty to sixty days. However, the firm expects that some of these debts will not be collected. Thus it has reduced its accounts receivables by a 5 percent

Current assets can be beautiful. Typical current assets include cash, marketable, securities, receivables, inventory, and prepaid expenses. For growers in Holland, tulips represent not only a beautiful current asset, but also a valuable one that is sold around the world.

allowance for doubtful accounts. The firm's *notes receivables* are receivables for which customers have signed promissory notes. They are generally repaid over a longer period of time than the firm's accounts receivables.

Northeast's *merchandise inventory* represents the value of goods that are on hand for sale to customers. These goods are listed as current assets because they will be sold in one year or less. Since Northeast Art Supply is a wholesale operation, the inventory listed in Figure 17.2 represents finished goods ready for sale to retailers. For a manufacturing firm, merchandise inventory can also represent raw materials that will become part of a finished product, or work in process that has been partially completed but requires further processing. For more information on the methods used to determine the dollar value of inventory, read Business Journal.

Northeast's last current asset is **prepaid expenses,** which are assets that have been paid for in advance but have not yet been used. An example is insurance premiums. They are usually paid at the beginning of the policy year for the next twelve months. The unused portion (say, for the last four months of the policy year) is a prepaid expense. For Northeast Art, all current assets total $182,000.

prepaid expenses assets that have been paid for in advance but have not yet been used

Fixed Assets   **Fixed assets** are assets that will be held or used for a period longer than one year. They generally include land, buildings, and equipment. Although Northeast owns no land or buildings, it does own *delivery equipment* that originally cost $110,000. It also owns *furniture and store equipment* that originally cost $62,000.

fixed assets assets that will be held or used for a period longer than one year

Note that the values of both fixed assets are decreased by their *accumulated depreciation.* **Depreciation** is the process of apportioning the cost of a fixed asset over the period during which it will be used. The amount

depreciation the process of apportioning the cost of a fixed asset over the period during which it will be used

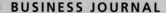

■ ■ ■ ■   **BUSINESS JOURNAL**

How Inventory Affects a Firm's Financial Statements

Question: What do Wal-Mart, Procter & Gamble, and ConAgra have in common?

Answer: All three companies have invested millions of dollars in inventory. At the end of 1994, Wal-Mart Stores, Inc.—the largest retailer in the United States—reported inventory valued at $11 billion. The Procter & Gamble Company—a leading supplier of laundry, cleaning, paper, beauty care, health care, and food products in more than 140 countries around the world—reported inventory valued at almost $3 billion. Finally, ConAgra—a diversified international food company that produces products ranging from prepared foods for today's busy consumers to supplies farmers need to grow their crops—reported inventory valued at $2.9 billion. These three corporations have invested vast sums of money for one simple reason: they must have merchandise to sell when their customers want it. And for all three, the dollar value of inventory represents a large part of each firm's total assets. Therefore, dollar values for inventory must be accurately reported to investors, lenders, suppliers, and government regulatory agencies.

METHODS USED TO EVALUATE INVENTORIES

Because the prices that a firm pays for the goods it sells (or for the materials it uses in manufacturing) are likely to change during an accounting period, one of four inventory methods can be used to determine the dollar value of the inventory. Under the *specific identification method,* the actual dollar cost of a particular item is assigned to the item. The *average-cost method* is based on the assumption that each inventory item carries an equal cost. To arrive at an average cost for each item, the total dollar cost of the goods available for sale is divided by the number of items. Under the *first-in, first-out (FIFO) method,* the accountant assumes that the costs of the first items purchased are assigned to the first items sold. With FIFO, the costs of the last items purchased are assigned to the items remaining in inventory. Under the *last-in, first-out (LIFO) method,* the accountant assumes that the cost of the last items purchased are assigned to the first items sold. With LIFO, the costs of the first items purchased are assigned to the items remaining in inventory.

WHICH INVENTORY METHOD IS BEST?

Each of the four methods of inventory valuation is based on a different set of assumptions. Though none is considered perfect, each method is acceptable for use in published financial statements, and each has advantages and disadvantages. A particular business firm choosing an inventory method should be sure to consider the effect the method will have on the firm's balance sheet and income statement, its taxes, and its management decisions.

allotted to each year is an expense for that year, and the value of the asset must be reduced by that expense amount. In the case of Northeast's delivery equipment, $20,000 of its value has been depreciated (or used up) since it was purchased. Its value at this time is thus $110,000 less $20,000, or $90,000. In a similar fashion, the original value of furniture and store equipment ($62,000) has been reduced by accumulated depreciation of $15,000.

Furniture and store equipment now has a reported value of $47,000. For Northeast Art, all fixed assets total $137,000.

Intangible Assets

intangible assets assets that do not exist physically but have a value based on legal rights or advantages that they confer on a firm

Intangible assets are assets that do not exist physically but have a value based on legal rights or advantages that they confer on a firm. They include patents, copyrights, trademarks, and goodwill. By their nature, intangible assets are long-term assets—they are of value to the firm for a number of years.

Northeast Art Supply lists two intangible assets. The first is a *patent* for an oil paint that the company has developed. The firm's accountants estimate the patent has a current market value of $6,000. The second intangible asset, **goodwill,** is the value of a firm's reputation, location, earning capacity, and other intangibles that make the business a profitable concern. Goodwill is not normally listed on a balance sheet unless the firm has been purchased from previous owners. In this case, the purchasers have actually paid an additional amount (over and above the value of the previous owners' equity) for this intangible asset. The firm's accountants included a $15,000 amount for goodwill. For Northeast Art, intangible assets total $21,000. Now it is possible to total all three types of assets for Northeast Art. As calculated in Figure 17.2, total assets are $340,000.

goodwill the value of a firm's reputation, location, earning capacity, and other intangibles that make the business a profitable concern

Liabilities and Owners' Equity

The liabilities and the owners' equity accounts complete the balance sheet. The firm's liabilities are separated into two categories—current and long-term—on the balance sheet.

current liabilities debts that will be repaid in one year or less

Current Liabilities

A firm's **current liabilities** are debts that will be repaid in one year or less. Northeast Art Supply purchased merchandise from its suppliers on credit. Thus its balance sheet includes an entry for accounts payable. **Accounts payable** are short-term obligations that arise as a result of making credit purchases.

accounts payable short-term obligations that arise as a result of making credit purchases

notes payable obligations that have been secured with promissory notes

Notes payable are obligations that have been secured with promissory notes. They are usually short-term obligations, but they may extend beyond one year. Only those that must be paid within the year are listed under current liabilities.

Northeast also lists *salaries payable* and *taxes payable* as current liabilities. These are both expenses that have been incurred during the current accounting period but will be paid in the next accounting period. Such expenses must be shown as debts for the accounting period in which they were incurred. For Northeast Art, current liabilities total $70,000.

long-term liabilities debts that need not be repaid for at least one year

Long-Term Liabilities

Long-term liabilities are debts that need not be repaid for at least one year. Northeast lists only one long-term liability—a $40,000 *mortgage payable.* Bonds and other long-term loans would be included here as well, if they existed. As you see in Figure 17.2, Northeast's current and long-term liabilities total $110,000.

Owners' Equity

For a sole proprietorship or partnership, the owners' equity is shown as the difference between assets and liabilities. In a partnership, each partner's share of the ownership is reported separately by each owner's name. For a corporation, the owners' equity is usually referred to as *stockholders' equity* or *shareholders' equity*. The dollar amount reported on the balance sheet is the total value of its stock, plus retained earnings that have accumulated to date.

Northeast Art Supply has issued only common stock. Its value is shown as its par value ($15) times the number of shares outstanding (10,000). In addition, $80,000 of Northeast's earnings have been reinvested in the business since it was founded. Thus, owners' equity totals $230,000.

As the two grand totals show, Northeast's assets and the sum of its liabilities and owners' equity are equal—at $340,000.

■■ THE INCOME STATEMENT

An **income statement** is a summary of a firm's revenues and expenses during a specified accounting period. The income statement is sometimes called the *earnings statement* or the *statement of income and expenses*. It may be prepared monthly, quarterly, semiannually, or annually. An income statement covering the previous year must be included in a corporation's annual report to its stockholders.

Figure 17.3 shows the income statement for Northeast Art Supply. Note that it consists of four sections. Generally, revenues *less* cost of goods sold *less* operating expenses *equals* net income from operations.

Revenues

As noted earlier, revenues are dollar amounts received by a firm. Northeast obtains its revenues solely from the sale of its products. The revenues section of its income statement begins with gross sales. **Gross sales** are the total dollar amount of all goods and services sold during the accounting period. From this amount are deducted the dollar amounts of

- *sales returns,* or merchandise returned to the firm by its customers;
- *sales allowances,* or price reductions offered to customers who accept slightly damaged or soiled merchandise;
- *sales discounts,* or price reductions offered by manufacturers and suppliers to customers who pay their bills promptly.

The remainder is the firm's net sales. **Net sales** are the actual dollar amounts received by the firm for the goods and services it has sold, after adjustment for returns, allowances, and discounts. For Northeast Art, net sales are $451,000.

Cost of Goods Sold

The standard method of determining the **cost of goods sold**—the cost of goods a firm has sold during an accounting period—by a retailing or wholesaling firm can be summarized as follows:

FIGURE 17.3
Income Statement
An income statement summarizes the firm's revenues and expenses during a specified accounting period—one month, three months, six months, or a year.

NORTHEAST ART SUPPLY, INC.

Income Statement
For the Year Ended
December 31, 199x

Revenues			
Gross sales		$465,000	
Less sales returns and allowances	$ 9,500		
Less sales discounts	4,500	14,000	
Net sales			$451,000
Cost of goods sold			
Beginning inventory, January 1, 199x		$ 40,000	
Purchases	$346,000		
Less purchase discounts	11,000		
Net purchases		335,000	
Cost of goods available for sale		$375,000	
Less ending inventory December 31, 199x		41,000	
Cost of goods sold			334,000
Gross profit on sales			117,000
Operating expenses			
Selling expenses			
Sales salaries	$ 20,000		
Advertising	6,000		
Sales promotion	2,500		
Depreciation—store equipment	3,000		
Miscellaneous selling expenses	1,500		
Total selling expenses		$ 33,000	
General expenses			
Office salaries	$ 28,500		
Rent	8,500		
Depreciation—delivery equipment	4,000		
Depreciation—office furniture	1,500		
Utilities expense	2,500		
Insurance expense	1,000		
Miscellaneous expense	500		
Total general expenses		46,500	
Total operating expenses			79,500
Net income from operations			$ 37,500
Less interest expense			2,000
Net income before taxes			$ 35,500
Less federal income taxes			5,325
Net income after taxes			$ 30,175

$$\text{cost of goods sold} = \text{beginning} + \text{net} - \text{ending}$$
$$\text{inventory} \quad \text{purchases} \quad \text{inventory}$$

A manufacturer must include raw materials inventories, work in progress inventories, and direct manufacturing costs in this computation.

According to Figure 17.3, Northeast began its accounting period on January 1 with a merchandise inventory that cost $40,000 (see *beginning inventory* under the *cost of goods sold* section). During the period, the firm purchased merchandise for resale valued at $346,000. But after taking advantage of *purchase discounts*, it paid only $335,000 for this merchandise.

Thus, during the year, Northeast had *goods available for sale* valued at $40,000 + $335,000 = $375,000.

At the end of the accounting period on December 31, Northeast had an *ending inventory* of $41,000. Thus it had sold all but $41,000 worth of the available goods. The cost of goods sold by Northeast was therefore $375,000 less $41,000, or $334,000. A firm's **gross profit on sales** is its net sales *less* the cost of goods sold. For Northeast, gross profit on sales was therefore $117,000.

gross profit on sales   a firm's net sales *less* the cost of goods sold

Operating Expenses

operating expenses   those costs that do not result directly from the purchase or manufacture of the products a firm sells

selling expenses   costs related to the firm's marketing activities

A firm's **operating expenses** are those costs that do not result directly from the purchase or manufacture of the products it sells. They are generally classed as either selling expenses or general expenses.

Selling expenses are costs related to the firm's marketing activities. They include salaries for members of the sales force, advertising and other promotional expenses, and the costs involved in operating stores. For Northeast Art, selling expenses total $33,000.

General expenses are costs incurred in managing a business. They are sometimes called *administrative expenses*. Typical general expenses are the salaries of office workers and the costs of maintaining offices. A catchall account called *miscellaneous expense* is usually included in the *general expenses* section of the income statement. For Northeast Art, general expenses total $46,500. Now it is possible to total both selling and general expenses for Northeast Art. As Figure 17.3 shows, total operating expenses for the accounting period are $79,500.

It costs money to operate a business. Salary expense is often the largest single expense for most firms. For Chrysler Corporation, it would be impossible to produce cars without assembly-line workers. It would also be impossible for Chrysler to attract qualified workers if the company didn't pay them.

Net Income

Net income is the profit earned (or the loss suffered) by a firm during an accounting period, after all expenses have been deducted from revenues. In Figure 17.3, Northeast's *net income from operations* is computed as gross profit on sales ($117,000) *less* total operating expenses ($79,500). For Northeast Art, net income from operations totals $37,500. From this amount, *interest expense* of $2,000 is deducted to obtain a *net income before taxes* of $35,500. The interest expense is deducted in this section of the income statement because it is not an operating expense. Rather, it is an expense that results from financing the business.

Northeast's *federal income taxes,* based on its pretax income, are $5,325. Although these taxes may or may not be payable immediately, they are definitely an expense that must be deducted from income. This leaves Northeast with a *net income after taxes* of $30,175. This amount may be used to pay a dividend to stockholders, retained or reinvested in the firm, used to reduce the firm's debts, or all three.

■ ■ THE STATEMENT OF CASH FLOWS

Cash generation is the life blood of business. In 1987 the Securities and Exchange Commission (SEC) and the Financial Accounting Standards Board (FASB) required all publicly traded companies to include a statement of cash flows along with their balance sheet and income statement in their annual report. The **statement of cash flows** illustrates the effect on cash of the operating, investing, and financing activities of a company for an accounting period. It provides information concerning a company's cash receipts and cash payments during the accounting period and is organized into three activities: operations, investing, and financing.

- *Cash flows from operating activities.* This first section of a statement of cash flows addresses the firm's primary revenue source—providing goods and services. The net income (from the income statement) is adjusted by adding back any noncash expenses (such as depreciation expense). Additional adjustments are made based on changes in selected current asset and current liability accounts. The end result gives the true cash flows from operating activities.
- *Cash flows from investing activities.* The second section is concerned with cash flow from investments. This includes the purchase and sale of land, equipment and other fixed assets, and long-term investments.
- *Cash flows from financing activities.* The third and final section deals with the cash flow from all financing activities. It reports changes in long-term liability and owners' equity accounts. This includes long-term borrowing and repayments, the sale and repurchase of the company's own stock, and cash dividends.

The totals of all three activities are added to the beginning cash balance to equal the ending cash balance. The cash flow statement, along with the balance sheet and income statement, illustrate the results of past business decisions and reflect the firm's ability to pay debts and dividends and to finance new growth or internal expansion.

■■ ANALYZING FINANCIAL STATEMENTS

LEARNING OBJECTIVE 6
Summarize why managers, lenders, and investors compare present financial statements with those prepared for past accounting periods.

As we have seen, a firm's balance sheet provides a "financial picture" of the firm at a particular time. Its income statement summarizes its operations during one accounting period. And its statement of cash flows provides information concerning a firm's cash receipts and cash payments during the accounting period. All three financial statements can provide answers to a variety of questions about the firm's ability to do business and stay in business, its profitability, its value as an investment, and its ability to repay its debts.

Comparing Data for Previous Accounting Periods

Even more information can be obtained by comparing present financial statements with those prepared for past accounting periods. Such comparisons permit managers, lenders and suppliers, and investors to (1) identify trends in growth, borrowing, and other business variables and (2) determine whether the firm is on track in terms of its long-term goals.

Most corporations include in their annual reports comparisons of the important elements from their financial statements for recent years. Typical comparisons for sales, long-term debt, earnings per share, and other important financial measures for the Allied Signal Corporation—a world leader in

FIGURE 17.4
Comparisons of Present and Past Financial Statements
Most corporations include in their annual reports comparisons of the important elements of their financial statements for recent years.

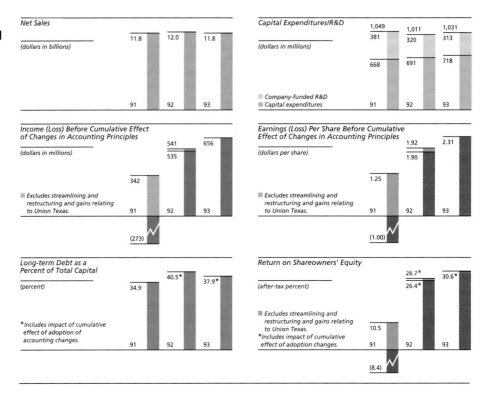

the aerospace and automotive industries—are shown in Figure 17.4. By examining these data, a marketing manager for Allied Signal can judge how fast annual sales are increasing. An operating manager can tell whether R&D expenditures are decreasing. And the vice president of finance can determine if the dollar amount of long-term debt is changing. Stockholders and potential investors, on the other hand, may be more concerned with increases or decreases for Allied Signal's earnings per share or return on owners' equity. For more information on how to use an annual report to analyze a company's financial health, read Business Journal.

Comparing Data with Other Firms' Data

Many firms also compare their financial results with those of competing firms and with industry averages. Comparisons are possible as long as accountants follow the basic rules of accounting, often referred to as *generally accepted accounting principles (GAAP)*. Except for minor differences in the format and terms used in each financial statement, the balance sheet and income statement for The Procter & Gamble Co. (Case 17.2) are similar to the balance sheet and income statement for similar large corporations in the industry. Comparisons give managers a general idea of a firm's relative effectiveness and its standing within the industry. For example, a manager at IBM would read the financial reports for Digital Equipment Corp., Hewlett-Packard Co., and Compaq Computer to get a sense of IBM's position within the office automation/computer fields. Competitors' financial

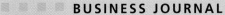

BUSINESS JOURNAL

Getting to the Basics of Annual Reports

One of the best resources that you as an investor can use to determine the soundness of an investment opportunity is a corporation's annual report. These reports, published every spring, are an excellent tool to use for learning about a company, its management, its past performance, and its goals. But you must always keep in mind while thumbing through these glossy publications that corporations use this medium to "toot their own horn." For some corporations, publishing an annual report is an exercise in public relations. The letter from the chairman of the board, the upbeat smiling faces of the employees, and the artistic layout and beautiful photographs are nice to look at, but it is the financial statements and footnotes that give the true picture of the financial health of a corporation. Understanding the items presented on those pages tucked away in the back of the report is the real key in determining if a company is making a profit. Once you know the basics of reading annual reports, you will be in a better position to evaluate all of your investment opportunities.

Before investing, experts recommend that you review and compare the annual reports a corporation has published over the last three years. Read the shareholders' letters to see if they met their goals each year. Are any areas of concern mentioned? Are the facts presented in a straightforward manner, or do you have to interpret their meaning? Learn to read between the lines in order to separate the hype from the truth. And watch for words like *except for, challenges,* and *contingencies.* Now, turn to the financial statements section of the report. This is where you will compare the corporation's financial position by noting changes in its current assets, current liabilities, inventories, total liabilities, and owners' equity. Information on the income statement will enable you to determine if the corporation earned a profit. Be sure to look at the amounts reported for sales, expenses, and profit or loss figures. And don't overlook the footnotes: they contain (and sometimes hide) important information. To help you discover how well the corporation is doing, calculate the following ratios (specific instructions on how to calculate each of these ratios are included at the end of this chapter):

- *Current ratio*—Measures a firm's ability to pay its current liabilities.

- *Debt-to-assets ratio*—Measures whether a company has too much debt.

- *Inventory turnover*—Measures how many times a firm sells its merchandise inventory during a twelve-month period.

- *Net profit margin*—Measures how effectively the firm is transforming sales into profits.

- *Earnings per share*—Measures the amount the firm earned for each share of stock owned by investors. For you, this may be the most important ratio of all!

statements can be obtained from their annual reports—if they are public corporations. Industry averages are published by reporting services such as The Dun & Bradstreet Corp. and Standard & Poor's, as well as by some industry trade associations.

Still another type of analysis involves computation of the financial ratios discussed in the next section.

■■ FINANCIAL RATIOS

LEARNING OBJECTIVE 7
Use financial ratios to reveal
how a business is doing.

financial ratio a number that
shows the relationship between
two elements of a firm's
financial statements

A **financial ratio** is a number that shows the relationship between two elements of a firm's financial statements. Many of these ratios can be examined, but only about a dozen or so have real meaning. Those that we discuss are generally grouped as profitability ratios, short-term financial ratios, activity ratios, and long-term debt ratios. The information required to form these ratios is found in the balance sheet and the income statement (or, in our examples, in Figures 17.2 and 17.3). Like the individual elements in the financial statements, these ratios can be compared with the firm's past ratios, with those of competitors, and with industry averages.

Profitability Ratios

A firm's net income after taxes indicates whether the firm is profitable. It does not, however, indicate how effectively the firm's resources are being used. For this latter purpose, three ratios can be computed.

net profit margin a financial
ratio that is calculated by
dividing net income after taxes
by net sales

Net Profit Margin   **Net profit margin** is a financial ratio that is calculated by dividing net income after taxes by net sales. For Northeast Art Supply,

$$\text{net profit margin} = \frac{\text{net income after taxes}}{\text{net sales}} = \frac{\$30,175}{\$451,000}$$
$$= 0.067, \text{ or } 6.7\%$$

The net profit margin indicates how effectively the firm is transforming sales into profits, and a higher net profit margin is better than a low one. Today, the average net profit margin for all business firms is between 4 and 5 percent. With a net profit margin of 6.7 percent, Northeast Art Supply is above average. A low net profit margin can be increased by reducing expenses, by increasing sales, or both.

return on equity a financial
ratio calculated by dividing net
income after taxes by owners'
equity

Return on Equity   **Return on equity,** sometimes called *return on investment*, is a financial ratio calculated by dividing net income after taxes by owners' equity. Again, for Northeast Art Supply,

$$\text{return on equity} = \frac{\text{net income after taxes}}{\text{owners' equity}} = \frac{\$30,175}{\$230,000}$$
$$= 0.13, \text{ or } 13\%$$

Return on equity indicates how much income is generated by each dollar of equity. Northeast is providing income of 13 cents per dollar invested in the business; the average for all businesses is between 12 and 15 cents. A higher return on equity is better than a low one, and the only practical way to increase return on equity is to increase net income after taxes. This means reducing expenses, increasing sales, or both.

earnings per share
a financial ratio that is
calculated by dividing net
income after taxes by the
number of shares of common
stock outstanding

Earnings per Share   From the point of view of stockholders, this is one of the most widely used indicators of a corporation's success. **Earnings per share** is calculated by dividing net income after taxes by the number of shares of common stock outstanding. For Northeast Art Supply,

$$\text{earnings per share} = \frac{\text{net income after taxes}}{\text{common-stock shares outstanding}} = \frac{\$30,175}{10,000}$$

$$= \$3.02 \text{ per share}$$

Earnings per share is, obviously, a measure of the amount earned (after taxes) per share of common stock owned by investors. There is no meaningful average for this measure, mainly because the number of outstanding shares of a firm's stock is subject to change via stock splits and stock dividends. As a general rule, however, an increase in earnings per share is a healthy sign for any corporation. For the stockholder, such an increase may mean that common-stock dividends will also be increased and that the market value for a share of stock may increase.

Short-Term Financial Ratios

Two short-term financial ratios permit managers (and lenders) to evaluate the ability of a firm to pay its current liabilities. Before we discuss these ratios, we should examine one other easily determined measure: working capital. Although it is not a ratio, it is an important indicator of a firm's ability to pay its short-term debts.

working capital the difference between current assets and current liabilities

Working Capital   **Working capital** is the difference between current assets and current liabilities. It indicates how much money would remain if a firm paid off all current liabilities with cash and other current assets. For Northeast Art Supply,

$$\textbf{current assets} - \textbf{current liabilities} = \textbf{working capital}$$
$$\$182,000 \quad - \quad \$70,000 \quad = \quad \$112,000$$

The "proper" amount of working capital depends on the type of firm, its past experience, and its particular industry. A firm with too little working capital may have to borrow money to finance its operations. A firm with too much—that is, more working capital than it needs to operate smoothly—may be able to invest excess working capital to earn interest over a short period of time.

current ratio a financial ratio that is computed by dividing current assets by current liabilities

Current Ratio   A firm's **current ratio** is computed by dividing current assets by current liabilities. For Northeast Art Supply,

$$\textbf{current ratio} = \frac{\textbf{current assets}}{\textbf{current liabilities}} = \frac{\$182,000}{\$70,000} = 2.6$$

This means that Northeast Art Supply has $2.60 of current assets for every $1 of current liabilities. The average current ratio for all industries is 2.0, but it varies greatly from industry to industry. Each firm should compare its current ratio with those of its own industry to determine whether it is high or low. A high current ratio indicates that a firm can pay its current liabilities. A low current ratio can be improved by repaying current liabilities, by converting current liabilities to long-term liabilities, or by increasing the firm's cash balance by reducing dividend payments.

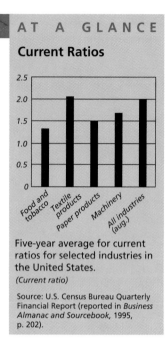

Current Ratios

Five-year average for current ratios for selected industries in the United States.
(Current ratio)

Source: U.S. Census Bureau Quarterly Financial Report (reported in *Business Almanac and Sourcebook*, 1995, p. 202).

acid-test ratio a financial ratio that is calculated by subtracting the value of inventory from the current asset amount and dividing the total by current liabilities

accounts receivable turnover a financial ratio that is calculated by dividing net sales by accounts receivable

inventory turnover a financial ratio that is calculated by dividing the cost of goods sold in one year by the average value of the inventory

Acid-Test Ratio   This ratio, sometimes called the *quick ratio,* is a measure of the firm's ability to pay current liabilities quickly—with its cash, marketable securities, and receivables. The **acid-test ratio** is calculated by subtracting the value of inventory from the current asset amount and dividing the total by current liabilities. It is similar to the current ratio, except that the value of the firm's inventory does not enter into the calculation. The value of inventory is "removed" from current assets because merchandise inventory is not converted into cash as easily as other current assets. For Northeast Art Supply,

$$\text{acid-test ratio} = \frac{\text{current assets} - \text{inventory}}{\text{current liabilities}}$$

$$= \frac{\$182,000 - \$41,000}{\$70,000} = \frac{\$141,000}{\$70,000} = 2.01$$

For all businesses, the desired acid-test ratio is 1.0. Northeast Art Supply is above average with a ratio of 2.01, and the firm should be well able to pay its current liabilities. To increase a low ratio, a firm would have to repay current liabilities, obtain additional cash from investors, or convert current liabilities to long-term debt.

Activity Ratios

Two activity ratios permit managers to measure how many times per year a company collects its accounts receivable or sells its inventory. Both activity ratios are described below.

Accounts Receivable Turnover   A firm's **accounts receivable turnover** is the number of times the firm collects its accounts receivable in one year. If the data are available, this ratio should be calculated using a firm's net credit sales. Since data for Northeast Art Supply's credit sales are unavailable, this ratio can be calculated by dividing net sales by accounts receivable. Then,

$$\text{accounts receivable turnover} = \frac{\text{net sales}}{\text{accounts receivable}} = \frac{\$451,000}{\$38,000}$$

$$= 11.9 \text{ times each year}$$

Northeast Art Supply collects its accounts receivable 11.9 times each year, or about every thirty days. If a firm's credit terms call for credit customers to pay up in twenty-five days, a collection period of thirty days is considered acceptable. There is no meaningful average for this measure, mainly because credit terms differ among companies. A high accounts receivable turnover is better than a low one. As a general rule, a low accounts receivable turnover ratio can be improved by pressing for payment of past-due accounts and by tightening requirements for prospective credit customers.

Inventory Turnover   A firm's **inventory turnover** is the number of times the firm sells and replaces its merchandise inventory in one year. It is approximated by dividing the cost of goods sold in one year by the average value of the inventory.

The average value of the inventory can be found by adding the beginning and ending inventory values (as given on the income statement) and dividing the sum by 2. For Northeast Art Supply, this comes out to $40,500. Then,

$$\textbf{inventory turnover} = \frac{\textbf{cost of goods sold}}{\textbf{average inventory}} = \frac{\$334,000}{\$40,500}$$

$$= 8.2 \text{ times each year}$$

Northeast Art Supply sells and replaces its merchandise inventory 8.2 times each year, or about once every month and a half.

The higher a firm's inventory turnover, the more effectively it is using the money invested in inventory. The average inventory turnover for all firms is about 9 times per year, but turnover rates vary widely from industry to industry. For example, supermarkets may have turnover rates of 20 or higher, whereas turnover rates for furniture stores are generally well below the national average. The quickest way to improve inventory turnover is to order merchandise in smaller quantities at more frequent intervals.

Long-Term Debt Ratios

Two financial ratios are of particular interest to lenders of long-term funds. They indicate the degree to which a firm's operations are financed through borrowing.

debt-to-assets ratio
a financial ratio that is calculated by dividing total liabilities by total assets

Debt-to-Assets Ratio   The **debt-to-assets ratio** is calculated by dividing total liabilities by total assets. It indicates the extent to which the firm's borrowing is backed by its assets. For Northeast Art Supply,

$$\textbf{debt-to-assets ratio} = \frac{\textbf{total liabilities}}{\textbf{total assets}} = \frac{\$110,000}{\$340,000} = 0.32, \text{ or } 32\%$$

Northeast's debt-to-assets ratio of 32 percent means that slightly less than one-third of its assets are financed by creditors. For all businesses, the average debt-to-assets ratio is 33 percent.

Most conservative managers try to keep the debt-to-assets ratio as low as possible. When this ratio is too high, a firm may have difficulty getting additional financing from lenders. Northeast has $3 in assets with which to repay each $1 of borrowing. A high debt-to-assets ratio can be reduced by restricting both short-term and long-term borrowing, by securing additional financing from stockholders, or by reducing dividend payments to stockholders.

debt-to-equity ratio
a financial ratio calculated by dividing total liabilities by owners' equity

Debt-to-Equity Ratio   The **debt-to-equity ratio** is calculated by dividing total liabilities by owners' equity. It compares the amount of financing provided by creditors with the amount provided by owners. For Northeast Art Supply,

$$\textbf{debt-to-equity ratio} = \frac{\textbf{total liabilities}}{\textbf{owners' equity}} = \frac{\$110,000}{\$230,000} = 0.48\%, \text{ or } 48\%$$

A debt-to-equity ratio of 48 percent means that creditors have provided about 48 cents of financing for every dollar provided by owners.

The debt-to-equity ratio for business in general ranges between 33 and 50 percent. The higher this ratio, the riskier the situation is for lenders. And like a high debt-to-assets ratio, a high debt-to-equity ratio may make borrowing additional money from lenders difficult. A high debt-to-equity ratio can be reduced by paying off debts or by increasing the owners' investment in the firm.

Northeast's Financial Ratios: A Summary

The formulas we used to analyze Northeast Art Supply's financial statements are listed in Table 17.3 along with the ratios we calculated. Northeast seems to be in good financial shape. Its net profit margin, current ratio, and acid-test ratio are all above average. Its other ratios are about average, although its inventory turnover could be improved. To do so, Northeast might consider ordering smaller quantities of merchandise at shorter intervals. Of course, the resulting decrease in inventory holding costs would have to be balanced against increased ordering costs and the possible cost of stock-outs.

TABLE 17.3   Summary of Financial Ratios for Northeast Art Supply

Ratio	Formula	Northeast Art Supply	Overall Business Average	Direction for Improvement
Profitability Ratios				
Net profit margin	$\dfrac{\text{net income after taxes}}{\text{net sales}}$	6.7%	4%–5%	Higher
Return on equity	$\dfrac{\text{net income after taxes}}{\text{owners' equity}}$	13%	12%–15%	Higher
Earnings per share	$\dfrac{\text{net income after taxes}}{\text{common-stock shares outstanding}}$	$3.02 per share	—	Higher
Short-Term Financial Ratios				
Working capital	current assets less current liabilities	$112,000	—	Higher
Current ratio	$\dfrac{\text{current assets}}{\text{current liabilities}}$	2.6	2.0	Higher
Acid-test ratio	$\dfrac{\text{current assets} - \text{inventory}}{\text{current liabilities}}$	2.01	1.0	Higher
Activity Ratios				
Accounts receivable turnover	$\dfrac{\text{net sales}}{\text{accounts receivable}}$	11.9	—	Higher
Inventory turnover	$\dfrac{\text{cost of goods sold}}{\text{average inventory}}$	8.2	9	Higher
Long-Term Debt Ratios				
Debt-to-assets ratio	$\dfrac{\text{total liabilities}}{\text{total assets}}$	32%	33%	Lower
Debt-to-equity ratio	$\dfrac{\text{total liabilities}}{\text{owners' equity}}$	48%	33%–50%	Lower

This chapter ends our discussion of accounting information. In Chapter 18, we begin our examination of business finances by discussing money, banking, and credit.

■ ■ ■ ■ CHAPTER REVIEW

Summary

1   Explain what accounting is and what accountants do.

Accounting is the process of systematically collecting, analyzing, and reporting financial information. A private accountant is employed by a specific organization to operate its accounting system. A public accountant performs these functions for various individuals or firms on a professional fee basis. Accounting information is used primarily by management, but it is also demanded by creditors, suppliers, stockholders, and government agencies.

2   Discuss the accounting equation and the concept of double-entry bookkeeping.

The accounting process is based on the accounting equation: *assets = liabilities + owners' equity*. Double-entry bookkeeping ensures that the balance shown by the accounting equation is maintained. The accounting process involves five steps: (a) Source documents are analyzed. (b) Each transaction is recorded in a journal. (c) Each journal entry is posted in the appropriate general ledger accounts. (d) At the end of each accounting period, a trial balance is prepared to make sure that the accounting equation is in balance. (e) Financial statements are prepared from the trial balance. Once statements are prepared, the books are closed. A new accounting cycle is then begun for the next accounting period.

3   Read and interpret a balance sheet.

A balance sheet is a summary of a firm's assets, liabilities, and owners' equity accounts at a particular time. This statement must demonstrate that the accounting equation is in balance. On the balance sheet, assets are categorized as current, fixed, or intangible. Similarly, liabilities can be divided into current liabilities and long-term liabilities. For a sole proprietorship or partnership, owners' equity is reported by each owner's name in the last section of the balance sheet. For a corporation, the values of common stock, preferred stock, and retained earnings are reported in the owners' equity section.

4   Read and interpret an income statement.

An income statement is a summary of a firm's financial operations during a specified accounting period. On the income statement, the company's gross profit on sales is computed by subtracting the cost of goods sold from net sales. Operating expenses are then deducted to compute net income from operations. Finally, nonoperating expenses and income taxes are deducted to obtain the firm's net income after taxes.

5   Describe business activities that affect a firm's cash flow.

Since 1987, the Securities and Exchange Commission (SEC) and the Financial Accounting Standards Board (FASB) have required all publicly traded companies to include a statement of cash flows in their annual report. This statement illustrates the effect on cash of the operating, investing, and financing activities of a company for an accounting period. The cash flow statement, along with the balance sheet and income statement, illustrate such variables as the results of past decisions and the business's ability to pay debts and dividends and to finance new growth.

6   Summarize why managers, lenders, and investors compare present financial statements with those prepared for past accounting periods.

The information contained in a firm's financial statements becomes more meaningful when it is compared with corresponding information for previous years, for competitors, and for the industry in which the firm operates. Such comparisons permit managers and other interested people to (a) pick out trends in growth, borrowing, income, and other business variables and (b) determine whether the firm is on the way to accomplishing its long-term goals. Comparisons are possible as long as accountants follow the basic rules of accounting, often referred to as *generally accepted accounting principles (GAAP)*.

7   Use financial ratios to reveal how a business is doing.

A number of financial ratios can be computed from the information contained on a firm's balance sheet and income statement. These ratios provide a picture of the firm's profitability, its short-term financial position, its activity in the area of accounts receivable and inventory, and its long-term debt financing. Like the information on the firm's financial statements, the ratios can and should be compared with those of past accounting periods, those of competitors, and those representing the average of the industry as a whole.

Key Terms

You should now be able to define and give an example relevant to each of the following terms:

accounting (534)

private (or nonpublic) accountant (534)

public accountant (535)

certified public accountant (CPA) (535)

assets (539)

liabilities (539)

owners' equity (539)

accounting equation (539)

revenues (539)

expenses (539)

double-entry bookkeeping (539)

general journal (541)

general ledger (542)

posting (542)

trial balance (542)

balance sheet (or statement of financial position) (542)

liquidity (542)

current assets (542)

prepaid expenses (544)

fixed assets (544)

depreciation (544)

intangible assets (546)

goodwill (546)

current liabilities (546)

accounts payable (546)

notes payable (546)

long-term liabilities (546)

income statement (547)

gross sales (547)

net sales (547)

cost of goods sold (547)

gross profit on sales (549)

operating expenses (549)

selling expenses (549)

net income (550)

statement of cash flows (550)

financial ratio (554)

net profit margin (554)

return on equity (554)

earnings per share (554)

working capital (555)

current ratio (555)

acid-test ratio (556)

accounts receivable turnover (556)

inventory turnover (556)

debt-to-assets ratio (557)

debt-to-equity ratio (557)

Questions

Review Questions

1. What is the difference between a private accountant and a public accountant?
2. What are certified public accountants? What functions do they perform?
3. List four groups that use accounting information, and briefly explain why each group has an interest in this information.
4. State the accounting equation, and list two specific examples of each term in the equation.
5. How is double-entry bookkeeping related to the accounting equation? Briefly, how does it work?
6. Briefly describe the five steps of the accounting cycle, in order.
7. What is the principal difference between a balance sheet and an income statement?
8. How are current assets distinguished from fixed assets?
9. Why are fixed assets depreciated on a balance sheet?
10. Can a single debt (for example, a promissory note) be part current liability and part long-term liability? Explain.
11. Explain how a retailing firm would determine the cost of goods sold during an accounting period.
12. How does a firm determine its net income after taxes?
13. What is the purpose of a statement of cash flows?
14. Explain the calculation procedure for and the significance of each of the following ratios:
    a. One profitability ratio
    b. One short-term financial ratio
    c. One activity ratio
    d. One long-term debt ratio

Discussion Questions

1. Like IDB Communications, many firms can and do "adjust" their financial statements to increase profits. Is this type of adjustment fair to investors, creditors, and government officials who may be evaluating or monitoring a firm's finances?
2. According to Jeffrey Sudikoff, IDB's chairman and chief executive officer, the confrontation between Deloitte & Touche and IDB was just a misunderstanding. What do you think?
3. Bankers usually insist that prospective borrowers submit audited financial statements along with a loan application. Why should financial statements be audited by a CPA?
4. What can be said about a firm whose owners' equity is a negative amount? How could such a situation come about?
5. Do the balance sheet, the income statement, and the statement of cash flows contain all the information you might want as a potential lender or stockholder? What other information would you like to examine?
6. Why is it so important to compare a firm's current financial statements with those of previous years, those of competitors, and the average of all firms in the industry in which the firm operates?
7. Which do you think are the two or three most important financial ratios? Why?

Exercises

1. Table 17.4 lists the ledger account balances for the Green Thumb Garden Shop, which was started just one year ago. From the information in the table, prepare a balance sheet and an income statement for the business.

2. Using the financial statements you prepared in Exercise 1 and the material on ratio analysis presented in this chapter, evaluate the financial health of the Green Thumb Garden Shop. Based on your calculations, explain how the firm's finances could be improved.

VIDEO CASE 17.1

The Arthur Andersen Worldwide Organization

According to Lawrence A. Weinbach, chairman, managing partner, and CEO for the Arthur Andersen Worldwide Organization, "It isn't how big you are but how well you serve your clients' needs." With annual revenues of more than $6 billion, this philosophy has enabled Arthur Andersen to become the largest

TABLE 17.4   Account Balances for Green Thumb Garden Shop

Accounts	Amounts
Cash	$ 7,500
Accounts receivables	3,500
Inventory	20,000
Equipment	15,000
Accumulated depreciation	2,000
Accounts payable	11,000
Long-term debt—equipment	10,000
Owners' equity	23,000
Sales	48,000
Cost of goods sold	23,000
Sales salaries expense	8,500
Advertising expense	1,500
Depreciation expense	2,000
Rent expense	6,000
Utilities expense	1,500
Insurance expense	1,000
Miscellaneous expense	500
Income taxes	600

accounting firm in the world. And although this philosophy certainly applies to all businesses, it is especially apt for an accounting firm. The basic product an accounting firm sells is information—information that must meet clients' needs.

Arthur Andersen may be the largest and one of the most respected accounting firms today, but it started small. Back in 1913, Arthur Andersen and Clarence Delany formed the public accounting firm, Andersen, Delany, and Company. Five years later, Delany left the firm and the name was changed to Arthur Andersen & Company. Although the new firm had little financial backing and few initial customers, Andersen had a vision. Orphaned at age sixteen and often described as a workaholic with a severe work ethic, Andersen wanted to create a different kind of accounting firm. Believing that accounting firms in the future would have to do more than just accounting work, he began a program that would eventually revolutionize the industry. For starters, he insisted on a business-oriented approach to auditing and focused heavily on consulting services. He also hired full-time, year-round staff personnel and created a system for recruiting college graduates. He adopted a five-day work week and paid for overtime work. And finally, he created a training regimen for all employees and established a program to build competence in specific industries. This willingness to innovate in an industry that most consider staid and unchanging has provided Arthur Andersen & Company with a firm foundation for more than eighty years.

Today, Arthur Andersen derives about 40 percent of its revenues from its U.S. operations, but attracting new business in North America has never been more difficult. As a result of burgeoning corporate mergers, the number of companies needing auditing has diminished. To keep current U.S. clients or attract new ones, most accounting firms have had to cut their fees. In response, Arthur Andersen is focusing on increasing the value of its services to clients and is initiating a wide range of financial consulting services, which are generating revenue growth.

At the same time, Arthur Andersen is continuing to concentrate on restructuring its global operations. First, the firm consolidated its worldwide operations into three geographic areas: Europe, India, Africa, and the Middle East; Asia Pacific; and the Americas. Then, Arthur Andersen realigned its services along distinct business lines reflecting the diverse client needs in the global marketplace. Two business units were established: Arthur Andersen, which provides audit, tax, and financial consulting services; and Andersen Consulting, which provides information technology and computer consulting services for firms around the globe.

As a result of increasing the value of the services that it provides to customers and restructuring its global operations, the Arthur Andersen Worldwide Organization is now in an excellent position to maintain its number 1 position well beyond the year 2000. And although many Arthur Andersen employees would argue that Andersen's 1913 vision of creating a different kind of company has already been fulfilled, that vision is in reality a continuing goal—one that will be around for years to come.[2]

Questions

1. According to Lawrence Weinbach, CEO for Arthur Andersen, an accounting firm must meet its clients' needs. How can Arthur Andersen or any accounting firm achieve this goal?
2. In your own words, describe what Arthur Andersen is doing to retain its number 1 ranking among accounting firms.

CASE 17.2

Financial News for Procter & Gamble

The Procter & Gamble Co. is one of the world's leading producers of packaged consumer goods. The company manufactures laundry and cleaning products, personal care products, food and beverage products, and pulp and chemicals. Based in Cincinnati, Ohio, the company markets its products in more than 140 countries around the world. For the fiscal year ended June 30, 1994, net sales were over $30 billion; net earnings after taxes were $2.2 billion.

The following are Procter & Gamble's consolidated (summarized) balance sheet and consolidated statement of earnings.[3]

Consolidated Balance Sheet

June 30 (Millions of Dollars)	1994

Assets

Current Assets	
Cash and cash equivalents	$ 2,373
Marketable securities	283
Accounts receivable	3,115
Inventories	2,877
Deferred income taxes	716
Prepaid expenses and other current assets	624
	9,988
Property, Plant, and Equipment	10,024
Goodwill and Other Intangible Assets	3,754
Other Assets	1,769
Total	$25,535

Liabilities and Shareholders' Equity

Current Liabilities	
Accounts payable—trade	$ 2,604
Accounts payable—other	660
Accrued liabilities	2,961
Taxes payable	440
Debt due within one year	1,375
	8,040
Long-Term Debt	4,980
Other Liabilities	3,336
Deferred Income Taxes	347
	16,703
Shareholders' Equity	
Convertible Class A preferred stock	1,942
Common stock—shares outstanding:	
1994—684,348,359	684
Additional paid-in capital	560
Currency translation adjustments	(63)
Reserve for employee stock ownership plan debt retirement	(1,787)
Retained earnings	7,496
	8,832
Total	$25,535

Consolidated Statement of Earnings

Year Ended June 30	1994
(Millions of Dollars Except Per Share Amounts)	
Net Sales	$30,296
Cost of products sold	17,355
Marketing, administrative, and other operating expenses	9,361
Provision for restructuring	—
Operating Income	3,580
Interest expense	482
Other income/expense, net	248
Earnings Before Income Taxes & Prior Years' Effect of Accounting Changes	3,346
Income taxes	1,135
Net Earnings Before Prior Years' Effect of Accounting Changes	2,211
Prior years' effect of accounting changes	—
Net Earnings	$ 2,211

Questions

1. Using the financial information provided in this case, calculate the following ratios for Procter & Gamble:
   a. Current ratio
   b. Acid-test ratio
   c. Net profit margin
   d. Return on equity
2. Based on your analysis of available information, how would you describe Procter & Gamble's current financial condition? What actions, if any, would you consider taking to improve it? Explain your recommendations.

CAREER PROFILE ■ ■ ■ ■ ■ ■ ■ ■ ■ ■ ■ ■

PART 5   Career Opportunities in Information, Computers, and Accounting

Job Title	Job Description	Salary Range
Accountant—corporate	Analyzes source documents and journalizes accounting entries for a private business; posts journal entries to ledger accounts; prepares a trial balance and financial statements for each accounting period; and closes the accounting books at the end of each accounting period	3–4
Accountant—private practice	Provides accounting services to businesses and individuals for a fee; offers accounting, auditing services, and help with taxes; consults with business owners and individuals on accounting and financial matters	4–5
Bookkeeper	Works for either a private business or accounting firm; talks with clients; uses computerized accounting systems to process daily accounting entries; posts journal entries to ledger accounts; prepares a trial balance at the end of the accounting period	1–2
Computer application engineer	Designs either hardware or software applications to perform a specific task; tests and debugs computer applications to ensure that programs or equipment do what they are supposed to do; communicates with other engineers, marketing personnel, and others involved in product development	3–4
Computer operator	Uses available software programs to process data into information; prepares reports based on original source documents; communicates with managers and other personnel who need processed information	1–2
Computer—repair technician	Provides repair service on either an in-house basis or for customers on a fee basis; analyzes and diagnoses problems with computer equipment; performs necessary repairs; completes accuracy checks to ensure equipment is correctly repaired	2–3
Computer—systems analyst	Serves as a communication link between managers and programmers; identifies needs that can be served by computers; develops computer applications that help managers achieve goals; determines hardware and software needs	4–5
Financial controller	Establishes company-wide financial and administrative goals and objectives; works with the company's stockholders; communicates the company's position on financial matters to all interested parties; approves the firm's annual operating budget; invests the company's excess funds in order to maintain the safety factor while maximizing financial return	3–5
Sales person—computer software or hardware	Analyzes customer needs; makes sales presentation to potential buyers; demonstrates hardware, software, or both; answers questions and overcomes objections; provides follow-up service after the sale	2–4

564

The figure in the salary column approximates the expected annual income after two or three years of service.
1 = $12,000–$15,000; 2 = $16,000–$20,000; 3 = $21,000–$27,000; 4 = $28,000–$35,000; 5 = $36,000 and up.

Educational Requirements	Skills Required	Prospects for Growth
Bachelor's degree in accounting; master's degree preferred	Computer; problem solving; quantitative; conceptual; critical thinking	Greatest
Bachelor's degree; state exam for Certified Public Accountant status; master's degree helpful	Computer; problem solving; quanitative; conceptual; critical thinking	Average
High school diploma; some college preferred	Computer; problem solving; quantitative	Limited
Bachelor's degree in business and computer science	Computer; problem solving; technical; conceptual; critical thinking	Average
Two years of college in data processing; on-the-job experience	Interpersonal; computer; problem solving; quantitative; technical; communication	Greatest
High school diploma; technical training required; on-the-job experience	Interpersonal; communication; problem solving; technical	Greatest
College degree; master's degree preferred; on-the-job experience	Computer; communication; problem solving; technical; conceptual; critical thinking	Above average
College degree in finance or accounting; master's degree helpful; on-the-job experience	Leadership; decision making; interpersonal; quantitative; computer; conceptual	Limited
Some college; degree helpful	Communication; computer interpersonal; technical; conceptual	Average

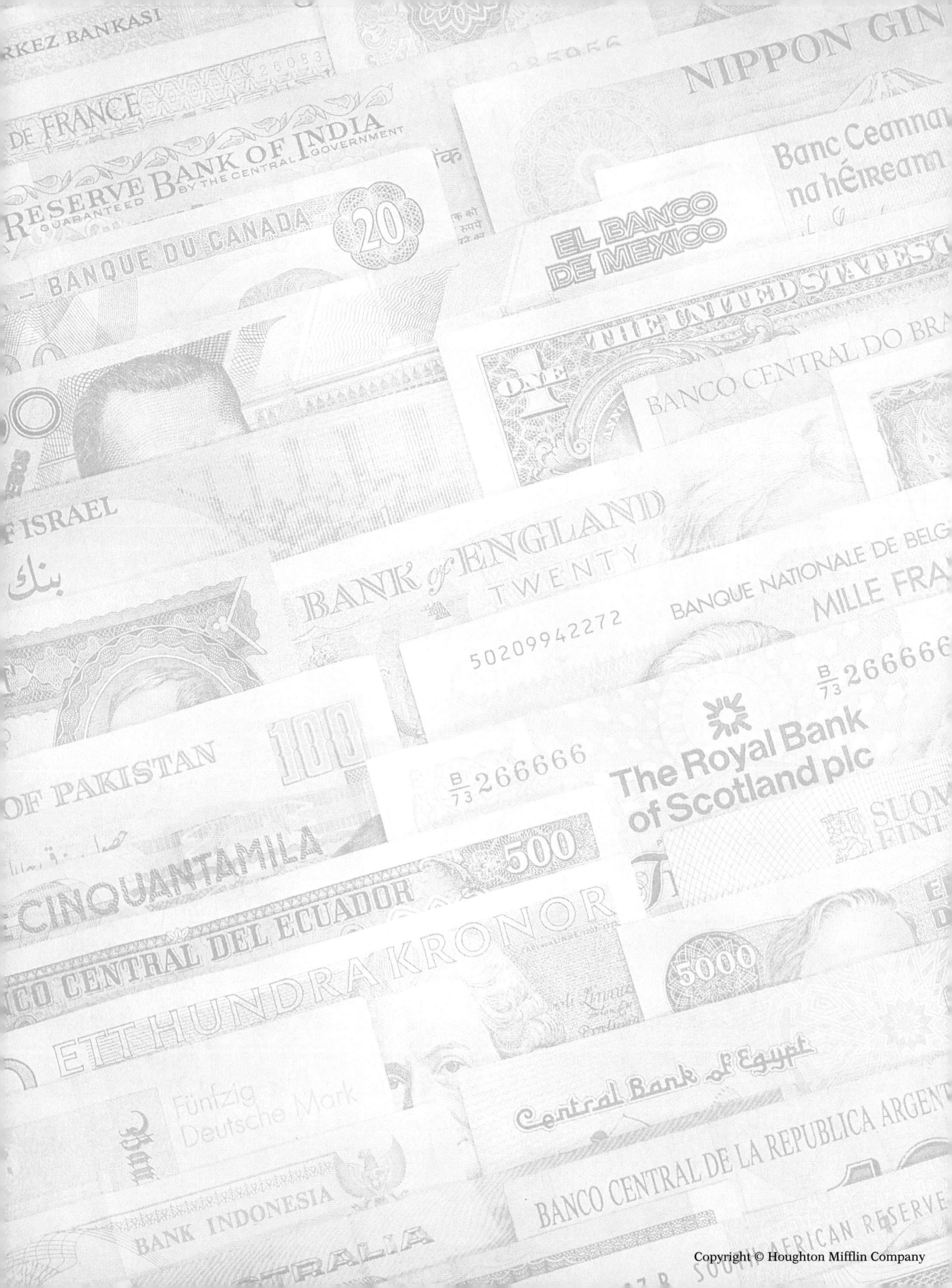

■■■■■ PART SIX

Finance and Investment

In this part, we are concerned with still another business resource—money. First we discuss the functions of money and the financial institutions that are part of the U.S. banking system. Then we examine the concept of financial management and investing, for both firms and individuals. Finally, we explore the means by which some types of financial losses can be minimized through insurance. Included in this part are

CHAPTER 18 Money, Banking, and Credit
CHAPTER 19 Financial Management
CHAPTER 20 Securities Markets and Investments
CHAPTER 21 Risk Management and Insurance

■ ■ ■ ■ **CHAPTER 18**

Money, Banking, and Credit

CHAPTER PREVIEW

In this chapter we take a good look at money and the financial institutions that create and handle it. We begin by outlining the purposes of money and the characteristics of money that make it an acceptable means of payment for products, services, and resources. Then we turn our attention to the banking industry—commercial banks, savings and loan associations, credit unions, and other institutions that offer financial services. Next we consider the role of the Federal Reserve System in maintaining a healthy economy. We also describe the safeguards established by the federal government to protect depositors against losses. In closing, we examine credit transactions, sources of credit information, and effective collection procedures.

NationsBank—A Financial Giant

NationsBank Corporation, with its 1,900 branches in nine states and the District of Columbia, is the third-largest bank in the United States. This banking giant began in 1988 when Hugh L. McColl, Jr., chairman of a small regional bank in Charlotte, North Carolina, submitted the successful bid at the FDIC's auction of the failed First Republic Bank, the largest bank in Texas. Since then McColl has not only acquired dozens of other failing banks, but he has also diversified NationsBank's holdings by merging with financial institutions that fall outside traditional banking functions. These mergers have allowed his branches to expand their product lines and the services they market to their customers and, in turn, have generated tremendous earnings for the corporation.

NationsBank is organized into three distinct businesses. Its original function as a commercial bank offers all the traditional bank products and services—savings and checking accounts, mortgage loans, automobile loans, credit cards, trust services, safe-deposit boxes, and so on. Over 7.6 million Americans use these services through NationsBank branches. Second is the institutional group, which provides corporate customers various products and services, markets mutual funds and bonds, and participates in the global-trading marketplace. And last, NationsBank operates NationsCredit, a consumer finance subsidiary, and Nations Financial Capital Corporation, a commercial finance subsidiary. These two operating units enable NationsBank to compete with companies in the financial world that are not regulated under government guidelines and thus to further diversify income sources.

The goal of Hugh J. McColl, Jr., is for NationsBank to provide products and services for its customers in a fast, dependable manner and at rates

both affordable and competitive in the marketplace. And he continues to look for other companies to add to this financial giant that has changed the face of the American banking industry. However, this phenomenal growth has not come without criticism from both inside and outside the banking community. McColl is known as an insider in Washington because of his friendship with President Clinton and his other political connections. His company contributed generously to congressional candidates and lobbyists in order to gain support for the passage of an interstate banking law. This 1994 legislation supersedes states' rights to place restrictions that protect their lending institutions from takeovers by larger banks. And McColl has antagonized stockholders and competitors alike because of questionable business dealings. NationsBank is currently under investigation for charges of unethical practices in persuading customers to buy into its bank-managed mutual funds. Furthermore, some corporations have claimed bank representatives use "tying" agreements, an illegal procedure that involves granting bank services dependent upon a customer's acquiring another service the bank offers.[1]

■ ■ ■ ■

569

■ ■ ■ ■ ■ ■ ■ ■ ■ ■ ■

In Chapter 1, a business was defined as the organized effort of individuals to produce and sell for a profit the goods and services that satisfy society's needs. NationsBank—the business profiled in Inside Business—fulfills the last part of this definition by providing financial products and services to its customers. And because NationsBank offers quality products and services that customers want, this North Carolina–based bank is expanding in a period when other financial institutions are barely able to stay afloat.

Most people regard a bank or similar financial institution as a place to deposit or borrow money. In return for depositing their money, they *receive* interest; when individuals borrow money, they must *pay* interest. They may borrow to buy a home, a car, or some other high-cost item. In this case, the resource that will be transformed into money to repay the loan is the individual's labor.

Businesses also transform resources into money. A business firm (even a new one) may have a valuable asset in the form of a product idea. If the firm (or its founder) has a good credit history and the idea is a good one, a bank will probably lend it the money to develop, produce, and market the product. The loan—with interest—will be repaid out of future sales revenue. In this way, both the firm and the bank will earn a reasonable profit.

In each of these situations, the borrower needs the money now and will have the ability to repay it later. But also, in each situation, the money will be used to *purchase something* and will be repaid through the use of *resources*.

■ ■ WHAT IS MONEY?

barter system a system of exchange in which goods or services are traded directly for other goods or services

The members of some remote societies exchange goods and services through barter, without using money. A **barter system** is a system of exchange in which goods or services are traded directly for other goods or services. One family may raise vegetables and herbs on a plot of land, and another may weave cloth. To obtain food, the family of weavers trades cloth for vegetables, provided that the farming family is in need of cloth.

The trouble with the barter system is that the two parties in an exchange must need each other's products at the same time, and the two products must be roughly equal in value. So even very isolated societies soon develop some sort of money to eliminate the inconvenience of trading by barter.

money anything used by a society to purchase products, services, or resources

Money is anything used by a society to purchase products, services, or resources. The members of the society receive money for their products or resources. Then they either hold that money or use it to purchase other products or resources. Different groups of people have used all sorts of objects as money—whales' teeth, stones, beads, copper crosses, clam shells, and gold and silver, for example. Today, the most commonly used objects are metal coins and paper bills, which together are called *currency*.

570

Sheets of pesos. Although you may not recognize the paper currency used in Argentina, the people who live there do. This currency inspector probably appreciates more than do most people the necessary attributes of currency. The pesos in these sheets must be durable, easily portable, and difficult to counterfeit.

The Functions of Money

LEARNING OBJECTIVE 1
Identify the functions and important characteristics of money.

medium of exchange
anything that is accepted as payment for products, services, and resources

measure of value   a single standard or "yardstick" that is used to assign values to, and compare the values of, products, services, and resources

We have already noted that money aids in the exchange of goods and services for resources. But that is a rather general (and somewhat theoretical) way of stating money's function. Let's look instead at three *specific* functions of money in any society.

Serves as a Medium of Exchange   A **medium of exchange** is anything that is accepted as payment for products, services, and resources. This definition looks very much like the definition of money. It is meant to, because the primary function of money is to serve as a medium of exchange. The key word here is *accepted*. As long as the owners of products, services, and resources accept money in an exchange, it is performing this function. Of course, these owners accept it because they know it is acceptable to the owners of other products, services, and resources, which *they* may wish to purchase. For example, the family in our earlier example can sell their vegetables and use the money to purchase cloth from the weavers. This eliminates the problems associated with the barter system.

Serves as a Measure of Value   A **measure of value** is a single standard or "yardstick" that is used to assign values to, and compare the values of, products, services, and resources. Money serves as a measure of value because the prices of all products, services, and resources are stated in terms of money. It is thus the "common denominator" we use to compare products and decide which we will buy. Imagine the difficulty you would have in deciding whether you could afford new shoes if they were priced in terms of yards of cloth or pounds of vegetables—especially if your employer happened to pay you in toothbrushes.

Represents a Store of Value   Money received by an individual or firm need not be used immediately. It may be held and spent later. Hence money serves as a **store of value,** or a means for retaining and accumulating wealth. This function of money comes into play whenever we hold on to money—in a pocket, a cookie jar, a savings account, or whatever.

Value that is stored as money is affected by *inflation.* As prices go up in an inflationary period, money loses value. Suppose you can buy a Sony stereo system for $1,000. Your $1,000 has a value equal to the value of that stereo system. But let us suppose that you wait a while and don't buy the stereo immediately. If the price goes up to $1,100 in the meantime because of inflation, you can no longer buy the stereo with your $1,000. Your money has *lost* value because it is now worth less than the stereo. To determine the effect of inflation on purchasing power, economists often refer to a consumer price index like the one illustrated in Figure 18.1.

store of value   a means for retaining and accumulating wealth

FIGURE 18.1
The Consumer Price Index and the Purchasing Power of the Consumer Dollar (Base Period: 1982–1984 = 100)
Inflation causes a loss of money's stored value. As the consumer price index goes up, the purchasing power of the consumer's dollar goes down. *(Source:* Economic Report of the President, *United States Printing Office, Washington, D.C., 1993, p. 339, and* Monthly Labor Review, *July 1994, p. 98.)*

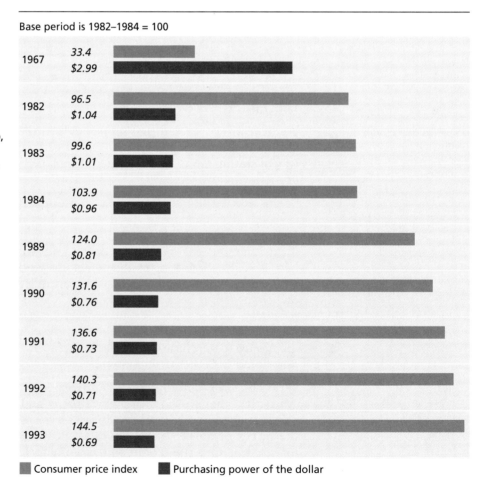

Base period is 1982–1984 = 100

Year	CPI	Purchasing power
1967	33.4	$2.99
1982	96.5	$1.04
1983	99.6	$1.01
1984	103.9	$0.96
1989	124.0	$0.81
1990	131.6	$0.76
1991	136.6	$0.73
1992	140.3	$0.71
1993	144.5	$0.69

■ Consumer price index   ■ Purchasing power of the dollar

Important Characteristics of Money

To be acceptable as a medium of exchange, money must be fairly easy to use, it must be trusted, and it must be capable of performing the three functions just mentioned. Together, these requirements give rise to five essential characteristics.

Divisibility   The standard unit of money must be divisible into smaller units to accommodate small purchases as well as large ones. In the United States, our standard is the dollar, and it is divided into pennies, nickels, dimes, quarters, and half-dollars. These coins allow us to make purchases of less than a dollar and of odd amounts greater than a dollar. Other nations have their own divisible currencies: the franc in France, the mark in Germany, and the yen in Japan, to mention a few.

Portability   Money must be small enough and light enough to be carried easily. For this reason, paper currency is issued in larger *denominations*— multiples of the standard dollar unit. Five-, ten-, twenty-, fifty-, and hundred-dollar bills make our money convenient for almost any purchase.

Stability   Money should retain its value over time. When it does not (during periods of high inflation), people tend to lose faith in their money. They may then turn to other means of storing value, such as gold and jewels, works of art, and real estate. In extreme cases, they may use such items as a medium of exchange as well. They may even resort to barter. During the recent upheavals in Eastern Europe, farmers have traded farm products for cigarettes because the value of cigarettes is more stable than each nation's money.

Durability   The objects that serve as money should be strong enough to last through reasonable usage. No one would appreciate (or use) dollar bills that disintegrated as they were handled or coins that melted in the sun. To increase the life expectancy of paper currency, most nations use special paper with a high fiber content.

Difficulty of Counterfeiting   If a nation's currency were easy to counterfeit—that is, to imitate or fake—its citizens would be uneasy about accepting it as payment. Even genuine currency would soon lose its value, because no one would want it. Thus countries do their best to ensure that it is very hard to reproduce their currency. Typically, countries use special paper and watermarks and print intricate designs on the currency to discourage counterfeiting.

The Supply of Money: M_1, M_2, and M_3

demand deposit   an amount that is on deposit in a checking account

How much money is there in the United States? Before we can answer that question, we need to define a couple of familiar concepts. A **demand deposit** is an amount that is on deposit in a checking account. It is called a *demand* deposit because it can be claimed immediately—on demand—by presenting a properly made-out check, withdrawing cash from an automated teller machine (ATM), or transferring money between accounts.

time deposit   an amount that
is on deposit in an interest-
bearing savings account

A **time deposit** is an amount that is on deposit in an interest-bearing savings account. Financial institutions generally permit immediate withdrawal of money from savings accounts. However, they can require written notice prior to withdrawal. The time between notice and withdrawal is what leads to the name *time* deposits. Time deposits are not immediately available to their owners, but they can be converted to cash easily. For this reason, they are called *near-monies*. Other near-monies include short-term government securities, government bonds, and the cash surrender values of insurance policies.

Now we can discuss the question of how much money there is in the United States. There are three main measures of the supply of money: M_1, M_2, and M_3.

The M_1 *supply of money* consists only of currency and demand deposits. (It is thus based on a narrow definition of money.) By law, currency must be accepted as payment for products, services, and resources. Checks are accepted as payment because they are convenient, convertible to cash, and generally safe.

The M_2 *supply of money* consists of M_1 (currency and demand deposits) plus certain specific securities and small-denomination time deposits of less than $100,000. Another common definition of money—M_3—consists of M_1 and M_2 plus large time deposits of $100,000 or more. The definitions of money that include the M_2 and M_3 supplies of money are based on the assumption that time deposits are easily converted to cash for spending. Figure 18.2 shows the elements of the M_1, M_2, and M_3 supplies. About 27 percent is coins, paper currency, and demand deposits; and the remaining 73 percent is time deposits and certain specific securities.

We have, then, at least three measures of the supply of money. (Actually, there are other measures as well, which may be broader or narrower than

FIGURE 18.2
The Supply of Money
Three measures of the money supply are M_1, which includes currency and demand deposits; M_2, which includes M_1 plus certain specific securities and small-denomination time deposits; and M_3, which includes M_1, M_2, plus time deposits of $100,000 or more. *(Source:* Federal Reserve Bulletin, *Oct. 1994, p. A14.)*

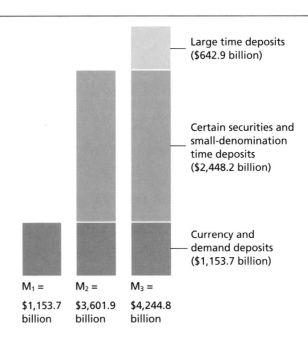

Large time deposits
($642.9 billion)

Certain securities and small-denomination time deposits
($2,448.2 billion)

Currency and demand deposits
($1,153.7 billion)

M_1 =

$1,153.7 billion

M_2 =

$3,601.9 billion

M_3 =

$4,244.8 billion

M_1, M_2, and M_3.) So the answer to our original question is that the amount of money in the United States depends very much on how we measure it. Generally, economists, politicians, and bankers tend to focus on M_1 or some variation of M_1.

We have seen that a very large part of the money that exists in this country is deposited in banks and other financial institutions. Let us now examine the banking industry.

■■ THE AMERICAN BANKING INDUSTRY

LEARNING OBJECTIVE 2
Describe the differences between commercial banks and other financial institutions in the banking industry.

Any banker you ask will tell you that—for the American banking industry—the first years of the 1990s have been exciting, to say the least. Competition among banks, savings and loan associations, credit unions, and other business firms that want to perform banking activities has never been greater. In addition, banks from Japan, Canada, France, and other foreign nations have thrown their hat into U.S. banking circles. As a result, major banks like Citicorp, BankAmerica, Chemical Bank, and J. P. Morgan & Company have begun to innovate and provide new services for their customers. Even smaller banks have adopted the full-service banking philosophy and compete aggressively for customers who expect more services than ever before.

Unfortunately, increased competition coupled with bad loans, fraud, and financial mismanagement has increased the number of banks, savings and loans associations, and credit unions that are in danger of failing. For the two-year period 1992–1993, more than 150 banks with approximately

For commercial banks, there's no such thing as national boundaries. Shown here is the lower-Manhattan branch office for the Banca Commerciale Italiana—just one of many foreign banks from Japan, Canada, France, Italy, and other foreign countries to throw their hat into U.S. banking circles.

$50 billion in assets went broke.[2] In addition to actual bank failures, the number of banks on the government's "problem list" has been hovering around 1,000 each year since 1991. Although no individual state is immune, most of the recent failures have occurred in either agricultural or oil-producing states. The New England states have also experienced a large number of closures since 1990.

The failure of any financial institution is an especially serious problem because of its effect on individuals, businesses, and other financial institutions. Yet, it is comforting to note three important facts. First, the majority of banks and financial institutions that perform banking functions are operating at a profit. Second, the government still provides deposit insurance to protect depositors. Finally, the current banking crisis is a strong reminder that, without a sound banking system, the nation and our economy would grind to a screeching halt.

Commercial Banks

commercial bank a profit-making organization that accepts deposits, makes loans, and provides related services to its customers

A **commercial bank** is a profit-making organization that accepts deposits, makes loans, and provides related services to its customers. Like other businesses, the bank's primary goal—its mission—is to earn a profit. Its input resource is money in the form of deposits, for which it pays interest. If the bank is successful, its income is greater than its expenses, and it will show a profit.

Because they deal with money belonging to individuals and other firms, banks are carefully regulated. They must also meet certain requirements before they are chartered, or granted permission to operate, by federal or state banking authorities. A **national bank** is a commercial bank that is chartered by the U.S. Comptroller of the Currency. There are approximately 3,600 national banks, accounting for about 53 percent of all bank deposits.[3] These banks must conform to federal banking regulations and are subject to unannounced inspections by federal auditors.

national bank a commercial bank that is chartered by the U.S. Comptroller of the Currency

state bank a commercial bank that is chartered by the banking authorities in the state in which it operates

A **state bank** is a commercial bank that is chartered by the banking authorities in the state in which it operates. State banks outnumber national banks by about two to one, but they tend to be smaller than national banks. They are subject to unannounced inspections by both state and federal auditors.

Table 18.1 lists the ten largest banks in the United States. All of these are classified as national banks.

Other Financial Institutions

In addition to commercial banks, at least seven other types of financial institutions perform either full or limited banking services for their customers. Included in this group are savings and loan associations, savings banks, credit unions, insurance companies, pension funds, brokerage firms, and finance companies.

savings and loan association (S&L) a financial institution that offers checking and savings accounts and certificates of deposit and that invests most of its assets in home-mortgage loans

Savings and Loan Associations and Savings Banks A **savings and loan association (S&L)** is a financial institution that offers checking and savings

TABLE 18.1   The Ten Largest U.S. Banks, Ranked by Total Assets

Rank	Commercial Bank	Assets (in billions)
1	Citicorp	$216.6
2	BankAmerica Corporation	186.9
3	NationsBank Corporation	157.7
4	Chemical Bank	149.9
5	J. P. Morgan & Company	133.9
6	The Chase Manhattan Bank	102.1
7	Bankers Trust New York Corp.	92.1
8	Banc One Corporation	79.9
9	First Union Corporation	70.8
10	PNC Bank Corporation	62.1

Source: Gary Hoover, ed., *Hoover's Handbook of American Business 1995.* Copyright © 1994. Published by The Reference Press, Inc., Austin, Texas, 800-486-8666.

accounts and certificates of deposit and that invests most of its assets in home-mortgage loans. Originally, S&Ls were permitted to offer their depositors *only* savings accounts. But since Congress passed the Depository Institutions Deregulation and Monetary Control Act, which became effective on January 1, 1981, they have been able to offer NOW accounts to attract depositors. A **NOW account** is an interest-bearing checking account. (*NOW* stands for Negotiable Order of Withdrawal.)

NOW account an interest-bearing checking account; *NOW* stands for Negotiable Order of Withdrawal

Today, there are approximately 2,000 savings and loan associations in the United States.[4] Federal associations are chartered under provisions of the Home Owners' Loan Act of 1933 and are supervised by the Office of Thrift Supervision, a branch of the U.S. Treasury. Savings and loan associations can also be chartered by state banking authorities in the state in which they operate. State-chartered S&Ls are subject to unannounced audits by state authorities.

During the 1980s, high interest rates, along with a reduced demand for homes, an increase in nonperforming loans and foreclosures, and fraud and corruption, led to record S&L failures. In fact, over 1,000 S&Ls failed during the 1980s and early 1990s. In this same period, U.S. taxpayers paid almost $120 billion to bail out failed S&Ls.[5] And the U.S. Congress expects to spend an additional $120 billion between now and 1998 to protect individuals and businesses that have deposited money in S&Ls that fail.[6] Experts still believe that the future of the industry will be determined by the ability of savings and loan associations to provide home mortgages and other financial services that their customers need.

savings bank a financial institution that offers many of the same services that are offered by savings and loan associations

In addition to savings and loan associations, approximately 400 savings banks operate primarily in the northeast section of the country.[7] **Savings banks** are financial institutions that offer many of the same services that are offered by savings and loan associations. They offer checking accounts, savings accounts, and certificates of deposit. And like S&Ls, they also fund home mortgages, commercial loans, and consumer loans. Savings banks are controlled by state banking authorities.

Credit Unions   Today, there are approximately 12,000 credit unions in the United States. A **credit union** is a financial institution that accepts deposits from, and lends money to, only those people who are its members. Usually the membership is composed of employees of a particular firm, people in a particular profession, or those who live in a community served by a local credit union. Some credit unions require that members purchase at least one share of ownership, at a cost of about $5 to $10. Credit unions generally pay higher interest on deposits than commercial banks and S&Ls, and they may provide loans at lower cost. Credit unions are regulated by the Federal Credit Union Administration.

Organizations That Perform Banking Functions   Four other types of financial institutions are involved in various banking activities. Though not actually banks, they offer customers limited bank services.

- *Insurance companies* provide long-term financing for office buildings, shopping centers, and other commercial real estate projects throughout the United States. The funds used for this type of financing are obtained from policyholders' insurance premiums.

- *Pension funds* are established by employers to guarantee their employees a regular monthly income on retirement. Contributions to the fund may come from the employer, the employee, or both. Pension funds earn additional income through generally conservative investments in certain corporate stocks, corporate bonds, and government securities, and through financing real estate developments.

- *Brokerage firms* offer combination savings and checking accounts that pay higher-than-usual interest rates (so-called money-market rates). Many people have switched to these accounts to get the higher rates. In the last few years, however, banks have instituted similar types of accounts, hoping to lure their depositors back.

- *Finance companies* provide financing to individuals and business firms that may not be able to get financing from banks, savings and loan associations, or credit unions. Lenders like Beneficial Finance or Household Finance provide short-term loans to individuals. Firms like Commercial Credit Corporation, Ford Motor Credit, GE Credit, and General Motors Acceptance Corporation provide debt financing to both individuals and business firms. Generally, the interest rates charged by these lenders are higher than the interest rates charged by other financial institutions.

■■ SERVICES PROVIDED BY FINANCIAL INSTITUTIONS

If it seems to you that banks and other financial institutions are competing for your business, you're right. Never before have so many different financial institutions offered such a tempting array of services to attract customers. The typical financial services provided by the banking industry are the following:

- Checking accounts
- Savings accounts
- Loans
- Credit cards
- Electronic transfer of funds
- Financial advice
- Payroll service
- Certified checks
- Trust services
- Safe-deposit boxes

The most important banking services for both individuals and businesses are described below.

Checking Accounts

check a written order for a bank or other financial institution to pay a stated dollar amount to the business or person indicated on the face of the check

Firms and individuals deposit money in checking accounts (demand deposits) so that they can write checks to pay for purchases. A **check** is a written order for a bank or other financial institution to pay a stated dollar amount to the business or person indicated on the face of the check. Today, most goods and services are paid for by check. Many financial institutions charge an activity fee (or service charge) for checking accounts. It is generally somewhere between $10 and $20 per month for individuals. For businesses, monthly charges are based on the average daily balance in the checking account and/or the number of checks written.

Today, most financial institutions offer interest-paying NOW accounts. With NOW accounts, the usual interest rate is between 2.5 and 4.5 percent. However, individual banks may impose certain restrictions on their NOW accounts, including the following:

- A minimum balance before any interest is paid
- Fees for accounts whose balances fall below a set minimum balance
- Restrictions on the number of checks that may be written each month

Some financial institutions offer Super NOW accounts. Super NOWs pay somewhat higher interest than NOW accounts and generally include unlimited check-writing privileges. But depositors may be required to maintain a higher minimum balance to avoid bank charges.

Savings Accounts

Savings accounts (time deposits) provide a safe place to store money and a very conservative means of investing. The usual *passbook savings account* earns between 3.5 and 5 percent in commercial banks and S&Ls, and slightly more in credit unions.

certificate of deposit (CD)   a document stating that the bank will pay the depositor a guaranteed interest rate for money left on deposit for a specified period of time

A depositor who is willing to leave money on deposit with a bank for a set period of time can earn a higher rate of interest. To do so, the depositor buys a certificate of deposit. A **certificate of deposit (CD)** is a document stating that the bank will pay the depositor a guaranteed interest rate for money left on deposit for a specified period of time. The interest rates paid on CDs change weekly; they once briefly exceeded 16 percent. Rates in the first part of the 1990s ranged from 3.5 to 6.5 percent. The rate always depends on how much is invested and for how long. Depositors are penalized for early withdrawal of funds invested in CDs.

Short- and Long-Term Loans

Commercial banks, savings and loan associations, credit unions, and other financial institutions provide short- and long-term loans to both individuals and businesses. *Short-term business loans* are those that are to be repaid within one year or less. For businesses, short-term loans are generally used to provide working capital that will be repaid with sales revenues. Typical uses for the money obtained through short-term loans include purchasing inventory, financing promotional needs, or meeting unexpected emergencies.

line of credit   a loan that is approved before the money is actually needed

To ensure that short-term money will be available when needed, many firms establish a line of credit. A **line of credit** is a loan that is approved before the money is actually needed. Because all the necessary paperwork is already completed and the loan is preapproved, the business can later obtain the money without delay, as soon as it is required. Even with a line of credit, a firm may not be able to borrow money if the bank does not have sufficient funds available. For this reason, some firms prefer a **revolving credit agreement,** which is a guaranteed line of credit.

revolving credit agreement   a guaranteed line of credit

Long-term business loans are loans that will be repaid over a period of years. In fact, the average length of a long-term business loan is generally three to seven years but sometimes as long as fifteen years. They are most often used to finance the expansion of facilities, replacement of equipment, or development of the firm's product mix.

collateral   real or personal property that is pledged as security for a loan

Most lenders require some type of collateral for long-term loans. **Collateral** is real or personal property (stocks, bonds, land, equipment, or any other asset of value) that is pledged as security for a loan. For example, when an individual obtains a loan to pay for a new Buick Riviera, the automobile is the collateral for the loan. If the borrower fails to repay the loan according to the terms specified in the loan agreement, the lender can repossess the car.

Repayment terms and interest rates for both short- and long-term loans are arranged between the lender and the borrower. For businesses, repayment terms may include monthly, quarterly, semiannual, or annual payments. Repayment terms (and interest rates) for personal loans vary, depending on how the money will be used and what type of collateral, if any, is pledged. Borrowers should always "shop" for a loan, comparing the repayment terms and interest rates offered by competing financial institutions.

Credit Card Transactions   "Charge it!" If those two words sound familiar, it is no wonder. Over 75 million Americans use credit cards to pay for every-

▶▶ **AT A GLANCE**

Loan Rates

Interest rates differ according to the type of loan and length of repayment period.
(Average annual percentage rate)

Source: HSH Associates, *Money*, Feb. 1995, p. 49.

■ ■ ■ ■ ETHICAL CHALLENGES

Do Banks Discriminate When Making Loans?

During the mid 1990s, the U.S. Justice Department initiated legal action against Connecticut-based Shawmut Mortgage Company and Maryland-based Chevy Chase Federal Savings Bank. In both cases, the Justice Department argued that the financial institutions were guilty of discriminating against minority borrowers. Lawyers for the Justice Department contended that the loan approval rates for African Americans and Hispanics for each bank were too low and should be higher. They also charged that the banks were guilty of red-lining—the practice of systematically eliminating entire neighborhoods because of racial makeup. As evidence of red-lining, the Justice Department argued that neither bank had sufficient branch offices in predominantly minority neighborhoods to service customers.

Both financial institutions denied any wrongdoing. They argued that loan approvals for any potential borrower are based not on race, but on sound business principles that include the borrower's credit record, employment history, income, and past payment history. Both banks also argue that at the time the lawsuit was filed,

each had special programs in place to encourage lending to minorities. Finally, the banks claimed that if they were subjecting minorities to higher standards, then the number of bad loans for minorities would be lower than the number of bad loans for whites. In fact, census data show that both groups have the same default rate as whites.

To avoid a lengthy court case, both Shawmut Mortgage Company and Chevy Chase Federal Savings Bank signed separate consent decrees designed to ensure that lending practices for both banks will not be biased against minorities in the future. In addition to signing the consent decree, Shawmut agreed to pay $1 million to people who had suffered mortgage discrimination. Shawmut also agreed to initiate special lending programs to attract loan applications from minority and low- and moderate-income individuals. Chevy Chase agreed to invest $11 million in the same neighborhoods that they were accused of discriminating against. Chevy Chase also agreed to make loans valued at $140 million at below-market interest rates to residents of those neighborhoods.

thing from tickets on American Airlines to Zenith computers. And the number of credit cardholders increases every month. In fact, most Americans receive at least two or three credit card applications in the mail every month. Why have credit cards become so popular?

For a merchant, the answer is obvious. By depositing charge slips in a bank or other financial institution, the merchant can convert credit card sales into cash. In return for processing the merchant's credit card transactions, the bank charges a fee that ranges between 1.5 and 5 percent. Actual bank fees are determined by the volume of credit card transactions, total dollar amount of credit sales, and how well the merchant can negotiate.

For the consumer, credit cards permit the purchase of goods and services even when funds are low. Today, most major credit cards are issued by

"There's gold in them there cards." "There's gold in them there hills" was a common saying in the wild west. And back in those days, gold ore could be used to purchase food, products, and services. Today, most consumers use *gold* credit cards issued by MasterCard or Visa to make the same type of purchases.

banks or other financial institutions in cooperation with Visa International or the Interbank Card Association, which issues MasterCard. The unique feature of bank credit cards is that they extend a line of credit to the cardholder, much as a bank's consumer loan department does. Thus, credit cards provide immediate access to short-term credit for the cardholder, who instructs the bank to pay the merchant immediately and reimburses the bank later. Refer to Business Journal for some helpful hints on using credit cards wisely. And see Video Case 18.1 on the Consumer Credit Counseling Service, an organization that provides help for individuals who "get in too deep."

Electronic Transfer of Funds

electronic funds transfer (EFT) system   a means for performing financial transactions through a computer terminal or telephone hookup

An **electronic funds transfer (EFT) system** is a means for performing financial transactions through a computer terminal or telephone hookup. Present EFT systems can be used in four ways.

1. *Automated teller machines (ATMs).* An ATM is an electronic bank teller—a machine that provides almost any service a human teller can provide. Once the customer is properly identified, the machine can dispense cash from the customer's checking or savings account or can make a cash advance charged to a credit card. ATMs are located in bank parking lots, supermarkets, drugstores, and even gas stations. Customers have access to them at all times of the day or night.

Using Credit Cards Wisely

Barbara Lindsey, home from college for Thanksgiving break, becomes very uncomfortable as the family excitedly talks about exchanging gifts for the upcoming holidays, since her bank account is close to empty. Then the idea occurs to her that a way for her to purchase the gifts she'd like to give would be to answer the pre-approved credit card letter that came in the mail last week. Should she answer the letter? The answer to that question will depend on Barbara's ability to use credit wisely. One of the most valuable assets a person can have is a good credit rating.

CREDIT TOOLS

The easiest way to begin your credit history is to open checking and savings accounts at your local bank. Then apply for a gasoline or store credit card. These cards are fairly easy to get because retailers want you to buy their goods and services. The third step, and the most dangerous one, is the acquisition of a major credit card like Visa, MasterCard, or American Express.

It is important to choose a credit card carefully because their terms and conditions vary widely. Look for a card with a low annual fee or none at all. The average fee these days is $16. If you will be one of the seven out of ten card users who don't pay off their credit transactions in full each month, look for the lowest interest rate. Today, the average interest rate for major credit cards is 17.3 percent.

YOUR FRIEND, THE CREDIT CARD

A credit card can be your *friend* because it can get you through unexpected emergencies. And if there is a problem with the goods and services you purchase with your credit card, you have an opportunity to withhold payment by asking the card company to "charge back" to the retailer until the dispute is settled. Monthly credit card statements can also help you keep your records in order. Finally, if you pay the full balance each month and do not incur interest charges, the card helps you to establish a good credit history.

YOUR ENEMY, THE CREDIT CARD

A credit card can be your *enemy* because it is an invitation to purchase items you really do not need. The credit card companies' continuous offers of low minimum payments, cash advances, and even months without payments may seem, on the surface, like a way to skate through a money crunch. In reality, your interest rates and fees only increase, and you go deeper into debt!

If you do find yourself in trouble, *do not* ignore the bills. Contact your creditors to explain your problem and express your desire to pay down your card balance. If that fails, a nonprofit organization like Consumer Credit Counseling Service can assist you in getting back on your financial feet.

A WORD OF CAUTION

Protect your card number and your credit history. *Never* give your card number and expiration date to someone you did not contact first. *Never* write your credit card number on a personal check. *Do not* answer every pre-approved credit card letter you receive (two or three cards are all you should need). Finally, *photocopy* your card, and if it is stolen, notify the credit card company immediately.

When convenience counts, use an ATM. Today more and more bank customers are using Automated Teller Machines (ATMs). Although they are machines, ATMs provide almost any service a human bank teller can provide. And ATMs provide service twenty-four hours a day, seven days a week, and are available in bank parking lots, supermarkets, drugstores, gas stations, and just about any place else that customers need banking services.

2. *Automated clearinghouses (ACHs).* Where ACHs are available, large companies can use them to transfer wages and salaries directly into their employees' bank accounts without making out individual paychecks. The ACH system saves time and effort for both employers and employees, and adds a measure of security to the transfer of these payments.

3. *Point-of-sale (POS) terminals.* A POS terminal is a computerized cash register that is located in a retail store and connected to a bank's computer. Here's how it works. You select your merchandise. At the cash register, you pull your bank card through a magnetic card reader and enter your four- to seven-digit personal identification number (PIN). A central processing center notifies a computer at your bank that you want to make a purchase. Next, the bank's computer immediately deducts the amount of the purchase from your bank account. Then, the amount of the purchase is added to the store's account. Finally, the store is notified that the transaction is complete, and the cash register prints out your receipt.

4. *Bill payment by telephone.* Individuals can use a touch-tone telephone to authorize their banks to make payments to various creditors. The customer simply punches in the required information, and the bank transfers the funds automatically.

Bankers and business owners are generally pleased with EFT systems. EFT is fast and it eliminates some costly processing of checks. However, many customers are reluctant to use EFT systems. Some customers simply don't like "the machine," whereas others fear the computer will garble their accounts. Congress has responded to consumer fears by passing the Electronic Funds Transfer Act (1978), which protects the customer in case the bank makes an error or the customer's EFT identification card is lost or stolen. This act is just one part of the set of regulations governing this industry. In fact, a network as diverse and influential as the banking industry must be, and is, subject to uniform regulations and controls.

■■ THE FEDERAL RESERVE SYSTEM

LEARNING OBJECTIVE 4
Summarize how the Federal Reserve System regulates the money supply.

Federal Reserve System the government agency responsible for regulating the U.S. banking industry

The **Federal Reserve System** (or simply "the Fed") is the government agency responsible for regulating the U.S. banking industry. It was created by Congress on December 23, 1913. Its mission is to maintain an economically healthy and financially sound business environment in which banks can operate. The Federal Reserve System is controlled by the seven members of its Board of Governors, who meet in Washington, D.C. Each governor is appointed by the president and confirmed by the Senate for a fourteen-year term. The president also selects the chairman and vice chairman of the board from among the board members for four-year terms. These terms may be renewed.

The Federal Reserve System comprises twelve Federal Reserve District Banks located in major cities throughout the United States, as well as twenty-five branch-territory banks (see Figure 18.3). Each Federal Reserve District Bank is actually owned—but not controlled—by the commercial banks that are members of the Federal Reserve System. All national (federally chartered) banks must be members of the Fed. State banks may join if they choose to and if they meet membership requirements.

The primary function of the Fed is to regulate the nation's supply of money in such a way as to maintain a healthy economy. It does so by controlling bank reserve requirements, regulating the discount rate, and running open-market operations.

Regulation of Reserve Requirements

reserve requirement the percentage of its deposits that a bank *must* retain, either in its own vault or on deposit with its Federal Reserve District Bank

When money is deposited in a bank, the bank must retain a portion of it to satisfy customers who may want to withdraw money from their accounts. The remainder is available to fund loans. The **reserve requirement** is the percentage of its deposits that a bank *must* retain, either in its own vault or on deposit with its Federal Reserve District Bank. For example, if a bank has deposits of $20 million and the reserve requirement is 10 percent, the bank must retain $2 million. The present reserve requirements range from 3 to 10 percent, depending on such factors as the total amount on deposit, average daily deposits, and the location of the particular member bank.

Through a process called *deposit expansion*, the bank can then use the remaining $18 million to actually create more money and make more loans. Here's how deposit expansion works. In the above example, the bank must retain $2 million in a reserve account. The remaining $18 million can be used to fund consumer and business loans. Assume that the bank lends all $18 million to different borrowers. Also assume that before using any of the borrowed funds, all borrowers deposit the $18 million in their bank

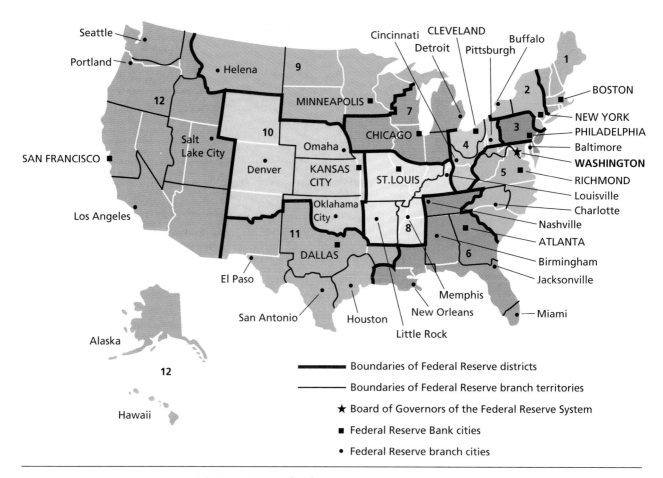

FIGURE 18.3   Federal Reserve System
The Federal Reserve System consists of twelve district banks and twenty-five branch banks. *(Source:* Federal Reserve Bulletin, *Oct. 1994, p. A78.)*

accounts at the lending institution. Now, the bank's deposits have increased by an additional $18 million. Since these deposits are subject to the same reserve requirement described above, the bank must maintain $1.8 million in a reserve account, and the bank can lend the additional $16.2 million to other bank customers. Of course, the bank's lending potential becomes steadily smaller and smaller as it makes more loans. And we should point out that, since bankers are usually very conservative by nature, they will not use deposit expansion to maximize their lending activities; they will take a more middle-of-the-road approach. Finally, the government allows banks to use the deposit-expansion process as long as the reserve requirement is maintained and the bank keeps enough cash on hand to meet the needs of depositors who want to withdraw money from their accounts.

The reserve requirement is set by the Board of Governors of the Fed. When the requirement is increased, banks have less money available for lending. Fewer loans are made, and the economy tends to slow. Thus, increasing the reserve requirement is a powerful anti-inflation weapon. On the other hand, by decreasing the reserve requirement, the Fed can make additional money available for lending to stimulate a slow economy. Because this means of controlling the money supply is so very potent and has such far-reaching effects, the Fed seldom changes the reserve requirement.

Regulation of the Discount Rate

Member banks may borrow money from the Fed to satisfy the reserve requirement and to make additional loans to their customers. The interest rate that the Federal Reserve System charges for loans to member banks is called the **discount rate.** It is set by the Fed's Board of Governors. In the past fifteen years, the discount rate has been as low as 3 percent and as high as 14 percent.[8]

discount rate   the interest rate that the Federal Reserve System charges for loans to member banks

When the Fed lowers the discount rate, money is easier to obtain. Member banks feel free to make more loans and to charge lower interest rates. This increases the money supply and generally stimulates the nation's economy. When the Fed raises the discount rate, banks begin to restrict loans. They increase the interest rates they charge and tighten their own loan requirements. The overall effect is to slow the economy—to check inflation—by making money more difficult and more expensive to obtain.

Open-Market Operations

The federal government finances its activities partly by selling U.S. government securities. These securities, which pay interest to owners, may be purchased by any individual, firm, or organization—including the Fed. **Open-market operations** are the buying and selling of U.S. government securities by the Federal Reserve System for the purpose of controlling the supply of money. They are the most frequently used tool of the Fed.

open-market operations   the buying and selling of U.S. government securities by the Federal Reserve System for the purpose of controlling the supply of money

To reduce the nation's money supply, the Fed simply *sells* government securities on the open market. The money it receives from purchasers is taken out of circulation. Thus less money is available for investment, purchases, or lending. To increase the money supply, the Fed *buys* government securities. The money that the Fed pays for the securities goes back into circulation, making more money available to individuals and firms.

Because the major purchasers of government securities are financial institutions, open-market operations tend to have an immediate effect on lending and investment. Moreover, this effect can be controlled and adjusted by varying the amount of securities that the Fed sells or buys at any given time.

Table 18.2 summarizes the effects of open-market operations and the other tools used by the Fed to regulate the money supply.

Other Fed Responsibilities

In addition to its regulation of the money supply, the Fed is also responsible for clearing checks, controlling and inspecting currency, and applying selective credit controls.

TABLE 18.2   Methods Used by the Federal Reserve System to Control the Money Supply and the Economy

Method Used	Immediate Result	End Result
Regulating reserve requirement		
1. Fed **increases** reserve requirement	Less money for banks to lend to customers—reduction in overall money supply	Economic slowdown
2. Fed **decreases** reserve requirement	More money for banks to lend to customers—increase in overall money supply	Increased economic activity
Regulating the discount rate		
1. Fed **increases** the discount rate	Less money for banks to lend to customers—reduction in overall money supply	Economic slowdown
2. Fed **decreases** the discount rate	More money for banks to lend to customers—increase in overall money supply	Increased economic activity
Open-market operations		
1. Fed **sells** government securities	Less money for banks to lend to customers—reduction in overall money supply	Economic slowdown
2. Fed **buys** government securities	More money for banks to lend to customers—increase in overall money supply	Increased economic activity

Clearing Checks   Today people use checks to pay for nearly everything they buy. A check written by a customer of one bank and presented for payment to another bank in the same town may be processed through a local clearinghouse. But the procedure becomes more complicated when the banks are not in the same town. That's where the Federal Reserve System comes in. The Fed is responsible for the prompt and accurate collection and crediting of intercity checking transactions.

The steps involved in clearing a check through the Federal Reserve System are outlined in Figure 18.4. About half of all the checks written in the United States are cleared in this way. The remainder are either presented directly to the paying bank or processed through local clearinghouses. Through the use of electronic equipment, most checks can be cleared within two or three days.

Control and Inspection of Currency   As paper currency is handled, it becomes worn or dirty. The typical one-dollar bill has a life expectancy of less than one year (larger denominations usually last longer because they are handled less). When member banks deposit their surplus cash in a Federal Reserve Bank, the currency is inspected. Bills that are unfit for further use are separated and destroyed.

FIGURE 18.4
Clearing a Check Through the Federal Reserve System
Approximately one-half of all U.S. checks are cleared this way, a process that usually takes two to three days.
(Source: Federal Reserve Bank of New York, The Story of Checks, 6th ed., 1983, p. 11.)

Suppose Ms. Henderson of Albany, New York, buys a painting from an art dealer in Sacramento, California. She sends her check. . .

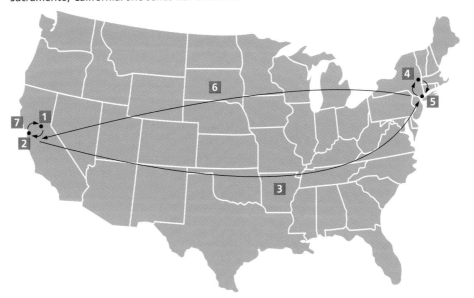

1 The dealer deposits the check in his account at a Sacramento bank.

2 The Sacramento bank deposits the check for credit in its account with the Federal Reserve Bank of San Francisco.

3 The Federal Reserve Bank of San Francisco sends the check to the Federal Reserve Bank of New York for collection.

4 The Federal Reserve Bank of New York forwards the check to the Albany bank, which deducts the amount of the check from Ms. Henderson's account.

5 The Albany bank authorizes the Federal Reserve Bank of New York to deduct the amount of the check from its deposit account with the Federal Reserve Bank.

6 The Federal Reserve Bank of New York pays the Federal Reserve Bank of San Francisco by payment from its share in the interdistrict settlement fund.

7 The Federal Reserve Bank of San Francisco credits the Sacramento bank's deposit account, and the Sacramento bank credits the art dealer's account.

Selective Credit Controls   The Federal Reserve System has the responsibility for implementing the Truth-in-Lending Act, which Congress passed in 1968. This act requires lenders to state clearly the annual percentage rate and total finance charge for a consumer loan. It also prohibits discrimination in lending based on race, color, sex, marital status, religion, or national origin.

The Federal Reserve System is also responsible for setting the margin requirements for certain stock transactions. The *margin* is the minimum portion of the purchase price that must be paid in cash. (The investor may borrow the remainder.) The current margin requirement is $2,000, or 50 percent, whichever is greater. Thus if an investor purchases $4,000 worth of stock, he or she must pay at least $2,000 in cash. The remaining $2,000 may be borrowed from the brokerage firm or some other financial institution.

LEARNING OBJECTIVE 5
Explain the function of the
Federal Deposit Insurance
Corporation (FDIC), Savings
Association Insurance Fund
(SAIF), Bank Insurance Fund
(BIF), and National Credit
Union Association (NCUA).

■■ THE FDIC, SAIF, BIF, AND NCUA

During the Depression, a number of banks failed and their depositors lost all their savings. To make sure that such a disaster does not happen again (and to restore public confidence in the banking industry), Congress organized the *Federal Deposit Insurance Corporation (FDIC)* in 1933. The primary purpose of the FDIC is to insure deposits against bank failure. All banks that are members of the Federal Reserve System are required to belong to the FDIC. Nonmember banks are allowed to join if they qualify. Insurance premiums are paid by the banks.

The FDIC insures all accounts in each member bank for up to $100,000 per individual at one bank. A depositor may obtain additional coverage by opening separate accounts in different banks. Individuals who deposit their money in savings and loan associations or credit unions receive similar protection. The newly created *Savings Association Insurance Fund (SAIF)*— funded by the FDIC—insures deposits in savings and loan associations. The FDIC has also created the Bank Insurance Fund (BIF) to insure deposits in savings banks. The *National Credit Union Association (NCUA)* insures deposits in credit unions. To see what happens to depositors when a bank fails, read Change in the Workplace.

The FDIC, SAIF, BIF, and NCUA have improved banking in the United States. When any one of these organizations insures an institution's deposits, it reserves the right to examine that institution's operations periodically. If a bank, S&L, savings bank, or credit union is found to be poorly managed, it is reported to the proper banking authority. In extreme cases,

Bank failures make depositors see red! Nothing worries bank customers more than the thought that they can't get their money out of an insolvent bank, savings and loan association, or credit union. Today, most financial institutions obtain federal deposit insurance to protect customers against bank failures.

■ ■ ■ ■ ■ CHANGE IN THE WORKPLACE

A Businessperson's Need for FDIC Coverage

Businesspeople must rely on a financial institution in which they can deposit funds to be used in facilitating cash flow and to make investments for business growth. In order to maintain confidence in the banking industry and to protect depositors, the Federal Deposit Insurance Company guarantees that monies deposited in a bank will be insured for up to $100,000 per depositor. Without this government-provided safety net, the solvency of any business would constantly be threatened by the possibility of bank failure.

EXCESS BALANCE AT RISK

After nineteen years with a Houston company, Neil Hill, age 48, was laid off and then forced to draw his entire pension and savings in order to support his family. On October 9, 1992, he deposited his $200,000 in the First City Bank of Texas, intending to withdraw the money from his bank account on November 4 to invest in mutual funds. Unfortunately, Hill found out what happens to balances that exceed $100,000 when the FDIC seized First City and its twenty branches on October 30, 1992, and declared the bank insolvent.

Hill's first $100,000 was insured and after all assets of the bank are liquidated over the next three to five years, the possibility does exist that he may retrieve 80 percent of the excess amount. Should that occur, Hill will be left with a loss of $20,000. At that, he would be lucky because the average depositor usually recovers only 50 to 60 percent of his or her uninsured funds. Regardless, Hill has lost the opportunity to invest his full retirement money and faces the uncertainty of recovering the uninsured funds.

BE WARNED

Remember that the FDIC insures each depositor, business, or individual, for only $100,000. With the mounting bank failures over the past few years, the get-tough policy adopted by government regulators for depositors of greater amounts can jeopardize the funds a businessperson deposits in any one financial institution. No matter how many different accounts a depositor may have in a given bank, the cap is applied to the total. When the option of depositing funds in multiple banks is impractical, a businessperson can achieve peace of mind by purchasing additional insurance through publicly owned insurance companies.

the FDIC, SAIF, BIF, or NCUA can cancel its insurance coverage. This is a particularly unwelcome action. It causes many depositors to withdraw their money from the institution and discourages most prospective depositors from opening an account.

Lending to individuals and firms is a vital function of banks. And deciding wisely to whom it will extend credit is one of the most important activities of any institution. The material in the next section explains the different factors that are used to evaluate credit applicants.

Installment Credit

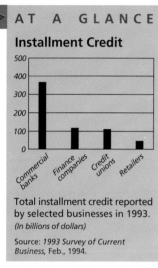

Total installment credit reported by selected businesses in 1993. *(In billions of dollars)*

Source: *1993 Survey of Current Business*, Feb., 1994.

credit immediate purchasing power that is exchanged for a promise to repay it, with or without interest, at a later date

LEARNING OBJECTIVE 6
Discuss the importance of credit and credit management.

■■ EFFECTIVE CREDIT MANAGEMENT

Credit is immediate purchasing power that is exchanged for a promise to repay it, with or without interest, at a later date. A credit transaction is a two-sided business activity that involves both a borrower and a lender. The borrower is most often a person or firm that wishes to make a purchase. The lender may be a bank, some other lending institution, or a business firm selling merchandise or services on credit.

For example, suppose you obtain a bank loan to buy a $40,000 Porsche automobile. You, as the borrower, obtain immediate purchasing power. In return, you agree to certain terms that are imposed by the bank. As the lender, the bank requires that you make a down payment, make monthly payments, pay interest, and purchase insurance to protect the car until the loan is paid in full.

Banks lend money because they are in business for that purpose. The interest they charge is what provides their profit. Other businesses extend credit to their customers for at least two reasons. First, some customers simply cannot afford to pay the entire amount of their purchase immediately, but they *can* repay credit in a number of smaller payments, stretched out over some period of time. Second, some firms are forced to sell goods or services on credit to compete effectively when other firms offer credit to their customers.

Credit terms can be used as a competitive weapon, and firms can realize a profit from interest charges. The major pitfall in granting credit is the possibility of nonpayment. However, if a firm follows the five Cs of credit management, it can minimize this possibility.

The Five Cs of Credit Management

When a business extends credit to its customers, it must face the fact that some customers will be unable or unwilling to pay for their credit purchases. With this in mind, credit managers must establish policies for determining who will receive credit and who will not. Most lenders build their credit policies around the five Cs of credit: character, capacity, capital, collateral, and conditions.

Character By *character* we mean the borrower's attitude toward credit obligations. Experienced credit managers often see this as the most important factor in predicting whether a borrower will make regular payments and ultimately repay a credit obligation. Typical questions to consider in judging a borrower's character include the following:

1. Is the borrower prompt in paying bills?
2. Have other lenders had to dun the borrower with overdue notices before receiving payment?
3. Have lenders been forced to take the borrower to court to obtain payment?

4. Has the customer ever filed for bankruptcy? If so, did the customer make an attempt to repay debts voluntarily?

Although it is illegal to discriminate, personal factors such as marital status and drinking or gambling habits may affect a lender's decision to loan money or extend credit to an individual.

Capacity   By *capacity* we mean the borrower's financial ability to meet credit obligations—that is, to make regular loan payments as scheduled in the credit agreement. If the customer is a business, the lender looks at the firm's income statement. For individuals, the lender checks salary statements and other sources of income, such as dividends and interest. The borrower's other financial obligations and monthly expenses are also taken into consideration before credit is approved.

Capital   The term *capital* as used here refers to the borrower's assets or net worth. In general, the greater the capital, the greater the borrower's ability to repay a loan. The capital position of a business can be determined by examining its balance sheet. For individuals, information on net worth can be obtained by requiring that the borrower complete a credit application like the one illustrated in Figure 18.5. The borrower must also authorize employers and financial institutions to release information to confirm the claims made in the credit application.

Collateral   For large amounts of credit—and especially for long-term loans—the lender may require some type of collateral. If the borrower fails to live up to the terms of the credit agreement, the lender can repossess the collateral and then sell it to satisfy the debt.

Conditions   Here we mean the *general economic conditions* that can affect a borrower's ability to repay a loan or other credit obligation. How well a business firm can withstand an economic storm may depend on the particular industry the firm is in, its relative strength within that industry, its earnings history, and its earnings potential. For individuals, the basic question focuses on security—of both the applicant's job and the firm that he or she works for.

Checking Credit Information

The five Cs of credit are concerned mainly with information supplied by the applicant. But how can the lender determine whether this information is accurate? That depends on whether the potential borrower is a business or an individual consumer.

Credit information concerning businesses can be obtained from the following four sources:

- *National credit-reporting agencies* that cover the entire country. Dun & Bradstreet is the most widely used credit-reporting agency in the United States. Its Dun & Bradstreet Reports present detailed credit information about specific companies. Its reference books include credit ratings for more than 20 million businesses worldwide.

Apply Today! Important: To ensure prompt processing, please print and fill out completely.
Note: If married, you may apply for a separate account in your own name.

Bank of America
Base Pln #40337 DDA Pln #37694
Sol #2279 (w/Bal Con) Sol #2269 (w/o Bal Con)

Type of Account (Please select one only) ☐ Visa® Account ☐ MasterCard® Account
Minimum Annual Income Requirement: $12,000 (*For Retirees or Permanently Disabled:* $8,400)

1 Please Tell Us About Yourself

First Name | Initial | Last Name | Jr./Sr.
Social Security Number – – | Date of Birth (MM/DD/YY) / /
Street Address | Apt #
City | State | Zip
Area Code & Home Phone ( ) –
Mo. Rent or Mortgage Pmt $ | How Long at Address? Yrs Mos | ☐Own ☐Rent | ☐Parents/Relative ☐Other
Previous Street Address (If less than 6 mos. at current address)
City | State | Zip
Nearest Relative Name | Area Code & Home Phone ( ) –
Are You a U.S. Citizen or a Permanent Resident of the U.S.?
☐Yes ☐No

2 Please Tell Us About Your Income

You need not list income from alimony, child support or separate maintenance unless you wish it considered for purposes of granting credit.

Current Job Title or Occupation | Gross Monthly Salary $
☐Self-Employed ☐Homemaker ☐Retired ☐Unemployed ☐Student
Name of Current Employer or Business
Street Address
City | State | Zip
Area Code & Work Phone ( ) – | How Long with Current Employer? Yrs Mos
Description of Any Other Income | Monthly Amount $
Name of Previous Employer (If at current job less than 6 mos.) | How Long? Yrs Mos

3 Your Current Accounts

Please check the boxes that apply.
Specify if the account is with Bank of America (BofA) or another institution.

Checking Account # | ☐BofA $ Amount | ☐Other
Savings/IRA/CD Account # | ☐BofA $ Amount | ☐Other
Money Market/NOW Account | ☐BofA $ Amount | ☐Other
Visa/MasterCard Account | ☐BofA | ☐Other (Name)
Other Credit Cards (Check all that apply)
☐Dept. Store ☐Gasoline ☐Discover ☐American Express/Diners Club ☐Other
Finance Co. (Name) 1 | Finance Co. (Name) 2

4 Co-Applicant's Information

Co-Applicant Name | Relationship
Social Security Number – – | Area Code & Phone Number ( ) –
Current Title or Occupation | Gross Monthly Salary $
Name of Co-Applicant's Employer | Area Code & Phone Number ( ) –

5 Yes, I Want a Free Additional Card

First Name | Initial | Last Name | Jr./Sr.

6 Signatures for Agreement

Note: Application cannot be processed without signature(s).
I have read and understand this application, and I agree to the terms as described.
Each person signing will have full and equal access to any credit line extended and will be individually and jointly liable for repayment of all amounts owing on the account.

X
Your Signature | Date

X
Co-Applicant's Signature | Date

7 Optional Payment Protection Plan

Form F583 794

Initial here to protect your BankAmericard account balance in the event of death, disability or involuntary unemployment by enrolling in the Group Credit Card Insurance Program. Enrollment is voluntary and you are free to cancel at any time. | YES Initial Here to Enroll | NO Initial Here to Decline

FOR BANK USE ONLY
DO NOT WRITE IN THIS SPACE | EMP. I.D.#
BCS-9519 (12/94)

© 1994 BANK OF AMERICA NA • MEMBER FDIC

FIGURE 18.5 Credit Application Form
Credit managers use the information on credit application forms to help determine which customers should be granted credit. *(Source: Bank of America National Trust and Savings Association)*

- *Local credit-reporting agencies,* which may require a monthly or yearly fee for providing information on a continual basis.
- *Industry associations,* which may charge a service fee.
- *Other firms* that have given the applicant credit.

Various credit bureaus provide credit information concerning individuals. The following are the three major consumer credit bureaus:

- TRW Credit Data—Dallas, Texas (800-682-7654)
- Trans Union—Philadelphia, Pennsylvania (800-851-2674)
- Equifax Credit Information Services—Atlanta, Georgia (800-685-1111)

Consumer credit bureaus are subject to the provisions of the Fair Credit Reporting Act, which became effective in 1971. This act safeguards consumers' rights in two ways. First, every consumer has the right to know what information is contained in his or her credit bureau file. In most cases, a consumer who has been denied credit on the basis of information provided by a credit bureau can obtain a credit report without charge. In other situations, the consumer may obtain the information for a $7 to $10 fee.

Second, a consumer who feels that some information in the file is inaccurate, misleading, or vague has the right to request that the credit bureau verify it. If the disputed information is found to be correct, the consumer can provide an explanation of up to one hundred words, giving his or her side of the dispute. This explanation must become part of the consumer's credit file. If the disputed information is found to be inaccurate, it must be deleted or corrected. Furthermore, any lender that has been supplied inaccurate information within the past six months must be sent a corrected credit report.

Sound Collection Procedures

The vast majority of borrowers follow the lender's repayment terms exactly. However, some accounts inevitably become overdue for a variety of reasons. Experience shows that such accounts should receive immediate attention.

Some firms handle their own delinquent accounts; others prefer to use a professional collection agency. (Charges for an agency's services are usually high—up to half of the amount collected.) Both tend to use the following standard collection techniques, generally in the order in which they are listed:

1. Subtle reminders, such as duplicate statements marked "Past Due"
2. Telephone calls to urge prompt payment
3. Personal visits to business customers to stress the necessity of paying overdue amounts immediately
4. Legal action, although the time, expense, and uncertain outcome of a lawsuit make this action a last resort

Good collection procedures should be firm, but they should also allow for compromise. Harassment is both illegal and bad business. Ideally, the borrower will be convinced to make up missed payments, and the firm will retain the borrower's goodwill.

In the next chapter, you will see why firms need financing, how they obtain the money they need, and how they ensure that funds are utilized efficiently, in keeping with their organizational objectives.

■ ■ ■ ■ CHAPTER REVIEW

Summary

1   Identify the functions and important characteristics of money.

Money is anything that is used by a society to purchase products, services, or resources. Money must serve as a medium of exchange, a measure of value, and a store of value. To perform its functions effectively, money must be divisible into units of convenient size, light and sturdy enough to be carried and used on a daily basis, stable in value, and difficult to counterfeit.

The M_1 supply of money is made up of coins and bills (currency) and deposits in checking accounts (demand deposits). The M_2 supply includes M_1 plus certain specific securities and small-denomination time deposits. Another common definition of the money supply—M_3—consists of M_1 and M_2 plus large time deposits of $100,000 or more.

2   Describe the differences between commercial banks and other financial institutions in the banking industry.

A commercial bank is a profit-making organization that accepts deposits, makes loans, and provides related services to customers. In the United States, commercial banks may be chartered by the federal government or state governments. Savings and loan associations, savings banks, and credit unions offer the same basic services that commercial banks provide. Insurance companies, pension funds, brokerage firms, and finance companies provide some limited banking services.

3   Identify the services provided by commercial banks and other financial institutions.

Banks and other financial institutions offer today's customers a tempting array of services. The most important and attractive banking services for both individuals and businesses are checking accounts, savings accounts, short- and long-term loans, credit card transactions, and electronic transfer of funds. Other services include financial advice, payroll services, certified checks, trust services, and safe-deposit boxes.

4   Summarize how the Federal Reserve System regulates the money supply.

The Federal Reserve System is responsible for regulating the U.S. banking industry and maintaining a sound economic environment. Banks with federal charters must be members of the Fed. State banks may join if they choose to and if they can meet the requirements for membership. Twelve district banks and twenty-five branch-territory banks compose the Federal Reserve System, whose seven-member Board of Governors is headquartered in Washington, D.C.

To control the supply of money, the Federal Reserve System regulates the reserve requirement, or the percentage of deposits that a bank must keep on hand. It also regulates the discount rate, or the interest rate the Fed charges member banks for loans. And it engages in open-market operations, in which it buys and sells government securities. The Fed is responsible for clearing checks, inspecting currency, enforcing the Truth-in-Lending Act, and setting margin requirements for stock transactions.

5   Explain the function of the Federal Deposit Insurance Corporation (FDIC), Savings Association Insurance Fund (SAIF), Bank Insurance Fund (BIF), and National Credit Union Association (NCUA).

The Federal Deposit Insurance Corporation (FDIC), Savings Association Insurance Fund (SAIF), Bank Insurance Fund (BIF), and National Credit Union Association (NCUA) insure accounts in member commercial banks, S&Ls, savings banks, and credit unions, respectively, for up to $100,000 per individual at one financial institution.

6   Discuss the importance of credit and credit management.

Credit is immediate purchasing power that is exchanged for a promise to repay it, with or without interest, at a later date. Businesses sell goods and services on credit because some customers cannot afford to pay cash and because they must keep pace with competitors who offer credit. Decisions on whether to grant credit to businesses and individuals are usually based on the five Cs of credit: character, capacity, capital, collateral, and conditions. Credit information can be obtained from various credit reporting agencies, credit bureaus, industry associations, and other firms. The techniques used to collect past-due accounts should be firm enough to prompt payment but flexible enough to maintain the borrower's goodwill.

Key Terms

You should now be able to define and give an example relevant to each of the following terms:

barter system (570)

money (570)

medium of exchange (571)

measure of value (571)

store of value (572)

demand deposit (573)

time deposit (574)

commercial bank (576)

national bank (576)

state bank (576)

savings and loan association (S&L) (576)

NOW account (577)

savings bank (577)

credit union (578)

check (579)

certificate of deposit (CD) (580)

line of credit (580)

revolving credit agreement (580)

collateral (580)

electronic funds transfer (EFT) system (582)

Federal Reserve System (585)

reserve requirement (585)

discount rate (587)

open-market operations (587)

credit (592)

Questions

Review Questions

1. How does the use of money solve the problems that are associated with a barter system of exchange?
2. What are the three functions that money must perform in a sound monetary system?
3. Explain why money must have each of the following characteristics.
   a. Divisibility
   b. Portability
   c. Stability
   d. Durability
   e. Difficulty of counterfeiting
4. What is included in the definition of the M_1 supply of money? of the M_2 supply? of the M_3 supply?
5. What is the difference between a national bank and a state bank? What other financial institutions compete with national and state banks?
6. Describe the major banking services provided by financial institutions today.
7. What is the major advantage of electronic banking? What is its major disadvantage?

8. What is the Federal Reserve System? How is it organized?
9. Explain how the Federal Reserve System uses each of the following to control the money supply.
   a. Reserve requirements
   b. The discount rate
   c. Open-market operations
10. The Federal Reserve is responsible for enforcing the Truth-in-Lending Act. How does this act affect consumers?
11. What is the basic function of the FDIC, SAIF, BIF, and NCUA? How do they perform this function?
12. List and explain the five Cs of credit management.
13. How would you check the information provided by an individual applicant for credit at a department store? by a business applicant at a heavy-equipment manufacturer's sales office?

Discussion Questions

1. NationsBank began as a small regional bank in Charlotte, North Carolina. How did it become the third largest bank in the United States?
2. What products and services does NationsBank offer its customers?
3. It is said that financial institutions "create" money when they make loans to firms and individuals. Explain what this means.
4. Is competition among financial institutions good or bad for the following?
   a. The institutions themselves
   b. Their customers
   c. The economy in general
5. Why would banks pay higher interest on money that is left on deposit for longer periods of time (for example, on CDs)?
6. How could an individual get in financial trouble by using a credit card?
7. Why does the Fed use indirect means of controlling the money supply, instead of simply printing more money or removing money from circulation when necessary?
8. Lenders are generally reluctant to extend credit to individuals with no previous credit history (and no outstanding debts). Yet they willingly extend credit to individuals who are in the process of repaying debts. Is this reasonable? Is it fair? Defend your answer.

Exercises

🖤 1. Devise a form of money, other than coins and bills, that fulfills the functions of money and has all the required characteristics of money.

✎ **2.** Obtain a credit application from a store or bank. Fill it out. Then answer the following questions:

a. Does the application ask for enough information so that a credit manager could apply the five Cs? What questions should be added to the application form?

b. Would you, as a credit manager, extend credit to yourself? Explain.

VIDEO CASE 18.1

Consumer Credit Counseling Service

For Betty and Mike Martin (not their real names), the last four years have been a nightmare. The couple got married right after they graduated from college, and both Betty and Mike got jobs as elementary school teachers. Everything seemed to be right on track when the Martins purchased their new $104,000 home. But when they began to furnish their home, the credit card bills began to mount. Soon their monthly payments totaled $4,300, even though their combined take-home pay was only $4,150.

To make ends meet, the Martins began to obtain cash advances on their credit cards. When they had reached their credit ceilings on their three bank cards, they could no longer get the cash advances they needed to exist. They began to use money that should have been paid on monthly bills to purchase food and other necessities. Within weeks, they began to receive telephone calls and letters from their creditors demanding payment. Stress began to take its toll, and the Martins began to argue over money and just about everything else. Finally, things got so bad that they considered filing for personal bankruptcy, but ironically they couldn't afford the legal fees. That's when Mike's brother suggested calling the local chapter of the Consumer Credit Counseling Service.

Unfortunately, Betty and Mike Martin are not alone. According to the Consumer Credit Counseling Service (CCCS)—a national network of nonprofit groups that help people with debt problems—over 500,000 Americans file for personal bankruptcy each year. CCCS counselors at more than 850 local offices help clients assess their current financial situation and create a plan for repaying outstanding debts.* Although each case is different, most CCCS counselors begin by establishing a realistic budget of income and expenditures. In addition to establishing a realistic budget, CCCS counselors also provide information on the wise use of credit and the real cost of credit purchases.

In more extreme cases, the counselor can recommend CCCS's debt-management program. With a debt-management program, the CCCS counselor works with the client's creditors to create a new debt-repayment schedule with lower monthly payments spread out over a longer period of time. The client then makes regular monthly payments to the CCCS, which in turn pays off creditors. In most cases, the debt-management program is designed to pay off the client's debt within two to three years.[9]

Questions

1. Americans consistently use credit cards to purchase everyday items. What are the advantages and disadvantages of using credit cards?

2. According to the experts, no more than 10 to 20 percent of your monthly budget should be used for short-term, credit card debt. Based on the experts' opinion, what is the maximum amount of credit card debt that a family with a $3,200 monthly budget should have?

3. What would you do if yours was the family in Question 2 and you found that your credit card debt was higher than 20 percent of your total budget? Explain your answer.

4. Because the CCCS is funded by contributions from local businesses, its credit counseling is usually free. Why would local businesses sponsor a service like the CCCS?

---

*To find a local Consumer Credit Counseling Service office near you, call 800-388-2227.

CASE 18.2

Are you investing in a Bank CD or a Mutual Fund?

During the 1980s, customers flocked to their local banks to invest their money in certificates of deposit that paid high interest. These investors enjoyed full confidence that in the event of a bank failure, their money was guaranteed against loss through the Federal Deposit Insurance Corporation (FDIC). Depositors also took advantage of the wide array of products and services that banks offer, like credit cards, home mortgage loans, automobile loans, and on and on. The banking industry prospered in that decade, and depositors earned a high return on their money. But as interest rates on CDs began to decline in the early 1990s, customers were lured away to investments like stocks, bonds, and mutual funds that carry more risk. Faced with the loss of these deposits, many banks formed alliances with brokerage and investment firms to market investment products directly to their own customers. Offering depositors the opportunity to purchase mutual funds might stem the tide of withdrawals, and the banks could generate tremendous income from the management fees and sales commissions. However, because mutual funds are outside the realm of commercial banking, they are not federally insured—nor are they risk-free.

Businesspeople such as certified public accountant James Jackson, who understands that mutual funds are speculative investments, are comfortable with the convenience of a one-stop approach to transacting all their financial affairs. Jackson relies on his local bank to manage his mutual fund portfolio, and he expects to pay fees for those services. But many depositors do not understand that investing in mutual funds through their banks involves risk. For example, Elizabeth Mooney, a widow, had most of her life savings in certificates of deposit. Just before they were ready to mature, she received a letter from Mrs. Lassiter, a bank officer, inviting her to come to the bank so they could discuss an alternative investment that might earn her high returns. Eager to improve her financial position, she met with her "trusted friend," who in turn introduced her to Mr. Johnson, an account executive for a brokerage firm. He explained to Mrs. Mooney that mutual funds currently were paying a higher rate of interest than her CDs and showed her a prospectus. When she agreed to invest in the fund he was recommending, he had her sign a paper written in fine print that explained the risks and fees involved. But she

really only heard the phrase "more income," and "knew" from past experience that her accounts at "her bank" were insured by the FDIC.

In reality, her mutual fund investment was not guaranteed by anyone. Because of such customers who have always had confidence and complete trust in their banking institution, some banks are now being accused of using unethical practices to entice clients into investing in bank-managed mutual funds. Although banks deny these charges claiming they give full disclosure to their customers, you can protect yourself, first, by learning everything you can about the mutual fund under consideration. Next, invest only what you can afford to lose. Finally, be fully prepared to pay a management fee or sales commission. If you still feel you are being pressured into investing—or if you are not informed of the risk—leave and take your money with you![10]

Questions

1. What motives would a bank have to lead a customer, intentionally or unintentionally, into investing in a mutual fund? Why would these motives appear to be unethical?

2. Money deposited in a certificate of deposit is federally insured; mutual fund investments are not. Which investment would you choose if you had $25,000 to invest? Explain your answer.

■ ■ ■ ■ CHAPTER 19

Financial Management

LEARNING OBJECTIVES

After studying this chapter you should be able to

1 Explain the need for financing and financial management in business.

2 Summarize the process of planning for financial management.

3 Describe the advantages and disadvantages of different methods of short-term financing.

4 Evaluate the advantages and disadvantages of equity financing and debt financing from the corporation's standpoint.

5 Discuss the importance of using funds effectively.

CHAPTER PREVIEW

In this chapter, we focus on two needs of business organizations: first, the need for money to start a business and keep it going and, second, the need to manage that money effectively. We also look at how firms develop financial plans and evaluate financial performance. Then we compare various methods of obtaining short-term financing—money that will be used for one year or less. We also examine sources of long-term financing, which a firm may require for expansion, new-product development, or replacement of equipment.

Goldman Sachs: A Trusted Investment Banker

When Goldman, Sachs and Company, a Wall Street investment banking firm that helps large corporations sell new stock and bond issues, recorded an estimated $2.7 billion in pretax profits for 1993, it rewarded each of its 160 partners with at least $5 million in year-end bonuses. In addition, every member of the staff, from the mail room clerks to the executive secretaries, received bonuses equal to 30 percent of their annual salaries. These dollar amounts seem astonishing, but as a private partnership, Goldman Sachs does not have to share its earnings with stockholders. This unusually generous bonus program promotes cooperation and is a major factor in attracting the top talent that contributes to the firm's success.

Today Goldman Sachs offers its clients a variety of services like managing assets, investment banking, real estate investing, and trading stocks, bonds, commodities, currency, and U.S. government securities. It also operates subsidiaries in Belgium, France, Germany, Japan, Singapore, and the United Kingdom.

Even though Goldman Sachs is considered to be the most stable, the best-managed, and the most profitable company in the investment banking industry, it has been deeply hurt by the bond market crash of 1994. When the Federal Reserve began to raise interest rates in February 1994, Wall Street investment firms were caught with enormous inventories of bonds that dropped in value. The resulting loss on the value of bonds caused a staggering decline in income for Wall Street firms. Goldman Sachs, as a partnership, is not required to disclose its finances publicly, but estimates are that its 1994 earnings—a mere $1.84 billion—were far short of its record-

breaking bonanza of 1993. Another indication of problems was the announcement that Stephen Friedman, the chairman who steered the company through its most successful years, was retiring at the end of November 1994. And now, forty other partners are rumored to be leaving the firm.

Taking over at the helm is Jon S. Corzine, the 47-year-old bond trader who led Goldman Sachs to prominence in the global bond markets. Joining him as vice chairman and chief operating officer is 48-year-old Henry M. Paulson, Jr., an investment banking specialist whose prestigious clients include Sears, Motorola, and Sara Lee. Corzine admits Goldman Sachs made a mistake when it failed to anticipate the last downturn in the bond market. But he envisions that his working partnership with Paulson will enable Goldman Sachs to accomplish the goals of the company and once again achieve record-breaking earnings.[1]

■■■■

601

■　■　■　■　■　■　■　■　■　■　■

oldman Sachs's commitment to helping its corporate clients raise capital by selling new stock and bond issues has made it one of the most respected and most profitable investment banking firms on Wall Street. As a result, when large corporations need help with financial management, they often turn to Goldman Sachs—a trusted investment firm. In the next section, we examine the topic of financial management and explain why today's managers are so concerned with how their firm's finances are managed.

■■　WHAT IS FINANCIAL MANAGEMENT?

LEARNING OBJECTIVE 1
Explain the need for financing and financial management in business.

financial management　all the activities that are concerned with obtaining money and using it effectively

Financial management consists of all the activities that are concerned with obtaining money and using it effectively. Within a business organization, the financial manager must not only determine the best way (or ways) to raise money. She or he must also ensure that projected uses are in keeping with the organization's goals. Effective financial management thus involves careful planning. That planning begins with a determination of the firm's financing needs.

The Need for Financing

Money is needed both to start a business and to keep it going. The original investment of the owners, along with money they may have borrowed, should be enough to open the doors. After that, it would seem that income from sales could be used to finance the firm's continuing operations and to provide a profit as well.

This is exactly what happens in a successful firm—over the long run. But income and expenses may vary from season to season or from year to year. Temporary financing may be needed when expenses are high or income is low. Then, too, situations, such as the opportunity to purchase a new facility or expand an existing plant, may require more money than is currently available within a firm. In either case, the firm must look for outside sources of financing.

short-term financing　money that will be used for one year or less and then repaid

Short-Term Financing Needs　**Short-term financing** is money that will be used for one year or less and then repaid.* As illustrated in Table 19.1, there are many short-term financing needs, but two deserve special attention. First, certain business practices may affect a firm's cash flow and create a

---

*Many financial managers define *short-term financing* as money that will be used for one year or one operating cycle of the business, whichever is longer. The operating cycle of the business may be longer than one year and is the amount of time between the purchase of raw materials and the sale of finished products that were manufactured from the raw materials to wholesalers, retailers, or in some cases, consumers.

602

Copyright © Houghton Mifflin Company

**TABLE 19.1
Comparison of Short-
and Long-Term Financing**
Whether a business seeks
short- or long-term financing
depends on what the money
will be used for.

Corporate Cash Needs	
Short-term financing needs	**Long-term financing needs**
Cash-flow problems	Business start-up costs
Current inventory needs	New-product development
Monthly expenses	Long-term marketing activities
Speculative production	Expansion of facilities
Short-term promotional needs	Replacement of capital assets
Unexpected emergencies	Mergers and acquisitions

cash flow the movement of
money into and out of an
organization

need for short-term financing. **Cash flow** is the movement of money into
and out of an organization. The ideal is to have sufficient money coming
into the firm in any period to cover the firm's expenses during that period.
But the ideal is not always achieved. For example, a firm that offers credit
to its customers will often have cash-flow problems. Such credit purchases
are generally not paid until thirty or sixty days (or more) after the transaction. Short-term financing may then be needed to pay the firm's bills until
customers have paid their bills. Unanticipated emergencies may also cause
a cash-flow problem.

A second major need for short-term financing that is related to a firm's
cash-flow problem is inventory. Inventory requires considerable investment
for most manufacturers, wholesalers, and retailers. Moreover, most goods
are manufactured four to nine months before they are actually sold to the
ultimate customer. Consider what happens when a firm like Black & Decker
begins to manufacture small appliances for sale during the Christmas season. Manufacturing begins in February, March, and April, and Black &
Decker negotiates short-term financing to buy materials and supplies, to pay
wages and rent, and to cover inventory costs until the appliances are eventually sold to wholesalers and retailers later in the year. Once payment is
received, usually 30 to 60 days after the merchandise is shipped, Black &
Decker can use these sales revenues to repay the borrowed money.

Retailers that range in size from Wal-Mart to the neighborhood drug-
store also need short-term financing to build up their inventories before
peak selling periods. For example, Dallas-based Calloway's Nurseries must
increase the amount of shrubs, trees, and flowering plants that it makes
available for sale during the spring and summer growing seasons. Much of
this merchandise is obtained from growers or wholesalers using short-term
financing. Again, Calloway repays the loan when the merchandise is sold.

long-term financing money
that will be used for longer than
one year

Long-Term Financing Needs   **Long-term financing** is money that will be
used for longer than one year. As illustrated in Table 19.1, long-term
financing is obviously needed to start a new business. It is also needed for
executing business expansions and mergers, for developing and marketing
new products, and for replacing equipment that has become obsolete or
inefficient.

The amounts of long-term financing needed by large firms can seem
almost unreal. Exxon spends about $10 million to drill an exploratory

offshore oil well—without knowing for sure whether oil will be found. Toyota Motor Corp. spent millions to develop, manufacture, and market the Lexus automobile. And both General Motors and Ford spend over $5 billion a year on research and development.[2]

The Need for Financial Management

Without financing there would be very little business. Financing gets a business started in the first place. Then financing supports the firm's production and marketing activities; pays its bills; and, when carefully managed, produces a reasonable profit.

Many firms have failed because their managers did not pay enough attention to finances. In fact, poor financial management was one of the major reasons why over 72,000 businesses filed for bankruptcy in 1993 (the most recent year for which complete statistics are available). In addition to businesses, some government entities have been forced to file for bankruptcy protection. To see what happened to Orange County, California, read Business Journal. Many fairly successful firms could be highly successful if they managed their finances more carefully. But business people often take finances for granted. Their first focus may be on production or marketing.

Anne Beiler, the self-proclaimed pretzel queen, borrowed $6,000 to open the first Auntie Anne's pretzel stand. Like most aspiring entrepreneurs, Ms. Beiler didn't have a lot of money when she opened her first store. And in order to obtain the needed financing, she borrowed $6,000 from her father-in-law. Now after eight years, a lot of hard work, and *more* financial capital, Anne Beiler's pretzel empire consists of 273 pretzel shops in 35 states.

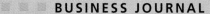

BUSINESS JOURNAL

Orange County's Star Has Faded

Orange County, California, stunned the investment world on December 6, 1994, when it filed for protection under Chapter 9 of the U.S. Bankruptcy Code. Recognized as an outstanding performer in the municipal bond market by such bond-rating agencies as Moody's and Standard & Poor's, this fifth-largest county in the United States, one of the nation's wealthiest, home to 2.5 million residents, and famous for Disneyland and Newport Beach, filed for bankruptcy when it lost $2 billion in the county's investment fund. By filing for bankruptcy protection, Orange County is buying time to evaluate its problems, consider its options, and liquidate some of its remaining investments. Now, the county's bond rating has sunk, making it nearly impossible to fund the shortages in its budget.

For two decades, under the aggressive investing leadership of the county treasurer Robert Citron, this fund was a star performer producing annual returns of 9 percent for Orange County. Betting that interest rates would fall during 1994, Citron invested $8 billion in derivatives, a complex form of investments whose returns are tied to interest rates, and other volatile investments. He also borrowed $14 billion in short-term loans. When the time came to repay the borrowed funds, the interest rates had gone up, and the county discovered it owed more on its loans than it earned on its investments. The result: bankruptcy. Citron's unchecked investing practices brought on the largest financial crisis ever in the world of municipal investments.

Orange County's investment fund, or pool as it is sometimes called, holds monies belonging to 180 cities in Southern California, 187 school districts, transportation authorities, and other county agencies. The expected earnings of $150 million in interest for 1995 to help fund the county's $3.7 billion annual budget had virtually disappeared, and all nonessential spending was suspended. This meant a reduction of services and/or higher taxes for its residents. Planned improvements to the emergency systems used by the police and fire departments were postponed. The school districts ran out of money before the school year ended. And negotiations for a proposed $3 billion expansion of Disneyland vanished.

Robert Citron resigned as treasurer several days before the bankruptcy announcement. But is he entirely to blame for this crisis?

- Where were the county's investment advisers?
- Did county officials become lax in monitoring the investments for the fund, relying solely on Citron's past performance?
- Why did the brokers at Merrill Lynch and other firms that sold those speculative investments allow a municipality to take on so many risks?

These questions and more will most likely be fought out in the courts for many years to come. The shock waves created by this crisis will certainly bring on intense regulation in the municipal bond market. Although there are very few regulations on municipalities' investments today, expect more at both the state and federal level in the near future.

As long as there is sufficient financing today, they don't worry about how well it is used or whether it will be there tomorrow.

Proper financial management, on the other hand, can ensure that

- Financing priorities are established in line with established organizational goals and objectives.
- Spending is planned and controlled in accordance with established priorities.
- Sufficient financing is available when it is needed, both now and in the future.
- Excess cash is invested in certificates of deposit (CDs), government securities, or conservative, marketable securities.

These functions define effective management as applied to a particular resource: money. And, like all effective management, financial management begins with goal setting and planning.

■■ PLANNING—THE BASIS OF SOUND FINANCIAL MANAGEMENT

LEARNING OBJECTIVE 2
Summarize the process of planning for financial management.

financial plan   a plan for obtaining and using the money that is needed to implement an organization's goals

In Chapter 6, we defined a plan as an outline of the actions by which an organization intends to accomplish its goals. A **financial plan,** then, is a plan for obtaining and using the money needed to implement an organization's goals. Once a financial plan is developed and put into action, the firm's performance must be monitored and evaluated. And, like any other plan, it must be modified if necessary.

Developing the Financial Plan

Financial planning (like all planning) begins with the establishment of a set of valid goals and objectives. Next, planners must determine how much money is needed to accomplish each goal and objective. Finally, financial planners must identify available sources of financing and decide which to use. In the process, they must make sure that financing needs are realistic and that sufficient funding is available to meet those needs. The three steps involved in financial planning are illustrated in Figure 19.1.

Establishing Organizational Goals and Objectives   As we have noted, establishing goals and objectives is an important and ongoing management task. A goal is an end state that the organization expects to achieve. Objectives are *specific* statements detailing what the organization intends to accomplish within a certain period of time. If goals and objectives are not specific and measurable, they cannot be translated into costs, and financial planning cannot proceed. Goals and objectives must also be realistic. Otherwise, they may be impossible to finance or achieve. One objective for General Motors in late 1994 was to develop an advertising campaign to introduce the new Oldsmobile Aurora. To fulfill this objective, management spent over $20 million on a dealer training program and over $30 million on advertising the Aurora.[3]

budget a financial statement that projects income and/or expenditures over a specified future period of time

Budgeting for Financial Needs   A **budget** is a financial statement that projects income and/or expenditures over a specified future period of time. Once planners know what the firm's goals and objectives are for a specific period of time—say, the next calendar year—they can estimate the various costs the firm will incur and the sales revenues it will receive. By combining these items into a companywide budget, financial planners can determine whether they must seek additional funding from sources outside the firm.

Usually the budgeting process begins with the construction of departmental budgets for sales and for each of the various types of expenses: production, human resources, promotion, administration, and so on. (A typical sales budget for Stars and Stripes Clothing, a California-based retailer, is shown in Figure 19.2.) Budgeting accuracy is improved when budgets are first constructed for separate departments and for shorter periods of time.

Financial managers can easily combine each department's budget for sales and expenses into a companywide cash budget, like the one in Figure 19.3. Notice in the cash budget for Stars and Stripes Clothing that cash sales and collections are listed at the top for each calendar quarter. Then, payments for purchases and routine expenses are listed in the middle section. Using this information, it is possible to calculate the anticipated cash gain or loss at the end of each quarter.

Most firms today use one of two approaches to budgeting. In the *traditional* approach, each new budget is based on the dollar amounts contained

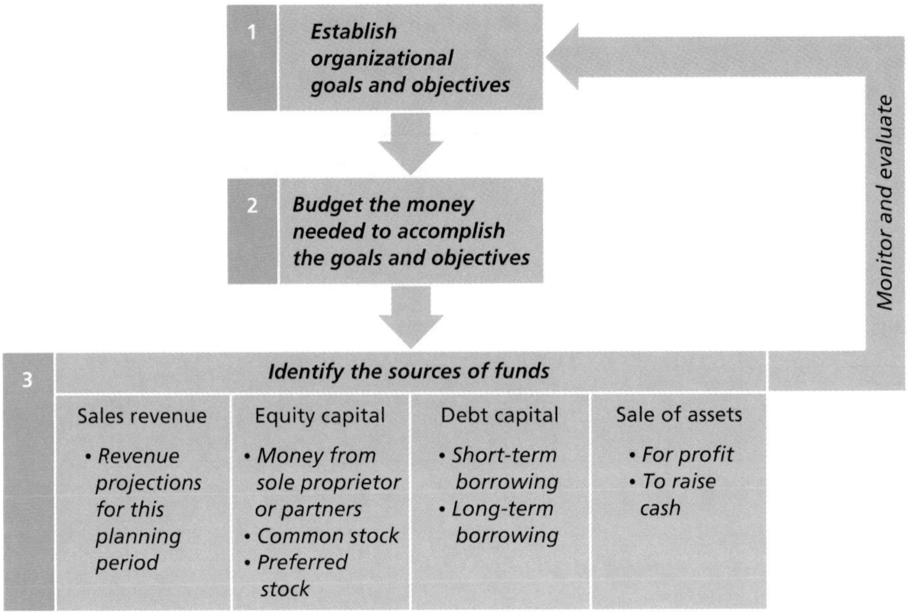

FIGURE 19.1
The Three Steps of Financial Planning
After a financial plan has been developed, it must be monitored continually to ensure that it actually fulfills the firm's goals and objectives.

FIGURE 19.1
The Three Steps of Financial Planning
After a financial plan has been developed, it must be monitored continually to ensure that it actually fulfills the firm's goals and objectives.

in the budget for the preceding year. These amounts are modified to reflect any revised goals, and managers are required to justify only new expenditures. The problem with this approach is that it leaves room for the manipulation of budget items to protect the (sometimes selfish) interests of the budgeter or his or her department.

This problem is essentially eliminated through zero-base budgeting. **Zero-base budgeting** is a budgeting approach in which every expense must be justified in every budget. It can dramatically reduce unnecessary spending because every budget item must stand on its own merits. However, some managers oppose zero-base budgeting on the grounds that it requires entirely too much time-consuming paperwork.

zero-base budgeting a budgeting approach in which every expense must be justified in every budget

Identifying Sources of Funds   The four primary sources of funds, as listed in Figure 19.1, are sales revenue, equity capital, debt capital, and proceeds from the sale of assets. Future sales generally provide the greatest part of a firm's financing. Figure 19.3 shows that, for Stars and Stripes Clothing, sales for the year are expected to cover all expenses and to provide a cash gain of about 16 percent of sales. However, Stars and Stripes has a problem in the first quarter, when sales are expected to fall short of expenses by $7,000. In fact, one of the primary reasons for financial planning is to provide management with adequate lead time to solve this type of problem.

A second type of funding is **equity capital.** For a sole proprietorship or partnership, equity capital is provided by the owner or owners of the business. For a corporation, equity capital is money received from the sale of shares of ownership in the business. Equity capital is used almost exclusively for long-term financing. Thus it might be used to start a business and to fund expansions or mergers. It would not be considered for short-term financing needs, such as Stars and Stripes' first-quarter $7,000 shortfall.

equity capital money received from the owners or from the sale of shares of ownership in the business

STARS AND STRIPES CLOTHING

Sales Budget   For January 1, 199x to December 31, 199x

Department	First quarter	Second quarter	Third quarter	Fourth quarter	Totals
Infants'	$ 50,000	$ 55,000	$ 60,000	$ 70,000	$235,000
Children's	45,000	45,000	40,000	40,000	170,000
Women's	35,000	40,000	35,000	50,000	160,000
Men's	20,000	20,000	15,000	25,000	80,000
Totals	$150,000	$160,000	$150,000	$185,000	$645,000

FIGURE 19.2   Sales Budget for Stars and Stripes Clothing
Usually the budgeting process begins with the construction of departmental budgets for sales.

debt capital   borrowed money obtained through loans of various types

A third type of funding is **debt capital,** which is borrowed money obtained through loans. Debt capital may be borrowed for either short- or long-term use—and a short-term loan seems made to order for Stars and Stripes Clothing. The firm would probably borrow the needed $7,000 (or perhaps a bit more) at some point during the first quarter and repay it from second-quarter sales revenue. In fact, Stars and Stripes Clothing might

FIGURE 19.3   Cash Budget for Stars and Stripes Clothing
A companywide cash budget projects sales and expenses for a given period of time to anticipate cash surpluses and deficits.

STARS AND STRIPES CLOTHING

Cash Budget   For January 1, 199x to December 31, 199x

	First quarter	Second quarter	Third quarter	Fourth quarter	Totals
Cash sales and collections	$150,000	$160,000	$150,000	$185,000	$645,000
Less payments					
Purchases	$110,000	$ 80,000	$ 90,000	$ 60,000	$340,000
Wages/salaries	25,000	20,000	25,000	30,000	100,000
Rent	10,000	10,000	12,000	12,000	44,000
Other expenses	4,000	4,000	5,000	6,000	19,000
Taxes	8,000	8,000	10,000	10,000	36,000
Total payments	$157,000	$122,000	$142,000	$118,000	$539,000
Cash gain or (loss)	$ (7,000)	$ 38,000	$ 8,000	$ 67,000	$106,000

already have established a line of credit—discussed in Chapter 18—at a local bank to cover just such periodic short-term needs.

The fourth type of funding is the proceeds from the sale of assets. A firm generally acquires assets because it needs them for its business operations. Therefore, selling assets is a drastic step. However, it may be a reasonable last resort when neither equity capital nor debt capital can be found.

Assets may also be sold when they are no longer needed or don't "fit" with the company's core business. To raise capital, Intelligent Electronics, Inc., the parent company of BizMart, sold 105 stores to Kmart for $270 million.[4] And in the early 1990s, management for Marriott Corporation decided to concentrate on its core business—hotels. As a result, Marriott sold its Roy Rogers fast-food restaurants to Hardees.[5]

In most cases, the particular funding need clearly suggests the best source of funding. (We discuss sources of equity and debt financing later in this chapter.) In all cases, though, the financial manager should identify and verify funding sources in advance to be sure they will be available when they are needed.

Monitoring and Evaluating Financial Performance

It is important to ensure that financial plans are being properly implemented and to catch minor problems before they become major problems. Accordingly, the financial manager should establish a means of monitoring and evaluating financial performance. Interim budgets (weekly, monthly, or quarterly) may be prepared for comparison purposes. These comparisons point up areas that require additional or revised planning—or at least those areas calling for a more careful investigation.

Figure 19.4 shows a quarterly comparison of budgeted and actual sales for Stars and Stripes Clothing. Sales of children's wear are about 7 percent over budget, and sales of infants' wear are about 9 percent below budget. Although neither discrepancy is a cause for immediate concern, the sales for both departments should be watched. And, such comparisons should be

FIGURE 19.4
Budget Comparison for Stars and Stripes Clothing
Budget comparisons can point out areas that require additional planning or careful investigation.

STARS AND STRIPES CLOTHING

Sales Budget Update   First Quarter, 199x

Department	First-quarter estimate	Actual sales	Dollar difference
Infants'	$ 50,000	$ 45,600	$-4,400
Children's	45,000	48,200	+3,200
Women's	35,000	36,300	+1,300
Men's	20,000	21,100	+1,100
Totals	$150,000	$151,200	$+1,200

routinely reported to department heads and upper-level managers. They may be used as the basis for budgeting, and they may reveal a need to take corrective action (such as promoting infants' wear more vigorously).

It is important to realize that the decision to borrow money does not necessarily mean that a firm is in financial trouble. On the contrary, astute financial management often means regular, responsible borrowing of many different kinds to meet different needs. In the next two sections we examine the sources of short- and long-term financing available to businesses.

■■ SOURCES OF SHORT-TERM DEBT FINANCING

LEARNING OBJECTIVE 3
Describe the advantages and disadvantages of different methods of short-term financing.

Short-term debt financing (money repaid in one year or less) is usually easier to obtain than long-term financing for three reasons:

1. The shorter repayment period means there is less risk of nonpayment for the lender.
2. The dollar amounts of short-term loans are usually smaller than those of long-term loans.
3. A close working relationship normally exists between the short-term borrower and the lender.

Most lenders do not require collateral for short-term financing. When they do, it is usually because they are concerned about the size of a particular loan, the borrowing firm's poor credit rating, or the general prospects of repayment. It may be the case that a financially weak firm will have difficulty obtaining short-term financing even when it is willing to pledge collateral to back up a loan.

Sources of Unsecured Short-Term Financing

unsecured financing
financing that is not backed by collateral

Unsecured financing is financing that is not backed by collateral. A company seeking unsecured short-term capital has several options. They include trade credit, promissory notes, bank loans, and commercial paper.

trade credit a type of short-term financing extended by a seller who does not require immediate payment after delivery of merchandise

Trade Credit   In Chapter 14, we noted that wholesalers sometimes provide financial aid to retailers by allowing them thirty to sixty days (or more) in which to pay for merchandise. This delayed payment, which may also be granted by manufacturers, is a form of short-term financing known as trade credit. More specifically, **trade credit** (sometimes referred to as an *open-book account*) is a type of short-term financing extended by a seller who does not require immediate payment after delivery of merchandise. And because 80 to 90 percent of all transactions between businesses involve some trade credit, it is the most popular form of short-term financing.

When trade credit is used, the purchased goods are delivered along with a bill (or invoice) that states the credit terms. Let's assume that a Barnes and Noble bookstore receives a shipment of books from the publisher Houghton Mifflin. Along with the merchandise, the publisher sends an invoice that states the terms of payment. Barnes and Noble now has two options for payment. First, the book retailer may pay the invoice promptly and take advantage of any cash discount Houghton Mifflin offers. Cash discount terms are specified on the invoice. For instance, "2/10, net 30" means that the customer—Barnes and Noble—may take a 2 percent discount if it pays the invoice within ten days of the invoice date. A second option is to wait until the end of the credit period before making payment. If Barnes and Noble does not have the cash available to take advantage of the cash discount, payment within the first ten days is out of the question. And if payment is made between eleven and thirty days, the customer must pay the entire (net) amount. As long as payment is made before the end of the credit period, the customer maintains the ability to purchase additional merchandise using the trade credit arrangement.

A variation of the trade credit arrangement occurs when a commercial draft is used. A **commercial draft** is a written order requiring a customer to pay a specified sum of money to a supplier for goods or services. It is often used when the supplier is unsure about the customer's credit standing. The commercial draft is similar to an ordinary check with one exception: the draft is filled out by the seller and not the buyer. If the information contained in the draft is correct and the merchandise has been received, an employee for the buyer marks the draft "accepted" and signs it. Then the draft is returned to the seller and can be processed for payment.

commercial draft   a written order requiring a customer to pay a specified sum of money to a supplier for goods or services

Promissory Notes Issued to Suppliers   A **promissory note** is a written pledge by a borrower to pay a certain sum of money to a creditor at a specified future date. Suppliers uneasy about extending trade credit may be less reluctant to offer credit to customers that sign promissory notes. Unlike trade credit, however, promissory notes usually require the borrower to pay interest. Although repayment periods may extend to one year, most promissory notes specify 60 to 180 days. A typical promissory note is shown in Figure 19.5. Note that the customer buying on credit (Richland Company) is called the *maker* and is the party that issues the note. The business selling the merchandise on credit (Shelton Company) is called the *payee*.

promissory note   a written pledge by a borrower to pay a certain sum of money to a creditor at a specified future date

A promissory note offers two important advantages to the firm extending the credit. First, a promissory note is a legally binding and enforceable document that has been signed by the individual or business borrowing the money. Second, most promissory notes are negotiable instruments that can be sold when the money is needed immediately. For example, the note shown in Figure 19.5 will be worth $820 at maturity. If it chose, the Shelton Company could discount, or sell, the note to its own bank. The price would be slightly less than $820, because the bank charges a fee for the service—hence the term *discount*. Shelton would have its money immediately, and the bank would collect the $820 when the note matured.

Unsecured Bank Loans   Commercial banks offer unsecured short-term loans to their customers at interest rates that vary with each borrower's credit rating. The **prime interest rate** (sometimes called the *reference rate*) is the lowest rate charged by a bank for a short-term loan. Figure 19.6 traces the fluctuations in the average prime rate charged by U.S. banks from 1986 to 1992. This lowest rate is generally reserved for large corporations with excellent credit ratings. Organizations with good to high credit ratings may pay the prime rate plus 2 percent. Firms with questionable credit ratings

prime interest rate   the lowest rate charged by a bank for a short-term loan

FIGURE 19.5
A Promissory Note
A promissory note is a borrower's written pledge to pay
a certain sum of money to a
creditor at a specified date.

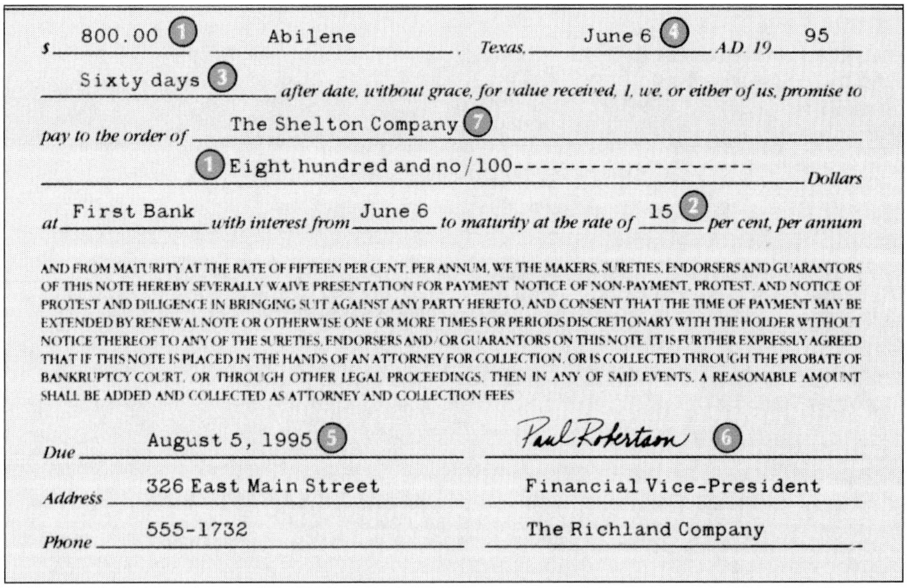

$ ___800.00___ ①   Abilene ___, _Texas_,___ June 6 ④ ___A.D. 19__ 95

___Sixty days___ ③ ___ _after date, without grace, for value received, I, we, or either of us, promise to_

pay to the order of ___The Shelton Company___ ⑦

①Eight hundred and no/100----------------- ___ _Dollars_

_at_ ___First Bank___ _with interest from_ ___June 6___ _to maturity at the rate of_ __15__ ② _per cent, per annum_

AND FROM MATURITY AT THE RATE OF FIFTEEN PER CENT, PER ANNUM, WE THE MAKERS, SURETIES, ENDORSERS AND GUARANTORS
OF THIS NOTE HEREBY SEVERALLY WAIVE PRESENTATION FOR PAYMENT, NOTICE OF NON-PAYMENT, PROTEST, AND NOTICE OF
PROTEST AND DILIGENCE IN BRINGING SUIT AGAINST ANY PARTY HERETO, AND CONSENT THAT THE TIME OF PAYMENT MAY BE
EXTENDED BY RENEWAL NOTE OR OTHERWISE ONE OR MORE TIMES FOR PERIODS DISCRETIONARY WITH THE HOLDER WITHOUT
NOTICE THEREOF TO ANY OF THE SURETIES, ENDORSERS AND/OR GUARANTORS ON THIS NOTE. IT IS FURTHER EXPRESSLY AGREED
THAT IF THIS NOTE IS PLACED IN THE HANDS OF AN ATTORNEY FOR COLLECTION, OR IS COLLECTED THROUGH THE PROBATE OF
BANKRUPTCY COURT, OR THROUGH OTHER LEGAL PROCEEDINGS, THEN IN ANY OF SAID EVENTS, A REASONABLE AMOUNT
SHALL BE ADDED AND COLLECTED AS ATTORNEY AND COLLECTION FEES

Due ___August 5, 1995___ ⑤   _Paul Robertson_ ⑥

Address ___326 East Main Street___   Financial Vice-President

Phone ___555-1732___   The Richland Company

1. The principal ($800.00) is the amount of the debt. It is the amount of the credit transaction.
2. The rate (15 percent) expresses the value paid for use of the borrowed money. It is usually stated in annual or yearly terms.
3. The time (60 days) is the period for which the money is borrowed.
4. The date (June 6) is the date the note was issued.
5. The maturity date (August 5) is the day the principal and interest are due. It is often called the due date.
6. The maker (The Richland Company) is the individual or company issuing the note and bor- rowing the money.
7. The payee (The Shelton Company) is the individual or company extending the credit.

may have to pay the prime rate plus 4 percent. Of course, if the banker believes loan repayment may be a problem, the borrower's loan application may be rejected.

Banks generally offer short-term loans through promissory notes, a line of credit, or a revolving credit agreement. _Promissory notes_ written to banks are similar to those discussed in the last section.

The _line of credit_—in essence, a prearranged short-term loan—is dis- cussed in Chapter 18. A bank that offers a line of credit may require that a _compensating balance_ be kept on deposit at the bank. This balance may be as much as 20 percent of the line-of-credit amount. Assume that North Carolina–based NationsBank requires a 20 percent compensating balance on short-term loans. If you borrow $50,000, at least $10,000 of the loan amount must be kept on deposit at the bank. In this situation, the actual interest rate you must pay on the original $50,000 loan increases because you have the use of only $40,000. The bank may also require that every com- mercial borrower _clean up_ (pay off completely) its line of credit at least once each year and not use it again for a period of thirty to sixty days. This

FIGURE 19.6
Average Prime Interest Rate Paid by U.S. Businesses Since 1986
The prime rate is the interest rate charged by U.S. banks when businesses with the "best" credit ratings borrow money. All other businesses pay interest rates higher than the prime rate.   *(Source:* Statistical Abstract of the United States, for 1993, *U.S. Government Printing Office, Washington, D.C., p. 520.)*

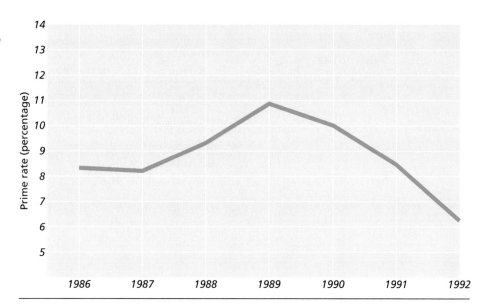

revolving credit agreement   a guaranteed line of credit

commercial paper   short-term promissory notes issued by large corporations

second requirement ensures that the money obtained through a line of credit is used only to meet short-term needs and that it doesn't gradually become a source of long-term financing.

Even with a line of credit, a firm may not be able to borrow on short notice if the bank does not have sufficient funds available. For this reason, some firms prefer a **revolving credit agreement,** which is a guaranteed line of credit. Under this type of agreement, the bank guarantees that the money will be available when the borrower needs it. In return for the guarantee, the bank charges a commitment fee ranging from 0.25 to 1.0 percent of the *unused* portion of the revolving credit agreement. The usual interest is charged for the portion that *is* borrowed.

Commercial Paper   Commercial paper is short-term promissory notes issued by large corporations. Commercial paper is secured only by the reputation of the issuing firm; no collateral is involved. It is usually issued in large denominations, ranging from $5,000 to $100,000. Corporations issuing commercial paper pay interest rates slightly below those charged by commercial banks. Thus, issuing commercial paper is cheaper than getting short-term financing from a bank. In reality, the interest rate that corporations pay when they issue commercial paper is tied to the corporation's credit rating and its ability to repay the commercial paper. Recently, the credit ratings for Digital Equipment, Woolworth, and Kmart were lowered by the major credit reporting agencies in the United States. As a result, these three firms will be required to pay higher interest rates on future commercial paper issues.

Large firms with excellent credit reputations can quickly raise large sums of money in this way. General Motors Acceptance Corporation (GMAC), for example, may issue commercial paper totaling millions of dollars. However, commercial paper is not without risks. If the issuing corporation later has severe financial problems, it may not be able to repay the promised amounts. Recently, Integrated Resources defaulted on commercial paper worth $276 million. And Wang Laboratories defaulted on commercial paper valued at $25 million.[6]

Sources of Secured Short-Term Financing

Financially secure firms prefer to reserve collateral for long-term borrowing needs. Yet if a business cannot obtain enough capital via unsecured financing, it must put up collateral to obtain the additional short-term financing it needs. Almost any asset can serve as collateral. However, *inventories* and *accounts receivable* are the assets most commonly pledged for short-term financing.

Loans Secured by Inventory   Normally, manufacturers, wholesalers, and retailers have large amounts of money invested in finished merchandise inventories. In addition, manufacturers carry raw materials and work-in-process inventories. All three types of inventory may be pledged as collateral for short-term loans. However, lenders prefer the much more salable finished goods to the other inventories.

A lender may insist that inventory used as collateral be stored in a public warehouse. In such a case, the receipt issued by the warehouse is retained by the lender. Without this receipt, the public warehouse will not release the merchandise. The lender releases the warehouse receipt—and the merchandise—to the borrower when the borrowed money is repaid. In addition to the interest on the loan, the borrower must also pay for storage in the public warehouse. As a result, this type of loan is more expensive than an unsecured short-term loan.

A special type of financing called floor planning is used by automobile, furniture, and appliance dealers. **Floor planning** is a method of financing in which title to merchandise is given to lenders in return for short-term financing. The major difference between floor planning and other types of secured short-term financing is that the borrower maintains control of the inventory. As merchandise is sold, the borrower repays the lender a portion of the loan. To ensure that the lender is being repaid a portion of the loan when the merchandise is sold, the lender will periodically check to ensure that the collateral is still in the borrower's possession.

floor planning method of financing in which title to merchandise is given to lenders in return for short-term financing

Loans Secured by Receivables   **Accounts receivable** are amounts owed to a firm by its customers. They arise primarily from trade credit and are usually due in less than sixty days. A firm can pledge its accounts receivable as collateral to obtain short-term financing. A lender may advance 70 to 80 percent of the dollar amount of the receivables. First, however, it conducts a thorough investigation to determine the *quality* of the receivables. (The quality of the receivables is the credit standing of the firm's customers coupled with the customers' ability to repay their credit obligations.) If a favorable determination is made, the loan is approved. When the borrowing firm collects from a customer whose account has been pledged as collateral, the money must be turned over to the lender as partial repayment of the loan.

accounts receivable amounts owed to a firm by its customers

An alternative approach is to notify the borrower's credit customers to make their payments directly to the lender.

Factoring Accounts Receivable

factor a firm that specializes in buying other firms' accounts receivable

Accounts receivable may be used in one other way to help raise short-term financing: they can be sold to a factoring company (or factor). A **factor** is a firm that specializes in buying other firms' accounts receivable. The factor buys the accounts receivable for less than their face value, but it collects the full dollar amount when each account is due. The factor's profit is thus the difference between the face value of the accounts receivable and the amount the factor has paid for them. Generally, the amount of profit the factor receives is based on the risk the factor assumes. Risk, in this case, is the probability that the accounts receivable will not be repaid when they mature.

Even though the firm selling its accounts receivable gets less than face value, it does receive needed cash immediately. Moreover, it has shifted both the task of collecting and the risk of nonpayment to the factor, which now owns the accounts receivable. In many cases, the factor may purchase only selected accounts receivable—usually those with the highest potential of repayment. In other cases, the firm selling its accounts receivable must check with the factor *before* selling merchandise on a credit basis. Thus, the firm receives instant feedback on whether the factor will purchase the account. Generally, customers whose accounts receivable have been factored are given instructions to make their payments directly to the factor.

A form of factoring called *forfaiting* is an increasingly popular method of financing international transactions. In fact, each year, U.S. businesses factor about $1 billion of accounts receivable that are the result of exporting goods to international markets.[7] When this method is used, the exporter avoids tying up working capital, eliminates the time required to manage accounts receivable, and eliminates the problem of nonpaying customers in a foreign land. For more information on financing exports, read Global Perspectives.

Cost Comparisons

Table 19.2 compares the various types of short-term financing. As you can see, trade credit is the least expensive. Generally, the less favorable a firm's credit rating, the more likely it is that the firm will have to use a higher-cost means of financing. Factoring of accounts receivable is the highest-cost method shown.

For many purposes, short-term financing suits a firm's needs perfectly. In other cases, however, long-term financing may be more appropriate.

■ ■ SOURCES OF LONG-TERM FINANCING

LEARNING OBJECTIVE 4
Evaluate the advantages and disadvantages of equity financing and debt financing from the corporation's standpoint.

Sources of long-term financing vary with the size and type of business. As mentioned earlier, if the business is a sole proprietorship or partnership, equity capital is acquired by the business when the owner or owners invest

■ ■ ■ ■ GLOBAL PERSPECTIVES

Financing an Export Sales Contract

Lawrence Thompson, president of the ABC Widget Company, has just returned from Europe with a contract in his pocket for a large order of widgets. Because this is ABC's first overseas order, Thompson telephones his local bank to set up an appointment to discuss his export trade–credit financing needs. He is surprised to learn that his bank does not provide financing, nor does it issue letters of credit in the international marketplace. Although Thompson has a contract, he is unable to secure the financing he needs to purchase materials, pay salaries, and meet everyday expenses until he receives payment from his overseas customer. What should he do?

In his search for an answer, Thompson will discover that many small to midsized companies have stalled at the same roadblock. Many banks are reluctant to venture into this area because they lack the expertise and manpower necessary for global trade financing. However, there are at least three options Thompson can pursue to obtain the needed financing to complete the contract with his overseas buyer.

1. Thompson could sell his export receivables right away to a factor or forfaiter at a discount for immediate cash. Factors and forfaiters have vast overseas contacts and extensive experience in the export business. They assume virtually all the risks involved, handle the interest and exchange rate, and perform all the administrative responsibilities in the collection of payments. The difference between the two is that factors want a large percentage of a company's export business, work with only short-term receivables of up to 180 days, and limit their services to companies that manufacture consumer goods. On the other hand, a forfaiter will assume a one-time sales agreement, work with medium-term receivables of 180 days to seven years, and deal in capital goods, commodities, and large projects.

2. Another alternative for Thompson is to let a trading company that specializes in the trading, managing, and financing of products from one industry take title to his goods and handle the shipment for him. Trading companies perform their services under the guarantees and insurance programs of the United States and foreign governments.

3. One final alternative for Thompson, since he lives in Illinois, is to take advantage of the state's export finance program. Illinois is one of the twenty-nine states that recognize the importance of exports to the local economy and have developed support programs that may include guarantees for commercial loans, direct loans from the state, and export credit insurance.

A FINAL NOTE

Because so many small-business people like Lawrence Thompson have met with difficulty when they approached their local bank for export financing, the U.S. Small Business Administration has set up a program for community bankers. Through this enterprise, cosponsored with the Bankers' Association for Foreign Trade, bankers who want to provide international services to their small-business customers can receive information and attend seminars on how to develop the expertise and contacts they need in the global marketplace.

TABLE 19.2   Comparison of Short-Term Financing Methods

Type of Financing	Cost	Repayment Period	Businesses That May Use It	Comments
Trade credit	Low, if any	30 to 60 days	All businesses	Usually no finance charge.
Promissory note issued to suppliers	Moderate	1 year or less	All businesses	Usually unsecured but requires legal document; issued by borrower.
Unsecured bank loan	Moderate	1 year or less	All businesses	A line of credit or revolving credit agreement may be used.
Commercial paper	Moderate	1 year or less	Large corporations with high credit ratings	Available only to large firms.
Secured loan	High	1 year or less	Firms with questionable credit ratings	Inventory or accounts receivable may be used as collateral.
Factoring	High	None	Firms that have large numbers of credit customers	Accounts receivable are sold to a factor.

money in the business. For corporations, equity-financing options include the sale of stock and the use of profits not distributed to owners. The available debt-financing options are the sale of corporate bonds and long-term loans.

Equity Financing

Some equity capital (money from the owners) is used to start every business—sole proprietorship, partnership, or corporation. In the case of corporations, equity capital is provided by stockholders who buy shares in the company.

There are at least two reasons why large corporations sell stock. First, the corporation need not repay money obtained from the sale of stock. Occasionally a corporation buys back its own stock, but only because such an investment is in its own best interest. In 1994 Toys "Я" Us announced plans to spend $1 billion to repurchase some of its own stock. According to management, purchasing its own stock was the best particular investment available to the firm at that particular time.[8] In addition to being a good investment, management often repurchases stock to increase the dollar value of shares still held by stockholders.

A second advantage of equity financing is that a corporation is under no legal obligation to pay dividends to stockholders. As mentioned in Chapter 4, a *dividend* is a distribution of earnings to the stockholders of a corporation. Investors purchase the shares of stock of many corporations primarily for the dividends they pay. However, for any reason (if a company has a bad year, for example), the board of directors can vote to omit dividend payments. Earnings are then retained for use in funding business operations. Thus a corporation need not even pay dividends for the use of equity capi-

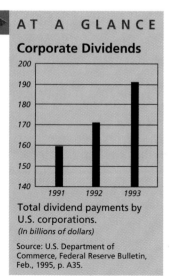

AT A GLANCE

Corporate Dividends

Total dividend payments by U.S. corporations.
(In billions of dollars)

Source: U.S. Department of Commerce, Federal Reserve Bulletin, Feb., 1995, p. A35.

tal. Of course, the corporate management may hear from unhappy stockholders if expected dividends are omitted too frequently.

There are two types of stock: common and preferred. Each type has advantages and drawbacks as a means of long-term financing.

common stock stock whose owners may vote on corporate matters, but whose claims on profits and assets are subordinate to the claims of others

Common Stock   A share of **common stock** represents the most basic form of corporate ownership. A common-stock certificate for Houghton Mifflin Company is shown in Figure 19.7. In return for the financing provided by selling common stock, management must make certain concessions to stockholders that may restrict or change corporate policies. By law, every corporation must hold an annual meeting, at which the holders of common stock may vote for the board of directors and approve (or disapprove) major corporate actions. Among such actions are

1. Amendments to the corporate charter or bylaws.
2. Sale of certain assets.
3. Mergers and acquisitions.
4. Issuing of preferred stock or bonds.
5. Changes in the amount of common stock issued.

pre-emptive rights the rights of current stockholders to purchase any new stock that the corporation issues before it is sold to the general public

Currently, forty-eight states require that a provision for pre-emptive rights be included in the charter of every corporation. **Pre-emptive rights** are the rights of current stockholders to purchase any new stock that the corporation issues before it is sold to the general public. By exercising their

FIGURE 19.7
A Common-Stock Certificate
Stockholders provide the company with capital when they purchase shares of stock (equity) in the company. *(Source: Used with permission of Houghton Mifflin Company.)*

pre-emptive rights, stockholders are able to maintain their current proportion of ownership of the corporation. This may be important when the corporation is small and management control is a matter of concern to stockholders.

Money acquired through the sale of common stock is thus essentially cost-free, but few investors will buy common stock if they cannot foresee some return on their investment. Information on how stockholders can make money with stock investments is provided in Chapter 20.

preferred stock   stock whose owners usually do not have voting rights, but whose claims on dividends and assets have precedence over those of common-stock owners

Preferred Stock   As noted in Chapter 4, the owners of **preferred stock** usually do not have voting rights, but their claims on dividends and assets precede those of common-stock owners. If the board of directors approves dividend payments, holders of preferred stock must receive their dividends before holders of common stock are paid dividends. And preferred stockholders have first claim (after creditors) on corporate assets if the firm is dissolved or declares bankruptcy. Even so, like common stock, preferred stock does not represent a debt that must be legally repaid.

The dividend to be paid on a share of preferred stock is known before the stock is purchased. It is stated on the stock certificate either as a percent

Would you give these two guys $10 million? Well, investors did! With the help of the Minneapolis brokerage firm R. J. Steichen & Co., Douglas Pihl and Duane Carlson raised $10 million to start a company called NetStar that manufactures computer peripherals. Investors who wanted to get in on the ground floor were willing to put up the cash to develop the company's first product—a gigarouter. A gigarouter is a piece of high-performance computer hardware that links electronic workstations to give them the power of a supercomputer at a fraction of the cost.

par value an assigned (and often arbitrary) dollar value printed on the stock certificate

of the par value of the stock or as a dollar amount of money. The **par value** of a stock is an assigned (and often arbitrary) dollar value printed on the stock certificate. For example, Pitney Bowes—a U.S. manufacturer of office and business equipment—issued 4 percent preferred stock with a par value of $50. The annual dividend amount is $2 per share (4 percent × $50 par value = $2 annual dividend).

A corporation usually issues one type of common stock, but it may issue many types of preferred stock with varying dividends or dividend rates. For example, Ohio Edison has one common-stock issue but ten preferred-stock issues with different dividend amounts for each type of preferred stock.

On occasion, a corporation may decide to call in or buy back an issue of preferred stock when management believes it can issue new preferred stock at a lower dividend rate—or possibly common stock with no specified dividend. When this occurs, management has two options. First, it can buy shares in the market—just like another investor purchases shares of the preferred-stock issue. Second, the corporation can buy back the stock, since practically all preferred stock is *callable* at the option of the corporation. When the corporation exercises a call provision, the investor usually receives a call premium. A **call premium** is a dollar amount over par value that the corporation has to pay an investor for redeeming either preferred stock or a corporate bond. (Corporate bonds are discussed later in this chapter.) When considering the two options, management will naturally obtain the preferred stock in the less costly way.

call premium a dollar amount over par value that the corporation has to pay an investor for redeeming either preferred stock or a corporate bond

convertible preferred stock preferred stock that can be exchanged *at the stockholder's option* for a specified number of shares of common stock

To make preferred stock more attractive to investors, some corporations include a conversion feature in various issues. **Convertible preferred stock** is preferred stock that can be exchanged *at the stockholder's option* for a specified number of shares of common stock. The Textron Corporation—a manufacturer of component parts for the automotive and aerospace industries—has issued convertible preferred stock. Each share of Textron preferred stock is convertible to 2.2 shares of the firm's common stock. This conversion feature provides the investor with the safety of preferred stock and the hope of greater speculative gain through conversion to common stock.

Retained Earnings   Most large corporations distribute only a portion of their after-tax earnings to shareholders. The remainder, the portion of a corporation's profits not distributed to stockholders, is called **retained earnings.** Because they are undistributed profits, retained earnings are considered a form of equity financing.

retained earnings the portion of a business's profits not distributed to stockholders

The amount of a firm's earnings that is to be retained in any year is determined by corporate management and approved by the board of directors. More mature corporations may distribute 40 to 60 percent of their after-tax profits as dividends. Utility companies and other corporations with very stable earnings often pay out as much as 80 to 90 percent of what they earn. For a large corporation, retained earnings can amount to a hefty bit of financing. For example, in 1993 the total amount of retained earnings for Ford Motor Company was in excess of $11 billion.[9] And for Exxon Corporation, 1993 retained earnings totaled more than $49 billion.[10] Most small and growing corporations pay no cash dividend—or a very small dividend—to their shareholders. All or most earnings are reinvested in the business for

You have to be sharp to manage something as important as a company's finances. Successful firms often use borrowed funds to increase the return on owners' equity. In most cases, the borrowed funds come from commercial banks, pension funds, *and* insurance companies. Here, one company, Principal Mutual Life Insurance Company, advertises how it can help businesses face financial problems by taking advantage of the services offered by one of its subsidiaries— The Principal Financial Group.

research and development, expansion, or to fund other major projects. Stockholders don't actually lose because of this. Reinvestment tends to increase the value of their stock while it provides essentially cost-free financing for the business.

Debt Financing

Most people think that for a business, borrowing money is a sign of weakness. And, to be sure, it *can be* a sign of financial weakness. But as we pointed out earlier in this chapter, businesses borrow money on a short-term basis for many valid reasons besides desperation. There are also valid reasons for long-term borrowing. In fact, successful businesses often use the financial leverage created by borrowing money to improve their financial performance. **Financial leverage** is the use of borrowed funds to increase the return on owners' equity. The principle of financial leverage works as long as a firm's earnings are larger than the interest charged for the borrowed money. Of course, if the firm's earnings should drop below the interest cost of borrowed money, the return on owners' equity will decrease.

To understand how financial leverage can increase a firm's return on owners' equity, study the financial information for Texas-based Cypress Springs Plastics presented in Table 19.3. Pete Johnston, the owner of the

financial leverage the use of borrowed funds to increase the return on owners' equity

TABLE 19.3   Analysis of the Effect of Additional Capital from Debt or Equity—Cypress Springs Plastics, Inc.

Additional Debt			Additional Equity		
Owners' equity		$500,000	Owners' equity		$500,000
Additional equity	+	– 0 –	Additional equity	+	100,000
Total equity		$500,000	Total equity		$600,000
Loan @ 9 percent	+	100,000	No loan	+	– 0 –
Total capital		$600,000	Total capital		$600,000

Year-end Earnings					
Gross profit		$95,000	Gross profit		$95,000
Less interest	–	9,000	No interest	–	– 0 –
Operating profit		$86,000	Operating profit		$95,000
Return on equity		17.2%	Return on equity		15.8%
($86,000 ÷ $500,000 = 17.2%)			($95,000 ÷ $600,000 = 15.8%)		

firm, is trying to decide how best to finance a $100,000 purchase of new high-tech manufacturing equipment. He could borrow the money and pay 9 percent annual interest. As a second option, Johnston could invest additional money in the firm. Assuming that the firm earns $95,000 a year and annual interest for this loan totals $9,000, the return on owners' equity for Cypress Springs Plastics would be higher if the firm borrowed the additional financing. Return on equity—a topic covered in Chapter 17—is determined by dividing a firm's net income by the dollar amount of owners' equity. For Cypress Springs Plastics, return on equity equals 17.2 percent ($86,000 ÷ $500,000 = .172, or 17.2 percent) if Johnston borrows the additional $100,000. The firm's return on owners' equity would decrease to 15.8 percent ($95,000 ÷ $600,000 = .158, or 15.8 percent) if Johnston invests an additional $100,000 in the business.

The most obvious danger when using financial leverage is that the firm's earnings could fall short of the cost of borrowing money. If this situation occurs, the fixed interest charge actually works to reduce or eliminate the return on owners' equity. Of course, borrowed money must eventually be repaid. Periodic payments for interest and debt reduction may be hard to manage for some businesses, especially if the firm has a bad year. Finally, because lenders always have the option to turn down a loan request, many managers are reluctant to rely on borrowed money.

For a small business, long-term debt financing is generally limited to loans. Large corporations have the additional option of issuing corporate bonds.

Long-Term Loans   Many businesses finance their long-range activities with loans from commercial banks, insurance companies, pension funds, and other financial institutions. Business start-up costs, new-product development, long-term marketing activities, expansion of facilities, purchase of new equipment, and mergers and acquisitions are likely to be partially or fully funded by long-term loans. Manufacturers and suppliers of heavy equipment and machinery may also provide long-term financing by granting extended credit terms to their customers.

When the loan repayment period is longer than one year, the borrower must sign a term-loan agreement. A **term-loan agreement** is a promissory note that requires a borrower to repay a loan in monthly, quarterly, semiannual, or annual installments.

Long-term business loans are normally repaid in three to seven years. The interest rate and other specific terms are often based on such factors as the reasons for borrowing, the borrowing firm's credit rating, and the value of collateral. Although long-term loans may occasionally be unsecured, in most cases the lender requires some type of collateral. Acceptable collateral includes real estate, machinery, and equipment. Lenders may also require that borrowers maintain a minimum amount of working capital.

term-loan agreement   a promissory note that requires a borrower to repay a loan in monthly, quarterly, semiannual, or annual installments

Corporate Bonds   Large corporations issue bonds in denominations of from $1,000 to $50,000, with the total face value of all the bonds in an issue usually running into the millions of dollars. A **corporate bond** is a corporation's written pledge that it will repay a specified amount of money, with interest. Most corporate bonds are debenture bonds. A **debenture bond** is a bond backed only by the reputation of the issuing corporation. To make its bonds more appealing to investors, a corporation may issue mortgage bonds. A **mortgage bond** is a corporate bond secured by various assets of the issuing firm. The corporation can also issue convertible bonds. A **convertible bond** can be exchanged, at the owner's option, for a specified number of shares of the corporation's common stock. Westinghouse Electric Corp.'s 2007 bond issue is convertible: each bond can be converted to 64.5 shares of Westinghouse common stock. The corporation can gain in two ways by issuing convertible bonds. Convertibles usually carry a lower interest rate than nonconvertible bonds. And once a bondholder converts a bond to common stock, the corporation is no longer obliged to redeem it.

corporate bond   a corporation's written pledge that it will repay a specified amount of money, with interest

debenture bond   a bond backed only by the reputation of the issuing corporation

mortgage bond   a corporate bond secured by various assets of the issuing firm

convertible bond   a bond that can be exchanged, at the owner's option, for a specified number of shares of the corporation's common stock

maturity date   the date on which the corporation is to repay the borrowed money

registered bond   a bond that is registered in the owner's name by the issuing company

Figure 19.8 shows a corporate bond for Baltimore Gas and Electric Company. Note that it includes the interest rate (8.40 percent) and the maturity date (October 15, 1999). The **maturity date** is the date on which the corporation is to repay the borrowed money. The bond also has spaces for the amount of its face value, the registration number, and the bondholder's name.

An individual or firm generally buys a corporate bond through a securities broker. Between the time of purchase and the maturity date, the corporation pays interest to the bond owner—usually every six months—at the stated rate. Owners of the Baltimore Gas and Electric bonds (Figure 19.8) receive 8.40 percent—or $84—a year for each $1,000 bond ($1,000 × .084 = $84). Because interest for corporate bonds is usually paid semiannually, bondowners receive $42 ($84 ÷ 2 = $42) every six months for each bond they own. The method used to pay bondholders their interest depends on whether they own registered or coupon bonds. A **registered bond**—like the Baltimore Gas and Electric bond—is a bond that is registered in the owner's name by the issuing company. Interest checks for registered bonds are mailed directly to the bondholder of record. When a

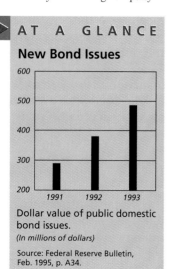

▶▶ **AT A GLANCE**

New Bond Issues

Dollar value of public domestic bond issues.
(In millions of dollars)

Source: Federal Reserve Bulletin, Feb. 1995, p. A34.

FIGURE 19.8
A Corporate Bond
A corporate bond is a corporation's written pledge that it will repay on the date of maturity a specified amount of money, with interest.
(Source: Used with permission of Baltimore Gas and Electric Company.)

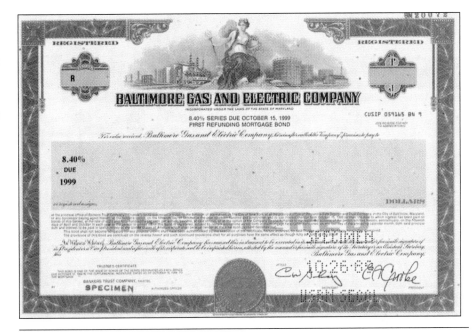

registered bond is sold, it must be endorsed by the seller before ownership can be transferred on the company books. A **coupon bond** is a bond issued with detachable coupons that the bondholder must present to a paying agent *or* the issuer to receive interest payments. At the maturity date, the bondowner returns both types of bonds to the corporation and receives cash equaling the face value.

coupon bond a bond issued with detachable coupons that the bondholder must present to a paying agent *or* the issuer to receive interest payments

Repayment Provisions for Corporate Bonds Maturity dates for bonds generally range from fifteen to thirty years after the date of issue. In the event that the interest is not paid or the firm becomes insolvent, bondowners' claims on the assets of the corporation take precedence over both common and preferred stockholders. Some bonds are callable before the maturity date. For these bonds, the corporation usually pays the bondowner a call premium. The amount of the call premium is specified, along with other provisions, in the bond indenture. The **bond indenture** is a legal document that details all the conditions relating to a bond issue.

bond indenture a legal document that details all the conditions relating to a bond issue

From the corporation's standpoint, financing through a bond issue differs considerably from equity financing. Bond interest must be paid periodically—usually every six months. In the eyes of the Internal Revenue Service, interest is a tax-deductible business expense. And because interest expense lowers corporate profits, the corporation pays less taxes. Furthermore, corporate bonds must be redeemed for their face value at maturity. If the corporation defaults on (does not pay) either of these interest or redemption payments, owners of bonds could force the firm into bankruptcy.

serial bonds   bonds of a single issue that mature on different dates

sinking fund   a sum of money to which deposits are made each year for the purpose of redeeming a bond issue

trustee   an independent firm or individual that acts as the bondowners' representative

A corporation may use one of three methods to ensure that it has sufficient funds available to redeem a bond issue. First, it can issue the bonds as **serial bonds,** which are bonds of a single issue that mature on different dates. For example, Seaside Productions used a twenty-five-year, $50-million bond issue to finance its expansion. None of the bonds mature during the first fifteen years. Thereafter, 10 percent of the bonds mature each year, until all the bonds are retired at the end of the twenty-fifth year. Second, the corporation can establish a sinking fund. A **sinking fund** is a sum of money to which deposits are made each year for the purpose of redeeming a bond issue. When H. J. Heinz sold a $50-million bond issue, the company agreed to contribute $3 million to a sinking fund each year until the bond's maturity in the year 2007. Third, a corporation can pay off an old bond issue by selling new bonds. Although this may appear to perpetuate the corporation's long-term debt, a number of utility companies and railroads use this repayment method. Business Journal explains why corporations buy back their own bonds.

A corporation that issues bonds must also appoint a **trustee,** which is an independent firm or individual that acts as the bondowners' representative. A trustee's duties are most often handled by a commercial bank or other large financial institution. The corporation must report to the trustee periodically regarding its ability to make interest payments and eventually redeem the bonds. In turn, the trustee transmits this information to the

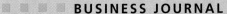

Corporations May Buy Back Their Bonds

Back in 1994, Shirley Clark—a 34-year-old office manager in Denver, Colorado—purchased ten corporate bonds issued by Ford Motor Company. Since 1994, the bonds have paid 8 7/8 percent annual interest or $88.75 per bond a year, and will until the bonds mature in 2022. At a time when interest rates on certificates of deposit were around 4 to 5 percent, Clark's bonds were still paying above-average returns compared with other quality investments. It was almost too good to be true—and it may be. What Clark didn't realize was that her Ford bonds are callable—at the option of the corporation—on or after November 15, 2002. At the time the corporation issued the bonds, the interest rate paid on this bond issue was less than what Ford would pay to obtain financing through other sources. But if interest rates in the overall economy should fall between now and the year 2002, Ford may decide to sell new bonds with a lower interest rate and call (redeem) Clark's high-interest bonds. The money that Ford needs to redeem Clark's bonds can also be obtained from selling common or preferred stock or from the sale of unwanted assets that are no longer needed. Regardless of where the money comes from, a firm's purpose in calling in a bond issue is always to replace high-cost financing with low-cost financing.

CALLING IN EXISTING BOND ISSUES

Because these Ford Motor Company bonds are callable, Ford can exercise its option to repurchase the bonds at a price that was specified at the time of issue. The call price is usually the face value of the bond (typically $1,000). In addition to paying the face value, the corporation may also agree to pay a small premium to the bondholder as compensation for calling the bond in before maturity. The fact that this Ford bond is callable is a risk that Clark assumed when she chose this particular bond. In return, she received a higher rate of interest compared with Ford bonds that were not callable.

BUYING BONDS ON THE OPEN MARKET

A second method that Ford can use to redeem outstanding bonds is simply to purchase bonds from the open market. According to financial managers, this method has at least three advantages over calling a bond issue. First, the corporation may pay less than face value for the bonds if the bond's current market value is less than $1,000. Second, the corporation doesn't have to pay a premium to redeem bonds. Finally, the corporation doesn't risk alienating bondholders by calling in its high-interest bonds.

bondowners, along with its own evaluation of the corporation's ability to pay.

Cost Comparisons

Table 19.4 compares the different types of long-term equity and debt financing. Obviously, the least expensive type of financing is through an issue of common stock. The most expensive is a long-term loan.

TABLE 19.4   Comparison of Long-Term Financing Methods

Type of Financing	Repayment?	Repayment Period	Interest/ Dividends	Businesses That May Use It
Equity				
1. Common stock	No	None	Dividends not required	All corporations that sell stock to investors
2. Preferred stock	No	None	Dividends not required but must be paid before common stockholders receive any dividends	Larger corporations that have an established investor base of common stockholders
Debt				
1. Long-term loan	Yes	Usually 3 to 7 years (up to 15 years)	Interest rates between 7% and 14%, depending on economic conditions and the financial stability of the company requesting the loan	All firms that can meet the lender's repayment and collateral requirements
2. Corporate bond	Yes	Usually 15 to 30 years	Interest rates between 7% and 12%, depending on economic conditions and the financial stability of the company issuing the bonds	Larger corporations that investors trust

■■ A WORD ABOUT THE USES OF FUNDS

LEARNING OBJECTIVE 5
Discuss the importance of using funds effectively.

In this chapter we have mentioned a variety of business uses of funds. They range from the payment of recurring expenses, such as rent, wages, and the cost of raw materials, to the payment of such one-time costs as plant expansions and mergers. In general, a business uses funds to pay for the resources it needs to produce and market its products.

The effective use of finances, as we have noted, is an important function of financial management. To some extent, financial management can be viewed as a two-sided problem. On one side, the uses of funds often dictate the type or types of financing needed by a business. On the other side, the activities that a business can undertake are determined by the types of financing available. Financial managers must ensure that funds are available when needed, that they are obtained at the lowest possible cost, and that they are used as efficiently as possible. And, finally, financial managers must ensure that funds are available for the repayment of debts in accordance with lenders' financing terms. Prompt repayment is essential to protect the firm's credit rating and its ability to obtain financing in the future.

To a great extent, firms are financed through the investments of individuals—money that people have deposited in banks or have used to purchase stocks, mutual funds, and bonds. In Chapter 20, we look at securities markets and how they help people invest their money in business.

■ ■ ■ ■ CHAPTER REVIEW

Summary

1 Explain the need for financing and financial management in business.

Financial management consists of activities that are concerned with obtaining money and using it effectively. Short-term financing is money that will be used for one year or less and then repaid. Although there are many short-term needs, cash flow and inventory are two for which short-term financing is often required. Long-term financing is money that will be used for more than one year. Such financing may be required for a business start-up or expansion, for new-product development, or for replacement of production facilities. Proper financial management can ensure that money is available when it is needed and that it is used efficiently, in keeping with organizational goals.

2 Summarize the process of planning for financial management.

A financial plan begins with the organization's goals and objectives. Next these goals and objectives are "translated" into budgets that detail expected income and expenses. From these budgets, which may be combined into an overall cash budget, the financial manager determines what funding will be needed and where it may be obtained. The four principal sources of financing are sales revenues, equity capital, debt capital, and proceeds from the sale of assets. Once the needed funds have been obtained, the financial manager is responsible for ensuring that they are properly used. This is accomplished through a system of monitoring and evaluating the firm's financial activities.

3 Describe the advantages and disadvantages of different methods of short-term financing.

Most short-term financing is unsecured; that is, no collateral is required. Sources of unsecured short-term financing include trade credit, promissory notes issued to suppliers, unsecured bank loans, and commercial paper. Sources of secured short-term financing include loans secured by inventory or accounts receivable. A firm may also sell receivables to factors. Trade credit is the least expensive source of short-term financing. The cost of financing through other sources generally depends on the source and on the credit rating of the firm that requires the financing. Factoring is generally the most expensive approach.

4 Evaluate the advantages and disadvantages of equity financing and debt financing from the corporation's standpoint.

Long-term financing may be obtained as equity capital or debt capital. For a corporation, equity capital is obtained by selling either common or preferred stock. Common stock is voting stock; holders of common stock elect the corporation's directors and must approve changes to the corporate charter. Holders of preferred stock must be paid dividends before holders of common stock are paid any dividends. Another source of equity funding is retained earnings, which is the portion of a business's profits that is reinvested in the corporation. Sources of long-term debt financing are long-term loans and sales of corporate bonds. The rate of interest for long-term loans usually depends on the financial status of the borrower, the reason for borrowing, and the kind of collateral pledged to back up the loan. Money realized from the sale of bonds must be repaid when the bonds mature. In addition, the firm must pay interest on that money from the time the bonds are sold until maturity.

5 Discuss the importance of using funds effectively.

Financial management is often viewed as a two-sided problem. On one side, the uses of funds often dictate the type or types of financing needed by a business. On the other side, the activities that a business can undertake are determined by the types of financing available. Financial managers must ensure that (1) funds are available when needed, (2) funds are obtained at the lowest possible cost, and (3) funds are available for the repayment of debts.

Key Terms

You should now be able to define and give an example relevant to each of the following terms:

financial management (602)

short-term financing (602)

cash flow (603)

long-term financing (603)

financial plan (606)

budget (607)

zero-base budgeting (608)

equity capital (608)

debt capital (609)

unsecured financing (611)

trade credit (611)

commercial draft (612)

promissory note (612)

prime interest rate (612)

revolving credit agreement (614)

commercial paper (614)

floor planning (615)

accounts receivable (615)

factor (616)

common stock (619)

pre-emptive rights (619)

preferred stock (620)

par value (621)

call premium (621)

convertible preferred stock (621)

retained earnings (621)

financial leverage (622)

term-loan agreement (624)

corporate bond (624)

debenture bond (624)

mortgage bond (624)

convertible bond (624)

maturity date (624)

registered bond (624)

coupon bond (625)

bond indenture (625)

serial bonds (626)

sinking fund (626)

trustee (626)

Questions

Review Questions

1. How does short-term financing differ from long-term financing? Give two business uses for each type of financing?
2. What is the function of budgets in financial planning?
3. What is zero-base budgeting? How does it differ from the traditional concept of budgeting?
4. How does a financial manager monitor and evaluate a firm's financing?

5. What are four general sources of funds?
6. How important is trade credit as a source of short-term financing?
7. What is the difference between a line of credit and a revolving credit agreement?
8. Why would a supplier require a customer to sign a promissory note?
9. Explain how factoring works. Of what benefit is factoring to a firm that sells its receivables?
10. What are the advantages of financing through the sale of stock?
11. From a corporation's point of view, how does preferred stock differ from common stock?
12. Where do a corporation's retained earnings come from? What are the advantages of this type of financing?
13. Describe how financial leverage can increase return on owners' equity.
14. For the corporation, what are the advantages of corporate bonds over long-term loans?
15. Describe the three methods used to ensure that funds are available to redeem corporate bonds at maturity.

Discussion Questions

1. When Goldman Sachs's earnings are high, it pays extremely high bonuses to its partners. What do you think are the advantages of a bonus program like the one at Goldman Sachs?
2. What services does an investment banking firm like Goldman Sachs offer its clients?
3. What does a financial manager do? How can she or he monitor a firm's financial success?
4. If you were the financial manager of Stars and Stripes Clothing, what would you do with the excess cash that the firm expects in the second and fourth quarters? (See Figure 19.3.)
5. Why would a supplier offer both trade credit and cash discounts to its customers?
6. Why would a lender offer unsecured loans when it could demand collateral?
7. In what circumstances might a large corporation sell stock rather than bonds to obtain long-term financing? In what circumstances would it sell bonds rather than stock?

Exercises

🖐 1. Suppose you are responsible for setting a bank's interest rates. Your prime rate is 7 percent. Determine the interest rate you would charge a new, medium-sized firm for

a. A six-month unsecured loan.

b. Loans on a revolving credit agreement. (Also specify the commitment fee.)

c. A three-month loan secured by the firm's accounts receivable.

d. A five-year loan secured by the firm's land and buildings.

Explain briefly how you arrived at each interest rate.

✎ **2.** You want to borrow funds to finance next year's college expenses. Set up a budget showing your expected income and expenses, and determine how much money you will need to borrow. Then outline a plan for repaying the borrowed funds. Provide enough detail to convince your financing source to lend you the money.

VIDEO CASE 19.1

Tyson Foods—From Eggs to Riches

Tyson Foods has its roots in the ingenuity of an Arkansas farmer, John Tyson, who developed a way to transport five hundred live chickens to the Chicago market in 1935. From this humble beginning, Tyson Foods has grown to become the world's largest producer of poultry products with annual sales of $8 billion. Tyson processes and markets its own chickens, as well as beef, pork, and Cornish game hens. In 1992, it took to the ocean by purchasing Arctic Alaska Fisheries and Louis Kemp Seafood. And Tyson also produces corn tortillas, animal feed, and pet food. It exports products to Canada, Russia, the Far East, the Middle East, and the Caribbean. Over half of Tyson's 6,000 different products are sold in restaurants and fast-food outlets: McDonald's Chicken McNuggets and the Colonel's Rotisserie Gold are just two of Tyson's many creations. Credit this phenomenal growth, in part, to the American consumer trend away from red meat and to families eating out more often. But the growth of this empire can also be attributed to Tyson's sound financial management, always remembering where it came from, focusing on where it is going, and having a clear strategy on how to get there.

The mission of the Tyson's finance department is to compile data, keep track of how the company is doing, provide statistical information to all functions of the company, be custodians of Tyson's assets, aggressively pursue financial interests, and to do all this in a manner that is profitable to the company and its stockholders. In order to fulfill this role, the department uses computers, sophisticated data processing programs, and of course people to operate the accounting systems. The finance department also provides the numbers needed to make informed decisions, for both inside management and outside sources, like stockholders and the banking community.

Money is considered a commodity at Tyson, like any of its raw materials. The company's cost of money is based on a lender's perception of Tyson—its reputation, its market strategies, its performance, and its credit-worthiness. The ongoing partnerships Tyson has built with the banking community has always enabled the food giant to acquire money at favorable terms and interest rates in order to expand production and distribution facilities in nineteen states and enter joint ventures in China and Mexico. It is Tyson's cost-effective purchasing controls and its ability to acquire money through creative financing that improves the bottom-line profits. And that bottom line is what attracts investors. For the past ten years, Tyson has reported the highest returns on investments among all the Fortune 500 companies.[11]

Questions

1. How does the finance department at Tyson Foods help the company achieve its goals?

2. What attributes does a lender consider when Tyson Foods needs financing? Why?

CASE 19.2

Dun & Bradstreet's Commercial Credit Reports

As the world's largest commercial credit bureau, The Dun & Bradstreet Corp. (known as D&B in the business community) maintains credit information on 20 million companies worldwide. And with more than 90 percent of the market, D&B has a virtual monopoly in the commercial credit-information industry. In fact, D&B receives over 90,000 requests each day for credit information to help business firms decide whether to extend short-term financing to another company or sell merchandise to another company on credit.

The most easily accessible source of information is the *Dun & Bradstreet Reference Book.* Information is given on a firm's line of business, net worth, and credit rating. The current D&B credit rating system is illustrated in Table 19.5. A firm with a *CC2* rating has estimated financial strength, based on net worth, of $75,000 to $125,000, with an overall composite credit appraisal of "Good." Dun & Bradstreet composite credit appraisals range from "High" to "Limited" and are based on a firm's repayment history, financial

TABLE 19.5 Dun & Bradstreet's Credit Rating System

Composite Credit Appraisal

High	Good	Fair	Limited
1	2	3	4

Estimated Financial Strength

5A	Over	$50,000,000
4A	$10,000,000 to	50,000,000
3A	1,000,000 to	10,000,000
2A	750,000 to	1,000,000
1A	500,000 to	750,000
BA	300,000 to	500,000
BB	200,000 to	300,000
CB	125,000 to	200,000
CC	75,000 to	125,000
DC	50,000 to	75,000
DD	35,000 to	50,000
EE	20,000 to	35,000
FF	10,000 to	20,000
GG	5,000 to	10,000
HH	Up to	5,000

Source: Key to Dun & Bradstreet ratings used by permission. Copyright Dun & Bradstreet.

strength, and management personnel. Although the prospects of repayment for firms in each category vary, firms rated "High" or "Good" generally repay their credit obligations. Firms rated "Fair" are less likely to repay credit obligations. Most lenders and suppliers are reluctant to extend credit to firms with a "Limited" credit rating.

It is also possible to obtain a more extensive credit report that includes all of the above plus additional information on a firm's sales, assets, debts, bank balances, number of employees, and facts relating to whether the firm is behind on its bills or not. Finally, there is a section on the company's history, with background information on its officers.

Users sometimes complain that the information in D&B reports is inaccurate, outdated, or incomplete. In addition, users complain that much of the information included in D&B's reports is self-reported by the business owners themselves. And, because a decision to sell merchandise on credit or extend short-term financing may be based entirely on the information contained in a D&B report, inaccuracies can have serious repercussions.

D&B counters that some mistakes are inevitable because it maintains credit information on 20 million businesses. To reduce customer complaints, D&B is developing a new quality-control system to monitor virtually all credit reports. Although the company cannot guarantee the accuracy, completeness, or timeliness of credit reports, D&B management insists that its theme is "Quality First."[12]

Questions

Assume that you are the owner of Mountain-Top Fashions, a small, Denver-based manufacturing company that specializes in women's sportswear. You receive an order for $22,500 worth of merchandise from a retailer in Seattle, Washington. You have never sold to this retailer before, and you have no idea whether the customer will pay for the merchandise.

1. If the Seattle retailer has an *FF3* rating in the *Dun & Bradstreet Reference Book*, would you sell your merchandise on a credit basis?
2. What type of information would you expect to find in an extensive D&B credit report on this retailer?
3. In the above situation, what other information would you obtain before making a decision to sell your merchandise on a credit basis? Where could you find this information?

■■■■■ CHAPTER 20

Securities Markets and Investments

LEARNING OBJECTIVES

After studying this chapter you should be able to

1 Describe how securities are bought and sold through the primary and secondary markets.

2 Develop a personal investment plan.

3 Explain how the factors of safety, risk, income, growth, and liquidity affect an individual's investment decisions.

4 Identify the advantages and disadvantages of the traditional investment alternatives: savings accounts, bonds, stocks, mutual funds, and real estate.

5 Describe the high-risk investment techniques, including buying on margin and selling short.

6 Use the various sources of financial information to evaluate potential investments.

7 Explain how federal and state authorities regulate trading in securities.

CHAPTER PREVIEW

To begin, we examine the process of buying and selling securities, noting the functions of securities exchanges and stock brokerage firms. Then we outline the reasons for developing a personal investment plan and point out several factors that should be considered before investing any money. Next, we present several types of traditional investments. In addition, we consider high-risk investment techniques—that is, investments that can lead to large gains but are also quite speculative. We also explain how to obtain and interpret financial information from newspapers, brokerage firms, corporate reports, and periodicals. Finally, we discuss the evolution of state and federal laws governing the sale of financial securities.

633

Home Depot: An Investment Opportunity Too Good to Pass Up

The Home Depot—the Atlanta-based home improvement store—originally sold shares of common stock for $0.47 when adjusted for stock splits. Today, that stock is worth more than $40 a share. Is this investment too good to be true? Not at all! It really happened; and as a result of the Home Depot phenomenon, stockholders like Charles and Barbara Thompson who bought stock during the ten-year period of 1981 to 1991 and then held onto their investment until 1995 have made a fortune. But be warned: for every investor like the Thompsons who made a fortune, there are countless others who lost their shirts investing in young and promising enterprises. The difference between The Home Depot and just any new, upstart company is that the Home Depot people did it right.

Back in 1991, the Thompsons—like many other small investors—didn't have a lot of money. Their combined annual income was just over $45,000. Nevertheless, Barbara talked Charles into saving about $1,000 with an eye toward beginning an investment program.

Their decision to purchase Home Depot stock was based on a short conversation between Barbara and her boss, Tony Mathers, in January 1991. It seems that Mathers had just made a sales call on The Home Depot and was "very impressed" with their operation. Their method of selling home improvement merchandise—hardware, lumber, paint, electrical products, plumbing, and just about anything else that professional contractors or the do-it-yourselfer could need, all at one location at discounted prices—was working. Mathers went on to say that since Home Depot had less than 8 percent of the national market for this type of merchandise, there was still "a lot of room for expansion." Based on this slim

information, Barbara and Charles decided to take a chance. On January 26, 1991, they bought one hundred shares of Home Depot stock at $8.25 per share for a total outlay of $890, including the broker's commission.

During the next eleven months, the Thompsons' stock increased to over $14 a share. Charles was tempted to sell their Home Depot stock because they had almost doubled their original investment. However, Barbara persuaded him that they should hold onto their investment a little longer.

Today, the Thompsons admit that their decision to hold their Home Depot stock "a little longer" was one of the best decisions they ever made. During the next three years (1992–1994), Home Depot opened an additional 156 new stores. Twelve-month sales for the calendar year 1994 (the last year for which complete financial results are available) increased to $9.2 billion. And the Thompsons' $890 investment—when adjusted for stock splits—was worth a staggering $15,000 in March 1995.[1]

■ ■ ■ ■

■　　■　　■　　■　　■　　■　　■　　■　　■　　■　　■

Back in 1981, The Home Depot sold stock to the general public for the very first time. Management used the money received from the sale of stock—almost $4 million—to open four new stores in southern Florida. Since then the company has continued to open new stores, to increase sales, and to report record profits each year. And because The Home Depot has been successful, investors like Barbara and Charles Thompson—the couple in Inside Business—who purchased Home Depot stock have made a lot of money. That's the way it's supposed to work. Simply put, investors provide the money; the corporation uses the money to generate sales and earn profits; and the stockholders earn a return on their investment. To better understand the mechanics of how corporations sell stock and why investors purchase that stock, read on.

■■ HOW SECURITIES ARE BOUGHT AND SOLD

To purchase a sweater, you simply walk into a store that sells sweaters, choose one, and pay for it. To purchase stocks, bonds, mutual funds, and many other investments, you have to work through a representative—your stockbroker. In turn, your broker must buy or sell for you in either the primary or secondary market.

The Primary Market

primary market a market in which an investor purchases financial securities (via an investment bank or other representative) directly from the issuer of those securities

investment banking firm an organization that assists corporations in raising funds, usually by helping sell new issues of stocks, bonds, or other financial securities

initial public offering (IPO) the first time a corporation sells common stock to the general public

The **primary market** is a market in which an investor purchases financial securities (via an investment bank or other representative) directly from the issuer of those securities. An **investment banking firm** is an organization that assists corporations in raising funds, usually by helping sell new issues of stocks, bonds, or other financial securities. An example of a financial security sold through the primary market is the common stock issue sold by the computer software developer Microsoft Corp. In 1986, investors bought those shares through the investment banking firm Goldman Sachs and paid $1.17 per share when adjusted for stock splits. Today, those same shares are worth $71.[2] And the money they paid for common stock (almost $60 million) flowed to Microsoft. Typically, this type of stock offering is referred to as an initial public offering or simply an IPO. An **initial public offering** occurs when a corporation sells common stock to the general public for the first time.

For a large corporation, the decision to sell securities is often complicated, time-consuming, and expensive. Such companies usually choose one of two basic methods. Large firms that need a lot of financing often use an investment banking firm to sell and distribute the new security issue. Analysts for the investment bank examine the corporation's financial condition to determine whether the company is financially sound and how difficult it will be to sell the new stock issue. If the analysts for the investment banking

635

firm are satisfied that the new security issue is a good risk, the bank will buy the securities and then resell them to the investment bank's customers—commercial banks, insurance companies, pension funds, mutual funds, and investors. The investment banking firm generally charges a fee of 2 to 12 percent of the proceeds received by the corporation issuing the securities. The size of the commission depends on the financial health of the corporation issuing the new securities and the size of the new security issue. The commission allows the investment bank to make a profit while guaranteeing that the corporation will receive the needed financing.

The second method used by a corporation trying to obtain financing through the primary market is to sell directly to current stockholders. Usually, promotional materials describing the new security issue are mailed to current stockholders. These stockholders may then purchase securities directly from the corporation. Why would a corporation try to sell securities on its own? The most obvious reason is to avoid the investment bank's commission. Of course, a corporation's ability to sell a new security issue without the aid of an investment banking firm is tied directly to the public's perception of the corporation's financial health.

The Secondary Market

secondary market a market for existing financial securities that are traded between investors

After securities are originally sold through the primary market, they are traded on a regular basis through the secondary market. The **secondary market** is a market for existing financial securities that are traded between investors. Usually, secondary-market transactions are completed through a securities exchange or the over-the-counter market.

securities exchange a marketplace where member brokers meet to buy and sell securities

Securities Exchanges   A **securities exchange** is a marketplace where member brokers meet to buy and sell securities. The securities sold at a particular exchange must first be *listed,* or accepted for trading, at that exchange. Generally, securities issued by larger, nationwide corporations are traded at the New York Stock Exchange. The securities of smaller corporations are traded at the American Stock Exchange or at *regional exchanges,* located in Chicago, San Francisco, Philadelphia, Boston, and several other cities. The securities of very large corporations may be traded at more than one of these exchanges. Securities of firms may also be listed on foreign securities exchanges—in Tokyo, London, or Paris, for example.

The largest and best-known securities exchange in the United States is the New York Stock Exchange (NYSE). It handles about 50 percent of all stock bought and sold in the United States. The NYSE lists stocks for over 2,000 corporations, with a total market value of $3 trillion.[3] The actual trading floor of the NYSE, where listed securities are bought and sold, is approximately the size of a football field. A glass-enclosed visitors' gallery lets people watch the proceedings below and, on a busy day, the floor of the NYSE can best be described as organized confusion. Yet, the system does work and enables brokers to trade over 200 million shares per day.

Before a corporation's stock is approved for listing on the New York Stock Exchange, the firm must meet five criteria (see Figure 20.1).

The American Stock Exchange handles about 5 percent of U.S. stock transactions. Regional exchanges and the over-the-counter market account

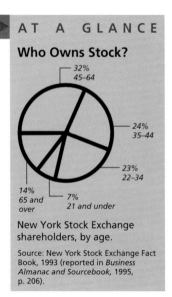

AT A GLANCE

Who Owns Stock?

32%
45–64

24%
35–44

23%
22–34

7%
21 and under

14%
65 and over

New York Stock Exchange shareholders, by age.

Source: New York Stock Exchange Fact Book, 1993 (reported in *Business Almanac and Sourcebook,* 1995, p. 206).

Organized confusion? To many investors, the floor of the New York Stock Exchange looks like organized confusion. In reality, the system works extremely well and enables brokers, representing clients who want to buy *or* sell stocks, to trade over 200 million shares per day.

for the remainder. The American and regional exchanges and the over-the-counter market have generally less stringent listing requirements than the NYSE.

over-the-counter (OTC) market a network of stockbrokers who buy and sell the securities of corporations that are not listed on a securities exchange

The Over-the-Counter Market The **over-the-counter (OTC) market** is a network of stockbrokers who buy and sell the securities of corporations that are not listed on a securities exchange. In an OTC stock transaction, your broker will fill your order for a specific OTC stock from his or her inventory of stocks if possible. Otherwise, your account executive must buy the OTC stock from a specialist who "makes a market" for a particular OTC stock. Your account executive will then sell the stock to you. The price that you pay for the stock is determined by the amount of stock that the specialist has in inventory, the prices of recent trades for the stock, and the demand for the

FIGURE 20.1 Criteria a Firm Must Meet Before Being Listed on the New York Stock Exchange
Approximately 2,000 corporations are currently listed on the New York Stock Exchange. (*Source: Nancy Dunnan,* Dun & Bradstreet Guide to Your Investment $$ 1994 *[New York: HarperCollins, 1994], p. 382.)*

CRITERIA				
Annual earnings before taxes: $2.5 million	Shares of stock held publicly: 1.1 million	Market value of publicly held stock: $18 million	Number of stockholders owning at least 100 shares: 2,000	Value of net tangible assets: $18 million

stock. Most OTC trading is conducted by telephone. Currently, about 5,000 stocks are traded over the counter. Since 1971, the brokers and dealers operating in the OTC market have used a computerized quotation system called *NASDAQ*—the National Association of Securities Dealers Automated Quotation system. NASDAQ displays current price quotations on terminals in subscribers' offices.

The Role of the Stockbroker

account executive an individual—sometimes called a *stockbroker* or *registered representative*—who buys or sells securities for clients

An **account executive**—sometimes called a *stockbroker* or *registered representative*—is an individual who buys or sells securities for clients. (Actually, *account executive* is the more descriptive title because account executives handle all securities—not only stocks. Choosing an account executive can be difficult for at least three reasons. First, you must exercise a shrewd combination of trust and mistrust when you approach an account executive. Remember that you are interested in the broker's recommendations to increase your wealth, but the account executive is interested in your investment trading as a means to swell commissions. Unfortunately, some account executives are guilty of *churning*—a practice that generates commissions by excessive buying and selling of securities.

Second, you must decide if you need a full-service broker or a discount broker. A full-service broker usually charges higher commissions but gives you personal investment advice. He or she can provide you with research reports from Moody's Investors Service, Standard & Poor's Corporation, and Value Line Inc.—all companies that specialize in providing investment information to investors. A full-service broker should also provide additional reports prepared by the brokerage firm's financial analysts. A discount broker simply executes buy and sell orders, usually over the phone.

Thriving on information! Many experts suggest that a stockbroker is only as good as the information that she or he can provide to clients. Here stockbrokers for Nikko Securities in New York City use computers to track global financial markets, make investment recommendations, and advise customers when to buy and sell stocks, bonds, and other securities.

Most discount brokers offer no investment advice; you must make your own investment decisions. Some discount brokers will supply research reports for a nominal fee.

Finally, you must consider the factor of compatibility. It is always wise to interview several potential account executives. During each interview, ask some questions to determine if you and the account executive understand each other. You must be able to communicate the types of investments that interest you, your expected rate of return, and the amount of risk you are willing to take to achieve your goals. If you become dissatisfied with your investment program, do not hesitate to discuss your dissatisfaction with the account executive. If your dissatisfaction continues, you may even find it necessary to choose another account executive.

Account executives are employed by stock brokerage firms, such as Merrill Lynch & Co., Dean Witter Reynolds, and Prudential Securities. To trade at a particular exchange, a brokerage firm must be a member of that exchange. The NYSE has a limited membership of 1,366 members, or "seats," as they are often called. Although seats on the NYSE are rarely sold, in the early 1990s a seat sold for $400,000.[4]

The Mechanics of a Transaction   Once investors have decided on a particular security, most simply telephone their account executive and place a market, limit, or discretionary order. A **market order** is a request that a security be purchased or sold at the current market price. The broker's representative on the exchange's trading floor will try to get the best possible price, and the trade will be completed as soon as possible.

> **market order** a request that a security be purchased or sold at the current market price

A **limit order** is a request that a security be bought or sold at a price equal to or better (lower for buying, higher for selling) than some specified price. Suppose you place a limit order to *sell* Home Depot common stock at $42 per share. Your broker's representative sells the stock only if the price is $42 per share or *more*. If you place a limit order to *buy* Home Depot at $42, the representative buys it only if the price is $42 per share or *less*. Limit orders may or may not be transacted quickly, depending on how close the limit price is to the current market price. Usually, a limit order is good for one day, one week, one month, or good until canceled (GTC).

> **limit order** a request that a security be bought or sold at a price that is equal to or better than some specified price

Investors can also choose to place a discretionary order. A **discretionary order** is an order to buy or sell a security that lets the broker decide when to execute the transaction and at what price. Financial planners advise against using a discretionary order for two reasons. First, a discretionary order gives the account executive a great deal of authority. If the account executive makes a mistake, it is the investor who suffers the loss. Second, financial planners argue that only investors (with the help of their account executives) should make investment decisions.

> **discretionary order** an order to buy or sell a security that lets the broker decide when to execute the transaction and at what price

A typical stock transaction includes the five steps shown in Figure 20.2. The entire process, from receipt of the selling order to confirmation of the completed transaction, takes about twenty minutes. Payment for stocks, bonds, and other financial securities is generally required within five business days of the transaction.

Commissions   Brokerage firms are free to set their own commission charges. Like other businesses, however, they must be concerned with the fees charged by competing firms.

FIGURE 20.2 **Steps in a Typical Stock Transaction**
A typical stock transaction takes about twenty minutes.

round lot a unit of 100 shares
of a particular stock

odd lot fewer than 100 shares
of a particular stock

On the trading floor, stocks are traded in round lots. A **round lot** is a unit of 100 shares of a particular stock. Table 20.1 shows typical commission charges for some round-lot transactions. Notice that commissions charged by full-service brokers are higher than the commissions charged by discount and super discount brokers. An **odd lot** is fewer than 100 shares of a particular stock. Brokerage firms generally charge higher per-share fees for trading in odd lots, primarily because several odd lots must be combined into round lots before they can actually be traded through the exchange.

Commissions for trading bonds, commodities, and options are usually lower than those for trading stocks. The charge for buying or selling a $1,000 corporate bond is typically $10. With the exception of some mutual funds, the investor generally pays a commission when buying *and* when selling securities.

■■ DEVELOPING AN INVESTMENT PLAN

personal investment the use
of one's personal funds to earn a
financial return

Personal investment is the use of one's personal funds to earn a financial return. Thus, in the most general sense, the goal of investing is to earn money with money. But that goal is completely useless for the individual, because it is so vague and so easily attained. If you place $100 in a savings account paying 4 percent annual interest, your money will earn 33 cents in one month. If your goal is simply to earn money with your $100, you will have attained that goal at the end of the month. Then what do you do?

TABLE 20.1   Typical Commissions Charged by Full-Service, Discount, and Super Discount Brokers

Brokerage Firm	Commission 100 shares of a $30 stock	Minimum commission for any transaction
Full-Service		
Dean Witter	$84	$50
A.G. Edwards	83	42
Kemper	88	50
Merrill Lynch	86	none
Paine Webber	89	none
Prudential	90	55
Smith Barney Shearson	91	50
Discount		
Charles Schwab	$55	$39
Fidelity	54	38
Quick & Reilly	49	38
Super Discount		
Pacific Brokerage	$25	$25
Waterhouse	25	35

Source: From "How the Brokers Stack Up," by Tricia Welsh, *1994 Investor's Guide/Fortune,* Autumn 1993. Copyright © 1993 Time Inc. All rights reserved. Used with permission.

Investment Goals

LEARNING OBJECTIVE 2
Develop a personal investment plan.

To be useful, an investment goal must be specific and measurable. It must be tailored to the individual so that it takes into account his or her particular financial circumstances and needs. It must also be oriented toward the future because investing is usually a long-term undertaking. Finally, an investment goal must be realistic in terms of the economic conditions that prevail and the investment opportunities that are available.

Some financial planners suggest that investment goals be stated in terms of money: "By January 1, 1999, I will have total assets of $80,000." Others believe that people are more motivated to work toward goals that are stated in terms of the particular things they desire: "By May 1, 1999, I will have accumulated enough money so that I can take a year off from work to travel around the world." Like the goals themselves, the way they are stated depends on the individual.

The following questions can be helpful in establishing valid investment goals:

1. What financial goals do I want to achieve?
2. How much money will I need, and when?
3. Is it reasonable to assume that I can obtain the amount of money I will need to meet my investment goals?

4. Do I expect my personal situation to change in a way that will affect my investment goals?

5. What economic conditions could alter my investment goals?

6. Am I willing to make the necessary sacrifices to ensure that my investment goals are met?

7. What are the consequences of not obtaining my investment goals?

A Personal Investment Plan

Once you have formulated specific goals, investment planning is similar to planning for a business. It begins with the assessment of different investment opportunities—including the potential return and risk involved in each. At the very least, this process requires some expert advice and careful study. Many investors turn to lawyers, accountants, bankers, or insurance agents. The problem of finding qualified help is compounded by the fact that many people who call themselves "financial planners" are in reality nothing more than salespersons for various financial investments, tax shelters, or insurance plans.

A true **financial planner** has had at least two years of training in securities, insurance, taxation, real estate, and estate planning and has passed a rigorous examination. As evidence of training and successful completion of the qualifying examination, the Institute of Financial Planning in Denver allows individuals to use the designation Certified Financial Planner (CFP). Similarly, the American College in Bryn Mawr, Pennsylvania, allows individuals who have completed the necessary requirements to use the designation Chartered Financial Consultant (ChFC). Most CFPs and ChFCs don't sell a particular investment product or charge commissions for their investment recommendations. Instead, they charge consulting fees that range from $100 to $250 an hour.

Many financial planners suggest that an investment program should begin with the accumulation of an "emergency fund"—a certain amount of money that can be obtained quickly in case of immediate need. This money should be deposited in a savings account at the highest available interest rate. The amount of money that should be salted away in the emergency fund varies from person to person. However, most financial planners agree that an amount equal to three to nine months' living expenses is reasonable.[5]

After the personal emergency account is established, the individual may invest additional funds according to his or her investment plan. Some additional funds may already be available, or money for further investing may be saved out of earnings. Then investment alternatives are chosen by a process of evaluation and elimination and combined into a comprehensive personal investment plan.

Once a plan has been put into operation, the investor must monitor it and, if necessary, modify it. The most successful investors spend hours each week evaluating their own investments and investigating new investment opportunities. An investor's circumstances and economic conditions are both subject to change. Hence all investment programs should be re-evaluated regularly.

financial planner an individual who has had at least two years of training in securities, insurance, taxation, real estate, and estate planning and has passed a rigorous examination

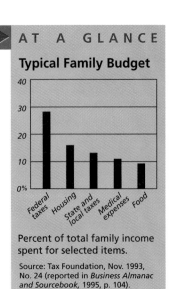

▶▶ A T   A   G L A N C E

Typical Family Budget

Percent of total family income spent for selected items.

Source: Tax Foundation, Nov. 1993, No. 24 (reported in *Business Almanac and Sourcebook*, 1995, p. 104).

Five Important Factors in Personal Investment

LEARNING OBJECTIVE 3
Explain how the factors of safety, risk, income, growth, and liquidity affect an individual's investment decisions.

How can the individual (or a financial planner) tell which investments are "right" for an investment plan and which are not? One way to start is to match potential investments with investment goals in terms of safety, risk, income, growth, and liquidity.

Safety and Risk   Safety and risk are two sides of the same coin. Safety in an investment means minimal risk of loss. On the other hand, risk in an investment means a measure of uncertainty about the outcome. Investors who want a steady increase in value over an extended period of time choose safe investments, such as savings accounts or certificates of deposit, highly rated corporate and municipal bonds, and the stocks of certain highly regarded corporations—sometimes called "blue-chip stocks." Corporations that are generally industry leaders and have provided their stockholders with stable earnings and dividends over a number of years include Abbott Labs, Kellogg, General Electric, and Sara Lee Corporation. Mutual funds and real estate may also be very safe investments.

To implement goals that stress higher dollar returns on their investments, investors must generally give up some safety. How much risk should they take in exchange for how much return? This question is almost impossible to answer for someone else, because the answer depends so much on the individual and his or her investment goals. However, in general, *the potential return should be directly related to the assumed risk*. That is, the greater the risk assumed by the investor, the greater the potential monetary reward should be. As we will see shortly, there are a number of risky—and potentially profitable—investments. They include some stocks and bonds, commodities, and stock options. The securities issued by new and growing corporations usually fall in this category. To measure the amount of risk you are comfortable with, take the risk test included in Enhancing Career Skills.

Investment Income   Savings accounts, certificates of deposit, corporate and government bonds, and certain stocks pay a predictable amount of interest or dividends each year. Such investments are generally used to implement investment goals that stress periodic income.

Investors in savings accounts, certificates of deposit, and bonds know exactly how much income they will receive each year. The dividends paid to stockholders can and do vary, even for the largest and most stable corporations. However, a number of corporations have built their reputations on a policy of paying dividends every three months. (The firms listed in Table 20.2 have paid dividends to their owners for at least ninety years.) The stocks of these corporations are often purchased primarily for income.

Investment Growth   To investors, *growth* means that their investments will increase or appreciate in value. For example, a corporation like Wal-Mart Stores, Inc., that is in the process of growing usually pays a small cash dividend or no dividend at all. Instead, profits are reinvested in the business (as retained earnings) to finance additional expansion. In this case, Wal-Mart's stockholders receive little or no income from their investments, but the value of their stock increases as the corporation grows and opens more retail outlets.

Measuring Investment Risk

Millions of Americans buy stocks or bonds, purchase mutual funds, or make even more speculative investments. These investments all have one thing in common—investment risk. The following brief quiz, adapted from one prepared by the T. Rowe Price group of mutual funds, can help you as an investor discover how comfortable you are with varying degrees of risk. Other things being equal, your risk tolerance score is a useful guide for decisions about the types of investments you include in a personal financial plan—while also allowing yourself a peaceful night's sleep. A primer on the ABCs of investing is available from T. Rowe Price, 100 East Pratt Street, Baltimore, MD 21202 (800-638-5600).

1. You're the winner on a TV game show. Which prize would you choose?

   ☐ $2,000 in cash (1 point).

   ☐ A 50 percent chance to win $4,000 (3 points).

   ☐ A 20 percent chance to win $10,000 (5 points).

   ☐ A 2 percent chance to win $100,000 (9 points).

2. You're down $500 in a poker game. How much more would you be willing to put up to win the $500 back?

   ☐ More than $500 (8 points).

   ☐ $500 (6 points).

   ☐ $250 (4 points).

   ☐ $100 (2 points).

   ☐ Nothing—you'll cut your losses now (1 point).

3. A month after you invest in a stock, it suddenly goes up 15 percent. With no further information, what would you do?

   ☐ Hold it, hoping for further gains (3 points).

   ☐ Sell it and take your gains (1 point).

   ☐ Buy more—it will probably go higher (4 points).

4. Your investment suddenly goes down 15 percent one month after you invest. Its fundamentals still look good. What would you do?

   ☐ Buy more. If it looked good at the original price, it looks even better now (4 points).

   ☐ Hold on and wait for it to come back (3 points).

   ☐ Sell it to avoid losing even more (1 point).

5. You're a key employee in a start-up company. You can choose one of two ways to take your year-end bonus. Which would you pick?

   ☐ $1,500 in cash (1 point).

   ☐ Company stock options that could bring you $15,000 next year if the company succeeds, but will be worthless if it fails (5 points).

Your total score: ____

Scoring

5–18 points:
More Conservative Investor. You prefer to minimize financial risks. The lower your score, the more cautious you are. When you choose investments, look for high credit ratings, well-established records, and an orientation toward stability. Avoid bonds with the very highest yields; they pay those yields because they involve bigger risks. In stocks and real estate, look for a focus on income.

19–30 points:
Less Conservative Investor. You are willing to take more chances in pursuit of greater rewards. The higher your score, the bolder you are. When you invest, look for high overall returns within the appropriate time category. You may want to consider bonds with the steepest yields and lower credit ratings, the stocks of newer companies, and real estate investments that use mortgage debt.

TABLE 20.2 Corporations That, Through Mid-1994, Had Made Consecutive Dividend Payments for at Least 90 Years

Corporation	Dividends Since	Type of Business
AT&T Corporation	1881	Telephone utility
Borden, Inc.	1899	Foods
Commonwealth Edison Company	1890	Electric utility
Du Pont (E.I.) de Nemours	1904	Chemicals
Exxon Corporation	1882	Chemical & petroleum products
General Electric Company	1899	Electrical equipment
Norfolk Southern Corp.	1901	Railroad
Procter & Gamble Company	1891	Soap products

Source: *Standard & Poor's Stock Market Encyclopedia,* August 1994, published by Standard & Poor's Corporation, a division of McGraw-Hill, Inc., 25 Broadway, New York, N.Y. 10004. Reprinted with permission.

Investment goals that stress growth, or an increase in the value of the investment, can be implemented by purchasing the stocks of such "growth corporations." During the 1980s, firms in the electronics, energy, and health-care industries showed the greatest growth. They are expected to continue growing in the 1990s. Of course, individual firms within these industries may grow at a slower or faster rate than the industry as a whole—or they may not grow at all.

For investors who carefully choose their investments, both mutual funds and real estate may offer substantial growth possibilities. More speculative investments like precious metals, gemstones, and collectibles (antiques and paintings) offer less predictable growth possibilities, whereas investments in commodities and stock options usually stress immediate returns as opposed to continued growth. Generally, corporate and government bonds are not purchased for growth.

Investment Liquidity   **Liquidity** is the ease with which an investment can be converted into cash. Investments range from cash or cash equivalents (like investments in government securities or money-market accounts) to the other extreme of frozen investments, where it is impossible to get your money. Checking and savings accounts are liquid investments because they can be quickly converted into cash. Another type of bank account—a certificate of deposit—is not as liquid as a checking or savings account. There are penalties for withdrawing money from this type of account before the maturity date.

Although you may be able to sell other investments quickly, you might not regain the amount of money you originally invested because of market conditions, economic conditions, or many other reasons. For example, the owner of real estate may have to lower the asking price to find a buyer for a

liquidity the ease with which an investment can be converted into cash

property. Finding a buyer for investments in certain types of collectibles may also be difficult.

Different kinds of investments offer different combinations of safety, risk, income, growth, and liquidity. Keep the nature of this important "mix" in mind as we consider the following investment alternatives.

■■ TRADITIONAL INVESTMENT ALTERNATIVES

LEARNING OBJECTIVE 4
Identify the advantages and disadvantages of the traditional investment alternatives: savings accounts, bonds, stocks, mutual funds, and real estate.

In this section and the next, we look at some investments that are available to investors. A number of the investments listed in Table 20.3 have already been discussed. Others have only been mentioned and will be examined in more detail. Still others may be completely new to you.

Bank Accounts

Bank accounts that pay interest—and are therefore investments—include passbook savings accounts, certificates of deposit, and NOW accounts. These were discussed in Chapter 18. They are the most conservative of all investments, and they provide safety and either income or growth. That is, the interest paid on bank accounts can be withdrawn to serve as income, or it can be left on deposit to earn additional interest and increase the size of the bank account. To ensure that money is available when needed, many investors deposit their emergency fund in an interest-bearing savings account.

Corporate and Government Bonds

In Chapter 19 we discussed the issuing of bonds by corporations to obtain financing. The U.S. government and state and local governments also issue bonds, for the same reason. In addition, many government and municipal bonds are tax free, which enables owners to earn income that is exempt from federal income taxes. Both corporate and government bonds may be purchased through brokers or, in some cases, directly from the issuer.

Because they are a form of long-term debt financing that must be repaid, bonds are generally considered a more conservative investment

TABLE 20.3   Investment Alternatives
Traditional investments involve less risk than high-risk investments.

Traditional	High Risk
Bank accounts	Margin transactions
Corporate and government bonds	Short transactions
	Options
Common stock	Commodities
Preferred stock	Precious metals
Mutual funds	Gemstones
Real estate	Coins
	Antiques/collectibles

than either stocks or mutual funds. They are primarily long-term, income-producing investments. Between the time of purchase and the maturity date, the bondholder will receive interest payments—usually semiannually, or every six months—at the stated interest rate. For example, assume you purchase a $1,000 bond issued by Westinghouse Electric and the interest rate for this bond is 9 percent. In this situation, you receive interest of $90 ($1,000 × .09 = $90) a year from the corporation. Westinghouse pays the interest every six months in $45 installments.

Most beginning investors think that a $1,000 bond is always worth $1,000. In reality, the price of corporate and government bonds may fluctuate until the bond's maturity date. Changes in the overall interest rates in the economy are the primary cause of most bond price fluctuations. For example, when overall interest rates in the economy are rising, the market value of existing bonds with a fixed interest rate typically declines. They may then be purchased for less than their face value. By holding such bonds until maturity or until interest rates decline (causing the bond's market value to increase), bond owners can realize some profit through the growth of their investments.

A typical bond transaction is illustrated in Table 20.4. Assume that on October 21, 1992, you purchased a 9.5 percent corporate bond issued by Revlon, Inc. Your cost for the bond was $880 plus a $10 commission, for a total investment of $890. Also assume that you held the bond until October 21, 1995, and then sold it at its current market value of $1,020. As illustrated in Table 20.4, your total return for this bond transaction including interest is $405.

We should point out that everything in the bond investment illustrated in Table 20.4 went "as planned." But remember that the price of a corporate bond can decrease and that interest payments and eventual repayment may

TABLE 20.4   Sample Corporate Bond Transaction for Revlon
Assumptions: interest, 9.5 percent; maturity date, 1999; purchased October 21, 1992, for $880; sold October 21, 1995, for $1,020

Costs When Purchased		Return When Sold	
1 bond @ $880	$880	1 bond @ $1,020	$1,020
Plus commission	+ 10	Minus commission	– 10
Total investment	$890	Total return	$1,010

Transaction Summary	
Total return	$1,010
Minus total investment	– 890
Profit from bond sale	$ 120
Plus interest (3 years)	+ 285
Total return for this transaction	$ 405

be a problem for a corporation that encounters financial difficulty or enters bankruptcy. When the LTV Corporation filed for reorganization under the provisions of the U.S. Bankruptcy Act, LTV bonds immediately dropped in value because of questions concerning the prospects of repayment. And back in the mid-1980s, Washington Public Power Supply was unable to pay off its debt on municipal bonds worth more than $2 billion; as a result, thousands of investors lost money.

Convertible Bonds   Some corporations prefer to issue convertible bonds because they carry a lower interest rate than nonconvertible bonds—by about 1 to 2 percent. In return for accepting a lower interest rate, holders of convertible bonds have the opportunity to benefit through investment growth. For example, assume an investor purchases a $1,000 corporate bond that is convertible to 40 shares of the company's common stock. This means the investor could convert the bond to common stock whenever the price of the company's stock is $25 (1,000 ÷ 40 = $25) or higher. In reality, there is no guarantee that bondholders will convert to common stock even if the market value of the common stock does increase to $25 or higher. The reason for not exercising the conversion feature is quite simple. As the market value of the common stock increases, the price of the convertible bond also increases. By not converting to common stock, bondholders enjoy interest income from the bond in addition to increased bond value caused by the price movement of the common stock.

Common Stock

How do you make money by buying common stock? Basically, there are three ways: through dividend payments, through an increase in the value of the stock, or through stock splits, which offer a potential for increased profits.

Dividend Payments   Most stockholders expect to receive *dividend income.* Although corporations are under no legal obligation to pay dividends, most corporate board members like to keep stockholders happy (and prosperous). Therefore, board members usually declare dividends if the corporation's after-tax profits are sufficient to do so. (Because dividends are a distribution of profits, intelligent investors must be concerned about after-tax profits.) A corporation may pay stock dividends in place of—or in addition to—cash dividends. A **stock dividend** is a dividend in the form of additional stock. It is paid to shareholders just as cash dividends are paid: in proportion to the number of shares owned. An individual stockholder may sell the additional stock to obtain income or retain it to increase the total value of her or his stock holdings.

stock dividend a dividend in the form of additional stock

Increase in Dollar Value   Stockholders can make money when the market value of their stock increases. The **market value** of a stock is the price of one share of the stock at a particular time. It is determined solely by the interaction of buyers and sellers in the various stock markets. (Note that *market value* is different from *par value,* which, as we noted in Chapter 19, is an arbitrary value the issuing corporation assigns to a share of stock.) If the

market value the price of one share of a stock at a particular time

Sometimes your customers really enjoy your products. Many financial analysts suggest that the way to pick a good stock is to look at the products you use on a daily basis. If you like the product, there's a good chance that other customers will, too. And the bottom line is quite simple: If customers like a firm's products, then sales, profits, *and* stock prices increase. Based on the smile on this child's face, he will continue to buy more Pepsi, pizza from Pizza Hut, and someday maybe even stock in Pepsico—the parent company of both Pepsi and Pizza Hut.

market value of a stock increases, the stockholder must decide whether to sell the stock at the higher price or to continue to hold it. If the stockholder decides to sell, the monetary difference between the purchase price and the selling price represents profit or loss. Let's assume that on October 11, 1994, you purchased 100 shares of Texaco at a cost of $59 a share and that your cost for this transaction was $5,900 plus $90 in commission charges, for a total investment of $5,990. Let's also assume that you hold your 100 shares until October 11, 1995, and then sell the Texaco stock for $67 a share. During the twelve months you owned Texaco stock, the company paid dividends totaling $3.20 a share. Your dollar return on investment is shown in Table 20.5. In this case you made a total of $910 because you received dividends totaling $3.20 a share and because the stock's market value increased by $8 a share. Of course, if the stock's market value had decreased, or if the firm's board of directors had voted to reduce or omit dividends, your return would have been much less than the total dollar return illustrated in the table.

Generally, the stock market is described as either a bull market or a bear market. A **bull market** is a market in which average stock prices are increasing. A **bear market** is a market in which average stock prices are declining. Similarly, a *bull* is an investor who expects prices to go up; a *bear* is an investor who expects prices to go down.

bull market a market in which average stock prices are increasing

bear market a market in which average stock prices are declining

Stock Splits   Directors of many corporations feel there is an optimal price range within which their firm's stock is most attractive to investors. When

TABLE 20.5   Sample Common-Stock Transaction for Texaco
Assumptions: purchased 100 shares of common stock on October 11, 1994, for $59 a share; sold 100 shares on October 11, 1995, for $67 a share; and annual dividends of $3.20 a share

Costs When Purchased		Return When Sold	
100 shares @ $59	$5,900	100 shares @ $67	$6,700
Plus commission	+ 90	Minus commission	– 120
Total investment	$5,990	Total return	$6,580

Transaction Summary	
Total return	$6,580
Minus total investment	– 5,990
Profit from stock sale	$ 590
Plus dividends (1 year)	+ 320
Total return for this transaction	$ 910

stock split the division of each outstanding share of a corporation's stock into a greater number of shares

the market value increases beyond that range, they may declare a *stock split* to bring the price down. A **stock split** is the division of each outstanding share of a corporation's stock into a greater number of shares. Although there are no guarantees that a stock's price will go up after a stock split, the investing public often feels that there is a potential for an increase because the stock is offered at a lower price.

The most common stock splits result in one, two, or three new shares for each original share. For example, in 1994 the board of directors for Lands' End, Inc., approved a two-for-one stock split. After this split, a stockholder who originally owned 100 shares owned 200 shares. The value of an original share was proportionally reduced. In the case of Lands' End, the market value per share was reduced to approximately half of the stock's value before the two-for-one stock split. Every shareholder retained his or her proportional ownership of the firm. But, at the lower price, the stock is more attractive to the investing public because there is a greater potential for a rapid increase in dollar value.

Preferred Stock

As we noted in Chapter 19, a firm's preferred stockholders must receive their cash dividends before common stockholders are paid any dividends. Moreover, preferred-stock dividends are specified on the stock certificates. And, compared with common stockholders, the owners of preferred stock have first claim, after bondholders and general creditors, on corporate assets if the firm is dissolved or enters bankruptcy. These features tend to provide the holders of preferred stocks with an added degree of safety and a predictable income compared to common stockholders.

In addition, owners of preferred stock may also gain through special features offered with some preferred stock issues. First, owners of *cumulative* preferred stocks are assured that omitted dividends will be paid to them before common stockholders receive any dividends. Second, owners of *participating* preferred stock may earn more than the specified dividend if the firm has a good year. The participating feature enables preferred stockholders to share in surplus profit, along with common stockholders, after the designated amounts have been paid to both classes of stockholders. Finally, owners of *convertible* preferred stock may profit through growth as well as from dividends. Thus, if the value of a firm's common stock increases, the market value of its convertible preferred stock also grows. Convertibility allows the owner of convertible preferred stock to combine the lower risk of preferred stock with the possibility of greater speculative gain through conversion to common stock.

Mutual Funds

mutual fund a professionally managed investment vehicle that combines and invests the funds of many individual investors

A **mutual fund** combines and invests the funds of many investors, under the guidance of a professional manager. The major advantages of a mutual fund are its professional management and its diversification, or investment in a wide variety of securities. Diversification spells safety, because an occasional loss incurred with one security is usually offset by gains from other investments.

How fragile is your nest egg? Most of us think that an egg is pretty fragile. And for a lot of people, their financial nest egg is even more fragile than the real thing. And yet professional help—as this advertisement for Kemper Mutual Funds illustrates—cannot only keep you from breaking your nest egg, but it can also help you use mutual funds to build and preserve your investment dollars for tomorrow.

Funny thing about a nest egg. You can't sit on it.

We understand the importance of your nest egg. You worked hard for it. You nurtured it. But sitting on it won't make it last. Your financial advisor can help you make the right decisions. At Kemper, our philosophy is that diligence and a disciplined plan will help you meet your retirement goals. For 40 years our Family of Funds have focused on a long-term investment approach that helps build and preserve tomorrows today.

Talk to your financial advisor. And, for ideas about making smart retirement investing choices, get our "Investing Your Nest Egg" brochure. It's free. Just call 1-800-KFS-5555, extension 400.

Kemper Mutual Funds

We're Building Tomorrows Today

Before you invest or send money, carefully read the Kemper Fund brochure and prospectus containing more complete information, including management fees and expenses. ©1995 Kemper Financial Services, Inc.   233940

Mutual-Fund Shares and Fees   A *closed-end* mutual fund sells shares (in the fund) to investors only when the fund is originally organized. And only a specified number of shares are made available at that time. Once all the shares are sold, an investor must purchase shares from some other investor who is willing to sell them. The mutual fund itself is under no obligation to buy back shares from investors. Shares of closed-end mutual funds are traded on the floor of stock exchanges like the New York Stock Exchange.

An *open-end* mutual fund issues and sells new shares to any investor who requests them. It also buys back shares from investors who wish to sell all or part of their holdings. The share value for any mutual fund is determined by calculating net asset value. **Net asset value (NAV)** per share is equal to the current market value of the mutual fund's portfolio minus the mutual fund's liabilities, divided by the number of outstanding shares. For most mutual funds, NAV is calculated at least once a day and is reported in newspapers and financial publications.

net asset value (NAV) current market value of the mutual fund's portfolio minus the mutual fund's liabilities, divided by the number of outstanding shares

With regard to costs, there are three types of mutual funds: load, low-load, and no-load funds. An individual who invests in a *load fund* pays a sales charge every time he or she purchases shares. This charge is typically 7 to 8.5 percent for investments under $10,000. A *low-load fund,* as the name implies, charges a lower commission than a load fund. Commissions for low-load funds range between 1 and 3 percent for investments under $10,000. The purchaser of shares in a *no-load fund* pays no sales charges at all. No-load funds offer the same type of investment opportunities that load funds and low-load funds offer. Because no-load funds offer the same investment opportunities, you should investigate them further before deciding which type of mutual fund is right for you. Most funds collect a management fee of about 0.5 to 1 percent of the total dollar amount of assets in the fund. In addition, some funds charge a redemption fee of 1 to 5 percent of the total amount withdrawn from a mutual fund.

Mutual-Fund Investments   The managers of mutual funds tailor their investment portfolios to provide growth, income, or a combination of both. Most mutual funds are fairly conservative and relatively safe, although there are some speculative mutual funds. The major categories of mutual funds, in terms of the types of securities they invest in, are listed below in alphabetical order:

- *Balanced funds,* which apportion their investments among common stocks, preferred stock, and bonds.
- *Bond funds,* which invest in municipal and corporate bonds that provide investors with interest income.
- *Global funds,* which invest in stocks, bonds, and other securities issued by foreign firms or countries.
- *Growth funds,* which invest in the common stock of well-managed, rapidly growing corporations.
- *Growth-income funds,* which invest in common and preferred stocks that pay good dividends *and* are expected to increase in market value.
- *Income funds,* which invest in stocks and bonds that pay high dividends and interest.

- *Index funds,* which invest in common stocks that react the same way the stock market as a whole does.
- *Industry funds,* sometimes called *specialty* or *sector funds,* which invest in common stocks of companies in the same industry.
- *Money-market funds,* which invest in short-term corporate obligations and government securities that offer high interest.

There are funds designed to meet just about any conceivable investment objective. Hundreds of funds trade daily under the headings "capital appreciation," "small-company growth," and "equity income." As a result, it is the investor's job to determine which is the right fund. For more information on evaluating global mutual funds, read Global Perspectives.

Real Estate

Real estate ownership represents one of the best hedges against inflation, but a piece of property in a poor location, for example, can actually decrease in value. And a number of people who bought land in the Florida Everglades were taken by unscrupulous promoters. Therefore, take a few moments and examine the real estate checklist in Table 20.6, which cites some of the many factors you should consider before investing in real estate.

There are, of course, disadvantages to any investment, and real estate is no exception. If you want to sell your property, you must find an interested buyer with the ability to obtain enough money to complete the transaction. Finding a qualified buyer can be difficult if loan money is scarce, the real estate market is in a decline, or you overpaid for a piece of property. If you are forced to hold your investment longer than you originally planned, taxes and installment payments must also be considered. As a rule, real estate increases in value and eventually sells at a profit, but there are no guarantees. The degree of your success depends on how well you evaluate different alternatives.

TABLE 20.6   Real Estate Checklist
Although real estate offers one of the best hedges against inflation, not all property increases in value. Many factors should be considered before investing in real estate.

Carefully evaluate all potential property.	Inspect the surrounding neighborhood.	Before making a final decision, answer the following questions:
Is the property priced competitively with similar property?	What are the present zoning requirements?	Why are the present owners selling the property?
What type of financing, if any, is available?	Is the neighborhood's population increasing or decreasing?	How long will you have to hold the property before selling it to someone else?
How much are the taxes?	What is the average income of people in the area?	How much profit can you reasonably expect to obtain?
	Evaluate the state of surrounding property. Do most of the buildings and houses need repair?	What are the risks involved?
		Is there a chance that the property value will decrease?

■ ■ ■ ■ GLOBAL PERSPECTIVES

Investments in Global Securities Are Booming!

In 1984 only 1 billion people were affected by free enterprise. But with the fall of communism and the enormous economic growth of many of the underdeveloped nations in the world, the free-market system and private enterprise are expected to expand dramatically. In the future, almost 5 billion people will live in countries with some form of free enterprise. As a result, the potential for the growth of global investments is enticing many U.S. investors to rush into the international securities market with the expectation of capitalizing on this new wave of opportunity. Between 1991 and 1994, Americans invested an estimated $230 billion in foreign markets— 7.5 times the amount that was invested between 1986 and 1990.

Investing in the international market is the same as investing at home—both offer opportunity and both incur risk. An investor can purchase shares of stock in individual foreign firms or, as most of the financial analysts recommend, purchase shares in a global mutual fund. For the small investor with less than $200,000 to invest and unaccustomed to the risks in foreign investments, global mutual funds offer more safety. More than one hundred stock funds and more than fifty bond funds invest partly or entirely abroad. And more than forty funds invest in stocks of a single nation or geographic region. Regardless of the type of investment you choose, financial analysts strongly agree that investors should not hold securities in just one country.

When building a conservative investment portfolio, most experts advise committing at least 10 percent of foreign investments to the emerging markets of the rapidly developing countries in Africa, Eastern Europe, the Far East, India, and Latin America. Even though they account for only 11 percent of the world's capitalization, these markets have the greatest potential for extraordinary growth in production and consumption, according to financial analysts. The remaining 90 percent should be invested in countries with more stable economies like Brazil, France, Germany, Great Britain, Japan, or Sweden.

With rising interest rates and a possible economic slowdown in the United States over the next few years, foreign investments are being hyped in the media, leading many investors to believe they can reduce the risks on their domestic portfolio by running to their broker and plunging into the global market. But these same investors must remember to evaluate foreign investments just as they would their U.S. investments. What drives the economy in the United States is often very different from what drives a foreign economy.

A major factor to consider when making foreign investments is the effect of currency fluctuations. Just as the buying power of our dollar increases or decreases, so does the currency of other nations. The foreign currency exchange factor is applied whenever securities are bought or sold and whenever dividends are paid. When the U.S. dollar is down, foreign investments may seem like a good buy, but on the other hand, when the U.S. dollar is rising, those same investments may decrease in value. And if a country devaluates its currency, as Mexico did to the peso in December 1994, an investment could evaporate overnight. The investor who wants to dip into the global market but is apprehensive of the exchange rate and other risks of foreign investments might consider investing in U.S. companies that operate successfully overseas.

■■ HIGH-RISK INVESTMENT TECHNIQUES

LEARNING OBJECTIVE 5
Describe the high-risk
investment techniques,
including buying on margin and
selling short.

high-risk investment   an
investment that is made in the
hope of earning a relatively
large profit in a short time

A **high-risk investment** is one that is made in the hope of earning a relatively large profit in a short time. (See the high-risk investment categories in Table 20.3.) Some securities may by their very nature be quite risky. (In this sense, a bet on a roulette wheel in a Las Vegas casino is a high-risk investment.) However, most high-risk investments become so because of the methods used by investors to earn a quick profit. These methods can lead to large losses as well as to impressive gains. They should not be used by anyone who does not fully understand the risks involved.

Buying Stock on Margin

margin requirement   the
proportion of the price of a
stock that cannot be borrowed

An investor buys stock *on margin* by borrowing part of the purchase price, usually from a stock brokerage firm. As we noted in Chapter 18, the **margin requirement** is the proportion of the price of a stock that cannot be borrowed. This requirement, which is set by the Federal Reserve Board, is currently 50 percent of the value of securities purchased.

Today, investors can borrow up to half the cost of a stock purchase. But why would they want to do so? Simply because they can buy twice as much stock by buying on margin. Suppose an investor expects the market price of Abbott Lab's common stock to increase in the next month or two. Let's say this investor has enough money to purchase 500 shares of the stock. But if she buys on margin, she can purchase an additional 500 shares. If the price of the Abbott Lab's stock increases by $5 per share, her profit will be $5 × 500, or $2,500, if she pays cash. But it will be $5 × 1,000, or $5,000, if she buys on margin. That is, by buying more shares on margin, she will earn double the profit (less the interest she pays on the borrowed money and customary commission charges).

Financial leverage—a topic covered in Chapter 19—is the use of borrowed funds to increase the return on an investment. When margin is used, the investor's profit is earned by both the borrowed money and the investor's own money. The investor retains all the profit and pays interest only for the temporary use of the borrowed funds. Note that the stock purchased on margin serves as collateral for the borrowed funds. Margin investors are subject to two problems. First, if the market price of the purchased stock does not increase as quickly as expected, interest costs mount and eventually drain the investor's profit. Second, if the price of the margined stock falls, the leverage works against the investor. That is, because the margin investor has purchased twice as much stock, he or she loses twice as much money.

Moreover, any decrease in the value of a stock bought using leverage is considered to come out of the investor's own funds, not out of the borrowed funds. If the stock's market value decreases to approximately half its original price, the investor will receive a *margin call* from the brokerage firm. The investor must then provide additional cash or securities to serve as collateral for the borrowed money. If he or she cannot provide additional collateral, the stock is sold and the proceeds are used to pay off the loan. Any funds remaining after the loan is paid off are returned to the investor.

Selling Short

Normally, investors buy stocks expecting that they will increase in value and can then be sold at a profit. This procedure is referred to as **buying long.** However, many securities decrease in value, for various reasons. More risk-oriented investors can use a procedure called *selling short* to make a profit when the price of an individual stock is falling. **Selling short** is the process of selling stock that an investor does not actually own but has borrowed from a brokerage firm and will repay at a later date. The idea is to sell at today's higher price and then buy later at a lower price.

To make a profit from a short transaction, the investor must proceed as follows:

1. Arrange to borrow a certain number of shares of a particular stock from a brokerage firm.
2. Sell the borrowed stock immediately, assuming that the price of the stock will drop in a reasonably short time.
3. After the price drops, buy the same number of shares that were sold in step 2.
4. Give the newly purchased stock to the brokerage firm in return for the stock borrowed in step 1.

The investor's profit is the difference between the amount received when the stock is sold in step 2 and the amount paid for the stock in step 3. For example, assume that you think that Sony Corp. stock is overvalued at $58 a share. You also believe the stock will decrease in value over the next three to four months. You call your broker and arrange to borrow 100 shares of Sony stock (step 1). The broker then sells your borrowed Sony stock for you at the current market price of $58 a share (step 2). Also assume that three months later, the Sony stock has dropped to $46 a share. You instruct your broker to purchase 100 shares of Sony stock at the current lower price (step 3). The newly purchased Sony stock is used to repay the borrowed stock (step 4). In this example, you made $1,200 by selling short ($5,800 selling price – $4,600 purchase price = $1,200 profit). Naturally, the $1,200 profit must be reduced by the commissions you paid to the broker for buying and selling the Sony stock.

People often ask where the broker obtains the stock for a short transaction. The broker probably borrows the stock from other investors who have purchased Sony stock through a margin arrangement or from investors who have left stock certificates on deposit with the brokerage firm. As a result, the person who is selling short must pay any dividends declared on the borrowed stock. The most obvious danger when selling short, of course, is that a loss can result if the stock's market value increases instead of decreases. If the market value of the stock increases after the investor has sold it in step 2, he or she loses money.

Other High-Risk Investments

We have already discussed two high-risk investments—margin transactions and selling short. Other high-risk investments include

buying long   buying stock with the expectation that it will increase in value and can then be sold at a profit

selling short   the process of selling stock that an investor does not actually own but has borrowed from a brokerage firm and will repay at a later date

Stock options	Gemstones
Commodities	Coins
Precious metals	Antiques and collectibles

Without exception, investments of this kind are normally referred to as high-risk investments for one reason or another. For example, the gold market has many unscrupulous dealers who sell worthless gold-plated lead coins to unsuspecting, uninformed investors. With each of the investments in this last category, it is extremely important that you deal with reputable dealers and recognized investment firms. It pays to be careful. *Although investments in this category can lead to large dollar gains, they should not be used by anyone who does not fully understand all of the potential risks involved.*

▪▪ SOURCES OF FINANCIAL INFORMATION

LEARNING OBJECTIVE 6
Use the various sources of financial information to evaluate potential investments.

A wealth of information is available to investors. Sources include newspapers, brokerage firm reports, business periodicals, corporate reports, and investors' services. For example, most local newspapers carry several pages of business news, including reports of securities transactions. The *Wall Street Journal* (published on weekdays) and *Barron's* (published once a week) are devoted almost entirely to financial and economic news. Both include complete coverage of transactions on all major securities exchanges. Most people prefer to evaluate their own investments; some investors, however, prefer to form investment clubs in order to evaluate different investment alternatives. Business Journal gives the inside story on investment clubs.

Newspaper Coverage of Securities Transactions

Securities transactions are reported as long tables of figures that tend to look somewhat forbidding. However, they are easy to decipher when you know how to read them. Because transactions involving stocks, bonds, and mutual funds are reported differently, we shall examine each type of report separately.

Common and Preferred Stocks   Transactions involving common and preferred stocks are reported together in the same table. This table usually looks like the top section of Figure 20.3. Parts of a dollar are traditionally quoted as fractions rather than as cents. Thus ⅛ means $0.125, or 12.5 cents, and ¾ means $0.75, or 75 cents. Stocks are listed alphabetically. Your first task is to move down the table to find the stock you're interested in. Then, to read the *stock quotation,* you read across the table. The third row in the table in Figure 20.3 gives detailed information about common stock issued by the Goodyear Company. (Each numbered entry in the list above the enlarged stock table refers to a numbered column of the stock table.)

If a corporation has more than one stock issue, the common stock is listed first. Preferred stock, as indicated by the letters *pf* in the stock column, is listed below the firm's common-stock issue.

Investment Clubs

We have all heard the saying, "Two heads are better than one." Well, that is basically the philosophy behind an investment club—a group of people who join together to invest in stocks and mutual funds. Working as a team, they research and discuss the financial performances of companies, use their individual talents to present differing points of view, share similar objectives, and then, by group consensus, pool their money to make investments. The more successful clubs say that research is the most important key to their success because members are usually small investors who want to not only *earn*, but they want to *learn* as well. And the clubs that invest in solid, long-term growth stocks do better than those who try to "beat the market."

SHOULD YOU JOIN AN INVESTMENT CLUB?

Your choice to join an investment club depends on your own personal goals. After you build your emergency fund, investing in stocks and mutual funds may well be part of your long-term financial plan. Today, many investors regard investment clubs as a way to help reach their financial goals. An investment club usually has twenty to thirty members who live within a reasonable distance of one another; they meet regularly and share similar goals. You commit yourself to do your share of the research, expend time and effort to monitor the performance of the group's investments, and are obligated to invest a set amount of money regularly, usually $10 to $100 per month. You must remember that investing in stocks and mutual funds entails a risk factor, so you should never invest more than you can afford to lose. If you would like more information on investment clubs, contact the National Association of Investors Corporation, Box 220, Royal Oak, Michigan 48068.

ON-LINE INVESTMENT CLUBS

With a computer, a modem, and an on-line service, you can belong to mutual fund investment clubs whose main purpose is to exchange information. The bulletin board service charges you for your time on-line, but the clubs themselves have no name or permanent address, do not charge dues or issue membership cards, and members do not actually invest through them. The service simply provides a means for people interested in investments either to participate by "lurking" (monitoring) or to communicate by joining in the dialogue. People with little investment experience are attracted to bulletin boards such as *Money Talk* on Prodigy. Writers and editors from *Kiplinger's Personal Finance Magazine* often participate, which can help the novice gain a better understanding of investing. Similar bulletin boards are available on CompuServe, America Online, and Delphi.

THE BEARDSTOWN LADIES CLUB

In 1983 a group of women in Beardstown, Illinois—all over sixty years of age and most of them widows—were discouraged by the way they were being treated by male brokers. These sixteen women agreed to form the Beardstown Business and Professional Women's Investment Club in order to learn as much as they could about investments. They meet one day a month to study and research companies, review corporate reports, and invest in stocks with growth potential. By reinvesting their dividends, the Ladies Club realized an average return of 23.5 percent on their investments each year from 1983 to 1993. This is very unusual, as most clubs do not experience such a high rate of annualized return. Because of their success, the Beardstown investors have been featured in magazine articles and appeared on the ABC television show *20/20* in January 1995.

FIGURE 20.3
Reading Stock Quotations for Listed Common Stocks
At the top of the figure, a portion of the stock quotations for the New York Stock Exchange as reported by the *Wall Street Journal* is reproduced. The same information is enlarged at the bottom of the figure. The itemized list in the middle explains what the numbers in each column of the figure mean. *(Source: Newspaper at the top of the figure is the* Wall Street Journal, *Oct. 11, 1994, p. C4)*

52 Weeks		Stock	Sym	Div	Yld %	PE	Vol 100s	Hi	Lo	Close	Net Chg
Hi	Lo										
48⅜	39	Goodrich	GR	2.20	5.3	11	244	41⅞	41½	41⅞	+ ⅜
52½	47½	Goodrich pfD		3.50	7.1	...	6	49⅜	49¼	49⅜	+ ¼
49¼	31⅝	Goodyear	GT	.80	2.3	10	6500	34⅜	33¼	34⅜	+1¼
13	7¼	Gottschks	GOT		...	dd	60	7¾	7½	7¾	+ ¼
46¾	34⅞	GraceWR	GRA	1.40	3.5	dd	1233	40¼	39½	40⅛	+ ⅞

1. Highest price paid for one share of Goodyear during the past 52 weeks: $49.25
2. Lowest price paid for one share of Goodyear during the past 52 weeks: $31.625
3. Name—often abbreviated—of the corporation: Goodyear
4. Ticker symbol or letters that identify a stock for trading: GT
5. Total dividends paid per share during the last 12 months: $0.80
6. Yield percentage, or the percentage of return based on the current dividend and current price of the stock: $0.80 ÷ $34.375 = 0.023 = 2.3%
7. Price-earnings (PE) ratio—the price of a share of stock divided by the corporation's earnings per share of stock outstanding over the last 12 months: 10. (The symbol "..." indicates that a company is operating at a loss and there are no earnings.)
8. Number of shares of Goodyear traded during the day, expressed in hundreds of shares: 650,000
9. Highest price paid for one share of Goodyear during the day: $34.375
10. Lowest price paid for one share of Goodyear during the day: $33.25
11. Price paid in the last transaction of the day: $34.375
12. Difference between the price paid for the last share today and the price paid for the last share on the previous day: 1¼, or $1.25 (In Wall Street terms, Goodyear "closed up 1¼" on this day.)

1	2	3	4	5	6	7	8	9	10	11	12
52 Weeks		Stock	Sym	Div	Yld %	PE	Vol 100s	Hi	Lo	Close	Net Chg
Hi	Lo										
48⅜	39	Goodrich	GR	2.20	5.3	11	244	41⅞	41½	41⅞	+ ⅜
52½	47½	Goodrich pfD		3.50	7.1	...	6	49⅜	49¼	49⅜	+ ¼
49¼	31⅝	Goodyear	GT	.80	2.3	10	6500	34⅜	33¼	34⅜	+1¼
13	7¼	Gottschks	GOT		...	dd	60	7¾	7½	7¾	+ ¼
46¾	34⅞	GraceWR	GRA	1.40	3.5	dd	1233	40¼	39½	40⅛	+ ⅞

Bonds   Purchases and sales of bonds are reported in tables like that shown at the top of Figure 20.4. In bond quotations, prices are given as a percentage of the face value, which is usually $1,000. Thus, to find the actual price paid, you must multiply the face value ($1,000) by the quotation listed in the newspaper. For example, a price quoted as 84 translates to a selling price of $840 ($1,000 × 84 percent, or .84, = $840). The first row of Figure 20.4 gives detailed information (again, by column number) for the Pennzoil bond that pays 4¾ percent interest and matures in 2003.

Mutual Funds   Purchases and sales of shares of mutual funds are reported in tables like the one shown at the top of Figure 20.5. As in reading stock and bond quotations, your first task is to move down the table to find the mutual fund you're interested in. Then, to find the mutual fund quotation, read across the table. The fourth row in the table in Figure 20.5 gives detailed information (again, by column number) for the Fidelity Select Biotech mutual fund.

FIGURE 20.4
Reading Bond Quotations
At the top of the figure, a portion of the bond quotations for the New York Bond Exchange as reported by the *Wall Street Journal* is reproduced. The same information is enlarged at the bottom of the figure. The itemized list at the top on the right side explains what the numbers in each column of the figure mean. *(Source: Newspaper at the top of the figure is the* Wall Street Journal, *Oct. 11, 1994, p. C18.)*

Bonds	Cur Yld	Vol	Close	Net Chg
Pennzl 4¾03	5.6	31	85	− 1
PeryDr 8½10	cv	5	87	− ½
Petrle 8s10	cv	51	115	+ ½
Pier1 6⅞02	cv	5	93¾	− ¼
PionFN 8s00	cv	3	97	...

1. Abbreviated name of the corporation (Pennzl), the bond's interest rate (4¾% of its face value, or $1,000 x 4.75%, or .0475 = $47.50), and the year of maturity (2003).
2. Current yield ($47.50 ÷ $850, or 5.6%), determined by dividing the dollar amount of annual interest by the current price of the bond. The "cv" for the Pier 1 bond indicates this bond is convertible into a specified number of shares of common stock.
3. Number (volume) of bonds traded during the day: 31.
4. Price paid in the last transaction for the day: $1,000 x 85% = $850.
5. Difference between the price paid for the last bond today and the price paid for the last bond on the previous day: $10 ($10 less than the day before). In Wall Street terms, the Pennzoil bond "closed down 1" on this day.

1 Bonds	2 Cur Yld	3 Vol	4 Close	5 Net Chg
Pennzl 4¾03	5.6	31	85	− 1
PeryDr 8½10	cv	5	87	− ½
Petrle 8s10	cv	51	115	+ ½
Pier1 6⅞02	cv	5	93¾	− ¼
PionFn 8s00	cv	3	97	...

Other Sources of Financial Information

In addition to newspaper coverage, other sources offer detailed and varied information about investment alternatives. Typical sources of information include brokerage firm reports, business periodicals, corporate reports, and investors' services.

Brokerage Firm Reports   Brokerage firms employ financial analysts to prepare detailed reports on individual corporations and their securities. Such reports are based on the corporation's sales, profits or losses, management, and planning, plus other information on the company, its industry, demand for its products, and its efforts to develop new products. The reports, which may include buy or sell recommendations, are usually provided free to the brokerage firm's clients. Firms offering this service include Paine Webber, Smith Barney Shearson, Rauscher Pierce, Merrill Lynch, and most other full-service brokerage firms.

Business Periodicals   Business magazines like *Business Week, Fortune, Forbes,* and *Harvard Business Review* provide not only general economic news but also detailed financial information about individual corporations. Trade or industry publications like *Advertising Age* and *Business Insurance* may include information about the firms in a specific industry. News magazines like *U.S. News & World Report, Time,* and *Newsweek* feature financial news regularly. Finally, *Money, Kiplinger's Personal Finance Magazine, Consumer Reports,* and similar magazines provide information and advice

FIGURE 20.5
Reading Mutual Fund Quotations
At the top of the figure, a portion of the mutual fund quotations as reported by the *Wall Street Journal* is reproduced. The same information is enlarged at the bottom of the figure. The itemized list in the middle explains what the numbers in each column of the figure mean.   *(Source: Newspaper at the top of the figure is the* Wall Street Journal, *Oct. 11, 1994, p. C24.)*

	Inv. Obj.	NAV	Offer Price	NAV Chg.	—Total Return— YTD	4 wks	1 yr
Fidelity Selects:							
Air r	SEC	13.32	13.73	+0.13	−17.1	−10.1	−12.1
AmGold r	SEC	23.18	23.90	−0.04	−1.6	+2.6	+13.8
Auto r	SEC	21.72	22.39	+0.51	−11.8	−2.3	−4.9
Biotech r	SEC	24.78	25.55	+0.08	−13.4	−1.2	−8.7
Broker r	SEC	15.19	15.66	−0.07	−17.0	−5.4	−12.1
Chem r	SEC	34.61	35.68	+0.34	+18.4	−2.4	+25.9
Comp r	SEC	27.46	28.31	+0.40	+12.8	−0.3	+24.3

1. The name of the mutual fund: Fidelity Select Biotech. The "r" after the fund name indicates that a redemption fee is charged to redeem shares in the fund.
2. The investment objective for the Biotech fund: Sector fund. A sector fund contains securities in only one particular industry.
3. The net asset value (NAV) of one share of the Biotech fund: $24.78.
4. The offer price for one share of the Biotech: $25.55. For load and low-load funds, the commission is added to the NAV to determine the offer price.
5. The difference between the net asset value today and the net asset value on the previous trading day: +0.08 (In Wall Street terms, Fidelity Select's Biotech fund closed up $0.08 on this day.)
6. The last three columns (YTD, 4 wks, and 1 yr) give the total return for Fidelity Select's Biotech mutual fund for the year to date, the last 4 weeks, and the last 12 months.

1	2	3	4	5	6		
	Inv. Obj.	NAV	Offer Price	NAV Chg.	—Total Return— YTD	4 wks	1 yr
Fidelity Selects:							
Air r	SEC	13.32	13.73	+0.13	−17.1	−10.1	−12.1
AmGold r	SEC	23.18	23.90	−0.04	−1.6	+2.6	+13.8
Auto r	SEC	21.72	22.39	+0.51	−11.8	−2.3	−4.9
Biotech r	SEC	24.78	25.55	+0.08	−13.4	−1.2	−8.7
Broker r	SEC	15.19	15.66	−0.07	−17.0	−5.4	−12.1
Chem r	SEC	34.61	35.68	+0.34	+18.4	−2.4	+25.9
Comp r	SEC	27.46	28.31	+0.40	+12.8	−0.3	+24.3

designed to improve the individual investor's skill. These periodicals are available at libraries and are sold at newsstands and by subscription.

Corporate Reports   Publicly held corporations must send their stockholders annual and quarterly reports. These reports include a description of the company's performance provided by the corporation's top management, information about the firm's products or services, and detailed financial statements that readers can use to evaluate the firm's actual performance. In addition, a corporation issuing a new security must—by law—prepare a prospectus and ensure that copies are distributed to potential investors. A **prospectus** is a detailed, written description of a new security, the issuing corporation, and the corporation's top management. Both prospectuses and annual and quarterly reports are available to the general public.

prospectus a detailed written description of a new security, the issuing corporation, and the corporation's top management

People who invest in United Inns can get a really good night's sleep. According to a 1995 survey published by *Fortune* magazine, United Inns was the best performing stock on the New York Stock Exchange. The total return to investors for 1994 was 158 percent. Here, hotel guests check into an Atlanta Holiday Inn—just one of many hotels owned and managed by United Inns.

Investors' Services   For annual fees ranging from $30 to $500 or more, various investors' services provide information about financial securities to subscribers. Three of the most widely accepted investors' services are provided by Standard & Poor's Corporation, Value Line, and Moody's Investors Services. Each of these services provides ratings for common and preferred stocks. They also provide more in-depth, detailed financial information, like the figures presented in the sample Moody's research report for Wal-Mart Stores, Inc., that is illustrated as part of Case 20.2 (see Figure 20.6.)

In addition, both Moody's and Standard & Poor's provide information that can be used to determine the quality and risk associated with bond issues. As Table 20.7 shows, bond ratings generally range from AAA (the highest) to D (the lowest). For both Moody's and Standard & Poor's, the first four individual categories represent investment-grade securities. Bonds in the next two categories are considered speculative in nature. Finally, the C and D categories are used to rank bonds that may be in default because of poor prospects of repayment or even of continued payment of interest.

A number of investors' services provide detailed information on mutual funds. Standard and Poor's Corporation, Lipper Analytical Services, and the Wiesenberger Investment Companies are three widely tapped sources of such information. In addition, various mutual fund newsletters supply financial information to subscribers for a fee.

All reports and services provided by these companies are fairly expensive, but they may be available from brokerage firms or libraries.

Stock Averages

stock average (or stock index) an average of the current market prices of selected stocks

Investors often gauge the stock market through the stock averages reported in newspapers and on television news programs. A **stock average** (or **stock index**) is an average of the current market prices of selected stocks. Over a

TABLE 20.7   Bond ratings provided by Moody's Investors Service and Standard & Poor's Corporation.
Today, bonds range from high-grade investments suitable for conservative investors to more speculative bond issues that offer both larger dollar gains *and* higher risk.

Quality	Moody's	Standard & Poor's	Description
High-grade	Aaa	AAA	Bonds that are judged to be of the best quality. They carry the smallest degree of investment risk and are generally referred to as *gilt edge*. Interest payments are protected by a large or exceptionally stable margin, and principal is secure.
	Aa	AA	Bonds that are judged to be of high quality by all standards. Together with the first group, they compose what are generally known as *high-grade* bonds. They are rated lower than the best bonds because their margins of protection may not be as large.
Medium-grade	A	A	Bonds that possess many favorable investment attributes and are to be considered upper medium-grade obligations. The factors giving security to principal and interest are considered adequate.
	Baa	BBB	Bonds that are considered medium-grade obligations; i.e., they are neither highly protected nor poorly secured.
Speculative	Ba	BB	Bonds that are judged to have speculative elements; their future cannot be considered well assured. Often, their protection of interest and principal payments may be very moderate.
	B	B	Bonds that generally lack characteristics of the desirable investment. Assurance of interest and principal payments or of maintenance of other terms of the contract over any long period of time may be small.
Default	Caa	CCC	Bonds that are of poor standing. Such issues may be in default, or elements of danger may be present with respect to principal or interest.
	Ca	CC	Bonds that represent obligations that are speculative to a high degree. Such issues are often in default or have other marked shortcomings.
	C		The lowest-rated class in Moody's designation. These bonds can be regarded as having extremely poor prospects of attaining any real investment standing.
		C	Rating given to income bonds on which interest is not currently being paid.
		D	Issues in default with arrears in interest and/or principal payments.

Sources: *Moody's Bond Survey,* Aug. 1994, Moody's Investors Service, 99 Church St., New York, NY 10007; and *Standard & Poor's Stock and Bond Guide,* 1994 Edition, Standard & Poor's Corporation, 25 Broadway, New York, NY 10004.

period of time, these averages indicate price trends, but they cannot predict the performance of individual stocks. At best, they can give the investor a "feel" for what is happening to stock prices generally.

The *Dow Jones Industrial Average,* established in 1897, is the oldest stock index in use today. This average is composed of the prices of the common stocks of thirty leading industrial corporations. (These firms are listed in Table 20.8.) In addition, Dow Jones & Co., Inc., publishes the following averages:

TABLE 20.8   The Thirty Corporations Whose Common Stocks Are Included in the Dow Jones Industrial Average

AT&T	Du Pont	Minnesota Mining & Mfg.
Alcoa	Eastman Kodak	Morgan (J. P.)
Allied-Signal	Exxon	Philip Morris
American Express	General Electric	Procter & Gamble
Bethlehem Steel	General Motors	Sears Roebuck
Boeing	Goodyear	Texaco
Caterpillar	IBM	Union Carbide
Chevron	International Paper	United Technologies
Coca-Cola	McDonald's	Westinghouse
Disney	Merck	Woolworth

Source: Reprinted by permission of the *Wall Street Journal.* Copyright © 1994 Dow Jones & Company, Inc. All rights reserved worldwide.

- A *transportation average,* computed from the prices of twenty transportation stocks.
- A *utility average,* computed from the prices of fifteen utility stocks.
- A *composite average,* computed from the prices of the sixty-five stocks included in the industrial, transportation, and utility averages.

The Standard & Poor's 500 Stock Index and the New York Stock Exchange Composite Index include more stocks than the Dow Jones averages. Thus they tend to reflect the stock market more fully. The *Standard & Poor's 500 Stock Index* is an average of the prices of 400 industrial, 60 transportation and utility, and 40 financial stocks. The *New York Stock Exchange Composite Index* is computed from the prices of all stocks listed on the NYSE, weighted to reflect the number and value of outstanding shares. The *American Stock Exchange (AMEX) Index* is an average of more than 1,300 stocks listed on the American Stock Exchange. Finally, the *NASDAQ Composite Index* includes the prices for 3,500 stocks that are traded over the counter.

It should be apparent that vast sums of money are involved in securities trading. In an effort to protect investors from unfair treatment, both federal and state governments have acted to regulate securities trading.

■■ REGULATION OF SECURITIES TRADING

LEARNING OBJECTIVE 7
Explain how federal and state authorities regulate trading in securities.

Government regulation of securities trading began as a response to abusive and fraudulent practices in the sale of stocks, bonds, and other financial securities. The states were the first to react, early in this century. Later, federal legislation was passed to regulate the interstate sale of securities.

State Regulation

The first state law regulating the sale of securities was enacted in Kansas in 1911. Within a few years, several other states had passed similar laws. Today, most states require that new issues be registered with a state agency and that brokers and securities dealers operating within the state be licensed. The states also provide for the prosecution of individuals accused of the fraudulent sale of stocks, bonds, and other securities.

blue-sky laws   state laws that regulate securities trading

The state laws that regulate securities trading are often called **blue-sky laws.** They are designed to protect investors from purchasing securities backed up by nothing but the "clear blue sky."

Federal Regulation

The *Securities Act of 1933,* sometimes referred to as the *Truth in Securities Act,* provides for full disclosure of important facts about corporations issuing new securities. Such corporations are required to file a *registration statement* containing specific information about the corporation's earnings, assets, and liabilities; its products or services; and the qualifications of its top management. Publication of a prospectus that can be given to prospective investors is also a requirement.

Securities and Exchange Commission (SEC)   the agency that enforces federal securities regulations

The *Securities Exchange Act of 1934* created the **Securities and Exchange Commission (SEC),** which is the agency that enforces federal securities regulations. The operations of the SEC are directed by five commissioners, who are appointed by the president of the United States. The 1934 act gave the SEC the power to regulate trading on all national securities exchanges. It also requires that corporations' registration statements be brought up-to-date periodically. Finally, this act requires brokers and securities dealers to register with the SEC.

Eight other federal acts have been passed primarily to protect investors.

National Association of Securities Dealers (NASD)   the organization responsible for the self-regulation of the over-the-counter securities market

- The *Maloney Act of 1938* made it possible to establish the **National Association of Securities Dealers (NASD)** to oversee the self-regulation of the over-the-counter securities market.

- The *Investment Company Act of 1940* placed investment companies that sell mutual funds under the jurisdiction of the SEC.

- The *Investment Advisers Act of 1940* required financial advisers with more than fifteen clients to register with the SEC.

- The *Federal Securities Act of 1964* extended the SEC's jurisdiction to include companies whose stock is sold over the counter, if they have total assets of at least $1 million or have more than 500 stockholders of any one class of stock.

- The *Securities Investor Protection Act of 1970* created the *Securities Investor Protection Corporation (SIPC).* The SIPC provides insurance of up to $500,000 per customer, including $100,000 for cash left on deposit with a brokerage firm that later fails. The SIPC is, in essence, the securities-market equivalent of the FDIC and the SAIF (discussed in Chapter 18).

- The *Securities Amendments Act of 1975* empowered the SEC to supervise the development of a national securities market system. In addition, the law prohibited fixed commissions.

- The *Insider Trading Sanctions Act of 1984* strengthened the penalty provisions of the Securities Exchange Act of 1934. Under the 1984 act, people are guilty of insider trading if they use information that is available only to account executives or other brokerage firm employees. This act also expanded the SEC's authority by empowering it to investigate such illegal acts.

- The *Insider Trading and Securities Fraud Enforcement Act of 1988* made the top management of brokerage firms responsible for reporting to the SEC any transaction that was based on inside information. In addition, this act empowered the SEC to levy fines of up to $1 million for failure to report such trading violations.

In Chapter 21, we discuss the protection of finances and other assets from the hazards involved in simply existing. As you will see, these hazards include fire, theft, accident, and the legal liability for injury to others. The potential effect of hazards on firms and individuals can be minimized through effective risk management.

■ ■ ■ ■ CHAPTER REVIEW

Summary

1 Describe how securities are bought and sold through the primary and secondary markets.

Stocks may be purchased in either the primary or the secondary market. The primary market is a market in which an investor purchases financial securities (via an investment bank or other representative) directly from the issuer of those securities. A corporation can also obtain financing by selling securities directly to current stockholders or bondholders. The secondary market involves transactions for existing securities that are currently traded between investors and are usually bought and sold through a securities exchange or the over-the-counter market.

If you invest in securities, chances are that you will use the services of an account executive who works for a brokerage firm. An investor should choose an account executive who is ethical, compatible, and able to provide the desired level of service.

2 Develop a personal investment plan.

Personal investment planning begins with formulating measurable and realistic investment goals. A personal investment plan is then designed to implement those goals. Many financial planners suggest, as a first step, that the investor establish an emergency fund equivalent to three to nine months' living expenses. Then additional funds may be invested according to the investment plan. Finally, all investments should be carefully monitored and, if necessary, the investment plan should be modified.

3 Explain how the factors of safety, risk, income, growth, and liquidity affect an individual's investment decisions.

Depending on their particular investment goals, investors seek varying degrees of safety, risk, income, growth, and liquidity from their investments. Safety is, in essence, freedom from the risk of loss. Generally, the greater the risk, the greater should be the potential return on an investment. Income is the periodic return from an investment. Growth is an increase in the value of the investment. Liquidity is defined as the ease with which an asset can be converted to cash.

4 Identify the advantages and disadvantages of the traditional investment alternatives: savings accounts, bonds, stocks, mutual funds, and real estate.

Although bank accounts and bonds can provide investment growth, they are generally purchased by investors who seek a predictable source of income.

With stock investments, investors can make money through dividend payments, an increase in the value of the stock, or stock splits. The major advantages of mutual fund investments are professional management and diversification. The success of real estate investments is often tied to how well each investment alternative is evaluated.

5   Describe the high-risk investment techniques, including buying on margin and selling short.

High-risk investment techniques can provide greater returns, but they also entail greater risk of loss. An investor buys stock on margin by borrowing part of the purchase price, usually from a stock brokerage firm. Because the investor can purchase up to twice as much stock by using margin, the investor can increase his or her return on investment as long as the stock's market value increases. Investors can also make money by selling short when the market value of a financial security is decreasing. Selling short is the process of selling stock that an investor does not actually own but has borrowed from a brokerage firm and will repay at a later date. Other high-risk investments include stock options, commodities, precious metals, gemstones, coins, and antiques and collectibles.

6   Use the various sources of financial information to evaluate potential investments.

Information on securities and the firms that issue them can be obtained from newspapers, brokerage firm reports, corporate reports, and investors' services. Most local newspapers report daily securities transactions and stock indexes, or averages. These averages indicate price trends but reveal nothing about the performance of individual stocks.

7   Explain how federal and state authorities regulate trading in securities.

State and federal regulations protect investors from unscrupulous securities trading practices. Federal laws, which are enforced by the Securities and Exchange Commission, require the registration of new securities, the publication and distribution of prospectuses, and the registration of brokers and securities dealers. These laws apply to securities listed on the national security exchanges, to mutual funds, and to some OTC stocks.

Key Terms

You should now be able to define and give an example relevant to each of the following terms:

primary market (635)
investment banking firm (635)
initial public offering (IPO) (635)
secondary market (636)
securities exchange (636)
over-the-counter (OTC) market (637)
account executive (638)
market order (639)
limit order (639)
discretionary order (639)
round lot (640)
odd lot (640)
personal investment (640)
financial planner (642)
liquidity (645)
stock dividend (648)
market value (648)
bull market (649)
bear market (649)
stock split (650)
mutual fund (651)
net asset value (NAV) (652)
high-risk investment (655)
margin requirement (655)
buying long (656)
selling short (656)
prospectus (661)
stock average (or stock index) (662)
blue-sky laws (665)
Securities and Exchange Commission (SEC) (665)
National Association of Securities Dealers (NASD) (665)

Questions

Review Questions

1. What is the difference between the primary market and the secondary market?
2. When a corporation decides to sell stock, what is the role of an investment banking firm?
3. What is the difference between a securities exchange and the over-the-counter market?

4. What steps are involved in purchasing a stock listed on the NYSE?

5. How would you go about developing a personal investment plan?

6. What is an "emergency fund," and why is it recommended?

7. What is meant by the safety of an investment? What is the tradeoff between safety and return on the investment?

8. In general, what kinds of investments provide income? What kinds provide growth?

9. How can the interest on savings accounts be used either as income or for growth?

10. Characterize the purchase of corporate bonds as an investment in terms of safety, risk, income, growth, and liquidity.

11. Describe the three methods by which investors can make money with stock investments.

12. An individual may invest in stocks either directly or through a mutual fund. How are the two investment methods different?

13. What are the risks and rewards of purchasing stocks on margin?

14. When would a speculator sell short?

15. In what ways are newspaper stock quotations useful to investors? In what ways are stock averages useful?

16. What is the Securities and Exchange Commission? What are its principal functions?

Discussion Questions

1. In 1994 *Fortune* magazine named The Home Depot America's most admired specialty retailer and second-most admired corporation. What factors led to The Home Depot's success?

2. Back in 1991, Barbara and Charles Thompson purchased one hundred shares of Home Depot stock for $8.25 a share; their total investment including commission was $890. In March 1995, this modest investment was valued at $15,000. If you were the Thompsons, would you sell your Home Depot stock and take your profits? Explain your answer.

3. What personal circumstances might lead some investors to emphasize income rather than growth in their investment planning? What might lead them to emphasize growth rather than income?

4. Suppose you have just inherited 500 shares of IBM common stock. What would you do with or about it, if anything?

5. For what reasons might a corporation's executives be *unwilling* to have their firm's securities listed on an exchange?

6. What kinds of information would you like to have before you invest in a particular common or preferred stock? From what sources can you get that information?

7. Federal laws prohibit corporate managers from making investments that are based on "inside information"—that is, special knowledge about their firms that is not available to the general public. Why are such laws needed?

Exercises

1. Assume that you are single and have graduated from college. Your monthly take-home pay is $2,100, and your monthly expenses total $1,800, which leaves you with a monthly surplus of $300. Based on this information, complete the following exercises.

   a. Develop at least three investment goals that you would like to achieve during the next ten years.

   b. Assume that you are going to seek the advice of a financial planner to help you achieve your investment goals. Prepare a list of questions that you could use to screen prospective financial planners.

   c. Choose three of the traditional investment alternatives presented in this chapter (bank accounts, bonds, common stocks, preferred stocks, mutual funds, and real estate) that could help you obtain your investment goals. Then rank the three investments on the factors of safety, risk, income, growth, and liquidity (1 is high; 2 is medium; and 3 is low).

2. Using recent newspaper stock quotations, fill in the following table for common stocks only.

Newspaper: _____

Date: _____

	Dividend	P-E Ratio	Closing Price	Net Change
American Express (AmExpress)	_____	_____	_____	_____
Boise Cascade (BoiseCasc)	_____	_____	_____	_____
General Motors (GenMotors)	_____	_____	_____	_____

a. Which of the three stocks would be the best investment for someone whose investment plan stresses income? Why?

b. Which stock would seem to be best for an investment plan that stresses growth? (If you need more information to answer this, explain what information you need.)

c. Can you tell from this information which stock offers the most safety? Explain.

VIDEO CASE 20.1

Buy and Sell Through Charles Schwab's Menu

It was a little over twenty years ago that a young man in San Francisco began to develop a dream of starting a company that would allow investors to manage their own finances without being influenced by commissioned salespeople who represent traditional Wall Street brokerage firms. He knew that many investors, like himself, were intelligent enough and more than capable of selecting investments that would help them attain their financial goals and would welcome the opportunity to do it in a cost-effective manner. He was right. Today, the Charles Schwab Corporation is the nation's largest discount brokerage firm with 208 branch offices in forty-six states offering over ninety convenient services at a fair price or cost-free. In addition to being cost-effective, Schwab provides investors with a wide menu of investment opportunities—mutual funds, money market funds, IRA accounts, computerized stock trading, specialized banking services, and fixed income securities, to name just a few.

Schwab's philosophy is to encourage customers to use the services that best meet their own needs and to obtain investing advice from independent advisers and financial periodicals. Schwab branch offices have trained representatives, free investing materials, and computers available for investors who want to research a company's historical data and its current share price. With the aid of technology, Schwab has introduced many innovative services; for example, TeleBroker, a 24-hour, toll-free telephone number with automated touchpad order entry in four languages, guarantees investors their transactions will be completed within one day. Schwab clients can also use StreetSmart for Windows, a software package that allows trading via computer, and Custom Broker, a phone-fax-pager alert for active traders.

Fifty percent of Schwab's investors take advantage of its OneSource program that offers 287 no-load mutual funds from twenty-seven fund families. This program is already attracting two thousand new accounts every day because it charges no transaction fees and makes it convenient to move in and out of the funds with just a phone call or a keystroke. And if the customer wants dividends reinvested, Schwab will set up an automatic reinvestment plan. Finally, Schwab sends OneSource customers quarterly consolidated statements that allow them to track the value of their investments. Customers can enroll in OneSource with a minimum investment of $1,000 and subsequent investments of at least $500.

Even the fund families included in OneSource like the program because it saves them marketing costs. Because Schwab sends out the prospectuses, quarterly guides with information on performance rankings, and the funds' newsletters, the fund families don't have to do as much marketing. Smaller fund families in particular like to be on Schwab's menu because they cannot afford their own brokerage offices and OneSource can reach a far wider audience of investors. Some top no-load families like Scudder, T. Rowe Price, and Vanguard have declined to be in the OneSource program. However, in order to accommodate its customers, Schwab will allow its investors to include these funds on their quarterly consolidated statements at no extra cost. And any customer who wants to buy into these funds can do so through Schwab for a small fee.

OneSource is attracting investors who want to make their own financial decisions. Older investors unhappy with full-time investment firms, as well as baby boomers looking ahead for financial security, have turned to Schwab for its low-cost, no-pressure, convenient services. Although Schwab shows what it has to offer, it is the investor who ultimately makes the final decision based on his or her own research. The people at Schwab are quick to point out that you should invest only what you can afford to lose and that all investments involve some potential risk. But after everything is said and done, Charles Schwab's original vision holds true: you, the investor, should decide how much risk is enough and ultimately which investments suit your financial goals.[6]

Questions

1. What makes the Charles Schwab Corporation different from the traditional Wall Street investment brokerage firms?

2. What services does the OneSource program offer investors? What services does OneSource offer the fund families included in the program?

FIGURE 20.6
Research Report on Wal-Mart Stores, Inc.
Detailed financial information about most major corporations is available from companies like Moody's Investors Service.   *(Source:* Moody's Handbook of Common Stock, *Summer 1994. Used by permission.)*

WAL-MART STORES, INC.

LISTED	SYM.	LTPS♦	STPS♦	IND. DIV.	REC. PRICE	RANGE (52-WKS.)	YLD.	DIV. ACH.
NYSE	WMT	110.1	93.5	$0.17	23½	30½ - 22⅜	0.7%	13 yrs.

HIGH GRADE. DESPITE A SLOWER RATE OF SALES GROWTH, WAL-MART SHOULD BENEFIT FROM SUPERCENTER EXPANSIONS.

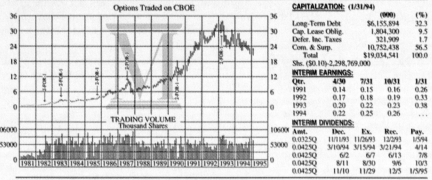

CAPITALIZATION: (1/31/94)

	(000)	(%)
Long-Term Debt	$6,155,894	32.3
Cap. Lease Oblig.	1,804,300	9.5
Defer. Inc. Taxes	321,909	1.7
Com. & Surp.	10,752,438	56.5
Total	$19,034,541	100.0

Shs. ($0.10)-2,298,769,000

INTERIM EARNINGS:

Qtr.	4/30	7/31	10/31	1/31
1991	0.14	0.15	0.16	0.26
1992	0.17	0.18	0.19	0.33
1993	0.20	0.22	0.23	0.38
1994	0.22	0.25	0.26	...

INTERIM DIVIDENDS:

Amt.	Dec.	Ex.	Rec.	Pay.
0.0325Q	11/11/93	11/26/93	12/2/93	1/5/94
0.0425Q	3/10/94	3/15/94	3/21/94	4/14
0.0425Q	6/2	6/7	6/13	7/8
0.0425Q	8/11	8/30	9/6	10/3
0.0425Q	11/10	11/29	12/5	1/5/95

BACKGROUND:

Wal-Mart Stores, Inc., as of 10/31/94, operated 2,102 discount department stores (including 119 Supercenter stores) and 437 Sam's Wholesale Clubs in 49 states, Puerto Rico and Canada. WMT also operates 52 Mexican units and 3 Hong Kong Value Clubs. Wal-Mart stores are designed to be one-stop shopping centers which provide a wide assortment of merchandise to satisfy most of the clothing, home recreational and convenience needs of the family. Supercenters combine food, general merchandise, and services including pharmacy, dry cleaning, portrait studios, photo finishing, hair salons, and optical shops. WMT also operates McLane and Western, a specialty distribution subsidiary, serving over 30,000 convenience stores and independent grocers.

RECENT DEVELOPMENTS:

For the quarter ended 10/31/94, net income was $588.1 million compared with $518.7 million a year ago. Sales grew 21% to $20.42 billion. As a percentage of sales, selling, general and administrative expenses increased to 16.4% from 16.2% a year ago. During the quarter, the Company opened 45 new discount stores, 32 new Supercenters, 3 Value Clubs in Hong Kong, and relocated or expanded 25 additional stores. For the nine months ended 10/31/94, net income was $1.65 billion versus $1.47 billion a year ago. Sales rose 23.5% to $58.05 billion.

PROSPECTS:

Earnings will continue to grow, but at a slower rate than previous years. Meanwhile, WMT plans to expand its Supercenter format, which should help boost margins due to its one-stop shopping concept. WMT also announced a joint venture with Cifra, SA (WMT's joint venture partner) and Dillard Department Stores to build and operate Dillard stores in Mexico. Under the agreement, the three companies will own (and Dillard will operate) department stores modeled after Dillard stores in the U.S., with the first store to be opened in Monterrey in late 1995.

STATISTICS:

YEAR	GROSS REVS. (&mil.)	OPER. PROFIT MARGIN %	RET. ON EQUITY %	NET INCOME (&mil.)	WORK CAP. (&mil.)	SENIOR CAPITAL (&mil.)	SHARES (000)	EARN. PER SH.&	DIV. PER SH.&	DIV. PAY. %	PRICE RANGE		P/E RATIO	AVG. YIELD %
a														
84	6,400.9	8.5	27.5	270.8	614	497.0	2,244,000	0.12	0.015	13	2⅞ -	1⅞	19.8	0.6
85	8,451.5	7.2	25.6	327.5	791	780.8	2,248,000	0.15	0.017	13	4⅜ -	2⅜	22.5	0.6
86	11,909.1	7.1	26.6	450.1	1,013	943.4	2,258,000	0.20	0.021	10	6¾ -	3⅝	25.9	0.4
87	15,959.3	6.8	27.8	627.6	1,161	1,052.6	2,260,000	0.28	0.028	11	10⅝ -	5	27.9	0.4
88	20,649.0	6.4	27.8	837.2	1,565	1,193.5	2,262,000	0.37	0.04	11	8½ -	6⅛	19.8	0.6
89	25,810.7	6.5	27.1	1,075.9	1,867	1,272.6	2,264,000	0.48	0.052	11	11¼ -	7½	19.5	0.6
90	32,601.6	6.0	24.1	1,291.0	2,424	1,898.9	2,284,000	0.57	0.067	12	18⅜ -	10⅛	25.0	0.5
91	43,886.9	5.5	23.0	1,608.5	3,572	3,277.9	2,298,000	0.70	0.082	12	30 -	14	31.4	0.4
92	55,483.8	5.4	22.8	1,994.8	3,443	4,845.0	2,299,638	0.87	0.10	11	33 -	25⅛	33.4	0.3
93	67,344.6	6.2	21.7	2,333.3	4,708	7,960.2	2,298,769	1.02	0.12	12	34⅛ -	23	28.0	0.4

♦Long-Term Price Score — Short-Term Price Score; see page 4a. STATISTICS ARE AS ORIGINALLY REPORTED. Adjusted for 100% stock dividends: 10/85, 7/87, 7/90 and 2/93. a-Fiscal year ends 1/31 of the following calendar year.

INCORPORATED:
October 1969 — DE

PRINCIPAL OFFICE:
702 S.W. 8th St.
P. O. Box 116
Bentonville, AR 72716
Tel.: (501) 273-4000

ANNUAL MEETING:
First Friday in June

NUMBER OF STOCKHOLDERS:
257,946

TRANSFER AGENT(S):
Boatmen's Trust Co.
St. Louis, MO

REGISTRAR(S):
Boatmen's Trust Co.
St. Louis, MO

INSTITUTIONAL HOLDINGS:
No. of Institutions: 1,034
Shares Held: 677,181,892

OFFICERS:
Chairman
S. R. Walton
President & C.E.O.
D. D. Glass
Exec. V.P. & C.F.O.
P. R. Carter
Sr. V.P., Gen. Coun. & Sec.
R. K. Rhoads
Treasurer
T. Bertschy

CASE 20.2

Wal-Mart Stores, Inc.

In this chapter, we have stressed the importance of evaluating potential investments. Now, you can test your skill at evaluating an investment in Wal-Mart Stores. Assume that on Tuesday, October 11, 1994, you prepared a personal investment plan and established an emergency fund equal to three months' living expenses. Also assume that you have saved $5,000, which you could use to purchase Wal-Mart's common stock. To help evaluate your investment in Wal-Mart, carefully examine the research report (Figure 20.6) taken from the Summer 1994 issue of *Moody's Handbook of Common Stocks*.

Questions

1. Based on the Moody's research report, would you buy Wal-Mart's common stock? Justify your answer.
2. What other information would you need in order to evaluate a Wal-Mart investment? Where would you obtain this information?
3. On Tuesday, October 11, 1994, the common stock for Wal-Mart Stores, Inc., was selling for $23⅜ a share. Using a recent newspaper, determine the current price for a share of Wal-Mart's common stock. Based on this information, would your Wal-Mart investment have been profitable had you purchased the common stock for $23⅜ a share in October 1994?

■■■■ CHAPTER 21

Risk Management and Insurance

LEARNING OBJECTIVES

After studying this chapter you should be able to

1 Explain what risk is, and understand the difference between a pure and a speculative risk.

2 Appraise the four general techniques of risk management: avoidance, reduction, assumption, and the shifting of risk to an insurer.

3 Discuss the principles underlying insurance and the insurability of risks.

4 Distinguish the types of insurance that can be used to protect businesses and individuals against property and casualty losses.

5 Describe the types of insurance available to individuals.

6 Analyze the advantages and disadvantages of term, whole, endowment, and universal life insurance.

CHAPTER PREVIEW

We open this chapter by defining two broad categories of risk: pure risks and speculative risks. Then we examine several methods of risk management available to individuals and businesses and consider situations for which each method is appropriate. Next we turn our attention to insurance companies—organizations that agree to assume responsibility for certain kinds of risks in exchange for payment of a fee. We see how insurance companies determine which risks they will cover and what prices they will charge for coverage. Then we list the major types of insurance against loss of property and losses owing to accidents. We close the chapter with a comparison of several kinds of life insurance.

Mutual of Omaha: Trust, Responsibility, Innovation

Mutual of Omaha began with the dream of a young medical student at Creighton University in Omaha, Nebraska, and has grown into an international organization that provides more individual health and accident insurance to Americans than any other company. Initially incorporated on March 5, 1909, as Mutual Benefit Health and Accident Association, the name was changed to Mutual of Omaha Insurance Company in 1962.

That visionary medical student, C. C. Criss, recognized the need for more comprehensive medical coverages than the very limited policies of his day. Under his leadership, Mutual of Omaha began to offer simplified, liberal policies to minimize an insured's liability from accident or illness. Underwriting rules were extended to provide disability coverage to the average person, including lifetime benefit periods. Innovative decisions like these, along with an emphasis on superior customer service, expanded Mutual of Omaha's policyholder base.

In 1949, a new president, V. J. Skutt, helped take the company from a small regional insurer to an international financial services organization. In 1949 the company collected $76 million in premiums; in 1994 premium income had grown to over $3.3 billion. Skutt was also responsible for beginning the company's corporate tradition of conservation education through the television program *Mutual of Omaha's Wild Kingdom*.

In the early 1950s, Mutual of Omaha took another innovative step and began to provide

group insurance coverages to employers. Employers, recognizing that offering low-cost, basic medical insurance benefits to employees would increase employee retention and improve morale, turned to Mutual of Omaha for group coverage. The company's Group Operation is now one of the largest group carriers in the country.

Today Mutual of Omaha, headquartered in Omaha, Nebraska, consists of a variety of companies offering a diverse line of products and services to meet the many and varied needs of its more than one million policyowners through approximately 2,700 agents.[1]

■ ■ ■ ■

■ ■ ■ ■ ■ ■ ■ ■ ■ ■ ■

Mutual of Omaha's emphasis on the personal, human side of insurance has succeeded in part because insurance satisfies a basic human need—the need for safety and protection from the unknown. (You may recall from Chapter 9 that Abraham Maslow considered safety a very basic human need, which he placed second only to the physiological needs for food and water, clothing, shelter, and sleep.) People worry about the risks in their lives and about the safety of their families, homes, cars, and investments. Insurance can't guarantee such safety, but it can limit the financial damage of an accident or tragedy. Therefore, when people worry about this basic need for safety and protection, they logically turn to a company they perceive as human and caring.

Today, American families spend more than $109 billion each year for automobile and home insurance.[2] The typical family purchases insurance coverage to protect its family members, home, car, and investments. Similarly, a business firm insures its resources and products against the hazards of doing business: damage, liability, theft, injury, and more. Today, businesses spend over $119 billion a year for such insurance coverage.[3]

Firms and individuals manage risks through other methods as well. One example is the periodic inspection of production facilities to discover and eliminate hazards that could lead to injury. Another is the use of smoke alarms in homes and businesses. Together, the various techniques of risk management are intended to reduce both the possibility of loss and the impact of any losses that do occur.

■■ THE ELEMENT OF RISK

LEARNING OBJECTIVE 1
Explain what risk is, and understand the difference between a pure and a speculative risk.

risk the possibility that a loss or injury will occur

Risk is the possibility that a loss or injury will occur. It is impossible to escape some types of risk in today's world. For individuals, driving an automobile, investing in stocks or bonds, and even jogging along a country road involve some risk. For businesses, risk is a part of every decision. In fact, the essence of business decision making is weighing the potential risks and gains involved in various courses of action.

There is obviously a difference between, say, the risk of losing money one has invested and the risk of being hit by a car while jogging. This difference leads to the classification of risks as either speculative or pure risks.

speculative risk a risk that accompanies the possibility of earning a profit

A **speculative risk** is a risk that accompanies the possibility of earning a profit. Most business decisions, such as the decision to market a new product, involve speculative risks. If the new product succeeds in the marketplace, there are profits; if it fails, there are losses. For example, Liquid Paper is a typewriter correction fluid invented and then marketed by Betty Graham. The product worked well, and the product's success eventually led Graham to form the Liquid Paper Corporation. In the beginning, however, there was a distinct possibility that office workers would reject the idea

674

Pure risk. The January 1994 San Fernando Valley, California, earthquake that measured 6.6 on the Richter scale killed 61 persons and injured over 8,000. Damage was estimated between $13 and 20 billion. Since 1989, insurance companies have paid out more than $44 billion in damage claims stemming from blizzards, hurricanes, earthquakes, tornadoes, floods, droughts, mud slides, wild fires, and other natural disasters.

of painting over typing errors with fluid from a bottle. Hence this was one speculative risk that accompanied the chance to earn a profit with the new product.

pure risk a risk that involves only the possibility of loss, with no potential for gain

A **pure risk** is a risk that involves only the possibility of loss, with no potential for gain. The possibility of damage due to hurricane, fire, or auto accident is a pure risk because there is no gain if such damage does not occur. Another pure risk is the risk of large medical bills resulting from a serious illness. Again, if there is no illness, there is no monetary gain.

Let us now look at the various techniques that are available for managing risk.

■■ RISK MANAGEMENT

LEARNING OBJECTIVE 2
Appraise the four general techniques of risk management: avoidance, reduction, assumption, and the shifting of risk to an insurer.

risk management the process of evaluating the risks faced by a firm or an individual and then minimizing the costs involved with those risks

Risk management is the process of evaluating the risks faced by a firm or an individual and then minimizing the costs involved with those risks. Any risk entails two types of costs. The first is the cost that will be incurred if a *potential* loss becomes an *actual* loss. An example is the cost of rebuilding and re-equipping an assembly plant that burns to the ground. The second type consists of the costs of reducing or eliminating the risk of potential loss. Here we would include the cost of purchasing insurance against loss by fire or the cost of not building the plant at all (this cost is equal to the profit that the plant might have earned). These two types of costs must be balanced, one against the other, if risk management is to be effective.

Most people think of risk management as simply buying insurance. But insurance, although an important part of risk management, is not the only means of dealing with risk. Other methods may be less costly in specific situations. And some kinds of risks are uninsurable—not even an insurance company will issue a policy to protect against them. In this section, we examine the four general risk-management techniques. Then, in the following sections, we look more closely at insurance.

Risk Avoidance

An individual can avoid the risk of an automobile accident by not riding in a car. A manufacturer can avoid the risk of product failure by refusing to introduce new products. Both would be practicing risk avoidance—but at a very high cost. The person who avoids automobile accidents by forgoing cars may have to give up his or her job to do so. The business that does not take a chance on new products will probably fail when the product life cycle, discussed in Chapter 13, catches up with existing products.

There are, however, situations in which risk avoidance is a practical technique. At the personal level, individuals who stop smoking or refuse to walk through a dark city park late at night are avoiding risks. Jewelry stores lock their merchandise in vaults at the end of the business day to avoid losses through robbery. And, to avoid the risk of a holdup, many gasoline stations accept only credit cards or the exact amount of the purchase for sales made during after-dark hours.

Obviously, no person or business can eliminate all risks. But, by the same token, no one should assume that all risks are unavoidable.

Risk Reduction

If a risk cannot be avoided, perhaps it can be reduced. An automobile passenger can reduce the risk of injury in an auto accident by wearing a seat belt. A manufacturer can reduce the risk of product failure through careful product planning and market testing. In both situations, the cost of reducing risk seems to be well worth the potential saving.

Businesses face risks as a result of their operating procedures and management decision making. An analysis of operating procedures—by company personnel or outside consultants—can often point out areas where risk can be reduced. Among the techniques that can be used are

- The establishment of an employee safety program to encourage awareness of safety among employees.
- The purchase *and* use of proper safety equipment, from hand guards on machinery to goggles and safety shoes for individuals.
- Burglar alarms, security guards, and even guard dogs to protect warehouses from burglary.
- Fire alarms, smoke alarms, and sprinkler systems to reduce the risk of fire and the losses due to fire.
- Accurate and effective accounting and financial controls to protect the firm's inventories and cash from pilfering.

Trying to reduce risk. All organizations will—and probably must—take on certain risks as part of doing business. If a risk cannot be prevented, perhaps it can be reduced. Here, hospital security guards can reduce the risks of unauthorized entry, theft and burglary, and fire, and can provide better protection to patients and employees by keeping a watchful eye twenty-four hours a day, seven days a week.

The risks involved in management decisions can be reduced only through effective decision making. These risks *increase* when a decision is made hastily or is based on less than sufficient information. However, the cost of reducing these risks goes up when managers take too long to make decisions. Costs also increase when managers require an overabundance of information before they are willing to decide.

Risk Assumption

An individual or firm will—and probably must—take on certain risks as part of living or doing business. Individuals who drive to work *assume* the risk of having an accident, but they wear a seat belt to reduce the risk of injury in the event of an accident. The firm that markets a new product *assumes* the risk of product failure—after first reducing that risk through market testing.

Risk assumption, then, is the act of taking responsibility for the loss or injury that may result from a risk. Generally, it makes sense to assume a risk when one or more of the following conditions exist:

1. The potential loss is too small to worry about.
2. Effective risk management has reduced the risk.
3. Insurance coverage, if available, is too expensive.
4. There is no other way of protecting against a loss.

self-insurance   the process of establishing a monetary fund that can be used to cover the cost of a loss

Large firms that own many facilities often find that a particular kind of risk assumption called self-insurance is a practical way to avoid high insurance costs. **Self-insurance** is the process of establishing a monetary fund that can be used to cover the cost of a loss. For instance, suppose there are approximately 8,000 7-Eleven convenience stores, each worth $200,000, scattered around the country. A logical approach to self-insurance against fire losses would be to collect a certain sum—say, $200—from each store every year. The funds are collected placed in an interest-bearing reserve fund and used as necessary to repair any fire damage that occurs to 7-Eleven stores. Money that is not used remains the property of the firm. Eventually, if the fund grows, the yearly contribution from each store can be reduced.

Self-insurance does not eliminate risks; it merely provides a means for covering losses. And it is, itself, a risky practice—at least in the beginning. 7-Eleven would suffer a considerable financial loss if more than eight stores were destroyed by fire in the first year the self-insurance program was in effect.

Shifting Risks

Perhaps the most commonly used method of dealing with risk is to shift, or transfer, the risk to an insurance company. An **insurer** (or **insurance company**) is a firm that agrees, for a fee, to assume financial responsibility for losses that may result from a specific risk. The fee charged by an insurance company is called the **premium.** A contract between an insurer and the person or firm whose risk is assumed is known as an **insurance policy.** Generally, an insurance policy is written for a period of one year. Then, if both parties are willing, it is renewed each year. It specifies exactly which risks are covered by the agreement, the dollar amounts that the insurer will pay in case of a loss, and the amount of the premium.

Insurance is thus the protection against loss that is afforded by the purchase of an insurance policy. Insurance companies will not, however, assume every kind of risk. A risk that insurance companies will assume is called an **insurable risk.** Insurable risks include the risk of loss by fire and theft, the risk of loss by automobile accident, and the risks of sickness and death. A risk that insurance companies will not assume is called an **uninsurable risk.**

In general, pure risks are insurable, whereas speculative risks are uninsurable (see Figure 21.1). An insurance company will protect a General Motors assembly plant against losses due to fire or tornadoes. It will not, however, protect General Motors Corp. against losses resulting from a lack of sales orders for automobiles.

The next section provides an overview of the basic principles of insurance and the kinds of companies that provide insurance.

insurer (or **insurance company**)   a firm that agrees, for a fee, to assume financial responsibility for losses that may result from a specific risk

premium   the fee charged by an insurance company

insurance policy   the contract between an insurer and the person or firm whose risk is assumed

insurance   the protection against loss that is afforded by the purchase of an insurance policy

insurable risk   a risk that insurance companies will assume

uninsurable risk   a risk that insurance companies will not assume

■■ INSURANCE AND INSURANCE COMPANIES

LEARNING OBJECTIVE 3
Discuss the principles underlying insurance and the insurability of risks.

An insurance company is a business. Like other businesses, an insurer provides a product—protection from loss—in return for a reasonable fee. Its sales revenues are the premiums it collects from the individuals and firms it insures. (Insurance companies typically invest the money they have on hand at any time; thus we should include interest and dividend income as part of

FIGURE 21.1
Insurable Risk for Businesses and Individuals
Generally, an insurance company will not protect against speculative risks such as lack of sales.

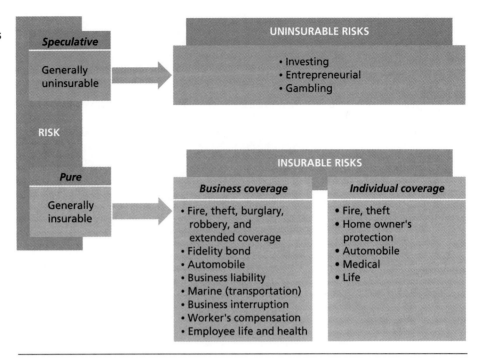

their revenues.) Its expenses are the costs of the various resources—salaries, rent, utilities, and so on—*plus* the amounts the insurance company pays out to cover its clients' losses.

Pricing and product are very important and exacting issues to an insurance company, primarily because it must set its price (its premiums) before knowing the specific cost of its product (the amount of money it will have to pay out in claims). For this reason, insurance companies employ mathematicians called *actuaries* to predict the likelihood of losses and to determine the premiums that should be charged. Let us look at some of the more important concepts on which insurance (and the work of actuaries) is based.

Basic Insurance Concepts

Insurance generally is based on several principles, including the principle of indemnity, insurability of the risk, and low-cost, affordable coverage.

The Principle of Indemnity   The purpose of insurance is to provide protection against loss; it is neither speculation nor gambling. This concept is expressed in the **principle of indemnity:** in the event of a loss, an insured firm or individual cannot collect, from the insurer, an amount greater than the actual dollar amount of the loss. Suppose you own a home valued at $150,000. However, you purchase $200,000 worth of fire insurance on your home. Even if it is destroyed by fire, the insurer will pay you only $150,000, the actual amount of your loss.

The premiums that are set by actuaries are based on the amount of risk involved and the amount to be paid in case of a loss. Generally, the greater the risk and the amount to be paid, the higher the premium.

principle of indemnity   in the event of a loss, an insured firm or individual cannot collect, from the insurer, an amount greater than the actual dollar amount of the loss

Fraud is expensive. At an estimated cost of $18 billion annually, insurance fraud is the number 2 crime in America, next to tax fraud. Who pays? We all do, in the form of increased costs for law enforcement and higher insurance premiums.

Fake an injury. Trick the insurance company into paying. Collect. Tempting, isn't it?

Insurability of the Risk   As we noted earlier, insurers will accept responsibility for risks that meet at least the following conditions:

1. *Losses must not be under the control of the insured.* Losses caused by fire, wind, or accident are generally insurable, but gambling losses are not. Nor will an insurer pay a claim for damage intentionally caused by the insured person. For example, a person who sets fire to an insured building cannot collect on a fire insurance policy.

2. *The insured hazard must be geographically widespread.* That is, the insurance company must be able to write many policies covering the same specific hazard throughout a wide geographic area. This condition allows the insurer to minimize its own risk: the risk that it will have to pay huge sums of money to clients within a particular geographic area in the event of a catastrophe caused, for example, by a tornado.

3. *The probability of a loss should be predictable.* Insurance companies cannot tell which particular clients will suffer losses. However, their actuaries must be able to determine, statistically, what *fraction* of their clients will suffer each type of loss. They can do so, for insurable risks, by examining records of losses for past years. They can then base their

premiums, at least in part, on the number and value of the losses that are expected to occur.

4. *Losses must be measurable.* Insured property must have a value that is measurable in dollars because insurance firms reimburse losses with money. Moreover, premiums are based partly on the measured value of the insured property. As a result of this condition, insurers will not insure an item for its emotional or sentimental value, but only for its actual monetary value.

5. *The policyholder must have an insurable interest.* That is, the individual or firm that purchases an insurance policy must be the one that would suffer from a loss. You can purchase insurance on your own home, but you cannot insure your neighbor's home in the hope of making a profit if it should burn down! Generally, individuals are considered to have an insurable interest in their family members. Therefore, a person can insure the life of a spouse, a child, or a parent. Corporations may purchase "key executive" insurance covering certain corporate officers. The proceeds from this insurance help offset the loss of the services of these key people if they die or become incapacitated.

Low-Cost, Affordable Coverage   Price is usually a marketing issue rather than a technical concept. However, the price of insurance is intimately tied to the risks and potential losses involved in a particular type of coverage. Insurers would like to "produce" insurance at a very low cost to their policyholders, but they must charge enough in premiums to cover their expected payouts. See Ethical Challenges to learn how insurance fraud costs American consumers billions of dollars in additional premiums.

Customers purchase insurance when they believe premiums are low in relation to the possible dollar loss. For certain risks, premiums can soar so high that insurance is simply not cost-effective. A $1,000 life insurance policy for a 99-year-old man would cost about $950 per year. Clearly, a man of that age would be better off if he invested the premium amount in a bank. By this means he would use self-insurance rather than shifting the risk. Although this is an extreme example, it illustrates the fact that insurers must compete, through their prices, with alternative methods of managing risk.

Ownership of Insurance Companies

Insurance companies are owned either by stockholders or by policyholders. A **stock insurance company** is owned by stockholders and is operated to earn a profit. Like other profit-making corporations, stock insurance companies pay dividends to stockholders from surplus of income (left over after benefit payments, operating expenses, and taxes have been paid). Most of the approximately 5,900 insurance companies in the United States are stock insurance companies.

A **mutual insurance company** is collectively owned by its policyholders and is thus a cooperative. Because a mutual insurance company has no stockholders, its policyholders elect the board of directors. The members of the board, in turn, choose the executives who manage the firm. Any surplus

stock insurance company an insurance company that is owned by stockholders and is operated to earn a profit

mutual insurance company an insurance company that is collectively owned by its policyholders and is thus a cooperative

ETHICAL CHALLENGES

Insurance Fraud: We All Pay

At an estimated cost of $18 billion annually, insurance fraud is the number 2 crime in America, next to tax fraud. Who pays? We all do, in the form of (1) increased costs for law enforcement and (2) higher insurance premiums.

Individuals and organized fraud rings commit fraud when they give false information about injuries, accidents, or losses. Some of the more common examples include staged car accidents, slip-and-fall accidents, faked car thefts, inflated medical or auto repair bills, and burglary or arson for profit.

By knowing the types of schemes that victimize the public financially and sometimes even physically, you can help reduce the opportunities for fraud. For example, if you're involved in an accident or witness one, report it to the authorities. Your statements can be important in determining the legitimacy of a claim. If someone gives you the name of a doctor or lawyer who can "make you some money," or if a body shop mechanic offers to inflate your damage estimate, don't just walk away. Contact your insurance agent and notify the police.

Today, insurance companies are fighting to take the profit out of insurance crime. Throughout the insurance industry, companies have special units investigating fraud. And many insurance firms have joined the Coalition Against Insurance Fraud. The insurance companies also work closely with the National Insurance Crime Bureau, an organization that has joined forces with police to investigate insurance fraud. If you suspect an insurance crime of any kind, call the National Insurance Crime Bureau at 1-800-TEL-NICB. Callers to this fraud hotline may be eligible for rewards of up to $1,000. By working together, we can help fight fraud and hold down everyone's insurance costs.

of income over expenses is distributed to policyholders as a return of part of their premiums. (This return may take the form of a reduced premium at the start of the policy year or of a "dividend" at the end of the policy year.) Although almost 95 percent of life insurance providers are stock companies, mutual companies account for about 45 percent of the industry's total assets and 36 percent of the total premiums received.[4]

Both stock and mutual insurance companies must maintain cash reserves to cover future obligations and policyholders' claims. Cash reserves are typically invested in certificates of deposit, stocks, bonds, and real estate. As Table 21.1 shows, four of the five largest life insurance firms are mutual companies. By prudent investment of reserves, insurance firms can develop sizable incomes for their owners.

Careers in Insurance

Insurance companies form one of the largest industries in the United States. The industry ranks in importance with banking and finance, manufactur-

TABLE 21.1   The Five Largest Life Insurance Companies in the United States, Ranked by Total Assets

Company Name	State	1993 Rank	1993 Assets (in 000s)	Type
The Prudential Insurance Co. of America	New Jersey	1	$165,741,911	Mutual
Metropolitan Life Insurance Co.	New York	2	128,225,204	Mutual
Teachers Ins. & Annuity Assoc. of America	New York	3	67,483,168	Mutual
New York Life Insurance Co.	New York	4	53,570,943	Mutual
Aetna Life Insurance Co.	Connecticut	5	51,535,383	Stock

Source: Best's Review L/H, "Assets of 100 Leading Life/Health Companies," Oct. 1994, p. 20. Used by permission.

ing, building, and electronics. Careers in insurance generally fall into two categories: sales and administration.

In the sales category, individuals can work as employees for insurance companies or as independent agents representing more than one insurance company. Recently, the insurance industry has placed increased emphasis on advanced training for sales personnel. Life insurance salespeople who pass examinations and meet other requirements are awarded the Chartered Life Underwriter (CLU) designation. The Chartered Property Casualty Underwriter (CPCU) designation is awarded to individuals who pass examinations and meet the requirements in all areas *except* life insurance.

Administrative employees work to meet the needs of the firm's customers. They must process policies and claims and handle an amazing amount of paperwork. Jobs in this category include actuary, claims adjuster, claims clerk, underwriter, and a number of other essential positions. In addition to meeting the needs of customers, administrative employees are responsible for investing funds for an insurance company.

■■ PROPERTY AND CASUALTY INSURANCE

LEARNING OBJECTIVE 4
Distinguish the types of insurance that can be used to protect businesses and individuals against property and casualty losses.

Insurance is available to cover most pure risks, but specialized or customized policies can be expensive. A part of effective risk management is to ensure that, when insurance is purchased, the coverage is proper for the individual situation. Three questions can be used as guidelines in this regard.

- What hazards must be insured against?
- Is the cost of insurance coverage reasonable in this situation?
- What other risk-management techniques can be used to reduce insurance costs?

Fire Insurance

fire insurance   insurance that covers losses due to fire

Fire insurance covers losses due to fire. The standard fire insurance policy provides protection against partial or complete loss of a building and/or its contents when that loss is caused by fire or lightning. Premiums depend on the construction of the building, its use and contents, whether risk-reduction devices (such as smoke and fire alarms) are installed in the building, and other factors. If a fire occurs, the insurance company reimburses the policyholder for either the actual dollar loss or the maximum amount stated in the policy, whichever is lower.

Coinsurance Clause   To reduce their insurance premiums, individuals and businesses sometimes insure property for less than its actual cash value. Their theory is that fire rarely destroys a building completely—thus they need not buy full insurance. However, if the building is partially destroyed, they expect their insurance to cover all the damage. This places an unfair burden on the insurance company, which receives less than the full premium but must cover the full loss. To avoid this problem, insurance companies include a coinsurance clause in most fire insurance policies.

coinsurance clause a part of a fire insurance policy that requires the policyholder to purchase coverage at least equal to a specified percentage of the replacement cost of the property to obtain full reimbursement for losses

A **coinsurance clause** is a part of a fire insurance policy that requires the policyholder to purchase coverage at least equal to a specified percentage of the replacement cost of the property to obtain full reimbursement for losses. In most cases, the required percentage is 80 percent of the replacement cost. Suppose the owners of a $600,000 building decide to purchase only $300,000 worth of fire insurance. If the building is totally destroyed, the insurance company must pay the policy's face value of $300,000. However, if the building is only partially destroyed, and the damage amounts to $200,000, the insurance company will pay only $125,000. This dollar amount is calculated in the following manner:

1. The coinsurance clause requires coverage of at least 80 percent of $600,000, or $480,000.
2. The owners have purchased only $300,000 of insurance. Thus they have insured themselves for only a portion of any loss. That portion is $300,000 ÷ $480,000 = 0.625, or 62.5 percent.
3. The insurance company will therefore reimburse the owner for only 62.5 percent of any loss. In the case of a $200,000 loss, the insurance company will pay 62.5 percent of $200,000, or $125,000.

If the owners of the building had insured it for $480,000, the insurance company would have covered the entire $200,000 loss.

extended coverage insurance protection against damage caused by wind, hail, explosion, vandalism, riots or civil commotion, falling aircraft, and smoke

Extended Coverage   **Extended coverage** is insurance protection against damage caused by wind, hail, explosion, vandalism, riots or civil commotion, falling aircraft, and smoke. Extended coverage is available as an *endorsement*, or addition, to some other insurance policy—usually a fire insurance policy. The premium for extended coverage is generally quite low (much lower than the total cost of separate policies covering each individual hazard). Normally, losses caused by war, nuclear radiation or contamination, and water (other than in storms and floods) are excluded from extended-coverage endorsements.

The importance of casualty insurance. Fire insurance covers losses due to fire. Without such insurance, many individuals and organizations would be ruined by the financial strains of rebuilding after fire damage.

Burglary, Robbery, and Theft Insurance

Burglary is the illegal taking of property through forcible entry. A kicked-in door, a broken window pane, or pry marks on a windowsill are evidence of a burglary or attempted burglary. *Robbery* is the unlawful taking of property from an individual by force or threat of violence. A thief who uses a gun to rob a gas station is committing robbery. *Theft* (or *larceny*) is a general term that means the wrongful taking of property that belongs to another. Insurance policies are available to cover burglary only, robbery only, theft only, or all three. Premiums vary with the type and value of the property covered by the policy.

Business owners must also be concerned about crimes that employees may commit. A **fidelity bond** is an insurance policy that protects a business from theft, forgery, or embezzlement by its employees. If such a crime does occur, the insurance company reimburses the business for financial losses up to the dollar amount specified in the policy. Individual employees or specific positions within an organization may be bonded. It is also possible to purchase a "blanket" policy that covers the entire work force. Fidelity bonds are most commonly purchased by banks, savings and loan associations, finance companies, and other firms whose employees handle cash on a regular basis.

Although business owners are concerned about shoplifting, they often find that insurance coverage, if available, is too expensive. And it is often difficult to collect on losses resulting from shoplifting because such losses are difficult to prove.

fidelity bond   an insurance policy that protects a business from theft, forgery, or embezzlement by its employees

Motor Vehicle Insurance

Individuals and businesses purchase automobile insurance because it is required by state law, because it is required by the firm financing the purchase of the vehicle, and/or because they want to protect their investment. Most types of automobile coverage can be broadly classified as either liability or physical damage insurance. Table 21.2 shows the distinction.

automobile liability insurance insurance that covers financial losses resulting from injuries or damages caused by the insured vehicle

Automobile Liability Insurance   **Automobile liability insurance** is insurance that covers financial losses resulting from injuries or damages caused by the insured vehicle. Most automobile policies have a split-liability limit that contains three numbers. For example, the liability limits stated on a typical policy are 50/100/50. The first two numbers indicate the maximum amounts, stated in thousands of dollars, the insurance company will pay for bodily injury. *Bodily injury liability coverage* pays medical bills and other costs in the event that an injury or death results from an automobile accident in which the policyholder is at fault. Bodily injury liability coverage protects the person in the other car and is usually specified as a pair of dollar amounts. In the above example, the policy limits are $50,000 for each person and $100,000 for each occurrence. This means the insurance company will pay up to $50,000 to each person injured in an accident and up to a total of $100,000 to all those injured in a single accident. Payment for additional damages above the policy limits is the responsibility of the insured. In view of the cost of medical care today, and considering the size of legal settlements resulting from automobile accidents, insurance companies recommend coverage of at least $100,000 per person and $300,000 per occurrence.

Property damage liability coverage pays for the repair of damage that the insured vehicle does to the property of another person. Such damage is covered up to the amount specified in the policy. In the above example, the third number (50) indicates that the insurance company will pay up to $50,000 for property damage. Insurance companies generally recommend at least $100,000 worth of property damage liability.

Along with other automobile liability insurance, most car owners also purchase protection for the passengers in their own cars. A *medical payments endorsement* can be included in automobile coverage for a small additional premium. This endorsement provides for the payment of medical bills, up to a specified amount, for passengers (including the policyholder) injured in the policyholder's vehicle.

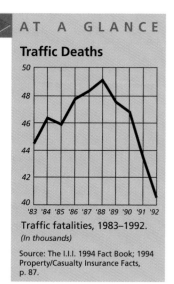

AT A GLANCE

Traffic Deaths

Traffic fatalities, 1983–1992.
(In thousands)

Source: The I.I.I. 1994 Fact Book; 1994 Property/Casualty Insurance Facts, p. 87.

TABLE 21.2   Automobile Insurance Coverage
Liability insurance covers financial losses resulting from injuries or damages caused by the insured vehicle; physical damage insurance covers damage to the insured vehicle.

Liability Insurance	Physical Damage Insurance
Bodily injury	Collision
Property damage	Comprehensive
Medical payments	Uninsured motorists

automobile physical damage insurance insurance that covers damage to the insured vehicle

Automobile Physical Damage Insurance

Liability insurance does not pay for the repair of the insured vehicle. **Automobile physical damage insurance** is insurance that covers damage to the insured vehicle. *Collision insurance* pays for the repair of damage to the insured vehicle as a result of an accident. Most collision coverages include a *deductible amount*—anywhere from $50 up—that the policyholder must pay. The insurance company then pays either the remaining cost of the repairs or the actual cash value of the vehicle (when the vehicle is "totaled"), whichever is less. For most automobiles, collision insurance is the most costly coverage. Premiums can, however, be reduced by increasing the deductible amount.

Comprehensive insurance covers damage to the insured vehicle caused by fire, theft, hail, dust storm, vandalism, and almost anything else that could damage a car, except collision and normal wear and tear. With the possible exception of CB radios and tape decks that are installed by the owner of the car, even the contents of the car are insured. For example, comprehensive coverage will pay for a broken windshield, stolen hubcaps, or small dents caused by a hailstorm. Like collision coverage, comprehensive coverage includes a deductible amount, usually $100 or $200.

Uninsured motorists insurance covers the insured driver and passengers from bodily injury losses (and, in some states, property damage losses) resulting from an accident caused by a driver with no liability insurance. It also covers damages caused by a hit-and-run driver. In some states and with some insurance companies, uninsured motorists coverage is not automatically included in a typical policy. And yet it is important coverage that is quite reasonable. Often, annual premiums are $20 to $25.

no-fault auto insurance a method of paying for losses suffered in an automobile accident; enacted by state law, requires that those suffering injury or loss be reimbursed by their own insurance companies, without regard to who was at fault in the accident

No-Fault Auto Insurance

No-fault auto insurance is a method of paying for losses suffered in an automobile accident. It is enacted by state law and requires that those suffering injury or loss be reimbursed by their own insurance companies, without regard to who was at fault in the accident. Although there are numerous exceptions, most no-fault laws also limit the rights of involved parties to sue each other.

Massachusetts enacted the first no-fault law in 1971 in an effort to reduce both auto insurance premiums and the crushing caseload in its court system. Since then, at least twenty-seven states have followed suit. Every state with a no-fault law requires coverage for all vehicles registered in the state.

Business Liability Insurance

Business liability coverage protects the policyholder from financial losses resulting from an injury to another person or damage to another person's property. During the past fifteen years or so, both the number of liability claims and the size of settlements have increased dramatically. The result has been heightened awareness of the need for liability coverage—along with quickly rising premiums for this coverage.

public liability insurance insurance that protects the policyholder from financial losses due to injuries suffered by others as a result of negligence on the part of a business owner or employee

Public liability insurance protects the policyholder from financial losses due to injuries suffered by others as a result of negligence on the part of a business owner or employee. It covers injury or death resulting from hazards at the place of business or from the actions of employees. For example, liability claims totaling more than $2 billion were filed on behalf of the victims of the 1981 skybridge collapse in the Hyatt Regency Hotel in Kansas City, Missouri. More recent examples in which damage claims totaled more than a billion dollars include the chemical accident at Union Carbide Corp.'s plant in Bhopal, India, and the 1987 Du Pont Hotel fire in San Juan, Puerto Rico. *Malpractice insurance,* which is purchased by physicians, lawyers, accountants, engineers, and other professionals, is a form of public liability insurance.

product liability insurance insurance that protects the policyholder from financial losses due to injuries suffered by others as a result of using the policyholder's products

Product liability insurance protects the policyholder from financial losses due to injuries suffered by others as a result of using the policyholder's products. Recent court settlements for individuals injured by defective products have been extremely large. A classic product liability case involved the Ford Motor Co. and Richard Grimshaw. Grimshaw was injured when he was a passenger in a Ford compact automobile that was hit from behind and burst into flames. He was so severely burned that more than fifty operations were required to treat him. He sued Ford Motor Co. and was awarded $128.5 million by a jury, which decided that his injuries resulted from poor design on the part of Ford. (Later, on appeal, the award was reduced to $6 million.)

Some juries have found manufacturers and retailers guilty of negligence even when the consumer used the product incorrectly. This development and the very large awards given to injured consumers have caused management to take a hard look at potential product hazards. As part of their risk-management efforts, most manufacturers now take the following precautions:

1. Include thorough and explicit directions with products.
2. Warn customers about the hazards of using products incorrectly.
3. Remove from the market those products that are considered hazardous.
4. Test products in-house to determine whether safety problems can arise from either proper *or* improper use.[5]

Such precautions can reduce both the risk of product liability losses and the cost of liability insurance. Where the risk of death, injury, or lawsuits cannot be eliminated or at least reduced, some manufacturers have simply discontinued the product. See Global Perspectives to learn how product liability has become a hot issue in Japan.

Marine (Transportation) Insurance

Marine, or transportation, insurance provides protection against the loss of goods that are being shipped from one place to another. It is the oldest type of insurance and originated with the ancient Greeks and Romans. The term *marine insurance* was coined at a time when only goods transported by ship were insured.

ocean marine insurance insurance that protects the policyholder against loss or damage to a ship or its cargo on the high seas

Today marine insurance is available for goods shipped over water or land. **Ocean marine insurance** protects the policyholder against loss or

Product Liability in Japan

A new product liability law? Some criticize it as "an unnecessary American import"; others praise it as "the most important consumer legislation of the decade." Controversy notwithstanding, the Japanese cabinet approved a product liability bill designed to protect consumers from faulty products. The bill will likely be ratified during the current Diet session and put into effect by summer 1995. It's been a long time coming. Despite nearly twenty years of studying the pros and cons of product liability legislation, Japan is still the only industrialized nation in which consumers lack adequate means to seek redress against manufacturers. The imminent passage of the new bill promises to ease the burden of proof for consumers in suits against manufacturers. As such, it represents another clear sign that Japan is shifting from a producer-driven to consumer-driven society.

THE HISTORICAL RECORD

Today's product liability regime stands on the legal foundation drawn up in Japan's Civil Code of 1968—consumers are responsible for proving that product defects are the result of intentional or overt negligence on the part of the manufacturer. Consumers find it nearly impossible to prove such negligence, however, given the proprietary nature of corporate information and the prohibitive costs of lawsuits. The proposed legislation is designed to reverse the situation. Based on the recommendations of a subcommittee to the prime minister and those of the Ministry of International Trade and Industry, the Ministry of

Health and Welfare, and the Ministry of Justice, the new legislation favors the adoption of European liability laws over those of the more stringent American regulations.

In essence, the proposals recommend that consumers need only demonstrate that a product is defective, rather than prove manufacturer negligence. But the definition of *defective* remains controversial and open to debate. Many believe that the term should be defined clearly so that manufacturers and consumers can act accordingly. Others want the definition to be left for the courts to decide.

CRITICS OF REFORM

Opponents say that product liability laws will lead to a flood of costly litigation from dissatisfied consumers and will play a limited role in improving consumer confidence and reducing product defects. According to Robert C. Weber, an expert on international product liability, "Product liability in Europe has proven to be largely irrelevant to the consumer because the citizenry there has not developed a reliance upon litigation as a way of life, the courts are not organized to be as supportive of claimants as in the United States and matters such as social insurance and product safety have traditionally been governed by regulatory tools other than litigation." He and others fear that a product liability law in Japan may distort the insurance markets, increase prices for consumers, and lead to overly cautious product engineering.

damage to a ship or its cargo on the high seas. **Inland marine insurance** protects against loss or damage to goods shipped by rail, truck, airplane, or inland barge. Both types cover losses from fire, theft, and most other hazards.

Business Interruption Insurance

Business interruption insurance provides protection for a business whose operations are interrupted because of a fire, storm, or other natural disaster. It is even possible to purchase coverage to protect the firm in the event that its employees go out on strike. For most businesses, interruption coverage is available as an endorsement to a fire insurance policy. Premiums are determined by the amount of coverage and the risks that are covered.

The standard business interruption policy reimburses the policyholder for both loss of profit and fixed costs in the event that it cannot operate. Profit payments are based on profits earned by the firm during some specified period. Fixed-cost payments cover expenses the firm incurs even when it is not operating. Employee salaries are normally not covered by the standard policy. However, they may be included for an increased premium.

■ ■ INSURANCE COVERAGE FOR INDIVIDUALS

LEARNING OBJECTIVE 5
Describe the types of insurance
available to individuals.

Both the government and private insurance companies offer a number of different types of coverage for individuals in the United States. In this section, we discuss Social Security, unemployment insurance, workers' compensation, 401(k) plans, and medical insurance.

Public Insurance

Federal and state governments offer insurance programs to meet the specific needs of individuals who are eligible for coverage. For example, the Social Security program was established when the Social Security Act was passed by Congress in 1935. Today, it provides benefits for more than 45 million people, almost one out of every six Americans. In reality, the Social Security program—financed by taxes paid by both employees and employers—is divided into four individual programs. First, *retirement* benefits are paid to eligible employees and self-employed individuals when they reach age 65. They can obtain reduced benefits at age 62. In 1993, the maximum retirement benefits were $1,147 per month. Second, *survivor* benefits are paid to a worker's spouse, dependent children, or in some cases dependent parents when a covered worker dies before retirement. Third, *disability* benefits are paid to workers who are severely disabled and unable to work. Benefits continue until it is determined that the individual is no longer disabled. When a disabled worker reaches age 65, the worker is then eligible for retirement benefits. Fourth, the *Medicare* program provides both hospital and medical coverage. Workers are eligible for coverage when they reach age 65. Persons who have received disability benefits for a period of at least twenty-four months are also eligible for Medicare coverage.

Unlike the federal Social Security program, *unemployment insurance* is a joint program between the federal and state governments. The purpose of the program is to provide benefits (employment services and money) to unemployed workers. The dollar amount and the duration of benefits are determined by state laws. The program is funded by a tax paid by employers.

401(k) Plans

401(k) plan a salary-reduction, employer-sponsored, pretax savings plan

A section **401(k) plan,** or salary-reduction savings plan, is an employer-sponsored, pretax savings plan. It allows employees to defer part of their pay and have it contributed to a retirement plan instead. The amount contributed, at a maximum of $9,240 in 1994, is excluded from current income for federal and state income taxes and Social Security tax purposes. Taxes on contributions and earnings are postponed until distributions begin (age 59½ at the earliest).

About 12 percent of workers in firms with fewer than 500 employees are offered a 401(k) plan, compared with more than 43 percent in large firms.[6] In 1993, 401(k) plans recorded $480 billion in plan assets, a 17 percent increase over 1992 levels. These plans, offered by almost 209,000 firms, have attracted over 17 million participants.[7] New government rules require employers to offer more investment choices for 401(k) plans, to provide more frequent performance reports, and to allow employees to change investment options more frequently.[8]

Workers' Compensation

workers' compensation insurance insurance that covers medical expenses and provides salary continuation for employees who are injured while at work

Workers' compensation insurance covers medical expenses and provides salary continuation for employees who are injured while at work. This insurance also pays benefits to the dependents of workers killed on the job. Every state now requires employers to provide some form of workers' compensation insurance, with benefits that are established by the state. This type of insurance may be purchased from insurance companies or, in some cases, from the state. Self-insurance can also be used to meet requirements in a few states. State laws do vary; some are more stringent than others. In fact, the low cost of workers' compensation is one of many reasons for locating or moving a business to a specific state.

Salary continuation benefits are paid to employees who are unable to work because of injuries sustained on the job. These payments normally range from 60 to 75 percent of an employee's usual wage, but they may be limited to a specified number of payments. In all cases, they stop when the employee is able to return to work.

Workers' compensation premiums are paid by the employer and are generally computed as a small percentage of each employee's wages. The percentage varies with the type of job and is, in general, higher for jobs that involve greater risk of injury.

Health-Care Insurance

Today, most employers pay, as an employee benefit, part or all of the cost of health-care insurance for employees. When the employer doesn't pay for

Shape up or pay. Doctors have long known that fitness affects health, and now many companies are making sure that their employees understand the connection. In an effort to combat rising health care costs, companies are telling their people to quit smoking and get in shape—or start paying a higher percentage of their health insurance premiums.

health-care insurance
insurance that covers the cost of medical attention, including hospital care, physicians' and surgeons' fees, prescription medicines, and related services

coverage, most individuals purchase their own health-care insurance when they can afford the coverage. **Health-care insurance** covers the cost of medical attention, including hospital care, physicians' and surgeons' fees, prescription medicines, and related services. In addition, some firms also provide employees with dental and life insurance. *Major medical insurance* can also be purchased to extend medical coverage beyond the dollar limits of the standard health-care insurance policy. In all cases, the types of coverage and amounts that are paid vary according to the provisions of the specific health-care policy, regardless of whether it is paid for by the employer or the individual.

The cost of medical care has been increasing at an alarming rate over the last twenty to thirty years. In 1965, the average American spent $181 on health care. In 1993 the Health Insurance Association of America (an industry trade association) estimated that the same individual would spend about $3,900.[9] In an attempt to keep medical insurance premiums from rising just as quickly, insurers have developed a variety of insurance plans that are less expensive than full-coverage plans. Some plans have deductibles of $500 to $1,000. Some require that the policyholder pay 20 to 30 percent of the first $1,000 to $3,000 in medical bills. And some pay the entire hospital bill but only a percentage of other medical expenses. One additional method that can reduce the cost of health-care coverage is the use of a health maintenance organization. A **health maintenance organization (HMO)** is an insurance plan that directly employs or contracts with selected physicians

health maintenance organization (HMO)   an insurance plan that directly employs or contracts with selected physicians and hospitals to provide health-care services in exchange for a fixed, prepaid monthly premium

and hospitals to provide health-care services in exchange for a fixed, prepaid monthly premium. Although there have been concerns about the quality of care provided by some health maintenance organizations, they are expected to grow in the 1990s because they offer a lower-cost alternative to traditional health-care plans.

preferred provider organization (PPO) an insurance plan that offers the services of doctors and hospitals at discount rates or gives breaks in copayments and deductibles

Preferred provider organizations (PPOs) offer the services of doctors and hospitals at discount rates or give breaks in copayments (the portion of the bill that the insured must pay each time services are used) and deductibles. An insurance company or an employer contracts with a PPO to provide specified services at predetermined fees to PPO members.

■■ LIFE INSURANCE

LEARNING OBJECTIVE 6
Analyze the advantages and disadvantages of term, whole, endowment, and universal life insurance.

life insurance insurance that pays a stated amount of money on the death of the insured individual

beneficiary individual or organization named in a life insurance policy as a recipient of the proceeds of that policy on the death of the insured

Life insurance pays a stated amount of money on the death of the insured individual. The money is paid to one or more beneficiaries. A **beneficiary** is a person or organization named in a life insurance policy as a recipient of the proceeds of that policy on the death of the insured.

Life insurance thus provides protection for the beneficiaries of the insured. The amount of insurance that is needed depends very much on *their* situation. A wage earner with three small children generally needs more life insurance than someone who is single. Moreover, the need for life insurance changes as a person's situation changes. When the wage earner's children are grown and on their own, they need less protection (through their parent's life insurance) than they did when they were young. Life insurance in the United States reached a record $11.3 trillion at the end of 1994.[10] That breaks down to about $41,600 per individual.

For a particular dollar amount of life insurance, premiums depend primarily on the age of the insured and on the type of insurance. The older a person is, the higher the premium. (On the average, older people are less likely to survive each year than younger people.) Finally, insurers offer several types of life insurance for customers with varying insurance needs. The price of each type depends on the benefits it provides.

Term Life Insurance

term life insurance life insurance that provides protection to beneficiaries for a stated period of time

Term life insurance provides protection to beneficiaries for a stated period of time. Because term life insurance includes no other benefits, it is the least expensive form of life insurance. It is especially attractive to young married couples who want as much protection as possible but cannot afford the higher premiums charged for other types of life insurance.

Most term life policies are in force for a period of one year. At the end of each policy year, a term life policy can be renewed at a slightly higher cost—to take into account the fact that the insured individual has aged one year. In addition, some term policies can be converted into other forms of life insurance at the option of the policyholder. This feature permits policyholders to modify their insurance protection to keep pace with changes in their personal circumstances.

AT A GLANCE

Life Insurance

Average size ordinary life insurance policy purchased in the U.S.
(*In thousands of dollars*)

Source: *1994 Life Insurance Fact Book,* American Council of Life Insurance, p. 11.

Whole Life Insurance

Whole life insurance, also called ordinary life insurance, provides both protection and savings. In the beginning, premiums are generally higher than those for term life insurance. However, premiums for whole life insurance remain constant for as long as the policy is in force.

A whole life policy builds up savings over the years. These savings are in the form of a **cash surrender value,** which is an amount that is payable to the holder of a whole life insurance policy if the policy is canceled. In addition, the policyholder may borrow from the insurance company, at a relatively low interest rate, amounts up to the policy's cash surrender value.

Whole life insurance policies are sold in these three forms:

- *Straight life insurance,* for which the policyholder must pay premiums as long as the insured is alive
- *Limited-payment life insurance,* for which premiums are paid for only a stated number of years
- *Single-payment life insurance,* for which one lump-sum premium is paid at the time the insurance is purchased

Which of these is best for a given individual depends, as usual, on that individual's particular situation and insurance needs.

Endowment Life Insurance

Endowment life insurance provides protection and guarantees the payment of a stated amount to the policyholder after a specified number of years. Endowment policies are generally in force for twenty years or until the insured person reaches age 65. If the insured dies while the policy is in force, the beneficiaries are paid the face amount of the policy. However, if the insured survives through the policy period, the stated amount is paid to the policyholder.

The premiums for endowment policies are generally higher than those for whole life policies. In return, the policyholder is guaranteed a future payment. Thus the endowment policy includes a sort of "enforced savings" feature. In addition, endowment policies have cash surrender values that are usually higher than those of whole life policies.

AT A GLANCE

Life Expectancy

Expectation of life at various ages in the U.S., 1993.
(*In years*)

Source: *1994 Life Insurance Fact Book,* American Council of Life Insurance, p. 114.

Universal Life Insurance

Universal life insurance combines insurance protection with an investment plan that offers a potentially greater return than that guaranteed by a whole life insurance policy. Universal life insurance is the newest product available from life insurance companies. It offers policyholders several options that are not available with other types of policies. For example, policyholders may choose to make larger or smaller premium payments, to increase or decrease their insurance coverage, or even to withdraw the policy's cash value without canceling the policy. Essentially, the purchase of

universal life insurance life insurance that combines insurance protection with an investment plan that offers a potentially greater return than that guaranteed by a whole life insurance policy

universal life insurance combines the purchase of annual term insurance with the buying and selling of investments.

Universal life generally offers lower premiums than whole life insurance. In fact, the premium is often called a "contribution." However, companies that offer universal life insurance may charge a fee when the policy is first purchased, each time an annual premium is paid, and when funds are withdrawn from the policy's cash value. Such fees tend to decrease the return on the savings account part of the policy.

This chapter concludes our discussion of finance and risk management for firms and individuals. Part 7 deals with the environment in which a business must operate. We begin our discussion in Chapter 22 with business law and how it affects day-to-day business operations.

■ ■ ■ ■ CHAPTER REVIEW

Summary

1   Explain what risk is, and understand the difference between a pure and a speculative risk.

Risk—or the possibility of loss or injury—is a part of everyday life for both businesses and individuals. Speculative risks are those that accompany the chance of earning a profit. Pure risks are those that involve only the possibility of loss, without any potential gain.

2   Appraise the four general techniques of risk management: avoidance, reduction, assumption, and the shifting of risk to an insurer.

Individuals and businesses must evaluate the risks they face, and they should minimize the costs involved with those risks. Four general techniques of risk management are risk avoidance, risk reduction, risk assumption, and the shifting of risk. Usually, pure risks that cannot be avoided or reduced and that are too large to be assumed can be shifted to insurance companies.

3   Discuss the principles underlying insurance and the insurability of risks.

Insurance companies, for a fee, assume risks that meet certain insurability criteria. They do so through contracts called insurance policies. An important condition in the issuing of an insurance policy is that

the insured individual or firm cannot profit from the policy. That is, the payment in the event of a loss cannot exceed the actual amount of the loss. Insurance company fees, or premiums, must be affordable. At the same time, they must be high enough to cover expected payouts and other expenses.

Stock insurance companies are profit-making corporations owned by stockholders. Mutual insurance companies are cooperatives owned by their policyholders.

4   Distinguish the types of insurance that can be used to protect businesses and individuals against property and casualty losses.

Property and casualty insurance protects the policyholder against loss of property and loss due to accidents. Included in this category is insurance that protects against loss of property due to fire, theft, and various natural hazards; against liability due to injury to employees or customers; and against damage and liability resulting from automobile accidents.

5   Describe the types of insurance available to individuals.

Both the government and private insurance companies offer a number of different types of coverage for individuals in the United States. The federal Social Security program offers retirement, survivor, disability, and Medicare benefits to people who are eligible. Unemployment insurance—a joint program sponsored by the federal and state governments—provides both employment services and money to people who are unemployed. Employers are required to provide workers' compensation insurance to protect the worker in case of injury. An increasing number of employers are making 401(k) salary-reduction savings plans available to their employees. And both employers and individuals purchase insurance to cover health-care costs.

6   Analyze the advantages and disadvantages of term, whole, endowment, and universal life insurance.

All life insurance provides a stated amount of money, paid to beneficiaries upon the death of the insured individual. Term insurance provides this single benefit. Whole life insurance provides some savings as well—in the form of a cash surrender value. Endowment insurance also provides a guaranteed payment at the end of some specified period of time. And universal life insurance combines protection with an investment plan.

Key Terms

You should now be able to define and give an example relevant to each of the following terms:

risk (674)
speculative risk (674)
pure risk (675)
risk management (675)
self-insurance (677)
insurer (or insurance company) (678)
premium (678)
insurance policy (678)
insurance (678)
insurable risk (678)
uninsurable risk (678)
principle of indemnity (679)
stock insurance company (681)
mutual insurance company (681)
fire insurance (683)
coinsurance clause (684)
extended coverage (684)
fidelity bond (685)
automobile liability insurance (686)
automobile physical damage insurance (687)
no-fault auto insurance (687)

public liability insurance (687)
product liability insurance (688)
ocean marine insurance (688)
inland marine insurance (690)
business interruption insurance (690)
401(k) plan (691)
workers' compensation insurance (691)
health-care insurance (692)
health maintenance organization (HMO) (692)
preferred provider organization (PPO) (693)
life insurance (693)
beneficiary (693)
term life insurance (693)
whole life insurance (694)
cash surrender value (694)
endowment life insurance (694)
universal life insurance (694)

Questions

Review Questions

1. What is the difference between a speculative risk and a pure risk? Why are speculative risks generally uninsurable?
2. List the four general risk-management techniques, and give an example of how each is used to manage risk.
3. Under what conditions is self-insurance a practical risk-management method?
4. How does the principle of indemnity affect the following?
   a. The amount an insurer will pay in the event of a loss
   b. The maximum amount for which property should be insured by its owner
5. What are the five principal conditions that determine whether a risk is insurable?
6. Distinguish between a stock insurance company and a mutual insurance company.
7. What is the general effect of the coinsurance clause in a fire insurance policy?
8. What is extended insurance coverage, and what does it usually "extend"?
9. What is the difference between automobile liability insurance and automobile physical damage insurance? List three liability coverages and three physical damage coverages.

10. What is the difference between public liability insurance and product liability insurance? Why would a business need these two coverages?

11. How are the premiums determined for workers' compensation insurance? Who pays them?

12. In what specific ways can an employer reduce the cost of health-care insurance?

13. What is a health maintenance organization (HMO)? How does an HMO plan differ from both a more traditional health-care insurance plan and a PPO?

14. List and briefly describe four different kinds of life insurance.

Discussion Questions

1. What need did C. C. Criss recognize, and how did he satisfy that need?

2. What innovative steps did Mutual of Omaha take in the early 1950s?

3. Suppose you were the owner of a retail clothing store. To what extent could you use risk avoidance, risk reduction, and risk assumption in your risk-management program? Cite specific applications of each of these three techniques.

4. As the owner of the retail store described in Question 3, which insurance coverages would you purchase for your business? How would you determine the amount of each type of coverage to purchase?

5. The principle of indemnity does not seem to apply to life insurance because people can, within reason, purchase as much or as little of this coverage as they wish. Why should this be so?

Exercises

1. Find and read an article or two on homeowner's or renter's insurance. From your reading, prepare a written report answering the following questions:

   a. Which hazards are generally covered by these policies?

   b. Which additional coverages are available as endorsements?

2. The owner of a $500,000 building has purchased $300,000 worth of fire insurance on the building. Assuming the insurance policy has an 80 percent coinsurance clause, how much will the owner collect from the insurance company under each of the following conditions?

a. The building is totally destroyed by fire

b. A fire does $300,000 worth of damage to the building

VIDEO CASE 21.1

Teens Who Didn't Make It Home

Sick with pneumonia and exhausted from a trip to Connecticut, Sarann Hackett was glad to see her husband Fred at the Florida airport that afternoon in February 1993. On the way home, she talked excitedly about the gifts she'd brought their son, sixteen-year-old Scott. "We were always playing tricks on each other in the van," Sarann recalls, "so I thought Scotty was hiding in the van when Fred picked me up at the airport. I do remember Fred telling me that Scott was with friends. I was basically running my mouth, and I didn't read anything in Fred at all, nothing. He told me he had something to tell me, and I thought maybe he lost his job. But he kept saying he had something else to tell me."

"He waited until we got the suitcases in the house and then he told me about the accident." Fred told his wife that Scott had died with two of his friends in a late-night crash when their sports car hit a utility pole at about 75 miles per hour. Scott and seventeen-year-old Mike Morgan had been making plans for that Saturday night for weeks. They were going to throw a bash for a friend home on leave from the U.S. Marines. It was to be a small get-together, but the party grew so large that police showed up to disperse the crowd.

That's when Scott, Mike, and another teenager took off in a Camaro with sixteen-year-old Jason Harrison at the wheel. They made it to Jason's house, where they got a phone call from a boy who'd been stranded at the party. "So the four boys piled back into the car, going back thinking they were only picking up one or two boys. When they got there, there were four," Mike's mother, Pam Barrett, explains. Now the Camaro was packed with eight teenagers, and Jason reportedly sped off at about 75 miles per hour. That's when he lost control of his car and hit a pole. The driver was one of three boys killed. A toxicology report showed he had a blood alcohol concentration of 0.11 percent. Mike Morgan and Scott Hackett hadn't been drinking, reports indicated, but they died with Jason.

"My husband works nights," Pam says, "so when the highway patrol came to the door at about six that morning, I just automatically assumed it was an accident with my husband. It was about the time he was on his way home from work, so I never even considered

Mike. When they told me it was him, I couldn't believe it. I don't remember anything very much after that." Mike's two sisters and four brothers are taking it hard. "To the two littlest ones, he really was their idol," Pam says. "They thought their big brother could do anything. They kind of worshiped the ground he walked on. He was real good with them."

Sarann Hackett reminds herself that Scott was with friends when he died. She finds comfort in donating his eyes. "When I watch the sun come up," she says, "I think, if Scotty can't see it himself, he helped someone else see it."

Intoxication is measured most accurately by tests for blood alcohol concentration (BAC). Although a BAC of 0.10 percent is the common measure of intoxication, ten states have taken a tougher stand and defined a BAC of 0.08 percent as being intoxicated. Even BAC as low as 0.02 percent affects a person's driving ability and can cause a crash. The Utah Citizens Council on Alcoholic Beverage Control has recommended that the state should adopt a zero tolerance, perhaps by June 1996. The reasoning behind this proposal is that any tolerance conveys the message that it is okay to drink and drive. With its current BAC of 0.08 percent, Utah already has one of the most restrictive laws in the country. A zero tolerance would make it the toughest in the world. The problem is that teens are inexperienced both at drinking and at driving, so even moderate amounts of alcohol before driving can cause more crash deaths. This is why most states have established very low legal blood alcohol concentrations for young drivers—lower than those for older drivers.

Questions

1. What factors might cause teenagers to drink? What, if anything, can be done to prevent teenagers from drinking and driving?
2. What feelings did you have as you watched the video? What moved you most?
3. Do you agree with the Utah Citizens Council's recommendation for a zero BAC tolerance? Explain your answer.

CASE 21.2

You're in Good Hands with Allstate

June 3, 1993, was a historic day for American business and for The Allstate Corporation. It marked the introduction of Allstate as a publicly traded corporation through the largest initial public offering ever for a U.S. company. Allstate likes its customers to think of its employees and agents as "The Good Hands People."

The company's ads often focus on an image of two capable, comforting hands, ready to assist the Allstate customer in need. Trying to live up to this caring image has led Allstate to consistent innovation in its customer service and has resulted in the company's holding a solid position as one of the nation's largest and most profitable insurance companies. In 1993 Allstate reported a record net income of $1.3 billion, with revenues of $20.95 billion. In 1994, the effects of the January 1994 earthquake in California dampened an otherwise good year; net income was $484 million, with revenues of $21.5 billion.

Allstate has always been different from other insurance companies. Sears, Roebuck and Co., the nation's third-largest retailer, established Allstate in 1931. Many Americans, especially those who lived outside urban areas, grew up buying virtually everything they needed from Sears. So when the time came for them to buy insurance, they felt confident buying it from the same people who had sold them toys, tires, and toasters. (In November 1994 Sears announced its intention to spin off its 80.2 percent ownership of Allstate to Sears shareholders, making Allstate a fully independent and 100 percent publicly owned company.)

Headquartered in Northbrook, Illinois, Allstate—the nation's largest publicly held property and casualty insurance company—provides a diverse blend of auto, property, life, and business insurance products and distribution systems throughout the United States and Canada. Through joint ventures, Allstate is engaged in insurance business in Japan and the Republic of Korea. It also is a worldwide reinsurer. (Reinsurance is insurance purchased by an insurance company from another insurer to reduce risk for the original insurer.) Allstate employs more than 45,000 people, including more than 14,500 full-time agents. In addition, Allstate offers its products through more than 2,000 independent agents in areas not served by Allstate agents.

With a reputation built on the familiarity and reliability of the local Sears store, Allstate has continued to expand its customer base and distinguish itself from its competitors through innovations. For example, agents are able to offer a remarkable level of service to the Allstate customer. Technological enhancements being introduced to agents countrywide include online field underwriting capability and a cross-line customer data bank. In addition, a proprietary database of approximately 58 million Sears/Allstate customer households can be used to profile and market to millions more potential customers. As part of its commitment to its agency system, Allstate has made an unprecedented investment in education, through a comprehensive job analysis and training initiative. By mid-1994, for example, 60 percent of agents and sales managers had completed testing and refresher courses in sales skills.

Today, Allstate stands tall as one of the most successful insurance companies in the nation. And that success is built on this notion: "Every employee encounter with a customer will be regarded as a moment of opportunity to reaffirm Allstate's reputation in the marketplace as a company of people who place the customer first."[12]

Questions

1. Allstate's sixty-four-year association with Sears was successful. Now that Allstate will become an independent, 100 percent publicly held corporation, what challenges does it face to succeed on its own?

2. How can Allstate best demonstrate that it is really alert to customers' needs?

CAREER PROFILE ■ ■ ■ ■ ■ ■ ■ ■ ■ ■ ■ ■

PART 6   Career Opportunities in Finance, Investment, and Insurance

Job Title	Job Description	Salary Range
Actuary	Determine probability of loss in specific situations; calculate premium amounts that provide enough revenue to cover losses and operating expenses, and provide reasonable profits for the company; communicate with managers, agents, and the firm's accounting staff	3–4
Bank officer and manager	Ensure that banking activities are carried out efficiently and without error; supervise employees; communicate with bank customers; approve both loans and expenditures; maintain financial records to ensure that the bank is in compliance with government regulations	3–4
Claims adjuster	Adjust claims when customers incur losses; maintain accurate insurance records; oversee disbursement of payments to customers; communicate with upper level managers and other insurance firm employees	2
Credit manager	Oversee activities of credit department employees; maintain control of credit records; communicate with credit applicants, other employees, and firms requesting credit information about credit applicants; ensure that the firm complies with government regulations	2–3
Financial analyst	Evaluate financial performance of corporations; write research reports that are distributed to brokerage firm customers; make predictions on which securities will increase or decrease in value; communicate with managers, stockbrokers, and other brokerage firm employees	4–5
Insurance agent	Communicate with customers; evaluate potential risks for customers; determine appropriate coverage to reduce or transfer customer risk to insurance company; follow up activities with both customers and insurance companies; maintain accurate records for each customer	3–4
Investment banker	Help corporations obtain both equity and debt financing; evaluate the financial health of corporations; ensure that a new security issue meets all government regulations; choose appropriate methods to advertise and distribute new security issues; maintain relations with prior customers that may desire additional financing in the future	5
Stockbroker (account executive)	Provide investment advice and recommendations to individual customers; evaluate the financial performance of stocks, bonds, mutual funds, and other investment alternatives; maintain accurate and complete financial records for individual customers; provide follow-up services for all customers; adhere to all government regulations that affect securities transactions	4–5

700

The figure in the salary column approximates the expected annual income after two or three years of service.
1 = $12,000 – $15,000; 2 = $16,000 – $20,000; 3 = $21,000 – $27,000; 4 = $28,000 – $35,000; 5 = $36,000 and up.

Educational Requirements	Skills Required	Prospects for Growth
Bachelor's or master's degree in math, business, or statistics	Computer; decision making; quantitative; conceptual; critical thinking	Average
College degree; master's degree preferred; on-the-job experience	Communication; leadership; decision making; interpersonal; quantitative; conceptual; critical thinking	Below average
Some college preferred; on-the-job training	Communication; computer; problem solving; technical; conceptual	Average
College degree; on-the-job experience	Communication; leadership; decision making; interpersonal; conceptual; critical thinking	Below average
College degree; on-the-job experience; master's degree helpful	Computer; problem solving; interpersonal; quantitative; analytical; critical thinking	Below average
Bachelor's degree preferred	Communication; computer; interpersonal; critical thinking	Below average
College degree; master's degree helpful; on-the-job experience	Computer; problem solving; interpersonal; quantitative; analytical; conceptual; critical thinking	Below average
Bachelor's degree; on-the-job experience	Communication; computer; quantitative; analytical; conceptual; critical thinking	Average

The Business Environment

This final part of *Business* covers three topics that affect the operations of every firm and every worker. First, the legal aspects of business and the relationship between business and government in the United States are explored. Then, the last chapter of the text provides information useful for planning your career, including career preparation, résumé writing, and interviewing. Included in this part are:

CHAPTER 22   Business Law and Government Regulation, Assistance, and Taxation

CHAPTER 23   Careers in Business

Business Law and Government Regulation, Assistance, and Taxation

LEARNING OBJECTIVES

After studying this chapter you should be able to

1 Explain how laws originate and how they are administered by courts.

2 Outline the requirements for a valid contract and the remedies for a broken contract.

3 Explain how property law, negotiable instruments, the agent-principal relationship, and bankruptcy affect business firms.

4 Discuss how federal, state, and local government laws and regulations affect the day-to-day operation of a business.

5 Analyze the current government deregulation movement.

6 Describe the ways in which government can assist business firms.

7 Identify the various taxes through which federal, state, and local governments are financed.

CHAPTER PREVIEW

Our initial task in this chapter is to examine the sources of law. We also describe the functions of federal and state court systems. Then we discuss the major categories of law that apply to business activities. These categories include (1) contract law, (2) property law, (3) negotiable instruments, (4) the agent-principal relationship, (5) and bankruptcy. We also examine several federal, state, and local laws and regulations that affect the day-to-day operations of a business firm. Next we describe how government supports business activities through providing information, funding research, and purchasing goods and services produced by business. We conclude the chapter with a discussion of federal, state, and local taxes—the primary means by which governments at all levels finance their activities.

Jenny Craig, Inc.: Fighting More Than Weight

Jenny and Sidney Craig opened their first weight-loss center in the United States in 1985. Today, Jenny Craig, Inc., has 608 company-owned and 202 franchised weight-loss centers in thirty-seven states, Australia, New Zealand, Canada, Mexico, and Puerto Rico. When Jenny Craig common stock sold for $34 per share in 1992, the company developed expansion plans to open an additional one hundred centers by 1996 in order to cater to the aging, health-conscious baby boomer generation. But plans for future growth are now threatened because Jenny Craig, the corporation, finds itself weighed down under the burden of investigations and lawsuits.

When the Federal Trade Commission began to probe into whether the advertising practices of weight-loss centers were deceptive, Jenny Craig—as well as Weight Watchers, Nutri/System, Diet Center, and Physician's Weight Loss Centers—asked the commission to issue industrywide standards. These requests were denied until the FTC concludes its investigation. Because of the publicity, former clients have filed lawsuits claiming that Jenny Craig's diets caused health problems ranging from stomach disorders to gall bladder disease.

To make matters worse, the Jenny Craig organization was sued by disgruntled shareholders. The class action lawsuits claimed that Jenny Craig expanded too fast at shareholder expense. Shareholders argued that the value of their shares decreased and that dividend payments were suspended because of corporate overexpansion.

Now—as a result of another class action lawsuit—even the balance of corporate power is under investigation. The Jenny Craig organization employs 4,300 employees nationwide. Ninety-one percent of those employees are

female, a statistic that has raised the question of whether males are prevented from climbing the corporate ladder. Eight former male employees have brought allegations of sex discrimination against Jenny Craig. Calling themselves the "Boston Eight," the men hired a team of female attorneys to represent them in reverse discrimination suits. In December 1994, the Massachusetts Commission Against Discrimination ruled there was probable cause that in three of the lawsuits the men were passed over for promotion. The commission has ordered that the men and the Jenny Craig organization submit their case to mediation in order to resolve the discrimination issue. The five remaining suits have been filed in the court system and are scheduled to be heard in January 1996.

In the meantime, Jenny Craig continues to operate its centers under the weight of litigation and controversy. The company would like to reduce the cost and time involved, so the corporation can return to its primary purpose—helping people to manage their weight.[1]

■ ■ ■ ■

705

■ ■ ■ ■ ■ ■ ■ ■ ■ ■ ■

L aws set standards of behavior for both businesses and individuals; they establish the rights of parties in exchanges and various types of agreements; and they provide remedies in the event that one business (or individual) believes it has been injured by another. For example, former clients, disgruntled stockholders, and one-time employees, all believing they had been injured by Jenny Craig, Inc., sued the company.

Two ideas are critical here. First, the lawsuits brought by clients, stockholders, and employees were based on existing laws. Second, each group sought a remedy to its complaint within the court system. We discuss both ideas in this chapter.

■■ LAWS AND THE COURTS

LEARNING OBJECTIVE 1
Explain how laws originate and how they are administered by courts.

law a rule developed by a society to govern the conduct of, and relationships among, its members

A **law** is a rule developed by a society to govern the conduct of, and relationships among, its members. In the United States, the supreme law of the land is the U.S. Constitution. No federal, state, or local law is valid if it violates the U.S. Constitution. In addition to the U.S. Constitution, laws are created and administered by federal, state, and local governments.

Sources of Laws

Each level of government derives its laws from two major sources: (1) judges' decisions, which make up common law, and (2) legislative bodies, which enact statutory laws.

common law the body of law created by the court decisions rendered by judges; also known as *case law* or *judicial law*

Common Law **Common law,** also known as *case law* or *judicial law,* is the body of law created by the court decisions rendered by judges. Common law began as custom and tradition in England. It was then transported to America during the colonial period and, since then, has been further enlarged by the decisions of American judges.

This growth of common law is founded on the doctrine of *stare decisis,* a Latin term that is translated as "to stand by a previous decision." The doctrine of *stare decisis* is a practical source of law for two reasons. First, a judge's decision in a case may be used by other judges as the basis for later decisions. The earlier decision thus has the strength of law and is, in effect, a source of law. Second, the doctrine of *stare decisis* makes law more stable and predictable. If someone brings a case to court *and* the facts are the same as those in a case that has already been decided, the court will make a decision based on the previous legal decision. The court may depart from the doctrine of *stare decisis* if the facts in the current case differ from those in an earlier case or if business practices, technology, or the attitudes of society have changed.

statute a law passed by the U.S. Congress, a state legislature, or a local government

statutory law all the laws that have been enacted by legislative bodies

Statutory Law A **statute** is a law passed by the U.S. Congress, a state legislature, or a local government. **Statutory law,** then, consists of all the laws

706

Uniform Commercial Code (UCC)   a set of laws designed to eliminate differences among state regulations affecting business and to simplify interstate commerce

that have been enacted by legislative bodies. For businesses, one very important part of statutory law is the Uniform Commercial Code. The **Uniform Commercial Code (UCC)** is a set of laws designed to eliminate differences among state regulations affecting business and to simplify interstate commerce. The UCC consists of eleven articles, or chapters, that cover sales, commercial paper, bank deposits and collections, letters of credit, transfers of title, securities, and transactions that involve collateral. It has been adopted with variations in all fifty states. The state statutes that were replaced by the UCC generally varied from state to state and caused problems for firms that did business in more than one state.

administrative law
the regulations created by government agencies established by legislative bodies

Today, most legal experts have expanded the concept of statutory law to include administrative law. **Administrative law** consists entirely of the regulations created by government agencies established by legislative bodies. The Nuclear Regulatory Commission, for example, has the power to set specific requirements for nuclear power plants. It can even halt the construction or operation of plants that do not meet such requirements. These requirements thus have the force and effect of law.

Most regulatory agencies hold hearings that are similar to court trials. Evidence is introduced, and the parties involved are represented by legal counsel. Moreover, the decisions of these agencies may be appealed in state or federal courts.

Improving the environment through cooperation between government agencies and private businesses. Although the Environmental Protection Agency (EPA) is a federal agency that has the power to create regulations to improve the environment, EPA officials would be the first to admit that voluntary compliance and alternative products are the preferred way of doing business. Here, a spokesperson for the National Consortium for Emissions Reductions in Lawn Care explains the benefits of using electric lawn mowers.

Public Law and Private Law: Crimes and Torts

public law   the body of law that deals with the relationships between individuals or businesses and society

crime   a violation of a public law

Public law is the body of law that deals with the relationships between individuals or businesses and society. A violation of a public law is called a **crime.** Among the crimes that can affect a business are the following:

- Burglary, robbery, and theft (these crimes were discussed in Chapter 21).
- Embezzlement, or the unauthorized taking of money or property by an employee, agent, or trustee.
- Forgery, or the false signing or changing of a legal document with the intent to alter the liability of another person.
- The use of inaccurate weights, measures, or labels.
- The use of the mails to defraud, or cheat, an individual or business.
- The receipt of stolen property.
- The filing of a false and fraudulent income tax return.

Those accused of violating public laws—or committing crimes—are prosecuted by a federal, state, or local government.

private law   the body of law that governs the relationships between two or more individuals or businesses

tort   a violation of a private law

negligence   a failure to exercise reasonable care, resulting in injury to another

Private law is the body of law that governs the relationships between two or more individuals or businesses. A violation of a private law is called a **tort.** In some cases, a single illegal act—such as fraud—can be both a crime and a tort.

Torts may result either from intentional acts or from negligence. Such acts as shoplifting and embezzlement are intentional torts. **Negligence,** on the other hand, is a failure to exercise reasonable care, resulting in injury to another. Suppose the driver of a delivery truck loses control at the wheel and rams into a building. A tort has been committed, and the owner of the building may sue both the driver and the driver's employer to recover the cost of repairing the damages. Among the torts that can affect a business are the following:

- *Slander,* or an oral statement that is false and injures a person's or business's reputation.
- *Libel,* or a written statement that is false and injures a person's or business's reputation.
- *Fraud,* or the misrepresentation of facts designed to take advantage of another individual or business.
- *Product liability,* or the manufacturer's responsibility for negligence in designing, manufacturing, or providing operating instructions for its products. (This topic was discussed in Chapter 21.)
- *Personal injury,* or damages caused by accidents, intentional acts, or defective products.
- *Unfair competitive practices,* a topic covered later in this chapter.

The purpose of private law is to provide a remedy for the party injured by a tort. In most cases, the injured party must bring a legal action and present the facts in a court of law. Then, either a judge or jury will render a decision. In most cases, the remedy consists of monetary damages to compensate the injured party and punish the person committing the tort. For example, the courts ruled in 1991 that Eastman Kodak Company was guilty of infringing on certain patent rights owned by Polaroid Corp. Thus Eastman Kodak committed a tort and was forced to pay Polaroid almost $900 million in damages. Because of the large dollar settlements that have become commonplace in the 1980s and 1990s, many business owners and politicians insist there is a need for tort reform. For more information about possible tort reforms, see Change in the Workplace.

The Court System

The United States has two separate and distinct court systems. The federal court system consists of the Supreme Court of the United States, which was established by the Constitution, and other federal courts that were created by Congress. In addition, each of the fifty states has established its own court system. Figure 22.1 shows the makeup of both the federal court system and a typical state court system.

The Federal Court System   Federal courts generally hear cases that involve

- Questions of constitutional law.
- Federal crimes or violations of federal statutes.
- Property valued at $50,000 or more between citizens of different states, or between an American citizen and a foreign nation.
- Bankruptcy; the Internal Revenue Service; the postal laws; or copyright, patent, and trademark laws.
- Admiralty and maritime cases.

The United States is divided into federal judicial districts. Each state includes at least one district court, and more populous states have two or more. A district court is a **court of original jurisdiction,** which is the first court to recognize and hear testimony in a legal action. In many cases, the

court of original jurisdiction
the first court to recognize and hear testimony in a legal action

FIGURE 22.1 The Court System
The United States has two separate and distinct court systems, as illustrated here by the federal court system and a typical state court system.

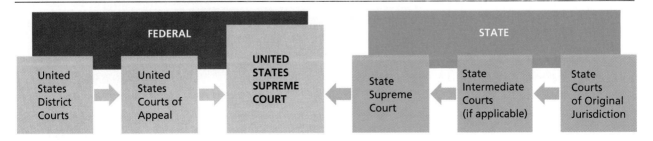

■ ■ ■ ■ CHANGE IN THE WORKPLACE

Is It Time for Tort Reform?

"Hurt?" "Injured?" "Free Injury Consultation!" These lead-ins for the innumerable advertisements by personal injury attorneys that appear in your Sunday TV supplement give you an idea of the widespread litigation fever rampant in the United States. In the last two decades, civil suits have burgeoned into a lawsuit lottery that is clogging our court systems and is costing businesses and the economy millions of dollars each year. We have become a nation in which people are quick to blame others and in which attorneys feed on the desire to make somebody pay. Too often, manufacturers must pay huge dollar amounts to settle personal injury lawsuits resulting not from poor product design but from the customer's incorrect use of the product. As a result, many manufacturers have been forced to discontinue product research and lay off workers just to be able to pay the tremendous legal costs incurred in defending themselves.

A NEED FOR TORT REFORM

When asked if we need tort reform, many Americans answer yes. For example, a recent Roper poll reported in the *Wall Street Journal* showed that 70 percent of the American people agree that liability suits give lawyers more money than they deserve, and 63 percent agree that some people start frivolous lawsuits because the awards are so big and there's so little to lose. Almost 70 percent would limit punitive damages (awards handed out for "pain and suffering") as well as a plaintiff's out-of-pocket expenses. Not only public opinion but also legal professionals are calling for tort reform. For example, the U.S. Judicial Conference, the administrative arm of the federal court system, will recommend a uniform set of federal reforms in 1995. These detailed changes are the result of a research study begun in 1990. And

many business and consumer groups also agree that ways must be found for the system to operate more quickly, more effectively, and more frugally.

TORT REFORM PROPOSALS

At the top of the list among many tort reform proposals is limiting punitive damages. In 1994, an Albuquerque woman won a judgment of $2.9 million against McDonald's: as she drove away from a golden arches drive-thru window, the cup of coffee she had just purchased and placed between her legs spilled and caused her extreme pain and suffering. The fast-food chain was found guilty of making its coffee "too hot."

Another proposal is the establishment of uniform standards for product liability cases. Too often, people ignore the warnings that manufacturers place on products that are known to be unsafe under certain conditions, and then they sue the makers for damages. Penalties for filing such lawsuits, firm trial dates, and a "loser pays" rule are just some of the options under consideration for reforming the present system.

WHAT IS BEING DONE NOW?

Many states are not waiting for federal reforms but are instead attempting to legislate reforms at the state level. In Texas, a major product liability reform statute has been enacted that deters product liability actions against consumer products known to be unsafe. In Mississippi, punitive damages for product liability may be awarded only if the maker is proven to have acted with malice. And Arizona has done away with multiple defendant lawsuits, in which a plaintiff seeks to collect from the defendant with the "deepest pockets," or the party with the most money.

appellate court a court that hears cases that are appealed from lower courts

decision reached in the district court may be appealed to a higher court. A court that hears cases that are appealed from lower courts is called an **appellate court.** If the appellate court finds the lower court's ruling to be in error, it may reverse that ruling, modify the decision, or return the case to the lower court for a new trial. Currently, there are thirteen U.S. courts of appeals.

The U.S. Supreme Court—the highest court in the land—consists of nine justices (the Chief Justice of the United States and eight associate justices). The Supreme Court has original jurisdiction in cases that involve ambassadors and consuls and in certain cases involving one or more states. However, its main function is to review decisions made by the U.S. courts of appeals and, in some cases, by state supreme courts.

The State Court Systems   The state court systems are quite similar to the federal system in structure. All have courts of original jurisdiction and supreme courts, and most have intermediate appellate courts as well. The decision of a state supreme court may be appealed to the U.S. Supreme Court if it involves a question of constitutional or federal law.

court of limited jurisdiction a court that hears only specific types of cases

Other Types of Courts   Other courts have been created to meet special needs at both the federal and state levels. A **court of limited jurisdiction** hears only specific types of cases. At the federal level, for example, Congress has created courts to hear cases that involve international trade, taxes and disputes with the IRS, and bankruptcy. At the state level, there are small-claims courts, which hear cases involving claims for less than a specified dollar amount (usually $500 or $5,000, depending on the state); traffic courts; divorce courts; juvenile courts; and probate courts.

In the next two sections, we briefly discuss the major categories of business law. These are contract law, property law, negotiable instruments, the agent-principal relationship, and bankruptcy.

■■ CONTRACT LAW

LEARNING OBJECTIVE 2
Outline the requirements for a valid contract and the remedies for a broken contract.

contract a legally enforceable agreement between two or more competent parties who promise to do, or not to do, a particular thing

Contract law is perhaps the most important area of business law because contracts are so much a part of doing business. Every business person should understand what a valid contract is and how a contract is fulfilled or violated.

A **contract** is a legally enforceable agreement between two or more competent parties who promise to do, or not to do, a particular thing. An *implied contract* is an agreement that results from the actions of the parties. For example, a person who orders dinner at a local Chili's restaurant assumes that the food will be served within a reasonable time and will be fit to eat. The restaurant owner, for his or her part, assumes that the customer will pay for the meal.

Most contracts are more explicit and formal than that between a restaurant and its customers. An *express contract* is one in which the parties involved have made oral or written promises about the terms of their agreement.

A contract is a contract is a contract. Today most people enter into more contracts than they realize. Even such everyday transactions such as leaving film for processing creates a contract between the owner of the film and a photo lab. And because a contract has been created, each party has certain legal rights. The customer assumes the film will be developed and the photo lab assumes the customer will pay for the processing.

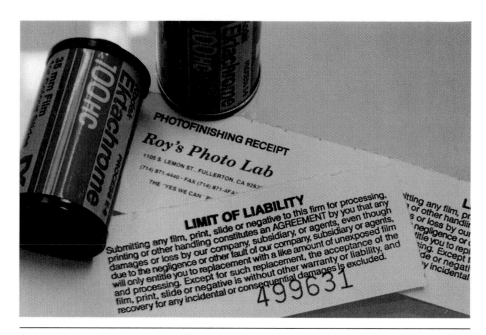

Requirements for a Valid Contract

To be valid and legally enforceable, a contract must meet five specific requirements, as follows: (1) voluntary agreement, (2) consideration, (3) legal competence of all parties, (4) lawful subject matter, and (5) proper form.

Voluntary Agreement   **Voluntary agreement** consists of both an *offer* by one party to enter into a contract with a second party and *acceptance* by the second party of all the terms and conditions of the offer. If any part of the offer is not accepted, there is no contract. And if it can be proved that coercion, undue pressure, or fraud was used to obtain a contract, it may be voided by the injured party.

voluntary agreement   a contract requirement consisting of an *offer* by one party to enter into a contract with a second party and *acceptance* by the second party of all the terms and conditions of the offer

Consideration   A contract is a binding agreement only when each party provides something of value to the other party. The value or benefit that one party furnishes to the other party is called **consideration.** This consideration may be money, property, a service, or the promise not to exercise a legal right. However, the consideration given by one party need not be equal in dollar value to the consideration given by the other party. As a general rule, the courts will not void a contract just because one party got a bargain.

consideration   the value or benefit that one party to a contract furnishes to the other party

Legal Competence   All parties to a contract must be legally competent to manage their own affairs *and* must have the authority to enter into binding agreements. The intent of the legal competence requirement is to protect individuals who may not have been able to protect themselves. The courts generally will not require minors, persons of unsound mind, or those who entered into contracts while they were intoxicated to comply with the terms of their contracts.

Lawful Subject Matter   A contract is not legally enforceable if it involves an unlawful act. Certainly, a person who contracts with an arsonist to burn down a building cannot go to court to obtain enforcement of the contract. Equally unenforceable is a contract that involves **usury,** which is the practice of charging interest in excess of the maximum legal rate. Other contracts that may be unlawful include promissory notes resulting from illegal gambling activities, contracts to bribe public officials, agreements to perform services without required licenses, and contracts that restrain trade or eliminate competition.

usury   the practice of charging interest in excess of the maximum legal rate

Proper Form of Contract   Businesses generally draw up all contractual agreements in writing so that differences can be resolved readily if a dispute develops. Figure 22.2 shows that a contract need not be complicated to be legally enforceable.

A written contract must contain the names of the parties involved, their signatures, the purpose of the contract, and all terms and conditions to which the parties have agreed. Any changes to a written contract should be made in writing, initialed by all parties, and attached to the original contract.

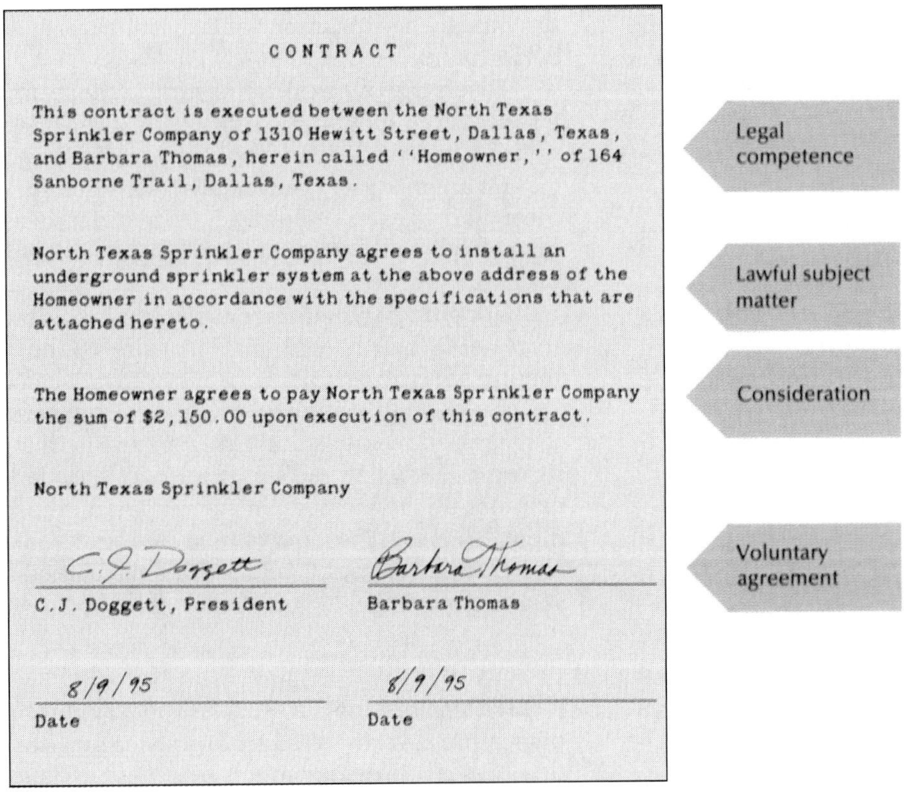

FIGURE 22.2
Contract Between a Business and a Customer
Notice that the requirements for a valid contract are satisfied and that the contract takes the proper form by containing the names of the parties involved, their signatures, the purpose of the contract, and all terms and conditions.

CONTRACT

This contract is executed between the North Texas Sprinkler Company of 1310 Hewitt Street, Dallas, Texas, and Barbara Thomas, herein called ''Homeowner,'' of 164 Sanborne Trail, Dallas, Texas.

Legal competence

North Texas Sprinkler Company agrees to install an underground sprinkler system at the above address of the Homeowner in accordance with the specifications that are attached hereto.

Lawful subject matter

The Homeowner agrees to pay North Texas Sprinkler Company the sum of $2,150.00 upon execution of this contract.

Consideration

North Texas Sprinkler Company

C.J. Dorsett   *Barbara Thomas*
C.J. Doggett, President   Barbara Thomas

Voluntary agreement

8/9/95   8/9/95
Date   Date

The *Statute of Frauds,* which has been passed in some form by all states, requires that certain types of contracts be in writing to be enforceable. These include contracts dealing with

- The exchange of land or real estate.
- The sale of goods, merchandise, or personal property valued at $500 or more.
- The sale of securities, regardless of the dollar amount.
- Acts that will not be completed within one year after the agreement is made.
- A promise to assume someone else's financial obligation.
- A promise made in contemplation of marriage.

Performance and Nonperformance

performance the fulfillment of all obligations by all parties to the contract

Ordinarily, a contract is terminated by **performance,** which is the fulfillment of all obligations by all parties to the contract. Occasionally, however, performance may become impossible. Death, disability, or bankruptcy, for example, may legally excuse one party from a contractual obligation. But what happens when one party simply does not perform according to a legal contract?

breach of contract the failure of one party to fulfill the terms of a contract when there is no legal reason for that failure

A **breach of contract** is the failure of one party to fulfill the terms of a contract when there is no legal reason for that failure. In such a case, it may be necessary for the other parties to the contract to bring legal action to discharge the contract, obtain monetary damages, or require specific performance.

discharge by mutual assent when all parties agree to void a contract

Discharge by mutual assent is the termination of a contract when all parties agree to void a contract. Any consideration received by the parties must be returned when a contract is discharged by mutual assent.

damages a monetary settlement awarded to a party injured through a breach of contract

Damages are a monetary settlement awarded to a party injured through a breach of contract. When damages are awarded, an attempt is made to place the injured party in the position it would be in if the contract had been performed.

specific performance the legal requirement that the parties to a contract fulfill their obligations according to the contract

Specific performance is the legal requirement that the parties to a contract fulfill their obligations according to the contract. Generally, the courts require specific performance if a contract calls for a unique service or product that cannot be obtained from another source.

Most individuals and firms enter into a contract expecting to live up to its terms. Very few end up in court. When they do, it is usually because one or more of the parties did not understand all the conditions of the agreement. Thus it is imperative to know what you are signing before you sign it. If you have any doubt, get legal help! A signed contract is very difficult—and often very costly—to void.

Sales Agreements

sales agreement a type of contract by which ownership is transferred from a seller to a buyer

A **sales agreement** is a special (but very common) type of contract by which ownership is transferred from a seller to a buyer. Article 2 of the UCC (entitled "Sales") provides much of our sales law, which is derived from both common and statutory law. Among the topics included in Article 2 are rights of the buyer and seller, acceptance and rejection of an offer, inspection of goods, delivery, transfer of ownership, and warranties.

Article 2 also provides that a sales agreement may be binding even when one or more of the general contract requirements are omitted. For example, a sales agreement is legally binding when the selling price is left out of the agreement. Article 2 requires that the buyer pay the reasonable value of the goods at the time of delivery. Key considerations in resolving such issues are the actions and business history of the parties and any customary sales procedures within the particular industry.

Finally, Article 2 deals with warranties—both express and implied. As we saw in Chapter 13, an **express warranty** is a written explanation of the responsibilities of the producer (or seller) in the event that a product is found to be defective or otherwise unsatisfactory. An **implied warranty** is a guarantee that is imposed or required by law. In general, the buyer is entitled to assume that

1. The merchandise offered for sale has a clear title and is not stolen.

2. The merchandise is as advertised.

3. The merchandise will serve the purpose for which it was manufactured and sold.

Any limitation to an express or implied warranty must be clearly stated so the buyer can understand any exceptions or disclaimers.

express warranty a written explanation of the responsibilities of the producer (or seller) in the event that a product is found to be defective or otherwise unsatisfactory

implied warranty a guarantee that is imposed or required by law

■■ OTHER LAWS THAT AFFECT BUSINESS

In addition to contract law, many other kinds of law affect the way a firm does business. In this section, we describe the impact of laws relating to property, negotiable instruments, the agent-principal relationship, and bankruptcy on the day-to-day operations of a business firm.

LEARNING OBJECTIVE 3
Explain how property law, negotiable instruments, the agent-principal relationship, and bankruptcy affect business firms.

Property Law

Property is anything that can be owned. The concept of private ownership of property is fundamental to the free-enterprise system. Our Constitution guarantees to individuals and businesses the right to own property and to use it in their own best interest.

property anything that can be owned

Kinds of Property Property is legally classified as either real property or personal property. **Real property** is land and anything permanently attached to it. The term also applies to water on the ground and minerals and natural resources beneath the surface. Thus, a house, a factory, a garage, and a well are all considered real property.

The degree to which a business is concerned with real-property law depends on its size and type of business. The owner of a small convenience store needs only a limited knowledge of real-property law. But a national grocery-store chain like Albertson's might employ several real estate experts with extensive knowledge of real-property law, property values, and real estate zoning ordinances throughout the country.

real property land and anything permanently attached to it

personal property all property other than real property

Personal property is all property other than real property. Personal property—such as inventories, equipment, store fixtures, an automobile, or a book—has physical or material value. It is referred to as *tangible personal property*. Thus, tangible personal property is movable and can be felt, tasted, or seen. Property that derives its value from a legal right or claim is called *intangible personal property*. Examples include stocks and bonds, receivables, trademarks, patents, and copyrights.

As we noted in Chapter 13, a trademark is a brand that is registered with the U.S. Patent and Trademark Office. Registration guarantees the owner the exclusive use of the trademark for ten years. At the end of that time, the registration can be renewed for additional ten-year periods. If necessary, the owner must defend the trademark from unauthorized use—usually through legal action. McDonald's was recently forced to do exactly that, when the trademark "Big Mac" was used by another fast-food outlet in a foreign country.

patent the exclusive right to make, use, or sell a newly invented product or process

A **patent** is the exclusive right to make, use, or sell, or to license others to make and sell, a newly invented product or process. Patents are granted by the U.S. Patent and Trademark Office for a period of seventeen years. After that time period has elapsed, the invention becomes available for general use.

copyright the exclusive right to publish, perform, copy, or sell an original work

A **copyright** is the exclusive right to publish, perform, copy, or sell an original work. Copyright laws cover fiction and nonfiction, plays, poetry, musical works, photographs, films, and computer programs. For example, the copyright on this textbook is held by the publisher, Houghton Mifflin Company. The copyright on the movie *The Lion King* is held by Walt Disney. A copyright is held by the creator of the work. It generally holds for the lifetime of the creator plus fifty years.

Valuable property. Trademarks and brands—like those pictured here—are valuable property. In each case, the corporations that own the trademarks and brands have invested a lot of money, time, and effort to develop symbols that their customers will recognize.

Transfer of Ownership   The transfer of ownership for both real property and personal property usually involves either a purchase, a gift, or an inheritance. As we noted earlier, the Statute of Frauds requires that exchanges of real estate be in writing. A **deed** is a written document by which the ownership of real property is transferred from one person or organization to another. The deed must contain the names of the previous owner and the new owner, as well as a legally acceptable description of the property being transferred. A **lease** is an agreement by which the right to use real property is temporarily transferred from its owner, the landlord, to a tenant. In return for the use of the property, the tenant generally pays rent on a weekly, monthly, or yearly basis. A lease is granted for a specific period of time, after which a new lease may be negotiated. If the lease is terminated, the right to use the real property reverts to the landlord.

Transfer of ownership for personal property depends on how payment is made. When the buyer pays the *full cash price* at the time of purchase, the title to personal property passes to the buyer immediately. When the buyer purchases goods on an *installment plan,* the title passes to the buyer when he or she takes possession of the goods. Although the full cash price has not been paid, the buyer has made a legally enforceable promise to pay it. This is sufficient consideration for the transfer of ownership. Moreover, if the purchased goods are stolen from the buyer, the buyer must still pay the full purchase price.

Laws Relating to Negotiable Instruments

A **negotiable instrument** is a written document that (1) is a promise to pay a stated sum of money and (2) can be transferred from one person or firm to another. In effect, a negotiable instrument is a substitute for money. Checks are the most familiar form of negotiable instruments. However, the promissory notes, drafts, certificates of deposit, and commercial paper discussed in Chapter 19 are also negotiable. Even a warehouse receipt can qualify as a negotiable instrument if certain conditions are met.

Requirements for Negotiability   The UCC establishes the following conditions for negotiability:

- The credit instrument must be in writing and signed.
- The instrument must contain an unconditional promise or order to pay a stated sum of money.
- The instrument must be payable on demand or at a definite future date.
- The instrument must be payable to a specified person or firm or to the bearer.

A financial document that does not meet all these requirements is not negotiable. It may still be valid and legally enforceable, but it cannot be transferred to another business or individual.

deed   a written document by which the ownership of real property is transferred from one person or organization to another

lease   an agreement by which the right to use real property is temporarily transferred from its owner, the landlord, to a tenant

negotiable instrument   a written document that (1) is a promise to pay a stated sum of money and (2) can be transferred from one person or firm to another

endorsement   the payee's
signature on the back of a
negotiable instrument

Endorsements   To transfer a negotiable instrument, the payee (the person named on the face of the document) must sign it on the back (see Figure 22.3, bottom). The payee's signature on the back of a negotiable instrument is called an **endorsement.** There are three types of endorsements, as shown at the bottom of Figure 22.3.

A *blank endorsement* consists only of the payee's signature. It is quick, easy, and dangerous because it makes the instrument payable to anyone who gets possession of it—legally or otherwise. A *restrictive endorsement* states the purpose for which the instrument is to be used. For example, the words "for deposit only" mean that this check *must* be deposited in the specified account.

A *special endorsement* identifies the person or firm to whom the instrument is payable. The words "Pay to the order of Robert Jones" means that the only person who can cash, deposit, or negotiate this check is Robert Jones.

FIGURE 22.3   Endorsements
The names of both the payee (Charles Hall) and the payor (Maria Martinez) are included on the front of the check. The payee's signature on the back of a negotiable instrument is called an *endorsement.* There are three types of endorsements.

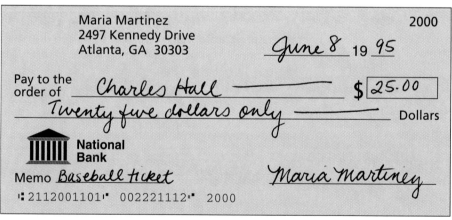

PERSONAL CHECK

ENDORSEMENTS

| Blank endorsement | Restrictive endorsement | Special endorsement |

Agency Law

agency a business relationship in which one party (called the *principal*) appoints a second party (called the *agent*) to act on behalf of the principal

An **agency** is a business relationship in which one party (called the *principal*) appoints a second party (called the *agent*) to act on behalf of the principal. Most agents are independent business people or firms. They are paid for their services with either set fees or commissions. Further, they are hired to use their special knowledge for a specific purpose. For example, real estate agents are hired to sell or buy real property. Insurance agents are hired to sell insurance. And theatrical agents are hired to obtain engagements for entertainers. The officers of a firm, lawyers, accountants, and stockbrokers also act as agents.

Almost any legal activity that can be accomplished by an individual can also be accomplished through an agent. (The exceptions are voting, giving sworn testimony in court, and making a will.) Moreover, under the law, the principal is bound by the actions of the agent. However, the principal may sue for damages an agent who performs an unauthorized act. For this reason, a written contract describing the conditions and limits of the agency relationship is extremely important to both parties.

power of attorney a legal document that serves as evidence that an agent has been appointed to act on behalf of a principal

A **power of attorney** is a legal document that serves as evidence that an agent has been appointed to act on behalf of a principal. In the majority of states in the United States, a power of attorney is required in agency relationships involving the transfer of real estate, as well as in other specific situations.

An agent is responsible for carrying out the principal's instructions in a professional manner, for acting reasonably and with good judgment, and for keeping the principal informed of progress according to their agreement. The agent must also be careful to avoid a conflict involving the interests of two or more principals. The agency relationship is terminated when its objective is accomplished, at the end of a specified time period, or in some cases, when either party renounces the agency relationship.

Bankruptcy Law

bankruptcy a legal procedure designed both to protect an individual or business that cannot meet its financial obligations and to protect the creditors involved

Bankruptcy is a legal procedure designed both to protect an individual or business that cannot meet its financial obligations and to protect the creditors involved. The Bankruptcy Reform Act was enacted in 1978 and was subsequently amended in July 1984. Under the act, bankruptcy proceedings may be initiated by either the person or the business in financial difficulty or by the creditors.

voluntary bankruptcy a bankruptcy procedure initiated by an individual or business that can no longer meet its financial obligations

involuntary bankruptcy a bankruptcy procedure initiated by creditors

Initiating Bankruptcy Proceedings **Voluntary bankruptcy** is a bankruptcy procedure initiated by an individual or business that can no longer meet its financial obligations. Individuals, partnerships, and most corporations may file for voluntary bankruptcy. **Involuntary bankruptcy** is a bankruptcy procedure initiated by creditors. The creditors must be able to prove that the individual or business has debts in excess of $5,000 and cannot pay its debts as they come due.

Today most bankruptcies are voluntary. Creditors are wary of initiating bankruptcy proceedings because they usually end up losing most of the money they are owed. They usually prefer to wait and to hope the debtor will eventually be able to pay.

Resolving a Bankruptcy Case A petition for bankruptcy is filed in a bankruptcy court. If the court declares the individual or business bankrupt, three means of resolution are available: liquidation, reorganization, and repayment.

Chapter 7 of the Bankruptcy Reform Act concerns *liquidation*, the sale of assets of a bankrupt individual or business to pay its debts (see Figure 22.4). In principle, the assets of the individual or business are sold to satisfy the claims of creditors. The debtor is then relieved of all remaining debts. Liquidation pursuant to Chapter 7 does not apply to railroads, banks, savings and loan associations, insurance companies, or government units. Chapter 7 also specifies the order in which claims are to be paid. First, creditors with secured claims are allowed to repossess (or assume ownership of) the collateral for their claims. Then, the remaining cash and assets—if any—are paid to unsecured creditors in the order prescribed by the bankruptcy act.

Chapter 11 of the Bankruptcy Reform Act outlines the procedure for *reorganizing* a bankrupt business. The idea is simple. The distressed business will be preserved by correcting or eliminating the factors that got the firm into financial trouble. To implement this idea, a plan to reorganize the business is developed. Only a debtor may file a reorganization plan for the first 120 days, unless a trustee has been appointed by the court. After 120 days, any interested party may file a reorganization plan. After the plan has been filed with the court, both the plan and a written disclosure statement are distributed to all individuals and businesses with claims against the bankrupt firm. These people and firms may testify at a hearing that is held for the purpose of confirming the plan. If the plan is confirmed by the court, the reorganized business emerges from bankruptcy with only the financial obligations that are imposed on it by the plan. This is exactly what

FIGURE 22.4 **Steps Involved in Chapter 7 (Liquidation) of the Bankruptcy Reform Act**
Chapter 7 of the Bankruptcy Reform Act concerns liquidation of assets.

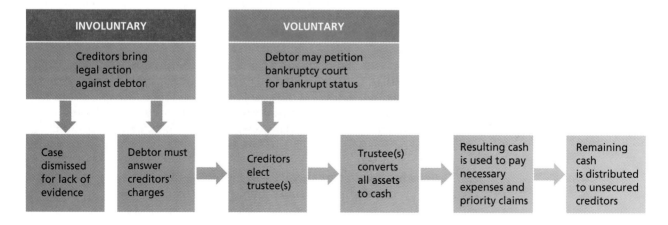

occurred when Colt Manufacturing Company, Federated Department Stores, Inc., Trans World Airlines, and Texaco Inc. filed for protection under Chapter 11.

Chapter 13 of the Bankruptcy Reform Act permits a bankrupt individual to file, with the courts, a plan for *repaying* specific debts. (Only individuals with a regular income, less than $100,000 in unsecured debts, and less than $350,000 in secured debts are eligible to file for repayment under Chapter 13.) The plan must provide for the repayment of specified amounts in up to three years. (In unusual circumstances, the court may extend the repayment period to five years.) If the plan is approved by the court, the individual usually pays the money to a court-appointed trustee in monthly installments. The trustee, in turn, pays the individual's creditors. For more information on personal bankruptcy, read Ethical Challenges.

■■ GOVERNMENT REGULATION OF BUSINESS

LEARNING OBJECTIVE 4
Discuss how federal, state, and local government laws and regulations affect the day-to-day operation of a business.

So far in this chapter, we have been concerned with the relationships among individuals and businesses—and, in particular, with the legal aspects of those relationships. In this section, we examine the relationship between business and the three levels of government in the United States.

Federal Regulations to Encourage Competition

Most states have laws to encourage competition, but for the most part, these laws duplicate federal laws. Therefore we discuss only federal legislation designed to encourage competition. A substantial body of federal law has been developed to guard against monopolies, price fixing, and other restraints on competition. These laws protect consumers by ensuring that they have a choice in the marketplace. The same laws protect businesses by ensuring that they are free to compete.

The need for such laws became apparent in the late 1800s, when monopolies, or trusts, developed in the sugar, whiskey, tobacco, shoe, and oil industries, among others. A **trust** is a business combination that is created when one firm obtains control of competing firms by purchasing their stock or their assets. Eventually, the trust gains control of the entire industry and can set prices and manipulate trade to suit its own interests. As a result, the government enacted antitrust laws to combat the stifling of competition by trusts.

trust a business combination that is created when one firm obtains control of competing firms by purchasing their stock or their assets

One of the most successful trusts was the Standard Oil Trust, created by John D. Rockefeller in 1882. Until 1911, the Standard Oil Trust controlled between 80 and 90 percent of the petroleum industry. The firm earned extremely high profits primarily because it had obtained secret price concessions from the railroads that shipped its products. Very low shipping costs, in turn, enabled the firm systematically to eliminate most of its competition by deliberately holding prices down. Once this was accomplished, Standard Oil quickly raised its prices.

In response to public outcry against such practices—and prices—Congress passed the Sherman Antitrust Act in 1890. Since then, Congress has

■ ■ ■ ■ ETHICAL CHALLENGES

Personal Bankruptcy: The "Ten-Year Mistake"

John and Susan Winslow have been advised by their family attorney to consider seeking protection under the U.S. Bankruptcy Code in order to obtain relief from the mounting pressure they are receiving from their creditors. The Winslows are in financial difficulty because of their reduced income, mounting medical bills, and overextension of credit card use. Many other people are in the same situation for other reasons—divorce, disability, or unemployment. The attorney explains that because so many people came to this country to escape the debtors' prisons in England, the United States Constitution and the Bill of Rights were drafted with special provisions that guarantee all individuals legal protection from their creditors. These laws are designed to give people like the Winslows relief from the burden of accumulated debt they can no longer manage. It is an opportunity for them to make a fresh start.

When individuals file for bankruptcy, they immediately receive an automatic stay that prohibits collection efforts from creditors, seizure of any assets, wage garnishments, evictions, or foreclosures. It does not release an individual from responsibility for alimony, child support, federal student loans, or federal income taxes. Because everyone needs to retain *something* in order to reestablish himself or herself, the law exempts certain types of assets, including a home, a car, or other essential items. These exemptions vary from state to state. The nonexempt items are then sold and the proceeds are divided among creditors. A discharge in a Chapter 7 bankruptcy case releases the debts entirely and is usually filed by an individual with no significant assets. People who sincerely want to pay their creditors, but at the same time want to be left alone while they work their way free of debt, can file Chapter 13, which sets up a repayment schedule. In either case, all creditors are forbidden to communicate directly with the debtor, nor may they take any action against the debtor's property.

Filing for bankruptcy is serious business and should not be regarded as an easy way out. A person with a minimum debt load and who is employed can work instead with a Consumer Credit Counseling Service to reduce his or her credit obligations. Because having credit is a basic necessity in our society, creditors call bankruptcy the "10-year mistake." Once someone has been granted a discharge in a bankruptcy filing, the information remains on their credit file for at least ten years, making it extremely difficult to obtain credit or anything else that calls for a review of personal credit history. Finding a lender to grant a home mortgage is almost impossible, and it is also difficult to obtain financing to purchase a car. Finally, it may be next to impossible to get a Visa or MasterCard credit card.

enacted a number of other laws designed to protect American businesses and consumers from monopolies.

The Sherman Antitrust Act (1890)   The objectives of the *Sherman Antitrust Act* are to encourage competition and to prevent monopolies. The act specifically prohibits any contract or agreement entered into for the purpose of restraining trade. Specific business practices prohibited by the Sherman Antitrust Act include price fixing, allocation of markets among competitors,

price fixing an agreement between two businesses as to the prices to be charged for goods

market allocation an agreement to divide a market among potential competitors

boycott in restraint of trade an agreement between businesses not to sell to or buy from a particular entity

and boycotts in restraint of trade. **Price fixing** is an agreement between two businesses as to the prices to be charged for goods. A **market allocation** is an agreement to divide a market among potential competitors. A **boycott in restraint of trade** is an agreement between businesses not to sell to or buy from a particular entity. Power to enforce the Sherman Antitrust Act was given to the Department of Justice, which may bring legal action against businesses suspected of violating its provisions.

Today, the Sherman Act is still the cornerstone of the federal government's commitment to encourage competition and to break up large businesses that monopolize trade. An amendment to the Sherman Antitrust Act, the *Antitrust Procedures and Penalties Act of 1974,* made violation of the Sherman Act a felony rather than a misdemeanor. It provides for fines of up to $100,000 and prison terms of up to three years for individuals convicted of antitrust violations. The act also provides that a guilty corporation may be fined up to $1 million and may be sued by competitors or customers for treble monetary damages plus attorneys' fees.

The Clayton Act (1914)   Because the wording of the Sherman Antitrust Act is somewhat vague, it could not be used to halt specific monopolistic tactics. Congress therefore enacted the *Clayton Act* in 1914. This legislation identifies and prohibits five distinct practices that had been used to weaken trade competition.

price discrimination the practice in which producers and wholesalers charge larger firms a lower price for goods than they charge smaller firms

tying agreement a contract that forces an intermediary to purchase unwanted products along with the products it actually wants to buy

binding contract an agreement that requires an intermediary to purchase products from a particular supplier, not from the supplier's competitors

interlocking directorate an arrangement in which members of the board of directors of one firm are also directors of a competing firm

community of interests the situation in which one firm buys the stock of a competing firm to reduce competition between the two

- **Price discrimination,** the practice in which producers and wholesalers charge larger firms a lower price for goods than they charge smaller firms. (The Clayton Act does, however, allow quantity discounts.)
- The **tying agreement,** which is a contract that forces an intermediary to purchase unwanted products along with the products it actually wants to buy. This practice was used to "move" a producer's slow-selling merchandise along with its more desirable merchandise.
- The **binding contract,** an agreement that requires an intermediary to purchase products from a particular supplier, not from the supplier's competitors. In return for signing a binding contract, the intermediary was generally given a price discount.
- The **interlocking directorate,** an arrangement in which members of the board of directors of one firm are also directors of a competing firm. Thus, for example, a person may not sit on the board of American Airlines and Delta Air Lines at the same time.
- The **community of interests,** the situation in which one firm buys the stock of a competing firm. If this type of merger substantially lessens competition or tends to create a monopoly, it is unlawful.

Federal Trade Commission (FTC) a five-member committee charged with the responsibility of investigating illegal trade practices and enforcing antitrust laws

The Federal Trade Commission Act (1914)   In 1914 Congress also passed the *Federal Trade Commission Act,* which states that "Unfair methods of competition in commerce are hereby declared unlawful." This act also created the **Federal Trade Commission (FTC),** a five-member committee charged with the responsibility of investigating illegal trade practices and enforcing antitrust laws.

At first, the FTC was limited to enforcement of the Sherman Antitrust, Clayton, and FTC Acts. However, in the 1938 *Wheeler-Lea Amendment* to the FTC Act, Congress gave the FTC the power to eliminate deceptive business practices—including those aimed at consumers rather than competitors. This early "consumer legislation" empowered the FTC to deal with a variety of unfair business tactics without having to prove that they endangered competition.

The Robinson-Patman Act (1936)   Although the Clayton Act prohibits price discrimination, it does permit quantity discounts. This provision turned out to be a major loophole in the law: it was used by large chain retailers to obtain sizable price concessions that gave them a strong competitive edge over independent stores. To correct this imbalance, the *Robinson-Patman Act* was passed by Congress in 1936. This law specifically prohibits

- Price differentials that "substantially" weaken competition, unless they can be justified by the actual lower selling costs associated with larger orders.
- Advertising and promotional allowances (a form of discount), unless they are offered to small retailers as well as large retailers.

The Robinson-Patman Act is more controversial than most antitrust legislation. Many economists believe the act tends to discourage price competition rather than to eliminate monopolies.

The Celler-Kefauver Act (1950)   The Clayton Act prohibited building a trust by purchasing the stock of competing firms. To get around that prohibition, however, a firm could still purchase the *assets* of its competitors. The result was the same: the elimination of competition. This gigantic loophole was closed by the *Celler-Kefauver Act*, which prohibits mergers through the purchase of assets if these mergers will tend to reduce competition. The act also requires all proposed mergers to be approved by both the FTC and the Justice Department.

The Antitrust Improvements Act (1976)   The laws we have discussed were enacted "after the fact"—to correct abuses. In 1976 Congress passed the *Antitrust Improvements Act* to strengthen previous legislation. This law provided additional time for the FTC and the Justice Department to evaluate proposed mergers, and it expanded the investigative powers of the Justice Department. It also authorized the attorneys general of individual states to prosecute firms accused of price fixing and to recover monetary damages for *consumers*.

The Present Antitrust Environment   The problem with antitrust legislation and its enforcement is that it is hard to define exactly what an appropriate level of competition is. For example, a particular merger may be in the public interest because it increases the efficiency of an industry. But at the same time it may be harmful because it reduces competition. There is really no rule of law (or of economics) that can be used to determine which of these two considerations is more important in a given case.

Three factors tend to influence the enforcement and effectiveness of antitrust legislation at the present time. The first is the growing presence of foreign firms in American markets. Foreign firms have increased competition in America and thus have made it more difficult for any firm to monopolize an industry. Second, most antitrust legislation must be interpreted by the courts because the laws are often vague and open-ended. Thus the attitude of the courts has a lot to do with the effectiveness of these laws. And third, political considerations often determine how actively the FTC and the Justice Department pursue antitrust cases.

Other Areas of Regulation

It is impossible to manage even a small business without being affected by local, state, and federal regulations. And it is just as impossible to describe all the government regulations that affect business. In addition to regulations that affect competition just discussed, we have examined a variety of regulations in other chapters. Chapter 2 discussed laws and regulations dealing with the physical environment, consumerism, and discrimination; Chapter 3, international trade; Chapter 4, organization of business entities; Chapter 10, personnel and employee relations; Chapter 11, union-management relations; Chapter 20, securities; and this chapter, trademarks, patents, and copyrights.

By now, you may think that there must be a government regulation to govern any possible situation. Actually, government regulations increased from the 1930s through the 1970s. The country then entered a deregulation period that lasted over twenty years. In the next section, we examine the effects of deregulation and the current status of the deregulation movement.

■■ THE DEREGULATION MOVEMENT

LEARNING OBJECTIVE 5
Analyze the current government deregulation movement.

deregulation   the process of removing existing regulations, forgoing proposed regulations, or reducing the rate at which new regulations are enacted

Deregulation is the process of removing existing regulations, forgoing proposed regulations, or reducing the rate at which new regulations are enacted. A movement to deregulate business began in the 1970s and continued into the 1990s.

The primary aim of the movement is to minimize the complexity of regulations that affect business and the cost of compliance. Today, many Americans believe the federal government is out of control and out of touch with the needs of average citizens. These same people often complain that the federal government has too many employees and spends too much money. At the time of publication, the U.S. government

- Employed approximately 3.1 million civilian workers (in addition to 1.7 million military personnel).
- Spent more than $1.5 trillion a year, which is approximately $6,000 for every person in the United States.

Critics also complain that too many government agencies regulate business activities. More than one hundred federal agencies are currently

How far should deregulation go? Deregulation of the airline industry began in 1978. Now after almost twenty years, even airline officials admit that some government regulations are needed to not only maintain an orderly market, but also to establish the best safety standards for any industry in the world.

responsible for enforcing a staggering array of regulations. And at least fifteen federal agencies now have a direct impact on business firms. These agencies and the activities they regulate are listed in Table 22.1.

The Cost of Regulation

Advocates of deregulation argue that the protest would be even louder if consumers really knew how much government regulations cost. One recent study found that government regulations cost the average American $725 each year.[2] And for some Americans who make large purchases, the total cost for government regulations is even higher. According to economist Robert Crandall, approximately $3,000 of the price of a new car pays for emissions and safety standards required by the federal government.[3]

Advocates of deregulation are also quick to point out that every business—both large and small—must obey an increasing number of government restrictions and directives. Large corporations can cope with government regulation. They have been doing so for some time. In essence, coping means passing the cost of regulation along to stockholders in the form of lower dividends and to consumers in the form of higher prices. Smaller firms bear a smaller regulatory burden, but they may find it harder to cope with that burden. Some may not have the staff necessary to comply with the various documentation requirements. And, for many small businesses, stiff competition for customers requires that they pass the cost of compliance directly to their owners.

TABLE 22.1   Government Agencies and What They Regulate

Government Agency or Commission	Regulates
Consumer Product Safety Commission	Consumer protection
Environmental Protection Agency	Pollution control
Equal Employment Opportunity Commission	Discrimination in employment practices
Federal Aviation Administration	Airline industry
Federal Communications Commission	Radio, television, telephone, and telegraph communications
Federal Energy Regulatory Commission	Electric power and natural gas
Federal Highway Commission	Vehicle safety
Federal Maritime Commission	Ocean shipping
Federal Mine Safety and Health Review Commission	Worker safety and health in the mining industry
Federal Trade Commission	Antitrust, consumer protection
Food and Drug Administration	Consumer protection
Interstate Commerce Commission	Railroads, bus lines, trucking, pipelines, and waterways
Nuclear Regulatory Commission	Nuclear power and nuclear industry
Occupational Safety and Health Administration	Worker safety and health
Securities and Exchange Commission	Corporate securities

Current Attempts at Deregulation

Back in 1981, President Reagan began a deregulation effort almost immediately after taking office. The principal guidelines for Reagan's deregulation efforts were as follows:

- Impose regulations only if their benefits exceed their costs.
- Choose the least expensive method of achieving the goals of regulation.
- Tailor regulatory burdens to the size and nature of the affected firms.
- Reduce unnecessary paperwork and regulatory delays.[4]

During the 1980s, the deregulation movement did help many industries post higher profits and improve financial performance. For example, the transportation industry—notably trucking, railroad, and air transportation firms—experienced tremendous gains as a result of deregulation. One study estimates the benefits of trucking deregulation at $39 billion to $63 billion annually, and another estimates the benefits of airline deregulation at $15 billion per year. Other successful results of deregulation include (1) the widespread introduction of money-market accounts that paid consumers higher interest rates and (2) increased pricing flexibility for stock commissions that reduced the cost of buying stocks and other securities. Finally, the relaxation of restrictions on overnight mail delivery led to dramatic increases for private companies providing next-day delivery services.[5]

The deregulation drive is continuing, but there is a question as to how far it can—or should—go. Continued deregulation may even create problems for the government and for business. For example, the government has been in the process of deregulating the airline industry since 1978. Now airline officials admit that some government regulations are needed to maintain an orderly market. Moreover, support for deregulation is mixed. Many politicians and consumers believe deregulation has gone far enough. They argue that further deregulation could result in inferior products, dangerous working conditions, polluted air, increased bank failures, and other problems that were prevalent during the 1980s and first part of the 1990s.

Perhaps what is needed now is not more deregulation but a fresh look at present regulation—its goals, costs, and effectiveness. Today, many experts suggest that any evaluation of government regulations should determine which regulations make sense, which should be modified, and which should be eliminated. Above all, any reworking of the regulatory environment should create a "livable" environment for consumers, workers, and businesses. For more information about current attempts to streamline government, read Business Journal.

■■ GOVERNMENT SUPPORT OF BUSINESS

LEARNING OBJECTIVE 6
Describe the ways in which government can assist business firms.

In the last two sections, we discussed government regulations and the current deregulation movement. Now, our focus turns to the ways government at the federal, state, and local levels supports and encourages business activities. In this section, we examine how government provides information and assistance, funds research, and acts as the largest customer of American business firms.

Providing Information and Assistance to Business

The U.S. government may be the world's largest collector and user of information. Much of this information is of value to businesses and is available at minimal cost. The U.S. Census Bureau, for example, collects and can provide a wealth of marketing data, such as

- Demographic data showing the population distribution by age, sex, race, geographic area, educational level attained, occupation, and income.
- Housing data by type and year of construction, size, building materials, and the like.

The Census Bureau also provides information on manufacturing and agricultural activity, government spending, and the availability of natural

Streamlining Government in the 1990s

In every presidential election since the 1970s, the candidates elected to office were sincere when they promised the American people they were prepared to declare war on the bureaucracy in Washington and cut unnecessary government spending from the federal budget. Presidents Carter, Nixon, Reagan, Bush, and Clinton all had their own ideas on how government should be reorganized. But each president found that government reform is often stymied by the overwhelming red tape in federal regulations, the duplication of services, the rigid rules in the civil service employment arena, and opposition from senators and representatives who seek to protect their favorite agencies or "pork barrel." Each president found that decades of growth and power in government cannot be swept away overnight.

REINVENTING GOVERNMENT

The latest attempt at cutting back government spending, led by Vice President Al Gore, is called "Reinventing Government." This program for reform, dubbed ReGo, was initiated in September 1993. Its goal is to make 800 changes to government programs that should result in saving American taxpayers $108 billion by 1998. Further, it calls for a 12 percent reduction in full-time federal employees, a move that will eliminate approximately 272,000 people from the civil service payroll. ReGo is aimed at making government work better and cost less by using tech-

nology and current management techniques to revamp existing government services.

INITIAL SUCCESS

One year after the program was initiated, Gore announced ReGo's efforts had resulted in saving more than $59 billion. This was accomplished by overhauling the government's purchasing system, consolidating the field offices for some agencies, and offering early retirement packages to almost 70,000 federal employees.

ROADBLOCKS

Congressional leaders in Washington may say they want reform, but when it comes to touching their pet projects or offending their constituents, they are reluctant to vote for drastic changes in the system—even when it comes to closing down agencies that have long outlived their original purpose and may be duplicating services available elsewhere. In order to get around this, the Reinventing Government plan asks all agencies to review their own operations and look for ways to cut waste in their own programs. And they have been requested to improve their communication lines with other agencies, so that a citizen who needs information or assistance can get it promptly. After all, citizens and taxpayers are the "real customers" of the government, and they deserve the best service possible.

resources. To inform businesses about the types of data and reports that are available, the bureau publishes an annual *Catalog of U.S. Census Publications.*

Other U.S. government publications that can be valuable sources of business information include the *Survey of Current Business* and *Business*

America from the Department of Commerce, the *Monthly Labor Review* from the Department of Labor, and the *Federal Reserve Bulletin.*

The Internal Revenue Service and the Small Business Administration provide not only information but also direct assistance. (As we saw in Chapter 5, the SBA provides management assistance and financial help to qualifying businesses.) Finally, state and local governments provide information and aid to firms that are, or expect to be, located within their borders.

Funding Research

Every year the federal government and private business each spend over $160 billion on research.[6] Some government-funded research is done at federal institutions such as the Centers for Disease Control in Atlanta. However, the greater portion of government-funded research is performed independently at colleges and universities under government grants.

For example, the federal government is (and has been, for some time) funding research into the causes of and potential cures for cancer. This research, which is taking place at a number of universities and medical schools around the country, is simply too expensive to be funded by individual firms. Because the research is being financed with public funds, the results it yields become part of the *public domain.* That is, they become the property of all citizens—and in particular, of those who can use the results to produce cancer-fighting drugs and apparatus.

Government funding is not limited to research into diseases. In the 1940s, for example, the federal government began to finance basic research into a phenomenon called semiconduction. This research eventually led to

A government priority: funding research. The U.S. government is the largest "researcher" in the world. Each year it spends over $160 billion to ensure that the research needed for scientific advancement is conducted at federal institutions such as the Centers for Disease Control and at colleges and universities that have government grants.

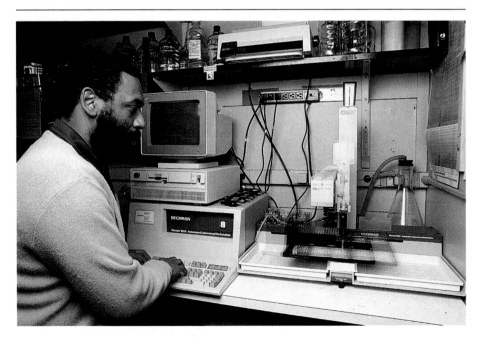

the development of the transistor, which you may recall from Chapter 16 is the basis of the modern computer industry. Present government-funded research may lead to entirely new industries and jobs in the decades to come.

Buying the Products of Business

The U.S. government is the largest single purchaser of goods and services in the world. A single purchase may range in size from a few hundred dollars for office supplies or furniture to more than a billion dollars for new aircraft. The federal government is the largest customer of many firms, and it is the only customer of some.

In addition, there are fifty state governments, 3,043 county governments, 19,296 cities, 16,666 townships, 14,556 school districts, and 33,131 special districts in this country.[7] Together, their total expenditures *exceed* the federal budget. Their needs run from paper clips to highways, from janitorial services to the construction of high-rise office buildings. And they purchase what they need from private businesses.

■■ GOVERNMENT TAXATION

LEARNING OBJECTIVE 7
Identify the various taxes through which federal, state, and local governments are financed.

Whether you believe there is too much government or too little, you are required to help pay for it. In one way or another, each of us helps pay for everything that government does—from regulating business to funding research into the causes and cures of cancer. We pay taxes to our local, state, and federal governments on the basis of what we earn, what we own, and even what we purchase.

Federal Taxes

It takes a lot of money to run something as big as the U.S. government. Each year vast sums are spent for human services, national defense, and interest on the national debt. In addition, the federal government must pay the salaries of its employees, cover its operating expenses, and purchase equipment and supplies that range from typewriter ribbons to aircraft carriers. Most of the money comes from taxes.

budget deficit an excess of spending over income

Taxes and Deficits   Figure 22.5 shows that the federal government had revenues of $1,249 billion in 1994. About 95 percent of that sum was obtained through taxation. However, the government actually spent more than it took in that year. In other words, there was a **budget deficit,** which is an excess of spending over income. In fact, the U.S. government has had budget deficits every year since 1960, with the exception of 1969 (see Figure 22.6).

What is disturbing about the information given in Figure 22.6 is the size of the budget deficits. Because deficits must be financed by borrowing, the outstanding debt of the U.S. government has grown to more than $4.6 trillion! The interest on this debt is enormous. As a result of continuing budget deficits, in 1985 politicians voted to enact the *Emergency Deficit Control Act,* commonly known as the Gramm-Rudman-Hollings Act, after its principal

FIGURE 22.5
Federal Revenues from Taxes
In 1994, the largest source of federal tax revenue was individual income taxes. Receipts are estimates for fiscal year 1994.   *(Source:* Statistical Abstract of the United States 1994, *114th ed., U.S. Department of Commerce, p. 331.)*

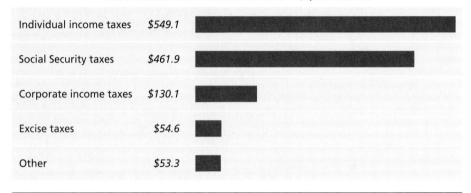

TOTAL FEDERAL REVENUES FOR 1994 — $1,249 BILLION

Individual income taxes	*$549.1*
Social Security taxes	*$461.9*
Corporate income taxes	*$130.1*
Excise taxes	*$54.6*
Other	*$53.3*

sponsors. The purpose of this act was to limit federal spending to total federal revenues. Then another piece of legislation, the Deficit Reduction Act of 1990, was enacted to replace the original Gramm-Rudman-Hollings Act. Since then, Congress has debated various pieces of legislation that could be used to limit spending and balance the federal budget. Since the ultimate goal of this type of legislation is to eliminate deficit spending, any act will either curtail government spending or lead to an increase in taxes. At the time of this book's publication, Congress had yet to pass a balanced budget amendment.

Individual Income Taxes   An individual's income tax liability is computed from his or her taxable income, which is gross income less various authorized deductions from income. In 1914, the federal government collected an average of 28 cents per taxpayer. Today that average is more than $2,100 per person.

The federal income tax is a progressive tax. A **progressive tax** requires the payment of an increasing proportion of income as the individual's income increases. For example, a single individual with a taxable income of $20,000 must currently pay a federal income tax of $3,004, or 15 percent of that taxable income. A single taxpayer with a taxable income of $40,000 must pay $8,250, or 21 percent of that income.

Taxpayers must file an annual tax return by April 15 of each year, for the previous calendar year. The return shows the income, deductions, and computations on which the taxpayer's tax liability is based.

Corporate Income Taxes   Corporate income taxes provide approximately 10 percent of total federal revenues. Corporations pay federal income tax only on their taxable income, which is what remains after deducting *all* legal business expenses from net sales. (This is net income before taxes, discussed in Chapter 17.) Currently, the federal corporate tax rate is

progressive tax   a tax that requires the payment of an increasing proportion of income as the individual's income increases

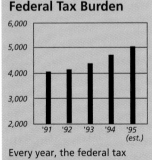

▶▶ A T   A   G L A N C E

Federal Tax Burden

Every year, the federal tax burden for the average American increases.
(Federal taxes, in dollars)

Source: Tax Foundation, *1995 Information Please Almanac, p. 47.*

Taxable income:	Tax is:
• Not over $50,000	15%
• Over $50,000 but not over $75,000	$7,500 + 25% of excess over $50,000

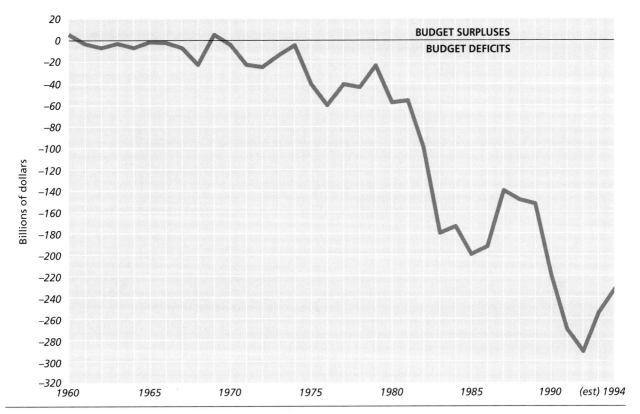

FIGURE 22.6   Federal Budgets—Surpluses and Deficits—1960–1994
The U.S. government has had budget deficits every year since 1960, except for 1969.
The budget deficit is estimated for 1994.   *(Source:* Statistical Abstract of the United
States 1994, *114th ed., U.S. Department of Commerce, p. 330.)*

- $75,000 but not over $100,000 $13,750 + 34% of excess over
                                            $75,000

- $100,000 but not over $335,000 $22,250 + 39% of excess over
                                            $100,000

- Special note: Corporate tax rates may increase or decrease depending
  on the amount of income in excess of $335,000.

Using the above tax rates, a corporation with a taxable income of $335,000
must pay a total of $113,900 to the federal government, as shown in
Table 22.2.

Other Federal Taxes   Additional sources of federal revenue include Social
Security, unemployment, and excise taxes, as well as customs duties. One
objective of all taxes is to raise money, but excise taxes and customs duties
are also designed to regulate the use of specific goods and services.

The second largest source of federal revenue is the *Social Security tax,*
which is collected under the Federal Insurance Contributions Act (FICA).

TABLE 22.2   Federal Corporate Income Tax on an Income of $335,000

According to the tax rate table, the tax is $22,250 + 39% of the excess over $100,000.

Step 1 Determine the excess over $100,000.

$335,000
− 100,000
$235,000

Step 2 Multiply the excess amount (step 1) by the tax rate (39%).
$235,000 × 0.39 = $91,650

Step 3 To determine the total tax, add the base amount to the additional tax determined in step 2.

$ 22,250
+ 91,650
$113,900

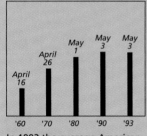
excise tax a tax on the manufacture or sale of a particular domestic product

This tax provides funding for retirement, disability, and death benefits for contributing employees. FICA taxes are paid by both the employer and the employee. The employee's share is withheld from his or her salary by the employer and sent to the federal government with the employer's share. The Social Security tax is broken into two components: (1) old age, survivors, and disability insurance and (2) Medicare. For old age, survivors, and disability insurance, the annual tax in 1995 is a total of 12.4 percent of the first $61,200 earned by an employee in 1995. For Medicare, the annual tax is a total of 2.9 percent on *all* wages an employee earns.

Under the provisions of the Federal Unemployment Tax Act (FUTA), employers must pay an *unemployment tax* equal to 6.2 percent of the first $7,000 of each employee's annual wages. Because employers are allowed credits against the 6.2 percent through participation in state unemployment programs, the actual unemployment rate paid by most employers is 0.8 percent. The tax is paid to the federal government to fund benefits for unemployed workers. Unlike the Social Security tax, the FUTA tax is levied only on employers.

An **excise tax** is a tax on the manufacture or sale of a particular domestic product. Excise taxes are used to help pay for government services directed toward the users of these products and, in some cases, to limit the use of potentially harmful products. For example, there are federal excise taxes on alcoholic beverages ($13.50 per gallon), cigarettes ($10 per 1,000), and gasoline (14.1 cents per gallon).[8] Alcohol and tobacco products are potentially harmful to consumers: they are taxed to raise the prices of these goods and thus discourage consumption. The federal excise tax on gasoline is a source of income that can be used to build and repair highways. Although manufacturers and retailers are responsible for paying excise taxes, these taxes are usually passed on to the consumer in the form of higher retail prices.

customs (or **import**) **duty** a tax on a particular foreign product entering a country

A **customs (or import) duty** is a tax on a particular foreign product entering a country. Import duties are designed to protect specific domestic industries by raising the prices of competing imported products. They are first paid by the importer, but the added costs are passed on to consumers through higher—and less competitive—prices.

State and Local Taxes

Like the federal government, state and local governments are financed primarily through taxes. As illustrated in Figure 22.7, sales taxes provide about 35 percent of state and local tax revenues. Most states and some cities also levy taxes on the incomes of individuals and businesses. Finally, many local and county governments also tax consumer sales, real estate, and some forms of personal property.

Sales Taxes   Sales taxes are levied by both states and cities and are paid by the purchasers of consumer products. Retailers collect sales taxes as a specified percentage of the price of each taxed product and then forward them to the taxing authority. A sales tax is a regressive tax. A **regressive tax** is one that takes a greater percentage of a lower income than of a higher income. The regressiveness of the sales tax stems from the fact that lower-income households generally spend a greater proportion of their income on taxable products such as food, clothing, and other essentials. Consider the impact of a 5 percent sales tax on food items purchased by a low-income family. A family that earns $10,000 a year and spends $3,000 on food will pay sales taxes of $150, or 1.5 percent of their total earnings. By comparison, a family that earns $40,000 a year and spends $5,000 on food will pay sales taxes of $250, or 0.625 percent of their total earnings. Not all states collect a sales tax on all items. In fact, many states exempt food from their sales tax.

regressive tax   a tax that takes a greater percentage of a lower income than of a higher income

Property Taxes   Many local governments use the property taxes that are levied on real estate and personal property owned by businesses and individuals to finance their ongoing activities.

FIGURE 22.7
Sources of Tax Revenues for State and Local Governments
Taxes are the primary source of revenues for state and local governments.   *(Source: Statistical Abstract of the United States 1994, U.S. Bureau of the Census, p. 302.)*

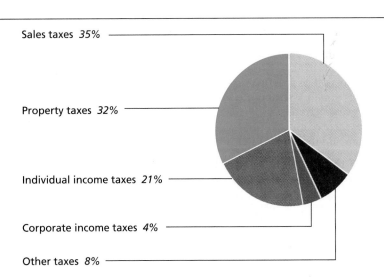

Sales taxes *35%*

Property taxes *32%*

Individual income taxes *21%*

Corporate income taxes *4%*

Other taxes *8%*

Real estate taxes are usually computed as a percentage of the assessed value of the real property. (The assessed value is determined by the local tax assessor as the fair market value of the property, a portion of its fair market value, or its replacement cost.) For example, suppose the city council has established a real estate tax rate of $2.10 per $100 of assessed valuation. Then the property tax bill for an office building with an assessed value of $200,000 will be $4,200 ($200,000 × $2.10/$100 = $4,200). This type of tax is called a proportional tax. A **proportional tax** is one whose percentage rate remains constant as the tax base increases. Therefore, if the tax rate remains constant at $2.10 per $100, a taxpayer who owns real estate valued at $10,000 pays $210 in taxes; a taxpayer who owns real estate valued at $100,000 pays $2,100 in taxes.

proportional tax a tax whose percentage rate remains constant as the tax base increases

Certain personal property owned by businesses and individuals is also subject to local taxation. For businesses, taxable personal property normally includes machinery, equipment, raw materials, and finished inventory. In some cases, local authorities also tax the value of stocks, bonds, mortgages, and promissory notes held by businesses. For individuals, such items as trucks, automobiles, and boats may be classified as personal property and taxed by local authorities.

In the next and final chapter of *Business*, we take a closer look at how you can apply the concepts presented in this text as you prepare to begin your own career.

■ ■ ■ ■ CHAPTER REVIEW

Summary

1 Explain how laws originate and how they are administered by courts.

In the United States, laws originate in judicial decisions (common law) and in the enactments of legislative bodies and government agencies (statutory law). An important body of statutory law is contained in the Uniform Commercial Code, which has been adopted with variations by all fifty states. Public law is concerned with the relationships between a society and its members. Private law is concerned with relationships among a society's members. To enforce both public and private laws, the United States has two separate and distinct court systems: the federal court system and the court systems of the fifty states.

2 Outline the requirements for a valid contract and the remedies for a broken contract.

A contract is a legally enforceable agreement. The conditions for a valid contract include voluntary agreement, consideration, the legal competence of all parties, subject matter that is legal, and proper contract form. A contract is usually terminated

through fulfillment of all obligations contained in the contract. Discharge by mutual assent occurs when all parties agree to void a contract. If one party to a contract does not fulfill its obligations, the other party may request the courts to discharge the contract, to award damages for nonperformance, or to require that the terms of the contract be fulfilled. A special type of contract is a sales agreement by which ownership is transferred from a seller to a buyer. Article 2 of the Uniform Commercial Code provides much of our sales law, including the difference between an express warranty and an implied warranty.

3 Explain how property law, negotiable instruments, the agent-principal relationship, and bankruptcy affect business firms.

Property is anything that can be owned and is classified as either real or personal. Real property is land and anything permanently attached to it. Personal property is all property other than real property. Personal property is also classified as either tangible or intangible. A negotiable instrument, the most common form of which is a check, is a written document that is a promise to pay a stated sum of money and can be transferred from one person or firm to another. An agency is a business relationship in which an agent acts on behalf of a principal. The principal is generally responsible for, and bound by, all actions of the agent. The agent is responsible for carrying out the instructions of the principal in a reasonable and professional manner. Bankruptcy laws are designed to protect either a person or a firm that cannot pay its debts and the creditors involved. Bankruptcy proceedings may be initiated by either the creditors (involuntary) or the person or firm that cannot cover its liabilities (voluntary). Bankruptcy proceedings may be resolved through liquidation of the debtor's assets (Chapter 7), reorganization of the bankrupt firm (Chapter 11), or repayment of specific debts incurred by a bankrupt individual (Chapter 13).

4   Discuss how federal, state, and local government laws and regulations affect the day-to-day operation of a business.

Congress passed the Sherman Antitrust Act in 1890 as a means of restoring a reasonable level of competition within industries that had become dominated by trusts. Later antitrust legislation was intended mainly to close loopholes in previous laws. Enforcement of these laws is the responsibility of the Federal Trade Commission and the U.S. Justice Department. In addition to antitrust regulations, a large number of other government regulations at the federal, state, and local level that affect day-to-day business operations are discussed in other chapters in this text.

5   Analyze the current government deregulation movement.

Government regulation extends to a wide range of business activities, and compliance can be very costly. Regulation increased from the 1930s through the 1970s. A period of deregulation followed, which has lasted more than twenty years and may continue. There is, however, a question as to how much regulation—or deregulation—is most effective in maintaining orderly markets. Many politicians and consumers argue that further deregulation could result in inferior products, dangerous working conditions, polluted air, increased bank failures, and other problems that were prevalent during the 1980s and first part of the 1990s.

6   Describe the ways in which government can assist business firms.

Government supports business by providing information and assistance to business, by funding much of the research that leads to new products and jobs, and by purchasing goods and services that businesses produce. At the same time, government regulates business activity in such a way as to promote competition and protect the interests of consumers.

7   Identify the various taxes through which federal, state, and local governments are financed.

Federal, state, and local governments finance their activities primarily by collecting taxes. Taxes may be progressive, regressive, or proportional. For the federal government, individual income taxes are the major source of funding. Other sources include corporate income, Social Security, unemployment, excise, and customs taxes. Sales taxes, which are levied on purchases of consumer goods, provide the largest portion of state and local tax revenues. In addition, state and local governments obtain revenues from taxes on property, individual income, corporate income, and other taxable property.

Key Terms

You should now be able to define and give an example relevant to each of the following terms:

law (706)
common law (706)
statute (706)
statutory law (706)
Uniform Commercial Code (UCC) (707)
administrative law (707)
public law (708)
crime (708)
private law (708)
tort (708)
negligence (708)
court of original jurisdiction (709)
appellate court (711)
court of limited jurisdiction (711)
contract (711)
voluntary agreement (712)
consideration (712)
usury (713)
performance (714)
breach of contract (714)
discharge by mutual assent (714)
damages (714)
specific performance (714)
sales agreement (714)

express warranty (715)

implied warranty (715)

property (715)

real property (715)

personal property (716)

patent (716)

copyright (716)

deed (717)

lease (717)

negotiable instrument (717)

endorsement (718)

agency (719)

power of attorney (719)

bankruptcy (719)

voluntary bankruptcy (719)

involuntary bankruptcy (719)

trust (721)

price fixing (723)

market allocation (723)

boycott in restraint of trade (723)

price discrimination (723)

tying agreement (723)

binding contract (723)

interlocking directorate (723)

community of interests (723)

Federal Trade Commission (FTC) (723)

deregulation (725)

budget deficit (731)

progressive tax (732)

excise tax (734)

customs (or import) duty (734)

regressive tax (735)

proportional tax (736)

Questions

Review Questions

1. What are the differences between common law and statutory law?
2. What is the difference between a crime and a tort? How does the law punish those who commit crimes? torts?
3. What are the three levels of courts in the federal and state court systems? What kinds of cases are heard at each level?
4. List and describe the conditions for a legally enforceable contract.

5. When a contract is breached, what remedies are available to the injured party or parties?
6. What are the differences between an express and an implied warranty? What does an implied warranty imply?
7. How does real property differ from personal property? Give a specific example of real property, intangible personal property, and tangible personal property, all owned by an independent service station.
8. What requirements must be met for a financial instrument to be negotiable? Why is negotiability important?
9. Identify the three types of endorsements discussed in this chapter. Explain the advantages and disadvantages of each.
10. What is the relationship between an agent and a principal?
11. Briefly describe the three means of resolving a bankruptcy case under current bankruptcy law.
12. How do federal antitrust regulations work to support American business?
13. In your own words define the following:
    a. Price fixing
    b. Market allocation
    c. Boycott in restraint of trade
14. The Clayton Act specifically prohibits five practices. List these practices and briefly explain how each weakens competition.
15. What principal reasons propelled the deregulation movement? What forces may slow it down?
16. In what ways does government provide assistance or support to business?
17. Which single tax provides the largest amount of income for the federal government? for state and local government?

Discussion Questions

1. What services does Jenny Craig, Inc., offer its clients?
2. Most likely, more women than men use the services of Jenny Craig weight-loss centers. What reasons would the Jenny Craig corporation give for employing more women than men? Why might women be more successful than men?
3. Why should the law specifically require written contracts for exchanges of real estate, sales over $500, and long-term obligations?
4. Suppose you are a party to a contract that has been breached by the other party. Under what circumstances would you sue for discharge? for damages? for specific performance?

5. Assume that you are the owner of a small business, and you must choose an agent to purchase a piece of real estate on your behalf. What specific conditions should be included in your contract of agency? Why?

6. In your opinion, is there a social stigma attached to bankruptcy today? Should there be?

7. What benefits and what problems might result from the requirement that the FTC and the Justice Department approve mergers before they take place?

8. How might legislators and regulatory agencies determine whether deregulation is needed in a particular area? How might they determine where additional regulation is needed?

9. Are budget deficits necessary, harmful, or both? Do you believe that a balanced budget amendment would eliminate deficit spending?

Exercises

1. Find two or more articles describing a recent court case that involved two or more businesses.
   a. State the exact nature of the issue or issues involved in the case.
   b. Describe how these issues were resolved.
   c. State whether the resolution seems fair, and justify your answer.

2. Draw up a standard contract form for a company that sells and installs burglar alarm systems in homes. The average cost of the alarm system, including installation, is $750. Include everything required for a valid contract.

3. Outline a plan for the removal of all graduation requirements (other than the number of credit hours required) at your school over the next two years. List three advantages and three disadvantages of such deregulation.

4. Suppose a certain state levies a 6 percent sales tax on all consumer products. Develop, in detail, a method for modifying the sales tax to make it less regressive. Explain how your method would be applied, and show that your tax would actually be less regressive than the present tax.

VIDEO CASE 22.1

The City of Indianapolis and KPMG Peat Marwick Join Forces to Eliminate Government Waste

What does it cost to fill a pothole? To change a bulb in a streetlight? To paint a white line down the middle of

a street? Although it would seem that any elected official or government employee should be able to answer such questions, in reality, most can't. Even in Indianapolis—a city that today is recognized as one of the most efficient in the nation—the questions would have gone unanswered until a few years ago. That's when Mayor Steven Goldsmith began exploring methods that would ultimately transform Indianapolis into a city that is run like a business. In his search for ways to reduce costs and make Indianapolis more entrepreneurial, Mayor Goldsmith eventually sought the help of KPMG Peat Marwick, one of the nation's six largest accounting firms.

The resulting three-way partnership between elected officials, government employees, and the accounting professionals at KPMG Peat Marwick has developed a state-of-the-art program designed to use available tax dollars more effectively. To develop this program, one of the first moves by the people at KPMG Peat Marwick was to implement an activity-based costing (often referred to simply as ABC) system. Although activity-based costing has been used by Boeing, Procter & Gamble, IBM, Dell Computer, Weyerhaeuser, and dozens of other large, successful U.S. corporations, its implementation by state and local governments is unusual.

The purpose of an ABC system, whether it is used by business or government, is to determine *all* of the costs associated with providing a product or service. Although traditional accounting systems examine costs, an ABC system digs deeper into hidden costs. For example, when determining the cost of street repairs for a city like Indianapolis, ABC looks not only at the obvious cash outlay required to repair a pothole, but also at the hidden cost of depreciation, overhead, and other expenses that governments traditionally do not measure.

Armed with information about the "true" cost of city services, Indianapolis officials could now decide whether it was more cost-effective to hire government employees or contract with outside private business firms to provide needed services. Some services, like the sewer billing function and window washing, went to private firms. Other services, including street repair, went to government employees who were willing to compete with the private business firms in order to keep their jobs.

Was the ABC system used by Indianapolis successful? You bet! Within two years, the city had saved more than $100 million by using KPMG Peat Marwick's ABC system. According to Mayor Goldsmith, costs are down *and* the city is providing more value-added services to the people of Indianapolis than it did two years ago.[9]

Questions

1. How can an activity-based costing system like the one that KPMG Peat Marwick introduced in Indianapolis help a state or local government become more cost-effective?
2. Steven Goldsmith, the mayor of Indianapolis, wants to run his city like a business. Do you believe that a city *should* be run like a business? Explain your answer.

CASE 22.2

Vlases v. *Montgomery Ward*

In this chapter, we discussed the basic principles of law that affect business transactions. Now it is your turn to apply those same principles. Here is the outline of a simple but typical court case.

> Plaintiff (Vlases) purchased 2,000 chickens from defendant (Montgomery Ward) to start a chicken-raising business. After a few weeks, the chickens showed signs of illness and were found to be suffering from avian leukosis, or bird cancer. Plaintiff brought a legal action based upon breach of implied warranties against the defendant. The defendant contended that there was no way of detecting the disease in baby chicks, and expert testimony bore this out. The defendant's position was that the birds might have contracted the disease after the sale was completed. The jury in the original court case returned a verdict in favor of the plaintiff. The defendant appealed.

Before you read on, put yourself in the position of the appeals court judge by answering the following questions.

Questions

1. Does the principle of implied warranty apply in this case? Explain.
2. Should the lower-court decision be upheld or reversed? Why?

In its decision, the appeals court judge noted that two implied warranties were involved: (1) the implied warranty of merchantability and (2) the implied warranty of fitness for a particular purpose. According to the court, the purpose of the implied warranty sections of the Uniform Commercial Code is to hold the seller responsible when inferior goods are passed along to an unsuspecting buyer. And the seller is responsible if the delivered goods are not salable or fit for their particular purpose. The seller's inability to detect the disease had no bearing on that responsibility; only the quality of the goods was of importance. The lower-court verdict was upheld.[10]

CHAPTER 23

Careers in Business

LEARNING OBJECTIVES

After studying this chapter you should be able to

1 Describe the factors that influence your career choice.

2 Identify trends in employment in today's changing job market.

3 Summarize occupational search activities used to find career opportunities.

4 Prepare a cover letter and résumé.

5 Identify the types of questions that are asked on employment applications.

6 Describe the interview process.

7 Summarize the factors that lead to career growth and advancement.

CHAPTER PREVIEW

In this chapter, we examine the factors that influence your career choices. We also look at trends in employment and at some methods that you can use to find job opportunities. Next we focus on the tools you can use to get a job: application letters, résumés, employment applications, and job interviews. Finally, we look at what it takes to be successful in today's changing job market.◣

741

Reality 101: Transition from College to Career

What a feeling! Clarence Wainwright finally made it! Four years of college courses, studying, and exams. Six months of job searching, writing letters and résumés, and preparing for interviews. And now, the work has finally paid off! After advancing through several interviews with the McKenna Corporation, Clarence has been offered a position and begins his new job three weeks after graduation. To ensure that the transition from college to the world of work is a smooth one, Clarence should keep the following pointers in mind.

First, Clarence was hired for his ability and the skills he learned in college. But in order to perform at his best and become the professional he envisions himself to be, he should not be afraid to ask questions. More important, he must learn to *listen* to what others have to say. Also, the image Clarence projects to others will be important to his success. His positive, businesslike manner can be demonstrated to others through his appearance and body language.

Second, every morning for the first few weeks of Clarence's new job will be exciting. But once he settles into the routine of his work environment, he may find himself feeling confined, doing the same thing at least eight hours a day, five days a week. Clarence will need to learn patience and look for ways to make his job more interesting. If he partied on a Wednesday night while he was in college, he could sleep in the next morning and miss a class and no one minded or cared. But that attitude doesn't work in the real world. A company expects its employees to be on time every day—not just when they feel like showing up.

Third, throughout Clarence's college years, he usually associated with people who were like him-

self with similar tastes and ideas. Now he will meet individuals of all ages, with different personalities, lifestyles, and backgrounds. In order to be a productive team member, it will be imperative for Clarence to keep an open mind and learn how to get along with others.

Fourth, in the real world, getting ahead is dependent on how employees manage their long-term relationships with their supervisors. It is critical that Clarence begin on a positive note by immediately adapting his work habits to the management style of his supervisor.

Clarence will begin his new position at the bottom of the organization chart. As he moves up the ladder to success, he will discover that employers want employees who not only do what is expected, but who also perform above and beyond what their job description calls for. It is up to Clarence to use this opportunity to gain all the experience he can, learn how to get along with a diverse assortment of people, and handle every assignment to the best of his ability.[1]

■ ■ ■ ■

742

■ ■ ■ ■ ■ ■ ■ ■ ■ ■ ■

Words like *excited, challenged, scared,* and *frustrated* have been used to describe someone involved in a job search. But the reality is that everyone who is employed must have looked for a job at one time or another, and survived. Clarence Wainwright, the individual profiled in Inside Business, spent six months searching for his first job. Now, Wainwright must make the transition from college to the world of work. Although first-time employees like Wainwright often think they will work for the same company for their entire career, most people change jobs and even careers during their lifetime. In fact, according to the Bureau of Labor Statistics, today's job applicants will change jobs over ten times during their career. And by the year 2000, graduates will experience at least four complete career changes. Therefore, the employment information that follows will be of lasting value. Let's begin our discussion with a look at the factors affecting an individual's career choices.

■ ■ THE IMPORTANCE OF CAREER CHOICES

LEARNING OBJECTIVE 1
Describe the factors that
influence your career choice.

Most people think that career planning begins with an up-to-date résumé and a job interview. In reality, it begins long before you prepare your résumé. It starts with *you* and what you want to become. In some ways, you have been preparing for a career since you started school back in the first grade. Everything that you have experienced during your lifetime you can now use as a resource to help define your career goals. Let's start with a basic assumption: it's likely that you will spend more time at work than at any other single place during your lifetime. It therefore makes sense to spend those hours doing something you enjoy. Unfortunately, some people just work at a *job* because they need money to survive. Other people choose a *career* because there is a commitment not only to a profession but also to their own interests and talents. Whether you are looking for a job or a career, you should examine your own priorities. Before reading the next section, you may want to evaluate your priorities by completing the exercise in Figure 23.1.

Personal Factors Influencing Career Choices

Before you choose your career or job, you need to have a pretty good idea what motivates you and what skills you can offer an employer. The following four questions may help you further refine what you consider to be important in life.

1. *What types of activities do you enjoy?* This question could be asked another way: what excites you? Although most people know what they enjoy in a general way, a number of interest inventories exist, which

743

FIGURE 23.1
Which Priorities Are Important to You?
Look over the following list of job and personal variables. In the left-hand column, number them in order of current priority to you. Now, renumber them in the right-hand column based on the priorities you anticipate having five or ten years down the road. *(Source: Susan D. Greene and Melanie C. L. Martel,* The Job Hunter's Guidebook *[Boston: Houghton Mifflin, 1992], p. 10.)*

PRIORITIES NOW	JOB AND PERSONAL VARIABLES	PRIORITIES IN 5 TO 10 YEARS
_____	Salary	_____
_____	Family (children/spouse/parents)	_____
_____	Personal time	_____
_____	Job location	_____
_____	Work-related travel	_____
_____	Potential for advancement	_____
_____	Commuting time	_____
_____	Friendly coworkers/boss	_____
_____	Job responsibilities	_____
_____	Personal hobbies	_____
_____	Prestige	_____
_____	Benefits	_____
_____	Vacation time	_____
_____	Retirement plan	_____
_____	Security/stability	_____

▷▷ **AT A GLANCE**

Job Choice Criteria

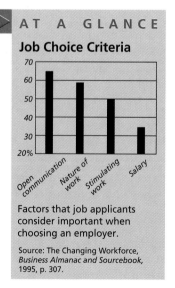

Factors that job applicants consider important when choosing an employer.

Source: The Changing Workforce, *Business Almanac and Sourcebook,* 1995, p. 307.

can help you determine specific interests and activities that can help you land a job leading to a satisfying career. In some cases, it may help just to list the interests or activities you enjoy, along with those you dislike. Watch for patterns that may influence your career choices.

2. *What do you do best?* All jobs in all careers require employees to be able to "do something." It is extremely important to assess what you do best. Be honest with yourself about your ability to succeed in a specific job. It may help to make a list of your strongest job-related skills. Also try looking at your skills from an employer's perspective. What can you do that an employer would be willing to pay for?

3. *What kind of education will you need?* The amount of education you need is determined by the type of career you choose. In some careers, it is impossible to get an entry-level position without at least a college degree. In other careers, technical or hands-on skills are more important than formal education. Generally, more education increases your potential earning power, as illustrated in Figure 23.2.

4. *Where do you want to live?* When you enter the job market, you may want to move to a different part of the country. According to the *Occupational Outlook Handbook,* the western and southern sections of the United States will experience the greatest population increase between now and the year 2000. The population in the midwestern section of the country will stay about the same, whereas the northeastern section will decrease slightly in population. These population changes will affect job prospects in each of those areas.

■ ■ ■ ■ ■ ENHANCING CAREER SKILLS

Handling Job Stress

You may think you are "exempt" from job stress, but are you? Management experts warn that stress is a much bigger problem today than most people think. In fact, stress is an unavoidable part of any job worth having. And although low productivity, high absenteeism, and frequent job changes are its most obvious symptoms, many workers suffer in silence.

Reducing job stress is difficult, but it can be done. And the people who are most successful are the ones who tackle the problem head on. Experts suggest that you begin by sitting down and analyzing each part of your job to isolate the specific causes of stress. Next, take specific steps—like those described below—to reduce the amount of stress you experience.

1. *Take charge.* Research indicates that people experience less job stress when they can identify what needs to be done and then follow specific steps to complete each task.

2. *Learn to work smarter.* Before starting your workday, take the time to plan the tasks that you want to accomplish. List important tasks on a "to-do" list; then when each task is completed, check it off.

3. *Share your problems with a friend.* Frequent talks with a friend or relative can provide an outlet for the stress you experience on the job. After explaining why you feel pressure on the job, ask for suggestions that you can use to reduce stress.

4. *Exercise on a regular basis.* Physical activity like jogging, walking, cycling, or swimming at least three times a week provides a change of pace and can reduce stress. Some people think you have to join a health club, but of course there are many other options: take a physical education course at a local college, join a tennis league at a public recreation center, or just walk at a climate-controlled shopping mall.

5. *Reward yourself for a job well done.* Once you have completed a difficult task, treat yourself to something special that is not part of your regular routine. Sometimes referred to as the carrot-and-stick approach, the promise of a dinner at your favorite restaurant, a weekend trip, or just a movie or a play can provide a pleasing incentive. Also, purchasing a new dress, shirt, or tie for yourself can serve as a reward for a job well done.

Finally, don't underestimate the connection between medical problems (heart attacks, high blood pressure, ulcers and stomach disorders, and more) and job stress. If all else fails, you may find that it is necessary to change jobs or even careers. Above all, take care of yourself and make sure that you don't become a victim of job stress. (For additional help with reducing job stress, you may want to read Enhancing Career Skills, "Managing a Scarce Resource: Your Time," on page 760.)

Before entering the job market, most people think they are free to move any place they want. In reality, job applicants may be forced to move to the town, city, or metropolitan area that has jobs available. Each of the ten cities listed in Table 23.1 received high scores not only on the economy factor but also on other factors that influence the overall quality of life for those who do obtain jobs there.

FIGURE 23.2
Education and Income
For most Americans, the average income they earn is tied to the number of years of education they have obtained. *(Source:* Statistical Abstract of the United States, *1994, p. 465.)*

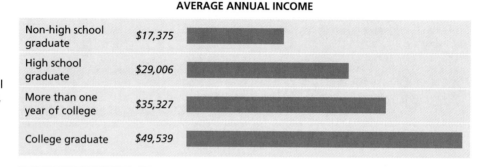

AVERAGE ANNUAL INCOME

Non-high school graduate	$17,375
High school graduate	$29,006
More than one year of college	$35,327
College graduate	$49,539

Trends in Employment

LEARNING OBJECTIVE 2
Identify trends in employment in today's changing job market.

Overall, the American work force is expected to increase by 22 percent by the year 2005. As you look ahead to your own career, you should consider the effects that the trends described below will have on employment and employment opportunities.

- Jobs in service industries will account for a larger proportion of total employment.
- Training—and retraining—will become increasingly important as firms require their employees to use the latest technology. Good jobs will require strong educational qualifications.

TABLE 23.1   The Best Places to Live
According to *Money* magazine the following ten cities are the best places to live in the United States. (*Note:* the higher the numbers in the table, the higher the ranking.)

	Health	Crime	Economy	Housing	Education	Transit	Weather	Leisure	Arts
1. Raleigh/Durham/Chapel Hill, North Carolina	88	20	93	88	95	41	38	4	28
2. Rochester, Minnesota	96	63	71	43	97	81	14	25	26
3. Provo/Orem, Utah	59	58	79	61	41	58	29	37	22
4. Salt Lake City/ Ogden, Utah	72	27	81	75	51	40	26	35	22
5. San Jose, California	82	35	37	25	40	27	83	93	91
6. Stamford/Norwalk, Connecticut	86	53	74	40	14	18	28	88	100
7. Gainesville, Florida	45	4	92	49	45	45	79	5	22
8. Seattle, Washington	79	20	67	28	62	28	47	94	52
9. Sioux Falls, South Dakota	71	54	96	43	6	75	9	2	14
10. Albuquerque, New Mexico	61	13	63	94	36	42	43	23	17

Source: Reprinted from the September, 1994, issue of *Money* by special permission; copyright © 1994, Time Inc.

Computer skills are a must for this job. Can you imagine trying to "map" population trends without a computer? Here an employee—with the help of a computer—determines which sections of a major metropolitan area are increasing in population, and which are decreasing.

- Automation of factories and offices will create new types of jobs. Many of these will be computer-related.
- The number of women, two-income families, and older workers in the work force will increase.
- There will be a greater emphasis on job sharing, flexible hours, and other innovative work practices to accommodate employees. In some cases, employees will be able to complete assignments at home on remote computer terminals.

College graduates with majors in business and management, computer science, education, engineering, and health professions will also be in high demand, according to human resources experts. There will be fewer manufacturing jobs, and those that remain will require high-tech skills.

The types of new jobs that will be created during the next decade or so will be related to technological advances and to the growth in the health professions and service industries. What specific jobs are expected to increase between now and the year 2005? According to a survey by the *Occupational Outlook Quarterly,* home health aides will be in greatest demand, followed closely by human services workers. Table 23.2 lists projections for the thirty fastest-growing U.S. occupations that will provide the best opportunities for employment.

■■ OCCUPATIONAL SEARCH ACTIVITIES

LEARNING OBJECTIVE 3
Summarize occupational search activities used to find career opportunities.

When most people begin to search for a job they immediately think of the classified ads in the local newspaper. Those ads are an important source of

TABLE 23.2   Fastest-Growing U.S. Occupations

Occupations Growing Much Faster Than Average	Percentage Increase in Employment, 1992–2005
Home health aides	138%
Human services workers	136
Personal and home care aides	130
Computer engineers and scientists	112
Systems analysts	110
Physical and corrective therapy assistants and aides	93
Physical therapists	88
Paralegals	86
Teachers, special education	74
Medical assistants	71
Corrections officers	70
Detectives except public	70
Travel agents	66
Childcare workers	66
Radiologic technologists and technicians	63
Nursery workers	62
Medical records technicians	61
Operations research analysts	61
Occupational therapists	60
Legal secretaries	57
Manicurists	54
Producers, directors, actors, and entertainers	54
Teachers, preschool and kindergarten	54
Flight attendants	51
Speech-language pathologists and audiologists	51
Guards	51
Insurance adjusters, examiners, and investigators	49
Respiratory therapists	48
Psychologists	48
Paving, surfacing, and tamping equipment operators	48

Source: *Occupational Outlook Quarterly*, Fall 1993, p. 38.

information about jobs in your particular area, but they are only one source. Many other sources can lead to employment and a satisfying career. As illustrated in Figure 23.3, there is a wealth of information about career planning. Therefore, you must be selective in both the type and the amount of information you use to guide your job search.

The four sources described below can be *especially* useful when trying to find the "perfect" job for you.

1. *Campus placement offices.* Colleges and universities have placement offices staffed by trained personnel specialists. In most cases, these offices serve as clearinghouses for career information. The staff may also be able to guide you in creating your résumé and preparing for your job interview.

FIGURE 23.3
Career Information Sources
Career information is available from the library, campus placement offices, professional sources, and employment agencies.

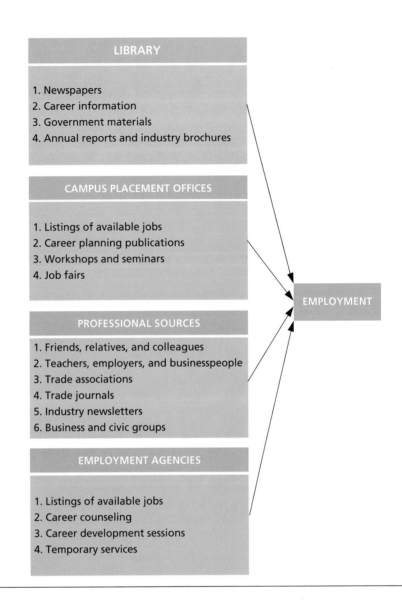

2. *Networks of friends and professionals.* A network is a group of friends, relatives, and professionals who are in a position to exchange information (including job openings) in your field of business. The National Self-Help Clearinghouse estimates that 15 million Americans are involved in some form of networking.[2] And according to many job applicants, networking is one of the best sources of career information and job leads. Start with as many people as you can think of to establish your initial network. Contact these individuals and ask specific questions about job opportunities that they may be aware of. Also, ask each of these individuals to introduce you or refer you to someone else who may be able to help you continue your job search.

Help is available. Looking for a job and planning a career can be among the most difficult and lonely experiences in a person's life. But job seekers are not as alone as they once were. One source of help is a college's or university's campus placement office. Here a trained personnel specialist helps a job applicant plan an occupational search.

For networking to work, you must continue this process. Remember that you must follow all leads. Even if you have referrals and introductions, *you* must still "get" the job. Finally, remember to thank the people who have helped you.

3. *Private employment agencies.* Private employment agencies charge a fee for helping people to find jobs. Typical fees can be as high as 15 to 20 percent of an employee's first-year salary. The fee may be paid by the employer or the employee. Like college placement offices, private employment agencies provide career counseling, help create résumés, and provide preparation for job interviews. Before you use a private employment agency, be sure that you understand the terms of any contract or agreement you sign. Above all, make sure you know who is responsible for paying the agency's fee.

4. *State employment agencies.* Another source of information about job openings in your immediate area is the local office of your state employment agency. Some job applicants are reluctant to use state agencies because the majority of jobs available through these agencies are for semiskilled or unskilled workers. From a practical standpoint, it can't hurt to consult state employment agencies. They will have information about some professional and managerial positions available in your area, and you will not be charged a fee if you obtain a job through a state employment agency.

Many people want a job immediately and are discouraged at the thought of an occupational search taking months. But in fact people seeking entry-level jobs should expect that their job search will take three to six months. Those job applicants that want higher-paying positions can expect to be looking for work for as long as a year, eighteen months, or more.[3] Of course, the state of the economy and whether employers are hiring or not can shorten or extend a job search for anyone.

Regardless of how long it takes, most people will tell you that a job search always takes too long. During a job search, you should use the same effective work habits that employees use on the job. When searching for a job, resist the temptation to "take the day off." Instead, make a master list of activities that you want to accomplish each day. If necessary, force yourself to make contacts, do job research, or schedule interviews that might lead to job opportunities. (Actually, many job applicants look at the job hunt as their job and work from eight to five, five days a week until they find the job they want.) Above all, realize that an occupational search requires patience and perseverance. And according to many individuals who have been through the process of trying to find a job, perseverance may be the most important trait that successful job-hunters need.

n n YOUR FUTURE IN BUSINESS

It is generally agreed that competition for the better jobs will get tougher and tougher. The key to landing the job you want is planning and preparation—and planning begins with goals. In particular, it is important to determine your *personal* goals, to decide on the role your career will play in reaching those goals, and then to develop your career goals. Once you know where you are going, you can devise a reasonable plan for getting there.

The time to begin planning is as early as possible. The career profiles at the ends of each part of this book can be helpful. You must, of course, satisfy the educational requirements for the occupational area you wish to enter. Early planning will give you the opportunity to do so. But those people with whom you will be competing for the better jobs will also be fully prepared. Can you do more?

The answer is yes. Corporate recruiters say that the following factors give job candidates a definite advantage.

- *Work experience*—You can get valuable work experience in cooperative work/school programs, during summer vacations, or in part-time jobs during the school year. Experience in your chosen occupational area carries the most weight, but even unrelated work experience is important.
- *The ability to communicate well*—Verbal and written communication skills are increasingly important in all aspects of business. Yours will be tested in your letters to recruiters, in your résumé, and in interviews. You will use these same communication skills throughout your career.
- *Clear and realistic job and career goals*—Recruiters feel most comfortable with candidates who know where they are headed and why they

are applying for a specific job. Women in particular must develop clear and realistic career goals if they want to break through the so-called glass ceiling, as you can see in Business Journal.

Here again, early planning can make all the difference in defining your goals; in sharpening your communication skills (through elective courses, if necessary); and in obtaining solid work experience.

Letter and Résumé

Preparation becomes important again when it is time to apply for a position. Your college placement office and various publications (including such directories as *Standard & Poor's Register of Corporations* and *Thomas Register*) can help you find firms to apply to for jobs. As already mentioned, help-wanted ads, networking, and employment agencies may also provide leads.

Your first contact with a prospective employer will probably be through the mail—in a letter in which you express your interest in working for that firm. This letter should be clear and straightforward, and it should follow proper business-letter form—see Figure 23.4. It (and any other letters you write to potential employers) will be considered part of your employment credentials.

This first letter should be addressed to the personnel or human resources manager, by name if possible. You may include in this letter, very briefly, some information regarding your qualifications and your reason for writing to that particular firm. If your source of information (newspaper advertisement, employment agency, current employee of the firm, and so on) indicates that this employer is looking for specific job skills, you may also want to state and describe in the cover letter the skills you possess. You should request an interview and, if the firm requires it, an employment application.

You should include a copy of your résumé with your first letter. (Most applicants do.) In any case, you should already have prepared the résumé, which is a summary of all your attention-getting employment achievements and capabilities. Your goal in preparing both the cover letter and the résumé is to give the potential employer the impression that you are someone who deserves an interview.

A résumé should highlight and summarize your abilities and work achievements. The résumé should fit on a single sheet of white, high-quality, bond letter paper. It should be carefully thought out—rework it as many times as necessary to get it right and put your best foot forward. Make your résumé concise, but be sure to note everything important. You need not include explanations or details; you will have an opportunity to discuss your qualifications during the interviews. It should be written to grab a potential employer's interest. The employer reading your résumé should want to meet you to find out more. Your résumé needs to show that, despite your current job title, you are qualified for the higher-level position you seek.

Remember that you are writing a résumé that will sell you to a potential employer. If necessary, ask former supervisors and colleagues to tell you what happened to projects or work that you produced. Then use action verbs to describe your major contributions. Words such as *managed, created,*

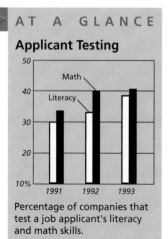

▷▷ **AT A GLANCE**

Applicant Testing

Percentage of companies that test a job applicant's literacy and math skills.

Source: American Management Association, *Business Almanac and Sourcebook,* 1995, p. 289.

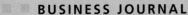

Women Moving Up Through the Glass Ceiling

Women executives and women who want to be executives face many obstacles. One particular difficulty is moving up through the "glass ceiling." The term *glass ceiling* refers to an imaginary barrier that separates women from top-management positions. According to an eighteen-month U.S. Labor Department study, the height of the glass ceiling varies from one company to the next, but it is often not much higher than entry level for women employees.

BARRIERS TO PROMOTION

According to the results of the Labor Department study, women are passed over for promotions to higher-level managerial positions for the following specific reasons:

1. Lack of early managerial training for prospective female managers.

2. Corporate recruiting practices that rely on word-of-mouth referrals from male managers, who recommend other males.

3. The use of executive search firms, sometimes referred to as *headhunters*, who fail to pursue qualified female managerial candidates.

4. The fact that female managers have often been passed over or have not volunteered for high-visibility projects that provide both exposure and the broad range of experience needed by the organization.

WHAT YOU CAN DO TO BREAK THROUGH

Today, more women than ever before are tapping on the glass ceiling, but to really break through, experts offer the following advice.

1. *Know where you want to go.* A woman manager who has clear-cut career goals is more likely to develop a strategy to obtain those goals. Simply put, where do you want to be in five or ten years?

2. *Evaluate your company.* What type of opportunities does your company offer women managers? Many large companies promote "just enough" women managers to be "respectable." If you feel your company doesn't provide equal career opportunities, you may want to begin searching for a new job with another employer. Many women have found that smaller, more entrepreneurial companies offer the best chance for advancement.

3. *Make sure you are in the loop.* Today, managers refer to anyone who is in the know as a person who is in "the loop." Are you invited to attend important meetings? Do managers ask for your advice? Do you receive feedback from suggestions you have made? If not, you should *tactfully* let your immediate supervisor know that you want to attend important meetings, are available to give advice, and expect feedback on your suggestions. In other words, put yourself in the loop.

4. *Find a mentor.* A mentor is a person who will "coach" you in ways that will help develop your career. A mentor can serve as a valuable role model or counselor, or can simply provide support. According to experts, mentoring may be the best way for women to fight the "old-boy network" that prevails in many organizations.

SHATTERING THE GLASS CEILING

Some women do indeed break through the glass ceiling and become important assets to their companies. Women are especially successful in high-tech, high-growth industries, where they seem to be promoted more quickly than in other fields. The publishing industry also has a history of being receptive to women executives. Health services, social services, the retail clothing business, and education have large numbers of women in executive positions. Certain other industries—such as steel, railroads, and mining—have a disproportionately low number of women in top management.

FIGURE 23.4
Letter of Application
A letter of application should give your qualifications and your reasons for applying to a given company.   *(Source: Adapted from Herb Rinehard and Bruce Moncrieff, "Résumé Preparation Guide," 6th printing, p. 21. College of DuPage, Glen Ellyn, Ill.)*

16 Wescott Lane
Collinsville, IL 62547

January 6, 1995

Mr. Clifford J. Ehrlich
Senior Vice President – Human Resources
Marriot Corporation
10400 Fernwood Road
Bethesda, MD 20058

Dear Mr. Ehrlich:

I am sending this letter and résumé in application for the position of Banquet Manager with your corporation. I think you will find my qualifications very compatible with those that you listed in the Hotel and Motel Journal.

For the last three years, I have been very excited about and involved in the restaurant training program at College of DuPage in Glen Ellyn, Illinois. Under the direction of George Macht, restaurant training coordinator, I became involved in both on- and off-campus educational experiences. After obtaining basic skills in the food service area, I supplemented my experience at various clubs, civic organizations, and trade shows (NRA). I feel confident that my practical experiences coupled with my educational background have well prepared me for the position you have available.

My interest in Marriot Corporation began years ago when Marriot's fine reputation was discussed in classes and has continued through my own dining experiences. I recognized your interest in cultivating good employees when I read about your six-month management training program. This program seems well designed to provide just the right exposure to the total operation of your banquet facility.

I would appreciate the opportunity to visit with you and further explain some of the information contained in the enclosed résumé. I'll be giving you a call within the next week to see if you have a few minutes to spend with me.

Sincerely yours,

Helen DeCarlis

Helen DeCarlis

Enclosure

developed, or *coordinated* sound high-powered. Passive words or phrases such as *was responsible for* or *performed* are not attention getting. Highlight your work achievements by using percentages, numbers, or dollar amounts. Such concrete details demonstrate just how important your contributions were. In some cases, personal traits or the ability to "do something" may be more important than technical skills. Employers may be looking for someone who has the ability to

1. Prepare letters, memos, and other written communications.
2. Answer the telephone and talk with customers.
3. Analyze and solve problems related to a specific job.
4. Work independently and make decisions.
5. Be flexible and get the job done.
6. Get along with others and be a team player.

These traits may be extremely important to some employers. And a job applicant who doesn't have a lot of occupational experience can use these traits to "beef up" a slim résumé.

Figure 23.5 shows an old-style résumé and a new-style résumé. Notice the new-style résumé highlights the applicant's job experience with action verbs. Regardless of the form used, a résumé should include the following: your name, address, and telephone number; your work experience and major accomplishments on the job; your educational background; and any awards you have won. Avoid all extraneous information (such as weight, age, marital status, and the names and addresses of references) that could be supplied during an interview. So that the "Employment" category gets top billing, place "Education" at the bottom of the résumé, along with awards entries. Reserve your employment and/or career objectives for mention in the one-page cover letters you send to potential employers with copies of your résumé.

Job Applications

LEARNING OBJECTIVE 5
Identify the types of questions that are asked on employment applications.

Once you have mailed your cover letter and résumé, the next step generally depends on the employer. Most interested prospective employers will ask that you complete an employment application, come in for a job interview, or both. Regardless of what happens next, you should view both the application and the job interview as opportunities to tell the prospective employer about any special skills and talents that will enable you to become the type of employee they are looking for. We discuss job applications in this section and job interviews in the next.

Many companies require that applicants complete an application form before being interviewed. Although employment applications vary in form and length, the typical application asks for the following information:

- Personal data
- Military record
- Criminal record
- Educational background
- Employment history
- Character references

When filling out an employment application, do the best job you can when answering questions in each of the above areas. Above all, completing

FIGURE 23.5
New Résumés for the 1990s
A résumé presents your work experience, major accomplishments, and education background.   *(Source: Adapted from Bruce Nussbaum, "A Career Survival Kit,"* Business Week, *Oct. 7, 1991, p. 104. Used by special permission. Copyright © 1991 by McGraw-Hill, Inc.)*

OLD RÉSUMÉ	NEW RÉSUMÉ
Lawrence Keenan, Accountant 1312 Hewitt Spring, TX 77135 713-555-3315	Jennifer Geraldo 11412 Bartlett Place Newton, MA 02109 617-555-1043
Career Objective To join a large corporation, become comptroller, and move up to treasurer.	**Summary** Skilled in bringing products to market. Proficient in financial analysis, negotiations, and dealmaking.
Education Bachelor of Science, Accounting, Leonard Stern School of Business, New York University, 1981–1985.	**Experience** **Startup Manufacturing Co. 1990–1995** Created business plan for startup. Developed marketing strategy, identified clients, and then became manager of business development.
Advanced accounting courses • Federal Tax Laws • Management Accounting • Quantitative Analysis	**Foodco Inc. 1989–1990** Led new-product development team to launch new shelf-stable stew that became a $36 million brand.
Experience **Standard Steel Co. 1985–1995** Junior accountant, worked in the comptroller's office on various projects. Desire a larger job and more responsibility to match education and abilities.	**LBO Inc., New York 1986–1989** Performed due diligence and valuation in M&A department. Participated in 12 acquisitions, 10 sales of operations, 7 common-stock offerings.
	Education • Harvard University Graduate School of Business Administration: MBA **1986** • University of Michigan: Bachelor of Arts **1984**

an application allows you to demonstrate your ability to follow directions and to communicate effectively. The suggestions listed in Table 23.3 can help you avoid some of the most common mistakes that applicants make.

The Job Interview

LEARNING OBJECTIVE 6
Describe the interview process.

Your résumé and cover letter are, in essence, an introduction. The deciding factor in the hiring process is the interview (or several interviews) with representatives of the firm. It is through the interview that the firm gets to know you and your qualifications. At the same time, the interview provides a chance for you to learn about the firm.

Here again, preparation is the key to success. Research the firm before your first interview. Learn all you can about its products, its subsidiaries, the markets it operates in, its history, the locations of its facilities, and so on. If possible, obtain and read the firm's most recent annual report. Be prepared

TABLE 23.3   Eight Tips for Completing Employment Applications

1. Do a "dry run" to practice answering the questions on a typical employment application.
2. If it is not possible to take the application home, complete the application in ink.
3. Follow the directions on the employment application.
4. Read all questions before you begin answering them.
5. Judge the amount of space that you have to answer each question.
6. Fill in every blank even if you must write *not applicable* (N/A) or *none.*
7. Read over the completed application, and look for grammatical or spelling errors.
8. Above all, answer all questions honestly.

Sources: Melanie A. Brown, *Get the Job You Want* (Boston: Houghton Mifflin, 1992), pp. 69–70; and Susan D. Greene and Melanie C. L. Martel, *The Job Hunter's Guidebook* (Boston: Houghton Mifflin, 1992), pp. 58–59.

to ask questions about the firm and the opportunities it offers. Interviewers welcome such questions. They expect you to be interested enough to spend some time thinking about your potential relationship with their firm.

Prepare also to respond to questions the interviewer may ask. Table 23.4 is a list of typical interviewer questions that job applicants often find difficult to answer. But don't expect interviewers to stick to the list given in the table or to the items appearing in your résumé. They will be interested in anything that helps them decide what kind of person and worker you are.

Job fairs: A good place to meet prospective employers. Your first contact with a prospective employer may be at a job fair like the one pictured here. Although different from a one-on-one interview, the same communication skills can be used at job fairs to convince would-be employers that you might be a valuable asset for their firm and that you deserve an in-depth interview.

TABLE 23.4   Interview Questions That Job Applicants Often Find Difficult to Answer

1. What can you tell me about yourself?
2. What are your strengths and weaknesses?
3. Have you ever been fired from a position?
4. What did you do in your last position?
5. How much did you earn in your last position?
6. How would you describe your previous supervisor?
7. Why do you want to switch jobs?
8. Are you willing to relocate?
9. What do you know about this company?
10. Why are you interested in this company?
11. Why should we hire you?
12. How long will it take you to make a contribution to this company?
13. What kind of manager would you be?
14. What are your salary requirements?
15. Why would you enjoy working for this company?

Sources: Susan D. Greene and Melanie C. L. Martel, *The Job Hunter's Guidebook* (Boston: Houghton Mifflin, 1992), pp. 77–78; Anita Gates, "How to Talk Your Way into a Hot Career," *Working Woman,* July 1991, p. 64; and Dan Moreau, "Answers That Get You Hired," *Changing Times,* Apr. 1989, pp. 53–55.

Make sure you are on time for your interview and are dressed and groomed in a businesslike manner. Punctuality and appearance, like other personal qualities, are judged as part of the interviewing process. Have a copy of your résumé with you, even if you have already sent one to the firm. You may also want to bring a copy of your course transcript and letters of recommendation. If you plan to furnish interviewers with the names and addresses of references rather than with letters of recommendation, make sure you have your references' permission to do so.

Consider the interview itself as a two-way conversation, rather than as a question-and-answer session. Volunteer any information that is relevant to the interviewer's questions. If an important point is skipped in the discussion, don't hesitate to bring it up. Be yourself, but emphasize your strengths. Good eye contact and posture are important, too. They should come naturally if you take an active part in the interview.

At the conclusion of the interview, thank the recruiter for taking the time to see you. Then, a day or two later, follow up by sending him or her a short letter of thanks. In this letter, you can ask a question or two that may have occurred to you after the interview or add pertinent information that may have been overlooked.

In most cases, the first interview is used to *screen* applicants, or choose those that are best qualified. These applicants are then given a second interview, and perhaps a third—usually with one or more department heads. If the job requires relocation to a different area, applicants may be invited there for these later interviews. After the interviewing process is complete, applicants are told when to expect a hiring decision.

Accepting an Offer

"We'd like to offer you the job" may be the best news a job applicant can hear. To accept the job, you should send the firm a letter in which you express your appreciation, accept the offer, and restate the conditions of employment as you understand them. These conditions should include the starting salary, employee benefits, and a general description of the job (responsibilities, training, the immediate supervisor's name, and such). If you have any concerns regarding the job, make sure they are cleared up before you send your letter of acceptance: the job offer and your acceptance constitute a contract between you and the firm.

Less exciting is the news that begins "We thank you for your interest in our firm, *but . . .*" The fact is, there are many more applicants for jobs than there are jobs. (This is because most people apply for several positions at the same time.) As a result, most people are turned down for some jobs during their careers. Don't be discouraged if you don't get the first position you apply for. Instead, think back over the application process, analyze it, and try to determine what you might improve. In other words, learn from your experience—and keep trying. Success will come if you persevere.

■■ A FINAL NOTE FROM THE AUTHORS

LEARNING OBJECTIVE 7
Summarize the factors that lead to career growth and advancement.

A job is for today, but a career can last a lifetime. Although most applicants are excited when they get their first job, the employment process doesn't

How do you measure success? Although different people measure success in different ways, it is true that success in a career means more than just knowing how to do a job. The doctor pictured here didn't spend four years in medical school just to learn how to give shots. And although giving shots may be an important part of the job, true success for any doctor is more likely to be measured by how many people she or he can help get well.

Managing a Scarce Resource: Your Time

"Do not squander time," said Benjamin Franklin, "for that is the stuff life is made of." According to time-management experts, that's good advice for anyone, and it's *excellent* advice for first-time employees. Once you land that "ideal" job, you may find that there aren't enough hours in the workday to accomplish all that needs to be done. No perfect—or magical—time-management system can increase the number of hours in the day, but experts offer the following hints to improve your productivity in the hours you do have.

1. *Plan the day's activities.* Invest ten minutes each morning to plan your day's activities. Think about what you want to accomplish each day. Then list each important activity on a master list.

2. *Prioritize each activity on your master list.* Successful people rank all activities that need to be accomplished. A typical scale might range from 1 (the highest priority) to 3 (the lowest priority). Once you have ranked your list, begin work on your number 1s. In some cases, the activities with the lowest priorities may end up in the wastebasket.

3. *Finish each activity you start.* Many people dance from one activity to the next without accomplishing anything. A much better approach is to *complete* one activity before starting the next one. And when you finish an activity, be sure to check it off the master list.

4. *Practice saying no.* Many people take on more jobs than they could possibly finish because they can't say no. Granted, it may be difficult or impossible to say no to your boss, but there are many other people who make demands on your time. Instead of saying yes to everyone who asks for your help, be selective. Take on the jobs in which you can really make a difference.

Like most skills, time management improves with practice. Unfortunately, today there are all too many opportunities to practice this skill. Project deadlines, smaller staffs handling larger workloads, and managers who are compulsive about getting more done—all these plus intense business competition combine to produce overly stressed workers. Those same stressed-out workers who learn to manage their time stand a much better chance not only of surviving but also of becoming more productive and finishing first.

stop with your first job—it continues throughout your career. Additional training and education, promotions and advancement, and even changing jobs or careers are all part of a continuing process.

Although different people measure success in different ways, it is true that success in a career means more than just knowing how to do a job. You must combine technical skills and managerial skills with the ability to get along with people. A number of traits that successful people usually possess are presented in Table 23.5. Generally, people who are promoted know how to make decisions, communicate well, and handle stress. These same people can also manage another valuable asset—their time. For more information on time management, read Enhancing Career Skills.

TABLE 23.5   Traits That Successful People Usually Possess

1. An ability to work well with others in a variety of settings.
2. A desire to do tasks better than they have to be done.
3. An interest in reading a wide variety and a large quantity of materials.
4. A willingness to cope with conflict and adapt to change.
5. An ability to anticipate problems.
6. A knowledge of technology and computer software such as word processing, spreadsheet, and database programs.
7. An ability to creatively solve problems.
8. A knowledge of research techniques and library resources.
9. Well-developed written and oral communication skills.
10. An understanding of both their own motivations and the motivations of others.

Source: Jack R. Kapoor, Les Dlabay, and Robert J. Hughes, Personal Finance, 3rd ed. (Homewood, Ill.: Richard D. Irwin, Inc., 1994), pp. 31–32. Used by permission.

In any career, there will be times when you need to re-evaluate your decisions and opportunities. It may be necessary to determine what you can do to get your career back on track. It may even be necessary to change jobs or careers to obtain a better or more rewarding position. Although there are no guarantees, workers who can adapt to change and who are willing to pursue further education and training are more likely to be successful. The world is changing, and it is your responsibility to make the right decisions. Your teachers, friends, and relatives are willing to help you make decisions, but it is your life and you must take charge. Good luck!

■ ■ ■ ■ ■ CHAPTER REVIEW

Summary

1   Describe the factors that influence your career choice.

Many people work at a job because they need money to survive. A career, on the other hand, is a commitment not only to a profession but also to an individual's own interests and talents. Before choosing a career, you must evaluate what you like to do, what you are good at, how much education you have, and where you want to live.

2   Identify trends in employment in today's changing job market.

Individuals should also consider future trends in employment before deciding on a career. It is expected that college graduates with degrees in business and management, computer science, education, engineering, and the health professions will be in high demand between now and the year 2005. It is also expected that there will be an increased emphasis on training, retraining, and automation and that job-seekers must incorporate each of these trends into their career plans. Finally, the experts predict that the number of women, two-income families, and older workers in the work force will increase between now and the year 2005.

3 Summarize occupational search activities used to find career opportunities.

When job applicants begin their career search, they usually obtain information from a number of sources—the library, campus placement offices, a network of friends and professionals, and employment agencies. Employment agencies may be divided into two categories: private and state. Both types help individuals obtain jobs, but private employment agencies do charge a fee for their services. Although most people want a job immediately, an occupational job search takes time. During the occupational search, you should use the same effective work habits that employees use on the job. Above all, you should realize that an occupational search requires patience and perseverance.

4 Prepare a cover letter and résumé.

The time to begin career planning is as early as possible. According to corporate recruiters, work experience, the ability to communicate well, and realistic job and career goals are essential. Preparation again becomes important when it is time to apply for a position. You should develop both your résumé and cover letter very carefully. Your goal in preparing both is to give the potential employer the impression that you are someone who deserves an interview.

5 Identify the types of questions that are asked on employment applications.

Once you have mailed your cover letter and résumé, the next step generally depends on the employer. If interested, most prospective employers will ask you to complete an employment application. Although employment applications vary in form and length, the typical application asks for the following information: personal data; military record; criminal record; educational background; employment history; and character references. You should always view the application as an opportunity to tell the prospective employer about your special skills and talents. Above all, completing an application allows you to demonstrate your ability to follow directions and to communicate effectively.

6 Describe the interview process.

Your cover letter, résumé, and application are, in essence, an introduction. The deciding factor in the hiring process is the interview with representatives of the firm. Once again, preparation is the key. Learn as much as you can about the firm and be prepared to ask questions about the firm and the opportunities it offers. Also prepare to answer questions that the interviewer may ask. In most cases, the first interview is used to screen applicants, or choose those that are best qualified. These applicants are then given a second interview, and perhaps a third—usually with one or more department heads. If a job is offered, you should send the firm a letter expressing your appreciation, accepting the offer, and restating the conditions of employment as you understand them.

7 Summarize the factors that lead to career growth and advancement.

To be competitive in today's world, you must realize that career planning doesn't stop when you get your first job. Additional training and education, promotions and advancement, and even changing jobs or careers are all part of a continuing process. In any career, there will be times when you need to re-evaluate your decisions and opportunities. The world is changing, and workers who can adapt to change and who are willing to pursue further education and training are much more likely to be successful.

Questions

Review Questions

1. How does a job differ from a career?
2. Describe at least four personal factors that influence career decisions.
3. Identify and briefly describe the employment trends presented in this chapter. How will these trends affect your own career?
4. Assume that you would like to be a computer programmer when you graduate. How can you find career information about this particular profession?
5. What services are provided by a campus placement office, a private employment agency, and a state employment agency? How do the services differ?
6. What is the purpose of networking?
7. What information should you include in a résumé? What information should you include in a cover letter?

8. Describe the types of information that are usually requested on an employment application.

9. What are some typical interview questions? How would you answer those questions if you were the job applicant?

10. Why should a job applicant restate the conditions of employment before accepting a job offer?

11. What type of activities would you recommend to individuals who desire career advancement and professional growth?

Discussion Questions

1. Based on the information presented in Inside Business, what steps help ensure a successful transition from college to the world of work?

2. In order to be a productive team member, Clarence Wainwright, the college graduate profiled in the chapter opening, must have mastered certain technical skills required to perform a specific job. What other qualities does an employee like Wainwright need?

3. How do the activities you enjoy and the skills you possess relate to success on the job?

4. According to this chapter, more education increases your earning power. Do you agree with this statement?

5. What factors are most important when choosing a city in which to live?

6. How can a person prepare for a job interview?

7. Under what conditions would you change jobs? Under what conditions would you change careers?

8. How do you define *success?* What specific traits make people successful?

Exercises

✎ **1.** Study the sample application letter illustrated in Figure 23.4 and the résumé illustrated in Figure 23.5. Then develop your own personal application letter and résumé that could be mailed to a prospective employer.

🗣 **2.** In a role-play situation with one of your classmates, answer the interview questions presented in Table 23.4. Then analyze your answers to determine those that need improvement.

3. Interview someone you consider to be a successful person. In the interview, determine how this person became successful and what personal traits made this person successful.

VIDEO CASE 23.1

Interview Techniques That Get Jobs

After weeks of searching for a job, Joan Martinez was sitting at home when the telephone rang. It was the call she had hoped for—a corporate recruiter for AT&T asking her to come in for an interview. AT&T, like all companies, receives many employment applications and usually interviews only those applicants it thinks will "fit" into the organization. There are a number of reasons that employers interview prospective employees: they may want to verify details on an individual's application; they may want to see the applicant demonstrate his or her ability to perform the job; or they may want to determine how professional and self-confident the prospect behaves under pressure.

You, like Joan Martinez, may be facing an upcoming interview. Most likely you opened the door for your interview appointment by preparing yourself for the job itself through education and training. You applied for the position because you saw the company's job announcement in a newspaper, read about the company in magazines or trade publications, or heard about the opening through your networking system. Or perhaps you just walked into the company's human resources department "cold turkey" and filled out a job application.

Once you are invited to come in for an interview, it's time to use all of your inner resources to prepare yourself carefully for your upcoming interview. According to employment counselors, the interview is the most important step in your job search. Therefore, you want to present yourself in the best possible manner. Before going to the interview, do your homework. Learn all you can about the company through library resources, annual reports, and trade publications so you are better able to discuss how you may help the company achieve its goals. Even try to learn something about the person who is going to interview you—his or her position within the organization, length of service with the company, and other important facts.

In addition to just gathering facts, you should also prepare yourself. Use a tape recorder to practice your communication skills by answering questions you think may come up during the interview. Play back your responses to hear how your voice and speech patterns sound to an interviewer. Maybe you can even have a friend videotape you while you are practicing, so you can see for yourself how you look to other people. The night before the interview you may even want to write down the four or five most important reasons why this company should hire you.

On the day of the interview, you should dress appropriately and arrive on time. Once the interview begins, try to relax and realize that the interview is a two-way communication between you and the interviewer. Take an active part in the conversation, and show your interest in the interviewer and the company. Try to describe why you are unique or what sets you apart from other applicants. You may also want to give examples of how you can get along with people or how you have solved difficult problems.

Usually the interviewer is the one who will end the interview. At this point, you should thank the interviewer for taking the time to talk with you. With a sentence or two, reinforce your interest in this company and this position. You might also ask when the interviewer will be calling people for a second interview or when a final decision will be made.

After the interview, you should analyze the interview process and learn from any mistakes. You may also want to send a note or letter not only to thank the interviewer for seeing you, but also to confirm your desire to work for this company. Regardless of the outcome, remember one important fact: persistence in a job search usually pays off.[4]

Questions

1. Assume that you have an interview appointment scheduled for next week with an interviewer for the Charles Schwab brokerage firm. Describe specific methods you could use to obtain information about this company.
2. According to employment counselors, most applicants are "too passive" in job interviews. With this warning in mind, describe how you as a job applicant could take an active role during an interview.

CASE 23.2

Employment Agency Scams Bilk Millions

After working three years for small companies in his home town of Erie, Pennsylvania, Bart Blackburn, a twenty-four-year-old computer programmer, dreamed of working for Apple Computer or one of California's other Silicon Valley computer firms. Intrigued by a newspaper ad for an employment agency that promised jobs with major computer firms, Blackburn called the toll-free telephone number for more information. The employment counselor with whom he talked promised the agency would prepare a résumé for Blackburn and would distribute it to the "right" people in the "right" companies. All he had to do was fill out an application and send a check for $295. Three months after sending the completed application and the money, Blackburn still hadn't heard a word, so he called the employment agency. The firm's telephone had been disconnected.

Unfortunately, Bart Blackburn is not the only job hopeful to be exploited by unethical employment agencies. Employment scams like this one are quite common—especially when unemployment rates are high and jobs are scarce. In fact, government authorities estimate that employment scams take in at least $100 million a year. To get you to sign up, phone "counselors" will promise jobs in the Caribbean, Europe, Asia, or Australia. In addition to a vacation paradise setting, many of these jobs also offer food, housing, and hospitalization. And all you have to do to get one of these "perfect" jobs is fill out an application *and* send in a "small" fee that ranges from $99 to $1,000. Some unethical agencies prey on white-collar executives by promising high-level management positions. Others entice blue-collar workers with high-salaried, exotic overseas jobs. In many cases, the only "help" job applicants receive is information that is easily available (for free) at the local library or through government sources.

Despite the large number of unethical and illegal employment agencies today, most firms in the employment industry are both ethical and legal. Most legitimate employment agencies don't ask for money up front. They begin by interviewing unemployed clients. Based on the information obtained in the interview, they match clients with prospective employers. The better employment agencies will also help prepare clients for employment interviews by giving them important information about job responsibilities, history of the prospective employer, the company's management style, future development plans, and the firm's dress code, if any.

When a client obtains a job, the employment agency collects a placement fee, either from the employer or from the new employee. In both cases, typical fees range from 15 to 20 percent of the applicant's first-year salary. When the applicant is responsible for the fee, it is usually paid in installments over a twelve-month period. Obviously, most employees would prefer that the employer pay the fee, and in fact that is the most common arrangement today.[5]

Questions

1. What types of questions could a job applicant like Bart Blackburn ask to evaluate an employment agency?

2. Although employment agencies can help you get your foot in the door, you are the one who must go through the interview process. How can you convince prospective employers that you are the best applicant for the job?

3. Why would an organization use an employment agency instead of recruiting and hiring its employees directly?

CAREER PROFILE ■ ■ ■ ■ ■ ■ ■ ■ ■ ■ ■

PART 7   Career Opportunities in Business Law, Government, and Career Placement

Job Title	Job Description	Salary Range
Career counselor	Helps job applicants find jobs; assesses current skills and provides recommendations for improving or updating skills; works with prospective employers	2–4
City manager	Coordinates the day-to-day operation of local governments; provides leadership for employees; appoints department heads and supervisors; prepares annual budgets	5
Economic analyst	Tracks economic data; assists senior analysts in the preparation of reports on the impact of economic changes in a community, state, or the nation; communicates information to politicians, business managers, and other interested parties	2–3
Economist	Analyzes the costs of producing and marketing goods and services; uses mathematical models to develop economic theories; prepares reports for profit and non-profit organizations; assesses economic conditions in the United States and abroad	3–4
Government chief executive	Appoints people to head departments, such as finance, highways, health, police, recreation; oversees the work of civil servants; prepares budgets; ensures that resources are used properly to encourage economic growth	4–5
Lawyer	Counsels and advises clients on legal matters; prepares wills, contracts, sales agreements, and similar documents; represents clients in criminal and civil trials; interprets the law and its application to personal and business situations	4–5
Paralegal or legal assistant	Performs all the functions of a lawyer other than accepting clients, setting legal fees, giving legal advice or presenting a case in court; investigates the facts of the case; prepares draft documents such as contracts, mortgages, separation agreements, and trust instruments	2–4
Tax attorney	Counsels clients as to their legal rights and obligations; suggests particular courses of action related to tax matters; represents clients in criminal and civil trials; interprets the law and its application; uses computers to make tax computations and explores alternative tax strategies for clients	4–5
Urban and regional planner	Develops programs to provide for growth and revitalization of urban, suburban, and rural communities; helps local officials make decisions on social, economic, and environmental problems; formulates capital improvement plans to construct new school buildings, housing, and other public projects	3–5

The figure in the salary column approximates the expected annual income after two or three years of service.
1 = $12,000–$15,000; 2 = $16,000–$20,000; 3 = $21,000–$27,000; 4 = $28,000–$35,000; 5 = $36,000 and up.

Educational Requirements	Skills Required	Prospects for Growth
Bachelor's degree in business (human resources management)	Interpersonal; conceptual; problem solving; critical thinking	Average
Bachelor's or master's degree in public administration; on the job experience	Interpersonal; conceptual; decision-making	Below average
Bachelor's degree in economics	Computer; interpersonal; problem solving; quantitative; critical thinking	Average
Bachelor's degree in economics	Computer; interpersonal; quantitative; conceptual; critical thinking	Above average
Bachelor's degree in public administration; financial management; master's degree preferred	Interpersonal; problem solving; leadership; decision making; conceptual; critical thinking	Average
Bachelor's degree plus at least three years of law school; on-the-job experience	Interpersonal; problem solving; conceptual; critical thinking	Above average
Associate's or bachelor's degree; on-the-job experience	Interpersonal; computer; problem solving; technical; conceptual	Above average
Bachelor's degree plus at least three years of law school; on-the-job experience	Interpersonal; computer; problem solving; conceptual; critical thinking	Average
Master's degree in urban or regional planning; on-the-job experience	Interpersonal; computer; decision making; problem solving; conceptual	Average

GLOSSARY ■ ■ ■ ■ ■ ■ ■ ■ ■ ■ ■

absolute advantage the ability to produce a specific product more efficiently than any other nation (3)

accessory equipment standardized equipment used in a variety of ways in a firm's production or office activities (13)

account executive (or **stock broker)** an individual who buys or sells securities for clients (20)

accountability the obligation of a worker to accomplish an assigned job or task (7)

accounting the process of systematically collecting, analyzing, and reporting financial information (17)

accounting equation the basis for the accounting process: *assets = liabilities + owners' equity* (17)

accounting program a software package that enables users to record and report financial information (16)

accounts payable short-term obligations that arise as a result of making credit purchases (17)

accounts receivable turnover a financial ratio that is calculated by dividing net sales by accounts receivable (17)

accounts receivables amounts that are owed to a firm by its customers (19)

acid-test ratio a financial ratio that is calculated by subtracting the value of inventory from the current asset amount and dividing the total by current liabilities (17)

Active Corps of Executives (ACE) a group of active managers who counsel small-business owners on a volunteer basis (5)

ad hoc committee a committee created for a specific short-term purpose (7)

administrative law the regulations created by government agencies that have been established by legislative bodies (22)

administrative manager a manager who is not associated with any specific functional area but who provides overall administrative guidance and leadership (6)

advertising a paid, nonpersonal message communicated to a select audience through a mass medium (15)

advertising agency an independent firm that plans, produces, and places advertising for its clients (15)

advertising media the various forms of communication through which advertising reaches its audience (15)

affirmative action program a plan designed to increase the number of minority employees at all levels within an organization (2)

agency a business relationship in which one party (called the principal) appoints a second party (called the agent) to act on behalf of the principal (22)

agency shop a workplace in which employees can choose not to join the union but must pay dues to the union anyway (11)

agent a middleman that facilitates exchanges, represents a buyer or a seller, and often is hired permanently on a commission basis (14)

alien corporation a corporation chartered by a foreign government and conducting business in the United States (4)

application software a computer program designed to solve business or personal information problems (16)

appellate court a court that hears cases that are appealed from lower courts (22)

arbitration the procedure by which a neutral third party hears the two sides of a dispute and renders a decision; the decision is binding when arbitration is part of the grievance procedure, but may not be binding when arbitration is used to settle labor-contract disputes (11)

arithmetic mean the sum of all the values of a set of data, divided by the number of items in the set (16)

arithmetic-logic unit the part of a computer that performs mathematical operations, comparisons of data, and other types of data transformations (16)

artificial intelligence a combination of computer hardware and software that exhibits the same type of intelligence as human beings (16)

assets the resources that a firm owns (17)

authoritarian leader one who holds all authority and responsibility, with communication usually moving from top to bottom (6)

authority the power, within the organization, to accomplish an assigned job or task (7)

automatic vending the use of machines to dispense convenience goods automatically when customers deposit money (14)

automobile liability insurance insurance that covers financial losses resulting from injuries or damages caused by the insured vehicle (21)

automobile physical damage insurance insurance that covers damage to the insured vehicle (21)

balance of payments the total flow of money into the country less the total flow of money out of the country, over some period of time (3)

A-1

balance of trade   the total value of a nation's exports less the total value of its imports, over some period of time (3)

balance sheet (or statement of financial position)   a summary of the dollar amounts for a firm's assets, liabilities, and owners' equity accounts at a particular time (17)

bankruptcy   a legal procedure designed both to protect an individual or business that cannot meet its financial obligations and to protect the creditors involved (22)

bargaining unit   the specific group of employees represented by a union (11)

barter   a system of exchange in which goods or services are traded directly for other goods and/or services—without using money (1)

barter system   a system of exchange in which goods or services are traded directly for other goods and/or services—without using money (1, 18)

bear market   a market in which average stock prices are declining (20)

behavior modification   use of a systematic program of reinforcement to encourage desirable behavior (9)

beneficiary   individual or organization named in a life insurance policy as recipient of the proceeds of that policy on the death of the insured (21)

binding contract   an agreement that requires an intermediary to purchase products from a particular supplier, not from the supplier's competitors (22)

blue-sky laws   state laws that regulate securities trading (20)

board of directors   the top governing body of a corporation, the members of which are elected by the stockholders (4)

bond indenture   a legal document that details all the conditions relating to a bond issue (19)

bonus   a payment in addition to wages, salary, or commissions, usually an extra reward for outstanding performance (10)

bookkeeping   the routine, day-to-day record keeping that is a necessary part of accounting (17)

boycott   a refusal to do business with a particular firm (11)

boycott in restraint of trade   an agreement between businesses not to sell to or buy from a particular entity (22)

brand   a name, term, symbol, design, or any combination of these that identifies a seller's products and distinguishes them from competitors' products (13)

brand mark   the part of a brand that is a symbol or distinctive design (13)

brand name   the part of a brand that can be spoken (13)

breach of contract   the failure of one party to fulfill the terms of a contract when there is no legal reason for that failure (22)

breakeven quantity   the number of units that must be sold for the total revenue (from all units sold) to equal the total cost (of all units sold) (13)

broker   a middleman that specializes in a particular commodity, represents either a buyer or a seller, and is likely to be hired on a temporary basis (14)

budget   a financial statement that projects income and/or expenditures over a specified future period of time (19)

budget deficit   an excess of spending over income (22)

bull market   a market in which average stock prices are increasing (20)

bureaucratic structure   a management system based on a formal framework of authority that is carefully outlined and precisely followed (7)

business   the organized effort of individuals to produce and sell, for a profit, the goods and services that satisfy society's needs (1)

business ethics   the application of moral standards to business situations (2)

business interruption insurance   insurance protection for a business whose operations are interrupted because of a fire, storm, or other natural disaster (21)

business plan   a carefully constructed guide for the person starting a business (5)

buying behavior   the decisions and actions of people involved in buying and using products (12)

buying long   buying stock with the expectation that it will increase in value and can then be sold at a profit (20)

call premium   the dollar amount over par value that the corporation has to pay an investor for redeeming either preferred stock or a corporate bond (19)

capacity   the amount of products or services that an organization can produce in a given time (8)

capital   all the financial resources, buildings, machinery, tools, and equipment that are used in an organization's operations (1)

capital-intensive technology   a process in which machines and equipment do most of the work (8)

capitalism   an economic system in which individuals own and operate the majority of businesses that provide goods and services (1)

captioned photograph   a picture accompanied by a brief explanation (15)

carrier   a firm that offers transportation services (14)

cash flow the movement of money into and out of an organization (19)

cash surrender value an amount that is payable to the holder of a whole life insurance policy if the policy is canceled (20)

catalog marketing marketing in which an organization provides a catalog from which customers make selections and place orders by mail or telephone (14)

catalog showroom a retail outlet that displays well-known brands and sells them at discount prices through catalogs within the store (14)

category killer a very large specialty store that concentrates on a single product line and competes on the basis of low prices and product availability (14)

caveat emptor a Latin phrase meaning "let the buyer beware" (2)

centralized organization an organization that systematically works to concentrate authority at the upper levels of the organization (7)

cents-off coupon a coupon that reduces the retail price of a particular item by a stated amount at the time of purchase (15)

certificate of deposit (CD) a document stating that the bank will pay the depositor a guaranteed interest rate for money left on deposit for a specified period of time (18)

certified public accountant (CPA) an individual who has met state requirements for accounting education and experience and has passed a rigorous two-day accounting examination (17)

chain of command the line of authority that extends from the highest to the lowest levels of an organization (7)

chain retailer a firm that operates more than one retail outlet (14)

channel of distribution (or marketing channel) a sequence of marketing organizations that directs a product from the producer to the ultimate user (14)

check a written order for a bank or other financial institution to pay a stated dollar amount to the business or person indicated on the face of the check (18)

close corporation a corporation whose stock is owned by relatively few people and is not traded in stock markets (4)

closed shop a workplace in which workers must join the union before they are hired, outlawed by the Taft-Hartley Act (11)

code of ethics a guide to acceptable and ethical behavior as defined by an organization (2)

coinsurance clause a part of a fire insurance policy that requires the policyholder to purchase coverage at least equal to a specified percentage of the replacement cost of the property to obtain full reimbursement for losses (21)

collateral real or personal property that is pledged as security for a loan (18)

collective bargaining the process of negotiating a labor contract with management (11)

combination store a store that carries food items and general merchandise (14)

commercial bank a profit-making organization that accepts deposits, makes loans, and provides related services to its customers (18)

commercial draft a written order requiring a customer to pay a specified sum of money to a supplier for goods or services (19)

commercial paper short-term promissory notes issued by large corporations (19)

commission a payment that is a percentage of sales revenue (10)

commission merchant a middleman that carries merchandise and negotiates sales for manufacturers but does not take title to the goods it sells (14)

common law (also known as case law or judicial law) the body of law created by the court decisions rendered by judges (22)

common stock stock owned by individuals or firms who may vote on corporate matters, but whose claims on profit and assets are subordinate to the claims of others (4, 19)

community of interests the situation in which one firm buys the stock of a competing firm to reduce competition between the two (22)

community shopping center a planned shopping center that includes one or two department stores and some specialty stores, along with convenience stores (14)

comparable worth a concept that seeks equal compensation for jobs requiring about the same level of education, training, and skills (10)

comparative advantage the ability to produce a specific product more efficiently than any other products (3)

compensation the payment that employees receive in return for their labor (10)

compensation system the policies and strategies that determine employee compensation (10)

competition a rivalry among businesses for sales to potential customers (1)

component part an item that becomes part of a physical product and is either a finished item ready for assembly or a product that needs little processing before assembly (13)

computer an electronic machine that can accept, store, manipulate, and transmit data in accordance with a set of specific instructions (16)

computer-aided design (CAD) the use of computers to aid in the development of products (8)

computer-aided manufacturing (CAM) the use of computers to plan and control manufacturing processes (8)

computer-integrated manufacturing (CIM) a computer system that not only helps design products but also controls the machinery needed to produce the finished product (8)

computer-interactive retailing a form of selling that presents products on customers' computer screens and allows customers to place orders by mail or telephone (14)

computer network a system in which several computers can either function individually or communicate with each other (16)

computer programmer a person who develops the step-by-step instructions that are contained in a computer program (16)

conceptual skill the ability to conceptualize and think in abstract terms (6)

consideration the value or benefit that one party to a contract furnishes to the other party (22)

consumer buying behavior the purchasing of products for personal or household use, not for business purposes (12)

consumer products goods and services purchased by individuals for personal consumption (1)

consumer sales promotion method a sales promotion method designed to attract consumers to particular retail stores and motivate them to purchase certain new or established products (15)

consumerism all those activities intended to protect the rights of consumers (2)

consumers individuals who purchase goods or services for their own personal use rather than to resell or to use in producing goods or services that will be sold (1)

contingency plan a plan that outlines alternative courses of action that may be taken if the organization's other plans are disrupted or become ineffective (6)

contract a legally enforceable agreement between two or more competent parties who promise to do, or not to do, a particular thing (22)

control unit the part of a computer that guides the entire operation of the computer (16)

controlling the process of evaluating and regulating ongoing activities to ensure that goals are achieved (6)

convenience product a relatively inexpensive, frequently purchased item for which buyers want to exert only minimal effort (13)

convenience store a small retail store that sells a limited variety of products but remains open well beyond the normal business hours (14)

convertible bond a bond that can be exchanged, at the owner's option, for a specified number of shares of the corporation's common stock (19)

convertible preferred stock preferred stock that may be exchanged *at the stockholder's option* for a specified number of shares of common stock (19)

cooperative an association of individuals or firms whose purpose it is to perform some business function for all its members (4)

cooperative advertising advertising whose cost is shared by a producer and one or more local retailers (15)

copyright the exclusive right to publish, perform, copy, or sell an original work (22)

corporate bond a corporation's written pledge that it will repay a specified amount of money, with interest (19)

corporate charter a contract between the corporation and the state, in which the state recognizes the formation of the artificial person that is the corporation (4)

corporate code of ethics a guide to acceptable and ethical behavior as defined by an organization (2)

corporate culture the inner rites, rituals, heroes, and values of a firm (6)

corporate officer the chairman of the board, president, executive vice president, corporate secretary and treasurer, or any other top executive appointed by the board of directors (4)

corporation an artificial person created by law, with most of the legal rights of a real person, including the right to start and operate a business, to own or dispose of property, to borrow money, to sue or be sued, and to enter into binding contracts (4)

cost of goods sold the cost of the goods a firm has sold during an accounting period; equal to beginning inventory *plus* net purchases *less* ending inventory (17)

countertrade an international barter transaction (3)

coupon bond a bond issued with detachable coupons that the bondholder must present to a paying agent *or* the issuer to receive interest payments (19)

court of limited jurisdiction a court that hears only specific types of cases (22)

court of original jurisdiction the first court to recognize and hear testimony in a legal action (22)

craft union an organization of skilled workers in a single craft or trade (11)

creative selling selling products to new customers and increasing sales to present customers (15)

credit immediate purchasing power that is exchanged for a promise to repay it, with or without interest, at a later date (18)

credit union a financial institution that accepts deposits from, and lends money to, only those people who are its members (18)

crime a violation of a public law (22)

cultural diversity the differences among people in a work force due to race, ethnicity, and gender (10)

currency devaluation the reduction of the value of a nation's currency relative to the currencies of other countries (3)

current assets cash and other assets that can be quickly converted into cash or that will be used in one year or less (17)

current liabilities debts that will be repaid in one year or less (17)

current ratio a financial ratio that is computed by dividing current assets by current liabilities (17)

customs (or import) duty a tax on a particular foreign product entering a country (22)

damages a monetary settlement awarded to a party that is injured through a breach of contract (22)

data numerical or verbal descriptions that usually result from measurements of some sort (16)

data processing the transformation of data into a form that is useful for a specific purpose (16)

database a single collection of data that are stored in one place and can be used by people throughout the organization to make decisions (16)

debenture bond a bond backed only by the reputation of the issuing corporation (19)

debt capital borrowed money obtained through loans (19)

debt-to-assets ratio a financial ratio that is calculated by dividing total liabilities by total assets (17)

debt-to-equity ratio a financial ratio that is calculated by dividing total liabilities by owners' equity (17)

decentralized organization an organization in which management consciously attempts to spread authority widely in the lower levels of the organization (7)

decision making the act of choosing one alternative from among a set of alternatives (6)

decisional role a role that involves various aspects of management decision making (6)

deed a written document by which the ownership of real property is transferred from one person or organization to another (22)

delegation assigning part of a manager's work and power to other workers (7)

demand the quantity of a product that buyers are willing to purchase at each of various prices (1, 13)

demand deposit an amount that is on deposit in a checking account (18)

democratic leader one who holds final responsibility but also delegates authority to others, who help determine work assignments; communication is active upward and downward (6)

department store a retail store that (1) employs twenty-five or more persons and (2) sells at least home furnishings, appliances, family apparel, and household linens and dry goods, each in a different part of the store (14)

departmentalization the process of grouping jobs into manageable units (7)

departmentalization by customer grouping activities according to the needs of the various customer populations (7)

departmentalization by function grouping jobs that relate to the same organizational activity (7)

departmentalization by location grouping activities according to a defined geographic area in which they are performed (7)

departmentalization by product grouping activities related to a particular product or service (7)

depreciation the process of apportioning the cost of a fixed asset over the period during which it will be used (17)

deregulation the process of removing existing regulations, foregoing proposed regulations, or reducing the rate at which new regulations are enacted (22)

design planning the development of a plan for converting a product idea into an actual commodity ready for marketing (8)

desktop publishing program a software package that allows users to prepare text and graphics in high-quality, professional looking reports, newsletters, and pamphlets (16)

direct-mail advertising promotional material that is mailed directly to individuals (15)

direct marketing the use of the telephone and nonpersonal media to introduce products to consumers, who can then purchase them by mail or telephone (14)

direct-response marketing a type of marketing that occurs when a retailer advertises a product and makes it available through mail or telephone orders (14)

direct selling the marketing of products to ultimate consumers through face-to-face sales presentations at home or in the workplace (14)

directing the combined processes of leading and motivating (6)

discharge by mutual assent when all parties agree to void a contract (22)

discount a deduction from the price of an item (13)

discount rate the interest rate that the Federal Reserve System charges for loans to member banks (18)

discount store a self-service, general-merchandise outlet that sells goods at lower-than-usual prices (14)

discretionary income disposable income less savings and expenditures on food, clothing, and housing (12)

discretionary order an order to buy or sell a security that lets the broker decide when to execute the transaction and at what price (20)

disposable income personal income less all additional personal taxes (12)

dividend a distribution of earnings to the stockholders of a corporation (4)

domestic corporation a corporation in the state in which it is incorporated (4)

domestic system a method of manufacturing in which an entrepreneur distributed raw materials to various homes, where families would process them into finished goods to be offered for sale by the merchant entrepreneur (1)

door-to-door retailer a retailer that sells directly to consumers in their homes (14)

double-entry bookkeeping a system in which each financial transaction is recorded as two separate accounting entries to maintain the balance shown in the accounting equation (17)

dumping exportation of large quantities of a product at a price lower than that of the same product in the home market (3)

earnings per share a financial ratio that is calculated by dividing net income after taxes by the number of shares of common stock outstanding (17)

economic community an organization of nations formed to promote the free movement of resources and products among its members and to create common economic policies (3)

economic model of social responsibility the view that society will benefit most when business is left alone to produce and market profitable products that society needs (2)

economics the study of how wealth is created and distributed (1)

economy the system through which a society answers the two economic questions—how wealth is created and distributed (1)

electronic funds transfer (EFT) system a means for performing financial transactions through a computer terminal or telephone hookup (18)

embargo a complete halt to trading with a particular nation or in a particular product (3)

employee benefit a reward in addition to regular compensation that is provided indirectly to employees—mainly a service (such as insurance) paid for by the employer or an employee expense (such as college tuition) reimbursed by the employer (10)

employee ownership practice of employees owning the company they work for by virtue of being stockholders (9)

employee training the process of teaching operations and technical employees how to do their present jobs more effectively and efficiently (10)

empowerment giving employees greater involvement in their jobs by increasing their participation in decision making (9)

endorsement the payee's signature on the back of a negotiable instrument (22)

endowment life insurance life insurance that provides protection and guarantees the payment of a stated amount to the policyholder after a specified number of years (21)

entrepreneur a person who risks time, effort, and money to start and operate a business (1)

entrepreneurship the willingness to take risks and the knowledge and ability to use the other factors of production efficiently (1)

Environmental Protection Agency (EPA) the federal agency charged with enforcing laws designed to protect the environment (2)

Equal Employment Opportunity Commission (EEOC) a government agency with the power to investigate complaints of employment discrimination and the power to sue firms that practice it (2)

equity capital money received from the owners or from the sale of shares of ownership in the business (19)

equity theory a theory of motivation based on the premise that people are motivated first to achieve and then to maintain a sense of equity (9)

esteem needs the human requirements for respect, recognition, and a sense of one's own accomplishment and worth (9)

ethics the study of right and wrong and of the morality of choices individuals make (2)

excise tax a tax on the manufacture or sale of a particular domestic product (22)

exclusive distribution the use of only a single retail outlet for a product in each geographic area (14)

expectancy theory a model of motivation based on the assumption that motivation depends on how much we want something and on how likely we think we are to get it (9)

expenses the costs incurred in operating a business (17)

Export-Import Bank of the United States an independent agency of the U.S. government whose function is to assist in financing the exports of American firms (3)

exporting selling and shipping raw materials or products to other nations (3)

express warranty a written explanation of the responsibilities of the producer (or seller) in the event that a product is found to be defective or otherwise unsatisfactory (13, 22)

extended coverage insurance protection against damage caused by wind, hail, explosion, vandalism, riots or civil commotion, falling aircraft, and smoke (21)

external recruiting the attempt to attract job applicants from outside the organization (10)

factor a firm that specializes in buying other firms' accounts receivable (19)

factors of production natural resources, labor, capital, and entrepreneurship (1)

factory system a system of manufacturing in which all of the materials, machinery, and workers required to manufacture a product are assembled in one place (1)

family branding the strategy in which a firm uses the same brand for all or most of its products (13)

feature article a piece (of up to 3,000 words) prepared by an organization for inclusion in a particular publication (15)

Federal Reserve System the government agency responsible for regulating the United States banking industry (18)

Federal Trade Commission (FTC) a five-member committee charged with the responsibility of investigating illegal trade practices and enforcing antitrust laws (22)

fidelity bond an insurance policy that protects a business from theft, forgery, or embezzlement by its employees (21)

financial leverage the use of borrowed funds to increase the return on owners' equity (19)

financial management all the activities that are concerned with obtaining money and using it effectively (19)

financial manager a manager who is primarily responsible for the organization's financial resources (6)

financial plan a plan for obtaining and using the money that is needed to implement an organization's goals (19)

financial planner an individual who has had at least two years of training in securities, insurance, taxation, real estate, and estate planning and has passed a rigorous examination (20)

financial ratio a number that shows the relationship between two elements of a firm's financial statements (17)

fire insurance insurance that covers losses due to fire (21)

first line manager a manager who coordinates and supervises the activities of operating employees (6)

fixed assets assets that will be held or used for a period longer than one year (17)

fixed cost a cost that is incurred no matter how many units of a product are produced or sold (13)

flexible benefit plan compensation plan whereby an employee receives a predetermined amount of benefit dollars to spend on a package of benefits that he or she has selected to meet individual needs (10)

flexible manufacturing system (FMS) a single production system that combines robotics and computer-aided manufacturing (8)

flextime a system in which employees set their own hours within employer-determined limits (9)

floor planning a method of financing where the title to merchandise is given to lenders in return for short-term financing (19)

flow chart a graphic description of the types and sequences of operations in a computer program (16)

foreign corporation a corporation in any state in which it does business except the one in which it is incorporated (4)

foreign-exchange control a restriction on the amount of a particular foreign currency that can be purchased or sold (3)

form utility utility created by converting raw materials, labor, and other resources into finished products (8, 12)

401(k) plan a salary-reduction, employer-sponsored, pretax savings plan (21)

franchise a license to operate an individually owned

business as though it were part of a chain of outlets or stores (5)

franchisee   a person or organization purchasing a franchise (5)

franchising   the actual granting of a franchise (4)

franchisor   an individual or organization granting a franchise (5)

free enterprise   the system of business in which individuals are free to decide what to produce, how to produce it, and at what price to sell it (1)

free-market economy   an economic system in which individuals and firms are free to enter and leave markets at will (1)

frequency distribution   a listing of the number of times each value appears in a set of data (16)

full-service wholesaler   a middleman that performs the entire range of wholesaler functions (14)

functional middleman   a middleman that helps in the transfer of ownership of products but does not take title to the products (14)

Gantt chart   a graphic scheduling device that displays the tasks to be performed on the vertical axis and the time required for each task on the horizontal axis (8)

General Agreement on Tariffs and Trade (GATT)   an international organization of 120 nations whose goal is to reduce or eliminate tariffs and other barriers to world trade (3)

general journal   a book of original entry in which typical transactions are recorded in order of their occurrence (17)

general ledger   a book of accounts that contains a separate sheet or section for each account (17)

general merchandise wholesaler   a middleman that deals in a wide variety of products (14)

general partner   a person who assumes full or shared responsibility for operating a business (4)

generic product (or brand)   a product with no brand at all (13)

goal   an end result that the organization is expected to achieve over a one-to-ten year period of time (6)

goodwill   the value of a firm's reputation, location, earning capacity, and other intangibles that make the business a profitable concern (17)

government-owned corporation   a corporation owned and operated by a local, state, or federal government (4)

grapevine   the informal communications network within an organization (7)

graphics program   a software package that enables the user to display and print pictures, drawings, charts, and diagrams (16)

grievance procedure   a formally established course of action for resolving employee complaints against management (11)

gross domestic product (GNP)   the total dollar value of all goods and services produced by citizens physically located within a country (1)

gross national product (GNP)   the total dollar value of all goods and services produced by all citizens of a country for a given time period (1)

gross profit on sales   a firm's net sales *less* the cost of goods sold (17)

gross sales   the total dollar amount of all goods and services sold during the accounting period (17)

hard-core unemployed   workers with little education or vocational training and a long history of unemployment (2)

hardware   the electronic equipment or machinery used in a computer system (16)

health maintenance organization (HMO)   an insurance plan that directly employs or contracts with selected physicians and hospitals to provide health-care services in exchange for a fixed, prepaid monthly premium (21)

health-care insurance   insurance that covers the cost of medical attention, including hospital care, physicians' and surgeons' fees, prescription medicines, and related services (21)

hierarchy of needs   Maslow's sequence of human needs in the order of their importance (9)

high-risk investment   an investment that is made in the hope of earning a relatively large profit in a short time (20)

hourly wage   a specific amount of money paid for each hour of work (10)

human resources management   all the activities involved in acquiring, maintaining, and developing an organization's human resources (10)

human resources manager   a person charged with managing the organization's human resources programs (6)

human resources planning   the development of strategies to meet a firm's human resources needs (10)

hygiene factors   job factors that reduce dissatisfaction when present to an acceptable degree, but do not necessarily result in high levels of motivation, according to the motivation-hygiene theory (9)

implied warranty   a guarantee that is imposed or required by law (22)

import duty (or tariff)   a tax that is levied on a particular foreign product entering a country (3)

import quota   a limit on the amount of a particular

good that may be imported into a country during a given period of time (3)

importing purchasing raw materials or products in other nations and bringing them into one's own country (3)

income statement a summary of a firm's revenues and expenses during a specified accounting period (17)

incorporation the process of forming a corporation (4)

independent retailer a firm that operates only one retail outlet (14)

individual branding the strategy in which a firm uses a different brand for each of its products (13)

industrial product a product bought for use in a firm's operations or to make other products (13)

industrial service an intangible product that an organization uses in its operations (13)

industrial union an organization of both skilled and unskilled workers in a single industry (11)

inflation a general rise in the level of prices (1)

infomercial a program-length televised commercial message resembling an entertainment or consumer affairs program (15)

informal group a group created by the members themselves to accomplish goals that may or may not be relevant to the organization (7)

informal organization the pattern of behavior and interaction that stems from personal rather than official relationships (7)

information data that are presented in a form that is useful for a specific purpose

information society a society in which large groups of employees generate or depend on information to perform their jobs (16)

informational role a role in which the manager either gathers or provides information (6)

initial public offering (IPO) the first time a corporation sells common stock to the general public (20)

injunction a court order requiring a person or group either to perform some act or to refrain from performing some act (11)

inland marine insurance insurance that protects against loss or damage to goods shipped by rail, truck, airplane, or inland barge (21)

input unit the device used to enter data into a computer (16)

inspection the examination of the quality of work in process (8)

institutional advertising advertising designed to enhance a firm's image or reputation (15)

insurable risk a risk that insurance companies will assume (21)

insurance the protection against loss that is afforded by the purchase of an insurance policy (21)

insurance policy the contract between an insurer and the person or firm whose risk is assumed (21)

insurer (or insurance company) a firm that agrees, for a fee, to assume financial responsibility for losses that may result from a specific risk (21)

intangible assets assets that do not exist physically but that have a value based on legal rights or advantages that they confer on a firm (17)

intensive distribution the use of all available outlets for a product (14)

interlocking directorate an arrangement in which members of the board of directors of one firm are also directors of a competing firm (22)

internal recruiting considering present employees as applicants for available positions (10)

international business all business activities that involve exchanges across national boundaries (3)

International Monetary Fund (IMF) an international bank with more than 150 member nations; makes short-term loans to countries experiencing balance-of-payment deficits (3)

interpersonal role a role in which the manager deals with people (6)

interpersonal skill the ability to deal effectively with other people (6)

intrapreneur an employee who pushes an innovative idea, product, or process through the organization (7)

inventory stocks of goods and materials (14)

inventory management the process of managing inventories in such a way as to minimize inventory costs, including both holding costs and potential stockout costs (8, 14)

inventory turnover a financial ratio that is calculated by dividing the cost of goods sold in one year by the average value of the inventory (17)

investment banking firm an organization that assists corporations in raising funds, usually by helping sell new issues of stocks, bonds, or other financial securities (20)

involuntary bankruptcy a bankruptcy procedure initiated by creditors (22)

job analysis a systematic procedure for studying jobs to determine their various elements and requirements (10)

job description a list of the elements that make up a particular job (10)

job enlargement expanding a worker's assignments to include additional but similar tasks (7, 9)

job enrichment a motivating technique that provides employees with more variety and responsibility in their jobs (7, 9)

job evaluation the process of determining the relative worth of the various jobs within a firm (10)

job redesign a type of job enrichment in which work is restructured to cultivate the worker-job match (9)

job rotation the systematic shifting of employees from one job to another (7)

job security protection against the loss of employment (11)

job sharing an arrangement whereby two people share one full-time position (9)

job specialization the separation of all organizational activities into distinct tasks and the assignment of different tasks to different people (7)

job specification a list of the qualifications required to perform a particular job (10)

joint venture a partnership that is formed to achieve a specific goal or to operate for a specific period of time (3, 4)

jurisdiction the right of a particular union to organize particular workers (11)

just-in-time inventory system a system designed to ensure that materials or supplies arrive at a facility just when they are needed (8)

labeling the presentation of information on a product or its package (13)

labor human resources such as managers and workers (1)

labor union an organization or workers acting together to negotiate their wages and working conditions with employers (11)

labor-intensive technology a process in which people must do most of the work (8)

laissez-faire capitalism an economic system characterized by private ownership of property, free entry into markets, and the absence of government intervention (1)

laissez-faire leader one who gives authority to employees and allows subordinates to work as they choose with a minimum of interference; communication flows horizontally among group members (6)

law a rule developed by a society to govern the conduct of, and relationship among, its members (22)

leadership the ability to influence others (6)

leading the process of influencing people to work toward a common goal (6)

lease an agreement by which the right to use real property is temporarily transferred from its owner, the landlord, to a tenant (22)

liabilities a firm's debts and obligations—what it owes to others (17)

licensing a contractual agreement in which one firm permits another to produce and market its product and use its brand name in return for a royalty or other compensation (3)

life insurance insurance that pays a stated amount of money on the death of the insured individual (21)

limit order a request that a stock be bought or sold at a price that is equal to or better than some specified price (20)

limited liability a feature of corporate ownership that limits each owner's financial liability to the amount of money he or she has paid for the corporation's stock (4)

limited partner a person who contributes capital to a business but is not active in managing it: this partner's liability is limited to the amount that he or she has invested (3)

limited-line wholesaler a middleman that stocks only a few product lines (14)

limited-service wholesaler a middleman that assumes responsibility for a few wholesale services only (14)

line management position a position that is part of the chain of command and that includes direct responsibility for achieving the goals of the organization (7)

line of credit a loan that is approved before the money is actually needed (18)

liquidity the ease with which an asset can be converted into cash (17, 20)

lockout a firm's refusal to allow employees to enter the workplace (11)

long-term financing money that will be used for longer than one year (19)

long-term liabilities debts that need not be repaid for at least one year (17)

lower-level manager a manager who coordinates and supervises the activities of operating employees (6)

lump-sum salary increase an entire pay raise taken in one lump sum (10)

mail-order retailer a retailer that solicits orders by mailing catalogs to potential customers (14)

maintenance shop a workplace in which an employee who joins the union must remain a union member as long as he or she is employed by the firm (11)

major equipment large tools and machines used for production purposes (13)

management the process of coordinating people and other resources of an organization to achieve the goals of the organization (6)

management by objectives (MBO) a motivation technique in which managers and subordinates collaborate in setting goals (9)

management development the process of preparing managers and other professionals to assume increased responsibility in both present and future positions (10)

management excellence an approach to management that promotes feelings of excellence in employees (6)

management information system (MIS) a system that provides managers with the information they need to perform their jobs as effectively as possible (16)

managerial hierarchy the arrangement that provides increasing authority at higher levels of management (7)

manufacturer (or producer) brand a brand that is owned by a manufacturer (13)

manufacturer's sales branch essentially a merchant wholesaler that is owned by a manufacturer (14)

manufacturer's sales office essentially a sales agent that is owned by a manufacturer (14)

margin requirement the proportion of the price of a stock that cannot be borrowed (20)

market a group of individuals, organizations, or both who have needs for products in a given category and who have the ability, willingness, and authority to purchase such products (12)

market allocation an agreement to divide a market among potential competitors (22)

market order a request that a stock be purchased or sold at the current market price (20)

market price in pure competition, the price at which the quantity demanded is exactly equal to the quantity supplied (1)

market segment a group of individuals or organizations, within a market, that share one or more common characteristics (12)

market segmentation the process of dividing a market into segments and directing a marketing mix at a particular segment or segments rather than at the total market (12)

market value the price of one share of a stock at a particular time (20)

marketing the process of planning and executing the conception, pricing, promotion, and distribution of ideas, goods, and services to create exchanges that satisfy individual and organizational objectives (12)

marketing concept the business philosophy that involves the entire organization in the process of satisfying customers' needs while achieving the organization's goals (12)

marketing information system a system for managing marketing information that is gathered continually from internal and external sources (12)

marketing manager a manager who is responsible for facilitating the exchange of products between the organization and its customers or clients (6)

marketing mix a combination of product, price, distribution, and promotion developed to satisfy a particular target market (12)

marketing research the process of systematically gathering, recording, and analyzing data concerning a particular marketing problem (12)

marketing strategy a plan that will enable an organization to make the best use of its resources and advantages to meet its objectives (12)

markup the amount that a seller adds to the cost of a product to determine its basic selling price (13)

materials handling the actual physical handling of goods, in warehousing as well as during transportation (14)

materials requirements planning (MRP) a computerized system that integrates manufacturing planning and inventory control (8)

matrix structure an organizational structure that combines vertical and horizontal lines of authority by superimposing product departmentalization on a functionally departmentalized organization (7)

maturity date the date on which the corporation is to repay the borrowed money (19)

measure of value a single standard or "yardstick" that is used to assign values to, and compare the values of, products, services, and resources (18)

median the value that appears at the exact middle of a set of data when the data are arranged in order (16)

mediation the use of a neutral third party to assist management and the union during their negotiations (11)

medium of exchange anything that is accepted as payment for products, services, and resources (18)

memory (or storage unit) that part of a computer that stores all data entered into the computer and processed by it (16)

merchant middleman a middleman that actually takes title to products by buying them (14)

merchant wholesaler a middleman that purchases goods in large quantities and then sells them to other wholesalers or retailers and to institutional, farm, government, professional, or industrial users (14)

merger the purchase of one corporation by another (4)

middle manager a manager who implements the strategy and major policies developed by top management (6)

middleman (or **marketing intermediary)** a marketing organization that links a producer and user within a marketing channel (14)

minority a racial, religious, political, national, or other group regarded as different from the larger group of which it is a part, often singled out for unfavorable treatment (2)

mission a statement of the basic purpose that makes a business different from other firms (6)

missionary salesperson a salesperson—generally employed by a manufacturer—who visits retailers to persuade them to buy the manufacturer's products (15)

mixed economy an economy that exhibits elements of both capitalism and socialism (1)

mode the value that appears most frequently in a set of data (16)

money anything used by a society to purchase products, services, or resources (18)

monopolistic competition a market situation in which there are many buyers along with relatively many sellers who differentiate their products from the products of competitors (1)

monopoly a market (or industry) with only one seller (1)

morale a person's attitude toward his or her job, superiors, and the firm itself (9)

mortgage bond a corporate bond that is secured by various assets of the issuing firm (19)

motivating the process of providing reasons for people to work in the best interests of the organization (6)

motivation the individual, internal process that energizes, directs, and sustains behavior; the personal "force" that causes us to behave in a particular way (9)

motivation factors job factors that increase motivation, but whose absence does not necessarily result in dissatisfaction according to the motivation-hygiene theory (9)

motivation-hygiene theory the idea that satisfaction and dissatisfaction are distinct and separate dimensions (9)

multilateral development bank (MDB) an internationally supported bank that provides loans to developing countries to help them grow (3)

multinational enterprise a firm that operates on a worldwide scale, without ties to any specific nation or region (3)

multiple-unit pricing the strategy of setting a single price for two or more units (13)

mutual fund a professionally managed investment vehicle that combines and invests the funds of many individual investors (20)

mutual insurance company an insurance company that is collectively owned by its policyholders and is thus a cooperative (21)

mutual savings bank a bank that is owned by its depositors (18)

National Alliance of Business (NAB) a joint business-government program to train the hardcore unemployed (2)

National Association of Securities Dealers (NASD) the organization responsible for the self-regulation of the over-the-counter securities market (20)

national bank a commercial bank that is chartered by the U.S. Comptroller of the Currency (18)

National Labor Relations Board (NLRB) the federal agency that enforces the provisions of the Wagner Act (11)

natural monopoly an industry requiring huge investments in capital and within which duplication of facilities would be wasteful and thus not in the public interest (1)

natural resources things in their natural state that can be used in production such as land, water, forests, and minerals (1)

need a personal requirement (9)

negligence a failure to exercise reasonable care, resulting in injury to another (22)

negotiable instrument a written document that (1) is a promise to pay a stated sum of money and (2) can be transferred from one person or firm to another (22)

neighborhood shopping center a planned shopping center consisting of several small convenience and specialty stores (14)

net asset value current market value of a mutual fund's portfolio minus the mutual fund's liabilities divided by the number of shares outstanding (20)

net income the profit earned (or the loss suffered) by a firm during an accounting period, after all expenses have been deducted from revenues (17)

net profit margin a financial ratio that is calculated by dividing net income after taxes by net sales (17)

net sales the actual dollar amount received by a firm for the goods and services it has sold, after adjustment for returns, allowances, and discounts (17)

news release a typed page of generally fewer than

300 words provided by an organization to the media as a form of publicity (15)

no-fault auto insurance a method of paying for losses suffered in an automobile accident; enacted by state law, requires that those suffering injury or loss be reimbursed by their own insurance companies, without regard to who was at fault in the accident (21)

nonprice competition competition that is based on factors other than price (13)

nonstore retailing a type of retailing where consumers purchase products without visiting a store (14)

nontariff barrier a nontax measure imposed by a government to favor domestic over foreign suppliers (3)

not-for-profit corporation a corporation that is organized to provide a social, educational, religious, or other service rather than to earn a profit (3)

notes payable obligations that have been secured with promissory notes (17)

NOW account an interest-bearing checking account; NOW stands for Negotiable Order of Withdrawal (18)

objective a specific statement detailing what the organization intends to accomplish over a shorter period of time (6)

ocean marine insurance insurance that protects the policyholder against loss or damage to a ship or its cargo on the high seas (21)

odd lot fewer than 100 shares of a particular stock (20)

odd pricing the strategy of setting prices at odd amounts that are slightly below a whole number of dollars (13)

off-price retailer a store that buys manufacturers' seconds, overruns, returns, and off-season merchandise for resale to consumers at deep discounts (14)

oligopoly a market situation (or industry) in which there are few sellers (1)

open corporation a corporation whose stock is traded openly in stock markets and can be purchased by any individual (4)

open-market operations the buying and selling of U.S. government securities by the Federal Reserve System for the purpose of controlling the supply of money (18)

operating expenses those costs that do not result directly from the purchase or manufacture of the products a firm sells (17)

operating system a set of programs that controls the basic operations of the computer (16)

operational plan a type of plan designed to implement tactical plans (6)

operations management all activities that managers engage in to produce goods and services (8)

operations manager a manager who manages the systems that convert resources into goods and services (6)

order getter a salesperson who is responsible for selling the firm's products to new customers and increasing sales to present customers (15)

order processing those activities that are involved in receiving and filling customers' purchase orders (14)

order taker a salesperson who handles repeat sales in ways that maintain positive relationships with customers (15)

organic structure a management system founded on cooperation and knowledge-based authority (7)

organization a group of two or more people working together to achieve a common set of goals (7)

organization chart a diagram that represents the positions and relationships within an organization (7)

organizational buying behavior the purchasing of products by producers, governmental units, institutions, and resellers (12)

organizational height the number of layers, or levels, of management in a firm (7)

organizing the grouping of resources and activities to accomplish some end result in an efficient and effective manner (6)

orientation the process of acquainting new employees with an organization (10)

outdoor advertising short promotional messages on billboards, posters, and signs (15)

output unit the mechanism by which a computer transmits processed data to the user (16)

over-the-counter (OTC) market a network of stockbrokers who buy and sell the securities of corporations that are not listed on securities exchange (20)

overtime time worked in excess of forty hours in one week; under some union contracts, it can be time worked in excess of eight hours in a single day (11)

owners' equity the difference between a firm's assets and its liabilities—what would be left over for the firm's owners if its assets were used to pay off its liabilities (17)

packaging all the activities involved in developing and providing a container for a product (13)

par value an assigned (and often arbitrary) dollar value printed on the face of a stock certificate (19)

part-time work   permanent employment in which individuals work less than a standard workweek (9)

partnership   an association of two or more persons to act as co-owners of a business for profit (4)

patent   the exclusive right to make, use, sell, or license others to make or sell a newly invented product or process (22)

penetration pricing   the strategy of setting a low price for a new product (13)

performance   the fulfillment of all obligations by all parties to the contract (22)

performance appraisal   the evaluation of employees' current and potential levels of performance to allow superiors to make objective human resource decisions (10)

personal income   the income an individual receives from all sources less the Social Security taxes that the individual must pay (12)

personal investment   the use of one's personal funds to earn a financial return (20)

personal property   all property other than real property (22)

personal selling   personal communication aimed at informing customers and persuading them to buy a firm's products (15)

PERT (Program Evaluation and Review Technique) a technique for scheduling a process or project and maintaining control of the schedule (8)

physical distribution   all those activities concerned with the efficient movement of products from the producer to the ultimate user (14)

physiological needs   the things human beings require for survival (9)

picketing   marching back and forth in front of the place of employment with signs informing the public that a strike is in progress (11)

piece-rate system   a compensation system under which employees are paid a certain amount for each unit of output they produce (9)

place utility   utility that is created by making a product available at a location where customers wish to purchase it (12)

plan   an outline of the actions by which an organization intends to accomplish its goals and objectives (6)

planned economy   an economy in which the answers to the basic economic questions are determined, to some degree, through centralized government planning (1)

planning   establishing organizational goals and deciding how to accomplish them (6)

planning horizon   the period during which a plan will be in effect (8)

plant layout   the arrangement of machinery, equipment, and personnel within a facility (18)

point-of-purchase display   promotional material that is placed within a retail store (15)

pollution   the contamination of water, air, or land through the actions of people in an industrialized society (2)

positioning   the development of a product image in buyers' minds relative to the images they have of competing products (15)

possession utility   utility that is created by transferring title (or ownership) of a product to the buyer (12)

posting   the process of transferring journal entries to the general ledger (17)

power of attorney   a legal document that serves as evidence that an agent has been appointed to act on behalf of a principal (22)

pre-emptive rights   the rights of current stockholders to purchase any new stock that the corporation issues before it is sold to the general public (19)

preferred provider organizations (PPOs)   offer the services of doctors and hospitals at discount rates or give breaks in copayments and deductibles (21)

preferred stock   stock whose owners usually do not have voting rights, but whose claims on dividends and assets have precedence over those of commonstock owners (4, 19)

premium   (promotion) a gift that a producer offers the customer in return for using its product (15)

premium   (insurance) the fee charged by an insurance company (21)

prepaid expenses   assets that have been paid for in advance but not yet used (17)

press conference   a meeting at which invited media personnel hear important news announcements and receive supplementary textual materials and photographs (15)

prestige pricing   the strategy of setting a high price to project an aura of quality and status (13)

price   the amount of money that a seller is willing to accept in exchange for a product, at a given time and under given circumstances (13)

price competition   an emphasis on setting a price equal to or lower than competitors' prices to gain sales or market share (13)

price discrimination   the practice in which producers and wholesalers charge larger firms a lower price for goods than they charge smaller firms (22)

price fixing   an agreement between two businesses as to the prices to be charged for goods (22)

price lining   the strategy of selling goods only at certain predetermined prices that reflect definite price breaks (13)

price skimming the strategy of charging the highest-possible price for a product during the introduction stage of its life cycle (13)

primary market a market in which an investor purchases financial securities (via an investment bank or other representative) from the issuer of those securities (20)

primary-demand advertising advertising whose purpose is to increase the demand for all brands of a product within a specific industry (15)

prime interest rate the lowest rate charged by a bank for a short-term loan (19)

principle of indemnity in the event of a loss, an insured firm or individual cannot collect, from the insurer, an amount greater than the actual dollar amount of the loss (21)

private accountant an accountant who is employed by a specific organization (17)

private law the body of law that governs the relationships between two or more individuals or businesses (22)

problem the discrepancy between an actual condition and a desired condition (6)

process material a material that is used directly in the production of another product and is not readily identifiable in the finished product (13)

product everything that one receives in an exchange, including all tangible and intangible attributes and expected benefits; it may be a good, service, or idea (13)

product deletion the elimination of one or more products from a product line (13)

product design the process of creating a set of specifications from which a product can be produced (8)

product differentiation the process of developing and promoting differences between one's product and all similar products (13)

product liability insurance insurance that protects the policyholder from financial losses due to injuries suffered by others as a result of using the policyholder's products (21)

product life cycle a series of stages in which a product's sales revenue and profit increase, reach a peak, and then decline (13)

product line a group of similar products that differ only in relatively minor characteristics (13)

product mix all the products that a firm offers for sale (13)

product modification the process of changing one or more of a product's characteristics (13)

production the process of converting resources into goods, services, or ideas (8)

productivity the average level of output per unit of time per worker (1, 8)

productivity the average output per hour for all workers in the private business sector (6)

profit what remains after all business expenses have been deducted from sales revenue (1)

profit sharing the distribution of a percentage of the firm's profit among its employees (10)

progressive tax a tax that requires the payment of an increasing proportion of income as the individual's income increases (22)

promissory note a written pledge by a borrower to pay a certain sum of money to a creditor at a specified future date (18)

promotion communication that is intended to inform, persuade, or remind an organization's target markets of the organization or its products (15)

promotion mix the particular combination of promotion methods that a firm uses to reach a target market (15)

promotional campaign a plan for combining and using the four promotion methods—advertising, personal selling, sales promotion, and publicity—in a particular promotion mix to reach one or more marketing goals (15)

property anything that can be owned (22)

proportional tax a tax whose percentage rate remains constant as the tax base increases (22)

prospectus a detailed written description of a new security, the issuing corporation, and the corporation's top management (20)

proxy a legal form that lists issues to be decided at a stockholders' meeting and requests that stockholders transfer their voting rights to some other individual or individuals (4)

public accountant an accountant whose services may be hired on a fee basis by individuals or firms (17)

public law the body of law that deals with the relationships between individuals or businesses and society (22)

public liability insurance insurance that protects the policyholder from financial losses due to injuries suffered by others as a result of negligence on the part of a business owner or employee (21)

public relations all activities whose objective is to create and maintain a favorable public image (15)

publicity a nonpersonal message delivered in news-story form through a mass medium, free of charge (15)

purchasing all the activities involved in obtaining required materials, supplies, and parts from other firms (8)

pure competition the market situation in which there are many buyers and sellers of a product, and no single buyer or seller is powerful enough to affect the price of that product (1)

pure risk a risk that involves only the possibility of loss, with no potential for gain (21)

quality circle a group of employees who meet on company time to solve problems of product quality (8)

quality control the process of ensuring that goods and services are produced in accordance with design specifications (8)

quasi-government corporation a business owned partly by the government and partly by private citizens or firms (4)

range the difference between the highest value and the lowest value in a set of data (16)

ratification approval of a labor contract by a vote of the union membership (11)

raw material a basic material that actually becomes part of a physical product; usually comes from mines, forests, oceans, or recycled solid wastes (13)

real gross national product the total dollar value, adjusted for price increases, of all goods and services produced by all the citizens of a country during a given time period (1)

real property land and anything that is permanently attached to it (22)

recruiting the process of attracting qualified job applicants (10)

refund a return of part of the purchase price of a product (15)

regional shopping center a planned shopping center containing large department stores, numerous specialty stores, restaurants, movie theaters, and sometimes even hotels (14)

registered bond a bond that is registered in the owner's name by the issuing company (19)

regressive tax a tax that takes a greater percentage of a lower income than of a higher income (22)

reinforcement theory a theory of motivation based on the premise that behavior that is rewarded is likely to be repeated, whereas behavior that is punished is less likely to recur (9)

replacement chart a list of key personnel and their possible replacements within the firm (10)

research and development (R&D) a set of activities intended to identify new ideas that have the potential to result in new goods and services (8)

reserve requirement the percentage of its deposits that a bank *must* retain, either in its own vault or on deposit with its Federal Reserve district bank (18)

responsibility the duty to do a job or perform a task (7)

retailer a middleman that buys from producers or other middlemen and sells to consumers (14)

retained earnings the portion of a business's profits that is not distributed to stockholders (19)

return on equity a financial ratio that is calculated by dividing net income after taxes by owners' equity (17)

revenues dollar amounts received by a firm (17)

revolving credit agreement a guaranteed line of credit (18, 19)

reward system the formal mechanism for defining, evaluating, and rewarding employee performance (9)

risk the possibility that a loss or injury will occur (21)

risk management the process of evaluating the risks faced by a firm or an individual and then minimizing the costs involved with those risks (21)

robotics the use of programmable machines to perform a variety of tasks by manipulating materials and tools (8)

round lot a unit of 100 shares of a particular stock (20)

S-corporation a corporation that is taxed as though it were a partnership (4)

safety needs the things human beings require for physical and emotional security (9)

salary a specific amount of money paid for an employee's work during a set calendar period, regardless of the actual number of hours worked (10)

sales agreement a type of contract by which ownership is transferred from a seller to a buyer (22)

sales forecast an estimate of the amount of a product that an organization expects to sell during a certain period of time, based on a specified level of marketing effort (12)

sales promotion the use of activities or materials as direct inducements to customers or salespersons (15)

sales support personnel employees who aid in selling but are more involved in locating prospects, educating customers, building goodwill for the firm, and providing follow-up service (15)

sample a free package or container of a product (15)

savings and loan association (S&L) a financial institution that offers checking and savings accounts and certificates of deposit and provides home-mortgage loans (18)

savings bank   a financial institution that offers many of the same services that are offered by savings and loan associations (18)

scheduling   the process of ensuring that materials are at the right place at the right time (8)

scientific management   the application of scientific principles to management of work and workers (9)

secondary market   a market for existing financial securities that are currently traded between investors (20)

Securities and Exchange Commission (SEC)   the agency that enforces federal securities regulations (20)

securities exchange   a marketplace where member brokers meet to buy and sell securities (20)

selection   the process of gathering information about applicants for a position and then using that information to choose the most appropriate applicant (10)

selective (or brand) advertising)   advertising that is used to sell a particular brand of product (15)

selective distribution   the use of only a portion or percentage of the available outlets for a product in each geographic area (14)

self-insurance   the process of establishing a monetary fund that can be used to cover the cost of a loss (21)

self-actualization needs   the needs to grow and develop as people and to become all that we are capable of being (9)

selling expenses   costs that are related to the firm's marketing activities (17)

selling short   the process of selling stock that an investor does not actually own but has borrowed from a stockbroker and will repay at a later date (20)

seniority   the length of time an employee has worked for the organization (11)

serial bonds   bonds of a single issue that mature on different dates (19)

Service Corps of Retired Executives (SCORE)   a group of retired business people who volunteer their services to small businesses through the SBA (5)

service economy   an economy in which the majority of the work force is involved in service industries and in which more effort is devoted to the production of services than to the production of goods (1, 8)

shop steward   an employee who is elected by union members to serve as their representative (11)

shopping product   an item for which buyers are willing to expend considerable effort on planning and making the purchase (13)

short-term financing   money that will be used for one year or less and then repaid (19)

sinking fund   a sum of money to which deposits are made each year for the purpose of redeeming a bond issue (19)

skills inventory   a computerized data bank containing information on the skills and experience of all present employees (10)

slowdown   a technique whereby workers report to their jobs but work at a slower pace than normal (11)

small business   one which is independently owned and operated for profit and is not dominant in its field (5)

Small Business Administration (SBA)   a governmental agency that assists, counsels, and protects the interests of small businesses in the United States (5)

Small Business Development Center (SBDC)   a university-based group that provides individual counseling and practical training to owners of small businesses (5)

Small Business Institute (SBI)   a group of senior and graduate students in business administration who provide management counseling to small businesses (5)

Small Business Investment Company (SBIC)   a privately owned firm that provides venture capital to small enterprises that meet its investment standards (5)

social audit   a comprehensive report of what an organization has done, and is doing, with regard to social issues that affect it (2)

social needs   the human requirements for love and affection and a sense of belonging (9)

social responsibility   the recognition that business activities have an impact on society and the consideration of that impact in business decision making (2)

socioeconomic model of social responsibility   the concept that business should emphasize not only profits but the impact of its decisions on society (2)

sole proprietorship   a business that is owned (and usually operated) by one person (4)

span of management (or **span of control)**   the number of workers who report directly to one manager (7)

specialization   the separation of a manufacturing process into distinct tasks and the assignment of different tasks to different individuals (1)

specialty product   an item that possesses one or more unique characteristics for which a significant group of buyers is willing to expend considerable purchasing effort (13)

specialty store   a retail outlet that sells a single category of merchandise (14)

specialty-line wholesaler   a middleman that carries a select group of products within a single line (14)

specific performance   the legal requirement that the parties to a contract fulfill their obligations according to the contract (22)

speculative investment   an investment that is made in the hope of earning a relatively large profit in a short time (20)

speculative risk   a risk that accompanies the possibility of earning a profit (21)

spreadsheet program   a software package that allows the user to organize numerical data into a grid of rows and columns (16)

staff management position   a position created to provide support, advice, and expertise within an organization (7)

standard of living   a loose, subjective measure of how well off an individual or a society is, mainly in terms of want satisfaction through goods and services (1)

standing committee   a relatively permanent committee charged with performing some recurring task (7)

state bank   a commercial bank that is chartered by the banking authorities in the state in which it operates (18)

statement of cash flows   a statement that illustrates the effect on cash of the operating, investing, and financing activities of a company for an accounting period (17)

statistic   a measure that summarizes a particular characteristic for an entire group of numbers (16)

statute   a law that is passed by the U.S. Congress, a state legislature, or a local government (22)

statutory law   all the laws that have been enacted by legislative bodies (22)

stock   the shares of ownership of a corporation (4)

stock average (or **stock index)**   an average of the current market prices of selected stocks (20)

stock dividend   a dividend in the form of additional stock (20)

stock insurance company   an insurance company that is owned by stockholders and is operated to earn a profit (21)

stock split   the division of each outstanding share of a corporation's stock into a greater number of shares (20)

stockholder   a person who owns a corporation's stock (4)

store (or **private) brand**   a brand that is owned by an individual wholesaler or retailer (13)

store of value   a means for retaining and accumulating wealth (18)

strategic alliance   partnership formed to create competitive advantage on a worldwide basis (3)

strategy   an organization's broadest set of plans, developed as a guide for major policy setting and decision making (6)

strike   a temporary work stoppage by employees, calculated to add force to their demands (11)

strikebreaker   a nonunion employee who performs the job of a striking union member (11)

supermarket   a large, self-service store that sells primarily food and household products (14)

superstore   a large retail store that carries not only food and nonfood products ordinarily found in supermarkets but also additional product lines (14)

supply   (product) an item that facilitates production and operations but does not become part of the finished product (13)

supply   (economics) the quantity of a product that producers are willing to sell at each of various prices (1)

syndicate   a temporary association of individuals or firms, organized to perform a specific task that requires a large amount of capital (4)

tabular display   a display used to present verbal or numerical information in columns and rows (16)

tactical plan   a smaller-scale plan developed to implement a strategy (6)

target market   a group of persons for whom a firm develops and maintains a marketing mix suitable for the specific needs and preferences of that group (12)

task force   a committee established to investigate a major problem or pending decision (7)

technical salesperson   a salesperson who assists the company's current customers in technical matters (15)

technical skill   a specific skill needed to accomplish a specialized activity (6)

telecommuting   working at home all of the time or for a portion of the workweek (9)

telemarketing   the performance of marketing-related activities by telephone (14)

television home shopping   selling in which products are displayed to television viewers, who can then order them by calling a toll-free number and paying by credit card (14)

term life insurance   life insurance that provides protection to beneficiaries for a stated period of time (21)

term-loan agreement   a promissory note that requires a borrower to repay a loan in monthly, quarterly, semiannual, or annual installments (19)

Theory X   a concept of employee motivation generally consistent with Taylor's scientific management; assumes that employees dislike work and will function only in a highly controlled work environment (9)

Theory Y   a concept of employee motivation generally consistent with the ideas of the human relations movement; assumes that employees accept responsibility and work toward organizational goals if by so doing they also achieve personal rewards (9)

Theory Z   the belief that some middle ground between Ouchi's Type A and Type J practices is best for American business (9)

time deposit   an amount that is on deposit in an interest-bearing savings account (18)

time utility   utility that is created by making a product available when customers wish to purchase it (12)

top manager   an upper-level executive who guides and controls the overall fortunes of the organization (6)

tort   a violation of a private law (22)

total cost   the sum of the fixed costs and the variable costs attributed to a product (13)

total market approach   a single marketing mix directed at the entire market for a particular product (12)

total quality management (TQM)   the coordination of efforts directed at improving customer satisfaction, increasing employee participation, strengthening supplier partnerships, and facilitating an organization atmosphere of continuous quality improvement (6)

total revenue   the total amount received from sales of a product (13)

trade credit   a type of short-term financing extended by a seller who does not require immediate payment after delivery of merchandise (19)

trade deficit   an unfavorable balance of trade (3)

trade name   the complete and legal name of an organization (13)

trade sales promotion method   a sales promotion method designed to encourage wholesalers and retailers to stock and actively promote a manufacturer's product (15)

trade salesperson   a salesperson—generally employed by a food producer or processor—who assists customers in promoting products, especially in retail stores (15)

trade show   an industrywide exhibit at which many sellers display their products (15)

trademark   a brand that is registered with the U.S. Patent and Trademark Office and is thus legally protected from use by anyone except its owner (13, 21)

trading company   provides a link between buyers and sellers in different countries (3)

traditional specialty store   a store that carries a narrow product mix with deep product lines (14)

transportation   the shipment of products to customers (14)

trial balance   a summary of the balances of all general ledger accounts at the end of the accounting period (17)

trust   a business combination that is created when one firm obtains control of competing firms by purchasing their stock or their assets (22)

trustee   an independent firm or individual that acts as the bond owners' representative (19)

tying agreement   a contract that forces an intermediary to purchase unwanted products along with the products it actually wants to buy (22)

Uniform Commercial Code (UCC)   a set of laws designed to eliminate differences among state regulations affecting business and to simplify interstate commerce (22)

uninsurable risk   a risk that insurance firms will not assume (21)

union security   protection of the union's position as the employees' bargaining agent (11)

union shop   a workplace in which new employees must join the union after a specified probationary period (11)

union-management (or labor) relations   the dealings between labor unions and business management, both in the bargaining process and beyond it (11)

universal life insurance   life insurance that combines insurance protection with an investment plan that offers a potentially greater return than that guaranteed by a whole life insurance policy (21)

unlimited liability a legal concept that holds a sole proprietor personally responsible for all the debts of his or her business (4)

unsecured financing financing that is not backed by collateral (19)

usury the practice of charging interest in excess of the maximum legal rate (22)

utility the ability of a good or service to satisfy a human need (8, 12)

variable cost a cost that depends on the number of units produced (13)

venture capital money that is invested in small (and sometimes struggling) firms that have the potential to become very successful (5)

vertical channel integration the combining of two or more stages of a distribution channel under a single firm's management (14)

vertical marketing system (VMS) a centrally managed distribution channel resulting from vertical channel integration (14)

visual display a diagram that represents several items of information in a manner that makes comparison easier (16)

voluntary agreement a contract requirement consisting of an offer by one party to enter into a contract with a second party and acceptance by the second party of all the terms and conditions of the offer (22)

voluntary bankruptcy a bankruptcy procedure initiated by an individual or business that can no longer meet its financial obligations (22)

wage survey a collection of data on prevailing wage rates within an industry or a geographic area (10)

warehouse club a large-scale, members-only establishment that combines features of cash-and-carry wholesaling with discount retailing (14)

warehouse showroom a retail facility in a large, low-cost building with on-premises inventories and minimal services (14)

warehousing the set of activities that are involved in receiving and storing goods and preparing them for reshipment (14)

wheel of retailing a hypothesis that suggests that new retail operations usually begin at the bottom—in price, profits, and prestige—and gradually evolve up the cost/price scale, competing with newer business (14)

whistle blowing informing the press or government officials about unethical practices within one's organization (2)

whole life insurance life insurance that provides both protection and savings (21)

wholesaler a middleman that sells products to other firms (14)

wildcat strike a strike that has not been approved by the strikers' union (11)

word processing program a software package that allows the user to store documents (letters, memos, reports) in the computer memory or on a disk (16)

work teams groups of employees with the authority and skills to manage themselves (9)

workers' compensation insurance insurance that covers medical expenses and provides salary continuation for employees who are injured while they are at work (21)

working capital the difference between current assets and current liabilities (17)

workplace diversity see **cultural diversity**

zero-based budgeting a budgeting approach in which every expense must be justified in every budget (19)

NOTES ■ ■ ■ ■ ■ ■ ■ ■ ■ ■ ■ ■

CHAPTER 1

1. Based on information from Faye Brookman, "Toy Fair Attracts 120,000 Products and 22,000 Buyers," *Drug Topics*, Mar. 21, 1994, pp. 65–66; Eric Schine, "Mattel's Wild Race to Market," *Business Week*, Feb. 21, 1994, pp. 62–63; Judy Feldman, "The Top 10 Boomer Toys," *Money*, May 1994, p. 159; Cyndee Miller, "Finding Next Big Toy Is Not Child's Play," *Advertising Age*, May 23, 1994, p. 2; Ann Marie Angebrandt, "An Old Friend Makes Good," *Asian Business*, Feb. 1994, p. 46; Seth Lubove, "Barbie Does Silicon Valley," *Forbes*, Sept. 26, 1994, pp. 84–85; "All Dolled Up," *The Economist*, Feb. 5, 1994, p. 66; and Gary Hoover, Alta Campbell, and Patrick J. Spain, eds., *Hoover's Handbook of American Business 1994* (Austin, Texas: Reference Press, 1993), pp. 736–737.
2. Adapted from "The Origins of Enterprise in America," *Exxon U.S.A.*, third quarter, 1976, pp. 8–11.
3. Based on information from the Bureau of National Affairs, Inc., *Daily Report for Executives*, Oct. 19, 1994, p. A–200; William H. Miller, "Success Isn't Enough," *Industry Week*, Apr. 4, 1994, pp. 62, 64; Dottie Enrico, "Winners of Top Awards Blow Their Own Horns," *USA Today*, Oct. 19, 1994, p. B1; Paul Wiseman and Micheline Maynard, "Bags Demming, Baldrige On Same Day," *USA Today*, Oct. 19, 1994, pp. B1–B2; and "Quest For Excellence," 1994 Baldrige Award Video, Jan. 26, 1995.
4. Based on information from James Bates, "Wayne's World," *Los Angeles Times*, June 6, 1993, p. D1; "Consumer Service: Blockbuster Entertainment," *Sales & Marketing Management*, Aug. 1993, p. 41; Peter Katel and Bob Andelman, "New Kid on the Block, Buster," *Newsweek*, Jan. 11, 1993, p. 48; Jeffery D. Zbar, "Recording Industry Hits Blockbuster," *Advertising Age*, May 17, 1993, p. 46; Michael Maurer, "Blockbuster Music Plans Upbeat," *Crain's Detroit Business*, June 20, 1994; "Blockbuster May Expand As Deal Fades," *Palm Beach (Florida) Post*, April 28, 1994, p. B8; Christopher Boyd, "Video King's Blockbuster New Theme Park Will Swamp Florida Neighbors, Critics Fear," *Chicago Tribune*, May 3, 1994, p. B1; and Gary Hoover, Alta Campbell, and Patrick J. Spain, eds., *Hoover's Handbook of American Business* (Austin, Texas: Reference Press, 1994), pp. 274–275.

CHAPTER 2

1. Based on information in Gary Hoover, Alta Campbell, and Patrick J. Spain, *Hoover's Handbook of American Business 1993* (Austin, Texas: Reference Press, 1994), pp. 250–251; Kenneth N. Gilpin, "Suit Against Bausch & Lomb Is Judged a Class Action," *New York Times*, Nov. 3, 1994, p. D5; "Bausch & Lomb Inc.," *Wall Street Journal*, Oct. 13, 1994, p. A8; and Lesley Alderman, "How to Save Dollars and Make Sense When You Buy Contact Lenses," *Money*, May 1994, pp. 156–157.
2. Barry Meier, "Settlement By Deloitte on S.&L.'s," *New York Times*, March 15, 1994, pp. 1, 16.
3. O. C. Ferrell and Larry G. Gresham, "A Contingency Framework for Understanding Ethical Decision Making in Marketing," *Journal of Marketing*, Summer 1985, pp. 87–96.
4. "Guns 'R' Us," *Business Ethics*, March/April 1994, p. 9.
5. "H. B. Fuller To Redesign Adhesives," *Business Ethics*, July/Aug. 1994, p. 9.
6. "Breakfast Of Champions," *Business Ethics*, Sept./Oct. 1993, p. 9.
7. "The Many Benefits of Drinking Coffee," *Business Ethics*, Sept./Oct. 1993, p. 9.
8. "Habitats for the Homeless," *Business Ethics*, July/Aug. 1993, p. 9.
9. "Hurricane Help," *Business Ethics*, Jan./Feb. 1993.
10. Jerry Urban, "145,00 Women Register To Join Implant Case Settlement," *Houston Chronicle*, Oct. 12, 1994, p. 18A.
11. Barbara Berish Brown, "EEOC Caseload Up, Issues Guidelines; DOL Acts On Glass Ceiling; DOJ on ADA," *Employment Relations Today*, Spring 1994, pp. 85–90.
12. "Water Pollution: Stronger Efforts Needed By EPA To Control Toxic Water Pollution," U.S. Congress. House Committee on Government Operations, *Report to the Chairman, Environment, Energy, and Natural Resources Subcommittee*, General Accounting Office (Washington, D.C., July 1991), p. 8.
13. Ibid.
14. Robert Steuteville, "The State of Garbage in America," *BioCycle*, April 1994, pp. 46–48.
15. Mary Beth Regan, "Can Clinton Clean Up The Superfund Morass?" *Business Week*, Feb. 14, 1994, p. 41.
16. Based on information from William Ecenbarger, "The Strange History of Tobacco," *Reader's Digest*, April 1992, pp. 139–142; Adrienne Ward, "Old Joe Lights Up AA Faxes," *Advertising Age*, March 23, 1992, pp. 3, 46; "Should Old Joe Stay Or Go?" *Advertising Age*, March 16, 1992, p. 52; Walecia Konrad, "I'd Toddle A Mile For A Camel," *Business Week*, Dec. 2, 1991, p. 34; Judann Dagnoli, " 'JAMA' Lights New Fire Under Camel's Ads," *Advertising Age*, Dec. 16, 1991, pp. 3, 32; Kim Foltz, "Old Joe Is Paying Off for Camel," *The New York Times*, Aug. 7, 1990; Gina Kolata, "Dr. Elders vs. Joe Uncool," *The New York Times*, Feb. 27, 1994; Kevin Goldman, "A Stable of Females Has Joined Joe Camel in Controversial Cigarette Ad Campaign," *The Wall Street Journal*, Feb. 18, 1994; Brett Shevack, "Ban Joe Camel Campaign? That's Unfair," *Advertising Age*, Sept. 20, 1993, p. 28; Stella M. Eisele, "Joe Camel Comes Out On Top," *Bryan-College Station Eagle*,

June 2, 1994, p. A5; and "American Heart Video Journal, Volume II, Tobacco Advertising," American Heart Association, 1987.

17. Based on information from Seema Nayyar, "The Big Chill," *Newsweek,* May 23, 1994, p. 51; Emily DeNitto, "Ben & Jerry & Spike & Smooth," *Advertising Age,* March 21, 1994, p. 3, 42; Barnaby J. Feder, "Ben Leaving as Ben & Jerry's Chief," *The New York Times,* June 14, 1994, p. D1, D5; Anne Murphy, "The Seven (Almost) Deadly Sins of High-Minded Entrepreneurs," *INC.,* July 1994, pp. 47–48, 51; and Fred Lager, *Ben & Jerry's: The Inside Scoop* (New York: Crown Publishers, 1994).

CHAPTER 3

1. Based on information from "Exporting Pays Off," *Business America,* January 1994, p. 38; "Exporting Pays Off," *Business America,* February 1994, p. 22; and Ford Motor Company, Annual Report, 1993, p. 50.
2. *Business America,* April 1994, p. 40.
3. James Bovard, "Free Trade in the 1990s," *Imprimis,* February 1993, p. 1.
4. "U.S. Pencil Makers Point to Thai, Chinese Imports," *Wall Street Journal,* January 24, 1993, p. A2.
5. James Bovard, "Free Trade in the 1990s," *Imprimis,* February 1993, p. 1.
6. William M. Pride and O. C. Ferrell, *Marketing,* 9th ed. (Boston: Houghton Mifflin, 1995), pp. 95–97.
7. James Bovard, "Torpedo Shipping Protection," *Wall Street Journal,* November 26, 1991, p. A14.
8. David M. Gould, "The Benefits of GATT for the U.S. and World Economies," *The Southwest Economy,* Federal Reserve Bank of Dallas, May 1994, p. 2.
9. "American Free Trade Policy: Rhetoric or Reality?" *Imprimis,* August 1989, p. 2.
10. Joseph B. White and Bob Davis, "U.S. Says Japan Is 'Dumping' in Minivan War," *Wall Street Journal,* December 23, 1991, p. B6.
11. Linda C. Hunter, "U.S. Trade Protection: Effects on the Industrial and Regional Composition of Employment," *Economic Review,* Federal Reserve Bank of Dallas, January 1990, pp. 1–11.
12. *Business America,* April 1994, p. 40.
13. *U.S. Industrial Outlook 1994,* pp. 15–16.
14. *IMF,* 1993.
15. *Business America,* June 1994, inside front cover.
16. Lewis T. Preston, "The Bank's Goal Is to Help Members Reduce Poverty and Raise Living Standards," *IMF Survey,* October 17, 1994, p. 310.
17. *Business America,* April 1994, p. 1.
18. Patricia S. Pollard, "Trade Between the United States and Eastern Europe," *Review,* The Federal Reserve Bank of St. Louis, July/August 1994, pp. 25–26.
19. Pride and Ferrell, p. 104.
20. Ibid.
21. Ibid.
22. *Business America,* June 1994, p. 11.
23. Annual Review 1993, Unilever, p. 6.
24. Colgate-Palmolive Company, Third Quarter Report, 1991, pp. 3–4.

25. Peter G. Peterson, "Japan's 'Invasion': A Matter of 'Fairness,'" *Wall Street Journal,* November 3, 1989, p. A12.
26. Pride and Ferrell, p. 113.
27. Ibid.
28. Carl A. Gerstacker, *A Look at Business in 1990* (Washington, D.C.: U.S. Government Printing Office, November 1990), pp. 274–275.
29. *Business Week,* May 23, 1994, p. 28.
30. Based on information from Colgate-Palmolive Company, 1993 Annual Report, pp. 6–7, 22; Howard Rudnitsky, "Making His Mark," *Forbes,* Sept. 26, 1994, p. 47; Jane A. Sasseen, "For Colgate-Palmolive, It's Time for Trench Warfare," *Business Week,* Sept. 19, 1994, p. 56; Sharen Kindel, "Selling by the Book," *Sales & Marketing Management,* Oct. 1994, p. 100; and "Colgate Buys Oral Hygiene Business in India," *The New York Times,* Aug. 18, 1994, p. C3.
31. Tracey Rosenthal, "American Harley-Davidson," *Business First of Buffalo,* May 9, 1994, p. 148; Harley-Davidson Japan, *Focus Japan,* Jan./Feb. 1994, p. 11; and Wendy F. Black, "Cashing in on Customization," *Dealernews,* May 1994, p. 26.

CHAPTER 4

1. Based on information from Gary S. Williams, "What Makes Entrepreneurs Tick?" *The Freeman,* October 1994, pp. 545–546.
2. *The State of Small Business: A Report of the President,* 1990, pp. 9–11.
3. Ibid., p. xii.
4. Small Business Administration, Annual Report, 1990, p. 16.
5. Based on information from General Motors Corporation, 1994 Annual Report, pp. 1–5; John Grettenberger's 1994 Annual Report Video presentation to shareholders on May 20, 1994; Charles W. L. Hill and Gareth R. Jones, *Strategic Management: An Integrated Approach,* 3rd ed. (Boston: Houghton Mifflin, 1995), pp. C271–C272, C274–C275; James Bennet, "Cadillac's New Campaign Reaches Out to Women and Minorities, Not Just the Older White Man," *The New York Times,* Aug. 8, 1994, p. C7; Tim Ward, "New Cadillacs for $31,000 Targets Younger Consumer," Sept. 20, 1994, p. A10; Cnydee Miller, "Cadillac Promo Targets African-Americans," *Marketing News,* May 23, 1994; and Fara Warner, "Caddy Comes Lately to Women, Blacks," *Adweek,* Eastern Edition, Feb. 29, 1994, p. 4.
6. Unilever United States, Inc., 1993 Report to Employees, p. 10, and Unilever Annual Review 1993, p. 4.

CHAPTER 5

1. Based on Small Business Administration, Annual Report, 1992, p. 49.
2. *The State of Small Business: A Report of the President,* 1990, pp. 9–11.
3. *The State of Small Business: A Report of the President, 1993,* pp. 36–38.
4. *State,* 1990, pp. 15–19.
5. Small Business Administration, Annual Report, 1992, p. 29.
6. Ibid., p. 71.

7. *State,* 1993, p. 63.

8. Small Business Administration, Annual Report, 1992, p. 70.

9. Ibid., p. 72.

10. *State,* 1993, p. 11.

11. Small Business Administration, Annual Report, 1992, p. 5.

12. Small Business Administration, Annual Report, 1990, p. 20.

13. John R. Emshwiller, "Enterprise," *Wall Street Journal,* December 26, 1990, p. B1.

14. Paul D. Lovett, "Meetings That Work: Plans Bosses Can Approve," *Harvard Business Review,* Nov.-Dec. 1988, pp. 38–41, 44.

15. Marc Leepsonn, "Building a Business: A Matter of Course," *Nation's Business,* April 1988, pp. 42–43.

16. Small Business Administration, Annual Report, 1992, p. 11.

17. Ibid., p. 53.

18. Ibid., p. 56.

19. *Small Business: Development Centers Meet Needs of Most Clients,* U.S. General Accounting Office, U.S. Senate Committee on Small Business, Brief Report to the Chairman, Washington, D.C., November 1989, p. 15.

20. Small Business Administration, Annual Report, 1992, pp. 27–28.

21. *The Universal Almanac,* 1991, p. 231.

22. Joan Oleck, "Franchise Finds: Buying a He-Man Franchise," *Executive Female,* July/Aug. 1994, p. 30.

23. Gregory Matusky, "The Franchise Hall of Fame," *Inc.,* April 1994, p. 86.

24. Al Urbanski, "The Franchise Option," *Sales and Marketing Management,* Feb. 1988, pp. 28–33.

25. "7-Eleven Franchises File for Lack of Support," *National Petroleum News,* May 1994, p. 17.

26. Jeanne Saddler, "Franchise Pacts Can End in Suits Over Contracts," *Wall Street Journal,* January 15, 1991, p. B1.

27. Barry M. Heller and Elaine A. Panagakos, "Territorial Encroachment: The Burger King and Taco Bell Cases," *Franchise Law Journal,* Summer 1994, p. 3.

28. Ibid.

29. Based on information from *Profiles in Franchise Leadership,* Sir Speedy, Inc., 1992, n.p.; Franchise Documents, Sir Speedy, Inc., Apr. 1994, pp. 1–13; *Franchise Opportunities Handbook,* U.S. Department of Commerce, June 1991, p. 233; David Yawn, "The Thrill Is Back," *Memphis Business Journal,* Sept. 12, 1994, p. 20; and author's personal interviews with Mr. Ted Malone, Regional Franchising Director, Sir Speedy, Inc., Westmont, Illinois, Feb. 1995.

30. Based on the Small Business Administration, Annual Report, 1992, p. 52.

CHAPTER 6

1. Based on information from Michael Treacy and Fred Wiersema, "How Market Leaders Keep Their Edge," *Fortune,* Feb. 6, 1995, pp. 88–90+; Gary Hoover, ed., *Hoover's Handbook of American Business 1995* (Austin, Texas: Reference Press, 1994), pp. 654–655; Brian O'Reilly, "J&J Is on a Roll," *Fortune,* Dec. 26, 1994, pp. 178–180+; Dan Moreau, "This Health Company's Share Price Is Hurting,"

Kiplinger's Personal Finance Magazine, Oct. 1994, p. 30; and Johnson & Johnson 1993 Annual Report, One Johnson & Johnson Plaza, New Brunswick, New Jersey.

2. Alan Farnham, "America's Most Admired Company, *Fortune,* Feb. 7, 1994, p. 51.

3. Henry Mintzberg, "The Manager's Job: Folklore and Fact," *Harvard Business Review,* July–August 1975, pp. 49–61.

4. Robert Kreitner, *Management,* 6th edition (Boston: Houghton Mifflin, 1995), p. 473.

5. Ricky Griffin, *Management,* 4th ed. (Boston: Houghton Mifflin, 1993), p. 202.

6. Kreitner, p. 247.

7. Gary Hoover, ed., *Hoover's Handbook of American Business 1994,* (Austin, Texas: Reference Press, 1993), p. 356.

8. Fred Steingraber, "Total Quality Management: A New Look at a Basic Issue," *Vital Speeches of the Day,* May 1990, pp. 415–416.

9. Based on information from Gary Hoover, ed., *Hoover's Handbook of American Business 1995* (Austin, Texas: Reference Press, 1994), pp. 514–515; Nancy Perry, "How to Mine Human Resources," *Fortune,* Feb. 21, 1994, p. 96; Michael Sivy, "Going Global with U.S. Stocks," *Money,* Jan. 1994, p. 152; Michael Sivy, "Top Bargains: Bank of N.Y., Fluor, Bristol and Alcoa," *Money,* Jan. 1993, p. 152; 1993 Fluor Annual Report, 3333 Michelson Dr., Irvine, CA 92730; and Eric Schine, "Cleaning Up at Fluor," *Business Week,* Oct. 5, 1992, pp. 112–113.

10. Based on information from Dan Moreau, "Midas of the Mundane," *Kiplinger's Personal Finance Magazine,* June 1994, pp. 34–35; Zachary Schiller, "No Bounce for Rubbermaid," *Business Week,* May 2, 1994, p. 36; Alan Farnham, "America's Most Admired Company," *Fortune,* Feb. 7, 1994, pp. 50–52+; Zachary Schiller, "At Rubbermaid, Little Things Mean a Lot," *Newsweek,* Nov. 11, 1991, p. 126; Brian O'Reilly, "Corporate Reputations: Quality of Products," *Fortune,* Jan. 29, 1990, pp. 42–43; Patricia Sellers, "Does the CEO Really Matter?" *Fortune,* Apr. 22, 1991, pp. 80–82+; and Brian Dumaine, "Who Needs a Boss?" *Fortune,* May 7, 1990, pp. 52–55+.

CHAPTER 7

1. Based on information from Jerry Flint, "Sometimes You're the Windshield, Sometimes You're the Bug," *Forbes,* Nov. 21, 1994, pp. 44–45; Alex Taylor III, "GM's $11,000,000,000 Turnaround," *Fortune,* Oct. 17, 1994, pp. 54+; Peter F. Drucker, "The Theory of the Business," *Harvard Business Review,* Sept.–Oct. 1994, pp. 95+; Gary Hoover, ed., *Hoover's Handbook of American Business 1995* (Austin, Texas: Reference Press, 1994), pp. 548–549; and Jerry Flint, "Revving Up," *Forbes,* Jan. 31, 1994, pp. 40–41.

2. Robert Kreitner, *Management,* 6th ed. (Boston: Houghton Mifflin, 1995), p. 309.

3. Michael Cieply, "Meanwhile, Back in Marysville," *Forbes,* March 12, 1984, p. 127.

4. Terrence Deal and Allan Kennedy, *Corporate Culture* (Reading, Mass.: Addison-Wesley, 1982).

5. Kreitner, *op. cit.,* p. 95.

6. Art Fry, "The Post-it Note: An Intrapreneurial Success,"

SAM Advanced Management Journal, Summer 1987, pp. 4–7.

7. Based on information from Gary Hoover, ed., *Hoover's Handbook of American Business 1994* (Austin, Texas: Reference Press, 1993), p. 780–781; *Moody's Handbook of Common Stocks,* Moody's Investors Service, Summer 1994; Kimberly Ryan, *Datamation,* June 15, 1993, pp. 76–77; Dan Moreau, "In Its Smokestack Business, 3M Is Driven by Productivity," *Kiplinger's Personal Finance Magazine,* Feb. 1993, p. 32; David Altany, "The New Bottom Line," *Industry Week,* Jan. 22, 1990, pp. 13–14+; "3M Co. Means Matrix, Matrix and More Matrix," *Computerworld,* June 17, 1991, p. 59; Ronald A. Mitsch, "Three Roads to Innovation," *The Journal of Business Strategy,* Sept.–Oct. 1990, pp. 18–21; and Barbara Burgower, "Sweetening the Lure of the Lab," *Business Month,* Aug. 1990, pp. 76–77.

8. Based on information from Ronald Henkoff, "Smartest & Dumbest Managerial Moves of 1994," *Fortune,* pp. 84–85; Gary Hoover, ed., *Hoover's Handbook of American Business 1995* (Austin, Texas: Reference Press, 1994), pp. 674–675; David Woodruff and Judith H. Dobrzynski, "Revolt? What Revolt?" *Business Week,* June 20, 1994, p. 42; Bill Saporito, "Bloody New Year for Retailers," *Fortune,* Feb. 7, 1994, pp. 19–20; James B. Treece, "Kmart: Slick Moves or Running in Place?" *Business Week,* Jan. 17, 1994, p. 28; Subrata N. Chakravarty, "The Best-Laid Plans," *Forbes,* Jan. 3, 1994, pp. 44–45; and Bill Saporito, "The High Cost of Second Best," *Fortune,* July 26, 1993, pp. 99+.

CHAPTER 8

1. Based on information from Gene Bylinsky, "The Digital Factory," *Fortune,* Nov. 14, 1994, pp. 92+; Ira Sager, "Lou Gerstner Unveils His Battle Plan," *Business Week,* Apr. 4, 1994, pp. 96–98; Ira Sager, "IBM Reboots—Bit By Bit," *Business Week,* Jan. 17, 1994, pp. 82–82; Judith H. Dobrzynski, "Rethinking IBM: An Exclusive Account of Lou Gerstner's First Six Months," *Business Week,* Oct. 4, 1993, pp. 86+.

2. *Monthly Labor Review,* Bureau of Labor Statistics, Nov. 1994; p. 80.

3. Robert Kreitner, *Management,* 6th ed. (Boston: Houghton Mifflin, 1995), pp. 108–109.

4. Gary Hoover, ed., *Hoover's Handbook of American Business 1994,* (Austin, Texas: Reference Press, 1993), p. 536.

5. Kreitner, *op. cit.,* p. 571.

6. Kreitner, *op. cit.,* p. 183.

7. Kreitner, *Management,* 5th ed. (Boston: Houghton Mifflin, 1992), p. 97.

8. *1994 Statistical Abstract of the United States,* U.S. Department of Commerce, p. 873.

9. "1995 Black Enterprise Auto Guide–Saturn," *Black Enterprise,* Nov. 1994, p. 196; "Planet Falls to Earth," *The Economist,* Mar. 12, 1994, pp. 74–75; David Woodruff, "Suddenly, Saturn's Orbit Is Getting Wobbly," *Business Week,* Feb. 28, 1994, p. 34; Frank Washington, "Saturn at 10: Happy Birthday?" *Newsweek,* Dec. 6, 1993, p. 43.

10. Based on information from Robert D. Haas, "Ethics—A Global Business Challenge," *Vital Speeches of the Day,* June 1, 1994, pp. 506–509; Nina Munk, "The Levi Straddle," *Forbes,* Jan. 17, 1994, pp. 44–45; Russell Mitchell, "Managing by Values," *Business Week,* Aug. 1, 1994, pp. 46–52; Margaret Price, "Pitfalls Are Plentiful in Hungarian Market," *Pensions and Investment,* Mar. 4, 1991, p. 1+; Natalia Wolniansky and Leon P. Garry, "A New Hungarian Spring?" *Management Review,* July 1991, pp. 37–40; Charles T. Powers, "Levi Strauss Sews Up Enthusiastic Support for Factory in Polish City," *Los Angeles Times,* July 9, 1991; "A Levi Strauss Plant in Poland," *USA Today,* Nov. 15, 1991; and Maria Shao, Robert Neff, and Jeffrey Ryser, "For Levi's, a Flattering Fit Overseas," *Business Week,* Nov. 5, 1990, pp. 76–77.

CHAPTER 9

1. Based on information from Pat Riley, "What Winners Know," *Reader's Digest,* Mar. 1994, pp. 177–178; "Executive Influences," *Training & Development,* June 1994, p. 10; Ira Berkow, "The Haunted Aspect of Coach Riley," *The New York Times,* Mar. 15, 1994; and Pat Riley, *The Winner Within* (New York: Putnam, 1993).

2. Douglas McGregor, *The Human Side of Enterprise* (New York: McGraw-Hill, 1960).

3. William Ouchi, *Theory Z* (Reading, Mass: Addison-Wesley, 1981).

4. Ricky W. Griffin, *Management,* 4th ed. (Boston: Houghton Mifflin, 1993), p. 169.

5. Paige Landsman, "Juggling Work and Family," *Business Insurance,* Aug. 8, 1994, p. 16.

6. Catherine Romano, "What's Your Flexibility Factor?" *Management Review,* Jan. 1994, p. 9.

7. Landsman, p. 16.

8. Penny Lunt, "Want to Share a Job? Some People Do," *ABA Banking Journal,* Mar. 1994, p. 88.

9. Gary Ritter and Stan Thompson, "The Rise of Telecommuting and Virtual Transportation," *Transportation Quarterly,* Summer 1994, pp. 235–248.

10. Mark Frohman, "The Aimless Empowered," *Industry Week,* April 20, 1992, pp. 64–66.

11. Richard C. Kearney and Steven W. Hays, "Labor Management Relations and Participative Decision-Making: Toward a New Paradigm," *Public Administration Review,* Jan./Feb. 1994, pp. 44–51.

12. Stewart L. Stokes, Jr., "Moving Toward Self-Directed Teams: An Action Plan for Self-Managed Teams," *Information Systems,* Winter 1994, pp. 40–44.

13. Susan G. Cohen and Gerald E. Ledford, Jr., "The Effectiveness of Self-managing Teams: A Quasi-Experiment," *Human Relations,* vol. 47, no. 1, 1994, pp. 13–41.

14. "The Inc. Network," *Inc.,* Aug. 1994, pp. 113–114.

15. Based on information from John Case, "Memo To Corporate America: Sometimes It's Best to Think Small," *Boston Globe,* Mar. 30, 1994; Gary Hoover, Alta Campbell, and Patrick J. Spain, eds., *Hoover's Handbook of American Business* (Austin, Texas: The Reference Press, 1994), pp. 462–463; Robin Yale Bergstrom, "Quietly and Without

Fanfare," Eaton Corporation press kit; and "Eaton Corporation: Excellence Through People," Eaton Corporation video.

16. Based on information from John Case, "Collective Effort," *Inc.,* Jan. 1992, pp. 32–35, 42–43; Sid de Boer, "Reflexite Glows Bright in Dark Economy," *New Britain (Conn.) Herald,* June 25, 1991; "Personal Safety Is Reflexite's Premium Concern," *Reflexite Corporation News,* Summer 1990, pp. 1, 4; "Reflexite AP1000 Makes a Safe Landing in Canada," *Reflexite Corporation News,* Summer 1991, pp. 1, 4; "From the President," *Reflexite Corporation News,* Summer 1991, p. 4; Reflexite Corporation, Annual Report, 1991; "Reflexite on the Move: New Technology Center Speeds Global Expansion," *Spectrum,* Winter 1993–1994, p. 1; "Brighter Buses Bring Children Safely Back to U.S. Schools," *Spectrum,* Winter 1993–1994, p. 1; "When the Lights Went Out in Florida, Reflexite Signs Kept Traffic Moving," *Spectrum,* Winter 1993–1994, p. 2; and Teri Lammers, "The Effective Employee-Feedback System," *Inc.,* Feb. 1993, pp. 109–111.

CHAPTER 10

1. Based on information from "Interview: Gun Denhart," *Business Ethics,* July/Aug. 1994, pp. 18–19, 20–21; Sarah Thomas, "Corporate Mission: Doing Business With Sense and Sensibility," *Horizon Air Magazine,* Apr. 1994, p. 64; Paula Lyons, "Doing Well By Doing Good," *Ladies' Home Journal,* Sept. 1994, pp. 112, 114; "Company Profile: Hanna Andersson Corporation," *The Bruce Report,* Apr. 28, 1994, pp. 2–3; Anne Murphy, "Too Good to Be True?" *Inc.,* July 1994, pp. 34–36, 38, 40, 42–43; and Hanna Andersson, press kit, 1994.

2. Faye Rice, "How To Make Diversity Pay," *Fortune,* Aug. 8, 1994, pp. 78–80, 82, 84, 86.

3. "HR and Government," *HRMagazine,* May 1994, pp. 43–45.

4. Brian H. Kleiner and Ann Sparks, "How Flexible Should Benefits Programs Be?" *Risk Management,* Feb. 1994, pp. 11–12, 17.

5. Ibid.

6. William Wiggenhorn, "Motorola U: When Training Becomes an Education," *Harvard Business Review,* July–Aug. 1990, pp. 71–83.

7. Robert Kreitner, *Management,* 5th ed. (Boston: Houghton Mifflin, 1992), pp. 327–328.

8. Based on information from Woolworth Corporation, Press Kit; Wade Lambert, "Law Helps Mentally Disabled Job Outlook," *Wall Street Journal,* Feb. 2, 1995, p. B6; Gary Hoover, Alta Campbell, and Patrick J. Spain, eds., *Hoover's Handbook of American Business 1994* (Austin, Texas: Reference Press, 1994), pp. 1132–1133; and Woolworth Corporation, "Employability," Video.

9. Based on information from Julia Lawlor, "Working with AIDS," *USA Today,* Dec. 11, 1991, pp. 1B–2B; Art Durity, "The AIDS Epidemic," *Personnel,* Apr. 1991, p. 1; Rhonda West and Art Durity, "Does My Company Need to Worry About AIDS?" *Personnel,* Apr. 1991, p. 5; Stuart Feldman, "When It Comes to AIDS, It's Survival of the Smartest,"

Personnel, Apr. 1991, p. 6; Eleanor Smith, "Train Supervisors to Be AIDS Savvy," *Personnel,* Apr. 1991, p. 7; Stuart Feldman, "A Job for Champions," *Personnel,* Apr. 5, 1991, p. 8; Charles Nau, "ADA Forces Employers to Respond," *Personnel,* Apr. 5, 1991, pp. 9–10; Stuart Feldman, "Three Successful Programs," *Personnel,* Apr. 5, 1991, p. 11; Julia Lawlor, "HIV-Infected Workers Get Little Support," *USA Today,* Nov. 11, 1991, p. B1.

CHAPTER 11

1. Based on information from "Cat Sinks Claws in Wildcat Strikers," *ENR,* June 20, 1994, p. 17; "A Cat Fight with No Winners," *Business Week,* July 4, 1994, p. 104; Ronald Grover, "Much Ado About Pettiness," *Business Week,* July 4, 1994, pp. 34–35; Kevin Kelly, "Cat Is Purring, But They're Hissing on the Floor," *Business Week,* May 16, 1994, p. 33; and Gary Hoover, Alta Campbell, and Patrick J. Spain, eds., *Hoover's Handbook of American Business 1994* (Austin, Texas: Reference Press, 1994), pp. 318–319.

2. Aaron Bernstein, "Why American Needs Unions, But Not the Kind It Has Now," *Business Week,* May 23, 1994, pp. 70–71, 74, 78, 82.

3. Based on information from Peter Lazes, et al., "Xerox and the ACTWU: Using Labor-Management Teams to Remain Competitive," *National Productivity Review,* Summer 1991, pp. 339–349; Norman E. Richard, Jr., "The Quest for Quality: A Race Without a Finish Line," *Industrial Engineering,* Jan. 1991, pp. 25–27; Anne Ritter, "Are Unions Worth the Bargain?" *Personnel,* Feb. 1990, pp. 12–14; Dan Dordtz, "Listening to Labor," *Financial World,* Sept. 2, 1991, pp. 44–47; "Company-Union Partnership Turns Xerox Around," *Personnel Journal,* Jan. 1994, p. 61; Dawn Anfuso, "Xerox Partners With the Union to Regain Market Share," *Personnel Journal,* Aug. 1994, pp. 46–53; and Xerox Corp., "The High Road: Union Management Partnership," Video 1994.

4. Based on information from Robert A. Mamis, "Man of Iron," *Inc.,* Jan. 1992, pp. 56–59; David Prizinsky, "Elyria Foundry Casts Success," *Cleveland Business,* Nov. 17, 1991, pp. 1, 10; Leslie Browka, "The Annual One-Page Company Game Plan," *Inc.,* June 1993, pp. 111–112; and "A Different Kind of Foundry," Elyria brochure.

CHAPTER 12

1. Based on information from James R. Healey, "Ford Begins Building Fresh Design Today," *USA Today,* Oct. 4, 1993, pp. 1B–2B; David C. Smith, "Saddling Up with the '94 Mustang," *WARD'S Auto World,* Mar. 1993, pp. 52–54, 59, 61, 63, 65, 71; Jon Lowell, "Mustang Fanatics Aren't from the Horsey Set," *WARD'S Auto World,* Mar. 1993, p. 54; Raymond Serafin, "New Mustang Ads Hope to Leap Generation Gap," *Advertising Age,* Nov. 22, 1993, p. 40; Raymond Serafin, "Mustang Love: Ford Revs Up Romantic Heritage to Sell New Model of Sports Car," *Advertising Age,* Oct. 4, 1993, p. 4; "The Best Products of 1993," *Time,* Jan. 3, 1994, p. 76; Ford Motor Company, Annual Report, 1993.

2. Michelle Dalton, "Technology Behind the Scenes," *Dealerscope*, May 1992, p. 74.

3. James F. Engel, Roger D. Blackwell, and Paul W. Miniard, *Consumer Behavior*, (Hinsdale, Ill.: Dryden Press, 1995), p. 3.

4. Consumer Expenditure Survey, Bureau of Labor Statistics, 1994.

5. Based on information from: Houghton Mifflin Company, *The American Heritage Dictionary*, 3rd ed., press kit; Joy Fleishhacker, "Book Review/Reference," *School Library Journal*, May 1994, p. 138; and Houghton Mifflin, "*The American Heritage Dictionary*," Video.

6. Based on information from Joseph Weber, Gail Schares, Stephen Hutcheon, Ian Katz, and Pete Engardio, "Campbell: Now It's M-M-Global," *Business Week*, Mar. 15, 1993, pp. 52–53; Jonathan Karp, "Soup for the Masses," *Far Eastern Economic Review*, Oct. 29, 1992, p. 80; Richard L. Holman, "Campbell Soup Varieties in China," *Wall Street Journal*, Nov. 13, 1992, p. A10; "New Mainstream: Hot Dogs, Apple Pie, and Salsa," *Supermarket Business*, May 1992, pp. 92, 94; Bickley Townsend, "Market Research That Matters," *American Demographics*, Aug. 1992, pp. 58–60; *Philadelphia Inquirer*, Apr. 7, 1994, p. C2; "Joint Venture Is Planned to Upgrade Sales in Japan," *Wall Street Journal*, Nov. 6, 1993, p. B4; Julie Liesse, "Campbell Turns Up Heat on Soup," *Advertising Age*, July 5, 1993, pp. 1, 36; and Pierce Hollingsworth, "Global Opportunities," *Food Technology*, Mar. 1994, pp. 65–68.

CHAPTER 13

1. Based on information from Birkenstock press kit, 1993; Jennifer Pendleton, "Margot Fraser: A Sure-Footed Business Woman," *Biz*, Mar. 1993, pp. 17–18; Morrison Shafroth, "Back to Birkenstocks," *Alaska Airlines Magazine*, Dec. 1992, p. 13; Richard Stengel, "Be It Ever So Birkenstock," *The New York Times*, Aug. 30, 1992; Brenda Paik Sunoo, "Birkenstock Braces to Fight the Competition," *Personnel Journal*, Aug. 1994, pp. 67–75; and Leslie Brokaw, "Feet, Don't Fail Me Now," *Inc.*, May 1994, pp. 69–78.

2. Peter D. Bennett, ed., *Dictionary of Marketing Terms* (Chicago: American Marketing Foundation, 1988), p. 18.

3. Based on information from Paula Lerner and Woodfin Camp, "Soleful Endeavor," *People*, Dec. 12, 1994, pp. 69–70; Glenn Rifkin, "Mix and Match: A Shoe For Women, A Survivor's Tale," *The New York Times*, July 3, 1994, p. 5; Ryka, Inc., press release, Jan. 30, 1995; and Ryka Shoes, Inc., Sales Training Video.

4. Based on information from Gary Hoover, Alta Campbell, and Patrick Spain, eds., *Hoover's Handbook of American Business 1994* (Austin, Texas: Reference Press, 1994), pp. 978–979; "Flying Straight with Southwest Airlines Chairman Herb Kelleher," *Brandweek*, Oct. 10, 1994, pp. 36, 38, 40; Jennifer Lawrence, "Southwest Setting the Rules in the Air Carrier Market," *Advertising Age*, Sept. 28, 1994, pp. 22, 38; Jennifer Lawrence, "Airlines Give Fliers Fleet of New Choices," *Advertising Age*, Sept. 12, 1994, p. 59; "Southwest Airlines Pressed by Its Rivals, Launches Fare Cuts," *Wall Street Journal*, Dec. 1, 1994, p. B4; Bridget O'Brian, "Southwest Airlines Fares Well Minus Some Reservations," *Wall Street Journal*, Aug. 8, 1994, p. 34; Jesus Sanchez, "A Sky Full of Imitators," *Los Angeles Times*, June 26, 1994, p. D1, D4; Michael Lyster, "We Hope to Have More," *Orange County (Calif.) Business Journal*, May 23, 1994; and Don Lee, "Southwest Lifting Airport's Business," *Los Angeles Times*, May 10, 1994, p. 12.

CHAPTER 14

1. Based on information from Dori Jones Yang, "The Starbucks Enterprise Shifts into Warp Speed," *Business Week*, Oct. 24, 1994, pp. 76, 78–79; "Delta Airlines To Introduce Starbucks Coffee on Shuttle Flights," *PR Newswire*, Sept. 7, 1994; "Starbucks to Buy Competitor for Northeast Push," *Nation's Restaurant News*, Mar. 28, 1994, p. 3; Bill McDowell, "Starbucks Coffee: 1994 Top Growth Companies: Company Profile," *Restaurants & Institutions*, Aug. 1, 1994, p. 53; and Martin Wolk, "Rising Coffee Prices Eat into Starbucks Sales," *The Reuter Business Report*, Sept. 30, 1994.

2. U.S. Statistical Abstract, 1991, p. 779.

3. U.S. Statistical Abstract, 1993.

4. Ibid.

5. Ibid. p. 775.

6. William M. Pride and O. C. Ferrell, *Marketing: Basic Concepts and Decisions*, 9th ed. (Boston: Houghton Mifflin, 1995), p. 448.

7. *Chain Store Age/Supermarkets*, July 1983, p. 11.

8. Stanley C. Hollander, "The Wheel of Retailing," *Journal of Marketing*, July 1960, p. 37.

9. Adapted from John F. Magee, *Physical Distribution Systems*, (New York: McGraw-Hill, 1967), p. 73.

10. Based on information from "Hot Shots: *HFD* Profiles 25 of the Industry's Most Influential Retail Buyers," *HFD*, July 20, 1992, pp. 47–48; Michael Hartnett, "Container Store Enjoys Steady Growth," *SCT Retailing Today*, Nov. 1992, pp. 67–68; Bob Weinstein, "Box Boys: The Container Store," *Entrepreneur*, June 1992, pp. 122–126; "Growth Plans for The Container Store," *Stores*, May 1992, p. 74; Trish Lichtenstein, "Find Something for Everything at Oak Brook Container Store," *Chicago Herald*, July 25, 1994; "Storage All Stars," *HFD*, July 18, 1994, pp. 49, 72; Julie Morse, "For the Organizationally Impaired," *Chicago Tribune*, July 31, 1994; John Schmeltzer, "Container Store Fills Gaps," *Chicago Tribune*, July 29, 1994, pp. 1–2; The Container Store, press kit; and *The Container Store*, video.

11. Based on information from "Retail Gain Clouds Rep's Horizon," *Industrial Distribution*, May 1992, pp. 10–11; Jennifer Reese, "What Sam Walton Taught America," *Fortune*, May 4, 1992, pp. 66–67; Jennifer Lawrence, "Wal-Mart Draws Fire," *Advertising Age*, Jan. 13, 1992, pp. 3, 43; Seema Nyyar, "Wal-Mart Move Confirms Shift in Retailer-Marketer Ties," *Brandweek*, Feb. 15, 1993, p. 8; Seema Nayyar, "Up Against the Wall," *Brandweek*, Feb. 8, 1992, pp. 1, 3; Zachary Schiller, Wendy Zellner, Ron Stodghill II, and Mark Maremont, "Clout! More and More, Retail Giants Rule the Marketplace," *Business Week*, Dec. 21,

1992, pp. 66–69, 72–73; Gerry Khermouch, "Wal-Mart Plan Hits Snag," *Brandweek*, May 10, 1993, p. 3; "Wal-Mart, Vendors Setting Category Management Plans," *Supermarket News*, Apr. 4, 1994, p. 42; Leslie Bayor, "Wal-Mart Exec Notes Need for Efficiency," *Advertising Age*, May 10, 1993, p. 3; and Gerry Ghermouch, "Kodak, Wal-Mart Price Stand-Off Is a Royal Rumble," *Brandweek*, Apr. 18, 1994, p. 1.

CHAPTER 15

1. Based on information from Dr Pepper USA, *Clockdial*, Winter 1994, pp. 10–11; Dr Pepper USA, *Clockdial*, Fall 1994, pp. 8–15; Karen Benezra, "Dr Pepper Girds for $150–$200M Market Blitz," *Brandweek*, Apr. 25, 1994, pp. 1, 6; and Stan Madden, "Jim Turner: A 'Pepper' on the Soft Drink Sea," *Baylor Business Review*, Spring 1994, pp. 2–5.
2. "Ad Gain of 5.2% in '93 Marks Downturn's End," *Advertising Age*, May 2, 1994, p. 4.
3. Nielsen Media Research, July 1994.
4. Ibid.
5. Terence A. Shimp, *Promotion Management and Marketing Communication* (Hinsdale, Ill.: Dryden Press, 1993), pp. 449–452.
6. Donnelley Marketing, Inc., *The 16th Annual Survey of Promotional Practices*, p. 9.
7. Jeanne Whalen, "Coupon Marketers Felt Chill in '93," *Advertising Age*, Jan. 17, 1994, p. S-4.
8. Fara Warner, "Hold the Comics, Sports, And Give Me That FSI," *Brandweek*, Mar. 21, 1994, p. 42.
9. Based on information from the Advertising Council, Annual Report, 1992; "Ad Council Targets Racism in Wake of L.A. Rioting," *Advertising Age*, May 11, 1992, pp. 1, 76; Ruth Ann Wooden, "Advertising Council Campaigns Make a Difference," *Broadcasting*, Nov. 2, 1992, p. 79; The Advertising Council, "New Radon PSAs to Help Prevent Carjacking," *Public Service Advertising Bulletin*, May–June 1993, pp. 1–2; Genine Babakain, "Russian Ad Council Gets Ready for Biz," *Adweek*, July 12, 1993, p. 15; Debra Aho, "Earth Share Finds Prodigy a Good Environment," *Advertising Age*, Oct. 18, 1993, p. 26; "Big Win For Ad Council," *Advertising Age*, Oct. 4, 1993, p. 32; and The Advertising Council, press releases.
10. Based on information from "When the Chips Were Down, Nabisco Didn't Crumble," *Sales and Marketing Management*, June 1990, pp. 64–76; "Inside Nabisco's Cookie Machine," *Adweek's Marketing Week*, Mar. 18, 1991, pp. 22–23; Megan Santosus, "Computer-Aided Bake Sales," *CIO*, May 1, 1993, p. 76; and Gary Hoover, Alta Campbell, and Patrick J. Spain, eds., *Hoover's Handbook of American Business 1994* (Austin, Texas: Reference Press, 1994), pp. 922–923.

CHAPTER 16

1. Based on information from Brent Schlender, "What Bill Gates Really Wants," *Fortune*, Jan. 16, 1995, pp. 34–37+; Gary Hoover, ed., *Hoover's Handbook of American Business, 1995* (Austin, Texas: Reference Press, 1994),

pp. 774–775; Amy Berstein, "Microsoft Goes Online," *U.S. News & World Report*, Nov. 21, 1994, p. 84; Paul M. Eng, "It's Getting Crowded On Line," *Business Week*, Nov. 7, 1994, p. 134+; and Tom Post, "Bill Gates's Soft Landing," *Newsweek*, July 25, 1994, p. 40.
2. Deidre A. Depke, "PCs: What the Future Holds," *Business Week*, Aug. 12, 1991, pp. 58–64.
3. Based on information from Gary Hoover, ed., *Hoover's Handbook of American Business, 1995* (Austin, Texas: Reference Press, 1994), pp. 864–865; PepsiCo, Inc., 1993 Annual Report, pp. 11–15; David Hage and Linda Grant, "How to Make America Work," *U.S. News & World Report*, Dec. 6, 1993, p. 52; Seth Lubove, "Report from the Front," *Forbes*, Sept. 13, 1993, p. 220; Bob Francis, "Frito-Lay's Network Recipe," *Datamation*, Jan. 15, 1991, pp. 57–58+; and Jeremy Main, "Frito-Lay Shortens Its Business Cycle," *Fortune*, Jan. 15, 1990, p. 11.
4. Based on information from Robert D. Hof, "The Education of Andrew Grove," *Business Week*, Jan. 16, 1995, pp. 60–62; Robert D. Hof, "The I-Way 'Will Be Paved with Silicon,'" *Business Week*, Jan. 9, 1995, p. 77; David Kirkpatrick, "The Fallout from Intel's Pentium Bug," *Fortune*, Jan. 16, 1995, p. 15; Gary Hoover, ed., *Hoover's Handbook of American Business, 1995* (Austin, Texas: Reference Press, 1994), pp. 634–635; and Ira Sager, "Bare Knuckles at Big Blue," *Business Week*, Dec. 26, 1994, pp. 60–62.

CHAPTER 17

1. Gary Hoover, ed., *Hoover's Handbook of American Business, 1995*, (Austin, Texas: Reference Press, 1994), pp. 426–427; Floyd Norris, "Market Place: Why Its Auditors Might Have Tired of Arguing with IDB," *The New York Times*, June 20, 1994, p. 4; Hubert B. Herring, "Business Diary: May 29–June 3," *The New York Times*, June 5, 1994, p. 2; "Company News; Auditors Resign at IDB Communications Group," *The New York Times*, June 1, 1994, p. 4; Brian Dumaine, "America's Smart Young Entrepreneurs," *Fortune*, Mar. 24, 1994, pp. 34+; and Gene G. Marcial, "Gathering News—and a Lot of Steam," *Business Week*, Feb. 22, 1993, p. 88.
2. Based on information from Gary Hoover, ed., *Hoover's Handbook of American Business, 1995*. (Austin, Texas: Reference Press, 1994), pp. 216–217; Alta Chai, ed., *Hoover's Handbook of World Business 1993*, (Austin, Texas: Reference Press, 1993), pp. 134–135; Rahul Jacob, "Can You Trust that Audit?" *Fortune*, Nov. 18, 1991, pp. 191–192+; "Civil War at Arthur Andersen," *The Economist*, Aug. 17, 1991, pp. 66–67; and Jeffrey M. Laderman, "When One Plus One Equals No. 1," *Business Week*, June 5, 1989, p. 94.
3. Procter & Gamble's consolidated statement of earnings and consolidated balance sheet are taken from the 1994 Procter & Gamble Annual Report, pp. 17–18.

CHAPTER 18

1. Based on information from Gregory Spears, "Bank Stocks That Are Headed Up," *Kiplinger's Personal Finance Magazine*, Jan. 1995, pp. 87–90; Matt Walsh, "Two Bankers,

Same Strategy," *Forbes*, Dec. 5, 1994, pp. 51–53; David Greising, "NationsBank, An Excess in Zeal?" *Business Week*, Nov. 28, 1994, pp. 104–106; Amy Barnett, "Alarms Are Going Off at the Banks," *Business Week*, Oct. 3, 1994, pp. 122+; Amy Barnett, "Right This Way, Mr. McColl. Your Hot Seat Is Ready," *Business Week*, Oct. 3, 1 994, p. 125; Linda Grant, "A Rebel Banker Battles On," *U.S. News & World Report*, Mar. 7, 1994, pp. 59+; and NationsBank Annual Report 1993, NationsBank Corporation, Nations-Bank Corporate Center, Charlotte, NC 28255.

2. Sheryl Nance-Nash, "Here's Why Bank Safety Still Matters," *Money*, Mar. 1994, pp. 38+.

3. Robert Farmighetti, ed., *The World Almanac and Book of Facts 1994.* (Mahwah, N.J.: Funk & Wagnalls, 1993), p. 106.

4. Sumner N. Levine, ed., *The Irwin Business and Investment Almanac 1994.* (Burr Ridge, Ill.: Irwin Professional Publishing, 1993), p. 29.

5. Tom Spring, "The Coming Banking Scandal," *USA Today*, Nov. 1993, p. 17.

6. Farmighetti, *op. cit.*, p. 107.

7. Levine, *op. cit.*, p. 30.

8. *Federal Reserve Bulletin*, Oct. 1994, p. A8.

9. Based on information from Richard A. Marini, "Never Had Credit? You Can Get It Now," *Good Housekeeping*, Sept. 1994, p. 237; "Do You Need Credit Counseling?" *Consumers' Research*, Sept. 1993, p. 27; Charles E. Cohen, "The Last Charge," *Ladies' Home Journal*, June 1991, pp. 118+; Guy Murdoch, "Credit Counseling," *Consumers' Research*, Mar. 1991, p. 2; and Theodore P. Roth, "Sorry, Your Card Is No Good," *Time*, Apr. 9, 1990, p. 62.

10. Based on information from David Greising, "Nationsbank: An Excess of Zeal?" *Business Week*, Nov. 28, 1994, pp. 104–106; Vanessa O'Connell, "A Whistle-Blower Tells How Banks Abuse Investors," *Money*, July 1994, pp. 31+; Virginia Munger Kahn, "Should You Invest Through Your Bank?" *Working Woman*, May 1994, pp. 33+; Mark Bautz, "We Find That Banks Often Give Bad Investment Advice," *Money*, May 1994, pp. 40+; Jeff Kosnett, "What Do Banks Know About Mutual Funds?" *Kiplinger's Personal Finance Magazine*, Oct. 1993, pp. 77–81.

CHAPTER 19

1. Based on information from Leah Nathans Spiro, Jeffrey M. Laderman, and Russell Mitchell, "So Many Securities Firms, So Little Security," *Business Week*, Feb. 27, 1995, p. 100; Gary Hoover, ed., *Hoover's Handbook of American Business, 1995*, (Austin, Texas: Reference Press, 1994), pp. 564–565; "Partners in Pain," *The Economist*, Dec. 3, 1994, pp. 89–90; Carol J. Loomis, "The Goldman Standard Slips," *Fortune*, Nov. 28, 1994, pp. 14–15; Leah Nathans Spiro, "Goldman's Deep Bench May Keep the Streak Alive," *Business Week*, Sept. 26, 1994, p. 109; "Dividing Up the Spoils," *Time*, Mar. 21, 1994, p. 60; Amey Stone with Leah Nathan Spiro, "Sorry, This Year Your Bonus Is Only . . . $5 Million," *Business Week*, Jan. 17, 1994, p. 27; and Phillip L. Zweig, "Goldman Sachs' Spectacular Road Trip," *Business Week*, Nov. 1, 1993, pp. 110–111.

2. Peter Coy, Neil Gross, Silvia Sansoni, and Kevin Kelly,

"What's the Word in the Lab? Collaborate," *Business Week*, June 27, 1994, p. 79.

3. Kathleen Kerwin, "GM's Aurora," *Business Week*, March 21, 1994, p. 89.

4. Gary Hoover, ed., *Hoover's Handbook of American Business 1994* (Austin, Texas: Reference Press, 1993), p. 634.

5. Ibid, p. 724.

6. David Zigas, "Junk Is Ripping Into Commercial Paper," *Business Week*, Mar. 26, 1990, pp. 84+.

7. Mary Ann Ring, "Innovative Export Financing: Factoring and Forfaiting," *Business America*, Jan. 11, 1993, pp. 12–13+.

8. Pam Black, "Buyback Doesn't Always Mean Buy," *Business Week*, Jan. 31, 1994, p. 82.

9. *Ford Motor Company, Annual Report*, 1993, p. 26.

10. *Exxon Corporation Annual Report*, 1993, p. F8.

11. Based on information from Gary Hoover, ed., *Hoover's Handbook of American Business 1995*, (Austin, Texas: Reference Press, 1994), pp. 1050–1051; Marcia Berss, "Protein Man," *Forbes*, Oct. 24, 1994, pp. 64+; and Dan McGraw, "The Birdman of Arkansas," *U.S. News & World Report*, July 18, 1994, pp. 42+.

12. Based on information from *Moody's Handbook of Common Stocks*, Summer 1994, Moody's Investors Service, 99 Church Street, New York, NY 10007; Gary Hoover, *Hoover's Handbook of American Business 1994* (Austin, Texas: Reference Press, 1993), pp. 458–459; Jeffrey Young, "Information Please," *Forbes*, Oct. 1993, pp. 222+; Anne Murphy, "How to Read a Credit Report," *Inc.*, June 1990, pp. 68–69; Jeffrey Rothfeder, "Damage Control at Dun & Bradstreet," *Business Week*, Nov. 27, 1989, pp. 187–188+; and Johnnie L. Roberts, "Dun's Credit Reports, Vital Tool of Business Can Be Off the Mark," *Wall Street Journal*, Oct. 5, 1989, pp. A1+.

CHAPTER 20

1. Based on information from Gary Hoover, ed., *Hoover's Handbook of American Business, 1995* (Austin, Texas: Reference Press, 1994), pp. 610–611; Monica D. Garrett and Samuel A. Young, eds. *Moody's Handbook of Common Stocks* (New York: Moody's Investors Service, 1994); Susan E. Kuhn, "Blue-Chip Stocks Offer Value in a Volatile Market," *Fortune*, July 25, 1994, pp. 29–30; Frank Wolfe, "Rearview Mirror," *Forbes*, June 20, 1994, p. 138; and Graham Button, "The Man Who Almost Walked Out on Ross Perot," *Forbes*, Nov. 22, 1993, pp. 68–69+.

2. James R. Norman, "Picking the Best New Issues," *Forbes*, June 20, 1994, p. 174.

3. Gary Hoover, et al., *Hoover's Handbook of American Business 1994*, (Austin, Texas: Reference Press, 1993), pp. 810–811.

4. Otto Johnson, et al., *Information Please Almanac 1993*, (Boston, Mass.: Houghton Mifflin, 1993), p. 50.

5. Nancy Dunnan, *Dun & Bradstreet Guide to Your Investment $$ 1994* (New York: HarperCollins, 1994), p. 18.

6. Based on information from Russell Mitchell, Jeffrey M. Laderman, Leah Nathans Spiro, Geoffrey Smith, and Sandra Atchison, "The Schwab Revolution," *Business Week*, Dec. 19, 1994, pp. 88+; Matthew Schifrin, "Fund Malls,"

Forbes, June 20, 1994, pp. 234+; Amey Stone, "Should You Buy Your No-Load from a Titan?" *Business Week,* June 13, 1994, pp. 88–89; Jeffrey M. Laderman, "Schwab Gets Mutually Exclusive," *Business Week,* May 2, 1994, p. 6; Vanessa O'Connell, "A Great Way to Shop for Funds," *Money,* Feb. 1994, pp. 150+; "Corporate Profile," *The Charles Schwab Corporation,* Feb. 28, 1994; and Charles R. Schwab, "The Vision and Values of Our Company," June 25, 1991.

7. Price information from *The Wall Street Journal,* Oct. 11, 1994, p. C6.

CHAPTER 21

1. Based on information from Mutual of Omaha Companies 1994 Annual Report, pp. 6 and 26, and Mutual of Omaha Companies Info/Brief, Sept. 1994, p. 1. Used by permission of Mutual of Omaha Companies.
2. *The Fact Book 1994: Property/Casualty Insurance Facts* (Insurance Information Institute), p. 21.
3. Ibid.
4. *U.S. Industrial Outlook 1991,* U.S. Department of Commerce, pp. 50–51.
5. "Proper Precautions Trim Product Liability Risks," *Inc.,* May 1980, p. 131.
6. *The State of Small Business: A Report of the President,* 1993, pp. 96–97.
7. Sue Burzawa, "401(k) Assets Grow 17 Percent Over 1992," *Employee Benefit Plan Review,* Mar. 1994, p. 10.
8. Gordon William, "Fiddling With 401(k)s," *Financial World,* Feb. 1, 1994, p. 64.
9. *Source Book of Health Insurance Data: 1991–1992* (Health Insurance of America).
10. *U.S. Industrial Outlook 1994,* p. 48–51.
11. Based on information from *Status Report,* Insurance Institute for Highway Safety, Dec. 17, 1994, pp. 7, 11; *The Fact Book 1994: Property/Casualty Insurance Facts,* Insurance Information Institute, p. 91; and *1994 Life Insurance Fact Book,* American Council of Life Insurance, pp. 115–116.
12. Based on information from Sears, Roebuck and Co. 1993 Annual Report, pp. 10–11; Sears, Roebuck and Co., *Sears Today,* n.d., n:p; Sears, Roebuck and Co. 1994 Annual Report, pp. 13–14; The Allstate Corporation 1994 Annual Report, pp. 1 and 8. Used by permission of The Allstate Corporation.

CHAPTER 22

1. Based on information from Colleen O'Connor, "Looking at Gender Bias," *Dallas Morning News,* Dec. 16, 1994, p. 1C; Margaret Carlson, "Female Chauvinist Pigs?" *Time,* Dec. 12, 1994, p. 62; Myriam Marquez, "Role Reversal Can Teach a Lesson," *Dallas Morning News,* Dec. 7, 1994, p. 25A; "Men Say Jenny Craig Discriminated," *Dallas Morning News,* Nov. 30, 1994, p. 12D; "Company News; Jenny Craig to Buy Back Some Common Stock," *The New York Times,* Aug. 16, 1994, p. D3; "Company News; Jenny Craig Stock Falls as Dividend Is Halted," *The New York Times,* June 21, 1994, p. D3; Amy Barrett, "How Can Jenny Craig Keep on Gaining?" *Business Week,* Apr. 12, 1993, pp. 52–53; and Phyllis Berman with Amy Feldman, "Fat City," *Forbes,* Feb. 17, 1992, pp. 72+.

2. John W. Merline, "Regulatory Rebound," *Consumers' Research,* Jan. 1991, p. 38.
3. Ibid.
4. "Deregulation: A Fast Start for the Reagan Strategy," *Business Week,* Mar. 9, 1981, p. 63.
5. *Economic Report of the President* (Washington, D.C.: U.S. Government Printing Office, 1989), p. 1+.
6. *Statistical Abstract of the United States 1994,* 114th ed., U.S. Department of Commerce, p. 606.
7. Ibid., p. 295.
8. Based on information from the Internal Revenue Service and the Alcohol, Tobacco, and Firearms Department of the U.S. Treasury Department on December 27, 1991.
9. Based on information from Peter F. Drucker, "The Information Executives Truly Need," *Harvard Business Review,* Jan.–Feb. 1995, pp. 54–62; Terence P. Pare, "A New Tool for Managing Costs," *Fortune,* June 14, 1993, pp. 124–126+; Kevin Kelly, "A Bean-Counter's Best Friend," *Business Week,* Oct. 25, 1991, pp. 42–43; and Robin Cooper and Robert S. Kaplan, "Profit Priorities from Activity-Based Costing," *Harvard Business Review,* May–June 1991, pp. 130–135.
10. Based on information from 377 F.2d 846 (3d Cir. 1967) as reported in *Daniel v. Davidson, et al., Business Law,* 3rd ed. (Boston: PWS-Kent Publishing Company, 1990), p. 366; and Robert N. Corley and William J. Robert, *Principles of Business Law,* 10th ed. (Englewood Cliffs, N.J.: Prentice-Hall, 1975), p. 343.

CHAPTER 23

1. Based on information from Gil Schwartz, "New And Improved!" *The Wall Street Journal,* Feb. 27, 1995, p. R15; Paul A. Grayson and Philip W. Meilman, "The Real World Is Waiting," Managing Your Career Supplement published by *The Wall Street Journal,* Spring/Summer 1993, pp. 7–8; Patsy Moore-Talbot, "Eek! The Real World!" Managing Your Career Supplement published by *The Wall Street Journal,* Spring/Summer 1993, pp. 13+; and Chris B. Bardwell, "Making the Transition from College to the World of Work," *Black Collegian,* Mar./Apr. 1993, pp. 87+.
2. Dave Ellis, Stan Lankowitz, Ed Stupka, and Doug Toft, *Career Planning* (Boston: Houghton Mifflin, 1993), p. 107.
3. Susan D. Greene and Melanie C. L. Martel, *The Job Hunter's Guidebook* (Boston: Houghton Mifflin, 1992), p. 95.
4. Based on information from Stephen M. Pollan and Mark Levine, "How to Ace a Tough Interview," *Working Woman,* July 1994, p. 49; Shena Crane, "How Not to Blow an Interview," *Glamour,* June 1994, p. 110; Adele Scheele, "Job-Hunting Advice for Executives," *Working Woman,* June 1993, pp. 26+; and Daniel P. Wiener, "A Road Map to that First Job," *U.S. News & World Report,* May 13, 1991, pp. 18+.
5. Based on information from Brigid McMenamin, "Don't Hang Up," *Forbes,* Nov. 7, 1994, p. 332; Cathy Booth, "Nice Work If You Can Get It," *Time,* Mar. 8, 1993, p. 57; "Don't Be Fooled by Job Scams," *Glamour,* May 1991, p. 92; and Sheila S. Harrison, "Star Search," *Black Enterprise,* Apr. 1990, pp. 74+.

CREDITS ■ ■ ■ ■ ■ ■ ■ ■ ■ ■ ■ ■ ■ ■

BOX CREDITS

CHAPTER 1

9 Based on information from Faye Rice, "How to Make Diversity Pay," *Fortune*, August 8, 1994, pp. 78–80, 82, 84, 86; Richard F. Federico, "Multiculturalism Makes Good Business Sense," *Compensation & Benefits Management*, Spring 1994, pp. 32–37; William Keenan, Jr., "Toward a More Diverse Sales Force," *Sales & Marketing Management*, March 1994, pp. 33–34; and Linda Deckard, "IAAM Panelists: Attitudes Must Change as Workplace Becomes Culturally Diverse," *Amusement Business*, February 28/March 6, 1994, pp. 3, 14. **13** Based on information from Sylvia Nasar, "F.B.I. Inquiry on Jet Engines: New Jolt to Company Image," *The New York Times*, July 18, 1994, pp. D1, D5; Terence P. Pare, "Jack Welch's Nightmare on Wall Street," *Fortune*, Sept. 5, 1994, pp. 40–43, 46, 48; John Greenwald, "Jack in the Box," *Time*, Oct. 3, 1994, pp. 56–58; and Zachary Schiller, "The Empty Chair at GE's Diamond Trial," *Business Week*, Oct. 24, 1994, p. 38. **25** Based on information from David Holley and James Bates, "MCA to Build Theme Park in Japan," *Los Angeles Times*, January 8, 1994; Jonathan Karp, "Disney's World of Fantasy," *Far Eastern Economic Review*, December 30, 1993, and January 6, 1994, p. 40; Stewart Toy and Paula Dwyer, "Is Disney Headed for the Euro-Trash Heap?" *Business Week*, January 24, 1994, p. 52; Jeff Giles and Andrew Murr, "The Ride Gets a Little Rougher," *Newsweek*, September 5, 1994, p. 43; and Michael Meyer, Stryker McGuire, Charles Fleming, Mark Miller, and Andrew Murr, "Of Mice and Men," *Newsweek*, September 5, 1994, pp. 41–47.

CHAPTER 2

35 Based on information from Robert F. O'Neil, "Economic Criteria Versus Ethical Criteria Toward Resolving a Basic Dilemma in Business," *Journal of Business Ethics*, Jan. 1994, pp. 71–78; Lucia E. Peek, George S. Peek, and Mary Horras, "Enhancing Arthur Andersen Business Ethics Vignettes: Group Discussions Using Cooperative/Collaborative Learning Techniques," *Journal of Business Ethics*, Jan. 1994, pp. 189–196; Nancy K. Austin, "The New Corporate Watchdogs," *Working Woman*, Jan. 1994, pp. 19–20; Gary Edwards and Rebecca Goodell, "Business Ethics," *Executive Excellence*, Feb. 1994, pp. 17–18; Charles P. Johnson, "A Free Market View of Business Ethics," *Supervision*, May 1994, pp. 14–17; and Shannon Bellamy, "Ethics Umbrella," *Executive Excellence*, Feb. 1994, pp. 11–12. **40** Based on information from Judith Nemes, "HFMA Toughens Policies on Law-Breakers," *Healthcare*, February 22, 1993, pp. 35–36; Gary R. Weaver, "Corporate Codes of Ethics: Purpose, Process, and Content Issues," paper presented at the International Association for Business and Society, Spring 1993; Ronald E. Anderson, Deborah G. Johnson, Donald Gotterbarn, and Judith Perrolle, "Using the New ACM Code of Ethics in Decision Making," *Communications of the ACM*, February 1993, pp. 98–107; and Gary Hoover, Alta Campbell, and Patrick J. Spain, eds., *Hoover's Handbook of American Business 1994* (Austin, Texas; Reference Press, 1994), pp. 658–659. **58** Based on information from Richard W. Stevenson, "Body Shop's Green Image is Attacked," *New York Times*, Sept. 2, 1994, p. D1; Betsy Pisik, "Questions Arise about Practices of Body-Care Chain," *Washington Times*, Sept. 3, 1994, p. D8; Jon Entine, "Shattered Image," *Business Ethics*, Sept./Oct. 1994, pp. 23–28.

CHAPTER 3

82 Based on information from Robert D. McTeer, Jr., "Is GATT a Good Deal," *The Southwest Economy*, Federal Reserve Bank of Dallas, May 1994, p. 1. **85** Source: *Consumer Bulletin*, Oct. 8, 1993, U.S. Department of Commerce, Office of Consumer Affairs, Washington, D.C. **87** Based on information from Cheryl Horst, "Watch Those Hands," *Daily Herald* (Carol Stream, IL), November 14, 1991, Sec. 8, pp. 1–2; "Blunders Abroad," *Nation's Business*, March 1989, pp. 54–55; "The Old Sexism in the New China," *U.S. News & World Report*, April 24, 1989, pp. 36–38; and "Understand and Heed Cultural Differences," *Business America*, vol. 112, no. 2, Special Edition, 1991, pp. 26–27. **89** Based on: "Success Story: Borland Company Ltd.", *Focus Japan*, July/August 1994, p. 10. Used with permission.

CHAPTER 4

107 Source: U.S. Small Business Administration, *Small Marketer's Aid*. **113** Based on information from William M. Pride and O. C. Ferrell, *Marketing: Concepts and Strategies*, 8th ed. pp. 100–101. Copyright © 1993 Houghton Mifflin Company. Used with permission; Maxine Lipner, "Ben & Jerry's: Sweet Ethics Evince Social Awareness," *COMPASS Readings*, July 1991, pp. 22–30; Eric J. Wieffering, "Trouble in Camelot," *Business Ethics*, Jan./Feb. 1991, pp. 16–19; and Erik Larson, "Forever Young," *INC.*, July 1988, pp. 50–62.

CHAPTER 5

142 Source: Your Personal Assessment, *Small Business Management Training Instructor's Handout* (Washington, D.C.: The U.S. Small Business Administration, Office of Business Development) n.p., n.d. **159** Source: U.S. Department of Commerce, *Franchise Opportunities Handbook* (Washington, D.C.: U.S. Government Printing Office, June 1991), pp. 11–12. **161** Based on Small Business Administration, Annual Report, 1992, p. 50.

CHAPTER 6

174 Based on information from Alan Deutschman, "Your Desktop in the Year 1996," *Fortune*, July 11, 1994, pp. 86–88+; Rick Tetzeli, "Surviving Information Overload," *Fortune*, July 11, 1994, pp. 60–62+; Thomas A. Stewart, "Managing in a Wired Company," *Fortune*, July 11, 1994, pp. 44+; and Michael Rothschild, "When You're Gagging on E-Mail," *Forbes ASAP*, June 6, 1994, pp. 25–26. **176** Based on information from Alan Farnham, "America's Most Admired Company," *Fortune*, Feb. 7, 1994, pp. 50–54; Tricia Welsh, "Best and Worst Corporate Reputations," *Fortune*, Feb. 7, 1994, pp. 58+; Monica D. Garrett and Samuel A. Young, eds., *Moody's Handbook of Common Stocks*, Summer 1994; Gary Hoover, Alta Campbell, and Patrick J. Spain, eds., *Hoover's Handbook of American Business*, 1994, pp. 360–361, 778–779. **184** Based on information from Laurence Lipsett and David Youst, "Develop Your Staffers with a Plan," *Supervisory Management*, May 1994, p. 6; Augusta C. Yrle and William P. Galle, "Using Interpersonal Skills to Manage More Effectively," *Supervisory Management*, Apr. 1993, p. 4; Stephen M. Pollan and Mark Levine, "Criticizing an Employee's Work," *Working Woman*, Nov. 1993, p. 80; and Martha E. Mangelsdorf, "The Dual-Purpose Sales Supervisor's Checklist," *Inc.*, July 1993, pp. 101–103.

CHAPTER 7

205 Based on information from Marilyn Moats Kennedy, "How To Get A Good Reference" and "Do You Need A New Job—Or a Whole New Career?" *Glamour*, Apr. 1993, p. 118; Sara Nelson, "Entry-Level Blues," *Glamour*, Nov. 1993, p. 160; and Stephen M. Pollan and Mark Levine, "You Are Your Own Business," *Working Woman*, Sept. 1993, pp. 50+. **213** Based on information from John A. Byrne, "Why Downsizing Looks Different These Days," *Business Week*, Oct. 10, 1994, p. 43; Rhonda Richards, "Preparing for a Layoff," *Essence*, Nov. 1994, p. 52; Kathleen Kerwin, "Rumble in Buick City," *Business Week*, Oct. 10, 1994, pp. 42–43; and Lee Smith, "Burned-Out Bosses," *Fortune*, July 25, 1994, pp. 44–46+. **220** Based on information from Thomas A. Stewart, "Managing in a Wired Company," *Fortune*, July 11, 1994, pp. 44+; Rick Tetzeli, "Surviving Information Overload," *Fortune*, July 11, 1994, pp. 60+; Alan Deutschman with Rick Tetzeli, "Your Desktop in the Year 1996," *Fortune*, July 11, 1994, pp. 86+.

CHAPTER 8

234 Based on information from Daniel Seymour, "The Baldrige Cometh," *Change*, Jan./Feb. 1994, pp. 16+; "1993 Winners of the Baldrige Quality Award: Eastman Chemical Co. and Ames Rubber Corp.," *Business America*, Nov. 1, 1993, pp. 20–21; George Harrar, "Baldrige Notwithstanding," *Forbes ASAP*, Oct. 28, 1994, pp. 44+; "Betting to Win on the Baldie Winners," *Business Week*, Oct. 18, 1993, p. 8. **239** Based on information from Michael Barrier and Amy Zuckerman, "Quality Standards the World Agrees On," *Nation's Business*, May 1994, pp. 71+; Ronald Henkoff, "The Hot New Seal of Quality," *Fortune*, June 28, 1993, pp. 116+, Bob Straetz, "U.S. Firms Are Told How to Develop Business Opportunities in the EC," *Business America*, June 14, 1993, p. 7; Mary Saunders, "U.S. Firms Doing Business in EC Have Options in Register-ing for ISO 9000 Quality Standards," *Business America*, June 14, 1993, p. 7; Leslie Brokaw, "ISO 9000: Making the Grade," *Inc.*, June 1993, pp. 98–99. **251** Based on information from John S. DeMott, "Look, World, No Hands!" *Nation's Business*, June 1994, pp. 41–42; Stephen Baker, "A Surgeon Whose Hands Never Shake," *Business Week*, Oct. 4, 1993, pp. 111–114; "Robot Farming," *The Futurist*, July–Aug. 1993, p. 54; Andrew Kupfer, "A Robot Inspector For Airplanes," *Fortune*, May 3, 1993, p. 93; Gregory T. Pope, "Homer Hoover," *Discover*, March 1993, p. 28.

CHAPTER 9

275 Based on information from Willa Bruce and Christine Reed, "Preparing Supervisors for the Future Work Force: The Dual-Income Couple and Work-Family Dichotomy," *Public Administration Review*, Jan./Feb. 1994, pp. 36–43; Michael A. Verespej, "Masters of Change," *Industry Week*, Mar. 7, 1994, p. 9; Julain M. Weiss, "Telecommuting Boosts Employee Output," *HR Magazine*, Feb. 1994, pp. 51–53; Penny Lunt, "Want To Share a Job?" *ABA Banking Journal*, Mar. 1994, p. 88; Catherine Romano, "What's Your Flexibility Factor?" *Management Review*, Jan. 1994, p. 9; and Michael J. O'Connor, "Authority," *Supermarket Business*, Apr. 1994, pp. 38–39, 41–47. **286** Based on information from "Levi Strauss & Company Implements New Pay and Performance System," *Employee Benefit Plan Review*, Jan. 1994, pp. 46–48; Robert D. Haas, "Ethics in the Trenches," *Across the Board*, May 1994, pp. 12–13; and Russell Mitchell and Michael Oneal, "Managing by Values," *Business Week*, Aug. 1, 1994, pp. 46–52. **288** Based on information from Stewart L. Stokes, Jr., "Moving Toward Self-Direction: An Action Plan for Self-Managed Teams," *Information Systems Management*, Winter 1994, pp. 40–46; Kevin B. Lowe, "Leading Self-Directed Work Teams: A Guide to Developing New Team Leadership Skills," *Organizational Dynamics*, Winter 1994, pp. 74–75; James A. Cusumano, "The Winning Team," *Chemical Marketing Reporter*, Apr. 11, 1994, pp. SR11–SR12; Erica Gordon Sorohan, "Managing Teams," *Training and Development*, Apr. 1994, p. 14; Mark Moon, "5 Steps for Team Selling Success," *Personal Selling Power*, Sept. 1994, pp. 56–57; and Brian Dumaine, "The Trouble with Teams," *Fortune*, Sept. 5, 1994, pp. 86–88, 90, 92.

CHAPTER 10

308 Based on information from Mary Baechler, "Death of a Marriage," *Inc.*, Apr. 1994, pp. 74–76, 78; Christine M. Reed and Willa M. Bruce, "Dual-Career Couples in the Public Sector: A Survey of Personnel Policies and Practices," *Public Personnel Management*, Summer 1993, pp. 187–199; and Anne B. Fisher, "Getting Comfortable with Couples in the Workplace," *Fortune*, Oct. 3, 1994, pp. 138–142, 144. **314** Based on information from "Be Careful Out There," *Training*, Jan. 1994, pp. 17, 19, 125; "Positive Steps for Screening Out Workplace Violence," *Restaurant Security Newsletter*, Feb. 1, 1994, p. 124; Michael J. McDermott, "Suits & Armor," *Profiles*, Oct. 1994, pp. 47, 49–51; and Bernard Baumohl, Sophfronia Scott Gregory, Scott Norvell, and Suneel Ratan, "Workers Who Fight Firing with Fire," *Time*, Apr. 25, 1994, pp. 34–37.

CHAPTER 11

334 Based on information from Aaron Bernstein, "Why America Needs Unions, But Not the Kind It Has Now," *Business Week*, May 23, 1994, pp. 70–71, 74, 78, 82; Robert L. Rose, "Companies, Unions Lengthen Contracts, Encouraged by Stable, Low Inflation," *Wall Street Journal*, Feb. 2, 1994, pp. A2, A6; Edward H. Phillips, "Union Approval Key to Buyout Plan," *Aviation Week & Space Technology*, Jan. 3, 1994, pp. 29–30; George J. Church, "Unions Arise—With New Tricks," *Time*, June 13, 1994, pp. 56–57; and Joel Rogers and Charles F. Sabel, "State of the Union (And Why You Should Care)," *Inc.*, Jan. 1994, p. 23. **344** Based on information from James H. Coil III and Charles M. Rice, "The Tip of the Iceberg: Early Trends in ADA Enforcement," *Employee Relations*, Spring 1994, pp. 485–506; Jay Finegan, "Law and Disorder," *Inc.*, Apr. 1994, pp. 64–68, 70, 72; Arthur F. Silbergeld, "Avoiding Wrongful Termination Claims: A Checklist for Employers," *Employment Relations Today*, Winter 1993/94, pp. 447–454; and Junda Woo, "Quirky Slander Actions Threaten Employers," *Wall Street Journal*, Nov. 26, 1993, pp. B1, B5. **349** Based on information from Robert L. Rose, "As Caterpillar Lures Picket-Line Crossers, A Striker's Mettle Is Put to a Severe Test," *Wall Street Journal*, July 6, 1994, pp. B1, B8; Cynthia L. Gramm and John F. Schnell, "Difficult Choices: Crossing the Picket Line During the 1987 National Football League Strike," *Journal of Labor Economics*, Vol. 12, No. 1, 1994, pp. 41–73; Michael H. LeRoy, "Multivariate Analysis of Unionized Employees' Propensity to Cross Their Union's Picket Line," *Journal of Labor Research*, Summer 1992, pp. 285–291; and "Nonunion Trucker Crossing Picket Line Is Severely Beaten," *The New York Times*, Apr. 18, 1994, p. A11.

CHAPTER 12

366 Based on information from David Greising, "Quality: How to Make It Pay," *Business Week*, Aug. 8, 1994, pp. 54–59; Susan J. Devlin and H. K. Dong, "Service Quality from the Customer's Perspective," *Marketing Research*, Winter 1994, pp. 4–13; Jill L. Sherer, "Hospitals Question the Return on Their TQM Investment," *Hospitals & Health Networks*, Apr. 5, 1994, p. 63; and Stanley C. Gault, "Reinventing the Wheel? The Consumer Will Decide," *Executive Speeches*, June/July 1994, pp. 48–51. **374** Based on information from Patricia Sellers, "Pepsi Opens a Second Front," *Fortune*, Aug. 8, 1994, pp. 70–76; Karen Benezra, "Double Entendre: The Life and The Life of Pepsi Max," *Brandweek*, Apr. 18, 1994, p. 40; and Karen Benezra, "Monkey See, Monkey No Can Do," *Brandweek*, Feb. 7, 1994, p. 8. **376** Based on information from William M. Pride and O. C. Ferrell, *Marketing: Strategies and Concepts* (Boston: Houghton Mifflin, 1995), pp. 692, 694–703.

CHAPTER 13

397 Based on information from Joshua Levine, "Bra Wars," *Forbes*, Apr. 25, 1994, p. 120; Elaine Underwood, "Victoria Pits Miracle vs. Sara," *Brandweek*, Sept. 19, 1994, p. 16; Judith Schoolman, "Cleavage Makes a Comeback as Underwear Takes Center Stage," *Reuter Business Report*, May 9, 1994; Lisa Anderson, "U.S. Next Beachhead in 'Bra Wars,'" *Chicago Tri-*bune, May 1, 1994; and Lisa Pollak, "Pair Pressure," *The News and Observer*, April 25, 1994. **406** Based on information from "Singapore: Bite-Size Market Shows a Taste for Snacks," *AgReporter*, Oct. 1994, pp. 4–7; "Marketing Tips For Consumer-Oriented Product Exporters," *AgReporter*, Oct. 1994, pp. 8–9; Richard Gibson, "Gerber Missed the Boat in Quest to Go Global, So It Turned to Sandoz," *Wall Street Journal*, May 24, 1994, pp. A1, A8; Peter Hollingsworth, "Global Opportunities," *Food Technology*, Mar. 1994, pp. 65–68; Amy Feldman, "Have Distribution, Will Travel," *Forbes*, June 20, 1994, pp. 44–45; and Cyndee Miller, "Going Overseas Requires Marketers to Learn More Than a New Language," *Marketing News*, Mar. 28, 1994, pp. 8, 13. **409** Based on information from Jerry Edgerton, "Steering Your Way to a Great Deal," *Money*, Mar. 1994, pp. 108–116; Peter Bohr, "Driving a Bargain on a New Car," *Working Woman*, Apr. 1994, pp. 32, 34; Walter L. Updegrave, "Capitalize on the Housing Recovery," *Money*, Forecast 1994, pp. 78–80; and Leslie Vreeland, "How to Be a Smart Shopper," *Black Enterprise*, Aug. 1993, pp. 85–86, 88, 90.

CHAPTER 14

435 Based on information from Judith Schwartz, "Searching for the Next Kiwi: Frieda's Branded Produce," *Brandweek*, May 2, 1994, pp. 46–48; Karen B. Caplan, 'Good Enough' Can Be Much Better," *Across the Board*, Sept. 1994, p. 55; "The Frieda's of the Future," *On the Cutting Edge*, Mar./Apr. 1992; Robert Johnson, "Thorny Question: Will the Prickly Pear Be Kiwi of the '90s?" *Wall Street Journal*, Jan. 26, 1993; and Frieda's Finest, press kit, 1993. **443** Based on information from Leslie P. Norton, "Avon Calls On China," *Barron's*, Jan. 17, 1994, pp. 40–41; Suein L. Hwang, "Avon Reorganizes European Businesses, Picks Cuello to Run Continental Market," *Wall Street Journal*, Aug. 4, 1994, p. B2; Ann Marsh, "Avon Is Calling On Eastern Europe," *Advertising Age International* (supplement to *Advertising Age*), June 20, 1994, p. I16; Veronica Byrd and Wendy Zellner, "The Avon Lady in the Amazon," *Business Week*, Oct. 24, 1994, pp. 93–94; and Gary Hoover, Alta Campbell, and Patrick J. Spain, eds., *Hoover's Handbook of American Business, 1993*, (Austin, Texas: Reference Press, 1994), pp. 228–229. **445** Based on information from Judith Waldrop, "The Business of Privacy," *American Demographics*, Oct. 1994, pp. 46–51, 54–55; Robin Raisfeld, "Telenuisances," *New York*, Jan. 31, 1994, p. 32; "Telemarketing and Consumer Fraud and Abuse Prevention Act," *Laws of the 103rd Congress*, Aug. 16, 1994, pp. 1545–1551; Gary Levin, "Learning Where to Draw the Line on Privacy Issue," *Advertising Age*, Feb. 15, 1993, pp. 35–36; "States Can Ban Autodial Calls," *Marketing News*, Apr. 26, 1993, p. 1; "Judge Voids Anti-Junk Call Law," *Marketing News*, June 21, 1993, p. 1; "Telemarketing Draws Lawsuit," *Marketing News*, Aug. 17, 1992, p. 1; Leah Fliter, "FCC Commissioner Addresses DMA Regarding Pending Rulemaking," *Telemarketing*, Aug. 1992, pp. 19–20; Anthony Ramirez, "Curbing Machines That Phone to Solicit," *The New York Times*, Nov. 5, 1992, p. C2; James P. Sterba, "In Your Ear: Telemarketing's Untold Story," *Wall Street Journal*, Oct. 22, 1992, p. A12; and Kristin Davis, "Why Not to Hang Up on Junk Calls," *Kiplinger's Personal Finance Magazine*, Dec. 1992, pp. 40, 42.

CHAPTER 15

471 Based on information from Carolyn Tripp, Thomas D. Jensen, and Les Carlson, "The Effects of Multiple Product Endorsements by Celebrities on Consumers' Attitudes and Intentions," *Journal of Consumer Research*, Mar. 1994, pp. 535–547; Larry Armstrong, "Still Starstruck," *Business Week*, July 4, 1994, p. 38; Cyndee Miller, "Celebrities Hot Despite Scandals," *Marketing News*, Mar. 28, 1994, pp. 1–2, 5; Cyndee Miller, "Well-Known Winners Will Reap More Olympic Gold," *Marketing News*, Mar. 28, 1994, pp. 2, 18; Laura Liebeck, "Celebrities Provide Halo For Store, Products," *Discount Store News*, Apr. 18, 1994, p. 37; Dottie Enrico, "Celebrity Endorsements: Women Take the Lead," *USA Today*, Dec. 20, 1994, p. 1C, 3C; and Kevin Goldman, "Catch a Falling Star: Big Names Plummet From List of Top 10 Celebrity Endorsers," *Wall Street Journal*, Nov. 8, 1994. **476** Based on information from Tony Seideman, "On the Cutting Age," *Sales & Marketing Management*, June 1994, pp. 18–23; Tony Seideman, "Reps' Needs Drive Gillette's System," *Sales & Marketing Management*, June 1994, p. 22; Tony Seideman, "Way Cool!" *Sales & Marketing Management*, June 1994, pp. 10–13; and Bruce K. Koepcke, "Automating Your Salesforce," *Small Business Reports*, Mar. 1994, pp. 14–17. **483** Based on information from Michael DeMarco, "The Collateral Effects of a Corporate Guilty Finding," *Federation of Insurance & Corporate Counsel Quarterly*, Spring 1994, pp. 335–353; Leah Richard, "Hoosier Tire's 'Rookie Mistake,'" *Advertising Age*, Mar. 7, 1994, p. 40; John Bissell, "How Do You Market an Image Brand When the Image Falls out of Favor?" *Brandweek*, June 6, 1994, p. 16; "Does Fleet Play Too Rough?" *CFO: The Magazine for Senior Financial Executives*, Mar. 1994, p. 33; Dale Johnson, "With a Little Help from My Friends," *Vital Speeches of the Day*, Aug. 15, 1994, pp. 666–669; and Beth Hogan Henthorne and Tony L. Henthorne, "The Tarnished Image: Anticipating and Minimizing the Impact of Negative Publicity in Health Services Organizations," *Journal of Consumer Marketing*, Vol. 11, No. 3, 1994, pp. 44–54.

CHAPTER 16

507 Based on information from "How to Buy a Computer: A Road Map to the Right Gear," *Consumer Reports*, Nov. 1994, pp. 689–693; M. F. Thompson, "Screening The New Computers," *Mademoiselle*, Sept. 1993, p. 154; Sue Berkman, "Guide to Buying a Computer," *Good Housekeeping*, May 1992, p. 248; "Buying a Computer for Your Kid Is Child's Play—Almost," *Business Week*, May 10, 1993, p. 89. **513** Based on information from William F. Allman, "Pioneering the Electronic Frontier," *U.S. News & World Report*, Dec. 6, 1993, pp. 57+; Diana Kunde, "Add Job-Hunting to Shopping List at the Supermarket," *Dallas Morning News*, Feb. 16, 1994, pp. D1, D11; Christopher Farrell and Michael J. Mandel, "What's Arriving on the Information Highway?" *Business Week*, Nov. 29, 1993, p. 40; Robert J. Samuelson, "Lost on the Information Highway," *Newsweek*, Dec. 20, 1993, p. 111; "A Hitch-Hiker's Guide," *The Economist*, Dec. 25, 1993–Jan. 7, 1994, p. 36 **521** Based on information from Carolyn Said, "Getting Women Wired," *Working Woman*, Mar. 1994, p. 12; Paul M. Eng, "It's Getting Crowded On Line," *Business Week*, Nov. 7, 1994, pp. 134, 136; Tom Holt, "Which On-Line Service for Your Family?" *Consumers' Research*, Aug. 1994, pp. 14–18; Phaedra Hise, "Networking on America Online," *Inc.*, Mar. 1994, p. 133; Andrew Kupfer, "A 'Whole New Medium' Online," *Fortune*, Jan. 16, 1995, p. 16; Steve Morgenstern, "A Guide For Computer Phobics," *Redbook*, Feb. 1995, pp. 53–56.

CHAPTER 17

538 Based on information from "Charges in Leslie Fay Case," *The New York Times*, Oct. 19, 1994, p. D16; Stephanie Strom, "Company News: Leslie Fay to be Revamped and Drop Career Clothing Line," *The New York Times*, Oct. 13, 1994, p. D4; Stephanie Strom, "Executives of Leslie Fay Are Cleared in Scandal," *The New York Times*, Aug. 17, 1994, p. D2; Mark Hoffman, "Contractors Go On Working for Troubled Leslie Fay," *Northeast Pennsylvania Business Journal*, May 1993, p. 8; "Leslie Fay Files for Bankruptcy," *Sun-Sentinel*, Apr. 6, 1993; and Elizabeth Lesly, "Who Played Dress-Up with the Books?" *Business Week*, Mar. 15, 1993, p. 34. **545** Based on information from Wal-Mart Stores, Inc., 1994 Annual Report, p. 18; The Procter & Gamble Company, 1994 Annual Report, p. 18; and ConAgra, Inc., 1994 Annual Report, p. 34. **553** Based on information from Carolyn M. Brown, "Understanding . . . Annual Reports," *Black Enterprise*, May 1994, p. 40; Julie Tilsner, "You Were Expecting Maybe John Grisham?" *Business Week*, Apr. 25, 1994, p. 40; and Grace M. Kang, "It's Corporate America's Spring Hornblowing Festival," *Business Week*, Apr. 12, 1993, p. 31.

CHAPTER 18

581 Based on information from Paul Craig Roberts, "Holding Banks Hostage Is a Rotten Way to Battle Bias," *Business Week*, Oct. 3, 1994, p. 22; "Reno Urges Banks to Market Services to Minority Areas," *Jet*, Sept. 12, 1994, p. 40; Paul Craig Roberts, "The Feds' Sham Settlement with Shawmut," *Business Week*, Jan. 24, 1994, p. 22; and "Eye of the Beholder," *National Review*, Sept. 20, 1993, p. 18. **583** Based on information from "Smart Debt, Dumb Debt," *Glamour*, June 1994, p. 114; "The Smart Way to Handle Creditors," *Good Housekeeping*, Aug. 1993, p. 161; "Never Had Credit? You Can Get It Now," *Good Housekeeping*, Sept. 1994, p. 237; "Pocket Guide to Money," *Consumer Reports*, Nov. 1993, p. 702; and "Keeping Your Record Error-Free," *Consumer Reports*, Dec. 1993, pp. 804–805. **591** Based on information from Frank Lalli, "It's Now Depositor Beware," *Money*, Jan. 1993, p. 5; Guy Murdoch, "Deposit Insurance," *Consumers' Research*, Feb. 1994, p. 2; Bruce G. Posner, ed., "Security for Bank Deposits," *Inc.*, July 1993, p. 32; and Sheryl Nance-Nash, "Here's Why Bank Safety Still Matters," *Money*, Mar. 1994, pp. 38+.

CHAPTER 19

605 Based on information from "Orange Craps Out," *Fortune*, Jan. 16, 1995, p. 97; "A Land of Beaches and Bankruptcy," *Newsweek*, Jan. 2, 1995, p. 13; Nanette Byrnes, "Orange County Is Looking Green Around the Gills," *Business Week*, Dec. 26, 1994; Marc Levinson, "Read It and Weep," *Newsweek*,

Dec. 19, 1994, pp. 46+; Leah Nathans Spiro, Nanette Byrnes, and Zachary Schiller, "Today, Orange County," *Business Week*, Dec. 19, 1994, pp. 28+; and Nanette Byrnes, "With Returns Like These, Why Ask Questions?" *Business Week*, Dec. 19, 1994, p. 30. **617** Based on information from Bill Holstein, "Congratulations, Exporter! Now About Getting Paid . . . ," *Business Week*, Jan. 17, 1994, p. 98; Mary Ann Ring, "Export Financing at the State Level," *Business America*, Nov. 15, 1993, pp. 2–5; Albert G. Holzinger, "SBA to Teach Bankers the Ins and Outs of Export Financing," *Nation's Business*, Aug. 1993, p. 12; and Mary Ann Ring, "Innovative Export Financing: Factoring and Forfaiting," *Business America*, Jan. 11, 1993, pp. 12–14. **627** Based on information from Gary Hoover, ed., *Hoover's Handbook of American Business*, 1995. (Austin, Texas: Reference Press, 1994), pp. 520–521; David P. Goldman, "A Bond Market Primer," *Forbes*, June 20, 1994, p. 158; and Zvi Bodie, Alex Kane, and Alan Marcus, *Essentials of Investments*, (Homewood, Ill: Irwin, 1992), pp. 347–349.

CHAPTER 20

644 "Asset-Mix Worksheet," T. Rowe Price, 100 Pratt Street, Baltimore, MD 21201. **654** Based on information from Carla Rapoport, "How to Win the Global Game," *Fortune*, Dec. 26, 1994, pp. 82+; David Dreman, "The Prudent Traveler," *Forbes*, July 18, 1994, p. 330; "Putting Your Tax Refund to Work," *Black Enterprise*, June 1994, p. 57; Marc Levison, "Strong Dollar, Sad Faces, Investing: Beware the Foreign Fund Bearing Gifts" *Newsweek*, Jan. 17, 1994, p. 37; and Michael Sivy, "Three Ways to Cash In on the Coming Boom in Europe," *Money*, June 1993, p. 164. **658** Based on information from William Giese, "When Investors Gather in Cyberspace, Anything Can Happen," *Kiplinger's Personal Finance Magazine*, Oct. 1994, pp. 47+; Richard A. Marini, "Should You Join an Investment Club?" *Good Housekeeping*, Apr. 1994, p. 194; Karen C. Holden, Ph.D., *The Gerontologist*, Apr. 1994, pp. 284–285; Melynda Dovel Wilcox, "A Clubby Approach to Beating the Market Year After Year," *Kiplinger's Personal Finance Magazine*, June 1993, p. 90.

CHAPTER 21

682 Based on information from "Insurance Fraud," *Good Neighbor*, State Farm Insurance; and Nationwide Insurance Annual Report 1991, Columbus, Ohio, p. 23. **689** Based on information from "Product Liability in Japan," *Focus Japan*, May 1995, p. 3.

CHAPTER 22

710 Based on information from Glenn W. Bailey, "Litigation Is Destroying American Companies," *USA Today*, Jan. 1994, pp. 76–77; David Warner, "Civil Courts on Trial," *Nation's Business*, Aug. 1993, pp. 56–57; David Frum, "Sanity Is Back in Style," *Forbes*, Aug. 2, 1993, p. 62; David Frum, "Unreformed," *Forbes*, Feb. 1, 1993, p. 82. **722** Based on information from Gracian Mack, "Bankruptcy; A Blessing in Disguise," *Black Enterprise*, Oct. 1994, p. 56; Alice Griffin, "Bankruptcy: A Debtor's Last Resort," *Consumers' Research*, June 1994, pp. 23+; and Denise M. Topolnicki and Elizabeth M. MacDonald, "The Bankruptcy Bonanza," *Money*, Aug. 1993, pp. 82+. **729** Based on information from David Warner, "Streamlining Yields Savings, Gore Says," *Nation's Business*, Nov. 1994, p. 8; Daniel Franklin, "Downsizing: Is It Aimed at the Right Targets?" *Washington Monthly*, Nov. 1994, pp. 22+; Susan B. Garland, with Amy Barrett, "Clinton Is Streamlining Government—But Voters May Not Care," *Business Week*, Sept. 19, 1994, p. 47; "Reinventing Government, Twelve Months Wiser," *The Economist*, Sept. 17, 1994; Howard Gleckman, "A Productive Junkie Takes On Fat City," *Business Week*, July 5, 1993, pp. 76+.

CHAPTER 23

745 Based on information from Glenn Rifkin, "Stress in the Workplace," *Harvard Business Review*, Sept. 1994, pp. 10–11; Armin A. Brott, "New Approaches to Job Stress," *Nation's Business*, May 1994, pp. 81–82; Marty Munson and Greg Gutfeld, "Undo Pressure," *Prevention*, Jan. 1994, pp. 16–17; and Joanne Cole, "Dealing with Job Pressure," *Supervisory Management*, Feb. 1993, p. 9. **753** Based on information from Charles E. Cohen, "Giving Your Company a Performance Review," *Working Woman*, Dec. 1994, pp. 40–43+; Elyse Mall, "Why Getting Ahead Is (Still) Tougher for Women," *Working Woman*, July 1994, p. 11; Maggie Mahar, "More Women Are Calling the Shots, But They're Still Making Less than the Guys," *Working Woman*, June 1994, p. 18; Terri Scandura, "Women Can Shatter Job Barriers," *USA Today*, May 1994, pp. 68–69; and Susan B. Garland, "How to Keep Women Managers on the Corporate Ladder," *Business Week*, Sept. 2, 1991, p. 64. **760** Based on information from Amy Feldman, "We'll Make You Scary," *Forbes*, Feb. 14, 1994, p. 96; Hyman Smith, "Control Time!" *Success*, Dec. 1993, p. 17; Jill Kirchner, "The Gift You Should Give Yourself," *McCall's*, Dec. 1993, pp. 80+; Nancy K. Austin, "Race Against Time—and Win," *Working Woman*, Nov. 1990, pp. 48+; and Peter Passell, "Time Is Money and Other Things," *New York Times*, Dec. 19, 1990, p. D2.

PHOTO CREDITS

PART 1 Murray Aloosser/The Image Bank

CHAPTER 1

2 Ed Honowitz/Tony Stone Images. **3** Reuters/Bettman. **4** Edward Gajdel. **7** Gale Zucker/Stock Boston. **14** O'Rourke/Image Works. **22** S. Gazin/Image Works. **25** Tony Stone Images.

CHAPTER 2

32 David Rickerd/The Image Bank. **33** Jay Freis/The Image Bank. **38** Courtesy of Martin Marietta Corporation.

42 Courtesy of British Airways. **43** The Granger Collection. **45** Courtesy of JCPenney. **55** Courtesy of Combibloc. **59** John Abbott.

CHAPTER 3

65 Grant Faint/The Image Bank. **66** Xinhua/Gamma Liaison. **72** Ymura Yama-Kurita/Gamma Liaison. **75** Mushni Ahmed. **83** (left) Halstead/Gamma Liaison; (right) Michael Schwartz/Image Works. **84** Kuala Lumpur/Stock Market.

CHAPTER 4

102 Mug Shots/The Stock Market. **103** Kenneth Redding/The Image Bank. **106** M. Siluk/Image Works. **109** Seth Resnick/Stock Boston. **123** John Neubauer/Photo Edit. **124** Cosmo Condina/Tony Stone Images. **125** Forest Anderson/Gamma Liaison.

CHAPTER 5

134 Steve Dunwell/The Image Bank. **135** Washington University in St. Louis. **137** Charles Gupton/Stock Boston. **140** Don Pitcher/Stock Boston. **145** Gabe Palmer/Stock Market. **148** Jeffrey W. Myers/Stock Boston. **158** Suzanne Opton.

PART 2 Lester Lefkowitz/Tony Stone Images

CHAPTER 6

170 Mug Shots/The Stock Market. **171** Churchill & Klehr. **173** Louis Psihoyos/Matrix. **185** Mark Richards/Photo Edit. **191** John Abbott. **193** Michael Newman/Photo Edit.

CHAPTER 7

199 Terry Vine/Tony Stone Images. **200** Joe Caputo/Gamma Liaison. **204** D. Richemond/Image Works. **206** Jeff Greenberg/Picture Cube. **216** John Abbott. **221** Mark Richards/Photo Edit. **222** David Young Wolff/Photo Edit.

CHAPTER 8

228 Steve Dunwell/The Image Bank. **229** IBM, Charlotte, N.C. **235** P. Gontier/Image Works. **239** The Image Works. **249** Bob Daemmrich/Image Works. **250** Photo Edit. **254** Tony Freeman/Photo Edit.

PART 3 Ken Fisher/Tony Stone Images

CHAPTER 9

264 Lori Adamski Peek/Tony Stone Images. **265** UPI/Bettmann. **267** Steven D. Starr/Stock Boston. **280** Chris Corsmeier. **282** Mark Peterson/SABA. **284** B. Mahoney/Image Works. **285** Andy Freeberg.

CHAPTER 10

293 Michel Tcherevkoff/The Image Bank. **294** Courtesy Hanna Andersson. **299** John Abbott. **303** Bob Daemmrich/Image Works. **312** John Abbott. **319** Daniel Nichols/Gamma Liaison. **321** J. Pickerel/Image Works.

CHAPTER 11

326 Mark Burnett/Stock Boston. **327** AP/Wide World Photos.

330 The Granger Collection. **335** Ben Van Hook/Gamma Liaison. **338** M. Siluk/Image Works. **348** Bill Aron/Photo Edit.

PART 4 Dennis O'Clair/Tony Stone Images

CHAPTER 12

360 Barry Rosenthal Studio Inc./FPG International Corp. **361** Reprinted courtesy of Ford Motor Company. **364** Courtesy of Chrysler Corporation. **368** Erin Hildebrandt/Gamma Liaison. **373** Courtesy of Canon. **375** Courtesy of Geographic Data Technology, Inc. **379** Amy C. Etra/Photo Edit.

CHAPTER 13

388 Jay Freis/The Image Bank. **389** Courtesy Birkenstock. **391** Mary Kate Denny/Photo Edit. **396** Bob Daemmrich/Stock Boston. **402** Farnsworth/Image Works. **411** Peter Menzel/Stock Boston. **413** M. Siluk/Image Works.

CHAPTER 14

424 Jeff Zaruba/Tony Stone Images. **425** Michael Newman/Photo Edit. **428** R. Lord/Image Works. **432** Joseph Nettis/Stock Boston. **440** R. Lord/Image Works. **444** Frank Siteman/Picture Cube. **450** Courtesy of DHL. **453** Billy Barnes/Photo Edit.

CHAPTER 15

459 Alese and Mort Pechter/The Stock Market. **460** Jonathan Nourok/Photo Edit. **462** Lee Snider/Image Works. **466** J. Sohm/Image Works. **468** Brent Jones/Stock Boston. **478** Peter Chapman/Stock Boston. **481** Jeff Greenberg/Photo Edit.

PART 5 Gabe Palmer/The Stock Market

CHAPTER 16

496 Dennis O'Clair/Tony Stone Images. **497** Microsoft Corporation. **503** Jeff Greenberg/Photo Edit. **509** Kip Brundage/Gamma Liaison. **514** Matthew McVay/Stock Boston. **519** Frank Pedrick/Image Works. **522** Tom McCarthy/Photo Edit.

CHAPTER 17

532 Dan Carstens/Folio. **533** Ted Horowitz/The Stock Market. **535** Bob Daemmrich/Image Works. **541** David Young Wolff/Photo Edit. **544** Nathan Benn/Stock Boston. **549** Stacy Pick/Stock Boston. **551** Courtesy of Arthur Andersen.

PART 6 Jeff Spielman/The Image Bank.

CHAPTER 18

568 Pierre-Yves Goavec/The Image Bank. **569** Joe Molear/Transparencies, Inc. **571** D. Goldberg/Sygma. **575** John Lei/Stock Boston. **582** Courtesy of the Bank of New York. **584** Amy Etra/Photo Edit. **590** NR Rowan/Stock Boston.

CHAPTER 19

600 Reza Estakhrian/Tony Stone Images. **601** Peter Steiner/The Stock Market. **604** Erica Freudenstein/SABA. **607** Courtesy of GE Capital. **620** Steve Woit. **622** Courtesy of

The Principal Financial Group. **625** Courtesy of Sprint Communications Company.

CHAPTER 20

633 Frank Saragnese/FPG International Corp. **634** Michael Newman/Photo Edit. **637** Jim Pickerell/Image Works. **638** Ed Hille/Stock Market. **649** Ron Haviv/SABA. **651** Courtesy of Kemper Mutual Funds. **662** Michael Schwarz.

CHAPTER 21

672 Peter M. Miller/The Image Bank. **673** Mutual of Omaha Public Affairs Division. **675** M. Justice/Image Works. **677** Mulvehill/Image Works. **680** Courtesy of Wausau Insurance. **685** Courtesy of Cigna. **692** Lincoln Russell/Stock Boston.

PART 7 Mug Shots/Stock Market

CHAPTER 22

704 Rich LaSalle/Tony Stone Images. **705** James Darrell/Tony Stone Images. **707** Gamma Liaison. **712** Tony Freeman/Photo Edit. **716** Susan Van Etten/Stock Boston. **726** John Neubauer/Photo Edit. **730** J. Griffin/Image Works.

CHAPTER 23

741 Michel Tcherevkoff/The Image Bank. **742** Laurence Dutton/Tony Stone Images. **747** Bob Daemmrich/Stock Boston. **750** Seth Resnick/Stock Boston. **757** Mark Richards/Photo Edit. **759** Robert Brenner/Photo Edit.

NAME INDEX ■ ■ ■ ■ ■ ■ ■ ■ ■ ■ ■ ■

A-37

SUBJECT INDEX ■ ■ ■ ■ ■ ■ ■ ■ ■ ■ ■

A-41